Child and
Adolescent Development

Child and Adolescent Development
An Advanced Course

Edited by

WILLIAM DAMON
RICHARD M. LERNER

WILEY

JOHN WILEY & SONS, INC.

Contents

PART VI: EMOTION AND MOTIVATION

PART VII: PROSOCIAL BEHAVIOR, ANTISOCIAL BEHAVIOR, AND MORAL DEVELOPMENT

PART VIII: ADOLESCENCE

CHAPTER 15 THE SECOND DECADE: WHAT DEVELOPS (AND HOW)?   **517**

Deanna Kuhn and Sam Franklin

CHAPTER 16 ADOLESCENT DEVELOPMENT IN INTERPERSONAL CONTEXT   **551**

W. Andrew Collins and Laurence Steinberg

PART IX: DIVERSITY IN DEVELOPMENT

CHAPTER 17 CULTURAL AND COGNITIVE DEVELOPMENT IN PHYLOGENETIC, HISTORICAL, AND ONTOGENETIC PERSPECTIVE   **593**

Michael Cole

Preface

Whatever else we—the two editors of this text—have done in our working lives, one thing is beyond doubt: We are veteran teachers of child and adolescent development. Combined, our years of teaching in this field total well over 70 years, or about the average life span of humans in most parts of the world today. What's more, each of us has taught child development in every corner of the university, from large lecture halls to intimate seminar rooms. We have taught (and learned from) student audiences ranging from first-semester freshmen to advanced postdocs in over a dozen colleges and universities in the United States and abroad.

Experience does not always improve performance—the aging literature is humbling on that matter—but it does allow us to make some observations from the perspectives of insiders. Our first and surest observation is that this is a delightful field to teach. The material is immediately fascinating and meaningful to students. It does not take much theatrical ability to get students to thrill to the first displays of attachment between caregiver and infant, or to the toddler's early mastery of symbolic speech, or the child's budding interests in close friendships, or the adolescent's discovery of new-found intellectual and personal powers. The field itself is built around a narrative of learning and growth, which students naturally find compelling, if not inspiring. Motivating students to read the material is not an instructor's primary problem in this particular field.

Yet that does not mean that teaching child development is a trivial exercise. To do justice to the dynamic interplay between nature and nurture, biology and culture, or the vast array of social and historical influences that shape a human life, demands a degree of conceptual complexity that requires students at any level to stretch and deepen their thinking. The primary task of any instructor in this field is to help students appreciate, and ultimately master, the complexity of how a child's life develops over time. Without working through the full complexity of this process, there can be little true understanding. For example, glance at a typical popular media account of child development, where extreme and untested explanations that often contradict one another are presented without any apparent awareness of the confusion. It is not that the writers of such accounts lack intelligence (far from it); instead, the case is that they have not studied this field in sufficient depth to unravel its many intricate laws and principles. We always like to point out that the study of human development in all its richness, dynamism, and contextual variation is not rocket science—it is actually far more challenging.

And the field of child development itself, in addition to the subjects it encompasses, is incredibly dynamic. In the $3\frac{1}{2}$ decades since we began teaching in this field, child development has become more interdisciplinary, contextual, and sophisticated, both methodologically and theoretically. Studies of the brain and studies of culture, each in their own way, have moved from the margins to the center of our field, informing us about the most fundamental questions of intellectual and social development. The purview of the field has expanded to diverse populations in the United States and to other parts of the world that were too long neglected in developmental study. New theoretical models that are better equipped to deal with the dynamic and systemic nature of human development have arisen and become strengthened.

From the point of view of two veteran (but still-aspiring) teachers, conveying this complex and dynamic field requires instructional materials that meet certain requirements.

For one thing, readings that we use must be up-to-date. The field has changed too rapidly to permit us to reuse old syllabuses. For another thing, readings must tackle, in ways that students can comprehend, the intricate interplay of all the biological and social forces that count in human development. To do this, the theoretical frameworks that are guiding current work in the field must inform the readings. Which brings us to why we put together the present advanced text.

In our view, there are a number of worthwhile basic textbooks for courses in child development. But to appreciate the field of child development in all its depth, students need more than a basic textbook. They need exposure to firsthand accounts of leading scientists who themselves are grappling with the most difficult, important, and exciting topics. Students need to hear the voices of these scientists as they discuss recent findings, explore new problems, use cutting-edge methods, and build new conceptual models. To really understand the field, students need access to the writings of those who are working at the boundaries of the field and inventing its future.

With the publication of the most recent edition of the *Handbook of Child Psychology,* we saw an opportunity to offer such access to students. In the present volume, we have brought together core readings from the *Handbook,* abridged and rewritten for advanced students. We believe our selections represent the range of major topics that define the field today, as understood by scholars who are creating much of the most influential work on those topics at the present time. In the pages of this volume, students encounter the full story of what is known and not known about child and adolescent development from many of the world's leading scholars. We are convinced that students will respond eagerly to these in-depth treatments of principal issues in child and adolescent development, and they deserve no less.

We believe also that students will share in the gratitude we have for the creativity and knowledge of the superb scientists who have contributed chapters to this book. We want to thank all the colleagues who have worked so hard to craft such useful and engaging chapters. It is their expertise that has made this book possible.

We are grateful as well to Jennifer Davison, managing editor at the Institute for Applied Research in Youth Development, and Lauren White, assistant editor at the Institute, for their expertise and impressive productivity in guiding the development of this work through all phases of the manuscript development and production processes. We appreciate as well the support of and the commitment to quality scholarship by our publisher, John Wiley & Sons, and, in particular, our editor, Patricia Rossi. Her enthusiasm for and expertise in publishing high-quality work in developmental science have been invaluable resources for us.

William Damon is grateful to the Thrive Foundation for Youth for its support of his scholarship during the period in which he worked on this book. Richard M. Lerner thanks both the National 4-H Council and the John Templeton Foundation for supporting his work during this period.

Finally, our work on the *Handbook of Child Psychology* and, in turn, on the present book was framed and inspired by our mentor, colleague, and friend—Paul H. Mussen. We dedicate this book to his memory.

WILLIAM DAMON
Stanford, California

RICHARD M. LERNER
Medford, Massachusetts

Contributors

John E. Bates
Department of Psychological and
    Brain Sciences
Bloomington, Indiana

Sheri A. Berenbaum
Department of Psychology
Pennsylvania State University
University Park, Pennsylvania

Julie C. Bowker
Department of Psychology
University at Buffalo
Buffalo, New York

William M. Bukowski
Department of Psychology
Concordia University
Montreal, Quebec

Raymond Buriel
Department of Psychology and
    Department of Chicano/a Latino/a Studies
Pomona College
Claremont, California

Joseph J. Campos
University of California, Berkeley
Berkeley, California

Linda A. Camras
Department of Psychology
DePaul University
Chicago, Illinois

Avshalom Caspi
Institute of Psychiatry
Kings College
London, England, and
Institute of Psychiatry
Duke University
Durham, North Carolina

John D. Coie
Department of Sociology and Health Science
Duke University
Durham, North Carolina

Michael Cole
Departments of Communication
    and Psychology
University of California
La Jolla, California

W. Andrew Collins
Institute of Child Development
University of Minnesota
Minneapolis, Minnesota

William Damon
Center on Adolescence
Stanford University
Stanford, California

Michelle de Haan
University of London
London, England

Kenneth A. Dodge
Duke University
Durham, North Carolina

Jacquelynne S. Eccles
Institute for Research on Women and Gender
University of Michigan
Ann Arbor, Michigan

Sam Franklin
Department of Human Development
Columbia University Teachers College
New York, New York

Susan A. Gelman
Department of Social Sciences
University of Michigan
Ann Arbor, Michigan

Susan Harter
Department of Psychology
University of Denver
Denver, Colorado

Charles W. Kalish
Waisman Center
University of Wisconsin-Madison
Madison, Wisconsin

Deanna Kuhn
Department of Human Development
Columbia University Teachers College
New York, New York

Richard M. Lerner
Institute for Applied Research in
    Youth Development
Tufts University
Medford, Massachusetts

Donald Lynam
Department of Psychological Sciences
Purdue University
West Lafayette, Indiana

Carol Lynn Martin
School of Social and Family Dynamics
Arizona State University
Tempe, Arizona

Charles A. Nelson III
Developmental Medicine Center
Harvard Medical School and
    Children's Hospital
Boston, Massachusetts

Ross D. Parke
Department of Psychology
University of California
Riverside, California

Jeffrey G. Parker
Department of Psychology
Pennsylvania State University
University Park, Pennsylvania

Robert W. Roeser
Institute for Applied Research in
    Youth Development
Tufts University
Medford, Massachusetts

Mary K. Rothbart
University of Oregon
Eugene, Oregon

Kenneth H. Rubin
Center for Children, Relationships,
    and Culture
University of Maryland
College Park, Maryland

Diane N. Ruble
Department of Psychology
New York University
New York, New York

Carolyn Saarni
Department of Counseling
Sonoma State University
Rohnert Park, California

Ulrich Schiefele
Department of Psychology
Universität Bielefeld
Bielefeld, Germany

Rebecca L. Shiner
Department of Psychology
Colgate University
Hamilton, New York

Margaret Beale Spencer
Department of Applied Psychology and
    Human Development
University of Pennsylvania
Philadelphia, Pennsylvania

Laurence Steinberg
Department of Psychology
Temple University
Philadelphia, Pennsylvania

Kathleen M. Thomas
Institute of Child Development
University of Minnesota
Minneapolis, Minnesota

Michael Tomasello
Max Planck Institute for
   Evolutionary Anthropology
Leipzig, Germany

Elliot Turiel
Graduate School of Education
University of California
Berkeley, California

Ellen Winner
Department of Psychology
Boston College
Chestnut Hill, Massachusetts

Allan Wigfield
Department of Human Development
University of Maryland
College Park, Maryland

David Witherington
Department of Psychology
University of New Mexico
Albuquerque, New Mexico

Part I

Introduction

Chapter 1

The Scientific Study of Child and Adolescent Development: Important Issues in the Field Today

WILLIAM DAMON and RICHARD M. LERNER

The purpose of this book is to offer students an advanced textbook that explores forefront issues in the study of child and adolescent development. The book's chapters are written as state-of-the-science reviews by leading scholars who themselves have been making groundbreaking contributions to the topics that they discuss. For this reason, the book is unique, both in the depth of its coverage and in the timeliness of the research that it presents. As a comprehensive collection of authored reviews, it conveys the field of child and adolescent development through the "primary source" of scientists who themselves are now shaping that field. The voices of the scientists add a lively energy to the important topics that they discuss.

The chapters in this book began as contributions to the most recent edition of the *Handbook of Child Psychology* (Damon & Lerner, 2006). For the purposes of the present text, we edited and abridged the chapters to make them maximally accessible to students wishing to master the current state of knowledge in this intricate and expanding field.

To create a text that would present a balanced representation of the field as a whole, we selected contributions that focused on the key processes and outcomes of child and adolescent development. Taken together, the book's 19 chapters cover development in the biological, cognitive, linguistic, social, cultural, moral, personality, emotional, and aesthetic domains. In addition, the chapters explore an extensive

The preparation of this chapter was supported in part by grants to Richard M. Lerner from the National 4-H Council and the John Templeton Foundation.

range of contemporary research topics, including the significance of diversity in development and the results of various social-policy and educational initiatives that attempt to foster gains in critical dimensions of youth development.

The core discipline represented by this text is psychology, but it would be inaccurate to claim that the text, or the field itself, stems purely from psychological science. Vital contributions have been made by other social and life-science disciplines such as anthropology, sociology, and biology, and by humanities disciplines such as history and philosophy. From its start, the study of child and adolescent development has been a multidisciplinary enterprise. The original 1933 edition of the *Handbook of Child Psychology,* despite the term "psychology" in its title, highlighted the work of biologists, physiologists, and educators, as well as a long chapter by the then-young anthropologist Margaret Mead. Today the boundaries of child study are expanding even further, pushed by recent advances in the cognitive and neurosciences as well as in social and cultural theory. The present text reflects the interplay of several disciplines that have taken an interest in the development of the child. It is a dynamic and productive interplay, yielding rich knowledge that no "bounded" discipline in isolation could achieve. Psychology, with its special focus on mind and self, is certainly at the center of this interplay, but virtually all the analytic frameworks in child and adolescent development have been enhanced by insights from other disciplines.

There are deep theoretical reasons why the study of children and adolescents—or for that matter, the investigation of individuals at any point across the life span—requires the integration of knowledge from multiple disciplines. Factors from all levels of human organization—biological factors; psychological and behavioral factors; social, cultural, ecological, and historical factors—all combine to influence the developmental course of every human life. As a consequence, understanding child and adolescent development requires more than a focus on psychological functioning. Such a focus is a necessary but not sufficient frame for describing, explaining, or optimizing the development of children and adolescents.

Scholars today approach the study of individuals across the life span within a framework that has been labeled "developmental science" (e.g., Magnusson & Stattin, 2006) because it involves the integrative use of the theoretical and methodological skills of scholars from the several disciplines that enable changes in all these levels to be understood. These disciplines include biology, neuroscience, psychology, sociology, anthropology, medicine, nursing, education, law, social work, engineering and computer science, economics, geography, ecology, the arts, and history. Scholars from these different fields focus on phenomena associated with the different levels of organizations noted previously—ranging from genes and neurons to social policy and culture. They work to understand the contributions to the development of people that are made by evolution; by the brain; by emotions, personality, cognition, motivation, and morality; by relations within the family or in peer groups and in the community; by the physical ecology; and by institutions of society, such as education, health care, business, and faith institutions.

These scholars do not see their contributions to the understanding of human development as isolated knowledge. To the contrary, in contemporary developmental science, the stress in both theory and research is on *relations* among variables within and across levels of organization (Overton, 2006). For instance, genes contribute to the development of mind and behavior but, at the same time, behavior and the broader ecology of human development influence the function and role in development of genes (Garcia Coll, Bearer, & Lerner, 2004; Gottlieb, Wahlsten, & Lickliter, 2006; Lewontin, 2000). Suomi (2004), for example, has found that variations in infant-mother and in peer group relations in rhesus monkeys accounts for whether specific genes are associated with aggression and poor social skills or with socially skilled and peaceful behaviors. Shiner and Caspi (Chapter 6, this volume) report that analogous interactions between genes and the social context have comparable outcomes in human development.

Accordingly, whether studying infancy, childhood, adolescence, or the adult and aging portions of the life span, the cutting edge of contemporary scholarship in human development is work attempting to integrate information from the several levels of organization involved in the ecology of human development (Bronfenbrenner & Morris, 2006). Such work aims to explain how mutually influential relations between individuals and their contexts provide the basis for behavior and development.

A primary goal of this book is to extract from the field of child and adolescent development the best scholarship currently available about how this individual-context relational process works. Each chapter addresses this relational process in its own way, with respect to the particular developmental phenomena that it examines.

Out of this dynamic relation between individual and context comes developmental change in all its glorious profusion: learning about the world and the self; acquiring skills, values, and knowledge; building biologic and neuronal capacities; gaining new powers of attention and memory; forming a unique personality; developing character; establishing emotional and behavioral regulation; learning how to communicate and collaborate with others; and a host of other achievements that lead to a fulfilled life. Parents, teachers, and other adults in all parts of the world value such developmental achievements in children, although they do not always know how to understand them, or how to foster them.

The story of change and progressive growth during the childhood and adolescent years is richly documented by the chapters in this text. The chapters in this text provide not only empirically driven descriptions of such change but also insightful explanations of the general course of change across the first 2 decades of life. In addition, many of the authors suggest ways in which theory and research may be applied to optimize the chances for positive, healthy development among children and adolescents. Not only is application of great interest scientifically, it is also of great interest personally to the families and communities that seek to nurture young people.

This text covers a diverse array of particular topics in childhood and adolescence. Within this diversity of topics, there are common themes that cut across the chapters and the field itself. Students seeking to understand the field may find it helpful to attend to, and master, each of the following key concepts as they appear in this text.

Developmental Systems Theory

The fundamental theme within contemporary developmental science involves a focus on *developmental systems theories*. These theories help scientists understand mutually influential (i.e., bidirectional, reciprocal, or fused; e.g., Thelen & Smith, 2006; Tobach & Greenberg, 1984) relations among variables from the multiple levels of organization involved in human development. To appreciate the use of developmental systems theories, it is useful to pose two questions that such models help address:

1. Why should developmental science focus on variables associated with, for instance, biology, psychology, culture, and history, to study children and adolescents?
2. Why should developmental science study the mutually influential relations among variables across these levels?

Quite specific answers to these questions, ones that are pertinent to numerous areas of development—emotions, personality, cognition, motivation, morality, or social relations within the family or with peers, to name a few instances—are found across this book. As a general way of answering these questions, however, we may note that over the course of its evolution as a field of scholarship, developmental science has found that approaches to development that pertain to one discipline or level of analysis, be it biology, psychology, or culture, are not adequate to explain the diverse ways in which human development occurs (Cairns & Cairns, 2006). Accordingly, across the past 30 years, approaches to development that seek to account for development by studying how variables from any one level of organization affect and are affected by variables from other levels have become of increasing interest and relevance to developmental science (Brandtstädter, 2006; Bronfenbrenner & Morris, 2006; Gottlieb et al., 2006; Magnusson & Stattin, 2006). Such approaches have been termed *developmental systems models* (Ford & Lerner, 1992; Gottlieb et al., 2006; Lerner, 2006).

These models, and the several concepts defining or derived from them, constitute a superordinate framework for all the work presented in this book. Table 1.1 presents the defining features of developmental systems theories. Inspection of this table will prepare the reader to appreciate how developmental systems theories frame all the other key themes of contemporary developmental science.

For instance, we may note that among the interrelated features of contemporary developmental systems theories are concepts such as relationism, the integration of levels of organization, historical embeddedness and temporality, relative plasticity, and diversity. These concepts are associated with additional concepts, such as reciprocal interaction, bidirectionality, plasticity, and biobehavioral organization. As explained in Table 1.1, these concepts lead to themes ranging from the importance of context for understanding human development through the ability to be optimistic that the application of developmental science may result in the promotion of positive development for diverse children and adolescents. To appreciate the import of development systems models for these other defining themes of contemporary developmental science, it is useful to discuss each of the other themes found in the chapters of this book.

Context of Human Development

Developmental science, when framed by developmental systems theories, does not just focus on the individual alone as a target of analysis to explain his or her development. Instead, developmental systems theories point to the fact that it is essential to consider the physical and social ecology within which human development occurs (Bronfenbrenner & Morris, 2006; Elder & Shanahan, 2006). As a consequence, interest in developmental systems ideas has made the role of *context* in human development a pervasive concern in the contemporary study of child and adolescent development.

All chapters in this book reflect this concern. For instance, variables at both the inner-biological and the social-cultural levels of organization provide proximal and distal contexts, respectively, of cognitive development (see Chapter 2 by Nelson, Thomas, & de Haan) and of personality development (see Chapter 3 by Rothbart & Bates and Chapter 6 by Shiner & Caspi). Similarly, characteristics of the psychological functioning of the child or adolescent is moderated by the family (see Chapter 4 by Parke & Buriel), by the peer group (see Chapter 5 by Rubin, Bukowski, Parker, &

TABLE 1.1   Defining Features of Developmental Systems Theories

A Relational Metamodel

Predicated on a postmodern philosophical perspective that transcends Cartesian dualism, developmental systems theories are framed by a relational metamodel for human development. There is, then, a rejection of all splits between components of the ecology of human development (e.g., between nature- and nurture-based variables, between continuity and discontinuity, or between stability and instability). Systemic syntheses or integrations replace dichotomizations or other reductionist partitions of the developmental system.

The Integration of Levels of Organization

Relational thinking and the rejection of Cartesian splits are associated with the idea that all levels of organization within the ecology of human development are integrated or fused. These levels range from the biological and physiological through the cultural and historical.

Developmental Regulation across Ontogeny Involves Mutually Influential
Individual ← → Context Relations

As a consequence of the integration of levels, the regulation of development occurs through mutually influential connections among all levels of the developmental system, ranging from genes and cell physiology through individual mental and behavioral functioning to society, culture, the designed and natural ecology, and ultimately, history. These mutually influential relations may be represented generically as Level 1 ← → Level 2 (e.g., Family ← → Community) and, in the case of ontogeny, may be represented as individual ← → context.

Integrated Actions, Individual ← → Context Relations, Are the Basic Unit of
Analysis within Human Development

The character of developmental regulation means that the integration of actions—of the individual on the context and of the multiple levels of the context on the individual (individual ← → context)—constitute the fundamental unit of analysis in the study of the basic process of human development.

Temporality and Plasticity in Human Development

As a consequence of the fusion of the historical level of analysis—and therefore temporality—within the levels of organization comprising the ecology of human development, the developmental system is characterized by the potential for systematic change, by plasticity. Observed trajectories of intra-individual change may vary across time and place as a consequence of such plasticity.

Plasticity Is Relative

Developmental regulation may both facilitate and constrain opportunities for change. Thus, change in individual ← → context relations is not limitless, and the magnitude of plasticity (the probability of change in a developmental trajectory occurring in relation to variation in contextual conditions) may vary across the life span and history. Nevertheless, the potential for plasticity at both individual and contextual levels constitutes a fundamental strength of all humans' development.

Intra-Individual Change, Interindividual Differences in Intra-Individual Change,
and the Fundamental Substantive Significance of Diversity

The combinations of variables across the integrated levels of organization within the developmental system that provide the basis of the developmental process will vary at least in part across individuals and groups. This diversity is systematic and lawfully produced by idiographic, group differential, and generic (nomothetic) phenomena. The range of interindividual differences in intra-individual change observed at any point in time is evidence of the plasticity of the developmental system and makes the study of diversity of fundamental substantive significance for the description, explanation, and optimization of human development.

(continued)

7

TABLE 1.1   *(Continued)*

Optimism, the Application of Developmental Science, and the Promotion of Positive Human Development
The potential for and instantiations of plasticity legitimate an optimistic and proactive search for characteristics of individuals and of their ecologies that, together, can be arrayed to promote positive human development across life. Through the application of developmental science in planned attempts (i.e., interventions) to enhance (e.g., through social policies or community-based programs) the character of humans' developmental trajectories, the promotion of positive human development may be achieved by aligning the strengths (operationalized as the potentials for positive change) of individuals and contexts.

Multidisciplinarity and the Need for Change-Sensitive Methodologies
The integrated levels of organization comprising the developmental system require collaborative analyses by scholars from multiple disciplines. Multidisciplinary knowledge and, ideally, interdisciplinary knowledge is sought. The temporal embeddedness and resulting plasticity of the developmental system requires that research designs, methods of observation, and measurement, and procedures for data analysis be change sensitive and able to integrate trajectories of change at multiple levels of analysis.

Bowker; and Chapter 16 by Collins & Steinberg), by the school (see Chapter 12 by Wigfield, Eccles, Roeser, & Schiefele), and by culture (see the Chapter 17 by Cole and Chapter 19 by Spencer).

Diversity

Because of the inevitable complexity of the combinations of individual and contextual variables that provide a basis of human development, the authors of the chapters in this book make clear that individual differences—*diversity*—constitute a fundamental, substantive feature of all human development. Indeed, estimates are that there are over 70 trillion potential human genotypes, and each of them may be coupled across life with an even larger number of physical and social contexts and interpersonal relationships and experiences (Hirsch, 2004). Therefore, the diversity of development is assured because of each person's singular history of individual-context relations. This history makes each person's trajectory of change across the life course unique and, indeed, as people age they become more different from each other (i.e., there is an increase in interindividual differences in intra-individual change; Baltes, Lindenberger, & Staudinger, 2006). Therefore, diversity becomes a fundamental substantive focus for developmental science.

Although, as noted, all chapters in this book focus on diversity—on both intra-individual change (which is the within-person instance of diversity) and on interindividual differences in intra-individual change (which is the between-person instance of diversity), several chapters in this book (Chapter 17 by Cole; Chapter 18 by Berenbaum, Martin, & Ruble; and Chapter 19 by Spencer) are focused specifically on the substantive importance of diversity in elucidating what is normative in regard to the structure and/or function of developmental change in children and adolescents.

Multidisciplinarity

Clearly, then, the approach to development found across the chapters in this volume involves an appraisal of how relations between diverse individuals and similarly diverse and changing proximal and distal contexts of the ecology of human development

(Bronfenbrenner & Morris, 2006) interrelate across life to constitute the basic process of development. What is also clear from this approach is that in order to either describe or explain the course of these changes, knowledge of the contributions made by variables from different levels of organization need to be integrated.

For example, the structure and function of genes, hormones, and neurons at the physiological level of organization need to be understood in relation to the structure and function of both the psychological level of organization (and, for instance, of cognitive, emotional, and motivational) and the social level of organization (involving, for example, family and peer relationships, and interactions with community organizations and cultural institutions). Chapter 2 in this book by Nelson, Thomas, and de Haan; Chapter 6 by Shiner and Caspi; Chapter 8 by Tomasello; and Chapter 17 by Cole illustrate this multidisciplinarity (see, too, Baltes et al., 2006; Elder & Shanahan, 2006; Gottlieb et al., 2006; Overton, 2006). In short, the theoretical and empirical scholarship in this book documents the importance of *a multidisciplinary approach* to studying children and adolescents.

Focus on Biological Development and Neuroscience

Across this book, there exist several specific substantive illustrations of the integration of multiple disciplines. A key case in point captures recently emerging interests within developmental science on brain-behavior relations and, as well, on a more general, dynamic approach to biology and physiological function. These emphases are illustrated by the chapters in the "Biological Foundations" section of the book (see Chapter 3 by Rothbart and Bates and Chapter 2 by Nelson, Thomas, & de Haan) and, as well, in other chapters (e.g., Chapter 6 by Shiner & Caspi). Stress is placed on understanding either cognitive development or behavioral individuality (temperament, personality) by understanding changes across childhood and adolescence in *biological development* (as compared to attempting to explain development by reference to the static possession of genes) and by a systems approach within the study of *developmental neuroscience.*

The importance of a developmental approach to biology and neuroscience cannot be overestimated. In prior historical eras within the study of human development, many scientists seeking to incorporate the contributions of biological level variables (e.g., genes, neurons) into the explanation of child and adolescent development sought to reduce the complexity of such development to what were regarded as either nonchanging features of genetic inheritance (i.e., genotypes; see for instance Plomin, 1986, 2000; Rowe, 1994) or to characteristics of physiological functioning (neural structure) that were construed as "hard wired" (e.g., see Edelman, 1987, 1988 for reviews). These approaches were actually antithetical to a developmental approach to the study of development (e.g., see Gottlieb, 1998, 2004; T. C. Schneirla, 1956, 1957; Tobach & Schneirla, 1968): They reduced development to characteristics of the individual that were seen to be fixed and unchanging. Simply, they sought to explain development by reference to characteristics that did not develop. However, as illustrated by chapters in this book, such nondevelopmental approaches have been superseded by theory and research that sees biological variables as products and producers of changes in variables at all other levels of the developmental system (e.g., see Gottlieb et al., 2006; Overton, 2006).

Accordingly, as illustrated by the chapters throughout this book, multidisciplinarity does not mean the addition of a biogenic view of the child with a psychogenic or a sociogenic view (Elder & Shanahan, 2006). Instead, developmental scientists work across levels to understand how both individual and contextual variables may combine to promote the development of, for instance, specific features of development, such as emotions (see Chapter 10 by Saarni, Campos, Camras, & Witherington), motivation (see Chapter 12 by Wigfield, Eccles, Roeser, & Schiefele), language (see Chapter 8 by Tomasello), concept development (see Chapter 9 by Gelman & Kalish), artistic development (see Chapter 10 by Winner), morality or problem behaviors (see Chapter 13 by Dodge, Coie, & Lynam and Chapter 14 by Turiel), or the self, personality, or gender characteristics (see Chapter 7 by Harter; Chapter 6 by Shiner & Caspi; and Chapter 18 by Berenbaum, Martin, & Ruble).

In addition, reliance on the contributions of variables from multiple levels of organization (and hence on the province of different disciplines) occurs when developmental scientists seek to elucidate development within a specific portion of the life span. This approach is illustrated in this book by the chapters on adolescent cognitive development (Chapter 15 by Kuhn & Franklin) and adolescent social development (Chapter 16 by Collins & Steinberg).

Diverse and Innovative Methodologies

How does such integrative developmental analysis happen? Certainly, theory must provide a frame for any useful empirical work undertaken to understand child and adolescent development. However, theory must be coupled with empirically useful methods. Given that developmental scientists are drawing from ideas across levels of organization, we see illustrated in this book the need for and the use of *diverse methodologies* across these different fields.

These tools often represent innovations in design, sampling, measurement, and data analysis. For instance, designs within contemporary developmental science are increasingly multimethod in character, seeking to triangulate information across time by combining both quantitative and qualitative methods of assessment. Neuroscience measurement, for instance, using brain functional magnetic imaging (fMRI) techniques may be combined with written or verbal assessment of cognitive or emotional functioning (see Chapter 2 by Nelson, Thomas, & de Haan). Similarly, qualitative, ethnographic understanding of the cultural values of diverse youth may be linked to quantitative measure of individual cognitive development (see Chapter 17 by Cole) or of identity and adjustment (see Chapter 19 by Spencer).

Moreover, while the study of change always requires longitudinal assessments, such designs have become increasing complex in developmental science. They may involve sequential strategies or time series analyses (e.g., Baltes, Reese, & Nesselroade, 1977) or, borrowing from multiple disciplines, cohort analyses, panel studies, program evaluation, or dynamic systems analysis (e.g., Teti, 2005; Thelen & Smith, 2006).

In addition, the data analysis techniques used to appraise dynamic, individual-context relations across time have also grown more complex. Quantitative techniques, such as structural equation modeling, hierarchical linear modeling, and pattern-centered analyses (that combine person-centered and variable-centered approaches) have been forwarded (e.g., see Card & Little, 2007; Duncan, Magnuson, & Ludwig, 2004; Laub & Sampson, 2004; Lerner, 2004; Little, Bovaird, & Card, 2007; McArdle & Nesselroade, 2003; Nesselroade & Ram, 2004; von Eye, 1990b; von Eye & Schuster, 2000; Willett, 2004). In turn, approaches that capitalize on new computer-based programs for understanding the substance and categorical characteristics or configurations of qualitative data (e.g., Atlas-ti or configural frequency analysis) have emerged in recent years to become effective tools for developmental scientists (e.g., Mishler, 2004; von Eye, 1990a). This qualitative research is especially useful as a means to identify the nature of an understudied phenomenon (e.g., as a sample case, see Damon, Menon, & Bronk, 2003, and Mariano & Damon, in press, in regard to the study of "noble purpose" in adolescents) and/or in triangulating quantitative appraisals of human development.

Application

Across the breadth of the chapters in this book it is clear that developmental science has come to value work that moves beyond description and explanation and toward attempts to optimize the course of life of diverse children and adolescents. As illustrated richly throughout this book, in the contemporary instantiation of developmental science, *application* is as important a goal of scholarship as is elucidation of basic features of developmental change.

Developmental science is aimed often then on proving its worth not only in the halls of academe but, as well, in the arena of public policy and in neighborhoods and communities nationally and internationally. Schools, youth-serving organizations, faith institutions, mental health clinics, foundations, industry, or government offices are places where developmental scientists are, today, likely to be found in large numbers.

Positive Child and Adolescent Development

In fact, whether working in laboratories on their campus, or in community-based organizations, educational settings, after-school programs, business, or government, there is considerable and growing commonality among developmental scientists in directing their work to enhancing the opportunities for health and successful development among diverse children and adolescents. Indeed, as illustrated in several chapters in this book (e.g., see Chapter 19 by Spencer, Chapter 14 by Turiel, and Chapter 10 by Winner), the promotion of *positive child and adolescent development* is of fundamental concern (Benson, Scales, Hamilton, & Sesma, 2006; Damon, 2004; Lerner, 2005).

Indeed, interest in the promotion of positive development may arise when work is focused on the study of basic issues in the description or explanation of a particular feature of development (e.g., the acquisition of linguistic constructions, as in Chapter 8 by Tomasello; the neural centers for specific cognitive functions, as in Chapter 2 by Nelson, Thomas, & de Haan, or the fundamental facets of musical understanding, as in Chapter 10 by Winner). In turn, interest in promoting positive development may obviously also occur in relation to highly applied concerns, such as bringing the "voice" of the community to bear on the planning of programs to enhance literacy among children and parents from immigrant families. Nevertheless, across the settings within which they work, developmental scientists are increasingly oriented to using their scholarship to inform policymakers, funders, and practitioners about ways to apply developmental science to enhance the probability that all youth will develop in positive ways.

In sum, reflecting the breadth and richness of contemporary developmental science, the chapters in this book elucidate eight key themes. Table 1.2 lists these themes. We

TABLE 1.2   Key Substantive Themes in Contemporary Developmental Science

1. Focus on developmental systems theories
2. Role of context in human development
3. Individual differences—diversity
4. Importance of a multidisciplinary approach
5. Study of biological development and of developmental neuroscience
6. Diverse methodologies
7. Application of developmental science
8. Promotion of positive child and adolescent development

believe that these themes all derive from and reflect the integrative ideas of the developmental systems models that, today, constitute the cutting edge of theory, research, and application in developmental science (e.g., see Cairns & Cairns, 2006; Damon, 2006; Lerner, 2006; Overton, 2006; Valsiner, 2006). In addition, together, these themes reflect the idea that all facets of the "job description" of developmental scientists—the description, explanation, and optimization of behavior and development—are today valued and essential components of the study of children and adolescents.

Conclusions

Contemporary developmental science—predicated on a relational model and focused on the use of developmental systems theories to frame research and application on dynamic relations between diverse individuals and contexts—constitutes an approach to understanding and promoting positive human development that is both complex and exciting. The approach, at the heart of the chapters in this book, also offers a productive means to do good science. Such work is informed by philosophically, conceptually, and methodologically useful information from the multiple disciplines having knowledge bases pertinent to the integrated, individual-context relations comprising the ecology of human development.

Indeed, and as illustrated eloquently by the work discussed across the chapters in this volume, the value of the science and the applications that constitute the contemporary study of children and adolescents are reasons for the growing interest in developmental science. The scholarship presented in this book shows the many ways in which children and adolescents, in dynamic exchanges with both natural and designed ecologies, can learn to thrive. In addition, the work discussed in this book documents how children and adolescents may themselves create opportunities for their own positive development. As Bronfenbrenner (2005) eloquently put it, it is these kinds of mutually beneficial relations among people and the world that make human beings fully human.

Scientific findings such as those presented in this text are needed to provide an understanding of how young people can learn to thrive in this world. The importance of sound scientific understanding has become especially clear in recent years, when news media broadcast story after story based on simplistic and biased popular speculations about the causes of human development. The careful and responsible discourse found in the chapters of this text contrasts sharply with most popular news stories about the role of parents, genes, or schools in children's growth and behavior. Students who read this text will have a sounder source of information about these vitally important issues. They will find in the chapters of this book the most solid, insightful and current set of scientific theories and findings available today in the field of child and adolescent development.

References

Baltes, P. B., Lindenberger, U., & Staudinger, U. M. (2006). Lifespan theory in developmental psychology. In W. Damon & R. M. Lerner (Series Eds.) & R. M. Lerner (Vol. Ed.), *Handbook of child psychology: Vol. 1. Theoretical models of human development* (6th ed., pp. 569–664). Hoboken, NJ: Wiley.

Baltes, P. B., Reese, H. W., & Nesselroade, J. R. (1977). *Life-span developmental psychology: Introduction to research methods.* Monterey, CA: Brooks/Cole.

Benson, P. L., Scales, P. C., Hamilton, S. F., & Semsa, A., Jr. (2006). Positive youth development: Theory, research, and applications. In W. Damon & R. M. Lerner (Series Eds.) & R. M. Lerner (Vol. Ed.), *Handbook of child psychology: Vol. 1. Theoretical models of human development* (6th ed., pp. 894–941). Hoboken, NJ: Wiley.

Brandtstädter, J. (2006). Action perspectives on human development. In W. Damon & R. M. Lerner (Series Eds.) & R. M. Lerner (Vol. Ed.), *Handbook of child psychology: Vol. 1. Theoretical models of human development* (6th ed., pp. 516–568). Hoboken, NJ: Wiley.

Bronfenbrenner, U. (2005). *Making human beings human.* Thousand Oaks, CA: Sage.

Bronfenbrenner, U., & Morris, P. A. (2006). The bioecological model of human development. In W. Damon & R. M. Lerner (Series Eds.) & R. M. Lerner (Vol. Ed.), *Handbook of child psychology: Vol. 1. Theoretical models of human development* (6th ed., pp. 793–828). Hoboken, NJ: Wiley.

Cairns, R. B., & Cairns, B. D. (2006). The making of developmental psychology. In W. Damon & R. M. Lerner (Series Eds.) & R. M. Lerner (Vol. Ed.), *Handbook of child psychology: Vol. 1. Theoretical models of human development* (6th ed., pp. 89–165). Hoboken, NJ: Wiley.

Card, N. A., & Little, T. D. (2007). Longitudinal modeling of developmental processes. *International Journal of Behavioral Development, 31*(4), 297–302.

Damon, W. (2004). What is positive youth development? *Annals of the American Academy of Political and Social Science, 591,* 13–24.

Damon, W. (2006). Preface. In W. Damon & R. M. Lerner (Eds.), *Handbook of child psychology* (6th ed., pp. xi–xix). Hoboken, NJ: Wiley.

Damon, W., & Lerner, R. M. (2006). *Handbook of child psychology* (6th ed., Vols. 1–4). Hoboken, NJ: Wiley.

Damon, W., Menon, J., & Bronk, K. C. (2003). The development of purpose during adolescence. *Applied Developmental Sciences, 7*(3), 119–128.

Duncan, G. J., Magnuson, K., & Ludwig, J. (2004). The endogeneity problem in developmental studies. *Research in Human Development, 1*(1/2), 59–80.

Edelman, G. M. (1987). *Neural Darwinism: The theory of neuronal group selection.* New York: Basic Books.

Edelman, G. M. (1988). *Topobiology: An introduction to molecular biology.* New York: Basic Books.

Elder, G. H., Jr., & Shanahan, M. J. (2006). The life course and human development. In W. Damon & R. M. Lerner (Series Eds.) & R. M. Lerner (Vol. Ed.), *Handbook of child psychology: Vol. 1. Theoretical models of human development* (6th ed., pp. 665–715). Hoboken, NJ: Wiley.

Ford, D. H., & Lerner, R. M. (1992). *Developmental systems theory: An integrative approach.* Newbury Park, CA: Sage.

Garcia Coll, C., Bearer, E., & Lerner, R. M. (Eds.). (2004). *Nature and nurture: The complex interplay of genetic and environmental influences on human behavior and development.* Mahwah, NJ: Erlbaum.

Gottlieb, G. (1998). Normally occurring environmental and behavioral influences on gene activity: From central dogma to probabilistic epigenesis. *Psychological Review, 105,* 792–802.

Gottlieb, G. (2004). Normally occurring environmental and behavioral influences on gene activity: From central dogma to probabilistic epigenesis. In C. Garcia Coll, E. L. Bearer, & R. M. Lerner (Eds.), *Nature and nurture: The complex interplay of genetic and environmental influences on human development and behavior* (pp. 85–106). Mahwah, NJ: Erlbaum.

Gottlieb, G., Wahlsten, D., & Lickliter, R. (2006). The significance of biology for human development: A developmental psychobiological systems perspective. In W. Damon & R. M. Lerner (Series Eds.) & R. M. Lerner (Vol. Ed.), *Handbook of child psychology: Vol. 1. Theoretical models of human development* (6th ed., pp. 210–257). Hoboken, NJ: Wiley.

Hirsch, J. (2004). Uniqueness, diversity, similarity, repeatability, and heritability. In C. Garcia Coll, E. Bearer, & R. M. Lerner (Eds.), *Nature and nurture: The complex interplay of genetic and environmental influences on human behavior and development* (pp. 127–138). Mahwah, NJ: Erlbaum.

Laub, J. H., & Sampson, R. J. (2004). Strategies for bridging the quantitative and qualitative divide: Studying crime over the life course. *Research in Human Development, 1*(1/2), 81–99.

Lerner, R. M. (2004). Innovative methods for studying lives in context: A view of the issues. *Research in Human Development, 1*(1/2), 5–7.

Lerner, R. M. (2005, September). *Promoting positive youth development: Theoretical and empirical bases.* Paper presented at the Workshop on the Science of Adolescent Health and Development, National Research Council/Institute of Medicine, Washington, DC.

Lerner, R. M. (2006). Developmental science, developmental systems, and contemporary theories of human development. In W. Damon & R. M. Lerner (Series Eds.) & R. M. Lerner (Vol. Ed.), *Handbook of child psychology: Vol. 1. Theoretical models of human development* (6th ed., pp. 1–17). Hoboken, NJ: Wiley.

Lewontin, R. C. (2000). *The triple helix: Gene, organism and environment.* Cambridge, MA: Harvard University Press.

Little, T. D., Bovaird, J. A., & Card, N. A. (Eds.). (2007). *Modeling contextual effects in longitudinal studies.* Mahwah, NJ: Erlbaum.

Magnusson, D., & Stattin, H. (2006). The person in the environment: Towards a general model for scientific inquiry. In W. Damon & R. M. Lerner (Series Eds.) & R. M. Lerner (Vol. Ed.), *Handbook of child psychology: Vol. 1. Theoretical models of human development* (6th ed., pp. 400–464). Hoboken, NJ: Wiley.

Mariano, J. M., & Damon, W. (in press). The role of spirituality and religious faith in supporting purpose in adolescence. In R. M. Lerner, R. W. Roeser, & E. Phelps (Eds.), *Positive youth development and spirituality: From theory to research.* Philadelphia: Templeton Foundation Press.

McArdle, J. J., & Nesselroade, J. R. (2003). Growth curve analysis in contemporary psychological research. In J. Shinka & W. Velicer (Eds.), *Research methods in psychology: Vol. 2. Comprehensive handbook of psychology* (pp. 447–480). Hoboken, NJ: Wiley.

Mishler, E. G. (2004). Historians of the self: Restorying lives, revising identities. *Research in Human Development, 1*(1/2), 101–121.

Nesselroade, J. R., & Ram, N. (2004). Studying intra-individual variability: What we have learned that will help us understand lives in context. *Research in Human Development, 1*, 9–29.

Overton, W. F. (2006). Developmental psychology: Philosophy, concepts, methodology. In W. Damon & R. M. Lerner (Series Eds.) & R. M. Lerner (Vol. Ed.), *Handbook of child psychology: Vol. 1. Theoretical models of human development* (6th ed., pp. 18–88). Hoboken, NJ: Wiley.

Plomin, R. (1986). *Development, genetics, and psychology.* Hillsdale, NJ: Erlbaum.

Plomin, R. (2000). Behavioural genetics in the 21st century. *International Journal of Behavioral Development, 24,* 30–34.

Rowe, D. C. (1994). *The limits of family influence: Genes, experience, and behavior.* New York: Guilford Press.

Schneirla, T. C. (1956). Interrelationships of the innate and the acquired in instictive behavior. In P. P. Grassé (Ed.), *L'instinct dans le comportement des animaux et de l'homme* (pp. 387–452). Paris, France: Mason et Cie.

Schneirla, T. C. (1957). The concept of development in comparative psychology. In D. B. Harris (Ed.), *The concept of development* (pp. 78–108). Minneapolis: University of Minnesota.

Suomi, S. (2004). How gene-environment interactions shape biobehavioral development: Lessons from studies with rhesus monkeys. *Research in Human Development, 1*(3), 205–222.

Teti, D. M. (Ed.). (2005). *Handbook of research methods in developmental science.* Cambridge, MA: Blackwell.

Thelen, E., & Smith, L. B. (2006). Dynamic systems theories. In W. Damon & R. M. Lerner (Series Eds.) & R. M. Lerner (Vol. Ed.), *Handbook of child psychology: Vol. 1. Theoretical models of human development* (6th ed., pp. 258–312). Hoboken, NJ: Wiley.

Tobach, E., & Greenberg, G. (1984). The significance of T. C. Schneirla's contribution to the concept of levels of integration. In G. Greenberg & E. Tobach (Eds.), *Behavioral evolution and integrative levels* (pp. 1–7). Hillsdale, NJ: Erlbaum.

Tobach, E., & Schneirla, T. C. (1968). The biopsychology of social behavior of animals. In R. E. Cooke & S. Levin (Eds.), *Biologic basis of pediatric practice* (pp. 68–82). New York: McGraw-Hill.

Valsiner, J. (2006). Developmental epistemology and implications for methodology. In W. Damon & R. M. Lerner (Series Eds.) & R. M. Lerner (Vol. Ed.), *Handbook of child psychology: Vol. 1. Theoretical models of human development* (6th ed., pp. 166–209). Hoboken, NJ: Wiley.

von Eye, A. (1990a). *Introduction to configural frequency analysis: The search for types and anitypes in cross-classifications.* Cambridge: Cambridge University Press.

von Eye, A. (1990b). *Statistical methods in longitudinal research: Principles and structuring change.* New York: Academic Press.

von Eye, A., & Schuster, C. (2000). The road to freedom: Quantitative developmental methodology in the third millennium. *International Journal of Behavioral Development, 24,* 35–43.

Willett, J. B. (2004). Investigating individual change and development: The multilevel model for change and the method of latent growth modeling. *Research in Human Development, 1*(1/2), 31–57.

PART II

BIOLOGICAL
FOUNDATIONS

Chapter 2

Neural Bases of Cognitive Development

Charles A. Nelson III, Kathleen M. Thomas, and Michelle de Haan

This chapter reviews what is known about the neural bases of cognitive development. We begin by discussing why developmental psychologists might be interested in the neural bases of behavior (with particular reference to cognitive development). Having established the value of viewing child development through the lens of the developmental neurosciences, we provide an overview of brain development. We then turn our attention to specific content areas, limiting ourselves to domains in which there is a corpus of knowledge about the neural underpinnings of cognitive development. We discuss learning and memory, face/object recognition, attention/executive functions, and spatial cognition, including illustrative examples from both typical and atypical development. We conclude the chapter with a discussion of the future of developmental cognitive neuroscience.

Why Developmental Psychologists Should Be Interested in Neuroscience

Prior to the ascendancy of Piagetian theory, the field of cognitive development was dominated by behaviorism (for discussion, see Goldman-Rakic, 1987; Nelson & Bloom, 1997). As students of the history of psychology are well aware, behaviorism eschewed the nonobservable; therefore, the study of the neural bases of behavior was not pursued for the simple reason that neural processes could not be observed. Through the 1950s and 1960s, Piagetian theory gradually came to replace behaviorism as the dominant theory of cognitive development. Despite being a biologist by training, Piaget, and subsequently his followers, primarily concerned themselves with developing a richly detailed cognitive architecture of the mind—albeit a brainless mind. We do not mean this in a pejorative sense, but rather, to imply that the zeitgeist of the time was to develop elegant models of cognitive structures, with little regard for (a) whether such structures were biologically plausible or (b) the neurobiological underpinnings of such structures. (At that time, there was no way to observe the living brain directly.) Throughout the late 1970s and into the last decade of the twentieth century, neo- and non-Piagetian approaches came into favor. Curiously, a prominent theme of a number of investigators writing during this time was that of nativism; we say curiously because inherent in nativism is the notion of biological determinism, yet those touting a nativist perspective rarely if ever grounded their models and data in biological reality. It was not until the mid-1990s that neurobiology began to be inserted into a discussion of cognitive development, as reflected in Mark Johnson's eloquent contribution to the *Handbook of Child Psychology's* fifth edition (Johnson, 1998). This perspective has become more commonplace, although the field of developmental cognitive neuroscience is still in its infancy. (For overviews of this field generally, see de Haan & Johnson, 2003a; Nelson & Luciana, 2001.) Moreover, we have observed that it is still not clear to many developmental psychologists why they should be interested in the brain. This is the topic to which we next direct our attention.

Our major argument in this regard is that our understanding of cognitive development will improve as the mechanisms that underlie development are elucidated. This, in turn, should permit us to move beyond the descriptive, black-box level to the level at which the actual cellular, physiologic, and eventually, genetic machinery will be understood—the mechanisms that underlie development.

A number of distinguished cognitive developmentalists and cognitive theorists have proposed or at least implied that elements of number concept (Wynn, 1992; Wynn, Bloom, & Chiang, 2002), object permanence (Baillargeon, 1987; Baillargeon, Spelke, & Wasserman, 1985; Spelke, 2000), and perhaps face recognition (Farah, Rabinowitz, Quinn, & Liu, 2000) reflect what we refer to as experience-independent functions; that is, they reflect inborn traits (presumably coded in the genome) that do not require experience to emerge. We see several problems with this perspective. First, these arguments seem biologically implausible because they represent sophisticated cognitive abilities; if they were coded in the genome, they would surely be polygenic traits and would not reflect the action of a single gene. Given that we now know the human genome consists of approximately 30,000 to 40,000 genes, it seems highly unlikely that we could spare the genes to separately code for number concept, object permanence, or face recognition. After all, those 40,000 genes must be involved in myriad other events (e.g., the general operation of the body as a whole) far more important than subserving these aspects of cognitive development.

A second concern about this nativist perspective is that it is not developmental. To say something is innate essentially closes the door to any discussion of mechanism. More problematic is that genes do not cause behaviors; rather, genes express proteins that in turn work their magic through the brain. It seems unlikely that behaviors that are not absolutely essential to survival (of the species, not the individual) have been directly coded in the genome, given the limited number of genes that are known to exist. Far more likely is that these behaviors are subserved by discrete or distributed neural circuits in the brain. And, these circuits, in turn, most likely vary in the extent to which they depend on experience or activity for their subsequent elaboration.

We make three general points:

1. The "value added" of thinking about behavior in the context of neurobiology is that doing so provides biological plausibility to our models of behavior (to be discussed further later).

2. Viewing behavioral development through the lens of neuroscience may shed light on the mechanism(s) underlying behavior and behavioral development, thereby moving us beyond the descriptive level to the process level.

3. When we insert the molecular biology of brain development into the equation, a more holistic view of the child becomes possible—genes, brain, and behavior. This, in turn, permits us to move beyond simplistic notions of gene-environment interactions to talk about the influence of specific experiences on specific neural circuits, which in turn influence the expression of particular genes, which influence how the brain functions and how the child behaves.

Brain Development

The construction and development of the human brain occurs over a very protracted period beginning shortly after conception and, depending on how we view the end of development, continuing through at least the end of adolescence.

Shortly after conception, embryonic tissue forms from the two-celled zygote (specifically, from the blastocyst, the ball of cells created through multiplying cells). The outer layer of the embryo gives rise to, among other things, the central (brain and spinal cord) and peripheral nervous systems. It is this outermost layer we will be concerned with in this chapter.

NEURAL INDUCTION AND NEURULATION

The process of transforming the undifferentiated tissue lining the dorsal side of the ectoderm into nervous system tissue is referred to as neural induction. In contrast, the dual processes called primary and secondary neurulation refer to the further differentiation of this neural tissue into, respectively, the brain and the spinal cord (for a review of neural induction and neurulation, see Lumsden & Kintner, 2003).

The thin layer of undifferentiated tissue that lines the ectoderm is gradually transformed into an increasingly thick layer of tissue that will become the neural plate. A class of chemical agents referred to as *transforming growth factors* is responsible for the subsequent transformation of this undifferentiated tissue into nervous system tissue (Murloz-Sanjuan & Brivanfou, 2002). What one observes morphologically is the shift from neural plate to neural tube. Specifically, the neural plate buckles, forming a crease down its longitudinal axis. The tissue then folds inward, the edges rise up, and a tube is formed. This process begins on approximately day 22 of gestation (Keith, 1948), fusing first at the midsection and progressing outward in either direction until approximately day 26 (Sidman & Rakic, 1982). The rostral portion of the tube eventually forms the brain, and the caudal portion develops into the spinal cord.

Cells trapped inside the tube typically go on to comprise the central nervous system (CNS); however, there is a cluster of cells trapped between the outside of the neural tube and the dorsal portion of the ectodermal wall that is referred to as the neural crest. Neural crest cells typically develop into the autonomic nervous system (ANS).

A fair amount is now known about the genes that regulate many aspects of brain development, including neurulation. Much of this knowledge is based on studies of invertebrates and vertebrates, in which alterations in morphogenesis are observed after genes are selectively deleted ("knock-out") or in a more recently developed method, added ("knock-in"). Although at first glance, one might be suspicious about the generalizability of such work to humans, reassurance can be found in the observation that humans share more than 61% of their genes with fruit flies and 81% with mice. Not everything we know is based on animal models: Increasingly our knowledge of the molecular biology of brain development is based on careful genetic analysis of nervous system tissue that has failed to develop correctly.

The patterning of the neuroaxis (i.e., head to tail) is for the most part completed by about the fifth prenatal week. Based on mouse studies, many of the transcription factors responsible for this process are well known. As reviewed by Levitt (2003), some of the genes involved in dorsal patterning include members of the emx, Pax, and ihx families of genes, whereas nkx and dlx gene families may play a role in ventral patterning.

PROLIFERATION

Once the neural tube has closed, cell division leads to a massive proliferation of new neurons (neurogenesis), generally beginning in the fifth prenatal week, and peaking between the third and fourth prenatal months (Volpe, 2000; for review, see Bronner-Fraser & Hatten, 2003). The term massive barely captures this process. It has been estimated, for example, that at its peak, several hundred thousand new nerve cells are generated each minute (Brown, Keynes, & Lumsden, 2001). Proliferation begins in the innermost portion of the neural tube, referred to as the ventricular zone (Chenn & McConnell, 1995), a region that is derived from the subependeymal location that lines the neural tube. In a process called interkinetic nuclear migration, new neural cells travel back and forth between the inner and outer portions of the ventricular zone. The new cell first travels toward the outer portion of the ventricular zone—the so-called S phase of mitosis—where DNA is synthesized, creating a duplicate copy of the cell. Once the S phase has been completed, the cell migrates downward toward the innermost portion of the ventricular zone where it divides into two cells (for a generally accessible description of these phases, see Takahashi, Nowakowski, & Caviness, 2001). Each of these new cells then begins the process again. As cells divide, a new zone is created, the marginal zone, which contains processes (axons and dendrites) from the cells of the ventricular zone. During the second phase of proliferation, neurons actually begin to form. However, for each dividing cell, only one daughter cell will continue to divide; the nondividing cell goes on to migrate to its final destination (Rakic, 1988).

Before turning to disorders of proliferation, three points should be noted. First, with the exception of cells that comprise the olfactory bulb, the dentate region of the hippocampus, and possibly regions of the neocortex, virtually every one of the estimated 100 billion neurons we possess (Naegele & Lombroso, 2001) are of prenatal origin (see section on postnatal neurogenesis); glia follow this same general pattern, although the development of glia (with the exception of radial glial cells; see section on migration that follows) lags somewhat behind neuronal development. What needs to be underscored about this observation is its importance in the context of plasticity: Unlike all other cells, the brain generally does not make new neurons after birth, which means that the brain does not repair itself in response to injury or disease by making new neurons.

Second, as cells continue to proliferate, the general shape of the neural tube undergoes a dramatic transformation—specifically, three distinct vesicles are formed: the proencephalon (forebrain), mesencephalon (midbrain), and rhombencephalon (hindbrain). Further proliferation leads to the proencephalon splitting into the telencephalon, which will give rise to the cerebral hemispheres, and the diencephalon, which gives rise to the thalamus and hypothalamus. The rhombencephalon will in turn give rise to the metencephalon (from which the pons and cerebellum are derived) and the myelencephalon (which will give rise to the medulla). The mesencephalon gives rise to the midbrain.

Finally, our knowledge of the molecular biology of cell proliferation is gradually advancing. The Foxg1 gene has been implicated in the process of cell proliferation (Hanashima, Li, Shen, Lai, & Fishell, 2004), but undoubtedly many other genes are involved as well.

CELL MIGRATION

The cortex proper (arguably the seat of cognition) is formed by a process whereby newly formed cells migrate out beyond their birthplace to ultimately give rise to a six-layered cortex. As discussed by Brown et al. (2001), the ventricular zone (the epithelium that lines the lateral ventricular cavities) gives rise to cells that undergo cell division, with the postmitotic cell migrating through the intermediate zone to its final point of destination. The cells born earliest take up residence in the preplate (the first layer of cortical neurons), which subsequently divides into the subplate and the marginal zone, both of which are derived from the cortical plate.

The postmitotic cells move in an inside-out (ventricular-to-pial) direction, such that the earliest migrating cells occupy the deepest layer of the cortex (and play an important role in the establishment of cortical connections), with subsequent migrations passing through the previously formed layer(s). (Note that this rule applies only to the cortex; the dentate gyrus and the cerebellum are formed in an outside-in pattern.) At approximately 20 weeks gestation, the cortical plate consists of three layers and by the seventh prenatal month the final contingent of six layers can be seen (Marin-Padilla, 1978).

There are two types of migratory patterns—radial and nonradial (generally tangential). Radial migration generally refers to the propagation of cells from the ventricular zone outward, or from the deepest to most superficial layers of the cortex. Approximately 70% to 80% of migrating neurons use this radial pathway. In contrast, cells adopting a tangential migratory pattern (generally interneurons for the cortex and nuclei of the brain stem) move along a tangential ("across") path. Pyramidal neurons, the major projection neurons in the brain, along with oligodendrocytes and astrocytes, enlist radial glial cells to migrate through the layers of cortex (Kriegstein & Götz, 2003), whereas cortical interneurons (for local connections) migrate via tangential migration within a cortical layer (Nadarajah & Parnavelas, 2002). Radial migration is particularly noteworthy for several reasons. First, there are different types of radial migration. Locomotion is characterized by migration along a radial glial fiber. In somal translocation, the cell body (soma) of a cell advances toward the pial surface by way of a leading process. Finally, cells that move from the intermediate zone (IZ) to the subventricular zone (SVZ) appear to migrate using multipolar migration (Tabata & Nakajima, 2003). A number of genes are involved in the regulation of migratory movement (see Hatten, 2002, and Ridley et al., 2003 for reviews).

SYNAPTOGENESIS

Synapses generally refer to the point of contact between two neurons. Depending on the receiving neuron, the resulting action can be excitatory (promoting an action potential) or inhibitory (reducing the likelihood of an action potential).

Development

The first synapses are generally observed by about the 23rd week of gestation (Molliver, Kostovic, & Van der Loos, 1973), although the peak of production does not occur until sometime in the first year of life (for review, see Webb, Monk, & Nelson, 2001). It is now well known that there is a massive overproduction of synapses distributed across broad regions of the brain, followed by a gradual reduction in synapses; it has been estimated that 40% more synapses are produced than exist in the final (adult) complement of synapses (see Levitt, 2003). The peak of the overproduction varies by brain area. For example, in the visual cortex, a synaptic peak is reached between roughly the fourth and eighth postnatal months (Huttenlocher & de Courten, 1987), whereas in the middle frontal gyrus (in the prefrontal cortex) the peak synaptic density is not obtained until after 15 postnatal months (Huttenlocher & Dabholkar, 1997).

There is evidence that the overproduction of synapses is largely under genetic control, although little is known about the genes that regulate synaptogenesis. For example, Bourgeois and colleagues (Bourgeois, Reboff, & Rakic, 1989) have reported that being born prematurely or even removing the eyes of monkeys prior to birth has little effect on the overproduction of synapses in the monkey visual cortex. Thus, in both cases the absolute number of synapses is the same as if the monkey experienced a typical, full-term birth. This suggests a highly regularized process with little influence by experience. As we demonstrate, however, the same cannot be said for synaptic pruning and the cultivating of synaptic circuits, both of which are strongly influenced by the environment.

Synaptic Pruning

The process of retracting synapses until some final (and presumably optimal) number has been reached is dependent in part on the communication among neurons. Pruning appears to follow the Hebbian principle of use/disuse: Thus, more active synapses tend to be strengthened and less active synapses tend to be weakened or even eliminated (Chechik, Meilijson, & Ruppin, 1999). Neurons organize and support synaptic contact through neurotransmitter receptors (both excitatory and inhibitory) on the presynaptic cell (the cell attempting to make contact) and through neurotrophins expressed by the postsynaptic cell (the cell on which contact is made). Synapses are modulated and stabilized by the distribution of excitatory and inhibitory inputs (Kostovic, 1990). The adjustments that are made in the pruning of synapses can either be quantitative (reducing the overall number of synapses) or qualitative (refining connections such that incorrect or abnormal connections are eliminated; for review, see Wong & Lichtman, 2003).

As has been thoroughly reported in both the lay and scientific press, the pruning of synapses appears to vary by area. Synapse numbers in the human occipital cortex peak between 4 and 8 months of age and are reduced to adult numbers by 4 to 6 years of age. In contrast, synapses in the middle frontal gyrus of the human prefrontal cortex reach their peak closer to 1 to 1.5 years of age, but are not reduced to adult numbers until mid- to late adolescence. Unfortunately, these data are based on relatively few brains (thus leaving open the question of the range of individual differences) and relatively old methods (i.e., density of synapses per unit area, which increases the risk that non-synaptic and even nonneuronal elements may be counted, such as glial cells). We should expect improved figures in the years to come with advances in new methods, a point that applies to much of the literature reviewed thus far.

MYELINATION

Myelin is a lipid/protein substance that wraps itself around an axon as a form of insulation and, as a result, increases conduction velocity. Oligodendroglia produce myelin in the CNS, whereas schwann cells produce myelin in the ANS. Myelination occurs in waves beginning prenatally and ending in young adulthood (and in some regions, as late as middle age; see Benes, Turtle, Khan, & Farol, 1994). Historically, myelin was examined in postmortem tissue using staining methods. From such work, it was revealed that myelination begins prenatally with the peripheral nervous system, motor roots, sensory roots, somesthetic cortex, and the primary visual and auditory cortices (in this chronological order). During the first postnatal year, regions of the brain stem myelinate, as does the cerebellum and splenium of corpus callosum; by 1 year, myelination of all regions of the corpus callosum is underway.

Although staining for myelin is undoubtedly the most sensitive metric for examining the course of myelination, an obvious disadvantage to this procedure is that it can only be done on a relatively small number of postmortem brains; in addition, as is the case with human synaptogenesis, it is also of concern how representative these brains are of the general population. Fortunately, advances in magnetic resonance imaging (MRI) have now made it possible to acquire detailed information about myelination in living children; importantly, several longitudinal studies have examined the course of myelination from early childhood through early adulthood (Giedd, Snell, et al., 1996; Giedd, Vatuzis, et al., 1996; Jernigan, Trauner, Hesselink, & Tallal, 1991; Paus et al., 1999; Sowell et al., 1999; Sowell, Thompson, Holmes, Jernigan, & Toga, 2000). The results of this work paint the following picture: The pre- through postadolescent period witnesses an increase in gray matter volume, followed by a decrease, whereas white matter shows first a decrease and then an increase. During this same age period (prepost adolescence), particular changes of note occur in the dorsal, medial, and lateral regions of the frontal lobes, whereas relatively smaller changes are observed in the parietal, temporal, and occipital lobes. This suggests, not surprisingly, that the most dramatic changes in myelination occur in the frontal lobes through the adolescent period (for a general overview, see Durston et al., 2001).

SUMMARY

Overall, brain development begins within weeks of conception and continues through the adolescent period. This general statement does not do justice to the age-specific changes that occur during the first 2 decades of life. Thus, the assembly of the basic architecture of the brain occurs during the first two trimesters of fetal life, with the last trimester and the first few postnatal years reserved for changes in connectivity and function. The most prolonged changes occur in the wiring of the brain (synaptogenesis) and in making the brain work more efficiently (myelination), both of which show dramatic, nonlinear changes from the preschool period through the end of adolescence.

Neural Bases of Cognitive Development

Having laid the foundation for how the human brain develops, we now turn our attention to the neural bases of specific cognitive functions. As is the case with many of the topics targeted for review in this chapter, the reader is encouraged to consult more comprehensive treatises (e.g., de Haan & Johnson, 2003b; Johnson, 2001; Nelson & Luciana, 2001). Also note that because the focus of our discussion is on the neural bases of cognitive development, we restrict our discussion to the literature that directly relates a specific cognitive ability to brain development; the basic cognitive developmental behavioral literature is thoroughly reviewed in other chapters contained in this and previous volumes.

MEMORY

Development of Memory Systems

Drawing on data from both juvenile and mature nonhuman primates, neuropsychological and neuroimaging data with adult humans, and the limited neuroimaging literature with developing humans, Nelson (1995) proposed that explicit qua explicit memory begins to develop some time after the first half year of life, as inferred from tasks such as deferred imitation, cross-modal recognition memory, delayed nonmatch-to-sample (DNMS), modified "oddball" designs in which event-related potentials (ERPs) are recorded, and preferential looking and habituation procedures that impose delays between familiarization (or habituation) and test. As is the case with the adult, this system depends on a distributed circuit that includes neocortical areas (such as the inferior temporal cortical area TE), the tissue surrounding the hippocampus (particularly the entorhinal cortex), and the hippocampus proper. However, Nelson also proposed that the development of explicit memory is preceded by an earlier form of memory referred to as *preexplicit memory*. What most distinguishes preexplicit from explicit memory is that the former (a) appears at or shortly after birth, (b) is most evident in simple novelty preferences (often reflected in the visual paired comparison procedure), and (c) is largely dependent on the hippocampus proper.

These proposals (subsequently updated and elaborated by Nelson & Webb, 2003) were built less on direct visualization of brain-behavior relations than on the integration of data from many sources. This renders the model a useful heuristic, albeit one that would benefit from more data and less speculation. The challenge is that relatively little is known about the development of the circuitry purported to be involved in different memory systems and different types of memory; similarly, there are relatively few investigators using neuroimaging tools of any sort to examine brain-memory relations. Nevertheless, advances over the past decade in the testing of developing nonhuman and human primates have provided much needed additional information.

Current Findings—Explicit Memory in the Developing Brain

It is critical to consider the task being used to evaluate memory in deriving an understanding of what structure or circuit is involved. As discussed by Nelson (1995), Nelson and Webb (2003), and most recently, Hayne (2004), the very same task, used in different ways, could impose different task demands on the subject and recruit different underlying circuitry (see discussion of the DNMS task later in this chapter).

There is now very good evidence from the monkey literature that lesions of the hippocampus lead to disruptions in visual recognition memory, at least under certain circumstances, and at least as inferred from novelty preferences. Pascalis and Bachevalier (1999) have reported that in monkeys, neonatal lesions of the hippocampus (but not amygdala; see Alvarado, Wright, & Bachevalier, 2002) impair visual recognition memory as tested in the Visual Paired Comparison (VPC) procedure, at least when the delay between familiarization and test is more than 10 seconds. Nemanic, Alvarado, and Bachevalier (2004) have reported similar effects in adult monkeys. Specifically, lesions of the hippocampus, perirhinal cortex, and the parahippocampal cortex all impair performance on the VPC, although differentially so. Thus, lesions of the perirhinal cortex, parahippocampal cortex, and hippocampus proper lead to impairments when the delay between familiarization and test exceeds 20 seconds, 30 seconds, and 60 seconds, respectively. These findings are consistent with those from the human adult, where, for example, individuals with known damage to the hippocampus also show deficits in novelty preferences under short delay conditions (McKee & Squire, 1993). Importantly, in the human adult work, the same individuals who hours later fail to show novelty preferences do show intact recognition memory (Manns, Stark, & Squire, 2000). Moreover, a patient with selective hippocampal damage shows impairments on the VPC task but relatively intact recognition memory (Pascalis, Hunkin, Holdstock, Isaac, & Mayes, 2004). Together, these results suggest that recognition memory per se may be mediated by extra-hippocampal tissue (a point to which we will return), whereas novelty preferences are likely mediated by the hippocampus proper. The monkey data are only partially consistent with this view, as they suggest that the hippocampus and surrounding cortex all play a role in novelty preferences, although differentially so, at least in the adult.

Further evidence for the role of the hippocampus in encoding the relations among stimuli (versus encoding individual stimuli, which may be the domain of the parahippocampal region) can be found in a paper by Robinson and Pascalis (2004). These authors tested groups of 6-, 12-, 18-, and 24-month-old infants using the VPC. Rather than evaluate memory for individually represented stimuli, the authors required infants to encode the properties of stimuli in context. During familiarization, stimuli were presented against one background, and during testing the same stimulus, paired with a novel stimulus, was presented against the same or a different background. The authors report that although all age groups showed strong novelty preferences when the background was the same, only the 18- and 24-month-olds showed novelty preferences when the backgrounds were changed. This would suggest that this particular function of the hippocampus—studying the relations among stimuli or encoding stimuli in context—is somewhat slower to develop than recognizing stimuli in which the context is the same. Support for this claim can be found in the developmental neuroanatomy literature. Specifically, although the hippocampus proper, the entorhinal cortex, and the connections between them are known to mature early in life (e.g., Serres, 2001), it is also known that the development of dentate gyrus of the hippocampus matures more slowly (see Serres, 2001), as does the perirhinal cortex (see Alvarado & Bachevalier, 2000). Thus, if Pascalis and colleagues are correct that their context-dependent task is dependent on the hippocampus, then in theory the delayed maturation observed on this task reflects the delayed maturation of some specific region of the hippocampus, such as the dentate gyrus.

This last observation underscores an important point, which is that although explicit memory emerges sometime between 6 and 12 months of life, it is far from fully developed by this age. The fact that even very young infants (i.e., a few months of age) do quite well on standard preferential looking paradigms suggests that there is either enough hippocampal function to subserve task performance (as would be inferred from the monkey work performed by Bachevalier and colleagues) or that perhaps the parahippocampal region (about which virtually nothing is known developmentally) is mediating task performance. Thus, consistent with the neuroscience literature, the full, adultlike expression of explicit memory awaits the subsequent development of subregions of the hippocampus along with the connections to and from associated neocortical areas.

NOVELTY PREFERENCES

Because of the prominent role novelty preferences have played in evaluating memory in infants and young children, it is worth discussing at some length the putative neural bases of such preferences. As stated, we have concluded from monkey data that the hippocampus plays a prominent role in novelty preferences, primarily based on the perturbations observed in such preferences when the hippocampus is lesioned. However, we need not restrict ourselves to data from monkeys. Neuroimaging studies with human adults have also reported that the hippocampus is involved in novelty preferences (see Dolan & Fletcher, 1997; Strange, Fletcher, Hennson, Friston, & Dolan, 1999; Tulving, Markowitsch, Craik, Habib, & Houle, 1996). In contrast, Zola et al. (2000) reported that hippocampal lesions in mature monkeys did not affect novelty preferences at 1-second delays, and thus, that impairment (i.e., decline in performance) at subsequent delays was due to problems in memory, not novelty detection. Similarly, Manns et al. (2000) have shown that among intact human adults, novelty preferences and recognition memory are both intact shortly after familiarization, although with increasing delay novelty preferences disappear, and recognition memory remains intact. This work, coupled with that from Zola et al. (2000), argues for a dissociation between novelty preferences and recognition memory and raises two questions. First, are novelty preferences truly mediated by the hippocampus or perhaps by extra-hippocampal tissue, and second, what does this dissociation say about the infancy literature in which recognition memory is typically inferred from novelty preferences?

First, it may be unwise to assume that all tasks that tap novelty preferences by default place the same demands on memory. For example, our view is that in tasks that require the subject to generalize discrimination across multiple exemplars of the same category of stimuli (e.g., to distinguish male faces from female faces), novelty preferences may depend on the ability to examine the relations among stimuli, and thus, depend disproportionately on the hippocampus. In contrast, if the task simply requires one to discriminate two individual exemplars (e.g., one female face from another), then perhaps the parahippocampal region is involved. Second, novelty preferences and recognition memory may not represent the same or different processes as much as related ones. Thus, in the VPC procedure, perceptual support is provided by presenting the familiar and novel stimuli simultaneously. In so doing, recognition may be facilitated at very short delays, perhaps due to some iconic store rather than the need to compare the novel stimulus to one stored in memory. This may occur in short-term memory and be supported by the parahippocampal region.

Whereas it is easy to dissociate novelty preferences from recognition memory in children or adults (in whom instructions can be given), the same is not true for infants, particularly when behavioral measures are employed. However, using ERPs, Nelson and Collins (1991, 1992) appeared to dissociate these processes to some degree. Four-through 8-month-old infants were initially familiarized to two stimuli; during the test trials, one of these stimuli was presented on a random 60% of the trials (frequent-familiar), the other on a random 20% of the trials (infrequent-familiar), and on each of the remaining 20% of the trials, a different novel stimulus (infrequent-novel) was presented. In theory, if recognition memory is independent of how often a stimulus is seen (i.e., its probability of occurrence), then all infants should treat the two familiar stimuli as equivalent, regardless of how often they are presented during the test trials. The authors reported that it was not until 8 months that infants responded equivalently to the two classes of familiar events and differently to the novel events. In contrast, at 6 months infants responded differently to the two classes of familiar events and differently yet again to the novel events. These findings were interpreted to reflect an improvement in memory from 6 to 8 months, specifically, the ability to ignore how often a stimulus is seen (inherent in novelty responses) from whether the stimulus is familiar (inherent in recognition memory).

At this point, it is difficult to say with certainty whether, in human children, it is the hippocampus or parahippocampal region that subserves novelty preferences and whether novelty preferences reflect a subroutine involved in recognition memory or reflect a proxy for recognition memory per se. These are questions that await further study.

DELAYED NON-MATCH-TO-SAMPLE

What about other tasks that have been thought to reflect explicit memory, such as the DNMS task? Here a subject is presented with a sample stimulus, and following some delay (during which the stimulus cannot be observed), the sample and a novel stimulus are presented side by side. In the case of monkeys, the animal is rewarded for retrieving the novel stimulus; in the case of humans, some investigators implement a similar reward system and essentially adopt the animal-testing model (e.g., see Overman, Bachevalier, Sewell, & Drew, 1993), whereas others have modified the task such that no reward is administered and looking at the novel stimulus rather than reaching for it serves as the dependent measure (see A. Diamond, 1995). In the classic DNMS task, it is generally reported that monkeys do not perform at adult levels until they approach 1 year of age, and performance among children does not begin to resemble adults until they are approximately 4 years of age (assuming the standard 1:4 ratio of monkey to human years, these data are remarkably consistent). Pascalis and Bachevalier (1999) have reported that neonatal lesions of the hippocampus do not impair performance on the DNMS task, suggesting that the DNMS likely depends on extra-hippocampal structures and does not depend on just novelty preferences (i.e., unlike the VPC task, the DNMS task requires the subject to coordinate action schemes with what is represented in memory, and as well, inhibit a response to the familiar stimulus). Support for this can be found in studies reported by Málková, Bachevalier, Mishkin, and Saunders (2001) and Nemanic et al. (2004), in which lesions of the perirhinal cortex in adult monkeys led to impairments in visual recognition memory as inferred from the DNMS; importantly, data from the Nemanic et al. (2004) study suggests that lesions of the hippocampus and parahippocampal regions have little effect on DNMS performance. Of note is the observation that these data contradict those reported by other groups (e.g., Zola et al., 2000), where hippocampal lesions in adult monkeys do lead to impairments on DNMS performance. Our group has reported hippocampal activation in human adults tested with the DNMS task (Monk et al., 2002). What is to account for these differences? First, it could be that there is a fundamental difference in structure function relations in young versus mature subjects thus, the same function could be subserved by a different structure in the developing versus the developed individual. Second, it could mean that the demands of the DNMS task differ (or are interpreted differently) depending on developmental age (e.g., the reward value of reinforcing stimuli could differ; how the child/juvenile monkey interprets the task demands could be different from how the adult/mature monkey interprets the task demands). Third, earlier studies of hippocampal lesions in adult monkeys could have included lesions of the surrounding cortex, thus making it difficult to distinguish between impairments due to the hippocampus or perirhinal cortex. Finally, in the Monk et al. (2002) neuroimaging work, it was difficult to distinguish the hippocampus from adjacent cortex, and therefore, it is possible that the surrounding cortex was most involved in performance on the DNMS task.

Summary

Piecing together heterogeneous sources of information, it appears that an early form of explicit memory emerges shortly after birth (assuming a full-term delivery). This pre-explicit memory is dependent predominantly on the hippocampus. As infants enter the second half of their first year of life, hippocampal maturation, coupled with development of the surrounding cortex, makes possible the emergence of explicit memory. A variety of tasks have been used to evaluate explicit memory, some unique to the human infant, others adopted from the monkey. Based on such tasks, one observes a gradual improvement in memory across the first few years of life, most likely due to changes in the hippocampus proper (e.g., dentate gyrus), to the surrounding cortex (e.g., parahippocampal cortex), and to increased connectivity between these areas. The changes one observes in memory from the preschool through elementary school years are likely due to changes in prefrontal cortex, and connections between the prefrontal cortex and the medial temporal lobe. Such changes make possible the ability to perform mental operations on the contents of memory, such as the ability to use strategies to encode and retrieve information. Finally, changes in long-term memory are likely due to the development of the neocortical areas that are thought to store such memories, and the improved communication between the neocortex and the medial temporal lobe (MTL). It is most likely these changes that usher in the end of infantile amnesia (for elaboration, see Nelson, 1998; Nelson & Carver, 1998).

Nondeclarative Memory

Nondeclarative or implicit forms of learning and memory functions represent an essential aspect of human cognition by which information and skills can be learned through mere exposure or practice, without requiring conscious intention or attention and eventually becoming automatic. Although controversy exists regarding the definition of nondeclarative memory or learning, performance on most nondeclarative tasks does not appear to depend on medial temporal lobe structures. Patients like H. M., mentioned earlier, demonstrate severe deficits in explicit memory consistent with known insults to or disruption of medial temporal lobe memory systems. However, these patients are not impaired on classic tests of implicit memory and learning, such as perceptual priming or serial reaction time (SRT) learning (Milner, Corkin, & Teuber,

1968; Shimamura, 1986; Squire, 1986; Squire & Frambach, 1990; Squire, Knowlton, & Musen, 1993; Squire & McKee, 1993).

A multitude of tasks have emerged in the cognitive literature to assess nondeclarative cognitive functions (see Seger, 1994; Reber, 1993). Reber (1993) proposes making a distinction between two broad categories of nondeclarative function: implicit memory (the end-state representation of knowledge available to an individual, of which he or she is unaware) and implicit learning (the unintentional and unconscious acquisition of knowledge). Implicit learning involves learning of underlying rules and structure in the absence of any conscious awareness of those regularities. Such learning is slow and requires repeated exposure to the information to be retained. In contrast, implicit memory may occur with a single exposure to a stimulus and results in an increased processing efficiency for subsequent presentations of that stimulus or closely related stimuli. Not only do these categories differ in their basic cognitive nature (representation versus acquisition of knowledge), but they seem to differ in their underlying neural substrates as well. In a now well-known classification of memory systems, Squire (1994) identified three primary forms of implicit learning and memory: priming, procedural learning (skills and habits), and classical conditioning (associative learning), each relying on separable neural systems.

IMPLICIT SEQUENCE LEARNING

In contrast to priming, implicit learning—also termed habit learning, skill learning, or procedural learning—involves the slow acquisition of a knowledge base or behavioral skill set over time. In everyday life, learning to ride a bicycle involves the gradual acquisition of a skill that is very difficult or impossible to describe verbally. Although intentionally trying to learn the skill, the learner is typically unaware of what exactly is being learned. Implicit learning has most frequently been tested using sequence learning (e.g., Nissen & Bullemer, 1987) or artificial grammar learning paradigms (Reber, 1993). In the SRT task, individuals are asked to map a set of spatial or object stimuli onto an equal number of response buttons. Reaction times to match the stimulus and the button are recorded. Unknown to the participant, whereas stimuli often appear in random order, at other times, the order of stimulus presentation follows a predictable and repeating sequence. Implicit learning is assumed when participants show reaction time improvements during the sequential trials compared with random trials, despite no conscious awareness of the underlying regularity.

Patients with temporal lobe amnesia perform normally on sequence learning tasks. However, patients with basal ganglia damage, such as those with Parkinson's or Huntington's diseases, have been shown to be impaired on the serial reaction time task (Ferraro, Balota, & Connor, 1993; Heindel, Salmon, Shults, Walicke, & Butters, 1989; Knopman & Nissen, 1991; Pascual-Leone et al., 1993). Importantly, these patients perform normally on measures of explicit memory as well as on measures of perceptual and conceptual priming (Schwartz & Hastroudi, 1991), providing support for the separability of implicit learning and implicit memory at the neural systems level. Neuroimaging data provide supporting evidence for the role of subcortical structures in serial reaction time learning. Common findings across a number of laboratories (Bischoff-Grethe, Martin, Mao, & Berns, 2001; Grafton, Hazeltine, & Ivry, 1995; Hazeltine, Grafton, & Ivry, 1997; Schendan, Searl, Melrose, & Ce, 2003) demonstrate differential activity in frontal—basal ganglia—thalamic circuits for sequential trials compared with random trials. Further evidence suggests that connections among these fronto-striatal loops and fronto-cerebellar loops may be an important aspect of implicit learning. Pascual-Leone et al. (1993) observed that, although adults with basal ganglia insults demonstrated significant reductions in implicit sequence learning, adults with cerebellar degeneration showed no evidence of learning on the SRT task.

Significant controversy exists regarding the developmental trajectory of implicit learning. In a study of SRT learning in 6- to 10-year-old children and adults, Meulemans, van der Linden, and Perruchet (1998) observed equivalent learning of a 10-step spatial sequence across age groups, despite overall reaction time differences with age. These data support the notion that implicit cognition may mature very early in infancy and show little variation or improvement with age (Reber, 1992). However, other measures of implicit pattern learning or contingency learning, as well as SRT data from an alternate group, are less clear. Maybery, Taylor, and O'Brien-Malone (1995) report age-related improvements in covariation learning, with older children showing larger learning effects than younger children. However, Lewicki (1986) found no evidence of age-related learning effects on the original version of the same task. Similarly, Thomas and Nelson (2001) found that, although the size of the implicit learning effect was similar between 4-, 7-, and 10-year-olds who showed evidence of sequence learning on an SRT task, older children were more likely to show learning. In fact, the probability of significant learning was inversely related to age, with fully one-third of the youngest age group showing no evidence of learning (whereas all 10-year-olds showed a learning effect). Evidence for age-related improvements in implicit sequence learning comes from an infant analogue of the SRT task: visual expectancy formation. In this task, infants are shown a repeating pattern of visual stimuli, and eye movements are recorded to determine whether the infant learns to anticipate the location of the upcoming stimuli over time. Although we cannot rule out the possibility that this behavior is explicitly learned, the task has many similarities to the adult SRT paradigm. Although infants as young as 2 and 3 months of age can show reliable visual expectancy formation (Canfield, Smith, Brezsnyak, & Snow, 1997; Haith, Hazan, & Goodman, 1988), older infants are able to learn more complicated sequential relationships than younger children (Clohessy, Posner, & Rothbart, 2002; Smith, Loboschefski, Davidson, & Dixon, 1997).

In a recent pediatric imaging study of the SRT task, Thomas et al. (in press) compared the neural systems subserving implicit sequence learning in 7- to 11-year-old children and adults. Overall, results from adults were consistent with previous neuroimaging studies implicating fronto-striatal circuitry in visuomotor sequence learning. In particular, activity in the basal ganglia was positively correlated with the size of the implicit learning effect (greater learning was associated with increased activity in the caudate nucleus). Although children and adults showed many of the same regions of activity, relative group differences were observed overall, with children showing greater subcortical activity and adults showing greater cortical activity. Consistent with findings from adult SRT studies (Schendan et al., 2003), both adults and children showed activity in the hippocampus despite no explicit awareness of the sequence. This activity is unlikely to be either necessary or sufficient for implicit sequence learning given the adult literature indicating spared performance following lesions to the hippocampus. Instead, this activity may reflect a sensitivity to stimulus novelty, a function of the hippocampus discussed earlier in this chapter. Children showed an inverse pattern of hippocampal activity as compared to adults (random trials elicited greater hippocampal activity than sequence trials for child participants). The SRT task used here produced significant developmental differences in the magnitude of the learning effect, with children demonstrating significantly less learning than adults. Unlike prior behavioral studies, this effect was not driven by a difference in the percentage of non-learners in the two age groups. Rather, despite significant individual learning in both groups, adults learned to a greater extent with the same degree of exposure.

Finally, some evidence exists to address the effects of basal ganglia insults early in development. Although early insults may lead to lasting impairments in functions subserved by the affected systems, the plastic nature of the developing brain may also allow for redistribution of function to other regions that are unaffected. Structural neuroimaging studies have identified childhood attention-deficit/hyperactivity disorder (ADHD), as well as perinatal complications such as intraventricular hemorrhage as risk factors for disrupted basal ganglia circuitry. Castellanos et al. (2001, 2002) have reported decreases in caudate volume in children with ADHD compared with nonaffected controls. Similarly, functional imaging studies of attentional control (see Executive Functions, later in this chapter) suggest a lack of typical basal ganglia activity in children with ADHD (Vaidya et al., 1998). A paper addressing reading disabilities suggests a possible link between reduced motor sequence learning and symptoms of ADHD (Waber et al., 2003). Thomas and colleagues reported evidence of significant decrements in sequence learning for 6- to 9-year-old children diagnosed with ADHD (Thomas, Vizueta, Teylan, Eccard, & Casey, 2003). These authors also examined implicit sequence learning in children with perinatal histories of intraventricular hemorrhage (IVH), or bleeding into the lateral ventricles at birth. Children whose IVH was moderate (bilateral grade II or more severe) evidenced significant decrements in the magnitude of the implicit learning effect. In contrast, children whose perinatal IVH had been relatively mild (unilateral grade II or less severe) showed no difference in learning from a full-term, age- and gender-matched control group. Together, these studies suggest a potential long-term deficit in implicit learning resulting from early insults to basal ganglia circuitry.

Object Recognition

FACE/OBJECT RECOGNITION

Among the numerous visual inputs that we receive each moment, the human face is perhaps one of the most salient. The importance of the many signals it conveys (e.g., emotion, identity, direction of eye gaze), together with the speed and ease with which adults typically process this information, are compelling reasons to suppose that there may exist brain circuits specialized for processing faces. Neuropsychological studies provided the first evidence to support this view, with reports of double dissociation of face and object processing. That is, there are patients who show impaired face processing but relatively intact general vision and object processing (with the occasional exception of color vision; reviewed in Barton, 2003), and other patients who show the opposite pattern of deficit (e.g., Moscovitch, Winocur, & Behrmann, 1997). These studies also hinted that damage to the right hemisphere might be necessary for the face-processing impairments to be observed. More recently, ERP, MEG, and fMRI methods have been used to identify the pathways involved in face processing in the intact brain. These studies have confirmed and extended findings from brain-injured patients, indicating that a distributed network of regions in the brain mediate face processing: occipito-temporal regions are important for the early perceptual stages of face processing, with more anterior regions, including areas of the temporal and frontal cortices and the amygdala, involved in processing aspects such as identity and emotional expression (Adolphs, 2002; Haxby, Hoffman, & Gobbini, 2002). In this section, we focus mainly on the involvement of occipito-temporal cortex and the amygdala, as these are the areas for which the most developmental data are available.

OCCIPITO-TEMPORAL CORTEX

In adults, a network including the inferior occipital gyrus, the fusiform gyrus, and the superior temporal sulcus is important for the early stages of face processing (Haxby et al., 2002). In this view, the inferior occipital gyrus is primarily responsible for early perception of facial features, while the fusiform gyrus and the superior temporal sulcus are involved in more specialized processing (Haxby et al., 2002). In particular, the fusiform gyrus is thought to be involved in the processing of invariant aspects of faces (such as the perception of unique identity), whereas the superior temporal sulcus is involved in the processing of changeable aspects (such as perception of eye gaze, expression, and lip movement; Haxby et al., 2002; Hoffman & Haxby, 2000).

Perhaps the most intensively studied of these regions is an area of fusiform gyrus labeled the fusiform face area (Kanwisher, McDermott, & Chun, 1997; Puce, Allison, Asgari, Gore, & McCarthy, 1996). This region is more activated to faces compared with other objects or body parts (Kanwisher et al., 1997; Puce et al., 1996). Although some investigators have argued against the view of face-specific patches of cortex and have instead emphasized the distributed nature of the representation of object feature information over the ventral posterior cortex (Haxby et al., 2001), even these authors acknowledge that the response to faces appears unique in certain ways (e.g., extent of activation, modulation by attention; Ishai, Ungerleider, Martin, & Haxby, 2000).

Although these studies appear to suggest that particular regions of cortex are devoted specifically to face processing, this interpretation has been questioned. In particular, it has been argued that the supposed face-specific cortical areas are not specific to faces per se, but instead are recruited for expert-level discrimination of complex visual patterns, whether faces or other classes of objects (R. Diamond & Carey, 1986; Gauthier, Skudlarski, Gore, & Anderson, 1999). In this view, the mechanisms active during development of face processing could be the same as those observed in adults learning an equally challenging visual perceptual task. In support of this view, studies have shown that the fusiform face area is also activated by nonface objects (e.g., cars) if the subjects are experts with that category (Gauthier et al., 2000), and activation in the fusiform face areas increases following training of expertise with a category of visual forms (Gauthier, Tarr, Anderson, Skudlarski, & Gore, 1999).

Developmental studies can provide important information to constrain the claims of the different sides of this debate. For example, by studying when and how face-specific brain responses emerge, developmental studies can provide some hints as to whether and how much experience might be needed for these responses to emerge. Behavioral studies provide a suggestion that face-processing pathways may be functional from very early in life: newborn babies move their eyes, and sometimes their heads, longer to keep a moving facelike pattern in view than several other comparison patterns (Johnson, Dziurawiec, Ellis, & Morton, 1991). While there is a debate as to whether this reflects a specific response to facelike configurations or a lower-level visual preference (e.g., for patterns with higher density of elements in the upper visual field, see Turati, Simion, Milani, & Umilta, 2002; see also Banks & Ginsburg, 1985; Banks & Salapatek, 1981), there is some agreement among the divergent views that the ultimate result is that facelike patterns are preferred to other arrangements from the first hours to days of life.

While this might seem to support the notion that face-specific cortical areas are active from birth, the prevailing view is that this early preferential orienting to faces is likely mediated by subcortical mechanisms (e.g., superior colliculus; for a review of the evidence, see Johnson & Morton, 1991), and that cortical mechanisms do not begin to emerge until 2 to 3 months of age. At this early age, cortical areas are thought to be relatively unspecialized (Johnson & Morton, 1991; Nelson, 2001). One possible role of the earlier-developing subcortical system is to provide a "face-biased" input to the slower-developing occipito-temporal cortical system, and to provide one mechanism whereby an initially more broadly tuned processing system becomes increasingly specialized to respond to faces during development (Johnson & Morton, 1991; Nelson, 2001).

The only functional neuroimaging study to investigate face processing in human infants confirms that occipito-temporal cortical pathways are involved by 2 to 3 months of age. In this study, 2-month-olds' positron emission tomography (PET) activation in the inferior occipital gyrus and the fusiform gyrus, but not the superior temporal sulcus, was greater in response to a human face than to a set of three light diodes (Tzourio-Mazoyer et al., 2002). These results demonstrate that areas involved in face processing in adults can also be activated in infants by 2 months of age, although they do not address the question of whether these areas are specifically activated by faces rather than by other visual stimuli. The superior temporal sulcus, suggested to be involved in the processing of information relevant to social communication, was not activated in this study. One possible explanation is that the stimuli (static and neutral) were not optimal for activating processing in the superior temporal sulcus. However, the observation that activation in the superior temporal sulcus has been found in adults even in response to static, neutral faces (e.g., Kesler-West et al., 2001) argues against this interpretation. It is possible that the superior temporal sulcus plays a different role in the face-processing network in infants than in adults, since in primates its connectivity with other visual areas is known to differ in infants compared with adult monkeys (Kennedy, Bullier, & Dehay, 1989).

Event-related potential studies support the idea that cortical mechanisms are involved in face processing from at least 3 months of age. However, these studies also suggest that when cortical mechanisms become involved in infants' processing of faces, they are less "tuned in" to faces than is the mature system. Two studies have shown that face-responsive ERP components are more specific to human faces in adults than in infants (de Haan, Pascalis, & Johnson, 2002; Halit, de Haan & Johnson, 2003). In adults, the N170, a negative deflection over occipito-temporal electrodes that peaks approximately 170 ms after stimulus onset, is thought to reflect the initial stage of the structural encoding of the face. Although the location in the brain of the generator(s) of the N170 remains a matter of debate, it is generally believed that regions of the fusiform gyrus (Shibata et al., 2002), the posterior inferior temporal gyrus (Shibata et al., 2002), lateral occipito-temporal cortex (Schweinberger, Pickering, Jentzsch,

Burton, & Kaufmann, 2002), and the superior temporal sulcus (Henson et al., 2003) are involved. The N170 is typically of larger amplitude and/or has a longer latency for inverted than upright faces (de Haan et al., 2002; Eimer, 2000; Itier & Taylor, 2002; Rossion et al., 2000), a pattern that parallels behavioral studies showing that adults are slower at recognizing inverted than upright faces (Carey & Diamond, 1994). In adults, the effect of inversion on the N170 is specific for human faces and does not occur for inverted compared with upright exemplars of nonface object categories (Rebai, Poiroux, Bernard, & Lalonde, 2001; Rossion et al., 2000), even animal (monkey) faces (de Haan et al., 2002).

Developmental studies have identified two components, the N290 and the P400, believed to be precursors of the N170. Both components are maximal over posterior cortex, with the N290 peaking at about 290 ms after stimulus onset and the P400 about 100 ms later. The N290 shows an adultlike modulation of amplitude by stimulus inversion by 12 months of age: inversion increases the amplitude of the N290 for human but not monkey faces (Halit et al., 2003). The P400 has a quicker latency for faces compared with objects by 6 months of age (de Haan & Nelson, 1999) and shows an adultlike effect of stimulus inversion on peak latency by 12 months of age: It is of longer latency for inverted than upright human faces but does not differ for inverted compared with upright monkey faces (Halit et al., 2003). At 3 and 6 months, the N290 is unaffected by inversion; and the P400, while modulated by inversion, does not show effects specific to human faces (de Haan et al., 2002; Halit et al., 2003). Overall, these findings suggest that there is a gradual emergence of face-selective response over the first year of life (and beyond). This finding is consistent with results of a behavioral study showing a decrease in discrimination abilities for nonhuman faces with age; 6-month-olds can discriminate between individual humans and monkeys, whereas 9-month-olds and adults tested with the same procedure discriminate only between individual human faces (Pascalis, de Haan, & Nelson, 2002). The results also suggest that the structural encoding of faces may be dispersed over a longer time in infants than in adults. It is possible that, as the processes become more automated, they are carried out more quickly and/or in parallel rather than in serial fashion.

The spatial distribution of the N170 and P400 both change from 3 to 12 months, with maxima shifting laterally for both components (de Haan et al., 2002; Halit et al., 2003). In addition, the maxima of these components appear more superior than in adults, a result consistent with studies in children finding a shift from superior to inferior maximum of the N170 with age (Taylor, Edmonds, McCarthy, & Allison, 2001). This might reflect a change in the configuration of generators underlying these components with age.

Investigations with older children also support the view of a gradual specialization of face processing. ERP studies suggest that there are gradual, quantitative improvements in face processing from 4 to 15 years of age rather than stage like shifts (Taylor, McCarthy, Saliba, & Degiovanni, 1999). The ERP studies also provide evidence that there is a slower maturation of configural than featural processing: Responses to eyes presented alone matured more slowly than responses to eyes presented in the configuration of the face (Taylor et al., 2001). There have not been many functional imaging studies of face processing during childhood, but one study examining facial identity processing suggests that changes in the network are activated in 10- to 12-year-olds compared with adults (Passarotti et al., 2003). Children showed a more distributed pattern of activation compared with adults. Within the fusiform gyrus, children tended to show more activation in lateral areas of the right hemisphere than did adults: In the left hemisphere, children showed greater lateral than medial activation, whereas adults showed no difference for the two areas. In addition, children showed twice as much activation of the middle temporal gyrus as adults. The authors interpret these results as suggesting that increased skill is associated with a more focal pattern of activation.

Studies of children with autistic spectrum disorders support the view that atypical activation of occipito-temporal cortex is related to impairments in face processing. Autistic spectrum disorders are characterized by impairments in processing of social information, including faces. Functional imaging studies indicate that when individuals with autism or Asperger syndrome view faces, they show a diminished response in the fusiform gyrus compared with controls (Hubl et al., 2003; Pierce, Muller, Ambrose, Allen, & Courchesne, 2001; Schultz et al., 2000) and show an increased activation of object-processing areas in the inferior temporal cortex (Hubl et al., 2003; Schultz et al., 2000). It is possible that this reflects a different processing strategy in which individuals with autism focus more on featural rather than configural information in the face. In other words, individuals with autism may rely more on general purpose object-processing pathways rather than specialized face-processing pathways when viewing faces.

AMYGDALA

The amygdala is a heterogeneous collection of nuclei located in the anterior temporal lobe. Several studies in adults have shown that lesions to the amygdala impair emotion recognition, even when they leave other aspects of face processing intact (e.g., identity recognition; Adolphs, Tranel, Damasio, & Damasio, 1994). Lesion studies also indicate that recognition of fearful expressions is particularly vulnerable to such damage (Adolphs et al., 1994, 1999; Broks et al., 1998; Calder et al., 1996). Functional imaging studies in healthy adults and school-age children complement these findings, with some studies showing that the amygdala responds to a variety of positive, negative, or neutral expressions (Thomas et al., 2001; Yang et al., 2002), and other studies suggesting that the amygdala is particularly responsive to fearful expressions (Morris et al., 1996; Whalen et al., 2001).

There is indirect evidence that the amygdala plays a role in processing facial expressions in infants. Balaban (1995) used the eye-blink startle response (a reflex blink initiated involuntarily by sudden bursts of loud noise) to examine the psychophysiology of infants' responses to facial expressions. In adults, these reflex blinks are augmented by viewing slides of unpleasant pictures and scenes, and they are inhibited by viewing slides of pleasant or arousing pictures and scenes (Lang, Bradley, & Cuthbert, 1990, 1992). Consistent with the adult findings, Balaban found that 5-month-old infants' blinks were augmented when they viewed angry expressions and were reduced when they viewed happy expressions, relative to when they viewed neutral expressions. Animal studies indicate that the fear potentiation of the startle response is mediated by the amygdala (Davis, 1989; Holstege, van Ham, & Tan, 1986), therefore, these results suggest that by 5 months of age, portions of the amygdala circuitry underlying the response to facial expressions may be functional.

There is evidence that early damage to the amygdala may have a more pronounced effect on recognition of facial expression than damage sustained later in life. For example, in one study of emotion recognition in patients who had undergone temporal lobectomy as treatment for intractable epilepsy, emotion recognition in patients with early, right mesial temporal sclerosis, but not those with left-sided damage or extratemporal damage, showed impairments on tests of recognition of facial expressions of emotion but not on comparison tasks of face processing (Meletti et al., 2003). This deficit was most pronounced for fearful expressions, and the degree of deficit was related to the age of first seizure and epilepsy onset.

ROLE OF EXPERIENCE

The preceding studies suggest that the cortical system involved in face processing becomes increasingly specialized for faces throughout the course of development. Several developmental theories propose that experience is necessary for this process of specialization to occur (e.g., Nelson, 2001). Only a few studies have directly examined the role of experience in development of face processing. In one series of studies, the face-processing abilities of patients with congenital cataracts who were deprived of patterned visual input for the first months of life were tested years after this period of deprivation. These patients show normal processing of featural information (e.g., subtle differences in the shape of the eyes and mouth), but show impairments in processing configural information (i.e., the spacing of features within the face; Le Grand, Mondloch, Maurer, & Brent, 2001a, 2001b; Geldart, Mondloch, Maurer, de Schonen, & Brent, 2002). This pattern was specific to faces in that both featural and configural aspects of geometric patterns were processed normally (Le Grand et al., 2001a, 2001b). Moreover, when patients whose visual input had been restricted mainly to one hemisphere during infancy were examined, it was found that visual input to the right hemisphere, but not the left hemisphere, was critical for an expert level of face processing to develop (Le Grand, Mondloch, Maurer, & Brent, 2003). These studies suggest that visual input during early infancy is necessary for the normal development of at least some aspects of face processing.

Another way in which the role of experience has been investigated is by studying children who experience atypical early emotional environments. For example, Pollak and colleagues have found that perception of the facial expression of anger, but not other expressions, is altered in children who are abused by their parents. Specifically, they report that, compared with nonabused children, abused children show a response bias for anger (Pollak, Cicchetti, Hornung, & Reed, 2000), identify anger based on less perceptual input (Pollak & Sinha, 2002), and show altered category boundaries for anger (Pollak & Kistler, 2002). These results suggest that atypical frequency and content of their emotional interactions with their caregivers result in a change in the basic perception of emotional expressions in abused children.

Executive Functions

Most high-level cognitive functions involve executive processes, or cognitive control functions, such as attention, planning, problem solving, and decision making. These processes are largely voluntary (as opposed to automatic) and are highly effortful. Such functions, including selective and executive attention, inhibition, and working memory, are hypothesized to improve with age and practice, and to vary with individual differences in motivation or intelligence. These cognitive control processes have been described as providing a "supervisory attention system" (Shallice, 1988)—a system for inhibiting or overriding routine or reflexive behaviors in favor of more controlled or situationally appropriate or adaptive behaviors. Desimone and Duncan (1995) describe this system as an attentional bias that provides a mechanism for attending to relevant information by simultaneously inhibiting irrelevant information (Casey, Durston, & Fossella, 2001). The ability to override a dominant response or ignore irrelevant information is critical in everyday life, as evidenced by the functional impairments associated with chronic inattention, behavioral impulsivity, or poor planning and decision making.

Classic lesion cases, such as the famous case of Phineas Gage, indicate that injury to the prefrontal cortex can result in difficulties in behavioral regulation, such as impulsivity and socially inappropriate behavior (Fuster, 1997), as well as disruptions in planning, working memory, and focused attention. Cognitive developmentalists will recognize these same functions as showing relatively protracted behavioral maturation, often not reaching adult levels of performance until late adolescence (Anderson, Anderson, Northam, Jacobs, & Catroppa, 2001). It is therefore not surprising that the prefrontal cortex shows one of the longest periods of development of any brain region (A. Diamond, 2002; Luciana, 2003, for reviews). In fact, the relations between prefrontal cortex development and the development of executive functions is probably one of the clearest relations in the developmental cognitive neuroscience literature. However, this does not imply that we fully understand the instantiation of attention, working memory, or inhibition in the brain. Instead, we have significant evidence from lesion and neuroimaging methods to relate subregions of prefrontal cortex to specific aspects of cognitive control in adulthood, as well as a growing body of literature addressing the normative and atypical function of these regions, and their connected networks of structures, in the development of cognitive control. For reasons of space, only illustrative examples from normative behavioral development, animal models, adult and pediatric neuroimaging studies, and atypical developmental populations are provided here (Casey, Durston, et al., 2001; A. Diamond, 2002; Luciana, 2003).

DOMAINS OF EXECUTIVE FUNCTION

Many researchers have identified working memory and behavioral inhibition as the primary functions of prefrontal cortex, and by extension, the basic components of executive function (e.g., A. Diamond, 2001). Working memory has typically been associated with dorsolateral prefrontal cortex (DLPFC; J. Cohen et al., 1994; Fuster, 1997; Levy & Goldman-Rakic, 2000), while more ventral regions have been implicated in inhibition of a prepotent behavioral response (Casey et al., 1997; Kawashima et al., 1996; Konishi et al., 1999). Other investigators have parsed their definition of executive functions somewhat differently in an effort to include the voluntary and effortful aspects of attentional control as well as response inhibition. Whatever scheme is used, it is apparent that the classic executive function tasks involve more than one of the preceding aspects of voluntary control or regulation. In the following sections, we provide examples of behavioral tasks thought to tap various aspects of executive function across development, as well as provide select examples that evidence the role of specific regions of prefrontal cortex in supporting cognitive control. Of course, prefrontal cortex does not act in isolation. Other brain regions are assumed to be integral to the executive function system, providing input and feedback, as well as receiving inputs from prefrontal cortex. Developmental improvements in executive function may arise as much from the development of such functional integration as from the architectural and physiological development of prefrontal cortex (Anderson et al., 2001; Anderson, Levin, & Jacobs, 2002).

WORKING MEMORY

Perhaps the task most clearly associated with both child development and prefrontal cortex is the classic A-not-B task. In this paradigm (or its close cousin, the delayed response task), an infant or animal watches an object being hidden at one of two identical locations, and after some delay is rewarded for retrieving the object. This task requires both holding information in mind across a delay and, on subsequent trials when the hiding location changes, inhibiting a prepotent tendency to return to a previously correct response location (A. Diamond, 1985). Animal lesion studies support the importance of DLPFC in successful performance on the A-not-B and delayed response tasks (A. Diamond & Goldman-Rakic, 1989; Fuster & Alexander, 1970; Goldman & Rosvold, 1970). In addition, electrophysiological studies indicate that cells in this region actively respond during the delay interval, suggesting that DLPFC is involved in the maintenance of information in working memory (Funahashi, Bruce, & Goldman-Rakic, 1989; Fuster & Alexander, 1971). Further investigation demonstrates that lesions to this region impair performance only under delay conditions and not during immediate object retrieval (A. Diamond & Goldman-Rakic, 1989). Functional imaging studies suggest that developmental differences in working memory function, at least in middle childhood, may be reflected in less efficient or less focal activation of DLPFC. That is, pediatric fMRI studies have demonstrated that children activate similar regions of DLPFC compared with adults during both verbal and spatial working memory tasks, but also may activate additional areas of prefrontal cortex, including ventral lateral regions (VLPFC; Casey et al., 1995; Nelson et al., 2000; Thomas et al., 1999).

INHIBITORY CONTROL

Although working memory has been associated with dorsolateral regions of the prefrontal cortex, the ability to inhibit inappropriate behaviors has typically been associated with ventral medial or orbital frontal cortex (Casey et al., 1997; Konishi et al., 1999). In adults, lesions to ventral prefrontal cortex lead to impulsive and socially inappropriate behavior (Barrash, Tranel, & Anderson, 1994; Damasio, Grabowski, Frank, Galaburda, & Damasio, 1994). One common developmental measure of response inhibition is the go/no-go paradigm. In this task, children are asked to respond to every stimulus except one (e.g., all letters except X). The task is designed such that the majority of trials are "go" trials, building up a compelling behavioral response tendency. The child's ability to refrain from making the response at the occurrence of the "no-go" stimulus is used as an index of inhibitory control. Performance on such tasks has been shown to improve across the preschool and school-age years (Casey, Durston, et al., 2001; Ridderinkhof, van der Molen, Band, & Bashore, 1997). Neuroimaging studies using the go/no-go paradigm have demonstrated signal increases in ventral PFC during periods high in inhibitory demand (Casey, Forman, et al., 2001; Casey et al., 1997), with correspondingly lower levels of activity during periods of low inhibitory demand. Konishi et al. (1999) observed increased ventral PFC activation during no-go trials in an event-related fMRI paradigm. Pediatric neuroimaging studies have demonstrated both developmental differences in activation of ventral prefrontal cortex (Bunge, Dudukovic, Thomason, Vaidya, & Gabrieli, 2002), with children showing reduced signal compared with adults, and increasing activation of ventral lateral PFC with increasing inhibitory load (Durston, Thomas, & Yang, 2002). Durston and colleagues (2002) showed that behavioral performance on the go/no-go task was significantly correlated with activity in inferior frontal cortex, as well as other prefrontal regions, including the anterior cingulate gyrus (ACC).

Importantly, these same studies highlight the importance of regions beyond the prefrontal cortex. In particular, basal ganglia structures have also been shown to be involved in response inhibition (e.g., Luna et al., 2001), perhaps particularly so for children (Bunge et al., 2002; Casey et al., 1997; Durston et al., 2002). Children with ADHD show significantly lower activity in basal ganglia regions during performance of a go/no-go task than typically developing children (Durston et al., 2003; Vaidya et al., 1998) and show high rates of false alarms on the task. Children with ADHD showed additional recruitment of dorsolateral PFC not observed for the control group who performed at a high rate of accuracy (Durston et al., 2003). When taking medication to treat their inattention and impulsivity, children with ADHD show basal ganglia activity equivalent to the typically developing group along with parallel improvements in behavioral performance (Vaidya et al., 1998). Other developmental disorders, such as Tourette syndrome, obsessive-compulsive disorder, and childhood-onset schizophrenia also have been associated with disruption of frontal-striatal circuitry (connections between basal ganglia and frontal cortex) and impaired performance on tasks involving attentional control.

ATTENTIONAL CONTROL

Beyond the general processes of working memory or inhibition, many real-world and experimental tasks require selectively focusing attention on relevant task information while simultaneously suppressing interference from salient but irrelevant or misleading information (Casey, Durston, et al., 2001). Perhaps the most studied adult task of this type is the color-word Stroop paradigm, in which participants are asked to identity the color of ink in which a word is written but, in the case of a color word, have to inhibit a natural tendency to read the word instead (e.g., the word "BLUE" presented in red ink). Neuroimaging data from the Stroop paradigm identify medial prefrontal cortex, specifically the anterior cingulate cortex, as particularly important in detecting (e.g., Botvinick, Braver, Barch, Carter, & Cohen, 2001; Bush et al., 1999; Bush, Luu, & Posner, 2000; Duncan & Owen, 2000; Fan, Flombaum, McCandliss, Thomas, & Posner, 2003; MacDonald, Cohen, Stenger, & Carter, 2000; Posner & Petersen, 1990) and perhaps even resolving this type of attentional conflict.

DLPFC and other regions of prefrontal cortex may also be activated during cognitive conflict depending on demands of the specific task. In the Simon task, a spatial conflict is created between the location of a stimulus (left or right side of the screen) and the required response (left or right button; Gerardi-Caulton, 2000). In a study by Fan et al. (2003), this conflict was associated with activation of superior frontal gyrus as well as anterior cingulate cortex, while conflict in the Stroop task was associated with activity in ventral lateral prefrontal cortex. When the same adult participants performed the Eriksen flanker task, which requires focusing attention on a central stimulus and actively ignoring competing flanking stimuli, these authors observed attention-related activity in premotor cortex. Despite these task-related differences in

MR signal, further analyses demonstrated overlapping regions of activity in the anterior cingulate gyrus and the left prefrontal cortex across all three tasks, suggesting some common activity related to cognitive control or management of cognitive conflict (Fan et al., 2003). Other neuroimaging studies of the Eriksen flanker task have indicated that prefrontal cortex is differentially activated based on the degree of cognitive conflict within the same task (Casey et al., 2000; Durston et al., 2003). Durston and colleagues (2003) found that parametric manipulations of conflict on the flanker task were associated with monotonic increases in both DLPFC and ACC. Of course, additional brain regions are activated beyond the prefrontal cortex, such as the superior parietal cortex, perhaps related to the spatial nature of the task. Applying the concept of a "spotlight of attention" (Posner & Raichle, 1997), the flanker task requires narrowing the spatial distribution of attentional focus to reduce interference or conflict from the irrelevant flanking stimuli. Activation of superior parietal cortex may be related to this spatial feature of the task (also see Orienting, later in this chapter).

Behaviorally, the cognitive control tasks previously described show significant developmental changes across early and middle childhood, and in some cases, even into adolescence. Casey et al. (2001) provide developmental data demonstrating that, for tasks such as the Eriksen flanker and Stroop, adult like performance is not achieved until early adolescence. A. Diamond (2002) has shown similar trajectories for Stroop-like tasks including the Simon task, with evidence of protracted development. Rueda and colleagues (2004) showed evidence of increased cognitive conflict in 6- and 7-year-olds compared with 8- to 10-year-olds and adults. Despite a significant literature demonstrating developmental improvements in cognitive control across early and middle childhood, fewer studies have addressed the brain bases of this development. A. Diamond (2001) has shown that children with presumed functional disruptions of prefrontal cortex (children treated for phenylketonuria or PKU) are impaired on their performance of Stroop-like and inhibitory control tasks like the go/no-go task, suggesting that typical developmental function is relying on this brain region that is continuing to develop across childhood. Similar effects on other executive function tasks have also been observed in this population (Luciana, Sullivan, & Nelson, 2001). Likewise Casey, Tottenham, and Fossella (2002) have demonstrated that children with psychiatric disorders associated with frontal-striatal circuitry show specific impairments on tests of cognitive conflict. Children with obsessive-compulsive symptomatology showed deficits when required to inhibit a well-learned response set, but no impairment in a Stroop-like task. In contrast, children with diagnoses of childhood onset schizophrenia were impaired on the Stroop-like task but not on the response selection task or on a go/no-go inhibition task, suggesting potential differences within prefrontal cortex.

A related aspect of cognitive control arises when the individual is required not only to ignore irrelevant information, but also to shift among multiple rules for responding. The classic adult task of this type is the Wisconsin Card Sorting Task (WCST), in which participants must discover the sorting rule simply on the basis of binary feedback received during card-sorting performance. Healthy adults show rapid acquisition of the initial sorting rule and quickly alter their behavior if and when the rule is changed. Lesions to the left DLPFC but not other regions of prefrontal cortex impair performance on switching tasks, resulting in perseverative errors (Keele & Rafal, 2000; Owen et al., 1993; Shallice & Burgess, 1991). Neuroimaging studies provide convergent evidence for the role of DLPFC and basal ganglia circuits in task switching and reversal learning (Cools, Clark, Owen, & Robbins, 2002; Cools, Clark, & Robbins, 2004).

Perhaps not surprisingly, typically developing 3-year-old children perform very similarly to adults with frontal lobe lesions. Zelazo, Frye, and Rapus (1996) have described a dramatic developmental shift in set-switching performance in the preschool years using the dimensional card sorting task. This task requires the child to first sort cards by one criterion (e.g., shape), and then to shift and sort the cards by another criterion (e.g., color). While 3-year-olds have no trouble sorting by the first criterion, whether it is shape or color, they frequently fail to shift their sorting behavior when the criterion changes despite being able to verbalize the rule, reminiscent of some patients with prefrontal cortex damage (REF). However, 5-year-olds generally have no difficulty with this task. Kirkham and colleagues have suggested that this developmental shift is predominantly the result of improved inhibitory control (A. Diamond, Kirkham, & Amso, 2002).

The developmental neuroimaging data in this domain are still sparse, although a number of groups are working in this direction. Additional work will be needed to assess developmental changes in the recruitment and efficiency of prefrontal cortex in such cognitive conflict or cognitive control tasks. It remains to be seen whether the normal developmental pattern of functional brain activity engages the same circuits known to be disrupted in adult lesion populations with executive dysfunctions.

Conclusions

Based on our extensive review of the literature, the field of developmental cognitive neuroscience has clearly advanced over the past decade. We know a considerable amount about the neural bases of a variety of cognitive abilities, although our knowledge base is uneven both between and within developmental periods. We know more about the neural bases of memory in infancy than we do in childhood, and we know more about some executive functions than others (e.g., working memory versus planning).

What does the future hold for those interested in this area? For starters, as our knowledge of brain development improves, our ability to ground behavior in the brain should similarly improve. This, in turn, should permit establishing more biologically plausible models of behavioral development (connectionist models, in particular, should benefit from this advance). Second, as our knowledge of neural plasticity and molecular biology increases, we will do a better job of designing studies that shed light on which behaviors are derived from experience-dependent versus experience-independent processes. This, in turn, should lead us away from strongly held nativist beliefs, at least in the context of higher-level cognitive functions. Third, we anticipate a judicious increase in the study of clinical populations; as such study has the potential to provide converging information on typical development. Fourth, given increased interest in using neuroimaging tools to study affective development, we anticipate increased interest in linking cognitive and emotional development in the context of brain development. Fifth, increased attention will be paid to the coregistration of imaging modalities, particularly ERPs with fMRI and optical imaging. Sixth, as investigators gain more experience in conducting fMRI studies with children, and as physicists and engineers improve MR scanning parameters, the field should experience a downward shift in the age at which such studies can be performed. Scanning infants will always prove difficult, but scanning preschool-age children may prove less challenging.

These are just a few of the areas of growth we anticipate in the coming decade—others will surface as the field evolves. But, we remain optimistic that interest in linking brain with behavior in the context of development is now firmly entrenched in developmental psychology.

References

Adolphs, R. (2002). Recognizing emotion from facial expressions: Psychological and neurological mechanisms. *Behavioural and Cognitive Neuroscience Reviews, 1,* 21–61.

Adolphs, R., Tranel, D., Damasio, H., & Damasio, A. (1994). Impaired recognition of emotion in facial expressions following bilateral damage to the human amygdala. *Nature, 372,* 669–672.

Adolphs, R., Tranel, D., Hamann, S., Young, A. W., Calder, A. J., Phelps, E. A., et al. (1999). Recognition of facial emotion in nine individuals with bilateral amygdala damage. *Neuropsychologia, 37,* 1111–1117.

Alvarado, M. C., & Bachevalier, J. (2000). Revisiting the maturation of medial temporal lobe memory functions in primates. *Learning and Memory, 7*(5), 244–256.

Alvarado, M. C., Wright, A. A., & Bachevalier, J. (2002). Object and spatial relational memory in adult rhesus monkeys is impaired by neonatal lesions of the hippocampal formation but not the amygdaloid complex. *Hippocampus, 12,* 421–433.

Anderson, V., Anderson, P., Northam, E., Jacobs, R., & Catroppa, C. (2001). Development of executive functions through late childhood and adolescence in an Australian sample. *Developmental Neuropsychology, 20*(1), 385–406.

Anderson, V., Levin, H., & Jacobs, R. (2002). Executive functions after frontal lobe injury: A developmental perspective. In D. Stuss & R. Knight (Eds.), *Principles of frontal lobe function* (pp. 504–527). New York: Oxford University Press.

Baillargeon, R. (1987). Object permanence in 3½- and 4½-month-old infants. *Developmental Psychology, 23,* 655–664.

Baillargeon, R., Spelke, E., & Wasserman, S. (1985). Object permanence in 5-month-old infants. *Cognition, 20,* 191–208.

Balaban, M. T. (1995). Affective influences on startle in 5-month-old infants: Reactions to facial expressions of emotion. *Child Development, 66,* 28–36.

Banks, M. S., & Ginsburg, A. P. (1985). Infant visual preferences: A review and new theoretical treatment. *Advances in Child Development and Behavior, 19,* 207–246.

Banks, M. S., & Salapatek, P. (1981). Infant pattern vision: A new approach based on the contrast sensitivity function. *Journal of Experimental Psychology, 31,* 1–45.

Barrash, J., Tranel, D., & Anderson, S. (1994). Assessment of dramatic personality changes after ventromedial frontal lesions. *Journal of Clinical and Experimental Neuropsychology, 18,* 355–381.

Barton, J. J. (2003). Disorders of face perception and recognition. *Neurologic Clinics, 21*(2), 521–548.

Benes, F., Turtle, M., Khan, Y., & Farol, P. (1994). Myelination of a key relay zone in the hippocampal formation occurs in the human brain during childhood, adolescence, and adulthood. *Archives of General Psychiatry, 51,* 477–484.

Bischoff-Grethe, A., Martin, M., Mao, H., & Berns, G. (2001). The context of uncertainty modulates the subcortical response to predictability. *Journal of Cognitive Neuroscience, 13*(7), 986–993.

Botvinick, M., Braver, T., Barch, D., Carter, C., & Cohen, J. (2001). Conflict monitoring and cognitive control. *Psychological Review, 108*(3), 624–652.

Bourgeois, J.-P., Reboff, P. J., & Rakic, P. (1989). Synaptogenesis in visual cortex of normal and preterm monkeys: Evidence from intrinsic regulation of synaptic overproduction. *Proceedings of the National Academy of Sciences, USA, 86,* 4297–4301.

Broks, P., Young, A. W., Maratos, E. J., Coffey, P. J., Calder, A. J., Isaac, C. L., et al. (1998). Face processing impairments after encephalitis: Amygdala damage and recognition of fear. *Neuropsychologia, 36*(1), 59–70.

Bronner-Fraser, M., & Hatten, M. B. (2003). Neurogenesis and migration. In L. R. Squire, F. E. Bloom, S. K. McConnell, J. L. Roberts, N. C. Spitzer, & M. J. Zigmond (Eds.), *Fundamental neuroscience* (2nd ed., pp. 391–416). New York: Academic Press.

Brown, M., Keynes, R., & Lumsden, A. (2001). *The developing brain.* Oxford: Oxford University Press.

Bunge, S., Dudukovic, N., Thomason, M., Vaidya, C., & Gabrieli, J. (2002). Immature frontal lobe contributions to cognitive control in children: Evidence from fMRI. *Neuron, 33*(2), 301–311.

Bush, G., Frazier, J., Rauch, S., Seidman, L., Whalen, P., Jenike, M., et al. (1999). Anterior cingulate cortex dysfunction in attention-deficit/hyperactivity disorder revealed by fMRI and the counting stroop. *Biological Psychiatry, 45*(12), 1542–1552.

Bush, G., Luu, P., & Posner, M. (2000). Cognitive and emotional influences in anterior cingulate cortex. *Trends in Cognitive Sciences, 4,* 215–222.

Calder, A. J., Young, A. W., Rowland, D., Perett, D. I., Hodges, J. R., & Etcoff, N. L. (1996). Facial emotion recognition after bilateral amygdala damage: Differentially severe impairment of fear. *Cognitive Neuropsychology, 13,* 699–745.

Canfield, R., Smith, E., Brezsnyak, M., & Snow, K. (1997). Information processing through the first year of life: A longitudinal study using the visual expectancy paradigm. *Monographs of the Society for Research in Child Development, 62*(2).

Carey, S., & Diamond, R. (1994). Are faces perceived as configurations more by adults than children? *Visual Cognition, 1,* 253–274.

Casey, B., Cohen, J., Jezzard, P., Turner, R., Noll, D., Trainor, R., et al. (1995). Activation of prefrontal cortex in children during a nonspatial working memory task with functional MRI. *Neuroimage, 2,* 221–229.

Casey, B., Durston, S., & Fossella, J. (2001). Evidence for a mechanistic model of cognitive control. *Clinical Neuroscience Research, 1,* 267–282.

Casey, B., Forman, S., Franzen, P., Berkowitz, A., Braver, T., Nystrom, L., et al. (2001). Sensitivity of prefrontal cortex to changes in target probability: A functional MRI study. *Human Brain Mapping, 13,* 26–33.

Casey, B., Thomas, K., Welsh, T., Badgaiyan, R., Eccard, C., Jennings, J., et al. (2000). Dissociation of response conflict, attentional control, and expectancy with functional magnetic resonance imaging (fMRI). *Proceedings of the National Academy of Sciences, USA, 97*(15), 8728–8733.

Casey, B., Tottenham, N., & Fossella, J. (2002). Clinical, imaging, lesion, and genetic approaches toward a model of cognitive control. *Developmental Psychobiology, 40*(3), 237–254.

Casey, B., Trainor, R., Orendi, J., Schubert, A., Nystrom, L., Cohen, J., et al. (1997). A pediatric functional MRI study of prefrontal activation during performance of a go-no-go task. *Journal of Cognitive Neuroscience, 9,* 835–847.

Castellanos, F., Giedd, J., Berquin, P., Walter, J., Sharp, W., Tran, T., et al. (2001). Quantitative brain magnetic resonance imaging in girls with attention-deficit/hyperactivity disorder. *Archives of General Psychiatry, 58,* 289–295.

Castellanos, F., Lee, P., Sharp, W., Jeffries, N., Greenstein, D., Clasen, L., et al. (2002). Developmental trajectories of brain volume abnormalities in children and adolescents with attention-deficit/hyperactivity disorder. *Journal of the American Medical Association, 288,* 1740–1748.

Chechik, G., Meilijson, I., & Ruppin, E. (1999). Neuronal regulation: A mechanism for synaptic pruning during brain maturation. *Neural Computation, 11*(8), 2061–2080.

Chenn, A., & McConnell, S. K. (1995). Cleavage orientation and the asymmetric inheritance of Notch1 immunoreactivity in mammalian neurogenesis. *Cell, 82,* 631–641.

Clohessy, A., Posner, M., & Rothbart, M. (2002). Development of the functional visual field. *Acta Psychologia, 106*(1/2), 51–68.

Cohen, J., Forman, S., Braver, T., Casey, B., Servan-Schreiber, D., & Noll, D. (1994). Activation of prefrontal cortex in a non-spatial working memory task with functional MRI. *Human Brain Mapping, 1,* 293–304.

Cools, R., Clark, L., Owen, A., & Robbins, T. (2002). Defining the neural mechanisms of probabilistic reversal learning using event-related functional magnetic resonance imaging. *Journal of Neuroscience, 22*(11), 4563–4567.

Cools, R., Clark, L., & Robbins, T. (2004). Differential responses in human striatum and prefrontal cortex to changes in object and rule relevance. *Journal of Neuroscience, 24*(5), 1129–1135.

Damasio, H., Grabowski, T., Frank, R., Galaburda, A., & Damasio, A. (1994). The return of Phineas Gage: Clues about the brain from the skull of a famous patient. *Science, 264,* 1102–1105.

Davis, M. (1989). The role of the amygdala and its efferent projections in fear and anxiety. In P. Tyrer (Ed.), *Psychopharmacology of anxiety* (pp. 52–79). Oxford: Oxford University Press.

de Haan, M., & Johnson, M. H. (2003a). *The cognitive neuroscience of development.* London: Psychology Press.

de Haan, M., & Johnson, M. H. (2003b). Mechanisms and theories of brain development. In M. de Haan & M. H. Johnson (Eds.), *The cognitive neuroscience of development* (pp. 1–18). London: Psychology Press.

de Haan, M., & Nelson, C. A. (1999). Brain activity differentiates face and object processing in 6-month-old infants. *Developmental Psychology, 35,* 1113–1121.

de Haan, M., Pascalis, O., & Johnson, M. H. (2002). Specialization of neural mechanisms underlying face recognition in human infants. *Journal of Cognitive Neuroscience, 14*(2), 199–209.

Desimone, R., & Duncan, J. (1995). Neural mechanisms of selective visual attention. *Annual Review of Neuroscience, 18,* 193–222.

Diamond, A. (1985). Development of the ability to use recall to guide action, as indicated by infants' performance on A-not-B. *Child Development, 56,* 868–883.

Diamond, A. (1995). Evidence of robust recognition memory early in life even when assessed by reaching behavior. *Journal of Experimental Child Psychology, 59,* 419–456.

Diamond, A. (2001). A model system for studying the role of dopamine in the prefrontal cortex during early development in humans: Early and continuously treated phenylketonuria. In C. Nelson & M. Luciana (Eds.), *Handbook of developmental cognitive neuroscience* (pp. 433–472). Cambridge, MA: MIT Press.

Diamond, A. (2002). Normal development of prefrontal cortex from birth to young adulthood: Cognitive functions, anatomy, and biochemistry. In D. Stuss & R. Knight (Eds.), *Principles of frontal lobe function* (pp. 466–503). New York: Oxford University Press.

Diamond, A., & Goldman-Rakic, P. (1989). Comparison of human infants and rhesus monkeys on Piaget's A-not-B task: Evidence for dependence on dorsolateral prefrontal cortex. *Experimental Brain Research, 74,* 24–40.

Diamond, A., Kirkham, N., & Amso, D. (2002). Conditions under which young children can hold two rules in mind and inhibit a prepotent response. *Developmental Psychology, 38,* 352–363.

Diamond, R., & Carey, S. (1986). Why faces are and are not special: An effect of expertise. *Journal of Experimental Psychology: General, 115,* 107–117.

Dolan, R. J., & Fletcher, P. C. (1997). Dissociating prefrontal and hippocampal function in episodic memory encoding. *Nature, 388*(6642), 582–585.

Duncan, J., & Owen, A. (2000). Common regions of the human frontal lobe recruited by diverse cognitive demands. *Trends in Neurosciences, 23,* 475–483.

Durston, S., Hulshoff Pol, H. E., Casey, B. J., Giedd, J. N., Buitelaar, J. K., & van Engeland, H. (2001). Anatomical MRI of the developing human brain: What have we learned? *Journal of the American Academy of Child and Adolescent Psychiatry, 40,* 1012–1020.

Durston, S., Thomas, K., & Yang, Y. (2002). The development of neural systems involved in overriding behavioral responses: An event-related fMRI study. *Developmental Science, 5,* 9–16.

Durston, S., Tottenham, N., Thomas, K., Davidson, M., Eigsti, I., Yang, Y., et al. (2003). Differential patterns of striatal activation in young children with and without ADHD. *Biological Psychiatry, 53*(10), 871–878.

Eimer, M. (2000). The face-specific N170 component reflects late stages in the structural encoding of faces. *NeuroReport, 11,* 2319–2324.

Fan, J., Flombaum, J., McCandliss, B., Thomas, K., & Posner, M. (2003). Cognitive and brain consequences of conflict. *NeuroImage, 18*(1), 42–57.

Farah, M. J., Rabinowitz, C., Quinn, G. E., & Liu, G. T. (2000). Early commitment of neural substrates for face recognition. *Cognitive Neuropsychology, 17,* 117–124.

Ferraro, F., Balota, D., & Connor, L. (1993). Implicit memory and the formation of new associations in nondemented Parkinson's disease individuals and individuals with senile dementia of the Alzheimer type: A serial reaction time (SRT) investigation. *Brain and Cognition, 21,* 163–180.

Funahashi, S., Bruce, C., & Goldman-Rakic, P. (1989). Mnemonic coding of visual space in the monkey's dorsolateral prefrontal cortex. *Journal of Neurophysiology, 61,* 1–19.

Fuster, J. (1997). *The prefrontal cortex: Anatomy, physiology, and neuropsychology of the frontal lobe* (3rd ed.). Philadelphia: Lippencott-Raven Press.

Fuster, J., & Alexander, G. (1970). Delayed response deficit by cryogenic depression of frontal cortex. *Brain Research, 61,* 79–91.

Fuster, J., & Alexander, G. (1971). Neuron activity related to short-term memory. *Science, 173,* 652–654.

Gauthier, I., Skudlarski, P., Gore, J. C., & Anderson, A. W. (2000). Expertise for cars and birds recruits brain areas involved in face recognition. *Nature Neuroscience, 3,* 191–197.

Gauthier, I., Tarr, M. J., Anderson, A. W., Skudlarski, P., & Gore, J. C. (1999). Activation of the middle fusiform "face area" increases with expertise in recognizing novel objects. *Nature Neuroscience, 2,* 568–573.

Geldart, S., Mondloch, C. J., Maurer, D., de Schonen, S., & Brent, H. P. (2002). The effect of early visual deprivation on the development of face processing. *Developmental Science, 5*(4), 490–501.

Gerardi-Caulton, G. (2000). Sensitivity to spatial conflict and the development of self-regulation in children 24 to 30 months of age. *Developmental Science, 3,* 397–404.

Giedd, J. N., Snell, J., Lange, N., Rajapakse, J., Casey, B., Kozuch, P., et al. (1996). Quantitative magnetic resonance imaging of human brain development: Ages 4 to 18. *Cerebral Cortex, 6,* 551–560.

Giedd, J. N., Vatuzis, A. C., Hamburger, S. D., Lange, N., Rajapakse, J. C., Matsen, D., et al. (1996). Quantitative MRI of the temporal lobe, amygdala, and hippocampus in normal human development: Ages 4 to 18 years. *Journal of Comparative Neurology, 366,* 223–230.

Goldman, P., & Rosvold, H. (1970). Localization of function within the dorsolateral prefrontal cortex of the rhesus monkey. *Experimental Neurology, 29,* 291–304.

Goldman-Rakic, P. S. (1987). Development of cortical circuitry and cognitive function. *Child Development, 58*(3), 601–622.

Grafton, S., Hazeltine, E., & Ivry, R. (1995). Functional mapping of sequence learning in normal humans. *Journal of Cognitive Neuroscience, 7*(4), 497–510.

Haith, M., Hazan, C., & Goodman, G. (1988). Expectation and anticipation of dynamic visual events by 3½-month-old babies. *Child Development, 59,* 467–479.

Halit, H., de Haan, M., & Johnson, M. H. (2003). Cortical specialization for face processing: Face sensitive-event related potential components in 3- and 12-month-old infants. *Neuroimage, 19,* 1180–1193.

Hanashima, C., Li, S. C., Shen, L., Lai, E., & Fishell, G. (2004). Foxg1 suppresses early cortical cell fate. *Science, 303,* 56–59.

Hatten, M. E. (2002). New directions in neuronal migration. *Science, 297,* 1660–1663.

Haxby, J. V., Gobbini, M. I., Furey, M. L., Ishai, A., Schouten, J. L., & Pietrini, P. (2001). Distributed and overlapping representations of faces and objects in ventral temporal cortex. *Science, 293,* 2425–2430.

Haxby, J. V., Hoffman, E. A., & Gobbini, M. I. (2002). Human neural systems for face recognition and social communication. *Biological Psychiatry, 51,* 59–67.

Hayne, H. (2004). Infant memory development: Implications for childhood amnesia. *Developmental Review, 24,* 33–73.

Hazeltine, E., Grafton, S., & Ivry, R. (1997). Attention and stimulus characteristics determined the locus of motor sequence encoding: A PET study. *Brain, 120,* 123–140.

Heindel, W., Salmon, D., Shults, C., Walicke, P., & Butters, N. (1989). Neuropsychological evidence for multiple implicit memory systems: A comparison of Alzheimer's, Huntington's, and Parkinson's disease patients. *Journal of Neuroscience, 9*(2), 582–587.

Henson, R. N., Goshen-Gottstein, Y., Ganel, T., Otten, L. J., Quayle, A., & Rugg, M. D. (2003). Electrophysiological and haemodynamic correlates of face perception, recognition and priming. *Cerebral Cortex, 13,* 795–805.

Hoffman, E., & Haxby, J. V. (2000). Distinct representations of eye gaze and identity in the distributed human neural system for face perception. *Nature Neuroscience, 3,* 80–84.

Holstege, G., van Ham, J. J., & Tan, J. (1986). Afferent projections to the orbicularis oculi motoneural cell group: An autoradiographical tracing study in the cat. *Brain Research, 374,* 306–320.

Hubl, D., Bolte, S., Feineis-Matthews, S., Lanfermann, H., Federspiel, A., Strik, W., et al. (2003). Functional imbalance of visual pathways indicates alternative face processing strategies in autism. *Neurology, 61,* 1232–1237.

Huttenlocher, P. R., & Dabholkar, A. S. (1997). Regional differences in synaptogenesis in human cerebral cortex. *Journal of Comparative Neurology, 387*(2), 167–178.

Huttenlocher, P. R., & de Courten, C. (1987). The development of synapses in striat cortex of man. *Human Neurobiology, 6,* 1–9.

Ishai, A., Ungerleider, L. G., Martin, A., & Haxby, J. V. (2000). The representation of objects in the human occipital and temporal cortex. *Journal of Cognitive Neuroscience, 12*(Suppl. 2), 35–51.

Itier, R. J., & Taylor, M. J. (2002). Inversion and contrast polarity reversal affect both encoding and recognition processes of unfamiliar faces: A repetition study using ERPs. *NeuroImage, 15*(2), 353–372.

Jernigan, T. L., Trauner, D. A., Hesselink, J. R., & Tallal, P. A. (1991). Maturation of human cerebrum observed in vivo during adolescence. *Brain, 114,* 2037–2049.

Johnson, M. H. (1998). The neural basis of cognitive development. In W. Damon (Series Ed.) & D. Kuhn & R. S. Siegler (Vol. Eds.), *Handbook of child psychology: Vol. 2. Cognition, perception and language* (5th ed., pp. 1–49). New York: Wiley.

Johnson, M. H. (2001). Functional brain development in humans. *Nature Reviews Neuroscience, 2,* 475–483.

Johnson, M. H., Dziurawiec, S., Ellis, H., & Morton, J. (1991). Newborns' preferential tracking of face-like stimuli and its subsequent decline. *Cognition, 40,* 1–19.

Johnson, M. H., & Morton, J. (1991). *Biology and cognitive development: The case of face recognition.* Oxford, England: Blackwell.

Kanwisher, N., McDermott, J., & Chun, M. M. (1997). The fusiform face area: A module in human extrastriate cortex specialized for face perception. *Journal of Neuroscience, 17,* 4302–4311.

Kawashima, R., Satoh, K., Itoh, H., Ono, S., Furumoto, S., Grotoh, R., et al. (1996). Functional anatomy of go/no-go discrimination and response selection: A PET study in man. *Brain Research, 728,* 79–89.

Keele, S., & Rafal, R. (2000). Deficits of task set in patients with left prefrontal cortex lesions. In S. Monsell & J. Driver (Eds.), *Control of cognitive processes, attention and performance* (Vol. 18, pp. 625–652). Cambridge, MA: MIT Press.

Keith, A. (1948). *Human embryology and morphology.* London: Edward Arnold.

Kennedy, H., Bullier, J., & Dehay, C. (1989). Transient projection from the superior temporal sulcus to area 17 in the newborn macaque monkey. *Proceedings of the National Academy of Sciences, USA, 86,* 8093–8097.

Kesler-West, M. L., Andersen, A. H., Smith, C. D., Avison, M. J., Davis, C. E., Kryscio, R. J., et al. (2001). Neural substrates of facial emotion processing using fMRI. *Brain Research: Cognitive Brain Research, 11,* 213–226.

Knopman, D., & Nissen, M. (1991). Procedural learning is impaired in Huntington's disease: Evidence from the serial reaction time task. *Neuropsychologia, 29*(3), 245–254.

Konishi, S., Nakajima, K., Uchida, I., Kikyo, H., Kameyama, M., & Miyashita, Y. (1999). Common inhibitory mechanism in human inferior prefrontal cortex revealed by event-related functional MRI. *Brain, 122,* 981–999.

Kostovic, I. (1990). Structural and histochemical reorganization of the human prefrontal cortex during perinatal and postnatal life. *Progress in Brain Research, 85,* 223–239.

Kriegstein, A. R., & Götz, M. (2003). Radial glia diversity: A matter of cell fate. *Glia, 43,* 37–43.

Lang, P. J., Bradley, M. M., & Cuthbert, B. N. (1990). Emotion, attention, and the startle reflex. *Psychological Review, 97,* 377–395.

Lang, P. J., Bradley, M. M., & Cuthbert, B. N. (1992). A motivational analysis of emotion: Reflex-cortex connections. *Psychological Science, 3,* 44–49.

Le Grand, R., Mondloch, C. J., Maurer, D., & Brent, H. P. (2001a). Early visual experience and face processing. *Nature, 410,* 890.

Le Grand, R., Mondloch, C. J., Maurer, D., & Brent, H. P. (2001b). Correction: Early visual experience and face processing. *Nature, 412,* 786.

Le Grand, R., Mondloch, C. J., Maurer, D., & Brent, H. P. (2003). Expert face processing requires input to the right hemisphere during infancy. *Nature Neuroscience, 6,* 1108–1112.

Levitt, P. (2003). Structural and functional maturation of the developing primate brain. *Journal of Pediatrics, 143*(Suppl. 4), S35–S45.

Levy, R., & Goldman-Rakic, P. (2000). Segregation of working memory functions within the dorsolateral prefrontal cortex. *Experimental Brain Research, 133*(1), 23–32.

Lewicki, P. (1986). Processing information about covariations that cannot be articulated. *Journal of Experimental Psychology: Learning, Memory, and Cognition, 12,* 135–146.

Luciana, M. (2003). The neural and functional development of human prefrontal cortex. In M. de Haan & M. H. Johnson (Eds.), *The cognitive neuroscience of development* (pp. 157–179). London: Psychology Press.

Luciana, M., Sullivan, J., & Nelson, C. A. (2001). Individual differences in phenylalanine levels moderate performance on tests of executive function in adolescents treated early and continuously for PKU. *Child Development, 72,* 1637–1652.

Lumsden, A., & Kintner, C. (2003). Neural induction and pattern formation. In L. R. Squire, F. E. Bloom, S. K. McConnell, J. L. Roberts, N. C. Spitzer, & M. J. Zigmond (Eds.), *Fundamental neuroscience* (2nd ed., pp. 363–390). New York: Academic Press.

Luna, B., Thulborn, K., Munoz, D., Merriam, E., Garver, K., Minshew, N., et al. (2001). Maturation of widely distributed brain function subserves cognitive development. *NeuroImage, 13,* 786–793.

MacDonald, A., Cohen, J., Stenger, V., & Carter, C. (2000). Dissociating the role of the dorsolateral prefrontal and anterior cingulate cortex in cognitive control. *Science, 288*(5472), 1835–1838.

Málková, L., Bachevalier, J., Mishkin, M., & Saunders, C. (2001). Neurotoxic lesions of perirhinal cortex impair visual recognition memory in rhesus monkeys. *NeuroReport, 12,* 1913–1917.

Manns, J. R., Stark, C. E., & Squire, L. R. (2000). The visual paired-comparison task as a measure of declarative memory. *Proceedings of the National Academy of Sciences, USA, 97*(22), 12375–12379.

Marin-Padilla, M. (1978). Dual origin of the mammalian neocortex and evolution of the cortical plate. *Anatomical Embryology, 152,* 109–126.

Maybery, M., Taylor, M., & O'Brien-Malone, A. (1995). Implicit learning: Sensitive to age but not to IQ. *Australian Journal of Psychology, 47,* 8–17.

McKee, R. D., & Squire, L. R. (1993). On the development of declarative memory. *Journal of Experimental Psychology: Learning, Memory, and Cognition, 19,* 397–404.

Meletti, S., Benuzzi, F., Rubboli, G., Cantalupo, G., Stanzani Maserati, M., Nichelli, P., et al. (2003). Impaired facial emotion recognition in early-onset right mesial temporal epilepsy. *Neurology, 60,* 426–431.

Meulemans, T., van der Linden, M., & Perruchet, P. (1998). Implicit sequence learning in children. *Journal of Experimental Child Psychology, 69,* 199–221.

Milner, B., Corkin, S., & Teuber, H. (1968). Further analysis of the hippocampal amnesic syndrome: 14-year follow-up study of HM. *Neuropsychologia, 6,* 215–234.

Molliver, M., Kostovic, I., & Van der Loos, H. (1973). The development of synapses in the human fetus. *Brain Research, 50,* 403–407.

Monk, C. S., Zhuang, J., Curtis, W. J., Ofenloch, I. T., Tottenham, N., Nelson, C. A., et al. (2002). Human hippocampal activation in the delayed matching- and nonmatching-to-sample memory tasks: An event-related functional MRI approach. *Behavioral Neuroscience, 116,* 716–721.

Morris, J. S., Frith, C. D., Perrett, K. I., Rowland, D., Young, A. W., Calder, A. J., et al. (1996). A differential neural response in the human amygdala to fearful and happy facial expressions. *Nature, 383,* 812–815.

Moscovitch, M., Winocur, G., & Behrmann, M. (1997). What is special about face recognition? Nineteen experiments on a person with visual object agnosia but normal face recognition. *Journal of Cognitive Neuroscience, 9,* 555–604.

Murloz-Sanjuan, I., & Brivanfou, A. H. (2002). Neural induction: The default model and embryonic stem cells. *Nature Reviews Neuroscience, 3*(4), 271–280.

Nadarajah, B., & Parnavelas, J. G. (2002). Models of neuronal migration in the developing cerebral cortex. *Nature Reviews Neuroscience, 3,* 423–432.

Naegele, J. R., & Lombroso, P. J. (2001). Genetics of central nervous system developmental disorders. *Child and Adolescent Psychiatric Clinics of North America, 10,* 225–239.

Nelson, C. A. (1995). The ontogeny of human memory: A cognitive neuroscience perspective. *Developmental Psychology, 31,* 723–738.

Nelson, C. A. (1998). The nature of early memory. *Preventive Medicine, 27,* 172–179.

Nelson, C. A. (2001). The development and neural bases of face recognition. *Infant and Child Development, 10,* 3–18.

Nelson, C. A., & Bloom, F. E. (1997). Child development and neuroscience. *Child Development, 68,* 970–987.

Nelson, C. A., & Carver, L. J. (1998). The effects of stress on brain and memory: A view from developmental cognitive neuroscience. *Development and Psychopathology, 10,* 793–809.

Nelson, C. A., & Collins, P. F. (1991). Event-related potential and looking time analysis of infants' responses to familiar and novel events: Implications for visual recognition memory. *Developmental Psychology, 27,* 50–58.

Nelson, C. A., & Collins, P. F. (1992). Neural and behavioral correlates of recognition memory in 4- and 8-month-old infants. *Brain and Cognition, 19,* 105–121.

Nelson, C. A., Lin, J., Carver, L. J., Monk, C. S., Thomas, K. M., & Truwit, C. L. (2000). Functional neuroanatomy of spatial working memory in children. *Developmental Psychology, 36*(1), 109–116.

Nelson, C. A., & Luciana, M. (Eds.). (2001). *Handbook of developmental cognitive neuroscience.* Cambridge, MA: MIT Press.

Nelson, C. A., & Webb, S. J. (2003). A cognitive neuroscience perspective on early memory development. In M. de Haan & M. H. Johnson (Eds.), *The cognitive neuroscience of development* (pp. 99–125). London: Psychology Press.

Nemanic, S., Alvarado, M. C., & Bachevalier, J. (2004). The hippocampal/parahippocampal regions and recognition memory: Insights from visual paired comparison versus object-delayed nonmatching in monkeys. *Journal of Neuroscience, 24,* 2013–2026.

Nissen, M., & Bullemer, P. (1987). Attentional requirements of learning: Evidence from performance measures. *Cognitive Psychology, 19,* 1–32.

Overman, W. H., Bachevalier, J., Sewell, F., & Drew, J. (1993). A comparison of children's performance on two recognition memory tasks: Delayed nonmatch-to-sample-versus-visual-paired-comparison. *Developmental Psychobiology, 26,* 345–357.

Owen, A., Roberts, A., Hodges, J., Summers, B., Polkey, C., & Robbins, T. (1993). Contrasting mechanisms of impaired attentional set shifting in patients with frontal lobe damage or Parkinson's disease. *Brain, 119,* 1597–1615.

Pascalis, O., & Bachevalier, J. (1999). Neonatal aspiration lesions of the hippocampal formation impair visual recognition memory when assessed by paired-comparison task but not by delayed nonmatching-to-sample task. *Hippocampus, 9,* 609–616.

Pascalis, O., de Haan, M., & Nelson, C. A. (2002). Is face processing species specific during the first year of life? *Science, 296,* 1321–1323.

Pascalis, O., Hunkin, N. M., Holdstock, J. S., Isaac, C. L., & Mayes, A. R. (2004). Visual paired comparison performance is impaired in a patient with selective hippocampal lesions and relatively intact item recognition. *Neuropsychologia, 42,* 1230–1293.

Pascual-Leone, A., Grafman, J., Clark, K., Stewart, M., Massaquoi, S., Lou, J.-S., et al. (1993). Procedural learning in Parkinson's disease and cerebellar degeneration. *Annals of Neurology, 34,* 594–602.

Passarotti, A. M., Paul, B. M., Bussiere, J. R., Buxton, R. B., Wong, E. C., & Stiles, J. (2003). The development of face and location processing: An fMRI study. *Developmental Science, 6,* 100–117.

Paus, T., Zijdenbos, A., Worsley, K., Collins, D. L., Blumenthal, J., Giedd, J. N., et al. (1999). Structural maturation of neural pathways in children and adolescents: In vivo study. *Science, 283,* 1908–1911.

Pierce, K., Muller, R. A., Ambrose, J., Allen, G., & Courchesne, E. (2001). Face processing occurs outside the fusiform "face area" in autism: Evidence from functional MRI. *Brain, 124,* 2059–2073.

Pollak, S. D., Cicchetti, D., Hornung, K., & Reed, A. (2000). Recognizing emotion in faces: Developmental effects of child abuse and neglect. *Developmental Psychology, 36*(5), 679–688.

Pollak, S. D., & Kistler, D. J. (2002). Early experience is associated with the development of categorical representations for facial expressions of emotion. *Proceedings of the National Academy of Sciences, USA, 99*(13), 9072–9076.

Pollak, S. D., & Sinha, P. (2002). Effects of early experience on children's recognition and facial displays of emotion. *Developmental Psychology, 38*(5), 784–791.

Posner, M., & Petersen, S. (1990). The attention system of the human brain. *Annual Review of Neuroscience, 13,* 25–42.

Posner, M., & Raichle, M. (1997). *Images of mind.* New York: Scientific American Library.

Puce, A., Allison, T., Asgari, M., Gore, J. C., & McCarthy, G. (1996). Differential sensitivity of human visual cortex to faces, letterstrings, and textures: A functional magnetic resonance imaging study. *Journal of Neuroscience, 16,* 5205–5215.

Rakic, P. (1988). Specification of cerebral cortical areas. *Science, 241,* 170–176.

Rebai, M., Poiroux, S., Bernard, C., & Lalonde, R. (2001). Event-related potentials for category-specific information during passive viewing of faces and objects. *Internal Journal of Neuroscience, 106*(3/4), 209–226.

Reber, A. (1992). The cognitive unconscious: An evolutionary perspective. *Consciousness and Cognition, 1,* 93–133.

Reber, A. (1993). *Implicit learning and tacit knowledge: Vol. 19. An essay on the cognitive unconscious.* New York: Oxford University Press.

Ridderinkhof, K., van der Molen, M., Band, G., & Bashore, T. (1997). Sources of interference from irrelevant information: A developmental study. *Journal of Experimental Child Psychology, 65,* 315–341.

Ridley, A. J., Schwartz, M. A., Burridge, K., Firtel, R. A., Ginsberg, M. H., Borisy, G., et al. (2003). Cell migration: Integrating signals from front to back. *Science, 302,* 1704–1709.

Robinson, A. J., & Pascalis, O. (2004). Development of flexible visual recognition memory in human infants. *Developmental Science, 7,* 527–533.

Rossion, B., Gauthier, I., Tarr, M. J., Despland, P., Bruyer, R., Linotte, S., et al. (2000). The N170 occipito-temporal component is delayed and enhanced to inverted faces but not inverted objects: An electrophysiological account of face-specific processes in the human brain. *NeuroReport, 11,* 69–74.

Rueda, M. R., Fan, J., McCandliss, B. D., Halparin, J. D., Gruber, D. B., Lercari, L. P., et al. (2004). Development of attentional networks in childhood. *Neuropsychologia, 42*(8), 1029–1040.

Schendan, H., Searl, M., Melrose, R., & Ce, S. (2003). An FMRI study of the role of the medial temporal lobe in implicit and explicit sequence learning. *Neuron, 37*(6), 1013–1025.

Schultz, R. T., Gauthier, I., Klin, A., Fulbright, K. A., Anderson, A. W., Volkmar, F., et al. (2000). Abnormal ventral temporal cortical activity during face discrimination among individuals with autism and Asperger syndrome. *Archives of General Psychiatry, 57,* 331–340.

Schwartz, B., & Hashtroudi, S. (1991). Priming is independent of skill learning. *Journal of Experimental Psychology: Learning, Memory and Cognition, 17*(6), 1177–1187.

Schweinberger, S. R., Pickering, E. C., Jentzsch, I., Burton, A. M., & Kaufmann, J. M. (2002). Event-related brain potential evidence for a response of inferior temporal cortex to familiar face repetitions. *Brain Research: Cognitive Brain Research, 14,* 398–409.

Seger, C. (1994). Implicit learning. *Psychological Bulletin, 115*(2), 163–196.

Serres, L. (2001). Morphological changes of the human hippocampal formation from midgestation to early childhood. In C. A. Nelson & M. Luciana (Eds.), *Handbook of developmental cognitive neuroscience* (pp. 45–58). Cambridge, MA: MIT Press.

Shallice, T. (1988). *From neuropsychology to mental structure.* New York: Cambridge University Press.

Shallice, T., & Burgess, P. (1991). Higher-order cognitive impairments and frontal lobe lesions in man. In H. Levin, H. Eisenberg, & A. Benton (Eds.), *Frontal lobe function and dysfunction* (pp. 125–138). Oxford: Oxford University Press.

Shibata, T., Nishijo, H., Tamura, R., Miyamoto, K., Eifuku, S., Endo, S., et al. (2002). Generators of visual evoked potentials for faces and eyes in the human brain as determined by dipole localization. *Brain Topography, 15,* 51–63.

Shimamura, A. (1986). Priming effects in amnesia: Evidence for a dissociable memory function. *Quarterly Journal of Experimental Psychology, 38A,* 619–644.

Sidman, R., & Rakic, P. (1982). Development of the human central nervous system. In W. Haymaker & R. D. Adams (Eds.), *Histology and histopathology of the nervous system* (pp. 3–145). Springfield, IL: Charles C Thomas.

Smith, P., Loboschefski, T., Davidson, B., & Dixon, W. (1997). Scripts and checkerboards: The influence of ordered visual information on remembering locations in infancy. *Infant Behavior and Development, 13,* 129–146.

Sowell, E. R., Thompson, P. M., Holmes, C. J., Batth, R., Jernigan, T. L., & Toga, A. W. (1999). Localizing age-related changes in brain structure between childhood and adolescence using statistical parametric mapping. *Neuroimage, 9,* 587–597.

Sowell, E. R., Thompson, P. M., Holmes, C. J., Jernigan, T. L., & Toga, A. W. (2000). In vivo evidence for post-adolescent brain maturation in frontal and striatal regions. *Nature Neuroscience, 2,* 859–961.

Spelke, E. S. (2000). Core knowledge. *American Psychologist, 55,* 1233–1243.

Squire, L. (1986). Mechanisms of memory. *Science, 232,* 1612–1619.

Squire, L. (1994). Declarative and nondeclarative memory: Multiple brain systems supporting learning and memory. In D. L. Schacter & E. Tulving (Eds.), *Memory systems* (pp. 203–231). Cambridge, MA: MIT Press.

Squire, L., & Frambach, M. (1990). Cognitive skill learning in amnesia. *Psychobiology, 18,* 109–117.

Squire, L., Knowlton, B., & Musen, G. (1993). The structure and organization of memory. *Annual Review of Psychology, 44,* 453–495.

Squire, L., & McKee, R. (1993). Declarative and nondeclarative memory in opposition: When prior events influence amnesic patients more than normal subjects. *Memory and Cognition, 21*(4), 424–430.

Strange, B. A., Fletcher, P. C., Hennson, R. N. A., Friston, K. J., & Dolan, R. J. (1999). Segregating the functions of the human hippocampus. *Proceedings of the National Academy of Sciences, USA, 96,* 4034–4039.

Tabata, H., & Nakajima, K. (2003). Multipolar migration: The third mode of radial neuronal migration in the developing cerebral cortex. *Journal of Neuroscience, 23*(31), 9996–10001.

Takahashi, T., Nowakowski, R. S., & Caviness, V. S. (2001). Neocortical neurogeneisis: Regulation, control points, and a strategy of structural variation. In C. A. Nelson & M. Luciana (Eds.), *Handbook of developmental cognitive neuroscience* (pp. 3–22). Cambridge, MA: MIT Press.

Taylor, M. J., Edmonds, G. E., McCarthy, G., & Allison, T. (2001). Eyes first! Eye processing develops before face processing in children. *NeuroReport, 12,* 1671–1676.

Taylor, M. J., McCarthy, G., Saliba, E., & Degiovanni, E. (1999). ERP evidence of developmental changes in processing of faces. *Clinical Neurophysiololgy, 110,* 910–915.

Thomas, K. M., Drevets, W. C., Whalen, P. J., Eccard, C. H., Dahl, R. E., Ryan, N. D., et al. (2001). Amygdala response to facial expressions in children and adults. *Biological Psychiatry, 49,* 309–316.

Thomas, K. M., Hunt, R., Vizueta, N., Sommer, T., Durston, S., Yang, Y., et al. (in press). Evidence of developmental differences in implicit sequence learning: An fMRI study of children and adults. *Journal of Cognitive Neuroscience.*

Thomas, K. M., King, S. W., Franzen, P. L., Welsh, T. F., Berkowitz, A. L., Noll, D. C., et al. (1999). A developmental functional MRI study of spatial working memory. *Neuroimage, 10,* 327–338.

Thomas, K. M., & Nelson, C. (2001). Serial reaction time learning in preschool- and school-age children. *Journal of Experimental Child Psychology, 79,* 364–387.

Thomas, K. M., Vizueta, N., Teylan, M., Eccard, C., & Casey, B. (2003, April). *Impaired learning in children with presumed basal ganglia insults: Evidence from a serial reaction time task.* Paper presented at the annual meeting of the Cognitive Neuroscience Society, New York.

Tulving, E., Markowitsch, H. J., Craik, F. E., Habib, R., & Houle, S. (1996). Novelty and familiarity activations in PET studies of memory encoding and retrieval. *Cerebral Cortex, 6,* 71–79.

Turati, C., Simion, F., Milani, I., & Umilta, C. (2002). Newborns' preferences for faces: What is crucial. *Developmental Psychology, 38,* 875–882.

Tzourio-Mazoyer, N., de Schonen, S., Crivello, F., Reutter, B., Aujard, Y., & Mazoyer, B. (2002). Neural correlates of woman face processing by 2-month-old infants. *NeuroImage, 15,* 454–461.

Vaidya, C., Austin, G., Kirkorian, G., Ridlehuber, H., Desmond, J., Glover, G., et al. (1998). Selective effects of methylphenidate in attention deficit hyperactivity disorder: A functional magnetic resonance study. *Proceedings of the National Academy of Sciences, USA, 95*(24), 14494–14499.

Volpe, J. J. (2000). Overview: Normal and abnormal human brain development. *Mental Retardation and Developmental Disabilities Research Reviews, 6,* 1–5.

Waber, D., Marcus, D., Forbes, P., Bellinger, D., Weiler, M., Sorensen, L., et al. (2003). Motor sequence learning and reading ability: Is poor reading associated with sequencing deficits? *Journal of Experimental Child Psychology, 84*(4), 338–354.

Webb, S. J., Monk, C. S., & Nelson, C. A. (2001). Mechanisms of postnatal neurobiological development in the prefrontal cortex and the hippocampal region: Implications for human development. *Developmental Neuropsychology, 19,* 147–171.

Whalen, P. J., Shin, L. M., McInerney, S. C., Fisher, H., Wright, C. I., & Rauch, S. L. (2001). A functional MRI study of human amygdala responses to facial expressions of fear versus anger. *Emotion, 1,* 70–83.

Wong, R. O., & Lichtman, J. W. (2003). Synapse elimination. In L. R. Squire, F. E. Bloom, S. K. McConnell, J. L. Roberts, N. C. Spitzer, & M. J. Zigmond (Eds.), *Fundamental neuroscience* (2nd ed., pp. 533–554). New York: Academic Press.

Wynn, K. (1992). Addition and subtraction by human infants. *Nature, 358,* 749–750.

Wynn, K., Bloom, P., & Chiang, W.-C. (2002). Enumeration of collective entities by 5-month-old infants. *Cognition, 83*(3), B55–B62.

Yang, T. T., Menon, V., Eliez, S., Blasey, C., White, C. D., Reid, A. J., et al. (2002). Amygdala activation associated with positive and negative facial expressions. *NeuroReport, 13*(14), 1737–1741.

Zelazo, P. D., Frye, D., & Rapus, T. (1996). An age-related dissociation between knowing rules and using them. *Cognitive Development, 11,* 37–63.

Zola, S. M., Squire, L. R., Teng, E., Stefanacci, L., Buffalo, E. A., & Clark, R. E. (2000). Impaired recognition memory in monkeys after damage limited to the hippocampal region. *Journal of Neuroscience, 20,* 451–463.

Chapter 3

Temperament

MARY K. ROTHBART and JOHN E. BATES

In this chapter, we describe recent advances in concepts of temperament. Early views on temperament as unchanging and stable have been replaced by more dynamic views of how temperament changes with development. An early focus on the period of infancy has been extended to childhood and adolescence, and research on temperament has burgeoned (Rothbart & Derryberry, 2002).

Definition of Temperament

We have defined temperament as constitutionally based individual differences in reactivity and self-regulation, in the areas of affect, activity, and attention (Rothbart & Bates, 1998; Rothbart & Derryberry, 1981). The term *constitutional* refers to the biological bases of temperament, influenced over time by heredity, maturation, and experience. *Reactivity* and *self-regulation* are umbrella terms that broadly organize the temperament domain. By *reactivity,* we mean responsiveness to change in the external and internal environment. Reactivity includes a broad range of reactions (e.g., the emotions of fear, cardiac reactivity) and more general tendencies (e.g., negative emotionality), and is not limited to general reactivity. Reactivity is measured by the latency, duration, frequency, and intensity of reactions (e.g., fear, anger, positive affect, or orienting; Rothbart & Derryberry, 1981). Emotional reactivity also includes action tendencies. Fear, for example, disposes freezing, attack, and/or inhibition, and positive affectivity disposes approach. Consequences of these behaviors can feed back to influence the ongoing emotional reaction. By *self-regulation,* we refer to processes such as effortful control and orienting that modulate reactivity.

Temperament dispositions require appropriate eliciting conditions for their expression. Fearful children, for example, are not continually distressed and inhibited. When they experience novelty, sudden change in stimulation, or signals of punishment, they are particularly prone to a fearful reaction.

Temperament represents the core of personality, whereas personality involves much more, including the content of thought, skills, habits, values, defenses, morals, beliefs, and social cognition. Social cognition, which includes the perception of the self, events, and others, and the relation of self to objects, events, and others, becomes increasingly important with development, eliciting and moderating temperamental processes. For example, anger comes to be elicited by judgments that others have broken the rules when we have been following them. Rutter (1987) has described personality as elaborations of temperament into the cognitive and social models we make of the world. Thus, temperament and experience, jointly, "grow" a personality (Rothbart, 2007).

In this chapter, we consider the recent history of temperament concepts and research, the structure of temperament as it has emerged from research on child development, neuroscience, and personality research, and methods and measures for the study of temperament. We consider the development of temperament, addressing issues of continuity and change. We discuss relations between temperament and behavioral adjustment. And finally, we indicate future directions for the study of temperament.

History of Temperament Research

The normative child psychologists of the 1920s and 1930s wished to establish the normal sequences of motor and mental development, and thereby noticed striking temperamental variability among the children (Gesell, 1928, as cited in Kessen, 1965; Shirley, 1933). Shirley described the infant's "core of personality" (p. 56), and devoted a full volume to it. Fifteen years later, Neilon (1948) had clinicians describe 15 of Shirley's 25 babies as adolescents, and found that judges matched Shirley's descriptions of infants with their descriptions as adolescents at a better-than-chance level of accuracy.

The early normative psychologists brought us three important concepts: First, temperament traits provide the core of personality and influence pathways of development. Second, although stability of temperament is expected across age, developmental outcomes also depend on the child's experiences in the social world. And third, different outcomes may occur for children with similar temperaments, and children who differ temperamentally may come to similar developmental outcomes via different pathways (see Kochanska, 1995).

CLINICAL RESEARCH

A second major line of research on temperament in childhood came from biologically oriented clinicians. Escalona's (1968) groundbreaking book, *The Roots of Individuality* proposed the concept of "effective experience," the idea that events in children's lives are experienced only as they are filtered through the individual child's nervous system. An adult's vigorous play, for example, may lead to pleasure in one child and distress in another.

Clinical investigators Thomas, Chess, Birch, Hertzig, and Korn (1963) published the first of their volumes on the influential New York Longitudinal Study (NYLS). Beginning when their sample of infants was 3 to 6 months of age, parents were interviewed about their children's behavior in varying contexts. Each infant reaction and its context was then typed on a separate sheet of paper, and Herbert Birch sorted the descriptions into categories that came to represent the nine NYLS temperament dimensions (Chess

& Thomas, personal communication, October 1992; Thomas et al., 1963): Activity Level, Approach/Withdrawal, Adaptability, Mood, Threshold, Intensity, Distractibility, Rhythmicity, and Attention Span/Persistence. Later, Michael Rutter suggested the term *temperament* to describe their area of study, and this term was adopted by the NYLS group (Chess & Thomas, personal communication, October 1992).

As reports from the NYLS emerged, researchers in social development were becoming increasingly aware of how individual children contribute to their own development (Bell, 1968; Sears, Maccoby, & Levin, 1957). Piagetian psychology also stressed children's influences on their own development via their mental representations of events (Kohlberg, 1969), and temperament ideas suggested that individual differences in children's *emotional* processing could affect children's representations of themselves and the social world.

Structure of Temperament

More recent research on temperament has led to revision of the original list of nine NYLS dimensions (Tables 3.1 and 3.2). Much of this research employed factor analysis of large sets of items within the temperament domain. Factor analysis allows researchers to see simultaneously the relations and nonrelations among large sets of behavior descriptions. Several broad dimensions of temperament have consistently emerged from different sets of data. We have identified six dimensions of infant temperament, as shown in Table 3.1 (Rothbart & Bates, 2006; Rothbart & Mauro, 1990). Individual differences in positive emotionality were differentiated from negative emotionality, and two kinds of negative emotion were identified: fear and anger/irritable distress. Infant scales with different names were also found to measure similar constructs (Goldsmith & Rieser-Danner, 1986).

Garstein and Rothbart (2003) studied the factor structure of an expanded number of infant scales (Table 3.2). Factor analysis of a large data set describing 3- to 12-month-old children yielded three broad dimensions: *Surgency/Extraversion,* defined primarily from scales of Approach, Vocal Reactivity, High Intensity Pleasure (stimulation seeking), Smiling and Laughter, Activity Level and Perceptual Sensitivity; *Negative Affectivity,* defined by Sadness, Frustration, Fear, and loading negatively, Falling Reactivity; and *Orienting/Regulation,* with loadings from Low Intensity Pleasure, Cuddliness, Du-

TABLE 3.1 Dimensions of Temperament in Infancy

Broad Factors	*Narrow Dimensions*	
Negative emotionality	Fear	Sadness
	Frustration/irritability	Falling reactivity
Surgency/extraversion	Approach	Smiling and laughter
	Vocal reactivity	Activity level
	High-intensity pleasure	Perceptual sensitivity
Orienting/regulation	Low-intensity pleasure	Cuddliness
	Duration of orienting	Soothability
Rhythmicity		

TABLE 3.2 Dimensions of Temperament in Childhood

Broad Factors	Narrow Dimensions	
Negative emotionality	Fear Shyness Frustration/irritability	Resistance to control Sadness Soothability Discomfort
Surgency/extraversion	Activity level High-intensity pleasure	Positive anticipation Sociability
Effortful control/self-regulation	Inhibitory control Attentional focusing Persistence	Low-intensity pleasure Perceptual sensitivity
Agreeableness/adaptability	Manageability	Affiliation

ration of Orienting, and Soothability and a secondary loading for Smiling and Laughter. As early as infancy, there is now evidence for at least three broad temperament dimensions.

This research indicates that temperament traits correspond to reactivity in the basic emotions and attention/regulation. In addition, bipolar constructs such as approach versus withdrawal and good versus bad mood have not held together; instead, unipolar constructs of infant temperament have gained support. Furthermore, these dimensions correspond to individual differences emerging from studies of nonhuman animals (Gosling & John, 1999), allowing links between temperament in humans and the psychobiology of individual differences.

In studying children past infancy, the Children's Behavior Questionnaire (CBQ; Rothbart, Ahadi, Hershey, & Fisher, 2001) has consistently yielded three broad factors, found in U.S. replications and in research performed in China and Japan (Ahadi, Rothbart, & Ye, 1993; Kochanska, DeVet, Goldman, Murray, & Putnam, 1993; Rothbart et al., 2001). The first, called *Surgency/Extraversion,* is defined primarily by the scales of Approach, High Intensity Pleasure (sensation-seeking), Activity Level, and a negative contribution from Shyness. The second, called *Negative Affectivity,* is defined by the scales of Discomfort, Fear, Anger/Frustration, Sadness, and loading negatively, Soothability. The third factor, labeled *Effortful Control,* is defined by the scales of Inhibitory Control, Attentional Focusing, Low Intensity Pleasure, and Perceptual Sensitivity. These three factors map well on the second-order factors identified by Sanson et al. (Sanson, Smart, Prior, Oberklaid, & Pedlow, 1994): Surgency/Extraversion on Sociability; Negative Affectivity on Negative Emotionality, and Effortful Control on self-Regulation. Similar factors have been identified by others (Hegvik, McDevitt, & Carey, 1982; McClowry, Hegvik, & Teglasi, 1993; Presley & Martin, 1994).

The factors emerging from research on temperament in childhood show strong conceptual similarities with the Big Three factors and three of the Big Five or Five Factor Model (FFM) factors that have been extracted from analyses of self- and peer descriptions of personality in adults (Goldberg, 1993) and children (Ahadi & Rothbart, 1994; Caspi & Shiner, 2006; Digman & Inouye, 1986). The *Negative Affectivity* factor is conceptually similar to the adult dimension of *Neuroticism* or *Negative Emotionality.* The *Surgency* and *Sociability* factors are similar to the adult dimension of *Extraversion* or

Positive Emotionality. The *Persistence, Self-Regulation,* or *Effortful Control* factors map onto the adult dimension of *Control/Constraint* (see Ahadi & Rothbart, 1994; Evans & Rothbart, 2007), and Martin et al.'s (Martin, Wisenbaker, & Huttunen, 1994) *Agreeableness/Adaptability* and our Affiliation are related to the adult dimension of *Agreeableness.*

In our research on adults, we have found strong correlations between temperament factor scores and Big Five measures (Evans & Rothbart, 2007), between Fearful Distress and Neuroticism, Positive Emotionality and Extraversion, and Effortful Control and Conscientiousness. In addition, Perceptual Sensitivity was related to Openness, and temperamental Affiliation and Anger (negatively) to Agreeableness. Neuroticism, however, often contains negative judgments about the self that may be strongly related to an individual's experiences with others; these may have a strong temperamental base, and research on the development of personality from temperament becomes very important.

SUMMARY

As noted earlier, work to date on temperament structure in infancy and in childhood suggests revisions of the original NYLS nine dimensions to include (with broad, aggregated constructs in parentheses): Positive Affect and Activity Level (Surgency/Extraversion), Fearful Distress, Irritable Distress (General Negative Emotionality), Effortful Control/Task Persistence, and Agreeableness/Adaptability. In the next section, we consider links between these constructs and information processing.

Neural Models of Temperament

Neural models and recent neuroimaging studies enhance our understanding of reactive and attentional temperament (see reviews by Rothbart, Derryberry, & Posner, 1994: Rothbart, Sheese, & Posner, in press).

EMOTION AS AN INFORMATION-PROCESSING SYSTEM

Emotions represent systems that order feeling, thought, and action and respond to the meaning or affective significance of events for the individual (LeDoux, 1989). Object recognition systems and spatial processing systems ask: "What is it?" and "Where is it?" Emotion processing networks ask: "What does it mean?" "Is it good for me?" "Is it bad for me?" and "What shall I do about it?"

In neural processing of emotion, thalamic connections route information about object qualities of a stimulus through sensory pathways (LeDoux, 1989). Simultaneously, information is routed to the limbic system and the amygdala, where memories of the affective meaning of the stimulus further influence the process. Later object processing can update the emotional analysis, but in the meantime, back projections from the amygdala can influence subsequent sensory processing. Output of the amygdala to organized autonomic reactions via the hypothalamus and to motor activation via the corpus striatum reflects the motivational aspect of the emotions (LeDoux, 1989). Reviews of neural models linked to temperament can be found in Rothbart and Posner (2006) and Whittle, Allen, Lubman, and Yucel (2006).

Models from neuroscience have been developed related to general dimensions of Approach, Fear/Inhibition or Harm Avoidance, Irritability (Fight/Flight or Rage), and Affiliativeness or Social Reward Dependence, Orienting, and executive attention as a basis of Effortful Control (see reviews by Rothbart & Bates, 2006; Rothbart & Posner, 2006). These dimensions offer a beginning for future work that will more finely differentiate the temperament domain, its development, and relation to the development of personality. We now discuss measurement issues in the study of temperament in childhood, with extensive evaluation of parent reports. We then discuss recent genetics research and other psychobiological approaches to the study of temperament.

Measurement of Temperament

Approaches to measuring temperament in children have included caregiver reports, self-reports for older children, naturalistic observations, and structured laboratory observations (see Table 3.3). Each approach has advantages and disadvantages, as discussed in greater detail by Bates (1994), Rothbart and Bates (1998, 2006) and Slabach, Morrow, and Wachs (1991). We focus on the issue of the scientific acceptability of caregiver reports, because the literature so often counsels against parent reports. We recognize limitations of caregiver reports (e.g., Bates, 1980), but argue that caregiver reports have broadly established validity (Rothbart & Bates, 1998).

Correlations between parent ratings and observer ratings are typically statistically significant but fairly small in size. Some conclude therefore that parent reports are not valid. However, low validity correlations could be due to problems with observer ratings as well as parent ratings. Measures are not simply valid or invalid, but valid in particular ways—with reference to particular criteria—and valid to a greater or lesser degree. Caregiver reports have demonstrated validity with respect to enough key criteria and in large enough degree that they are of definite scientific value.

CAREGIVERS' VANTAGE POINT VERSUS BIAS AND INACCURACY

Temperament dimensions are by definition general patterns of responses by the child, and parents are in a good position to observe the child's behavior on multiple, ecologically important occasions, including infrequent ones, such as distress to the vacuum cleaner, that may be critical to defining a particular temperament dimension. Parent observations also avoid ethical concerns about creating aversive situations to assess temperament in the laboratory.

Bias and inaccuracy in parent report are real concerns, but they have been extensively dealt with in personality research. The major conclusion has been that traits can be reliably assessed by ratings of knowledgeable informants, including the self, friends, and parents (Kenrick & Funder, 1988; Moskowitz & Schwarz, 1982). In addition, validity is a problem for structured and naturalistic observational measures of temperament as well as for parent reports, and we have summarized potential sources of measurement error in three temperament assessment methods in Table 3.3.

Kagan (1994) argued that the language of an individual item on a temperament questionnaire is subject to multiple interpretations. This ambiguity, however, is the main reason why researchers use scales rather than individual items to measure temperament. Attempts are made to write the best possible items, but by doing this, the researcher does not expect that all sources of error will be eliminated. Basic psychometric theory

TABLE 3.3   Potential Sources of Measurement Error in Three Child Temperament Assessment Methods

	A. Rater Characteristics Relatively independent of child behavior	B. Bias in Assessment As a function of child behavior or rater-child interaction	C. Method Factors Relatively independent of both child and rater characteristics
I. Parent questionnaires	1. Comprehension of instructions, questions, and rating scales 2. Knowledge of child's behavior (and general impression rater has of the child) 3. Inaccurate memory: recency effects, selective recall 4. State when completing rating task (e.g., anxiety) 5. Response sets (e.g., social desirability and acquiescence) 6. For ratings, knowledge of implicit reference groups 7. Accuracy in detecting and coding rare but important events 8. Kind of impression (if any) raters want child/self to make on researcher	1. Observed child behavior occurring in response to parental behavior 2. Parents' interpretations of observed behavior a function of parental characteristics	1. Need to inquire about rarely observed situations 2. Adequacy of item selection, wording, and response options
II. Home observation measures (in vivo coding)	1. Limited capacity of coder to process all relevant behavior 2. Coding of low-intensity ambiguous behaviors 3. State of coder during observation 4. Limits of precision of coding 5. For ratings, knowledge of implicit reference groups	1. Caregiver-child interaction moderating behavior coded (including I.8) 2. For ratings, halo effects	1. Change in child and caregiver behavior due to presence of coder (e.g., decreased conflict) 2. Difficulties of sensitively coding the context of behavior 3. Limitations of number of instances of behavior (especially rare ones) that can be observed 4. Lack of normative data 5. Lack of stability in observational time windows—limited sample of behavior

TABLE 3.3   *(Continued)*

	A. Rater Characteristics Relatively independent of child behavior	B. Bias in Assessment As a function of child behavior or rater-child interaction	C. Method Factors Relatively independent of both child and rater characteristics
III. Laboratory measures (objective measures scored from videotape in episodes designed to elicit temperament related reactions)	1. Scoring of low-intensity ambiguous reactions 2. For ratings, knowledge of implicit reference groups 3. Limited capacity of coder to process all relevant behavior 4. State of coder during observation 5. Limits of precision of coding 6. Accuracy in detecting and coding of rare but important events	1. Effects of uncontrolled caregiver behavior or other experience prior to or during testing 2. Selection of sample, including completion of testing on the basis of child reactions (e.g., distress-prone infants not completing procedures) 3. Subtle variations in experimenter reactions to different children (e.g., more soothing behavior toward distress-prone infant)	1. Lack of adequate normative data 2. Limitations of number of instances of behavior that can be recorded 3. Carryover effects in repeated testing 4. Constraints on range of behavioral options 5. Novelty of laboratory setting 6. Adequate identification of episodes appropriate to evoking temperamental reactions

holds that the reason a set of convergent, but imperfectly correlated items tends to have better test-retest reliability, better stability over time, and better validity is that the error components of individual items tend to cancel each other out when the item scores are added to each other, yielding a closer approximation to a "true" score. This same principle applies to aggregation across multiple observations. Analytical tools such as the computer programs EQS and AMOS can also explicitly model links between items' and scales' error components, creating latent constructs that more precisely control for measurement error. Other approaches are validity scale filters, as in the Minnesota Multiphasic Personality Inventory (MMPI), and studies of how parents construe child behavior and the items researchers present to them (Bates, 1994).

As one example of the value of aggregation, Asendorpf (1990) used multiple measures on multiple occasions to assess children's behavioral inhibition to strangers (shyness) across a 4-year period beginning at age 3. Measures included a parent-report assessment as well as observations of children's behavior with strange adults and children. Of all the measures taken by Asendorpf, parent report consistently showed the strongest relations with the other measures; for example, parent reported shyness predicted observed latency to talk to a stranger at 3 years with $r = .67$; the overall average r between parent-report and other shyness measures across the 4 years ranged from .43 to .53. Bishop, Spence, and McDonald (2003) also reported convergence between parent ratings, teacher ratings, and structured observation, using a new behavioral inhibition questionnaire. Forman et al. (2003) also showed that aggregating laboratory measures of temperament across multiple tasks enhances convergence with mother-report questionnaire measures.

Laboratory measures have been found to be positively related to the Infant Behavior Questionnaire (IBQ) and Toddler Behavior Assessment Questionnaire (TBAQ; see

Goldsmith & Rothbart, 1991) and between temperament measures and tasks designed to reflect underlying brain function; for example, a positive relation was found between a laboratory spatial conflict task designed to measure executive attention and the Children's Behavior Questionnaire (CBQ) measure of inhibitory control ($r = .66$) for 36-month-old children (Gerardi-Caulton, 2000).

Hagekull, Bohlin, and Lindhagen (1984) asked parents to directly record infant behavior, such as infants' reactions to loud sounds, over extended periods in specific situations. Parent data converged strongly with independent observers' data: Correlations between parents' and observers' direct observation data for two, 4-hour visits ranged from .60 (for attentiveness) to .83 (for sensory sensitivity). This suggests that parents were not deficient or strongly biased in their powers of observation, especially since their training for the task was minimal. For an open time frame, general questionnaire scales completed by the parents converged to a modest to moderately strong degree with scales based on independent direct observation, with correlations ranging from .21 to .63.

USING PARENT REPORTS

Evidence to date supports the careful use of parent-report measures of temperament. Two basic reasons to use parent-report measures are (1) that they provide a useful perspective on the temperament of children because parents can see a wide range of child behaviors, and (2) that they possess a fair degree of objective validity. In addition, parent-report measures have contributed to substantial empirical advances, including our understanding of the structure of temperament in relation to the Big Five or Big Three models, as described earlier, and their parallels in psychophysiological systems (Bates, Wachs, & Emde, 1994; Rothbart, Derryberry, et al., 1994). A further reason for using parent reports is that the social relationship aspects of temperament obtained from parents may in themselves be important to understanding development. Nevertheless, we do recognize such concerns as:

- Caregiver reports must be carefully interpreted as reflecting a combination of subjective and objective factors (Bates & Bayles, 1984; Seifer, 2003).
- Improvements in caregiver-report measures should recognize possible sources of bias, such as parents' tendency to contrast one child with another in rating temperament (Saudino, 2003) on some, but not all, parent report questionnaires (Hwang & Rothbart, 2003).

We should also develop subscales to detect specific biases in reporters and improve the generalizability of the observational measures we use to validate caregiver reports (Goldsmith & Hewitt, 2003). Observational and laboratory measures are appealing and can be used in temperament studies; however, they should not at this time be the sole measure of temperament.

Psychobiological Research Approaches

Many interesting approaches to the biological bases of temperament traits have been explored, including psychophysiological, neuroimaging, and neurohormonal approaches. These have been reviewed in detail in Rothbart and Bates (2006) and other sources (Gunnar, 1990). Here, we focus on just one psychobiological approach—genetics.

BEHAVIORAL GENETICS

The pathways to personality that run through temperament include genetic contributions (Bouchard & Loehlin, 2001; Caspi & Shiner, 2006; Goldsmith, Losoya, Bradshaw, & Campos, 1994; Plomin, Chipuer, & Loehlin, 1990). Heritability estimates from behavioral genetics studies show that about half of phenotypic (observable) variance in most temperament and personality traits is attributable to genetic variation in a population (Bouchard & Loehlin, 2001).

These results do not tell us what might be accomplished via environmental intervention. They also do not reveal the specific developmental processes involved in temperament and personality outcomes. To learn more about the latter questions, studies of temperament and development are essential. Zuckerman (1995) addressed the question of "What is inherited?" and proposed this answer:

We do not inherit personality traits or even behavior mechanisms as such. What is inherited are chemical templates that produce and regulate proteins involved in building the structure of nervous systems and the neurotransmitters, enzymes, and hormones that regulate them. . . . How do these differences in biological traits shape our choices in life from the manifold possibilities provided by environments? . . . Only cross-disciplinary, developmental, and comparative psychological research can provide the answers. (pp. 331–332)

We now recognize that experiential and environmental processes themselves build changes in brain structure and functioning (Posner & Raichle, 1994), both before and after birth (Black & Greenough, 1991).

MOLECULAR GENETICS

The mapping of the human genome has provided a promising new direction for studying genes and environment in development (Carcy, 2003; Plomin & Caspi, 1999). One example is the association between the 7-repeat allele of the dopamine D4 receptor (DRD4) and novelty seeking in adults, which was reported in 1996 (Benjamin, Ebstein, & Belmaker, 1996; Ebstein et al., 1996), although its replication has been inconsistent. Another is the short polymorphism of the serotonin transporter gene, found to be associated with susceptibility to fear and distress (Auerbach et al., 1999).

Ebstein and his colleagues used a longitudinal sample to investigate these two genetic polymorphisms in relation to neonatal and later infant behavior (Auerbach et al., 1999; Ebstein et al., 1998). Ebstein and Auerbach used the Neonatal Behavioral Assessment Scale (NBAS) to measure temperament in newborns, and the IBQ (Rothbart, 1981) to measure temperament at 2 months (Auerbach et al., 1999; Ebstein et al., 1998). The DRD4 long variant that has been linked to sensation seeking in adults was associated with newborns' orientation, range of state, regulation of state, and motor organization. An interaction was also found between DRD4 and the 5-HTTLPR polymorphisms. The serotonin transporter gene s/s polymorphism that has been linked to fear and distress in adults was related to lower orientation scores, but only for newborns who did not have the long repeat variant of DRD4. For those who did, presence of the 5-HTTLPR s/s genotype had no effect. Newborns with high orientation and motor organization showed lower negative emotionality at 2 months. In addition, 2-month-old infants with long repeat DRD4 alleles had lower scores on IBQ negative emotionality and distress to limitations. Finally, at 1 year of age, infants with the long DRD4 allele had lower negative emotionality scores, and showed less fear and less social inhibition (Auerbach et al., 1999).

Schmidt and Fox (2002) found a relation between the long repeat form of DRD4 and high scores on observed disruptive behavior and parent-reported aggressive behavior in 4-year-olds. Schmidt, Fox, Perez-Edgar, Hu, and Hamer (2001) also found a link between the long repeat form and mothers' reports of attention problems. Children with the long 7-repeat allele of DRD4 show behavioral aspects of ADHD, but no deficits in conflict performance as measured by the color-word Stroop task (Swanson et al., 2000). Evidence from evolutionary studies suggests that the 7-repeat allele may confer an advantage during human evolution (Ding et al., 2002), and an interaction has been found between the 7-repeat and parenting in sensation-seeking outcomes (Sheese, Voelker, Rothbart, & Posner, 2007).

Dopamine genes pertain to individual differences in attention (Posner & Fan, in press; Posner, Rothbart, & Sheese, 2007). The anterior cingulate, associated with executive attention, has five types of DA receptor, and is only one synapse away from the ventral tegmental area, a major source of DA. The DRD4 gene and the monoamine oxidase A (MAOA) gene, related to the synthesis of DA and norepinepherine, were related to executive attention as measured by the Attention Network Task (ANT), which assesses efficiency of alerting, orienting, and executive attention (Fossella, Posner, Fan, Swanson, & Pfaff, 2002). Presence of the more common 4 repeat allele, rather than the long repeat allele of DRD4 that has been related to sensation seeking, was associated with greater difficulty in resolving conflict (Fossella et al., 2002). It will be particularly exciting in the future to look at genetic relationships at different ages and in connection with different life experiences. Human studies have also identified significant interactions between genes and environment in maladaptive outcomes, and we discuss these in the Temperament and Adjustment section.

Temperament and Development

Early theorists of temperament stressed that temperament was stable over time, even from infancy to adulthood (Buss & Plomin, 1975). We have now learned, however, that temperament itself develops, and our study of this development lets us consider different pathways of individual differences (Goldsmith, Buss, & Lemery, 1997; Rothbart, 1989; Rothbart & Derryberry, 1981). Temperamental measures may change over time, for example, but genetically related individuals can show strong similarities in their patterns of change (Eaton, 1994; Matheny, 1989).

Expressions of temperament also change over time. For example, 6-year-olds spend much less time crying than do 6-month-olds, but they worry a good deal more. To assess stability of temperamental characteristics, there must be conceptual continuity in the temperament constructs studied. A meta-analysis by Roberts and DelVecchio (2000), using the Big Five conceptual model, showed considerable stability in measures of temperament and personality after about the age of 3 years, with estimated cross-time correlations for 0 to 2.9 years = .35; 3 to 5.9 years = .52; 6 to 11.9 years = .45; and 12 to 17.9 years = .47. In the next section, we consider issues of temperament stability and change in social-emotional and personality development. We review research in the areas of positive affect/approach and inhibition, distress proneness, activity level, and two forms of control of reactivity (reactive) fear and effortful control.

CONTRIBUTIONS OF TEMPERAMENT TO DEVELOPMENT

Some children are temperamentally high in responsiveness to reward, others to punishment, and some children are highly responsive to both (Rothbart, Ahadi, & Hershey, 1994). Temperament is also linked to the development of coping strategies. If one child experiences high distress to strangers, for example, and another child little distress, coping involving avoidance of strangers may be elicited for the first child, but not for the second. If the second child also experiences delight in the interaction with a stranger, increasingly rapid and confident approach to interactions with strangers is likely. Thus, the practice and reinforcement of children's temperamentally based responses may serve to magnify initial differences through positive feedback. Temperament differences also promote the child's active seeking of environments, or "niche picking" (Scarr & McCartney, 1983). The child who stays at the edge of a nursery school class or a party is selecting a different experience than the child who goes directly to the center of social excitement.

In Gray's (1991) theory, extraverts, high in positive affect and approach (the BAS), are seen as more susceptible to reward, and introverts, high in fear and shyness, to punishment (the BIS). Other models, optimal level theories (e.g., Bell, 1974; Strelau, 1983), stress individual preferences for high or low levels of stimulation. A child easily overwhelmed by stimulation will try to keep things quiet, whereas a child who requires high levels of stimulation for pleasure will attempt to keep things exciting. Mismatches between child stimulation preferences and environments may lead to developmental challenges for both child and caregiver.

A child's temperamental characteristics can also elicit reactions from others that may influence the child's development (Scarr & McCartney, 1983). Thus, a positive and outgoing disposition may serve as a protective factor by eliciting the support of others in a high-risk environment (Werner, 1985). Radke-Yarrow and Sherman (1990) noted that in a high-risk situation, a buffering effect can occur when the child's characteristics somehow meet the needs of the parent. This notion is similar to Thomas and Chess's (1977) "goodness-of-fit" argument.

Because temperament itself develops (Rothbart, 1989), new systems of behavioral organization (e.g., smiling and laughter, frustration, fear, executive attention) will also come "online" over time. When these new systems modulate characteristics that were previously present, there will likely be instability of temperament across the developmental transition. In addition to the direct effects of later developing control systems of fear and effortful control, children who develop a given control system early in life may have quite different experiences from children who develop the system later (Rothbart & Derryberry, 1981). For example, the child who develops fear-related inhibition late will likely experience a greater number of interactions with potentially threatening objects or situations than the child who develops fearful inhibition early. The child who is fearful and inhibited by threats early in development may spend more time watching and making sense of events in the environment than the less inhibited child. We now consider a selection of dimensions of temperament in a developmental context. For a more detailed discussion of this topic, see Rothbart and Bates (2006).

EXTRAVERSION/SURGENCY VERSUS SHYNESS AND BEHAVIORAL INHIBITION

By 2 to 3 months, infants show a pattern of smiling, vocalization, and motor cycling of the limbs to social and nonsocial stimuli. These reactions appeared to increase in duration and decrease in latency into the second and third months of life (Kistiakovskaia, 1965). This cluster of intercorrelated behaviors (smiling and laughter; vocal and motor activity) is also found in parents' reports of temperament and in home observations (Rothbart, 1986).

Beyond 3 to 4 months, positive affect shows normative increases in probability and duration across the first year of life, both in home observation and parent-report data (Rothbart, 1981, 1986). Continuity over 3 to 9 months has also been found for a composite positive emotionality measure assessed by parent report and home observation, including smiling and laughter, motor and vocal activity, and stability of a laboratory measure of smiling and laughter has been found between 3 and 13.5 months of age (Rothbart, 1986). Smiling and laughter in infancy observed in the laboratory predicted both concurrent (Rothbart, 1988) and 6- to 7-year-old approach tendencies (Rothbart et al., 2001). Pedlow, Sanson, Prior, and Oberklaid (1993) also found stability from infancy to 7 to 8 years on their dimension of Approach/Sociability.

An important form of control over approach develops in the second half of the first year because some infants who were highly approaching at 5 or 6 months now inhibit their approach responses when stimuli are unfamiliar and/or intense, such as novel or intense toys (Rothbart, 1988; Schaffer, 1974). Infants' approach latency to low-intensity stimuli showed stability from 6.5 months to later ages (10 and 13.5 months), but to high-intensity stimuli, it did not (Rothbart, 1988). Once inhibition of approach is established, it will be a relatively enduring aspect of temperament and an important social trait. This has been shown in a number of studies, following children from infancy to late adolescence (Bayley & Schafer, 1963), early to later childhood (Asendorpf, 1993; Gest, 1997), early childhood to adolescence and adulthood (Honzik, 1965; Kagan & Moss, 1962), and adolescence to adulthood (Tuddenham, 1959). Further evidence of stability of behavioral inhibition and outgoingness has been provided by Caspi and Silva (1995), Kagan (1998), Kagan and Fox (2006), and Pfeifer, Goldsmith, Davidson, and Rickman (2002). These results can be added to evidence from Kagan (1998; Kagan & Fox, 2006) on stability of behavioral inhibition, and to Caspi and Silva's (1995) and Pfeifer et al.'s (2002) work on stability of outgoingness and inhibition.

In summary, evidence for approach tendencies related to positive affect can be seen early in development. Later in infancy, behavioral inhibition related to fear develops. Once established, tendencies toward approach versus inhibition demonstrate significant stability over relatively long developmental periods, with important implications for social development and for the measurement of temperament (Rothbart & Sheese, 2007).

ATTENTIONAL ORIENTING AND EFFORTFUL CONTROL

Attention has both reactive and self-regulative aspects. Reactive attention and its development in the early months of life are considered in some detail in Rothbart and Bates (2006) and Rothbart, Derryberry, et al. (1994). Here, we focus on the self-regulative aspects of attention, which begins its development late in the first year of life (Kagan, Kearsley, & Zelazo, 1978; Kochanska, Murray, & Harlan, 2000; Posner & Rothbart, 2007a, 2007b; Rothbart & Rueda, 2005; Ruff & Rothbart, 1996).

Effortful control—the ability to activate and inhibit action, thought and emotion—is based on the efficiency of executive attention, including the ability to inhibit a dominant response and/or to activate a subdominant response, to plan, and to detect errors, also appears to be linked to the child's developing ability to maintain a sustained focus of attention. Krakow, Kopp, and Vaughn (1981) studied sustained attention to a set of toys in 12- to 30-month-old infants. Duration increased across this period, with stability of individual differences between 12 and 18 months, and between 24 and 30 months. Sustained attention was also positively related to self-control measures, independent of developmental quotient, at 24 months.

Emerging differences in effortful control also appear to be linked to differences in children's emotional expression. In a major longitudinal study, Kochanska (Kochanska & Knaack, 2003; Kochanska et al., 2000) used multiple methods to assess effortful control and emotionality. Mother report of effortful control was aggregated with laboratory measures, which included delay, slowing motor activity, lowering the voice, suppressing and initiating activity to a signal, and effortful attention at 22, 33, and 45 months of age. Focused attention at 9 months predicted children's later effortful control (Kochanska et al., 2000). Between 33 and 45 months, stability was equivalent to that of IQ. Children who showed more regulated anger and joy and more fear-related inhibition at 22 months demonstrated later higher levels of effortful control (Kochanska & Knaack, 2003). The link between inhibition and later effortful control was further supported by Aksan and Kochanska (2004).

In our research using spatial conflict tasks, children began to demonstrate effective management of conflict at 30 months, and 36-month-old children who showed greater interference in reaction time for conflicting responses were reported by their mothers as exhibiting lower levels of inhibitory control (Rothbart, Ellis, & Posner, 2004). Less accurate children were also reported as showing higher levels of anger/frustration in the IBQ (Gerardi-Caulton, 2000), suggesting attentional control over emotion as well as action.

Direct links have also been found between children's disengagement of attention and decreases in negative affect (Stifter & Braungart, 1995), and infants' use of self-regulation in anger inducing situations has predicted their early childhood ability to delay responses (Calkins & Williford, 2003). Mechanisms used to cope with negative emotion may later be transferred to control of cognition and behavior (see also Posner & Rothbart, 1998). Further support of this idea was found by Mischel and his colleagues (Sethi, Mischel, Aber, Shoda, & Rodriguez, 2000). Toddlers were briefly separated from their mothers and children's coping strategies coded. Later, at age 5, their behavior was observed in a situation where they could delay gratification for a more valued reward. Children who used more distraction strategies during the maternal separation at the younger age were later able to delay longer.

Long-term stability in the ability to delay gratification and later attentional and emotional control has been reported (Mischel, 1983). In Mischel's work, the number of seconds delayed by preschool children while waiting for rewards that were physically present (a conflict situation) significantly predicted parent-reported attentiveness and ability to concentrate when the children were adolescents (Shoda, Mischel, & Peake, 1990). Children less able to delay in preschool were also reported as more likely to "go to pieces" under stress as teenagers, and to show lower academic competence in SAT scores, even when controlling for intelligence (Shoda et al., 1990). In follow-up studies, preschool delay predicted goal setting and self-regulatory abilities when the participants reached their early 30s (Ayduk et al., 2000), suggesting remarkable continuity in self-regulation.

In Caspi and Silva's (1995) study, preschool children characterized as "well adjusted" were described as flexible in orientation, and "capable of reserve and control when it was demanded of them" (p. 492). These children's flexibility of responsiveness may have been linked to greater executive attention and effortful control. At age 18, children earlier identified as "well adjusted" by Caspi and Silva had high scores on Social Potency, including leadership and low social shyness. Studies are now underway exploring contributions of both temperament and parent treatment to the development of self-control, and Olson, Bates, and Bayles (1990) have found relationships between parent-child interaction at 13 months and 2 years (but not at 6 months) and children's self-control at age 6. Attention thus shows major developments over the first years of life, with a more self-regulative system added to a more reactive one (Rothbart, Posner, & Rosicky, 1994).

TWO CONTROL SYSTEMS

Early individual differences in motor and emotional reactivity thus appear to be influenced by development of at least two temperament-related control systems: One is part of an emotional reaction (fear and behavioral inhibition), the other is more strictly self-regulatory (effortful control), with the first system developing earlier than the second. This view is related to the two control systems of Block and Block (1980): *ego-control,* involving fearful or inhibitory control over impulsive approach; and *ego-resiliency,* defined by flexible adaptation to changing circumstances. Eisenberg et al. (1996) found a relationship between ego-resiliency and CBQ attentional control in kindergarten to third-grade children. Eisenberg et al. (2004) also studied parent- and teacher-reported effortful control and impulsivity in relation to ego resiliency in children 4.5 to 8 years, with a 2-year follow-up. At both ages, effortful control and impulsivity directly predicted resiliency and externalizing problems, and temperament also predicted internalizing problems indirectly, through resiliency. All relations held in predictions from Time 1 to Time 2, except the path from impulsivity to externalizing.

Where there is high ego-control, fear and its correlates may develop into a relatively constricted life, with approach tendencies strongly opposed, and rigid functioning a likely result. Ego-resiliency, alternatively, is strengthened by a set of life experiences that build on capacities for both expression and control of impulses. Effortful control appears to provide an important underlying system for the development of ego resiliency, as seen also in the research of Kochanska summarized earlier. Block and Block (1980) stress the importance of experience in the development of adaptation, with endogenous control systems allowing cultural influences on the particular behavior, thoughts, and emotions to be controlled, as well as on the self-regulatory capacities and strategies used by the child.

SUMMARY

Early reactive systems of emotionality and approach are modulated by the development of at least two temperamental control systems. The first, fearful inhibition, is linked to developments in fearfulness late in the first year of life. The second, effortful control, develops across the preschool period and later shows considerable stability. Another likely control mechanism for the support of socialization is the development of a social reward system, connected with children's desires to please and to refrain from hurting their parents and other persons, likely linked to temperamental affiliation. Any failure of these controls may be linked to the development of behavior problems. Because these temperamental systems are open to experience, high quality socialization will be necessary for positive outcomes.

Temperament and the Development of Personality

Life experiences influence connections between children's emotional reactions, their understanding of events, and their use of coping strategies to deal with these events. Coping strategies, which may have been originally based on temperamental predispositions, become part of mental affective and cognitive units linked to particular situations. Mischel and Ayduk (2004) give the example of individual differences in rejection sensitivity (RS). RS is a disposition leading to coding of ambiguous events in interpersonal situations (e.g., when a friend doesn't say hello) as a sign of rejection. Signs of rejection are then responded to with sadness or anger. As RS becomes habitual, the person's attention may become quite narrowly focused on the likelihood of rejection, and defensive behaviors (e.g., anger or preventive rejection of the other) may be used to fend off expected rejection. Thus, the experience of early criticism and rejection, which may have its strongest impact on children prone to distress, can have long-term consequences for habitual mental units and problems in development.

Mischel and Ayduk's (2004) analysis of RS describes an anxious or defensive set, but alternatively, children's experiences with others may be generally of acceptance. If so, the child will be less likely to be on guard about rejection or to show a defensive perceptual set. Instead, the child's attention can be directed more broadly, allowing greater conscious awareness of the state and needs of others. More distress prone, fearful, and irritable children may be more likely to develop such habits as RS, but after experiencing high levels of rejection, even a low distress-prone child is likely to develop RS. Surgent and approaching children may also be more likely to expect acceptance, but if even distress-prone children never learn about the possibility of rejection, they would not develop RS.

When repeatedly exercised, habitual activations of clusters of thoughts, emotions, and action tendencies become more likely to occur and difficult to change, especially when they involve fear and distress. When mental habits involve distress, how might they be changed? In Eastern traditions, this is done partly through diminishing the role of the ego so that situations become less threatening to the self. Mental discipline and meditation also allow weakening of links between thoughts and emotions or thoughts and action tendencies. Western therapies similarly work through the clients' patterns of reaction, attempting to reconstruct previously consolidated patterns and provide new frameworks for meaning. Developmental psychologists, however, would desire that children be given the kinds of experiences that form favorable mental habits in the first place.

In a temperament view, the biological equipment underlying temperament is similar across cultures, but specific mental habits and representations of self, the world and other, will vary from culture to culture, and from context to context. By the time a child is a well-socialized member of the society, more biologically based temperament will have been shaped into a set of values, goals, and representations of the self and others that specify what is good and bad for the person. Even for children who are not well-socialized, values stressed by the culture may nevertheless have an effect. Children in the United States, for example, may still attempt to promote a positive self-concept, but pursue it though a delinquent peer group, even when the goals and values followed may not be socially acceptable ones.

Several longitudinal studies have described the continuity of personality from childhood to adulthood. Shiner and her colleagues considered the period of 8 to 12 to 20 years (Shiner, Masten, & Tellegen, 2002). They found that positive emotionality at age 20 was moderately predicted by childhood mastery motivation, surgent engagement, and self-assurance (Shiner et al., 2002). Negative emotionality at 20, however, was predicted by low adaptation in all areas in childhood, and was linked to all 20-year-old adaptation measures except romantic competence. Lower academic achievement and greater conduct problems in childhood predicted adult negative emotionality, and childhood mastery motivation and surgent engagement were related to low adult negative emotionality. Positive emotionality may be more closely linked to current adaptation, whereas negative emotionality shows more continuity with earlier adaptation. In our section on adjustment, we note other strong links between negative emotionality and psychopathology, particularly when negative emotionality is associated with low effortful control (Caspi, 2000; Eisenberg, Fabes, Guthrie, & Reiser, 2000).

Shiner et al. (2002) note that adults high on negative emotionality tend to be upset by daily problems (Suls, Martin, & David, 1998). How might the development of mental habits contribute to these findings? First, when a habit is related to distress, there may be numerous attempts to decrease distress through thinking about the problem, which when repeated may make distress even more likely. Positive experiences are less of a challenge and thus less likely to be rehearsed. When thoughts have been tied to distress in difficult and painful situations in the past, one faces not only problems of the moment, but also stored thoughts and affects related to them. Each time they are rehearsed, the negative affect, cognition, and action links become stronger. Thus, early failure, such as poor achievement in school, may create the possibility of long-term negative affect or neuroticism that extends to achievement situations later in life.

Caspi, Harrington, et al. (2003) related children's characteristics at age 3 to their self-reported personality at age 26: Undercontrolled children (10% of the sample) had been temperamentally impulsive, restless, distractible, and negativistic at age 3; Confident children (28%) were friendly, eager, and somewhat impulsive; Inhibited children (8%) were fearful, reticent, and easily upset; Reserved children (15%) were timid but not extreme in shyness; Well-adjusted children (40%) appeared to be capable of self-control, were adequately self-confident, and did not become upset during testing. Undercontrolled children, who combined extraversion/surgency, negative affect, and low attentional control at age 3, showed neurotic and alienated tendencies as 26-year-old adults. Confident extraverted children were confident and unfearful as adults. More shy and fearful Inhibited and Reserved children maintained their caution and fearfulness into adulthood and were also low in social potency, whereas the more extremely Inhibited children were also high in Constraint (a mixture of fearfulness and self-control) and low in positive emotionality and social support. Kubzansky, Martin, and Buka (2004) related children's temperament and personality at age 7 to self-ratings at age 35. Children's behavioral inhibition did not predict adult functioning, but their anger proneness (Distress) predicted adult hostility/anger, and children who showed low interpersonal self-regulation were low in interpersonal sensitivity in adulthood. Strong relations were found between child distress proneness and adult somatization, another very intriguing finding.

Temperament and Adjustment

In the preceding section, we began to consider temperament and some aspects of adjustment. Now we consider in more detail theoretical models and research findings relating temperament to adjustment. The term *adjustment* means not only psychopathology but also positive behaviors, including the development of conscience. We consider dimensions of adjustment rather than categorical diagnostic systems, and think of adjustment as adaptation to particular contexts and related experiences. A child may carry temperament traits from one context to another, but their implications for adjustment will depend on the specific context and expectations of the parent, peer, or teacher (Chess & Thomas, 1984; Lerner & Lerner, 1994), as well as on the child's specific mental habits, as described in preceding paragraphs.

DOES TEMPERAMENT PREDICT ADJUSTMENT?

Meaningful patterns of relationship exist between constructs of temperament and constructs of adjustment in children's development. This was clear by the late 1980s (Bates, 1989) and has become more firmly established since then, with many studies showing temperament links with psychopathology (e.g., see reviews by Eisenberg, Guthrie, et al., 2000; Lonigan, Vasey, Phillips, & Hazen, 2004; Rothbart, 2007; Rothbart & Bates, 1998; Rothbart & Posner, 2006; Sanson, Hemphill, & Smart, 2004; Wachs & Bates, 2001). In these studies, temperament has been measured in a variety of ways, including parent reports, teacher reports, and direct observation. Adjustment has been assessed at home and at school, using cross-sectional and longitudinal designs. In this review, we focus mainly on a differentiated view of how temperament might contribute to the child's adjustment. We mention two methodological and conceptual issues before describing findings.

One issue is measurement *contamination.* Sanson, Prior, and Kyrios (1990) argued that relations between a temperament measure and an adjustment measure might be an artifact of content overlap between the two scales. Items in a temperament scale, for example, might concern behaviors that are the same as those indicating psychopathology or vice versa. Bates (1990) argued that adjustment and temperament should actually have some conceptual overlap. The child's adjustment could reflect a component of temperament, and psychopathology could be, at least in part, an extreme point on a temperament dimension. For theoretical reasons, however, we tend to regard temperament and adjustment as separate. One support for this distinction comes from studies where expert raters and psychometric principles are used to remove items with overlapping content. Findings demonstrate links between temperament and psychopathology even after "decontamination" (Lemery, Essex, & Smider, 2002; Lengua, West, & Sandler, 1998; Oldehinkel, Hartman, de Winter, Veenstra, & Ormel, 2004). A second way of supporting a distinction between temperament and adjustment is shown by studies on change and development. One study, for example, found that therapy led to changes in parents' descriptions of their children's psychopathology but not their descriptions of the child's temperament (Sheeber, 1995). Other studies address the question of the developmental processes through which temperament and adjustment are related, and these are discussed after considering the second methodological issue.

This issue is called *source bias*. As we have argued, caregivers' reports do show validity. However, when a relation is inferred from two constructs measured via the same source, for example, parents, it is possible that relations are due to preconceptions in the minds of the informant rather than the behavior of the subject. Bates and Bayles (1984) have nevertheless argued, on the basis of many different tests of subjective and objective components in parents' perceptions of their children, that measures of subjective bias do not account for more of the variance than measures of objective phenomena. In addition, as is discussed later, the different measures are related to one another within and across time in a differentiated pattern. For example, early novelty distress (fear) predicts later novelty distress or internalizing problems more than externalizing problems. Studies have also shown objectivity in caregivers' descriptions of children's temperament, even when subjective factors, such as depression, play some role (e.g., Bishop et al., 2003; Forman et al., 2003). Thus, source biases are not as powerful as one might have feared, and caregivers perceive children's behavioral traits in a relatively differentiated rather than global or unitary ways. This brings us to the central question: How does temperament predict adjustment?

Temperament might be involved in the development of behavior problems in a number of ways. Clark, Watson, and Mineka (1994) listed four ways in which mood and anxiety disorders might be related to personality characteristics (also see Shiner & Caspi, 2003):

1. A *vulnerability model,* where there is a predisposition to the development of disorders (e.g., distress in response to stressors)
2. The *pathoplasty model,* in which personality shapes the course of a disorder (e.g., by producing an environment that maintains the disorder)
3. The *scar hypothesis,* in which a disorder produces enduring changes in personality (e.g., increased levels of insecurity)
4. The *spectrum or continuity hypothesis* where the psychopathological condition is an extreme manifestation of the underlying temperament or personality trait

These four models need not be mutually exclusive. Generally, available evidence does not allow for a choice among the models, but in recent years, behavioral and molecular genetics research is offering the promise of choices (e.g., Eaves, Silberg, & Erkanli, 2003).

DIRECT LINKAGE

Most studies of the relations between temperament and adjustment have considered direct, linear effects, where a particular temperament trait contributes to the development of an adjustment pattern. Additive effects of multiple temperament traits are also possible, as when two or more temperament traits increase the risk of some disorder, such as negative affectivity and lack of impulse control predicting behavior problems (Eisenberg et al., 1996), negative emotionality and fearfulness predicting levels of young boys' internalizing problems (Gilliom & Shaw, 2004), and both impulsivity and negative emotionality associated with adolescents' antisocial behavior (Stice & Gonzales, 1998).

In evaluating direct linkage models, studies examining multiple temperament traits in relation to multiple dimensions of adjustment are critical. According to current theories of psychopathology, individual differences in specific temperament-related brain circuits are linked to specific forms of motivation or functioning (Table 3.4; Bates et al., 1994; Clark et al., 1994; Fowles, 1994; Gray, 1991; MacDonald, 1988; Rothbart, Derryberry, et al., 1994; Rothbart & Posner, 2006). There are systems controlling inhibition to novelty and signals of punishment and nonreward, as well as unconditioned fear, positive affectivity and reward seeking, sensitivity to social rewards, and attentional control. We now use these systems as general constructs to organize the evidence on temperament and adjustment. At present, only a limited number of studies permit a differentiated view of links between temperament and adjustment, and none are methodologically strong enough to stand alone in support or rejection of a psychobiological systems model. However, enough convergence exists that we are confident about the broad outlines of direct linkage models.

THEORETICAL EXPECTATIONS

Direct linkage models will become more detailed as neurobehavioral systems are better understood and as measures of adjustment are meaningfully differentiated. For now, we would expect early irritability, or general tendencies toward negative affect, to predict a wide variety of adaptive difficulties, including internalizing (anxiety problems), and externalizing (conduct problems), as well as deficits in social competencies. As measures of irritability are more finely differentiated, however, more clearly defined pathways to later adjustment may be identified. For example, sensitivity to minor aversive stimuli might predispose a child to both internalizing (e.g., whining and withdrawal) and externalizing (e.g., reactive aggression) behavior problems, whereas irritability to frustration of reward or of stimulation-seeking behavior (Rothbart, Derryberry, et al., 1994) would likely be more related to externalizing tendencies than to internalizing ones.

Temperamental tendencies toward fearfulness in novel or potentially punishing situations should predict internalizing-type adjustments most directly, although they may also serve to predict externalizing problems in inverse or interactive ways, as discussed later. A finer differentiation of fearfulness will ultimately be important for predicting different kinds of internalizing adjustment. For example, separation distress may differ in some ways from novelty fear. See Fowles' (1994) discussion of theories placing separation fear in a panic or fight/flight brain system and novelty fear in a behavioral inhibition system, and Panksepp's (1998) psychobiological theory.

Positive affectivity or surgency, involving activity, stimulation seeking, assertiveness, and possibly some aspects of manageability, should be more involved in externalizing than in internalizing problems, except that depression has a strong component of low positive affectivity (Tellegen, 1985). However, a trait of prosocial tendency, affiliation and agreeableness, perhaps involving sensitivity to social rewards (MacDonald, 1992), might prove separable from the more general extraversion or surgency (positive affectivity) system, as Rothbart and Victor's (2004) findings suggest. Low levels of prosocial interest and concern would be expected to be associated with the

TABLE 3.4   Processes that May Link Temperament and Adjustment

Processes	Examples
A. Direct, Linear Effects	
1. Temperament extreme constitutes psychopathology or positive adaptation.	Extreme shyness, attention deficit disorder, high attentional control
2. Temperament extreme predisposes to a closely related condition.	Fearfulness → general anxiety disorder, agoraphobia/panic disorder; high attentional control → good social adjustment
3. Temperament characteristics affect particular symptomatology of a disorder.	Anxiety versus hopelessness in depression
B. Indirect, Linear Effects	
1. Temperament structures the immediate environment, which then influences development of positive adjustment or psychopathology.	High stimulation seeking → leaving home early, marrying poorly; high attentional control → planning → good school adjustment
2. Temperament biases others to behave in ways that provide experiences leading to risk factors, pathology, or more positive outcome.	High positive affect → attention from caregivers in institutional situations; infant irritability → coercive cycles in parent-child interactions
3. Temperament biases processing of information about self and others, predisposing to cognitively based psychopathology or positive adjustment.	Negative affectivity → negatively biased social information processing → aggression; positive affectivity → positively biased social information processing → optimism about others
C. Temperament × Environment Interactions	
1. Temperament buffers against risk factors or stressors.	Fear protecting against aggression or criminal socialization; positive affect protecting against peer or parent rejection
2. Temperament heightens response to event.	Negative affectivity augmenting response to stress, increasing risk of depression or likelihood of posttraumatic stress disorder; attentional orienting augmenting response to teachersÅf instructions
D. Temperament × Temperament Interactions	
1. Self-regulation of a temperament extreme qualitatively changes its expression.	High surgency with nonregulation → ADHD, high surgency with good regulation → high competence; high negative emotionality with low attentional control → sensitization and increasing anxiety; high negative emotionality plus high attentional control → no maladjustment
2. One temperament trait protects against risk consequences of another temperament-based trait.	Fearfulness or higher attentional control protecting against impulsivity
E. Miscellaneous	
1. Different temperament characteristics may predispose to similar outcomes.	Shyness, impulsivity, lack of affiliativeness, and negativity may each predispose to development of social isolation
2. Temperament or personality may be shaped by psychopathological disorder.	Anxiety disorder → increased dependency

Note: Some of the wording and examples have been changed. Note that many of the examples are theoretically plausible, but not based on empirical evidence.

From "Temperament" (p. 137), by M. K. Rothbart, and J. E. Bates, in *Handbook of child psychology: Vol. 3. Social, emotional, and personality development,* sixth edition, W. Damon and R. M. Lerner (Series Eds.) and N. Eisenberg (Vol. Ed.), 2006, Hoboken, NJ: Wiley. Adapted with permission.

development of externalizing but not internalizing problems, and perhaps with failure to acquire positive social competencies independent of behavioral problems.

Finally, systems controlling attention, especially the executive attention system described earlier, would be expected to be related to both externalizing and internalizing, but to have more to do with externalizing problems than with internalizing ones. As with fear systems, attentional control should also play an additive or interactive role with other temperament characteristics. In addition, a well-functioning set of attentional controls is likely to be linked to more positive developmental outcomes.

EMPIRICAL FINDINGS OF DIRECT LINKAGE

A number of studies provide support for the models just described. In general, predictive relations between temperament and adjustment are of modest to moderate size. Correlations between infancy measures and adjustment in late preschool and middle childhood tend to be smaller, and those between preschool or middle childhood and later periods larger. Even though the correlations may be modest to moderate, they have been well replicated, and are clearly not chance findings. Moreover, the size of the relations is usually not less than and sometimes greater than predictions from other theoretically linked variables, such as parenting quality. Lytton (1995), for example, performed a meta-analysis of studies predicting conduct disorder (a diagnosis of extreme externalizing problems) and criminality, finding child temperament variables to be the single most powerful predictor of the outcomes, even in comparison with qualities of parenting.

In the Bloomington Longitudinal Study (BLS), infancy and toddlerhood temperamental difficultness (frequent and intense negative affect and attention demanding) predicted later externalizing and internalizing problems as seen in the mother-child relationship, from preschool to the middle-childhood periods (Bates & Bayles, 1988; Bates, Bayles, Bennett, Ridge, & Brown, 1991; Bates, Maslin, & Frankel, 1985; Lee & Bates, 1985). Early negative reactivity to novel situations (unadaptability) predicted less consistently, but when it did, it predicted internalizing problems more than externalizing problems. Early resistance to control (perhaps akin to the manageability dimension of Hagekull, 1989, and perhaps at least partly related to the construct of effortful control) predicted externalizing problems more than internalizing problems. This was also found in predicting externalizing problems at school in both the BLS and a separate longitudinal study, the Child Development Project (CDP; Bates, Pettit, Dodge, & Ridge, 1998).

In a structural modeling analysis of CDP data, dealing with the overlap in externalizing and internalizing symptoms, Keiley, Lofthouse, Bates, Dodge, and Pettit (2003) separated mothers' and teachers' reports of behavior problems across 5 to 14 years into pure externalizing, pure internalizing, and covarying factors, and then considered their early childhood predictors. Resistant temperament (unmanageability) predicted the pure factors of mother- and teacher-rated externalizing, but not the pure internalizing factors. Unadaptable temperament (novelty distress) predicted both mother and teacher pure internalizing factors, and to a lesser degree, and *negatively,* the pure mother and teacher externalizing factors. It is reasonable that fearfulness and sensitivity would be likely to inhibit externalizing behavior (Bates, Pettit, & Dodge, 1995). Finally, difficult temperament (negative emotionality and demandingness) predicted, in the multivariate analysis, none of the pure factors, but only the covarying externalizing plus internalizing factor in mothers' reports.

These findings are all consistent with models where temperament extremes either constitute pathology themselves or predispose to risk for these conditions. The linkages are modest, but they obtain from early in life. They are also not eliminated when family and parenting characteristics are included in the prediction, so they are not simply artifacts of family functioning. Also supporting the general pattern, Gilliom and Shaw (2004) found that, in a sample of preschool-age boys from low-income families, high negative emotionality was associated with initial levels of both externalizing and internalizing problems, whereas high fearfulness was associated with decreases in externalizing problems over time. High initial internalizing was also associated with increases in internalizing problems over time. Russell, Hart, Robinson, and Olsen (2003), however, found that negative emotionality as measured by parent report on the EAS did not predict preschoolers' adjustment as rated by teachers. However, EAS shyness was related to both lower prosocial behavior and lower aggressive behavior at preschool.

Lemery et al. (2002) also provide support for a differential linkage model. Mother-rated child anger on the CBQ at ages 3 to 4 predicted mother and father reports of externalizing problems at age 5 more strongly than it predicted age 5 internalizing problems. Early fear and sadness predicted later internalizing problems more strongly than they predicted later externalizing problems. Early inhibitory control also inversely predicted later externalizing or Attention-Deficit/Hyperactivity Disorder (ADHD) problems more strongly than it predicted later internalizing problems. These studies provide support for a differential linkage between specific temperament dimensions and particular dimensions of later adjustment. For a review of additional studies on this, see Rothbart and Bates (2006).

SUMMARY

The literature on temperament and adjustment supports a direct linkage model. With a few exceptions, specific temperament dimensions also relate in a differentiated way to internalizing and externalizing, with early inhibition relating more to later internalizing, and early unmanageability to later externalizing, and with early negative affect relating to both outcomes.

Evidence does not yet answer the question of which of the direct linkage models listed previously applies best to the observed relations between temperament and adjustment. Given generally modest predictive relations, we would favor a vulnerability or predisposition model; a spectrum/continuity model might also apply. However, early individual differences likely become transformed, via developmental processes that include experience, into the more complex forms of adjustment in later years, and these processes must shape adjustment outcomes. Many child temperament researchers agree with Thomas, Chess, and Birch (1968) that temperament in itself does not constitute a negative versus positive adjustment, but that it conditions developmental processes that determine adjustment. This concept fits a vulnerability model better than a simpler continuity or spectrum model.

EMPIRICAL AND THEORETICAL LIMITS ON CONTINUITY

Predictive correlations tend to be modest to moderate in size, especially when temperament is assessed in early life. Several factors may influence this result. Measurement error is almost always a problem, but when power is sufficient, it can be controlled in structural models. However, even with a statistical control for measurement error, there will be limited predictive power (e.g., see Keiley et al., 2003). Limited predictiveness can also occur because of conceptual limitations in the measure of either temperament or adjustment. For example, the sample of situations used in a set of items may not be sufficient to capture the relevant construct. One particular problem involves the lower levels of prediction from temperament at home to adjustment at school. This is sometimes ascribed to parental rating biases, but many differences in incentive conditions are present at home and school, and even if a child's temperament is measured accurately, the child's expression of that temperament could differ in the two settings. For example, the same child could be resistant and angry with the mother and yet inhibited and adequately compliant at school, a pattern seen empirically by Dumas and LaFreniere (1993) and clinically in some young children in our treatment program for oppositional behavior problems. It is not that the child is inconsistent in temperament, but rather that a child with a disposition toward anxiety can be quite uncooperative and disruptive in familiar situations and more reserved in the highly stimulating and more novel school setting.

Alternatively, a child with an anxiety-prone temperament could be angry as a way to reduce anxiety aroused in a chaotically stressful home, by gaining a sense of control, and be calm in a more well-ordered, supportive school environment. The habit model described earlier (linking thoughts, emotions, and actions) allows for different experiences across situations. These situations differ in the constraints they offer for temperament expression and allow for different histories of experience that may be relatively idiosyncratic.

Another factor in limiting prediction is that temperament itself can change with development, as a result of either experience or later-emerging traits such as effortful control. It remains an interesting possibility that we may discover laws to account for *changes* in temperament. The adaptive behavior of shy children who were highly intelligent improved more over development than that of shy children who were less intelligent (Asendorpf, 1994). Negatively reactive infants, at high risk for behavioral inhibition, were more likely to show behavioral inhibition across age 14 months to 4 years if they also showed right frontal EEG asymmetry (indicating in another way a strong disposition to negative affect; Fox, Henderson, Rubin, Calkins, & Schmidt, 2001). They were also more likely to be continuously inhibited if they were exclusively in the care of their parents rather than receiving some nonparental care.

The limited size of prediction from temperament to adjustment may also be due to other major factors in development such as parenting, family stress, or school environment. In other words, temperament might be linked to adjustment through indirect processes. These include mediator models, as when a child's negative temperament influences negative parenting, which, in turn, plays the dominant role in producing the child's aggressive behavior problems, or moderator models, as when a child's negative temperament has one implication for development of adjustment in the context of negative parenting and another in the context of positive parenting. We next consider such processes, most sharply focusing on temperament X environment moderator models.

MODERATED LINKAGE

Rothbart and Bates (1998) discussed two possible indirect processes by which temperament and adjustment could be related. The first was mediated linkage in which temperament influences transactions with the environment, which in turn shape the child's developing adjustment. For example, a child's negative emotional reactivity might evoke hostile responses from caregivers, which build habitual frustration and hostility in the child. Research, especially longitudinal research, on such temperament-parenting-adjustment processes has been relatively sparse. Given space limitations, we will not discuss this work.

Another indirect process was a moderated linkage in which one temperament trait interacted with another in accounting for an adjustment outcome. Temperament X temperament interaction findings are not numerous, but would be worth a detailed review. For example, relations between effortful control and externalizing and prosocial behavior are stronger for children high in negative emotionality than for children low in negative emotionality (Belsky, Friedman, & Hsieh, 2001; Diener & Kim, 2004; Eisenberg, Fabes, et al., 2000; Eisenberg, Guthrie, et al., 2000; Stifter, Spinrad, & Braungart-Rieker, 1999). However, review of this topic will not be done here.

Another indirect process was moderated linkage in which we address how temperament and a feature of the environment might interact in the development of adjustment. For example, a child with high temperamental negative emotionality exposed to stress might be more likely to develop behavior problems than a less reactive child. There has been a striking growth in studies of moderated linkage, and this research direction is especially exciting because developmental theory has emphasized the likelihood of temperament-environment interaction. Although these connections have been posited for decades, they are just now beginning to take empirical shape.

Researchers sometimes focus on environmental moderation of how a temperament trait is associated with adjustment, as in parental hostility moderating the relation between child negative emotionality and adjustment. They also focus on how an environmental feature is moderated by the child's temperament, as when self-regulation tendencies moderate the adjustment implications of family stress. Choice between these two perspectives reflects the basic interests of the researchers, but an interaction from one perspective could often have also been described from the other perspective.

A bigger methodological challenge, however, is simply to find the interaction effect. Nonexperimental studies typically have to deal with correlated predictor and moderator variables, problems in the joint distributions of the variables, and insufficient statistical power for detecting effects (McClelland & Judd, 1993; Stoolmiller, 2001; Wachs & Plomin, 1991). Sometimes, interaction effects may be present but not found by statistical tests, or statistically significant effects may be specific to a sample or spurious. For these reasons, we focus especially on effects that have been replicated in some fashion. Many, but not all of the findings we review consider the interaction of temperament and environment in the context of the main effects, which is typically preferred by methodologists. We concentrate more on the substantive patterns of results than on methodological features (see Bates & McFadyen-Ketchum, 2001, for more discussion of methods).

Most of the emerging literature concerns three kinds of temperament trait: Those related to (a) low self-regulation, including low effortful control, unmanageability, and resistance to control, probably related to the Big Five personality dimensions of agreeableness and conscientiousness; (b) negative emotional reactivity, sometimes called difficult temperament; and (c) novelty distress, fear, or unadaptability. Each of these areas is reviewed in detail in Rothbart and Bates (2006) and Bates and Pettit (2007). Here we focus only on interactions involving low self-regulation. We are especially drawn to studies showing temperament X environment interaction effects in longitudinal studies of development of adjustment, but some useful cross-sectional findings have also emerged.

INTERACTIONS BETWEEN SELF-REGULATION AND ENVIRONMENT

Temperamental tendencies toward dysregulation, such as impulsivity or resistance to control, may be rooted not only in underdeveloped effortful control systems, but also in strong behavioral approach systems, or surgency. Such tendencies have shown direct associations with adjustment, especially with externalizing problems. At least 20 studies show traits in this broad domain interacting with characteristics of the rearing environment in the development of adjustment, and most of these consider the effects of temperament and parenting.

One emerging theme is that a disposition to dysregulation is more highly associated with problem behavior when parenting is negative or harsh rather than gentle. Calkins (2002) found that 18-month-old children high on distress and resistant in frustrating situations were likely to be high on angry and aggressive behavior in similar situations at 24 months when their mothers were low in positive parenting, but not when their mothers were highly positive. Rubin, Burgess, Dwyer, and Hastings (2003) measured children's self-regulation in laboratory tasks at age 2 and mother reports on the TBAQ at age 2. They also measured intrusive and hostile mothering in a snack situation and by mother report. Poor child self-regulation predicted mother-reported externalizing behavior problems at age 4 to a greater extent for children who at age 2 received higher levels of intrusive and hostile mothering. This pattern was found cross-sectionally at age 2 in the same study, but only for boys (Rubin, Hastings, Chen, Stewart, & McNichol, 1998).

Other cross-sectional examples include the finding that positive parenting as measured by interview and incidental observations matters more for temperamentally unmanageable children's adjustment in preschool than for less resistant children (Bates, Viken, & Williams, 2003). Morris et al. (2002) found that children rated by their mothers as low in effortful control (CBQ) showed an especially strong relationship between mother hostility (child report) and teacher-reported externalizing behavior, whereas Patterson and Sanson (1999) reported that mother-rated temperamental inflexibility (negative emotionality and resistance to demands) was more strongly associated with mother-reported externalizing problems when the mothers described themselves as relatively high in harsh punishment.

The general pattern also extends to a prosocial behavior—expression of sympathy. Valiente et al. (2004) found that parents' expressivity of negative emotion (self-rated and observed) was associated with children's self-reported sympathetic responses, but only when the child was high in effortful control (parent and teacher ratings on the CBQ and observation). This was true for self-rated general dispositions and personal distress to an empathy-inducing film, but not for sympathy responses to the film. A number of other studies show this general pattern (see Rothbart & Bates, 2006; Bates & Pettit, 2007).

A second emerging theme is supported by fewer studies, but it raises the possibility that disciplinary responses by parents can have *positive* rather than adverse implications for children with tendencies toward dysregulation. Adolescents' ratings of parental control and support were positively correlated and, for highly impulsive youth, high parental control and support were more associated with low levels of adolescent antisocial behavior than for nonimpulsive youth (Stice & Gonzales, 1998). Even more clearly showing the effectiveness of control for dysregulated children, boys who were highly unmanageable (disposed to have tantrums) in their early years showed a stronger relationship between mothers' unskilled discipline techniques and higher externalizing problems (as rated by teachers from elementary school to middle school) than boys who were low or medium in their unmanageability (Stoolmiller, 2001).

In two studies with community samples, early childhood temperamental resistance to control (mother report on the ICQ) better predicted externalizing problems in middle childhood (mother and teacher reports) for children who received low levels of parent control (observed in the home) than for children receiving high levels of control (Bates et al., 1998). Parent control was measured as reactions to misbehavior, and these reactions were sometimes but not always negative, for example, scolding. The researchers almost never saw harsh discipline such as spanking. Although hostile parenting and lack of warmth might well lead dysregulated temperament traits to become acting-out problems, the findings of Stice and Gonzales (1998) and Bates et al. (1998) suggest that parent control might also lessen the likelihood that dysregulated temperament will lead to problem behavior. However, high levels of parental control may not be ideal for all children: high levels of maternal control with highly manageable children sometimes resulted in higher externalizing behavior than would have been predicted by temperament alone, suggesting that mothers' control somehow prevented the development of truly internalized self-control (Bates et al., 1998).

A third emerging theme concerns a trait not usually discussed in the temperament literature—the core psychopathy trait, *callous-unemotional,* nonempathic, manipulative, and lacking anxiety and guilt. This pattern seems likely to be a form of temperamental dysregulation, even though its regulatory core appears to involve low prosocial orientation more than impulsivity to reward or low effortful control. It may also be related to very low levels of fear, but this does not seem likely to be the dominant component. In a combined clinical and normal sample when children were described by parents and teachers as low on the callous-unemotional scale, less positive parenting, as described by parent and child, was associated with greater conduct problems as measured by parent and teacher report (Wootton, Frick, Shelton, & Silverthorn, 1997). When high on the callous-unemotional scale, however, children were high on conduct problems whether the parenting was positive or not. This pattern was replicated, in essence, by O'Connor and Dvorak (2001) in a community sample, and by Oxford, Cavell, and Hughes (2003) in a sample more similar to that of Wootton et al. (1997).

It has been encouraging to see the emerging body of interactions between temperament and parenting environment in the development of adjustment. However, the studies do not provide sufficient evidence on developmental processes. The parent and child are also genetically related, and interaction effects might be confounded or obscured by gene-environment correlations. This makes it valuable to have relevant findings from studies considering variables other than standard temperament/personality, behavioral adjustment, and parenting. One example is the Hart, Atkins, and Fegley (2003) study, which shows, among other things, Head Start experience was especially beneficial in developing academic skills for children with resilient (well-regulated) personalities living in highly stressful family environments. Other examples include Lengua and Long (2002), considering the interaction of family stress and child effortful control, Fabes et al. (1999), considering the interaction of intensity of peer interactions and child effortful control, and Goodnight, Bates, Newman, Dodge, and Pettit (2006), considering the interaction of the deviance of friends of teens and the teens' impulsivity. Even further examples include El-Sheikh, Harger, and Whitson (2001), evaluating the interaction of parental marital quarrels and child vagal tone (a measure of self-regulation via the parasympathetic nervous system), and Caspi et al. (2002) and Caspi, Sugden, et al. (2003), showing the interaction between stressful experiences and alleles for two different genes related to self-regulation.

FUTURE DIRECTIONS IN RESEARCH ON TEMPERAMENT MODERATOR EFFECTS

Research has begun to demonstrate that child characteristics related to low behavioral regulation interact with a range of environmental qualities in the development of competencies and problems. In general, negative experiences and the absence of positive experiences appear to have less adverse effect on the development of children with stronger self-regulation, and greater effects on the development of children with weaker self-regulation. Ten years ago, this pattern was essentially undiscovered. Now, after an inspiring flurry of studies on interactions involving self-regulation, reviewed here, as well as negative emotionality and fearfulness (see Bates & Pettit, 2007; Rothbart & Bates, 2006), we can begin to envision research on the actual developmental processes by which temperament and environment moderate one another's effects on child adjustment. What are the limits of these phenomena? More precisely, which environmental factors interact with which particular child characteristics? What are the developmental processes by which these effects are found? What are the psychological products of the temperament and environment?

It may also be valuable to more extensively explore interactions between multiple temperament variables and environmental variables simultaneously. About 10 years ago, the typical limit of complexity found in research was considering temperament and environment variables' main effects as linear, additive contributors to a developmental outcome. Currently, the typical limit considers main effects plus the interaction of one temperament variable and one environment variable as predictors of an outcome, or main effects plus the interaction of two temperament variables (e.g., between negative emotionality and effortful control) as predictors. Where the meaning of a given temperament variable in isolation is not always clear, however, it might be helpful to consider the effect of a profile of temperament variables as moderating or moderated by an environmental variable (see also Rothbart & Sheese, 2007).

Conclusions

There has been considerable progress in identifying both broad outlines and more specific dimensions of temperament in childhood. The general framework includes broad dimensions of Positive Affect and Approach, Negative Affectivity, including differentiated subconstructs of Irritability and Fear, Effortful Control, and possibly Affiliation or Social Orientation. These broad dimensions share similarities with four of the Big Five Factors of Personality (Extraversion, Neuroticism, Conscientiousness, and Agreeableness), and with all of the Big Three broad factors of personality (Extraversion, Neuroticism, and Conscientiousness), but are by no means identical. Research establishing links between measures of these early temperament dimensions and later personality has now begun to appear, and will continue to be one of the major continuing projects for our area, along with further differentiating temperament and personality measures.

DIFFERENTIATING TEMPERAMENT DIMENSIONS

It is important to differentiate between fearful and irritable distress, and both biological and clinical studies have benefited from this distinction. Further evidence links anger and early surgency/extraversion to the development of externalizing problems and indicates that fear may be a protective factor against aggression and other externalizing problems as well as a contributor to the early development of conscience. A great deal of recent research has established connections between effortful control and the regulation of both affect and behavior. Future research will consider the limits of fearful and effortful control on adaptation, in connection with the Blocks' (Block & Block, 1980) construct of overcontrol, and allow us to study the way in which effortful control may become part of a resilient approach to life's challenges.

Probably the most striking new findings involve interactions between temperament and environment. The child's effortful control, manageability, and agreeableness have been found to moderate the effects of adverse environments. Not reviewed here (see Rothbart & Bates, 2006), but important, are patterns of findings in which negative emotionality amplifies the effects of adverse experience, and in which more fearful or inhibited children appear to benefit from early challenge, at least in measures of the later strength of this system, whereas they appear to benefit in early conscience development in the context of gentle socialization methods.

MEASURES

Good measures of temperament are crucial to our theoretical understanding. Further advances in defining the structure of temperament and understanding its neural and developmental substrates will continue to rely on advances in measurement. For this reason, we advocate the further development of sound measures, using parent-report, naturalistic observation, and structured or laboratory observation measures in converging and complementary ways.

Aside from the important future work of comparing results of alternative methods, another important focus in research should be identification of nonrelationships among constructs—tests for discriminant as well as convergent validity. Partly on the basis of differential, discriminating patterns of correlations between parent-reports of temperament and other measures, we are able to argue for the validity of parent-reports. The use of brain marker tasks in the study of development of executive attention and effortful control has also made significant strides in the past 5 years. We encourage the continued use of marker tasks to link performance to the development of brain functioning.

DEVELOPMENT

As the dimensions of temperament have been further delineated and measures improved, real advances have occurred in our understanding of temperament-environment interactions. Future research is needed to examine the processes supporting these effects. There may also be times when emotionality or effortful control systems are more sensitive to environmental conditions than others, or times when the child's irritable and frustrative distress might be most easily directed toward or away from coercive responses and tendencies to aggressive action. These are basic developmental questions with profound implications for our understanding of the nature of temperament and the development of personality.

Establishing closer links with our understanding of the developing neurophysiological substrate of temperament is a related task for our area, where findings from each domain illuminate the other. Thus, behavioral research on the developing structure of temperament helps to specify the operations necessary to link the psychology of temperament to its neurophysiology. Scholars who relate parallel research carried out in these two domains will aid in this work. The use of physiological assays, behavioral measures in research designs and the use of marker tasks will lead to further advances.

Finally, we have identified possible trajectories in the development of social and personality traits from early temperamental characteristics, most strongly in Kochanska's (1995) work on multiple routes to conscience. The task of identifying routes to other significant outcomes requires progress in all of the tasks described earlier. The study of developmental pathways or trajectories requires establishing stronger links between our work and more environmentally oriented areas of our field such as social learning and social cognition research. Temperament constructs do not conflict with these areas of research: The temperament dimensions we have described are open to experience, although some systems are likely more open than others. In addition, the functioning of control systems will be highly dependent on what the culture indicates should be controlled. Prospects for effective longitudinal research will be much improved by integrating research on individual differences, cross-cultural psychology, social learning, and social cognition.

Developmental research in our area may also eventually answer questions like the following: To what degree is temperament plastic and susceptible to change? To what degree does experience alter only the expression of temperamental characteristics? If distress and maladaptive social cognitions can result from a painful life history, how much of early temperament may have been overlain by these negative experiences? Could the original core of temperament be uncovered by imaginative assays, intervention, further social experience, or even by further changes in social or physical development? We know someone who, through the aging process, lost many of her memories, including information that had troubled her over many years and led to major conflicts in herself and with others. What remained after her memory loss was a positive and expressive person, loved by all who met her. Was this the child she once was? If so, could other less serious interventions have uncovered it? Better yet, could developmental research inform both child rearing and children's prospects in society so that the accumulating pain might never have occurred? We have made much progress in our field in the past decades, but a number of questions remain. Many of these questions are hopeful about a future for our parents, our children, and us.

References

Ahadi, S. A., & Rothbart, M. K. (1994). Temperament, development and the big five. In C. F. Halverson, G. A. Kohnstamm, & R. P. Martin (Eds.), *The developing structure of temperament and personality from infancy to adulthood* (pp. 189–207). Hillsdale, NJ: Erlbaum.

Ahadi, S. A., Rothbart, M. K., & Ye, R. (1993). Children's temperament in the United States and China: Similarities and differences. *European Journal of Personality, 7,* 359–378.

Aksan, N., & Kochanska, G. (2004). Links between systems of inhibition from infancy to preschool years. *Child Development, 75*(5), 1477–1490.

Asendorpf, J. B. (1990). Development of inhibition during childhood: Evidence for situational specificity and a two-factor model. *Developmental Psychology, 26,* 721–730.

Asendorpf, J. B. (1993). Social inhibition: A general-developmental perspective. In H. C. Traue & J. W. Pennebaker (Eds.), *Emotion inhibition and health* (pp. 80–99). Ashland, OH: Hogrefe & Huber.

Asendorpf, J. B. (1994). The malleability of behavioral inhibition: A study of individual developmental functions. *Developmental Psychology, 30,* 912–919.

Auerbach, J., Geller, V., Letzer, S., Shinwell, E., Levine, J., Belmaker, R. H., et al. (1999). Dopamine D4 receptor (D4DR) and serotonin transporter promoter (5-HTTLPR) polymorphisms in the determination of temperament in 2-month-old infants. *Molecular Psychiatry, 4,* 369–374.

Ayduk, O., Mendoza-Denton, R., Mischel, W., Downey, G., Peake, P. K., & Rodriguez, M. (2000). Regulating the interpersonal self: Strategic self-regulation for coping with rejection sensitivity. *Journal of Personality and Social Psychology, 79,* 776–792.

Bates, J. E. (1980). The concept of temperament. *Merrill-Palmer Quarterly, 26,* 299–319.

Bates, J. E. (1989). Applications of temperament concepts. In G. A. Kohnstamm, J. E. Bates, & M. K. Rothbart (Eds.), *Temperament in childhood* (pp. 321–355). Chichester, West Sussex, England: Wiley.

Bates, J. E. (1990). Conceptual and empirical linkages between temperament and behavior problems: A commentary on the Sanson, Prior, and Kyrios study. *Merrill-Palmer Quarterly, 36,* 193–199.

Bates, J. E. (1994). Parents as scientific observers of their children's development. In S. L. Friedman & H. C. Haywood (Eds.), *Developmental follow-up: Concepts, domains, and methods* (pp. 197–216). New York: Academic Press.

Bates, J. E., & Bayles, K. (1984). Objective and subjective components in mothers' perceptions of their children from age 6 months to 3 years. *Merrill-Palmer Quarterly, 30,* 111–130.

Bates, J. E., & Bayles, K. (1988). The role of attachment in the development of behavior problems. In J. Belsky & T. Nezworski (Eds.), *Clinical implications of attachment* (pp. 253–299). Hillsdale, NJ: Erlbaum.

Bates, J. E., Bayles, K., Bennett, D. S., Ridge, B., & Brown, M. M. (1991). Origins of externalizing behavior problems at eight years of age. In D. Pepler & K. Rubin (Eds.), *Development and treatment of childhood aggression* (pp. 93–120). Hillsdale, NJ: Erlbaum.

Bates, J. E., Maslin, C. A., & Frankel, K. A. (1985). Attachment security, mother-child interaction, and temperament as predictors of behavior-problem ratings at age three years. *Monographs of the Society for Child Development, 50*(1/2, Serial No. 209), 167–193.

Bates, J. E., & McFadyen-Ketchum, S. (2001). Temperament and parent-child relations as interacting factors in children's behavioral adjustment. In V. J. Molfese & D. L. Molfese (Eds.), *Temperament and personality across the life span* (pp. 141–176). Mahwah, NJ: Erlbaum.

Bates, J. E., & Pettit, G. S. (2007). Temperament, parenting, and socialization. In J. E. Grusec & P. D. Hastings (Eds.), *Handbook of socialization* (pp. 153–177). New York: Guilford Press.

Bates, J. E., Pettit, G. S., & Dodge, K. A. (1995). Family and child factors in stability and change in children's aggressiveness in elementary school. In J. McCord (Ed.), *Coercion and punishment in long-term perspectives* (pp. 124–138). New York: Cambridge University Press.

Bates, J. E., Pettit, G. S., Dodge, K. A., & Ridge, B. (1998). The interaction of temperamental resistance to control and restrictive parenting in the development of externalizing behavior. *Developmental Psychology, 34,* 982–995.

Bates, J. E., Viken, R. J., & Williams, N. (2003, April). *Temperament as a moderator of the linkage between sleep and preschool adjustment.* Paper presented at the meeting of the Society for Research in Child Development, Tampa, FL.

Bates, J. E., Wachs, T. D., & Emde, R. N. (1994). Toward practical uses for biological concepts of temperament. In J. E. Bates & T. D. Wachs (Eds.), *Temperament: Individual differences at the interface of biology and behavior* (pp. 275–306). Washington, DC: American Psychological Association.

Bayley, N., & Schafer, E. S. (1963). Maternal behavior, child behavior, and their intercorrelations from infancy through adolescence. *Monographs of the Society for Research in Child Development, 28,* 127.

Bell, R. Q. (1968). A reinterpretation of the direction of effects in studies of socialization. *Psychological Review, 75,* 81–95.

Bell, R. Q. (1974). Contributions of human infants to caregiving and social interaction. In M. Lewis & L. A. Rosenblum (Eds.), *The effect of the infant on its caregiver* (pp. 1–19). New York: Wiley.

Belsky, J., Friedman, S., & Hsieh, K. (2001). Testing a core emotion-regulation prediction: Does early attentional persistence moderate the effect of infant negative emotionality on later development? *Child Development, 72,* 123–133.

Benjamin, J., Ebstein, R. P., & Belmaker, R. H. (Eds.). (1996). *Molecular genetics and the human personality.* Washington, DC: American Psychiatric Press.

Bishop, G., Spence, S. H., & McDonald, C. (2003). Can parents and teachers provide a reliable and valid report of behavioral inhibition? *Child Development, 74,* 1899–1917.

Black, J. E., & Greenough, W. T. (1991). Developmental approaches to the memory processes. In J. L. Martinez Jr. & R. P. Kesner (Eds.), *Learning and memory: A biological view* (2nd ed., pp. 61–91). San Diego, CA: Academic Press.

Block, J. H., & Block, J. (1980). The role of ego-control and ego-resiliency in the organization of behavior. In W. A. Collins (Ed.), *Minnesota Symposia on Child Psychology* (Vol. 13, pp. 39–101). Hillsdale, NJ: Erlbaum.

Bouchard, T. J., Jr., & Loehlin, J. C. (2001). Genes, evolution, and personality. *Behavior Genetics, 31*(3), 243–273.

Buss, A. H., & Plomin, R. (1975). *A temperament theory of personality development.* New York: Wiley.

Calkins, S. D. (2002). Does aversive behavior during toddlerhood matter? The effects of difficult temperament on maternal perceptions and behavior. *Infant Mental Health Journal, 23,* 381–402.

Calkins, S. D., & Williford, A. P. (2003, April). *Anger regulation in infancy: Consequences and correlates.* Paper presented at the meeting of the Society for Research in Child Development, Tampa, FL.

Carey, G. (2003). *Human genetics for the social sciences.* London: Sage.

Caspi, A. (2000). The child is father of the man: Personality continuities from childhood to adulthood. *Journal of Personality and Social Psychology, 78,* 158–172.

Caspi, A., Harrington, H., Milne, B., Amell, J. W., Theodore, R. F., & Moffitt, T. E. (2003). Children's behavioral styles at age 3 are linked to their adult personality traits at age 26. *Journal of Personality, 71,* 495–513.

Caspi, A., McClay, J., Moffitt, T., Mill, J., Martin, J., Craig, I. W., et al. (2002). Role of genotype in the cycle of violence in maltreated children. *Science, 297,* 851–854.

Caspi, A., & Shiner, R. L. (2006). Personality development. In W. Damon & R. M. Lerner (Series Eds.) & N. Eisenberg (Vol. Ed.), *Handbook of child psychology: Vol. 3. Social, emotional, and personality development* (6th ed., pp. 300–365). Hoboken, NJ: Wiley.

Caspi, A., & Silva, P. A. (1995). Temperament qualities at age three predict personality traits in young adulthood: Longitudinal evidence from a birth cohort. *Child Development, 66,* 486–498.

Caspi, A., Sugden, K., Moffitt, T. E., Taylor, A., Craig, I. W., Harrington, H., et al. (2003). Influence of life stress on depression: Moderation by a polymorphism in the 5-HTT gene. *Science, 301,* 386–389.

Chess, S., & Thomas, A. (1984). *Origins and evolution of behavior disorders.* New York: Brunner/Mazel.

Clark, L. A., Watson, D., & Mineka, S. (1994). Temperament, personality, and the mood and anxiety disorders. *Journal of Abnormal Psychology, 103,* 103–116.

Diener, M. L., & Kim, D.-Y. (2004). Maternal and child predictors of preschool children's social competence. *Applied Developmental Psychology, 25,* 3–24.

Digman, J. M., & Inouye, J. (1986). Further specification of the five robust factors of personality. *Journal of Personality and Social Psychology, 50,* 116–123.

Ding, Y. C., Chi, H. C., Grady, D. L., Morishima, A., Kidd, J. R., Kidd, K. K., et al. (2002). Evidence of positive selection acting at the human dopamine receptor D4 gene locus. *Proceedings of the National Academy of Sciences, USA, 99,* 309–314.

Dumas, J. E., & LaFreniere, P. J. (1993). Mother-child relationships as sources of support or stress: A comparison of competent, average, aggressive, and anxious dyads. *Child Development, 64,* 1732–1754.

Eaton, W. O. (1994). Temperament, development, and the five-factor model: Lessons from activity level. In C. F. Halverson Jr., G. A. Kohnstamm, & R. P. Martin (Eds.), *The developing structure of temperament and personality from infancy to adulthood* (pp. 173–187). Hillsdale, NJ: Erlbaum.

Eaves, L., Silberg, J., & Erkanli, A. (2003). Resolving multiple epigenetic pathways to adolescent depression. *Journal of Child Psychology and Psychiatry, 44,* 1006–1014.

Ebstein, R. P., Levine, J., Geller, V., Auerbach, J., Gritsenko, I., & Belmaker, R. H. (1998). Dopamine D4 receptor and serotonin transporter promoter in the determination of neonatal temperament. *Molecular Psychiatry, 3,* 238–246.

Ebstein, R. P., Novick, O., Umansky, R., Priel, B., Osher, Y., Blaine, D., et al. (1996). Dopamine D4 receptor (D4DR) exon III polymorphism associated with the human personality trait of novelty seeking. *Nature Genetics, 12*(1), 78–80.

Eisenberg, N., Fabes, R. A., Guthrie, I. K., Murphy, B. C., Poulin, R., & Shepard, S. (1996). The relations of regulation and emotionality to problem behavior in elementary school children. *Development and Psychopathology, 8,* 141–162.

Eisenberg, N., Fabes, R. A., Guthrie, I. K., & Reiser, M. (2000). Dispositional emotionality and regulation: Their role in predicting quality of social functioning. *Journal of Personality and Social Psychology, 78,* 136–157.

Eisenberg, N., Guthrie, I. K., Fabes, R. A., Shepard, S., Losoya, S., Murphy, B. C., et al. (2000). Prediction of elementary school children's externalizing problem behaviors from attentional and behavioral regulation and negative emotionality. *Child Development, 71*(5), 1367–1382.

Eisenberg, N., Spinrad, T. L., Fabes, R. A., Reiser, M., Cumberland, A., Shepard, S. A., et al. (2004). The relations of effortful control and impulsivity to children's resiliency and adjustment. *Child Development, 75*(1), 25–46.

El-Sheikh, M., Harger, J., & Whitson, S. M. (2001). Exposure to interparental conflict and children's adjustment and physical health: The moderating role of vagal tone. *Child Development, 72,* 1617–1636.

Escalona, S. K. (1968). *The roots of individuality: Normal patterns of development in infancy.* Chicago: Aldine.

Evans, D., & Rothbart, M. K. (in press). Developing a model for adult temperament. *Journal for Research in Personality.*

Fabes, R. A., Eisenberg, N., Jones, S., Smith, M., Guthrie, I., Poulin, R., et al. (1999). Regulation, emotionality, and preschoolers' socially competent peer interactions. *Child Development, 70,* 432–442.

Forman, D. R., O'Hara, M. W., Larsen, K., Coy, K. C., Gorman, L. L., & Stuart, S. (2003). Infant emotionality: Observational methods and the validity of maternal reports. *Infancy, 4,* 541–565.

Fossella, J., Posner, M. I., Fan, J., Swanson, J. M., & Pfaff, D. W. (2002). Attentional phenotypes for the analysis of higher mental function. *Scientific World Journal, 2,* 217–223.

Fowles, D. C. (1994). A motivational theory of psychopathology. In W. Spaulding (Ed.), *Nebraska Symposium on Motivation: Vol. 41. Integrated views of motivation and emotion* (pp. 181–238). Lincoln: University of Nebraska Press.

Fox, N. A., Henderson, H. A., Rubin, K. H., Calkins, S. D., & Schmidt, L. A. (2001). Continuity and discontinuity of behavioral inhibition and exuberance: Psychophysiological and behavioral influences across the first four years of life. *Child Development, 72,* 1–21.

Gartstein, M. A., & Rothbart, M. K. (2003). Studying infant temperament via the revised Infant Behavior Questionnaire. *Infant Behavior and Development, 26,* 64–86.

Gerardi-Caulton, G. (2000). Sensitivity to spatial conflict and the development of self-regulation in children 24 to 36 months of age. *Developmental Science, 3,* 397–404.

Gest, S. D. (1997). Behavioral inhibition: Stability and associations with adaptation from childhood to early adulthood. *Journal of Personality and Social Psychology, 72*(2), 467–475.

Gilliom, M., & Shaw, D. (2004). Codevelopment of externalizing and internalizing problems in early childhood. *Development and Psychopathology, 16,* 313–333.

Goldberg, L. R. (1993). The structure of phenotypic personality traits. *American Psychologist, 48,* 26–34.

Goldsmith, H. H., Buss, K. A., & Lemery, K. S. (1997). Toddler and childhood temperament: Expanded content, stronger genetic evidence, new evidence for the importance of environment. *Developmental Psychology, 33,* 891–905.

Goldsmith, H. H., & Hewitt, E. C. (2003). Validity of parental report of temperament: Distinctions and needed research. *Infant Behavior and Development, 26,* 108–111.

Goldsmith, H. H., Losoya, S. H., Bradshaw, D. L., & Campos, J. J. (1994). Genetics of personality: A twin study of the five-factor model and parental-offspring analyses. In C. Halverson, R. Martin, & G. Kohnstamm (Eds.), *The developing structure of temperament and personality from infancy to adulthood* (pp. 241–265). Hillsdale, NJ: Erlbaum.

Goldsmith, H. H., & Rieser-Danner, L. (1986). Variation among temperament theories and validation studies of temperament assessment. In G. A. Kohnstamm (Ed.), *Temperament discussed: Temperament and development in infancy and childhood* (pp. 1–9). Lisse, The Netherlands: Swets & Zeitlinger.

Goldsmith, H. H., & Rothbart, M. K. (1991). Contemporary instruments for assessing early temperament by questionnaire and in the laboratory. In A. Angleitner & J. Strelau (Eds.), *Explorations in temperament: International perspectives on theory and measurement* (pp. 249–272). New York: Plenum Press.

Goodnight, J. A., Bates, J. E., Newman, J. P., Dodge, K. A., & Pettit, G. S. (2006). The interactive influences of friend deviance and disinhibition on the development of externalizing behavior during middle adolescence. *Journal of Abnormal Child Psychology, 34*(5), 573–583.

Gosling, S. D., & John, O. P. (1999). Personality dimensions in nonhuman animals: A cross-species review. *Current Directions in Psychological Science, 8,* 69–75.

Gray, J. A. (1991). The neuropsychology of temperament. In J. Strelau & A. Angleitner (Eds.), *Explorations in temperament: International perspectives on theory and measurement* (pp. 105–128). New York: Plenum Press.

Gunnar, M. R. (1990). The psychobiology of infant temperament. In J. Colombo & J. Fagen (Eds.), *Individual differences in infancy: Reliability, stability, prediction* (pp. 387–409). Hillsdale, NJ: Erlbaum.

Hagekull, B. (1989). Longitudinal stability of temperament within a behavioral style framework. In G. A. Kohnstamm, J. E. Bates, & M. K. Rothbart (Eds.), *Temperament in childhood* (pp. 283–297). Chichester, West Sussex, England: Wiley.

Hagekull, B., Bohlin, G., & Lindhagen, K. (1984). Validity of parental reports. *Infant Behavior and Development, 7,* 77–92.

Hart, D., Atkins, R., & Fegley, S. (2003). Personality and development in childhood: A person-centered approach. *Monographs of the Society for Research in Child Development, 68,* 74–85.

Hegvik, R. L., McDevitt, S. C., & Carey, W. B. (1982). The Middle Childhood Temperament Questionnaire. *Developmental and Behavioral Pediatrics, 3,* 197–200.

Honzik, M. P. (1965). Prediction of behavior from birth to maturity [Review of the book *Birth to maturity* by J. Kagan & H. Moss]. *Merrill-Palmer Quarterly, 11,* 77–88.

Hwang, J., & Rothbart, M. K. (2003). Behavior genetics studies of infant temperament: Findings vary across parent-report instruments. *Infant Behavior and Development, 26,* 112–114.

Kagan, J. (1994). *Galen's prophecy: Temperament in human nature.* Cambridge, MA: Harvard University Press.

Kagan, J. (1998). Biology and the child. In W. Damon (Series Ed.) & N. Eisenberg (Vol. Ed.), *Handbook of child psychology: Vol. 3. Social, emotional, and personality development* (5th ed., pp. 177–235). New York: Wiley.

Kagan, J., & Fox, N. A. (2006). Biology, culture, and temperamental biases. In W. Damon & R. M. Lerner (Series Eds.) & N. Eisenberg (Vol. Ed.), *Handbook of child psychology: Vol. 3. Social, emotional, and personality development* (6th ed., pp. 167–225). Hoboken, NJ: Wiley.

Kagan, J., Kearsley, R. B., & Zelazo, P. R. (1978). *Infancy: Its place in human development.* New York: Wiley.

Kagan, J., & Moss, H. A. (1962). *Birth to maturity.* New York: Wiley.

Keiley, M. K., Lofthouse, N., Bates, J. E., Dodge, K. A., & Pettit, G. S. (2003). Differential risks of covarying and pure components in mother and teacher reports of externalizing and internalizing behavior across ages 5 to 14. *Journal of Abnormal Child Psychology, 31,* 267–283.

Kenrick, D. T., & Funder, D. C. (1988). Profiting from controversy: Lessons from the person-situation debate. *American Psychologist, 43,* 23–34.

Kessen, W. (1965). *The child.* New York: Wiley.

Kistiakovskaia, M. I. (1965). Stimuli evoking positive emotions in infants in the first months of life. *Soviet Psychology and Psychiatry, 3,* 39–48.

Kochanska, G. (1995). Children's temperament, mothers' discipline, and security of attachment: Multiple pathways to emerging internalization. *Child Development, 66,* 597–615.

Kochanska, G., DeVet, K., Goldman, M., Murray, K. T., & Putnam, S. P. (1993). Maternal reports of conscience development and temperament in young children. *Child Development, 65,* 852–868.

Kochanska, G., & Knaack, A. (2003). Effortful control as a personality characteristic of young children: Antecedents, correlates, and consequences. *Journal of Personality, 71,* 1087–1112.

Kochanska, G., Murray, K. T., & Harlan, E. T. (2000). Effortful control in early childhood: Continuity and change, antecedents, and implications for social development. *Developmental Psychology, 36,* 220–232.

Kohlberg, L. (1969). Stage and sequence: The cognitive developmental approach to socialization. In D. A. Goslin (Ed.), *Handbook of socialization theory and research* (pp. 347–480). Chicago: Rand McNally.

Krakow, J. B., Kopp, C. B., & Vaughn, B. E. (1981, April). *Sustained attention during the second year: Age trends, individual differences, and implications for development.* Paper presented at the meeting of the Society for Research in Child Development, Boston.

Kubzansky, L. D., Martin, L. T., & Buka, S. L. (2004). Early manifestations of personality and adult emotional functioning. *Emotion, 4,* 364–377.

LeDoux, J. E. (1989). Cognitive-emotional interactions in the brain. *Cognition and Emotion, 3,* 267–289.

Lee, C. L., & Bates, J. E. (1985). Mother-child interaction at two years and perceived difficult temperament. *Child Development, 56,* 1314–1325.

Lemery, K. S., Essex, M. J., & Smider, N. A. (2002). Revealing the relation between temperament and behavior problem symptoms by eliminating measurement confounding: Expert ratings and factor analyses. *Child Development, 73,* 867–882.

Lengua, L. J., & Long, A. C. (2002). The role of emotionality and self-regulation in the appraisal-coping process: Tests of direct and moderating effects. *Applied Developmental Psychology, 23,* 471–493.

Lengua, L. J., West, S. G., & Sandler, I. N. (1998). Temperament as a predictor of symptomatology in children: Addressing contamination of measures. *Child Development, 69,* 164–181.

Lerner, J. V., & Lerner, R. M. (1994). Explorations of the goodness-of-fit model in early adolescence. In W. B. Carey & S. C. McDevitt (Eds.), *Prevention and early intervention: Individual differences as risk factors for the mental health of children—A festschrift for Stella Chess and Alexander Thomas* (pp. 161–169). New York: Brunner/Mazel.

Lonigan, C. J., Vasey, M. W., Phillips, B. M., & Hazen, R. A. (2004). Temperament, anxiety, and the processing of threat-relevant stimuli. *Journal of Clinical Child and Adolescent Psychology, 33,* 8–20.

Lytton, H. (1995, March). *Child and family factors as predictors of conduct disorder and criminality.* Paper presented at the meeting of the Society for Research in Child Development, Indianapolis, IN.

MacDonald, K. (1988). *Social and personality development: An evolutionary synthesis.* New York: Plenum Press.

MacDonald, K. (1992). Warmth as a developmental construct: An evolutionary analysis. *Child Development, 63,* 753–773.

Martin, R. P., Wisenbaker, J., & Huttunen, M. (1994). The factor structure of instruments based on the Chess-Thomas model of temperament: Implications for the big five model. In C. F. Halverson, G. A. Kohnstamm, & R. P. Martin (Eds.), *The developing structure of temperament and personality from infancy to adulthood* (pp. 339–347). Hillsdale, NJ: Erlbaum.

Matheny, A. P., Jr. (1989). Children's behavioral inhibition over age and across situations: Genetic similarity for a trait during change. *Journal of Personality, 57,* 215–235.

McClelland, G. H., & Judd, C. M. (1993). Statistical difficulties of detecting interactions and moderator effects. *Psychological Bulletin, 114*(2), 376–390.

McClowry, S. G., Hegvik, R., & Teglasi, H. (1993). An examination of the construct validity of the middle childhood temperament questionnaire. *Merrill-Palmer Quarterly, 39,* 279–293.

Mischel, W. (1983). Delay of gratification as process and as person variable in development. In D. Magnusson & V. P. Allen (Eds.), *Human development: An interactional perspective* (pp. 149–165). New York: Academic Press.

Mischel, W., & Ayduk, O. (2004). Willpower in a cognitive-affective processing system: The dynamics of delay of gratification. In R. F. Baumeister & K. D. Vohs (Eds.), *Handbook of self-regulation: Research, theory, and applications* (pp. 99–129). New York: Guilford Press.

Morris, A. S., Silk, J. S., Steinberg, L., Sessa, F. M., Avenevoli, S., & Essex, M. J. (2002). Temperamental vulnerability and negative parenting as interacting predictors of child adjustment. *Journal of Marriage and Family, 64,* 461–471.

Moskowitz, D. S., & Schwarz, J. C. (1982). Validity comparison of behavior counts and ratings by knowledgeable informants. *Journal of Personality and Social Psychology, 42,* 518–528.

Neilon, P. (1948). Shirley's babies after 15 years. *Journal of Genetic Psychology, 73,* 175–186.

O'Connor, B. P., & Dvorak, T. (2001). Conditional associations between parental behavior and adolescent problems: A search for personality-environment interactions. *Journal of Research in Personality, 35,* 1–26.

Oldehinkel, A. J., Hartman, C. A., de Winter, A. F., Veenstra, R., & Ormel, J. (2004). Temperamental profiles associated with internalizing and externalizing problems in preadolescence. *Development and Psychopathology, 16,* 421–440.

Olson, S. L., Bates, J. E., & Bayles, K. (1990). Early antecedents of childhood impulsivity: The role of parent-child interaction, cognitive competence, and temperament. *Journal of Abnormal Child Psychology, 18,* 317–334.

Oxford, M., Cavell, T. A., & Hughes, J. N. (2003). Callous/unemotional traits moderate the relation between ineffective parenting and child externalizing problems: A partial replication and extension. *Journal of Clinical Child and Adolescent Psychology, 32,* 577–585.

Panksepp, J. (1998). *Affective neuroscience: The foundations of human and animal emotions.* New York: Oxford University Press.

Patterson, G., & Sanson, A. (1999). The association of behavioural adjustment to temperament, parenting and family characteristics among 5-year-old children. *Social Development, 8,* 293–309.

Pedlow, R., Sanson, A. V., Prior, M., & Oberklaid, F. (1993). The stability of temperament from infancy to eight years. *Developmental Psychology, 29,* 998–1007.

Pfeifer, M., Goldsmith, H. H., Davidson, R. J., & Rickman, M. (2002). Continuity and change in inhibited and uninhibited children. *Child Development, 73,* 1474–1485.

Plomin, R., & Caspi, A. (1999). Behavioral genetics and personality. In L. A. Pervin & O. P. John (Eds.), *Handbook of personality: Theory and research* (2nd ed., pp. 251–276). New York: Guilford Press.

Plomin, R., Chipuer, H. M., & Loehlin, J. C. (1990). Behavioral genetics and personality. In A. L. Pervin (Ed.), *Handbook of personality theory and research* (pp. 225–243). New York: Guilford Press.

Posner, M. I., & Fan, J. (in press). Attention as an organ system. In J. Pomerantz (Ed.), *Neurobiology of perception and communication: From synapse to society* (The 4th De Lange Conference). Cambridge: Cambridge University Press.

Posner, M. I., & Raichle, M. E. (1994). *Images of the mind.* New York: Scientific American Library.

Posner, M. I., & Rothbart, M. K. (1998). Attention, self-regulation, and consciousness. *Philosophical Transactions of the Royal Society of London, B, 353,* 1915–1927.

Posner, M. I., & Rothbart, M. K. (2007a). *Educating the human brain.* Washington DC: American Psychological Association.

Posner, M. I., & Rothbart, M. K. (2007b). Research on attention networks as a model for the integration of psychological science. *Annual Review of Psychology, 58,* 1–23.

Posner, M. I., Rothbart, M. K., & Sheese, B. E. (2007). Attention genes. *Developmental Science, 10*(1), 24–29.

Presley, R., & Martin, R. P. (1994). Toward a structure of preschool temperament: Factor structure of the temperament assessment battery for children. *Journal of Personality, 62,* 415–448.

Radke-Yarrow, M., & Sherman, T. (1990). Hard growing: Children who survive. In J. Rolf, A. S. Masten, D. Cicchetti, K. H. Neuchterlin, & S. Weintraub (Eds.), *Risk and protective factors in the development of psychopathology* (pp. 97–119). New York: Cambridge University Press.

Roberts, B. W., & DelVecchio, W. F. (2000). The rank-order consistency of personality traits from childhood to old age: A quantitative review of longitudinal studies. *Psychological Bulletin, 126,* 3–25.

Rothbart, M. K. (1981). Measurement of temperament in infancy. *Child Development, 52,* 569–578.

Rothbart, M. K. (1986). Longitudinal observation of infant temperament. *Developmental Psychology, 22,* 356–365.

Rothbart, M. K. (1988). Temperament and the development of inhibited approach. *Child Development, 59,* 1241–1250.

Rothbart, M. K. (1989). Temperament and development. In G. Kohnstamm, J. Bates, & M. K. Rothbart (Eds.), *Temperament in childhood* (pp. 187–248). Chichester, West Sussex, England: Wiley.

Rothbart, M. K. (2007). Temperament, development and personality. *Current Directions in Psychological Science, 16,* 207–212.

Rothbart, M. K., Ahadi, S. A., & Hershey, K. L. (1994). Temperament and social behavior in childhood. *Merrill-Palmer Quarterly, 40,* 21–39.

Rothbart, M. K., Ahadi, S. A., Hershey, K., & Fisher, P. (2001). Investigations of temperament at 3 to 7 years: The Children's Behavior Questionnaire. *Child Development, 72,* 1394–1408.

Rothbart, M. K., & Bates, J. E. (1998). Temperament. In W. Damon (Series Ed.) & N. Eisenberg (Vol. Ed.), *Handbook of child psychology: Vol. 3. Social, emotional, and personality development* (5th ed., pp. 105–176). New York: Wiley.

Rothbart, M. K., & Bates, J. E. (2006). Temperament. In W. Damon & R. M. Lerner (Series Eds.) & N. Eisenberg (Vol. Ed.), *Handbook of child psychology: Vol. 3. Social, emotional, and personality development* (6th ed., pp. 99–166). Hoboken, NJ: Wiley.

Rothbart, M. K., & Derryberry, D. (1981). Development of individual differences in temperament. In M. E. Lamb & A. L. Brown (Eds.), *Advances in developmental psychology* (Vol. 1, pp. 37–86). Hillsdale, NJ: Erlbaum.

Rothbart, M. K., & Derryberry, D. (2002). Temperament in children. In C. von Hofsten & L. Bäckman (Eds.), *Psychology at the turn of the millennium: Vol. 2. Social, developmental, and clinical perspectives* (pp. 17–35). East Sussex, England: Psychology Press.

Rothbart, M. K., Derryberry, D., & Posner, M. I. (1994). A psychobiological approach to the development of temperament. In J. E. Bates & T. D. Wachs (Eds.), *Temperament: Individual differences at the interface of biology and behavior* (pp. 83–116). Washington, DC: American Psychological Association.

Rothbart, M. K., Ellis, L. K., & Posner, M. I. (2004). Temperament and self-regulation. In R. F. Baumeister & K. D. Vohs (Eds.), *Handbook of self-regulation: Research, theory, and applications* (pp. 357–370). New York: Guilford Press.

Rothbart, M. K., & Mauro, J. A. (1990). Questionnaire approaches to the study of infant temperament. In J. W. Fagen & J. Colombo (Eds.), *Individual differences in infancy: Reliability, stability, and prediction* (pp. 411–429). Hillsdale, NJ: Erlbaum.

Rothbart, M. K., & Posner, M. I. (2006). Temperament, attention, and developmental psychopathology. In D. Cicchetti (Ed.), *Handbook of developmental psychopathology.* Hoboken, NJ: Wiley.

Rothbart, M. K., Posner, M. I., & Rosicky, J. (1994). Orienting in normal and pathological development. *Development and Psychopathology, 6,* 635–652.

Rothbart, M. K., & Rueda, M. R. (2005). The development of effortful control. In U. Mayr, E. Awh, & S. W. Keele (Eds.), *Developing individuality in the human brain: A tribute to Michael I. Posner* (pp. 167–188). Washington, DC: American Psychological Association.

Rothbart, M. K., & Sheese, B. E. (2007). Temperament and emotion regulation. In J. J. Gross (Ed.), *Handbook of emotion regulation* (pp. 331–350). New York: Guilford Press.

Rothbart, M. K., Sheese, B. E., & Posner, M. I. (in press). Development of self-regulation in childhood. *Child Development Perspectives.*

Rothbart, M. K., & Victor, J. (2004, October). *Temperament and the development of personality.* Paper presented at the Occasional Temperament Conference, Athens, GA.

Rubin, K. H., Burgess, K. B., Dwyer, K. M., & Hastings, P. D. (2003). Predicting preschoolers' externalizing behaviors from toddler temperament, conflict, and maternal negativity. *Developmental Psychology, 39,* 164–176.

Rubin, K. H., Hastings, P., Chen, X., Stewart, S., & McNichol, K. (1998). Intrapersonal and maternal correlates of aggression, conflict, and externalizing problems in toddlers. *Child Development, 69,* 1614–1629.

Ruff, H. A., & Rothbart, M. K. (1996). *Attention in early development: Themes and variations.* New York: Oxford University Press.

Russell, A., Hart, C. H., Robinson, C. C., & Olsen, S. F. (2003). Children's sociable and aggressive behavior with peers: A comparison of the U.S. and Australia, and contributions of temperament and parenting styles. *International Journal of Behavioral Development, 27,* 74–86.

Rutter, M. (1987). Continuities and discontinuities from infancy. In J. D. Osofsky (Ed.), *Handbook of infant development* (pp. 1150–1198). New York: Wiley.

Sanson, A., Hemphill, S. A., & Smart, D. (2004). Connections between temperament and social development: A review. *Social Development, 13,* 142–170.

Sanson, A., Prior, M., & Kyrios, M. (1990). Contamination of measures in temperament research. *Merrill-Palmer Quarterly, 36,* 179–192.

Sanson, A., Smart, D. F., Prior, M., Oberklaid, F., & Pedlow, R. (1994). The structure of temperament from 3 to 7 years: Age, sex, and sociodemographic influences. *Merrill-Palmer Quarterly, 40,* 233–252.

Saudino, K. J. (2003). Parent ratings of infant temperament lessons from twin studies. *Infant Behavior and Development, 26,* 100–107.

Scarr, S., & McCartney, K. (1983). How people make their own environments: A theory of genotype-environment effects. *Child Development, 54,* 242–435.

Schaffer, H. R. (1974). Cognitive components of the infant's response to strangeness. In M. Lewis & L. A. Rosenblum (Eds.), *The origins of fear* (pp. 11–24). New York: Wiley.

Schmidt, L. A., & Fox, N. A. (2002). Molecular genetics of temperamental differences in children. In J. Benjamin, R. P. Ebstein, & R. H. Belmaker (Eds.), *Molecular genetics and the human personality* (pp. 245–255). Washington, DC: American Psychiatric Press.

Schmidt, L. A., Fox, N. A., Perez-Edgar, K., Hu, S., & Hamer, D. H. (2001). Association of DRD4 with attention problems in normal childhood development. *Psychiatric Genetics, 11,* 25–29.

Sears, R. R., Maccoby, E. E., & Levin, H. (1957). *Patterns of child rearing.* Evanston, IL: Row, Peterson.

Seifer, R. (2003). Twin studies, biases of parents, and biases of researchers. *Infant Behavior and Development, 26,* 115–117.

Sethi, A., Mischel, W., Aber, J. L., Shoda, Y., & Rodriguez, M. L. (2000). The role of strategic attention deployment in development of self-regulation: Predicting preschoolers' delay of gratification from mother-toddler interactions. *Developmental Psychology, 6,* 767–777.

Sheeber, L. B. (1995). Empirical dissociations between temperament and behavior problems: A response to the Sanson, Prior, and Kyrios study. *Merrill-Palmer Quarterly, 41,* 554–561.

Sheese, B. E., Voelker, P. M., Rothbart, M. K., & Posner, M. I. (2007). Parenting quality interacts with genetic variation in dogamine receptor D4 to influence temperament in early childhood. *Development and Psychopathology, 19,* 1039–1046.

Shiner, R. L., & Caspi, A. (2003). Personality differences in childhood and adolescence: Measurement, development, and consequences. *Journal of Child Psychology and Psychiatry, 44,* 2–32.

Shiner, R. L., Masten, A. S., & Tellegen, A. (2002). A developmental perspective on personality in emerging adulthood: Childhood antecedents and concurrent adaptation. *Journal of Personality and Social Psychology, 83,* 1165–1177.

Shirley, M. M. (1933). *The first two years: A study of 25 babies.* Minneapolis: University of Minnesota Press.

Shoda, Y., Mischel, W., & Peake, P. K. (1990). Predicting adolescent cognitive and self-regulatory competencies from preschool delay of gratification: Identifying diagnostic conditions. *Developmental Psychology, 26,* 978–986.

Slabach, E. H., Morrow, J., & Wachs, T. D. (1991). Questionnaire measurement of infant and child temperament: Current status and future directions. In J. Strelau & A. Angleitner (Eds.), *Explorations in temperament: International perspectives on theory and measurement* (pp. 205–234). New York: Plenum Press.

Stice, E., & Gonzales, N. (1998). Adolescent temperament moderates the relation of parenting to antisocial behavior and substance use. *Journal of Adolescent Research, 13,* 5–31.

Stifter, C. A., & Braungart, J. M. (1995). The regulation of negative reactivity in infancy: Function and development. *Developmental Psychology, 31,* 448–455.

Stifter, C. A., Spinrad, T. L., & Braungart-Rieker, J. M. (1999). Toward a developmental model of child compliance: The role of emotion regulation in infancy. *Child Development, 70,* 21–32.

Stoolmiller, M. (2001). Synergistic interaction of child manageability problems and parent-discipline tactics in predicting future growth in externalizing behavior for boys. *Developmental Psychology, 37,* 814–825.

Strelau, J. (1983). *Temperament personality activity.* New York: Academic Press.

Suls, J., Martin, R., & David, J. P. (1998). Person-environment fit and its limits: Agreeableness, neuroticism, and emotional reactivity to interpersonal conflict. *Personality and Social Psychology Bulletin, 24,* 88–98.

Swanson, J. M., Flodman, P., Kennedy, J., Spence, M. A., Moyzis, R., Schuck, S., et al. (2000). Dopamine genes and ADHD. *Neuroscience and Biobehavioral Reviews, 24,* 21–25.

Tellegen, A. (1985). Structures of mood and personality and their relevance to assessing anxiety, with an emphasis on self-report. In A. H. Tuma & J. D. Maser (Eds.), *Anxiety and the anxiety disorders* (pp. 681–706). Hillsdale, NJ: Erlbaum.

Thomas, A., & Chess, S. (1977). *Temperament and development.* New York: New York University Press.

Thomas, A., Chess, S., & Birch, H. G. (1968). *Temperament and behavior disorders in children.* New York: New York University Press.

Thomas, A., Chess, S., Birch, H. G., Hertzig, M. E., & Korn, S. (1963). *Behavioral individuality in early childhood.* New York: New York University Press.

Tuddenham, R. D. (1959). The constancy of personality ratings over 2 decades. *Genetic Psychology Monographs, 60,* 3–29.

Valiente, C., Eisenberg, N., Fabes, R. A., Shepard, S. A., Cumberland, A., & Losoya, S. (2004). Prediction of children's empathy-related responding from their effortful control and parents' expressivity. *Developmental Psychology, 40,* 911–926.

Wachs, T. D., & Bates, J. E. (2001). Temperament. In G. Bremner & A. Fogel (Eds.), *Blackwell handbook of infant development: Handbooks of developmental psychology* (pp. 465–501). Malden, MA: Blackwell.

Wachs, T. D., & Plomin, R. (1991). Overview of current models and research. In T. D. Wachs & R. Plomin (Eds.), *Conceptualization and measurement of organism-environment interaction* (pp. 1–8). Washington, DC: American Psychological Association.

Werner, E. E. (1985). Resilient offspring of alcoholics: A longitudinal study from birth to age 18. *Journal of Studies on Alcohol, 47,* 34–40.

Whittle, S., Allen, N. B., Lubman, D. I., & Yucel, M. (2006). The neurobiological basis of temperament: Towards a better understanding of psychopathology. *Neuroscience and Biobehavioral Reviews, 30*(4), 511–525.

Wootton, J. M., Frick, P. J., Shelton, K. K., & Silverthorn, P. (1997). Ineffective parenting and childhood conduct problems: The moderating role of callous-unemotional traits. *Journal of Consulting and Clinical Psychology, 65,* 301–308.

Zuckerman, M. (1995). Good and bad humors: Biochemical bases of personality and its disorders. *Psychological Science, 6*(6), 325–332.

PART III

PARENTAL AND PEER RELATIONS

Chapter 4

Socialization in the Family: Ethnic and Ecological Perspectives

Ross D. Parke and Raymond Buriel

Socialization is a process in which an individual's standards, skills, motives, attitudes, and behaviors change to conform to those regarded as desirable and appropriate for his or her present and future role in society. Many agents and agencies play a role in the socialization process, including family, peers, schools, and the media. Moreover, it is recognized that these various agents function together rather than independently. Families have been recognized as an early pervasive and highly influential context for socialization. Children are dependent on families for nurturance and support from an early age, which accounts, in part, for their prominence as a socialization agent.

Our goal is to expand our framework for conceptualizing the family's role in socialization. This takes several forms, including treating the family as a social system in which parent-child, marital, and sibling subsystems, among others, are recognized. The diversity of family forms has increased in the past several decades and a second goal is to explore the implications of various family configurations for the socialization process. Cultural and ethnic variations in family traditions, beliefs, and practices are increasingly being recognized, and a further aim of this chapter is to explore how ethnic diversity informs our understanding of socialization. A further goal is to locate family socialization in an ecological context to appreciate how family environments shape and constrain their socialization practices. We demonstrate the value of a life-course perspective on socialization that recognizes the importance of both developmental changes in adult lives and the historical circumstances under which socialization unfolds. Finally, we recognize that families are increasingly diverse in their organization, form, and lifestyle. Some issues are beyond the scope of the chapter including the work

Preparation of this chapter was facilitated by National Science Foundation grants BNS 8919391 and SBR 9308941 and NICHD grand HD 32391 to Parke. Finally, thanks to Faye Harmer for her preparation of the manuscript.

on gay and lesbian families and research on adopted children (see Brodzinsky & Pinderhughes, 2002; C. J. Patterson, 2002, for reviews).

Contemporary Theoretical Approaches to Socialization in the Family

Several themes are evident in current theoretical approaches to socialization. First, systems theory (Sameroff, 1994) has transformed the study of socialization from a parent-
child focus to an emphasis on the family as a social system (Parke, 2004a). To
understand fully the nature of family relationships, it is necessary to recognize the interdependence among the roles and functions of all family members. For example, as men's
roles in families shift, changes in women's roles in families must also be monitored.

Second, family members—mothers, fathers, and children—influence each other
both directly and indirectly (Minuchin, 2002). Examples of fathers' indirect impact include various ways in which fathers modify and mediate mother-child relationships. In
turn, women affect their children indirectly through their husbands by modifying both
the quantity and the quality of father-child interaction. Children may indirectly influence the husband-wife relationship by altering the behavior of either parent and that, in
turn, changes the interaction between spouses.

Third, different units of analysis are necessary to understand families. Although the
individual—child, mother, and father—remains a useful level of analysis, recognition
of relationships among family members as units of analysis is necessary. The marital
relationship, the mother-child relationship, and the father-child relationship require
separate analysis (Parke et al., 2001). Finally, the family as a unit that is independent of
the individual or dyads in the family requires recognition (Cook, 2001).

A fourth shift is from unidirectional to transactional models of relationships among
family members. There have been various phases in the conceptual thinking in this domain. First, scholars traditionally were guided by unilateral models of parent-child relations in which the direction of causality was unidirectional, from parent to child. The
child's role was relatively passive, the focus was on individuals rather than relationships, and power relations were relatively static. A bilateral model has emerged as the
dominant paradigm in the parent-child relationship domain (Kuczynski, 2003) in which
the direction of causality is bidirectional, equal agency on the part of parent and child is
recognized, and power relations are characterized as "interdependent asymmetry."

Fifth, under the influence of Bronfenbrenner's ecological theory (1989), recognition
is being given to the embeddedness of families in other social systems as well as the
cultures in which they exist (Parke & Kellam, 1994). These include a range of extrafamilial influences, such as extended families, and informal community ties such as
friends and neighbors, work sites, and social, educational, and medical institutions
(Repetti, 1994).

Sixth, the importance of considering family relationships from a developmental perspective is now recognized. Although developmental changes in child capacities continue to represent the most commonly investigated aspect of development, other
aspects of development are viewed as important too. Under the influence of life-course
and life-span perspectives (Elder, 1998), examination of developmental changes in
adults is gaining recognition because parents continue to change and develop during
adult years. This involves an exploration of the tasks faced by adults such as self-

identity, education, and career, and an examination of the relation between these tasks and parenting. Developmental analysis need not be restricted to the individual level since relationships (e.g., the marital, the mother-child, or the father-child relationship) may follow separate and partially independent developmental courses over childhood (Parke, 1988). In turn, the mutual impact of different sets of relationships on each other will vary as a function of the nature of the developmental trajectory. Families change their structure (e.g., through the addition of a new child or the loss of a member through death or divorce), norms, rules, and strategies over time. Tracking the family unit itself over development is an important and neglected task (Cook, 2001).

Seventh, a major shift over the past 2 decades is the challenge to the universality of socialization theories. As cross-cultural work accumulated, it became evident that generalizations from a single culture (e.g., American) may not be valid in other cultural contexts (Rogoff, 2003). Social class differences in socialization challenged the generality of findings even in one cultural or national context (Gauvain, 2001; Hoff, Laursen, & Tardif, 2002). Currently, there is an increased awareness of the importance of both recognizing and studying variations in families and family socialization strategies in both other cultures (Rogoff, 2003) and across ethnic groups in our own culture (Parke, 2004b). It is important not only to examine the diversity of familial organization, goals, and strategies across ethnic groups but it is equally critical to explore variations within different ethnic groups (Garcia Coll & Magnuson, 1999).

An eighth assumption involves the recognition of the impact of secular shifts on families. There have been many social changes in American society that have had an impact on families including the decline in fertility and family size, changes in the timing of the onset of parenthood, increased participation of women in the workforce, rise in the divorce rate, and the subsequent increase in single-parent families and remarried step families (Elder, 1998; Hetherington & Kelly, 2001). The ways in which these societal changes impact relationships between parents and children merit examination. A related theme involves the recognition of the importance of historical time periods that provide the social conditions for individual and family transitions. Examples include the 1960s (the Vietnam War era), the 1930s (the Great Depression), or the 1980s (Farm Belt Depression; Conger & Elder, 1994; Elder & Conger, 2000). Across these periods, family interaction may be quite different due to the unique conditions of each era. The distinctions among different developmental trajectories, as well as social change and historical period effects, are important because these different forms of change do not always harmonize (Modell & Elder, 2002). For example, a family event such as the birth of a child may have different effects on a man early rather than later in his career. Moreover, individual and family developmental trajectories are embedded in both the social conditions and the values of the historical time in which they exist.

Ninth, renewed interest in the biological bases of behavior has altered our views of socialization. Recognition of the role of genetics across development has produced a more sophisticated understanding of the potential role genetics can play in the onset of certain behaviors and also in the unfolding of behavior across development. Moreover, the reformulation of genetic questions has led to studies of the effects of nonshared family environment on children's development (O'Connor, 2003); this work has suggested that individual differences between children—some of which are genetically based—play a central role in eliciting and shaping parent's socialization strategies. Studies of hormones and behavior, especially during infancy and adolescence (Corter & Fleming, 2002) have illuminated another biological aspect of socialization. The increased use of psychophysiological and neurological assessments with families represents a further instance of how the study of biological processes is changing socialization studies (Eisenberg, 2000). In addition, the resurgence of interest in evolutionary approaches to socialization is producing new and provocative hypotheses and research directions (Geary & Bjorklund, 2000).

Tenth, affect and cognition are increasingly viewed as central socialization processes. The study of affect includes the development of emotion regulation (Denham, 1998), emotional production, and understanding of the role of emotion in the enactment of the parenting role (Dix, 1991). Cognition comes in many guises, including the child's own cognitive capacities as determinants of socialization strategies and parents' cognitions, beliefs, values, and goals as constraints on their socialization practices (Goodnow, 2002). These processes are interdependent, mutually influencing each other with cognition and affect often operating together in determining parenting practices (Dix & Branca, 2003).

Eleventh, just as processes are viewed as interdependent, there is a new appreciation of the need for multidisciplinary perspectives to understand the family socialization process. Beyond developmental psychology, the family socialization field includes history, anthropology, sociology, demography, pediatrics, psychiatry, and economics (Parke, 2004b).

Finally, methodological rigor has increased in recent years. Instead of sole reliance on cross-sectional and/or correlational studies, greater weight is being given to carefully designed longitudinal studies (Gottfried, Gottfried, & Bathurst, 2002) and experimental studies (Cowan & Cowan, 2002) because these approaches allow more confidence in interpreting direction of effects. Recent studies avoid the problems of shared method or reporter variance by reliance on either multiple reporters and/or methods. There is recognition of rival explanations of apparent socialization effects (Harris, 1998; Plomin, 1994). There is a move beyond description by the emergence of theories that specify the mediating and moderating variables that can account for the relation between parenting and child outcomes (Parke, McDowell, Kim, & Leidy, 2006) and the moderating influences, such as social context, ethnicity, or family structure that alter socialization processes (Mounts, 2002). Throughout our review, we focus on work that meets these new standards of scientific rigor whenever possible.

Family Systems Approach to Socialization

Consistent with a family systems viewpoint, recent research has focused on a variety of subsystems, including parent-child, marital, and sibling-sibling systems. We focus on each of these subsystems as contexts for socialization and examine conceptualizations of the family as a unit of analysis.

PARENT-CHILD SUBSYSTEM: A TRIPARTITE APPROACH

In this section, we consider the parent-child subsystem and the relation between this parent-child subsystem and children's social adaptation. Although traditional paradigms focus on the impact of the parent-child relationship or parental child-rearing styles, according to the Parke, Burks, Carson, Neville, and Boyum tripartite model (1994), this represents only one pathway (see Figure 4.1). In addition, this scheme posits that parents may influence their children through a second pathway namely as

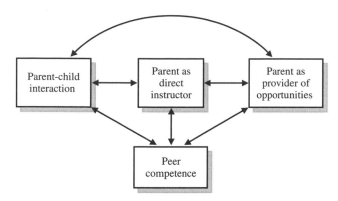

FIGURE 4.1   A Tripartite Model of Family-Peer Relationships. (*Source:* "Family-Peer Relationships: A Tripartite Model" (pp. 115–145), by R. D. Parke, V. M. Burks, J. V. Carson, B. Neville, and L. A. Boyum in *Exploring Family Relationships with Other Social Contexts: Family Research Consortium—Advances in Family Research,* R. D. Parke and S. Kellam (Eds.), 1994, Hillsdale, NJ: Erlbaum.)

direct instructor, educator, or consultant. In this role, parents may explicitly set out to educate their children concerning appropriate norms, rules, and mores of the culture. According to this second socialization pathway, parents may serve as coaches, teachers, and supervisors who provide advice, support, and directions about strategies for managing new social situations or negotiating social challenges. In a third role, parents function as managers of their children's social lives and serve as regulators of opportunities for social contacts and cognitive experiences. Although the model has been largely applied to the issue of family peer relationships, it is useful for explaining a wide range of socialization outcomes such as gender roles and aggression (see S. M. McHale, Crouter, & Whiteman, 2003, for an application to gender roles).

Parent-Child Relationships: Interaction and Child-Rearing Styles

Two approaches to the issue of the effect of parent-child interaction on children's socialization outcomes have been used in research. One adopts a typological approach and examines styles of child-rearing practices. The other employs a social interaction approach and focuses on the nature of the interchanges between parent and child.

Typological Approach.   The most influential typology was offered by Baumrind (1973), who distinguished between three types of parental child-rearing typologies, namely authoritative, authoritarian, and permissive. Baumrind (1991) followed her authoritarian, authoritative, and permissive parents and their children from the preschool period through adolescence in a longitudinal study and found that authoritative parenting continued to be associated with positive outcomes for adolescents as with younger children and that responsive, firm parent-child relationships were especially important in the development of competence in sons. Moreover, authoritarian child rearing had more negative long-term outcomes for boys than for girls. Sons of authoritarian parents were low in both cognitive and social competence.

Maccoby and Martin (1983) extended the Baumrind typology based on combinations of the warm/responsive, unresponsive/rejecting dimension and the restrictive/demanding, permissive/undemanding dimension and included a fourth type of parenting style—disengaged—which is characterized by neglect and lack of involvement. These parents are "motivated to do whatever is necessary to minimize the costs in time and effort of interaction with the child" (p. 11). Such parents keep the child at a distance and focus on their own rather than their child's needs. They are parent rather than child centered. With older children, this is associated with the parents' failure to monitor the child's activity or to know where the child is, what the child is doing, and who the child's companions are. In infants, such a lack of parental involvement is associated with disruptions in attachment; in older children, it is associated with impulsivity, aggression, noncompliance, moodiness, and low self-esteem (Baumrind, 1991). Older children also show disruptions in peer relations and in cognitive development, achievement, and school performance (Hetherington & Clingempeel, 1992). It is the combined impact of not having the skills to be able to gain gratification in either social or academic pursuits that frequently leads to delinquency in children with neglecting parents (Reid, Patterson, & Snyder, 2002). Parental involvement plays an important role in the development of both social and cognitive competence in children.

A major concern about the focus on parental style is the limited attention to the delineation of the processes that account for the effects of different styles on children's development. Throughout the history of socialization research, there has been a tension between molar (Baumrind, 1991; Steinberg, Dornbusch, & Brown, 1992) and molecular levels of analysis (Reid et al., 2002). Over the past 3 decades, the pendulum has swung back and forth between these levels of analysis. Currently, these two strands of research coexist and are seldom united in a single study. However, Hetherington and Clingempeel (1992) have used parenting style in combination with sequential analyses of children's levels of compliance to parental control in a useful bridging of the two levels of analyses.

In an attempt to resolve this issue, Darling and Steinberg (1993) argued that parental style and parental practices need to be distinguished. Parenting style is "a constellation of attitudes toward the child that are communicated to the child and create an emotional climate in which parents' behaviors are expressed" (p. 493). In contrast to style, "parenting practices are behaviors defined by specific content and socialization goals" (p. 492) such as attending school functions and spanking. Style is assumed to be independent of both the content of parenting behavior and the specific socialization content. Critical to their model is the assumption that parenting style has its impact on child outcomes indirectly. First, style transforms the nature of parent-child interaction and thereby moderates the impact of specific practices. Second, style modifies the child's openness to parental influence, which, in turn, moderates the association between parenting practices and child outcomes.

A second concern is the issue of direction of effects. It is unclear whether the styles described by Baumrind are, in part, responses to the child's behavior. Placing the typology work in a transactional framework (Sameroff, 1994) would argue that children with certain temperaments and/or behavioral characteristics would determine the nature of the parental style.

A third concern is the universality of the typological scheme. Recent studies have raised questions about the generalizability of these styles across either socioeconomic status (SES) or ethnic/cultural groups. Two issues are involved here. First, does the rate of utilization of different styles vary across groups? Second, are the advantages of positive social outcomes associated with a particular style (e.g., authoritative) similar across groups? The answer to both questions seems to be negative. In lower-SES families, parents are more likely to use an authoritarian as opposed to an authoritative style, but this style is often an adaptation to the ecological conditions, such as increased danger and threat, which may characterize the lives of poor families (Furstenberg, Cook, Eccles, Elder, & Sameroff, 1999). Moreover, studies find that the use of authoritarian strategies under these circumstances may be linked with more positive outcomes for children (Dodge, McLoyd, & Lansford, 2005). A second challenge to the presumed universal advantage of authoritative child-rearing styles comes from cross-ethnic studies. Accumulating evidence underscores the nonuniversality of these stylistic distinctions and suggests the importance of developing concepts that are based on an indigenous appreciation of the culture in question (Chao, 1994). Both contextual and cultural considerations need more attention in typological approaches to child rearing.

Parent-Child Interactional Approach.   Research in this tradition is based on the assumption that face-to-face interaction with parents may provide the opportunity to learn, rehearse, and refine social skills that are common to successful social interaction with other social partners. This work has yielded several conclusions. First, the style of the interaction between parent and child is linked to a variety of social outcomes. To illustrate this approach, studies of children's social competence are considered. Parents who are responsive, warm, and engaging are more likely to have children who are more socially competent (Grimes, Klein, & Putallaz, 2004). Moreover, high levels of positive synchrony and low levels of nonsynchrony in patterns of mother-child interaction are related to school adjustment rated by teachers, peers, and observers (Harrist, Pettit, Dodge, & Bates, 1994). In contrast, parents who are hostile and controlling have children who experience more difficulty with age-mates in the preschool period (Harrist et al., 1994) and middle childhood.

Although there is an overlap between mothers and fathers, fathers make a unique and independent contribution to their children's social development since fathers continue to contribute to children's social behavior with peers—after accounting for the mothers' contribution (Isley, O'Neil, & Parke, 1996). Although father involvement is quantitatively less than mother involvement, fathers have an important impact on their offspring's development. Quality rather than quantity of parent-child interaction is the important predictor of cognitive and social development.

Beyond Description: Processes Mediating Relations between Parent-Child Interaction and Children's Social Competence

Several processes have been hypothesized as mediators between parent-child interaction and peer outcomes. These include emotion-encoding and decoding skills, emotional regulatory skills, cognitive representations, attributions and beliefs, as well as problem-solving skills and attention-deployment abilities (Eisenberg, 2000; Ladd, 1992; Parke et al., 2006). These abilities or beliefs are acquired in parent-child interchanges during development and, in turn, guide the nature of children's behavior with their peers. We focus on three sets of mediating processes that are promising: (1) affect-management skills, (2) cognitive representational processes, and (3) attention regulatory processes (see Figure 4.2).

Affect-Management Skills as a Mediating Mechanism.   Children learn more than specific affective expressions, such as anger, sadness, or joy in the family. They learn a cluster of processes associated with the understanding and regulation of affective

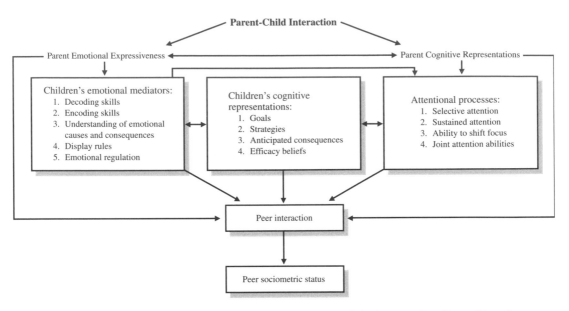

FIGURE 4.2   Emotional, Cognitive, and Attentional Mediating Links between Family and Peer Systems.

displays, which we term affect-management skills (Parke, Cassidy, Burks, Carson, & Boyum, 1992). These skills are acquired during the course of parent-child interaction and are available to the child for use in other relationships. Moreover, it is assumed that these skills play a mediating role between family and children's social competence.

One set of skills that is relevant to successful peer interaction and may, in part, be acquired in the context of parent-child play, especially arousing physical play, is the ability to encode emotional signals and to decode others' emotional states. Through physically playful interaction with their parents, especially fathers, children may learn how to use emotional signals to regulate the social behavior of others. In addition, they learn to accurately decode the social and emotional signals of social partners. Several studies have found positive relations between children's ability to encode emotional expressions and children's social competence with peers (Halberstadt, Denham, & Dunsmore, 2001). Successful peer interaction requires not only the ability to recognize and produce emotions but also a social understanding of emotion-related experiences, of the meaning of emotions, of the cause of emotions, and of the responses appropriate to others' emotions (Cassidy, Parke, Butkovsky, & Braungart, 1992) .

Research suggests that parental support and acceptance of children's emotions is related to children's ability to manage emotions in a constructive fashion. Several investigators (Eisenberg, 2000; Parke et al., 2006) have found links between the ability to regulate emotional arousal and social competence. Similarly, children who either have limited knowledge of emotional display rules (Saarni, 1999) or are poor at utilizing display rules are less well accepted by their peers (McDowell, O'Neil, & Parke, 2000; McDowell & Parke, 2000). Parental comforting of children when they experience negative emotion has been linked with constructive anger reactions (Eisenberg & Fabes, 1992) and children's emotional regulation and their knowledge of and use of display rules are linked with high positive parental affect and low levels of parental control (McDowell & Parke, 2005).

These studies suggest that various aspects of emotional development—encoding, decoding, cognitive understanding, and emotional regulation—play a role in accounting for variations in peer competence and serve as mediators between the parents and peers. At the same time, the contribution of genetics to individual differences in emotionality and emotional regulation probably plays a role in the emergence of these emotional processes (Eisenberg, 2000; Kochanska, 1993).

Cognitive Representational Models: A Second Mediating Mechanism.   How do children transfer the strategies they acquire in the family to their peer relationships? Several theories assume that individuals possess internal mental representations that guide their social behavior. Attachment theorists offer working models (Bretherton & Munholland, 1999), while social and cognitive psychologists suggest that scripts or cognitive maps serve as guides for social action (Grusec & Ungerer, 2003). Attachment researchers have found support for Bowlby's argument that representations vary as a function of child-parent attachment history (Bretherton & Munholland, 1999). Children who had been securely attached infants were more likely to represent their family in their drawings in a coherent manner, with a balance between individuality and connection, than were insecurely attached children (Carlson, Sroufe, & Egeland, 2004). Research in a social interactional tradition reveals links between parent and child cognitive representations of social relationships. McDowell, Parke, and Spitzer (2002) found that the cognitive representations of social behavior of both fathers and mothers were related to their children's representations. Moreover, fathers' but not mothers' cognitive models of relationships were linked to children's social competence. Fathers' strategies that were related high on confrontation and instrumental qualities were associated with low teacher ratings of children's social competence. Fathers with relational-prosocial goals have children who are rated as more competent by teachers and peers.

These studies suggest that cognitive models of relationships may be transmitted across generations and these models, in turn, may serve as mediators between family contexts and children's relationships with others outside of the family. Finally, this work implies that both children and parents actively construct their own dyadic relationships and other social relationships and both are influenced in their behavior with each other by these cognitive constructions. Coordination and coregulation rather than simply a bidirectional pattern of influence probably increasingly characterizes the parent-child relationship in middle childhood and adolescence (Kuczynski, 2003).

Attention Regulation: A Third Mediating Mechanism.   Attentional regulatory processes have come to be viewed as another mechanism through which familial socialization experiences influence children's social competence. These processes include the ability to attend to relevant cues, to sustain attention, to refocus attention through such processes as cognitive distraction and cognitive restructuring. Evidence suggests that attentional regulation may have direct effects on children's social functioning (Eisenberg, 2000) and, in some circumstances, attentional control may function in interaction with dimensions of emotionality and social information processing. Other work (Eisenberg & Fabes, 1992) suggests that attentional control and emotional negativity may interact when predicting social competence. Attention regulatory skills appear to be more critical among children who experience higher levels of emotional negativity (Eisenberg, 2000).

The role of attention in a laboratory task as a mediator between parenting and peer outcomes was examined in the National Institute of Child Health and Human Development (NICHD) Study of Child Care and Youth Development (NICHD Child Care Research Network, 2003b). Children who had fewer errors of omission in a lab task of attention had greater ability to sustain attention; children with errors of commission were more impulsive. Sustained attention and less impulsivity were associated with higher social competence scores while impulsivity served as a mediator between family- and social-outcome measures. In a follow-up (NICHD Early Child Care Research Network, 2008), attention regulation mediated between mother and father sensitivity measures and children's peer competence in first and third grade. Together these studies provide evidence for the role of attention as a mediator of the links between family and peer systems.

Parental Instruction, Advice Giving, Consultation, and Monitoring

Learning about relationships through interaction with parents can be viewed as an indirect pathway because the goal is often not explicitly to influence children's social relationships with extrafamilial partners such as peers. In contrast, parents may influence children's relationships directly in their role as a direct instructor, educator, or advisor.

In research with preschool (Russell & Finnie, 1990) and elementary school age children (Mize & Pettit, 1997) the quality of parental advice was positively related to children's peer competence. As children grow, caregiver forms of management shift from direct involvement or supervision of the ongoing activities of children and their peers to consultation, a less public form of management, involving advice or consultation concerning appropriate ways of handling peer problems (Ladd & Pettit, 2002). Parents use verbal guidance (e.g., discussion about future consequences, talk of values, and offering their advice) more often than direct interventions (e.g., limiting the adolescent's activities with peers or inviting friends over to the house to shape peer influence; Mounts, 2000). These indirect forms of supervision that emerge as the child reaches adolescence are linked with positive outcomes.

Another way in which parents can affect their children's social relationships is through monitoring of their children's social activities. This form of management is particularly evident as children move into adolescence and is associated with the relative shift in importance of family and peers as sources of social influence. Moreover, direct monitoring is more common among younger children, whereas distal monitoring is more evident among adolescents. Monitoring refers to a range of activities, including the supervision of children's choice of social settings, activities, and friends. Parents of delinquent and antisocial children engage in less monitoring and supervision of their children's activities than parents of nondelinquent children (G. R. Patterson & Stouthamer-Loeber, 1984; Xiaoming, Stanton, & Feigelman, 2000).

Although monitoring has been viewed as a parent to child effect, Kerr and Stattin (2000) have reconceptualized this issue and argued that monitoring is a process that is jointly co-constructed by the parent and child. Monitoring may be a function of the extent to which children share information about their activities and companion choices with their parents. Given this reconceptualization, prior research could be reinterpreted to suggest that children with poorer social adjustment discussed their activities with parents less than did well-adjusted children. Parental attempts to learn more about their children's activities must be met with the child's own willingness to discuss such information (Mounts, 2000).

Parents as Managers of Children's Opportunities

Parents influence their children's social relationships not only through their direct interactions with their children but also as managers of their children's social lives (Furstenberg et al., 1999; Parke et al., 2003). This parental role is of theoretical importance given the recent claims that parents' impact on children's development is limited and peer group-level processes account for major socialization outcomes (Harris, 1998). In contrast, we conceptualize the parental management of access to peers as a further pathway through which parents influence their children's development. Parents make choices about neighborhoods and schools as well as the formal and informal activities in which their children can participate. In these ways, "parents act as designers when they seek to control or influence the settings in which children are likely to meet and interact with peers" (Ladd & Pettit, 2002, p. 286). These design decisions can influence children's social and academic outcomes. Instead of viewing parents as acting alone in their designer roles, we view parents and children as co-designers. Many decisions—even in the designer domain—are influenced by children's and parents' needs, wishes, and decisions.

Neighborhoods as Determinants of Peer Contact.   Although it is assumed that parents choose their neighborhoods, many constraints limit the range of locations from which to choose, especially economic (i.e., cost) and geographic (i.e., distance from work or transportation). Choice of neighborhood is not equally available to parents; lower-SES and minority group parents have a more restricted set of options than higher SES and nonminority parents. However, there is considerable variability in "neighborhood effects" on children because of the ways in which parents manage their children's access to aspects of their neighborhood setting. A second conceptual assumption about neighborhoods concerns children's role in neighborhood selection. Although children—especially young children—are not usually direct participants in the choice of neighborhoods, parents generally consider children's needs (safety, access to other children) in their choice of neighborhood. Adolescents may be more active participants by articulating their concerns about moving to a new neighborhood that, for example, involves loss of community-based friendships and shifts in school district.

What is the impact of neighborhood variations on peer competence? Youngsters in areas with high levels of poverty differed from those in low-poverty areas on several outcomes, including reading scores, birth weight, infant death, and juvenile delinquency (Coulton & Pandey, 1992). A related Australian study (Homel & Burns, 1989) found that children in the most disadvantaged neighborhoods, reported higher loneliness, feelings of rejection by peers, worry, and lower life satisfaction compared to children in less disadvantaged neighborhoods. The effects of neighborhoods on children's outcomes are often mediated by parenting practices such as supervision and monitoring. When mothers and fathers perceived their neighborhoods as dangerous and low in social control, they placed more restrictions on their fourth grade children's activities, which was related to higher peer competence for their children (O'Neil, Parke, & McDowell, 2001).

Parents and Children as Partners in Schooling.   Parents choose not only neighborhoods but also the type and quality of day care and elementary schools that their children will attend. The quality and amount of time in child care are linked to children's cognitive and social development (Clarke-Stewart & Allhusen, 2005). Social behavior, despite the opportunity to have increased peer contact, is not consistently linked with day-care quality: Some evidence suggests that children who are in day care for more than 40 hours per week may show some increases in aggression (NICHD Early Childcare Research Network, 2003a). As children develop, parents especially middle-class parents who have options, select neighborhoods as a function of quality of the schools that are available (Furstenberg et al., 1999). Moreover, the ability to choose is not inconsequential because exercising the ability to choose a school has been linked to adolescent academic outcome (Furstenberg et al., 1999). The extent of parental involvement in school-related activities (e.g., parent-teacher associations or school conferences) is positively related to children's academic outcomes. Practices of partnerships between parents and schools decline across development; in recognition of adolescents' need for autonomy and independence, parental involvement decreases in high school, but young adolescents still want their families to support their learning and activities at home (Epstein & Sanders, 2002). These developmental changes suggest that the child is active in shaping the form that the parent-school partnership will assume at different points in the child's educational career.

Parents and children are frequently active in religious organizations. Parental facilitation of children's involvement in religious institutions is another important way in which parents manage their children's lives. It is important to distinguish between the issue of involvement in religious institutions and religious beliefs because these two aspects of religion may have partially independent effects on family functioning and child outcomes (see Mahoney, Pargament, Tarakeshwar, & Swank, 2001, for a review). When both parents attended church on a regular basis, children were more likely to be involved in religious organizations (Elder & Conger, 2000). Involvement in church activities was associated with higher endorsement of school, good grades, and—especially for boys—community activities. Religiously involved youth perceived their friends as less involved in deviance and less likely to encourage deviant activities.

Both parents and children are active players in the process of involvement in religious activities. Although parents—through their own involvement and through their introduction of the child to religious beliefs and functions—play an important initial role, children, and especially adolescents, themselves are central agents in choosing to continue their regular participation in religious institutions. These findings are most easily understood through the lens of the bilateral model that guides our chapter. Finally, parental religiousness (frequency of church attendance and importance of religion) was associated with better child adjustment as well (Brody, Stoneman, & Flor, 1996). The relative importance of beliefs or involvement in organized religious activities in accounting for these effects remains unclear.

Interdependence among Components of the Tripartite Socialization Model. Although we have treated parental style and/or parent-child interaction, advice giving, and parental management as separate influences, these components often operate together during children's socialization. Similarly, Grusec and Goodnow (1994) suggested that parental strategies vary in their effectiveness as a function of the quality of the parent-child relationship. These three components can be usefully viewed as a cafeteria model (Parke et al., 1994). Two issues need to be addressed. First, are there natural occurring combinations of these components? Second, do the different components moderate the relative effectiveness of each component depending on the level of the other components? Mounts (2002) examined the co-occurrence of different types of parenting management practices—prohibiting, guiding, monitoring, supporting—with various parenting styles (authoritarian, authoritative, permissive, and uninvolved). She found that all parents, regardless of their parenting style, use prohibiting and guiding as management strategies. In contrast, monitoring and supporting are more common in authoritative style homes relative to the other parenting style environments. When mothers were low in parental responsiveness (parental style), higher levels of constructive coaching (parental practices) aimed at improving peer relationships were linked to lower levels of aggression than when mothers had low levels of responsiveness and low levels of constructive coaching (Mize & Pettit, 1997). In contrast, when mothers had moderate or high levels of responsiveness, their level of coaching was unrelated to the level of children's aggression. In this case, coaching compensated for a less adequate parenting style. These studies illustrate the interdependence among the components of our tripartite model and the importance of moderating effects among the components.

Co-Parenting as a Socialization Strategy

Co-parenting recognizes that mothers and fathers operate as a parenting team and as individual parents (J. P. McHale & Rasmussen, 1998). Co-parenting alliances include "a pattern signifying antagonistic and adult centered or hostile competitive, a pattern marked by significant imbalance or parenting discrepancy in levels of parental engagement with the child and a pattern reflecting cooperation, warmth, cohesion, and child centeredness or high family harmony" (J. P. McHale, Lauretti, Talbot, & Pouquette, 2002, p. 142). These patterns have been observed with infants, preschoolers, and school-age children, and in European and African American families (Brody, Flor, & Neubaum, 1998; Fivaz-Depeursinge & Corboz-Warnery, 1999). J. P. McHale and Rasmussen (1998) found that hostile-competitive co-parenting during infancy was related to aggression, whereas large parenting discrepancies were related to parent-rated anxiety. Others have found links between problematic family alliances in the first year and insecure mother-child attachments and clinical symptomatology in the preschool years (Fivaz-Depeursinge & Corboz-Warnery, 1999; J. P. McHale et al., 2002). Finally, co-parenting accounts for unique variance in child measures and clearly needs to be distinguished from traditional parent-child and marital level processes.

BEYOND THE PARENT-CHILD DYAD: THE MARITAL SUBSYSTEM AS A CONTRIBUTOR TO CHILDREN'S SOCIALIZATION

Children's experiences in families extend beyond their interactions with parents and their understanding of relationships is shaped through their active participation in other family subsystems (e.g., child-sibling) and through exposure to the interactions of other dyadic subsystems (e.g., parent-parent) or participation in triadic relationships (e.g., child-sibling-parent, child-parent-parent).

Influence of Marital Satisfaction and Discord on Child Outcomes

Marital functioning is related to children's short-term coping and long-term adjustment. Exposure of children to marital discord and conflict is related to poorer quality of interpersonal relationships with siblings and peers and more internalizing and externalizing behavior problems (Cummings & Davies, 1994; Grych & Fincham, 2001).

Two alternative, but not mutually exclusive, models have been proposed to account for the impact of marital relations on children's developmental outcomes. Until recently, theoretical frameworks typically conceptualized marital discord as an indirect influence on children's adjustment that operated through its effect on the quality of parenting (Fauber & Long, 1991). Factors such as affective changes in the quality of the parent-child relationship, lack of emotional availability, and adoption of less optimal parenting styles have been implicated as potential mechanisms through which marital discord disrupts parenting processes In their meta-analytic review, Erel and Burman (1995) found a positive relation between the quality of the marital relationship and the quality of the parent-child relationship. Theoretically, two models have been offered to account for these effects—the spillover hypothesis and the compensatory hypothesis. According to the spillover hypothesis, mood or behavior in one subsystem transfers to another subsystem (e.g., from marital subsystem to parent-child subsystem). In contrast, the compensatory hypothesis suggests that positive parent-child relationships can be maintained even in the face of martial conflict and can serve as a buffer on children. The meta-analysis clearly supported the spillover hypothesis and underscores the difficulty of buffering children from marital conflict. Although much of the prior work has focused on the transfer of negativity between marital and parent-child subsystems, some evidence suggests that marital satisfaction is a predictor of positive parenting (Russell, 1997).

A second model (Cummings & Davies, 1994; Grych & Fincham, 2001) focuses on the direct effects of witnessed marital conflict on children's outcomes. Recent lab analog studies show that the form of expression of marital conflict plays a role in how children react. More frequent interparental conflict and more intense or violent forms of conflict have been found to be particularly disturbing to children and likely to be associated with externalizing and internalizing difficulties (Cummings, Goeke-Morey, & Raymond, 2004). Conflict that was child-related in content was more likely than conflict involving other content to be associated with behavior problems in children (Grych & Cardoza-Fernandez, 2001). Resolution of conflict, even when it was not viewed by the child, reduces children's negative reactions to exposure to interadult anger and conflict. Exposure to unresolved conflict is associated with negative affect and poor coping responses in children (Kerig, 1996).

Conflict is inevitable in most parental relationships and is not always detrimental to family relationships and children's functioning. When conflict is expressed constructively, is moderate in degree, is expressed in the context of a warm and supportive family environment, and shows evidence of resolution, children may learn valuable lessons regarding how to negotiate conflict and resolve disagreements (Cummings & Davies, 1994).

Siblings and Children's Socialization

Sibling relationships have been hypothesized to contribute to children's socialization in a number of significant ways. A social-learning framework analogous to the one posited to explain parental contributions to the development of children's social competence (Parke & O'Neil, 1999) predicts that through their interactions with siblings children develop specific interaction patterns and social-understanding skills that generalize to relationships with other children. Relationships with siblings also may provide a context in which children can practice the skills and interaction styles that have been learned from parents or others. Older siblings function as tutors, managers, or supervisors of their younger brother's or sister's behavior during social interactions (Edwards & Whiting, 1993) and may function as gatekeepers who extend or limit opportunities to interact with other children outside of the family (Zukow-Goldring, 2002). Also paralleling the indirect influence that the observation of parent-parent interaction has on children, a second avenue of influence on children's development is their observation of parents interacting with siblings (Dunn, 1993). These interactions have been hypothesized to serve as an important context in which children deal with issues of differential treatment and learn about complex social emotions such as rivalry and jealousy.

Children's experiences with siblings provide a context in which interaction patterns and social skills and understanding may generalize to relationships with other children but evidence of straightforward "carryover" of interaction styles between children's relationships is limited. When associations emerge, they may be complicated by birth-order effects and other processes (Dunn, 1993, 2004). Moreover, sibling relationships may play a role in compensating for other problematic relationships by providing an alternative context for experiencing satisfying social relationships and protecting children from adjustment difficulties. East and Rook (1992) found that children who were socially isolated in their peer relationships were buffered from adjustment problems when they reported positive relationships with a favorite sibling. Similarly, Stocker (1994) reported support for the compensatory role of at least one positive relationship (sibling, friend, or mother) as protection from the development of behavioral conduct difficulties. In view of our focus on bidirectionality of influence, it is important to consider the impact of friendships on sibling relationships. Kramer and Gottman (1992) examined the role that positive relationships with peers play in children's adaptation to the birth of a new sibling. Children who displayed a more positive interaction style with a best friend and who were better able to manage conflict and negative affect, behaved more positively toward their new sibling at 6 and 14 months. Management of conflict, a valuable skill when interacting with siblings, may be more likely to be learned in interactions with peers than in direct interactions with parents. Kramer (2004) developed a social skills training program aimed at improving children's relationships with their siblings. In comparison to a control group of 4- to 6-year-olds, children with a younger sibling who received social skills training showed more positive and less negative sibling relationships.

The challenge is to discover the contexts under which strong, weak, or compensatory connections may be expected between relationship systems and the processes through which children's experiences with siblings are translated into skills that are used in other relationships. There is a need to examine the moderating and mediating influences of these factors to uncover normative patterns of associations between siblings and peer relationships.

Family Unit as a Contributor to Children's Socialization

Consistent with our systems theory perspective (Sameroff, 1994), the properties, functions, and effects of the family unit cannot necessarily be inferred from these smaller units of analysis such as the parent-child, marital or sibling-sibling dyads. Families as units change across development in response to changes in the individual members, life circumstances, and scheduled and unscheduled transitions. Families develop distinct "climates" (Moos & Moos, 1981), "styles" of responding to events (Reiss, 1989) and distinct "boundaries" (Boss, 1999), which provide differing socialization contexts for the developing child. Several investigators (Fiese, 2006; Reiss, 1989) have argued that the family regulates the child's development through a range of processes, including myths, stories, and rituals. Family myths refer to beliefs that influence family process, provide continuity across generations, and are generally not open to discussion or debate (Sameroff, 1994). Family-of-origin experiences may be transmitted across generations through stories and shared memories and shape contemporary interactions among family members (Fiese, 2006) as well as children's social competence (Putallaz, Costanzo, & Smith, 1991). Rituals and routines are associated with better child health and better behavioral regulation in intact families (Fiese, 2006).

PUTTING THE PIECES TOGETHER: TOWARD A MULTIPLE SOURCES MODEL OF SOCIALIZATION

Our family systems' viewpoint argues for the construction of a comprehensive model in which the contribution of parent-child, parent-parent, and sibling relationships are all recognized. Figure 4.3 outlines a comprehensive model of family socialization that includes the influence of all family members. Few studies have simultaneously addressed how these subsystems combine to produce their impact on children's relationship learning. Little is known about the relative weighting of parent-child relationships versus other family relationships (Parke & O'Neil, 1999). Nor do we understand how the impact of these different relationships changes as the child develops. The most crucial issue remains the specification of the pathways through which these different relationships exert their influence. In our model, multiple pathways are possible and there is support for both direct and mediated effects. As noted earlier, marital relationships exert both direct (e.g., witnessed effects) and indirect effects (e.g., marital relationships influence parent-child patterns). Similarly, parent-child relationships could influ-

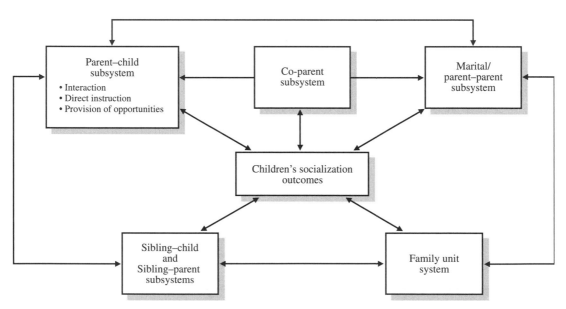

FIGURE 4.3   Model Indicating the Hypothesized Relations among Family Subsystems and Children's Socialization Outcomes.

ence marital but less is known about the impact of parent-child relationships on marital interactions than the reverse. Do all combinations produce equally socially competent children, or are some ingredients in this mix more important than others? Do different combinations produce children who are different, but equally well-adjusted in their social relationships? Can children in a family with a poor marriage compensate by investing "relationship energy" into another subsystem such as the sibling-sibling or parent-child system? Studies of divorce suggest that a close sibling-sibling relationship can help buffer children during a stressful divorce (Hetherington & Kelly, 2001).

Determinants of Family Socialization Strategies

A major advance in the field has been recognition of the importance of understanding the determinants of parenting behavior. Belsky (1984) proposed a three-domain model of the determinants of parenting, which included the characteristics of the child, the personal resources of the parents, and the contextual sources of stress and support.

CHILD CHARACTERISTICS

Child characteristics take two forms: (1) universal predispositions that are shared by all children and (2) individual differences in particular characteristics. Consistent with an evolutionary approach (Geary & Bjorklund, 2000), infants are biologically prepared for social, cognitive, and perceptual challenges and these prepared responses play a significant role in facilitating children's adaptation to their environment. Under the influence of behavior genetics (Plomin, 1994), there is a recognition of the role of individual differences in a wide variety of behavioral characteristics in shaping parental socialization strategies. The most well-researched determinant of parenting behavior is child temperament. Infants with difficult temperaments elicit more arousal and distress from caregivers than less-difficult infants (Putnam, Sanson, & Rothbart, 2002). Children who are more difficult may elicit increasingly coercive strategies from parents (Reid et al., 2002). Alternatively, fearful children may respond optimally to subtle parental socialization strategies (Kochanska, 1997). Other characteristics have been examined, including activity level, social responsiveness, and compliance level. In general, more active, less responsive, and more noncompliant children elicit more negative parenting and more negative parental arousal and affect (Crouter & Booth, 2003). The impact of these individual differences on parental socialization behavior depends on environmental conditions. Crockenberg and Leerkes (2003) showed that the impact of a difficult infant temperament on the parent-infant attachment relationship varied with the degree of social support available to the mother, which underscores the modifiability of temperament-based influences.

PERSONAL RESOURCES

Personal resources—conceptualized as knowledge, ability, and motivation to be a responsible caregiver—alter parenting behaviors (Belsky, 1984). Parental psychopathology, such as depression, will alter parenting behavior from infancy onward (Goodman & Gotlib, 2002). Patterns of interaction between depressed and nondepressed parents (usually mothers) and their offspring are less positive, less stimulating, and less contingent and infants show less attentiveness, more fussiness, and lower activity levels (Field, 1992) especially when depression is protracted and not merely transient (Campbell, Cohn, & Meyers, 1995). Infants and preschoolers of depressed mothers are more likely to develop insecure attachments, including disorganized attachment behavior (Lyons-Ruth, Lyubchik, Wolfe, & Bronfman, 2002). Other personal problems (e.g., antisocial personality disorder or schizophrenia, limited education, poverty) contribute to poorer parenting (Cummings et al., 2004). However, positive personal characteristics (e.g., high intelligence and self-regulation) and a transpersonal orientation (i.e., a focus on family, work, and child rearing) are linked to better quality parenting (Pulkkinen, Nurmi, & Kokko, 2002). Some have argued that some of these individual differences across parents, such as depression and proneness to abuse or coerciveness, may, in part, be genetically based (Caspi et al., 2002).

SOCIALIZATION AND SOCIAL CAPITAL

The concept of social capital considers the relations among people, institutions, and organizations of the community outside the immediate family structure. Social capital is both the flow of information and the sharing of norms and values that serve to facilitate or constrain the actions of people who interact in the community's social structures (e.g., schools, places of worship). Children benefit from the presence of norm and value consensus among members of their family and the wider community (Coleman, 1988). Monitoring of children is facilitated, as is their socialization, through multiple efforts of network members who hold shared family-community norms and values (Elder & Conger, 2000). Moreover, if a child's own family is negligent in fulfilling the socialization role, other adults are available to assume the responsibility.

Community networking has implications for youth development. Adolescent boys have better school performance and attendance and more positive social behavior when their social networks include large numbers of nonrelated adults (Cochran & Bo, 1989). When parents as well as nonrelated adults (adolescent's friends' parents) were perceived as authoritative in their parenting style, adolescents were lower in delinquency and substance abuse (Fletcher, Darling, Steinberg, & Dornbusch, 1995). When both parents and their children are acquainted with other parents and their children, they form network closure that involves more shared values and more social control over their offspring that is related to better social outcomes (Darling, Steinberg, Gringlas, & Dornbusch, 1995).

In sum, the social capital can aid parents' socialization of their children through several pathways. First, when parents and children have community ties, more social support is available. Second, parental awareness of community services and their participation in shaping community institutions promote the maintenance of values and norms that influence their children. Third, parental participation with their children enables closer child supervision and reduces children's time with peers. Parenting is a community enterprise and both children and adults are active players in the distribution of social capital.

SOCIOECONOMIC STATUS

There is a long history of research concerning the links between socioeconomic status (SES) and parenting. Although the debate concerning the best strategy for measuring SES continues (Bornstein & Bradley, 2003), most scholars agree that SES is multiply determined, and therefore the links with parenting are likely to be multiple as well. In contrast to traditional assumptions that SES is a static state, most argue that SES is a dynamic concept (Hoff et al., 2002). Over the course of childhood and adolescence, families change social class and change is greatest in the youngest ages. Over 50% of American children change social class prior to entering school (Featherman, Spenner, & Tsunematsu, 1988). There are SES differences in parental socialization practices and beliefs; lower-SES parents are more authoritarian and more punitive than higher-SES families (Hoff et al., 2002). Additionally, there are more SES differences on language measures than on nonverbal measures with higher-SES mothers being more verbal than lower-SES mothers (Hoff et al., 2002). Some SES differences are independent of race and income. In China, where there are relatively small differences in income across groups who vary in terms of education, Tardif (1993) found that less-educated parents used more imperatives with their toddlers than better-educated mothers. Similarly, Hess and Shipman (1965) in their studies of cognitive socialization found clear SES differences in African American lower-class and middle-class families.

Social Change and Family Socialization

Families are continuously confronted by challenges, changes, and opportunities. A number of societywide changes have produced shifts in family relationships. Fertility rates and family size have decreased, the percentage of women in the workforce has increased, the timing of onset of parenthood has shifted, divorce rates and the number of single-parent families have increased. These social trends provide an opportunity to explore how families change in response to these shifting circumstances and represent natural experiments in family adaptation. Moreover, they challenge our traditional assumption that families can be studied at a single point in time because the historical contexts are constantly shifting. Our task is to establish how socialization processes operate similarly or differently under varying historical circumstances. In this section, the effects of recent shifts in family employment and unemployment patterns is explored to illustrate the impact of social change on family relationships (for reviews of timing of parenthood, see Moore & Brooks-Gunn, 2002; of divorce, see Clarke-Stewart & Brentano, 2006). Some of these changes are scheduled or planned, such as reentry into the workforce or delaying the onset of parenthood; other changes, such as job loss or divorce, are unscheduled or nonnormative transitions. According to a life-course view, both scheduled and unscheduled transitions need to be examined to fully appreciate how these different types of change alter family socialization strategies (Elder, 1998). These family transitions are adult-focused in contrast to child-focused transitions (e.g., entry to day care or junior high school) and underscore our assumption that adult developmental issues need to be directly addressed to understand how these transitions alter parental socialization beliefs and behaviors. At the same time, child developmental status plays a major role in determining how adults respond to these transitions. It is insufficient to focus on individual levels of analysis—either adult or child since individual, dyadic, triadic, and family units each follow their own developmental trajectory and the interplay among these separate developmental trajectories can produce a diverse set of effects on children. The role of these units (i.e., individual, dyad, or family) in modifying the impact of family transitions will vary as a result of these interlocking developmental curves. Both the timing and nature of family transitions and reactions to these alterations will be determined by the points at which particular individuals, dyads, triads, or families fall along their respective developmental life-course trajectories. Moreover, individual families can vary widely in the particular configuration of life-course trajectories. The particular configurations of these multiple sets of developmental trajectories needs to be considered to understand the impact of societal change on families.

WOMEN'S AND MEN'S EMPLOYMENT PATTERNS AND FAMILY SOCIALIZATION

Since the 1960s, there has been a dramatic shift in the participation rate of women in the labor force, especially married women with children. In the United States in 1998, over 75% of married women with school-age children and over 63% of mothers with children under age 6 were in the paid workforce (U.S. Census Bureau, 1998). In 1960, fewer than 19% of mothers with children were employed. How does maternal employment alter mother-child involvement? There is little difference in the amount of time that mothers spend with their children or in the types of activities engaged in dual or father-only employed families (Gottfried et al., 2002). Between 1981 and 1997, there was little change in mother's time with children even though there were dramatic increases in maternal employment (Bianchi, 2000). Not surprisingly, there are few negative outcomes of maternal employment on children across age (infancy to age 17), developmental domain, and gender, in part, because "there has been reallocation of mothers' time and priorities, delegation of family work to others, increased preschool enrollment of children of employed and nonemployed mothers, and redefinition of parenting roles" (Gottfried et al., 2002, p. 214). Maternal employment is associated with more egalitarian views of sex roles by their children and higher educational and occupational goals in children (Hoffman & Youngblade, 1999) and duration of employment among African American mothers is associated with longer school attendance in their daughters (Wolfer & Moen, 1996). However, the effects of maternal employment can be evaluated only in relation to other factors, such as the reason why the mother is working, the mother's satisfaction with her role, the demands placed on other family members, the attitudes of the other family members toward the mother's employment, and the quality of substitute care and supervision provided for the children.

QUALITY OF MOTHER'S AND FATHER'S WORK AND FAMILY SOCIALIZATION

In addition to examining whether one or both parents are employed, researchers have addressed the impact of the quality of work on parenting behavior. This shift in focus is due to the fact that many workers experienced an increase in work hours, a decrease in job stability, a rise in temporary jobs, and, especially among low-wage workers, a decrease in income (Mishel, Bernstein, & Schmitt, 1999). There are two types of linkage between family and work (Crouter, 1994). One type focuses on work as an "emotional climate," which may have short-term carryover effects to the enactment of roles at home. A second type focuses on the kinds of skills, attitudes, and perspectives that adults acquire in their work settings and how these variations in job experience alter their behavior in family contexts. In the first tradition, Repetti (1994) studied the impact of working in a high-stress job (air-traffic controller) on subsequent family interaction patterns. Male air traffic controllers were behaviorally and emotionally withdrawn during interactions with their children after high-stress shifts. Distressing social experiences at work were associated with higher expressions of anger and greater use of discipline during interaction with the child later in the day. Similarly, Crouter, Bumpus, Maguire, and McHale (1999) found that parents who reported high work pressure and role overload had more conflicts with their adolescents.

Research in the second tradition has focused on the outcomes of job characteristics for children's development. Children had fewer behavior problems when their mother's work involved more autonomy working with people and more problem-solving opportunities (Cooksey, Menaghan, & Jekielek, 1997). Similarly, fathers with greater job complexity and autonomy were less authoritarian (Grimm-Thomas & Perry-Jenkins, 1994). The process operates in both directions: The home experience of parents affects their job performance as well. Arguments at home with a wife or with a child were negatively related to work performance (Frone, Yardley, & Markel, 1997). It is important to move beyond employment status per se to a detailed exploration of the nature of work in studies of family work linkages.

Single versus Multiple Transitions

To date, societal changes, such as shifts in the timing of parenting, work participation, or divorce, have been treated relatively independently, but these events co-occur rather than operate in any singular fashion. As work on the impact of multiple transitions, such as the onset of puberty and entry into junior high school, on children's adjustment has found, co-occurrence of several changes can have a cumulative impact on the adolescent's adaptation (Simmons & Blyth, 1987). Similarly, as the number of environmental risk variables increases, the level of family functioning and child outcomes decrease (Sameroff, 1994). We would expect that the co-occurrence of the arrival of a new infant accompanied by job loss would have different effects than either of these events occurring singly. Moreover, the impact of any historical change may be different as a result of its occurrence in the same period as another change or changes. For example, women's increased presence in the workplace and delay in the onset of parenthood covary, and probably each event has different meaning without the other change. Multivariate designs are needed to capture the simultaneous impact of multiple events on family socialization strategies.

Children and Families of Color in the United States: Issues of Race, Ethnicity, and Culture

The term *ethnic minority* does not accurately capture the most salient aspects in the lives of non-Whites, which distinguish them from the White population—skin color and physical appearance. Therefore, the term *people of color* has gained greater acceptance as the preferred designation for groups typically considered ethnic minorities—American Indians, African Americans, Latinos, and Asian Americans. Nationally, people of color comprise approximately 35% of the U.S. population, and by the year 2020, about 40% of all children will be African American or Latino. Ethnicity refers to an individual's membership in a group sharing a common ancestral heritage based on nationality, language, and culture. Ethnic identity or the psychological attachment to the group is also a dimension of ethnicity (Phinney, 2003). Culture is a multidimensional construct referring to the shared values, behaviors, and beliefs of a people that are transmitted from one generation to the next. Unlike ethnicity and race, which are usually self- and other-ascribed attributes, respectively, culture is learned behavior and can vary both across and within ethnic and racial groups. It is invalid to equate ethnicity and race with culture. The terminology regarding race, ethnicity, and culture is changing as a result of demographic shifts and more informed awareness of how these factors contribute to development. However, to maintain consistency between past and present group designations, the terms *minority group, ethnic minority,* and *people of color* will be used interchangeably.

CONCEPTUAL AND METHODOLOGICAL ISSUES FOR STUDYING CHILDREN AND FAMILIES OF COLOR

Cross-cultural and intracultural theories have emphasized the importance of socialization goals, values, and beliefs as organizing principles for understanding cultural variations (Harkness & Super, 1995). In contrast to older cultural deficit models of socialization, recent models emphasize how ecological demands shape socialization goals, values, and practices, and are viewed as adaptive strategies to meet the demands of the ecological settings. Ecological and family systems perspectives have been useful in explaining how socialization goals for children derive from their parents' experiences with adaptive strategies that have helped them meet the challenges faced as people of color (Harrison, Wilson, Pine, Chan, & Buriel, 1990).

Earlier cultural deficit perspectives were reinforced by the popularity of two-group studies that compared European Americans with ethnic/racial minorities and assumed that differences between the groups were cultural in nature. Ethnicity and race were equated with culture as if all members of an ethnic/racial group were equally involved with the culture of their group. It was assumed that people of color needed to assimilate or become like European Americans to correct deficiencies in their development (Ramirez & Castaneda, 1974). More recently, the focus on families of color has shifted away from majority-minority comparisons toward within-group studies (Garcia Coll & Magnuson, 1999; Parke, 2004b) which tell us how within-group variations account for differences in outcomes among children of the same ethnic/racial group.

The complexity of diversity means that some children of color belong to two or more ethnic/racial groups or claim an identity that is not consistent with our ethnic/racial categorization system based primarily on color. Thus, some Afro-Latinos from Puerto Rico or the Dominican Republic may self-identify as Latinos, whereas they are identified as African Americans on the basis their skin color. Researchers need to allow children and families of color to self-identify rather than to assume membership in a racial/ethnic group on the basis of phenotype or surname.

One of the problems in cross-cultural or intracultural research about different ethnic groups is the issue of the equivalence of measures across groups. Because most standard measures of family functioning are developed and standardized in White middle-class populations, efforts have been made to develop culturally and linguistically equivalent measures. Focus groups consisting of members of the ethnic/racial group of interest to generate items and issues that are culturally relevant are common (DeMent, Buriel, & Villanueva, 2005; Vazquez-Garcia, Garcia Coll, Erkut, Alarcon, & Tropp, 1995). Another innovation is the use of translation and back translation to ensure that the meaning is retained in the translation process.

Socialization of Children of Color

As with most children, the socialization of children of color usually takes place in a family setting that includes adult caregivers who are usually biological parents but may include grandparents, relatives, godparents, and other nonbiologically related adults. An important goal of socialization in ethnic minority families is teaching children how to interact effectively in dual cultural contexts: the context of their ethnic/racial group and the context of the larger European American society. Harrison et al. (1990) have adopted an ecological orientation that views the socialization of ethnic/racial minority children by the interconnectedness between the status of ethnic/racial minority families, adaptive strategies, socialization goals, and child outcomes. Family status involves socioeconomic resources such as housing, employment, health care, and education. Despite considerable within-group diversity in SES, a growing number of ethnic minority children live in poverty (National Center for Children in Poverty, 2000). Adaptive strategies are the cultural patterns that promote the well-being of group members. Some are adaptations of the original ethnic/racial culture to life circumstances in the United States while other patterns arise as a result of coping with the conflicting demands of being an ethnic/racial minority in a predominately European American society. Thus, biculturalism (the simultaneous adoption of two cultural orientations), which arose in response to conflicting cultural demands, is now part of the ethnic minority/racial culture. Other adaptive strategies include role flexibilities and ancestral worldviews. Emerging out of the adults' adaptive strategies are socialization goals for children to help them meet the ecological challenges they face as ethnic/racial minorities. Ethnic/racial pride and interdependence are two goals that enable ethnic/racial minority children to function competently as members of both minority and majority cultures (Harrison et al., 1990).

Families of Color

Between 1990 and 2000, all groups of people of color increased in size, whereas the number of Whites decreased from 80% to 75% of the U.S. population (U.S. Census Bureau, 2000); Latinos now are the largest minority group in the United States. Whites have a higher median age and a smaller percentage of children under the age of 18 (37.7 years and 23.5%, respectively) than all groups of people of color: African Americans (30.2 years and 31.4%, respectively); American Indians (28 years and 33.9%, respectively); Asian Americans (32.7 years and 24%, respectively); and Latinos (25.8 years and 35%, respectively; U.S. Census Bureau, 2002). In public schools, approximately 40% of students in kindergarten through 12th grade are children of color (Young, 2002).

The growth of the Asian American and Latino populations was due in large measure to increases in immigration. As immigrant groups, Latinos and Asian Americans share common characteristics, including diverse subpopulations with distinct histories, non-English native languages, and relatively young age. Both groups include economic immigrants who seek a better quality of life and political immigrants who seek refuge from persecution in their countries of origin. The influx of Latino and Asian immigrants into this country means that these two groups will constantly be characterized by within-group differences in generational status and degree of acculturation. The importance of generational status and acculturation to diversity in family ecologies is illustrated with the following example using Mexican Americans.

Generational Differences in Family Ecologies.   The first generation includes those persons born in Mexico who later immigrated to the United States. Some parents immigrate with only some of their children, leaving the other children in Mexico under the care of relatives. As the parents' economic condition improves, children are brought to the United States. These children often experience multiple socializing influences in both Mexico and the United States which gives rise to a dual frame of reference for these parents and children (Perez, 2004; Valenzuela, 1999). Socialization goals related to the immigrant experience are self-reliance, productive use of time, biculturalism, a Mexican ethnic identity, and use of Spanish as their primary home language (Buriel, 1993a, 1993b).

The second generation represents the U.S. born children of immigrant parents. Their family environments are similar to those of their first-generation peers owing to the foreign-born status of their parents. Although Spanish is usually the native language of second-generation children, English becomes their dominant language after the onset of schooling. However, Spanish continues as the primary language of parents and they stress the retention of Spanish as the home language. Socialization of first- and second-generation children is similar, particularly in areas such as respect for adults, *personalismo* (Valdes, 1996), and family obligation (Fuligni, Tseng, & Lam, 1999). The second generation's exposure to European American culture impacts on their child-rearing practices as adults and the longer families live in the United States, the more socialization practices and child behavior shift in an individualistic direction (Delgado-Gaitan, 1994). Foreign-born parents prefer a Mexican identity, whereas their second-generation children prefer either a Mexican American or Chicano identity (Buriel & Cardoza, 1993).

The third generation refers to persons of Mexican descent whose parents were born in the United States, including persons in the fourth and subsequent generations whose grandparents and great grandparents were born in this country. This generation is socialized in homes where all family members are U.S. citizens, where English is the primary language, where parental schooling has taken place in the United States, and where children and parents express a Mexican American ethnic identity (Buriel & Cardoza, 1993). Buriel (1993b) found that among parents of third-generation children, parental schooling was associated with a child-rearing style involving more support, control, and equality. Although family incomes are higher in the third generation, schooling outcomes are often lower than in the previous generation. Second-generation children complete more years of schooling and have higher educational aspirations than their third-generation peers (Buriel, 1987, 1994; Valenzuela, 1999).

Acculturation

Acculturation is the process of learning a new culture and is typically measured by increasing English proficiency, English media preferences, and European American friendships (Cuellar, Arnold, & Maldonado, 1995). The measurement of acculturation has included culturally related values, attitudes, and identity in acknowledgment of the multidimensional nature of this construct (Felix-Ortiz de la Garza, Newcomb, & Meyers, 1995). Acculturation across generations is not a uniform process. In each generation, there is diversity in individuals' involvement with both native and European American culture. In addition, acculturation is not a unidirectional process such that movement toward European American culture is necessarily associated with a corresponding loss of the native culture. Ecological variables such as societal discrimination, educational and employment opportunities, and participation in native culture can all contribute to variations in both the rate and direction of acculturation across generations.

Bicultural Adaptation

Many ethnic/racial minority group members strive for a bicultural orientation that allows for selective acculturation to European American culture while simultaneously retaining aspects of the native culture. Using Mexican Americans as an example, Figure 4.4 illustrates a bidirectional model of cultural adaptation. This bidirectional model posits four acculturation adaptation styles for Mexican immigrants and their descendants, depending on their involvement with both Mexican immigrant culture and European American culture. The four acculturation styles are: (1) the bicultural orientation, (2) the Mexican orientation, (3) the marginal orientation, and (4) the European American orientation. Ramirez (1983) has defined biculturalism as the simultaneous adoption of the language, values, and social competencies of two cultures. Ethnic/racial minorities who develop bicultural competencies have better physical and psychological health than those who do not (Buriel & Saenz, 1980; LaFromboise, Coleman, & Gerton, 1993).

EMIC DEVELOPMENTAL RESEARCH ISSUES

Immigrants and their children face many sociocultural adaptation challenges that have implications for parenting and child development. Three experiences common to immigrant families and children include language and cultural brokering, children as family workers, and dual frames of reference.

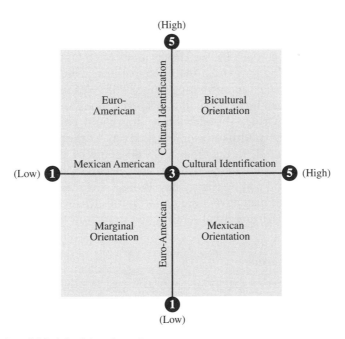

FIGURE 4.4   Bicultural Model of Acculturation.

Language and Cultural Brokers

Approximately one in every five children in the United States comes from a home where at least one parent is of foreign birth (Federal Interagency Forum on Child and Family Statistics, 2002). Most of these children are the first in their families to learn English and attend U.S. schools. As a result, these children are often delegated adult-like responsibilities by their parents, such as interpreting and making decisions with English-speaking agents that affect the whole family (Chao, 2001; DeMent et al., 2005; Orellana, Dorner, & Pulido, 2003; Tse, 1996; Valdes, 2003). Children who serve as interpreters for their non-English speaking parents are referred to as "language brokers" and as the links between their parents' culture and European American society; they are also "cultural brokers."

Child cultural brokers are unique because in addition to the stress related to their own acculturation, they experience additional stressors arising from their role as mediators between their parents and U.S. society. In public, child cultural brokers act with adult authority on behalf of their parents, but at home they are expected to behave as children and show deference and respect to parents. The stress connected to language brokering may be particularly pronounced among young children because their cognitive and social capacities are not fully developed (Weisskirch & Alva-Alatorre, 2002). However, among adolescents, there is little evidence that language brokering is associated with psychological distress (Buriel, Love, & DeMent, 2006), particularly among girls. A strong affective parent-child bond buffers adolescents against stress connected to language brokering (Buriel et al., 2006). Among Latino adolescents, more language brokering was associated with greater biculturalism and more social self-efficacy (Buriel et al., 1998). Children who broker in diverse settings such as stores, banks, hospitals, and schools have more opportunities to develop accelerated linguistic, cognitive, and interpersonal skills and have higher school grades.

Children as Family Workers

Family obligation and duty are strong values among immigrant children from collectivist cultures (Fuligni et al., 1999). These values often take the form of young children devoting time assisting parents in their occupations, which is viewed not so much as helping parents as much as contributing to the welfare of the entire family. These work-related experiences can influence children's perceptions and values about work, family relations, and gender roles. In addition to household chores, children in immigrant families often assume adultlike responsibilities as workers whose labor is beneficial, and sometimes essential, to the financial well-being of the family (Orellana, 2001). Many immigrants in manual and service labor occupations "bring children along" to help with the work and make extra money. From a social learning perspective, children in family worker roles may have more opportunities to develop personal responsibility, autonomy, and self-efficacy by observing and modeling their parents in work-related activities.

Dual Frames of Reference

The immigrant adaptation experience may give rise to a dual frame of reference that allows immigrant children to compare their socioeconomic and cultural status in the United States to their past situation in their country of origin. A dual frame of reference is an enabling quality that gives foreign-born children higher expectations and feelings of positive self-worth relative to their native-born counterparts (Suarez-Orozco &

Suarez-Orozco, 1995). By having been raised in a culturally supportive environment in their native country, immigrant children have a frame of reference to counter the negative stereotypes ascribed to many immigrant groups (Perez, 2004). A dual frame of reference is a useful psychological mechanism for understanding generational differences in school achievement, motivation, and feelings of self-worth.

SOCIALIZATION CONCERNS IN ETHNIC MINORITY FAMILIES

African American Families

The focus on African American family research has shifted from a pathological/disorganizational model to a strength/resilient model, characterized by (a) an examination of African Americans in an African American sociocultural context, (b) a consideration of the role of grandmothers and other extended family members in child-rearing activities, (c) an analysis of the presence of fathers rather than their absence in the family, and (d) the role of grandfathers in the transmission of family values and beliefs (McWright, 2002; Wilson, 1992).

Characteristics of African American extended-kin systems include: (a) a high degree of geographical propinquity; (b) a strong sense of family and familial obligations; (c) fluidity of household boundaries, with great willingness to absorb relatives, both real and fictive; (d) frequent interaction with relatives; (e) frequent extended-family get-togethers; and (f) a system of mutual aid (Harrison et al., 1990; Hatchett & Jackson, 1993). The extended family is important because of the large number of female-headed households that require child-rearing assistance and economic support (Wilson, 1992). The proportion of African American households with elderly heads that have young family members is also high, numbering about one in three families (Pearson, Hunter, Ensminger, & Kellam, 1990). When coupled with the fact that many African American grandparents live in close proximity to their married children and families, grandparents have many opportunities to influence the development of their grandchildren. Pearson et al. (1990) found that in multigenerational households, mothers were the primary caregivers, followed by grandmothers and then fathers. Grandmothers also showed more supportive behaviors in mother-grandmother families than in mother-father-grandmother families. In mother-absent families, grandmothers were more involved in control and punishment of children. Tolson and Wilson (1990) found that the presence of grandmothers increases the moral-religious emphasis in the household. Grandfathers also play an important role. Given that two-parent households were the plurality in the African American community before 1980, many grandfathers are currently involved in the socialization of grandchildren. In a study of the transmission of family values through the use of proverbs, McWright (2002) found that grandfathers' influence was greatest in the area of family connectedness.

Working-class African American fathers use more physical than verbal discipline and focus on the transgression's consequences rather than the child's intent (Dodge et al., 2005). However, they rarely couple physical discipline with love withdrawal, which may reduce some of the anxiety and resentment associated with this method. Because African American socialization stresses obedience to adults, parents have been described as harsh, rigid, and strict (Portes, Dunham, & Williams, 1986) and as being parent-centered rather than child-centered (Kelley, Power, & Wimbush, 1992). However, these parents often raise children in dangerous neighborhoods having greater risks of involvement in antisocial behavior. Under these circumstances, strict obedience to parental authority is an adaptive strategy that parents may endeavor to maintain through physical discipline (Dodge et al., 2005; Kelley et al., 1992). This disciplinary method underscores for children the importance of following societal rules and the consequences of rule breaking as a member of an ethnic/racial group that is unfairly stereotyped as violent (Willis, 1992). A socialization goal of many ethnic minority parents is fostering a sense of ethnic/racial pride in children (Harrison et al., 1990) in order to confront the hostility they will encounter as African Americans. Parents of successful African American children emphasized ethnic pride, self-development, awareness of racial barriers, and egalitarianism in their socialization practices (Bowman & Howard, 1985). African American youth exposed to race empowerment strategies were higher in racial identity and self-concept than those exposed to a race-defensiveness strategy, which taught dislike of other groups and the usefulness of acting White (Murray & Mandara, 2002).

American Indian Families

Although American Indians were known as the "Vanishing Americans," the American Indian population has increased at every census count since 1940. American Indians are a socioculturally diverse group of over 450 distinct tribal units who speak over 100 different languages (Trimble & Medicine, 1993). Today, approximately 70% of American Indians live away from reservations (Banks, 1991), mostly in urban areas, although most research focuses on those living on reservations.

American Indian families may be characterized as a collective cooperative social network that extends from the mother and father union to the extended family, the community, and the tribe (Burgess, 1980). A strong extended-family system and tribal identity characterizes many urban and rural American Indian families (Harrison et al., 1990). Extended families include several households representing significant relatives that give rise to village-like characteristics even in urban areas. In such families, grandparents retain an official symbolic leadership role. Children seek daily contact with grandparents, who monitor children's behavior and have a voice in child rearing (Lum, 1986). Despite the many social problems faced by these families (e.g., poverty, alcoholism, accidents, and adolescent suicide), the majority (68%) are two parent families. Base year data from the early childhood longitudinal study (Flanagan & Park, 2005), shows that 45% of American Indian children live with both of their married biological parents, and 27% live with cohabitating biological parents. The remaining 24% live with one parent.

Although there are variations among tribes, some common American Indian values include (a) present-time orientation—a primary concern for the present and acceptance of time as fluid and not segmented; (b) respect for elders; (c) identity with group so that the interests of the family and tribe are the same as one's own self-interest; (d) cooperation ("Help each other so the burden won't be so heavy," a Pueblo Indian saying; Suina & Smolkin, 1994, p. 121); (e) the concept of partnership as the desirable way of conducting most activities; and (f) living in harmony with nature. In traditional-oriented Indian culture, knowledge and learning are prescribed to help individuals live fulfilling lives as fully integrated members of the family and tribe. Among the Navajo, knowledge is organized around three life goals: (1) lifetime knowledge concerns language, kinship, religion, customs, values, beliefs, and the purpose of life; (2) occupational knowledge, which involves an apprenticeship with teaching experts such as herders, weavers, and hunters, is gained through listening, modeling and practice (Suina & Smolkin, 1994); and (3) healing and leadership knowledge is restricted to a few and involves specialized instruction that is usually in addition to learning other means of livelihood (Joe, 1994).

Two major tribal concerns are infant health and the child-rearing abilities of adolescents, which are critical for the tribes' survival (Berlin, 1987). American Indian teens are nearly two and a half times more likely to become pregnant before reaching their 18th birthday. Although infant death at birth is among the lowest of any racial/ethnic group, the rate of sudden infant death syndrome (SIDS) is three times the national average and infants have a 500% greater chance of being born with Fetal Alcohol Syndrome (Fuller, 2004). Indian Health Services and greater tribal self-determination in the areas of education (the Indian Self-Determination and Education Assistance Act of 1975), family life (The Indian Child Welfare Act of 1978), and culture (The American Indian Religious Freedom Act of 1978) have made it possible for some tribes to sustain healthy families and to recover traditional child-rearing practices. Zimmerman, Ramirez, Washienko, Walter, and Dyer (1998) have proposed an "enculturation hypothesis" to explain how involvement with American Indian culture buffers children from the negative effects of acculturation, such as alcohol and substance abuse. In their research with Odawa and Ojibwa tribes, they found that cultural affinity positively predicted youths' self-esteem. Youth with the highest levels of self-esteem and cultural identity had the lowest levels of alcohol and substance abuse, which was consistent with the enculturation hypothesis.

Asian American Families

The Asian American population includes people from 28 Asian countries or ethnic groups. It is a very diverse group in terms of languages, cultures, number of generations in the United States, and reasons for immigrating to the United States. Today, the largest groups, are Chinese Americans (2.7 million), Filipino Americans (2.4 million), Asian Indians (1.9 million), Vietnamese Americans (1.2 million), Korean Americans (1.2 million), and Japanese Americans (1.1 million; U.S. Census Bureau, 2002). Little research exists on the structure and process of Asian American families. Most studies have sampled from Chinese and Japanese American populations with the goal of identifying the family characteristics that contribute to children's academic performance (Huntsinger, Jose, & Larson, 1998) with less focus on the socioemotional development of children. Discussions of Asian American families usually invoke Confucian principles to explain family structure and roles. Confucius developed a hierarchy defining a person's roles, duties, and moral obligations in the state. This hierarchical structure is also applied to the family, and each member's role is dictated by age and gender. Typically, Asian American families are seen as patriarchal, with the father maintaining authority and emotional distance from other members (Wong, 1995). Traditionally, the family exerts control over family members, who are taught to place family needs before individual needs. Children show obedience and loyalty to their parents and, especially male children, are expected to take care of elderly parents (filial piety). Confucian influences on family life are stronger in some Asian American populations (e.g., Chinese and Vietnamese) than others (e.g., Japanese) due to differences in immigration patterns and degree of Westernization of the country of origin. Length of U.S. residence and acculturation also contribute to extensive within-group differences in family structure and roles. Kibria (1993) found that large Vietnamese families varying in age and gender fared better economically than smaller nuclear families by sharing a variety of social and economic resources.

Chao (1994) has argued that the traditional view of Chinese parents as authoritarian, restrictive, and controlling is misleading because these parenting behaviors do not have cross-cultural equivalence for European Americans and Chinese: these child-rearing concepts are rooted in European American culture and do not reflect the socialization styles and goals of Chinese parents. Chinese parenting should be viewed from the concepts of *chiao shun,* which means training or teaching appropriate behaviors by exposing children to examples of proper behavior and limiting their view of undesirable behaviors in the context of a supportive parent-child relationship and *guan* which means to govern, to care for or to love. Thus, control and governance have positive connotations for the Chinese. Chao (1994) compared European American and immigrant Chinese American mothers on standard measures of control and authoritarian parenting, as well as measures of *chiao shun* and *guan.* Chinese American mothers scored higher on both standard measures of parental control and authoritarian parenting and on measures of *chiao shun* and *guan.* Thus, Chinese American parenting style could not be captured using European American concepts. Instead, parenting of Chinese American mothers is conceptualized as a type of training performed by parents who are deeply concerned and involved in the lives of their children. Future research should take into account within-group difference in child-rearing practices due to generation and acculturation since larger acculturation gaps between Asian immigrant parents and their children are associated with more parental difficulties and communication problems and lower parenting satisfaction (Buki, Ma, Strom, & Strom, 2003).

Latino Families

The term *Latino* is used here to describe those persons often referred to as Hispanics, a word coined by the Department of Commerce to enumerate persons in the United States whose ancestry derives from the Spanish-speaking countries and peoples of the Americas. Mexican Americans make up the majority of Latinos (67%), followed by Central and South Americans (14%), Puerto Ricans (9%), and Cuban Americans (4%; U.S. Census Bureau, 2002). Ramirez and Castaneda (1974) have divided cultural values of Latinos into four conceptual categories: (1) identification with family, community, and ethnic group; (2) personalization of interpersonal relationships; (3) status and roles based on age and gender; and (4) Latino Catholic ideology.

Identification with Family, Community, and Ethnic Group.   Latino child-rearing practices encourage the development of a self-identity embedded firmly in the context of the family. One's individual identity is therefore part of a larger identity with the family. For many Latinos, family refers to a combination of nuclear and extended family members, including fictive kin such as godparents. The desire for closeness often results in many members of the same family living in the same community. The family network extends further into the community through kinships formed by intermarriage among families and *el compadrazco,* which is the cultural practice of having special friends become godparents of children in baptisms.

Personalization of Interpersonal Relationships.   Latino culture socializes children to be sensitive to the feelings and needs of others and to personalize interpersonal relationships (*personalismo*). This socialization goal encourages the development of cooperative social motives while discouraging individual competitive behaviors that set apart the individual from the group (Kagan, 1984). The importance of the social domain is reflected in the term *bien educado* (well educated), a term referring not only to someone with a good formal education but also to someone who can function interpersonal situations without being disrespectful. Children in particular are expected to be *bien educado* in their relations with adults (Valdes, 1996; e.g., by addressing adults in Spanish with the formal "you" [*usted*] rather than the informal "you" [*tu*]).

Status and Roles Based on Age and Gender.   Latino culture has clearly defined norms governing an individual's actions in the family and the community. Age and gender are important determinants of status and respect. Children are expected to be obedient and respectful toward their parents, even after they are grown and have children of their own. Grandparents and older persons in general receive respect and have considerable status owing to their knowledge of life. Males are expected to have more knowledge about politics and business, whereas females are expected to know more about child rearing, health care, and education. However, Latino husbands and wives most often share responsibility for major family decisions (Zavella, 1987).

Latino Catholic Ideology.   Religion strongly influences the lives of Latinos because Latino Catholicism, a synthesis of Spanish European Catholicism and indigenous religious beliefs and practices supports cultural values. Identity with family and community is facilitated through religious practices, such as weddings and *el compadrazco,* which help extend family networks. The emphasis on respect, group harmony, and cooperation is in line with the religious themes of peace, community, and self-denial. Many cultural events and developmental milestones are celebrated in religious contexts, such as a *quinceañera*—a coming-of-age celebration that marks the beginning of adulthood for a young girl on her fifteenth birthday.

Role of Family in Latino Adaptation.   The longer immigrants live in the United States, the more their family networks expand through marriage and birth and from continued immigration of family members. Thus, even as individual family members become acculturated, their local extended family becomes larger. Second- and third-generation Mexican Americans have larger and more integrated extended families than immigrants (Keefe & Padilla, 1987). Buriel (1993b) found that early assumption of responsibility was a dominant socialization goal of Mexican immigrant parents that persists into adolescence. He also found greater similarity in socialization styles among immigrant mothers and fathers than among native-born mothers and fathers. Consensus in socialization styles may reflect an area of domestic interdependence conditioned by the immigrant experience. Because immigrants lack extended kinship networks, parents may depend more on each other for socialization of children, which encourages agreement in parents' socialization styles.

Researchers are beginning to examine how traditional theories of parenting and socialization "fit" with family relations and child outcomes in Latino families. In both Mexican American and European American families, those with low levels of conflict and hostile control had children with fewer conduct problems and depressive symptoms (Hill, Bush, & Roosa, 2003). In the Mexican American sample, lower acculturation was associated with a stronger negative relationship between maternal acceptance and child conduct problems. Moreover, among Spanish-speaking parents, hostile control co-occurred with acceptance. The combination of hostile control and acceptance may represent an adaptive parenting strategy for families living in culturally unfamiliar environments involving high levels of acculturative stress.

Parke et al. (2004) found that for both Mexican American and European American families, feelings of economic hardship were positively related to depression for both parents while paternal hostile parenting was related to higher levels of children's internalizing and externalizing behaviors. However, among Mexican American families, maternal acculturation was associated with higher levels of marital problems and lower levels of both maternal and paternal hostile parenting. Although higher maternal acculturation may disrupt traditional male-centered authority patterns in the family, it may also serve as the catalyst for altering parenting styles in a less hostile direction.

A widely misunderstood issue is the role of Latino fathers and grandparents in socialization. The stereotype of *machismo* has characterized Latino fathers as neither caring nor involved with their spouses and children. However, less-acculturated Mexican American men supervise and engage their children in conventionally feminine activities more than their more acculturated counterparts (Coltrane, Parke, & Adams, 2004). Paternal participation in family rituals, which are often cultural in nature, is positively associated with monitoring and interacting with children in these families (Coltrane et al., 2004). Father involvement may represent an important dimension of *familism,* which is the most important value in Latino culture.

Research on grandparent involvement, particularly grandmothers, suggests that grandmothers are often the symbolic heads of extended families and are sought after for advice and support in child rearing (Ramos-McKay, Comas-Diaz, & Rivera, 1988). Using a Puerto Rican sample, Contreras et al. (1999) found grandmother support was related to less symptomatology and parenting stress among less-acculturated adolescent mothers. When mothers were more unidirectionally acculturated, greater grandmother support was associated with more symptomatology and parenting distress. This research, like the work with fathers, illustrates the moderating role of acculturation in family relationships with Latinos.

PERSPECTIVES ON ETHNIC INFLUENCES ON FAMILY SOCIALIZATION

At present, and for the foreseeable future, the growth of minority families will be due primarily to immigration from Latin America and Asia. Research with families of these groups needs to take into account the acculturation level and generational status of parents and children and the effects these factors have on family processes and child outcomes. Together with acculturation, recognition of biculturalism as both an adaptation strategy and socialization goal should guide future research. The effects of prejudice and discrimination on ethnic minorities, in areas such as social and emotional development, ethnic/racial identity, and achievement motivation, deserve more attention. Language development research should also give greater attention to second-language acquisition (usually English) and bilingualism and their relation to cognitive development and school achievement. More attention must be given to the role of fathers, grandparents, and extended family members in the socialization of children.

Remaining Issues and Future Trends

A number of issues remain to be examined in future research if we are to describe fully the complexities, specify the determinants and processes, and outline the consequences of family-child relationships. These include the effects of family variation, types of developmental change, the role of historical change, and methodological issues.

One advance of the past decade is recognition of the importance of individual differences in children; one of the next advances will be the recognition of individual differences among families and the expansion of sampling procedures. Despite greater awareness of family diversity, the range of family types that are studied is still relatively narrow. Although progress has been made in describing parents and children in different cultures (Rogoff, 2003) and in different ethnic groups in the United States (Contreras, Kerns, & Neal-Barnett, 2002; McLoyd, Hill, & Dodge, 2005), this work represents only a beginning. Particularly critical is an examination of other subsystems such as the marital, sibling, and family systems in families with different ethnic backgrounds, organizations, and structure. Developmental issues need to be addressed more fully to include children at a wider range of ages. We are only beginning to map developmental changes in parental socialization strategies. Moreover, we need to move beyond childhood and examine more closely parental relationships with their adult children—if we are to achieve a life-span view of family socialization. Parents' management of a variety of life-course tasks, such as marriage, work, and personal identity, will clearly determine how they will execute parental tasks; in turn, these differences may find expression in measures of parent-child interaction. The description of the interplay between child and adult developmental curves is necessary to capture adequately the nature of developmental changes in a families' role in the socialization process.

There is a continuing need to monitor secular trends and to describe their impact on family relationships (Modell & Elder, 2002). Secular change is complex and clearly does not affect all individuals equally or all behavior patterns to the same extent. Moreover, better guidelines are necessary to illuminate which particular processes in families are most likely to be altered by historical events and which processes are less amenable to change (Parke, 2004a).

No single methodological strategy will suffice to understand the development of family socialization. Instead, a wide range of designs and data collection and data analysis strategies is necessary. There is still little information concerning interrelations across molar and molecular levels of analysis or when each level is most useful. Ethnographic approaches can play a role in family research as well, particularly to gain a better understanding of contextual factors that affect parental functioning (see Burton & Price-Spratlen, 1999). Reliance on nonexperimental strategies are insufficient to address the important issue of direction of effects in work on the impact of parents on children and families. Experimental strategies have been underutilized in studies of families. By experimentally modifying either the type of parental behavior or the level of involvement, firmer conclusions concerning the direct causative role that parents play in modifying their children's and their spouse's development will be possible. As Cowan and Cowan (2002) argued, intervention studies provide the "gold standard" for testing causal hypotheses. In addition to intervention designs, natural experiments continue to be a useful tool for aiding us in sorting out causal issues For example, work on adopted Romanian children has shown that the length of institutionalization is a major predictor of later functioning (Rutter, Pickles, Murray, & Eaves, 2001).

Under the influence of the behavior geneticists, there has been an increased focus on the value of nonshared environmental designs, which allow measurement of the differential impact of families on different children in the same family. The field has progressed beyond the simple environment-gene partitioning argument toward a conceptual framework that reframes the debate as gene × environment interactions. According to this view (Reiss, 2003), family processes mediate genetic influence in children's outcomes, and the future challenge is to determine how this gene × environment family model plays out across development. Several designs, including cross-fostering studies with nonhuman primates (Suomi, 2000), modified sibling designs (Reiss, Neiderhiser, Hetherington, & Plomin, 2000), and prospective adoption designs (Reiss, 2003) are promising new approaches for addressing this issue.

A major challenge is to determine the unique contribution of families to socialization outcomes and the limits of family effects (Harris, 1998). However, our recognition of the family as a partner with other institutions, such as peers, schools, media, religious institutions, and government policy makers that together influence children's development, has significantly expanded our view of the family's role in the socialization process and suggests that the family—directly and indirectly—may have a larger impact on children's outcomes than previously thought. However, our understanding of the ways in which families influence their children's socialization through their links with other institutions is still poorly understood.

Conclusion

Families continue to play a central role in the socialization process but their role has undergone dramatic change during the past several decades. To maintain our understanding, it is critical to monitor how changing ecologies of families of different ethnic backgrounds are modifying the socialization of families. Only by a better understanding of these changes will we be able to offer meaningful assistance and support for families. And only by achieving these goals will we be able to fulfill our goal of providing optimal conditions for promoting children's development.

References

Banks, J. A. (1991). *Teaching strategies for ethnic studies* (5th ed.). Boston: Allyn & Bacon.

Baumrind, D. (1973). The development of instrumental competence through socialization. In A. D. Pick (Ed.), *Minnesota Symposia on Child Psychology* (Vol. 7, pp. 3–46). Minneapolis: University of Minnesota Press.

Baumrind, D. (1991). Parenting styles and adolescent development. In R. Lerner, A. C. Peterson, & J. Brooks-Gunn (Eds.), *The encyclopedia of adolescence* (pp. 746–758). New York: Garland Press.

Belsky, J. (1984). The determinants of parenting: A process model. *Child Development, 55,* 83–96.

Berlin, I. N. (1987). Effects of changing Native American cultures on child development. *Journal of Community Psychology, 15,* 299–306.

Bianchi, S. M. (2000). Maternal employment and time with children: Dramatic change or surprising continuity? *Demography, 37,* 401–414.

Bornstein, M. H., & Bradley, R. H. (Eds.). (2003). *Socioeconomic status, parenting, and child development.* Mahwah, NJ: Erlbaum.

Boss, P. (1999). *Ambiguous loss: Learning to live with unresolved grief.* Cambridge, MA: Harvard University Press.

Bowman, P. J., & Howard, C. (1985). Race-related socialization, motivation and academic achievement: A study of Black youths in three-generation families. *Journal of the American Academy of Child Psychiatry, 24,* 134–141.

Bretherton, I., & Munholland, K. A. (1999). Internal working models in attachment relationships: A construct revisited. In J. Cassidy & P. R. Shaver (Eds.), *Handbook of attachment: Theory, research, and clinical applications* (pp. 89–111). New York: Guilford Press.

Brody, G. H., Flor, D. L., & Neubaum, E. (1998). Coparenting processes and child competence among rural African-American families. In M. Lewis & C. Feiring (Eds.), *Families, risk and competence* (pp. 227–243). Mahwah, NJ: Erlbaum.

Brody, G. H., Stoneman, Z., & Flor, D. (1996). Parental religiosity, family processes and youth competence in rural two-parent African American families. *Developmental Psychology, 32,* 696–706.

Brodzinsky, D. M., & Pinderhughes, E. (2002). Parenting and child development in adoptive families. In M. H. Bornstein (Ed.), *Handbook of parenting: Vol. 1. Children and parenting* (2nd ed., pp. 279–311). Mahwah, NJ: Erlbaum.

Bronfenbrenner, U. (1989). Ecological systems theory. In R. Vasta (Ed.), *Six theories of child development: Revised formulations and current issues* (pp. 187–249). Philadelphia: Jessica Kingsley.

Buki, L. P., Ma, T.-C., Strom, R. D., & Strom, S. K. (2003). Chinese immigrant mothers of adolescents: Self-perceptions of acculturation effects on parenting. *Cultural Diversity and Ethnic Minority Psychology, 9,* 127–140.

Burgess, B. J. (1980). Parenting in the Native American community. In M. D. Fantini & R. Cardenas (Eds.), *Parenting in a multicultural society: Practice and policy* (pp. 63–73). New York: Longman.

Buriel, R. (1987). *Academic performance of foreign- and native-born Mexican Americans: A comparison of first-, second-, and third-generation students and parents* (New Directions for Latino Public Policy Research, Working Paper No. 14). New York: Inter-University Program for Latino Research and the Social Science Research Council.

Buriel, R. (1993a). Acculturation, respect for cultural differences and biculturalism among three generations of Mexican American and Euro-American school children. *Journal of Genetic Psychology, 154,* 531–543.

Buriel, R. (1993b). Childrearing orientations in Mexican American families: The influence of generation and sociocultural factors. *Journal of Marriage and the Family, 55,* 987–1000.

Buriel, R. (1994). Immigration and education of Mexican Americans. In A. Hurtado & E. E. Garcia (Eds.), *The educational achievement of Latinos: Barriers and successes* (pp. 197–226). Santa Cruz: Regents of the University of California.

Buriel, R., & Cardoza, D. (1993). Mexican American ethnic labeling: An intrafamilial and intergenerational analysis. In M. E. Bernal & G. P. Knight (Eds.), *Ethnic identity: Formation and transmission among Hispanics and other minorities* (pp. 197–210). Albany: State University of New York Press.

Buriel, R., Love, J. A., & DeMent, T. L. (2006). The relation of language brokering to depression and parent-child bonding among Latino adolescents. In M. H. Bornstein & L. R. Cote (Eds.), *Acculturation and parent-child relationships* (pp. 249–270). Mahwah, NJ: Erlbaum.

Buriel, R., Perez, W., DeMent, T. L., Chavez, D. V., & Moran, V. R. (1998). The relationship of language brokering to academic performance, biculturations, and self-efficacy among Latino adolescents. *Hispanic Journal of Behavioral Sciences, 20,* I, 283–297.

Buriel, R., & Saenz, E. (1980). Psychocultural characteristics of college-bound and noncollege-bound Chicanas. *Journal of Social Psychology, 110,* 245–251.

Burton, L. M., & Price-Spratlen, T. (1999). Through the eyes of children: An ethnographic perspective on neighborhoods and child development. In A. S. Masten (Ed.), *Minnesota Symposia on Child Psychology: Vol. 29. Cultural processes in child development* (pp. 77–96). Mahwah, NJ: Erlbaum.

Campbell, S. B., Cohn, J. F., & Meyers, T. (1995). Depression in first-time mothers: Mother-infant interaction and depression chronicity. *Developmental Psychology, 31,* 349–357.

Carlson, E. A., Sroufe, L. A., & Egeland, B. (2004). The construction of experience: A longitudinal study of representation and behavior. *Child Development, 75,* 66–83.

Caspi, A., McClay, J., Moffitt, T., Mill, J., Martin, J., Craig, I. W., et al. (2002). Role of genotype in the cycle of violence in maltreated children. *Science, 297,* 851–854.

Cassidy, J., Parke, R. D., Butkovsky, L., & Braungart, J. M. (1992). Family-peer connections: The role of emotional expressiveness within the family and children's understanding of emotions. *Child Development, 63,* 603–618.

Chao, R. K. (1994). Beyond parental control and authoritarian parenting style: Understanding Chinese parenting through the cultural notion of training. *Child Development, 65,* 1111–1119.

Chao, R. K. (2001, April). *The role of children's linguistic bordering among immigrant Chinese and Mexican families.* Paper presented at the biennial meeting of the Society for Research in Child Development, Minneapolis, MN.

Clarke-Stewart, K. A., & Allhusen, V. (2005). *What we know about childcare.* Cambridge, MA: Harvard University Press.

Clarke-Stewart, K. A., & Brentano, C. (2006). *Divorce: Causes & consequences.* New Haven, CT: Yale University Press.

Cochran, M., & Bo, I. (1989). The social networks, family involvement and pro and anti-social behavior of adolescent males in Norway. *Journal of Youth and Adolescence, 18,* 377–398.

Coleman, J. (1988). Social capital in the creation of human capital. *American Journal of Sociology, 94*(Suppl.), S95–S120.

Coltrane, S., Parke, R. D., & Adams, M. (2004). Complexity of father involvement in low-income Mexican American families. *Family Relations: Interdisciplinary Journal of Applied Family Studies, 53,* 179–189.

Conger, R., & Elder, G. H., Jr. (Eds.). (1994). *Families in troubled times: Adapting to change in rural America.* Hawthorn, NY: Aldine de Gruyter.

Contreras, J. M., Kerns, K. A., & Neal-Barnett, A. M. (Eds.). (2002). *Latino children and families in the United States.* Westport, CT: Praeger.

Contreras, J. M., Lopez, I. R., Rivera-Mosquera, E. T., Raymond-Smith, L., & Rothstein, K. (1999). Social support and adjustment among Puerto Rican adolescent mothers: The moderating effects of acculturation. *Journal of Family Psychology, 13,* 228–243.

Cook, W. L. (2001). Interpersonal influence in family systems: A social relations model analysis. *Child Development, 72,* 1179–1197.

Cooksey, E. C., Menaghan, E. G., & Jekielek, S. M. (1997). Life course effects of work and family circumstances on children. *Social Forces, 76,* 637–667.

Corter, C. M., & Fleming, A. S. (2002). Psychobiology of maternal behavior in human beings. In M. H. Bornstein (Ed.), *Handbook of parenting: Vol. 2. Biology and ecology of parenting* (2nd ed., pp. 141–82). Mahwah, NJ: Erlbaum.

Coulton, C. V., & Pandey, S. (1992). Geographic concentration of poverty and risk to children in urban neighborhoods. *American Behavioral Scientist, 35,* 238–257.

Cowan, P. A., & Cowan, C. P. (2002). Interventions as tests of family systems theories: Marital family relationships in children's development and psychopathology. *Development and Psychopathology, 14,* 731–759.

Crockenberg, S. C., & Leerkes, E. M. (2003). Parental acceptance, postpartum depression, and maternal sensitivity: Mediating and moderating processes. *Journal of Family Psychology, 17,* 80–93.

Crouter, A. C. (1994). Processes linking families and work: Implications for behavior and development in both settings. In R. D. Parke & S. G. Kellam (Eds.), *Exploring family relationships with other social contexts* (pp. 9–28). Hillsdale, NJ: Erlbaum.

Crouter, A. C., & Booth, A. (Eds.). (2003). *Children's influence on family dynamics: The neglected side of family relationships.* Mahwah, NJ: Erlbaum.

Crouter, A. C., Bumpus, M. F., Maguire, M. C., & McHale, S. M. (1999). Linking parents' work pressure and adolescents' well being: Insights into dynamics in dual-earner families. *Developmental Psychology, 35,* 1453–1461.

Cuellar, I., Arnold, B., & Maldonado, R. (1995). Acculturation rating scale for Mexican Americans-II: A revision of the original ARSMA scale. *Hispanic Journal of Behavioral Sciences, 17,* 275–304.

Cummings, E. M., & Davies, P. (1994). *Children and marital conflict: The impact of family dispute and resolution.* New York: Guilford Press.

Cummings, E. M., Goeke-Morey, M. C., & Raymond, J. A. (2004). Fathers in family context: Effects of marital quality and marital conflict. In M. E. Lamb (Ed.), *The role of the father in child development* (4th ed., pp. 196–221). Hoboken, NJ: Wiley.

Darling, N., & Steinberg, L. (1993). Parenting style as context: An integrative model. *Psychological Bulletin, 113,* 487–496.

Darling, N., Steinberg, L., Gringlas, B., & Dornbusch, S. (1995). *Community influences on adolescent achievement and deviance: A test of the functional community hypothesis.* Unpublished manuscript, Philadelphia, Temple University.

Delgado-Gaitan, C. (1994). Socializing young children in Mexican-American families: An intergenerational perspective. In P. M. Greenfield & R. R. Cocking (Eds.), *Cross-cultural roots of minority child development* (pp. 55–86). Hillsdale, NJ: Erlbaum.

DeMent, T., Buriel, R., & Villanueva, C. (2005). Children as language brokers: Recollections of college students. In S. Farideh (Eds.), *Language in multicultural education* (pp. 255–272). Greenwich, CT: Information Age.

Denham, S. A. (1998). *Emotional development in young children.* New York: Guilford Press.

Dix, T. (1991). The affective organization of parenting: Adaptive and maladaptive processes. *Psychological Bulletin, 110,* 3–25.

Dix, T., & Branca, S. H. (2003). Parenting as a goal-regulation process. In L. Kuczynski (Eds.), *Handbook of dynamics in parent-child relations* (pp. 167–187). Thousand Oaks, CA: Sage.

Dodge, K. A., McLoyd, V. C., & Lansford, J. E. (2005). The cultural context of physically disciplining children. In V. C. McLoyd, N. E. Hill, & K. A. Dodge (Eds.), *African American family life* (pp. 245–263). New York: Guilford Press.

Dunn, J. (1993). *Young children's close relationships: Beyond attachment.* Thousand Oaks, CA: Sage.

Dunn, J. (2004). *Children's friendships: The beginnings of intimacy.* London: Blackwell.

East, P. L., & Rook, K. S. (1992). Compensatory patterns of support among children's peer relationships: A test using school friends, nonschool friends, and siblings. *Developmental Psychology, 28,* 163–172.

Edwards, C. P., & Whiting, B. B. (1993). "Mother, older sibling and me": The overlapping roles of caregivers and companions in the social world of 2- to 3-year-olds in Ngeca, Kenya. In K. MacDonald (Ed.), *Parent-child play: Descriptions and implications* (pp. 305–329). Albany: State University of New York Press.

Eisenberg, N. (2000). Emotion, regulation, and moral development. *Annual Review of Psychology, 51,* 665–697.

Eisenberg, N., & Fabes, R. A. (1992). Emotion, regulation and the development of social competence. In M. S. Clark (Ed.), *Emotion and social behavior: Vol. 14. Review of personality and social psychology* (pp. 119–150). Thousand Oaks, CA: Sage.

Elder, G. H., Jr. (1998). The life course as developmental theory. *Child Development, 69,* 1–12.

Elder, G. H., Jr., & Conger, R. D. (2000). *Children of the land: Adversity and success in rural America.* Chicago: University of Chicago Press.

Epstein, J. L., & Sanders, M. G. (2002). Family, school, and community partnerships. In M. H. Bornstein (Ed.), *Handbook of parenting: Vol. 5. Practical issues in parenting* (pp. 407–438). Mahwah, NJ: Erlbaum.

Erel, O., & Burman, B. (1995). Interrelatedness of marital relations and parent-child relations: A meta-analytic review. *Psychological Bulletin, 118,* 108–132.

Fauber, R. L., & Long, N. (1991). Children in context: The role of the family in child psychotherapy. *Journal of Consulting and Clinical Psychology, 59,* 813–820.

Featherman, D. L., Spenner, K. I., & Tsunematsu, N. (1988). Class and the socialization of children: Constancy, change, or irrelevance. In E. M. Hetherington, R. M. Lerner, & M. Perlmutter (Eds.), *Child development in life-span perspective* (pp. 67–90). Hillsdale, NJ: Erlbaum.

Federal Interagency Forum on Child and Family Statistics. (2002). *America's children: Key national indicators of well-being.* Washington, DC: Author.

Felix-Ortiz de la Garza, M., Newcomb, M. D., & Meyers, H. F. (1995). A multidimensional measure of cultural identity for Latino and Latina adolescents. In A. M. Padilla (Ed.), *Hispanic psychology: Critical issues in theory and research* (pp. 26–42). Thousand Oaks, CA: Sage.

Field, T. (1992). Infants of depressed mothers. *Development and Psychopathology, 4,* 49–66.

Fiese, B. H. (2006). *Family routines and rituals: Promising prospects for the 21st century.* New Haven, CT: Yale University Press.

Fivaz-Depeursinge, E., & Corboz-Warnery, A. (1999). *The primary triangle: A developmental systems view of mothers, fathers, and infants.* New York: Basic Books.

Flanagan, K., & Park, J. (2005). *American Indian and Alaska Native children: Findings from the base year of the early childhood longitudinal study, birth cohort* (ECLS-B; NCES-116). Washington, DC: U.S. Department of Education, National Center for Educational Statistics.

Fletcher, A. C., Darling, N. E., Steinberg, L., & Dornbusch, S. (1995). The company they keep: Relation of adolescents' adjustment behavior to their friends' perceptions of authoritative parenting in the social network. *Developmental Psychology, 31,* 300–310.

Frone, M. R., Yardley, J. K., & Markel, K. S. (1997). Developing and testing an intergrative model of the work-family interface. *Journal of Vocational Behavior, 50,* 145–167.

Fuligni, A. J., Tseng, V., & Lam, M. (1999). Attitudes toward family obligations among American adolescents with Asian, Latin American, and European backgrounds. *Child Development, 70,* 1030–1044.

Fuller, G. (2004). *A snapshot report on American Indian youth and families.* Retrieved October 10, 2004, from www.ocbtracker.com/007/snapshot.html.

Furstenberg, F. F., Jr., Cook, T. D., Eccles, J., Elder, G. H., Jr., & Sameroff, A. (1999). *Managing to make it: Urban families and adolescent success.* Chicago: University of Chicago Press.

Garcia Coll, C. T., & Magnuson, K. (1999). Cultural influences on child development: Are we ready for a paradigm shift. In A. S. Masten (Ed.), *Minnesota Symposia on Child Psychology: Vol. 29. Cultural processes in child development* (pp. 1–24). Mahwah, NJ: Erlbaum.

Gauvain, M. (2001). *The social context of cognitive development.* New York: Guilford Press.

Geary, D. C., & Bjorklund, D. F. (2000). Evolutionary developmental psychology. *Child Development, 71,* 57–65.

Goodman, S. M., & Gotlib, I. (Eds.). (2002). *Children of depressed parents: Mechanisms of risk and implications for treatment.* Washington, DC: American Psychological Association.

Goodnow, J. J. (2002). Parents' knowledge and expectations: Using what we know. In M. H. Bornstein (Ed.), *Handbook of parenting: Vol. 3. Being and becoming a parent* (2nd ed., pp. 439–460). Mahwah, NJ: Erlbaum.

Gottfried, A. E., Gottfried, A. W., & Bathurst, K. (2002). Maternal and dual-earner employment status and parenting. In M. H. Bornstein (Ed.), *Handbook of parenting: Vol. 2. Biology and ecology of parenting* (2nd ed., pp. 207–230). Mahwah, NJ: Erlbaum.

Grimes, C. L., Klein, T. R., & Putallaz, M. (2004). Parents' relationships with their parents and peers: Influences on children's social development. In J. B. Kupersmidt & K. Dodge (Eds.), *Children's peer relations: From development to intervention* (pp. 141–158). Washington, DC: American Psychological Association.

Grimm-Thomas, K., & Perry-Jenkins, M. (1994). All in a day's work: Job experiences, self-esteem and fathering in working-class families. *Family Relations: Interdisciplinary Journal of Applied Family Studies, 43,* 174–181.

Grusec, J. E., & Goodnow, J. J. (1994). Impact of parental discipline methods on the child's internalization of values: A reconceptualization of current points of view. *Developmental Psychology, 30,* 4–19.

Grusec, J. E., & Ungerer, J. (2003). Effective socialization as problem solving and the role of parenting cognitions. In L. Kuczynski (Ed.), *Handbook of dynamics in parent-child relations* (pp. 211–228). Thousand Oaks, CA: Sage.

Grych, J. H., & Cardoza-Fernandez, S. (2001). Understanding the impacts of interparental conflict on children: The role of social cognitive processes. In J. H. Grych & F. D. Fincham (Eds.), *Interparental conflict and child development: Theory, research, and applications* (pp. 157–187). New York: Cambridge University Press.

Grych, J. H., & Fincham, F. D. (Eds.). (2001). *Child development and interparental conflict: Theory, research, and applications.* New York: Cambridge University Press.

Halberstadt, A. G., Denham, S. A., & Dunsmore, J. C. (2001). Affective social competence. *Social Development, 10,* 79–119.

Harkness, S., & Super, C. M. (1995). Culture and parenting. In M. H. Bornstein (Ed.), *Handbook of parenting: Vol. 2. Biology and ecology of parenting* (pp. 211–234). Hillsdale, NJ: Erlbaum.

Harris, J. R. (1998). *The nurture assumption: Why children turn out the way they do.* New York: Free Press.

Harrison, A. O., Wilson, M. N., Pine, C. J., Chan, S. Q., & Buriel, R. (1990). Family ecologies of ethnic minority children. *Child Development, 61,* 347–362.

Harrist, A. W., Pettit, G. S., Dodge, K. A., & Bates, J. E. (1994). Dyadic synchrony in mother-child interaction: Relation with children's subsequent kindergarten adjustment. *Family Relations: Interdisciplinary Journal of Applied Family Studies, 43,* 417–424.

Hatchett, S. J., & Jackson, J. S. (1993). African American extended kin systems: An assessment. In H. P. McAdoo (Ed.), *Family ethnicity: Strength in diversity* (pp. 90–108). Thousand Oaks, CA: Sage.

Hess, R. D., & Shipman, V. C. (1965). Early experience and the socialization of cognitive modes in children. *Child Development, 36,* 869–886.

Hetherington, E. M., & Clingempeel, W. G. (Eds.). (1992). Coping with marital transitions: A family systems perspective. *Monographs of the Society for Research in Child Development, 57*(2/3, Serial No. 227), 1–242.

Hetherington, E. M., & Kelly, J. (2001). *For better or for worse: Divorce reconsidered.* New York: Norton.

Hill, N. E., Bush, K. R., & Roosa, M. W. (2003). Parenting and family socialization strategies and children's mental health: Low income, Mexican-American and Euro-American mothers and children. *Child Development, 74,* 189–204.

Hoff, E., Laursen, B., & Tardif, T. (2002). Socioeconomic status and parenting. In M. H. Bornstein (Ed.), *Handbook of parenting: Vol. 2. Biology and ecology of parenting* (2nd ed., pp. 231–252). Mahwah, NJ: Erlbaum.

Hoffman, L. W., & Youngblade, L. M. (1999). *Mothers at work: Effects on children's well-being.* New York: Cambridge University Press.

Homel, R., & Burns, A. (1989). Environmental quality and the well-being of children. *Social Indicators Research, 21,* 133–158.

Huntsinger, C. S., Jose, P. E., & Larson, S. L. (1998). Do parent practices to encourage academic competence influence the social adjustment of young European American and Chinese American children? *Developmental Psychology, 34,* 747–756.

Isley, S., O'Neil, R., & Parke, R. D. (1996). The relation of parental affect and control behaviors to children's classroom acceptance: A concurrent and predictive analysis. *Early Education and Development, 7,* 7–23.

Joe, J. R. (1994). Revaluing Native-American concepts of development and education. In P. M. Greenfield & R. R. Cocking (Eds.), *Cross-cultural roots of minority child development* (pp. 107–113). Hillsdale, NJ: Erlbaum.

Kagan, S. (1984). Interpreting Chicano cooperativeness: Methodological and theoretical considerations. In J. L. Martinez Jr. & R. H. Mendoza (Eds.), *Chicano psychology* (2nd ed., pp. 289–333). Orlando, FL: Academic Press.

Keefe, S. E., & Padilla, A. M. (1987). *Chicano ethnicity.* Albuquerque: University of New Mexico Press.

Kelley, M. L., Power, T. G., & Wimbush, D. D. (1992). Determinants of disciplinary practices in low-income Black mothers. *Child Development, 63,* I, 573–582.

Kerig, P. K. (1996). Assessing the links between interparental conflict and child adjustment: The conflict and problem-solving scales. *Journal of Family Psychology, 10,* 454–473.

Kerr, M., & Stattin, H. (2000). What parents know, how they know it, and several forms of adolescent adjustment: Further support for a reinterpretation of monitoring. *Developmental Psychology, 36,* 366–380.

Kibria, N. (1993). *Family tightrope: The changing lives of Vietnamese Americans.* Princeton, NJ: Princeton University Press.

Kochanska, G. (1993). Toward a synthesis of parental socialization and child temperament in early development of conscience. *Child Development, 64,* 325–347.

Kochanska, G. (1997). Multiple pathways to conscience for children with different temperaments: From toddlerhood to age 5. *Developmental Psychology, 33,* 228–240.

Kramer, L. (2004). Experimental interventions in sibling relationships. In R. D. Conger, F. O. Lorenz, & K. A. S. Wickrama (Eds.), *Continuity and change in family relations: Theory, methods and empirical findings* (pp. 345–380). Mahwah, NJ: Erlbaum.

Kramer, L., & Gottman, J. M. (1992). Becoming a sibling: "With a little help from my friends." *Developmental Psychology, 28,* 685–699.

Kuczynski, L. (Ed.). (2003). *Handbook of dynamics in parent-child relations.* Thousand Oaks, CA: Sage.

Ladd, G. W. (1992). Themes and theories: Perspective on processes in family-peer relationships. In R. D. Parke & G. W. Ladd (Eds.), *Family-peer relationships: Modes of linkage* (pp. 3–34). Hillsdale, NJ: Erlbaum.

Ladd, G. W., & Pettit, G. (2002). Parenting and the development of children's peer relationships. In M. H. Bornstein (Ed.), *Handbook of parenting: Vol. 5. Practical issues in parenting* (2nd ed., pp. 269–309). Mahwah, NJ: Erlbaum.

LaFromboise, T., Coleman, H. L., & Gerton, J. (1993). Psychological impact of biculturalism: Evidence and theory. *Psychological Bulletin, 114,* 395–412.

Lum, D. (1986). *Social work practice and people of color: A process-stage approach.* Monterey, CA: Brooks/Cole.

Lyons-Ruth, K., Lyubchik, A., Wolfe, R., & Bronfman, E. (2002). Parental depression and child attachment: Hostile and helpless profiles of parent and child behavior among families at risk. In S. H. Goodman & I. H. Gotlib (Eds.), *Children of depressed parents: Mechanisms of risk and implications for treatment* (pp. 89–120). Washington, DC: American Psychological Association.

Maccoby, E. E., & Martin, J. A. (1983). Socialization in the context of the family: Parent-child interaction. In E. M. Hetherington (Ed.), *Handbook of child psychology: Vol. 4. Socialization, personality, and social development* (4th ed., pp. 1–101). New York: Wiley.

Mahoney, A., Pargament, K. I., Tarakeshwar, N., & Swank, A. B. (2001). Religion in the home in the 1980s and 1990s: A meta-analytic review and conceptual analysis of links between religion, marriage, and parenting. *Journal of Family Psychology, 15,* 559–596.

McDowell, D. J., O'Neil, R., & Parke, R. D. (2000). Display rule application in a disappointing situation and children's emotional reactivity: Relations with social competence. *Merrill-Palmer Quarterly, 46,* 306–324.

McDowell, D. J., & Parke, R. D. (2000). Differential knowledge of display rules for positive and negative emotions: Influences from parents, influences on peers. *Social Development, 9,* 415–432.

McDowell, D. J., & Parke, R. D. (2005). Parental control and affect as predictors of children's display rule use and social competence with peers. *Social Development, 14,* 440–457.

McDowell, D. J., Parke, R. D., & Spitzer, S. (2002). Parent and child cognitive representations of social situations and children's social competence. *Social Development, 4,* 486–496.

McHale, J. P., Lauretti, A., Talbot, J., & Pouquette, C. (2002). Retrospect and prospect in the psychological study of coparenting and family group process. In J. P. McHale & W. S. Grolnick (Eds.), *Retrospect and prospect in the psychological study of families* (pp. 127–165). Mahwah, NJ: Erlbaum.

McHale, J. P., & Rasmussen, J. L. (1998). Coparental and family group-level dynamics during infancy: Early family precursors of child and family functioning during preschool. *Development and Psychopathology, 10,* 39–58.

McHale, S. M., Crouter, A. C., & Whiteman, S. D. (2003). The family contexts of gender development in childhood and adolescence. *Social Development, 12,* 125–148.

McLoyd, V. C., Hill, N. E., & Dodge, K. A. (Eds.). (2005). *African American family life.* New York: Guilford Press.

McWright, L. (2002). African American grandmothers' and grandfathers' influence in the value socialization of grandchildren. In H. P. McAdoo (Ed.), *Black children: Social, educational, and parental environments* (2nd ed., pp. 27–44). Thousand Oaks, CA: Sage.

Minuchin, P. (2002). Looking toward the horizon: Present and future in the study of family systems. In J. P. McHale & W. S. Grolnick (Eds.), *Retrospect and prospect in the psychological study of families* (pp. 259–278). Mahwah, NJ: Erlbaum.

Mishel, L., Bernstein, J., & Schmitt, J. (1999). *The state of working America.* Ithaca, NY: Cornell University Press.

Mize, J., & Pettit, G. S. (1997). Mothers' social coaching, mother-child relationship style, and children's peer competence: Is the medium the message? *Child Development, 68,* 312–332.

Modell, J., & Elder, G. H. (2002). Children develop in history: So what's new. In W. W. Hartup & R. A. Weinberg (Eds.), *Minnesota Symposia on Child Psychology: Vol. 32. Child psychology in retrospect and prospect* (pp. 173–206). Mahwah, NJ: Erlbaum.

Moore, M. R., & Brooks-Gunn, J. (2002). Adolescent parenthood. In M. H. Bornstein (Ed.), *Handbook of parenting: Vol. 3. Being and becoming a parent* (2nd ed., pp. 173–214). Mahwah, NJ: Erlbaum.

Moos, R. H., & Moos, B. S. (1981). *Family environment scales manual.* Palo Alto, CA: Consulting Psychologists Press.

Mounts, N. S. (2000). Parental management of adolescent peer relationships: What are its effect on friend selection. In K. A. Kerns, J. M. Contreras, & A. M. Neal-Barnett (Eds.), *Family and peers: Linking two social worlds* (pp. 169–194). Westport, CT: Praeger.

Mounts, N. S. (2002). Parental management of adolescent peer relationships in context: The role of parenting style. *Journal of Family Psychology, 16,* 58–69.

Murray, C. B., & Mandara, J. (2002). Racial identity development in African American children: Cognitive and experiential antecedents. In H. P. McAdoo (Ed.), *Black children: Social, educational, and parental environments* (2nd ed., pp. 73–96). Thousand Oaks, CA: Sage.

National Center for Children in Poverty. (2000, Fall). *News and Issues, 10* (NDRI Monograph No. 3). New York: Columbia University, Mailman School of Public Health.

National Institute of Child Health and Human Development Early Child Care Research Network. (2003a). Does amount of time spent in child care predict socioemotional adjustment during the transition to kindergarten? *Child Development, 74,* 976–1005.

National Institute of Child Health and Human Development Early Child Care Research Network. (2003b). Do children's attention processes mediate the link between family predictors and school readiness? *Developmental Psychology, 39,* 581–593.

National Institute of Child Health and Human Development Early Child Care Research Network. (2008). *Family-peer linkages: Attentional processes as mediators.* Unpublished manuscript, National Institute of Child Health and Human Development, Bethesda, MD.

O'Connor, T. G. (2003). Behavioral genetic contributions to understanding dynamic processes in parent-child relationships. In L. Kuczynski (Ed.), *Handbook of dynamics in parent-child relations* (pp. 145–163). Thousand Oaks, CA: Sage.

O'Neil, R., Parke, R. D., & McDowell, D. J. (2001). Objective and subjective features of children's neighborhoods: Relations to parental regulatory strategies and children's social competence. *Journal of Applied Developmental Psychology, 22,* 135–155.

Orellana, M. F. (2001). The work kids do: Mexican and Central American children's contributions to households and schools in California. *Harvard Educational Review, 71,* 366–389.

Orellana, M. F., Dorner, L., & Pulido, L. (2003). Accessing assets: Immigrant youth's work as family translators or "para-phrasers." *Social Problems, 50,* 505–524.

Parke, R. D. (1988). Families in life-span perspective: A multi-level developmental approach. In E. M. Hetherington, R. M. Lerner, & M. Perlmutter (Eds.), *Child development in life-span perspective* (pp. 159–190). Hillsdale, NJ: Erlbaum.

Parke, R. D. (2004a). Development in the family. *Annual Review of Psychology, 55,* 365–399.

Parke, R. D. (2004b). The Society for Research in Child Development at 70: Progress and promise. *Child Development, 75,* 1–24.

Parke, R. D., Burks, V. M., Carson, J. V., Neville, B., & Boyum, L. A. (1994). Family-peer relationships: A tripartite model. In R. D. Parke & S. Kellam (Eds.), *Exploring family relationships with other social contexts* (pp. 115–145). Hillsdale, NJ: Erlbaum.

Parke, R. D., Cassidy, J., Burks, V. M., Carson, J. L., & Boyum, L. (1992). Family contributions to peer relationships among young children: The role of affective and interactive processes. In R. D. Parke & G. W. Ladd (Eds.), *Family-peer relationships: Modes of linkage* (pp. 107–134). Hillsdale, NJ: Erlbaum.

Parke, R. D., Coltrane, S., Duffy, S., Buriel, R., Dennis, J., Powers, J., et al. (2004). Economic stress, parenting and child adjustment in Mexican American and European American families. *Child Development, 75,* 1632–1656.

Parke, R. D., & Kellam, S. (Eds.). (1994). *Exploring family relationships with other social contexts.* Hillsdale, NJ: Erlbaum.

Parke, R. D., Killian, C. M., Dennis, J., Flyr, M. V., McDowell, D. J., Simpkins, S., et al. (2003). Managing the external environment: The parent and child as active agents in the system. In L. Kuczynski (Ed.), *Handbook of dynamics in parent-child relations* (pp. 247–270). Thousand Oaks, CA: Sage.

Parke, R. D., Kim, M., Flyr, M., McDowell, D. J., Simpkins, S., Killian, C. M., et al. (2001). Managing marital conflict: Links with children's peer relationships. In J. H. Grych & F. D. Fincham (Eds.), *Interparental conflict and child development: Theory, research, and applications* (pp. 291–314). New York: Cambridge University Press.

Parke, R. D., McDowell, D. J., Kim, M., & Leidy, M. S. (2006). Family-peer relationships: The role of emotional regulatory processes. In D. Snyder, J. A. Simpson, & J. N. Hughes (Eds.), *Emotional regulation in families: Pathways to dysfunction and health.* Washington, DC: American Psychological Association.

Parke, R. D., & O'Neil, R. (1999). Social relationships across contexts: Family-peer linkages. In W. A. Collins & B. Laursen (Eds.), *Minnesota Symposia on Child Psychology: Vol. 30. Relationships as developmental contexts* (pp. 211–239). Hillsdale, NH: Erlbaum.

Patterson, C. J. (2002). Lesbian and gay parenthood. In M. H. Bornstein (Ed.), *Handbook of parenting: Vol. 3. Being and becoming a parent* (2nd ed., pp. 317–338). Mahwah, NJ: Erlbaum.

Patterson, G. R., & Stouthamer-Loeber, M. (1984). The correlation of family management practices and delinquency. *Child Development, 55,* 1299–1307.

Pearson, J. L., Hunter, A. G., Ensminger, M. E., & Kellam, S. G. (1990). Black grandmothers in multigenerational households: Diversity in family structure and parenting involvement in the Woodlawn community. *Child Development, 61,* 434–442.

Perez, W. (2004). *Is there a dual frame of reference in Mexican immigrant adolescents?* Unpublished doctoral dissertation, Stanford University, CA.

Phinney, J. S. (2003). Ethnic identity and acculturation. In K. M. Chun, P. B. Organista, & G. Marin (Eds.), *Acculturation: Advances in theory, measurement and applied research* (pp. 63–82). Washington, DC: American Psychological Association.

Plomin, R. (1994). The Emanuel Miller Memorial Lecture 1993: Genetic research and identification of environmental influences. *Journal of Child Psychology and Psychiatry, 35,* 817–834.

Portes, P. R., Dunham, R. M., & Williams, S. (1986). Assessing child-rearing style in ecological settings: Its relation to culture, social class, early age intervention, and scholastic achievement. *Adolescence, 21,* 723–735.

Pulkkinen, L., Nurmi, J.-E., & Kokko, K. (2002). Individual differences in personal goals in mid-thirties. In L. Pulkkinen & A. Caspi (Ed.), *Paths to successful development: Personality in the life course* (pp. 331–352). New York: Cambridge University Press.

Putallaz, M., Costanzo, P. R., & Smith, R. B. (1991). Maternal recollections of childhood peer relationships: Implications for their children's social competence. *Journal of Social and Personal Relationships, 8,* 403–422.

Putnam, S. P., Sanson, A. V., & Rothbart, M. K. (2002). Child temperament and parenting. In M. H. Bornstein (Ed.), *Handbook of parenting: Vol. 1. Children and parenting* (pp. 255–278). Mahwah, NJ: Erlbaum.

Ramirez, M. III. (1983). *Psychology of the Americas: Mextizo perspectives on personality and mental health.* New York: Pergamon Press.

Ramirez, M., III, & Castaneda, A. (1974). *Cultural democracy, bicognitive development and education.* New York: Academic Press.

Ramos-McKay, J. M., Comas-Diaz, L., & Rivera, L. A. (1988). Puerto Ricans. In L. Comas-Diaz & E. E. H. Griffith (Eds.), *Clinical guidelines in cross-cultural mental health* (pp. 204–232). New York: Wiley.

Reid, J. B., Patterson, G. R., & Snyder, J. (Eds.). (2002). *Antisocial behavior in children and adolescents: A developmental analysis and model for intervention.* Washington, DC: American Psychological Association.

Reiss, D. (1989). The represented and practicing family: Contrasting visions of family continuity. In A. J. Sameroff & R. N. Emde (Eds.), *Relationship disturbances in early childhood: A developmental approach* (pp. 191–220). New York: Basic Books.

Reiss, D. (2003). Child effects on family systems: Behavioral genetic strategies. In A. C. Crouter & A. Booth (Eds.), *Children's influence on family dynamics: The neglected side of family relationships* (pp. 3–25). Mahwah, NJ: Erlbaum.

Reiss, D., Neiderhiser, J. M., Hetherington, E. M., & Plomin, R. (2000). *The relationship code: Deciphering genetic and social influences on adolescent development.* Cambridge, MA: Harvard University Press.

Repetti, R. V. (1994). Short-term and long-term processes linking job stressors to father-child interactions. *Social Development, 3,* 1–15.

Rogoff, B. (2003). *The cultural nature of human development.* London: Oxford University Press.

Russell, A. (1997). Individual and family factors contributing to mothers' and fathers' positive parenting. *International Journal of Behavioral Development, 21,* 111–132.

Russell, A., & Finnie, V. (1990). Preschool children's social status and maternal instructions to assist group entry. *Developmental Psychology, 26,* 603–611.

Rutter, M., Pickles, A., Murray, R., & Eaves, L. (2001). Testing hypotheses on specific environmental causal effects on behavior. *Psychological Bulletin, 127,* 291–324.

Saarni, C. (1999). *The development of emotional competence.* New York: Guilford Press.

Sameroff, A. (1994). Developmental systems and family functioning. In R. D. Parke & S. G. Kellam (Eds.), *Exploring family relationships with other social contexts* (pp. 199–214). Hillsdale, NJ: Erlbaum.

Simmons, R. G., & Blyth, D. A. (1987). *Moving into adolescence: The impact of pubertal change and school context.* Hawthorne, NY: Aldine de Gruyter.

Steinberg, L., Dornbusch, S. M., & Brown, B. B. (1992). Ethnic differences in adolescent achievement: An ecological perspective. *American Psychologist, 47,* 723–729.

Stocker, C. M. (1994). Children's perceptions of relationships with siblings, friends, and mothers: Compensatory processes and links with adjustment. *Journal of Child Psychology and Psychiatry, 35,* 1447–1459.

Suarez-Orozco, C., & Suarez-Orozco, M. (1995). *Transformations: Migration, family life, and achievement motivation among Latino adolescents.* Stanford, CA: Stanford University Press.

Suina, J. H., & Smolkin, L. B. (1994). From natal culture to school culture to dominant society culture: Supporting transitions for Pueblo Indian students. In P. M. Greenfield & R. R. Cocking (Eds.), *Cross-cultural roots of minority child development* (pp. 115–130). Hillsdale, NJ: Erlbaum.

Suomi, S. J. (2000). A biobehavioral perspective on developmental psychopathology: Excessive aggression and serotonergic dysfunction in monkeys. In A. J. Sameroff, M. Lewis, & S. M. Miller (Ed.), *Handbook of developmental psychopathology* (2nd ed., pp. 237–256). Dordrecht, The Netherlands: Kluwer Press.

Tardif, T. (1993). *Adult-to-child speech and language acquisition in Mandarin Chinese.* Unpublished doctoral dissertation, Yale University, New Haven, CT.

Tolson, T. F., & Wilson, M. N. (1990). The impact of two- and three-generational Black family structure on perceived family climate. *Child Development, 61,* 416–428.

Trimble, J. E., & Medicine, B. (1993). Diversification of American Indians: Forming an indigenous perspective. In U. Kim & J. W. Berry (Eds.), *Indigenous psychologies: Research and experience in cultural context* (pp. 133–151). Thousand Oaks, CA: Sage.

Tse, L. (1996). Who decides? The effects of language brokering on home-school communication. *Journal of Educational Issues of Language Minority Students, 16,* 225–234.

U.S. Census Bureau. (1998, March). *Households and family characteristics* (Current population reports, P2–215). Washington, DC: U.S. Department of Commerce.

U.S. Census Bureau. (2000). *USA statistics in brief: Population and vital statistics.* Washington, DC: U.S. Department of Commerce. Retrieved January 15, 2004, from www.census.gov./statab/www/poppart.htm.

U.S. Census Bureau. (2002, March). *Census, 2000,* Summary File 1. Retrieved January 10, 2004, from www.census.gov/population/cen2000/Phc-TQ8/.

Valdes, G. (1996). *Con respeto: Bridging the distances between culturally diverse families and schools—An ethnographic portrait.* New York: Teachers College Press.

Valdes, G. (2003). *Expanding definitions of giftedness: The case of young interpreters from immigrant communities.* Mahwah, NJ: Erlbaum.

Valenzuela, A. (1999). *Subtractive schooling: U.S.-Mexican youth and the politics of caring.* Albany: State University of New York Press.

Vazquez-Garcia, H. A., Garcia Coll, C., Erkut, S., Alarcon, O., & Tropp, L. (1995, April). *An instrument for the assessment of family values and functioning of Latin parents.* Poster presented at the biennial meeting of the Society for Research in Child Development, Indianapolis, IN.

Weisskirch, R. S., & Alva-Alatorre, S. (2002). Language brokering and acculturation of Latino children. *Hispanic Journal of Behavioral Sciences, 24,* 369–378.

Willis, W. (1992). Families with African American roots. In E. W. Lynch & M. J. Hanson (Eds.), *Developing cross-cultural competence: A guide for working with young children and their families* (pp. 121–150). Baltimore: Paul H. Brookes.

Wilson, M. N. (1992). Perceived parental activity of mothers, fathers, and grandmothers in three-generational Black families. In A. K. H. Burlew, W. C. Banks, H. P. McAdoo, & D. A. Azibo (Eds.), *African American psychology: Theory, research, and practice* (pp. 87–104). Thousand Oaks, CA: Sage.

Wolfer, L. T., & Moen, P. (1996). Staying in school: Maternal employment and the timing of Black and White daughters' school exit. *Journal of Family Issues, 17,* 540–560.

Wong, M. G. (1995). Chinese Americans. In P. G. Min (Ed.), *Asian Americans: Contemporary trends and issues* (pp. 58–94). Thousand Oaks, CA: Sage.

Xiaoming, L., Stanton, B., & Feigelman, S. (2000). Impact of perceived parental monitoring on adolescent risk behavior over 4 years. *Journal of Adolescent Health, 27,* 49–56.

Young, B. A. (2002, April). *Public school students, staff, and graduate counts by state: School year 2000–2001.* Washington, DC: National Center for Education Statistics.

Zavella, P. (1987). *Women's work and Chicano families: Cannery workers of the Santa Clara Valley.* Ithaca, NY: Cornell University Press.

Zimmerman, M. A., Ramirez, J., Washienko, K. M., Walter, B., & Dyer, S. (1998). Enculturation hypothesis: Exploring direct and protective effects among Native American youth. In H. I. McCubbins, E. A. Thompson, A. I. Thompson, & J. E. Fromer (Eds.), *Resiliency in family series: Vol. 2. Resiliency in Native American and immigrant families* (pp. 199–220). Thousand Oaks, CA: Sage.

Zukow-Goldring, P. (2002). Sibling caregiving. In M. H. Bornstein (Ed.), *Handbook of parenting: Vol. 3. Being and becoming a parent* (pp. 253–286). Mahwah, NJ: Erlbaum.

PART IV

PERSONALITY, SELF, AND SELF-CONCEPT

Chapter 5

Peer Interactions, Relationships, and Groups

KENNETH H. RUBIN, WILLIAM M. BUKOWSKI,
JEFFREY G. PARKER, and JULIE C. BOWKER

Experiences with peers constitute an important developmental context for children wherein they acquire a wide range of behaviors, skills, and attitudes that influence their adaptation during the life span. In this chapter, we review current research on children's peer experiences while distinguishing between processes and effects at different levels of analysis—namely individual characteristics, social interactions, dyadic relationships, and group membership and composition. Our thesis is that interactions, relationships, and groups reflect social participation at different interwoven orders of complexity. Our goal, in introducing these levels of analysis, is to establish a framework for further discussion of the origins, development, and significance of children's peer experiences. Moreover, discussion of the interaction, relationships, and group levels of social complexity allows subsequent commentary on conceptual issues that pertain to individual differences in children's behavioral tendencies and peer relationships.

Orders of Complexity in Children's Peer Experiences

Over the past 25 years, recognition and articulation of the multiple levels of analysis and perspectives that comprise the peer system have greatly increased. Especially significant in this regard has been the contribution of Robert Hinde (e.g., 1987, 1995) who has articulated the features and dialectical relations between successive levels of

The writing of this chapter was supported, in part, by a grant from the National Institute of Mental Health (MH-58116) to Kenneth H. Rubin and by grants from the Social Sciences and Humanities Research Council of Canada and the Fonds Québécois de la Recherche sur la Société et la Culture to William M. Bukowski.

social complexity. Borrowing heavily from Hinde, in this section we discuss the nature of three successive levels of complexity in children's experiences with peers—interactions, relationships, and groups.

INTERACTIONS

The simplest order of complexity of peer experience involves interactions. Interaction refers to the social exchange between two individuals. Behaviors that simply (and only) complement one another (like riding on either end of a teeter-totter) would ordinarily not be considered true interaction unless it was clear that they were jointly undertaken. Instead, the term *interaction* is reserved for dyadic behavior in which the participants' actions are interdependent such that each actor's behavior is both a response to, and stimulus for, the other's behavior. Conversational turn-taking is a quintessential illustration: Child A requests information from Child B ("What's your name?"), Child B responds ("My name is Julius. What's yours?"), Child A replies ("Elodie."), and so on.

Such a simple exchange as that of Julius and Elodie belies the richness and complexity of the ways that children of most ages communicate with and influence one another. Thus, besides introducing themselves, children in conversation may argue, gossip, self-disclose, and joke, among other things. And during interaction, children also cooperate, compete, fight, withdraw, respond to provocation, and engage in a host of other behaviors that includes everything from ritualized sexual contact to rough-and-tumble (R&T) play to highly structured sociodramatic fantasy. Typically, researchers have been less interested in cataloguing the myriad of interactional experiences than in understanding the origins and consequences of three broad childhood behavioral tendencies: (1) moving toward others, (2) moving against others, and (3) moving away from others. As a consequence, our understanding of children's experiences at the interactional level may be disproportionately organized around the constructs of sociability and helpfulness, aggression, and withdrawal.

Although many social exchanges have their own inherent logic (as in the question-answer sequence of Julius and Elodie), it is also the case that the forms and trajectories of episodes of interaction are shaped by the relationships in which they are embedded. For example, friends are more committed to resolving conflict with each other than nonfriends, are more likely than nonfriends to reach equitable resolutions, and continue to interact following a disagreement (Laursen, Finkelstein, & Betts, 2001; Laursen, Hartup, & Koplas, 1996). Beyond this, children engaged in interaction vary their behavior as a function of such factors as their short-term and long-term personal goals, their understanding of their partner's thoughts and feelings in the situation, the depth of their repertoire of alternative responses, and various "ecological" features of the context of the interactions (such as the presence of bystanders). It is precisely the demonstration of such range and flexibility in responding to the challenges of interpersonal interaction that many writers think of as social competence (e.g., Bukowski, Rubin, & Parker, 2001).

RELATIONSHIPS

Relationships introduce a second and higher-order level of complexity to children's experiences with peers. Relationships refer to the meanings, expectations, and emotions that derive from a succession of interactions between two individuals known to each other. Because the individuals are known to each other, the nature and course of each interaction is influenced by the history of past interactions between the individuals as well as by their expectations for interactions in the future. It has been suggested that the degree of closeness of a relationship is determined by such qualities as the frequency and strength of influence, the diversity of influence across different behaviors, and the length of time the relationship has endured. In a close relationship, influence is frequent, diverse, strong, and enduring. Alternatively, relationships can be defined with reference to the predominant emotions that participants typically experience in them (e.g., affection, attachment, or enmity).

As a form of social organization, dyadic relationships share features with larger social organizations, such as a family, a class, or a team. For instance, dyads, like larger organizational structures, undergo role differentiation, specialization, and division of labor (McCall, 1988). However, there are certain features of dyadic relationships that are distinct to this level of social organization and vital to understanding its functioning and impact on interactions and individuals. Unlike most social organizations, dyadic relationships do not vary in membership size. This makes the dyad peculiarly vulnerable, for the loss of a single member terminates the dyad's existence. Because members appreciate this vulnerability, issues of commitment, attachment, and investment loom larger in dyadic relationships than in other forms of social organization. Indeed, an understanding of the surface behavior of members of relationships can be elusive unless the deeper meaning of behavior in relation to the relationship's mortality is considered.

A final point is that relationships must be understood according to their place in the network of other relationships. For example, children's friendships are influenced by the relationships they have at home with parents and siblings (Belsky & Cassidy, 1995).

Friendship

In the literature on children's peer experiences, one form of dyadic relationship has received attention above all others—friendship. The issue of what constitutes friendship is a venerable philosophical debate beyond the scope of this chapter. However, some points from this debate warrant noting here because of their operational significance.

First, there is widespread agreement that friendship is a reciprocal relationship that must be affirmed or recognized by both parties. Reciprocity is the factor that distinguishes friendship from the nonreciprocal attraction of only one partner to another. A second point of consensus is that reciprocity of affection represents an essential, though not necessarily exclusive, tie that binds friends together (Hays, 1988). Similarities or complementarities of talents and interests may lead to friendships and can help sustain them; however, they do not constitute the basis of the friendship itself. The basis is reciprocal affection. Third, friendships are voluntary, not obligatory or prescribed. In some cultures and in some circumstances, children may be assigned their "friends," sometimes even at birth (Krappmann, 1996). Although these relationships may take on some of the features and serve some of the same interpersonal ends as voluntary relationships, most scholars would agree that their involuntary nature argues against confusing them with friendship.

GROUPS

A group is a collection of interacting individuals who have some degree of reciprocal influence over one another. Hinde (1987) suggests that a group is the structure that emerges from the features and patterning of the relationships and interactions present in a population of children. Accordingly, groups possess properties that arise from the manner in which the relationships are patterned but are not present in the individual relationships themselves. Examples of such properties include cohesiveness, or the degree of unity and inclusiveness exhibited by the children or manifest by the density of the interpersonal relationships; hierarchy, or the extent of intransitivity in the ordering of the individual relationships along interesting dimensions (e.g., If Fred dominates Brian and Brian dominates Peter, does Fred dominate Peter?); and homogeneity, or consistency across members in the ascribed or achieved personal characteristics (e.g., sex, race, age, or attitudes toward school). Finally, every group has norms, or distinctive patterns of behaviors and attitudes that characterize group members and differentiate them from members of other groups.

Many of our most important means for describing groups speak to these core characteristics or processes. Thus, researchers may address the degree to which the relationships and interactions in a group are segregated along sex or racial lines (e.g., Killen, Lee-Kim, McGlothlin, & Stangor, 2002); they may compare the rates of social isolation among groups that differ in composition; or they may investigate the extent to which a group's hierarchies of affiliation, dominance, and influence are linear and interrelated. In addition, group norms can be used as a basis for distinguishing separate "crowds" in the networks of relationships among children in high school (e.g., Brown, 1989).

It is worth noting that the construct that has dominated the peer literature during the past 25 years, namely that of popularity, is both an individual- and a group-oriented phenomenon. Measures of popularity refer to the group's view of an individual in relation to the dimensions of liking and disliking. In this regard, popularity is a group construct and the processes of rejection and acceptance are group processes. Yet, despite this reality, most peer researchers treat popularity as characteristic of the individual (e.g., Newcomb, Bukowski, & Pattee, 1993).

SUMMARY

To understand children's experiences with peers, researchers have focused on children's interactions with other children and on their involvements in peer relationships and groups. Analyses in each level—interactions, relationships, groups—are scientifically legitimate and raise interesting questions. However, until recently, studying individual, dyadic, and group measures was challenging, both conceptually and statistically. Advances in multilevel modeling techniques and in the availability of more-or-less user-friendly software have given researchers the tools to examine the effects of group, dyadic, and individual variables simultaneously. These procedures can be used to assess how the effects of variables describing individual tendencies (e.g., aggressiveness, sociability, or inhibition) on an outcome (e.g., one's subsequent aggressiveness, sociability, or reticence) will vary as a function of dyadic-relationship characteristics (e.g., quality of friendship; quality of the mother-child relationship). In turn, a researcher can assess variations in dyadic effects due to the characteristics of the groups in which they are embedded. These techniques have been used with success already (e.g., Kochenderfer-Ladd & Wardrop, 2001).

Culture

It is important to recognize that each of the social levels described earlier falls under the all-reaching umbrella of culture. Culture is defined as "the set of attitudes, values, beliefs, and behaviors shared by a group of people, communicated from one generation to the next" (Matsumoto, 1997, p. 5). Cultural beliefs and norms help interpret the acceptability of individual characteristics and the types and ranges of interactions and relationships that are likely or permissible.

Given that the majority of the world's inhabitants do not reside in culturally Westernized countries, the cross-cultural work on peer interactions, relationships, and groups requires careful review: Child development is influenced by many factors. In any culture, children are shaped by the physical and social settings in which they live as well as culturally regulated customs, childrearing practices, and culturally based belief systems (Harkness & Super, 2002). The bottom line is that the psychological "meaning" attributed to any given social behavior is, in large part, a function of the ecological niche in which it is produced. If a given behavior is viewed as acceptable, then parents (and significant others) will attempt to encourage its development; if the behavior is perceived as maladaptive or abnormal, then parents (and significant others) will attempt to discourage its growth and development. And the very means by which people go about encouraging or discouraging the given behavior may be culturally determined and defined. Thus, in some cultures, the response to an aggressive act may be to explain to the child why the behavior is unacceptable; in others, physical discipline may be the accepted norm; in yet others, aggression may be ignored or perhaps even reinforced (for a discussion, see Bornstein & Cheah, 2006). It would appear most sensible for the international community of child development researchers not to generalize to other cultures their own culture-specific theories of normal and abnormal development. In this regard, we describe relevant extant research pertaining to cross-cultural similarities and differences in children's peer interactions and relationships throughout this chapter.

Peer Interactions, Relationships, and Groups: A Developmental Perspective

Children's peer experiences become increasingly diverse, complex, and integrated with development. In some cases, the impetus for these developments rests in children (i.e., changes in interpersonal understanding), while others derive from situational or contextual phenomena. In the following sections, we review many developmental mileposts in the interactional, relational, and group levels of children's involvement with other children.

THE INFANT AND TODDLER YEARS

Interactions

Infants do have obvious social limitations. Babies are unable, for example, to comprehend the social and cognitive needs, capacities, or zones of proximal development of their age-mates (Hay, 1985). Yet, careful observation of infants reveals remarkable strides taken during the 1st year of life. These include (a) the careful observation of peers and seemingly intentional direction of smiles, frowns, and gestures to their play partners (Hay, Nash, & Pederson, 1983); and (b) the response, often in kind, to their play partner's behaviors (Mueller & Brenner, 1977). With the emergence of locomotion and the ability to use words to communicate during the second year of life, interactive bouts become lengthier, and toddler play becomes organized around particular themes or games. Often, these toddler games are marked by reciprocal imitative acts (Ross, 1982).

These developments promote more effective social commerce between toddlers and contribute a generally positive affective quality to their interaction (Hay, Castle, Davies, Demetriou, & Stimson, 1999). However, toddler social interaction is also marked by conflict (e.g., Hay & Ross, 1982; Rubin, Hastings, Chen, Stewart, & McNichol, 1998). Rubin et al. (1998) found that over 70% of 25-month-old children participated in a conflict situation at least once in a 50-minute laboratory setting. In a comparable setting, Hay and Ross (1982) observed 87% of 21-month-old toddlers engaged in at least one conflict. As such, it appears that conflict is neither infrequent nor limited to a small percentage of toddlers.

Importantly, it appears as if many of those toddlers who frequently instigate conflicts with peers are the most socially outgoing and initiating (National Institute of Child Health and Human Development Early Child Care Research Network, 2001). It is also the case that toddlers are highly attentive to, and are more likely to imitate and initiate interactions with, highly sociable age-mates (Howes, 1988). Taken together, these data suggest that during the second year of life, toddlers do display social skills of modest complexity.

Relationships

It has been demonstrated that toddlers are more likely to initiate play, direct positive affect to, and engage in complex interactions with familiar than unfamiliar playmates (Howes, 1988). But can familiarity be equated with the existence of a relationship? Ross and colleagues have demonstrated that toddlers do develop reciprocal relationships with familiar others that are characterized not only by the mutual exchange of positive overtures, but also by agonistic interactions. Positive interactions are directed specifically to those who have directed positive initiations to the child beforehand; conflict is initiated specifically with those who have initiated conflictual interactions with the child beforehand (e.g., Ross, Conant, Cheyne, & Alevizos, 1992).

To the extent that reciprocal interchanges of positive overtures may characterize particular dyads, it may be said that toddlers do have friendships. Howes (1988) defined toddler friendship as encompassing the response to a peer's overture at least once, the production of at least one complementary or reciprocal dyadic exchange, and the demonstration of positive affect during at least one such exchange. Vandell and Mueller (1980) identified toddler friends as those who initiated positive social interaction more often with each other than with other potential partners. Thus, during the toddler period, friendships, as defined earlier, do exist; however, it is doubtful that they carry the same strength of psychological meaning as the friendships of older children. Nevertheless, these early relationships may lay the groundwork for the establishment and maintenance of friendships throughout the childhood years.

Groups

Even young toddlers spend much of their time in small groups such as with day-care mates. But there is little empirical evidence that this level of social organization is salient to, or influential on, these young children. Nevertheless, some authors (e.g., Legault & Strayer, 1991) have observed dominance hierarchies in small groups of young toddlers, as well as in subsets of children who invest greater attention and inter-action to one another than to outside nonmembers. Interestingly, some members of these groups appear more central to their functioning than others, perhaps illustrating the earliest examples of individual differences in popularity and influence.

EARLY CHILDHOOD

Interaction

From 24 months to 5 years, the frequency of peer interaction increases and becomes more complex. To begin with, children at these ages engage in a variety of different types of play behaviors and activities, including unoccupied, onlooking (the child ob-serves others but does not participate in the activity), solitary, parallel (the child plays beside but not with other children), and group activities (Rubin, Watson, & Jambor, 1978). Importantly, the categories of solitary, parallel, and group behavior comprise a variety of play forms that differ in cognitive complexity. Thus, whether alone, near, or with others, children may produce simple sensorimotor behaviors (functional play, e.g., aimlessly bouncing a ball), construct structures from blocks or draw with crayons (con-structive play), or engage in some form of pretense (dramatic play). The examination of these cognitive forms of play reveals interesting developmental trends. For example, solitary-sensorimotor behaviors become increasingly rare over the preschool years, while the relative frequency of solitary-construction or exploration remains the same (Rubin et al., 1978). Furthermore, the only types of social interactive activity to in-crease over the preschool years are sociodramatic play and games with rules (Goncu, Patt, & Kouba, 2002).

Perhaps the most complex form of group interactive activity during the preschool years is sociodramatic play (Goncu et al., 2002). The ability to engage easily in this form of social activity represents mastery of one of the essential tasks of early child-hood—the will and skill to share and coordinate decontextualized and substitutive ac-tivities. Researchers have reported that by the 3rd year of life, children are able to share symbolic meanings through social pretense (e.g., Howes, 1988). This is a remarkable accomplishment, as it involves the capacity to take on complementary roles, none of which matches real-world situations, and to agree on the adoption of these imaginary roles in a rule-governed context. The ability to share meaning during pretense has been referred to as intersubjectivity (Goncu, 1993), which research findings suggest reflect the increasing sophistication of preschooler's naive "theory of mind" (Watson, Nixon, Wilson, & Capage, 1999). Researchers have also demonstrated that engaging in socio-dramatic play is associated with social perspective-taking skills and the display of skilled interpersonal behavior (Howes, 1992).

Several other significant advances are made during the preschool period. For one, prosocial caring, sharing, and helping behaviors become more commonplace with in-creasing age. Four-year-olds direct prosocial behavior to their peers more often than 3-year-olds (e.g., Benenson, Markovits, Roy, & Denko, 2003). Importantly, aggression increases until age 3 and then declines, and the nature of conflict changes from the tod-dler to the preschool period. During toddlerhood, most conflict appears to center on toys and resources; during the preschool years, conflict becomes increasingly centered on differences of opinion (e.g., D. W. Chen, Fein, & Tam, 2001)—a reflection of the child's growing ability to focus on others' ideas, attitudes, and opinions.

Relationships

During early childhood, children express preferences for some peers over others as playmates. It appears that one important influence on this process is that preschoolers are attracted to peers who are similar to them in some noticeable regard. For example, similarities in age and sex draw young children together. Furthermore, preschoolers appear to be attracted to, and become friends with peers whose behavioral tendencies are similar to their own, a phenomenon known as behavioral homophily (e.g., Rubin, Lynch, Coplan, Rose-Krasnor, & Booth, 1994).

Once preschoolers form friendships, their behavior with these individuals is distinctive from their behavior with other children who are familiar but not friends. Children as young as 3.5 years direct more social overtures, engage in more social interactions, and play in more cooperative and prosocial ways with friends than nonfriends (e.g., Dunn & Cutting, 1999). Compared to nonfriends, preschool friends also demonstrate more quarreling and more active (assaults and threats) and reactive hostility (refusals and resistance; Dunn & Cutting, 1999). Moreover, Hartup, Laursen, Stewart, and Eastenson (1988) demonstrated that preschool children engage in more conflicts with their friends than with neutral associates. These differences are best understood by recognizing that friends spend much more time actually interacting with each other than do nonfriends. Hartup and his colleagues also reported qualitative differences in how preschool friends and nonfriends resolve conflicts and in what the outcomes of these conflicts are likely to be. Friends, as compared with nonfriends, make more use of negotiation and disengagement, relative to standing firm, in their resolution of conflicts. In conflict outcomes, friends are more likely to have equal resolutions, relative to win or lose occurrences. Also, following conflict resolution, friends are more likely than neutral associates to stay in physical proximity and continue to engage in interaction.

While approximately 75% of preschoolers have reciprocally nominated best friendships (Dunn, 1993), not all young children have a best friend. And, Ladd, Kochenderfer, and Coleman (1996) have shown that not all friendships in early childhood are equally stable. Those friendships that involve higher levels of positive friendship qualities (e.g., validation) and lower levels of negative friendship qualities (e.g., low conflict) are most likely to be stable. Importantly, during this period of early childhood, the ability to make friends, friendship quality, and stability of young children's friendships are associated with, and predicted by, social-cognitive and emotional maturity. For example, the abilities to understand emotional displays and social intent and to perspective-take are associated with friendship formation, maintenance, and friendship quality (Dunn & Cutting, 1999; Ladd & Kochenderfer, 1996). Furthermore, the young child's ability to regulate emotions is associated with and predictive of both the number of mutual friends and friendship quality (Walden, Lemerise, & Smith, 1999).

Groups

Many researchers have found that the social dominance hierarchy is an important organizational feature of the preschool peer group (e.g., Vaughn, Vollenweider, Bost, Azria-Evans, & Snider, 2003). And researchers have argued that dominance hierarchies develop naturally in groups to serve adaptive functions. In the case of preschool-aged children, dominance hierarchies appear to reduce overt aggression among members of the group. Observations of exchanges between children in which physical attacks, threats, and object conflicts occur reveal a consistent pattern of winners and losers.

And children who are losers in object struggles rarely initiate conflict with those who have proven "victorious" over others or who have been victorious over them (Strayer & Strayer, 1976).

MIDDLE CHILDHOOD AND EARLY ADOLESCENCE

The school-age years represent a dramatic shift in social context for most children in Western cultures. During this time, the proportion of social interaction that involves peers increases. The peer group also grows in size, and peer interaction becomes less closely supervised by adults. The settings of peer interaction also change. Preschool children's peer contacts are centered in the home and in day-care centers, whereas school-age children come into contact with peers in a wide range of settings (e.g., "hanging out" at school or after-school, talking on the telephone; Zarbatany, Hartmann, & Rankin, 1990).

Interaction

During middle childhood, verbal and relational aggression (insults, derogation, threats, gossip) gradually replace direct physical aggression. Further, relative to preschoolers, the aggressive behavior of 6- to 12-year-olds is less frequently directed toward possessing objects or occupying specific territory and more specifically hostile toward others (Dodge, Coie, & Lynam, 2006). With regard to positive social behavior, Eisenberg, Fabes, and Spinrad (2006) report the levels of generosity, helpfulness, or cooperation that children direct to their peers increases somewhat during the primary and middle school years. The frequency of "pretend" or "nonliteral" aggression, or R&T play increases in early elementary school, and thereafter declines in middle childhood and early adolescence. Interestingly, it has been proposed that the primary function of R&T, especially among young adolescent boys, is to establish dominance status and thereby delimit aggression among peers (Pellegrini, 2002).

Children's concerns about acceptance in the peer group rise sharply during middle childhood, and these concerns appear related to an increase in the salience and frequency of gossip (Kuttler, Parker, & La Greca, 2002). Gossip, at this age, reaffirms children's membership in important same-sex social groups and reveals, to its constituent members, the core attitudes, beliefs, and behaviors comprising the basis for inclusion in or exclusion from these groups. Thus, gossip may play a role in fostering friendship closeness and in promulgating children's social reputations.

One additional form of interaction has received specific attention in the recent literature. Deviancy training occurs when children model and reward aggressive behaviors in each other; the process by which these exchanges take place is thought to increase individual tendencies in aggressiveness and to strengthen ties to aggressive and substance-abusing friends and delinquent peer groups. In this regard, deviancy training "hits" at all levels of the social enterprise (Dishion, McCord, & Poulin, 1999).

Yet another form of interaction emerging fully blown during middle childhood and early adolescence is bullying and victimization (Espelage, Bosworth, & Simon, 2000). *Bullying* refers to acts of verbal and physical aggression on the part of an individual that are chronic and directed toward particular peers (victims). Bullying accounts for a substantial portion of the aggression that occurs in the peer group (Olweus, 1978, 1993). The dimension that distinguishes bullying from other forms of aggressive behavior is its specificity—bullies direct their behavior toward only certain peers, comprising approximately 10% of the school population (National Institute of Child Health and Human Development Early Child Care Research Network, 2001). Research on bullying suggests that bullies are characterized by strong tendencies toward aggressive behavior, relatively weak control over their aggressive impulses, and a tolerance for aggressive behavior (Olweus, 1978, 1993).

Children who are greatest risk for victimization are those who have elevated scores on measures of either aggression or social withdrawal. Nearly every study that has assessed the association between aggressiveness and victimization has revealed a positive correlation (e.g., Hanish & Guerra, 2004; Snyder et al., 2003). These findings appear to be culturally universal; victimization and aggression have been found to be positively associated in North American, Southern Asian (Khatri & Kupersmidt, 2003) and East Asian (Schwartz, Farver, Chang, & Lee-Shin, 2002) samples. Finally, there is evidence that anxious and socially reticent children are also victims of bullying behavior (Kochenderfer-Ladd, 2003; Olweus, 1993).

There are at least two explanations for the observation that aggression and social withdrawal are associated with victimization. First, a withdrawn child is likely to be victimized because she or he is an easy prey who is unlikely to retaliate when provoked (e.g., the construct of "whipping boy"; Olweus, 1978, 1993); alternatively, an aggressive child is victimized because his or her behavior is irritating and likely to provoke victimization from others ("the provocative victim"; Olweus, 1993). According to this view different mechanisms underlie victimization for different types of children. Another view uses a single model to explain victimization. It claims that children victimize peers who do not promote the basic group goals of coherence, harmony, and evolution. According to this view, aggressive and withdrawn children do not promote these positive aspects of group functioning and as a result they are victimized.

Relationships

The period of middle childhood and early adolescence brings marked changes in children's understanding of friendship. For example, children's friendship conceptions at the start of middle childhood (7 to 8 years) involve rewards and costs—friends are rewarding to be with, whereas nonfriends are difficult or uninteresting to be with. At this age, a friend is also someone who is convenient (i.e., who lives nearby), has interesting toys or possessions, and shares the child's expectations about play activities. By about 10 to 11 years, children recognize the importance of shared values and social understanding, and friends are expected to stick up for and be loyal to one another. Later, at 11 to 13 years, children acquire the view that friends share similar interests, are required to make active attempts to understand each other, and are willing to engage in self-disclosure (Bigelow, 1977).

Changes in the understanding of friendship are accompanied by changes in the patterns and nature of involvement in friendships. Children's friendship choices are more stable and more likely to be reciprocated in middle childhood than at earlier ages (Berndt & Hoyle, 1985). Friendships that are high in relationship quality are more likely to persist over time, and this is also true in early childhood. Furthermore, stable friendships in middle childhood and early adolescence are more likely to comprise dyads in which the partners are sociable and altruistic; friendships that dissolve during the course of a school year are more likely to comprise partners who are aggressive and victimized by peers (Hektner, August, & Realmuto, 2000; Wojslawowicz Bowker, Rubin, Burgess, Booth-LaForce, & Rose-Krasnor, 2006).

With respect to the features of friendships in middle childhood and early adolescence, Newcomb and Bagwell (1995) reported that children are more likely to behave in positive ways with friends than nonfriends or to ascribe positive characteristics to their interactions with friends. Although the effect size of this difference may, in some cases, be small, this pattern of findings is observed across a broad range of studies using a variety of methods, including direct observations (e.g., Simpkins & Parke, 2002), and interviews (Berndt, Hawkins, & Hoyle, 1986). More important, Newcomb and Bagwell's (1995) meta-analysis showed that the expression of affect varied considerably for pairs of friends and nonfriends. In their interactions with friends, relative to interaction with nonfriends, children show more affective reciprocity and emotional intensity, and enhanced levels of emotional understanding. Moreover, young adolescent friends use distraction to keep their friends from potentially harmful rumination about social attributions that may induce guilt or shame (Denton & Zarbatany, 1996). In this regard, friendship is a socially and positive relational context, and it provides opportunities for the expression and regulation of affect. Friend-nonfriend differences are stronger during early adolescence than during either middle childhood or during the preschool years.

One of the few dimensions of interaction in which there are no differences between friends and nonfriends is that of conflict. Research has shown repeatedly that after early childhood, pairs of friends engage in about the same amount of conflict as pairs of nonfriends (Laursen et al., 1996). There is a major difference, however, in the conflict resolution strategies that friends and nonfriends adopt. In particular, friends are more likely than nonfriends to resolve conflicts in a way that will preserve or promote the continuity of their relationship (Laursen et al., 2001). The beneficial effects of friendship are qualified by the characteristics of the best friend: Young adolescents with aggressive friends, compared with those who have nonaggressive friends, adopt increasingly aggressive solutions to conflicts; young adolescents who are nonaggressive and who have nonaggressive friends use more prosocial solutions (Brendgen, Bowen, Rondeau, & Vitaro, 1999).

There appear to be consistent qualitative differences in boys' and girls' best friendships in the middle childhood and early adolescent years. For example, girls' friendships are marked by greater intimacy, self-disclosure, and validation and caring than those of boys (e.g., Zarbatany, McDougall, & Hymel, 2000). Ironically, it is because of the intimacy of girls' best friendships that they appear to be less stable and more fragile than those of boys (e.g., Benenson & Christakos, 2003). According to Benenson and Christakos, intimate disclosure between female friends may become hazardous when best friends have a conflict. In such cases, the conflicting friends can divulge personal information to outsiders (Crick & Grotpeter, 1995). Intimate disclosure within the friendships of girls also appears hazardous to psychological well-being when conducted in a "co-ruminative" fashion (Rose, 2002). Significantly, when boys' best friendships are with girls rather than boys, intimacy is higher, thus suggesting that there may be two different "worlds" of relationships defined by context and activity (Zarbatany et al., 2000).

Throughout this age period, children are attracted to and become best friends with those who resemble them in age, sex, ethnicity, and behavioral status (Hartup & Abecassis, 2002). Researchers in both Western and Eastern cultures have reported that greater behavioral similarities exist between friends than nonfriends, and children share friendships with other children who resemble themselves in terms of prosocial and antisocial behaviors (e.g., Haselager, Hartup, van Lieshout, & Riksen-Walraven, 1998; Poulin & Boivin, 2000), shyness and internalized distress (e.g., Rubin, Wojslaw-owicz, Burgess, Booth-LaForce, & Rose-Krasnor, 2006), sociability, peer popularity, and academic achievement and motivation (e.g., Altermatt & Pomerantz, 2003).

Finally, researchers have begun to study enmity and mutual antipathies (e.g., Abecassis, Hartup, Haselager, Scholte, & van Lieshout, 2002). Whereas the topic of disliking is certainly not new (e.g., Hayes, Gershman, & Bolin, 1980), the emphasis of recent research has been on the frequency of mutual antipathies, their correlates, and their developmental significance. Abecassis et al. (2002) have shown that rates vary across classrooms, with the frequencies of dyadic enmity being as high as 58% in some classrooms. Although all children experience mutual antipathies, they are most common among rejected children and they are more common among boys than girls, especially during middle childhood compared with adolescence (Rodkin & Hodges, 2003). Children in such relationships tend to be more depressed than are other children, and the presence of a mutual antipathy appears to exacerbate the effect of other negative experiences, such as peer rejection.

Nevertheless, the developmental significance of mutual antipathies is unclear, and many issues related to the study of mutual antipathies require further exploration. Perhaps the most important concerns the issue of how we define and measure the concept of enemy. To paraphrase the important discussions provided by Hartup and Abecassis (2002), having an enemy implies warfare. Consequently, researchers would do well to examine whether children who nominate each other as "Someone I do not like," actually interact. It may be that mutual antipathies merely capture an affective dimension, not an interactional one. "True" enemies may be proactive about their relationship. They may spread gossip about one another and engage in relational or other forms of aggression. At present, there are virtually no data indicating how and whether those who mutually nominate each other as "Someone I do not like" actually have a clearly defined relationship.

Groups

During the upper elementary school and middle school years, the structure of the peer group changes from a relatively unified whole to a more differentiated structure. In this new structure, children organize themselves into social groups, clusters, networks, or cliques (e.g., Bagwell, Coie, Terry, & Lochman, 2000). Peer networks and cliques are voluntary, friendship-based groups, and stand in contrast to the activity or work groups to which children can be assigned by circumstance or by adults. Cliques generally include three to nine same-sex children of the same race (X. Chen, Chang, & He, 2003; Kindermann, McCollom, & Gibson, 1995). By 11 years of age, most of children's peer interaction takes place in the context of the clique, and nearly all children report being a member of one. With respect to group size, boys, compared with girls, show a preference for larger groups (Benenson, Apostoleris, & Parnass, 1997).

Peer networks, whether identified observationally (e.g., Gest, Farmer, Cairns, & Xie, 2003) or via peer reports (e.g., Bagwell et al., 2000), or whether identified in or out of school (Kiesner, Poulin, & Nicotra, 2003), are typically organized to maximize within-group homogeneity (Rodkin, Farmer, Pearl, & Van Acker, 2000). Thus, in studies of preadolescents conducted in both Western (e.g., Canada, Finland, United States) and Eastern (e.g., China) cultures, group membership has been found to comprise children similar with regard to the following characteristics: aggression (Espelage, Holt, & Henkel, 2003; Gest et al., 2003; Xie, Cairns, & Cairns, 1999), bullying (e.g.,

Espelage et al., 2003), and school motivation and performance (e.g., X. Chen et al., 2003; Kindermann, 1993).

Apart from cliques, the other primary organizational feature of children's groups in middle childhood and early adolescence is the popularity hierarchy. There have been recent attempts to distinguish between sociometric popularity and perceived popularity. In the case of sociometric popularity or peer acceptance, the questions asked of children are "Who do you most like?" and "Who do you most dislike?" In the case of perceived popularity, the child is asked who he or she believes is the most popular in the classroom, grade, or school (Parkhurst & Hopmeyer, 1998; LaFontana & Cillessen, 2002). Whereas being liked or accepted occurs at the dyadic level (i.e., one person has affection for someone else), the perception of someone as being popular in a classroom or school reflects a group level of analysis (i.e., the person is perceived according to her/his position in the group). Thus, in the study of peer group relationships, the word (and traditional measurement of) "acceptance" is most properly taken as a direct assessment of the extent to which a child is liked by his or her peers, whereas the word *popularity* refers to a child's perceived standing or status in the group.

More recently, researchers have focused on the study of such negative characteristics as aggression to clarify the distinction between the meanings and measurement of peer acceptance and perceived popularity. Findings show that children whose level of aggression is moderately above the mean and who use aggression for instrumental reasons are perceived as more popular in their groups than are children who are low in aggression or whose aggression is high and undifferentiated (e.g., Hawley, 2003; Vaughn at al., 2003). Although the association between aggression and popularity may be seen even during the preschool period (Vaughn et al., 2003), this association appears to be stronger during early adolescence (Cillessen & Mayeux, 2004; Prinstein & Cillessen, 2003). Yet, whereas aggression is positively associated with measures of popularity during early adolescence, it is not related to acceptance. Moderately aggressive children may be given status and power in the peer group; however, this does not mean they are well-adjusted or that they will receive or benefit from the affection or kindness from their peers.

These findings are consistent with ideas about how groups function and reward persons who promote the group's functioning (see Bukowski & Sippola, 2001). Whereas the main reward that one can provide at the level of the dyad is affection, the main rewards that can be provided at the level of the group are power, attention, and status. And whereas group members victimize peers who impede the group's evolution and coherence, groups give power, attention, and status to group members who promote the group's well-being. Given that group leaders may, at times, have to be forceful, strong, assertive, indeed Machiavellian, their behavior may include a larger coercive or aggressive component than is seen among other children. This tendency to ascribe power and status to moderately aggressive individuals may be more pronounced in adolescence when aggression is seen as a more normative entity than among younger children (Moffitt, 1993).

ADOLESCENCE

Interaction

The trend of spending increasingly substantial amounts of time with peers that begins in middle childhood continues in adolescence (e.g., Csikszentmihalyi & Larson, 1984). Moreover, adolescent peer interaction takes place with less adult guidance and control than peer interaction in middle childhood, and is more likely to involve individuals of the opposite-sex (Brown & Klute, 2003). These phenomena are largely consistent across cultural groups.

Relationships

As they enter adolescence, both boys and girls already understand a great deal about the reciprocal operations and obligations of friendship, about the continuity of friendships, and about the psychological grounds that evoke behavior. During adolescence, however, youngsters begin to accept the other's need to establish relationships with others and to grow through such experiences. Thus, adolescents' discussions of friendship and friendship issues show fewer elements of possessiveness and jealousy, and more concern with how the relationship helps the partners enhance their respective self-identities (Berndt & Hoyle, 1985).

During adolescence, friendships are relatively stable and best maintained when the partners have similar attitudes, aspirations, and intellect (Berndt et al., 1986). Same-sex friends account for an increasingly larger proportion of adolescents' perceived primary social network, and friends equal or surpass parents as sources of support and advice to adolescents in many significant domains (e.g., Furman & Buhrmester, 1992). One hallmark of friendship in adolescence is its emphasis on intimacy and self-disclosure: adolescents report greater levels of intimacy in their friendships than do younger children (Buhrmester & Furman, 1987).

Romantic relationships are first seen during early adolescence with approximately 25% of 12-year-olds claiming they have had a romantic relationship during the past 18 months (Carver, Joyner, & Udry, 2003). This frequency increases in a largely linear fashion during adolescence with roughly 70% of boys and 75% of girls making this claim at age 18 (Carver et al., 2003; Seiffge-Krenke, 2003). The average duration of a romantic relationship has been observed to be 3.9 months at age 13, and 11.8 months at age 17 months (Seiffge-Krenke, 2003). Importantly, adolescent boys and girls have clear conceptions of the properties that distinguish romantic relationships from friendships (Connolly, Craig, Goldberg, & Pepler, 2004). Whereas romantic relationships are conceived in terms of passion and commitment, other-sex friendships are largely characterized by affiliation.

There are large differences between those adolescents who do and do not participate in romantic relationships. These differences vary during the adolescent period and they are often characterized by complex patterns. Early involvement in romantic relationships has been linked to problem behaviors and emotional difficulties during adolescence, although this difference appears to be strongest among boys and girls who are unpopular among their same-sex peers (Brendgen, Vitaro, Doyle, Markiewicz, & Bukowski, 2002). It has been reported also that early daters show lower levels of scholastic achievement (Seiffge-Krenke, 2003), especially among girls (Brendgen et al., 2002). Among older adolescents, however, participation in romantic relationships is associated with positive experiences among same-sex peers and emotional and behavioral well-being (Seiffge-Krenke, 2003). Connolly, Furman, and Konarski (2000) reported that being part of a small group of close same-sex friends predicted being involved in other-sex peer networks, which, in turn, predicted the emergence of future romantic relationships. There is evidence also that the quality of a child's same-sex friendships predicts the quality of their concurrent and subsequent romantic relationships (Connolly et al., 2000).

Although there appears to be some inter-relatedness between romantic relationships and other relationship experiences, this association is often complex. Using an attachment framework, Furman, Simon, Shaffer, and Bouchey (2002) studied adolescents' internal working models for their relationships with parents, friends, and romantic partners. Adolescents' perceived support in relationships with their parents tended to be related to their perceived support in romantic relationships and friendships; support in friend and romantic relationships, however, were not related to each other. Nevertheless, self and other controlling behaviors in friendships were related to corresponding behaviors in romantic relationships. Perceived negative interactions in the three types of relationships were also significantly associated with each other. This pattern of results indicates greater generalizability of negative than positive features across relationship types.

Groups

As in middle childhood, cliques are readily observed in adolescence, and group membership comprises individuals who are similar with regard to school achievement (Kindermann, 1995), substance use (cigarettes and alcohol; Urberg, Degirmencioglu, & Pilgrim, 1997), and delinquency (Kiesner et al., 2003). Whereas cliques represent small groups of individuals linked by friendship selections, the concept of peer subcultures, or "crowds" (Brown & Klute, 2003), is a more encompassing organizational framework for segmenting adolescent peer social life. A crowd is a reputation-based collective of similarly stereotyped individuals who may or may not spend much time together. Crowds are defined by the primary attitudes or activities their members share. Thus, crowd affiliation is assigned through the consensus of the peer group and is not selected by the adolescents themselves. Brown (1989) listed the following as common crowd labels among American high school students: jocks, brains, eggheads, loners, burnouts, druggies, populars, nerds, and greasers.

Crowd membership is an especially salient feature of adolescent social life and children's perceptions of crowds change in important ways with age. For example, between the ages of 13 and 16 years, adolescents alter the ways that they identify and describe the crowds in their school (O'Brien & Bierman, 1987). Whereas young adolescents focus on the specific behavioral proclivities of group members, older adolescents center on members' dispositional characteristics and values. This observation reflects broader changes that characterize developmental shifts in person-perception between the childhood and adolescent years.

The stigma that is placed on members of a particular crowd channels adolescents into relationships and dating patterns with those sharing a similar crowd label. This may prevent adolescents from the exploration of new identities and discourage shifts to other crowd memberships. There is evidence that the stigma associated with some large peer groups or crowds influences the judgments that adolescents form about their peers (Horn, 2003). In particular, Horn (2003) found that adolescents are biased in their use of reputational or stereotypical information about particular groups, particularly when presented with ambiguous situations. It is likely that these crowd-specific evaluations help to perpetuate group stereotypes and the structure of peer groups in a school.

Despite the differences that exist in the structures of peer groups, all of them inevitably disintegrate by late adolescence. This is largely due to the integration of the sexes that accompanies this period. To begin with, mixed-sex cliques emerge. Eventually, the larger groups divide into couples, and by late adolescence, girls and boys feel comfortable enough to approach one another directly without the support of the clique. Another contributing factor to the decline in importance of crowds results from adolescents creating their own personal values and morals. In this regard, they no longer see it as necessary to broadcast their membership in a particular social group and are therefore content to be separate and apart from particular crowds.

Summary

In this chapter, we have outlined developmental differences that mark the changing nature of social interactions and peer relationships from infancy to adolescence. Hopefully, this review provides a normative basis for the discussion that follows concerning the development of individual differences in children's social behaviors and peer relationships.

Proximal Correlates and Distal Predictors of Children's Peer Relationships

The literature on individual differences in popularity and friendship can be divided into two domains. First, the largest concentration of investigations center on the individual characteristics associated with (a) acceptance or rejection in the peer group at large, (b) the ability to make and keep friends, and (c) the quality of friendship. A second body of research is concerned with the associations between peer acceptance and rejection and friendship and both the child's family relationship experiences and the social environments in which the child functions. This literature deals with the distal correlates of peer acceptance and friendship. We focus on these proximal correlates and distal predictors next.

Proximal Correlates—Peer Acceptance

In studies involving play groups (e.g., Coie & Kupersmidt, 1983) and/or peer-assessment techniques (Newcomb & Bukowski, 1984), researchers interested in behavioral explanations for peer acceptance and rejection typically examine differences between children classified as sociometrically popular, rejected, and average. A thorough review of the voluminous literature on the concomitants of popularity is presented in Rubin, Bukowski, and Parker (1998). Whereas some reviews of research serve as renaissances that renew the study of a topic, the reviews of the sociometric classification studies served as a requiem. Although many of the basic questions of sociometric classification remain unanswered, research on the differences between children in the different sociometric groups has waned. Herein we provide a cursory discussion of the literature.

Popular Children

Popular children are high in acceptance and low in rejection. Relative to other children, those of popular status are skilled at initiating and maintaining qualitatively positive relationships. When entering new peer situations, popular children do not talk exclusively or overbearingly about themselves and their own social goals or desires, and they are not disruptive of the group's activity (Dodge, McClaskey, & Feldman, 1985). Popular children are seen as cooperative, friendly, sociable, and sensitive by peers, teachers, and observers (e.g., Newcomb & Bukowski, 1984; Parkhurst & Hopmeyer, 1998).

In a meta-analysis of research on popularity, Newcomb et al. (1993) distinguished between assertive/agonistic behaviors and behaviors that reflected disruptiveness. Popular children did not differ from others on the former category of behavior whereas they did on the latter. Popular children, it appears, do engage in some forms of assertive behavior, but they rarely engage in behaviors that are likely to interfere with the actions and goals of others.

Rejected Children

The most commonly cited behavioral correlate of peer rejection is aggression, regardless of whether aggression is indexed by peer evaluations, teacher ratings, or observations (e.g., McNeilly-Choque, Hart, Robinson, Nelson, & Olsen, 1996). The association between rejection and aggression appears to be rather broad; Newcomb et al. (1993) revealed that rejected children, relative to average popular and neglected children, showed elevated levels on three forms of aggression—specifically, disruptiveness, physical aggression, and negative behavior (e.g., verbal threats). A small number of studies provide evidence of a causal link between aggression and rejection. In groundbreaking play group studies (Dodge, 1983; Coie & Kupersmidt, 1983), the interactions between unfamiliar peers in small groups were observed in a laboratory context over several days. Gradually, some of the children became popular and others became rejected. The behavior that most clearly predicted peer rejection was aggression. With increasing age, however, it appears as if aggression becomes decreasingly associated with rejection, especially among boys (e.g., Sandstrom & Coie, 1999). Also, aggressive behavior may not lead to rejection if it is balanced by a set of positive qualities (e.g., social skill) that facilitate links with other children (Farmer, Estell, Bishop, O'Neal, & Cairns, 2003).

Indeed, researchers have found that there is a high level of heterogeneity among the behavioral tendencies of rejected children. Detailed analyses indicate that aggressive children comprise 40% to 50% of the rejected group; children who are highly withdrawn, timid, and wary comprise 10% to 20% of the rejected group (e.g., Cillessen, van IJzendoorn, van Lieshout, & Hartup, 1992). Finally, victimization has been observed to be associated with peer rejection, either as a correlate (e.g., Kochenderfer-Ladd, 2003), as a mediator that explains the association between withdrawal and victimization, or as a moderator that increases the stability of victimization (e.g., Hanish & Guerra, 2004).

VARIATIONS IN THE BEHAVIORAL CORRELATES OF POPULARITY: SEX, GROUP, AND CULTURAL DIFFERENCES

Groups have norms, or standards, regarding the "goodness" of particular acts. The acceptability of a behavior, and of the child who displays that behavior, is determined by whether the behavior conforms to the group's norms. If a behavior is universally valued, it should correlate with peer acceptance; if the normalcy of a behavior varies across groups, the extent to which the behavior is linked to popularity should vary across these groups also. It is this logic that has provided the basis for much of the research on group variations in the correlates of popularity.

Sex Differences

Given the widespread concern with sex differences in the literature on child development, it seems surprising to discover how little work exists on the topic of sociometric peer acceptance. Typically, researchers have failed to examine whether general findings are equally valid for boys and girls. Further, sex differences have been neglected despite (a) the long-standing view that the relationships formed and maintained by females are qualitatively distinct from those of males (Leaper, 1994) and (b) the evidence that some aspects of social behavior may be differentially normative for boys and girls (e.g., Humphreys & Smith, 1987). This gap in the literature is striking and it severely compromises our current understanding of the peer system (see Ruble, Martin, & Berenbaum, 2006).

Variations across Groups

The argument that a child's popularity will be associated with particular peer group norms has been the central focus of a number of investigations. Boivin, Dodge, and Coie (1995), for example, reported that reactive aggression, proactive aggression, and solitary play were more negatively linked to a measure of social preference when high levels of these specific behaviors were nonnormative and unrelated to preference when high levels on these behaviors were normative. Stormshak et al. (1999) also found support for the person-group similarity model. These researchers reported that for boys, social withdrawal was associated with peer acceptance in those classrooms in which withdrawal was normative; for boys, aggression was linked to peer preference in those classrooms in which aggression was more normative. Findings for girls were, complex and in some cases not supportive of the person-group similarity model. For example, in classrooms marked by high aggression, aggressive girls were not better liked than nonaggressive girls.

These studies show clearly that the association between a particular form of behavior and popularity depends on whether the behavior is normative for a group. Considering the importance of group norms as moderators of the associations between behaviors and popularity, researchers should be cautious about drawing broad conclusions about the correlates of popularity. Indeed, researchers would do well to assess the person/group interaction and similarity as a major determinant of peer acceptance and rejection.

Variations across Culture

Cross-cultural research on the correlates of peer acceptance and rejection has been aimed at asking whether given behaviors known to be associated with acceptance or rejection in North American samples demonstrate similar relations in other cultures. One shortcoming in this work may be that investigators have taken measures originally developed for use in a Western cultural context, and have employed them in other cultural milieus. The general conclusion from this research has been that aggression and helpfulness are associated with rejection and popularity respectively in a wide range of cultures (e.g., Chang et al., 2005; Cillessen et al., 1992). Alternatively, researchers have found that among young Chinese children, sensitive, cautious, and inhibited behavior are positively associated with competent and positive social behavior and with peer acceptance (e.g., X. Chen, Rubin, & Sun, 1992). However, Hart and colleagues (2000) found that social reticence, defined as unoccupied and onlooking behavior, was associated with a lack of peer acceptance, not only in young American children, but also among Russian and Chinese youngsters. Relatedly, X. Chen, Cen, Li, and He (2005) reported that over the years, since the early 1990s, shy, reserved behavior among Chinese elementary school children has increasingly become associated with negative peer reputations. Chen and colleagues have argued that the changing economic and political climate in China is being accompanied by preferences for more assertive, yet competent, social behavior. In short, researchers would do well not to generalize findings drawn from children of one cultural group to children from another context. Moreover, changing socioeconomic climates may prove to have significant influences on that which is deemed acceptable behavior by significant peers and adults in the child's environment.

Social Cognitive Correlates of Peer Acceptance and Rejection

In this section, we review research in which social cognition has been associated with sociometric status. The majority of this research has been guided by social information-processing models, such as those of Rubin and Rose-Krasnor (1992), Crick and Dodge (1994), and Lemerise and Arsenio (2000). For a complete description of these models and others, see Dodge et al. (2006).

Much research on social cognition and peer relationships has focused on rejected children's deficits or qualitative differences in performance at various stages of these social information-processing models. For instance, when considering the motives or intentions of others, rejected-aggressive children are more disposed than their popular counterparts to assume that negative events are the product of malicious, malevolent intent on the part of others (e.g., Dodge et al., 2003). This bias is evident when children are asked to make attributions for others' behaviors in situations where something negative has happened but the motives of the instigator are unclear. In these ambiguous situations, rejected-aggressive children appear unwilling to give a provocateur the benefit of the doubt—for example, by assuming that the behavior occurred by accident. This "intention cue bias" is often suggested as an explanation for why it is that aggressive and oppositional-defiant children choose to solve their interpersonal problems in hostile and agonistic ways (e.g., see Orobio de Castro, Veerman, Koops, Bosch, & Monshouwer, 2002, for a review).

But why would aggressive children think that when negative, but ambiguously caused events befall them, the protagonist means them harm? In keeping with Lemerise and Arsenio (2000), a transactional perspective would suggest that aggressive children, many of whom are already rejected (and victimized) by their peers, believe that certain others do not like them, those others have a history of rejecting of them or acting mean toward them, and thus the negative act must be intentionally caused. This conclusion of intentional malevolence is posited to elicit anger and a rapid fire response of reactive aggression. Many researchers have found that when asked how they would react to an ambiguously caused negative event, aggressive children respond with a choice of agonistic strategies (Orobio de Castro et al., 2002). And aggressive children also regard aggression to be an effective and appropriate means to meet their interactive goals (Vernberg, Jacobs, & Hershberger, 1999). The processes leading to the enactment of aggression and the behavioral display itself no doubt reinforces an already negative peer profile.

By the elementary and middle school years, many socially withdrawn children are also rejected by their peers. Thus, one may ask whether these children view their social worlds in ways that vary from those of nonwithdrawn and/or nonrejected children. To begin with, when socially withdrawn 4- and 5-year-olds are asked how they would go about obtaining an attractive object from another child, they produce fewer alternative solutions, display more rigidity in generating alternative responses, and are more likely to suggest adult intervention to aid in the solution of hypothetical social problems when compared to their more sociable age-mates (Rubin, Daniels-Beirness, & Bream, 1984).

Rubin, Burgess, Kennedy, and Stewart (2003) have argued that as a result of frequent interpersonal rejection by peers, withdrawn children may begin to attribute their social failures to internal causes. Supporting these notions, Rubin and Krasnor (1986) found that extremely withdrawn children tended to blame social failure on personal, dispositional characteristics rather than on external events or circumstances. These results are in keeping with findings by Wichmann, Coplan, and Daniels (2004) who reported that when 9- to 13-year-old withdrawn children were presented with hypothetical social situations in which ambiguously caused negative events happened to them, they attributed the events to internal and stable "self-defeating" causes. Moreover, withdrawn children suggested that when faced with such negative situations, they were more familiar with failure experiences and that a preferred strategy would be to withdraw and escape.

Given the earlier noted conceptual associations between social withdrawal, victimization, and peer rejection, the findings by Wichmann et al. (2004) are reminiscent of work by Graham and Juvonen (1998). These latter researchers reported that youngsters who identified themselves as victimized by peers tended to blame themselves for their peer relationship problems. And Nolen-Hoeksema, Girgus, and Seligman (1992) have argued that self-blame can lead to a variety of negative outcomes of an internalizing nature, such as depression, low self-esteem, and withdrawal, thereby suggesting a self-reinforcing cycle of negative socioemotional functioning.

SELF-SYSTEM CORRELATES OF PEER ACCEPTANCE AND REJECTION

An important repercussion that has been ascribed to negative experiences with peers is their effect on the self-concept. Indeed, researchers have consistently reported that it is mainly rejected-withdrawn children who believe they have poor social skills and relationships (Hymel, Bowker, & Woody, 1993). Rejected-aggressive children do not report thinking poorly about their social competencies or their relationships with peers (Zakriski & Coie, 1996).

Given rejected-withdrawn children's negative perceptions of their social competencies and relationships, and given their negative experiences in the peer group, it is not surprising that these children report more loneliness and social detachment than popular children or children who are rejected but aggressive (e.g., Gazelle & Ladd, 2003). These relations have been reported throughout childhood and early adolescence (e.g., Crick & Ladd, 1993). A further distinction between rejected children is the chronicity of their peer problems. Whereas rejection is temporary for some children, it is an enduring experience for others. Ladd and Troop-Gordon (2003) showed that chronic rejection was related to subsequent views of the self and that these negative self-perceptions partially mediated the relation between peer difficulties and internalizing problems and loneliness.

CHILDREN'S FRIENDSHIPS: CORRELATES AND INDIVIDUAL DIFFERENCES

Beginning with the correlates of friendship involvement, researchers have found that the lack of a best friendship, whether at a given point in time or chronically, can be accompanied by numerous risks. Friendless children are more likely to be lonely and victimized by peers (e.g., Brendgen, Vitaro, & Bukowski, 2000). Chronic friendlessness during childhood has been associated contemporaneously with social timidity, sensitivity, and the lack of social skills (Parker & Seal, 1996; Wojslawowicz Bowker et al., 2006), and predictively with subsequent internalizing problems (Ladd & Troop-Gordon, 2003).

Friendship dissolution may have a serious impact on children's adjustment. Disruptions of close peer relationships have been associated with depression, loneliness, guilt, and anger (e.g., Laursen et al., 1996; Parker & Seal, 1996). In addition, friendship loss in early adolescence may be particularly painful, due to the special role of friends' loyalty during this developmental period (Buhrmester & Furman, 1987). Wojslawowicz Bowker et al. (2006) reported that 10- and 11-year-old children who had a best friend at the beginning of the school year but who lost that friendship and failed to replace it by the end of the school year were at increased risk for victimization by peers. Thus, it may be that if a dissolved best friendship is not replaced, the "advantages" of once having a best friend may quickly vanish.

Individual child characteristics are also related to the prevalence of friendship and the quality of their dyadic relationships with peers. Given that many rejected children appear to be aggressive and/or withdrawn, it is surprising to note that few investigators have examined the friendships of these children. Not all aggressive and withdrawn children and certainly not all rejected children experience later adjustment difficulties. Thus, the best friendships of these children may function protectively and buffer them from later problems. Alternately, some best friendships may actually serve to exacerbate existing problems. An example of the protective role that friendship may play for children who have difficulties in the peer group may be drawn from research by Hodges, Boivin, Vitaro, and Bukowski (1999). These researchers found that peer victimization predicted increases in internalizing and externalizing difficulties during the school year for those children who lacked a mutual best friendship. The relation between peer victimization, internalizing, and externalizing problems was nonsignificant for children who possessed a mutual best friendship, thereby suggesting that friendship may function protectively for children who are victimized by their peers.

We now compare the friendships of those children who appear at greatest risk for peer rejection (i.e., those who have been identified as aggressive or socially withdrawn) with their age-mates who have do not evidence such behavioral or psychological difficulties.

Friendship Prevalence and Quality

Investigators have shown that the majority of aggressive children have a mutual best friendship and are as likely as well-adjusted children to have mutual friends (e.g., Vitaro, Brendgen, & Tremblay, 2000). Aggression, however, does seem to be negatively related to friendship stability (e.g., Hektner et al., 2000). Moreover, aggressive children have friends who are more aggressive and their relationships are more confrontational and antisocial in quality (e.g., Dishion, Eddy, Haas, Li, & Spracklen, 1997). High levels of relational aggression (e.g., threatening friendship withdrawal) within the friendship, and high levels of exclusivity/jealously, and intimacy characterize the friendships of relationally aggressive children. In contrast, overtly aggressive children direct their overt aggression outside their friendship dyads, and report low levels of intimacy (Grotpeter & Crick, 1996).

The prevalence of best friendships among young socially withdrawn children is not significantly different from that among nonwithdrawn children (Ladd & Burgess, 1999), and approximately 60% of withdrawn 8-, 9-, and 10-year-olds have reciprocated, stable friendships (e.g., Rubin et al., 2006). These data suggest that social withdrawal and shyness are individual characteristics that do not influence the formation, prevalence, and maintenance of friendship in childhood. In terms of relationship quality, however, it has been shown that the friendships of withdrawn children are viewed as relatively lacking in fun, intimacy, helpfulness and guidance, and validation and caring (Rubin et al., 2006). These findings suggest a "misery loves company" scenario for withdrawn children and their best friends. We may conjure up images of victimized friends coping poorly in the world of peers, images reflected in media accounts of peer victimization and its untimely consequences.

There is some evidence to suggest that socially withdrawn children are more likely than their age-mates to be chronically friendless. In a summer camp study conducted by Parker and Seal (1996), chronically friendless children were rated by their peers to be more shy and timid, to spend more time playing alone, and to be more sensitive than children who possessed a mutual best friendship during the summer camp program. Additionally, counselors rated these friendless children as less mature, less socially skilled, and as displaying more withdrawn and anxious behaviors than children with friends.

DISTAL PREDICTORS OF CHILDREN'S SOCIAL SKILLS AND PEER RELATIONSHIPS

The quality of children's extrafamilial social lives is likely a product of factors internal and external to the child. Drawing from Hinde (1987), for example, it seems reasonable to suggest that such individual characteristics as biological or dispositional factors (e.g., temperament; self-regulatory mechanisms) may influence children's peer interactions and relationships. It is equally plausible that the interactions and relationships children experience with their parents are important.

Temperament

Temperament has been construed as constitutionally based individual differences in emotional, motoric, and attentional reactivity and the regulation thereof (Rothbart, Ellis, & Posner, 2004). Researchers who study temperament report that individuals differ not only in the ease with which positive and negative emotions may be aroused (emotionality) but also in the ease with which emotions, once aroused, can be regulated (Rothbart et al., 2004). In some respects, a better term for emotionality is reactivity because most research on the phenomenon is focused on the extent to which children react to situations or events with anger, irritability, or fear. And again, most contemporary researchers have been interested in the ways in which reactive responses can be self-regulated. Thus, researchers have centered on the effortful self-control of emotional, behavioral, and attentional processes (Sanson, Hemphill, & Smart, 2004).

The constructs of difficult temperament, activity level, inhibition, and sociability merit special attention in the study of peer interactions and relationships. Difficult temperament refers to the frequent and intense expression of negative affect (Thomas & Chess, 1977). Fussiness and irritability would be characteristic of a "difficult" infant or toddler. In reactivity/regulation terminology, the difficult child is one whose negative emotions are easily aroused and difficult to soothe or regulate. The highly active baby/toddler is one who is easily excited, motorically facile, and highly reactive. Inhibited infants/toddlers are timid, vigilant, and fearful when faced with novel social stimuli; like the other groups of children, their emotions are easily aroused and difficult to regulate. Finally, children who are outgoing and open in response to social novelty are described as sociable (Kagan, 1999).

Each of these temperamental characteristics is relatively stable, and each is related to particular constellations of social behaviors that we described earlier as characteristic of either popular or rejected children. Infants and toddlers who have been identified as having difficult and/or active temperament, or as emotionally reactive are more likely to behave in aggressive, impulsive ways in early childhood (e.g., Rubin, Burgess, Dwyer, & Hastings, 2003). Contemporaneous and predictive connections between negative emotionality and/or difficult temperament and children's aggressive and oppositional behavior have been discovered by researchers the world over (e.g., Russell, Hart, Robinson, & Olson, 2003). And, as we noted earlier, undercontrolled, impulsive, and aggressive behavior is associated contemporaneously and predictively with peer relationships characterized by rejection.

Similarly, behavioral inhibition, an individual trait identified in toddlerhood predicts the display of shyness and socially reticent behavior in early childhood (Rubin, Burgess, & Hastings, 2002). Shy, socially reticent children display less socially competent and prosocial behaviors, employ fewer positive coping strategies, and are more likely to develop anxiety problems than their nonreticent age-mates (e.g., Coplan, Rubin, Fox, Calkins, & Stewart, 1994). Moreover, reticence and social withdrawal predict peer rejection and victimization from as early as the preschool years (e.g., Gazelle & Ladd, 2003).

It has been suggested that dispositional characteristics related to emotion regulation may lay the basis for the emergence of children's social behaviors and relationships. For example, Rubin, Coplan, Fox, and Calkins (1995) have argued that the social consequences of emotion dysregulation vary in accord with the child's behavioral tendency to approach and interact with peers during free play. They found that sociable children whose approach behaviors lacked regulatory control were disruptive and aggressive; those who were sociable but able to regulate their emotions were socially competent. Unsociable children who were good emotion regulators appeared to suffer no ill effects from their lack of social behavior. Yet, unsociable children who were poor emotion regulators were more behaviorally anxious and wary and more reticent than constructive when playing alone. Thus, emotionally dysregulated preschoolers may behave in ways that will elicit peer rejection and inhibit the development of qualitatively adaptive friendships. Further, this is the case for emotionally dysregulated sociable as well as unsociable children (see also Eisenberg, Cumberland, et al., 2001; Fabes, Hanish, Martin, & Eisenberg, 2002). Relatedly, researchers have found that the abilities to regulate negative emotions and to inhibit the expression of undesirable affect and behavior (regulatory control) are associated with, and predictive of, social competence and peer acceptance (e.g., Eisenberg, Pidada, & Liew, 2001), findings that are consistent across cultures (e.g., Zhou, Eisenberg, Wang, & Reiser, 2004).

It is important to note that very little is known about the associations between temperament and aspects of friendship. When compared to highly emotional children, some findings indicate that sociable children have more positive relationships with friends (e.g., Pike & Atzaba-Poria, 2003). Dunn and Cutting (1999), in a study of young children, found that negative emotionality was associated with the observed frequency of failed social bids and with less amity directed to the best friend; as a counterpoint, children showed less amity to friends who were inhibited or shy.

Parent-Child Attachment Relationship

A basic premise of attachment theory is that the early mother-infant relationship lays the groundwork for children's understanding of, and participation in, subsequent extrafamilial relationships. And, since the quality of attachment relationships with the mother may vary, subsequent social success and relationships with peers is expected to vary as well. For a thorough review of attachment theory in relation to peer relationships, see Rubin and Burgess (2002).

Studies of attachment and peer relationships have demonstrated that securely attached infants are more likely than their insecure counterparts to demonstrate socially competent behaviors amongst peers during the toddler (e.g., Pastor, 1981), preschool (e.g., Booth, Rose-Krasnor, & Rubin, 1991), and elementary school periods (e.g., Elicker, Englund, & Sroufe, 1992). Insecure babies, especially those classified as avoidant, later exhibit more hostility, anger, and aggressive behavior in preschool settings than their secure counterparts (e.g., Burgess, Marshall, Rubin, & Fox, 2003). Insecure-ambivalent infants are more easily frustrated, and socially inhibited at 2 years than their secure age-mates (e.g., Fox & Calkins, 1993). Finally, evidence that disorganized/disoriented attachment status in infancy predicts the subsequent display of aggression amongst preschool and elementary school peers derives from several sources (e.g., Lyons-Ruth, Easterbrooks, & Cibelli, 1997).

It is also the case that secure and insecure attachments, as assessed in early and middle childhood, as well as in early adolescence are associated contemporaneously with and predictive of adaptive and maladaptive social behaviors respectively. For example, children who experience a secure relationship with their mothers (and fathers) have been found to be more sociable and competent than their insecure counterparts, whilst insecure children exhibit more aggression and withdrawal (Allen, Moore, Kuperminc, & Bell, 1998; Rose-Krasnor, Rubin, Booth, & Coplan, 1996).

If the quality of the attachment relationship is associated with, and predictive of, patterns of social interaction, it seems logical to propose a relation between attachment status and the child's standing in the peer group. In a meta-analysis of the extant literature on links between attachment and peer acceptance, Schneider, Atkinson, and Tardif (2001) found a small-to-moderate effect size between these domains. Importantly however, these researchers found a larger effect size linking attachment security with friendship than with peer relationships more generally. Booth, Rubin, Rose-Krasnor, and Burgess (2004), argue that although associations between attachment security and social competence and peer acceptance are theoretically meaningful, there is an even more compelling rationale for the link between attachment security and friendship. From attachment theory, one would expect that the trust and intimacy characterizing secure child-parent relationships should produce an internalized model of relationship expectations that affects the quality of relationships with friends. In support, secure parent-child attachment in late childhood and early adolescence is associated positively (and contemporaneously) with positive qualities of children's close peer relationships (Lieberman, Doyle, & Markiewicz, 1999).

Parental Beliefs and Children's Social Behaviors and Peer Relationships

Parents' ideas, beliefs, and perceptions about the development and maintenance of children's social behaviors and relationships predict, and presumably partially explain the development of socially adaptive and maladaptive interactive behaviors and peer relationships in childhood. This is true because parents' child-rearing practices represent a behavioral expression of their ideas about how children become socially competent, how family contexts should be structured to shape children's behaviors, and how and when children should be taught to initiate and maintain relationships with others (Bugental & Happaney, 2002). These ideas about child rearing and about what is acceptable and unacceptable child behavior in the social world are culturally determined. Extended discussions of such cultural determination may be found in Rubin and Chung (2006).

Investigators have shown that parents of socially competent children believe that, in early childhood, they should play an active role in the socialization of social skills via teaching and providing peer interaction opportunities (Rubin, Mills, & Rose-Krasnor, 1989). They believe also that when their children display maladaptive behaviors, it is due to transitory and situationally caused circumstances. Parents whose preschoolers display socially incompetent behaviors, alternatively, are less likely to endorse strong beliefs in the development of social skills. Furthermore, they are more likely to attribute the development of social competence to internal factors, to believe that incompetent behavior is difficult to alter, and to believe that interpersonal skills are best taught through direct instructional means.

Child as Parental Belief Evocateur

There is growing evidence that parental beliefs may be evoked by child characteristics and behavior, and that parental beliefs and child characteristics influence each other in a reciprocal manner (Bornstein, 2002). For example, in the case of aggressive children, any hostile behavior, whether directed at peers, siblings, or parents may evoke (a) strong parental feelings of anger and frustration (Eisenberg, Gershoff, et al., 2001) and (b) biased attributions that "blame" the child's noxious behavior on traits, intentions, and motives internal to the child (e.g., Strassberg, 1995). These parental cognitions and emotions, predict the use of power assertive and restrictive disciplinary techniques (Coplan, Hastings, Lagace-Seguin, & Moulton, 2002). This type of low warmth-high control parental response, mediated by affect and beliefs/cognitions about the intentionality of the child behavior, the historical precedence of child aggression, and the best means to control child aggression, is likely to evoke negative affect and cognitions in the child. The result of this interplay between parent and child beliefs, affects, and behavior may be the reinforcement and extension of family cycles of hostility (e.g., Granic & Lamey, 2002).

Parental reactions to social wariness and fearfulness are less well understood. Researchers have found that when children produce a high frequency of socially wary, withdrawn behaviors their parents (a) recognize this as a problem; (b) express feelings of concern, sympathy, guilt, embarrassment, and, with increasing child age, a growing sense of frustration; and (c) are more inclined than parents of nonwary children to attribute their children's social reticence to dispositional traits (Hastings & Rubin, 1999). Perhaps in an attempt to regulate their own expressed guilt and embarrassment emanating from their children's ineffectual behaviors, mothers of socially withdrawn preschoolers indicate that they would react to their children's displays of social withdrawal by providing them with protection and direct instruction (Mills & Rubin, 1998).

Parenting Behaviors, Children's Social Skills, and Peer Relationships

Parental discipline of unacceptable, maladaptive peer-directed behaviors has also been associated with their children's peer relationships. Parents (usually mothers) of unpopular and/or peer-rejected children use inept, intrusive, harsh, and authoritarian disciplinary and socialization practices more frequently than those of their more popular counterparts (e.g., McDowell & Parke, 2000). Alternately, parents of popular children use more feelings-oriented reasoning and induction, responsivity, warm control (authoritative), and positivity during communication than their unpopular counterparts (e.g., Mize & Pettit, 1997).

With regard to parenting behavior and children's socially incompetent behaviors, researchers have shown consistently that aggressive children have parents who model and inadvertently reinforce aggressive and impulsive behavior, and who are cold and rejecting, physically punitive, and inconsistent in their disciplinary behaviors. In addition to parental rejection and the use of high power-assertive and inconsistent disciplinary strategies, parental permissiveness, indulgence, and lack of supervision have often been found to correlate with children's aggressive behavior (see Rubin & Burgess, 2002 for a review). Importantly, these findings appear to have cross-cultural universality (e.g., Cheah & Rubin, 2004).

Research concerning the parenting behaviors and styles associated with social withdrawal focuses clearly on two potential socialization contributors—overcontrol and overprotection. Parents who use high power-assertive strategies and who place many constraints on their children tend to rear shy, reserved, and dependent children. Thus, the issuance of parental commands combined with constraints on exploration and independence may hinder the development of competence and deprive the child of opportunities to interact with peers. It should not be surprising that children who are socially withdrawn are on the receiving end of parental overcontrol and overprotection (e.g., Rubin et al., 2002). These findings concerning parental overcontrol and restriction stem from very few studies, most of which center on young children. Furthermore, the contexts in which parents of socially withdrawn children display overcontrol and overprotection have not been well specified.

Parenting Behaviors and Children's Social Competence: A Model

There is some support for the contention that parental behavior is associated, not only with the development of children's social competence, but also with their peer relationships. The assumption has been that parenting leads to social competence or incompetence, which in turn leads to peer acceptance or rejection. This causal model has been tested in a number of studies.

Dishion (1990) examined the relations among grade-school boys' sociometric status, academic skills, antisocial behavior, and several elements of parental discipline practices and family circumstances. Causal modeling suggested that the relation between inept parenting and peer rejection was mediated by boys' antisocial behavior and academic difficulties: Lower levels of parental skill were associated with higher levels of antisocial behavior and lower levels of academic performance; antisocial behavior and poor academic performance, in turn, were associated with higher levels of peer rejection. These findings have been replicated and extended in a similar study conducted in the People's Republic of China (X. Chen & Rubin, 1994).

There is also the possibility that the link between parenting and child outcomes of an adaptive or maladaptive nature can be attenuated by the quality of the child's status in the peer group or the quality of his or her friendships. For example, the longitudinal relation between harsh parenting and negative outcomes of an externalizing nature is augmented when children have poor peer relationships (e.g., Lansford, Criss, Pettit, Dodge,

& Bates, 2003). Research findings also indicate that an insecure attachment relationship may predict difficulties of an externalizing or internalizing nature, but only for those children or young adolescents who lack friendship or qualitatively rich friendship (e.g., Rubin et al., 2004). Thus, in recent models pertaining to the links between parenting and adaptive or maladaptive outcome, it appears as if, by middle to late childhood, children's friendships may buffer or exacerbate the statistical associations.

Childhood Peer Experiences and Later Adjustment

Our goal, in this section, is to provide a summary of research in which the primary focus has been to identify aspects of childhood peer relationship experiences at the dyadic and group levels that predict subsequent adaptation and maladaptation. Here, we focus only on studies in which prospective, follow-forward designs have been employed. A lengthy overview of retrospective studies may be found in Rubin, Bukowski, and Parker (1998).

ACADEMIC ADJUSTMENT

It has been shown that adjustment to school derives from several aspects of children's relationships with peers. Wentzel and Asher (1995) found that popular children were viewed as helpful, good students. Rejected/aggressive students, relative to average and rejected/submissive children, showed little interest in school, were perceived by teachers as dependent, and were seen by peers and teachers as inconsiderate, noncompliant, and prone to causing trouble in school. These findings were consistent with longitudinal findings reported by Ollendick, Weist, Borden, and Greene (1992) who showed that children who were actively disliked by their peers were anywhere from two to seven times more likely to fail a subsequent grade than better accepted children. Similarly, higher levels of rejection predict later grade retention and poorer adjustment after the transition to middle school (Coie, Lochman, Terry, & Hyman, 1992). Given these longitudinal connections between peer rejection and later poor school performance, it is not surprising to learn that children who have troubled relationships with their peers are more likely to drop out of school than are other children (Ollendick et al., 1992).

Factors other than peer rejection appear to be important also. Most notably friendships appear to influence school adjustment. For example, children typically associate with peers who had a motivational orientation similar to their own (Kindermann, 1993). Adolescents who drop out of school are more likely than other students to have associated with peers who do not regard school as useful and important (Hymel, Comfort, Schonert-Reichl, & McDougall, 2002). These findings are important because they show that friendships via peer group norms can influence academic adjustment.

In two studies, the effect of early adolescent friendship was demonstrated clearly and in richer ways than seen previously. Berndt, Hawkins, and Jiao (1999) showed that adjustment to junior high school was facilitated by engagement in friendships that were stable and of high quality (e.g., rated as high in closeness and support). Wentzel, McNamara-Barry, and Caldwell (2004) also examined friendship and the adjustment to a junior high school. They showed that friendless children were lower in prosocial behavior and higher in affective distress both concurrently and 2 years later. They noted that friends' characteristics can act as a form of social motivation that can either increase or decrease an early adolescent's adjustment to school.

Similar friendship factors seem to be important with younger children also. Children with many friends at the time of elementary school entry develop more favorable attitudes toward school in the early months than children with fewer friends (Ladd, 1990, 1991; Ladd, Kochenderfer, & Coleman, 1996, 1997). Those who maintained their friendships also liked school better as the year went by. Findings also revealed positive associations between children's perceptions of best friendship quality in kindergarten and later indices of scholastic adjustment (school-related affect, perceptions, involvement, and performance) in grade school.

PSYCHOLOGICAL ADJUSTMENT

Externalizing Problems

Results of longitudinal studies have indicated that peer rejection in childhood predicts a wide range of externalizing problems in adolescence, including delinquency, conduct disorder, attention difficulties, and substance abuse (e.g., Ollendick et al., 1992). These findings are not particularly surprising given the well-established link between aggression and peer rejection, and especially given that aggressive-rejected children are more likely to remain rejected over time. Importantly, research has shown that early peer rejection provides a unique increment in the prediction later antisocial outcomes, even when controlling for previous levels of aggression and externalizing problems (e.g., Laird, Jordan, Dodge, Pettit, & Bates, 2001; Miller-Johnson, Coie, Maumary-Gremaud, Bierman, & Conduct Problems Prevention Research, 2002).

Given the less than perfect stability of rejected status, it would seem reasonable to ask whether psychological risk status is equivalent for children with chronic versus episodic and transient rejection by peers. To address this question, Miller-Johnson et al. (2002) showed that peer rejection in first grade added incrementally to the prediction of early starting conduct problems in third and fourth grades, over and above the effects of aggression. Similarly, Dodge and colleagues (2003) reported that peer rejection predicted longitudinal "growth" in aggression over time from early to middle childhood, and from middle childhood to adolescence. These researchers also found a developmental pathway in which peer rejection led to more negative information processing patterns (i.e., hostile cue interpretation), which led to increased aggression. Certainly part of the association between rejection and externalizing involves the network of peer involvement experiences by rejected children. Rejected children were more likely than other boys and girls to associate with delinquent peers and these associations accounted for their subsequent delinquency (Brendgen, Vitaro, & Bukowski, 1998). Consistent with expectations related to the process of deviancy training, at-risk children, especially boys, who have aggressive friends appear to influence each other with reinforcements and enticements (Bagwell & Coie, 2004), which increase each other's aggression. These mechanisms also appear to account for the development of substance abuse problems (e.g., Dishion, Capaldi, & Yoerger, 1999).

Internalizing Problems

Results from a growing number of studies have indicated that anxious-withdrawal is contemporaneously and predictively associated with internalizing problems during the life span, including low self-esteem, anxiety problems, loneliness, and depressive symptoms (e.g., Coplan, Prakash, O'Neil, & Armer, 2004). In a longitudinal study from kindergarten (age 5 years) to the ninth grade (age 14 years), Rubin and colleagues reported that withdrawal in kindergarten and second grade predicted peer rejection, self-reported feelings of depression, loneliness, and negative self-worth and teacher ratings of anxiety in the fifth grade (Hymel, Rubin, Rowden, & LeMare, 1990; Rubin & Mills, 1988). In turn, social withdrawal in the fifth grade predicted self-reports of loneliness, depression, negative self-evaluations of social competence, the lack of perceived peer social support, and parental assessments of internalizing problems in the ninth grade (Rubin, Chen, McDougall, Bowker, & McKinnon, 1995).

Researchers have also begun to explore the unique role of peer rejection in the prediction of internalizing problems. For example, Kraatz-Keily, Bates, Dodge, and Pettit (2000) reported that peer rejection predicted increases in both internalizing and externalizing problems from kindergarten to seventh grade. Children's self-perceived rejection has been associated with increases in internalizing problems over time (e.g., Kistner, Balthazor, Risi, & Burton, 1999). Relatedly, Gazelle and Ladd (2003) found that shy-anxious kindergarteners who were also excluded by peers displayed a greater stability in anxious solitude through the fourth grade and had elevated levels of depressive symptoms as compared to shy-anxious peers who did not experience peer exclusion. Further, Gazelle and Rudolph (2004) found that in the fifth and sixth grades, high exclusion by peers led anxious solitary youth to maintenance or exacerbate the extent of social avoidance and depression; increased social approach and less depression resulted from the experience of low exclusion.

The majority of the research regarding friendship and subsequent internalizing problems has considered the effects of friendship as either a moderator or as a mediator. In addition to the previously described study by Hodges, Boivin, et al. (1999), Rubin et al. (2004) demonstrated that when 10- to 11-year-olds reported difficulties in their relationships with their mothers and fathers, having a strong supportive best friendship buffered them from negative self-perceptions and internalizing problems.

The notion that friendship may buffer rejected children from negative outcomes has been examined in a number of studies. However, the findings in these studies have been somewhat counterintuitive. For example, Hoza, Molina, Bukowski, and Sippola (1995) and Kupersmidt, Burchinal, and Patterson (1995) reported that having a best friend actually augmented negative outcomes for children who were earlier identified as rejected and aggressive. One explanation for these findings emanates from findings indicating that the friendship networks of aggressive-rejected children comprise other aggressive children; the existence of a friendship network supportive of maladjusted behavior may actually exacerbate the prospects of a negative developmental outcome for rejected children (e.g., Cairns, Gariepy, & Kindermann, 1989).

Conclusions

In this chapter, we examined the remarkable progress that has been made in describing and explaining the features, processes, and effects of children's experiences with their age-mates. A consequence of this progress is that peer research must now answer new questions and deal with new challenges. An additional repercussion of our progress is that the gaps in our understanding of the peer system become clear. We address these concerns in this concluding section. Specifically, we identify two current challenges and opportunities for peer research, and we identify two topics that deserve more attention than they have received in the past.

TWO CRITICAL CHALLENGES

First, we propose that the efforts to study peer relationships as a system need to be continued and intensified. The study of peer relationships has been frequently predicated on the concept that peer relationships, however construed, must be viewed as either an antecedent or consequence. Consistent with the view that development is a dynamic, multidirectional process (Sameroff & MacKenzie, 2003), the study of peer relationships needs to be understood as a complex system. Children bring various behaviors, needs, and cognitions into their peer experiences at the dyadic and group level. In turn, these individual characteristics affect the features of these experiences and the provisions that children derive from these experiences leading to changes, for better or worse, in the child's subsequent short-term and long-term functioning. Although the study of transactional models of development has been aided by the evolution of statistical procedures (e.g., structural equation modeling, growth curve analyses, hierarchical linear modeling), the number of investigations incorporating these models and techniques remains lower than one might expect.

Second, the features and effects of experiences with peers need to be understood according to the larger systems in which they are embedded and according to how they interface with other systems. Opportunities for peer interaction and relationships vary from one culture to another and different cultures ascribe different degrees of significance to them. The "content" of peer interactions and relationships is likely to vary, for example, as a function of how much power is ascribed to kinship structures and by who makes primary decisions about allowable extrafamilial relationships. Because the defining features or characteristics of what it means to be adapted to one's social context will differ across contexts, the impact on adaptation of particular characteristics of peer relationships is likely to vary also. Finally, in a culture, the effect of the peer system is likely to vary according to differences between children in provisions they obtain in their families.

TWO QUESTIONS IN SEARCH OF ANSWERS

In spite of its diversity and breadth, at least two fundamental aspects of peer interactions, relationships, and groups are nearly absent from our review. First, what aspects of peer interactions, relationships, and groups affect boys and girls differently? The study of sex differences is covered sporadically throughout this chapter. There are many exemplary studies of how peer interactions and relationships differ for boys and for girls. A central gap in the literature is the understanding of whether some aspects of peer interactions and relationships affect boys and girls differently. This question is not about whether there are differences between the features of peer interactions and relationships of boys and girls. Instead, it is concerned with potential differences in the functions and the developmental significance of peer experiences for boys and girls. Knowing if and how the peer system works differently for boys and girls would certainly add to our understanding of peer relationships; it would augment our understanding of sexual differentiation as well.

Second, what are the provisions of peer relationships? Friendship, acceptance, and popularity have been studied extensively. We know how to measure these constructs, and we know a good deal about their antecedents and their consequences. Yet, we know little about what it is that children and adolescents "get" from these relationships. To be sure there have been theoretical propositions about why friendship is important and how acceptance and rejection can influence child and adolescent development. But there have been few studies of the specific opportunities and experiences that are afforded by friendship, acceptance, and popularity. And there have been fewer studies of the significance of friendship and/or peer acceptance and rejection for children who vary with regard to sex, ethnicity, and behavioral characteristics. Certainly, the role of culture remains to be fully explored. This question is not simply one of description. Research on friendship, for example, is based on claims about the putative provisions of this relationship. Similar comments can be offered about acceptance and, to a lesser extent, popularity. Further inquiries into what these experiences provide for children would help us better understand the value of the theories we have relied on.

References

Abecassis, M., Hartup, W. W., Haselager, G. J. T., Scholte, R. H. J., & van Lieshout, C. F. M. (2002). Mutual antipathies and their significance in middle childhood and adolescence. *Child Development, 73,* 1543–1556.

Allen, J. D., Moore, C., Kuperminc, G., & Bell, K. (1998). Attachment and adolescent psychosocial functioning. *Child Development, 69,* 1406–1419.

Altermatt, E. R., & Pomerantz, E. M. (2003). The development of competence-related and motivational beliefs: An investigation of similarity and influence among friends. *Journal of Educational Psychology, 95,* 111–123.

Bagwell, C. L., & Coie, J. D. (2004). The best friendships of aggressive boys: Relationship quality, conflict management, and rule-breaking behavior. *Journal of Experimental Child Psychology, 88*(1), 5–24.

Bagwell, C. L., Coie, J. D., Terry, R. A., & Lochman, J. E. (2000). Peer clique participation and social status in preadolescence. *Merrill-Palmer Quarterly, 46,* 280–305.

Belsky, J., & Cassidy, J. (1995). Attachment: Theory and evidence. In M. Rutter, D. Hay, & S. Baron-Cohen (Eds.), *Developmental principles and clinical issues in psychology and psychiatry.* Oxford, England: Blackwell.

Benenson, J. F., Apostoleris, N. H., & Parnass, J. (1997). Age and sex differences in dyadic and group interaction. *Developmental Psychology, 33,* 538–543.

Benenson, J. F., & Christakos, A. (2003). The greater fragility of female's versus male's closest same-sex friendships. *Child Development, 74,* 1123–1129.

Benenson, J. F., Markovits, H., Roy, R., & Denko, P. (2003). Behavioural rules underlying learning to share: Effects of development and context. *International Journal of Behavioural Development, 27,* 116–121.

Berndt, T. J., Hawkins, J. A., & Hoyle, S. G. (1986). Changes in friendship during a school year: Effects on children's and adolescents' impressions of friendship and sharing with friends. *Child Development, 57,* 1284–1297.

Berndt, T. J., Hawkins, J. A., & Jiao, Z. (1999). Influences of friends and friendships on adjustment to junior high school. *Merrill-Palmer Quarterly, 45,* 13–41.

Berndt, T. J., & Hoyle, S. G. (1985). Stability and change in childhood and adolescent friendships. *Developmental Psychology, 21,* 1007–1015.

Bigelow, B. J. (1977). Children's friendship expectations: A cognitive developmental study. *Child Development, 48,* 246–253.

Boivin, M., Dodge, K. A., & Coie, J. D. (1995). Individual-group behavioral similarity and peer status in experimental play groups of boys: The social misfit revisited. *Journal of Personality and Social Psychology, 69,* 269–279.

Booth, C. L., Rose-Krasnor, L., & Rubin, K. H. (1991). Relating preschoolers' social competence and their mothers' parenting behaviors to early attachment security and high-risk status. *Journal of Social and Personal Relationships, 8,* 363–382.

Booth, C. L., Rubin, K. H., Rose-Krasnor, L., & Burgess, K. (2004). Attachment and friendship predictors of psychosocial functioning in middle childhood and the mediating roles of social support and self-worth. In

K. Kerns & R. A. Richardson (Eds.), *Attachment in middle childhood* (pp. 161–188). New York: Guilford Press.

Bornstein, M. H. (2002). Parenting infants. In M. H. Bornstein (Ed.), *Handbook of parenting: Vol. 1. Children and parenting* (2nd ed., pp. 3–43). Mahwah, NJ: Erlbaum.

Bornstein, M. H., & Cheah, C. S. L. (2006). The place of "culture and parenting" in the ecological contextual perspective on developmental science. In K. H. Rubin & O. Boon Chung (Eds.), *Parental beliefs, parenting, and child development in cross-cultural perspective.* London: Psychology Press.

Brendgen, M., Bowen, F., Rondeau, N., & Vitaro, F. (1999). Effects of friends' characteristics on children's social cognitions. *Social Development, 8,* 41–51.

Brendgen, M., Vitaro, F., & Bukowski, W. M. (1998). Affiliation with delinquent friends: Contributions of parents, self-esteem, delinquent behavior, and rejection by peers. *Journal of Early Adolescence, 18*(3), 244–265.

Brendgen, M., Vitaro, F., & Bukowski, W. M. (2000). Deviant friends and early adolescents' emotional and behavioral adjustment. *Journal of Research on Adolescence, 10*(2), 173–189.

Brendgen, M., Vitaro, F., Doyle, A. B., Markiewicz, D., & Bukowski, W. M. (2002). Same-sex peer relations and romantic relationships during early adolescence: Interactive links to emotional, behavioral, and academic adjustment. *Merrill-Palmer Quarterly, 48,* 77–103.

Brown, B. B. (1989). The role of peer groups in adolescents' adjustment to secondary school. In T. J. Berndt & G. W. Ladd (Eds.), *Peer relationships in child development* (pp. 188–216). New York: Wiley.

Brown, B. B., & Klute, C. (2003). Friends, cliques, and crowds. In G. R. Adams & M. D. Berzonsky (Eds.), *Blackwell handbook of adolescence* (pp. 330–348). Malden, MA: Blackwell.

Bugental, D., & Happaney, K. (2002). Parental attributions. In M. Bornstein (Ed.), *Handbook of parenting: Vol. 3. Being and becoming a parent* (2nd ed., pp. 509–535). Mahwah, NJ: Erlbaum.

Buhrmester, D., & Furman, W. (1987). The development of companionship and intimacy. *Child Development, 58,* 1101–1103.

Bukowski, W. M., Rubin, K. H., & Parker, J. (2001). Social competence. In N. J. Smelser, P. B. Baltes, & N. Eisenberg (Eds.), *International encyclopedia of social and behavioral sciences* (pp. 14258–14264). Oxford, England: Elsevier Science.

Bukowski, W. M., & Sippola, L. K. (2001). Groups, individuals, and victimization: A view of the peer system. In J. Juvonen & S. Graham (Eds.), *Peer harassment in school: The plight of the vulnerable and victimized* (pp. 355–377). New York: Guilford Press.

Burgess, K. B., Marshall, P., Rubin, K. H., & Fox, N. A. (2003). Infant attachment and temperament as predictors of subsequent behavior problems and psychophysiological functioning. *Journal of Child Psychology and Psychiatry and Allied Disciplines, 44,* 1–13.

Cairns, R. B., Gariepy, J. L., & Kindermann, T. (1989). *Identifying social clusters in natural settings.* Unpublished manuscript, University of North Carolina at Chapel Hill, Social Development Laboratory.

Carver, K., Joyner, K., & Udry, J. R. (2003). National estimates of adolescent romantic relationships. In P. Florsheim (Ed.), *Adolescent romantic relations and sexual behavior: Theory, research, and practical implications* (pp. 23–56). Mahwah, NJ: Erlbaum.

Chang, L., Lei, L., Li, K., Liu, H., Guo, B., Wang, Y., et al. (2005). Peer acceptance and self perceptions of verbal and behavioral aggression and social withdrawal. *International Journal of Behavioral Development, 29,* 48–57.

Cheah, C. S. L., & Rubin, K. H. (2004). A cross-cultural examination of maternal beliefs regarding maladaptive behaviors in preschoolers. *International Journal of Behavioral Development, 28,* 83–94.

Chen, D. W., Fein, G., & Tam, H. P. (2001). Peer conflicts of preschool children: Issues, resolution, incidence, and age-related patterns. *Early Education and Development, 12,* 523–544.

Chen, X., Cen, G., Li, D., & He, Y. (2005). Social functioning and adjustment in Chinese children: The imprint of historical time. *Child Development, 76,* 182–195.

Chen, X., Chang, L., & He, Y. (2003). The peer group as a context: Mediating and moderating effects on the relations between academic achievement and social functioning in Chinese children. *Child Development, 74,* 710–727.

Chen, X., & Rubin, K. H. (1994). Family conditions, parental acceptance, and social competence and aggression in Chinese children. *Social Development, 3,* 269–290.

Chen, X., Rubin, K. H., & Sun, Y. (1992). Social reputation and peer relationships in Chinese and Canadian children: A cross-cultural study. *Child Development, 63,* 1336–1343.

Cillessen, A. H., & Mayeux, L. (2004). From censure to reinforcement: Developmental changes in the association between aggression and social status. *Child Development, 75,* 147–163.

Cillessen, A. H., van IJzendoorn, H. W., van Lieshout, C. F., & Hartup, W. W. (1992). Heterogeneity among peer-rejected boys: Subtypes and stabilities. *Child Development, 63,* 893–905.

Coie, J. D., & Kupersmidt, J. (1983). A behavioral analysis of emerging social status in boys' groups. *Child Development, 54,* 1400–1416.

Coie, J. D., Lochman, J. E., Terry, R., & Hyman, C. (1992). Predicting early adolescent disorder from childhood aggression and peer rejection. *Journal of Consulting and Clinical Psychology, 60,* 783–792.

Connolly, J., Craig, W., Goldberg, A., & Pepler, D. (2004). Mixed-gender groups, dating, and romantic relationships in early adolescence. *Journal of Research on Adolescence, 14,* 185–207.

Connolly, J., Furman, W., & Konarski, R. (2000). The role of peers in the emergence of heterosexual romantic relationships in adolescence. *Child Development, 71*(5), 1395–1408.

Coplan, R. J., Hastings, P. D., Lagace-Seguin, D. G., & Moulton, C. E. (2002). Authoritative and authoritarian mothers' parenting goals, attributions, and emotions across different childrearing contexts. *Parenting: Science and Practice, 2,* 1–26.

Coplan, R. J., Prakash, K., O'Neil, K., & Armer, M. (2004). Do you "want" to play? Distinguishing between conflicted shyness and social disinterest in early childhood. *Developmental Psychology, 40*(2), 244–258.

Coplan, R. J., Rubin, K. H., Fox, N. A., Calkins, S., & Stewart, S. L. (1994). Being alone, playing alone, and acting alone: Distinguishing between reticence and passive- and active-solitude in young children. *Child Development, 65,* 129–138.

Crick, N. R., & Dodge, K. A. (1994). A review and reformulation of social information processing in children's social adjustment. *Psychological Bulletin, 115,* 74–101.

Crick, N. R., & Grotpeter, J. K. (1995). Relational aggression, gender, and social-psychological adjustment. *Child Development, 66,* 710–722.

Crick, N. R., & Ladd, G. W. (1993). Children's perceptions of their peer experiences: Attributions, loneliness, social anxiety, and social avoidance. *Development Psychology, 29,* 244–254.

Csikszentmihalyi, M., & Larson, R. (1984). *Being adolescent.* New York: Basic Books.

Denton, K., & Zarbatany, L. (1996). Age differences in support processes in conversations between friends. *Child Development, 67,* 1360–1373.

Dishion, T. J. (1990). The family ecology of boys' peer relations in middle childhood. *Child Development, 61,* 874–892.

Dishion, T. J., Capaldi, D. M., & Yoerger, K. (1999). Middle childhood antecedents to progressions in male adolescent substance use: An ecological analysis of risk and protection. *Journal of Adolescent Research, 14*(2), 175–205.

Dishion, T. J., Eddy, M., Haas, E., Li, F., & Spracklen, K. (1997). Friendships and violent behavior during adolescence. *Social Development, 6*(2), 207–223.

Dishion, T. J., McCord, J., & Poulin, F. (1999). When interventions harm: Peer groups and problem behavior. *American Psychologist, 54*(9), 755–764.

Dodge, K. A. (1983). Behavioral antecedents of peer social status. *Child Development, 54,* 1386–1399.

Dodge, K. A., Coie, J. D., & Lynam, D. (2006). Aggression and antisocial behavior. In W. Damon & R. M. Lerner (Series Eds.) & N. Eisenberg (Vol. Ed.), *Handbook of child psychology: Vol. 3. Social, emotional, and personality development* (6th ed., pp. 719–788). Hoboken, NJ: Wiley.

Dodge, K. A., Lansford, J. E., Burks, V. S., Bates, J. E., Pettit, G. S., Fontaine, R., et al. (2003). Peer rejection and social information-processing factors in the development of aggressive behavior problems in children. *Child Development, 74*(2), 374–393.

Dodge, K. A., McClaskey, C. L., & Feldman, E. (1985). A situational approach to the assessment of social competence in children. *Journal of Consulting and Clinical Psychology, 53,* 344–353.

Dunn, J. (1993). *Young children's close relationships: Beyond attachment.* London: Sage.

Dunn, J., & Cutting, A. (1999). Understanding others and individual differences in friendship interactions in young children. *Social Development, 8,* 201–219.

Eisenberg, N., Cumberland, A., Spinrad, T. L., Shepard, S. A., Reiser, M., Murphy, B. C., et al. (2001). The relations of regulation and emotionality to children's externalizing and internalizing problem behavior. *Child Development, 72,* 1112–1134.

Eisenberg, N., Fabes, R. A., & Spinrad, T. L. (2006). Prosocial behavior. In W. Damon & R. M. Lerner (Series Eds.) & N. Eisenberg (Vol. Ed.), *Handbook of child psychology: Vol. 3. Social, emotional, and personality development* (6th ed., pp. 646–718). Hoboken, NJ: Wiley.

Eisenberg, N., Gershoff, E. T., Fabes, R. A., Shepard, S. A., Cumberland, A. J., Losoya, S. H., et al. (2001). Mothers' emotional expressivity and children's behavior problems and social competence: Mediation through children's regulation. *Developmental Psychology, 37,* 475–490.

Eisenberg, N., Pidada, S., & Liew, J. (2001). The relations of regulation and negative emotionality to Indonesian children's social functioning. *Child Development, 72,* 1747–1763.

Elicker, J., Englund, M., & Sroufe, L. A. (1992). Predicting peer competence and peer relationships in childhood from early parent-child relationships. In R. Parke & G. Ladd (Eds.), *Family-peer relationships: Modes of linkage* (pp. 77–106). Hillsdale, NJ: Erlbaum.

Espelage, D., Bosworth, K., & Simon, T. R. (2000). Examining the social context of bullying behaviors in early adolescence. *Journal of Counseling and Development, 78,* 326–333.

Espelage, D., Holt, M., & Henkel, R. (2003). Examination of peer-group contextual effects on aggression during early adolescence. *Child Development, 74,* 205–220.

Fabes, R. A., Hanish, L. D., Martin, C. L., & Eisenberg, N. (2002). Young children's negative emotionality and social isolation: A latent growth curve analysis. *Merrill-Palmer Quarterly, 48,* 284–307.

Farmer, T., Estell, D., Bishop, J., O'Neal, K., & Cairns, B. (2003). Rejected bullies or popular leaders? The social relations of aggressive subtypes of rural African American early adolescents. *Developmental Psychology, 39*(6), 992–1004.

Fox, N. A., & Calkins, S. D. (1993). Pathways to aggression and social withdrawal: Interactions among temperament, attachment, and regulation. In K. H. Rubin & J. Asendorpf (Eds.), *Social withdrawal, inhibition, and shyness in childhood* (pp. 81–100). Hillsdale, NJ: Erlbaum.

Furman, W., & Buhrmester, D. (1992). Age and sex differences in perceptions of networks and personal relationships. *Child Development, 63,* 103–115.

Furman, W., Simon, V. A., Shaffer, L., & Bouchey, H. A. (2002). Adolescents' working models and styles for relationships with parents, friends, and romantic partners. *Child Development, 73,* 241–255.

Gazelle, H., & Ladd, G. W. (2003). Anxious solitude and peer exclusion: A diathesis-stress model of internalizing trajectories in childhood. *Child Development, 74,* 257–278.

Gazelle, H., & Rudolph, K. D. (2004). Moving toward and moving away from the world: Social approach and avoidance trajectories in anxious youth. *Child Development, 75*(3), 829–849.

Gest, S. D., Farmer, T., Cairns, B., & Xie, H. (2003). Identifying children's peer social networks in school classrooms: Links between peer reports and observed interactions. *Social Development, 12*(4), 513–529.

Goncu, A. (1993). Development of intersubjectivity in the dyadic play of preschoolers. *Early Childhood Research Quarterly, 8,* 99–116.

Goncu, A., Patt, M. B., & Kouba, E. (2002). Understanding young children's pretend play in context. In P. K. Smith & C. H. Hart (Eds.), *Blackwell handbook of childhood social development* (pp. 418–437). Malden, MA: Blackwell.

Graham, S., & Juvonen, J. (1998). Self-blame and peer victimization in middle school: An attributional analysis. *Developmental Psychology, 34,* 587–599.

Granic, I., & Lamey, A. V. (2002). Combining dynamic systems and multivariate analyses to compare the mother-child interactions of externalizing subtypes. *Journal of Abnormal Child Psychology, 30,* 265–283.

Grotpeter, J. K., & Crick, N. R. (1996). Relational aggression, overt aggression, and friendship. *Child Development, 67,* 2328–2338.

Hanish, L. D., & Guerra, N. G. (2004). Aggressive victims, passive victims, and bullies: Developmental continuity or developmental change. *Merrill-Palmer Quarterly, 50,* 17–38.

Harkness, S., & Super, C. M. (2002). Culture and parenting. In M. H. Bornstein (Ed.), *Handbook of parenting: Vol. 2. Biology and ecology of parenting* (2nd ed., pp. 253–280). Mahwah, NJ: Erlbaum.

Hart, C. H., Yang, C., Nelson, L. J., Robinson, C. C., Olsen, J. A., Nelson, D., et al. (2000). Peer acceptance in early childhood and subtypes of socially withdrawn behavior in China, Russia, and the United States. *International Journal of Behavioral Development, 24,* 73–81.

Hartup, W. W., & Abecassis, M. (2002). Friends and enemies. In P. K. Smith & C. H. Hart (Eds.), *Blackwell handbook of childhood social development* (pp. 286–306). Malden, MA: Blackwell.

Hartup, W. W., Laursen, B., Stewart, M. A., & Eastenson, A. (1988). Conflicts and the friendship relations of young children. *Child Development, 59,* 1590–1600.

Haselager, G. J. T., Hartup, W. W., van Lieshout, C. F. M., & Riksen-Walraven, J. M. A. (1998). Similarities between friends and nonfriends in middle childhood. *Child Development, 69,* 1198–1208.

Hastings, P., & Rubin, K. H. (1999). Predicting mothers' beliefs about preschool-aged children's social behavior: Evidence for maternal attitudes moderating child effects. *Child Development, 70*(3), 722–741.

Hawley, P. H. (2003). Strategies of control, aggression and morality in preschoolers: An evolutionary perspective. *Journal of Experimental Child Psychology, 85*(3), 213–235.

Hay, D. F. (1985). Learning to form relationships in infancy: Parallel attainments with parents and peers. *Developmental Review, 5,* 122–161.

Hay, D. F., Castle, J., Davies, L., Demetriou, H., & Stimson, C. (1999). Prosocial action in very early childhood. *Journal of Child Psychology and Psychiatry, 40,* 905–916.

Hay, D. F., Nash, A., & Pedersen, J. (1983). Interaction between 6-month-old peers. *Child Development, 54,* 557–562.

Hay, D. F., & Ross, H. (1982). The social nature of early conflict. *Child Development, 53,* 105–113.

Hayes, D. S., Gershman, E., & Bolin, L. J. (1980). Friends and enemies: Cognitive bases for preschool children's unilateral and reciprocal friendships. *Child Development, 51,* 1276–1279.

Hays, R. B. (1988). Friendship. In S. W. Duck (Ed.), *Handbook of personal relationships: Theory, research, and interventions* (pp. 391–408). London: Wiley.

Hektner, J. M., August, G. J., & Realmuto, G. M. (2000). Patterns and temporal changes in peer affiliation among aggressive and nonaggressive children participating in a summer school program. *Journal of Clinical Child Psychology, 29*(4), 603–614.

Hinde, R. A. (1987). *Individuals, relationships and culture.* Cambridge: Cambridge University Press.

Hinde, R. A. (1995). A suggested structure for a science of relationships. *Personal Relationships, 2,* 1–15.

Hodges, E. V. E., Boivin, M., Vitaro, F., & Bukowski, W. M. (1999). The power of friendship: Protection against an escalating cycle of peer victimization. *Developmental Psychology, 35,* 94–101.

Horn, S. (2003). Adolescents' reasoning about exclusion from social groups. *Developmental Psychology, 39,* 11–84.

Howes, C. (1988). Peer interaction of young children. *Monographs of the Society for Research in Child Development, 53*(217).

Howes, C. (1992). *The collaborative construction of pretend.* Albany: State University of New York Press.

Hoza, B., Molina, B., Bukowski, W. M., & Sippola, L. K. (1995). Aggression, withdrawal and measures of popularity and friendship as predictors of internalizing and externalizing problems during early adolescence. *Development and Psychopathology, 7,* 787–802.

Humphreys, A. P., & Smith, P. K. (1987). Rough-and-tumble, friendship, and dominance in school children: Evidence for continuity and change with age. *Child Development, 58,* 201–212.

Hymel, S., Bowker, A., & Woody, E. (1993). Aggressive versus withdrawn unpopular children: Variations in peer and self-perceptions in multiple domains. *Child Development, 64,* 879–896.

Hymel, S., Comfort, C., Schonert-Reichl, K., & McDougall, P. (2002). Academic failure and school dropout: The influence of peers. In K. Wentzel & J. Juvonen (Eds.), *Social motivation: Understanding children's school adjustment* (pp. 313–335). Cambridge: Cambridge University Press.

Hymel, S., Rubin, K. H., Rowden, L., & LeMare, L. (1990). Children's peer relationships: Longitudinal predictions of internalizing and externalizing problems from middle to late childhood. *Child Development, 61,* 2004–2021.

Kagan, J. (1999). The concept of behavioral inhibition. In L. A. Schmidt & J. Schulkin (Eds.), *Extreme fear, shyness, and social phobia: Origins, biological mechanisms, and clinical outcomes* (pp. 3–13). London: Oxford University Press.

Khatri, P., & Kupersmidt, J. B. (2003). Aggression, peer victimization, and social relationships among Indian youth. *International Journal of Behavioral Development, 27,* 87–95.

Kiesner, J., Poulin, F., & Nicotra, E. (2003). Peer relations across contexts: Individual network homophily and network inclusion in and after school. *Child Development, 74,* 1328–1343.

Killen, M., Lee-Kim, J., McGlothlin, H., & Stangor, C. (2002). How children and adolescents evaluate gender and racial exclusion. *Monographs of the Society for Research in Child Development, 67*(4).

Kindermann, T. A. (1993). Natural peer groups as contexts for individual development: The case of children's motivation in school. *Developmental Psychology, 29,* 970–977.

Kindermann, T. A. (1995). Distinguishing "buddies" from "bystanders": The study of children's development within natural peer contexts. In T. A. Kindermann & J. Valsiner (Eds.), *Development of person-context relations* (pp. 205–226). Hillsdale, NJ: Erlbaum.

Kindermann, T. A., McCollom, T. L., & Gibson, E., Jr. (1995). Peer networks and students' classroom engagement during childhood and adolescence. In K. Wentzel & J. Juvonen (Eds.), *Social motivation: Understanding children's school adjustment* (pp. 279–312). New York: Cambridge University Press.

Kistner, J., Balthazor, M., Risi, S., & Burton, C. (1999). Predicting dysphoria from actual and perceived acceptance in childhood. *Journal of Clinical Child Psychology, 28,* 94–104.

Kochenderfer-Ladd, B. (2003). Identification of aggressive and asocial victims and the stability of their peer victimization. *Merrill-Palmer Quarterly, 49*(4), 401–425.

Kochenderfer-Ladd, B., & Wardrop, J. L. (2001). Chronicity and instability of children's peer victimization experiences as predictors of loneliness and social satisfaction trajectories. *Child Development, 72,* 134–151.

Kraatz-Keily, M., Bates, J. E., Dodge, K. A., & Pettit, G. S. (2000). A cross-domain analysis: Externalizing and internalizing behaviors during 8 years of childhood. *Journal of Abnormal Child Psychology, 28,* 161–179.

Krappmann, L. (1996). Amicitia, drujba, shin-yu, philia, freundschaft, friendship: On the cultural diversity of a human relationship. In W. M. Bukowski, A. F. Newcomb, & W. W. Hartup (Eds.), *The company they keep: Friendship in childhood and adolescence* (pp. 19–40). Cambridge: Cambridge University Press.

Kupersmidt, J. B., Burchinal, M., & Patterson, C. J. (1995). Developmental patterns of childhood peer relations as predictors of externalizing behavior problems. *Development and Psychopathology, 7,* 649–668.

Kuttler, A. F., Parker, J. G., & La Greca, A. M. (2002). Developmental and gender differences in preadolescents' judgments of the veracity of gossip. *Merrill-Palmer Quarterly, 48,* 105–132.

Ladd, G. W. (1990). Having friends, keeping friends, making friends, and being liked by peers in the classroom: Predictors of children's early school adjustment? *Child Development, 61,* 312–331.

Ladd, G. W. (1991). Family-peer relations during childhood: Pathways to competence and pathology? *Journal of Social and Personal Relationships, 8,* 307–314.

Ladd, G. W., & Burgess, K. B. (1999). Charting the relationship trajectories of aggressive, withdrawn, and aggressive/withdrawn children during early grade school. *Child Development, 70,* 910–929.

Ladd, G. W., & Kochenderfer, B. (1996). Linkages between friendship and adjustment during early school transitions. In W. M. Bukowski, A. F. Newcomb, & W. W. Hartup (Eds.), *The company they keep: Friendship in childhood and adolescence* (pp. 322–345). Cambridge: Cambridge University Press.

Ladd, G. W., & Kochenderfer, B. J., & Coleman, C. C. (1996). Friendship quality as a predictor of young children's early school adjustment. *Child Development, 67,* 1103–1118.

Ladd, G. W., & Kochenderfer, B. J., & Coleman, C. C. (1997). Classroom peer acceptance, friendship, and victimization: Distinct relational systems that contribute uniquely to children's school adjustment? *Child Development, 68,* 1181–1197.

Ladd, G. W., & Troop-Gordon, W. (2003). The role of chronic peer difficulties in the development of children's psychological adjustment problems. *Child Development, 74*(5), 1344–1367.

LaFontana, K. M., & Cillessen, A. H. N. (2002). Children's perceptions of popular and unpopular peers: A multimethod assessment. *Developmental Psychology, 38,* 635–647.

Laird, R. D., Jordan, K. Y., Dodge, K. A., Pettit, G. S., & Bates, J. E. (2001). Peer rejection in childhood, involvement with antisocial peers in early adolescence, and the development of externalizing behavior problems. *Development and Psychopathology, 13,* 337–354.

Lansford, J. E., Criss, M. M., Pettit, G. S., Dodge, K. A., & Bates, J. (2003). Friendship quality, peer group affiliation, and peer antisocial behavior as moderators of the link between negative parenting and adolescent externalizing behavior. *Journal of Research on Adolescence, 13,* 161–184.

Laursen, B., Finkelstein, B. D., & Betts, N. T. (2001). A developmental meta-analysis of peer conflict resolution. *Developmental Review, 21,* 423–449.

Laursen, B., Hartup, W. W., & Koplas, A. L. (1996). Towards understanding peer conflict. *Merrill-Palmer Quarterly, 42,* 76–102.

Leaper, C. (1994). Exploring the consequences of gender segregation on social relationships. In C. Leaper (Ed.), *Childhood gender segregation: Causes and consequences* (pp. 67–86). San Francisco: Jossey-Bass.

Legault, F., & Strayer, F. F. (1991). The emergence of sex-segregation in preschool peer groups. *Behaviour, 119,* 285–301.

Lemerise, E. A., & Arsenio, W. F. (2000). An integrated model of emotion processes and cognition in social information processing. *Child Development, 71,* 107–118.

Lieberman, M., Doyle, A. B., & Markiewicz, D. (1999). Developmental patterns in security of attachment to mother and father in late childhood and early adolescence: Associations with peer relations. *Child Development, 70,* 202–213.

Lyons-Ruth, K., Easterbrooks, M. A., & Cibelli, C. D. (1997). Infant attachment strategies, infant mental lag, and maternal depressive symptoms: Predictors of internalizing and externalizing problems at age seven. *Developmental Psychology, 33,* 681–692.

Matsumoto, D. (1997). *Culture and modern life.* Pacific Grove, CA: Brooks/Cole.

McCall, G. J. (1988). The organizational life cycle of relationships. In S. W. Duck (Ed.), *Handbook of personal relationships* (pp. 467–484). New York: Wiley.

McDowell, D. J., & Parke, R. D. (2000). Differential knowledge of display rules for positive and negative emotions: Influences from parents, influences on peers. *Social Development, 9,* 415–432.

McNeilly-Choque, M. K., Hart, C. H., Robinson, C. C., Nelson, L. J., & Olsen, S. F. (1996). Overt and relational aggression on the playground: Correspondence among different informants. *Journal of Research in Childhood Education, 11,* 47–67.

Miller-Johnson, S., Coie, J. D., Maumary-Gremaud, A., Bierman, K., & Conduct Problems Prevention Research Group. (2002). Peer rejection and aggression and early starter models of conduct disorder. *Journal of Abnormal Child Psychology, 30,* 217–230.

Mills, R. S. L., & Rubin, K. H. (1998). Are behavioral control and psychological control both differentially associated with childhood aggression and social withdrawal? *Canadian Journal of Behavioral Sciences, 30,* 132–136.

Mize, J., & Pettit, G. S. (1997). Mothers' social coaching, mother-child relationship style and children's peer competence: Is the medium the message? *Child Development, 68,* 312–332.

Moffitt, T. E. (1993). Adolescence-limited and life-course-persistent antisocial behavior: A developmental taxonomy. *Psychological Review, 100,* 674–701.

Mueller, E., & Brenner, J. (1977). The origins of social skills and interaction among playgroup toddlers. *Child Development, 48,* 854–861.

National Institute of Child Health and Human Development Early Child Care Research Network. (2001). Child care and children's peer interaction at 24 and 36 months: The National Institute of Child Health and Human Development Study of Early Child Care. *Child Development, 72,* 1478–1500.

Newcomb, A. F., & Bagwell, C. (1995). Children's friendship relations: A meta-analytic review. *Psychological Bulletin, 117,* 306–347.

Newcomb, A. F., & Bukowski, W. M. (1984). A longitudinal study of the utility of social preference and social impact sociometric classification schemes. *Child Development, 55,* 1434–1447.

Newcomb, A. F., Bukowski, W. M., & Pattee, L. (1993). Children's peer relations: A meta-analytic review of popular, rejected, neglected, controversial, and average sociometric status. *Psychological Bulletin, 113,* 99–128.

Nolen-Hoeksema, S., Girgus, J. S., & Seligman, M. E. (1992). Predictors and consequences of childhood depressive symptoms: A 5-year longitudinal study. *Journal of Abnormal Psychology, 101*(3), 405–422.

O'Brien, S. F., & Bierman, K. L. (1987). Conceptions and perceived influence of peer groups: Interviews with preadolescents and adolescents. *Child Development, 59,* 1360–1365.

Ollendick, T. H., Weist, M. D., Borden, M. G., & Greene, R. W. (1992). Sociometric status and academic, behavioral, and psychological adjustment: A 5-year longitudinal study. *Journal of Consulting and Clinical Psychology, 60,* 80–87.

Olweus, D. (1978). *Aggression in the schools: Bullies and whipping boys.* Oxford, England: Hemisphere.

Olweus, D. (1993). Victimization by peers: Antecedents and long-term outcomes. In K. H. Rubin & J. B. Asendorpf (Eds.), *Social withdrawal, inhibition and shyness in childhood* (pp. 315–341). Hillsdale, NJ: Erlbaum.

Orobio de Castro, B., Veerman, J. W., Koops, W., Bosch, J. D., & Monshouwer, H. J. (2002). Hostile attribution of intent and aggressive behavior: A meta-analysis. *Child Development, 73*(3), 916–934.

Parker, J. G., & Seal, J. (1996). Forming, losing, renewing, and replacing friendships: Applying temporal parameters to the assessment of children's friendship experiences. *Child Development, 67,* 2248–2268.

Parkhurst, J. T., & Hopmeyer, A. (1998). Sociometric popularity and peer-perceived popularity: Two distinct dimensions of peer status. *Journal of Early Adolescence, 18,* 125–144.

Pastor, D. L. (1981). The quality of mother-infant attachment and its relationship to toddlers' initial sociability with peers. *Developmental Psychology, 17,* 326–335.

Pellegrini, A. D. (2002). Rough-and-tumble play from childhood through adolescence: Development and possible functions. In P. K. Smith & C. H. Hart (Eds.), *Blackwell handbook of childhood social development* (pp. 438–453). London: Blackwell.

Pike, A., & Atzaba-Poria, N. (2003). Do sibling and friend relationships share the same temperamental origins? A twin study. *Journal of Child Psychology and Psychiatry and Allied Disciplines, 44,* 598–611.

Poulin, F., & Boivin, M. (2000). The role of proactive and reactive aggression in the formation and development of boys' friendships. *Developmental Psychology, 36,* 233–240.

Prinstein, M. J., & Cillessen, A. (2003). Forms and functions of adolescent peer aggression associated with high levels of peer status. *Merrill-Palmer Quarterly, 49*(3), 310–342.

Rodkin, P. C., Farmer, T. W., Pearl, R., & Van Acker, R. (2000). Heterogeneity of popular boys: Antisocial and prosocial configurations. *Developmental Psychology, 36,* 14–24.

Rodkin, P. C., & Hodges, E. V. E. (2003). Bullies and victims in the peer ecology: Four questions for psychological and school professionals. *School Psychology Review, 32,* 384–401.

Rose, A. (2002). Co-rumination in the friendships of girls and boys. *Child Development, 73,* 1830–1843.

Rose-Krasnor, L., Rubin, K. H., Booth, C. L., & Coplan, R. J. (1996). Maternal directiveness and child attachment security as predictors of social competence in preschoolers. *International Journal of Behavioral Development, 19,* 309–325.

Ross, H. S. (1982). The establishment of social games amongst toddlers. *Developmental Psychology, 18,* 509–518.

Ross, H. S., Conant, C., Cheyne, J. A., & Alevizos, E. (1992). Relationships and alliances in the social interactions of kibbutz toddlers. *Social Development, 1,* 1–17.

Rothbart, M. K., Ellis, L., & Posner, M. I. (2004). Temperament and self-regulation. In R. F. Baumeister & K. D. Vohs (Eds.), *Handbook of self-regulation: Research, theory, and applications* (pp. 357–370). New York: Guilford Press.

Rubin, K. H., Bukowski, W., & Parker, J. G. (1998). Peer interactions, relationships, and groups. In W. Damon (Series Ed.) & N. Eisenberg (Vol. Ed.), *Handbook of child psychology: Vol. 3. Social, emotional, and personality development* (5th ed., pp. 619–700). New York: Wiley.

Rubin, K. H., & Burgess, K. (2002). Parents of aggressive and withdrawn children. In M. Bornstein (Ed.), *Handbook of parenting* (2nd ed., Vol. 1, pp. 383–418). Hillsdale, NJ: Erlbaum.

Rubin, K. H., Burgess, K. B., Dwyer, K. D., & Hastings, P. (2003). Predicting preschoolers' externalizing behaviors from toddler temperament, conflict, and maternal negativity. *Developmental Psychology, 39,* 164–176.

Rubin, K. H., Burgess, K. B., & Hastings, P. D. (2002). Stability and social-behavioral consequences of toddlers' inhibited temperament and parenting. *Child Development, 73,* 483–495.

Rubin, K. H., Burgess, K. B., Kennedy, A. E., & Stewart, S. (2003). Social withdrawal in childhood. In E. Mash & R. Barkley (Eds.), *Child psychopathology* (2nd ed., pp. 372–406). New York: Guilford Press.

Rubin, K. H., Chen, X., McDougall, P., Bowker, A., & McKinnon, J. (1995). The Waterloo longitudinal project: Predicting internalizing and externalizing problems in adolescence. *Development and Psychopathology, 7,* 751–764.

Rubin, K. H., & Chung, O. B. (Eds.). (2006). *Parental beliefs, parenting, and child development in cross-cultural perspective.* London: Psychology Press.

Rubin, K. H., Coplan, R. J., Fox, N. A., & Calkins, S. (1995). Emotionality, emotion regulation, and preschoolers' social adaptation. *Development and Psychopathology, 7,* 49–62.

Rubin, K. H., Daniels-Beirness, T., & Bream, L. (1984). Social isolation and social problem solving: A longitudinal study. *Journal of Consulting and Clinical Psychology, 52,* 17–25.

Rubin, K. H., Dwyer, K. M., Booth, C. L., Kim, A. H., Burgess, K. B., & Rose-Krasnor, L. (2004). Attachment, friendship, and psychosocial functioning in early adolescence. *Journal of Early Adolescence, 24,* 326–356.

Rubin, K. H., Hastings, P., Chen, X., Stewart, S., & McNichol, K. (1998). Intrapersonal and maternal correlates of aggression, conflict, and externalizing problems in toddlers. *Child Development, 69,* 1614–1629.

Rubin, K. H., & Krasnor, L. R. (1986). Social-cognitive and social behavioral perspectives on problem solving. In M. Perlmutter (Ed.), *Minnesota Symposia on Child Psychology: Vol. 18. Cognitive perspectives on children's social and behavioral development* (pp. 1–68). Hillsdale, NJ: Erlbaum.

Rubin, K. H., Lynch, D., Coplan, R., Rose-Krasnor, L., & Booth, C. L. (1994). "Birds of a feather . . .": Behavioral concordances and preferential personal attraction in children. *Child Development, 65,* 1778–1785.

Rubin, K. H., & Mills, R. S. L. (1988). The many faces of social isolation in childhood. *Journal of Consulting and Clinical Psychology, 6,* 916–924.

Rubin, K. H., Mills, R. S. L., & Rose-Krasnor, L. (1989). Maternal beliefs and children's social competence. In B. Schneider, G. Attili, J. Nadel, & R. Weissberg (Eds.), *Social competence in developmental perspective* (pp. 313–331). Dordrecht, The Netherlands: Kluwer Press.

Rubin, K. H., & Rose-Krasnor, L. (1992). Interpersonal problem solving. In V. B. Van Hasselt & M. Hersen (Eds.), *Handbook of social development* (pp. 283–323). New York: Plenum Press.

Rubin, K. H., Watson, K., & Jambor, T. (1978). Free play behaviors in pre-school and kindergarten children. *Child Development, 49,* 534–536.

Rubin, K. H., Wojslawowicz, J. C., Burgess, K. B., Booth-LaForce, C., & Rose-Krasnor, L. (2006). The best friendships of shy/withdrawn children: Prevalence, stability, and relationship quality. *Journal of Abnormal Child Psychology, 34,* 139–153.

Ruble, D. N., Martin, C. L., & Berenbaum, S. A. (2006). Gender development. In W. Damon & R. M. Lerner (Series Eds.) & N. Eisenberg (Vol. Ed.), *Handbook of child psychology: Vol. 3. Social, emotional, and personality development* (6th ed., pp. 858–932). Hoboken, NJ: Wiley.

Russell, A., Hart, C. H., Robinson, C. C., & Olsen, S. F. (2003). Children's sociable and aggressive behavior with peers: A comparison of the U.S. and Australia, and contributions of temperament and parenting styles. *International Journal of Behavioral Development, 27,* 74–86.

Sameroff, A. J., & MacKenzie, M. J. (2003). Research strategies for capturing transactional models of development: The limits of the possible. *Development and Psychopathology, 15,* 613–640.

Sandstrom, M. J., & Coie, J. D. (1999). A developmental perspective on peer rejection: Mechanisms of stability and change. *Child Development, 70,* 955–966.

Sanson, A., Hemphill, S. A., & Smart, D. (2004). Connections between temperament and social development: A review. *Social Development, 13,* 142–170.

Schneider, B. H., Atkinson, L., & Tardif, C. (2001). Child-parent attachment and children's peer relations: A quantitative review. *Developmental Psychology, 37*(1), 86–100.

Schwartz, D., Farver, J. M., Chang, L., & Lee-Shin, Y. (2002). Victimization in South Korean children's peer groups. *Journal of Abnormal Child Psychology, 30,* 113–125.

Seiffge-Krenke, I. (2003). Testing theories of romantic development from adolescence to young adulthood: Evidence of a developmental sequence. *International Journal of Behavioral Development, 27,* 519–531.

Simpkins, S. D., & Parke, R. D. (2002). Do friends and nonfriends behave differently? A social relations analysis of children's behavior. *Merrill-Palmer Quarterly, 48,* 263–283.

Snyder, J., Brooker, M., Patrick, M. R., Snyder, A., Schrepferman, L., & Stoolmiller, M. (2003). Observed peer victimization during early elementary school: Continuity, growth, and relation to risk for child antisocial and depressive behavior. *Child Development, 74,* 1881–1898.

Stormshak, E. A., Bierman, K. L., Bruschi, C., Dodge, K. A., Coie, J. D., & the Conduct Preventions Research Group. (1999, January/February). The relation between behavior problems and peer preference in different classroom contexts. *Child Development, 70*(1), 169–182.

Strassberg, Z. (1995). Social information processing in compliance situations by mothers of behavior-problem boys. *Child Development, 66*(2), 376–389.

Strayer, F. F., & Strayer, J. (1976). An ethological analysis of social agonism and dominance relations among preschool children. *Child Development, 47,* 980–989.

Thomas, A., & Chess, S. (1977). *Temperament and development.* New York: Brunner/Mazel.

Urberg, K. A., Degirmencioglu, S. M., & Pilgrim, C. (1997). Close friend and group influence on adolescent cigarette smoking and alcohol use. *Developmental Psychology, 33,* 834–844.

Vandell, D. L., & Mueller, E. (1980). Peer play and friendships during the first 2 years. In H. Foot, A. Chapman, & J. Smith (Eds.), *Friendship and social relations in children* (pp. 181–208). New York: Wiley.

Vaughn, B. E., Vollenweider, M., Bost, K. K., Azria-Evans, M. R., & Snider, J. B. (2003). Negative interactions and social competence for preschool children in two samples: Reconsidering the interpretation of aggressive behavior for young children. *Merrill-Palmer Quarterly, 49,* 245–278.

Vernberg, E. M., Jacobs, A. K., & Hershberger, S. L. (1999). Peer victimization and attitudes about violence during early adolescence. *Journal of Clinical Child Psychology, 28*(3), 386–395.

Vitaro, F., Brendgen, M., & Tremblay, R. E. (2000). Influence of deviant friends on delinquency: Searching for moderator variables. *Journal of Abnormal Child Psychology, 28*(4), 313–325.

Walden, T., Lemerise, E., & Smith, M. C. (1999). Friendship and popularity in preschool classrooms. *Early Education and Development, 10,* 351–371.

Watson, A. C., Nixon, C. L., Wilson, A., & Capage, L. (1999). Social interaction skills and theory of mind in young children. *Developmental Psychology, 35,* 386–391.

Wentzel, K. R., & Asher, S. R. (1995). The academic lives of neglected, rejected, popular, and controversial children. *Child Development, 66,* 754–763.

Wentzel, K. R., McNamara-Barry, C., & Caldwell, K. A. (2004). Friendships in middle school: Influences on motivation and school adjustment. *Journal of Educational Psychology, 96*(2), 195–203.

Wichmann, C., Coplan, R. J., & Daniels, T. (2004). The social cognitions of socially withdrawn children. *Social Development, 13,* 377–392.

Wojslawowicz Bowker, J. C., Rubin, K. H., Burgess, K. B., Booth-LaForce, C., & Rose-Krasnor, L. R. (2006). Behavioral characteristics associated with stable and fluid best friendship patterns in middle childhood. *Merrill-Palmer Quarterly, 52*(4), 671–693.

Xie, H., Cairns, R. B., & Cairns, B. D. (1999). Social networks and configurations in inner-city schools: Aggression, popularity, and implications for students with EBD. *Journal of Emotional and Behavioral Disorders, 7,* 147–155.

Zakriski, A., & Coie, J. (1996). A comparison of aggressive-rejected and nonaggressive rejected children's interpretations of self-directed and other-directed rejection. *Child Development, 67,* 1048–1070.

Zarbatany, L., Hartmann, D., & Rankin, D. (1990). The psychological functions of preadolescent peer activities. *Child Development, 61,* 1067–1080.

Zarbatany, L., McDougall, P., & Hymel, S. (2000). Gender-differentiated experience in the peer culture: Links to intimacy in preadolescence. *Social Development, 9,* 62–79.

Zhou, Q., Eisenberg, N., Wang, Y., & Reiser, M. (2004). Chinese children's effortful control and dispositional anger/frustration: Relations to parenting styles and children's social functioning. *Developmental Psychology, 40,* 352–366.

Chapter 6

Personality Development

REBECCA L. SHINER and AVSHALOM CASPI

Differences among individuals are the most remarkable feature of human nature. After all, in both genetic and cultural evolution, selection pressures operate on differences among people. Not surprisingly, individual differences pervade all aspects of life, and they demand scientific inquiry: What are the most salient personality differences between people? What gives rise to these differences? Do personality differences shape important life outcomes? Answers to these questions are crucial for those who wish to describe, explain, and predict the nature of individual lives across time. Given the slow progress of soft psychology (Meehl, 1978), it is heartening to recognize that there have been significant advances in research on personality development over the past decade. In this chapter, we reflected these advances and anticipated future directions. In reflecting on the past decade of research, we are struck that debates pitting the person versus the situation, nature versus nurture, and continuity versus change are increasingly being brought to a halt. These three tired debates have given way to a more nuanced understanding of personality development.

At the heart of the person-situation debate was the ontological status of personality traits: Are traits real? Over the past decade, researchers have gained a much deeper understanding of the biological, emotional, and social-cognitive processes underlying personality traits. The first two sections of this chapter review this new evidence in detail. We delineate a taxonomy of measurable individual differences in temperament and personality in childhood and introduce a process-focused analysis of personality traits that details what is known about their psychological and biological underpinnings. A personality taxonomy serves at least three research purposes: First, it improves research

Work on this chapter was supported by grants from the National Institute of Mental Health (MH-45070 and MH-49414), the Medical Research Council, the William T. Grant Foundation, and the Colgate Research Council. We thank Terrie E. Moffitt, Brent W. Roberts, William G. Graziano, and Nancy Eisenberg for their helpful comments and ideas. This chapter reviews material available to us through July 2004.

communication; connecting multiple and different measures of personality to an established and validated personality structure helps to organize and integrate diffuse research findings. Second, it helps researchers to develop new measures of personality; locating new measures in relation to what is already known eliminates redundancy and elucidates psychological constructs. Third, it enables researchers to connect personality measures to more elaborate nomological networks and thereby to interpret research and generate new hypotheses about individual differences in personality. As becomes evident, the personality taxonomy discussed in the second section organizes the remaining sections of our review.

A second, related debate has pitted nature versus nurture. This is the longest-lived controversy in psychology, and there are signs that it too is dissipating. We begin the fourth section with an overview of research showing a genetic contribution to personality. The use of genetic techniques is helping to replace the nature-nurture conjunction "versus" with the more appropriate conjunction "and."

A third debate has focused on continuity versus change, which also subsumes the question of whether personality traits matter. Trait models are often caricatured as static, nondevelopmental conceptions of personality. This misapprehension arises because personality traits are thought to represent stable and enduring psychological differences between persons; therefore, they are static. Few personality researchers subscribe to this conclusion. Rather, contemporary personality research has sought to formulate the ways in which personality differences, in transaction with environmental circumstances, organize behavior in dynamic ways over time. Personality traits are thus organizational constructs; they influence how individuals organize their behavior to meet environmental demands and new developmental challenges. As Allport (1937) noted, personality traits are "modi vivendi, ultimately deriving their significance from the role they play in advancing adaptation within, and mastery of, the personal environment" (p. 342). The third, fifth, and sixth sections review new and accumulating evidence about the pathways through which personality traits develop over time, stability and change in personality development from childhood to adulthood, and the impact of personality differences on various life outcomes.

Developing Structure of Personality

In this first section, we address two issues that are central to the study of temperament and personality across the life course: (1) How should we conceptualize temperament and personality, and what is similar and distinctive about these two types of individual differences? and (2) How are temperament and personality differences structured from infancy through adulthood? It is important that we address these foundational issues from the outset before turning to questions of how individual differences develop and affect the life course.

TEMPERAMENT AND PERSONALITY: HOW ARE THEY SIMILAR? HOW ARE THEY DISTINCT?

Humans display a wide range of individual differences during the life span—from birth to old age. Both child psychologists and adult personality researchers study these individual differences, but historically the two groups have done so in different research traditions: Child psychologists have typically studied temperament traits, whereas adult personality researchers have typically studied personality traits.

The contemporary empirical study of early temperament was spurred largely by Thomas and Chess, who initiated the New York Longitudinal Study to examine the significance of biologically based temperament traits in infancy and childhood (Thomas, Chess, Birch, Hertzig, & Korn, 1963). Thomas and Chess challenged the way that social development was studied at the time because they emphasized that children are not merely the products of their rearing environments; rather, infants come into the world with biologically based behavioral tendencies. Like Thomas and Chess, most temperament researchers continue to focus on individual differences that emerge early in life, include differences in emotional processes, and have a presumed biological basis (Goldsmith et al., 1987). However, most contemporary researchers also recognize that temperament is shaped by both hereditary and environmental influences and that temperament includes components of self-regulation and emotion (Rothbart & Bates, 2006).

Personality is typically seen as including a wider range of individual differences in feeling, thinking, and behaving than is temperament. Personality differences include personality traits such as Extraversion and Neuroticism, but they also encompass goals, coping styles, defensive styles, motives, attachment styles, life stories, identities, and various other processes (McAdams, 1995). Although much of the research on children's individual differences has focused on traits labeled temperament, a great deal of productive research has already been done on childhood traits that could rightly be considered personality. Developmentalists have investigated a vast array of children's traits—aggression, delay of gratification, dominance, achievement strivings, empathy, anxiousness, and the list goes on—but sometimes have not explicitly labeled these traits aspects of children's emerging personalities per se (Shiner, 1998).

Empirical work has demonstrated a number of striking similarities between temperament traits and personality traits. First, although temperament differences between nonhuman animals have been recognized at least as long as humans have bred animals, important aspects of personality traits can be observed in nonhuman animals as well (Gosling, 2001). Second, like temperament traits, nearly all self-reported and observed personality traits show moderate genetic influence (Bouchard, 2004). Third, like personality traits, temperament traits are affected by experience: Behavioral genetic studies have established that temperament in infancy and early childhood is only partially heritable and is influenced by environmental events (Emde & Hewitt, 2001), including both pre- and postnatal experiences. Occasionally, researchers claim that individual differences measured later in childhood are not temperament because such traits have already been affected by environmental experiences, implying that only individual differences at birth represent genetically influenced temperament. The behavioral genetic findings reviewed later in this chapter reveal the fallacy of such a claim: From infancy through adulthood, to varying degrees and at varying times, genetic and environmental influences are at work shaping both temperament and personality traits. A fourth key similarity between temperament and personality traits is that many traits from both domains are characterized by specific habitual positive and negative emotions (reviewed later in the chapter). Thus, emotional experience and expression are associated with a wide variety of traits across the life span. In short, many of the distinctions between temperament and personality traits seem to be breaking down. Because temperament and personality traits share so much in common, we discuss temperament and personality systems together throughout this review.

PERSONALITY STRUCTURE ACROSS THE LIFE SPAN

One of the most striking points of convergence between temperament and personality is their similar structure across most periods of the life span; by structure, we mean the reliable patterns of covariation of traits across individuals. We later describe research findings on the structure of individual differences in infants and toddlers and the structure observed in young children, adolescents, and adults. The establishment of a personality structure for describing adult personality has been a complicated, contentious enterprise; work on the structure of young children's individual differences is inherently even more complex. As children's motor, cognitive, emotional, and language abilities develop, the range of traits they can express similarly expands. For example, although infants may differ in temperament traits that are likely to be related to later aggression, infants cannot exhibit differences in aggression until they develop the motor and language skills necessary to direct aggressive actions toward others. Similar rapid growth occurs in children's emotional development. Thus, the structure of individual differences is likely to change over the course of childhood because of children's increasing capacities. Like many other aspects of development, children's individual differences are likely to become increasingly differentiated and complex over development. Despite the challenges in mapping the structure of individual differences in infancy and childhood, substantial progress has been made in this area.

As we illustrate in our description of temperament and personality structure, individual differences are organized hierarchically across the life span. Covariation among specific behavioral descriptors (e.g., talkative or friendly) is explained by lower-order traits, and the covariation among these narrower, lower-order traits (e.g., sociability or social potency) is explained by broad, higher-order traits (e.g., Extraversion). Individual differences exhibit such a hierarchical structure in infancy and early childhood (Putnam, Ellis, & Rothbart, 2001), middle childhood and adolescence (Shiner & Caspi, 2003), and adulthood (Markon, Krueger, & Watson, 2005). We now turn to a discussion of the traits that can be observed (a) during infancy and early childhood and (b) during the preschool through adult years.

Structure of Individual Differences in Infancy and Early Childhood

During infancy and early childhood, children display a limited range of traits. Current models of temperament in infancy and early childhood derive from research on caregiver-report questionnaires, structured laboratory tasks, and home observational systems. Taken together, these sources provide the strongest support for the following lower-order temperament traits in the infant and toddler years (Kochanska, Coy, Tjebkes, & Husarek, 1998; Lemery, Goldsmith, Klinnert, & Mrazek, 1999; R. P. Martin, Wisenbaker, & Huttunen, 1994; Rothbart & Bates, 2006):

- *Positive emotions/pleasure:* This trait measures the child's propensity toward the expression of positive emotions, including smiling and laughter as well as pleasure and excitement in social interaction.
- *Fear/inhibition:* This trait addresses the child's tendency to withdraw and express fear in the face of stressful or novel situations (both social and nonsocial). This

trait expresses itself in fearful, withdrawn, and avoidant behavior in situations with strangers and unfamiliar, unpredictable objects (Kagan, 1998; Kochanska et al., 1998).

- *Irritability/anger/frustration:* In early childhood, this trait includes fussing, anger, and poor toleration of frustration and limitations. Fear and irritability each appear to be influenced by unique genetic and environmental sources, demonstrating the distinct nature of these two traits (Goldsmith, Lemery, Buss, & Campos, 1999).
- *Discomfort:* Infants and toddlers differ in the extent of their negative emotional reactions to irritating or painful sensory stimulation (e.g., loud noises, cold touches, or sour tastes; Kochanska et al., 1998).
- *Attention:* Between the 4- and 8-month periods, infants vary in their attentiveness to environmental stimuli (Rothbart, Chew, & Garstein, 2001). Questionnaire measures of this trait tap infants' duration of attention to stimuli and their ability to notice environmental variation. In toddlers, this trait also includes the ability to sustain attention over time and persist at a task (R. P. Martin et al., 1994).
- *Activity level:* Activity level is an important component of most temperament models; however, the meaning of this trait is likely to change with development. Motor movement in infancy is associated with both anger and positive emotions, whereas motor movement in the toddler years is linked in complex ways with early markers of high Extraversion and low self-control (Eaton, 1994). When activity level is defined as positive activity, it is already highly correlated with markers of Extraversion by the toddler years (Lamb, Chuang, Wessels, Broberg, & Hwang, 2002).

Most research on early temperament has focused on narrowly defined, lower-order traits. Rothbart and colleagues have more recently explored the structure of higher-order temperament traits in infancy and the toddler years by examining the factor structure of two newly expanded caregiver-report temperament questionnaires (Rothbart & Bates, 2006). In samples of American infants and toddlers, three factors emerge. In infancy and the toddler years, a Surgency factor taps children's tendencies toward an eager, positive approach to potentially pleasurable activities; vocal reactivity (in infants) and sociability (in toddlers); expression of positive emotions; enjoyment of high-intensity activities; and high activity level. In infancy and the toddler years, a Negative Affectivity factor taps children's tendencies toward sadness, irritability and frustration, and fear, as well as their abilities to quiet themselves after high arousal (reversed). The third factor differs in the two periods. In infancy the third factor measures soothability, cuddliness, ability to sustain attention, and pleasure in low-intensity situations, whereas in the toddler years this factor (labeled Effortful Control) includes these traits and more sophisticated self-regulatory abilities. The third factor appears to tap young children's emerging behavioral constraint and regulation. As described in the next section, these three higher-order traits are highly similar to three higher-order temperament and personality traits observed among older children and adults.

Structure of Individual Differences from Childhood through Adulthood

One of the great achievements in the study of adult personality over the past 2 decades is greater clarity about the higher-order structure of personality. Prior to this emerging consensus, debate raged about which traits are most valid and important. Researchers were prone to the "jingle-jangle" fallacy of studying the same trait under different names (jingle) or using the same name to describe different traits (jangle; Block, 1996). Research on adult personality has been energized by emerging consensus about personality structure because researchers can now focus their attention on a common set of traits.

The most widespread support has been obtained for a five-trait structure in adulthood, dubbed the Big Five or the Five-Factor Model (John & Srivastava, 1999; McCrae & Costa, 1999); these traits include Extraversion, Neuroticism, Conscientiousness, Agreeableness, and Openness to Experience/Intellect. Extraversion describes the extent to which the person actively engages the world or avoids intense social experiences. Neuroticism describes the extent to which the person experiences the world as distressing or threatening. Conscientiousness describes the extent and strength of impulse control in task-focused domains, whether the person is able to delay gratification in the service of more distant goals or is unable to modulate impulsive expression. Agreeableness describes a person's interpersonal nature on a continuum from warmth and compassion to antagonism. Agreeable persons are empathic, altruistic, helpful, and trusting, whereas antagonistic persons are abrasive, ruthless, manipulative, and cynical. Openness to Experience (also called Intellect) describes the complexity, depth, and quality of a person's mental and experiential life.

Consensus about the structure of adult personality traits has important implications for developmental research: We now have greater clarity about the adult personality traits that childhood studies should be trying to predict over time. Developmental researchers have explored the possibility that childhood personality structure might map onto the structure observed in adults, and there is now evidence (from the preschool years through adolescence) from a variety of sources that such is the case. First, factor analyses of questionnaires, adjective lists, and the California Child Q-Set have often produced factors similar to the Big Five traits in studies of children from approximately age 3 through late adolescence (Caspi, Roberts, & Shiner, 2005; Shiner & Caspi, 2003). Second, further support for several of the Big Five traits derives from temperament research in older children and adolescents. In Rothbart and colleagues' work on temperament structure, they have found evidence for the same three higher-order traits observed in early childhood—Surgency, Negative Emotionality, and Effortful Control—as well as a trait named Affiliativeness in early adolescence (Rothbart & Bates, 2006). Third, a variety of behavioral-task and observational measures provide support for traits similar to the Big Five (Shiner & Caspi, 2003). To illustrate the meaning of the factors, Table 6.1 lists items defining the Big Five traits in three types of child measures: (1) teacher reports using a list of trait descriptors (Digman & Shmelyov, 1996), (2) parent reports using the California Child Q-Sort (John, Caspi, Robins, Moffitt, & Stouthamer-Loeber, 1994; van Lieshout & Haselager, 1993, 1994), and (3) children's self-reports using a puppet interview (Measelle, John, Ablow, Cowan, & Cowan, 2005).

Temperament and Personality Traits in Childhood and Adolescence: A Process-Focused, Developmental Taxonomy

In this section, we elaborate a taxonomy of personality traits in children and adolescents. It is important to include lower-order traits in our proposed taxonomy. The Big Five are too broad to capture all the interesting variations in human personality, and distinctions at the level of more specific traits are necessary. In this taxonomy, we integrate what is known about diverse aspects of each trait. First, we present a description

TABLE 6.1 Examples of Trait Descriptors, California Child Q-Sort Items, and Self-Report Puppet Interview Items for Five Higher-Order Personality Traits in Children

Higher-Order Personality Trait	Trait Descriptors[a]	Sample Items	
		Child Q-Sort Items[b]	Puppet Interview Items[c]
Extraversion	Gregarious	Emotionally expressive	I'm not shy when I meet new people.
	Cheerful	A talkative child	It's easy for me to make new friends.
	Energetic	Fast paced; moves and reacts to things quickly	If kids are playing, I ask if I can play too.
	Withdrawn (rev.)	Inhibited or constricted (rev.)	
Neuroticism	Afraid	Fearful and anxious	I'm sad a lot.
	Touchy	Tends to go to pieces under stress; becomes rattled and disorganized	I get nervous when my teacher calls on me.
	Tearful	Appears to feel unworthy	I don't like myself.
	Steady (rev.)	Self-reliant, confident (rev.)	
Conscientiousness	Diligent	Attentive and able to concentrate	I think it's important to do well in school.
	Planful	Planful; thinks ahead	I try my best in school.
	Careful	Persistent in activities; does not give up easily	When I can't figure something out, I don't give up.
	Focused	Reflective; thinks and deliberates before speaking or acting	
Agreeableness	Considerate	Warm and kind toward others	I don't get mad at kids at school.
	Trusting	Helpful and cooperative	If someone is mean to me, I don't hit them.
	Spiteful (rev.)	Tends to give, lend, and share	I don't pick on other kids.
	Rude (rev.)	Teases and picks on others (rev.)	
Openness to experience	Original	Curious and exploring	I learn things well.
	Perceptive	Appears to have high intellectual capacity (whether expressed in achievement or not)	I have good ideas.
	Knowledgeable	Creative in perception, thought, work, or play	I'm a smart kid.
	Curious	Has an active fantasy life	

Note: Rev. = Item is scored in the reversed direction.

[a] Items defining the factor in a study of 480 Russian children aged 8 to 10 whose teachers rated them. From "The Structure of Temperament and Personality in Russian Children," by J. M. Digman and A. G. Shmelyov, 1996, *Journal of Personality and Social Psychology, 71,* pp. 341–351. Copyright 1996 by the American Psychological Association. Adapted with permission.

[b] Abbreviated California Child Q-sort items defining the factor in two independent studies: (1) a study of 720 Dutch boys and girls who were Q-sorted by parents and teachers and (2) a study of 350 African American and Caucasian boys aged 12 to 13 enrolled in the Pittsburgh Youth Study who were Q-sorted by their mothers. From "Personality Development across the Life Course" (pp. 311–388), by A. Caspi, in *Handbook of Child Psychology: Vol. 3. Social, Emotional and Personality Development,* fifth edition, N. Eisenberg (Ed.), 1998, New York: Wiley.

[c] Berkley Puppet Interview items defining the factor in a study of 95 children aged 5 to 7. From "Can Children Provide Coherent, Stable, and Valid Self-Reports on the Big Five Dimensions?" by J. Measelle et al., 2005, *Journal of Personality and Social Psychology, 89,* pp. 90–106. Copyright 2005 by the American Psychological Association. Adapted with permission.

TABLE 6.2   A Proposed Taxonomy of Higher-Order and Lower-Order Personality Traits in Childhood and Adolescence

Higher-order traits	Extraversion (E)	Neuroticism (N)	Conscientiousness (C)	Agreeableness (A)	Openness to experience (O)
Lower-order traits	Sociability	Anxiety	Attention	Prosocial tendencies	Intellect
	Energy/Activity level	Sadness	Self control	Antagonism	Creativity
			Achievement Motivation Orderliness	Willfulness	Curiosity
	E + N	N + low A	C + A		
	Social inhibition	Anger/Irritability Alienation/Mistrust	Responsibility		

Note: The lower-order traits shown at the bottom of the table typically load on more than one higher-order trait.

of the Big Five traits and the lower-order traits likely to be subsumed by them (see Table 6.2). Next, we survey theories and evidence about the processes underlying each trait. One of the great benefits of a consensually agreed-on taxonomy of traits is that it allows researchers to train their lenses on how personality traits express themselves in everyday life and on the fundamental processes underlying variations in these traits. We thus review some of the most interesting current work on the psychological and biological underpinnings of each Big Five trait.

EXTRAVERSION

Children vary in their tendencies to be vigorously, actively, and surgently engaged with the world around them. Extraverted children and adolescents are described in Big Five studies as sociable, expressive, high-spirited, lively, socially potent, physically active, and energetic. In contrast, introverted youths are quiet, inhibited, and lethargic. Observations of preschoolers reveal a similar, coherent set of behaviors: high positive affect, energy and zestful engagement, and eager anticipation of enjoyable events (Buckley, Klein, Durbin, Hayden, & Moerk, 2002). Based on observational measures, extraverted children indeed are more talkative, more dominant, and more involved and engaged in interaction than their introverted peers (Markey, Markey, & Tinsley, 2004).

Extraversion encompasses the lower-order traits of sociability and energy/activity level. Another lower-order trait—social inhibition—is related to both Extraversion and Neuroticism. Sociability (or gregariousness) is the most prototypical lower-order component of Extraversion. It includes the preference for being with others rather than alone and a variety of behaviors that suggest vigorous, active ways of making connections with others: talkativeness, friendliness, vivaciousness, and expressiveness (Peabody & De Raad, 2002). Sociability can be distinguished conceptually and empirically from social inhibition, feelings of discomfort and reluctance to act in novel situations. As noted previously, fear/inhibition is a trait readily identified in infants and toddlers. Shyness appears to be one aspect of a broader inhibition trait in older children. Inhibition consists of a number of related but distinct behaviors: hesitance with new peers and adults, wariness in physically challenging and unfamiliar situations, difficulty with separation from parents, and acute discomfort in performance situations (Bishop, Spence, & McDonald, 2003). Sociability and social inhibition represent distinct traits: Sociability is a pure marker of Extraversion, whereas social inhibition appears to be a more complex blend of low Extraversion and high fear or anxiety in the presence of novel situations (Markon et al., 2005; Nigg, 2000). Energy and activity level are aspects of Extraversion that are easily observed among children. Energetic engagement with pleasurable tasks is a component of Extraversion by around age 2 or 3 (Halverson et al., 2003; Lamb et al., 2002).

Two main models have been advanced to explain the basis of the Extraversion trait. First, Extraversion is often conceptualized as the predisposition to experience positive emotions (Tellegen, 1985; Watson & Clark, 1997). The expression of positive emotions in infancy is predictive of later markers of Extraversion. These links between Extraversion and the experience of positive emotions are robust in adulthood as well; a meta-analysis obtained an average correlation of .37 between Extraversion and the concurrent experience of positive affect (Lucas & Fujita, 2000). Why are Extraversion and positive affect linked so consistently? One possibility is that more extraverted individuals engage in activities that promote positive affect, such as spending time with friends. Extraverted adults do engage in more social activity, which results in positive affect, but social activity alone does not account for the Extraversion-positive affect link (Watson, Clark, McIntyre, & Hamaker, 1992). An additional explanation is a temperamental view of Extraversion—that there are endogenous links between Extraversion and positive affect. Second and relatedly, Extraversion has been conceptualized as a biologically based behavioral activation, approach, or appetitive system. The most influential framework for understanding this approach system has been Gray's (1987, 1990) model of the Behavioral Activation System (BAS). According to Gray, the BAS is a neurobiological system that responds to incentives for appetitive behavior, including signals of reward, nonpunishment, and escape from punishment. Individuals with a stronger BAS should be highly attentive to such incentives: When this system is activated, individuals begin to approach or pursue goals. Biological evidence for an approach system derives from Davidson and colleagues' work demonstrating that specialized neural substrates for behavioral approach exist in the left anterior cerebral cortex (Davidson, Pizzagalli, Nitschke, & Kalin, 2003).

NEUROTICISM

Just as children vary in their predisposition toward positive emotions, they vary in their susceptibility to negative emotions and general distress. In the Big Five studies, children and adolescents who are high on Neuroticism are described as anxious, vulnerable, tense, easily frightened, "falling apart" under stress, guilt-prone, moody, low in frustration tolerance, and insecure in relationships with others. Fewer descriptors define the lower end of this dimension; these include traits such as stability, being "laid back," adaptability in novel situations, and the ability to "bounce back" after a bad experience. As these descriptions of childhood Neuroticism illustrate, the trait appears to include both the child's experience of negative emotions and the child's effectiveness at self-regulating such negative emotions. Neurotic individuals tend to be self-critical, insecure, and sensitive to criticism and teasing. Neurotic adults tend to be dissatisfied with major aspects of their lives, including their relationships, work, and health (Heller, Watson, & Ilies, 2004). Behavioral observations confirm the questionnaire descriptions of children high on this trait; childhood Neuroticism is associated with behaviors such as making self-critical statements, expressing a sense of self-pity and guilt, acting irritated, and showing signs of physical tension (Markey et al., 2004). Higher Neuroticism may also be linked with a variety of aversive interpersonal behaviors in childhood. In an observational study of parent-child interaction, higher Neuroticism was correlated with keeping parents at a distance, seeming detached, speaking sarcastically, and exhibiting low levels of upbeat, enthusiastic behavior (Markey et al., 2004).

Neuroticism is likely to include a number of lower-order traits, including anxiety and sadness (Muris, Schmidt, Merckelbach, & Schouten, 2001). Anxiety taps tendencies toward nervous apprehension, general distress, worry, and physical tension when there is no imminent threat. Sadness includes behaviors associated with depression, including lowered mood, hopelessness, and dejection arising from experiences of disappointment and loss. Two other lower-order traits appear to be related to both high Neuroticism and low Agreeableness: (1) anger/irritability and (2) alienation/mistrust. Anger/irritability taps outer-directed, hostile emotions such as anger, jealousy, frustration, and irritation (Halverson et al., 2003); in children, such hostility is often evoked by limits set by adults. A final lower-order trait, alienation/mistrust, taps an individual's tendency to mistrust others and to feel mistreated (Tellegen & Waller, 1992). Individual differences in interpersonal alienation and mistrust have been identified in research on social information processing in youths (Crick & Dodge, 1994) and in the attachment literature (Sroufe, Carlson, Levy, & Egeland, 1999).

Research with adults has helped to characterize the cognitive style, daily experiences, and interpersonal functioning of individuals high on Neuroticism. Adults high on trait anxiety show attentional biases toward information relevant to their personal fears; such biases are consistent with a model of anxiety as helping to prepare individuals for potentially dangerous situations by rapidly focusing attention on threatening material (Mineka, Rafaeli, & Yovel, 2003). In contrast, tendencies toward depression are associated with biases toward remembering and ruminating over past negative experiences (Mineka et al., 2003). Adults high on trait anxiety and adults high on depression are biased toward assuming they will encounter unduly negative experiences in the future. Thus, there is good evidence that Neuroticism and its lower-order components are associated, at least in adulthood, with biases toward processing negative information, though the biases may vary somewhat for different lower-order components. Just as Neuroticism is associated with negative cognitive biases, it is also linked with more negative daily life events in adults (Magnus, Diener, Fujita, & Pavot, 1993). Neurotic adults have stronger negative emotional reactions to everyday problems, including both interpersonal conflicts and stress at work and at home (Suls, Martin, & David, 1998). More neurotic individuals also exhibit more disagreeable and submissive behavior and less agreeable and dominant behavior (Cote & Moskowitz, 1998). The interpersonal behaviors associated with Neuroticism in adults are consistent with the previously described aversive interaction style observed in more neurotic children. In summary, the process-oriented studies with adults have demonstrated that Neuroticism is associated with a variety of difficulties in emotional and behavioral regulation.

All of these findings regarding Neuroticism are consistent with the claim that individual differences in Neuroticism are associated with variation in a biologically based withdrawal, inhibition, or avoidance system. As with Extraversion, one of the most important frameworks for understanding this system has been a model developed by Gray (1987, 1990). According to Gray, individuals differ in the sensitivity of a neurobiological Behavioral Inhibition System (BIS), which serves to inhibit behavior in the face of potential punishment, nonreward, and novelty. Thus, individuals with a strong BIS should be sensitive to signals of threats and should be quick to withdraw or inhibit their behavior when they perceive such signals. As with Extraversion, Davidson and colleagues have shown that there are specialized neural substrates for behavioral withdrawal, in this case in the right anterior cerebral cortex (Davidson et al., 2003). The findings on the biological and psychological processes associated with Neuroticism should provide impetus to study similar processes associated with the development of Neuroticism in children.

CONSCIENTIOUSNESS

An overarching Conscientiousness trait taps children's individual differences in self-control, in large part as control is used in service of completing tasks and striving to meet standards. In Big Five studies, highly Conscientious children and adolescents are described as responsible, attentive, persistent, orderly and neat, planful, possessing high standards, and thinking before acting. Children low on this trait are depicted as irresponsible, unreliable, careless, distractible, and quitting easily. There is evidence from at least one study that some of these more complex manifestations of self-control can be measured with moderate reliability in children as young as ages 3 and 4 years (Halverson et al., 2003). As noted previously, Rothbart and colleagues have identified in children a similar temperament trait labeled Effortful Control, which includes children's capacities to plan behavior, inhibit inappropriate responses, focus and shift attention, take pleasure in low intensity situations, and perceive subtle external stimuli (Rothbart & Bates, 2006). In a series of studies, Kochanska and colleagues have developed a battery of tasks to measure children's emerging Effortful Control (Kochanska & Knaack, 2003): All of the tasks require a child to exert self-control by suppressing a dominant response in favor of carrying out a subdominant response. Although temperament and personality models both include dimensions related to self-control, the content of these traits differs somewhat. Temperament models tend to emphasize attention and impulse control. In contrast, personality models include not only impulse control but also traits that children do not exhibit until they are older, such as orderliness, dependability, and motivation to meet goals and complete work. More work will be needed to clarify the similarities and differences between the personality and temperament conceptions of this higher-order trait.

Conscientiousness in children includes a number of lower-order components: attention, self-control, achievement motivation, orderliness, and responsibility (Goldberg, 2001; Halverson et al., 2003; Peabody & De Raad, 2002; Roberts, Bogg, Walton, Chernyshenko, & Stark, 2004; Rothbart, Ahadi, Hershey, & Fisher, 2001). Attention versus distractibility taps children's capacity to focus attention, regulate attention by shifting mental sets, and persist at tasks in the face of distractions. Self-control taps tendencies to be planful, cautious, deliberate, and behaviorally controlled. Achievement motivation (also called work or industriousness) taps the tendency to strive for high standards, to work hard and be productive, and to pursue goals over time in a determined, persistent manner. Orderliness (or organization) reflects a propensity to be neat, clean, and organized rather than sloppy, disorganized, and disorderly. Responsibility ranges from the tendency to be reliable and dependable to the tendency to be irresponsible and unreliable; this subcomponent appears to measure Conscientiousness manifested in relation to other people and may be a blend of Conscientiousness and Agreeableness.

Conscientiousness indexes a child's or adult's active engagement with various tasks; an individual high on this trait invests greater energy in completing work, upholding commitments, and maintaining order. The adaptive profile associated with Conscientiousness is consistent with such a view of the trait. As we review later in this chapter, childhood Conscientiousness predicts better academic achievement and improvement in academic achievement over time, and adult Conscientiousness is the best personality trait predictor of work success. Conscientious adults tend to set higher goals for themselves, are more committed to meeting those goals, and have greater confidence that they can meet those goals (Judge & Ilies, 2002). The importance of Conscientiousness is not restricted to task-focused endeavors; rather, Conscientiousness is often associated with effective social functioning as well. For example, a study of observed interactions between school-age children and their parents showed that child Conscientiousness was (unsurprisingly) associated with greater exhibited intelligence and ambition and (unexpectedly) with better social skills, warmth, and cooperativeness (Markey et al., 2004). One straightforward reason that Conscientiousness may be linked with effective social functioning is that self-regulation is clearly important for maintaining social relationships (Eisenberg, Fabes, Guthrie, & Reiser, 2000). A second, deeper reason for these links between Conscientiousness and social functioning may that Conscientiousness reflects children's and adults' adoption of society's norms for regulated behavior (Hogan & Ones, 1997). Consistent with this model, Effortful Control in childhood is associated with toddlers' and preschoolers' "committed compliance" or internalization of parental rules (Kochanska, Coy, & Murray, 2001). Researchers studying the biological basis of self-regulation have pointed to the importance of the prefrontal cortex for a variety of self-regulatory skills, including working memory, emotional processing, planning, novelty detection, resolving conflicting information, initiating action, and inhibiting inappropriate responses (Banfield, Wyland, Macrae, Munte, & Heatherton, 2004; Nigg, 2000). Posner, Rothbart, and colleagues (Posner & Rothbart, 2000; Rueda, Posner, & Rothbart, 2004) consider many of these capacities to reflect individual differences in an overarching executive attention capacity, which they likewise link with the development of the frontal cortex, particularly the anterior cingulate cortex. Based on this model, children's manifest differences in Effortful Control may be driven in large part by differences in executive attention.

AGREEABLENESS

Agreeableness includes a variety of traits seen as very important by developmental psychologists; yet, historically, these traits have been left out of temperament models. The high end of Agreeableness includes descriptors such as warm, considerate, empathic, generous, gentle, protective of others, and kind. The low end of Agreeableness includes tendencies toward being aggressive, rude, spiteful, stubborn, bossy, cynical, and manipulative. In studies with both children and adults, Agreeableness also includes being willing to accommodate others' wishes rather than forcing one's own desires and intentions on others; for children this aspect of the trait also involves how manageable the child is for parents and teachers. Observations of Agreeable children interacting with their parents are consistent with questionnaire descriptions of such children (Markey et al., 2004): Children's high Agreeableness is positively associated with expressing agreement and warmth, seeking agreement from parents, and seeming to like parents and is negatively associated with competitiveness, condescending behavior, and criticalness. In short, Agreeableness is linked with a variety of behaviors that are likely to foster congenial relationships with both peers and adults. Given the adaptive significance of this trait, it is not surprising that parents from many countries spontaneously offer a large number of traits from this domain when they are asked to describe their children (Havill, Besevegis, & Mouroussaki, 1998).

In our discussion of Neuroticism, we already noted two lower-order traits that are linked with both Neuroticism and Agreeableness: (1) anger/irritability and (2) alienation/mistrust. A number of other lower-order traits appear to be aspects of Agreeableness in childhood: prosocial tendencies, antagonism, and willfulness. Prosocial tendencies (also called helpfulness or nurturance) encompass children's individual differences in traits that demonstrate concern for other people rather than interest only in themselves. Children differ in their tendencies to be empathic, kind, and nurturant (Eisenberg, Fabes, & Spinrad, 2006). Individual differences in prosocial behavior are moderately stable during the preschool- and school-age years (Graziano & Eisenberg, 1997). Antagonism ranges from the tendency to be peaceful and gentle to the tendency to be aggressive, spiteful, quarrelsome, and rude: Children who are high on this trait express hostility openly toward others. Willfulness refers to the extent to which an individual attempts to assert his or her will over others through domineering behavior. Children and adults who are high on this trait are described as bossy, manipulative, overbearing, and defiant rather than accommodating and flexible (Halverson et al., 2003; Peabody & De Raad, 2002). Children high on this trait are likely to pose significant management problems for parents and teachers.

A number of researchers have argued that Agreeableness reflects individual differences in the motivation to maintain harmonious relationships with others; from this point of view, Agreeableness taps differences in the willingness to forgo individual interests out of concern for others (Graziano & Eisenberg, 1997). A number of studies have provided evidence that Agreeableness does reflect individual differences in the motivation to maintain harmonious relationships. Based on data from experience-sampling studies, high-Agreeable adults are more distressed than low-Agreeable adults when they face interpersonal conflicts (Suls et al., 1998) and report more negative affect when they themselves behave in a quarrelsome manner (Cote & Moskowitz, 1998). They also report more positive affect when they engage in warm, agreeable behavior than do low-Agreeable adults (Cote & Moskowitz, 1998). Further, the motivation to maintain harmonious relationships manifests itself in stronger endorsement of fewer destructive and more constructive tactics for handling conflicts in youth and adults (Jensen-Campbell, Gleason, Adams, & Malcolm, 2003; Jensen-Campbell & Graziano, 2001). Teachers and parents describe high-Agreeable children as negotiating conflict better (Jensen-Campbell et al., 2003), whereas peers describe low-Agreeable adolescents as more aggressive (Gleason, Jensen-Campbell, & Richardson, 2004). When children are observed in conflict situations in the lab, low Agreeableness is associated with higher levels of conflict and tension, as well as more destructive conflict tactics such as stand-offs, name-calling, and withdrawals (Jensen-Campbell et al., 2003). Interestingly, greater Agreeableness does not predict more observed submissive behavior in children and adults (Cote & Moskowitz, 1998; Jensen-Campbell et al., 2003); apparently, Agreeable people do not simply solve their interpersonal problems by giving in to other people. In short, more Agreeable youths and adults appear to generate fewer conflicts for themselves and have a greater capacity for handling the interpersonal conflicts that do arise.

There is increasing research interest in understanding the biological systems underlying individual differences in Agreeableness. Differences in empathy, warmth, and

nurturance may arise from a biological system designed to promote parental investment in offspring and close family bonds. Some researchers (e.g., MacDonald, 1995)
have argued that evolution yielded a human biological system that typically ensures
that an intimate relationship and the care of close others is inherently rewarding and
pleasurable and that the loss of such relationships is painful and distressing. Such a
system would confer adaptive benefits because it would promote successful care of
offspring through the establishment of strong attachment relationships between infants
and their caregivers. Research with animals has pointed to several potential biological
substrates of this affectional system, including endogenous opioids and the neuropep-
tide oxytocin (Carter, 1998; Taylor et al., 2000). Further, there is some preliminary evidence in humans that affectional bonds may activate brain areas that support positive
emotions and deactivate brain areas that are linked with aggression, fear, and sadness
(Diamond, 2004); this finding is consistent with the emotional profile associated with
Agreeableness.

OPENNESS TO EXPERIENCE/INTELLECT

Openness to Experience/Intellect is perhaps the most debated and least understood
of the Big Five traits, yet it includes a number of potentially important characteristics. This trait does not appear in temperament models, despite parents from a
number of countries spontaneously using words from this domain of individual differences to describe their children (Mervielde, De Fruyt, & Jarmuz, 1998). In the Big
Five studies, children who are high on this trait are described as eager and quick to
learn, clever, knowledgeable, perceptive, imaginative, curious, and original. The
lower-order components of Openness in childhood are not yet clear, but intellect
(Halverson et al., 2003) and curiosity and creativity (Goldberg, 2001) have received
some support.

McCrae and Costa (1997) suggested that Openness includes two particularly important processes: Openness as a psychic structure and Openness as a motivation to pursue
new, complex experiences. First, "open individuals have access to more thoughts, feelings, and impulses in awareness, and can maintain many of these simultaneously"
(McCrae & Costa, 1997, p. 838). Openness is associated with numerous indicators of
greater access to varied inner experiences in adults: more differentiated self-reports
of emotions (Terracciano, McCrae, Hagemann, & Costa, 2003) and reduced tendencies
to screen out previously irrelevant stimuli (Peterson, Smith, & Carson, 2002). This
greater access to inner experience may be a mixed blessing; for example, in one study
of women undergoing a major move, greater Openness predicted both heightened self-
esteem and increased depression (Kling, Ryff, Love, & Essex, 2003). More highly
open adults are more creative, at least in supportive circumstances (George & Zhou,
2001); it seems likely that a very important source of this creativity is access to a complex world of inner ideas and emotions. Second, open individuals are motivated to seek
out interesting new experiences. This view of Openness is consistent with some of the
markers of Openness in children, including eagerness to learn new things (both academic and nonacademic). Among adults, Openness expresses itself in a wide variety of
observable behaviors and attitudes. More open adults tend to be more politically lib-
eral, less authoritarian in their attitudes, and less traditional in their beliefs (Jost,
Glaser, Kruglanski, & Sulloway, 2003). In contrast, we know strikingly little about the
behaviors associated with Openness in children.

Developmental Elaboration of Personality Traits

The process of developmental elaboration refers to the mechanisms by which those temperament attributes that are part of each individual's genetic heritage accumulate response strength through their repeated reinforcement and become elaborated into cognitive and affective representations that are quickly and frequently activated—into personality traits. This elaboration may involve at least six processes (Table 6.3), which we now describe in the order of their hypothesized emergence. For example, learning processes and environmental elicitation are hypothesized to influence the course of personality development in the first few months of life; environmental construal and social comparison processes can influence personality development only following the emergence of necessary cognitive functions in early and middle childhood; and environmental selection and manipulation generally require the emergence of self-regulatory functions in childhood and are likely to become particularly important as youths move into adolescence. Before describing these six processes, we remind you that examples of these processes appear in nearly all sections of this chapter. The ubiquitous presence of process-focused personality analysis in this chapter is not an accident. As we noted in the beginning of the chapter, personality research is increasingly based on the recognition that traits are not merely semantic labels but rather reflect organizing and motivating biological and psychological processes. The purpose of this section is to provide an organizing framework for thinking about and studying the processes by which personality traits develop and increasingly shape behavior.

TABLE 6.3   Processes through which Early Temperament/Personality Shapes the Development of Later Personality and Adaptation

Process	Definition	Example
Learning processes	Temperament shapes the child's experience of classical and operant conditioning.	Children high on Openness may find complex and novel stimuli to be reinforcing.
Environmental elicitation	Temperament shapes the response of adults and peers to the child.	Children high on Extraversion may attract peers to play with them.
Environmental construal	Temperament shapes the ways that children interpret the environment and their experiences.	Children low on Agreeableness may interpret requests from adults as hostile impositions on their freedom.
Social and temporal comparisons	Temperament shapes the ways children evaluate themselves relative to others and to themselves across time.	Children high on Neuroticism may wrongly view themselves as inadequate relative to their peers.
Environmental selection	Temperament shapes children's choices about their everyday environments.	Children high on Conscientiousness may pursue challenging activities.
Environmental manipulation	Temperament shapes the ways that children alter, modify, and manipulate their environments.	Children high on Extraversion may actively persuade other children to choose them as leaders of school groups.

LEARNING PROCESSES

Temperament differences may influence several learning processes that are involved in the elaboration process, including positive and negative reinforcement, punishment, discrimination learning, and extinction. In the second section, we described current models positing that Extraversion and Neuroticism reflect individual differences in a BAS and BIS, respectively (Gray, 1987, 1990). In essence, proponents of these models argue that Extraversion and Neuroticism reflect differences in various learning mechanisms (i.e., Extraversion indexes sensitivity to potential rewards and Neuroticism indexes sensitivity to potential threats). Other traits in addition to Extraversion and Neuroticism should affect learning processes as well. For example, as we have reviewed, children differ strikingly in their persistence and attention, two temperament traits that are likely to influence learning. Agreeableness may be related to sensitivities to anger- or frustration-inducing stimuli, whereas Openness may be associated with attraction to complex or novel stimuli. All of these differences in learning processes should be amenable to investigation through behavioral and neuroscience methods.

ENVIRONMENTAL ELICITATION

Through a process of environmental elicitation, temperament differences evoke different reactions from the environment and influence how other people react to children, beginning in the first few months of life. Research on evocative effects of children's temperament on parents is especially well developed in relation to infants and young children with "difficult" temperaments (i.e., children who are irritable, hostile, prone to cry, and hard to soothe). Many studies have documented that mothers of difficult infants experience lower confidence, greater depression, and lower self-efficacy than do mothers of more temperamentally easy infants (Crockenberg & Leerkes, 2003). The evidence for child effects on parents is the most robust in relation to individual differences in negative emotions, but other temperament traits appear to predict parental responses as well (Putnam et al., 2002). In addition, it is important to recognize that the effects of children's temperaments extend beyond the family environment to other caregivers, teachers, and peers. In turn, the responses that children evoke from others are likely to be internalized as part of children's emerging self-concepts. Temperament characteristics elicit not only behaviors on the part of others but also expectations. Adults have implicit theories about developmental trajectories that they associate with particular temperament attributes. As such, children's temperament-based behaviors may elicit expectancy-based reactions from adult caregivers (Graziano, Jensen-Campbell, & Sullivan-Logan, 1998). Finally, it is important to recognize that children's effects on others are likely to be moderated by the characteristics of the interaction partner. Even among parents of emotionally negative children, there are some parents in some contexts who respond with heightened attention and sensitivity (Crockenberg & Leerkes, 2003), which suggests the presence of important moderators of parental responses.

ENVIRONMENTAL CONSTRUAL

With the emergence of belief systems and expectations, temperament differences may also begin to influence environmental construal, thus shaping each person's effective experience of the environment. Research about the construal process stems from the cognitive tradition in personality psychology, which emphasizes each person's subjective experience and unique perception of the world. This research focuses on what people "do" mentally (Cervone & Mischel, 2002), demonstrating that social information processing—including attention, encoding, retrieval, and interpretation—is a selective process shaped by individual differences in temperament and personality (Derryberry & Reed, 2003). The role of cognitive factors in personality and psychopathology has been detailed by Crick and Dodge (1994), whose social information-processing model of children's social adjustment includes six steps: (1) to encode information about the event, (2) to interpret the cues and arrive at some decision about their meaning and significance, (3) to clarify goals, (4) to search for possible responses to the situation, (5) to consider the consequences of each potential response and to select a response from the generated alternatives, and (6) to carry out the selected response. Temperament and personality have the potential to shape social information processing at each of these steps. Another important reason that temperament is likely to influence cognitive processing is that temperament involves emotional processes that are known to shape cognition (Derryberry & Reed, 2003).

SOCIAL AND TEMPORAL COMPARISONS

With increased cognitive sophistication (e.g., role-taking skills), two social-psychological processes are hypothesized to influence self-evaluations and identity development: Children learn about themselves by comparing and contrasting themselves to others (social comparisons) as well as to themselves over time (temporal comparisons). Age-related changes in social cognition and social roles make it likely that social comparisons may be especially influential from childhood to adolescence and into adulthood and that temporal comparisons may become increasingly important during the adult years. The micro processes through which personality may shape social and temporal comparisons also deserve attention. Temperament and personality may shape a range of relevant processes (Cassidy, Ziv, Mehta, & Feeney, 2003; Derryberry & Reed, 2003), including (a) the kinds of feedback that people deliberately seek out about themselves, (b) attentional biases to comparison information, (c) standards used for comparison, and (d) emotional responsivity to comparison information.

ENVIRONMENTAL SELECTION

As self-regulatory competencies increase with age, individuals begin to make choices and display preferences that may reinforce and sustain their characteristics; thus, environmental selection comes into play. Children's emerging personalities shape the environments they select, whether consciously or unconsciously. Processes of environmental selection are likely to become increasingly important across the years from childhood to adulthood (Scarr & McCartney, 1983). Even among very young children, temperament is likely to shape the spheres children occupy in the environments chosen for them by adults (e.g., inhibited toddlers may avoid interactions with other children in child care, or children high on intellect may choose more stimulating activities at home). As children move into middle childhood, they are given greater freedom to choose the environments in which they spend their time (Cole & Cole, 1996). During childhood and adolescence, youths' personalities may help determine the activities in which they participate and the ways in which they choose to spend their free time. Personality effects on children's peer relationships may be particularly important. Children's individual differences also predict the life events they experience; for example, children with externalizing behavior problems experience a greater number of controllable negative life events than children without these problems (Masten, Neeman, & Andenas, 1994). In adulthood, individuals make personality-based choices regarding education, occupation, and intimate relationships (reviewed in a later section); all of these choices shape individuals' everyday environments. Indeed, by adulthood the most striking personality differences between individuals are to be found not by studying their responses to the same situation but by studying how they choose and construct new situations. A person's selection and creation of environments is thus one of the most individualizing and pervasive expressions of his or her personality.

ENVIRONMENTAL MANIPULATION

Once the self-concept is firmly established, and with the development of more sophisticated self-regulatory capacities, through a process of environmental manipulation, individuals also begin to alter and modify the environments in which they find themselves (Buss, 1987). These processes may become particularly important as children become more skilled in regulating their own behavior and more insightful into the causes of others' behaviors. Like adults, children vary in the goals that they pursue in various circumstances (Rose & Asher, 1999), and these goals are likely to influence the ways that children attempt to modify their environments. The ways that individuals select and shape their environments may be especially relevant for self-regulation. Individuals regulate their behavior in the midst of an ongoing emotional experience. But individuals also regulate their behavior and others' behavior proactively by anticipating potential situations and selecting how to handle those situations according to their goals.

The Origins of Individual Differences in Personality

In this section, we review what is known about genetic influences on personality variation between people.

To estimate the relative roles that genes and environments play in personality development, behavioral geneticists employ two basic research designs: (1) twin studies and (2) adoption studies. The logic behind using the twin method to estimate heritable influences is straightforward, and it has three parts. First, a genetic contribution to personality is indicated when the similarity of monozygotic (MZ) twins' personalities is greater than the similarity of dizygotic (DZ) twins' personalities. This inference is based on the fact that MZ twins share all their genes, but DZ twins, like all siblings, share on average only half of their polymorphic genes. Quantitative model fitting usually labels this "A," for additive genetic effects. To use this logic, researchers must test the critical assumption that all of the greater similarity between MZ and DZ twins can safely be ascribed to MZ twins' greater genetic similarity. This is called the "equal environments assumption." In other words, researchers must show that MZ twins have not been treated more alike than DZ twins in ways that are related to their personality outcomes. Research into this question suggests that MZ and DZ twins are not perfectly equal on some environmental experiences. However, some part of the greater MZ than DZ twin similarity in treatment arises because MZ twins' genetically influenced similar behavior evokes similar treatment. Evoked similar treatment does not violate the assumption unless it further exacerbates MZ twin similarity. Moreover, despite the fact that such inequality may have inflated some heritability estimates by a small amount, it has not done so enough to invalidate the inference that genes influence personality differences.

Second, twin studies can show whether environmental experiences influence twin similarity over and above genetic influences. MZ twins' genetic similarity is twice that of DZ twins, and therefore, if nothing more than genes were influencing their personalities, MZ twins' personalities should be at least twice as similar as DZ twins'. If not, this indicates that something more than genes has made the twins similar (i.e., environments that the siblings share in common must have enhanced their similarity). In model fitting, this yields a significant variance component called family wide, shared, or common environmental variance, often labeled "C." It indexes environmental effects on personality that can be detected because they have increased the personality similarity between family members in the study and because the family members shared the experience for reasons completely apart from their genetic similarity.

Third, twin studies also address the perennial question of why family members differ from each other (Plomin & Daniels, 1987), by using the following logic. If MZ twins, despite sharing all their genes, are not perfectly identical in their personality, this indicates that nonshared experience unique to each family member has reduced their similarity. In model fitting, this yields a significant variance component called child-specific, nonshared, or unique environmental variance, often labeled "E." It indexes environmental effects on personality that can be detected because they have created differences between family members in the study. Phenotype measurement errors can produce such effects, too, because errors in measurement produce scores that look different for twins in a pair.

The fundamental logic behind using the adoption method to estimate heritable influences is also straightforward. The correlation between adoptee and biological parent personality represents genetic transmission, whereas the correlation between adoptee and adoptive parent personality represents social (i.e., environmental) transmission. To use this logic researchers must test the critical assumptions that adoptees share no more than random genes with their adoptive parents (i.e., adoption was extrafamilial and the adoption agency did not try to match the adoptive and birth family's characteristics), and adoptees share not more than random environments with their biological parents (e.g., the quality of prenatal and orphanage care were uncorrelated with adoptees' biological backgrounds). Like twin data, adoption data can be modeled to ascertain A, C, and E components of variance.

With data from large studies throughout the world (Boomsma, Busjahn, & Peltonen, 2002), research has uncovered increasingly reliable and robust evidence that personality traits are substantially influenced by genetic factors. Bouchard and Loehlin (2001; Bouchard, 2004) provide a comprehensive review of this research, pointing to heritability estimates across the Big Five factors in the range of .50 + .10. There are some fluctuations from study to study, but in general (a) all five superfactors appear to be influenced by genetic factors to the same extent and (b) genetic and environmental factors also affect individual differences in men's and women's personalities to the same extent.

Three clarifications and qualifications deserve special notice. First, twin studies using peer ratings of personality, rather than self-report personality questionnaires show genetic influences similar to those found in self-report studies (Reimann, Angleiter, & Strelau, 1997). It does not appear to be the case that heritability estimates derived from twin studies are simply an artifact of self-report methodologies in which MZ and DZ twins are asked to rate themselves. Some studies using observational measures of behavior (e.g., empathy; Emde & Hewitt, 2001) yield lower heritability estimates than have been found using questionnaire measures. However, there are still too few such observational studies to know if this is a robust methodological difference.

A second, related methodological challenge has been levied at temperament and personality research with children. Twin studies of younger age groups have relied primarily on ratings by parents, which have yielded an odd result: Correlations for identical (MZ) twins are high, and correlations for fraternal (DZ) twins are very low, sometimes even negative (Saudino & Cherny, 2001). The suggestion is that parents may provide biased ratings of their twins and that behavioral genetic studies that rely on parents for data may not yield valid estimates of genetic and environmental influences on personality functioning. However, the situation is rather less alarming than often claimed. Parents sometimes contrast their twins in ways that generate greater than expected differences between MZ versus DZ twins, but this problem may be restricted to some traits (e.g., symptoms of hyperactivity, temperament ratings of activity level; Simonoff et al., 1998) and may be attenuated by different rating measures (Goldsmith, Buss, & Lemery, 1997).

Third, family and adoption studies of personality yield lower estimates of genetic influences than twin studies (M. Martin, Boomsma, & Machin, 1997; Plomin, Corley, Caspi, Fulker, & DeFries, 1998). Specifically, parent-child and biological sibling correlations for personality traits average about .1 to .2, with corresponding heritabilities of .3 that are considerably lower than the heritabilities of .5 obtained in twin studies. One possibility is that the discrepant findings result from the fact that parent-offspring and sibling-sibling correlations are derived from different-age pairs and thus (dis)similarity is confounded by age and cohort differences. Another possibility is that nonadditive genetic effects play a larger role in personality than suggested by MZ and DZ correlations. Nonadditive genetic effects refer to effects of genes that interact to influence a trait, in contrast to additive genetic effects in which genes "add up." Nonadditive effects only contribute slightly to the resemblance of DZ twins and other first-degree relatives, whereas MZ twins are identical for all (additive and nonadditive) genetic effects. Although adoption studies are far fewer and much smaller than twin studies of personality, it is noteworthy that they suggest less genetic influence than twin studies, and the lack of correspondence, at least in relation to personality research, between the results of twin and adoption/family studies merits further scrutiny.

Personality Continuity and Change

The assertion that an individual's personality has changed or remained the same over time is ambiguous. The boy who has daily temper tantrums when he is age 2 but weekly tantrums when he is age 9 has increased his level of emotional control; he has changed in absolute terms. But if he ranks first in temper tantrums among his peers at both ages, he has not changed in relative terms. Further ambiguity arises if the form of the behavior changes. If this boy emerges into adulthood as a man who is irritable and moody, we may grant that the phenotype has changed but claim that the underlying personality has not. A third ambiguity arises when a claim of continuity rests on observations not of an individual but of a sample of individuals. The continuity of an attribute at the group level may be masking large but mutually canceling changes at the individual level. There are several meanings denoted by the term *continuity*. The purpose of this section is to disentangle those meanings. First, we review evidence about two types of continuity and change observed in longitudinal research: differential and mean-level. Second, we review the conceptual challenge of testing and documenting coherence in personality functioning across time and in diverse circumstances.

DIFFERENTIAL CONTINUITY AND CHANGE

Continuity and change are most often indexed by correlations between personality scores across two points in time (i.e., test-retest correlations). These differential, or rank-order stability correlations, reflect the degree to which the relative ordering of individuals on a given trait is maintained over time. Two contradictory predictions have been proposed about the rank-order stability of personality traits. The classical trait perspective argues that personality traits in adulthood are biologically based temperaments that are not susceptible to the influence of the environment and thus do not change over time (McCrae et al., 2000). From this essentialist perspective, we would expect the test-retest correlations to be high, even early in life. In contrast, the radical contextual perspective emphasizes the importance of life changes and role transitions in personality development and suggests that personality should be fluid and prone to change and should yield low test-retest correlation coefficients, especially during developmental periods characterized by rapid physical, cognitive, and social changes (Lewis, 2001). Existing longitudinal studies do not support either of these positions. A meta-analysis of the rank-order stability of personality (organized according to the five-factor model) revealed six major conclusions (Roberts & DelVecchio, 2000):

1. Test-retest correlations over time are moderate in magnitude, even from childhood to early adulthood.
2. Rank-order stability increases with age. Test-retest correlations (unadjusted for measurement error) increased from .41 in childhood to .55 at age 30, and then reached a plateau around .70 between ages 50 and 70.
3. Rank-order stability decreases as the time interval between observations increases.
4. Rank-order stability does not vary markedly across the Big Five traits.
5. Rank-order stability does not vary markedly according to assessment method (i.e., self-reports, observer ratings, and projective tests).
6. Rank-order stability does not vary markedly by gender.

Several implications can be drawn from this meta-analysis. First, the level of continuity in childhood and adolescence is much higher than originally expected (Lewis, 2001), especially after age 3. Even more impressive is the fact that the level of stability increases in a relatively linear fashion through adolescence and young adulthood. Young adulthood has been described as demographically dense, in that it involves more life-changing roles and identity decisions than any other period in the life course (Arnett, 2000). Despite these dramatic contextual changes, personality differences remain remarkably consistent during this time period. Second, personality continuity in adulthood peaks later than expected. According to one prominent perspective, personality traits are essentially fixed and unchanging after age 30 (McCrae & Costa, 1994). However, the meta-analytic findings show that rank-order stability peaks some time after age 50, but at a level well below unity. Thus, individual differences in personality traits continue to change throughout adulthood, but only modestly after age 50. Third, the magnitude of differential stability of personality traits, although not as high as essentialists would claim, is still remarkably high.

MEAN-LEVEL CONTINUITY AND CHANGE

Mean-level change refers to changes in the average trait level of a population. This type of change is thought to result from maturational processes shared by a population and is typically assessed by mean-level differences in specific traits over time, which indicate whether the sample as a whole is increasing or decreasing on a trait. Contradictory perspectives—similar to those guiding predictions about differential stability—have also guided expectations about mean-level changes in personality traits. Proponents of the five-factor model of personality argue that personality traits do not demonstrate mean-level changes after adulthood is reached (Costa & McCrae, 1997). In contrast, proponents of a life-span developmental perspective emphasize the importance of life changes and role transitions in personality development and suggest that mean-level changes do occur and often at ages much later than young adulthood (Helson, Kwan, John, & Jones, 2002).

A meta-analysis synthesized and organized (according to the Five-Factor Model) data from 92 longitudinal studies spanning the period from age 10 to 101 years (Roberts, Walton, & Viechtbauer, 2006). The pattern of change in the first domain of the Big Five, Extraversion, was complex until this superfactor was divided into constituent elements of social dominance (assertiveness, dominance) and social vitality (talkativeness, sociability). Traits associated with social dominance increased from adolescence through early middle age, whereas traits associated with social vitality increased in adolescence and then showed decreases in young adulthood and old age. Consistent with evidence from cross-sectional comparisons of different age groups (McCrae et al., 2000), traits belonging to the domains of Agreeableness and Conscientiousness increased in young adulthood and middle age. Traits belonging to the domain of Neuroticism decreased mostly in young adulthood. Finally, traits from the Openness to Experience domain showed increases in adolescence and young adulthood and a tendency to decrease in old age. Overall, the results suggest that, on average, individuals change in the direction of having greater capacity to be productive and involved contributors to society, in that people tend to become more planful, deliberate, and decisive, but also more considerate and charitable (traits encompassed by lower Neuroticism and higher Conscientiousness and Agreeableness).

Three additional aspects of these longitudinal findings deserve note. First, there are no discernible sex differences in patterns of mean-level continuity and change across the Big Five. Apparently, men and women change in the same ways over the life course, although mean-level differences between the sexes are maintained over time. This suggests that the causes of personality continuity and change across the life course are likely to be the same for the sexes. Second, the majority of mean-level personality change occurs in young adulthood not in adolescence, as we might suspect given traditional theories of psychological development. This pattern of change is not simply a recent phenomenon because it was observed in different cohorts across the twentieth century. This finding suggests that the causes of normative personality change are likely to be identified by narrowing research attention to the study of young adulthood. Third, for select trait categories, change occurs well past young adulthood, demonstrating the continued plasticity of personality well beyond typical age markers of maturity.

PERSONALITY COHERENCE

The kinds of continuity discussed so far refer to homotypic continuity—continuity of similar behaviors or phenotypic attributes over time. The concept of coherence enlarges the definition of continuity to include heterotypic continuity—continuity of an inferred attribute presumed to underlie diverse phenotypic behaviors. Specific behaviors in childhood may not predict phenotypically similar behavior later in adulthood but may still be associated with behaviors that are conceptually consistent with the earlier behavior. Kagan (1969) noted that heterotypic continuities are most likely to be found from the earlier years of life, when children go through numerous rapid changes. In contrast, homotypic continuities are more likely to be found after puberty, when psychological organization nears completion. With the coming of age of various longitudinal samples, examples of heterotypic continuities now abound in the psychological literature. But it is important to emphasize that coherence and heterotypic continuity refer to conceptual rather than a literal continuity among behaviors: "The notion of coherence refers to a pattern of findings where a construct, measured by several different methods, retains its psychological meaning as revealed in relationships to a variety of other measures" (Ozer, 1986, p. 52) across time and in different contexts. Accordingly, the investigator who claims to have discovered coherence must have a theory—no matter how rudimentary or implicit—that specifies the basis on which the diverse behaviors and attributes can be said to belong to the same equivalence class. We now review three conceptual approaches to the problem of studying personality coherence across the life course. Each of these social-developmental approaches provides a framework for understanding coherence by focusing on the distinctive ways in which individuals organize their behavior to meet new environmental demands and developmental challenges.

An organizational-adaptational perspective focuses on tasks and milestones that are encountered during the course of development and on how these are met by different personalities (Masten & Coatsworth, 1995). According to this perspective, personality traits influence problem-solving modalities that individuals use when meeting new developmental challenges at different points in the life course (e.g., developing competent peer relationships in childhood, establishing appropriate cross-sex relationships in adolescence, learning to parent in early adulthood, or providing for dependent parents in middle age). Some of these developmental tasks are universal, whereas others are specific to a sociocultural context and historical period.

Beyond childhood the search for coherence becomes more complicated, and it may be that a purely psychological approach is insufficient for the analysis of personality continuity and change as the individual increasingly negotiates social roles defined by the culture. Some researchers have found it useful to adopt a sociocultural perspective and to conceive of the life course as a sequence of culturally defined, age-graded roles (e.g., marriage, work, and parenting) that the individual enacts over time (Caspi, 1987; Helson, Mitchell, & Moane, 1984). In this fashion, the life course can be charted as a sequence of age-linked social roles, and personality coherence can be explored by investigating consistencies in the ways different persons select and perform different sociocultural roles; for example, in whether they opt for conventional or unconventional career paths or in whether they are "off-time" in relation to normative, age-graded tasks such as getting married.

Bouchard (1995) correctly argued that a purely sociocultural perspective on the life course "ignores the fact that life-histories themselves are complex evolved adaptations" (p. 91). An evolutionary psychology perspective on the life course complements the sociocultural perspective by exploring how personality variation is related to those adaptively important problems with which human beings have had to repeatedly contend: It focuses research on the genetically influenced strategies and tactics that individuals use for survival and reproduction. Evolutionary psychology thus focuses attention on the coherence of behavioral strategies that people use in, for example, mate selection, mate retention, reproduction, parental care, kin investment, status attainment, and coalition building (Buss, 1999). Evolutionary psychology may thus hold promise for organizing longitudinal-developmental data on personality coherence.

These three approaches, or road maps for studying personality across the life course, share an important assumption: Continuities of personality across the life course are expressed not only through the constancy of behavior across time and in diverse circumstances but also through the consistency over time in the ways that persons characteristically modify their changing contexts as a function of their behavior. We now review evidence of such continuities across the life course.

Personality and the Life Course: How Early-Emerging Personality Differences Shape Developmental Pathways

Two events have served to make research on personality trait development more vibrant over the past 10 years. First, developmental psychologists have begun to measure personality traits rather than ignore them. Second, personality psychologists have become increasingly interested in relating measures of personality traits to something besides other personality measures. The result is robust evidence that early emerging individual differences in personality shape how individuals experience, interpret, and respond to the developmental tasks they face across the life course. In this section, we review longitudinal evidence about how personality traits shape (a) the cultivation of social relationships, (b) the mastery of educational and work tasks, and (c) the promotion and maintenance of physical health. For each developmental task, we identify the most relevant personality variables and outline the mechanisms by which these personality traits are hypothesized to exert their influence.

CULTIVATING RELATIONSHIPS: HOW PERSONALITY SHAPES FRIENDSHIPS AND INTIMATE RELATIONSHIPS

One of the most important tasks faced by children and adolescents is the establishment of friendships and acceptance among peers. Among children, all of the higher-order

Big Five traits except Openness are important predictors of social competence. Perhaps so many aspects of personality predict social competence because social functioning requires a wide array of skills, including emotional expression, emotional understanding, and emotional and behavioral regulation (Rubin, Bukowski, & Parker, 2006). Agreeable and Extraverted children show better social competence concurrently and across time and experience growth in perceived social support from early to late adolescence (Asendorpf & van Aken, 2003; Branje, van Lieshout, & van Aken, 2004; Shiner & Masten, 2002). Children high on Negative Emotionality or low on aspects of Conscientiousness (e.g., attention and self-control) have a variety of social difficulties concurrently and across time (Eisenberg et al., 2000); the interaction of high Negative Emotionality and low self-regulation may be especially problematic for social functioning (Eisenberg et al., 2000).

Personality continues to be an important predictor of relationships in adulthood. Extraversion predicts positive romantic relationships and friendships (Shiner, Masten, & Tellegen, 2002), whereas Neuroticism and Disagreeableness are the strongest and most consistent personality predictors of negative relationship outcomes (Karney & Bradbury, 1995; Roberts, Kuncel, Shiner, Caspi, & Goldberg, 2007). These effects of Neuroticism and low Agreeableness have been uncovered in long-term studies following samples of children into adulthood and in shorter-term longitudinal studies of adults. The potential contribution of personality differences to shaping abusive relationships has been further underscored by longitudinal studies that find associations between early developing aggressive traits in childhood and subsequent abusive behavior in adult romantic relationships (Ehrensaft, Moffitt, & Caspi, 2004). One study that followed a large sample of adolescents across their multiple relationships in early adulthood discovered that the influence of Neuroticism and low Agreeableness on relationship quality showed cross-relationship generalization: It predicted the same abusive relationship experiences across relationships with different partners (Robins, Caspi, & Moffitt, 2002). Increasingly, sophisticated studies that include dyads (not just individuals) and multiple methods (not just self reports) demonstrate that the link between personality traits and relationship processes is more than simply an artifact of shared method variance in the assessment of these two domains (Donnellan, Conger, & Bryant, 2004).

An important research goal is to uncover the proximal relationship-specific processes that mediate these personality effects on relationship outcomes. Personality traits affect relationships by influencing and altering micro-interactional processes. First, individuals select their interactional contexts by choosing partners who resemble them. Second, personality differences influence people's exposure to relationship events, such as daily conflicts. Third, personality differences shape people's reactions to the behavior of their partners. Fourth, personality differences evoke behaviors from partners that contribute to relationship quality.

STRIVING AND ACHIEVING: HOW PERSONALITY SHAPES PERFORMANCE IN SCHOOL AND WORK SETTINGS

During the life course, individuals assume multiple performance tasks (e.g., pursuing an education, assuming a job, or managing and allocating resources). Personality traits from the domain of Conscientiousness are the most important noncognitive predictors of educational achievement and occupational attainment (Judge, Higgins, Thoresen, &

Barrick, 1999; Roberts et al., 2007). In fact, childhood Conscientiousness predicts improvements in academic achievement across time into adulthood (Shiner & Masten, 2002). Similarly, adult Conscientiousness predicts job performance across a wide variety of measures and across nearly all types of jobs (Barrick, Mount, & Judge, 2001). Conscientiousness encompasses many traits that are necessary for completing work effectively: the capacities to sustain attention, to strive toward high standards, and to inhibit impulsive behavior. In contrast, childhood Neuroticism predicts lower adult occupational attainment (Judge et al., 1999). Adult Neuroticism appears to have small negative effects on job performance (Barrick et al., 2001; Hurtz & Donovan, 2000). Links between the other Big Five traits and academic and work achievement are less consistent and robust but are still found. Openness to Experience/Intellect predicts academic achievement in samples of school-age children, adolescents, and college students (Farsides & Woodfield, 2003; Graziano, Jensen-Campbell, & Finch, 1999), and child and adult Agreeableness sometimes do as well (Shiner & Masten, 2002). Meta-analyses reveal that Extraversion, Agreeableness, and Openness predict some more limited aspects of work performance in a subset of occupations (Barrick et al., 2001). Research with children, adolescents, and adults demonstrates that many of the links between personality traits (especially Conscientiousness) and various indices of achievement remain significant after controlling for individual differences in ability (Judge et al., 1999; Shiner & Masten, 2002), but sometimes the links disappear (Schmidt & Hunter, 2004). The predictive associations between temperament and personality traits and achievement are apparent early in life, at the time that children first enroll in school (Miech, Essex, & Goldsmith, 2001).

The personality processes involved may vary across different stages of development, and at least four candidate processes deserve research scrutiny (see Schneider, Smith, Taylor, & Fleenor, 1998). First, the personality-achievement associations may reflect "attraction" effects, or "active niche-picking," whereby people actively choose educational and work experiences whose qualities are concordant with their own personalities. Second, personality-achievement associations reflect "recruitment" effects, whereby people are selected into achievement situations and are given preferential treatment on the basis of their personality characteristics. Third, some personality-achievement associations emerge as consequences of "attrition" or "deselection pressures," whereby people leave achievement settings (e.g., schools or jobs) that do not fit with their personality or are released from these settings because of their trait-correlated behaviors. Fourth, personality-achievement associations emerge as a result of direct, proximal effects of personality on performance. Personality traits may promote certain kinds of task effectiveness, interpersonal interactions at work, and performance motivation.

HEALTH PROMOTION AND MAINTENANCE: HOW PERSONALITY SHAPES HEALTH TRAJECTORIES

The lifelong interplay between psyche and soma is nowhere more apparent than in research documenting that personality traits contribute to the maintenance of physical integrity and health. Especially impressive are life-span studies documenting associations between personality traits related to Conscientiousness with longevity (Roberts et al., 2007). Individuals high in traits related to Disagreeableness (e.g., anger and hostility) appear to be at greatest risk of disease (e.g., cardiovascular illness; Miller, Smith,

Turner, Guijarro, & Hallet, 1996). The evidence for the involvement of Neuroticism in ill health is more mixed, with some research pointing to links with increased risk of actual disease and other studies documenting links with illness behavior only (Smith & Spiro, 2002). The study of health also serves to illustrate the utility of hierarchical structural models of personality in integrating and interpreting research findings. For example, some of the inconsistency that has been observed in studies of hostility and cardiovascular disease may be due to the fact that hostility is a facet or component of both Neuroticism and Agreeableness (versus Antagonism). Measures of hostility that reflect overt interpersonal expressions of anger are facets of Agreeableness that may be the lethal personality risk factor for coronary heart disease, whereas measures of hostility that tap irritation and self-focused negativity are facets of Neuroticism and may be better predictors of health complaints rather than actual health outcomes. A taxonomic model of personality can help researchers to make conceptual and measurement refinements in testing psychosomatic hypotheses.

Personality health associations may reflect at least three distinct processes (Contrada, Cather, & O'Leary, 1999; Rozanski, Blumenthal, & Kaplan, 1999). First, personality differences may be related to pathogenesis—mechanisms that promote disease. Second, personality differences may be related to physical-health outcomes because they are associated with health-promoting or health-damaging behaviors. Third, personality differences may be related to reactions to illness. This includes a wide class of behaviors, including the possibility that personality differences affect the selection and execution of coping behaviors (e.g., Scheier & Carver, 1993), modulate distress reduction, and shape treatment adherence (Kenford et al., 2002).

PREDICTING ALL OF BEHAVIOR ALL OF THE TIME

Although personality traits have been shown to shape developmental outcomes in multiple domains and in different age groups, a common refrain is that these predictive associations only account for a fraction of the variance in outcomes of interest. This observation must be balanced by four considerations. First, it seems necessary to periodically reissue the reminder that even small effect sizes are of theoretical and practical significance (Roberts et al., 2007). By way of comparison, epidemiological and clinical studies repeatedly uncover associations whose effect sizes range between .1 and .3. Second, debates about the size of personality effects are based on the implicit assumption that every behavior is the product of a single trait. This is implausible, because each individual is characterized by a personal pattern of multiple traits working additively and interactively to influence behavior. This multiple-trait perspective has important implications for effect-size estimates: Simulation studies demonstrate that it is unreasonable and statistically inconceivable in multiply determined systems for any single trait to explain much more than 10% of the variance (Ahadi & Diener, 1989). Third, social behavior is a product of multiple personalities acting in concert and influencing one another. Consider the case of relationship outcomes. If personality effects are additive across partners, the true impact of a personality trait on a relationship should be regarded as the summed effect of two personalities not a single individual's trait (Moffitt, Robins, & Caspi, 2001). Fourth, because the effects of personality differences accumulate over a lifetime, a focus on a single outcome variable measured at a single point in time may underestimate the contribution of personality to the course of developmental trajectories. Abelson

(1985) makes this point in noting that differences between baseball players are trivial if considered on the basis of a single at-bat but become meaningful over the course of a game, a season, and a career. These observations are not intended to breed smug self-satisfaction. Rather, they are meant to foster reasonable expectations and aspirations for research on personality development.

Conclusions

Throughout this chapter, we summarized definitive findings, identified promising research leads and hypotheses, and underscored existing methodological limitations. Our concluding comments are thus devoted to sketching the requirements for improved research.

Longitudinal research is the lifeblood of developmental psychology, but simply tracking people over time is not good enough. There is room for improvement on three fronts. Longitudinal research on personality can be improved through better trait measurement. The availability of a taxonomy of measurable individual differences in temperament and personality is an indispensable aid to developmental research. However, few off-the-shelf measures assess the full range of higher- and lower-order traits described in this chapter: The development of reliable, valid, and comprehensive measures of child and adolescent personality remains an important task.

Longitudinal research is not always developmental research and, conversely, many developmental questions require different types of research designs. In particular, little is known about how early emerging individual differences become elaborated into the consistent ways of behaving, thinking, and feeling that we call personality. Throughout this chapter, we listed some ideas and working hypotheses about these processes. These will need to be examined using traditional observational methods and, increasingly, the tools of neuroscience as well. To the extent that the most important sources of influence on the processes of developmental elaboration are to be found in interpersonal settings, the ideal study of individual development ought to be conceived of as a study of social relationships, one in which longitudinal participants are successively studied alongside their significant others at different points in the life course. These types of studies will include both global ratings of individual differences and minute-to-minute assessments of social interactions to document how behavior patterns are evoked and sustained. Just as research in social cognition inspired deeper understanding of personality dynamics in the latter part of the twentieth century, the fusion of differential psychology and neuroscience will lead the way to a fuller understanding of how personality traits are linked to processing emotional stimuli.

Finally, research into personality development will need to embrace genetics. Questions about the extent to which genetic factors influence individual differences in personality are increasingly less interesting, if only because it is by now so well established that genetic factors do have a large influence. But this does not mean that behavioral genetics research has served its purpose and worn out its welcome. To the contrary, discoveries about the human genome open up new research possibilities in which measured genotypes will be used to study the origins of personality differences and the links between personality and psychopathology. To ignore genetics is not only irresponsible but also a missed opportunity.

These concluding observations are intended to stimulate new research into personality development and also to promote discussion about the kind of multidisciplinary (re)training that is increasingly required of new students (and seasoned researchers), spanning psychometric theory, epidemiology, neuroscience, and genetics. It is a daunting and exciting task.

References

Abelson, R. (1985). A variance explanation paradox: When a little is a lot. *Psychological Bulletin, 97,* 129–133.

Ahadi, S., & Diener, E. (1989). Multiple determinants and effect sizes. *Journal of Personality and Social Psychology, 56,* 398–406.

Allport, G. W. (1937). *Personality: A psychological interpretation.* New York: Holt.

Arnett, J. J. (2000). Emerging adulthood: A theory of development from the late teens through the twenties. *American Psychologist, 55,* 469–480.

Asendorpf, J. B., & van Aken, M. A. G. (2003). Personality-relationship transaction in adolescence: Core versus surface personality characteristics. *Journal of Personality, 71,* 629–666.

Banfield, J. F., Wyland, C. L., Macrae, C. N., Munte, T. F., & Heatherton, T. F. (2004). The cognitive resolution of self-regulation. In R. F. Baumeister & K. D. Vohs (Eds.), *Handbook of self regulation: Research, theory, and applications* (pp. 62–83). New York: Guilford Press.

Barrick, M. R., Mount, M. K., & Judge, T. A. (2001). Personality and performance at the beginning of the new millennium: What do we know and where do we go next? *International Journal of Selection and Assessment, 9,* 9–30.

Bishop, G., Spence, S. H., & McDonald, C. (2003). Can parents and teachers provide a reliable and valid report of behavioral inhibition? *Child Development, 74,* 1899–1917.

Block, J. (1996). Some jangly remarks on Baumeister and Heatherton. *Psychological Inquiry, 7,* 28–32.

Boomsma, D., Busjahn, A., & Peltonen, L. (2002). Classical twin studies and beyond. *Nature Reviews Genetics, 3,* 872–882.

Bouchard, T. J. (1995). Longitudinal studies of personality and intelligence: A behavior genetic and evolutionary psychology perspective. In D. Saklofske & M. Zeidner (Eds.), *International handbook of personality and intelligence* (pp. 81–106). New York: Plenum Press.

Bouchard, T. J. (2004). Genetic influence on human psychological traits: A survey. *Current Directions in Psychological Science, 13,* 148–151.

Bouchard, T. J., & Loehlin, J. C. (2001). Genes, evolution, and personality. *Behavior Genetics, 31,* 243–274.

Branje, S. J. T., van Lieshout, C. F. M., & van Aken, M. A. G. (2004). Relations between big five personality characteristics and perceived support in adolescent families. *Journal of Personality and Social Psychology, 86,* 615–628.

Buckley, M. E., Klein, D. N., Durbin, E., Hayden, E. P., & Moerk, K. C. (2002). Development and validation of a q-sort procedure to assess temperament and behavior in preschool-age children. *Journal of Clinical Child and Adolescent Psychology, 31,* 525–539.

Buss, D. M. (1987). Selection, evocation, and manipulation. *Journal of Personality and Social Psychology, 53,* 1214–1221.

Buss, D. M. (1999). *Evolutionary psychology.* Boston: Allyn & Bacon.

Carter, C. S. (1998). Neuroendoicrine perspectives on social attachments and love. *Psychoneuroendicrinology, 23,* 779–818.

Caspi, A. (1987). Personality in the life course. *Journal of Personality and Social Psychology, 53,* 1203–1213.

Caspi, A. (1998). Personality development across the life course. In W. Damon (Series Ed.) & N. Eisenberg (Vol. Ed.), *Handbook of child psychology: Vol. 3. Social, emotional, and personality development* (5th ed., pp. 311–388). New York: Wiley.

Caspi, A., Roberts, B. W., & Shiner, R. (2005). Personality development: Stability and change. *Annual Review of Psychology, 56,* 453–484.

Cassidy, J., Ziv, Y., Mehta, T. G., & Feeney, B. C. (2003). Feedback seeking in children and adolescents: Associations with self-perceptions, attachment representations, and depression. *Child Development, 74,* 6121–6628.

Cervone, D., & Mischel, W. (2002). Personality science. In D. Cervone & W. Mischel (Eds.), *Advances in personality science* (pp. 1–26). New York: Guilford Press.

Cole, M., & Cole, S. R. (1996). *The development of children* (3rd ed.). New York: Freeman.

Contrada, R. J., Cather, C., & O'Leary, A. (1999). Personality and health: Dispositions and processes in disease susceptibility and adaptation to illness. In L. A. Pervin & O. P. John (Eds.), *Handbook of personality* (2nd ed., pp. 576–604). New York: Guilford Press.

Costa, P. T., & McCrae, R. R. (1997). Longitudinal study of adult personality. In R. Hogan, J. Johnson, & S. Briggs (Eds.), *Handbook of personality psychology* (pp. 269–292). San Diego, CA: Academic Press.

Cote, S., & Moskowitz, D. S. (1998). On the dynamic covariation between interpersonal behavior and affect: Prediction from neuroticism, extraversion, and agreeableness. *Journal of Personality and Social Psychology, 75,* 1032–1046.

Crick, N. R., & Dodge, K. A. (1994). A review and reformulation of social information processing mechanisms in children's social adjustment. *Psychological Bulletin, 115,* 74–101.

Crockenberg, S., & Leerkes, E. (2003). Infant negative emotionality, caregiving, and family. In A. C. Crouter & A. Booth (Eds.), *Children's influence on family dynamics: The neglected side of family relationships* (pp. 57–78). Mahwah, NJ: Erlbaum.

Davidson, R. J., Pizzagalli, E., Nitschke, J. B., & Kalin, N. H. (2003). Parsing the subcomponents of emotion and disorders of emotion: Perspectives from affective neuroscience. In R. J. Davidson, K. R. Scherer, & H. H. Goldsmith (Eds.), *Handbook of affective sciences* (pp. 8–24). New York: Oxford University Press.

Derryberry, D., & Reed, M. A. (2003). Information processing approaches to individual differences in emotional reactivity. In R. J. Davidson, K. R. Scherer, & H. H. Goldsmith (Eds.), *Handbook of affective sciences* (pp. 681–697). New York: Oxford University Press.

Diamond, L. M. (2004). Emerging perspectives on distinctions between romantic love and sexual desire. *Current Directions in Psychological Science, 13,* 116–119.

Digman, J. M., & Shmelyov, A. G. (1996). The structure of temperament and personality in Russian children. *Journal of Personality and Social Psychology, 71,* 341–351.

Donnellan, M. B., Conger, R. D., & Bryant, C. M. (2004). The big five and enduring marriages. *Journal of Research in Personality, 38,* 481–504.

Eaton, W. O. (1994). Temperament, development, and the five-factor model: Lessons from activity level. In C. F. Halverson, G. A. Kohnstamm, & R. P. Martin (Eds.), *The developing structure of temperament and personality from infancy to adulthood* (pp. 173–187). Hillsdale, NJ: Erlbaum.

Ehrensaft, M., Moffitt, T. E., & Caspi, A. (2004). Clinically abusive relationships in an unselected birth cohort: Men's and women's participation and developmental antecedents. *Journal of Abnormal Psychology, 113,* 258–270.

Eisenberg, N., Fabes, R. A., Guthrie, I. K., & Reiser, M. (2000). Dispositional emotionality and regulation: Their role in predicting quality of social functioning. *Journal of Personality and Social Psychology, 78,* 136–157.

Eisenberg, N., Fabes, R. A., & Spinrad, T. L. (2006). Prosocial development. In W. Damon & R. M. Lerner (Series Eds.) & N. Eisenberg (Vol. Ed.), *Handbook of child psychology: Vol. 3. Social, emotional, and personality development* (6th ed., pp. 646–718). Hoboken, NJ: Wiley.

Emde, R. N., & Hewitt, J. (Eds.). (2001). *Infancy to early childhood: Genetic and environmental influences on developmental change.* New York: Oxford University Press.

Farsides, T., & Woodfield, R. (2003). Individual differences and undergraduate success: The roles of personality, intelligence, and application. *Personality and Individual Differences, 34,* 1225–1243.

George, J. M., & Zhou, J. (2001). When openness to experience and conscientiousness are related to creative behavior: An interactional approach. *Journal of Applied Psychology, 86,* 513–524.

Gleason, K. A., Jensen-Campbell, L. A., & Richardson, D. S. (2004). Agreeableness as a predictor of aggression in adolescence. *Aggressive Behavior, 30,* 43–61.

Goldberg, L. R. (2001). Analyses of Digman's child-personality data: Derivation of big five factor scores from each of six samples. *Journal of Personality, 69,* 709–743.

Goldsmith, H. H., Buss, A. H., Plomin, R., Rothbart, M. K., Thomas, A., Chess, S., et al. (1987). Roundtable: What is temperament? *Child Development, 67,* 218–235.

Goldsmith, H. H., Buss, K. A., & Lemery, K. S. (1997). Toddler and childhood temperament: Expanded content, stronger genetic evidence, new evidence for the importance of environment. *Developmental Psychology, 33,* 891–905.

Goldsmith, H. H., Lemery, K. S., Buss, A., & Campos, J. J. (1999). Genetic analyses of focal aspects of infant temperament. *Developmental Psychology, 35,* 972–985.

Gosling, S. D. (2001). From mice to men: What can we learn about personality from animal research? *Psychological Bulletin, 127,* 45–86.

Gray, J. A. (1987). *The psychology of fear and stress* (2nd ed.). New York: McGraw-Hill.

Gray, J. A. (1990). Brain systems that mediate both emotion and cognition. *Cognition and Emotion, 4,* 269–288.

Graziano, W. G., & Eisenberg, N. (1997). Agreeableness: A dimension of personality. In R. Hogan, J. Johnson, & S. Briggs (Eds.), *Handbook of personality psychology* (pp. 795–824). San Diego, CA: Academic Press.

Graziano, W. G., Hair, E. C., & Finch, J. F. (1997). Competitiveness mediates the link between personality and group performance. *Journal of Personality and Social Psychology, 73,* 1394–1808.

Graziano, W. G., Jensen-Campbell, L. A., & Finch, J. F. (1999). The self as mediator between personality and adjustment. *Journal of Personality and Social Psychology, 73,* 392–404.

Graziano, W. G., Jensen-Campbell, L. A., & Sullivan-Logan, G. (1998). Temperament, activity, and expectations for later personality development. *Journal of Personality and Social Psychology, 74,* 1266–1277.

Halverson, C. F., Havill, V. L., Deal, J., Baker, S. R., Victor, J. B., Pavlopoulos, V., et al. (2003). Personality structure as derived from parental ratings of free descriptions of children: The inventory of child individual differences. *Journal of Personality, 71,* 995–1026.

Havill, V. L., Besevegis, E., & Mouroussaki, S. (1998). Agreeableness as a diachronic human trait. In C. S. Kohnstamm, C. F. Halverson, I. Mervielde, & V. L. Havill (Eds.), *Parental descriptions of child personality: Developmental antecedents of the big five* (pp. 49–64). Mahwah, NJ: Erlbaum.

Heller, D., Watson, D., & Ilies, R. (2004). The role of person versus situation in life satisfaction: A critical examination. *Psychological Bulletin, 130,* 574–600.

Helson, R., Kwan, V. S. Y., John, O. P., & Jones, C. (2002). The growing evidence of personality change in adulthood: Findings from research with personality inventories. *Journal of Research in Personality, 36,* 287–306.

Helson, R., Mitchell, V., & Moane, G. (1984). Personality and patterns of adherence and nonadherence to the social clock. *Journal of Personality and Social Psychology, 46,* 1079–1096.

Hogan, J., & Ones, D. S. (1997). Conscientiousness and integrity at work. In R. Hogan, J. Johnson, & S. Briggs (Eds.), *Handbook of personality psychology* (pp. 849–870). San Diego, CA: Academic Press.

Hurtz, G. M., & Donovan, J. J. (2000). Personality and job performance: The big five revisited. *Journal of Applied Psychology, 85,* 869–879.

Jensen-Campbell, L. A., Gleason, K. A., Adams, R., & Malcolm, K. T. (2003). Interpersonal conflict, agreeableness, and personality development. *Journal of Personality, 71,* 1059–1085.

Jensen-Campbell, L. A., & Graziano, W. G. (2001). Agreeableness as a moderator of interpersonal conflict. *Journal of Personality, 69,* 323–362.

John, O. P., Caspi, A., Robins, R. W., Moffitt, T. E., & Stouthamer-Loeber, M. (1994). The "little five": Exploring the five-factor model of personality in adolescent boys. *Child Development, 65,* 160–178.

John, O. P., & Srivastava, S. (1999). The big five trait taxonomy: History, measurement, and theoretical perspectives. In L. A. Pervin & O. P. John (Eds.), *Handbook of personality: Theory and research* (2nd ed., pp. 102–138). New York: Guilford Press.

Jost, J. T., Glaser, J., Kruglanski, A. W., & Sulloway, F. J. (2003). Political conservatism as motivated social cognition. *Psychological Bulletin, 129,* 339–375.

Judge, T. A., Higgins, C. A., Thoresen, C. J., & Barrick, M. R. (1999). The big five personality traits, general mental ability, and career success across the life-span. *Personnel Psychology, 52,* 621–652.

Judge, T. A., & Ilies, R. (2002). Relationship of personality to performance motivation: A meta-analytic review. *Journal of Applied Psychology, 87,* 797–807.

Kagan, J. (1969). The three faces of continuity in human development. In D. A. Goslin (Ed.), *Handbook of socialization theory and research* (pp. 983–1002). Chicago: Rand McNally.

Kagan, J. (1998). Biology and the child. In W. Damon (Series Ed.) & N. Eisenberg (Vol. Ed.), *Handbook of child psychology: Vol. 3. Social, emotional and personality development* (5th ed., pp. 177–235). New York: Wiley.

Karney, B. R., & Bradbury, T. N. (1995). The longitudinal course of marital quality and stability: A review of theory, method and research. *Psychological Bulletin, 118,* 3–34.

Kenford, S. L., Smith, S. S., Wetter, D. W., Jorenby, D. E., Fiore, M. C., & Baker, T. B. (2002). Predicting relapse back to smoking: Contrasting affective and physical models of dependence. *Journal of Consulting and Clinical Psychology, 70,* 216–227.

Kling, K. C., Ryff, C. D., Love, G., & Essex, M. (2003). Exploring the influence of personality on depressive symptoms and self-esteem across a significant life transition. *Journal of Personality and Social Psychology, 85,* 922–932.

Kochanska, G., Coy, K. C., & Murray, K. T. (2001). The development of self-regulation in the first 4 years of life. *Child Development, 72,* 1091–1111.

Kochanska, G., Coy, K. C., Tjebkes, T. L., & Husarek, S. J. (1998). Individual differences in emotionality in infancy. *Child Development, 64,* 375–390.

Kochanska, G., & Knaack, A. (2003). Effortful control as a personality characteristic of young children: Antecedents, correlates, and consequences. *Journal of Personality, 71,* 1087–1112.

Lamb, M. E., Chuang, S. S., Wessels, H., Broberg, A. G., & Hwang, C. P. (2002). Emergence and construct validation of the big five factors in early childhood: A longitudinal analysis of their ontogeny in Sweden. *Child Development, 73,* 1517–1524.

Lemery, K. S., Goldsmith, H. H., Klinnert, M. D., & Mrazek, D. A. (1999). Developmental models of infant and childhood temperament. *Developmental Psychology, 35,* 189–204.

Lewis, M. (2001). Issues in the study of personality development. *Psychological Inquiry, 12,* 67–83.

Lucas, R. E., & Fujita, F. (2000). Factors influencing the relation between extraversion and pleasant affect. *Journal of Personality and Social Psychology, 79,* 1039–1056.

MacDonald, K. (1995). Evolution, the five-factor model, and levels of personality. *Journal of Personality, 63,* 525–567.

Magnus, K., Diener, E., Fujita, F., & Pavot, W. (1993). Extraversion and neuroticism as predictors of objective life events: A longitudinal analysis. *Journal of Personality and Social Psychology, 65,* 525–567.

Markey, P. M., Markey, C. N., & Tinsley, B. J. (2004). Children's behavioral manifestations of the five-factor model of personality. *Personality and Social Psychology Bulletin, 30,* 423–432.

Markon, K. E., Krueger, R. F., & Watson, D. (2005). Delineating the structure of normal and abnormal personality: An integrative hierarchical approach. *Journal of Personality and Social Psychology, 88,* 139–157.

Martin, M., Boomsma, D., & Machin, G. (1997). A twin-pronged attack on complex traits. *Nature Genetics, 17,* 387–392.

Martin, R. P., Wisenbaker, J., & Huttunen, M. (1994). Review of factor analytic studies of temperament measures based on the Thomas-Chess structural model: Implications for the big five. In C. F. Halverson, G. A. Kohnstamm, & R. P. Martin (Eds.), *The developing structure of temperament and personality from infancy to adulthood* (pp. 157–172). Hillsdale, NJ: Erlbaum.

Masten, A. S., & Coatsworth, J. D. (1995). Competence, resilience, and psychopathology. In D. Cicchetti & D. Cohen (Eds.), *Developmental psychopathology: Vol. 2. Risk, disorder, and adaptation* (pp. 715–752). New York: Wiley.

Masten, A. S., Neeman, J., & Andenas, S. (1994). Life events and adjustment in adolescents: The significance of event independence, desirability, and chronicity. *Journal of Research on Adolescence, 4,* 71–97.

McAdams, D. P. (1995). What do we know when we know a person? *Journal of Personality, 63,* 365–376.

McCrae, R. R., & Costa, P. T. (1994). The stability of personality: Observation and evaluations. *Current Directions in Psychological Science, 3,* 173–175.

McCrae, R. R., & Costa, P. T. (1997). Conceptions and correlates of openness to experience. In J. Hogan, J. Johnson, & S. Briggs (Eds.), *Handbook of personality: Theory and research* (pp. 825–847). San Diego, CA: Academic.

McCrae, R. R., & Costa, P. T. (1999). A five-factor theory of personality. In L. A. Pervin & O. P. John (Eds.), *Handbook of personality: Theory and research* (pp. 139–153). New York: Guilford Press.

McCrae, R. R., Costa, P. T., Ostendorf, F., Angleitner, A., Hrebickova, H., Avia, M. D., et al. (2000). Nature over nurture: Temperament, personality, and life span development. *Journal of Personality and Social Psychology, 78,* 173–186.

Measelle, J., John, O. P., Ablow, J., Cowan, P. A., & Cowan, C. P. (2005). Can children provide coherent, stable, and valid self-reports on the big five dimensions? *Journal of Personality and Social Psychology, 89,* 90–106.

Meehl, P. E. (1978). Theoretical risks and tabular asterisks: Sir Karl, Sir Roland, and the slow progress of soft psychology. *Journal of Consulting and Clinical Psychology, 46,* 806–834.

Mervielde, I., De Fruyt, F., & Jarmuz, S. (1998). Linking openness and intellect in childhood and adulthood. In C. S. Kohnstamm, C. F. Halverson, I. Mervielde, & V. L. Havill (Eds.), *Parental descriptions of child personality: Developmental antecedents of the big five?* (pp. 105–142). Mahwah, NJ: Erlbaum.

Miech, R., Essex, M. J., & Goldsmith, H. H. (2001). Self-regulation as a mediator of the status-attainment process: Evidence from early childhood. *Sociology of Education, 74,* 102–120.

Miller, T. Q., Smith, T. W., Turner, C. W., Guijarro, M. L., & Hallet, A. J. (1996). A meta-analytic review of research on hostility and physical health. *Psychological Bulletin, 119,* 322–348.

Mineka, S., Rafaeli, E., & Yovel, I. (2003). Cognitive biases in emotional disorders: Information processing and social-cognitive perspectives. In R. J. Davidson, K. R. Scherer, & H. H. Goldsmith (Eds.), *Handbook of affective sciences* (pp. 976–1009). New York: Oxford University Press.

Moffitt, T. E., Robins, R. W., & Caspi, A. (2001). A couples analysis of partner abuse with implications for abuse prevention. *Criminology and Public Policy, 1,* 401–432.

Muris, P., Schmidt, H., Merckelbach, H., & Schouten, E. (2001). The structure of negative emotions in adolescents. *Journal of Abnormal Child Psychology, 29,* 331–337.

Nigg, J. T. (2000). Inhibition/disinhibition in developmental psychopathology: Views from cognitive and personality psychology and a working inhibition taxonomy. *Psychological Bulletin, 126,* 220–246.

Ozer, D. J. (1986). *Consistency in personality: A methodological framework.* New York: Springer.

Peabody, D., & De Raad, B. (2002). The substantive nature of psycholexical personality factors: A comparison across languages. *Journal of Personality and Social Psychology, 83,* 983–997.

Peterson, J. B., Smith, K. W., & Carson, S. (2002). Openness and extraversion are associated with reduced latent inhibition: Replication and commentary. *Personality and Individual Differences, 33,* 1137–1147.

Plomin, R., Corley, R., Caspi, A., Fulker, D. W., & DeFries, J. C. (1998). Adoption results for self-reported personality: Evidence of non-additive genetic effects? *Journal of Personality and Social Psychology, 75,* 211–218.

Plomin, R., & Daniels, D. (1987). Why are children in the same family so different from one another? *Behavioral and Brain Sciences, 10,* 1–16.

Posner, M. I., & Rothbart, M. K. (2000). Developing mechanisms of self-regulation. *Development and Psychopathology, 12,* 427–441.

Putnam, S. P., Ellis, L. K., & Rothbart, M. K. (2001). The structure of temperament from infancy through adolescence. In A. Eliasz & A. Angleneiter (Eds.), *Advances in research on temperament* (pp. 165–182). Miami, FL: Pabst Science.

Putnam, S. P., Sanson, A. V., & Rothbart, M. K. (2002). Child temperament and parenting. In M. Bornstein (Ed.), *Handbook of parenting: Vol. 1. Children and parenting* (2nd ed., pp. 255–277). Mahwah, NJ: Erlbaum.

Reimann, R., Angleitner, A., & Strelau, J. (1997). Genetic and environmental influences on personality: A study of twins reared together using the self- and peer report NEO-FFI scales. *Journal of Personality, 65,* 449–476.

Roberts, B. W., Bogg, T., Walton, K. E., Chernyshenko, O. S., & Stark, S. E. (2004). A lexical investigation of the lower-order structure of conscientiousness. *Journal of Research in Personality, 38,* 164–178.

Roberts, B. W., & DelVecchio, W. F. (2000). The rank-order consistency of personality traits from childhood to old age: A quantitative review of longitudinal studies. *Psychological Bulletin, 126,* 25–30.

Roberts, B. W., Kuncel, N. R., Shiner, R. L., Caspi, A., & Goldberg, L. R. (2007). The power of personality: The comparative validity of personality traits, socioeconomic status, and cognitive ability for predicting important life outcomes. *Perspectives in Psychological Science, 2,* 313–345.

Roberts, B. W., Walton, K., & Viechtbauer, W. (2006). Patterns in mean-level change in personality traits across the life-course: A meta-analysis of longitudinal studies. *Psychological Bulletin, 132,* 1–25.

Robins, R. W., Caspi, A., & Moffitt, T. E. (2002). It's not just who you're with, it's who you are: Personality and relationship experiences across multiple relationships. *Journal of Personality, 70,* 925–964.

Rose, A. J., & Asher, S. R. (1999). Children's goals and strategies in response to conflicts within a friendship. *Developmental Psychology, 35,* 69–79.

Rothbart, M. K., Ahadi, S. A., Hershey, K. L., & Fisher, P. (2001). Investigation of temperament at 3 to 7 years: The Children's Behavior Questionnaire. *Child Development, 72,* 1394–1408.

Rothbart, M. K., & Bates, J. E. (2006). Temperament. In W. Damon and R. M. Lerner (Series Eds.) & N. Eisenberg (Vol. Ed.), *Handbook of child psychology: Vol. 3. Social, emotional, and personality development* (6th ed., pp. 99–166). Hoboken, NJ: Wiley.

Rothbart, M. K., Chew, K. H., & Garstein, M. A. (2001). Assessment of temperament in early development. In L. T. Singer & P. S. Zeskind (Eds.), *Biobehavioral assessment of the infant* (pp. 190–208). New York: Guilford Press.

Rozanski, A., Blumenthal, J. A., & Kaplan, J. (1999). Impact of psychological factors on the pathogenesis of cardiovascular disease and implications for therapy. *Circulation, 99,* 2217.

Rubin, K. H., Bukowski, W. M., & Parker, J. G. (2006). Peer interactions, relationships, and groups. In W. Damon & R. M. Lerner (Series Eds.) & N. Eisenberg (Vol. Ed.), *Handbook of child psychology: Vol. 3. Social, emotional, and personality development* (6th ed., pp. 571–645). Hoboken, NJ: Wiley.

Rueda, M. R., Posner, M. I., & Rothbart, M. K. (2004). Attentional control and self-regulation. In R. F. Baumeister & K. D. Vohs (Eds.), *Handbook of self-regulation: Research, theory, and applications* (pp. 283–300). New York: Guilford Press.

Saudino, K. J., & Cherny, S. C. (2001). Parental ratings of temperament in twins. In R. N. Emde & J. Hewitt (Eds.), *Infancy to early childhood: Genetic and environmental influences on developmental change* (pp. 73–88). Oxford: Oxford University Press.

Scarr, S., & McCartney, K. (1983). How people make their own environments: A theory of genotype-environment effects. *Child Development, 54,* 424–435.

Scheier, M. F., & Carver, C. S. (1993). On the power of positive thinking. *Current Directions in Psychological Science, 2,* 26–30.

Schmidt, L. A., & Hunter, J. (2004). General mental ability in the world of work: Occupational attainment and job performance. *Journal of Personality and Social Psychology, 86,* 162–173.

Schneider, B., Smith, D. B., Taylor, S., & Fleenor, J. (1998). Personality and organizations: A test of the homogeneity of personality hypothesis. *Journal of Applied Psychology, 83,* 4.

Shiner, R. L. (1998). How shall we speak of children's personalities in middle childhood? A preliminary taxonomy. *Psychological Bulletin, 124,* 308–332.

Shiner, R. L., & Caspi, A. (2003). Personality differences in childhood and adolescence: Measurement, development, and consequences. *Journal of Child Psychology and Psychiatry, 44,* 2–32.

Shiner, R. L., & Masten, A. S. (2002). Transactional links between personality and adaptation from childhood through adulthood. *Journal of Research in Personality, 36,* 580–588.

Shiner, R. L., Masten, A. S., & Tellegen, A. (2002). A developmental perspective on personality in emerging adulthood: Childhood antecedents and concurrent adaptation. *Journal of Personality and Social Psychology, 83,* 1165–1177.

Simonoff, E., Pickles, A., Hervas, A., Silberg, J. L., Rutter, M., & Eaves, L. (1998). Genetic influences on childhood hyperactivity: Contrast effects imply parental rating bias, not sibling interaction. *Psychological Medicine, 4,* 825–834.

Smith, T. W., & Spiro, A. (2002). Personality, health, and aging: Prolegomenon for the next generation. *Journal of Research in Personality, 36,* 363–394.

Sroufe, L. A., Carlson, E. A., Levy, A. K., & Egeland, B. (1999). Implications of attachment theory for developmental psychopathology. *Development and Psychopathology, 11,* 1–13.

Suls, J., Martin, R., & David, D. P. (1998). Person-environment fit and its limits: Agreeableness, neuroticism, and emotional reactivity to interpersonal conflict. *Personality and Social Psychology Bulletin, 24,* 88–98.

Taylor, S. E., Klein, L. C., Lews, B. P., Gruenewald, T. L., Gurung, R. A. R., & Updegraff, J. A. (2000). Biobehavioral responses to stress in females: Tend-and-befriend, not fight-or-flight. *Psychological Review, 107,* 411–429.

Tellegen, A. (1985). Structure of mood and personality and their relevance to assessing anxiety, with an emphasis on self-report. In A. H. Tuma & J. D. Maser (Eds.), *Anxiety and the anxiety disorders* (pp. 681–706). Hillsdale, NJ: Erlbaum.

Tellegen, A., & Waller, N. G. (1992). *Exploring personality through test construction: Development of the Multi-Dimensional Personality Questionnaire* (MPQ). Unpublished manuscript.

Terracciano, A., McCrae, R. R., Hagemann, D., & Costa, P. T. (2003). Individual difference variables, affective differentiation, and the structures of affect. *Journal of Personality, 71,* 669–703.

Thomas, A., Chess, S., Birch, H., Hertzig, M., & Korn, S. (1963). *Behavioral individuality in early childhood.* New York: New York University Press.

van Lieshout, C. F. M., & Haselager, G. J. T. (1993). *The big five personality factors in the Nijmegen California Child Q-Set* (NCCQ). Nijmegen, The Netherlands: University of Nijmegen.

van Lieshout, C. F. M., & Haselager, G. J. T. (1994). The big five personality factors in Q-sort descriptions of children and adolescents. In C. F. Halverson, G. A. Kohnstamm, & R. P. Martin (Eds.), *The developing structure of temperament and personality from infancy to adulthood* (pp. 293–318). Hillsdale, NJ: Erlbaum.

Watson, D., & Clark, L. A. (1997). Extraversion and its positive emotional core. In J. Hogan, J. Johnson, & S. Briggs (Eds.), *Handbook of personality psychology* (pp. 767–793). San Diego, CA: Academic Press.

Watson, D., Clark, L., McIntyre, C. W., & Hamaker, S. (1992). Affect, personality, and social activity. *Journal of Personality and Social Psychology, 63,* 1011–1025.

Chapter 7

The Developing Self

SUSAN HARTER

Interest in self-processes has recently burgeoned in many branches of psychology. Cognitive-developmentalists of a neo-Piagetian persuasion have addressed normative changes in the emergence of a sense of self (e.g., Case, 1992; Fischer, 1980; Harter, 1997; Higgins, 1991). Developmentalists interested in memory processes have described how the self is crafted through the construction of narratives that provide the basis for autobiographical memory (see Fivush, 1987; Snow, 1990). Contemporary attachment theorists, building on the earlier efforts of Ainsworth (1979) and Bowlby (1980), have provided new insights into how interactions with caregivers shape the representations of self and others that young children come to construct (e.g., see Bretherton, 1993; Rutter & Sroufe, 2000; Sameroff, 2000). Clinicians in the psychodynamic tradition have also contributed to our understanding of how early socialization experiences come to shape the structure and content of self-evaluations and contribute to psychopathology (e.g., Bleiberg, 1984; Winnicott, 1965). Moreover, social and personality theorists have devoted considerable attention to those processes that produce individual differences in perceptions of self, particularly among adults (e.g., see Baumeister, 1993; Epstein, 1991; Steele, 1988).

Although there is a new look to many of these contemporary formulations, the field has also witnessed a return to many of the classic issues that captured the attention of historical scholars of the self. New life has been breathed into James's (1890, 1892) distinction between the I-self as subject, agent, knower and the Me-self as object, as known. In addition, James's analysis of the causes of self-esteem is alive and well. There has also been a resurgence of interest in symbolic interactionists, such as Baldwin (1897), Cooley (1902), and Mead (1934), who placed heavy emphasis on how interactive processes with caregivers shape the developing self.

The first part of this chapter deals with six stages of self-development, during three periods of childhood, very early, middle, and late childhood, and three periods of adolescence, early, middle, and late adolescence. In each of these six periods, three issues are covered.

First, the normative-developmental features of self-description and self-evaluation are presented.

Second, the normative-developmental *liabilities* that mark the emergence to each period or stage are described. The very fabric of development involves advances to new stages that may bring with them normative liabilities that should not be interpreted as pathological, liabilities that will dissipate as more advanced developments and skills are acquired. Movement to a new stage of cognitive development inevitably leads to liabilities given that the individual lacks "cognitive control" (see Fischer, 1980) over emerging new skills. Because the self is not only a cognitive construction but also a social construction (Harter, 1999) crafted in the crucible of interactions with significant others, normative-developmental manifestations of the self will necessarily be affected by socialization at the hands of parents and peers.

At each developmental period there are individual differences that can result in maladaptive outcomes. These are to be distinguished from normative-developmental liabilities in their severity and the extent to which they compromise the functioning of the child or adolescent. (They are described in detail, in the *Handbook of Child Psychology* [Harter, 2006].)

First, several general themes are presented as background: (a) antecedents of the self as a cognitive and social construction, (b) distinctions between the I-self and the Me-self, (c) recent perspectives on the differentiation of the self and the creation of multiple selves during adolescence, (d) historical formulations and contemporary perspectives, and (e) recent genetic positions on the heritability of self-esteem.

Antecedents of the Self as a Cognitive and Social Construction

This chapter focuses on the antecedents of self-representations as well as on their consequences. With regard to antecedents, the self is a cognitive and a social construction—two major themes around which the material to be presented is organized. From a cognitive-developmental perspective, changes in self-representations are inevitable. As neo-Piagetians (e.g., Case, 1992; Fischer, 1980) and self theorists (e.g., Epstein, 1991; Kelly, 1955; Markus, 1980; Sarbin, 1962) have forcefully argued, our species has been designed to actively create theories about our world, to make meaning of our experiences, including the construction of a theory of self. Thus, the self is, first and foremost, a cognitive construction.

As a result, the self will develop over time as cognitive processes undergo normative-developmental change. Thus, because the self is a cognitive construction, the particular cognitive abilities and limitations of each developmental period will dictate the features of the self-system or how self-representations are conceptually organized. As such, emphasis is given to the processes responsible for those normative-developmental changes that result in similarities in self-representations at a given developmental level.

In addition to an exploration of the cognitive-developmental antecedents of the self, emphasis is placed on the self as a social construction. Thus, attention is devoted to how socialization experiences in children's interactions with caregivers, peers, teachers, and in the wider sociocultural context will influence the particular content and valence of their self-representations. Those building on the symbolic interactionist perspective (Baldwin, 1897; Cooley, 1902; Mead, 1934), as well as those of an attachment theory persuasion (Bretherton & Munholland, 1999), have focused on how socialization experiences with caregivers produce individual differences in the content of self-representations, including whether self-evaluations are favorable or unfavorable. The reactions of significant others determine whether the child comes to view the self as competent versus incapable, as lovable versus undeserving of others' affection and esteem. Although cognitive-developmentalists emphasize the fact that children are active agents in their own development, including the construction of self, the symbolic inter-actionist and attachment perspectives alert us to the fact that children are also at the mercy of the particular caregiving hand they have been dealt.

THE I-SELF AND THE ME-SELF

In addressing these themes, we can draw on a distinction in the literature between the I-self and the Me-self. The majority of scholars who have devoted thoughtful attention to the self have come to a similar conclusion: Two distinct but intimately intertwined aspects of self can be meaningfully identified: (1) self as subject (the I-self) and (2) self as object (the Me-self). William James (1890) introduced this distinction defining the I-self as the actor or knower, whereas the Me-self was the object of one's knowledge, "an empirical aggregate of things objectively known" (p. 197) such as the "material me," the "social me," and the "spiritual me." We will come to appreciate how, in contemporary models, this translates into new domains of the self-concept and supports the current multidimensional approaches to the self (see Harter, 1999).

Lewis (1994) adopted new terminology. He refers to the I-self as the "machinery of the self," the basic biological, perceptual, and cognitive processes that allow for the construction of the Me-self as the "idea of me." Such cognitive representations of the self begin to emerge in rudimentary form in the second half of the second year. Both the "machinery of the self" as well as the "idea of me" undergo considerable change during the course of development.

Historically, major attention has been devoted to the Me-self (to the study of the self as an object of one's knowledge and evaluation) as evidenced by myriad studies on self-concept and self-esteem (see Harter, 1983; Wylie, 1989). More recently, the I-self, which James himself regarded as an elusive if not incorrigible construct, has become more prominent in accounts of self-development. As we come to appreciate, both the structure and content of the Me-self at any given developmental level depend on the particular I-self capabilities (those cognitive processes that define the knower). Thus, cognitive-developmental changes in I-self processes will directly influence the nature of the self-theory that the child is constructing.

Most scholars conceptualize the self as a theory that must be cognitively constructed. Those theorists in the tradition of adult personality and social psychology have suggested that the self-theory should possess the characteristics of any formal theory, defined as a hypothetico-deductive system. Such a personal epistemology should, therefore, meet those criteria by which any good theory is evaluated: that it is parsimonious, empirically valid, internally consistent, coherently organized, testable, and useful. From a developmental perspective, however, the self-theories created by children cannot meet these criteria, given numerous cognitive limitations that have been identified in Piagetian (1960) and neo-Piagetian formulations (e.g., Case, 1992; Fischer, 1980). The I-self in its role as constructor of the Me-self does not, in childhood, possess the capacities to create a hierarchically organized system of postulates that are internally consistent, coherently organized, testable, or empirically valid. It is not until late adolescence or early adulthood that the cognitive abilities to construct a self-portrait meeting the criteria of a good formal theory potentially emerge. Therefore, it is essential to examine how the changing characteristics of the I-self processes that define each developmental stage directly impact the Me-self (the self-theory that is being constructed).

GLOBAL VERSUS DOMAIN-SPECIFIC EVALUATIONS

The increasing ability with development to differentiate self-domains, as well to integrate self-perceptions into a larger global concept of self, has led contemporary scholars to separate domain-specific perceptions from a global concept of a person's worth or self-esteem. Thus, it has become increasingly important to distinguish between self-evaluations that represent global characteristics of the individual (e.g., "I am a worthwhile person") from those that reflect the individual's sense of adequacy across particular domains such as their cognitive competence (e.g., "I am smart"), social competence (e.g., "I am well liked by peers"), athletic competence (e.g., "I am good at sports"), and so forth (e.g., see Harter, 1998a, 2006; Marsh, 1986; Rosenberg, 1979).

With regard to terminology, global self-evaluations have typically been referred to as self-esteem (Rosenberg, 1979), self-worth (Harter, 1983, 1999) or general self-concept (Marsh, 1986). In each case, the focus is on the overall evaluation of one's worth or value as a person. In this chapter, the terms *self-esteem* and *self-worth* are employed interchangeably. It is important to appreciate that this general evaluation is tapped by a separate set of items that explicitly tap one's perceived worth as a person (e.g., "I feel that I am a worthwhile person"). It is not a summary statement of self-evaluations across specific domains. In this chapter, the term *self-concept* is primarily reserved for evaluative judgments of attributes in discrete domains, such as cognitive competence, social acceptance, physical appearance, and so forth, or "domain-specific self-evaluations."

HISTORICAL PERSPECTIVES

These contemporary themes find their roots in the writings of historical scholars of the self. William James clearly contributed with regard to his formulations regarding the origins of our self-esteem, to the differentiation of domains of the self, and to what he labeled the "conflict of the different Me's" across differing relational constructs. The symbolic interactionists, such as Cooley (1902), Baldwin (1895), and Mead (1934), articulated the role of social processes in constructing the self.

The field has witnessed a return to classic issues that captured the attention of historical scholars of the self. The history of interest in the self can be traced back to ancient Greek philosophy, as revealed in the injunction to "know thyself." However, contemporary scholars of the self-concept typically pay major intellectual homage to James (1890, 1892) and to the previously listed symbolic interactionists such as Cooley, Mead, and Baldwin.

For James, we find many themes that anticipate contemporary issues about the self. First and foremost is the distinction between "I" and "Me" selves. James's multidimensional view of the Me-self has been modernized in recent treatments of the self-structure, where investigators have sought to examine the particular relationships among global and domain-specific self-evaluations. Moreover, the potential conflict between different Me-selves that James observed has served as a springboard to contemporary interest in the construction of multiple selves. As we come to see, differing attributes across role-related selves that appear contradictory (e.g., depressed with parents but cheerful with friends) usher in the potential for conflict. Finally, James's formulation concerning the causes of self-esteem has been revived.

In contrast to James, the symbolic interactionists placed primary emphasis on how social interactions with others profoundly shaped the self. For Cooley (1902), Mead (1934), and Baldwin (1895), the self is viewed as a social construction, crafted through linguistic exchanges (symbolic interactions) with others. Several themes have found their way into contemporary theorizing. For example, beginning in childhood, the child (a) engages in the imitation of significant others' behaviors, attitudes, and values or standards; (b) adjusts his or her behavior to garner the approval of salient socializing agents; (c) comes to adopt the opinions that significant others are perceived to hold toward them (these reflected appraisals come to define one's self as a person).

Charles Horton Cooley was perhaps the most influential. His formulation was the most metaphorical, given his postulation of the "looking glass self." For Cooley, significant others constituted a social mirror into which the individual gazes to detect their opinions toward the self. These opinions, in turn, are incorporated into one's sense of self. Cooley contended that what becomes the self is what we imagine that others think of us, including our appearance, motives, deeds, character, and so on: We come to own these reflected appraisals. These appear to gradually become psychologically removed from their initial social sources through an implied internalization process.

Cooley's views on the internalization of others' opinions about the self paved the way for a more developmental perspective on how the opinions of others are incorporated into the self. Moreover, his looking glass self-perspective provides an alternative to James's contentions regarding the determinants of global self-esteem. James focused largely on those cognitive processes in which an individual actively compares particular aspirations to perceived successes in corresponding domains. For Cooley, the antecedents were far more social in nature, and less consciously driven, in that children inevitably internalized the opinions that they believed significant others held toward the self.

SELF-PSYCHOLOGY IN THE SECOND HALF OF THE TWENTIETH CENTURY

During the eras of James and Cooley, inquiry into topics concerning the self and psyche flourished. However, with the emergence of radical behaviorism, such constructs were excised from the scientific vocabularies of many theorists and the writings of James and the symbolic interactionists gathered dust on the shelf. It is of interest to ask why the self became an unwelcome guest at the behaviorists' table. Why did constructs such as self, including self-esteem, ego strength, sense of omnipotence, narcissistic injury, and so on, do little to whet the behaviorists' appetite? Several reasons appear responsible.

The very origins of the behaviorist movement rested on the identification of observables. Thus, hypothetical constructs were both conceptually and methodologically unpalatable. Cognitions, in general, and self-representations, in particular, could not be operationalized as observable behaviors. Moreover, self-report measures designed to tap self-constructs were not included on the methodological menu because people were assumed to be very inaccurate judges of their own behavior. Those more accepting of introspective methodologies found the existing measures of self-concept ungratifying because their content was overly vague. Finally, self-constructs were not satisfying to the behaviorist's palate because their functions were not clearly specified. The very cornerstone of behavioral approaches rested on a functional analysis of behavior. In contrast, approaches to the self did little more than implicate self-representations as correlates of behavior, affording them little explanatory power as causes or mediators of behavior.

Several shifts in emphasis, later in the twentieth century, allowed self-constructs to become more palatable. Hypothetical constructs, in general, gained favor as parsimonious predictors of behavior, often far more economical in theoretical models than a multitude of discrete observables. Moreover, we witnessed a cognitive revolution in both child and adult psychology (Bruner, 1990). For developmentalists, Piagetian and neo-Piagetian models came to the forefront. For experimental and social psychologists, numerous cognitive models found favor. In this revolution, self theorists jumped on the bandwagon, resurrecting the self as a cognitive construction, as a mental representation that constitute a theory of self (e.g., Case, 1985; Fischer, 1980; Greenwald, 1980; Kelly, 1955; Markus, 1980; Sarbin, 1962). Finally, self-representations gained increased legitimacy as behaviorally oriented therapists were forced to acknowledge that the spontaneous self-evaluative statements of their clients seemed powerfully implicated in their pathology.

The discussion thus far has focused on psychological mechanisms that account for a child's level of self-esteem, describing the contribution of cognitive-developmental and social determinants. For many years, these have been the prevailing approaches. Neurological and genetic models have come to the forefront, the 1990s were declared the decade of the brain, and it became obvious that our splintered subfields needed to be integrated if we are truly to understand development and human behavior. These new approaches to self-esteem and their interpretations are presented in the Handbook of Child Psychology.

Developmental Differences in Self-Representations during Childhood

In the sections that follow, we examine the nature of self-representations and self-evaluations at three periods of childhood: (1) toddlerhood to very early childhood, (2) early to middle childhood, and (3) middle to late childhood. For each period, there is a prototypical self-descriptive cameo that reflects the cardinal features of the content and structure of the self at that developmental level. Discussion focuses on the normative-developmental changes that are critical as a backdrop and against which we can judge whether a child's self-representations are age-appropriate including the normative-developmental liabilities for the self at this period. (Deviations that can be considered more maladaptive for others are discussed in *the Handbook of Child Psychology.*)

TODDLERHOOD TO EARLY CHILDHOOD: VERBAL CAMEO OF NORMATIVE SELF-REPRESENTATIONS AND SELF-EVALUATIONS

I'm almost 3 years old and I live in a big house with my mother and father and my brother, Jason, and my sister, Lisa. I have blue eyes and a kitty that is orange and a television in my own room. I know all of my ABCs, listen: A, B, C, D, E, F, G, H, J, L, K, O, P, Q, R, X, Y, Z. I can run real fast. I like pizza and I have a nice teacher at preschool. I can count up to 100, want to hear me? I love my dog Skipper. I can climb to the top of the jungle gym, I'm not scared! I'm never scared! I'm always happy. I have brown hair and I go to preschool. I'm really strong. I can lift this chair, watch me! (adapted from Harter, 1999, p. 37)

Such descriptions will typically be observed in 3- to 4-year-olds. Noteworthy is the nature of the attributes selected to portray the self. Theory and evidence (e.g., see Fischer, 1980; Griffin, 1992; Harter, 1999, 2006; Higgins, 1991) indicate that the young child can only construct concrete cognitive representations of observable features of the self (e.g., "I know my ABC's," "I can count," "I live in a big house"). Damon and Hart (1988) label these as categorical identifications; the young child understands the self only as separate, taxonomic attributes that are physical (e.g., "I have blue eyes"), active (e.g., "I can run real fast, climb to the top"), social (e.g., "I have a brother, Jason, and a sister, Lisa"), or psychological (e.g., "I am happy"). Particular skills are touted (running, climbing) rather than generalizations about being athletic or good at sports. Moreover, often these behavioral descriptions will spill over into actual demonstrations of one's abilities ("I'm really strong. I can lift this chair, watch me!"), suggesting that these emerging self-representations are still directly tied to behavior. From a cognitive-developmental perspective, they do not represent higher-order conceptual categories through which the self is defined. In addition to concrete descriptions of behaviors, the young child defines the self by preferences (e.g., "I like pizza; I love my dog Skipper") and possessions ("I have an orange kitty and a television in my own room"). Those with rudimentary ownership understanding provide richer self-representations than those who do not possess such knowledge. On balance, as Rosenberg (1979) cogently observes, the young child acts as a demographer or radical behaviorist in that his or her self-descriptions are limited to characteristics that are potentially observable by others.

From the standpoint of organization, the self-representations of this period are highly differentiated or isolated from one another. The young child is incapable of integrating these compartmentalized representations of self, and thus self-descriptive accounts appear quite disjointed. This lack of coherence is a general cognitive characteristic that pervades the young child's thinking across a variety of domains (Fischer, 1980; Harter, 1999). As Piaget (1960) observed, young children's thinking is transductive in that they reason from particular to particular in no logical order.

Neo-Piagetians have elaborated on these processes. Case (1992) refers to this level as "Interrelational," in that young children can forge rudimentary links in the form of discrete structures that are defined by physical dimensions, behavioral events, or habitual activities. However, they cannot coordinate two such structures (Griffin, 1992), in part, because of working memory constraints that prevent young children from holding several features in mind simultaneously. Fischer's (1980) formulation is very similar. He labels these initial structures "Single Representations." Such structures are highly differentiated from one another because the cognitive limitations at this stage render the child incapable of integrating single representations into a coherent self-portrait.

Moreover, self-evaluations during this period are typically unrealistically positive (e.g., "I know all of my ABCs"—which he or she doesn't) because young children have difficulty distinguishing between their desired and their actual competence, which is a confusion initially observed by both Freud (1952) and Piaget (1932). Thus, young children cannot yet formulate an ideal self-concept that is differentiated from a real self-concept. Rather, their descriptions represent a litany of talents that may transcend reality (Harter & Pike, 1984). For contemporary cognitive-developmentalists, such overstated virtuosity stems from another cognitive limitation of this period: The inability of young children to bring social comparison information to bear meaningfully on their perceived competencies (e.g., Frey & Ruble, 1990). The ability to use social comparison toward the goals of self-evaluation requires that the child be able to relate one concept (e.g., his or her own performance) to another (e.g., someone else's performance), a skill that is not sufficiently developed in the young child. Thus, self-descriptions typically represent an overestimation of personal abilities. It is important to appreciate, however, that these apparent distortions are normative in that they reflect cognitive limitations rather than conscious efforts to deceive the listener.

Another manifestation of the self-structure of very young children is their inability to acknowledge that they can possess attributes of opposing valence, for example, good and bad or nice and mean (Fischer, Hand, Watson, Van Parys, & Tucker, 1984). This all-or-none thinking can be observed in the cameo, in that all of the attributes appear to be positive. Self-representations may also include emotion descriptors (e.g., "I'm always happy"). However, children at this age do not acknowledge that they can experience both positive and negative emotions, particularly at the same time. The majority will deny that they have negative emotions (e.g., "I'm never scared!") as salient features of their descriptive self-portrait. Other procedures reveal that they do have rudimentary concepts of such single negative emotions as mad, sad, and scared (e.g., see Dunn, 1988; Harter & Whitesell, 1989). Evidence now indicates that young children report that they cannot experience seemingly opposing emotional reactions simultaneously (see other references in *Handbook of Child Psychology.*) For Fischer and colleagues (e.g., Fischer & Ayoub, 1994), this dichotomous thinking represents the natural fractionation of the mind. Such "affecting splitting" constitutes a normative form of dissociation that is the hallmark of very young children's thinking about both self and other.

Cognitive limitations of this period extend to the inability of young children to create a concept of their overall worth as a person: a representation of their global self-esteem (Harter, 1990). This self-representation requires a higher-order integration of domain-specific attributes that have first been differentiated. Young children do describe themselves in terms of concrete cognitive or physical abilities, how they behave, how they look, and the friendships they have formed (Harter, 1999). However, these domains are not clearly differentiated from one another, as revealed through factor-analytic procedures.

Young children cannot cognitively or verbally formulate a general concept of their worth as a person. However, this does not dictate that they lack the experience of self-esteem. Rather, our findings (see Haltiwanger, in Harter, 1999) indicate that young children manifest self-esteem in their behavior, what we have labeled "behaviorally presented self-esteem." These efforts and results are presented in the *Handbook of Child Psychology.*

ADDITIONAL FUNCTIONS OF THE SOCIALIZING ENVIRONMENT

Higgins (1991), building on the efforts of Case (1985), Fischer (1980), and Selman (1980), focuses on how self-development during this period involves the interaction between the young child's cognitive capacities and the role of socializing agents. He provides evidence for the contention that at Case's stage of "interrelational develop-ment" and Fischer's stage of "single representations," the very young child can place him- or herself in the same category as the parent who shares his or her gender, form-ing an initial basis for identification with that parent. Thus, the young boy can evaluate his overt behavior with regard to the question: "Am I doing what Daddy is doing?" Similarly, the young girl evaluates her behavior, asking "Am I doing what Mommy is doing?" Attempts to match that behavior impact which attributes become incorporated into the young child's self-definition. Thus, these processes represent one way in which socializing agents impact the self.

Higgins (1991) observes that at the interrelational stage, young children can also form structures allowing them to detect the fact that their behavior evokes a reaction in others, notably parents, which causes psychological reactions in the self. These experi-ences shape the self to the extent that the young child chooses to engage in behaviors designed to please the parents. Stipek, Recchia, and McClintic (1992) have provided empirical evidence for this observation, demonstrating that slightly before the age of 2, children begin to anticipate adult reactions, seeking positive responses to their suc-cesses and attempting to avoid negative responses to failure. At this age, they also find that young children show a rudimentary appreciation for adult standards, for example, by turning away from adults in seeming distress and hunching their shoulder in the face of failures (see also Kagan, 1984). For Mascolo and Fischer (1995), such reactions constitute rudimentary forms of shame. Shame at this period, like self-esteem, can only be behaviorally manifest. Children do not understand the concept at a verbal level (see Harter, 1999). Moreover, although young children are beginning to recognize that their behavior has an impact on others, their perspective-taking skills are extremely limited (see Harter, 1999; Selman, 1980). Thus, they are unable to incorporate others' opinions of the self into a realistic self-evaluation that can be verbalized.

THE ROLE OF NARRATIVE IN THE CO-CONSTRUCTION OF THE SELF

Another arena in which parental figures, in particular, impact children's self-development involves the role of narratives in promoting the young child's autobio-graphic memory: a rudimentary story of the self. The infantile amnesia that one observes before the age of approximately 2 can only be overcome by learning from adults how to formulate their own memories as narratives. Initially, parents recount to the child stories about his or her past and present experiences. With increasing lan-guage facility, children come to take on a more active role in that parent and child co-construct the memory of a shared experience (e.g., Eisenberg, 1985; Snow, 1990). However, for the young child, such narratives are still highly scaffolded by the parents, who reinforce aspects of experience that they feel are important to codify and remem-ber (Fivush & Hudson, 1990; Nelson, 1989). Through these interactions, an autobio-graphic account of the self is created. Of further interest are findings demonstrating individual differences in maternal styles of narrative construction (e.g., see Bretherton, 1993). For example, Tessler (1991) has distinguished between an elaborative style (where mothers present an embellished narrative) and a pragmatic style (focusing more on useful information). Elaborative mothers were more effective in establishing and eliciting memories with their young children.

Linguistic interactions with parents also impact the developing child's representation of self in semantic memory (e.g., Bowlby, 1973; Snow, 1990). As Bowlby first noted, early semantic memory is conferred by caregivers. Parents convey considerable descriptive and evaluative information about the child, including labels to distinguish one from others (e.g., "You're a big boy"), evaluative descriptors of the self (e.g., "You are so smart"; "You're a good girl"), as well as rules and standards and the extent to which the child has met parental expectations ("Big boys don't cry"). Consistent with Cooley's (1902) model of the looking glass self, children incorporate these labels and evaluations into their self-definition in the form of general trait knowledge (represented in semantic memory). Thus, the linguistic construction of the self is a highly interpersonal process, with caregivers making a major contribution to its representation in both autobiographical and semantic memory.

NORMATIVE LIABILITIES FOR SELF-DEVELOPMENT DURING VERY EARLY CHILDHOOD

Infantile amnesia precludes a conscious sense of self for the toddler. Even once very young children are able to verbally describe the self, their self-representations are still limited in that they reflect concrete descriptions of behaviors, abilities, emotions, possessions, and preferences that are potentially observable by others. These attributes are also highly differentiated or isolated from one another, leading to rather disjointed accounts, because at this age, young children lack the ability to integrate such characteristics. For some, this lack of a logical self-theory may be cause for concern if not consternation. However, these features are normative in that the I-self processes (i.e., the cognitive structures available at this developmental period) preclude a more logical rendering of the Me-self.

Self-representations are also likely to be unrealistically positive for several reasons (see Harter, 1999). First, they lack the cognitive ability to engage in social comparison, for the purpose of self-evaluation. From a cognitive-developmental perspective, this skill, like many of the abilities that are unavailable to the preoperational child as Piaget (1960) revealed, requires that one be able to simultaneously hold two dimensions in mind to compare them (cf. conservation tasks). We apply this analysis to the inability to hold in mind an evaluation of one's own attributes while simultaneously thinking about another's attributes and comparing them.

Second, and for similar reasons, the very young child is unable to distinguish between their actual self-attributes and their ideal self-attributes. This requires making a discrimination between the two, holding each in mind simultaneously, and comparing the two judgments, a cognitive ability that the very young child lacks. As a result, self-evaluations are unrealistically positive because the fusion of the two favors the ideal or desirable self-concept. When we are dealing with older children, we might interpret such a tendency to reflect socially desirable responding (i.e., the conscious distortion of one's self-evaluation) to be favorable. Cognitive-developmental interpretations lead to a different conclusion: that the very young child's positive evaluations reflect cognitive limitations rather than a conscious attempt to deceive.

Third, young children lack the perspective-taking ability to understand and therefore incorporate the perceived opinions of significant others toward the self (Harter, 1999; Selman, 1980). As becomes evident in the discussion of middle childhood, the ability to appreciate others' evaluations of the self becomes a powerful determinant of a child's sense of worth as he or she emerges in middle childhood.

Cognitive limitations also lead to young children's inability to acknowledge that they can possess both positive and negative self-attributes. The all-or-none, black-and-white thinking that is characteristic of the preoperational child extends to his or her conceptualizations of self: One must be one or the other. To the extent that the majority of socializing agents are relatively benevolent and supportive, the psychological scale will tip toward the imbalance of positive self-attributes. Thus, the young child will bask in the glow of overall virtuosity (even if it is unrealistic).

The inability to possess a verbalizable concept of self-esteem can also be explained by the cognitive limitations of this period. As is documented, the subsequent ability to compare one's actual self-attributes with one's ideal self-attributes will become an important determinant of one's level of self-esteem. Perspective-taking abilities will also become critical given that the internalization of the opinions of significant others becomes a powerful predictor of a child's overall sense of personal worth. It was noted that behavioral manifestations of self-esteem do emerge during early childhood, as has been documented. However, it is an interesting empirical question as to whether level of self-esteem as so displayed parallels or predicts the concept of a child's self-esteem that will emerge in middle childhood.

The description of the normative liabilities that impact conceptions and manifestations of the self during early childhood follow from normative cognitive limitations. One may question, however, the extent to which these reflect psychological liabilities. Many of the cognitive limitations of this period may serve as protective factors, to the extent that the very young child maintains very positive perceptions of self, even if potentially unrealistic. Positive self-views may serve as motivating factors and emotional buffers, contributing to the young child's development. They may propel the child toward growth-building mastery attempts, they may instill a sense of confidence, and they may lead the child to rebuff perceptions of inadequacy, all of which may foster positive future development. From an evolutionary perspective, such "liabilities" may represent critical strengths, at this developmental level. This issue is revisited as we move up the ontogenetic ladder of representations and evaluations of the self.

INDIVIDUAL DIFFERENCES: ADAPTIVE AND MALADAPTIVE OUTCOMES DURING TODDLERHOOD AND EARLY CHILDHOOD

In the previous two sections on the period of toddlerhood to early childhood, the focus was on normative self development, including normative liabilities. An important goal of the *Handbook of Child Psychology* is to distinguish between normative liabilities in the formation of the self and more maladaptive or pathological processes and outcomes at each developmental level. The original chapter describes the effects of abuse that can seriously compromise a very young child's psychological development. Typically, the causes of severe maladjustment involve an interaction between the child's level of cognitive development and chronic, negative abusive treatment at the hands of caregivers.

Language and False-Self Behavior

Language clearly promotes heightened levels of relatedness and allows for the creation of a personal narrative. Stern (1985) also alerts us to the liabilities of language. He argues that language can drive a wedge between two simultaneous forms of interpersonal experience: as it is lived and as it is verbally represented. The very capacity for objectifying the self through verbal representations allows us to transcend, and potentially distort, our immediate experience and to create a fantasized construction of the self. As noted earlier, there is the potential for incorporating the biases of caregivers' perspectives on the self, because initially, adults dictate the content of narratives incorporated in autobiographical memory (e.g., Bowlby, 1980; Bretherton, 1987). Children may receive subtle signals that certain episodes should not be retold or are best forgotten (Dunn, Brown, & Beardsall, 1991). Bretherton describes another manifestation (defensive exclusion) in which negative information about the self or the other is not incorporated because it is too psychologically threatening. Wolf (1990) further describes several mechanisms, such as deceit and fantasy, whereby the young child, as author of the self, can select, edit, or change the facts in the service of personal goals, hopes, or wishes (see also Dunn, 1988).

Such distortions may well contribute to the formation of a self that is perceived as unauthentic if a person accepts the falsified version of experience. Winnicott's (1958) observations alert us to the fact that intrusive or overinvolved mothers, in their desire to comply with maternal demands and expectations, lead infants to present a false outer self that does not represent their own inner experiences. Moreover, such parents may reject the infant's "felt self," approving only of the falsely presented self (Crittenden, 1994). As Stern (1985) notes, the display of false-self, incurs the risk of alienating a person from those inner experiences that represent their true self. Thus, linguistic abilities not only allow a person to share his or her experiences with others but also to withhold them as well.

Early to Middle Childhood: Verbal Cameo of Normative Self-Representations and Self-Evaluations

I have a lot of friends, in my neighborhood, at school, and at my church. I'm good at schoolwork, I know my words, and letters, and my numbers. I can run fast, and I can climb high, a lot higher than I could when I was little and I can run faster, too. I can also throw a ball real far, I'm going to be on some kind of team when I am older. I can do lots of stuff real good. Lots! It makes me really happy and excited when they watch me! (adapted from Harter, 1999, p. 41)

Such self-descriptions are typical of children ages 5 to 7. Some of the features of the previous stage persist in that self-representations are still typically very positive, and the child continues to overestimate his or her virtuosity. References to various competencies, for example, social skills, cognitive abilities, and athletic talents are common self-descriptors. With regard to the advances of this age period, children begin to display a rudimentary ability to intercoordinate concepts that were previously compartmentalized (Case, 1985; Fischer, 1980; Harter, 1999). For example, they can form a category or representational set that combines a number of their competencies (e.g., good at running, jumping, schoolwork, having friends in the neighborhood, at school, and at church). However, all-or-none thinking persists. In Case's (1985) model and its application to the self (Griffin, 1992), this stage is labeled "unidimentional" thinking. Such black-and-white thinking is supported by another new cognitive process that emerges at this stage. The novel acquisition is the child's ability to link or relate representational sets to one another, to "map" representations onto one another, to use Fischer's (1980) terminology. Of particular interest to self-development is one type of representational mapping that is extremely common in the thinking of young children—a link in the form of opposites. For example, in the domain of physical concepts, young children can oppose up versus down, tall versus short, and thin versus wide or fat.

Opposites can also be observed in the realm of the descriptions of self and others, where the child's ability to oppose "good" to "bad" is especially relevant. As observed earlier, the child develops a rudimentary concept of the self as good at a number of skills. Given that good is defined as the opposite of bad, this cognitive construction typically precludes the young child from being "bad," at least at the same time. Thus, the oppositional mapping takes the necessary form of "I'm good and therefore I can't be bad." However, other people may be perceived as bad at these skills, as the cameo description reveals ("I know other kids who are bad at things but not me!"). Therefore, the structure of such mappings typically leads the child to overdifferentiate favorable and unfavorable attributes, as demonstrated by findings revealing young children's inability to integrate attributes such as nice and mean (Fisher et al., 1984) or smart and dumb (Harter, 1986). Moreover, the mapping structure leads to the persistence of self-descriptions laden with virtuosity.

These principles also apply to children's understanding of their emotions, in that they cannot integrate emotions of opposing valence such as happy and sad (Harter & Buddin, 1987). There is an advance over the previous period in that children come to appreciate the fact that they can have two emotions of the same valence (e.g., "I'm happy and excited when my parents watch me"). However, the representational set for positive emotions is cognitive separate from negative emotions (e.g., sad, mad, or scared). Thus, children at this stage cannot yet integrate the sets of positive and negative emotions sets that are viewed as conceptually opposites and therefore incompatible. The inability to acknowledge that a person can possess both favorable and unfavorable attributes, or experience both positive and negative emotions, represents a cognitive liability that is a hallmark of this period of development. Unlike the previous period, the child is now, due to greater cognitive and linguistic abilities, able to verbally express his or her staunch conviction that a person cannot possess both positive and negative characteristics at the same time. As one 5-year-old vehemently put it, "Nope, there is no way you could be smart and dumb at the same time. You only have one mind!"

THE ROLE OF THE SOCIALIZING ENVIRONMENT

Socializing agents also have an impact on self-development, in interaction with cognitive acquisitions. Thus, children acquire an increasing cognitive appreciation for the perspective of others that influences self-development. The child at this level comes to realize that socializing agents have a particular viewpoint (not merely a reaction) toward them and their behavior (Higgins, 1991). As Selman (1980) also observes, the improved perspective-taking skills at this age permit children to realize that others are actively evaluating the self (although children have not yet internalized these evaluations sufficiently to make independent judgments about their attributes). At this age level, cognitive-developmental limitations preclude the internalization of others' standards and opinions about the self, which will, with later advances, allow the child to personally come to own such standards and opinions.

There are additional forms of interaction between cognitive-developmental level and the socializing environment that affect the self, including certain advances in the ability to utilize social comparison information. Frey and Ruble (1990) as well as Suls and Sanders (1982) provide evidence that at this stage children first focus on temporal comparisons (how I am performing now, compared to when I was younger) and age norms rather than individual difference comparisons with age-mates. As our prototypical subject tells us, "I can climb a lot higher than when I was little and I can run faster, too." Suls and Sanders observe that such temporal comparisons are particularly gratifying to young children given the rapid skill development at this age level. As a result, such comparisons contribute to the highly positive self-evaluations that typically persist at this age level.

Evidence (reviewed in Ruble & Frey, 1991) reveals that younger children do engage in certain rudimentary forms of social comparison; however, it is directed toward different goals than for older children. For example, young children use such information to determine if they have received their fair share of rewards. However, they cannot yet utilize such information for the purposes of self-evaluation, in large part due to the cognitive limitations of this period; thus, their evaluations continue to be unrealistic.

NORMATIVE LIABILITIES FOR SELF-DEVELOPMENT BETWEEN EARLY AND MIDDLE CHILDHOOD

Many of the features of the previous stage persist, in that self-representations are typically very positive, and the child continues to overestimate his or her abilities. Moreover, the child at this period still lacks the ability to develop an overall concept of his or her worth as a person. With regard to advances, children do begin to display a rudimentary ability to intercoordinate self-concepts that were previously compartmentalized; for example, they can construct a representational set that combines a number of their competencies (e.g., good at running, jumping, and schoolwork). However, all-or-none thinking persists due to a new cognitive acquisition in which different valence attributes are verbally conceptualized as opposites (e.g., good versus bad or nice versus mean). Typically this all-or-none structure leads to self-attributes that are all positive, these beliefs are even more intractable than in the previous period given cognitive and linguistic advances that bring such beliefs into consciousness to the extent that the socializing environment supports such positivity.

Rudimentary processes allow the child to appreciate the fact that others are evaluating the self, although cognitive-developmental limitations preclude the child from internalizing these evaluations. Advances include the ability to make temporal comparisons between one's past performance. Given the rapid skill development during these years, such comparisons contribute to the highly positive self-evaluations that typically persist at this age level. The failure to use social comparison information for the purpose of self-evaluation, however, contributes to the persistence of unrealistically favorable self-attributes. As noted in describing the previous period, children at this stage are not consciously distorting their self-perceptions. Rather, they have not yet acquired the cognitive skills to develop more realistic self-perceptions.

Patterns That Are More Maladaptive

In the attachment literature (e.g., see Bretherton, 1991; Cassidy & Shaver, 1999; Crittenden, 1990; Main, 1995), there have been further distinctions between less than optimal parenting styles that are associated with three patterns of insecurely attached children, which have implications for the self-development of children described as (1) having an avoidance attachment style, (2) being ambivalently attached, and (3) being disorganized (a style identified by Main, 1995).

The (anxious) avoidant style leads the young child to perceive that the mother is unavailable, nonnurturing, and not sharing positive affect. She is viewed as nonsoothing in times of need, as turning away when the child is distressed, and sometimes angry.

Not feeling loved, the child cuts the self off from emotionally threatening situations. Given this working model of the mother, the working model of the self follows directly. Thus, the child does not feel lovable, nor does he or she feel capable of getting people to meet his or her needs. Sensitivity to being rebuffed leads to occasional periods of anger and hostility. Moreover, the precursors of this style lead the child to eventually feel ineffective in the social domain with peers.

The (anxious) ambivalent child, also labeled as "resistant" by some, perceives the mother to be inconsistently available, sometimes there, sometimes not, leading to the inability to predict and therefore to trust whether she will meet basic and psychological needs. Therefore, distress is expressed in the absence of assurance, leading to a sense that one is not loved and that the mother is not there to support the mastery of new skills. Sometimes, when the mother is present, the child feels good. When she is not available, fussiness and resistance are expressed.

Those identified as disorganized-disoriented infants (Main, 1995) seem to have a combination of negative child-rearing that represents a combination of avoidant and ambivalent tendencies, including signs of fear and confusion, crying, depression, freezing, and numbing that reflect more severe disturbances in the self, including negativity and inconsistencies in their manifestation of the self.

Abuse at the hands of socializing agents can also continue to derail the self-system. In chronic and severe abuse, the major coping strategy is "dissociation" in which the individual attempts to cognitively split off the traumatic event from consciousness—to detach the self from the traumatic event (e.g., Herman, 1992; Putnam, 1993). When such abuse occurs at this period of childhood, it conspires with the natural or normative penchant for cognitive dissociation, splitting, or fragmentation (Fischer & Ayoub, 1994). Moreover, the very construction of cognitive structures that consciously lead the child of this age to think in opposites, one must be all good or all bad, lead to a painful awareness that one must be all bad or that the self is totally flawed. This can lead to compromising symptoms of depression.

Briere (1992), based on clinical cases, provides a complementary analysis of the sequential "logic" that governs the abused child's attempt to make meaning of his or her experiences. Given maltreatment at the hands of a parent or family member, the child first surmises that either "I am bad or my parents are bad." However, the assumption of young children that parents or adult authority figures are always right leads to the conclusion that parental maltreatment must be due to the fact that they, as children, are bad (that the acts were their fault), and that therefore they deserve to be punished. When children are repeatedly assaulted, they come to conclude that they must be "very bad" contributing to the sense of fundamental badness at their core.

MIDDLE TO LATE CHILDHOOD: VERBAL CAMEO OF NORMATIVE SELF-REPRESENTATIONS AND SELF-EVALUATIONS

I'm in fourth grade this year, and I'm pretty popular, at least with my girl friends. That's because I'm nice to people and helpful and can keep secrets. Mostly I am nice to my friends, although if I get in a bad mood I sometimes say something that can be a little mean. I try to control my temper, but when I don't, I'm ashamed of myself. I'm usually happy when I'm with my friends, but I get sad if there is no one to do things with. How I look and how popular I am are more important. I also like myself because I know my parents like me and so do other kids. That helps you like yourself. (adapted from Harter, 1999, p. 48)

Such self-descriptions are typically observed in children ages 8 to 11. In contrast to the more concrete self-representations of younger children, older children are much more likely to describe the self as popular, nice, helpful, mean, smart, and dumb. Children moving into late childhood continue to describe themselves in terms of their competencies (e.g., "smart," "dumb"). However, self-attributes become increasingly interpersonal as relations with others, particularly peers, become an increasingly salient dimension of the self (see also Damon & Hart, 1988; Rosenberg, 1979).

From the standpoint of emerging cognitive-developmental (I-self) processes, these attributes represent traits in the form of higher-order generalizations, integrating more specific behavioral features of the self (see Fischer, 1980; Siegler, 1991). Thus, in the cameo, the higher-order generalization that she is "smart" is based on the integration of scholastic success in both language arts and social studies. That she also feels "dumb" represents a higher-order construction based on her math and science performance. "Popular" also combines several behaviors: being nice, helpful, and keeping secrets.

SOCIAL PROCESSES

A more balanced view of self in which positive as well as negative attributes of the self are acknowledged is also fostered by new social comparison skills. As our prototypical subject reports, "I'm feeling pretty dumb in math and science, especially when I see how well the other kids are doing." A number of studies conducted in the 1970s and early 1980s presented evidence revealing that it is not until middle childhood that the child can apply comparative assessments with peers in the service of self-evaluation. From a cognitive-developmental perspective, the ability to use social comparison information toward the goal of self-evaluation requires that the child have the ability, which is not sufficiently developed at younger ages, to relate one concept to another simultaneously. In addition to the contribution of advances in cognitive development (see also Moretti & Higgins, 1990), age stratification in school stimulates greater attention to individual differences between age-mates (e.g., Higgins & Bargh, 1987). More recent findings reveal that the primary motive for children in this age period to utilize social comparison is for personal competence assessment.

The ability to utilize social comparison information for the purpose of self-evaluation is founded on cognitive-developmental advances or the ability to simultaneously compare representations of self and others. However, it is also supported by the socializing environment. For example, evidence reveals that as children move up the academic ladder, teachers make increasing use of social comparison information (Eccles & Midgley, 1989) and that students are well aware of these educational practices (Harter, 1996). Moreover, parents may contribute to the increasing salience of social comparison, to the extent that they make comparative assessments of how their child is performing relative to siblings, friends, or classmates.

NORMATIVE LIABILITIES FOR SELF-DEVELOPMENT DURING MIDDLE TO LATE CHILDHOOD

A cardinal thesis of this chapter is that cognitive advances bring about, paradoxically, normative liabilities for the self-system. The ability to be able to construct a global perception of one's worth as a person represents a major developmental acquisition—a milestone, as it were—in terms of a shift from mere domain-specific self-perceptions to an integrated sense of one's overall self-esteem. However, other cognitive-developmental acquisitions can serve to lower the valence of this global perception of self, leading to lowered self-esteem. Beginning in middle childhood self-perceptions become more negative, normatively, compared to the very positive self-perceptions of the majority of young children (see Harter, 1999). The emergence of three cognitive skills is noteworthy in this regard: (1) the ability to use social comparison for the purpose of self-evaluation, (2) the ability to differentiate real from ideal self-perceptions, and (3) increases in social perspective-taking skills.

The ability to employ social comparison for the purpose of self-evaluation (e.g., see Maccoby, 1980; Ruble & Frey, 1991) leads many, with the exception of the most competent or adequate in any given domain, to fall short in their self-evaluations. If a child therefore judges him- or herself deficient, compared to others, in domains that are deemed important to the self and others, global self-esteem will be eroded. Thus, the very ability and penchant, supported by the culture (e.g., family, peers, schools, and the media) to compare oneself with others makes one vulnerable in valued domains (e.g., appearance, popularity, scholastic competence, athletic performance, and behavioral conduct).

A second newfound cognitive ability to emerge in middle to late childhood involves the capacity to make the distinction between one's real and one's ideal self. From a Jamesian perspective, this skill involves the ability to distinguish between one's actual competencies or adequacies and those to which they aspire and deem important. The cognitive realization that one is not meeting one's expectations (an ability that young children do not possess) will necessarily lower one's overall level of self-esteem, as James's formulation accurately predicts. Moreover, parents, teachers, and peers may normatively raise the bar in terms of their expectations, leading to higher self-ideals.

Increased perspective-taking skills can also directly impact self-perceptions, leading them to be more realistic. Protected by limitations in the ability to divine what others truly think of the self, younger children can maintain very positive self-perceptions. The developing ability to more accurately assess the opinions that others hold about one's characteristics, coupled with increasing concern about the importance of the views of others toward the self, normatively leads many older children to realistically lower their self-evaluations.

INDIVIDUAL DIFFERENCES: ADAPTIVE AND MALADAPTIVE OUTCOMES IN MIDDLE TO LATE CHILDHOOD

Several formulations, supported by empirical evidence, speak to the emergence of individual differences in self-representations and associated self-evaluations. From a Jamesian perspective, those who are genetically blessed with talents and/or who are praised for competence in domains deemed important to success will fare the best in terms of positive self-evaluations.

Moreover, child-rearing practices continue to be critical during middle to late childhood. Parental or caregiver approval is particularly critical in the child's domain-specific sense of competence and adequacy as well as global self-worth. Coopersmith (1967), in his seminal efforts to unravel the causes of high and low self-esteem in children, described how the socialization practices of parents impact children's self-esteem. Parents of children with high self-esteem were more likely to (a) be accepting, affectionate, and involved in their child's activities; (b) enforce rules consistently and encourage children to uphold high standards of behavior; (c) prefer noncoercive disciplinary practices, discussing the reasons why the child's behavior was inappropriate; and (d) be democratic in considering the child's opinion around certain family decisions.

Evidence also reveals that parental support, particularly in the form of approval and acceptance, is associated with high self-esteem and the sense that one is lovable (see review by Feiring & Taska, 1996). Other studies have built on Baumrind's (1989) typology of parenting styles, linking them to child and adolescent self-evaluations. For example, Lamborn, Mounts, Steinberg, and Dornbusch (1991) reported that those with more authoritative or democratic parents reported significantly higher self-evaluations in the domains of social and academic competence than did those with authoritarian or neglectful parenting.

These findings are consistent with the theorizing of Cooley (1902) and attachment theorists (e.g., Bretherton, 1991). Benevolent socializing agents who readily provide nurturance, approval sensitivity, emotional availability, and support for mastery attempts will produce children who mirror and eventually internalize this support in the form of positive self-evaluations. However, in their search for their image in the social mirror, other children may well gaze through a glass darkly. Caregivers lacking in responsiveness, nurturance, encouragement, and approval, as well as socializing agents who are rejecting, punitive, or neglectful, will both cause their children to develop tarnished images of self, feeling unlovable, incompetent, and generally unworthy.

Thus, there is considerable evidence that support from parents as significant others in the child's life will have a powerful influence on self-evaluations (be they domain-specific or global in nature) or overall self-esteem (see Harter, 1999). Our own research documents the fact that parental or caregiver support is a major predictor of global self-worth throughout the childhood years. However, as the child moves up the developmental ladder, other sources of support emerge, where peer support becomes increasingly important. Thus, one can ask the question "Mirror, mirror on the wall, whose opinion is the most critical of all?" At this particular developmental level, we have documented in numerous studies that there are four primary sources of support: (1) parents, (2) teachers, (3) classmates, and (4) close friends. Parental and classmate support correlate most highly with global self-esteem. Why is close friend support not more predictive? We have argued (Harter, 1999) that, by definition, close friend support must be high. Furthermore, when one examines the various functions of support from different significant others, support from close friends typically manifests itself in the form of empathy, caring, and sensitivity to emotions and solutions to personal problems. Classmate support in the form of approval represents more seemingly objective feedback about one's competencies, adequacy, and worth as a person.

To return to the theme of the importance of parental child rearing, and more pathological implications in the extreme, children subjected to severe and chronic abuse continue to create images of the self that are despicable, given the difficulty overcoming Posttraumatic Stress Disorder (PTSD), including the psychological pain and symptoms that endure in the form of flashbacks and dissociative symptoms (e.g., Fischer & Ayoub, 1994; Harter, 1998b, 2006). More than constructing negative self-perceptions, they view the self as fundamentally flawed. Often excessively high and unrealistic parental standards that are unattainable contribute to these negative views of the self. Thus, the Me-self, both at the level of domain-specific self-perceptions and one's sense of global self-esteem, may be irrevocably damaged. In reaction to low self-esteem, depression and suicidal behavior may result. Finally, negative perceptions of one's appearance can lead to a variety of easting disorders (see original chapter in the *Handbook of Child Psychology*).

In addition to the incorporation of the opinions of significant others, children come to internalize the standards and values of the larger society. Perceptions of one's physical attractiveness, in relation to the importance that is attached to meeting cultural standards of appearance, contribute heavily to one's overall sense of worth as a person (see Harter, 1999). Those few who feel they have attained the requisite physical attributes will experience relatively high levels of self-esteem. Conversely, those who feel that they fall short of the punishing standards of appearance that represent the cultural ideal will suffer from low self-esteem and depression. Moreover, a related liability can be observed in the eating-disordered behavior of females, in particular, many of whom display symptoms (e.g., associated with anorexia) that are life threatening (Harter, 1999). Our own findings (Kiang & Harter, 2004) provide support for a model in which endorsement of the societal standards of appearance leads to low self-esteem that predicts both depression and eating-disordered behavior. Finally, genetic factors leading to physical characteristics that do not meet cultural standards of attractiveness can also contribute to this pattern that may be particularly resistant to change.

DEVELOPMENTAL DIFFERENCES IN SELF-REPRESENTATIONS DURING ADOLESCENCE

The period of adolescence represents a dramatic developmental transition, given pubertal and related physical changes, cognitive-developmental advances, and changing social expectations. With regard to cognitive-developmental acquisitions, adolescents develop the ability to think abstractly (e.g., Case, 1985; Fischer, 1980; Harter, 1999; Higgins, 1991). From a Piagetian (1960) perspective, the capacity to form abstractions emerges with the stage of formal operations in early adolescence. These newfound acquisitions, according to Piaget, should equip the adolescent with the hypothetico-deductive skills to create a formal theory. This observation is critical to the topic of self-development, given the claims of many (e.g., Epstein, 1981; Kelly, 1955; Markus, 1980; Sarbin, 1962) that the self is a personal epistemology, a cognitive construction, or a theory that should possess the characteristics of any formal theory. Therefore, a self-theory should meet those criteria by which any good theory is evaluated. Such criteria include the degree to which it is parsimonious, empirically valid, internally consistent, coherently organized, testable, and useful. From a Piagetian perspective, entry into the period of formal operations should supposedly make the construction of such a theory possible—be it a theory about elements in the world or a theory about the self.

However, as becomes apparent, the self-representations during early and middle adolescence fall far short of these criteria. The self-structure of these periods is not coherently organized, nor are the postulates of the self-portrait internally consistent. Moreover, many self-attributes fail to be subjected to tests of empirical validity; as a result, they can be extremely unrealistic. Nor are self-representations particularly parsimonious. Thus, the Piagetian framework fails to provide an adequate explanation for the dramatic developmental changes in the self-structure that can be observed across the substages of adolescence. Rather, as in our analysis of how self-representations change during childhood, a neo-Piagetian approach is needed to understand how changes in cognitive-developmental I-self processes result in very different Me-self organizational and content at each three age levels: early adolescence, middle adolescence, and late adolescence. As in our examination of self-development during childhood, for each age level we first provide a cameo self-description. What follows is (a) an analysis of the normative-developmental changes in self-representations and self-evaluations, (b) the exploration of the normative liabilities of each age period, and (c) the mention of the implications for adaptive and maladaptive self-development at each period of adolescence which are elaborated in the *Handbook of Child Psychology*.

EARLY ADOLESCENCE: VERBAL CAMEO OF NORMATIVE SELF-REPRESENTATIONS AND SELF-EVALUATIONS

I'm an extrovert with my friends: I'm talkative, pretty rowdy, and funny. I'm fairly good-looking if I do say so. All in all, around people I know pretty well I'm awesome, at least I think my friends think I am. I'm usually cheerful when I'm with my friends, happy and excited to be doing things with them. I like myself a lot when I'm around my friends. With my parents, I'm more likely to be depressed. I feel sad as well as mad and also hopeless about ever pleasing them. They think I spend too much time at the mall with my friends, and that I don't do enough to help out at home. They tell me I'm lazy and not very responsible, and it's hard not to believe them. I get real sarcastic when they get on my case. The fact of the matter is that what they think about is still really important. So when they are on my case, it makes me dislike myself as a person. At school, I'm pretty intelligent. I know that because I'm smart when it comes to how I do in classes, I'm curious about learning new things, and I'm also creative when it comes to solving problems. My teacher says so. I get better grades than most, but I don't brag about it because that's not cool. I can be a real introvert around people I don't know well. I'm shy, uncomfortable, and nervous. Sometimes I'm simply stupid, I mean I act really dumb and say things that are just plain stupid. I worry a lot about what others my age who are not my closest friends must think of me, probably that I'm a total dork. I just hate myself when that happens, because what they think is really important. (adapted from Harter, 1999)

With regard to the content of the self-portraits of young adolescents, interpersonal attributes, and social skills that influence interactions with others or one's social appeal are typically quite salient, as findings by Damon and Hart (1988) indicate. Thus, our prototypical young adolescent admits to being talkative, rowdy, funny, good-looking, and downright awesome, characteristics that may enhance acceptance by peers. In addition to social attributes, self-representations also focus on competencies such as one's scholastic abilities (e.g., "I'm intelligent") and affects (e.g., "I'm cheerful" and "I'm depressed").

From a developmental perspective, there is considerable evidence that the self becomes increasingly differentiated (see Harter, 1998a, 1999). During adolescence, there is a proliferation of selves that vary as a function of social context. These include self with father, mother, close friends, romantic partners, peers, as well as the self in the role of student, on the job, and as an athlete (e.g., Harter, Bresnick, Bouchey, & Whitesell, 1997; Harter & Monsour, 1992; Smollar & Youniss, 1985). For example, as the cameo reveals, the adolescent may be cheerful and rowdy with friends, depressed and sarcastic with parents, intelligent, curious, and creative as a student, and shy and uncomfortable around people whom he or she does not know. A critical developmental task, therefore, is the construction of multiple selves that will undoubtedly vary across different roles and relationships, as James (1892) observed over 100 years ago.

Many of the self-descriptions to emerge in early adolescence represent abstractions about the self, based on the newfound cognitive ability to integrate trait labels into higher-order self-concepts (e.g., see Case, 1985; Fischer, 1980; Harter, 1983; Higgins, 1991). For example, as the prototypical cameo reveals, one can construct an abstraction of the self as "intelligent" by combining such traits as smart, curious, and creative. Alternatively, one may create an abstraction that the self is an "airhead" given situations where one feels dumb and "just plain stupid." Similarly, an adolescent could construct abstractions that he or she is an "extrovert" (integrating the traits of rowdy, talkative, and funny) and that he or she is also an "introvert" in certain situations (when one is shy, uncomfortable, and nervous).

Although the ability to construct such abstractions reflects a cognitive advance, these representations are highly compartmentalized; that is, they are quite distinct from one another (Case, 1985; Fischer, 1980; Higgins, 1991). For Fischer, these "single abstractions" are overdifferentiated, and therefore the young adolescent can only think about each of them as isolated self-attributes. When the adolescent first moves to the level of abstract thought, he or she lacks the ability to integrate the many single abstractions that are constructed to define the self in different relational contexts. As a result, adolescents will engage in all-or-none thinking at an abstract level. For Fischer, movement to a qualitatively new level of thought brings with it lack of "cognitive control," and, as a result, adolescents at the level of single abstractions can only think about isolated self-attributes. Thus, contrary to earlier models of mind (Piaget, 1960), which focus on integration of the self, fragmentation of self-representations during early adolescence is more the rule than the exception (Fischer & Ayoub, 1994; Harter, 1998b; Harter & Monsour, 1992).

Another manifestation of the compartmentalization of these abstract attributes can be observed in the tendency for the young adolescent to be unconcerned about the fact that across different roles, certain postulates appear inconsistent, as the prototypical self-description implies (in contrast, at middle adolescence, there is considerable concern). However, during early adolescence, the inability to integrate seemingly contradictory characteristics of the self (e.g., intelligent versus airhead, extrovert versus introvert, or depressed versus cheerful) has the psychological advantage of sparing the adolescent conflict over opposing attributes in his or her self-theory (Harter & Monsour, 1992).

Our own findings (Harter et al., 1997) suggest that young adolescents do not yet have the cognitive ability to simultaneously compare these attributes to one another, and therefore they tend not to detect, or be concerned about, self-representations that are potential opposites. As one young adolescent put it, when confronted with the fact that he had indicated that he was both caring and rude, "Well, you are caring with your friends and rude to people who don't treat you nicely. There's no problem. I guess I just think about one thing about myself at a time and don't think about the other until the next day." When another young adolescent was asked why opposite attributes did not bother her, she succinctly exclaimed, "That's a stupid question. I don't fight with myself!" As becomes apparent, this pattern changes dramatically during middle adolescence.

In addition to their sensitivity to feedback from others, young adolescents continue to make use of social comparison information. However, with increasing age, children shift from more conspicuous to more subtle forms of social comparison as they become more aware of the negative social consequences of overt comparisons; for example, they may be accused of boasting about their superior performance (Pomerantz,

Ruble, Frey, & Greulich, 1995). As the prototypical young adolescent describes in the cameo, "I get better grades than most, but I don't brag about it because that's not cool."

NORMATIVE LIABILITIES FOR SELF-DEVELOPMENT DURING EARLY ADOLESCENCE

As with the entry into any new developmental level, there are liabilities associated with these emerging self-processes. For example, although abstractions are developmentally advanced cognitive structures, they are removed from concrete, observable behaviors and therefore more susceptible to distortion. The adolescent's self-concept, therefore, becomes more difficult to verify and is often less realistic. As Rosenberg (1986) observes, when the self comes to be viewed as a collection of abstractions, uncertainties are introduced because there are "few objective and unambiguous facts about one's sensitivity, creativity, morality, dependability, and so on" (p. 129). Moreover, the necessary skills to apply hypothetico-deductive thinking to the postulates of one's self-system are not yet in place. Although the young adolescent may have multiple hypotheses about the self, he or she does not yet possess the ability to correctly deduce which are true, leading to distortions in self-perceptions.

The all-or-none thinking of this period, in the form of overgeneralizations that the young adolescent cannot cognitively control (Fischer, 1980), also contributes to unrealistic self-representations, in that at one point in time one may feel totally intelligent or awesome, whereas at another point in time one may feel like a complete dork. Thus, the adolescent sense of self will vacillate, given the inability to cognitively control one's self-representations.

In describing this "barometric self" during adolescence, Rosenberg (1986) points to a different set of more social causes. He cites considerable literature revealing that adolescents experience an increased concern with what their peers think of them, findings that are relevant to Cooley's looking glass self model. This heavy dependence on the perceptions of other's opinions tends to set the stage for volatility in one's assessment of the self. However, there is inevitable ambiguity about others' attitudes toward the self because one can never have direct access to the mind of another. Thus, attributions about others' thought processes may change from one time period to another. The second reason for fluctuating self-evaluations inheres in the fact that different significant others have different opinions of the self, depending on the situation or moment in time. Third, adolescents' concern with what others think of them leads to efforts at impression management, provoking variations in the self across relational contexts. Finally, at times, adolescents are treated as more adultlike (e.g., on a job) whereas at other times, they are treated as more childlike (e.g., with parents at home). Thus, the self fluctuates in tandem.

Finally, there are domain-specific normative liabilities that are associated with educational transitions. Young adolescents all shift from an elementary school to either a middle school or junior high school that typically draws on several elementary feeder schools. Thus, they must now move into a group of peers, many of whom they have previously not known (typically two-thirds to three-fourths of the peer group will be new). Given the young adolescent's heightened concern with how others view the self, an important source of global self-esteem, there may be understandable shifts in global self-esteem, if individuals perceive that their social acceptance is higher or lower than when they were in elementary school.

Eccles and Midgley (1989) have also pointed to different emphases in the educational system during the transition to middle school or elementary school that have implications for perceptions of a child's scholastic competence. They note that there is considerably more emphasis on social comparison (e.g., public posting of grades, ability grouping, or teachers, in their feedback to classes, verbally acknowledging the personal results of competitive activities). These educational practices represent a mismatch given the adolescent's needs. At a time when young adolescents are painfully self-conscious, the school system heightens the salience of social comparison in conjunction with publicizing each student's performance. In addition to the greater emphasis on social comparison, the standards for performance shift from effort to ability, according to Eccles and colleagues. They note that in elementary school, there is more emphasis on effort: "Try harder and you can do better." In middle and junior high schools, however, poorer performance is attributed to lack of scholastic ability, leading the young adolescent to feel that he or she does not have the aptitude to succeed or that he or she lacks intelligence. For those not performing well, these practices can lead to declines in self-perceptions of academic ability, shifts that will be exacerbated in contexts of high public feedback and greater social comparison.

INDIVIDUAL DIFFERENCES: ADAPTIVE AND MALADAPTIVE OUTCOMES DURING EARLY ADOLESCENCE

The frameworks of James (1892) and Cooley (1902), in conjunction with attachment theory, provide perspectives on the tremendous individual differences that one can observe in self-evaluations beginning in adolescence. From a Jamesian perspective, the congruence or discrepancy between one's perceptions of competence in age-appropriate domains and the importance of success attached to each domain have been demonstrated to be a major determinant of one's global self-esteem or self-worth (1890). Thus, those who are able to positively evaluate their successes in domains deemed important to the self will report high self-esteem. A parallel process is the ability to tout the importance of those domains in which one is succeeding. Conversely, those reporting failures in domains of importance will report low self-esteem. Such individuals appear unable to discount the importance of domains in which they are not successful.

Cooley's (1902) looking glass formulation and attachment theorists' explorations into working models of the self (see Bretherton & Munholland, 1999), bolster the social framework for viewing individual differences in self-worth, particularly as young adolescents are becoming more cognizant of their own thinking about themselves. However, "more cognizant," as our earlier developmental analysis reveals, does not necessarily translate into more "realistic." The more abstract self-evaluations are further removed from behavioral reality (see Harter, 1999). In early to middle adolescence, teenagers do not have the ability to engage in hypothetico-deductive thinking to arrive at realistic conclusions about the self. It is for this reason that more recent findings (reviewed in Harter, 1999) and more classic reviews (see Shrauger & Schoeneman, 1979) have concluded that self-perceptions of approval from significant others will be a better predictor of constructs such as self-esteem than actual measures of support from significant others.

Therefore, beginning in early adolescence, there is a heightened concern with how others view the self, a normative process that has implications for the salience of those determinants of self-esteem that have been articulated in Cooley's (1902) looking glass self-formulation. If significant others provide support for whom the young adolescent is as a person, for those attributes that the young adolescent feels truly define the self, he or she will experience the self as authentic. However, the construction of a self that is too highly dependent on the internalization of the opinions of others can, under some circumstances, lead to the creation of a false self that does not mirror his or her authentic experience. In our own research (Harter, 1999), we have found that it is not until early adolescence that the concept of acting as a false self becomes very salient in the consciousness of young teenagers. The detection of hypocrisy, not only in others but also in the self, emerges as a critical filter in evaluating others as well as the self. Our own findings (Harter, Marold, Whitesell, & Cobbs, 1996) reveal that unhealthy levels of false-self behavior are particularly likely to emerge if caregivers make their approval contingent on the young adolescent living up to unrealistic standards of behavior, based on unattainable standards dictated by parents.

Chronic and severe abuse continues to put an adolescent at even more extreme risk for suppressing his or her true self and displaying various forms of inauthentic or false-self behavior. Such a process has its origins in childhood, given the very forms of parenting that constitute psychological abuse. As described earlier, parenting practices that represent lack of attunement to the child's needs, empathic failure, lack of validation, threats of harm, coercion, and enforced compliance all cause the true self to go underground (e.g., Stern, 1985; Winnicott, 1965) and lead to what Sullivan (1953) labeled as "not me" experiences.

Our findings (see Harter, 1999) document that while peer support increases in its predictability of global self-esteem between late childhood and early adolescence, the impact of parental support does not decline. Previous textbook portrayals of adolescence imply that parental influences decline as a child moves into adolescence. However, nothing is further from the truth when we examine the impact of parental support, including conditionality, on self-processes including false-self behavior, global self-esteem, and the related correlates of depressed affect, hopelessness, and suicidal ideation.

PEER REJECTION, HUMILIATION, AND IMPLICATIONS FOR THE HIGH PROFILE SCHOOL SHOOTINGS

More recently, we have become focused on the role of peer rejection, not merely the lack of peer approval. Our initial interest in this construct came from an analysis of the emerging profiles of the, now, eleven high-profile cases in which White, middle-class older children and adolescents, from small cities or suburbs, have gone on shooting sprees killing peers, and in a few cases, school officials who were random targets rather than specifically identified individuals. What became evident, in the analysis of media reports, is that all of these male youth killers had a history of peer rejection and humiliation. As a psychologist who for many years has contributed to (and kept up with) the literature on emotional development in children and adolescents, it was astounding to learn that we have no literature on humiliation. There is ample literature on shame, guilt, embarrassment, but virtually nothing about humiliation. Yet, we can all appreciate the fact (be it from our own experience or the experience of our children) that humiliation is a daily event in schools for many children. For the school shooters, extreme feelings of chronic humiliation by peers, due to excessive teasing, taunting, and physical insults, eventually led them to psychologically "snap," leading to random deaths and in the case of the Columbine teens to suicide.

An examination of the media accounts of the school shooters made it obvious that many of the determinants in our model could be found in the lives of these adolescents (see Harter, Low, & Whitesell, 2003). As a result, we examined a revised model in which we added angry aggression as well as violent ideation. We examined this model in a normative sample of middle school students. Through path-analytic techniques, we demonstrated that the data fit the model exceedingly well: The antecedents in the model, domain-specific perceived inadequacies predicted lack of approval from peers and parents alike. These determinants, in turn, predicted low self-esteem, depressed affect, angry affect, and hopelessness, all of which predicted both suicidal ideation and violent ideation. Consistent with the clinical literature on the comorbidity of internalizing and externalizing symptoms, we found a correlation of $R = .55$ between suicidal and violent ideation toward others. Thus, the determinants in our model, if negative, put adolescents at pathological risk for endangering their own and others' lives.

We have also pursued the emotion of humiliation and its role in contributing to violent ideation. In the Harter, Low, et al. study (2003), we wrote vignettes that simulated some of the types of humiliating events that were experienced by the school shooters. We then asked middle school students what other emotions they might experience (e.g., anger or depression) and what behaviors they might exhibit, along a continuum from doing nothing to acting violently toward the perpetrators or toward anyone (given the randomness of the actual school shooting events). While the majority of students reported that they would be humiliated (given that the vignettes were designed to be humiliating) we identified a group of violent ideators (in the minority) and a group who did not report that they would think about violent revenge. We then sought to determine what distinguished the two groups, finding that those entertaining violent thoughts expressed higher levels of anger and depression. In addition, the violent ideators reported higher levels of negative determinants in the model, such as more peer rejection, less parental support, lower self-concept scores (e.g., appearance or peer likability), lower self-worth, and greater hopelessness. Thus, certain factors in histories of violent ideators propel them to thoughts of seriously harming others and themselves, which are pathological outcomes that may require clinical interventions given that they may be putting themselves and others at serious risk.

In a subsequent study, we sought to more specifically investigate what were some of the factors that lead humiliation to result in violent ideation as well as suicidal ideation, given the paucity of work on the emotion of humiliation. Our findings have documented that teasing and taunting and bullying, particularly in the presence of an audience who mocks the victim, lead to humiliation. Humiliation, in turn, serves to provoke prototypical reactions, including revenge, wanting to hide, or attempts to minimize the humiliation (Harter, Kiang, Whitesell, & Anderson, 2003). We are pursuing this prototypical approach to humiliation currently.

Pathological Eating—Disordered Behavior

Our model identifies one self-concept domain that robustly affects global self-esteem across ages and cultures, namely, perceived physical appearance or attractiveness. In reviewing the inextricable link between perceived appearance and self-esteem, between the outer self and the inner self (see Harter, 1999), it became very apparent that this link is profoundly impacted by cultural standards of appearance for each gender. That cultures tout physical attractiveness as the measure of one's worth as a person has been amply demonstrated in contemporary society, as well as historically (Hatfield &

Sprecher, 1986). The empirical findings (reviewed in Harter, 1999) indicate that Pearson correlations range from the .40s to the .80s. Moreover, investigators have revealed that these relationships are not merely statistical but are very much embedded in the consciousness of individuals who are aware of this link. In our own work (Kiang & Harter, 2004), we have found strong support for a model in which awareness of current cultural values (e.g., being attractive will lead to higher self-esteem, meeting standards of appearance will make people more popular, and people who are overweight are discriminated against) are highly endorsed. However, there is enough variability in these scores to relate such awareness to perceptions of one's own appearance, which, in turn, predict level of self-esteem and eating-disordered perceptions and behaviors. Specifically, those endorsing these cultural values or links reported more negative views of their appearance, lower self-esteem, more psychological correlates of eating disorders and more eating-disordered behaviors.

MIDDLE ADOLESCENCE: VERBAL CAMEO OF NORMATIVE SELF-REPRESENTATIONS AND SELF-EVALUATIONS

What am I like as a person? You're probably not going to understand. I'm complicated! With my really close friends, I am very tolerant. I mean, I'm understanding and caring. With a group of friends, I'm rowdier. I'm also usually friendly and cheerful but I can get pretty obnoxious and intolerant if I don't like how they're acting. I'd like to be friendly and tolerant all of the time, that's the kind of person I want to be, and I'm disappointed in myself when I'm not. At school, I'm serious, even studious every now and then, but on the other hand, I'm a goof-off too, because if you're too studious, you won't be popular. So I go back and forth, which means I don't do all that well in terms of my grades. But that causes problems at home, where I'm pretty anxious when I'm around my parents. I can't be my real self with my parents. They don't understand me. What do they know about what it's like to be a teenager? They treat me like I'm still a kid. At least at school, people treat you more like you're an adult. That gets confusing, though. I mean, which am I? When you're 15, are you still a kid or an adult? I have a part-time job and the people there treat me like an adult. I want them to approve of me, so I'm very responsible at work, which makes me feel good about myself there. But then I go out with my friends and I get pretty crazy and irresponsible. So, which am I, responsible or irresponsible? How can the same person be both? So I think a lot about who is the real me, and sometimes I try to figure it out when I write in my diary, but I can't resolve it. There are days when I wish I could just become immune to myself! (adapted from Harter, 1999)

Self-descriptions are likely to increase in length during this period, as adolescents become increasingly introspective and morbidly preoccupied with what others think of them (e.g., Broughton, 1978; Elkind, 1967; Erikson, 1968; Rosenberg, 1979). The unreflective self-acceptance of earlier periods of development vanishes, and, as Rosenberg observes, what were formerly unquestioned self-truths now become problematic self-hypotheses. The tortuous search for the self involves a concern with what or who am I (Broughton, 1978), a task made more difficult given the multiple Me's that crowd the self-landscape. There is typically a further proliferation of selves as adolescents come to make finer differentiations; in the cameo, the adolescent describes a self with really close friends (e.g., tolerant) versus with a group of friends (e.g., intolerant) and a self with mother (e.g., close) versus father (e.g., distant). The acquisition of new roles, for example, self at a job, may also require the construction of new context-specific attributes (e.g., responsible).

Moreover, additional cognitive I-self processes emerge that give the self-portrait a very new look (Case, 1985; Fischer, 1980). Whereas, in the previous stage, single abstractions were isolated from one another, during middle adolescence one acquires the ability to make comparisons between single abstractions, namely, between attributes in the same role-related self or across role-related selves. Fischer labels these new structures "abstract mappings," in that the adolescent can now "map" constructs about the self onto one another or directly compare them. Therefore, mappings force the individual to compare and contrast different attributes. It should be noted that abstract mappings have features in common with the "representational" mappings of childhood, in that the cognitive links that are initially forged often take the form of opposites. During adolescence, these opposites can take the form of seemingly contradictory abstractions about the self (e.g., tolerant versus intolerant, extrovert versus introvert, responsible versus irresponsible, and good-looking versus unattractive as in the cameo).

However, the abstract mapping structure has limitations as a means of relating two concepts to one another in that the individual cannot yet truly integrate such self-representations in a manner that would resolve apparent contradictions. Therefore, at the level of abstract mappings, the awareness of these opposites causes considerable intrapsychic conflict, confusion, and distress (Fischer et al., 1984; Harter & Monsour, 1992; Higgins, 1991), given the inability to coordinate these seemingly contradictory self-attributes. For example, our prototypical adolescent agonizes over whether she is an extrovert or an introvert ("Am I just acting like an extrovert, am I just trying to impress them, when really I'm an introvert?" "So which am I, responsible or irresponsible? How can the same person be both?"). Such cognitive-developmental limitations contribute to the emergence of what James (1892) identified as the "conflict of the different Me's."

In addition to such confusion, these seeming contradictions lead to very unstable self-representations (e.g., "I don't really understand how I can switch so fast from being cheerful with my friends, then coming home and feeling anxious, and then getting frustrated and sarcastic with my parents. Which one is the real me?"). The creation of multiple selves, coupled with the emerging ability to detect potential contradictions between self-attributes displayed in different roles, naturally ushers in concern and confusion over which attributes define the true self. However, from a normative perspective, the adolescent at this level is not equipped with the cognitive skills to fully solve the dilemma (e.g., "So I think a lot about who is the real me, and sometimes try to figure it out when I write in my diary, but I can't resolve it").

Across three different studies (see Harter et al., 1997), we have found that the number of opposing self-attribute pairs, as well as the number of opposites in conflict, increases between early and middle adolescence. This pattern of findings supports the hypothesis that the abstract mapping structures that emerge in middle adolescence allow one to detect, but not to meaningfully integrate, these apparent contradictions. Thus, they lead to the phenomenological experience of intrapsychic conflict. We have asked teenagers to verbally elaborate on the opposites and conflicts that they reported on our task. As one 14-year-old put it, "I really think I am a happy person and I want to be that way with everyone, not just my friends; but I get depressed with my family, and it really bugs me because that's not what I want to be like." Another 15-year-old, in describing a conflict between self-attributes in the realm of romantic relationships, exclaimed, "I hate the fact that I get so nervous! I wish I wasn't so inhibited. The real me is talkative. I just want to be natural, but I can't." Another 15-year-old girl explained, "I really think of myself as friendly and open to people, but the way the other girls act, they force me to become an introvert, even though I know I'm not." In exasperation, one ninth-grader observed of the self-portrait she had constructed, "It's not right, it should all fit together into one piece!" These comments suggest that at this age level, there is a need for coherence; there is a desire to bring self-attributes into harmony with one another, yet in mid-adolescence, the cognitive abilities to create such a self-portrait are not yet in place. In the larger chapter we present robust gender differences revealing that, at every age level, females detect more contradictory attributes than do males. These findings replicate two other studies in which similar gender differences were obtained (see Harter et al., 1997).

The challenges posed by the need to create different selves are also exacerbated for ethnic minority youth in this country who must bridge "multiple worlds," as Cooper and her colleagues point out (Cooper, Jackson, Azmitia, Lopez, & Dunbar, 1995). Minority youth must move between multiple contexts, some of which may be with members of their own ethnic group, including family and friends, and some of which may be populated by the majority culture, including teachers, classmates, and other peers who may not share the values of their family of origin. Rather than assume that all ethnic minority youth will react similarly to the need to cope with such multiple worlds, these investigators highlighted several different patterns of adjustment. Some youth are able to move facilely across the borders of their multiple worlds, in large part, because the values of the family, teachers, and peers are relatively similar. Others, for whom there is less congruence in values across contexts, adopt a bicultural stance, adapting to the world of family and to that of the larger community. Others find the transition across these psychological borders more difficult, and some find it totally unmanageable. Particularly interesting is the role that certain parents play in helping adolescents navigate these transitions, leading to more successful adaptations for some than others.

NORMATIVE LIABILITIES DURING MIDDLE ADOLESCENCE

Middle-adolescence brings a preoccupation with what significant others think of the self, a task that is made more challenging given the proliferation of roles that demand the creation of multiple selves. The addition of new role-related selves can be observed in the fact that adolescents make finer discriminations (e.g., self with a close friend versus self with a group of friends, and self with mother versus self with father). Moreover, there is relatively little overlap in the personal attributes that define the self in each role. The proliferation of multiple selves ushers in the potential for such attributes to be viewed as contradictory. The emergence of new cognitive processes, such as abstract mappings, forces the adolescent to compare and contrast different attributes, exacerbating the likelihood that contradictions will be detected. Mappings, in the form of the identification of opposites, are problematic in that the individual cannot yet truly integrate such self-representations in a manner that would resolve the contradictions. Thus, the adolescent is likely to experience conflict, confusion, and distress. Opposites and associated conflict are particularly likely to occur for attributes in different roles rather than in the same role. Females are particularly likely to display these negative outcomes. Opposing self-attributes also lead to unstable self-representations, in addition to concern over which characteristics represent one's true self.

With regard to the impact of the socializing environment, adolescents gaze intently into the social mirror for information about what standards and attributes to internalize. However, contradictory messages from different significant others can lead to confusion about just what characteristics to adopt. Differential support, in the form of approval or validation, will also lead to differing levels of self-worth across relational contexts. The contradictory feedback that adolescents may receive from different sources will, therefore, lead to volatility in self-esteem across interpersonal contexts. Contradictory standards and feedback can also contribute to a lowering of global self-esteem between early and middle adolescence (see findings reviewed by Harter, 2006), to the extent that one cannot meet the expectations of everyone in each relational context.

Cognitive-developmental advances during mid-adolescence also represent limitations that can lead to distortions in the interpretation of the opinions of significant others. As observed earlier, with the advent of any new cognitive capacities comes difficulty in controlling and applying them effectively. For example, teenagers have difficulty differentiating their own mental preoccupations from what others are thinking, leading to a form of adolescent egocentrism that Elkind (1967) has labeled the "imaginary audience." Adolescents falsely assume that others are as preoccupied with their behavior and appearance as they themselves are. As our prototypical respondent exclaims, "Everybody, I mean everybody else is looking at me like they think I am totally weird!" With regard to lack of cognitive control, this phenomenon represents overgeneralization (or failure to differentiate) in that adolescents project their own concerns onto others.

The liabilities of this period, therefore, are legion with regard to potential conflict and confusion over contradictory attributes and messages, concern over which characteristics define the true self, distortions in the perception of self versus others, and a preoccupation with discrepancies between the real and ideal self-concepts, all of which can lead to lowered self-worth. Some of these processes would appear to be problematic for particular subgroups of adolescents, for example, females who adopt a feminine gender orientation or ethnic minority youth who are challenged by the need to create selves that bridge "multiple worlds," with one's family, ethnic peers and in the mainstream majority culture.

An appreciation for the ramifications of these normative processes is critical in interpreting the unpredictable behaviors, shifting self-evaluations, and mood swings that are observed in many adolescents during this age period. Such displays are less likely to be viewed as intentional or pathological, and more likely to meet with empathy and understanding to the extent that normative cognitive-development changes can be invoked as in part responsible. For many parents, as well as other adults working closely with teenagers, these seemingly inexplicable reactions often lead to perplexity, exasperation, and anger, provoking power struggles and altercations that strain the adolescent-adult relationship. The realization that this is a normative part of development that should not persist forever may provide temporary comfort to adults who feel beleaguered and ineffectual in dealing with adolescents of this age. Indeed, it gives a more charitable rendering to this period of development.

INDIVIDUAL DIFFERENCES: ADAPTIVE AND MALADAPTIVE OUTCOMES IN MIDDLE ADOLESCENCE

With regard to the focus on meeting cultural standards appearance, females are much more likely to suffer from processes that move into the realm of pathology, including depression and eventual eating disorders. From the perspective of our own model of the causes and correlates of self esteem, an intense preoccupation with attempts to meeting the impossible standards of beauty, coupled with very negative perceptions of one's body image, can lead to extremely low self-esteem, depression, and in the extreme, eating-disordered behaviors. We have documented the links between the high importance attached to physical appearance and negative perceptions of one's body image, leading to extremely negative reports of self-esteem and depression among those in mid-adolescence. In the subsequent section on later adolescence and emerging adulthood, we provide further documentation about how these processes can lead to pathological eating-disordered behaviors.

However, numerous findings (e.g., reviewed by Harter, 1999; Nolen-Hoeksema & Girgus, 1994) reveal that dramatic gender differences in depression emerge in middle adolescence. The discrepancy between impossible ideals for appearance and one's perception of one's own body image contributes to very low self-esteem for some, particularly those who are overweight, which leads to profound depression that can require clinical intervention.

While the potential for such internalizing symptoms looms large for girls during middle adolescence, the potential for the escalation of violence and males, as in the case of the high profile cases of school shootings by White, middle-class adolescents is apparent. Intense rejection by peers, at a time when self-consciousness and the need for approval are so salient, sets the stage for violent ideation that can turn to action. The fragile and vacillating self-structures of this particular period can, in the face of humiliation, lead to lack of control, both over cognitions about the self (Harter, 1999) and behaviors that these cognitions may drive. Given the lack of cognitive control (Fischer, 1980), the adolescent during this period may act more impulsively on his thoughts. Recent work on the adolescent brain supports the view that the frontal cortex is not yet completely developed, leading to gaps in executive functions that could serve to curb such impulsive, violent intentions and behaviors.

While the fragmented self is a normative liability of this period of middle adolescence, interactions with a history of severe and chronic physical and sexual abuse may lead to pathological outcomes that can continue as PTSD symptoms even though the abuse occurred in early childhood. The effects of abuse on the self-system are legion (see review in Harter, 1999). From a developmental perspective, a history of abuse can lead to dissociative symptoms that serve to further fragment the fragile multiple selves in the process of psychological construction (e.g., see also Putnam, 1993) at a time when adolescents have normative challenges to integrating their various selves. As a result, there is no core self at the helm, there is little communication between multiple selves that become "alters," comprising the ability to develop an integrated self. As a result, there is the risk for dissociative identity disorders that represent severe pathological conditions that may require years of treatment.

LATE ADOLESCENCE: VERBAL CAMEO OF NORMATIVE SELF-REPRESENTATIONS AND SELF-EVALUATIONS

I'm a pretty conscientious person, particularly when it comes to things like doing my homework. It's important to me because I plan to go to college next year. Eventually I want to go to law school, so developing good study habits and getting top grades are both essential. (My parents don't want me to become a lawyer; they'd rather I go into teaching, but law is what I want to pursue.) Every now and then I get a little lackadaisical and don't complete an assignment as thoroughly or thoughtfully as I could, particularly if our high school has a big football or basketball game that I want to go to with my friends. But that's normal, I mean, you can't just be a total "grind." You'd be pretty boring if you were. You have to be flexible. I've also become more religious as I have gotten older, not that I am a saint or anything. Religion gives me a sense of purpose, in the larger scheme of things, and it provides me with personal guidelines for the kind of adult I'd like to be. Basically, I like who I am, so I don't stay depressed for long. Usually, I am pretty upbeat and optimistic. I guess you could say that I'm a moody person. I'm not as popular as a lot of other kids. You have to look a certain way, have the right body image, wear the right clothes, to be accepted. At our school, it's the jocks who are looked up to. I'm pretty much being the kind of person I want to be. I'm doing well at things that are important to me like getting good grades. That's what is probably most important to me right now. I'm looking forward to leaving home and going to college, where I can be more independent, although I'm a little ambivalent. I'll probably always be somewhat dependent on my parents. How can you escape it? But I'm also looking forward to being on my own. (adapted from Harter, 1999)

With regard to the content of the self-representations that emerge in late adolescence and early adulthood, typically, many of the attributes reflect personal beliefs, values, and moral standards that have become internalized, or alternatively, constructed from their own experiences (see findings by Damon & Hart, 1988). These characteristics are exemplified in the prototypical cameo, in that the adolescent expresses the personal desire to go to college, which requires good grades and discipline in the form of study habits. Although classmates tout athletics as the route to popularity, there is less concern at this age with what others think ("I used to care but now what I think is important"). In addition, there is a more realistic focus on one's future selves (e.g., not only becoming a lawyer, but also an ethical lawyer, as a personal goal). Noteworthy in this narrative is the absence of an explicit reference to the potential origins of these goals; for example, parental encouragement or expectations that one pursue such a career. Moreover, this adolescent's career choice does not conform to the parents' occupational goals for their child.

The failure to acknowledge the socialization influences that might have led to these choices does not necessarily indicate that significant others, such as peers and parents, had no impact. Findings (see Steinberg, 1990) reveal that the attitudes of adolescents and their parents are quite congruent when it comes to occupational, political, and religious decisions or convictions. That the impact of significant others is not acknowledged suggests that older adolescents and young adults have come to "own" various values as personal choices, rather than attribute them to the sources from which they may have been derived (Damon & Hart, 1988). In Higgins' (1991) terminology, older adolescents have gone through a process in which they have actively selected among alternative "self-guides" and are no longer merely buffeted about by the expectations of significant others; that is, self-guides become increasingly internalized and less tied to their social origins. Moreover, there is a greater sense of direction as the older adolescent comes to envisage future or "possible" selves (Markus & Nurius, 1986) that function as ideals toward which one aspires.

Another feature of the self-portrait of the older adolescent can be contrasted with the period before, in that many potentially contradictory attributes are no longer described as characteristics in opposition to one another. Thus, being conscientious as a student does not appear to conflict with one's lackadaisical attitude toward schoolwork: "That's normal, I mean, you can't just be a total 'grind.' You'd be pretty boring if you were. You have to be flexible." Nor does introversion conflict with extroverted behaviors. "You have to be adaptive around other people. It would be weird to be the same kind of person on a date and with my friends at a football game!"

There are cognitive acquisitions that allow the older adolescent to overcome some of the liabilities of the previous period, where potentially opposing attributes were viewed as contradictory and as a cause of internal conflict. The general cognitive advances during this period involve the construction of higher-order abstractions that involve the meaningful intercoordination of single abstractions (e.g., see Case, 1985; Fischer, 1980). For example, the fact that one is both introverted and extroverted can be integrated through the construction of a higher-order abstraction that defines the self as "adaptive." The observation that one is both depressed and cheerful or optimistic can be integrated under the personal rubric of "moody." Similarly, "flexible" can allow one to coordinate conscientiousness with the tendency to be lackadaisical. The higher-order concept of "ambivalence" integrates the desire to be independent yet still remain connected to parents. Moreover, "bittersweet" reflects a higher-order abstraction combining excitement over going to college with sadness over leaving one's parents. Such higher-order abstractions provide self-labels that bring meaning and therefore legitimacy to what formerly appeared to be troublesome contradictions in the self.

Neo-Piagetians, such as Case (1985), Fischer (1980), and colleagues, observe that developmental acquisitions at these higher levels typically require greater scaffolding by the social environment in the form of support, experiences, instruction, and so on for individuals to function at their optimal level. If these new skills are fostered, they will help the adolescent to integrate opposing attributes in a manner that does not produce conflict or distress. Thus, efforts to assist the adolescent in realizing that it is normal to display seemingly contradictory traits, and perhaps quite appropriate, may alleviate perceptions of conflict. Moreover, helping teenagers to provide higher-order labels that integrate opposing attributes (e.g., flexible, adaptive, moody, and inconsistent) may avert some of the distress that was salient during middle adolescence. The original chapter in the *Handbook of Child Psychology* provides speculation on why gender differences persist during late adolescence.

Finally, with regard to developmental changes in the self, evidence from longitudinal studies documents that self-esteem or global self-worth improves in later adolescence (e.g., see O'Malley & Bachman, 1983; Rosenberg, 1986). Several interpretations of these gains have been suggested (see Harter, 2006; McCarthy & Hoge, 1982). Reductions in the discrepancy between one's ideal self and one's real self, between one's aspirations and one's successes, according to James's (1892) formulation, may be in part responsible. As the prototypical adolescent indicates, he or she has more self-respect now, compared to a few years ago and observes that "I'm pretty much being the kind of person I want to be. I'm doing well at things that are important to me like getting good grades and being ethical." Gains in personal autonomy and freedom of choice may also play a role, in that the older adolescent may have more opportunity to select performance domains in which he or she is successful. Such freedom may also provide one with more opportunity to select those support groups that will provide the positive regard necessary to promote or enhance self-esteem, consistent with the looking glass self-formulation. Increased role-taking ability may also lead older teenagers to behave in more socially acceptable ways that enhance the evaluation of the self by others, such that the favorable attitudes of others toward the self are internalized as positive self-worth.

NORMATIVE LIABILITIES DURING LATE ADOLESCENCE

Many of the limitations of the preceding period of mid-adolescence would appear to be overcome as a result of changes during late adolescence. Attributes reflecting personal beliefs, values, and standards become more internalized, and the older adolescent would appear to have more opportunity to meet these standards, thereby leading to enhanced self-esteem. The focus on future selves also gives the older adolescent a sense of direction. A critical cognitive advance can be observed in the ability to construct higher-order abstractions that involve the meaningful integration of single abstractions that represent potential contradictions in the self-portrait (e.g., depressed and cheerful do not conflict because they are both part of being moody). The older adolescent can also resolve potentially contradictory attributes by asserting that he or she is flexible or adaptive, thereby subsuming apparent inconsistencies under more generalized abstractions about the self. Moreover, older adolescents are more likely to normalize potential contradictions, asserting that it is desirable to be different across relational contexts and that it would be weird or strange to be the same with different people.

Nevertheless, conflict between role-related attributes does not totally abate in later adolescence. Conflict will be more likely to occur if the new skills that allow for an integration of seeming contradictions are not fostered by the socializing environment. Furthermore, opposing attributes across particular role combinations, notably self with mother versus self with father, continue to be problematic in late adolescence, especially for girls. To the extent that one's mother and father elicit or reinforce opposing attributes, cognitive solutions for integrating seeming contradictions would appear to be more difficult to invoke.

Last, although the internalization of standards and opinions that the adolescent comes to own as personal choices and attitudes toward the self represents a developmental advance, there are liabilities as well associated with this process. As Rosenberg (1986) observes, the shift in the locus of self-knowledge from an external to internal source can introduce uncertainty. As long as major truths about the self derive from omniscient and omnipotent adults, then there is little doubt about their veracity. However, when the locus of self-knowledge shifts inward and adolescents must rely on their own autonomous judgment and insight to reach conclusions about the self, the sense of certainty can be compromised.

INDIVIDUAL DIFFERENCES: ADAPTIVE AND MALADAPTIVE SELF-PROCESSES AND OUTCOMES IN LATE ADOLESCENCE/EARLY ADULTHOOD

Many of the pathological processes that have been described in the earlier periods of adolescence can be observed, even if in a somewhat different form, due to developmental advances. Preoccupation with impossible cultural standards of attractiveness looms even larger as the older adolescent anticipates emerging adulthood, making it even more critical to attain these standards to be socially acceptable and successful in the new adult world order (Harter, 2004). For females, failure to meet these standards can lead to more pathological processes that may include eating disorders (see *Handbook of Child Psychology* for empirical findings).

Male adolescents are at continued risk for violence, particularly the type of violence that emanates from peer rejection and humiliation. Chronic rejection and humiliation are likely culprits for violent ideation (Harter, 2004) and for violent action, as in the case of the school shooters. Unlike the impulsive acts of the school shooters in middle adolescence, the acts of those (e.g., Eric Harris and Dylan Kleibold from Columbine) who were older teens were far more planful. For over a year, they had developed their strategies, some of which were revealed in Harris's written manifesto. While speculative, at this point, in examining the media accounts of the 11 high-profile school shooting cases, it would appear that the dynamics may be different from what we normally consider to be delinquent, conduct-disordered behavior that had come to the attention of teachers, school officials, school psychologists, peers, and parents. There had been few warning signs with regard to the male shooters having been in trouble with the law, having been identified as troublemakers in the school, having clinical diagnoses, or being placed in special classes for student with a penchant for acting out. As noted earlier, Harter and McCarley, 2004, found that 33% of those in a normative sample reporting to us that they had serious thoughts of harming others who humiliated them went undetected by their classroom teachers who were given parallel rating forms. Thus, there is a need to discriminate the form of violence that has recently emerged from previous acts that have been committed by known delinquents and conduct-disordered youth who have come to the attention of school and mental health professional, and who commit different types of crimes; for example, drive-by shootings to target one individual versus the random shooting of as many classmates as possible.

The construction of multiple selves, while a normative process, can also have pathological implications. It was pointed out in the section on middle adolescence that the effects of abuse can lead to dissociative symptoms that prevent one's multiple selves from being integrated. In the severest cases, this can lead to dissociative identity disorder (what used to be termed multiple personality disorder). Abuse has also been found to impact the valence (positive or negative) of those attributes judged to be one's core self (versus more peripheral attributes). Normatively, we have found that when asked to rate the attributes across multiple relational context with regard to whether they are central core characteristics or more peripheral, less important attributes that define the self, normative samples of older attributes will define their most important attributes as positive and assign their more negative characteristics (less important attributes) to the periphery of the self (Harter & Monsour, 1992). This self-protective strategy has been defined, normatively, as "beneffectance" by Greenwald (1980); namely, seeing one's positive attributes as central to the self and one's negative attributes as more peripheral.

Our colleagues Fischer and Ayoub (1994) employed our multiple selves procedure with an inpatient sample of seriously abused older adolescent girls, finding just the opposite pattern. Compared to a normative sample, the abused patients identified negative attributes as their core self, relegating what few positive characteristics they could identify as peripheral. Herein, we can detect another deleterious effect of abuse on self-processes leading to potential pathological outcomes that require clinical intervention that can hopeful restore a more positive balance of self-perceptions.

Stability versus Change in Self-Representations

Initially, it is important to address the question of whether concepts of self are immutable or subject to change. If self-representations are relatively stable, then practitioners should be less sanguine about the possibility of promoting positive self-evaluations in individuals with negative self-images. Alternatively, if self-representations are potentially malleable, practitioners can be more optimistic, particularly if there is a cogent analysis of the particular causes of a given individual's negative self-evaluations.

With regard to normative-developmental change, the evidence reveals that self-evaluative judgments become less positive as children move into middle childhood (Frey & Ruble, 1990; Harter & Pike, 1984). Investigators attribute such a decline to the greater reliance on social comparison information and external feedback, leading to more realistic judgments about one's capabilities. Studies suggest that there is another decline at early adolescence (ages 11 to 13), after which global evaluations of worth and domain-specific self-evaluations gradually become more positive over the course of adolescence (e.g., O'Malley & Bachman, 1983; Rosenberg, 1986; Savin-Williams & Demo, 1993).

Many of the changes reported coincide with the educational transition to junior high school. Eccles and colleagues (Wigfield, Eccles, Mac Iver, Reuman, & Midgley, 1991), and Simmons and colleagues (e.g., Blyth, Simmons, & Carlton-Ford, 1983; Simmons & Blyth, 1987) have postulated that differences in the school environments of elementary and junior high schools are in part responsible. Junior high school brings more emphasis on social comparison and competition, stricter grading standards, more teacher control, less personal attention from teachers, and disruptions in social networks, all of which lead to a mismatch between the structure of the school environment and the needs of young adolescents. The numerous physical, cognitive, social, and emotional changes further jeopardize the adolescent's sense of continuity, which may, in turn, threaten self-esteem.

The magnitude of the decline in perceptions of overall worth is also related to the timing of school shifts and to pubertal change (Brooks-Gunn, 1988; Simmons & Blyth, 1987). Those making the shift from sixth to seventh grade show greater losses of self-esteem than those who make the school transition a year later, from seventh to eighth grade. Moreover, students making the earlier change, particularly girls, do not recover these losses during the high school years. Early-maturing girls fare the worst. They are the most dissatisfied with their bodies, in part, because they tend to be somewhat heavier and do not fit the cultural stereotype of female attractiveness emphasizing thinness, as is discussed further in the section on the link between self-esteem and perceived appearance. This, in turn, has a negative effect on their self-worth. Furthermore, according to the developmental readiness hypothesis (Simmons & Blyth, 1987), early maturing girls are not yet emotionally prepared to deal with the social expectations that surround dating or with the greater independence that early maturity often demands (see Lipka, Hurford, & Litten, 1992, for a general discussion of the effects of being "off-time" in one's level of maturational development).

Several interpretations have been offered for the gradual gains in self-esteem that follow from eighth grade through high school (McCarthy & Hoge, 1982). Gains in personal autonomy may provide more opportunity to select performance domains in which one is competent, is consistent with a Jamesian analysis. Increasing freedom may allow more opportunities to select support groups that will provide esteem-enhancing approval, is consistent with the looking glass self-formulation. Increased role-taking ability may also lead teenagers to behave in more socially acceptable ways that garner the acceptance of others.

INDIVIDUAL DIFFERENCES

Considerable attention has been given to the issue of whether self-esteem is best viewed as a state or trait (see Trzesniewski, Donnellan, & Robins, 2003, for a review of this issue). Our own position (see Harter, 2004), addresses whether self-esteem is stable over time for individuals (is it a trait?) or is it subject to fluctuations (more state-like) and therefore the question is false and misguided. We have taken the stance (based on several strands of research) that the construct of self-esteem (or self-worth), in and of itself, is neither a trait nor a state per se. Rather for some individuals self-esteem is stable, whereas for others self-esteem is subject to change. Among adolescents, we have found evidence for this position with regard to self-esteem during the transition to junior high school. Some students enhance their self-esteem, others decline in self-esteem, and for a third group self-esteem remains stable. We linked changes versus stability to change or stability in the competence to important relationship (from James) and to stability or change in social support (from Cooley). Thus, if one feels more competent in domain, of importance and/or more social support, self-esteem will increase. If one feels less competent or garners less support, self-esteem will decline.

Gender Differences in Global and Domain-Specific Self-Evaluations

There is an emerging body of literature that has examined gender differences in subscale scores among older children, adolescents, and college students. For the most part, the findings are quite consistent with regard to a number of gender differences as well as similarities (see our own work and others' reviewed in Harter, 1999). A major and consistent finding is that females, at every age beginning in middle to late childhood report lower global self-worth than do males. We find this across the life span; however, differences are greatest in middle to late adolescence. An impressive meta-analysis on gender differences in self-esteem by Kling, Hyde, Showers, and Buswell (1999) confirms this finding in that the largest mean effect size favoring boys is in the 15- to 18-year-old group.

Kling et al. (1999) speculate on several reasons for these gender differences. One potential cause involves the gender role stereotypes that are reinforced in the school setting. Boys are socialized to use dominance, whereas girls are oriented toward shared social activities. Kling et al. (1999) also suggest that different opportunities for athletic participation could contribute to gender differences in self-esteem. Although Title IX certainly opened more doors for female children and adolescents to participate in sports, more emphasis and status has been given to male athletes and male sports programs. Furthermore, despite greater opportunities for girls, many do not take advantage of the options, fearing it will undermine their femininity. However, studies do show that males and females who do participate in sports report higher self-esteem.

Kling et al. (1999) put forth a powerful explanation for gender differences in self-esteem, consistent with our own interpretation on the inextricable link between perceived physical appearance and global self-worth, where we have found that correlations range from .66 to .82 across numerous studies (see Harter, 1999). We have argued elsewhere that the combination of the importance of appearance for females combined with the punishing standards of appearance for females profoundly contributes to their devaluation of their looks. Movies, magazines, and TV all tout the importance of good looks that are impossible to achieve, in part, because many of these looks are due to air-brushing, computer simulation, and the combining of body parts from models or movie stars to "achieve the look." Very few ads tout the importance of a physically fit female as desirable but rather showcase thinness combined with height and large breasts as the contemporary ideal.

Moreover, when both genders are considered, evidence indicates that girls and boys experience pubertal changes differently (Graber, Peterson, & Brooks-Gunn, 1996). Boys express greater satisfaction with the changes (e.g., becoming taller, more muscular, and lower voice) changes that signal masculinity (Nolen-Hoeksema & Girgus, 1994). In contrast, girls lose their prepubertal body (an image currently valued in our society with regard to thinness) and can be distressed by their new sexual status. Body dissatisfaction becomes critical to the extent that it leads to other mental health concerns such as eating-disordered behavior. There is overwhelming evidence that it is also associated with depression (see review, Harter, 1999).

The playing field has shifted for men in recent years. In former years, males could be judged attractive not only on the basis of their physical features, where they was much more latitude than for females, but by virtue of the fact that they have money, status, or power. (A magazine poll of women just after the Gulf War ended revealed that General Norman Schwartzkopf was judged to be the sexiest man in America.) This observation was made 15 years ago. It is my conjecture, as I look around my world and steep myself in gender literature on appearance and contemporary magazine articles and advertisements that trends are changing rapidly and the bar has been raised for men. Standards of appearance for men have become more important, more salient in our culture as well as more difficult to obtain. Muscles, abs, calves, the V-body shape, and hair (both facial hair and head hair or its absence) all must conform to new and punishing expectations for males, beginning in childhood. Workout centers and plastic surgeons are reaping big benefits given that the focus has become so much more on the outer, physical self than on the inner, psychological self.

Cross-Cultural Comparisons

It has become increasingly common for investigators in other countries to administer self-concept scales, such as our own, to children and adolescents in their own culture. However, there are potential pitfalls in administering measures developed for a given culture to those from other countries. At a minimum, any meaningful interpretation requires that these instruments show comparable psychometric properties. However, attention must also be directed to culturally relevant content, because domains and/or items in a given subscale may need to be tailored to each culture.

There are particular concerns about the use of our instruments in countries such as China and Japan. For example, the concept of global self-worth as defined in the American mainstream culture may not be an appropriate construct to include on an instrument examining meaningful self-perceptions among the Chinese. Other studies have reported relatively low reliabilities across all subscales (ranging from .44 to .61) suggesting that there exist items that are inappropriate for each of the domains (see Harter, 1999, for a review of these studies with Asian populations). There are additional domains of relevance to Chinese children that are not included on our American instruments (e.g., willingness to help others) and respect for parental and teacher authority.

Of further concern is that in Chinese, Japanese, and Korean samples, the means are considerably lower than are scores in United States, Canadian, Australian, and European samples. (The domain of social acceptance is perhaps the only exception.) One interpretation is that the Chinese appear to display a self-effacing style that leads them to be more modest in their report of personal qualities. The second is that our structured alternative format, in which we contrast statements about "Some kids" versus "Other kids," implicitly demands a form of social comparison with others. Such social comparison is frowned on in China, where individual differences in competence are downplayed. Thus, Chinese children's unwillingness to report that they may be superior to others leads to a pattern of low scores that may not truly reveal their private perceptions of personal adequacy. These same interpretations may well apply to other Asian countries such as Japan and Korea.

Ethnic Differences in Our Own Culture

Most of the work on ethnic differences has been comparisons between the self-esteem of African Americans and Europeans in this country. For many years it was merely assumed that Blacks, as they were called at the time, would have lower self-esteem due to their initial status as slaves, their treatment by White society, their status as second-class citizens, and therefore their cultural marginalization. However, with the advent of attention to the Black community by psychologists, using appropriate methodologies, these myths and assumptions were challenged. Two excellent meta-analyses (Gray-Little & Hafdahl, 2000; Twenge & Crocker, 2002) have clearly documented that African Americans in our culture have higher self-esteem than European-Americans, and these and other investigators have developed trenchant analyses of why this might be the case.

Gray-Little and Hafdahl (2000) form two related questions that capture the reader's attention. From a Cooley, symbolic-interactionist perspective, a social framework on reflected self-appraisals, one needs to ask to whom do Blacks turn as the significant others. It has been suggested that Blacks do not turn to the larger White society as their reference groups but rather turn to the Black community as their source of support and acceptance; these are the people whose opinions are most important to them. Adhering to these values, accepting them, makes them less vulnerable to their marginalization by the White culture, and allows them to develop a sense of meeting the expectations of their ethnic in-group, thereby experiencing high self-esteem (as the Jamesian hypothesis would predict). Moreover, social comparison looms large as a factor in impacting an individual's self-esteem. To the extent that Blacks are comparing themselves to other Blacks, rather than White norms for success, this potentially enhances their self-esteem.

It should be noted that the basic processes underlying self-esteem formation among African Americans appears to be similar to that of White adolescents (see review in Harter, 1999). Given the notion that an individual incorporates the attitudes of significant others toward the self, the context for self-esteem development in African Americans involves the African American family, peers, and community. Thus, African American children and adolescents internalize the opinions of parents and siblings, as well as African American friends, teachers, and coaches, who serve as their primary social reference groups. Interestingly, the relationship between the attitudes of significant others toward the self and self-esteem has been found to be somewhat stronger among African Americans than among European-Americans (Rosenberg & Simmons, 1972). It has been suggested that the African American community is a source of positive self-concept in African American children and that, under certain conditions, the African American family can filter out destructive racist messages from the White community, supplanting such messages with more positive feedback that will enhance self-esteem (Barnes, 1980).

A Jamesian analysis can also be applied to the level of self-esteem in African American youth. To the extent that African American values differ from those of Whites, different domains will be judged important. For example, there is a stronger correlation between school grades and self-esteem among European Americans than among African Americans, suggesting that the two racial groups may well base their self-esteem on different attributes. If we assume that people value those things at which they do well, and try to do well in those domains that they value, we see that African American adolescents may come to value those nonacademic arenas in which they feel they excel and over which they have some control and devalue their negative academic experiences. African American male youth, in particular, may substitute compensatory values in areas where they can perform more successfully. For example, athletic prowess, musical talent, acting ability, sexuality, and certain antisocial behaviors may become more highly valued than academic performance.

Conclusions

The study of self-development continues to thrive as new theoretical, methodological, and empirical perspectives emerge. There continues to be an interesting marriage between historical formulations about the self, attachment perspectives, and many other contemporary perspectives. Historical perspectives have concentrated more heavily on the social construction of the self. Cognitive-developmental differences, given the impetus of neo-Piagetians, have heightened our appreciation for how more subtle and discrete changes in cognitive advances and limitations influence self-development. The I-self has been transmitted into those changing cognitive processes that determine how the Me-self (one's verbalizable sense of self) will necessarily change with age. The field has far more appreciation for how broad stages, previously conceived as childhood and adolescence, must be broken down into the mini-substages in each broad categories of development. With regard to changes in self-development, we have identified three substages in childhood and three substages in adolescence, where self-development makes major leaps in content and organization. Normative cognitive advances and limitations clearly define the self, as have social influences by caregivers, significant other adults, and peers.

Our explorations need to extend beyond normative developmental differences, to include gender and ethnic differences in our own cultural and cross-cultural considerations. Sensitivity to gender and cultural differences are critical in understanding how the self is constructed. These are the future directions that the study of self-development must take.

References

Ainsworth, M. (1979). Infant-mother attachment. *American Psychologist, 34,* 932–937.

Baldwin, J. M. (1897). *Social and ethical interpretations in mental development: A study in social psychology.* New York: Macmillan.

Barnes, E. J. (1980). The Black community as a source of positive self-concept for Black children: A theoretical perspective. In R. Jones (Ed.), *Black psychology* (pp. 231–250). New York: Harper & Row.

Baumeister, R. F. (1993). Understanding the inner nature of low self-esteem: Uncertain, fragile, protective, and conflicted. In R. F. Baumeister (Ed.), *Self-esteem, the puzzle of low self-regard* (pp. 201–218). New York: Plenum Press.

Baumrind, D. (1989). Rearing competent children. In W. Damon (Ed.), *Child development today and tomorrow* (pp. 349–378). San Francisco: Jossey-Bass.

Bleiberg, E. (1984). Narcissistic disorders in children. *Bulletin of the Menninger Clinic, 48,* 501–517.

Blyth, D. A., Simmons, R. G., & Carlton-Ford, S. (1983). The adjustment of early adolescents to school transitions. *Journal of Early Adolescence, 3,* 105–120.

Bowlby, J. (1973). *Attachment and loss: Vol. 2. Separation.* New York: Basic Books.

Bowlby, J. (1980). *Attachment and loss: Vol. 3. Loss, sadness, and depression.* New York: Basic Books.

Bretherton, I. (1987). New perspectives on attachment relations: Security, communication, and internal working models. In J. D. Osofsky (Ed.), *Handbook of infant development* (2nd ed., pp. 1061–1101). New York: Wiley.

Bretherton, I. (1991). Pouring new wine into old bottles: The social self as internal working model. In M. R. Gunnar & L. A. Sroufe (Eds.), *Minnesota Symposia on Child Development: Vol. 23. Self processes and development* (pp. 1–41). Hillsdale, NJ: Erlbaum.

Bretherton, I. (1993). From dialogue to internal working models: The co-construction of self in relationships. In C. A. Nelson (Ed.), *Minnesota Symposia on Child Psychology: Vol. 26. Memory and affect* (pp. 237–363). Hillsdale, NJ: Erlbaum.

Bretherton, I., & Munholland, K. A. (1999). Internal working models in attachment relationships. In J. Cassidy & P. Shaver (Eds.), *Handbook of attachment* (pp. 89–111). New York: Guilford Press.

Briere, J. (1992). *Child abuse trauma: Theory and treatment of the lasting effects.* Newbury Park, CA: Sage.

Brooks-Gunn, J. (1988). Antecedents and consequences of variations in girls' maturational timing. *Journal of Adolescent Health Care, 9,* 365–373.

Broughton, J. (1978). The development of the concepts of self, mind, reality, and knowledge. In W. Damon (Ed.), *Social cognition* (pp. 75–100). San Francisco: Jossey-Bass.

Bruner, J. (1990). *Acts of meaning.* Cambridge, MA: Harvard University Press.

Case, R. (1985). *Intellectual development: Birth to adulthood.* New York: Academic Press.

Case, R. (1992). *The mind's staircase.* Hillsdale, NJ: Erlbaum.

Cassidy, J., & Shaver, P. R. (Eds.). (1999). *Handbook of attachment.* New York: Guilford Press.

Cooley, C. H. (1902). *Human nature and the social order.* New York: Charles Scribner & Sons.

Cooper, C. R., Jackson, J. F., Azmitia, M., Lopez, E., & Dunbar, N. (1995). Bridging students' multiple worlds: African American and Latino youth in academic outreach programs. In R. F. Marcias & R. G. Garcia-Ramos (Eds.), *Changing schools changing students: An anthology of research on language minorities* (pp. 211–234). Santa Barbara: University of California Linguistic Minority Research Institute.

Coopersmith, S. A. (1967). *The antecedents of self-esteem.* San Francisco: Freeman.

Crittenden, P. M. (1990). Internal representational models of attachment relationships. *Infant Mental Health Journal, 11,* 259–277.

Crittenden, P. M. (1994). Peering into the black box: An exploratory treatise on the development of self in young children. In D. Cicchetti & S. L. Toth (Eds.), *Rochester Symposium on Developmental Psychopathology: Vol. 5. Disorders and dysfunctions of the self* (pp. 79–148). Rochester, NY: University of Rochester Press.

Damon, W., & Hart, D. (1988). *Self-understanding in childhood and adolescence.* New York: Cambridge University Press.

Dunn, J. (1988). *The beginnings of social understanding.* Cambridge, MA: Harvard University Press.

Dunn, J., Brown, J., & Beardsall, L. (1991). Family talk about feeling states and children's later understanding of others' emotions. *Developmental Psychology, 27,* 445–448.

Eccles, J. P., & Midgley, C. (1989). State/environment fit: Developmentally appropriate classrooms for early adolescents. In R. Ames & C. Ames (Eds.), *Research on motivation in education* (Vol. 3, pp. 139–181). New York: Academic Press.

Eisenberg, A. (1985). Learning to describe past experiences in conversations. *Discourse Processes, 8,* 177–204.

Elkind, D. (1967). Egocentrism in adolescence. *Child Development, 38,* 1025–1034.

Epstein, S. (1981). The unity principle versus the reality and pleasure principles, or the tale of the scorpion and the frog. In M. D. Lynch, A. A. Norem-Hebeisen, & K. Gergen (Eds.), *Self-concept: Advances in theory and research* (pp. 82–110). Cambridge, MA: Ballinger.

Epstein, S. (1991). Cognitive-experiential self-theory: Implications for developmental psychology. In M. Gunnar & L. A. Sroufe (Eds.), *Minnesota Symposium on Child Development: Vol. 23. Self-processes and development* (pp. 111–137). Hillsdale, NJ: Erlbaum.

Erikson, E. H. (1968). *Identity, youth, and crisis.* New York: Norton.

Feiring, C., & Taska, L. S. (1996). Family self-concept: Ideas on its meaning. In B. Bracken (Ed.), *Handbook of self-concept* (pp. 317–373). New York: Wiley.

Fischer, K. W. (1980). A theory of cognitive development: The control and construction of hierarchies of skills. *Psychological Review, 87,* 477–531.

Fischer, K. W., & Ayoub, C. (1994). Affective splitting and dissociation in normal and maltreated children: Developmental pathways for self in relationships. In D. Cicchetti & S. Toth (Eds.), *Rochester Symposium on Developmental Psychopathology: Vol. 5. Disorders and dysfunctions of the self* (pp. 149–222). Rochester, NY: University of Rochester Press.

Fischer, K. W., Hand, H. H., Watson, M. W., Van Parys, M., & Tucker, J. (1984). Putting the child into socialization: The development of social categories in preschool children. In L. Katz (Ed.), *Current topics in early childhood education* (Vol. 5, pp. 27–72). Norwood, NJ: Ablex.

Fivush, R. (1987). Scripts and categories: Inter-relationships in development. In U. Neisser (Ed.), *Concepts and conceptual development: Ecological and intellectual factors in categorization* (pp. 223–248). Cambridge: Cambridge University Press.

Fivush, R., & Hudson, J. A. (Eds.). (1990). *Knowing and remembering in young children.* New York: Cambridge University Press.

Freud, S. (1952). *A general introduction to psychoanalysis.* New York: Washington Square Press.

Frey, K. S., & Ruble, D. N. (1990). Strategies for comparative evaluation: Maintaining a sense of competence across the life span. In R. J. Sternberg & J. Kolligian Jr. (Eds.), *Competence considered* (pp. 167–189). New Haven, CT: Yale University Press.

Graber, J. A., Peterson, A. C., & Brooks-Gunn, J. (1996). Pubertal processes: Methods, measures, and models. In J. A. Graber (Ed.), *Transitions through adolescence: Interpersonal domains and context* (pp. 23–53). Mahwah, NJ: Erlbaum.

Gray-Little, B., & Hafdahl, A. R. (2000). Factors influencing racial comparisons of self-esteem: A quantitative review. *Psychological Bulletin, 126,* 26–54.

Greenwald, A. G. (1980). The totalitarian ego: Fabrication and revision of personal history. *American Psychologist, 7,* 603–618.

Griffin, S. (1992). Structural analysis of the development of their inner world: A neo-structured analysis of the development of intrapersonal intelligence. In R. Case (Ed.), *The mind's staircase* (pp. 189–206). Hillsdale, NJ: Erlbaum.

Harter, S. (1983). Developmental perspectives on the self-system. In P. Mussen (Series Ed.) & E. M. Hetherington (Vol. Ed.), *Handbook of child psychology: Vol. 4. Socialization, personality, and social development* (4th ed., pp. 275–385). New York: Wiley.

Harter, S. (1986). Cognitive-developmental processes in the integration of concepts about emotions and the self. *Social Cognition, 4,* 119–151.

Harter, S. (1990). Causes, correlates and the functional role of global self-worth: A life-span perspective. In R. Sternberg & J. Kolligian Jr. (Eds.), *Competence considered* (pp. 67–98). New Haven, CT: Yale University Press.

Harter, S. (1996). Teacher and classmate influences on scholastic motivation, self-esteem, and choice. In K. Wentzel & J. Juvonen (Eds.), *Social motivation: Understanding children's school adjustment* (pp. 11–42). Cambridge: Cambridge University Press.

Harter, S. (1997). The personal self in social context: Barriers to authenticity. In R. D. Ashmore & L. Jussim (Eds.), *Self and identity: Fundamental issues* (pp. 81–105). New York: Oxford University Press.

Harter, S. (1998a). The development of self-representations. In W. Damon (Series Ed.) & N. Eisenberg (Vol. Ed.), *Handbook of child psychology: Vol. 3. Social, emotional, and personality development* (5th ed., pp. 553–617). New York: Wiley.

Harter, S. (1998b). The effects of child abuse on the self-system. In B. B. Rossman & M. S. Rosenberg (Eds.), *Multiple victimization of children: Conceptual, developmental, research, and treatment issues* (pp. 147–170). New York: Haworth Press.

Harter, S. (1999). *The construction of the self.* New York: Guilford Press.

Harter, S. (2004). The developmental emergence of self-esteem: Individual differences in change and stability. In D. Mroczek & T. Little (Eds.), *The handbook of personality* (pp. 44–59). New York: Erlbaum.

Harter, S. (2006). The self. In W. Damon & R. M. Lerner (Series Eds.) & N. Eisenberg (Vol. Ed.) *Handbook of child psychology: Vol. 3. Social, emotional, and personality development* (6th ed., pp. 505–570). Hoboken, NJ: Wiley.

Harter, S., Bresnick, S., Bouchey, H. A., & Whitesell, N. R. (1997). The development of multiple role-related selves during adolescence. *Development and Psychopathology, 9,* 835–854.

Harter, S., & Buddin, B. J. (1987). Children's understanding of the simultaneity of two emotions: A five-stage developmental acquisition sequence. *Developmental Psychology, 23,* 388–399.

Harter, S., Kiang, L., Whitesell, N. R., & Anderson, A. V. (2003, April). *A prototype approach to the emotion of humiliation in college students.* Poster presented at the biennial meeting of the Society for Research in Child Development, Tampa, FL.

Harter, S., Low, S., & Whitesell, N. R. (2003). What have we learned from Columbine: The impact of the self-system on suicidal and violent ideation among adolescents. *Journal of Youth Violence, 2,* 3–26.

Harter, S., Marold, D. B., Whitesell, N. R., & Cobbs, G. (1996). A model of the effects of parent and peer support on adolescent false self behavior. *Child Development, 55,* 1969–1982.

Harter, S., & McCarley, K. (2004, April). *Is there a dark side to high self-esteem leading to adolescent violence?* Poster presented at the American Psychological Association Convention, Honolulu, HI.

Harter, S., & Monsour, A. (1992). Developmental analysis of conflict caused by opposing attributes in the adolescent self-portrait. *Developmental Psychology, 28,* 251–260.

Harter, S., & Pike, R. (1984). The pictorial scale of perceived competence and social acceptance for young children. *Child Development, 55,* 1969–1982.

Harter, S., & Whitesell, N. R. (1989). Developmental changes in children's understanding of single, multiple and blended emotion concepts. In C. Saarni & P. L. Harris (Eds.), *Children's understanding of emotion* (pp. 81–116). Cambridge: Cambridge University Press.

Hatfield, E., & Sprecher, S. (1986). *Mirror, mirror: The importance of appearance in everyday life.* New York: State University of New York Press.

Herman, J. (1992). *Trauma and recovery.* New York: Basic Books.

Higgins, E. T. (1991). Development of self-regulatory and self-evaluative processes: Costs, benefits, and tradeoffs. In M. R. Gunnar & L. A. Sroufe (Eds.), *Minnesota Symposia on Child Development: Vol. 23. Self processes and development* (pp. 125–166). Hillsdale, NJ: Erlbaum.

Higgins, E. T., & Bargh, J. A. (1987). Social cognition and social perception. *Annual Review of Psychology, 38,* 369–425.

James, W. (1890). *Principles of psychology.* Chicago: Encyclopedia Britannica.

James, W. (1892). *Psychology: The briefer course.* New York: Henry Holt.

Kagan, J. (1984). *The nature of the child.* New York: Basic Books.

Kelly, G. A. (1955). *The psychology of personal constructs.* New York: Norton.

Kiang, L., & Harter, S. (2004). *Socialcultural values or appearance and attachment processes: An integrated model of eating disorder symptomatology.* Manuscript submitted for publication.

Kling, K. C., Hyde, J. S., Showers, C. J., & Buswell, B. N. (1999). Gender differences in self-esteem: A meta-analysis. *Psychological Bulletin, 125,* 470–500.

Lamborn, S. D., Mounts, N. S., Steinberg, L., & Dornbusch, S. M. (1991). Patterns of competence and adjustment among adolescents from authoritative, authoritarian, indulgent and neglectful families. *Child Development, 62,* 1049–1065.

Lewis, M. (1994). Myself and me. In S. T. Parker, R. W. Mitchell, & M L. Boccia (Eds.), *Self-awareness in animals and humans: Developmental perspectives* (pp. 20–34). New York: Cambridge University Press.

Lipka, R. P., Hurford, D. P., & Litten, M. J. (1992). Self-in school: Age and school experience effects. In R. P. Lipka & T. M. Brinthaupt (Eds.), *Self-perspectives across the life span* (Vol. 3, pp. 93–115). Albany: State University of New York Press.

Maccoby, E. (1980). *Social development.* New York: Wiley.

Main, M. (1995). Recent studies in attachment: Overview with selected implications for clinical work. In S. Goldberg, R. Muir, & J. Kerr (Eds.), *Attachment theory: Social, developmental, and clinical implications* (pp. 407–474). Hillsdale, NJ: Analytic Press.

Markus, H. (1980). The self in thought and memory. In D. M. Wegner & R. R. Vallacher (Eds.), *The self in social psychology* (pp. 42–69). New York: Oxford University Press.

Markus, H., & Nurius, P. (1986). Possible selves. *American Psychologist, 41,* 954–969.

Marsh, H. W. (1986). Global self-esteem: Its relation to specific facets of self-concept and their important. *Journal of Personality and Social Psychology, 51,* 224–1236.

Mascolo, M. F., & Fischer, K. W. (1995). Developmental transformations in appraisals for pride, shame, and guilt. In J. P. Tangney & K. W. Fischer (Eds.), *Self-conscious emotions: The psychology of shame, guilt, embarrassment, and pride* (pp. 64–113). New York: Guilford Press.

McCarthy, J., & Hoge, D. (1982). Analysis of age effects in longitudinal studies of adolescent self-esteem. *Developmental Psychology, 18,* 372–379.

Mead, G. H. (1934). *Mind, self, and society from the standpoint of a social behaviorist.* Chicago: University of Chicago Press.

Moretti, M. M., & Higgins, E. T. (1990). The development of self-esteem vulnerabilities: Social and cognitive factors in developmental psychopathology. In R. J. Sternberg & J. Kolligian Jr. (Eds.), *Competence considered* (pp. 286–314). New Haven, CT: Yale University Press.

Nelson, K. (Ed.). (1989). *Narratives from the crib.* Cambridge, MA: Harvard University Press.

Nolen-Hoeksema, S., & Girgus, J. S. (1994). The emergence of gender differences in depression during adolescence. *Psychological Bulletin, 115,* 424–443.

O'Malley, P., & Bachman, J. (1983). Self-esteem: Change and stability between 13 and 23. *Developmental Psychology, 19,* 257–268.

Piaget, J. (1932). *The moral judgment of the child.* New York: Harcourt, Brace & World.

Piaget, J. (1960). *The psychology of intelligence.* Patterson, NJ: Littlefield-Adams.

Pomerantz, E. V., Ruble, D. N., Frey, K. S., & Greulich, F. (1995). Meeting goals and confronting conflict: Children's changing perceptions of social comparison. *Child Development, 66,* 723–738.

Putnam, F. W. (1993). Dissociation and disturbances of the self. In D. Cicchetti & S. Toth (Eds.), *Rochester Symposium on Developmental Psychopathology: Vol. 5. Disorders and dysfunctions of the self* (pp. 251–266). Rochester, NY: University of Rochester Press.

Rosenberg, M. (1979). *Conceiving the self.* New York: Basic Books.

Rosenberg, M. (1986). Self-concept from middle childhood through adolescence. In J. Suls & A. G. Greenwald (Eds.), *Psychological perspective on the self* (Vol. 3, pp. 107–135). Hillsdale, NJ: Erlbaum.

Rosenberg, M., & Simmons, R. G. (1972). *Black and White self-esteem: The urban school child.* Washington, DC: American Psychological Association.

Ruble, D. N., & Frey, K. S. (1991). Changing patterns of comparative behavior as skills are acquired: A functional model of self-evaluation. In J. Suls & T. A. Wills (Eds.), *Social comparison: Contemporary theory and research* (pp. 70–112). Hillsdale, NJ: Erlbaum.

Rutter, M., & Sroufe, L. A. (2000). Developmental psychopathology: Concepts and challenges. *Development and Psychopathology, 12,* 265–296.

Sameroff, A. (2000). Development systems and psychopathology. *Development and Psychopathology, 12,* 297–312.

Sarbin, T. R. (1962). A preface to a psychological analysis of the self. *Psychological Review, 59,* 11–22.

Savin-Williams, R. C., & Demo, P. (1993). Situational and transitional determinants of adolescent self-feelings. *Journal of Personality and Social Psychology, 44,* 820–833.

Selman, R. L. (1980). *The growth of interpersonal understanding.* New York: Academic Press.

Shrauger, J. S., & Schoeneman, T. J. (1979). Symbolic interactionist view of self-concept: Through the looking glass darkly. *Psychological Bulletin, 86,* 549–573.

Siegler, R. S. (1991). *Children's thinking* (2nd ed.). Englewood Cliffs, NJ: Prentice-Hall.

Simmons, R. G., & Blyth, D. A. (1987). *Moving into adolescence: The impact of pubertal change and school context.* New York: Aldine de Gruyter.

Smollar, J., & Youniss, J. (1985). Adolescent self-concept development. In R. L. Leahy (Ed.), *The development of self* (pp. 247–266). New York: Academic Press.

Snow, K. (1990). Building memories: The ontogeny of autobiography. In D. Cicchetti & M. Beeghly (Eds.), *The self in transition: Infancy to childhood* (pp. 213–242). Chicago: University of Chicago Press.

Steele, C. M. (1988). The psychology of affirmation: Sustaining the integrity of the self. In L. Berkowitz (Ed.), *Advances in experimental social psychology* (Vol. 21, pp. 261–302). San Diego, CA: Academic Press.

Steinberg, L. (1990). Interdependency in the family: Autonomy, conflict, autonomy in the parent-adolescent relationship. In S. Feldman & G. Elliot (Eds.), *At the threshold: The developing adolescent* (pp. 255–276). Cambridge, MA: Harvard University Press.

Stern, D. (1985). *The interpersonal world of the infant.* New York: Basic Books.

Stipek, D., Recchia, S., & McClintic, S. (1992). Self-evaluation in young children. *Monographs of the Society for Research in Child Development, 57,* 1–84.

Sullivan, H. S. (1953). *The interpersonal theory of psychiatry.* New York: Norton.

Suls, J., & Sanders, G. (1982). Self-evaluation via social comparison: A developmental analysis. In L. Wheeler (Ed.), *Review of personality and social psychology* (Vol. 3, pp. 67–89). Beverly Hills, CA: Sage.

Tessler, M. (1991). *Making memories together: The influence of mother-child joint encoding on the development of autobiographical memory style.* Unpublished doctoral dissertation, City University of New York Graduate Center, New York.

Trzesniewski, K. H., Donnellan, M., & Robins, R. W. (2003). Stability of self-esteem across the life span. *Journal of Personality and Social Psychology, 84,* 205–220.

Twenge, J. M., & Crocker, J. (2002). Race and self-esteem: Meta-analyses comparing Whites, Blacks, Hispanics, Asians, and American Indians and comment on Gray-Little and Hafdahl (2000). *Psychological Bulletin, 128,* 371–408.

Wigfield, A., Eccles, J. S., Mac Iver, D., Reuman, D. A., & Midgley, C. (1991). Transitions during early adolescence: Changes in children's domain-specific self-perceptions and general self-esteem across the transition to junior high school. *Developmental Psychology, 27,* 552–565.

Winnicott, D. W. (1958). *From paediatrics to psychoanalysis.* London: Hogarth Press.

Winnicott, D. W. (1965). *The maturational processes and the facilitating environment.* New York: International Universities Press.

Wolf, D. P. (1990). Being of several minds: Voices and version of the self in early childhood. In D. Cicchetti & M. Beeghly (Eds.), *The self in transition: Infancy to childhood* (pp. 183–212). Chicago: University of Chicago Press.

Wylie, R. C. (1989). *Measures of self-concept.* Lincoln: University of Nebraska Press.

PART V

LANGUAGE AND THOUGHT

Chapter 8

Acquiring Linguistic Constructions

MICHAEL TOMASELLO

Human linguistic communication differs from the communication of other animal species in three main ways. First, and most importantly, human linguistic communication is symbolic. Linguistic symbols are social conventions by means of which one individual attempts to share attention with other individuals by directing their attentional or mental states to something in the outside world. Other animal species do not communicate with one another using linguistic symbols, most likely because they do not understand that conspecifics have attentional or mental states that they could attempt to direct or share (Tomasello, 1999). This mental dimension of linguistic symbols gives them unparalleled communicative power, enabling their users to refer to and to predicate all kinds of diverse perspectives on objects, events, and situations in the world.

The second main difference is that human linguistic communication is grammatical. Human beings use their linguistic symbols together in patterned ways, and these patterns, known as linguistic constructions, come to take on meanings themselves—deriving partly from the meanings of the individual symbols but, over time, at least partly from the pattern itself. The process by which this occurs over historical time is called *grammaticalization,* and grammatical constructions add still another dimension of communicative power to human languages by enabling all kinds of unique symbol combinations. Grammatical constructions are also uniquely human, of course, because if a species does not use symbols, the question of grammar is moot.

Third, unlike all other animal species, human beings do not have a single system of communication used by all members of the species. Rather, different groups of humans have conventionalized over historical time different, mutually unintelligible systems of communication (there are more than 6,000 natural languages in the world). This means that children, unlike other animal species, must learn the communicative conventions used by those around them—indeed they take several years to acquire the many tens of thousands, perhaps even hundreds of thousands, of linguistic symbols and constructions of their natal group(s). This is much more learning in this domain—by many orders of magnitude—than is characteristic of any other species.

This chapter is about the way children master a language, the way they learn to communicate using the linguistic conventions used by those around them in both their symbolic and grammatical dimensions. We begin with some background history and theory of the field, proceed in the next two sections to outline the major ontogenetic steps of language acquisition, and conclude with a focus on the cognitive and social processes involved in becoming a competent user of a natural language.

Theory

There are two basic theories of how young children acquire grammatical competence in their native language. One derives from researchers who take a formal approach to language and its acquisition—a more adult-centered approach emanating from Chomsky's theory of generative grammar—and the other derives from researchers who take a more functional, usage-based approach to language and its acquisition—a potentially more child-centered approach with room for serious developmental change. These two basic orientations structure the most fundamental theoretical debates in the modern study of child language acquisition.

Chomskian generative grammar is a *formal* theory, meaning that it is based on the supposition that natural languages are like formal languages (e.g., algebra, predicate logic). Natural languages are thus characterized in terms of: (a) a unified set of abstract algebraic rules that are both meaningless themselves and also insensitive to the meanings of the elements they algorithmically combine, and (b) a lexicon containing meaningful linguistic elements that serve as variables in the rules. Principles governing the way the underlying algebra works constitute a universal grammar, the core of linguistic competence. The linguistic periphery involves such things as the lexicon, the conceptual system, irregular constructions and idioms, and pragmatics.

With regard to language acquisition, Chomskian generative grammar begins with the assumption that children innately possess a universal grammar abstract enough to structure any language of the world. Acquisition then consists of two processes: (1) Acquiring all the words, idioms, and quirky constructions of the particular language being learned (by "normal" processes of learning); and (2) Linking the particular language being learned, that is, its core structures, to the abstract universal grammar. This is the so-called *dual process* approach—also sometimes called the *words and rules* approach (Pinker, 1999)—since the "periphery" of linguistic competence is learned but the "core" is innately given in universal grammar. Because it is innate, universal grammar does not develop ontogenetically but is the same throughout the life span: This is the so-called continuity assumption (Pinker, 1984). This assumption allows generativists to use adultlike formal grammars to describe children's language and so to assume that the first time a child utters, for example, "I wanna play" that she has an adultlike understanding of infinitival complement sentences and so can generate similar infinitival complement sentences *ad infinitum*.

In sharp contrast is the group of theories most often called *Cognitive-Functional Linguistics,* but which are sometimes also called *Usage-Based Linguistics* to emphasize their central processing tenet that language structure emerges from language use (e.g., Bybee, 1985, 1995; Croft, 1991, 2001; Givón, 1995; Goldberg, 1995; Langacker, 1987, 1991; see Tomasello, 1998, 2003, for other similar approaches). Usage-based theories hold that the essence of language is its symbolic dimension, with grammar being derivative. The ability to communicate with conspecifics symbolically (conventionally, intersubjectively) is a species-specific biological adaptation. The grammatical dimension of language derives from historical processes of grammaticalization, which create various grammatical constructions (e.g., the English passive construction, noun phrase construction, or -*ed* past tense construction). As opposed to linguistic rules conceived as algebraic procedures for combining words and morphemes that do not contribute to meaning, linguistic constructions are meaningful linguistic symbols. They are nothing other than the patterns in which meaningful linguistic symbols are used in communication (e.g., the passive construction is used to communicate about an entity to which something happens). In this approach, mature linguistic competence is conceived as a structured inventory of meaningful linguistic constructions—including both the more regular and the more idiomatic structures in a given language (and all structures in between).

According to the usage-based theory, there is no such thing as universal grammar and so the theoretical problem of how a child links it to a particular language does not exist. It is a single-process theory of language acquisition, in the sense that children are thought to acquire the more regular and rule-based constructions of a language in the same way they acquire the more arbitrary and idiosyncratic constructions: They learn them. And, as in the learning of all complex cognitive activities, they then construct abstract categories and schemas out of the concrete things they have learned. Thus, in this view, children's earliest acquisitions are concrete pieces of language—words (e.g., *cat*), complex expressions (e.g., *I-wanna-do-it*), or mixed constructions (e.g., *Where's-the-_____*, which is partially concrete and partially abstract)—because early in development they do not possess the fully abstract categories and schemas of adult grammar. Children construct these abstractions only gradually and in piecemeal fashion, with some categories and constructions appearing much before others that are of a similar type from an adult perspective—due quite often to differences in the language that individual children hear ("input"). Children construct their language using general cognitive processes falling into two broad categories: (1) intention-reading (joint attention, understanding communicative intentions, cultural learning), by which they attempt to understand the communicative significance of an utterance; and (2) pattern-finding (categorization, schema formation, statistical learning, analogy), by which they create the more abstract dimensions of linguistic competence.

In this chapter, we adopt a usage-based theoretical perspective on the process of language acquisition. We thus assume that what children are learning initially is concrete pieces of language, of many different shapes and sizes, across which they then generalize to construct more abstract linguistic constructions—which underlies their ability to generate creative new utterances. The central theoretical construct is therefore the construction. A linguistic construction is prototypically a unit of language that comprises multiple linguistic elements used together for a relatively coherent communicative function, with subfunctions being performed by the elements as well. Consequently, constructions may vary in their complexity depending on the number of elements involved and their interrelations. For example, the English regular plural construction (N + *s*) is relatively simple, whereas the passive construction (X *was* VERB*ed by* Y) is relatively complex. Independent of complexity, however, constructions may also vary in their abstractness. For example, the relatively simple English regular plural construction and the more complex English passive construction are both highly (though not totally) abstract. To repeat, even these most abstract constructions are still symbolic, as they possess a coherent, if abstract, meaning in relative independence of the lexical items involved (Goldberg, 1995). Thus, in the utterance *Mary sneezed John the football,* our construal of the action is influenced more by the transfer of possession meaning of the ditransitive construction than it is by the verb *sneeze* (since sneezing is not normally construed as transferring possession). Similarly, we know that the nonce noun *gazzers* very likely indicates a plurality without even knowing what a gazzer is.

Importantly, however, some complex linguistic structures are not based on abstract categories, but rather on particular linguistic items (Fillmore, 1988, 1989; Fillmore, Kaye, & O'Conner, 1988). The limiting case is totally fixed expressions such as the idiom *How do you do?* which is a structure of English with an idiosyncratic meaning that dissolves if any of the particular words is changed. (One does not normally, with the same intended meaning, ask *How does she do?*) Other clear examples are such well-known idioms as *kick the bucket* and *spill the beans,* which have a little more flexibility and abstractness as different people may kick the bucket and they may do so in past, present, or future tense—but we cannot, with the same meaning, kick the pail or spill the peas. It turns out that, on inspection, a major part of human linguistic competence—much more than previously believed—involves the mastery of all kinds of routine formulas, fixed and semi-fixed expressions, idioms, and frozen collocations. Indeed one of the distinguishing characteristics of native speakers of a language is their control of these semi-fixed expressions as fluent units with somewhat unpredictable meanings (e.g., I wouldn't *put it past* him; He's *getting to me* these days; *Hang in there;* That won't *go down well* with the boss; She *put me up to* it; etc.; Pawley & Syder, 1983).

Early Ontogeny

It is widely believed that young children begin their linguistic careers by learning words, which they then combine together by means of rules. But this is not exactly accurate. Children hear and attempt to learn whole adult utterances, instantiating various types of constructions used for various communicative purposes. Sometimes children only learn parts of these complex wholes, and so their first productions may correspond to adult words. But these are always packaged in conventional intonational patterns indicating such things as requests, comments, or questions—which correspond to the general communicative functions for which adults use more complex constructions. From the beginning, children are attempting to learn not isolated words, but rather communicatively effective speech forms corresponding to whole adult constructions. Learning words—which will not be a topic of this chapter is essentially a process of extracting elements (including their function) from these larger wholes.

In this section, our account of the early ontogeny of language focuses first, on the language children hear; then on their early holophrases (single words or phrases that have a larger, holistic meaning); then on their early word combinations, pivot schemas, and item-based constructions; and finally on the linguistic devices they use early in development for marking basic syntactic roles such as agent and patient.

THE LANGUAGE CHILDREN HEAR

To understand how children acquire a language, we must know something about the language they hear—both in terms of specific utterances and in terms of the constructions these instantiate. Surprisingly, very few studies have attempted to document the full range of linguistic expressions and constructions that children hear in their daily lives. The majority of studies of child-directed-speech (CDS) have focused on specific aspects (for classic studies, see the papers in Galloway & Richards, 1994; Snow & Ferguson, 1977).

Cameron-Faulkner, Lieven, and Tomasello (2003) examined all the CDS of 12 English-speaking mothers during samples of their linguistic interactions with their 2- to 3-year-old children. The overall findings were that:

- Children heard an estimated 5,000 to 7,000 utterances per day.
- Between one-quarter and one-third of these were questions.
- More than 20% of these were not full adult sentences, but instead were some kind of fragment (most often a noun phrase or prepositional phrase).
- About one-quarter of these were imperatives and utterances structured by the copula.
- Only about 15% of these had the canonical English SVO form (i.e., transitive utterances of various kinds) supposedly characteristic of the English language; and over 80% of the SVOs had a pronoun subject.

In a second analysis, these investigators looked at the specific words and phrases with which mothers initiated utterances in each of these general construction types, including such item-based frames as *Are you . . . , I'll . . . , It's . . . , Can you . . . , Here's . . . , Let's . . . , Look at . . . , What did . . . ,* and so on. It was found that more than half of all maternal utterances began with one of 52 highly frequent item-based frames (i.e., frames used more than an estimated 40 times per day for more than half the children), mostly consisting of 2 words or morphemes. Further, using the same kind of analysis, more than 65% of all of the mothers' utterances began with one of just 156 item-based frames. And perhaps most surprising, approximately 45% of all maternal utterances began with one of just 17 words: *What* (8.6%), *That* (5.3%), *It* (4.2%), *You* (3.1%), *Are/Aren't* (3.0%), *Do/Does/Did/Don't* (2.9%), *I* (2.9%), *Is* (2.3%), *Shall* (2.1%), *A* (1.7%), *Can/Can't* (1.7%), *Where* (1.6%), *There* (1.5%), *Who* (1.4%), *Come* (1.0%), *Look* (1.0%), and *Let's* (1.0%). Interestingly, the children used many of these same item-based frames in their speech, in some cases at a rate that correlated highly with their own mother's frequency of use.

The language-learning child is thus faced with a prodigious task: acquiring simultaneously many dozens and dozens (perhaps hundreds) of constructions based on input in which all of the many different construction types are semi-randomly strewn. On the other hand, the task is made a bit easier by the fact that many of, indeed the majority of, the utterances children hear are grounded in highly repetitive item-based frames that they experience dozens, in some cases hundreds, of times every day. Indeed, many of the more complex utterances children hear have as a major constituent some well-practiced item-based frame. This means that the more linguistically creative utterances that children hear every day constitute only a small minority of their linguistic experience, and even these quite often rest on the foundation of many highly frequent and relatively simple item-based utterance frames.

EARLIEST LANGUAGE

Most Western, middle-class children begin producing conventional linguistic symbols in utterances in the months following their first birthdays. By the time they begin doing this, they typically have been communicating with other people gesturally and vocally for some months. Children's first linguistic expressions are learned and used in the context of these prior forms of nonlinguistic communication and for the same basic motives—declarative (statements) and imperative (requests)—and children soon learn to ask things interrogatively (questions) as well. There is typically a distinctive intonational pattern for each of these three speech act types. Children's first declarative utterances are sometimes about shared, topical referents and sometimes aimed at focusing the listener's attention on something new (typically assessed only from their own egocentric point of view; Greenfield & Smith, 1976).

At this early age, the communicative functions of children's early single-word utterances are an integral aspect of their reality for the child, and initially these functions (e.g., imperative or interrogative) may not be well differentiated from the more referential aspects of the utterance (Ninio, 1992, 1993). That is to say, children's early one-word utterances may be thought of as *holophrases* that convey a holistic, undifferentiated communicative intention, most often the same communicative intention as that of the adult expression from which it was learned (Barrett, 1982; Ninio, 1992). Many of children's early holophrases are relatively idiosyncratic and their uses can change and evolve over time in a somewhat unstable manner. Some holophrases, however, are a bit more conventional and stable. Children speaking all the languages of the world use their holophrases to do such things as:

- Request or indicate the existence of objects (e.g., by naming them with a requestive or neutral intonation).
- Request or describe the recurrence of objects or events (e.g., *More, Again, Another*).
- Request or describe dynamic events involving objects (e.g., as described by *Up, Down, On, Off, In, Out, Open, Close*).
- Request or describe the actions of people (e.g., *Eat, Kick, Ride, Draw*).
- Comment on the location of objects and people (e.g., *Here, Outside*).
- Ask some basic questions (e.g., *Whats-that?* or *Where-go?*).
- Attribute a property to an object (e.g., *Pretty* or *Wet*).
- Use performatives to mark specific social events and situations (e.g., *Hi, Bye, Thank you,* and *No*).

An important issue for later language development is what parts of adult expressions children choose for their initial holophrases. The answer lies in the specific language they are learning and the kinds of discourse in which they participate with adults, including the perceptual salience of particular words and phrases in adults' speech (Slobin, 1985). Thus, in English, most beginning language learners acquire so-called relational words such as *more, gone, up, down, on,* and *off,* presumably because adults use these words in salient ways to talk about salient events (Bloom, Tinker, & Margulis, 1993; McCune, 1992). Many of these words are verb particles in adult English, and so the child at some point must learn to talk about the same events with phrasal verbs such as *pick up, get down, put on, take off,* and so forth. In Korean and Mandarin Chinese, on the other hand, children learn fully adult verbs from the onset of language development because this is what is most salient in adult speech to them (Gopnik & Choi, 1995; Tardif, 1996). When they begin with an adult verb as a holophrase, children must then at some point learn, at least for some discourse purposes, to fill in linguistically the nominal participants involved in the scene (e.g., "Take-off *shirt!*"). Children in all languages also learn object labels for some events, for example, "Bike!" as a request to ride a bicycle or "Birdie" as a comment on a passing flight, which means that they still need to learn to linguistically express the activity involved (e.g., "*Ride* bike!" or "*See* birdie").

In addition, most children begin language acquisition by learning some unparsed adult expressions as holophrases—such things as "I-wanna-do-it," "Lemme-see," and "Where-the-bottle." The prevalence of this pattern in the early combinatorial speech of English-speaking children has been documented by Pine and Lieven (1993), who found that almost all children have at least some of these so-called frozen phrases in their early speech. This is especially true of some children (especially later-born children who observe siblings; Barton & Tomasello, 1994; Bates, Bretherton, & Snyder, 1988). In these cases, there is different syntactic work to do if the child is to extract productive linguistic elements that can be used appropriately in other utterances, in other linguistic contexts, in the future. For this, the child must engage in a process of segmentation, with regard not only to the speech stream but also to the communicative intentions involved—so as to determine which components of the speech stream go with which components of the underlying communicative intention. Functionally speaking, then, children's early one-unit utterances are entire semantic-pragmatic packages—holophrastic expressions—that express a single relatively coherent, yet undifferentiated, communicative intention. Why children begin with only one-unit expressions—either individual words or holistic expressions—is not known at this time. But it is presumably the case that in many instances they initially only attend to limited parts of adult utterances, or can only process one linguistic unit at a time.

ITEM-BASED CONSTRUCTIONS

Children produce their earliest multiword utterances to talk about many of the same kinds of things they talked about previously with their holophrases—since indeed many, though not all, early multiword constructions may be traced back to earlier holophrases. From the point of view of linguistic form, the utterance-level constructions underlying these multiword utterances come in three types: word combinations, pivot schemas, and item-based constructions.

Word Combinations

Beginning at around 18 months of age, many children combine two words or holophrases in situations in which they both are relevant—with both words having roughly equivalent status. For example, a child has learned to name a ball and a table and then spies a ball on a table and says, "Ball table." Utterances of this type include both "successive single-word utterances" (with a pause between them; Bloom, 1973) and "word combinations" or "expressions" (under a single intonational contour). The defining feature of word combinations or expressions is that they partition the experiential scene into multiple symbolizable units—in a way that holophrases obviously (by definition) do not—and they are totally concrete in the sense that they are comprised only of concrete pieces of language, not categories.

Pivot Schemas

Beginning at around this same age, however, many of children's multiword productions show a more systematic pattern. Often there is one word or phrase that seems to structure the utterance in the sense that it determines the speech act function of the utterance as a whole (often with help from an intonational contour), with the other linguistic item(s) simply filling in variable slot(s)—the first type of linguistic abstraction. Thus, in many of these early utterances, one event-word is used with a wide variety of object labels (e.g., "More milk," "More grapes," "More juice") or, more rarely, something like a pronoun or other general expression is the constant element (e.g., *I* _____ *or it* or even *It's* _____ or *Where's* _____). Following Braine (1963), we may call these pivot schemas.

Braine (1976) established that this is a widespread and productive strategy for children acquiring many of the world's languages. And Tomasello, Akhtar, Dodson, and Rekau (1997) found that 22-month-old children who were taught a novel name for an object knew immediately how to combine this novel name with other pivot-type words already in their vocabulary. That is, when taught a novel object label as a single word utterance (e.g., "Look! A wug!"), children were able to use that new object label in combination with their existing pivot-type words in utterances such as "Wug gone" or "More wug." This productivity suggests that young children can create linguistic categories at this young age, specifically categories corresponding to the types of linguistic items that can play particular roles in specific pivot schemas (e.g., "things that are gone," "things I want more of"). However, these same children do not make generalizations across the various pivot schemas. Thus, Tomasello et al. (1997) also found that when taught a novel verb as a single-word utterance for a novel scene (e.g., "Look! Meeking!" or "Look what she's doing to it. That's called meeking."), these same 22-month-old children were not then able to say creative things like "Ernie meeking!"—because they had never heard how *meeking* structured a pivot schema with an actor. Each pivot schema is thus at this point a constructional island, and so at this stage of development, children do not have an overarching grammar of their language.

Item-Based Constructions

Not only are pivot schemas organized locally, but even within themselves they do not have syntax; that is, "Gone juice" does not mean something different from "Juice gone" (and there is no other marking to indicate syntactic role for elements in pivot schemas). The consistent ordering patterns in many pivot schemas are very likely direct reproductions of the ordering patterns children have heard most often in adult speech, with no communicative significance. This means that although young children are using their early pivot schemas to partition scenes conceptually with different words, they are not using syntactic symbols—such as word order or case marking—to indicate the different roles being played by different participants in that scene.

On the other hand, item-based constructions go beyond pivot schemas in having syntactic marking as an integral part of the construction. The evidence that children have, from fairly early in development, such syntactically marked item-based constructions is solid. Most important are a number of comprehension experiments in which children barely 2 years of age respond appropriately to requests that they "Make the bunny push the horse" (reversible transitives) that depend crucially and exclusively on a knowledge of canonical English word order (e.g., Bates et al., 1984; DeVilliers & DeVilliers, 1973; Roberts, 1983). Successful comprehension of word order with familiar verbs is found at even younger ages if preferential looking techniques are used (Hirsh-Pasek & Golinkoff, 1991, 1996). In production as well, many children around their second birthdays are able to produce transitive utterances with familiar verbs that respect canonical English word order marking (Tomasello, 2000).

However, there is abundant evidence from many studies of both comprehension and production that the syntactic marking in these item-based constructions is still verb specific, depending on how a child has heard a particular verb being used. For example, Tomasello (1992) found that almost all of his daughter's early multiword utterances during her second year of life revolved around the specific verbs or predicative terms involved. The lexically specific pattern of this phase of combinatorial speech was evident in the patterns of participant roles with which individual verbs were used. Thus, during exactly the same developmental period, some verbs were used in only one type of construction and that construction was quite simple (e.g., *Cut _____*), whereas other verbs were used in more complex frames of several different types (e.g., *Draw _____, Draw _____ on _____, Draw _____ for _____, _____ draw on _____*). Interestingly and importantly, within any given verb's development, there was great continuity such that new uses of a given verb almost always replicated previous uses and then made one small addition or modification (e.g., the marking of tense or the adding of a new argument). In general, by far the best predictor of this child's use of a given verb on a given day was not her use of other verbs on that same day, but rather her use of that same verb on immediately preceding days. (See Lieven, Pine, & Baldwin, 1997; Pine & Lieven, 1993; Pine, Lieven, & Rowland, 1998, for some very similar results in a sample of 12 English-speaking children from 1 to 3 years of age. For additional findings of this same type in other languages, see Allen, 1996, for Inuktitut; Behrens, 1998, for Dutch; Berman, 1982, for Hebrew; Gathercole, Sebastián, & Soto, 1999, for Spanish; Pizzuto & Caselli, 1992, for Italian; Rubino & Pine, 1998, for Portugese; Serrat, 1997, for Catalan; and Stoll, 1998, for Russian.)

Similarly, in experimental studies, when children who are themselves producing many transitive utterances are taught a new verb in any one of many different constructions, they mostly cannot transfer their knowledge of word order from their existing item-based constructions to this new item until after their third birthdays—and this finding holds for comprehension as well (Tomasello, 2000). These findings would seem to indicate that young children's early syntactic marking—at least with English word order—is only local, learned for different verbs on a one-by-one basis (see next section for a review of these studies). What little experimental evidence we have from nonce verb studies of case-marking languages (e.g., Berman, 1993; Wittek & Tomasello, 2005) is in general accord with this developmental pattern.

The main point is that unlike in pivot schemas, in item-based constructions children use syntactic symbols such as morphology, adpositions, and word order to syntactically mark the roles participants are playing in these events, including generalized slots that include whole categories of entities as participants. But all of this is done on an item-specific basis; that is, the child does not generalize across scenes to syntactically mark similar participant roles in similar ways without having heard those participants used and marked in adult discourse for each verb specifically. This limited generality is presumably due to the difficulty of categorizing or schematizing entire utterances, including reference to both the event and the participant roles involved, into more abstract constructions—especially given the many different kinds of utterances children hear and must sort through. Early syntactic competence is therefore best characterized as a semi-structured inventory of relatively independent verb island constructions that pair a scene of experience and an item-based construction, with very few structural relationships among these constructional islands.

Processes of Schematization

From a usage-based perspective, word combinations, pivot schemas, and item-based constructions are things that children construct out of the language they hear around them using general cognitive and social-cognitive skills. It is thus important to establish that, at the necessary points in development, children have the skills they need to comprehend, learn, and produce each of these three types of early constructions.

First, to produce a word combination under a single intonation contour, children must be able to create a multiple-step procedure toward a single goal, assembled conceptually ahead of time (what Piaget, 1952, called "mental combinations"). They are able to do this in nonlinguistic behavior quite readily, from about 14 to 18 months of age in their own problem solving, and, moreover, they are also able to copy such sequences from the behavior of other persons at around this same age. Thus, Bauer (1996) found that 14-month-old infants were quite skillful at imitatively learning both 2- and 3-step action sequences from adults—mostly involving the constructing of complex toy objects (e.g., a toy bell) that they saw adults assembling. Children were sensitive to the order of the steps involved as well. These would seem to be the right skills at the right time for constructing word combinations.

Second, the process by which pivot schemas are formed—as abstractions across individual word combinations—is presumably very similar to the way 1-year-olds form other kinds of sensory-motor schemas, including those learned through observation of others' behavior: what may be called schematization. Thus, Piaget (1952) reports that when infants repeatedly enact the same action on different objects, they form a sensory-motor schema consisting of (a) what is general in all of the various actions and (b) a kind of slot for the variable component. As one example, A. Brown and Kane (1988) taught 2-year-old children to use a certain kind of action with a particular object (e.g., pull a stick) and then gave them transfer problems in which it was possible for them to use the same action but with a different object creatively (e.g., they learned to pull stick, pull rope, pull towel). Their skill at doing this demonstrates exactly the kind of cognitive ability needed to create a pivot schema across different utterances so as to yield something like *Pull X*. Ultimately, if the child forms a generalized action or event schema with a variable slot for some class of items (e.g., *Throw X*), that slot and class of items are defined by their role in the schema, which is why Nelson (1985) calls them slot-filler categories. This means that in the case of pivot schemas such as *Throw X, X gone,* and *Want X,* the slot could be thought of as something like "throwable things," "things that are gone," "things I want more of," and so forth. This primacy of the schema in defining the slot leads to the kinds of coercion evidenced in creative uses of language in which an item is used in a schema that requires us to interpret it in an unusual way. For example, under communicative pressure, a child might say "I'm juicing it" as she pours juice onto something, or "Where's-the swimming?" as she looks for a picture of a swimming activity in a book. This process of "functional coercion" is perhaps the major source of syntactic creativity in the language of 1- and 2-year-old children.

Third and finally, it is not clear how young children learn about syntactically marking their utterance-level constructions, so creating item-based constructions. Essentially what they need to learn is that whereas some linguistic symbols are used for referring and predicating things about the world, others (including word order) are used for more grammatical functions. These functions are many and various but they all share the property that they are parasitic on the symbols that actually carry the load of referring and predicating. Thus, with special reference to utterance-level constructions, an accusative case marker (or an immediate postverbal position) can only function symbolically if there is some referential expression to indicate the entity that is the object of some action; we may thus call syntactic markers second-order symbols (Tomasello, 1992). Although children do engage in nonlinguistic activities that have clear and generalized roles, there is really nothing in nonlinguistic activities that corresponds to such second-order symbols. (The closest might be the designation of participant roles in some forms of pretend play—but that is typically a much later developmental achievement.) Children presumably learn to deal with such symbols when they hear such things as, in English, *X is pushing Y* and then on another occasion *Y is pushing X,* each paired with its own real world counterpart. From this, they begin to see that the verb island construction involving *push* is structured so that the "pusher" is in the preverbal position and "pushee" is in the postverbal position regardless of the specific identity of that participant.

MARKING SYNTACTIC ROLES

From a psycholinguistic point of view, linguistic constructions are comprised of four and only four types of symbolic elements: words, morphological markers on words, word order, and intonation/prosody (Bates & MacWhinney, 1982). Of special importance for utterance-level constructions are the syntactic devices used for marking the participant roles (typically expressed as noun phrases, NPs) to indicate the basic "who-did-what-to-whom" of the utterance, what are sometimes called agent-patient relations. The two major devices that languages use for this purpose are (1) word order (mainly of NPs) and (2) morphological marking (casemarking on NPs and agreement marking between NPs and verb).

Word Order

In their spontaneous speech, young English-speaking children use canonical word order for most of their verbs, including transitive verbs, from very early in development (Bloom, 1992; Braine, 1971; R. Brown, 1973). And as reported, in comprehension tasks, children as young as 2 years of age respond appropriately to requests that they "Make the doggie bite the cat" (reversible transitives) that depend crucially and exclusively on a knowledge of canonical English word order (e.g., DeVilliers & DeVilliers, 1973). But to really discover the nature of children's underlying linguistic representations, we need to examine utterances we know children are producing creatively; this means overgeneralization errors (which they could not have heard from adults) and the use of novel words introduced in experiments.

First, children's overgeneralization errors—indicating a more abstract understanding of word order and constructional patterns—include such things as *She falled me down* or *Don't giggle me* in which the child uses intransitive verbs in the SVO transitive frame productively. Pinker (1989) compiled examples from many sources and found that children produce a number of such overgeneralizations, but few before about 3 years of age. Second, production experiments focused on the marking of agent-patient relations by word order in English typically introduce young children to a novel verb in a syntactic construction such as an intransitive or passive and then see if they can later use that verb in the canonical SVO transitive construction. Cues to syntactic roles other than word order (e.g., animacy of the S and O participants, use of case-marked pronouns) are carefully controlled and/or monitored. Experiments of this type have clearly demonstrated that by 3.5 or 4 years of age most English-speaking children can readily assimilate novel verbs to an abstract SVO schema that they bring to the experiment. For example, Maratsos, Gudeman, Gerard-Ngo, and DeHart (1987) taught children from 4.5 to 5.5 years of age the novel verb *fud* for a novel transitive action (human operating a machine that transformed the shape of Play-Doh). Children were introduced to the novel verb in a series of intransitive sentence frames such as "The dough finally fudded," "It won't fud," and "The dough's fudding in the machine." Children were then prompted with questions such as "What are you doing?" (which encourages a transitive response such as "I'm fudding the dough"). The general finding was that the vast majority of children from 4.5 to 5.5 years of age could produce a canonical transitive SVO utterance with the novel verb, even though they had never heard it used in that construction.

But the same is not true for younger children. Over a dozen studies similar to that of Maratsos et al. (1987) have been done with 2- and 3-year-olds, and they are generally not productive (see Tomasello, 2000, for a review). When findings across all ages are compiled and quantitatively compared, we see a continuous developmental progression in which children gradually become more productive with novel verbs in the transitive SVO construction during their third and fourth years of life and beyond, evidencing a growing understanding of the working of canoncial English word order (see Figure 8.1).

Akhtar (1999) used a different novel verb methodology to investigate young children's knowledge of English word-order conventions. An adult modeled novel verbs for novel transitive events for young children at 2;8, 3;6, and 4;4 years of age. One verb

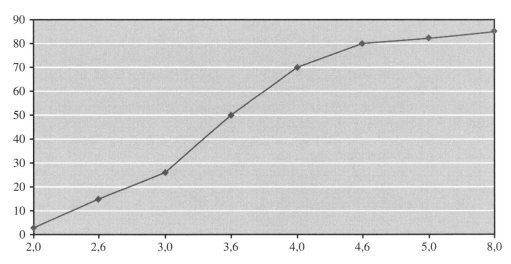

FIGURE 8.1 Percentage of Children Who Produce Transitive Utterances Using Novel Verbs in Different Studies. (From "Do Young Children Have Adult Syntactic Competence?" by M. Tomasello, 2000, *Cognition, 74*, pp. 209–253. Adapted with permission.)

was modeled in canonical English SVO order, as in *Ernie meeking the car,* whereas two others were in noncanonical orders, either SOV (*Ernie the cow tamming*) or VSO (*Gopping Ernie the cow*). Children were then encouraged to use the novel verbs with neutral questions such as *What's happening?* Almost all of the children at all three ages produced exclusively SVO utterances with the novel verb when that is what they heard. However, when they heard one of the noncanonical SOV or VSO forms, children behaved differently at different ages. In general, the older children used their verb-general knowledge of English transitivity to correct the noncanonical uses of the novel verbs to canonical SVO form. The younger children, in contrast, much more often matched the ordering patterns they had heard with the novel verb, no matter how bizarre that pattern sounded to adult ears. Abbot-Smith, Lieven, and Tomasello (2001) have extended this methodology to younger ages (children at 2;4, using intransitives) and found that even fewer children (less than half as many as Akhtar's youngest children) corrected the adult's strange word order utterances. The results of these two studies combined are depicted in Figure 8.2.

Perhaps surprisingly, young children also fail to show a verb-general understanding of canonical English word order in comprehension studies using novel verbs in which they must act out (with toys) a scene indicated by an SVO utterance. Thus, Akhtar and

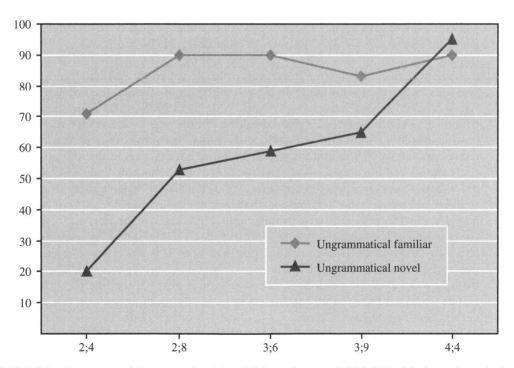

FIGURE 8.2 Percentage of Utterances in which Children "Corrected" Weird Word Order to Canonical English SVO with Familiar and Unfamiliar Verbs in Two Studies. (*Sources:* "Acquiring Basic Word Order: Evidence for Data-Driven Learning of Syntactic Structure," by N. Akhtar, 1999, *Journal of Child Language, 26,* pp. 339–356. Reprinted with permission; "What Children Do and Do Not Do with Ungrammatical Word Orders," by K. Abbot-Smith et al., 2001, *Cognitive Development, 16,* pp. 1–14. Reprinted with permission.)

Tomasello (1997) exposed young children to many models of *This is called dacking* used to describe a canonical transitive action. They then, using novel characters, asked the children to *Make Cookie Monster dack Big Bird.* All 10 of the children 3;8 were excellent in this task, whereas only 3 of the 10 children at 2;9 were above chance in this task—even though most did well on a control task using familiar verbs. In a second type of comprehension test, children just under 3 years of age first learned to act out a novel action on a novel apparatus with two toy characters, and only then (their first introduction to the novel verb) did the adult hand them two new characters and request *Can you make X meek Y* (while pushing the apparatus in front of them)? In this case, children's only exposure to the novel verb was in a very natural transitive sentence frame used for an action they already knew how to perform. Since every child knew the names of the novel characters and on every trial attempted to make one of them act on the other in the appropriate way, the only question was which character should play which role. These under-3-year-old children were, as a group, at chance in this task, with only 3 of the 12 children performing above chance as individuals. Similar results, using a different comprehension methodology (a token placement task), were found by Bridges (1984). Using a comprehension methodology in which children had to point to the agent of an utterance—the main clue to which was word order, Fisher (1996) found positive results for children averaging 3;6 years of age (and Fisher, 2002, found somewhat weaker evidence for the same effect in children at 2;6).

Another technique used to assess children's comprehension of various linguistic items and structures is so-called preferential looking. In this technique, a child is shown two displays (often on two television screens) and hears a single utterance (through a centrally located loudspeaker) that describes only one of the pictures felicitously. The question is which picture she will look at longer. The relevant studies are those using novel or very low frequency verbs, so we know that children have had no previous experience with them. In almost all of these studies, the comparison is between transitives and intransitives. Thus, Naigles (1990) found that when they hear canonical SVO utterances English-speaking children from 2;1 prefer to look at one participant doing something to another (causative meaning) rather than two participants carrying out synchronous independent activities. This study shows that in the preferential looking paradigm young 2-year-old children know enough about the simple transitive construction to know that it goes with asymmetrical activities (one participant acting on another) rather than symmetrical activities (two participants engaging in the same activity simultaneously). What it does *not* show, as is sometimes claimed, is an understanding of word order. That is, it does not show that young children can connect the preverbal position with the agent (or subject) and the postverbal position with the patient (or object) in a transitive utterance—which would be required for a full-blown representation of the transitive construction, and which is indeed required of children in both act-out comprehension tasks and novel verb production tasks.

The overall conclusion is thus that in both production and comprehension the majority of English-speaking children do not fully understand word order as a verb-general, productive syntactic device for marking agents and patients (subjects and objects) until after 3 years of age (although some minority of children may understand it before). In some cases, even the presence of animacy cues (agents were animate, patients inanimate) does not help. But, of course, most English-speaking children are hearing SVO utterances with one or more case-marked pronouns (*I-me, he-him, they-them, we-us,* etc.), and so we now turn to an investigation of their understanding of case marking—which is much more important in some other languages than it is in English.

Case and Agreement

In the 1960s and 1970s, a number of investigators speculated that word order should be easier than case and agreement for children to learn as a syntactic device because canonical ordering is so fundamental to so many sensory-motor and cognitive activities (Braine, 1976; Bruner, 1975; McNeill, 1966; Pinker, 1981). However, cross-linguistic research has since exploded this word order myth (Weist, 1983). That is, cross-linguistic research has demonstrated that in their spontaneous speech, children learning many different languages—regardless of whether their language relies mainly on word order, case marking, or some combination of both—generally conform to adult usage and appear to mark agent-patient relations equally early and appropriately. Indeed, on the basis of his review, Slobin (1982) concluded that children learning languages that mark agent-patient relations clearly and simply with morphological (case) markers, such as Turkish, comprehend agent-patient syntax earlier than children learning word order languages such as English. In support of his argument, Slobin cited the fact that some children learning case marking languages overgeneralize case markers in ways indicating productive control while they are still only 2 years old (Slobin, 1982, 1985).

In comprehension experiments, children learning morphologically rich languages, in which word order plays only a minor role in indicating agent-patient relations, comprehend the syntactic marking of agent-patient relations as early or earlier than children learning word order languages such as English. Representative studies are reported by Slobin and Bever (1982) for Turkish, Hakuta (1982) for Japanese, and Weist (1983) for Polish (see Slobin, 1982, and Bates & MacWhinney, 1989, for reviews). But it should be noted that in neither comprehension nor production do we have the kind of nonce word studies that could provide the most definitive evidence of children's productive knowledge of case marking. The few nonce verb studies we have of case-marking languages (e.g., Berman, 1993; Wittek & Tomasello, 2005) show a very slow and gradual developmental pattern of increasing productivity, just as with word order marking in English and similar languages.

For English, most of the discussion of case marking has centered around pronoun case errors, such as *me do it* and *him going*. About 50% of English-speaking children make such errors, most typically in the 2- to 4-year age range, with much variability across children. The most robust phenomenon is that children often substitute accusative forms for nominative forms ("Me going") but very seldom do the reverse ("Billy hit I"). Rispoli (1994, 1998) notes that the particular pronouns that English-speaking children overgeneralize proportionally most often are the objective forms *me* and *her* (and not the subjective forms *I* and *she*). Rispoli attributes these facts to the morphophonetic structure of the English personal pronoun paradigm:

I	she	he	they
me	her	him	them
my	her	his	their

It is easily seen that *he-him-his* and *they-them-their* each has a common phonetic core (*h-* and *th-*, respectively) whereas *I-me-my* and *she-her-her* do not. And indeed, the errors that are made most often are ones in which children in these latter two cases use the forms that have a common initial phoneme (*me-my* and *her-her*) to substitute for the odd-man-out (*I* and *she*), with the *her*-for-*she* error having the overall highest rate (because of the fact, according to Rispoli, that *her* occurs as both the objective and genetive form; the so-called double-cell effect). The overall idea is thus that children are making retrieval errors based on both semantic and phonological factors.

Currently, there is no widely accepted explanation of children's pronoun case errors in English, and it is likely that several different factors play a role. Of most importance to resolve the issue in a theoretically interesting way is cross-linguistic research enabling the examination of pronoun paradigms with different morphophonemic and syntactic properties.

Cue Coalition and Competition

In all languages, there are multiple potential cues indicating agent-patient relations. For example, in many languages, both word order and case marking are at least potentially available, even though one of them might most typically be used for other functions (e.g., in many morphologically rich languages, word order is used primarily for pragmatic functions such as topicalization). In addition, in attempting to comprehend adult utterances, children might also attend to information that is not directly encoded in the language; for example, they may use animacy to infer that in an utterance containing the lexical items *man, ball,* and *kick,* the most likely interpretation is that the man kicked the ball, regardless of how those items are syntactically combined.

In an extensive investigation of language acquisition in a number of different languages, Slobin (reviewed in 1982) identified some of the different comprehension strategies that children use to establish agent-patient relations, depending on the types of problems their particular language presents to them. A central discovery of this research, as noted, was that children can more easily master grammatical forms expressed in "local cues" such as bound morphology as opposed to more distributed cues such as word order and some forms of agreement. This accounts for the fact that Turkish-speaking children master the expression of agent-patient relations at a significantly earlier age than do English-speaking children. In addition, Turkish is especially "child friendly," even among languages that rely heavily on local morphological cues. Slobin (1982) outlines 12 reasons why Turkish agent-patient relations are relatively easy to learn. An adaptation of that list (focusing on nominal morphology) follows. Turkish nominal grammatical morphemes are:

- Postposed, syllabic, and stressed, which makes them perceptually more salient.
- Obligatory and employ almost perfect one-to-one mapping of form to function (no fusional morphemes or homophones), which makes them more predictable.
- Bound to the noun, rather than freestanding, which makes them more local.
- Invariably regular across different nominals and pronominals, which makes them readily generalizable.

All of these factors coalesce to make Turkish agent-patient relations especially easy to learn, and their identification is a major step in discovering the basic processes of language acquisition that are employed by children in general.

A central methodological problem, however, is that in natural languages many of these cues go together naturally, and so it is difficult to evaluate their contributions separately. Therefore, Bates and MacWhinney (summarized in 1989) conducted an extensive set of experimental investigations of the cues children use to comprehend agent-patient relations in a number of different languages. The basic paradigm is to ask children to act out utterances using toy animals, with agent-patient relations indicated in different ways—sometimes in semi-grammatical utterances with conflicting cues. For example, an English-speaking child might be presented with the utterance "The spoon kicked the horse." In this case, the cue of word order is put in competition with the most likely real-world scenario in which animate beings more often kick inanimate things than the reverse. From an early age, young English-speaking children make the spoon "kick" the horse, which simply shows the power of word order in English. Interestingly, when presented with an equivalent utterance, Italian-speaking children ignore word order and make the horse kick the spoon. This is because word order is quite variable in Italian, and so, since there is no case marking (and in this example agreement is no help because both the horse and the spoon are third-person singular), semantic plausibility is the most reliable cue available. German-speaking children gradually learn to ignore both word order and semantic plausibility (animacy) and simply look for nominative and accusative marking on the horse and the spoon (Lindner, 2003).

Later Ontogeny

During the preschool years, English-speaking children begin to be productive with a variety of abstract utterance-level constructions, including such things as: transitives, intransitives, ditransitives, attributives, passives, imperatives, reflexives, locatives, resultatives, causatives, and various kinds of question constructions. Many of these are so-called argument-structure constructions, and they are used to refer to experiential scenes of the most abstract kind, including such things as: people acting on objects, objects changing state or location, people giving people things, people experiencing psychological states, objects or people being in a state, things being acted on, and so forth (Goldberg, 1995). It is presumably the case that these abstract constructions represent children's generalizations across many dozen (or more) item-based constructions, especially verb island constructions.

Children also construct smaller constructions that serve as the major internal constituents of utterance-level constructions. Most especially, they construct nominal constructions (NPs) in order to make reference to things in various ways (*Bill, my father, the man who fell down*) and verbal constructions (VPs) in order predicate for something about those things (*is nice, sleeps, hit the ball*). Children also create, a bit later in development, larger and more complex constructions containing multiple predicates such as infinitival complements (*I want him to go*), sentential complements (*I think it will fall over*), and relative clauses (*That's the doggy I bought*). These smaller and larger constructions also are important components in children's later linguistic competence.

Theoretically, we are concerned here again with the nature of the cognitive processes that enable young children to generalize from their linguistic experience and so build up these highly abstract constructions. In addition, in this section, we also address the difficult question of why children make just the generalizations they do, and not some others that might be reasonable from an adult point of view.

ABSTRACT CONSTRUCTIONS

The most abstract constructions that English-speaking children use early in development have mostly been studied from an adult perspective—using constructions defined from an adult model. We follow suit here, but the truth is that many of the constructions listed here probably should be differentiated in a more fine-grained way (as families of subconstructions) once the necessary empirical work is done.

Identificationals, Attributives, and Possessives

Among the earliest utterance-level constructions used by many English-speaking children are those that serve to identify an object or to attribute to it some property, including a possessor or simple location (Lieven, Pine, & Dresner-Barnes, 1992). In adult language, these would almost invariably require some form of the coplua, *to be,* although children do not always supply it. Quite often, these constructions revolve around one or a few specific words. Most common for the identification function are such things as *It's a/the X; That's a/the X;* or *This's a/the X.* Most common for the attributive function are such things as: *Here's a/the X; There's a/the X.* Most common for the possessive function are such things as: *(It's) X's _____; That's X's/my _____; This is X's/your _____.* Clancy (2000) reports some very similar constructions for Korean-speaking children, and a perusal of the studies in Slobin's cross-linguistic volumes reveals many other languages in which these are frequently used child constructions for focusing attention on, or attributing a property to, an external entity.

Simple Transitives, Simple Intransitives, and Imperatives

The simple transitive construction in English is used for depicting a variety of scenes that differ greatly from one another. The prototype is a scene in which there are two participants and one somehow acts on the other. English-speaking children typically produce utterances of this type in their spontaneous speech early in language development for various physical and psychological activities that people perform on objects—everything from pushing to having to dropping to knowing. The main verbs young children use in the transitive construction are such things as *get, have, want, take, find, put, bring, drop, make, open, break, cut, do, eat, play, read, draw, ride, throw, push, help, see, say,* and *hurt.*

The simple intransitive construction in English is also used for a wide variety of scenes. In this case, the only commonality is that they involve a single participant and activity. The two main types of intransitives are the so-called unergatives, in which an actor does something (e.g., *John smiled*) and the so-called unaccusatives, in which something happens to something (e.g., *The vase broke*). English-speaking children typically produce utterances of both of these types early in language development, with unergatives such as *sleep* and *swim* predominating (unaccusatives occurring most often with the specific verbs *break* and *hurt*). The main verbs young children use in the intransitive construction—including imperative uses—are such things as *go, come, stop, break, fall, open, play, jump, sit, sing, sleep, cry, swim, run, laugh, hurt,* and *see.*

Ditransitives, Datives, and Benefactives

All languages of the world have utterance-level constructions for talking about the transfer of objects (and other things) between people. In English, there is a constellation of three related constructions for doing this: the *to*-dative, the *for*-dative (or benefactive), and the double-object dative (or ditransitive). Many verbs occur in both the *to*-dative and the double-object dative constructions (e.g., *give, bring, offer*), with the choice of which construction to use jointly affected by the semantic and discourse status of the participants (Erteschik-Shir, 1979). Most clearly, the prepositional form is most appropriate when the recipient is new information and what is being transferred is known (compare the natural "Jody sent it to Julie" with the unnatural "Jody sent Julie it"). However, the selection of a construction is only partially determined by discourse because a great many English verbs occur only in the prepositional form (e.g., *donate*) and a few occur only in the ditransitive (e.g., *cost, deny, fine*). The main verbs young children use in the ditransitive construction are such things as *get, give, show, make, read, being, buy, take, tell, find,* and *send* (see Campbell & Tomasello, 2001).

Locatives, Resultatives, and Causatives

Beginning with their first words and pivot schemas, English-speaking children use a variety of locative words to express spatial relationships in utterance-level constructions. These include prepositions such as *X up, X down, X in, X out, on X, off X, over X,* and *under X,* and verb + particle constructions such as *pick X up, wipe X off,* and *get X down.* Once children start producing more complex structures designating events with two or more participants, two-argument locative constructions are common. For Tomasello's (1992) daughter, these included such utterances as "Draw star on me" and "Peoples on there boat" which were produced at 20 months of age. By 3 years of age, most children have sufficient flexibility with item-based constructions to talk explicitly about locative events with three participants, most often an agent causing a theme to move to some object-as-location (e.g., "He put the pen on the desk").

The resultative construction (as in "He wiped the table clean") is used, most typically, to indicate both an action and the result of that action. Although no experimental studies of the resultative construction have yet been conducted with novel verbs, the occurrence of novel resultatives in spontaneous speech attests to the productivity of the construction from sometime after the third birthday. In Bowerman's (1982) study of her two daughters, the following developmental progression was observed. At around 2 years of age, the two children learned various combinations of "causing verb + resulting effect" such as *pull + up* and *eat + all gone.* For the next year or so, each child accumulated an assortment of these forms that were used in an apparently adultlike manner. Subsequently, each child, at some point after her third birthday, seemed to reorganize her knowledge of the independently learned patterns and extract a more abstract schema. Evidence for this reorganization came from each child's production of a number of novel resultative utterances such as "And the monster would eat you in pieces" and "I'll capture his whole head off."

Causative notions may be expressed in English utterance-level constructions either lexically or phrasally. Lexical causatives are simply verbs with a causative meaning used in the transitive construction (e.g., "He killed the deer"). Phrasal causatives are important because they supply an alternative for causativizing an intransitive verb that cannot be used transitively. Thus, if Bowerman's daughter had been skillful with phrasal causatives, she could have said, instead of "Don't giggle me," "Don't make me giggle"; and instead of "Stay this open" she could have said "Make this stay open." *Make* is thus the direct causation matrix verb in English, but an important related verb—that is in fact the most frequent such verb for young English learners—is *let,* as in "Let her do it," or "Let me help you." Another common matrix verb that follows this same pattern is *help,* as in "Help her get in there" or "Help him put on his shoes." It is unknown whether young children see any common pattern among the utterances in which these three different matrix verbs are used.

Passives, Middles, and Reflexives

The English passive construction consists of a family of related constructions that change the perspective from the agent of a transitive action (relative to active voice constructions) to the patient and what happened to it. Thus, "Bill was shot by John" takes the perspective of Bill and what happened to him, rather than focusing on John's act of shooting (with the truncated passive "Bill was shot" serving to strengthen this perspective further). In addition to this general function of the passive, Budwig (1990) has shown that the "get" and "be" forms of the passive are themselves associated with distinct discourse perspectives. Thus, the prototypical "get" passive in "Spot got hit by a car" or "Jim got sick from the water" tends to be used when there is a negative consequence, which occurs when an animate patient is adversely affected by an inanimate entity or a nonagent source. In contrast, the "be" passive construction in "The soup was heated on the stove" is used when there is a neutral outcome of an inanimate entity undergoing a change of state where the agent causing the change of state is unknown or irrelevant. In general, actional transitive verbs can be used in passive constructions quite readily, whereas many stative verbs seem to fit less well (e.g., *She was loved by him*). This was demonstrated experimentally by Sudhalter and Braine (1985), who found that preschoolers were much better at comprehending passive utterances containing actional verbs (e.g., *kick, cut, dress*) than they were at comprehending passive utterances containing experiential verbs (e.g., *love, see, forget*).

English-speaking children typically do not produce full passives in their spontaneous speech until 4 or 5 years of age, although they produce truncated passives (often with *get*) and adjectival passives much earlier (e.g., "He got dunked" or "He got hurt"). Israel, Johnson, and Brooks (2000) analyzed the development of children's use of the passive participle. They found that children tended to begin with stative participles (e.g., *Pumpkin stuck*), then use some participles ambiguously between stative and active readings (e.g., *Do you want yours cut?*—do you want it to undergo a cutting action or, alternatively, do you want to receive it already in a cut state), then finally use the active participles characteristic of the full passive (e.g., *The spinach was cooked by Mommy*). Although passive utterances are infrequent in English-speaking children's spontaneous speech, a number of researchers have observed that older preschoolers occasionally create truncated passives with verbs that in adult English do not passivize, for example, "It was bandaided," "He will be died and I won't have a brother anymore," indicating some productivity with the construction (Bowerman, 1982, 1988; Clark, 1982).

It is important to note that children acquiring certain non-Indo-European languages typically produce passive sentences quite early in development. This result has been obtained for children learning Inuktitut (Allen & Crago, 1996), K'iche' Mayan (Pye & Quixtan Poz, 1988), Sesotho (Demuth, 1989, 1990), and Zulu (Suzman, 1985). Allen and Crago (1996) report that a child at age 2.0 to 2.9 (as well as two slightly older children) produced both truncated and full passives quite regularly. Although a majority of these were with familiar actional verbs, they also observed passives with experiential predicates and several clearly innovative forms with verbs that do not passivize in adult Inuktitut. The reasons for this precocity relative to English-speaking children are hypothesized to include the facts that: (a) Inuktitut passives are very common in child-directed speech; and (b) passive utterances are actually simpler than active voice constructions in Inuktitut because the passivized verb has to agree only with the subject, whereas the transitive verb has to agree with both subject and object.

There is very little research on English-speaking children's use of so-called middle voice constructions (medio-passives) such as "This bread cuts easily" or "This piano plays like a dream" (see Kemmer, 1993). The prototype of this construction involves an inanimate entity as subject, which is held responsible for the predicate (i.e., why the adverb is typically needed; "This bread cuts" or "This piano plays" by themselves are scarcely grammatical). Budwig, Stein, and O'Brien (2001) looked at a number of utterances of young children involving inanimate subjects and found that the most frequent constructions of this type in young English-speaking children's speech were such things as "This doesn't pour good." Reflexives are also not common in English-speaking children's early language (or in adult English), although they do produce a few things such as "I hurt myself." However, reflexives are quite common in the speech of young children learning languages in which these constructions are frequent in child-directed speech. For example, most Spanish-speaking youngsters hear and use quite early such things as *Se cayó* (It fell down), *Me siento* (I sit down), *Levántate* (Stand up!), and *Me lavo las manos* (I wash my hands).

Questions

Questions are used primarily to seek information from an interlocutor. In many languages, this is done quite simply through a characteristic intonation ("He bought a *house?*") or by the replacement of a content word with a question word ("He bought a *what?*"). Although both of these are possible in English, two other forms are more common: wh- questions and yes/no questions. In the classic structural linguistic analysis, English questions are formed by subject-auxiliary inversion (sometimes with do-support) and wh- movement. These rules assume that the speaker has available a simple declarative linguistic representation, which she then transforms into a question by moving, rearranging, or inserting grammatical items. Thus, "John kicked the ball" becomes either "Did John kick the ball?" or "What did John kick?"

But this rule-based analysis is highly unlikely initially in development for two main reasons. First, some English-speaking children learn some wh- question constructions before they learn any other word combinations. For instance, Tomasello's (1992) daughter learned to ask where-questions (e.g., "Where's-the bottle?") and what-questions (e.g., "What's that"?) as her first multiword constructions. Second, everyone who has studied children's early questions has found that their earliest constructions are tied quite tightly to a small number of formulae. For example, in their classic analysis, Klima and Bellugi (1966) suggested that almost all the wh- questions of Adam, Eve, and Sarah emanated from two formulae: *What NP (doing)?* and *Where NP (going)?* Fletcher's (1985) subject produced almost all of her early questions with one of three formulae: *How do . . . , What are . . . ,* and *Where is. . . .* More recently, Dabrowska (2001) looked in detail at one child's earliest uses of wh- questions in English and found that 83% of her questions during her third year of life came from one of just 20 formulas such as *Where's THING? Where THING go? Can I ACT? Is it PROPERTY?*

One phenomenon that bears on this issue is so-called inversion errors. English-speaking children sometimes invert the subject and auxiliary in wh- questions and sometimes not—leading to errors such as *Why they're not going?* A number of fairly complex and abstract rule-based accounts have been proposed to account for these errors, and, as usual, some researchers have claimed that children know the rules but apply them only optionally or inconsistently (e.g., Ingram & Tyack, 1979). However, in a more detailed analysis, Rowland and Pine (2000) discovered the surprising fact that the child they studied from age 2 to age 4 consistently inverted or failed to invert particular wh-word-auxiliary combinations on an item-specific basis. He thus consistently said such incorrect things as *Why I can . . . ? What she will . . . ? What you can . . . ?* but at the same time, he also said such correct things as *How did . . . ? How do . . . ? What do . . . ?* In all, of the 46 particular wh-word auxiliary pairs this child produced, 43 of them were produced either 100% correctly or 100% incorrectly (see also Erreich, 1984, who finds equal number of inversion errors in wh- and yes/no questions). Again, the picture is that children learn questions as a collection of item-based constructions, moving only gradually to more abstract representations.

ANALOGY

Children begin to form abstract utterance-level constructions by creating analogies among utterances emanating from different item-based constructions. The process of analogy is very like the process of the schematization for item-based schemas/constructions; it is just that analogies are more abstract. Thus, whereas all instances of a particular item-based schema have at least one linguistic item in common (e.g., the verb in a verb island schema), in totally abstract constructions (such as the English ditransitive construction) the instances need have no items in common. So the question is: On what basis does the learner make the alignments among constituents necessary for an analogy among complex structures?

The answer is that the learner must have some understanding of the functional interrelationship that makes up the two structures being aligned. In the most systematic research program on the topic, Gentner and colleagues (Gentner & Markman, 1995; Gentner & Medina, 1998) stress that the essence of analogy is the focus on relations. When an analogy is made, the objects involved are effaced; the only identity they retain is their role in the relational structure. Gentner and colleagues have much evidence that young children focus on relations quite naturally and so are able to make analogies quite readily. An example is as follows. Children are shown two pictures: one of a car towing a boat (hitched to its rear) and one of a truck towing a car (hitched to its rear), and this car is identical in appearance to the car in the other picture. After some training in making analogies, the experimenter then points to the car in the first picture and asks the child to find the one doing the same thing in the second picture. Children have no trouble ignoring the literal match of cars across the two pictures and choosing the truck. In essence, they identify in both pictures the "tow-er," or the agent, based on the role it is playing in the entire action depicted.

Gentner and colleagues also stress what they call the systematicity principle: In making analogies structures are aligned as wholes, as "interconnected systems of relations." In the current context, this simply means that learners align whole utterances or constructions, or significant parts thereof, and attempt to align all the elements and relations in one comparison. In doing this, learners search for "one-to-one correspondence" among the elements involved and "parallel connectivity" in the relations involved. In the current context, this means that the learner makes an analogy between utterances (or constructions) by aligning the arguments one to one, and in making this alignment, she is guided by the functional roles these elements play in the larger structure. For example, in aligning *the car is towing the boat* and *the truck is towing the car,* the learner does not begin to match elements on the basis of the literal similarity between the two *cars,* but aligns *the car* and *the truck* because they are doing the same job from the perspective of the functional interrelations involved. This analysis implies that an important part of making analogies across linguistic constructions is the meaning of the relational words, especially the verbs, involved—particularly in terms of such things as the spatial, temporal, and causal relations they encode. But there is basically no systematic research relevant to the question of how children might align verb meanings in making linguistic analogies across constructions.

Gentner and colleagues also have some specific proposals relevant to learning. For example, they propose that even though in some sense neutralized, the object elements that children experience in the slots of a structure can facilitate analogical processes. In particular, they propose that in addition to type variability in the slots, also important is consistency of the items in the slots (i.e., a given item occurs only in one slot and not in others). When all kinds of items occur promiscuously in all of the slots in two potentially analogous relational structures, structure mapping is made more difficult (Gentner & Medina, 1998). For example, children find it even easier to make the analogy cited earlier if in the two pictures a car is towing a boat and a car is towing a trailer, so that the tow-er is identical in the two cases. This principle explains why children begin with item-based constructions. They find it easier to do structural alignments when more of the elements and relations are not just similar functionally but also similar, or even identical, perceptually—the process of schematization as it works in, for example, verb island constructions. Children then work their way up to the totally abstract analogies gradually. There are also some proposals from the morphological domain, that a certain number of exemplars is needed—a "critical mass"—before totally abstract analogies can be made (Marchman & Bates, 1994). But if this is true, the nature of this critical mass (e.g., verb types versus verb tokens) is not known at this time; there is no research.

It is thus possible that abstract linguistic constructions are created by a structural alignment across different item-based constructions, or the utterances emanating from them. For example, some verb island constructions that children have with the verbs *give, tell, show, send,* and so forth, share a "transfer" meaning, and appear in the form: NP1 + V + NP2 + NP3. In the indicated transfer, NP1 is the giver, NP2 is the receiver, and NP3 is the gift. So the aligning must be done on the basis of *both* form and function: Two utterances or constructions are analogous if a "good" structure mapping is found both on the level of linguistic form (even if these are only categorically indicated) and on the level of communicative function. This consideration is not really applicable in nonlinguistic domains. It may also be that in many cases particular patterns of grammatical morphology in constructions (e.g., X *was* VERB*ed*)—which typically designate abstract relations of one sort or another—facilitate, or even enable, recognition of an utterance as instantiating a particular abstract construction.

The only experimental study of children's construction of an abstract linguistic construction (as tested by their ability to assimilate a nonce verb to it) was conducted by Childers and Tomasello (2001). In this training study, 2.5-year-old English-speaking children heard several hundred transitive utterances, such as *He's kicking it,* involving 16 different verbs across three separate sessions. Half the children learned new English verbs (and so increased their transitive verb vocabularies during training—toward a critical mass) whereas the other half heard only verbs they already knew. Within these groups, some children heard all the utterances with full nouns as agent and patient, whereas others heard utterances with both pronouns (i.e., *He's VERB-ing it*) and also full nouns as agent and patient. They were then tested to see if they could creatively produce a transitive utterance with a nonce verb. The main finding was that children were best at generalizing the transitive construction to the nonce verb if they had been trained with pronouns and nouns, regardless of the familiarity of the trained verbs (and few children in a control condition generalized to the novel verb at all). That is, the consistent pronoun frame *He's VERB-ing it* (in combination with type variation in the form of nouns as well) seemed to facilitate children's formation of a verb-general transitive construction to a greater degree than the learning of additional transitive verbs with nouns alone, in the absence of such a stabilizing pronominal frame.

The results of this study are consistent with Gentner's more general analysis of the process of analogy in several ways. First, they show that children can make generalizations, perhaps based on analogy, across different item-based constructions. Second and more specifically, they also show that the material that goes in the slots, in this case NP slots, plays an important role (see also Dodson & Tomasello, 1998). In English, the pronoun *he* only goes in the preverbal position, and, although the pronoun *it* may occur in either position in spontaneous speech, it occurs most frequently in postverbal position in child-directed speech, and that is the only position in which the children heard it during training. These correspondences between processes in the creation of nonlinguistic analogies and in the creation of abstract linguistic constructions constitute impressive evidence that the process is basically the same in the two cases.

CONSTRAINING GENERALIZATIONS

Importantly, there must be some constraints on children's linguistic abstractions, and this is a problem for both of the major theories of child language acquisition. Classically, a major problem for generative theories is that as the rules and principles are made more elegant and powerful through theoretical analyses, they become so abstract that they generate too large a set of grammatical utterances; and so constraints (e.g., the subjacency constraint) must be posited to restore empirical accuracy. In usage-based theories, children are abstracting as they learn, but they cannot do this indiscriminately; they must make just those generalizations that are conventional in the language they are learning and not others. It is thus clear that any serious theory of syntactic development, whatever its basic assumptions, must address the question of why children make just the generalizations they do and not others.

We may illustrate the basic problem with so-called dative alternation constructions. The situation is this: Some verbs can felicitously appear in both ditransitive and prepositional dative constructions, but others cannot; for example:

He gave/sent/bequeathed/donated his books to the library.

He gave/sent/bequeathed/*donated the library his book.

Why should the other three verbs be felicitous in both constructions, but *donate* be felicitous only in the prepositional dative? The four verbs have very similar meanings, and so it would seem likely that they should all behave the same. Another example is:

She said/told something to her mother.

She *said/told her mother something.

Again, the meanings of the verbs are very close, and so the difference of behavior seems unprincipled and unpredictable (Bowerman, 1988, 1996). Other similar alternations are the causative alternation (*I rolled the ball; The ball rolled*) and the locative alternation (*I sprayed paint on the wall; I sprayed the wall with paint*)—both of which also apply only to limited sets of verbs.

One solution is quite simple. Perhaps children only learn verbs for the constructions in which they have heard them. Based on all of the evidence reviewed here, this is very likely the case at the earliest stages of development. But it is not true later in development, especially in the 3- to 5-year age period. Children at this age overgeneralize with some regularity, as documented most systematically by Bowerman (1982, 1988; see Pinker, 1989, for a summary of evidence). As reported earlier, her two children produced things like: "Don't giggle me" (at age 3.0) and "I said her no" (at age 3.1). It is thus not the case that children are totally conservative throughout development, and so this cannot be the whole answer.

A second solution is also simple. When children make overgeneralization errors, adults may correct them, and so children's overgeneralization tendencies are constrained by the linguistic environment. But this is not true in the sense that adults do not explicitly correct child utterances for their grammatical correctness (R. Brown & Hanlon, 1970). Adults, at least Western middle-class adults, do respond differently to well-formed and ill-formed child utterances, however. For example, they continue conversing to well-formed utterances, but they revise or recast ill-formed utterances (e.g., Bohannon & Stanowicz, 1988; Farrar, 1992). But this kind of indirect feedback is generally not considered by most theorists sufficient to constrain children's overgeneralization tendencies because it is far from consistent. It is also not clear that this type of feedback is available to all children learning all languages. Nevertheless, it is still possible that linguistic feedback from adults may play some role—although neither a necessary nor a sufficient role—in constraining children's overgeneralization tendencies.

Given the inadequacy of these simple solutions, three factors have been most widely discussed. First, Pinker (1989) proposed that there are certain very specific and (mostly) semantic constraints that apply to particular English constructions and to the verbs that may or may not be conventionally used in them. For example, a verb can be used felicitously with the English transitive construction if it denotes "manner of locomotion" (e.g., *walk* and *drive* as in *I walked the dog at midnight* or *I drove my car to New York*), but not if it denotes a "motion in a lexically specified direction" (e.g., *come* and *fall* as in *He came her to school* or *She falled him down*). How children learn these verb classes—and they must learn them since they differ across languages—is unknown at this time. Second, it has also been proposed that the more frequently children hear a verb used in a particular construction (the more firmly its usage is entrenched), the less likely they will be to extend that verb to any novel construction with which they have not heard it used (Bates & MacWhinney, 1989; Braine & Brooks, 1995; Clark, 1987; Goldberg, 1995). And third, if children hear a verb used in a linguistic construction that serves the same communicative function as some possible generalization, they may infer that the generalization is not conventional—the heard construction preempts the generalization. For example, if a child hears *He made the rabbit disappear,* when she might have expected *He disappeared the rabbit,* she may infer that *disappear* does not occur in a simple transitive construction—since the adult seems to be going to some lengths to avoid using it in this way (the periphrastic causative being a more marked construction).

Two experimental studies provide evidence that indeed all three of these constraining processes—entrenchment, preemption, and knowledge of semantic subclasses of verbs—

are at work. First, Brooks, Tomasello, Lewis, and Dodson (1999) modeled the use of a number of fixed-transitivity English verbs for children from 3;5 to 8;0 years—verbs such as *disappear* that are exclusively intransitive and verbs such as *hit* that are exclusively transitive. There were four pairs of verbs, one member of each pair typically learned early by children and typically used often by adults (and so presumably more entrenched) and one member of each pair typically learned later by children and typically used less frequently by adults (less entrenched). The four pairs were: *come-arrive, take-remove, hit-strike, disappear-vanish* (the first member of each pair being more entrenched). The finding was that, in the face of adult questions attempting to induce them to overgeneralize, children of all ages were less likely to overgeneralize the strongly entrenched verbs than the weakly entrenched verbs; that is, they were more likely to produce *I arrived it* than *I comed it.*

Second, Brooks and Tomasello (1999) taught novel verbs to children 2.5, 4.5, and 7.0 years of age. They then attempted to induce children to generalize these novel verbs to new constructions. Some of these verbs conformed to Pinker's (1989) semantic criteria, and some did not. Additionally, in some cases, experimenters attempted to preempt generalizations by providing children with alternative ways of using the new verb (thus providing them with the possibility of answering *What's the boy doing?* with *He's making the ball tam*—which allows the verb to stay intransitive). In brief, the study found that both of these constraining factors worked, but only from age 4.5. Children from 4.5 years showed a tendency to generalize or not generalize a verb in line with its membership in one of the key semantic subclasses, and they were less likely to generalize a verb to a novel construction if the adult provided them with a preempting alternative construction. But the younger children showed no such tendency.

Overall, entrenchment seems to work early, from 3;0 or before, as particular verb island constructions become either more or less entrenched depending on usage. Preemption and semantic subclasses begin to work sometime later, perhaps not until 4 years of age or later, as children learn more about the conventional uses of verbs and about all of the alternative linguistic constructions at their disposal in different communicative circumstances. Thus, just as verb-argument constructions become more abstract only gradually, so also are they constrained only gradually.

Processes of Language Acquisition

From a cognitive science point of view, the central issue in the study of language development is the nature of children's underlying linguistic representations and how these change during ontogeny. Summarizing all that has gone before in this chapter, we now address directly these two issues.

THE GROWING ABSTRACTNESS OF CONSTRUCTIONS

Based on all the available evidence, it would appear that children's early linguistic representation are highly concrete, based in concrete and specific pieces of language not in abstract categories (although they have some open slot-filler categories as well). We have cited: (a) analyses of children's spontaneous productions showing very restricted ranges of application of many early linguistic items and structures, asynchronous development of item-based constructions that from an adult point of view should have similar structures, and gradual and continuous development within specific item-based structures; (b) production experiments in which young children use nonce verbs in the way adults have used them, failing to generalize them to other of their existing constructions—suggesting that these existing constructions are item-based and not verb-general; and (c) comprehension experiments in which young children, who know the activity they are supposed to act out in response to a nonce verb, fail to assign the correct agent-patient roles to the characters involved based on canonical word order cues (in English)—again suggesting that their constructions at this point are item-based and not totally general.

There is one other recent finding that supports this same conclusion further. Savage, Lieven, Theakston, and Tomasello (2003) primed English-speaking children with either active or passive sentences, in some cases with high lexical overlap between the priming sentence and the sentence the child was likely to produce (i.e., the prime used some pronouns and grammatical morphemes that the child could use in her target utterance even though different objects and actions were involved) and in some cases with very low lexical overlap (i.e., the prime used only nouns, which the child could not use in her target utterance since different objects were involved). In some ways, this method could be considered the most direct test yet of children's early syntactic representations because successful priming in the high lexical overlap condition would suggest that their linguistic knowledge is represented more in terms of specific lexical items, whereas priming in the low lexical overlap condition would suggest that their linguistic knowledge is represented more abstractly. The answer is that the older children, around 6 years of age, could be structurally primed to produce a particular construction such as the passive. The younger children, who had just turned 3 years old, could not be primed structurally; but they were primed by the more lexically specific primes. Four-year-old children fell somewhere in between these two extremes. So once more—in this case using a very different method, widely accepted in the adult psycholinguistic community—we find that children's early linguistic representations are very likely based in specific item-based constructions (with some abstract slots), and it is only in the late preschool period that their utterance-level constructions take on adultlike abstractness.

But rather than thinking of children's utterance-level constructions as either concrete or abstract, it is probably better to think of them as growing gradually in abstractness over time as more and more relevant exemplars are encountered and assimilated to the construction. One reasonable interpretation of all of the studies directly aimed at children's underlying linguistic representation—as reviewed here—is thus as follows. From about 2 or 2.5 years of age children have only very weak verb-general representations of their utterance-level constructions, and so these show up only in preferential looking tasks that require weak representations. But over the next months and years, their linguistic representations grow in strength and abstractness, based on both the type and token frequency with which they hear certain linguistic structures. These now begin to show themselves in tasks requiring more active behavioral decision making or even language production requiring require stronger representations. This hypothesis is in the general spirit of a number of proposals suggesting that, if cognitive representations retain information about the variety of individual instances, they may be felicitously described as being either weaker or stronger based mainly on their type and token frequency (e.g., Munakata, McClleland, Johnson, & Siegler, 1997). It is also consonant with the view that linguistic knowledge and linguistic processing are really just different aspects of the same thing. Thus, things like frequency and the probabilistic distribution of lexical items in the input not only play a crucial role in how children build up their linguistic representations, but also form an integral part of those representations in the end state (see the papers in Barlow & Kemmer, 2000; Elman et al., 1996).

PSYCHOLINGUISTIC PROCESSES OF DEVELOPMENT

In accounting for how children learn linguistic constructions and make generalizations across them, we have argued and presented evidence for the operation of certain general cognitive processes. Tomasello (2003) argues that we may segregate these into the two overall headings: intention-reading, comprising the species-unique social cognitive skills responsible for symbol acquisition and the functional dimensions of language; and pattern-finding, the primate-wide cognitive skills involved in the abstraction process. More specifically, these two kinds of general cognitive abilities interact in specific acquisition tasks to yield the processes we have outlined in various places previously. Thus, we have previously made reference to four specific sets of processes:

1. *Intention-Reading and Cultural Learning,* which account for how children learn linguistic symbols in the first place (discussed here very little).
2. *Schematization and Analogy,* which account for how children create abstract syntactic constructions (and syntactic roles such as subject and direct object) out of the concrete pieces of language they have heard.
3. *Entrenchment and Competition,* which account for how children constrain their abstractions to those that are conventional in their linguistic community.
4. *Functionally Based Distributional Analysis,* which accounts for how children form paradigmatic categories of various kinds of linguistic constituents (e.g., nouns and verbs).

These are the processes by which children construct a language, that is, a structured inventory of linguistic constructions. But for a full account, we also need to look briefly at the processes by which children actually produce utterances.

If children are not putting together creative utterances with meaningful words and meaningless rules, then how exactly do they do it? In the current view, what they are doing is constructing utterances out of various already mastered pieces of language of various shapes, sizes, and degrees of internal structure and abstraction—in ways appropriate to the exigencies of the current usage event. To engage in this process of symbolic integration, in which the child fits together into a coherent whole such things as an item-based construction and a novel item to go in the slot, the child must be focused on both form and function. The growth of working memory is an integral part of this process (Adams & Gathercole, 2000).

Lieven, Behrens, Speares, and Tomasello (2003) recorded a 2-year-old child learning English using extremely dense taping intervals: 5 hours per week for 6 weeks. To investigate this child's constructional creativity, all her utterances produced during the last one-hour taping session at the end of the 6-week period were designated as target utterances. Then, for each target utterance, there was a search for similar utterances produced by the child (not the mother) in the previous 6 weeks of taping. The main goal was thus to determine for each utterance recorded on the final day of the study what kinds of syntactic operations were necessary for its production, that is to say, in what ways did the child have to modify things she had previously said (her stored linguistic experience) to produce the thing she was now saying. We may call these operations *usage-based syntactic operations* since they explicitly indicate that the child does not put together each of her utterances from scratch, morpheme by morpheme, but rather, she puts together her utterances from a motley assortment of different kinds of preexisting psycholinguistic units.

What was found by this procedure was that (a) about two-thirds of the multiword utterances produced on the target day were exact verbatim repetitions of utterances the child had said before (only about one-third were novel utterances); (b) of the novel multiword utterances, about three-quarters consisted of repetition of some part of a previously used utterance with only one small change, for example, some new word was filled into a slot or added on to the beginning or end. For example, the child had said many hundreds of times previously *Where's the _____?* and on the target tape she produced the novel utterance *Where's the butter?* The majority of the item-based, utterance-level constructions that the child used on the last day of the study had been used by the child many times during the previous 6 weeks; (c) only about one-quarter of the novel multiword utterances on the last tape (a total of 5% of all utterances during the hour) differed from things this child had said before in more than one way. These mostly involved the combination of filling in and adding onto an established utterance-level construction, but there were several utterances that seemed to be novel in more complex ways.

There was also very high functional consistency across different uses of this child's utterance-level constructions, that is, the child filled a given slot with basically the same kind or kinds of linguistic items or phrases across the entire 6-week period of the study. Based on these findings, we might say that children have three basic options for producing an utterance on a particular occasion of use (1) they might retrieve a functionally appropriate concrete expression and just say it as they have heard it said; (2) they might retrieve an utterance-level construction and simultaneously "tweak" it to fit the current communicative situation by filling a new constituent into a slot in the item-based construction, adding a new constituent onto the beginning or end of an utterance-level construction or expression, or inserting a new constituent into the middle of an utterance-level construction or expression; or (3) they might produce an utterance by combining constituent schemas without using an utterance-level construction on the basis of various kinds of pragmatic principles governing the ordering of old and new information.

These processes of utterance production may be called usage-based syntactic operations because the child does not begin with words and morphemes and glue them together with contentless rules; rather, she starts with already constructed pieces of language of various shapes, sizes, and degrees of abstraction (and whose internal complexities she may control to varying degrees), and then "cuts and pastes" these together in a way appropriate to the current communicative situation. It is important to note in this metaphor that to cut and paste effectively, a speaker is always making sure that the functions of the various pieces fit together functionally in the intended manner—one does not cut and paste indiscriminately in a word-processing document but in ways that fit. These processes may also work at the level of utterance constituents and their internal structure.

Conclusions

Acquiring a language is one of the most complicated tasks facing developing children. To become competent users of natural language, children must, at the very least, be able to comprehend communicative intentions as expressed in utterances; segment communicative intentions and ongoing speech and so extract individual words from these utterances; create linguistic schemas with slots; mark syntactic roles in item-based constructions; form abstract constructions across these schemas via analogy; perform distributional analyses to form paradigmatic categories; learn to take their current listener's perspective into account in both forming and choosing appropriately among conventional nominal and clausal constructions; learn to comprehend and express different modalities and negation (speaker attitude); acquire competence with complex constructions containing two or more predicates; learn to manage conversations and narratives, keeping track of referents over long stretches of discourse; cut and paste together stored linguistic units to produce particular utterances appropriate to the current communicative context; and on and on.

There are no fully adequate theoretical accounts of how young children do all of this. One problem has been that quite often the study of language acquisition has been cut off from the study of children's other cognitive and social skills with linguistic theories that barely make reference to these other skills. But in the current view, our best hope for unraveling some of the mysteries of language acquisition rests with approaches that incorporate multiple factors, that is, with approaches that incorporate not only some explicit linguistic model, but also the full range of biological, cultural, and psycholinguistic processes involved. Specifically, it has been argued here that children need to be able (a) to read the intentions of others to acquire the productive use of meaningful linguistic symbols and constructions and (b) to find patterns in the way people use symbols and thereby to construct the grammatical dimensions of language. The outstanding theoretical question in the field is whether, in addition, children's language learning also incorporates an innate universal grammar and, if so, what functions this additional element might serve.

In the meantime, there is much to be done empirically. We know very little about how children segment the communicative intentions behind utterances into their subcomponents. We know very little about how children form analogies across complex linguistic constructions. Perhaps the weakest part of all theories of language acquisition is how children come to constrain the generalizations that they make to just those generalizations that are conventional in their linguistic community. And how children use their mind-reading skills to take into account listener perspective is only now being seriously studied. The utterance production process is also one that requires much more intensive investigation. In general, the way forward in the study of language acquisition involves both more intensive empirical investigations of particular phenomena and more breadth in the range of theoretical and methodological tools utilized.

References

Abbot-Smith, K., Lieven, E., & Tomasello, M. (2001). What children do and do not do with ungrammatical word orders. *Cognitive Development, 16,* 1–14.

Adams, A. M., & Gathercole, S. E. (2000). Limitations in working memory: Implications for language development. *International Journal of Language and Communication Disorders, 35,* 95–116.

Akhtar, N. (1999). Acquiring basic word order: Evidence for data-driven learning of syntactic structure. *Journal of Child Language, 26,* 339–356.

Akhtar, N., & Tomasello, M. (1997). Young children's productivity with word order and verb morphology. *Developmental Psychology, 33,* 952–965.

Allen, S. E. M. (1996). *Aspects of argument structure acquisition in Inuktitut.* Amsterdam: Benjamins.

Allen, S. E. M., & Crago, M. B. (1996). Early passive acquisition in Inuktitut. *Journal of Child Language, 23,* 129–156.

Barlow, M., & Kemmer, S. (Eds.). (2000). *Usage based models of language acquisition.* Stanford, CA: CSLI Publications.

Barrett, M. (1982). The holophrastic hypothesis: Conceptual and empirical issues. *Cognition, 11,* 47–76.

Barton, M., & Tomasello, M. (1994). The rest of the family: The role of fathers and siblings in early language development. In C. Gallaway & B. Richards (Eds.), *Input and interaction in language acquisition* (pp. 109–134). Cambridge: Cambridge University Press.

Bates, E., Bretherton, I., & Snyder, L. (1988). *From first words to grammar: Individual differences and dissociable mechanisms.* Cambridge: Cambridge University Press.

Bates, E., & MacWhinney, B. (1982). A functionalist approach to grammatical development. In E. Wanner & L. Gleitman (Eds.), *Language acquisition: The state of the art.* Cambridge: Cambridge University Press.

Bates, E., & MacWhinney, B. (1989). Functionalism and the competition model. In B. MacWhinney & E. Bates (Eds.), *The cross-linguistic study of sentence processing.* Cambridge: Cambridge University Press.

Bates, E., MacWhinney, B., Caselli, C., Devoscovi, A., Natale, F., & Venza, V. (1984). A cross-linguistic study of the development of sentence comprehension strategies. *Child Development, 55,* 341–354.

Bauer, P. (1996). What do infants recall of their lives? Memory for specific events by 1- to 2-year-olds. *American Psychological Association, 51,* 29–41.

Behrens, H. (1998). *Where does the information go?* Paper presented at Max-Planck-Institute Workshop on Argument Structure, Nijmegen, The Netherlands.

Berman, R. (1982). Verb-pattern alternation: The interface of morphology, syntax, and semantics in Hebrew child language. *Journal of Child Language, 9,* 169–191.

Berman, R. (1993). Marking verb transitivity in Hebrew-speaking children. *Journal of Child Language, 20,* 641–670.

Bloom, L. (1973). *One word at a time.* The Hague, The Netherlands: Mouton.

Bloom, L. (1992). *Language development from 2 to 3.* Cambridge: Cambridge University Press.

Bloom, L., Tinker, E., & Margulis, C. (1993). The words children learn: Evidence for a verb bias in early vocabularies. *Cognitive Development, 8,* 431–450.

Bohannon, N., & Stanowicz, L. (1988). The issue of negative evidence: Adult responses to children's language errors. *Developmental Psychology, 24,* 684–689.

Bowerman, M. (1982). Reorganizational processes in lexical and syntactic development. In L. Gleitman & E. Wanner (Eds.), *Language acquisition: The state of the art.* Cambridge: Cambridge University Press.

Bowerman, M. (1988). The "no negative evidence" problem: How do children avoid constructing an overgeneral grammar. In J. A. Hawkins (Ed.), *Explaining language universals.* Oxford, England: Basil Blackwell.

Bowerman, M. (1996). Learning how to structure space for language: A cross-linguistic perspective. In P. Bloom, M. Peterson, L. Nadel & M. Garret (Eds.), *Language and space.* Cambridge, MA: MIT Press.

Braine, M. (1963). The ontogeny of English phrase structure. *Language, 39,* 1–14.

Braine, M. (1971). On two types of models of the internalization of grammars. In D. I. Slobin (Ed.), *The ontogenesis of grammar.* New York: Academic Press.

Braine, M. (1976). Children's first word combinations. *Monographs of the Society for Research in Child Development, 41*(1).

Braine, M., & Brooks, P. (1995). Verb-argument structure and the problem of avoiding an overgeneral grammar. In M. Tomasello & W. Merriman (Eds.), *Beyond names for things: Young children's acquisition of verbs.* Hillsdale, NJ: Erlbaum.

Bridges, A. (1984). Preschool children's comprehension of agency. *Journal of Child Language, 11,* 593–610.

Brooks, P., & Tomasello, M. (1999). How young children constrain their argument structure constructions. *Language, 75,* 720–738.

Brooks, P., Tomasello, M., Lewis, L., & Dodson, K. (1999). Children's overgeneralization of fixed transitivity verbs: The entrenchment hypothesis. *Child Development, 70,* 1325–1337.

Brown, A., & Kane, M. (1988). Preschool children can learn to transfer: Learning to learn and learning from example. *Cognitive Psychology, 20,* 493–523.

Brown, R. (1973). *A first language: The early stages.* Cambridge, MA: Harvard University Press.

Brown, R., & Hanlon, C. (1970). Derivational complexity and order of acquisition in child speech. In J. R. Hayes (Ed.), *Cognition and the development of language.* New York: Wiley.

Bruner, J. (1975). The ontogenesis of speech acts. *Journal of Child Language, 2,* 1–20.

Budwig, N. (1990). The linguistic marking of nonprototypical agency: An exploration into children's use of passives. *Linguistics, 28,* 1221–1252.

Budwig, N., Stein, S., & O'Brien, C. (2001). Non-agent subjects in early child language: A crosslinguistic comparison. In K. Nelson, A. Aksu-Ko, & C. Johnson (Eds.), *Children's language: Vol. 11. Interactional contributions to language development.* Mahwah, NJ: Erlbaum.

Bybee, J. (1985). *Morphology: A study of the relation between meaning and form.* Amsterdam: Benjamins.

Bybee, J. (1995). Regular morphology and the lexicon. *Language and Cognitive Processes, 10,* 425–455.

Cameron-Faulkner, T., Lieven, E., & Tomasello, M. (2003). A construction based analysis of child directed speech. *Cognitive Science, 27,* 843–873.

Campbell, A., & Tomasello, M. (2001). The acquisition of English dative constructions. *Applied Psycholinguistics, 22,* 253–267.

Childers, J., & Tomasello, M. (2001). The role of pronouns in young children's acquisition of the English transitive construction. *Developmental Psychology, 37,* 739–748.

Clancy, P. (2000). The lexicon in interaction: Developmental origins of preferred argument structure in Korean. In J. DuBois (Ed.), *Preferred argument structure: Grammar as architecture for function.* Amsterdam: Benjamins.

Clark, E. V. (1982). The young word maker: A case study of innovation in the child's lexicon. In E. Wanner & L. R. Gleitman (Eds.), *Language acquisition: The state of the art.* New York: Cambridge University Press.

Clark, E. V. (1987). The principle of contrast: A constraint on language acquisition. In B. MacWhinney (Ed.), *Mechanisms of language acquisition.* Hillsdale, NJ: Erlbaum.

Croft, W. (1991). *Syntactic categories and grammatical relations: The cognitive organization of information.* Chicago: University of Chicago Press.

Croft, W. (2001). *Radical construction grammar.* Oxford: Oxford University Press.

Dabrowska, E. (2001). Learning a morphological system without a default: The Polish genitive. *Journal of Child Language, 28,* 545–574.

Demuth, K. (1989). Maturation and the acquisition of the Sesotho passive. *Language, 65,* 56–80.

Demuth, K. (1990). Subject, topic, and Sesotho passive. *Journal of Child Language, 17,* 67–84.

DeVilliers, J., & DeVilliers, P. (1973). Development of the use of word order in comprehension. *Journal of Psycholinguistic Research, 2,* 331–341.

Dodson, K., & Tomasello, M. (1998). Acquiring the transitive construction in English: The role of animacy and pronouns. *Journal of Child Language, 25,* 555–574.

Elman, J. L., Bates, E., Johnson, M., Karmiloff-Smith, A., Parisi, D., & Plunkett, K. (1996). *Rethinking innateness: A connectionist perspective on development.* Cambridge, MA: MIT Press.

Erreich, A. (1984). Learning how to ask: Patterns of inversion in yes-no and wh-questions. *Journal of Child Language, 11,* 579–592.

Erteschik-Shir, N. (1979). Discourse constraints on dative movements. In T. Givón (Ed.), *Syntax and semantic 12: Discourse and syntax.* New York: Academic Press.

Farrar, J. (1992). Negative evidence and grammatical morpheme acquisition. *Developmental Psychology, 28,* 90–98.

Fillmore, C. (1988). The mechanisms of construction grammar. *Berkeley Linguistics Society, 14,* 35–55.

Fillmore, C. (1989). Grammatical construction theory and the familiar dichotomies. In R. Dietrich & C. F. Graumann (Eds.), *Language processing in social context.* Amsterdam: North-Holland/Elsevier.

Fillmore, C., Kaye, P., & O'Conner, M. (1988). Regularity and idiomaticity in grammatical constructions: The case of let alone. *Language, 64,* 501–538.

Fisher, C. (1996). Structural limits on verb mapping: The role of analogy in children's interpretations of sentences. *Cognitive Psychology, 31,* 41–81.

Fisher, C. (2002). Structural limits on verb mapping: The role of abstract structure in 2½-year-old's interpretations of novel verbs. *Developmental Science, 5*(1), 55–64.

Fletcher, P. (1985). *A child's learning of English.* Oxford, England: Blackwell.

Galloway, C., & Richards, B. J. (1994). *Input and interaction in language acquisition.* Cambridge: Cambridge University Press.

Gathercole, V., Sebastián, E., & Soto, P. (1999). The early acquisition of Spanish verbal morphology: Across-the-board or piecemeal knowledge? *International Journal of Bilingualism, 3,* 133–182.

Gentner, D., & Markman, A. (1995). Similarity is like analogy: Structural alignment in comparison. In C. Cacciari (Ed.), *Similarity in language, thought and perception.* Brussels: BREPOLS.

Gentner, D., & Medina, J. (1998). Similarity and the development of rules. *Cognition, 65,* 263–297.

Givón, T. (1995). *Functionalism and grammar.* Amsterdam: Benjamins.

Goldberg, A. (1995). *Constructions: A construction grammar approach to argument structure.* Chicago: University of Chicago Press.

Gopnik, A., & Choi, S. (1995). Names, relational words, and cognitive development in English and Korean speakers: Nouns are not always learned before verbs. In M. Tomasello & W. E. Merriman (Eds.), *Beyond names for things: Young children's acquisition of verbs.* Hillsdale, NJ: Erlbaum.

Greenfield, P. M., & Smith, J. H. (1976). *The structure of communication in early language development.* New York: Academic Press.

Hakuta, K. (1982). Interaction between particles and word order in the comprehension and production of simple sentences in Japanese children. *Developmental Psychology, 18,* 62–76.

Hirsh-Pasek, K., & Golinkoff, R. M. (1991). Language comprehension: A new look at some old themes. In N. Krasnegor, D. Rumbaugh, M. Studdert-Kennedy, & R. Schiefelbusch (Eds.), *Biological and behavioral aspects of language acquisition.* Hillsdale, NJ: Erlbaum.

Hirsh-Pasek, K., & Golinkoff, R. M. (1996). *The origins of grammar: Evidence from early language comprehension.* Cambridge, MA: MIT Press.

Ingram, D., & Tyack, D. (1979). The inversion of subject NP and aux in children's questions. *Journal of Psycholinguistic Research, 4,* 333–341.

Israel, M., Johnson, C., & Brooks, P. J. (2000). From states to events: The acquisition of English passive participles. *Cognitive Linguistics, 11*(1/2), 103–129.

Kemmer, S. (1993). *The middle voice.* Amsterdam: Benjamins.

Klima, E., & Bellugi, U. (1966). Syntactic regularities in the speech of children. In J. Lyons & R. J. Wales (Eds.), *Psycholinguistic papers.* Edinburgh, Scotland: Edinburgh University Press.

Langacker, R. (1987). *Foundations of cognitive grammar* (Vol. 1). Stanford, CA: Stanford University Press.

Langacker, R. (1991). *Foundations of cognitive grammar* (Vol. 2). Stanford, CA: Stanford University Press.

Lieven, E., Behrens, H., Speares, J., & Tomasello, M. (2003). Early syntactic creativity: A usage based approach. *Journal of Child Language, 30,* 333–370.

Lieven, E., Pine, J., & Baldwin, G. (1997). Lexically-based learning and early grammatical development. *Journal of Child Language, 24,* 187–220.

Lieven, E., Pine, J., & Dresner-Barnes, H. (1992). Individual differences in early vocabulary development. *Journal of Child Language, 19,* 287–310.

Lindner, K. (2003). The development of sentence interpretation strategies in monolingual German-learning children with and without specific language impairment. *Linguistics, 41*(2), 213–254.

Maratsos, M., Gudeman, R., Gerard-Ngo, P., & DeHart, G. (1987). A study in novel word learning: The productivity of the causative. In B. MacWhinney (Ed.), *Mechanisms of language acquisition.* Hillsdale, NJ: Erlbaum.

Marchman, V., & Bates, E. (1994). Continuity in lexical and morphological development: A test of the critical mass hypothesis. *Journal of Child Language, 21,* 339–366.

McCune, L. (1992). First words: A dynamic systems view. In C. Ferguson, L. Menn, & C. Stoel-Gammon (Eds.), *Phonological development: Models, research, and implications.* Parkton, MD: York Press.

McNeill, D. (1966). The creation of language by children. In J. Lyons & R. J. Wales (Eds.), *Psycholinguistic papers: Proceedings of the 1966 Edinburgh Conference.* Edinburgh, Scotland: Edinburgh University Press.

Munakata, Y., McClelland, J. L., Johnson, M. H., & Siegler, R. S. (1997). Rethinking infant knowledge: Toward an adaptive process account of successes and failures in object permanence tasks. *Psychological Review, 104,* 686–713.

Naigles, L. (1990). Children use syntax to learn verb meanings. *Journal of Child Language, 17,* 357–374.

Nelson, K. (1985). *Making sense: The acquisition of shared meaning.* New York: Academic Press.

Ninio, A. (1992). The relation of children's single word utterances to single word utterances in the input. *Journal of Child Language, 19,* 87–110.

Ninio, A. (1993). On the fringes of the system: Children's acquisition of syntactically isolated forms at the onset of speech. *First Language, 13,* 291–314.

Pawley, A., & Syder, F. (1983). Two puzzles for linguistic theory. In J. Richards & R. Smith (Eds.), *Language and communication.* New York: Longman.

Piaget, J. (1952). *The origins of intelligence in children.* New York: Norton. (Original work published 1935)

Pine, J., & Lieven, E. (1993). Reanalysing rote-learned phrases: Individual differences in the transition to multi word speech. *Journal of Child Language, 20,* 551–571.

Pine, J., Lieven, E., & Rowland, G. (1998). Comparing different models of the development of the English verb category. *Linguistics, 36,* 4–40.

Pinker, S. (1981). A theory of graph comprehension. In R. Freedle (Ed.), *Artificial intelligence and the future of testing.* Hillsdale, NJ: Erlbaum.

Pinker, S. (1984). *Language learnability and language development.* Cambridge, MA: Harvard University Press.

Pinker, S. (1989). *Learnability and cognition: The acquisition of verb-argument structure.* Cambridge, MA: Harvard University Press.

Pinker, S. (1999). *Words and rules.* New York: Morrow Press.

Pizzuto E., & Caselli, M. C. (1992). The acquisition of Italian morphology: Implications for models of language development. *Journal of Child Language, 19,* 491–557.

Pye, C., & Quixtan Poz, P. (1988). Precocious passives and antipassives in Quiche Mayan. *Papers and Reports on Child Language Development, 27,* 71–80.

Rispoli, M. (1994). Structural dependency and the acquisition of grammatical relations. In Y. Levy (Ed.), *Other children, other languages: Issues in the theory of language acquisition.* Hillsdale, NJ: Erlbaum.

Rispoli, M. (1998). Patterns of pronoun case error. *Journal of Child Language, 25,* 533–544.

Roberts, K. (1983). Comprehension and production of word order in stage 1. *Child Development, 54,* 443–449.

Rowland, C., & Pine, J. M. (2000). Subject-auxiliary inversion errors and wh-question acquisition: "What children do know?" *Journal of Child Language, 27,* 157–181.

Rubino, R., & Pine, J. (1998). Subject-verb agreement in Brazilian Portugese: What low error rates hide. *Journal of Child Language, 25,* 35–60.

Savage, C., Lieven, E., Theakston, A., & Tomasello, M. (2003). Testing the abstractness of young childrens linguistic representations: Lexical and structural priming of syntactic constructions? *Developmental Science, 6,* 557–567.

Serrat, E. (1997). *Acquisition of verb category in Catalan.* Unpublished doctoral dissertation, Barcelona, Spain.

Slobin, D. (1982). Universal and particular in the acquisition of language. In L. Gleitman & E. Wanner (Eds.), *Language acquisition: The state of the art.* Cambridge: Cambridge University Press.

Slobin, D. (1985). Crosslinguistic evidence for the language-making capacity. In D. I. Slobin (Ed.), *The crosslinguistic study of language acquisition: Vol. 2. Theoretical issues.* Hillsdale, NJ: Erlbaum.

Slobin, D., & Bever, T. (1982). Children use canonical sentence schemas: A crosslinguistic study of word order and inflections. *Cognition, 12,* 229–265.

Snow, C. E., & Ferguson, C. A. (1977). *Talking to children.* Cambridge: Cambridge University Press.

Stoll, S. (1998). The acquisition of Russian aspect. *First Language, 18,* 351–378.

Sudhalter, V., & Braine, M. (1985). How does comprehension of passives develop? A comparison of actional and experiential verbs. *Journal of Child Language, 12,* 455–470.

Suzman, S. M. (1985). Learning the passive in Zulu. *Papers and Reports on Child Language Development, 24,* 131–137.

Tardif, T. (1996). Nouns are not always learned before verbs: Evidence from Mandarin speakers' early vocabularies. *Developmental Psychology, 32*(3), 492–504.

Tomasello, M. (1992). *First verbs: A case study of early grammatical development.* Cambridge: Cambridge University Press.

Tomasello, M. (1998). Reference: Intending that others jointly attend. *Pragmatics and Cognition, 6,* 229–244.

Tomasello, M. (1999). *The cultural origins of human cognition.* Cambridge, MA: Harvard University Press.

Tomasello, M. (2000). Do young children have adult syntactic competence? *Cognition, 74,* 209–253.

Tomasello, M. (2003). *Constructing a language: A usage-based theory of language acquisition.* Cambridge, MA: Harvard University Press.

Tomasello, M., Akhtar, N., Dodson, K., & Rekau, L. (1997). Differential productivity in young children's use of nouns and verbs. *Journal of Child Language, 24,* 373–387.

Weist, R. (1983). Prefix versus suffix information processing in the comprehension of tense and aspect. *Journal of Child Language, 10,* 85–96.

Wittek, A., & Tomasello, M. (2005). German-speaking children's productivity with syntactic constructions and case morphology: Local cues help locally. *First Language, 25,* 103–125.

Chapter 9

Conceptual Development

SUSAN A. GELMAN and CHARLES W. KALISH

There are more things in heaven and earth, Horatio,
Than are dreamt of in your philosophy.

—*Hamlet,* Act I, Scene V

Concepts organize experience. When an infant smiles at a human face, a 2-year-old points to the family pet and says "Doggy!," a 10-year-old plays a card-game, or a scientist identifies a fossil, each is making use of concepts. One hallmark of human cognition is that we organize experience *flexibly*—at different levels of abstraction, and in cross-cutting ways. Although theorists often equate concepts and categories (concepts are the mental representations that correspond to categories of things in the world, such as *dogs* or *chairs*; Oakes & Rakison, 2003), concepts also include properties (*red*), events or states (*running*), individuals (*Mama*), and abstract ideas (*time*). Concepts are generally understood to be the building blocks of ideas; thus, to form the thought "Fido is a happy dog," a child must possess the constituent concepts. At the same time, concepts are embedded in larger knowledge structures. An important goal of this chapter is to provide a framework for understanding how the full range of human concepts develops.

Background and Overview

Although concepts deeply reflect our experiences of structure in the world, concepts do not reduce fully to world structure. Certainly there is structure to the world, and there

Preparation of this chapter was supported by NICHD grant RO1 HD36043 from NICHD to the first author. We thank Sandra Waxman for helpful discussions and Deanna Kuhn for detailed comments on an earlier draft.

are important perceptual clues that correlate with concepts. Rosch (1978) showed that object categories capture feature clusters—for example, the distinction between birds and mammals is overdetermined: birds (generally) have wings, feathers, and beaks, whereas mammals (generally) have legs, fur, and mouths. However, it would be a mistake to equate concepts with experience. Instead, concepts are *interpretations* of experience. Piaget illustrated this vividly by showing us how different interpretations of even mundane experiences are possible: what we identify as the same object over time could instead be construed as a series of distinct objects; what we view as unthinking and inert (such as a stone) could instead be construed as living and feeling.

A related point is that concept learning includes a crucial inductive component. That is, a concept extends beyond an instance presented at a given point in time, and includes other instances (in the case of categories) or other manifestations over time (in the case of individuals). One of the inductive problems children face is how to extend a concept to novel instances (e.g., if I tell you that this is a hamster, how do you decide what other instances are also hamsters?). Another of the inductive problems children face is figuring out when to use concepts. For example, if a child sees her pet hamster eating a lettuce leaf, is this an idiosyncratic event, or an event that can be applied to future instances? If the latter, has she learned something about her hamster, about hamsters in general, or about animals in general? Thus, another theme of this chapter is that concepts entail active inductive processes, and that human heuristics, frameworks, and biases influence the form of concepts that children develop.

WHY CONCEPTUAL DEVELOPMENT IS IMPORTANT

Concepts play a central role in children's cognition. They are an efficient means of representing and storing experience (obviating the need to track each and every individual interaction or encounter), and they encourage people to extend knowledge and learn about the world by means of inductive inferences (e.g., E. E. Smith, 1989). Children's memory, reasoning, problem solving, and word learning all powerfully reflect their concepts (Bruner, Olver, & Greenfield, 1966; Rakison & Oakes, 2003). By studying concepts, we learn about the representation of experience and about reasoning by induction.

Studies of conceptual development also enable a detailed portrait of children's knowledge and beliefs about the world. Equally important, the study of concepts allows us to examine numerous issues at the heart of the study of cognitive development: Are there innate concepts? Are cognitive systems modular? Can complex concepts emerge out of perceptually based associative learning mechanisms? How domain-general versus domain-specific is human cognition? Does children's thinking undergo qualitative reorganizations with age? These questions are not unique to the study of conceptual development, but studying conceptual development can provide unique insights into these questions.

Finally, understanding children's concepts has implications for many other developmental issues, both basic and applied. For example, in the field of education, providing children with appropriate instruction requires first understanding their conceptual errors, in order to revise misconceptions rather than superimpose new ways of understanding on these misconceptions (Carey, 1986). The need to do so becomes evident when trying to teach children (and adults!) evolutionary theory. Children first need to *unlearn* that categories are stable, unchanging, and fixed, before they can fully grasp that species can evolve (Evans, 2000; Mayr, 1991).

CURRENT APPROACHES TO CHILDREN'S CONCEPTS

Currently there are three broad theoretical approaches to understanding concept acquisition, dating back to long-standing philosophical debates: nativist, empiricist, and *naïve* theory approaches.

Nativist accounts range from innate attentional biases due to perceptual limits in the infant (Mandler, 2004), to the possibility of innate concepts of *cause, animate,* and so on (Spelke, 1994), to the extreme claim that all lexicalized concepts are innate (including *dog, cup, car;* Fodor, 1981). Innate conceptual structure may also be characterized as a set of skeletal principles (R. Gelman & Williams, 1998) or biases that provide initial conditions for conceptual development but may be modified, and even superseded, during development (Gopnik, Meltzoff, & Kuhl, 1999).

Empiricist accounts assume that knowledge derives from our senses. Concepts are therefore either direct representations of perceptual/sensory experience, or combinations of such experiences. Theories of similarity provide formal empiricist accounts of concept representation and acquisition (see Hahn & Ramscar, 2001; Rakison & Oakes, 2003; Sloutsky, 2003). Empiricist approaches have had a resurgence in recent years, in part due to the demonstration that infants can track low-level statistical cues with much greater accuracy than had been thought (Saffran, Aslin, & Newport, 1996), and in part due to new empiricist models that provide a more detailed and realistic appreciation of children's concepts (Sloutsky & Fisher, 2004; Yoshida & Smith, 2003).

Naïve theory approaches come in a wide variety. The shared commitment is to some inferential processes of conceptual development. Roughly, concepts are acquired based on their meaningful relations with existing concepts and beliefs. In most cases, these inferential processes are seen as supplements to either nativist or associationist mechanisms or both. That is, theory-based views are compatible with some amount of innate structure. However, the claim is that innate structure is supplemented and revised in the face of evidence and attempts to explain and make predictions. Nature may provide initial conditions or general constraints, but there is room for substantial conceptual development and change (R. Gelman, 2002). Theory-based views also admit processes of association-based learning (S. A. Gelman & Medin, 1993; Keil, Smith, Simons, & Levin, 1998). Intuitive theories connect with data. People experience surprising outcomes, notice new connections, and realize failures of predictions. Associations are therefore important data for theory-building.

Theory-based views are often taken as committed to the position that children are little scientists (or scientists are big children, Gopnik et al., 1999). Different strands of theory-based approaches take this connection more or less literally, though all acknowledge important differences between scientists and children in the *process* of constructing theories (see Gopnik & Wellman, 1994). The basic point may be that just as scientists have means of forming new concepts that go beyond maturation and association learning, so too do laypeople—including children. A way of posing the central research question for theory-based approaches is to ask whether the kinds of thinking demonstrated by scientists and other experts are unprecedented in everyday experience, or whether such "advanced" forms of thinking are somewhat continuous with basic processes of conceptual development. Research in the field often takes the form of demonstrating that associationist or maturational processes are not sufficient to account for some aspect of cognitive development, and thus theory-building must be admitted.

The approach we assume in this chapter is a naïve theory approach because we find that it is best able to account for the widest range of evidence. However, ideas from both nativist and empiricist traditions continue to have important influences. For example, the theory approach assumes some innate starting points (Carey & Spelke, 1994) as well as the importance of associative mechanisms. Likewise, some (though not all) who espouse an empiricist or associationist approach recognize the need for innate constraints to get the system off the ground (Rakison, 2003a). And anyone who posits innate mechanisms also acknowledges the need for appropriate environmental input and support, as well as the mechanisms to enable environmental learning (Chomsky, 1975). We find most merit in a framework that assumes some role for each of these approaches. Specifically, the naïve theory approach assumes (1) important innate frameworks to give children a conceptual grounding, (2) sophisticated associationist and statistical learning procedures to acquire new information and detect regularities in the environment, as well as (3) theory-building impulses and capacities, to enable fundamental reorganizations of the input over developmental time.

Conceptual Diversity

What is involved in learning a concept? This question is difficult to answer in part because not all concepts are alike. How college students acquired a concept of "red triangles" in a classic learning experiment of the 1950s would appear to differ in important ways from how infants acquire a concept of animacy. At minimum, the concepts children learn in the first few years of life include (but are not limited to):

- Concepts corresponding to words, including not just concrete nouns (dog) but also mass nouns (water), abstract nouns (furniture), collective nouns (family), verbs (jump), adjectives (good, happy, alive), and a range of other word types (three, because, mine).
- Concepts reflected in grammatical usage (e.g., singular versus plural; gender; Whorf, 1956).
- Ontological distinctions that may or may not be encoded in language but lead to important predictions (e.g., animate versus inanimate entities).
- Concepts for individuals (including significant people, animals, or even individual objects such as a favorite blanket).
- Systems for organizing concepts with respect to one another (e.g., hierarchies; scripts).

Concepts vary from one another in content (e.g., natural kinds versus artifacts), process (e.g., learned explicitly in school versus implicitly in ordinary interactions), structure (e.g., basic versus superordinate level), and function (e.g., quick identification versus inductive inferences). Strikingly, studies of these varied concepts often reach rather different conclusions regarding children's skills and abilities.

We review this conceptual variety by considering three key contrasts that have far-reaching implications for how children reason. Specifically, we consider: concepts encoded in language versus those that are not encoded in language; natural kinds versus arbitrary groupings; and individuals versus categories. In no case are we proposing developmental *dichotomies* (e.g., children can't do X but they can do Y). Rather, in each case, children have access to multiple sorts of concepts, but the nature of the concept influences processing.

CONCEPTS ENCODED IN LANGUAGE VERSUS THOSE THAT ARE NOT

Many concepts correspond to a word in a language (e.g., *shoes*), whereas others do not (e.g., *objects that begin with the letter* s). The former are also called "lexicalized" concepts. Generally, we can assume that lexicalized concepts are important to speakers of the language: they are shared by a community and passed down from one generation to the next. However, important concepts are not necessarily lexicalized. For example, the concept "living thing" is rarely lexicalized across the world's languages (Waxman, in press).

There has been an upswing in research on the role of language in conceptual development (e.g., Bowerman & Levinson, 2001; Gentner & Goldin-Meadow, 2003). A classic question is how language influences concepts. Piaget's proposal that language is simply a vehicle for thought is no longer tenable. Nor do concepts require a conventional language system: witness the impressive conceptual abilities of preverbal infants, nonhuman primates, and deaf children with no language input (Goldin-Meadow, 2003; Tomasello, 1999). Rather, we must ask about the nature of the relation between words and concepts, and how they are coordinated in development.

One starting point is that speakers of different languages possess different concepts, particularly early in development. For example, whereas English distinguishes containment (in) versus support (on) relations, Korean distinguishes loose-fitting containment (*nehta*) versus tight-fitting containment (*kkita*). The relevant developmental evidence is that children, from their earliest word productions, use spatial language in a manner that conforms to the system presented by their language (Bowerman & Choi, 2003). Thus, English-speaking children and Korean-speaking children use spatial terms in cross-cutting ways, thereby apparently demonstrating contrasting conceptual frameworks.

One question raised by this work is whether the speakers of the two languages have acquired *only* the language-relevant system (i.e., support for language influencing initial concepts), or instead whether they have access to a wider range of spatial relations, including those of the other language, but choose to use only the conventional ones when talking because language is a conventional system (a weaker claim, according to which language influences "thinking for speaking"; Slobin, 1996). Recent work with adults provides more support for the first interpretation. When English-speaking adults are given a task that requires them to group spatial relations in the Korean way (i.e., loose- versus tight-fitting), they have great difficulty (McDonough, Choi, & Mandler, 2003). Interestingly, 5-month-old infants exposed to English were able to categorize both contrasts (Hespos & Spelke, 2004). It appears that children are initially more open to a wider range of conceptual possibilities, which become narrowed as a function of language experience.

Relatedly, speakers of different languages seem to notice different aspects of experience, and to draw conceptual boundaries differently from one another. For example, Lucy and Gaskins (2003) studied speakers of Yucatec Mayan, who use a classifier system such that different-shaped things can receive the same name but with a different classifier attached. In Yucatec, the word for banana, banana leaf, and banana tree are all the same root word, varying only in the classifier. This pattern contrasts with the English system of naming, for which shape is a fairly good predictor of how a count noun is used (e.g., bananas are all crescent-shaped). Correspondingly, when asked to group objects on the basis of either shape or substance in a nonlinguistic sorting task, English speakers are more likely to use shape whereas Yucatec Mayan speakers are more likely to use substance.

Similarly, Imai and Gentner (1997) and Yoshida and Smith (2003) found that Japanese-speaking children draw the boundary between objects and substances differently than English-speaking children. Whereas both English- and Japanese-speaking children agree that a complex object (such as a clock) is an individual and a continuous boundless mass (such as milk) is a substance, they differ when it comes to simple objects. A molded piece of plastic, for example, would be an object for the English-speaker but a substance for the Japanese-speaker. These findings do not suggest radically different ontologies for speakers of English and Japanese, but rather subtle effects at the margins.

One difficult question that remains is whether language can effect change or just direct attention. For example, can language create concepts that weren't there to begin with? Or does language serve to draw attention and highlight available concepts? Boroditsky (2001) shows that, for adults, time concepts in Chinese are conceptualized differently than time concepts in English, in ways that can be traced to differences in how English- and Chinese-speakers *talk* about time (either horizontally or vertically, respectively). However, she also finds that these differences can be readily reversed with a simple priming task, thus suggesting that the language effects are not deeply entrenched.

An example of the difficulty determining the effects of language can be seen by considering the effects of labeling on inductive inferences. Some researchers have proposed that hearing the word "bird" for a wide variety of dissimilar birds (hummingbirds, eagles, ostriches) signals to the child that something other than surface similarity must bind these instances together (Hallett, 1991; Mayr, 1991). On this view, labels have a powerful causal force in directing children to look for underlying similarities that category members share. Consistent with this view, experimental work with children demonstrates that they draw more inferences to items that share a label than to instances that do not (S. A. Gelman & Markman, 1986; Jaswal, 2004; Welder & Graham, 2001) and more generally respond differently to items that are labeled than to items that are not (Markman & Hutchinson, 1984; Waxman & Markow, 1995; Xu, 1999). Moreover, hearing a label for a concept does provoke a more stable, immutable construal (e.g., a person who is "a carrot-eater" is assumed to eat carrots more consistently and persistently than someone who "eats carrots whenever she can"; S. A. Gelman & Heyman, 1999).

However, these findings do not unambiguously locate the source of the labeling effect. Is the relevant factor the label per se, or does the label work as a cue because it activates other assumptions, such as essentialism? We would argue the latter. One problem with assigning too central a role to language is that not all names promote inductive inferences. Children learn homonyms (Lily as a name versus lily as a flower), adjectives (sleepy), and nonkind nouns (pet), and these words do not seem to work in the same way as category labels such as "bird." When learning novel words, children do not automatically assume that the words promote inferences, if perceptual cues compete (S. A. Gelman, 2003).

These examples suggest that language may provide important cues to children regarding their concepts, without necessarily being the mechanism by which concepts emerge to begin with. Despite this caveat, there is also reason to suspect that language may play a broader role in conceptual change. Spelke (2003) argues that language may provide a mechanism for acquiring concepts that go beyond those innately specified.

She notes that innate concepts in humans are highly similar and overlapping with innate concepts in a range of other species: object constancy, number tracking, and so on. What seems to distinguish humans from nonhumans is the ease with which we combine concepts across domains. For example, in navigating space, we can combine geometric concepts (e.g., "to the left") with nongeometric concepts (e.g., "blue") to arrive at novel combinations ("to the left of the blue wall"). Strikingly, preverbal infants and nonhuman animals seem to lack the ability to construct such cross-domain concepts. When faced with a task that requires this sort of conceptual combination, only language-using humans can solve it. In further studies, Spelke found that manipulating the use of language (either training children on a new linguistic expression, or preventing internal or external use of language in adults) directly affects a person's capacity to use these combinations.

NATURAL KINDS VERSUS ARBITRARY GROUPINGS

Kalish (2002) describes several senses in which concepts may be "natural": they may refer to objects that are naturally occurring (versus construed by humans), they may possess clusters of co-occurring features (rather than single, arbitrary features), or they may be acquired easily and automatically (rather than via formal instruction). One foundational sense of "natural" is the realist assumption that certain categories truly exist in the world—they are discovered (not invented); they carve up nature at its joints. Just as an individual tiger has a reality beyond our perception of it, so too does the *category* of tigers. Natural kinds contrast with artificial or nominal kinds. Nominal kinds are arbitrary collections having no basis outside the mind. The natural/nominal distinction is often traced back to Locke (1671/1959) and is at the center of contemporary philosophy of language, particularly causal theories of reference (Kripke, 1972; Putnam, 1975).

Much of the older developmental work seemed to treat concepts as nominal kinds. Inhelder and Piaget (1964), for example, thought about categories as starting with a rule, and extending via logical application of that rule. A category might be something like "green triangles," and the challenge for children was to hold onto that rule and apply it with logical precision (a challenge that young children find quite difficult). In contrast, natural kinds do not seem to fit that model. Rather than starting with a defining rule, a natural kind category is a placeholder for properties that have not yet been learned.

One goal of more recent research is to explore when in development children begin to form natural kind concepts. One theory is that children's early concepts are simple tabulations of feature co-occurrences, and that only with the development of content knowledge and causal intuitions do children seek the explanations behind the experiential groupings (e.g., Quine, 1977). Keil (1989) describes this as the doctrine of "original sim" (where "sim" is short for "similarity"). He notes that although there is evidence for developmental shifts in conceptual representation, it is also the case that young children have very basic and fundamental intuitions about conceptual kinds (Keil et al., 1998).

An alternative perspective is that children start out assuming that concepts represent natural kinds, and only over time come to appreciate the arbitrary or conventional nature of some categories. S. A. Gelman and Kalish (1993) describe this position as "categorical realism": labels and kinds pick out real objectively significant groups. Some evidence for this position comes from Kalish's (1998) finding that young children are more likely to treat category membership as an objective matter of fact. Whereas adults treat the distinction between a pot and a can as an arbitrary convention, children seem to feel there is a real difference that needs to be identified. Adults accept that the distinction is a matter of convention, so that people in other cultures could legitimately form different concepts. Young children seem to feel there is a fact to the matter; different categorization practices are errors.

Even quite young children treat concepts as natural. S. A. Gelman (2003) describes the inordinate power that names have for children; to label something is to say something very deep about its nature (also Markman, 1989). Thus, if one member of a natural kind is found to have a novel property, children assume that other members of the kind will share the property. This kind of category-based induction is characteristic even of toddlers (S. A. Gelman & Coley, 1990; Jaswal & Markman, 2002; Welder & Graham, 2001), and extends to reasoning about categories in the social domain (Heyman & Gelman, 2000) and to children in varying cultural contexts (Diesendruck, 2001).

CATEGORIES VERSUS INDIVIDUALS

The study of concepts typically focuses on categories (e.g., dogs, chairs), but children also develop rich concepts of individuals. Among the most studied are the object concept (e.g., whether an infant realizes that an object continues to exist when out of sight) and the self-concept. Children are sensitive to linguistic differences that indicate whether an act of naming refers to a kind (e.g., dogs) or an individual (e.g., Fido; Hall, Waxman, & Bredart, 2003; Macnamara, 1982). For example, "This is a fep" implies a kind, whereas "This is Fep" implies an individual—especially if the entity is animate. One of the central intuitions underlying concepts of individuals is persistence across time and transformations. Individual identity may persist despite changes in characteristic properties (Gutheil & Rosengren, 1996) and even material composition (Hall, 1998). For example, if a doll wearing a distinctive green cloth cape is named "Daxy," and the doll is then moved to a new location and the distinctive cape is removed while a new doll is placed in the old location with the distinctive cape added, 3-year-olds report that the original doll—not the new doll—is Daxy (Sorrentino, 2001). Moreover, individual identity may persist across changes in category identity and labeling. Young children realized that a change in name did not necessarily signal a change in individual identity (Gutheil & Rosengren, 1996). Similarly, the same individual may change from a caterpillar to a butterfly (Rosengren, Gelman, Kalish, & McCormick, 1991). What is crucial to determining individual identity is historical path, not the location, appearance, or even name that was present at the original naming.

Critically, individual identity is not independent of categories; for an individual to persist over time, it would typically retain at least some kinds of category identity (fictional frogs turning into princes notwithstanding). Thus, a table ground to dust and reconstituted at some later time in a similar form is a new table. Categories that function as conditions for individual persistence are called "sortals," and are typically encoded in common nouns such as "dog" or "table" (Hirsch, 1982). Macnamara (1986) notes that sortals are required for individuating entities. For example, the question "How many?" makes no sense without supplying the sortal—how many *what* (e.g., dogs? legs? molecules?). Likewise, sortals are required for making judgments of identity. "Are these two things the same?" makes no sense without supplying the sortal—the same *what* (see also Carey, Xu, Jackendoff, Bloom, & Wynn, 1999).

Sortal concepts have become significant in the developmental literature because of suggestions that the set of sortals may undergo fundamental developmental change;

specifically, infants may appreciate only very global sortal concepts. Xu and Carey (1996) note that infants are often insensitive to radical changes in the appearance of individuals. If a cup moves behind a screen and a ball emerges from the other side, 10-month-old infants appear to construe this event as involving a single individual, whereas adults (and 12-month-olds) construe the event as involving two distinct individuals (but see Wilcox & Baillargeon, 1998, for an alternative interpretation). Carey and Xu argue that the concept "object" functions as a sortal for young children (allows tracking of individuals), but more specific kinds do not.

There is a further way in which the distinction between categories and individuals is of great interest, and this concerns the uses to which concepts are put. Although most developmental studies of concepts focus on categories, they do not examine children's concepts of categories per se, but rather of individuals as instances of these categories. For example, consider the category "dog." Most typically, a word-learning researcher might ask which things get called "dog" ("Is this *a* dog?"). A categorization researcher might ask a child to sort instances ("Put *the dogs* in this box"), or make inferences ("Does *this dog* have an omentum inside?"). In all of these cases, the category is considered with respect to the classification of individual instances (this dog, the dogs, a dog). However, a different type of use entails thinking about the category as a whole—so-called "generic" uses of the category. "Is this a dog?" refers to an individual; "Dogs have four legs" refers to the larger category.

Generic knowledge is vital to human reasoning. Thinking about generic categories leads children to make rich inferences about the world (Shipley, 1993). "Category-based" reasoning is predicated on kinds (Osherson, Smith, Wilkie, Lopez, & Shafir, 1990). More generally, "semantic" (versus episodic) memory (e.g., Collins & Quillian, 1969) tends to be generic. Despite the centrality of this form of reasoning, it poses a challenging learning problem for children (see S. A. Gelman, 2003). Generics are never directly instantiated in the world, but can only be theorized. You cannot show a child the generic class of dogs. Furthermore, as noted, generic knowledge is not disconfirmed by counterexamples (e.g., birds lay eggs, even though a majority of birds—males and infants—do not; McCawley, 1981). Thus, the puzzle, concisely framed by Prasada, is an extension of the classic riddle of induction: "How do we acquire knowledge about kinds of things if we have experience with only a limited number of examples of the kinds in question?" (2000, p. 66).

Sensitivity to generics in language seems to develop by about 2.5 to 3 years of age (S. A. Gelman & Raman, 2003). For example, young preschoolers interpret a generic noun phrase as referring to an abstract kind—even when it conflicts with the instances present during testing (e.g., when presented with a picture of two penguins, they report that "birds fly," but "the birds don't fly"). However, it is not until about 4 years of age that children showed sensitivity to a distinction between generics ("birds") and quantified predications ("all birds," "some birds"; Hollander, Gelman, & Star, 2002). Although more research is needed in this area, it may be during the preschool years that children come to represent fully the notion of a kind as distinct from its instances.

IMPLICATIONS FOR CHILDREN'S CONCEPTS

We suspect that some of the disagreements between theories of conceptual development stem from taking different kinds of concepts as paradigmatic. As already discussed, children acquire a wealth of different kinds of concepts; these likely develop in different ways. Certain concepts may have an innate basis; others may be readily acquired on the basis of perceptual learning; still others require causal reasoning and integration of facts within a growing commonsense "theory." Furthermore, certain concepts are important in organizing others, and can be called "foundational" concepts. A concept such as "alive" is one such example, having implications for how one thinks about a range of other concepts, including plants (and how they are similar to animals) and clouds (and how they differ from animals, despite being apparently self-moving). In contrast, other concepts (e.g., "green triangles") are unlikely to have implications for much other knowledge.

We therefore cannot rely on a monolithic model of children's concepts (Siegler, 1996). The importance of naïve theories can be overestimated when focusing exclusively on natural kind concepts and providing a task that requires children to make biological inferences. Likewise, children's reliance on outward appearances can be overrated when focused on nonlexicalized categories for which children have little prior knowledge (Landau, Smith, & Jones, 1988).

More controversially, Keil et al. (1998) propose that *even when considering a single concept,* children consider multiple kinds of information: on the one hand, associations and feature tabulations; on the other hand, propositions that interpret features and relations. Perceptual and conceptual are tightly linked—the salient perceptual features are those that give us conceptual purchase. Different conceptual structures also reflect task variability and conceptual variability. Rather than possessing a global or stable conceptual preference at any age, children and adults apparently have multiple kinds of categorization available to them (Lin & Murphy, 2001; Waxman & Namy, 1997).

In addition to conceptual differences, different tasks tap into different ways of thinking. Categorization serves many different functions, and children recruit different sorts of information depending on the task at hand. Rapid identification calls for one kind of process; reasoning about genealogy calls for another. Even when the task is restricted to object identification, people make use of different sorts of information depending on the task instructions (Yamauchi & Markman, 1998)—at times even in parallel on the same trial (Allen & Brooks, 1991).

Though there are many different kinds of concepts, and different acquisitional accounts may be appropriate for different concepts, we focus on a particularly important set of concepts, those characterized as foundational. As noted, foundational concepts organize domains and influence development of many other concepts. For example, the foundational concept "living thing" organizes the domain of intuitive biology and is critical for learning about specific types of plants and animals (Carey, 1985). An approach that considers children's naïve "theories" provides the most compelling account of the acquisition and development of foundational concepts. We turn next to this approach.

Concepts Embedded in Theories

Lin and Murphy (2001) make a distinction between the *internal structure* of a concept and its *external relations.* Much research has focused on questions of internal structure: Do concepts have definitions, are they characterized by prototypes, are they based on perceptual or conceptual features, and so on. In contrast, concepts also have relations to entities outside themselves: larger bodies of knowledge, theories, functions, relations, goals, and so on. These external relations are, in a sense, the whole point of concepts: we construct them in order to use them in these larger knowledge systems. This section concerns these external relations—how concepts relate to larger bodies of knowledge.

Consider the concept "planet," which has a long history in scientific thinking. There is continuity over time: in English, the planets are still identified by their Roman names (derived from the Greek). Yet, the twenty-first century understanding of planets is radically different from that of ancient celestial observers. How has the concept changed? One could point to definitional changes: modern planets must orbit stars, whereas ancient planets could include stars and moons (and exclude earth). Yet any such definitional differences would understate the conceptual differences. Modern and ancient concepts were located in radically incommensurate theories (T. Kuhn, 1963). It is only given the larger background of ancient belief systems that we can make sense of the old concepts. The general point here is that internal (definitional) properties are not sufficient to characterize concepts.

As this example illustrates, concepts are embedded in larger explanatory structures, often described as theories (Wellman & Gelman, 1998). Thus a full account of foundational concepts such as *force, living thing,* and *belief*—or even a full account of more mundane concepts such as *drop, hamster,* or *afraid*—would require a discussion of the nature and development of children's thinking about physics, biology, and psychology (respectively). It is beyond the scope of this chapter to consider the domain-specific factors underlying development of the full range of children's concepts. Rather, in this section we present evidence for the link between concepts and theories, drawing many of the examples from the specific domain of intuitive biology.

ONTOLOGY

Keil (1979, p. 1) defines ontological knowledge as "one's conception of the basic categories of existence, of what sorts of things there are." Ontologies form the foundation of intuitive framework theories. For example, physics deals with masses, velocities, and energy. Psychology deals with thoughts, desires, and beliefs. Biology deals with species, genes, and reproduction. The same entity can be construed in different theories: thus, a person is at once a *physical* mass, possessing *psychological* states, and undergoing *biological* processes. The difference between an ontological distinction and other categorical distinctions is that, with ontologies, predicates assigned to the wrong ontological category are not false—they are nonsensical. For example, "The cow is green" is false but sensible; in contrast, "the cow is one hour long" is an ontological category error (Sommers, 1963).

When do children begin to honor ontological distinctions, in their categories and in their language? There is a rich literature demonstrating that children honor at least two ontological distinctions quite early in life, that of mental versus physical (Wellman, 1990), and that of animate versus inanimate (Rakison & Poulin-Dubois, 2001). We focus primarily on the latter, as its relevance for categorization is especially clear.

Animacy is clearly a central concern by the time children can talk. Children are aware that subject nouns are typically animate and object nouns tend to be inanimate (Golinkoff, Harding, Carlson, & Sexton, 1984). For children learning English, animacy is an important factor in learning the passive construction (Lempert, 1989), and in the types of implicit causal attributions children make when interpreting verbs (Corrigan & Stevenson, 1994). A key question is whether children's animacy distinction can be reduced to lower-level perceptual features. Cues such as spatial distribution of facial features, irregular contour, dynamic patterns of movement, and so forth, are all low-level correlates of animacy to which infants are sensitive (Bertenthal, Proffitt, Spetner, & Thomas, 1985; Bornstein & Arterberry, 2003; Rakison, 2003b). An infant who distinguishes horses from airplanes (Mandler & McDonough, 1998) may not have an abstract concept of animacy, but rather sensitivity to critical perceptual features.

One way to examine whether animacy is wholly a perceptually based distinction or one with ontological significance is to determine what meaning it has for the child (Legerstee, 1992). Some of the earliest evidence that infants distinguish people from inanimate objects comes from infants' socioemotional reactions: for example, gazing, smiling, and cooing (Legerstee, Pomerleau, & Malcuit, 1987) as well as infants' novel inferences (Mandler & McDonough, 1998). Furthermore, several researchers have proposed that infants imbue animates (particularly people) with important psychological characteristics, and that infants distinguish "surface" behaviors from "deeper" psychological interpretations of those behaviors (Baron-Cohen, 1995; Legerstee, Barna, & DiAdamo, 2000; Woodward, 1998).

A further piece of evidence is that, in children's classifications, ontology can trump other salient information, such as object shape. By 9 months of age, infants group together different basic-level animal categories (e.g., dogs and fish) and separate birds-with-outspread-wings from airplanes (Mandler & McDonough, 1993). By age 2 years, children weight substance more heavily than shape on a match-to-sample task on which the items are nonsolid masses (Soja, Carey, & Spelke, 1991). By 3 and 4 years of age, children treat plants and animals as belonging to a single category (things that grow and self-heal), despite the extreme differences in shape between, say, a cow and a tree (Inagaki & Hatano, 2002). Conversely, children treat humans and apes as belonging to distinctly different categories, despite their greater similarity (K. Johnson, Mervis, & Boster, 1992). A further argument is that the perceptual cues that do correlate with animacy are insufficient. Prasada (2003) suggests that so-called "animate motion" in fact is not perceptually given, nor can it be represented as a correlation between properties, but rather requires "an appropriate relational structure" (p. 18; see also R. Gelman & Williams, 1998). For example, self-motion (in the sense of self-generated movement) is not simply a matter of detecting whether an object moves without a visible causal agent, because wind and magnets can be (and indeed sometimes are) imputed as causal agents in such cases (e.g., S. A. Gelman & Gottfried, 1996; R. Gelman, Durgin, & Kaufman, 1995; Subrahmanyam, R. Gelman, & Lafosse, 2002). How to represent such relational structures on a perceptual-learning account is not clear (though see Yoshida & Smith, 2003, for suggestions).

CAUSATION

Some years ago, we proposed that, if children's categories are theory-based, then causes should be crucial to their category representations (S. A. Gelman & Kalish, 1993). Similarly, Ahn (1998) formulated the "causal status hypothesis," in which causal features are more central than effect features (see also Rehder, 2003). Ahn, Gelman, Amsterlaw, Hohenstein, and Kalish (2000) found evidence for the causal status effect in children 7 to 9 years of age. Children learned descriptions of novel animals, in which one feature caused two other features. When asked to determine which test item was more likely to be an example of the animal they had learned, children preferred an animal with a cause feature and an effect feature rather than an animal with two effect features.

Other studies add to the support for the importance of cause in children's concepts. Barrett, Abdi, Murphy, and Gallagher (1993) find that, when asked to categorize novel birds into one of two categories, children of elementary-school age noticed correlations that were supported by causal links, and used such correlations to categorize new members (e.g., correlation between brain size and memory). The children did not make use of features that correlated equally well but were unsupported by a theory (e.g., the correlation between structure of heart and shape of beak). Krascum and Andrews (1998) likewise found beneficial effects of causal information on category learning in children as young as 4 and 5 years of age.

Causal relations are central to concepts in theories because they involve explanatory as well as associative relations. For example, preschool children recognize that baby animals tend to resemble their parents (Springer, 1996; S. A. Gelman & Wellman, 1991). They also recognize that there is a highly regular and constrained pattern of development across the lifetime of an individual animal (Rosengren et al., 1991). The two facts can be explained and integrated via the idea of some sort of intrinsic species essence. Similarly, young children recognize that many behaviors can lead to illness, including getting sneezed on, sharing a toothbrush, or eating a dirty piece of food. What links these apparently dissimilar events is a common underlying mechanism, transmission of germs (Kalish, 1996).

The detail with which children represent mechanisms remains an open question (Au & Romo, 1999; R. Gelman & Williams, 1998; Keil et al., 1998). Consider the concept of "inheritance." Some researchers have argued that young children recognize a physical or biological mechanism mediating parent-offspring resemblance (Hirschfeld, 1996; Springer & Keil, 1991). This sort of representation links inheritance to a set of other beliefs and concepts, an intuitive theory of biology. Alternatively, if children assume that intentional or social mechanisms underlie inheritance (Solomon, Johnson, Zaitchik, & Carey, 1996; Weissman & Kalish, 1999), then the conceptually central links would be quite different. Use of a concept (e.g., "mother," "sick") involves, in part, coming to appreciate which mechanism is operative.

NONOBVIOUS PROPERTIES

The importance of nonobvious properties can be seen in several respects. It is implicit in children's understanding of causation and ontology, as discussed previously. It can also be seen more directly in children's formulation of domain-specific theories that posit nonvisible constructs: mental states in a naïve theory of mind (Wellman, 2002), physical force and gravity in a naïve theory of physics (Wellman & Inagaki, 1997), and a wealth of constructs in children's formulation of biological theories, including germs (Kalish, 1996; Siegal & Share, 1990), vital powers (Inagaki & Hatano, 2002; Morris, Taplin, & Gelman, 2000), elements of reproduction (Springer, 1996), and cooties (Hirschfeld, 2002). That children appear to learn and accept such constructs readily would argue against the notion that their concepts depend on concrete, perceptually apparent properties.

Furthermore, studies that focus specifically on nonobvious properties, such as internal parts or substance, find that children rely on such properties for categorizing (see also R. R. Gelman & Williams, 1998). In a by-now classic series of studies, Keil (1989) asked children to consider animals and objects that had undergone transformations leading them to appear to be something else—for example, a raccoon that underwent an operation so that it looked and acted like a skunk. Second graders realized that animal identity was unaffected by superficial transformations (e.g., the animal was judged to be a raccoon despite its skunk-like properties). Even younger children demonstrated a similar understanding when considering items that were transformed to resemble something from a different ontological category (e.g., preschoolers reported that a porcupine that was transformed to look like a cactus was still a porcupine), or that were transformed by means of a costume. Preschool children similarly appreciated that for some objects, insides are more important than outsides for judgments of identity and functioning (e.g., a dog without its insides cannot bark and is not a dog, whereas a dog without its outsides can bark and is a dog; S. A. Gelman & Wellman, 1991). Moreover, when asked what differentiates pairs of identical-looking animals that differ in kind (e.g., real dog versus toy dog; dog versus wolf), both 5-year-olds and adults are more likely to invoke internal parts/substance than the irrelevant property of age (S. A. Gelman, 2003; Lizotte & Gelman, 1999).

Interestingly, children appreciate *that* insides are important at an age when they do not yet know much about *what* insides objects have. For example, although 4-year-olds recognize that insides are crucial to object identity and expect that animal insides differ in consistent ways from machine insides, they cannot accurately identify whether a photograph depicts the insides of an animal or the insides of a machine (Simons & Keil, 1995). This result led Simons and Keil to suggest that children's grasp of insides is an abstract appreciation that precedes a concrete, detailed understanding. This is a surprising reversal of the usual developmental story (that concrete understandings precede abstractions), and implies that children may be predisposed to consider nonobvious properties important, even in the absence of direct evidence.

An example of a nonobvious construct is that of an "essence" (S. A. Gelman, 2003). Essentialism is the view that categories have an underlying reality or true nature that one cannot observe directly but that gives an object its identity (S. A. Gelman, 2003; Locke, 1671/1959; Schwartz, 1977). Essentialism requires no specialized knowledge, and people may possess an "essence placeholder" without knowing what the essence is (Medin, 1989). For example, a child might believe that girls have some inner, nonobvious quality that distinguishes them from boys and that is responsible for the many observable differences in appearance and behavior between boys and girls, before ever learning about chromosomes or human physiology.

Evidence for essentialism is indirect but extensive. It includes several expectations children hold about certain categories: that they permit rich underlying structure, have innate potential, and have sharp and immutable boundaries (S. A. Gelman, 2003). Essentialism is a hypothesized construct based on indirect evidence, and so cannot be demonstrated definitively. Not surprisingly, then, there are debates as to whether this is the most apt characterization. One set of questions concerns whether there is a single essentialist "stance" (Keil, 1994), or instead an amalgamation of a variety of tendencies (S. A. Gelman, 2003). If the latter, then how coherent are essentialist beliefs? Do different strands (e.g., nativism, inductive potential, boundary intensification) all "hang together," or do they develop piecemeal? Another set of issues was raised by Strevens (2000), who suggested that the data taken as evidence for psychological essentialism could instead be accounted for if people simply assume that there are causal laws connecting kind membership with observable properties. Strevens's account, though eschewing essentialism, overlaps with the current model in emphasizing that people treat surface features as caused and constrained by deeper features of concepts.

Other scholars have argued that the essentialist model cannot account for certain experimental findings with adults (Braisby, Franks, & Hampton, 1996; Malt, 1994; Sloman & Malt, 2003). For example, the extent to which different liquids are judged to be water is independent of the extent to which they share the purported essence of water, H_2O. At issue are questions such as: What is meant by "essentialism"? (See S. A. Gelman & Hirschfeld, 1999, for several distinct senses that have been conflated in the literature.) Which concepts are essentialized? Can there be a mismatch between language and concepts (e.g., an essentialized concept of "pure water" that does not map neatly onto uses of the word "water")? Whether these findings undermine (or even conflict with) psychological essentialism is a matter of current debate (S. A. Gelman, 2003; Rips, 2001).

DISCUSSION

Any developmental theory needs to account not only for the acquisition of simple concepts ("cup") but also complex knowledge. By the time children are 2.5 to 3 years of age, many of their concepts incorporate properties that cannot be readily captured by perceptual description. We reviewed several types of evidence to support this claim: the centrality of ontology, of causal features, and of nonobvious constructs (including function, intentionality, and internal parts). Children are not simply stringing together observed properties, but rather are searching for underlying causes and explanations. The resulting concepts are often called "theory-based." In some cases, concepts are embedded in an identifiable, articulated theory (e.g., "beliefs" and "desires" in a theory of mind). In other cases, such a theory has not yet been identified, but the components of a theory (ontology, causation, nonobvious features) are present from an early age.

Theories are argued to *contribute to* concept development rather than to *result from* concept development (see Wellman & Gelman, 1998). Murphy (1993) argues that theories help concept learners in three respects: (1) Theories help identify those features that are relevant to a concept; (2) theories constrain how (e.g., along which dimensions) similarity should be computed; and (3) theories can influence how concepts are stored in memory.

However, these data and arguments do not imply that perceptual features are unimportant to early concepts. Even within a "concepts-in-theories" framework, appearances provide crucial cues regarding category membership (S. A. Gelman & Medin, 1993). Similarity plays an important role in fostering comparisons of representations and hence discovery of new abstractions and regularities (Gentner & Medina, 1998). Rather than suggesting that perceptual cues are irrelevant, we suggest that many concepts have two distinct though interrelated levels: the level of observable reality and the level of explanation and cause.

It is this two-tier structure that may in fact serve to motivate further development, leading children to develop deeper, more thoughtful understandings (Wellman & Gelman, 1998). Most developmental accounts of cognitive change include something like this structure, such as equilibration (Inhelder & Piaget, 1958), competition (MacWhinney, 1987), theory change (Carey, 1985), analogy (Goswami, 1996), and cognitive variability (Siegler, 1996). In all these cases, children consider contrasting representations. Not surprisingly, children also look beyond observable features when forming concepts.

Theory-based approaches argue for the interdependence of categorization and other cognitive processes, such as causal reasoning or reading of intentionality (Murphy, 2002). However, the extent of this interdependence has not yet been sufficiently plumbed. It would be intriguing to know, for example, how categorization changes (if at all) for those people with impairments that affect other high-level reasoning processes. We need more fine-grained studies of categorization in autism (which devastates theory of mind) or Williams syndrome (which seems to undercut theory construction; see S. C. Johnson & Carey, 1998).

At this point, the greatest challenge for the concepts-in-theories approach is to describe mechanisms of theory change. Various investigators have argued that low-level associative mechanisms can account for children's seemingly sophisticated concepts, so that there is no need to appeal to higher-order processing. For example, Smith and Yoshida (L. B. Smith, Colunga, & Yoshida, 2003; Yoshida & Smith, 2003) argue that foundational concepts (i.e., animacy) may be extracted from regularities in language. Syntactic structures are associated with conceptual distinctions between objects and substances (e.g., count nouns versus mass nouns in English) and between animates and inanimate (e.g., plural marking is more common for animates than inanimates, in Japanese). For the young child (on this view), animacy falls out of those perceptual and linguistic correlations that can be found in the input, thereby leading to different conceptualizations of "animacy" depending on the language being learned (English versus Japanese). Similar arguments have been provided to explain children's use of shape as an organizing principle in their early concepts (Samuelson & Smith, 2000), and the use of similarity in young children's representations of animal kinds (Sloutsky, 2003). Processes of general induction, based on association learning and similarity assessment, are undoubtedly potent tools for acquiring categories. However, we suggest that such processes are insufficient to provide a complete account for concept acquisition and conceptual change (including, for example, the context-sensitivity of similarity, and children's ability to make novel inferences that are supported by theoretical assumptions rather than prior associations).

Conclusions

INTERLEAVING MECHANISMS

As suggested earlier, there is no principled reason why different theoretical approaches could not be combined to account for conceptual learning even within a particular domain. R. Gelman (2002) reminds us that "innate" and "learning" can go hand-in-hand. This point is unquestionable in other species. For example, white-crowned sparrows typically produce a characteristic song that has an innate template (acquired only by birds of this species) yet requires appropriate input between 10 and 50 days of age (Marler, 1991). In short, the song is both innate and learned.

An example that is closer to the current case can be seen in the domain of word learning, which overlaps considerably with concept learning. Woodward (2000) proposes that different levels of explanation work together when children acquire word meanings. Although theorists often argue for a particular single position (e.g., social-constructivist, constraints-based, or associationist), she notes that each position explains different developmental phenomena.

We also have a sketch of how such coordination among levels might look, when considering the acquisition of intentions (i.e., the purposes that underlie actions). "Intention" is a concept informed by theory of mind. There are certainly many examples of intentions that are hidden, nonobvious, in conflict with surface cues, and that require understanding a web of motives, goals, and desires. Much of legal reasoning entails attempting to discern intentional from accidental action, on the basis of ambiguous behaviors for which multiple stories can be told. Nonetheless, despite the theoretical richness of the concept, Baldwin (2003) outlines how low-level patterns in the available percepts could form a basis for children's initial ability to detect intentions. She proposes that domain-general skills for covariation detection, sequence learning, and structure mapping may give rise to the detection of intentions (i.e., judging whether something was purposeful). For example, subtle cues regarding the acceleration of limbs toward goal objects might provide characteristic information regarding the beginning and end-points of intentional sequences (Baldwin & Baird, 2001, p. 174). Initial evidence suggests that infants are sensitive to some of these low-level cues (Baldwin, Baird, & Saylor, 2001; Behne, Carpenter, Call, & Tomasello, in press). Importantly, the proposal is *not* that intention-detection reduces to low-level pattern detection, but rather that pattern detection "jump-starts and facilitates" intention detection. This integration of approaches seems to hold great promise for a full understanding of conceptual development.

BEYOND INITIAL UNDERSTANDINGS

Much of the research on children's concepts that we have reviewed focuses on initial states and early frameworks—in other words, concepts in the first few years of life: in infants, toddlers, and preschool children. This is so for very good reason. Some researchers focus on this period to uncover developmental primitives; others do so to reveal developmental change. These initial states and early frameworks are critical to any understanding of concept acquisition. If nothing else, research on cognitive development over the past 30 years convinces us of the sophistication of conceptual processes in the ages of 0 to 5 years. The process of acquiring concepts in young children cannot simply reduce to the models for adding on new concepts in adults (Rakison, 2003a; Markman & Jaswal, 2003). This central early period of concept development remains a highly fertile ground for future research.

In addition, later developments are also critical—and perhaps even less well understood. Conceptual development is open-ended: we do not acquire all our concepts by age 5, or 10, or even 45. Issues of conceptual change can continue throughout a person's life. We have seen glimpses of the complexities children face in trying to integrate bits of conceptual knowledge, adjudicate domain boundaries, and wrestle with incommensurate conceptual systems. Children also must consider larger cultural messages (Astuti, Solomon, & Carey, 2004; Coley, 2000; Lillard, 1999). Furthermore, later childhood raises important practical issues of the implications of basic research on conceptual development to issues of education and instruction (e.g., Au & Romo, 1999; Evans, 2000; Vosniadou, Skopeliti, & Ikospentaki, 2004). Schooling is only the most formal context in which conceptual change takes place. Any sort of communication (e.g., hearing a story, reading a newspaper) or informal learning (visiting a museum or zoo, tending a garden) depends on, and potentially modifies, existing concepts. To return to the metaphor that opened the chapter, if concepts are the building blocks of thought, manipulating these blocks is not mere child's play. Understanding the full complexity of concepts and conceptual change are fundamental issues, and many puzzles remain.

References

Ahn, W. (1998). The role of causal status in determining feature centrality. *Cognition, 69*, 135–178.

Ahn, W., Gelman, S. A., Amsterlaw, J. A., Hohenstein, J., & Kalish, C. W. (2000). Causal status effect in children's categorization. *Cognition, 76*, B35–B43.

Allen, S. W., & Brooks, L. R. (1991). Specializing the operation of an explicit rule. *Journal of Experimental Psychology: General, 120*, 3–19.

Astuti, R., Solomon, G. E. A., & Carey, S. (2004). Constraints on conceptual development. *Monographs of the Society for Research in Child Development, 69*.

Au, T. K., & Romo, L. F. (1999). Mechanical causality in children's 'folkbiology'. In D. L. Medin & S. Atran (Eds.), *Folkbiology*. Cambridge, MA: MIT Press.

Baldwin, D. (2003). *Socio-cognitive foundations for language acquisition and how they are acquired*. Third biennial meeting of the Cognitive Development Society, Park City, UT.

Baldwin, D. A., & Baird, J. A. (2001). Discerning intentions in dynamic human action. *Trends in Cognitive Sciences, 5*, 171–178.

Baldwin, D. A., Baird, J. A., & Saylor, M. M. (2001). Infants parse dynamic action. *Child Development, 72*, 708–717.

Baron-Cohen, S. (1995). *Mindblindness: An essay on autism and theory of mind*. Cambridge, MA: MIT Press.

Barrett, S. E., Abdi, H., Murphy, G. L., & Gallagher, J. M. (1993). Theory-based correlations and their role in children's concepts. *Child Development, 64*, 1595 1616.

Behne, T., Carpenter, M., Call, J., & Tomasello, M. (in press). Unwilling or unable? Infants' understanding of intentional action. *Developmental Psychology*.

Bertenthal, B. I., Proffitt, D. R., Spetner, N. B., & Thomas, M. A. (1985). The development of infant sensitivity to biomechanical motions. *Child Development, 56*, 531–543.

Bornstein, M. H., & Arterberry, M. (2003). Recognition, discrimination, and categorization of smiling by 5-month-old infants. *Developmental Science, 6*, 585–599.

Boroditsky, L. (2001). Does language shape thought? Mandarin and English speakers' conceptions of time. *Cognitive Psychology, 43*, 1–22.

Bowerman, M., & Choi, S. (2003). Space under construction: Language-specific spatial categorization in first language acquisition. In D. Gentner & S. Goldin-Meadow (Eds.), *Language in mind: Advances in the study of language and thought* (pp. 389–427). Cambridge, MA: MIT Press.

Bowerman, M., & Levinson, S. C. (Eds.). (2001). *Language acquisition and conceptual development*. New York: Cambridge University Press.

Braisby, N. R., Franks, B., & Hampton, J. A. (1996). Essentialism, word use, and concepts. *Concepts, 59*, 247–274.

Bruner, J. S., Olver, R. R., & Greenfield, P. M. (1966). *Studies in cognitive growth*. New York: Wiley.

Carey, S. (1985). *Conceptual development in childhood*. Cambridge, MA: MIT Press.

Carey, S. (1986). Cognitive science and science education. *American Psychologist, 41*, 1123–1130.

Carey, S., & Spelke, E. (1994). Domain-specific knowledge and conceptual change. In L. A. Hirschfeld & S. A. Gelman (Eds.), *Mapping the mind: Domain specificity in cognition and culture* (pp. 169–200). New York: Cambridge University Press.

Carey, S., Xu, F., Jackendoff, R., Bloom, P., & Wynn, K. (1999). Sortals and kinds: An appreciation of John Macnamara. In *Language, logic, and concepts: Essays in memory of John Macnamara* (pp. 311–335). Cambridge, MA: The MIT Press.

Chomsky, N. (1975). *Reflections on language*. New York: Random House.

Coley, J. D. (2000). On the importance of comparative research: The case of folkbiology. *Child Development, 71*, 82–90.

Collins, A. M., & Quillian, M. R. (1969). Retrieval time from semantic memory. *Journal of Verbal Learning and Verbal Behavior, 8,* 240–247.

Corrigan, R., & Stevenson, C. (1994). Children's causal attributions to states and events described by different classes of verbs. *Cognitive Development, 9,* 235–256.

Diesendruck, G. (2001). Essentialism in Brazilian children's extensions of animal names. *Developmental Psychology, 37,* 49–60.

Evans, E. M. (2000). Beyond Scopes: Why creationism is here to stay. In K. S. Rosengren, C. N. Johnson, & P. L. Harris (Eds.), *Imagining the impossible* (pp. 305–333). New York: Cambridge University Press.

Fodor, J. (1981). The present status of the innateness controversy. In *Representations: Philosophical essays on the foundations of cognitive science.* Cambridge, MA: MIT Press.

Gelman, R. (2002). *Cognitive development.* In H. Pashler & D. L. Medin (Eds.), *Stevens' handbook of experimental psychology* (3rd ed., Vol. 2). Hoboken, NJ: Wiley.

Gelman, R., Durgin, F., & Kaufman, L. (1995). Distinguishing between animates and inanimates: Not by motion alone. In D. Sperber, D. Premack, & A. Premack (Eds.), *Causal cognition: A multidisciplinary debate* (pp. 150–184). New York: Clarendon Press.

Gelman, R., & Williams, E. (1998). Enabling constraints for cognitive development and learning: Domain specificity and epigenesis. In W. Damon (Series Ed.) & D. Kuhn & R. S. Siegler (Vol. Eds.), *Handbook of child psychology: Vol. 2. Cognition, perception and language* (5th ed., pp. 575–630). New York: Wiley.

Gelman, S. A. (2003). *The essential child: Origins of essentialism in everyday thought.* New York: Oxford University Press.

Gelman, S. A., & Coley, J. D. (1990). The importance of knowing a dodo is a bird: Categories and inferences in 2-year-old children. *Developmental Psychology, 26,* 796–804.

Gelman, S. A., & Gottfried, G. (1996). Causal explanations of animate and inanimate motion. *Child Development, 67,* 1970–1987.

Gelman, S. A., & Heyman, G. D. (1999). Carrot-eaters and creature-believers: The effects of lexicalization on children's inferences about social categories. *Psychological Science, 10,* 489–493.

Gelman, S. A., & Hirschfeld, L. A. (1999). How biological is essentialism. In D. L. Medin & S. Atran (Eds.), *Folkbiology* (pp. 403–446). Cambridge, MA: MIT Press.

Gelman, S. A., & Kalish, C. W. (1993). Categories and causality. In R. Pasnak & M. L. Howe (Eds.), *Emerging themes in cognitive development: Vol. 2. Competencies* (pp. 3–32). New York: Springer-Verlag.

Gelman, S. A., & Markman, E. M. (1986). Categories and induction in young children. *Cognition, 23,* 183–209.

Gelman, S. A., & Medin, D. L. (1993). What's so essential about essentialism? A different perspective on the interaction of perception, language, and conceptual knowledge. *Cognitive Development, 8,* 157–167.

Gelman, S. A., & Raman, L. (2003). Preschool children use linguistic form class and pragmatic cues to interpret generics. *Child Development, 74,* 308–325.

Gelman, S. A., & Wellman, H. M. (1991). Insides and essences: Early understandings of the non-obvious. *Cognition, 38,* 213–244.

Gentner, D., & Goldin-Meadow, S. (2003). *Language in mind: Advances in the study of language and thought.* Cambridge, MA: MIT Press.

Gentner, D., & Medina, J. (1998). Similarity and the development of rules. *Cognition, 65,* 263–297.

Goldin-Meadow, S. (2003). *The resilience of language: What gesture creation in deaf children can tell us about how all children learn language.* New York: Psychology Press.

Golinkoff, R. M., Harding, C. G., Carlson, V., & Sexton, M. E. (1984). The infant's perception of causal events: The distinction between animate and inanimate objects. In L. P. Lipsitt (Ed.), *Advances in infancy research* (Vol. 3, pp. 145–151). Norwood, NJ: Ablex.

Gopnik, A., Meltzoff, A. N., & Kuhl, P. K. (1999). *The scientist in the crib: Minds, brains, and how children learn.* New York: HarperCollins.

Gopnik, A., & Wellman, H. (1994). The theory theory. In L. A. Hirschfeld & S. A. Gelman (Eds.), *Mapping the mind: Domain specificity in cognition and culture* (pp. 257–293). New York: Cambridge University Press.

Goswami, U. (1996). Analogical reasoning and cognitive development. In H. W. Reese (Ed.), *Advances in child development and behavior* (Vol. 26, pp. 92–138). San Diego, CA: Academic Press.

Gutheil, G., & Rosengren, K. S. (1996). A rose by any other name: Preschooolers' understanding of individual identity across name and appearance changes. *British Journal of Developmental Psychology, 14,* 477–498.

Hahn, U., & Ramscar, M. (2001). *Similarity and categorization.* New York: Oxford University Press.

Hall, D. G. (1998). Continuity and the persistence of objects: When the whole is greater than the sum of the parts. *Cognitive Psychology, 37,* 28–59.

Hall, D. G., Waxman, S. R., & Bredart, S. (2003). Preschoolers' use of form class cues to learn descriptive proper names. *Child Development, 74,* 1547–1560.

Hallett, G. L. (1991). *Essentialism: A Wittgensteinian critique.* Albany: State University of New York Press.

Hespos, S. J., & Spelke, E. S. (2004). Conceptual precursors to language. *Nature, 430,* 453–456.

Heyman, G. D., & Gelman, S. A. (2000). Preschool children's use of traits labels to make inductive inferences about people. *Journal of Experimental Child Psychology, 77,* 1–19.

Hirsch, E. (1982). *The concept of identity.* New York: Oxford University Press.

Hirschfeld, L. A. (1996). *Race in the making: Cognition, culture, and the child's construction of human kinds.* Cambridge: MIT Press.

Hirschfeld, L. A. (2002). Why don't anthropologists like children? *American Anthropologist, 104.*

Hollander, M. A., Gelman, S. A., & Star, J. (2002). Children's interpretation of generic noun phrases. *Developmental Psychology, 38,* 883–894.

Imai, M., & Gentner, D. (1997). A cross-linguistic study of early word meaning: Universal ontology and linguistic influence. *Cognition, 62,* 169–200.

Inagaki, K., & Hatano, G. (2002). *Young children's naïve thinking about the biological world.* New York: Psychology Press.

Inhelder, B., & Piaget, J. (1958). *The growth of logical thinking from childhood to adolescence.* New York: Basic Books.

Inhelder, B., & Piaget, J. (1964). *The early growth of logic in the child.* New York: Norton.

Jaswal, V. K. (2004). Don't believe everything you hear: Preschoolers' sensitivity to speaker intent in category induction. *Child Development, 75,* 1871.

Jaswal, V. K., & Markman, E. M. (2002). Children's acceptance and use of unexpected category labels to draw non-obvious inferences. In W. Gray & C. Schunn (Eds.), *Proceedings of the twenty-fourth annual conference of the Cognitive Science Society* (pp. 500–505). Hillsdale, NJ: Erlbaum.

Johnson, K., Mervis, C., & Boster, J. (1992). Developmental changes within the structure of the mammal domain. *Developmental Psychology, 28,* 74–83.

Johnson, S. C., & Carey, S. (1998). Knowledge enrichment and conceptual change in folkbiology: Evidence from Williams syndrome. *Cognitive Psychology, 37,* 156–200.

Kalish, C. W. (1996). Preschoolers' understanding of germs as invisible mechanisms. *Cognitive Development, 11,* 83–106.

Kalish, C. W. (1998). Natural and artificial kinds: Are children realists or relativists about categories? *Developmental Psychology, 34,* 376–391.

Kalish, C. (2002). Gold, jade, and emeruby: The value of naturalness for theories of concepts and categories. *Journal of Theoretical and Philosophical Psychology, 22,* 45–67.

Keil, F. C. (1979). *Semantic and conceptual development: An ontological perspective.* Cambridge, MA: Harvard University Press.

Keil, F. C. (1989). *Concepts, kinds, and cognitive development.* Cambridge, MA: Bradford Book/MIT Press.

Keil, F. C. (1994). The birth and nurturance of concepts by domains: The origins of concepts of living things. In L. A. Hirschfeld & S. A. Gelman (Eds.), *Mapping the mind: Domain specificity in cognition and culture* (pp. 234–254). New York: Cambridge University Press.

Keil, F. C., Smith, W. C., Simons, D. J., & Levin, D. T. (1998). Two dogmas of conceptual empiricism: Implications for hybrid models of the structure of knowledge. *Cognition, 65,* 103–135.

Krascum, R. M., & Andrews, S. (1998). The effects of theories on children's acquisition of family-resemblance categories. *Child Development, 69,* 333–346.

Kripke, S. (1972). Naming and necessity. In D. Davidson & G. Harman (Eds.), *Semantics of natural language*. Dordrecht, The Netherlands: Reidel.

Kuhn, T. S. (1963). *The structure of scientific revolutions*. Chicago: University of Chicago Press.

Landau, B., Smith, L. B., & Jones, S. S. (1988). The importance of shape in early lexical learning. *Cognitive Development, 3,* 299–321.

Legerstee, M. (1992). A review of the animate-inanimate distinction in infancy: Implications for models of social and cognitive knowing. *Early Development and Parenting, 1,* 59–67.

Legerstee, M., Barna, J., & DiAdamo, C. (2000). Precursors to the development of intention at 6 months: Understanding people and their actions. *Developmental Psychology, 36,* 627–634.

Legerstee, M., Pomerleau, A., & Malcuit, G. (1987). The development of infants' responses to people and a doll: Implications for research in communication. *Infant Behavior and Development, 10,* 81–95.

Lempert, H. (1989). Animacy constraints on preschool children's acquisition of syntax. *Child Development, 60,* 327–245.

Lillard, A. (1999). Developing a cultural theory of mind: The CIAO approach. *Current Directions in Psychological Science, 8,* 57–61.

Lin, E. L., & Murphy, G. L. (2001). Thematic relations in adults' concepts. *Journal of Experimental Psychology: General, 130,* 3–28.

Lizotte, D. J., & Gelman, S. A. (1999). *Essentialism in children's categories.* Poster presented at the Cognitive Development Society, Chapel Hill, NC.

Locke, J. (1959). *An essay concerning human understanding* (Vol. 2). New York: Dover. (Original work published in 1671)

Lucy, J. A., & Gaskins, S. (2003). Interaction of language type and referent type in the development of nonverbal classification preferences. In D. Gentner & S. Goldin-Meadow (Eds.), *Language in mind: Advances in the study of language and thought*. Cambridge, MA: MIT Press.

Macnamara, J. (1982). *Names for things: A study of human learning*. Cambridge, MA: MIT Press.

Macnamara, J. (1986). *A border dispute*. Cambridge, MA: MIT Press.

MacWhinney, B. (1987). The competition model. In B. MacWhinney (Ed.), *Mechanisms of language acquisition* (pp. 249–308). Hillsdale, NJ: Erlbaum.

Malt, B. C. (1994). Water is not H_2O. *Cognitive Psychology, 27,* 41–70.

Mandler, J. M. (2004). *The foundations of mind*. New York: Oxford University Press.

Mandler, J. M., & McDonough, L. (1993). Concept formation in infancy. *Cognitive Development, 8,* 291–318.

Mandler, J. M., & McDonough, L. (1998). Studies in inductive inference in infancy. *Cognitive Psychology, 37,* 60–96.

Markman, E. M. (1989). *Categorization and naming in children: Problems in induction*. Cambridge, MA: Bradford Book/MIT Press.

Markman, E. M., & Hutchinson, J. E. (1984). Children's sensitivity to constraints on word meaning: Taxonomic versus thematic relations. *Cognitive Psychology, 16,* 1–27.

Markman, E. M., & Jaswal, V. K. (2003). Commentary on Part II: Abilities and assumptions underlying conceptual development. In D. H. Rakison & L. M. Oakes (Eds.), *Early category and concept development: Making sense of the blooming, buzzing confusion* (pp. 384–402). New York: Oxford University Press.

Marler, P. (1991). The instinct to learn. In S. Carey & R. Gelman (Eds.), *Epigenesis of mind: Essays on biology and cognition* (pp. 37–66). Hillsdale, NJ: Erlbaum.

Mayr, E. (1991). *One long argument: Charles Darwin and the genesis of modern evolutionary thought*. Cambridge, MA: Harvard University Press.

McCawley, J. D. (1981). *Everything that linguists have always wanted to know about logic*. Chicago: University of Chicago Press.

McDonough, L., Choi, S., & Mandler, J. M. (2003). Understanding spatial relations: Flexible infants, lexical adults. *Cognitive Psychology, 46,* 229–259.

Medin, D. (1989). Concepts and conceptual structure. *American Psychologist, 44,* 1469–1481.

Morris, S. C., Taplin, J. E., & Gelman, S. A. (2000). Vitalism in naive biological thinking. *Developmental Psychology, 36,* 582–595.

Murphy, G. L. (1993). Theories and concept formation. In I. Van Mechelen, J. Hampton, R. Michalski, & P. Theuns (Eds.), *Categories and concepts: Theoretical views and inductive data analysis* (pp. 173–200). New York: Academic Press.

Murphy, G. L. (2002). *The big book of concepts.* Cambridge, MA: MIT Press.

Oakes, L. M., & Rakison, D. H. (2003). Issues in the early development of concepts and categories: An introduction. In D. H. Rakison & L. M. Oakes (Eds.), *Early category and concept development: Making sense of the blooming, buzzing, confusion* (pp. 3–23). New York: Oxford University Press.

Osherson, D. N., Smith, E. E., Wilkie, O., Lopez, A., & Shafir, E. (1990). Category-based induction. *Psychological Review, 97,* 185–200.

Prasada, S. (2000). Acquiring generic knowledge. *Trends in Cognitive Sciences, 4,* 66–72.

Prasada, S. (2003). Conceptual representation of animacy and its perceptual and linguistic reflections. *Developmental Science, 6,* 18–19.

Putnam, H. (1975). The meaning of "meaning." In H. Putnam (Ed.), *Mind, language, and reality* (pp. 215–271). Cambridge: Cambridge University Press.

Quine, W. V. (1977). Natural kinds. In S. P. Schwartz (Ed.), *Naming, necessity, and natural kinds* (pp. 155–175). Ithaca, NY: Cornell University Press.

Rakison, D. H. (2003a). Free association? Why category development requires something more. *Developmental Science, 6,* 20–22.

Rakison, D. H. (2003b). Parts, motion, and the development of the animate-inanimate distinction in infancy. In D. H. Rakison & L. M. Oakes (Eds.), *Early category and concept development: Making sense of the blooming, buzzing confusion* (pp. 159–192). New York: Oxford University Press.

Rakison, D. H., & Oakes, L. M. (2003). *Early category and concept development: Making sense of the blooming, buzzing confusion.* New York: Oxford University Press.

Rakison, D. H., & Poulin-Dubois, D. (2001). The developmental origin of the animate-inanimate distinction. *Psychological Bulletin, 127.*

Rehder, B. (2003). Categorization as causal reasoning. *Cognitive Science, 27,* 709–748.

Rips, L. J. (2001). Necessity and natural categories. *Psychological Bulletin, 127,* 827–852.

Rosch, E. (1978). Principles of categorization. In E. Rosch & B. B. Lloyd (Eds.), *Cognition and categorization* (pp. 27–48). Hillsdale, NJ: Erlbaum.

Rosengren, K., Gelman, S. A., Kalish, C., & McCormick, M. (1991). As time goes by: Children's early understanding of biological growth. *Child Development, 62,* 1302–1320.

Saffran, J. R., Aslin, R. N., & Newport, E. L. (1996). Statistical learning by 8-month-old infants. *Science, 274,* 1926–1928.

Samuelson, L. K., & Smith, L. B. (2000). Children's attention to rigid and deformable shape in naming and non-naming tasks. *Child Development, 71,* 1555–1570.

Schwartz, S. P. (Ed.). (1977). *Naming, necessity, and natural kinds.* Ithaca, NY: Cornell University Press.

Shipley, E. F. (1993). Categories, hierarchies, and induction. In D. Medin (Ed.), *The psychology of learning and motivation* (Vol. 30, pp. 265–301). New York: Academic Press.

Siegal, M., & Share, D. L. (1990). Contamination sensitivity in young children. *Developmental Psychology, 26,* 455–458.

Siegler, R. S. (1996). *Emerging minds: The process of change in children's thinking.* New York: Oxford University Press.

Simons, D. J., & Keil, F. C. (1995). An abstract to concrete shift in the development of biological thought: The insides story. *Cognition, 56,* 129–163.

Slobin, D. I. (1996). From "thought and language" to "thinking for speaking." In J. J. Gumperz & S. C. Levinson (Eds.), *Rethinking linguistic relativity* (pp. 70–96). New York: Cambridge University Press.

Sloman, S. A., & Malt, B. C. (2003). Artifacts are not ascribed essences, nor are they treated as belonging to kinds. *Language and Cognitive Processes, 18,* 563–582.

Sloutsky, V. M. (2003). The role of similarity in the development of categorization. *Trends in Cognitive Sciences, 7,* 246–251.

Sloutsky, V. M., & Fisher, A. V. (2004). Induction and categorization in young children: A similarity-based model. *Journal of Experimental Psychology: General, 133,* 166–188.

Smith, E. E. (1989). Concepts and induction. In M. I. Posner (Ed.), *Foundations of cognitive science* (pp. 501–526). Cambridge, MA: MIT Press.

Smith, L. B., Colunga, E., & Yoshida, H. (2003). Making an ontology: Cross-linguistic evidence. *Cognitie Creier Comportament, 7,* 61–90.

Springer, K. (1996). Young children's understanding of a biological basis for parent-offspring relations. *Child Development, 67,* 2841–2856.

Springer, K., & Keil, F. C. (1991). Early differentiation of causal mechanisms appropriate to biological and nonbiological kinds. *Child Development, 62,* 767–781.

Soja, N. N., Carey, S., & Spelke, E. S. (1991). Ontological categories guide young children's inductions of word meaning: Object terms and substance terms. *Cognition, 38,* 179–211.

Solomon, G. E. A., Johnson, S. C., Zaitchik, D., & Carey, S. (1996). Like father, like son: Young children's understanding of how and why offspring resemble their parents. *Child Development, 67,* 151–171.

Sommers, F. (1963). Types and ontology. *The Philosophical Review, 72,* 327–363.

Sorrentino, C. M. (2001). Children and adults represent proper names as referring to unique individuals. *Developmental Science, 4,* 399–407.

Spelke, E. S. (1994). Initial knowledge: Six suggestions. *Cognition, 50,* 431–445.

Spelke, E. S. (2003). What makes humans smart. In D. Gentner & S. Goldin-Meadow (Eds.), *Advances in the investigation of language and thought.* Cambridge, MA: MIT Press.

Strevens, M. (2000). The naïve aspect of essentialist theories. *Cognition, 74,* 149–175.

Subrahmanyam, K., Gelman, R., & Lafosse, A. (2002). Animate and other separably moveable things. In E. Fordes & G. Humphreys (Eds.), *Category-specificity in brain and mind* (pp. 341–373). London: Psychology Press.

Tomasello, M. (1999). *The cultural origins of human cognition.* Cambridge, MA: Harvard University Press.

Vosniadou, S., Skopeliti, I., & Ikospentaki, K. (2004). Modes of knowing and ways of reasoning in elementary astronomy. *Cognitive Development, 19,* 203–222.

Waxman, S. R. (in press). The gift of curiosity. In W. Ahn, R. L. Goldstone, B. C. Love, A. B. Markman, & P. Wolff (Eds.), *Categorization inside and outside the lab: Essays in honor of Douglas L. Medin.* Washington, DC: American Psychological Association.

Waxman, S. R., & Markow, D. B. (1995). Words as invitations to form categories: Evidence from 12- to 13-month-old infants. *Cognitive Psychology, 29,* 257–302.

Waxman, S. R., & Namy, L. L. (1997). Challenging the notion of a thematic preference in young children. *Developmental Psychology, 33,* 555–567.

Weissman, M. D., & Kalish, C. W. (1999). The inheritance of desired characteristics: Children's view of the role of intention in parent-offspring resemblance. *Journal of Experimental Child Psychology, 73,* 245–265.

Welder, A. N., & Graham, S. A. (2001). The influence of shape similarity and shared labels on infants' inductive inferences about nonobvious object properties. *Child Development, 72,* 1653–1673.

Wellman, H. M. (1990). *The child's theory of mind.* Cambridge, MA: MIT Press.

Wellman, H. M. (2002). Understanding the psychological world: Developing a theory of mind. In U. Goswami (Ed.), *Blackwell handbook of childhood cognitive development* (pp. 167–187). Malden, MA: Blackwell.

Wellman, H. M., & Gelman, S. A. (1998). Knowledge acquisition. In W. Damon (Series Ed.) & D. Kuhn & R. S. Siegler (Eds.), *Handbook of child psychology: Cognitive development* (5th ed., pp. 523–573). New York: Wiley.

Wellman, H. M., & Inagaki, K. (Eds.). (1997). *The emergence of core domains of thought: Children's reasoning about physical, psychological, and biological phenomena.* San Francisco: Jossey-Bass.

Whorf, B. L. (1956). *Language, thought, and reality.* Cambridge, MA: MIT Press.

Wilcox, T., & Baillargeon, R. (1998). Object individuation in infancy: The use of featural information in reasoning about occlusion events. *Cognitive Psychology, 37,* 97–155.

Woodward, A. L. (1998). Infants selectively encode the goal object of an actor's reach. *Cognition, 69,* 1–34.

Woodward, A. L. (2000). Constraining the problem space in early word learning. In *Becoming a word learner: A debate on lexical acquisition* (pp. 81–114). New York: Oxford University Press.

Xu, F. (1999). Object individuation and object identity in infancy: The role of spatiotemporal information, object property information, and language. *Acta Psychologica, 102,* 113–136.

Xu, F., & Carey, S. (1996). Infants' metaphysics: The case of numerical identity. *Cognitive Psychology, 30,* 111–153.

Yamauchi, T., & Markman, A. B. (1998). Category learning by inference and classification. *Journal of Memory and Language, 39,* 124–148.

Yoshida, H., & Smith, L. B. (2003). Shifting ontological boundaries: How Japanese- and English-speaking children generalize names for animals and artifacts. *Developmental Science, 6,* 1–34.

Chapter 10

Development in the Arts: Drawing and Music

ELLEN WINNER

Participation in the arts is central to human behavior. The earliest humans made art and traces of artistic ability can be seen in nonhuman animals. The arts are critical to the development of cognitive, social, and affective capacities in children and were included in the *Handbook of Child Psychology* for the first time in the present edition.

This chapter reviews the developmental course of the comprehension and production of two major nonverbal art forms, drawing and music, focusing on typical development in the absence of formal training. Research on individual differences and on giftedness in the arts is not covered (but see Moran & Gardner, 2006, for a discussion of giftedness). Unfortunately, almost all of the research on drawing and music has been conducted in Western settings, with a few exceptions.

Research on drawing has focused on production whereas research on music has focused on perception. This asymmetry may be due to the fact that the earliest music children produce is song rather than notated compositions. Songs are fleeting, while drawings are permanent and thus perhaps more amenable to study.

For each art form, I consider the following questions: What does an investigation into the evolutionary roots of this art form tell us? What historical, theoretical, and methodological approaches have been taken in the study of this art form? What are the major milestones in the development of comprehension and production of this art form?

For both art forms, I also consider one of the most enduring and provocative questions in the developmental study of the arts—whether development improves linearly with age, or whether some artistic abilities decline with age or are U-shaped, with young children responding more like adult artists than older children. This question is far more acute with respect to the arts than for logical, mathematical, scientific, or moral reasoning, where linear development is the normal expectation.

322

Drawing

Drawing is a complex activity that involves motoric, perceptual, and conceptual skills, including the use of schemas and rules specific to pictures (Gombrich, 1977; Thomas, 1995). Adults with no special training in drawing are able to translate a three-dimensional scene into a recognizable two-dimensional representation. While their drawings may not look highly skilled or accurate, their accomplishment is impressive: They can represent objects in a recognizable manner even though there is little actual similarity between a real-world scene and its small two-dimensional representation.

Pictures pervade our lives—we see them not only in art museums but also in magazines, billboards, cereal boxes, and so on. Pictures can be nonrepresentational (as in designs, abstractions) or representational, and, if the latter, they can be either realistic or nonrealistic. Nonrealistic representations are as easily recognized as realistic ones (witness cartoons, caricatures, and children's drawings). When we read a picture as a work of art (e.g., rather than as a diagram or scientific illustration), we attend to aesthetic properties—specifically we attend to what the picture expresses (properties not literally present such as sadness, agitation, loudness), the style of the work (the artist's individual handprint), and its composition (the organization of its parts and its balance or lack thereof; Arnheim, 1974; Goodman, 1976).

We can speculate about the evolutionary base of the visual arts from what we know about early human art as well as nonhuman capacities in picture-making and picture-responding.

EVOLUTIONARY BASE

The drawings of the earliest humans, from over 30,000 years ago, are extraordinarily realistic, capturing the fluid contours of the animals they hunted. Cave paintings have been likened in skill to the most highly prized human drawings (e.g., to drawings by Picasso). Cave art testifies to the drive to create art in humans: The earliest humans crawled through tunnels into deep recesses in caves to paint. The function of cave art has been debated (Was it to encourage hunters? Was it religious?), and we will only be able to speculate on this question. Perhaps the function was purely aesthetic, perhaps it was ritualistic, most likely it was poly functional. We also will never know what proportion of the population was able to draw in this way.

The visual arts extend to the nonhuman realm but only in a very limited manner. Apes and monkeys can recognize two-dimensional depictions of objects (Davenport & Rogers, 1971; Zimmerman & Hochberg, 1970; but see Winner & Ettlinger, 1979). Chimps have shown a sense of visual balance: Given a page with a small figure off-center, chimps added marks in a location that balanced the marks (Schiller, 1951). Morris (1967) gave painting materials to Congo, a laboratory chimp, and noted certain resemblances between Congo's spontaneous paintings and those by very young children. Paintings by chimps in the laboratory have been confused with abstract expressionist paintings, though surely the intentions behind the chimp and adult works were not comparable (Hussain, 1965). Chimps trained in sign language have shown the ability to make a rudimentary drawing and then, using sign language, label the object drawn, revealing an understanding that a mark on a page can stand for something in the three-dimensional world (R. Gardner & Gardner, 1978; Patterson, 1978). And when Premack (1975) gave three chimps a photograph of a chimpanzee head with the face blanked out and offered them the cutout eyes, nose, and mouth, one of the three chimps was able to place these parts in correct position. But no nonhuman animals draw spontaneously, and even when given drawing and painting materials, chimps make only nonrepresentational marks (with the possible exception of those trained in sign language). The achievements of humans in the realm of visual arts are far more impressive, even in infancy.

HISTORICAL AND THEORETICAL APPROACHES TO THE STUDY OF DRAWING DEVELOPMENT

The study of children's drawings began at the end of the nineteenth century with the rise of the field of child development. The many oddities of children's drawings were seen as deficiencies indicative of children's oversimplified concepts of the objects they were drawing (Figure 10.1).

The French art historian Luquet (1913, 1927) proposed three phases in the development of realism—a claim that remains influential yet controversial. At ages 3 to 4, Luquet theorized, children are in the phase of failed realism, unable to capture spatial relationships among objects. From 5 to 8, children are in the phase of intellectual realism in which objects are depicted in canonical position rather than from the viewpoint of the child drawing. At this phase, he argued, children draw what they know rather than what they see. Drawings are based on children's internal models (i.e., a tabletop is drawn as a rectangle because the child knows it to be rectangular). After age 9, children become visual realists, drawing what they see. They base their drawings on how things look from a single viewpoint, even if this means distorting an object by making it partially occluded or by altering its shape (e.g., drawing a tabletop as a parallelogram despite knowing it is in reality a rectangle).

Piaget and Inhelder's (1956) studies of children's drawings were influenced by Luquet (1913, 1927), and exemplify this "deficiency/progressing toward realism" tradi-

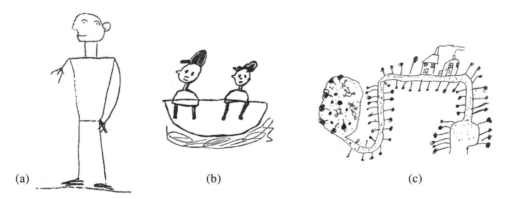

(a)   (b)   (c)

FIGURE 10.1 Odd Features of Children's Drawings. (a) Two-eyed profile; (b) Transparent boat; (c) Trees folded out from a street and drawn from mixed viewpoints. (*Sources:* (a) The Viktor Lowenfeld Papers, Penn State University Archives, Special Collections, Pennsylvania State University Libraries. Reprinted with permission. (b) *L'arte dei Bambini* [The Art of Children], by C. Ricci, 1887, Bologna, Italy: Zanichelli; (c) *Die Entwicklung der zeichnerischen,* by G. Kerschensteiner,1905, Begabung, Munich: Gerber.)

tion. They saw the development of drawing as guided by the child's developing understanding of space. Following Luquet, they described a progression characterized at age 3 to 4 by bounded objects (e.g., a closed circle) with no attention to capturing size or shape. Children at this age draw the human figure as a tadpole, reflecting deficiencies in spatial representation. From age 4 to 7 or 8, children were said to enter the stage of intellectual realism where they draw what they know, not what they see. At the concrete operational stage, children were said to be able to draw in a realistic way, reflecting their understanding of Euclidean geometry and emergence from spatial egocentrism. Piaget and Inhelder argued that at this stage the child could represent the third dimension (through occlusion and perspective, even if not with perfectly correct perspective). Thus, they saw drawing stages as progressive and assumed the desired endpoint to be visual realism.

Piaget and Inhelder's (1956) deficiency view pervaded theories of children's drawings for many years. But the assumption that the errors children make in their drawings are direct windows into their level of conceptual understanding is wrong. Even adults know far more about an object that they can show in a drawing (Golomb, 1973; Morra, 1995; Thomas, 1995).

Although the study of children's drawings began with the emergence of the study of child development, this topic was gradually relegated to a minor area of developmental psychology. By the 1970s, children's drawings went unmentioned in many developmental textbooks (Thomas & Silk, 1990). Freeman's (1980) experimental approach to children's drawings helped to revive the study of child art. Willats's (1995) information-processing theory of picture production (based on Marr's, 1982, theories of the visual system) also brought the study of child art into the arena of experimental cognitive development. Both Willats and Freeman (1980) distinguished between object-centered descriptions (in which shapes are not distorted) and viewer-centered descriptions (in which shapes are distorted to show how they look rather than how they actually are). What develops for Willats is a set of different drawing systems, from topological relations to various kinds of projection systems, with the final one being linear perspective. He also argued that denotation systems develop with two-dimensional regions first standing for volumes and later for surfaces of objects, and with one-dimensional lines ultimately standing for edges and contours. Willats's and Freeman's view that drawings develop from object-centered to viewer-centered descriptions parallels Piaget's view of the movement from intellectual to visual realism.

In contrast to the deficit models of children's drawings was a more positive view put forth by artists and art educators at the beginning of the twentieth century championing the resemblance between child art and Western modernism (Fineberg, 1997; Golomb, 2002; Viola, 1936). Arnheim (1974), the leading spokesperson for the aesthetic view, argued that children's art had its own aesthetics and was not just a sign of children's underdevelopment. He pointed out that many of the distortions and oddities found in children's drawings (e.g., fold-out drawings, lack of depth, transparencies) can be found in non-Western or pre-Renaissance Western art, showing us how many ways there are to represent and how much tolerance we have for lack of realism (cf. Deregowski, 1984, pp. 120–122). Arnheim (1974) argued that children's drawings are not failed attempts at realism but instead are intelligent solutions to the problem of depicting a three-dimensional world on paper.

PICTURE RECOGNITION, COMPREHENSION, AND PREFERENCE: MAJOR MILESTONES

Understanding pictures requires that one recognize pictures as representations. Understanding pictures also requires the ability to perceive the illusion of the third dimension in a two-dimensional picture, as well as the ability to perceive aesthetic properties of pictures.

Understanding the Representational Nature of Pictures: Four Components

The representational information carried by pictures is far more impoverished than information available in the ordinary environment: Objects are smaller than in real life, color is frequently lacking, and edges of objects are often represented by lines despite the fact that objects in the real world do not come with outlines. In addition, pictorial information is contradictory: Certain depth cues suggest the third dimension, while other information (e.g., from binocular and motion parallax) shows the surface of the picture to be flat.

Understanding the representational nature of pictures is four-part: A person must recognize (1) the similarity between a picture and what it represents, (2) the difference between a picture and what it represents, (3) the dual reality of a picture as both a flat object and a representation of the three-dimensional world, and (4) the fact that pictures are made with intentionality and are to be interpreted. Infants are excellent at the first two understandings while the third and fourth kinds develop later.

Recognizing the Similarity between a Picture and What It Represents.   Hochberg and Brooks (1962) kept their child from seeing any representational images until the age of 2, and then presented him with pictures of familiar objects such as a shoe or key (drawings, then black-and-white photos). The child labeled the pictures correctly, showing that no one needed to teach him to recognize objects represented in pictures. Twelve-month-olds can even recognize line drawings of common objects when much of their contour has been deleted (Rose, Jankowski, & Senior, 1997). Thus, understanding what a picture represents is an untutored skill.

Recognizing the Difference between a Picture and What It Represents.   Piaget argued that children confuse the sign with the thing signified, referring to this trait as "realism" (Piaget, 1929). If children are realists, they should succeed at recognizing what a picture represents but fail to distinguish a picture from its referent. In one sense, children are not realists about pictures. Infants discriminate between photographs and their referents between 3 to 6 months of age (Beilin, 1991; DeLoache, Pierroutsakos, & Uttal, 2003; DeLoache, Strauss, & Maynard, 1979).

But in another sense, children are realists about pictures. Despite their ability to discriminate pictures from objects, they sometimes see pictures as "substandard" versions of real objects possessing some of the properties that only the real objects possess (Thomas, Nye, & Robinson, 1994). Pierroutsakos and DeLoache (2003) described 9-month-olds manually exploring pictures of objects as if they were the real thing (see also Ninio & Bruner, 1978). This behavior occurred despite infants' ability to select the actual object when given a choice between the pictured versus real object (DeLoache et al., 2003). By 19 months, the infants had stopped grasping at pictures and now pointed to them.

Recognizing the Representational Status of Pictures.   Children under 2.5 years of age do not grasp that a picture *stands for* its referent. Callaghan (1999) showed 2-, 3-, and 4-year-olds several balls differing in size and features. The experimenter held up a picture to show which ball should be dropped down a tunnel. Two-year-olds could not use the pictures as symbolic objects and thus selected balls randomly rather than selecting the one that matched the picture. Sometimes they even put the picture down the tunnel instead of the object, showing that they treated the pictures as objects.

By 2.5 years, children can understand the representational status of pictures. DeLoache (1987) showed children color photos of a room, each indicating where a toy was hidden in the actual room. The experimenter pointed to one of the photos to show the child where to search for a toy hidden in the room. Children aged 2.5 years could use the photos to find the toys, showing that they recognized the photos as representational objects.

But children may succeed on DeLoache's (1987) task simply by attending to what the picture represents. Attending to the *dual* identity of a picture (i.e., recognizing that a picture of a flower is both a flower and a flat piece of paper) is not tested by her task and remains more difficult for children. Thomas et al. (1994) showed children an actual flower, a color photo of a flower, and a plastic replica of a flower and asked them to label and handle each one. The alternative identity of the plastic and pictured flower was then explained (e.g., it does not really grow in the ground), and children were then asked an appearance question (Does it look like a flower?) and a reality question (Is it really a flower?). Four-year-olds made some errors when asked about the plastic and pictured flower, and most errors were realist ones in which they confused the representation with the referent (saying it both looked like a flower and was a flower). Thus, while infants recognize pictures, it is not until at least 4 years of age that children grasp the dual identity of a picture.

Acquisition of an Intentional Theory of Pictures.   Full understanding of pictures requires the realization that pictures are made by someone with a mind. The "artist" interprets what is seen and puts it on paper. Thus, beauty is not directly transferred from world to paper but is a matter of the artist's interpretation of what he or she sees. Moreover, the beholder too has a mind, and this affects how the picture is perceived (Freeman, 1995; H. Gardner, Winner, & Kircher, 1975).

Richert and Lillard (2002) found that children under age 8 are easily confused about the role of the artist's intention in determining what a picture represents. Even if they are told that an artist had no knowledge of a certain object, if the drawing produced looks like that object, children say that this is what the artist was drawing. Studies have not pinpointed what causes the emergence of understanding of the role of intention in drawing. However, one likely catalyst is the experience of having one's own drawings misinterpreted, which could lead children to reflect about how their intentions determine the meaning of their drawings.

Freeman and Sanger (1993) found that subtle misunderstandings about the role of the artist in picture making persist until adolescence. When children were asked whether an ugly thing would make a worse picture than a pretty thing, most 11-year-olds said yes (revealing a belief that beauty flows directly from the world to the picture), but most 14-year-olds said no (they said that whether the picture is pretty or not depends on the artist's skill). Thus, the older children recognized that the artist determines whether a picture is beautiful. These findings about pictures are but one of many manifestations of a developmental progression in epistemological understanding by which children gradually come to understand that knowledge has its origin not only in the external world but also in the mind (see Kuhn & Franklin, 2006).

Perceiving Depth in Pictures

To perceive depth in a picture, one must overlook three kinds of cues that indicate that the picture is flat. First, binocular disparity is a cue resulting from small differences in how a scene looks to each eye. The farther away an object, the less disparity between the two views. In a picture, objects meant to appear far away are the same distance from our eyes as objects meant to appear near, which is why binocular disparity tells us that the two objects are on the same plane. Second, binocular convergence is a cue given by the fact that our eyes converge on what we focus on. For near objects, the angle of convergence is greater than for distant objects. This angle of convergence is interpreted by the brain as information about distance. But when we look at a picture, the angle of convergence is identical for images meant to be near and far in the picture because all of the objects are on the same flat picture plane. Third, motion parallax is a cue yielded by moving our head as we view a scene. When we do so, nearer objects are displaced faster than farther ones. But when we move our head in front of a picture, near and far represented objects move at the same rate, declaring the surface to be flat.

These three cues tell us that a three-dimensional scene is three-dimensional, and that a picture is only two-dimensional. How then do we perceive depth in two-dimensional pictures? We do so by ignoring these cues in favor of pictorial depth cues. These include occlusion (near objects partially occlude far ones), linear perspective (receding lines converge toward a vanishing point), size diminution (distant objects are smaller than near ones of the same absolute size), relative height (distant objects are drawn farther up on the picture plane), and texture gradients (textures get denser in the distance).

Infants perceive depth in the three-dimensional world when the nonpictorial cues of motion parallax and binocular cues are available, but fail to read depth in pictures (Bower, 1965, 1966; Campos, Langer, & Krowitz, 1970). Children between the ages of 2 and 3, however, can judge which of two houses in a picture is farther away using either occlusion cues or the cue of relative height, two pictorial cues to depth (Olson & Boswell, 1976). Like the ability to recognize what is represented in a picture, the ability to perceive depth in a picture may develop simply as a function of experience perceiving the actual world.

PERCEIVING AESTHETIC PROPERTIES OF PICTURES: EXPRESSION, STYLE, AND COMPOSITION

Expression

Pictures can express properties they do not literally possess. They can express nonvisual properties (loudness) and moods, doing so via representational content (a dying tree expresses sadness) or formal properties (dark colors express sadness; note that the depiction of a sad face is a literal rather than an expressive way to depict sadness). Because expressive properties are not literally present in pictures, reading expression in pictures can be considered a form of metaphorical thinking, and expression in art has been referred to as "metaphorical exemplification" (Goodman, 1976).

Preschoolers are sensitive to the expressive properties of abstract (nonrepresentational) stimuli, such as angular lines versus softly curving lines and bright colors versus dark colors (H. Gardner, 1974; Lawler & Lawler, 1965; Winston, Kenyon, Stewardson, & Lepine, 1995), and to expressive properties of certain kinds of representational content (e.g., a dying tree as sad; Winston et al., 1995). Shown abstract paintings, 5-year-olds respond with the same mood labels as do adults (Blank, Massey, Gardner, & Winner, 1984; Callaghan, 1997; Jolley & Thomas, 1994, 1995; Jolley, Zhi, & Thomas, 1998a). And even 3-year-olds can reliably select paintings that express happy, sad, excited, and calm after seeing adults modeling such judgments (Callaghan, 2000).

On more challenging expression tasks, young children do not succeed. When simply asked to select an appropriate completion for a picture, one of which matched the mood in the picture (e.g., a wilted tree versus a blooming tree to complete a sad picture), children did not succeed until 10 to 11 years of age (Carothers & Gardner, 1979; Jolley & Thomas, 1995; see also Winner, Rosenblatt, Windmueller, Davidson, & Gardner, 1986).

Style

Children's ability to detect style in works of art has been studied through paradigms in which children are asked to match works by the same artist. Whenever it is possible to match on the basis of representational content, representation trumps style (H. Gardner, 1970; Jolley, Zhi, & Thomas, 1998b). In matching tasks in which the choices vary in style but not subject matter, preschoolers and even 3-year-olds can perceive which paintings are by the same artist, though they justify such matches only in global terms such as looking alike (H. Gardner, 1970; Hardiman & Zernich, 1985; O'Hare & Westwood, 1984; Steinberg & DeLoache, 1986; Walk, Karusitis, Lebowitz, & Falbo, 1971).

In a more difficult style perception task, children were asked to complete a drawing by adding a person the way the artist would have done it (Carothers & Gardner, 1979). They were given a choice of two drawings of people, one of which used the same line quality as the target drawing. Six-year-olds chose at random, but 9-year-olds selected the completion in the appropriate style of line. Thus, when only line quality was varied, 6-year-olds failed to match by style.

Composition

Infants pay attention to the external contour of a pattern but not to the internal organization of its parts (Bond, 1972); sensitivity to the internal structure of a pattern develops gradually between the ages of 4 and 8 (Chipman & Mendelson, 1975). This was demonstrated by asking children to judge which of two patterns identical in external contour was simpler. The ability to look through the content of a painting to perceive its structure develops only by late childhood and early adolescence: When asked to sort groups of four paintings two of which had similar composition and two of which had similar content, classification by subject matter decreased with age with the main decline between ages 11 to 14, and classification by composition increased, with the main increase between ages 7 to 11 (H. Gardner & Gardner, 1973).

Taken together, studies of children's perception of aesthetic properties of pictures show that by age 3 or 4, children have the ability to perceive aspects of expression, style, and composition. However, when representational content is pitted against one of these nonrepresentational properties and competes for the child's attention, representation wins out and children ignore the aesthetic property.

MAKING PICTURES: MAJOR MILESTONES

Action Representations

The first milestone in drawing is the emergence, sometime between the ages of 1 to 2, of scribbling. Kellogg (1969) believed that representation emerges only after extensive practice with mark-making and only when adults respond to the child's "meaningless" forms by pointing out a resemblance to objects in the world (e.g., showing the child how the circle with lines radiating out looks like a person). But children and adults with no previous drawing experience can rapidly arrive at drawings of humans that children in our culture achieve only after much practice with scribbling (Alland, 1983; Harris, 1971; Kennedy, 1993; Millar, 1975). Thus, scribbling may not be a necessary precursor to graphic representation (see Golomb, 2004, chap.1). Figure 10.2 shows the first drawings of a 5-year-old boy from the South American Andes who progressed rapidly to human figures (Harris, 1971).

Evidence that scribbling often carries representational meaning comes from watching the process of the child scribbling (Matthews, 1984, 1997, 1999; Wolf & Perry, 1988). Children may symbolize an object's motion as they scribble (e.g., mimicking the action of a rabbit hopping by making the marker hop along the page leaving dots and saying "hop hop"; Wolf & Perry, 1988), but the resultant static marks do not capture the action and thus do not reveal to the naive eye what the child has intended to symbolize. Figure 10.3 shows such an "action representation" by a 2-year-old who moved the brush in circular motions while labeling his painting an airplane.

Graphic Representations

The first spontaneous graphic representations (depicting recognizable objects) emerge between 3 to 4 years of age (Golomb, 2004). Even in cultures with almost no pictorial tradition, children make graphic representational drawings when asked by researchers to draw (Alland, 1983). Thus, children do not need to be instructed to arrive at graphic representation, nor do they first need models of representational drawings to do so.

Tadpoles.   One of the first graphic representations 3-year-olds attempt is the human figure (Cox & Parkin, 1986; Golomb, 2004). Children's early attempts to represent the human figure have been described as "tadpoles" because these representations consist of a circle with arms and legs (or just legs) emanating from it, as shown in Figures 10.4a and 10.4b. These figures appear to have heads but no trunks (Luquet, 1913, 1927; Piaget & Inhelder, 1956; Ricci, 1887).

Tadpoles should not be seen as reflecting a limited understanding of the human body. When asked to construct a person out of given geometric shapes, only 2 out of 27 3-year-olds made tadpoles; when asked to complete a drawing consisting of a head with facial features, or when asked to model a person out of Play-Doh, many of the same children who drew tadpoles included a trunk (Golomb, 2004). Figure 10.5 shows drawings by a 4-year-old: When asked just to draw a person she drew an armless tadpole (the two figures on the left); when asked to draw a person with a tummy she drew a body (third figure from the left); and when asked to draw a person with a flower, she included a body and an arm. Thus while children may not draw what they see, their drawings do not tell us all that they know about what they draw.

According to Freeman's (1980) production deficit view of children's drawings, tadpoles are defective not because of the child's limited knowledge of the human form but

FIGURE 10.2 First Drawings by a 5-Year-Old from the South American Andes Who Had Never Drawn Before. (*Source:* "The Case Method in Art Education" (pp. 29–49), by D. B. Harris, in *A Report on Preconference Education Research Training Program for Descriptive Research in Art Education,* G. Kensler (Ed.), 1971, Reston, VA: National Art Education Association.)

FIGURE 10.3 Action Representation of an Airplane by a Child Age Two Years and Two Months. (*Source: The Art of Childhood and Adolescence: The Construction of Meaning* (p. 34, figure 11), by J. Matthews, 1999, London: Falmer Press. Reprinted with permission of Taylor & Francis Books.)

rather because of children's planning and memory deficits. Freeman argues that drawing is a serially ordered performance. When children draw the figure, they begin with the head and end with the legs, forgetting what comes in the middle (trunk and arms). But there are problems with this performance explanation. Experiments by Golomb and Farmer (1983) show that while children do draw the human starting at the top and moving down, 40% of the 3-year-olds also moved back up, adding arms, facial features, and so on. When asked to list the parts needed to draw a person, children were far more likely to include arms and a trunk than they were when asked to draw a person. As mentioned, when given global instructions (draw a person), 3- to 5-year-olds produced tadpoles, but when given more specific instructions (e.g., draw a person with a tummy, with a flower), these same children were able to add a torso and an arm (Golomb, 1981, 2004). And when children who spontaneously draw tadpoles were asked to construct a person out of cutout pieces of paper such as circles and rectangles, they often included a torso, showing that they are aware of the torso but just did not know how to include it in their spontaneous drawings (see also Bassett, 1977; Cox &

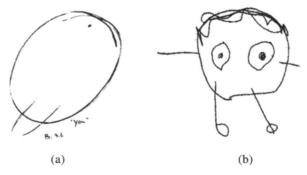

(a)   (b)

FIGURE 10.4 (a) Armless tadpole by a child aged three years and three months. (b) Tadpole with legs and arms by a three and a half year old. (*Source: The Child's Creation of a Pictorial World,* second edition, (p. 29, figures 16a and 16b), by C. Golomb, 2004, Mahwah, NJ: Erlbaum. Reprinted with permission.)

FIGURE 10.5 Drawings by a 4-Year-Old Showing the Effect of Instructions on Presence/Absence of Arms in Tadpoles. (*Source: The Child's Creation of a Pictorial World,* second edition, (p. 46, figure 25a), by C. Golomb, 2004, Mahwah, NJ: Erlbaum. Reprinted with permission.)

Mason, 1998). These findings fail to support Freeman's position that failure to remember the trunk and the arms explains why these are omitted from tadpole humans.

Taken together, the evidence shows that defects of knowledge, memory, or understanding do not explain tadpoles. The tadpole is a simple, undifferentiated form that is, in Arnheim's (1974) terms, a clear structural equivalent for a human reflecting the difficulty of the drawing task, but not reflecting all that the child can do when pushed, prodded, and stimulated by clever tasks and instructions.

Transition from Intellectual to Visual Realism

Because of the assumption of a universal trajectory from object-centered representation toward viewer-centered optical realism, the dominant question in the study of children's drawings has been how realism develops. Luquet's (1913, 1927) and Piaget and Inhelder's (1956) claim that children do not draw what they see (visual realism) but instead what they know (intellectual realism), is consistent with a nineteenth-century demonstration by Clark (1897) who showed that 6-year-olds drew an apple with a pin stuck in it so that the pin (which the child knew was inside the apple) was visible inside the apple, which thus appeared transparent. Piaget and Inhelder (1956) demonstrated the same phenomenon by asking children to draw a stick shown either from a side view or a foreshortened end view. Children under ages 7 to 8 drew a line or long region for both orientations. It would have been correct to depict the foreshortened stick as a circle, and circles are just as easy for the child to draw as a straight line, but children's depictions of the foreshortened stick were presumed to reflect their knowledge that the stick was long.

Do children draw in an intellectually realistic way because their knowledge interferes or because they can't figure out how to translate a three-dimensional object into a two-dimensional representation? Evidence for the first of these explanations comes from a study showing that when children copied drawings of cubes, they drew much less accurately than when they copied designs, which were matched to the cubes in number of lines and regions (Phillips, Hobbs, & Pratt, 1978). When children knew they were copying a cube, their knowledge that a cube has square faces interfered with realism and they did not distort the faces of the cube by drawing them as parallelograms. Figure 10.6 shows the two models children were given to copy, and an example

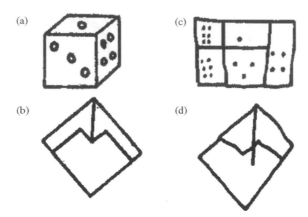

FIGURE 10.6   Children Copy Pictures of Cubes More Accurately than They Copy Designs. (a) Cube model that children copied. (b) Design that children copied. (c) Intellectually realistic copy of cube. (d) Visually realistic correct copy of design. (*Source:* "Intellectual Realism in Children's Drawings of Cubes," by W. A. Phillips, S. B. Hobbs, and F. R. Pratt, 1978, *Cognition, 6*(1), pp. 15–33. Copyright © 1978 by Elsevier. Reprinted with permission from Elsevier.)

of an intellectually realistic copy of the cube and a fairly correct copy of the design. The fact that they were copying pictures of cubes rather than drawing from a three-dimensional model shows that in this case intellectual realism was not due to the difficulty of translating a three-dimensional image into a two-dimensional one because the drawing they were copying solved that problem for them. Presumably, their knowledge of a cube's actual shape interfered. Phillips et al. (1978) suggest that young children have graphic-motor schemata for specific objects (e.g., when drawing a cube, they draw square faces). When they begin to draw a particular object, they select its corresponding schema; the observation of the object being copied then no longer influences the drawing.

Representing Depth

Willats (1977, 1995) uncovered a series of stages that children go through as they acquire the graphic rules for creating the illusion of depth in a drawing. He asked children ages 5 to 17 to draw, from observation, a table with objects resting on it (Figure 10.7a). Five kinds of projective systems and five different sets of drawing rules for mapping objects onto the page were found. Drawings with no projection system were more common among the 5- to 7-year-olds than at older ages (Figure 10.7b). The most common strategy for 7- to 12-year-olds was to draw the table in orthographic projection, in which the tabletop was drawn as a line with objects resting on it, with the third dimension completely ignored (Figure 10.7c). This is a visually realistic way of depicting a table, and captures the view from eye level. The most common strategy for 12- to 13-year-olds was to use vertical oblique projection (Figure 10.7d), which is a system used in Indian, Islamic, and Byzantine art and never taught in Western art classes. Here the vertical dimension on the page represents the third dimension in the scene (vertical lines represent edges receding into depth). Vertical oblique projection allows children to show their knowledge that a tabletop is rectangular, but the drawing is no longer vi-

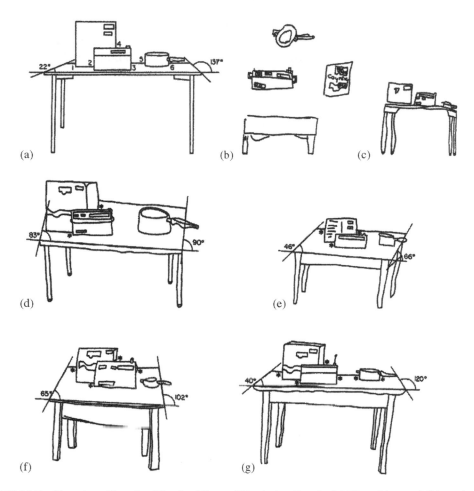

FIGURE 10.7 Drawings Showing Varying Ways of Depicting Depth. (a) The tabletop children drew. (b) No projections system and objects float. (c) Orthographic projection with no indication of depth. (d) Vertical oblique projection where depth is ambiguously represented by vertical lines. (e) Oblique projection where depth is unambiguously represented by diagonal lines. (f) Naive perspective where lines converge but not at the correct angles. (g) Correct perspective. (*Source:* "How Children Learn to Draw Realistic Pictures," by J. Wallats, 1977, *Quarterly Journal of Experimental Psychology, 29,* pp. 367–382. Reprinted with permission from the Experimental Psychology Society, www.psypress.co.uk/journals.asp.)

sually realistic. Moreover, this system results in ambiguity because it does not disambiguate between high up versus receding into depth in the actual scene.

Only a minority of 13- to 14-year-olds figured out that one can resolve this ambiguity by using diagonal lines to indicate depth (Figure 10.7e; called oblique perspective—a system used in Asian art for centuries). Children using this system drew the tabletop as a parallelogram with diagonal lines representing edges receding into depth. The price they paid for creating a less ambiguous drawing is that they had to distort the rectangular shape of the table into a parallelogram. Forty percent of the drawings were in oblique projection, despite the fact that children rarely see drawings of this sort in illustrations.

The lines of true perspective drawings converge on a vanishing point; those of naive perspective do not converge sufficiently. Only a few children, between fifteen and a half and seventeen and a half, drew in naive perspective (Figure 10.7f); even fewer at this age drew in true perspective (Figure 10.7g). Consistent with Willats's findings, early collections of children's drawings included few perspective drawings even at adolescence (e.g., Kerschensteiner, 1905). Children in our culture do not naturally begin to draw in perspective, even though perspectival images are everywhere. Those who do draw in perspective have probably had training, or they are gifted in the visual arts.

Willats's stages show the complexity of the development of the ability to represent depth. The stages do not increase linearly in visual realism because the orthographic projections of stage 2 are actually more realistic than the vertical oblique projections that come next. Willats (1977) argued that perspective drawing develops not as a function of increasingly accurate observation of the world or of pictures, but rather due to the desire to reduce ambiguity. This view is consistent with Karmiloff-Smith's (1992) studies of children's overmarking in various domains (including drawing) to reduce ambiguity, and would explain the shift from vertical oblique to oblique perspective. Willats (1984, 1995) goes on to argue, in a manner that echoes Luquet (1927), that development away from object- to viewer-centered descriptions occurs as children begin to notice that their drawings do not fully capture how the scene really looks and begin to judge their drawings self-consciously in these terms. Children invent increasingly complex systems when they become aware of the limitations of the system they are using.

AESTHETIC PROPERTIES: EXPRESSION, COMPOSITION, AND STYLE

Expression

While preschoolers' drawings appear expressive to adults, we cannot tell from spontaneous drawings whether the expressive properties are intentional. Some intervention is called for. When children were asked to draw a tree to complete a picture that was either gloomy or cheery, they were unable to add expressively appropriate trees (e.g., drooping or dying tree versus blooming tree) until the age of about 11 (Carothers & Gardner, 1979). However, when instructions make it clear that children are to attend to expression, children succeed at a much younger age. Asked directly to make a sad, happy, and angry tree, and a sad, happy, and angry line, even 4-year-olds succeed 37% of the time (Ives, 1984; see also Winner et al., 1986; and Winston et al., 1995). These findings are consistent with ones reported earlier showing that preschoolers can, under certain conditions, perceive expressive properties.

Composition

Studies of compositional principles in children's drawings show a development toward order and balance (Golomb, 1987, 2004; Golomb & Dunnington, 1985). Golomb and Farmer (1983) analyzed compositional principles found in over 1,000 drawings of about 600 children ranging from 3 to 13 years of age. The most primitive compositional strategy, seen only infrequently in the drawings of 3-year-olds, was an aspatial one in which figures were placed arbitrarily across the page. This strategy was followed by a proximity strategy in which objects were clustered together. Both of these strategies gave way to alignment and centering.

The alignment principle was seen as young as age 3, with objects partially aligned side by side along an imaginary horizontal axis. The alignment is only partial because objects still appear to float about in space. Partial alignment was used by 3-year-olds 55% of the time in Golomb's (2004) samples. By age 4, figures were aligned carefully and evenly across the horizontal axis. Five- and 6-year-olds continued this strategy, but clearly located the figures at the bottom of the page, with the empty space on top representing the sky, thus defining up and down (see also Eng, 1931).

The centering principle can be seen in drawings of 3-year-olds. The earliest use of centering consists of a single figure placed in the middle of the page. This results in symmetry (recall that by 12 months of age children prefer vertical symmetry over asymmetry; Bornstein, Ferdinandsen, & Gross, 1981). Golomb (2004) found this kind of simple centering in 15% of 3-year-olds' drawings. By age 4, several figures may be balanced around the center (36% of 4-year-olds' drawings were centered). By age 5 and 6, symmetry was created by equal spacing of figures and repetition of elements. An increase in symmetry with age was also reported by Winner, Mendelsohn, and Garfunkel (1981).

Balance can also be achieved without symmetry, when different qualities counterbalance each other (e.g., a small bright form may be balanced by a larger pale form because brightness lends weight; Arnheim, 1974). This kind of "dynamic balance" was found by Winner et al. (1981) in 25% of drawings by children aged 4, 6, and 10. In contrast, dynamic balance was seen rarely by Golomb (2004), who found little change in compositional strategies after the ages of 9 to 13, perhaps due to children's competing interest in realistic depiction.

Style

Some children have recognizable drawing styles by age 5. This was demonstrated in a study in which adults judged the similarity relationships among pairs of drawings by three 5-year-old children (Hartley, Somerville, Jensen, & Elifjua, 1982). Their judgments showed that drawings by two of these children were cohesive, meaning they had a distinctive style. Judges were also able to recognize new drawings by the same two children drawn at the same time as well as 9 months later. An even stronger demonstration that children have persistent drawing styles was reported by Pufall and Pesonen (2000) who found that adults who learned to recognize the style of three 5-year-olds could identify drawings by these children done 4 years later. But Watson and Schwartz (2000) showed that only about a third of the children in their sample showed a distinctive style, with younger ones (5- to 8-year-olds) showing greater distinctiveness than older children (9- to 10-year-olds). Perhaps this decline is due to drawings in middle childhood becoming conventional, stereotyped, and less playful than those in the preschool years, as is discussed later.

DOES DRAWING SKILL IMPROVE LINEARLY WITH AGE?

While all would agree that technical drawing skills improve steadily with age, including the ability to draw realistically, researchers disagree about whether aesthetic properties of children's drawings improve linearly with age. Some aspects of drawing ability have been shown to be U-shaped, declining after the preschool years, only to return again in those children with talent and interest in drawing. Resemblances between the art of twentieth-century masters and drawings by young children (in terms of playfulness, simplicity, expressivity, and aesthetic appeal) have been noted (Arnheim, 1974; H. Gardner, 1980; M. A. Hagen, 1986; Schaefer-Simmern, 1948; Winner & Gardner, 1981).

Children draw less frequently as they grow older (Cox, 1992; Dennis, 1991; Golomb, 2002) and drawings become conventional and lose their playfulness by age 9 or 10 (H. Gardner, 1980). And young children are more willing to violate realism than are older children (Winner, Blank, Massey, & Gardner, 1983). Children ages 6 through 12 were given copies of black-and-white line drawings by artists varying in level of realism (e.g., a realistic Picasso versus a nonrealistic Picasso) and each with a small portion of the drawing deleted. Children were asked to finish the drawings the way the artist would have done. When the drawings were representational, children were told to add the "hair" or the "arm" and were shown where the drawing was incomplete. Responses were scored by whether the level of realism in the drawing was matched in the completion. Six-year-olds performed better than both 8- and 10-year-olds and did as well as the 12-year-olds. Thus, for example, 6-year-olds completed a schematic, nonrealistic Picasso drawing with a missing arm by adding an arm with a nonrealistic, schematic hand; they completed a realistic Picasso, also with a missing hand, with a far more realistic hand. In contrast, 8- and 10-year-olds completed all works in an equally realistic way. They were preoccupied with trying to draw realistically and thus were unable or unwilling to draw nonrealistically even when this tactic was called for by the criterion of stylistic consistency. Because the 6- to 12-year-olds performed equally well and better than the 8- to 10-year-olds, the willingness to violate realism was found to be U-shaped.

Davis (1997) provided the strongest evidence for U-shaped development in drawing. She elicited drawings by the following groups: Those presumed to be at the high end of the U-curve in aesthetic dimensions of their drawings (5-year-olds), those presumed to be in the depths of the literal, conventional stage (8-, 11-, 14-year-olds and adults, all nonartists), and those presumed to have moved beyond the literal stage (14-year-old self-declared artists and professional adult artists). Participants were asked to make three drawings under the following instructions: Draw happy, draw sad, and draw angry. Judges blind to group scored the drawings for overall expression, overall balance, appropriate use of line as a means of expression (e.g., sharp angled lines to express anger), and appropriate use of composition as a means of expression (e.g., asymmetrical composition as more expressive of sadness than a symmetrical composition). The results were clear: Scores for the adult artists' drawings were significantly higher than scores for the works of children ages 8, 11, 14 (nonartists), and adults (nonartists), but did not differ from the scores of two other groups—the youngest children (age 5) and the adolescents who saw themselves as artists. Thus, only the 5-year-olds' drawings were similar to those by adult and adolescent artists, revealing a U-shaped developmental curve for aesthetic dimensions of drawing. While the adult artists often depicted a mood through nonrepresentational drawings, all but one of the 5-year-olds drew representational works. Thus, artists and young children used different means to achieve equally clear expression.

Pariser and van den Berg (1997) countered that the U-shaped curve is culturally determined—a product of the Western expressionist aesthetic. They found that while Westerners judged preschool art as more aesthetic than that of older children, Chinese American judges, influenced by their own more traditional, nonmodernist artistic tradition, awarded higher scores to older than younger children's art. This finding, if replicated in other studies, shows that the U-curve is a manifestation of how we judge children's art, and could be a product a Western modernist expressionist aesthetic.

The loss of interest in drawing, and the loss of expressiveness in drawing (as perceived by Westerners) in the middle childhood years, may not be inevitable. Arts education plays a very small role in our schools. It is certainly possible (though yet untested) that if the visual arts were taught seriously throughout the school years, no decline in interest or expressiveness would be found.

Music

Music is a near-constant presence in our lives, whether on the radio, television, elevator, or concert hall, and almost all people love some kind of music. While we may not be able to talk explicitly about what it is that we hear when we listen to music, we have a great deal of implicit knowledge about music, based on certain innate sensitivities (to be discussed later) and years of exposure to the music of our culture.

Because almost all of the developmental research on music has been conducted on Western children exposed to Western tonal music, we know little about development in non-Western musical traditions. However, many musical universals exist. For example, all cultures have a systematic way of organizing pitches that repeat over octaves, and all scales have a limit of about seven pitches within an octave (Dowling & Harwood, 1986). Individuals from different musical traditions share the ability to perceive notes separated by octaves as equivalent (octave equivalence); and there is a weaker tendency to perceive the perfect fifth as having a special status (Dowling, 1991). Almost all scales divide the octave into five to seven pitches with unequal steps between them (A to A sharp is a half step, A to B is a whole step; the Western diatonic major scale is made up of seven notes; Sloboda, 1985). This property, which leads to a sense of motion and rest or tension and resolution is not found in the regularity of chromatic scales, which have 12 equally spaced notes (and in which, therefore, every tone has equal status), and might account for why chromatic scales have never been widespread (Shepard, 1982).

Although musical universals exist (as do universals in drawing), we also know that exposure to the music of a person's culture has a profound effect on musical development. Western music, whether folk, rock, classical, or songs sung to infants, consists of a fairly small set of musical relationships, which form the basis of all of our music, and from which composers often deliberately deviate to create tension and affect (Lerdahl & Jackendoff, 1983; Meyer, 1956, 1973). How we hear music is constrained by our years of exposure to these basic relationships. Adults in Western culture have internalized tonal structure and tonality organizes our perception of music (Bartlett, 1996; Dewar, Cuddy, & Mewhort, 1977; Frances, 1988; Krumhansl, 1979). For example, the major scale is the most common structure found in Western European music, and Western listeners find it easier to recall melodies in the major scale than in any other kind of scale (Cuddy, Cohen, & Mewhort, 1981).

EVOLUTIONARY BASE

Evidence of music making exists in every known human culture, from hunter gatherers to industrial cultures (Miller, 2000). Evidence that Neanderthals had music comes from the discovery of a flute carved out of the bone of a bear and dated between 42,000 and 82,000 years ago (Wallin, Merker, & Brown, 2001). This bone had three holes, with the distance between the second and third hole twice that of the distance between the third and fourth, indicating that this flute played music based on the Western diatonic scale. We should not be too quick to conclude from this discovery that the diatonic scale is the most "natural," however, because Neanderthals or early humans may also certainly have used other scales.

Some have argued that music evolved for mate selection (Miller, 2000) or for group cohesion (E. H. Hagen & Bryant, 2003). Scholars may never resolve the question of whether music is a complex adaptation that occurred during evolution (Miller, 2000) or a byproduct of other abilities that themselves evolved for adaptive purposes (Hauser & McDermott, 2003).

Comparative studies of musical abilities in nonhumans can help to clarify the evolutionary history of music. Here we must make a clear distinction between music production (either singing or with instruments) and music perception. No nonhuman primates sing (Hauser & McDermott, 2003), although one (Kanzi, a bonobo) showed controlled drumming on an object and bobbed his head rhythmically as he drummed (Kugler & Savage-Rumbaugh, 2002). Aside from Kanzi, the only nonhumans known to produce music are birds and birdsong is far more constrained than is human music (Hauser & McDermott, 2003).

With respect to music perception, some striking similarities have been found between human and nonhuman primate abilities. Wright, Rivera, Hulse, Shyan, and Neiworth (2000) trained rhesus monkeys to make same/different judgments of melodies and found that they treated a melody as the same when it was transposed by 1 to 2 octaves in the same key. However, if the transposition was only half or one and a half octaves from the original, the transposition (which was then in a new key) was not heard as the same as the original. This finding shows that monkeys hear two Cs as the same, even though they are separated by eight notes (octave generalization), but they hear a C and a G as different even though they are closer on the scale. Wright et al. also found that the perception of similarity between two notes an octave or two apart occurred only when the notes were part of melodies based on the diatonic scale, and not when atonal melodies were used (melodies whose notes are chosen from the 12 tones of the chromatic scale). We can conclude that nonhuman primates are sensitive to tonality and octave relationships (and we will see that human infants are as well).

Although monkeys show a humanlike sensitivity to musical structure, they do not create music. Hauser and McDermott (2003) argue that this frees us from the burden of explaining the evolutionary function of music. Human musical capacities (or at least some of them) may not have evolved as a special music faculty but instead may have drawn on auditory sensitivities that evolved for other purposes. Domain-general auditory capacities likely evolved before humans began to make music, and at least some basic human musical capacities depend on these more general auditory capacities. The same kind of argument holds for speech perception: Chinchillas perceive some speech sounds categorically, as do human infants, and from this it has been argued that the mechanisms underlying speech perception originally evolved for auditory perception and were later co-opted for speech perception (Hauser, Chomsky, & Fitch, 2002).

Hauser and McDermott (2003) suggest that the human music faculty may also have co-opted another mechanism for music—the mechanism by which human and nonhuman animals express emotion via vocalization, and the sensitivity that young children have to the emotional message in others' voices. Sensitivity to rhythm may also have evolved for nonmusical reasons. Ramus, Hauser, Miller, Morris, and Mehler (2000) showed that human infants and cotton-top tamarin monkeys could discriminate Dutch from Japanese sentences (languages that have different rhythmic properties). Thus, the ability to perceive rhythm may initially have served purposes other than musical or linguistic ones (given that monkeys have neither music nor language).

HISTORICAL AND THEORETICAL APPROACHES TO THE STUDY OF MUSICAL DEVELOPMENT

Early music psychologists conflated music perception with acoustics and acoustical tests of musical ability. Seashore, the author of the Seashore Measures of Musical Talent (Seashore, 1919), assumed musical ability to be adequately measured by atomistic acoustical tests, views criticized by Farnsworth (1928) and Mursell (1937). Psychologists of music have now begun to connect their work closely to the work of music theorists (e.g., Meyer, 1956). Music theorists have developed models of musical grammar that offer predictions for cognitive psychologists to test, with perhaps the most influential model being the grammar of music initially proposed by Lerdahl and Jackendoff (1983). For reviews of theory-driven research in the cognitive psychology of music with the goal of determining the mental structures involved in the perception and interpretation of music, see Deutsch (1982) and Sloboda (1985).

MUSIC PERCEPTION AND COMPREHENSION: MAJOR MILESTONES

Infant Music Perception: Sensitivity to Simple Musical Structures

In many ways, infants process music in adult-like fashion, consistent with Meyer's (1994) view that "the central nervous system . . . predisposes us to perceive certain pitch relationships, temporal proportions, and melodic structures as well shaped and stable" (p. 289, cited in Trehub, Schellenberg, & Hill, 1997, p. 122). However, because infants are exposed to music in utero and from the first day they are born, experience may play a role.

Music processing in infancy is analogous to speech processing in several ways: (a) Infants must process complex sound patterns with affective rather than referential meaning; (b) there are special forms of music and speech directed to infants; and (c) infants' lack of acculturation allows them to make certain discriminations in music and speech that adults fail to make, as shown later (Trehub, Trainor, & Unyk, 1993).

Universals in Songs Sung to Infants. In all known cultures, children are exposed to music from early on, particularly in the form of songs sung to them by adults (Trehub & Schellenberg, 1995). Just as infants are exposed to child-directed-speech with certain universal properties, they are also exposed to child-directed-songs with universal properties (Trehub & Trainor, 1998).

Songs directed to infants are soothing, repetitive, remain in the same key, and have simple, descending contours (Dowling, 1988). Nursery songs repeat strongly tonal patterns and thus may be particularly helpful for Western children's learning of the Western tonal scale system (Dowling, 1988). Songs directed to infants are higher in pitch, slower in tempo, and more emotionally expressive than songs directed to older children or to adults (Bergeson & Trehub, 1999; Trainor, Clark, Huntley, & Adams, 1997; Trehub, Unyk, & Henderson, 1994; Trehub, Unyk, & Trainor, 1993a, 1993b).

Infants listen longer to songs in the maternal style than to songs sung by the same singers in their usual style (Masataka, 1999; Trainor, 1996) and prefer higher to lower pitched versions of songs (Trainor & Zacharias, 1998). These attention-getting universal aspects of songs sung to infants probably help to mold infants' musical sensitivities.

Relational Processing of Rhythm and Melody.   Like adults, infants perceive rhythms and melodies as coherent patterns rather than sequences of unrelated sounds (Dowling, 1978; Trehub et al., 1997). For instance, 7- to 9-month-olds perceive simple rhythmic patterns differing in speed as the same rhythm—they recognize the rhythm despite the change in speed (Trehub & Thorpe, 1989; see also Chang & Trehub, 1977b).

Relational processing also occurs for melodies. Contours—the pattern of ups and downs in a melody—are defining properties of melodies for adults (Dowling & Fujitani, 1971) and for infants (Dowling, 1999; Trehub, 2001; Trehub et al., 1997). Infants perceive two melodies as the same when one is transposed to a new octave, as long as the relations among tones (and hence the melodic contour) are maintained (Chang & Trehub, 1977a). Thus, in both rhythm and melody, infants perceive simple musical gestalts, whether these be rhythmic groupings or melodic contours.

Sensitivity to "Good" Melody Structure or "Good" Intervals.   Infants show better processing for melodies that Western music theory considers well-structured. Cohen, Thorpe, and Trehub (1987) showed that 7- to 11-month-olds were better able to detect a semitone change in a transposition of a melody if the transposition resulted in a well-structured melody based on the major triad (CEGEC) than if it resulted in a less well-structured melody based on the augmented triad (CEG# EC). Similarly, Trehub, Thorpe, and Trainor (1990) found that 7- to 10-month-olds detected a semitone change (in a transposition) only when the original melody was a "good" Western melody in which all the notes belonged to a major scale (in contrast to a "bad" Western melody with notes not in any scale or to a non-Western melody with intervals less than one semitone apart). And Trainor and Trehub (1993) showed that infants have a processing advantage for transpositions related by a perfect fifth. The most likely explanation for infants' better performance with certain types of melodies and intervals that are privileged in Western music is that these infants have already acquired a sensitivity to Western musical structure. Yet, we cannot rule out the possibility that certain structures in Western music are intrinsically easier to process than are violations of these structures. To test this, we need to administer these same tasks to infants from a culture whose music does not follow these structures.

Preference for Consonance.   Zentner and Kagan (1996, 1998) played 4-month-olds two unfamiliar melodies in both a consonant and a dissonant version. The consonant version was played in parallel thirds (the third is the interval that adults judge as consonant); the dissonant version was played in parallel minor seconds (the interval judged by adults as most dissonant). Infants looked significantly longer at the source of the music and showed significantly less motor activity when they heard the consonant version, showing that they distinguished consonance from dissonance. Zentner and Kagan speculate that the findings also show that infants prefer consonance to dissonance because the dissonant version promoted more motor activity (including more fretting and turning away) and less fixation time, indicating a distressed state of arousal.

Zentner and Kagan's (1996, 1998) research confounded consonance with pitch distance (the consonant intervals were wider), but a study by Trainor and Heinmiller (1998) kept interval size constant and again reported a preference for consonance.

Numerous other studies have also shown a preference for consonant over dissonant intervals in infancy. For example, infants as young as 6 months detect quarter semitone changes in intervals when the first interval heard is an octave, a "perfect fifth," and a perfect fourth (Schellenberg & Trehub, 1996), but they cannot detect such subtle changes when the first interval heard is a tritone, a chord considered to be unpleasing and nonharmonious. And octave intervals, the most consonant of all intervals, are clearly perceived by infants. Like adults, infants perceive octave equivalence of pitch: They can tell the difference between a pair of tones separated precisely by one octave versus a pair separated by almost an octave (Demany & Armand, 1984).

Post-Infancy: Sensitivity to Higher-Level Musical Structures

Sensitivity to Diatonic Structure. Almost all Western tonal music (e.g., not only classical but also folk, jazz, and rock) is written within a particular key. Though Western music typically modulates from one key to another over time, at any point in time tonal music is made up primarily of the notes of a particular scale. In the context of a given key, the notes of a scale are perceived as closely related and tones outside of this key sound less related. The relationship among the seven notes of a key is referred to as "diatonic structure."

In tonal music, the notes in a key have varying functions. The first note of the scale is called the tonic (e.g., in the key of G, the tonic is G). The tonic is heard as the most stable note in a tune and as the central tone toward which the others are drawn (Krumhansl, 1979). Melodies often end on the tonic, resulting in a feeling of stability. If the tune ends on the second note of the scale, it feels incomplete, hanging in midair and unresolved.

As a piece modulates from one key to another, the tonic or tonal center also shifts. In twentieth-century Western atonal music, there is neither key nor tonal center. Atonal music lacks the organizing framework provided by a key because the notes are not limited to one scale (Krumhansl, 1979).

Adults can distinguish tonal from atonal music (Dowling, 1982), and recall tonal melodies better than atonal ones (Cuddy, Cohen, & Miller, 1979; Dewar et al., 1977; Krumhansl, 1979). The ability to hear tonal structure (which is an abstraction) is critically important to understanding music, but the ability to distinguish tonal from atonal music is not present in infancy. Zenatti (1969) showed that by age 6 (but not before), children recall tonal sequences better than atonal ones. Children heard tonal and atonal melodies of three, four, and six notes followed by a comparison melody with one of the notes altered by one or two semitones. The task was to indicate which note had been changed. When the melodies had only three notes, 5-year-olds performed the same (and above chance) for both tonal and atonal melodies. By age 6, children performed better on tonal melodies, showing that they had acquired Western scale structure. By age 12, performance on atonal melodies improved and the tonal melodies did not facilitate performance. However, when the melodies were four or six notes long, the tonal framework remained easier even for adults.

Sensitivity to Key Changes. Perception of key is also late to develop. Trainor and Trehub (1992) investigated the ability to detect changes in melodies when the altered pitch was either within or outside the key of the melody. Adults found changes that violated key much easier to detect than ones that remained within key. But 8-month-olds not only performed identically in both conditions (showing a lack of sensitivity to key) but also performed better than adults in detecting within-key changes. Thus, years of listening to Western music impose a structure on what adults hear, such that note changes that remain in key are not heard as changes.

By age 5, children can distinguish keys that are tonally near versus far, a distinction that is independent of geographical distance, because geographically near keys (e.g., C and D) are more remote than tonally near keys (e.g., C and G). Bartlett and Dowling (1980, Experiment 4) played children and adults a melody followed by either a transposition or a same-contour imitation, either in a key near to the original melody (and hence sharing many pitches) or in a key far from the original melody (sharing few pitches). Adults heard the transpositions as the same as the original melody, and the same-contour imitations as different. Five-year-olds responded in terms of key: Near key changes (whether transpositions or same-contour imitations) were heard as the same as the original melody, far key changes as different. Thus, 5-year-olds could distinguish near from far keys but could not detect interval size changes when the contour was preserved. By age 8, children were more likely to hear a far-key transposition as the same, and a near-key imitation as different, showing that, like adults, they attend both to key distance and interval changes.

Sensitivity to the Hierarchy of Notes within a Key.   Children show a growing awareness of the proper structure of melodies (in Western tonal music), recognizing the importance of the tonic note for the ending of a melody. Krumhansl and Keil (1982) asked children to judge the goodness of six-note melodies that began with the tonic triad (C-E-G) and ended on a randomly chosen pitch. When adults were asked to judge the goodness of the final note, notes that are part of the tonic triad (C-E-G) were more highly rated than notes that are outside this triad (Krumhansl, 1990). However, 6- and 7-year-olds only distinguished between endings that were within key versus outside of key. Only by ages 8 to 9 did children begin to distinguish among the pitches of the key, ranking those in the tonic triad as better endings than other notes. When the task was simplified by using five- rather than six-note melodies, sensitivity to this hierarchy of notes within the scale was found by ages 6 to 7 (Cuddy & Badertscher, 1987; see also Sloboda, 1985, pp. 211–212).

The diatonic tonal scale, with its key structure and its hierarchy of notes, is specific to Western tonal music. Thus, it is not surprising that sensitivity to tonality is a late development. Acquisition of sensitivity to tonality occurs implicitly: Such acquisition depends on exposure to Western music but not on formal music instruction.

Perceiving Aesthetic Properties of Music

Expression.   Whether or not they are musically trained, adults agree in general on the emotions expressed by music (Crowder, 1984; Hevner, 1936). Young children agree with adults in their interpretation of musical passages of happy or sad (Dolgin & Adelson, 1990; Kratus, 1993), though there is mixed evidence about how early the ability to recognize emotion in music emerges. Cunningham and Sterling (1988) found that children aged 5 (but not 4) agreed with adults about which pieces are happy, sad, or angry. Gentile, Pick, Flom, and Campos (1994) found that 3-year-olds agreed with adults on which pieces communicated happiness and which sadness, but only for five out of eight musical passages. Because these studies used actual segments of music, they do not allow us to determine which aspects of the music (e.g., mode, tempo, pitch, and volume) contributed to the emotion attribution.

Kastner and Crowder (1990) played 3- to 12-year-olds tunes in minor and major modes and asked them to point to the face that went with the tune (choosing among a happy, content, sad, and angry face). Even 3-year-olds matched positive faces to pieces played in the major mode (though performance improved with age). It is possible that children actually heard the major/minor distinction as a happy/sad one. But it is equally possible that children heard the major/minor distinction as a familiar/unfamiliar one, and gave positive choices when they heard something familiar. It is also possible that correct scores for the major mode were inflated by the selection of the "content" face which looked neutral (and children called it "plain"). A similar study used only a happy versus sad face, and found that 5-year-olds could not reliably match the minor melodies with the sad face and the major melodies with the happy face (Gerardi & Gerken, 1995). Thus, it may be that the perception of the minor mode as negative in affect and the major mode as positive emerges only with experience—perhaps the experience of hearing songs that pair sad lyrics or sad movies with the minor mode.

Style.   A few studies have examined children's ability to attend to the style of musical passages. H. Gardner (1973) asked children ages 6 to 19 to decide whether two passages from classical music came from the same piece and found that all children could succeed on this task though accuracy increased with age. When popular music was used along with classical music and children were asked to decide whether two passages came from the same piece of music, Castell (1982) found that 8-year-olds succeeded remarkably well, confirming Gardner's findings. Both studies however showed that correct perceptual choices emerged earlier than the ability to verbalize what two passages deemed to be from the same piece had in common. Hargreaves (1982) documented the development of the ability to verbalize how two pieces are alike or different, and found that even 7- to 8-year-olds (the youngest he studied) were able to offer what he called "objective-analytic" responses describing the properties of the music.

MAKING MUSIC THROUGH SONG: MAJOR MILESTONES

Infant Song

Infants possess the rudimentary ability needed to make music: They vocalize and vary and imitate pitch. This early "singing" is much like scribbling and babbling.

Pitch Matching.   Newborn cries have musical qualities and involve a wide range of pitches (Ostwald, 1973), but there is no reason to consider these cries as evidence of intentional music making. Kessen, Levine, and Wendrich (1979) provided evidence of intentional music making in infancy by showing that 3- to 6-month-olds could match isolated pitches sung to them on a pitch pipe. The ability to imitate sequences of two notes did not emerge prior to 1 year of age. See also Révész (1954) and Platt (1933) for earlier studies showing infants' ability to match pitches.

Babbled Songs.   Even though 9- to 12-month-olds can imitate discrete pitches, when children this age sing they do so in continuous pitches on a single breath (sometimes called song babbling). This results in an undulating siren-like sound in which pitches are blurred. This kind of sound is rarely heard in Western adult music. Babbled songs are not based on the diatonic system and have no clear rhythmic organization (McKernon, 1979; Moog, 1976; Moorhead & Pond, 1978).

Rhythm.   In striking contrast to the evidence that children can imitate pitches, there is no evidence of intentional production of rhythm in the 1st year of life (Sloboda, 1985). To count as evidence of production of rhythm, it is not enough to see a child bang something over and over. One must look for subdivision of a beat so that there are two or more events within a regular superordinate pulse; omission of a beat with the picking up of the pulse at the correct time after a pause; imitation of a rhythmic pattern; and moving or beating in time to music (Sloboda, 1985).

Post-Infancy: Invented Songs

When it comes to language, children reach the level of the typical adult by age 5 or 6, with no explicit training; similarly, children sing at the level of the untrained adult by age 6. They have overcome three hurdles: (1) pitch has become discrete, (2) intervals have widened, and (3) their songs now have a metric and tonal organization.

Pitch Becomes Discrete.   The undulating pitches of babbled song give way, at around 18 months, to an essential element of Western music—discrete pitches and discrete pitch intervals (Davidson, McKernon, & Gardner, 1981; McKernon, 1979; Werner, 1961). When children first begin to sing in discrete pitches, they do not yet use adult pitch categories—children do not yet sing in a diatonic scale (Dowling, 1988). In addition, pitches wander in and out of tune, interval sizes are not precise, and there is no tonal center (Dowling, 1984). At this age, children are not trying to imitate songs that they have heard; rather, they are inventing their own songs (Davidson et al., 1981; Moog, 1976).

Intervals Widen.   The first intervals that children sing are very small, and development is characterized by a gradual expansion of interval size (Jersild & Bienstock, 1934; McKernon, 1979; Nettl, 1956a; Werner, 1961). McKernon found that major seconds were the most commonly produced intervals between 17 to 23 months. A third of the intervals sung at this age were of this type, and major seconds are among the most common intervals in songs across cultures (Nettl, 1956b). Between 1.5 to 2.5 years, the kinds of intervals increased and widened.

Children first expand their intervals and later fill them in a stepwise fashion (Davidson, 1985). Davidson refers to these early tonal structures as contour schemes—they are the stable intervals that the child possesses. These schemes are imposed on any song that a child acquires, reducing the range of a song's contour if necessary, and sometimes expanding the range to match the size of a new contour scheme just being constructed.

Melodies Gain Rhythmic and Tonal Organization.   Rather than following a primarily rising or falling pattern, the contours of early songs undulate up and down (McKernon, 1979). Adult songs do this, too: Undulating contours are the most common types in adult songs across cultures (Nettl, 1956b). In this respect, as with the most common intervals produced, early songs resemble adult songs. But in their lack of either rhythmic or tonal organization, early songs are qualitatively different from adult songs (McKernon, 1979; Moorhead & Pond, 1978).

The melodic contours of children's early songs are narrow despite the fact that children can vocalize across a wide range (Fox, 1990): And almost all contours range between middle C and the B seven notes above it. Early songs consist of atonal groups of pitches: They are chromatic rather than diatonic, based on any or all of the notes in an octave rather than on the notes of a particular scale, and thus they lack the tonal center heard in Western music (McKernon, 1979; Moorhead & Pond, 1978). The lack of melodic and rhythmic structure in children's first invented songs makes these songs very different from the songs (written by adults) to which they are constantly exposed. By age 3, children are able to sing songs in a single key, though they do not do so reliably at first (McKernon, 1979).

Dowling (1984) described the invented songs his two daughters produced over a 5-year period, beginning in infancy. These children produced an average of 2.23 songs a week. The phrases of the songs had steady beats, but the beat did not always carry across phrases, consistent with findings by Moorhead and Pond (1978) and Moog (1976). Between ages 1 to 2, these two children produced songs with one repeated contour. By age 3, their songs had two to three different contours and often had a "coda," a contour that occurs only at the end of the song. The use of a coda may well have been due to having heard nursery rhymes because this form is found more often in nursery rhymes than in other kinds of songs.

Post-Infancy: Conventional Songs

Imitated Songs. At around the age of 2, children attempt to sing the songs of their culture (Davidson, 1985; Davidson et al., 1981; McKernon, 1979). These early attempts to reproduce conventional songs sound very much like spontaneous songs in their lack of a metric and tonal organization. In both spontaneous songs and early renditions of standard songs, a narrow range of pitches and contours undulates in groups of two or three notes. The first property of a standard song imitated successfully is the lyrics—and these are simply imported into the child's spontaneous musical repertoire without their accompanying tonal and rhythmic structure (McKernon, 1979; Moog, 1976). Next to be reproduced is a song's rhythm. By 28 months, children studied by Davidson et al. (1981) could imitate the rhythmic structure of the alphabet song and fit the words appropriately into the rhythm. Last to develop is the ability to reproduce correct intervals and remain within a key. Adults pass through a similar sequence when learning a new song (Davidson et al., 1981).

By 29 months, children's spontaneous tunes have diverged in sophistication from invented tunes (McKernon, 1979). By the age of 3 or 4, children's standard songs have a clear underlying Western metric structure, even though their invented songs at this age lack this structure (McKernon, 1979). By age 5, spontaneous invented songs have declined and children become self-conscious and concerned with singing "correctly" according to the culture's norms (H. Gardner & Wolf, 1983; Moog, 1976).

Children are able to reproduce rhythm before pitch. Five- to 7-year-olds were followed over 3 years as they learned the song, Row, Row, Row Your Boat (Davidson & Scripp, 1988). Accurate rhythm production requires that a person match the number of units, keep a steady underlying pulse, capture the surface grouping, and coordinate the underlying pulse with the surface notes. Accurate pitch production requires matching the initial pitch, the melodic contour, the interval boundary (highest and lowest notes), and the key. Most (85%) of the 5-year-olds got the rhythm right, but only about half got the pitch right. The ability to reproduce pitch developed rapidly so that by age 7 the gap between rhythm and pitch had narrowed considerably.

We can conclude that musically untrained children show quite sophisticated singing abilities. By the age of 2 or 3, they can reproduce the general contour of a melody even though they cannot reproduce pitches exactly. By age 4, they can maintain intervals but cannot sing in a stable key (because they shift keys at phrase boundaries; McKernon, 1979). They are sensitive to melodic contours very early but the acquisition of a stable tonal center is not present until age 5 or 6, when they can maintain a key. Thus, in both perception and production of music, tonality is a late-developing structure.

Intentional Expression in Singing.   Children as young as age 4 can intentionally vary how they sing a song to convey emotion. Adachi and Trehub (1998) asked 4- to 12-year-olds to sing a familiar song (e.g., "Twinkle, Twinkle, Little Star") to make a listener happy or sad. Children at all ages primarily used devices that express emotion in both speech and music—they sang faster, louder, and at a higher pitch for happy and slower, softer, and lower for sad. Devices for emotion expression that are specific to music (e.g., mode or articulation) were infrequent at all ages.

Post-Infancy: Invented Notations

By asking children to invent ways of notating music that they hear, we can learn whether children understand that music cannot be captured by words or pictures and requires its own system of representation. This understanding emerges at least at early as age 5. In the longitudinal study mentioned earlier in which 5- to 7-year-olds without musical training heard "Row, Row, Row Your Boat," children were asked to write down "the song" so that another person could sing it back (Davidson & Scripp, 1988). The most common kind of notation system at age 5 was one in which abstract symbols were used to represent the notes (e.g., increasingly long lines used to represent increasingly low notes). Forty-three percent of the 5-year-olds used some kind of invented abstract system. The second most common solution at age 5 (26%) was simply to draw a representational picture that captured nothing of the musical information (e.g., a picture of a boat in water). By age 7, 56% of the children still used an invented abstract notation, though half of these combined the abstract notations with words (and almost no children used representational pictures).

The task of notating music is one that these children have probably never encountered before. What is notable is that 5-year-olds did not all rely on pictures; many invented abstract symbols. By age 5, children have learned to write letters, and also know quite a bit about pictorial representation (as shown earlier in the discussion of drawing). When asked to represent music, they invent a symbol system that is independent of both language and pictorial representation. This finding shows that young children are not only inventive when it comes to symbolizing but also recognize that neither words nor pictures do an adequate job of representing music, and that music needs its own form of representational system.

DOES MUSICAL SKILL IMPROVE LINEARLY WITH AGE?

In two areas, development in music does not steadily improve: (1) Absolute pitch capacity may decline with age and (2) young children demonstrate a "figural" understanding of music—a kind of understanding as sophisticated as that of adult musicians.

Absolute Pitch

Absolute pitch refers to the ability to recognize pitches when heard in isolation. This incidence of absolute pitch is estimated at 1/1,500 to 1/10,000 (Bachem, 1955; Miyazaki, 1988; Profita & Bidder, 1988; Takeuchi & Hulse, 1993) though it is difficult to test for absolute pitch in nonmusicians because they have not learned about the names of musical notes.

The incidence of absolute pitch declines with age. Sergeant and Roche (1973) found that absolute pitch is more common in 3- than 6-year-olds. Children were taught to sing three tunes. One week after the last lesson, they were asked to sing the tunes. While the older children were able to sing back the song with the correct contour and precise intervals, it was the younger children who sang back the pitches most precisely. Saffran and Griepentrog (2001) showed that when only one kind of pitch cue (absolute or relative) is available, 8-month-olds discriminate tone patterns on the basis of absolute but not relative pitch. Adults responded in opposite fashion, succeeding only on the relative pitch task. Thus, the ability to store and reproduce pitches precisely may decline with age, giving way to the ability to grasp the overall gestalt of a tune. It is possible that absolute pitch becomes "unlearned" with age as children begin to focus on the distance between tones rather than the tones themselves. Without the ability to represent relative distance, we could not grasp musical structure.

Figural Understanding

Children's invented notations of music demonstrate that they hear music in an intuitive "figural" manner akin to how adult musicians are able to hear music. Bamberger (1991) asked a classroom of 8- and 9-year-olds to make drawings of a clapped rhythm so that someone else could clap back the rhythm. The rhythm had been invented by one of the children in the class and matched the rhythm of the familiar nursery tune, "Three, four, shut the door; five, six, pick up sticks; seven, eight, shut the gate." Eight- and 9-year-olds invented two kinds of notations, which Bamberger refers to as figural and metric (or formal).

In the figural notation in Figure 10.8a, claps 3-4-5 are shown to be alike. Clap 5 is like the two previous ones because all three form one rapidly clapped bounded figure. Figural drawings reveal that children are classifying claps in terms of gestures—the three small circles feel like they are all part of one gesture. In the formal notation in Figure 10.8b, claps 5-6-7 are shown to be alike. Clap 5 is like 6 and 7, revealing that

(a)

(b)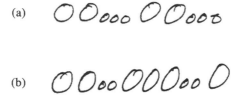

FIGURE 10.8 (a) Figural notation of rhythm. (b) Metric notation of rhythm. (*Source: The Mind Behind the Musical Ear: How Children Develop Musical Intelligence* (p. 24), by Jeanne Bamberger, 1991, Cambridge, MA: Harvard University Press. Copyright © 1991 by the President and Fellows of Harvard College. Reprinted with permission.)

these children are classifying each clap in terms of duration from one clap to the next. To do this they must step back from the performance of clapping and compare claps.

Children who drew one kind of drawing could not understand how the other kind could be right. However, both can be considered right because each captures a different aspect of the rhythm (Bamberger, 1991). Metric notations capture the relative durations of claps—just what standard music notation captures. Figural notations are intuitive phrasings of what the rhythm sounds like—and they capture what musicians refer to as phrasing. For example, a musical performance of the previously mentioned rhythm might involve making claps 3, 4, and 5 louder or softer than the first two to indicate that they form a unit. Children who invented metric notations had managed to transform the continuous flow of the physical act of clapping into static and discrete symbols. These symbols are qualitatively different from the figural ones that capture the bodily flow of making music. In a further study with a large number of 7- to 12-year-olds, Upitas (1987) found that even with formal music training, children favor figural notations (though once they were shown the metric form, children with training were more able to switch to this form than were musically untrained children).

Musicians are able to perceive music both metrically and figurally: They would not be able to impose phrasing on a score without figural understanding. Musical scores often do not contain phrase markings, leaving phrasing up to the musician's interpretation. Thus, children's early and untrained understanding of rhythms as figures is an understanding that is not discarded by experts but instead is maintained. Figural drawings are too often considered less developed than metric ones. Yet, figural drawings capture what is important for musical expression—playing musically and achieving musical coherence (Bamberger, 1982). Thus, the child's earliest intuitive understanding of rhythm represents a way of knowing that remains important and ought to be retained even after more formal modes have been achieved. The challenge is for formal understanding to exist alongside figural understanding rather than have the formal replace the intuitive figural understanding.

Conclusions

A basic premise of developmental psychology holds that we can only study a developmental process of an implicitly or explicitly defined end state (Kaplan, 1967). Freud assumed the normal healthy personality; along with most cognitive-developmentalists, Piaget presupposed the full-blown logical scientific formal-operational thinker. But norms of mental health differ across groups and cultures, and the kind of scientific thought valued by Piaget has emerged only in recent centuries.

The arts address and sometimes answer issues that are less visible in other spheres. Among these issues are why humans persist in activities with nonobvious survival value, to what extent skills develop and even flower in the absence of formal training, and in which ways development may proceed in nonlinear and even regressive directions. In addition, it is particularly in the arts that links between early and adult end states can be seen: Both child and adult artist are experimenters. Artists deliberately violate rules they have mastered; children have not yet mastered the rules and are therefore willing to be playful.

Even though the arts are universal in the way that science is not, I would not go so far as to claim that development perceived from a musical or visual artistic perspective provides the more important perspective. But our understanding of development is enhanced if we can probe and synthesize findings from these various prized developmental end states.

References

Adachi, M., & Trehub, S. E. (1998). Children's expression of emotion in song. *Psychology of Music, 26*(2), 133–153.

Alland, A. (1983). *Playing with form.* New York: Columbia University Press.

Arnheim, R. (1974). *Art and visual perception: A psychology of the creative eye.* Berkeley: University of California Press.

Bachem, A. (1955). Absolute pitch. *Journal of Acoustical Society of America, 27,* 1180–1185.

Bamberger, J. (1982). Revisiting children's drawings of simple rhythms: A function for reflection in action. In S. Strauss (Ed.), *U-shaped behavioral growth* (pp. 191–226). New York: Academic Press.

Bamberger, J. (1991). *The mind behind the musical ear.* Cambridge, MA: Harvard University Press.

Bartlett, D. L. (1996). Tonal and musical memory. In D. A. Hodges (Ed.), *Handbook of music psychology* (pp. 177–195). San Antonio, TX: IMR Press.

Bartlett, J. C., & Dowling, W. J. (1980). The recognition of transposed melodies: A key distance effect in developmental perspective. *Journal of Experimental Psychology: Human Perception and Performance, 6,* 501–515.

Bassett, E. M. (1977). Production strategies in the child's drawing. In G. Butterworth (Ed.), *The child's representation of the world* (pp. 49–59). New York: Plenum Press.

Beilin, H. (1991). Developmental aesthetics and the psychology of photography. In R. M. Downs, L. S. Liben, & D. S. Palermo (Eds.), *Visions of aesthetics, the environment, and development: The legacy of Joachim F. Wohlwill* (pp. 45–86). Hillsdale, NJ: Erlbaum.

Bergeson, T. R., & Trehub, S. E. (1999). Mothers: Singing to infants and preschool children. *Infant Behavior and Development, 22*(11), 51–64.

Blank, P., Massey, C., Gardner, H., & Winner, E. (1984). Perceiving what paintings express. In W. R. Crozier & A. J. Chapman (Eds.), *Cognitive processes in the perception of art* (pp. 127–143). Amsterdam: Elsevier.

Bond, E. (1972). Perception of form by the human infant. *Psychological Bulletin, 77,* 225–245.

Bornstein, M. H., Ferdinandsen, K., & Gross, C. G. (1981). Perception of symmetry in infancy. *Developmental Psychology, 17,* 82–86.

Bower, T. G. R. (1965). Stimulus variables determining space perception in infants. *Science, 149,* 88–89.

Bower, T. G. R. (1966). The visual world of infants. *Scientific American, 215,* 80–92.

Callaghan, T. C. (1997). Children's judgments of emotions portrayed in museum art. *British Journal of Developmental Psychology, 15,* 515–529.

Callaghan, T. C. (1999). Early understanding and production of graphic symbols. *Child Development, 70,* 1314–1324.

Callaghan, T. C. (2000). The role of context in preschoolers' judgments of emotion in art. *British Journal of Developmental Psychology, 18,* 465–474.

Campos, J. J., Langer, A., & Krowitz, A. (1970). Cardiac responses on the visual cliff in prelocomotor human infants. *Science, 170,* 196.

Carothers, T., & Gardner, H. (1979). When children's drawings become art: The emergence of aesthetic production and perception. *Developmental Psychology, 15,* 570–580.

Castell, K. C. (1982). Children's sensitivity to stylistic differences in "classical" and "popular" music [Special issue]. *Psychology of Music,* 22–25.

Chang, H. W., & Trehub, S. E. (1977a). Auditory processing of relational information by young infants. *Journal of Experimental Child Psychology, 24,* 324–331.

Chang, H. W., & Trehub, S. E. (1977b). Infants' perception of temporal grouping in auditory patterns. *Child Development, 48,* 1666–1670.

Chipman, S., & Mendelson, M. (1975). The development of sensitivity to visual structure. *Journal of Experimental Child Psychology, 20,* 411–429.

Clark, A. B. (1897). The child's attitude towards perspective problems. In E. Barnes (Ed.), *Studies in education* (Vol. 1). Stanford, CA: Stanford University Press.

Cohen, A. J., Thorpe, L. A., & Trehub, S. E. (1987). Infants' perception of musical relations in short transposed tone sequences. *Canadian Journal of Psychology, 41,* 33–47.

Cox, M. V. (1992). *Children's drawings.* London: Penguin.

Cox, M. V., & Mason, S. (1998). The young child's pictorial representation of the human figure. *International Journal of Early Years Education, 6*(1), 31–38.

Cox, M. V., & Parkin, C. E. (1986). Young children's human figure drawings: Cross sectional and longitudinal studies. *Educational Psychology, 6,* 353–368.

Crowder, R. G. (1984). Perception of the major/minor distinction: Pt. 1. Historical and theoretical foundations. *Psychomusicology, 4,* 3–10.

Cuddy, L. L., & Badertscher, B. (1987). Recovery of the tonal hierarchy: Some comparisons across age and levels of musical experience. *Perception and Psychophysics, 41,* 609–620.

Cuddy, L. L., Cohen, A. J., & Mewhort, D. J. K. (1981). Perception of structure in short melodic sequences. *Journal of Experimental Psychology: Human Perception and Performance, 7,* 869–883.

Cuddy, L. L., Cohen, A. J., & Miller, J. (1979). Melody recognition: The experimental application of musical rules. *Canadian Journal of Psychology, 33,* 148–157.

Cunningham, J. G., & Sterling, R. S. (1988). Developmental change in the understanding of affective meaning of music. *Motivation and Emotion, 12,* 399–413.

Davenport, R. K., & Rogers, C. M. (1971). Perception of photographs by apes. *Behavior, 39,* 318–320.

Davidson, L. (1985). Tonal structures of children's early songs. *Music Perception, 2*(3), 361–373.

Davidson, L., McKernon, P., & Gardner, H. (1981). *The acquisition of song: A developmental approach* (Documentary report of the Ann Arbor Symposium: Applications of Psychology to the Teaching and Learning of Music). Reston, VA: Music Educators National Conference.

Davidson, L., & Scripp, L. (1988). Young children's musical representations: Windows on music cognition. In J. Sloboda (Ed.), *Generative processes in music* (pp. 195–230). Oxford: Oxford University Press.

Davis, J. H. (1997). The what and the whether of the U: Cultural implications of understanding development in graphic symbolization. *Human Development, 40,* 145–154.

DeLoache, J. S. (1987). Rapid change in the symbolic functioning of very young children. *Science, 238,* 1556–1557.

DeLoache, J. S., Pierroutsakos, S. L., & Uttal, D. H. (2003). The origins of pictorial competence. *Current Directions in Psychological Science, 12*(4), 114–117.

DeLoache, J. S., Strauss, M. S., & Maynard, J. (1979). Picture perception in infancy. *Infant Behavior and Development, 2,* 77–89.

Demany, L., & Armand, F. (1984). The perceptual reality of tone chroma in early infancy. *Journal of the Acoustical Society of America, 76,* 57–66.

Dennis, S. (1991). Stage and structure in children's spatial representations. In R. Case (Ed.), *The mind's staircase* (pp. 229–245). Hillsdale, NJ: Erlbaum.

Deregowski, J. B. (1984). *Distortion in art: The eye and the mind.* London: Routledge & Kegan Paul.

Deutsch, D. (Ed.). (1982). *The psychology of music.* New York: Academic Press.

Dewar, K. M., Cuddy, L. L., & Mewhort, D. J. K. (1977). Recognition memory for single tones with and without context. *Journal of Experimental Psychology: Human Learning and Memory, 3,* 60–69.

Dolgin, K. G., & Adelson, E. H. (1990). Age changes in the ability to interpret affect in sung and instrumentally-presented melodies. *Psychology of Music, 18,* 87–98.

Dowling, W. J. (1978). Scale and contour: Two components of a theory of memory for melodies. *Psychological Review, 85,* 341–354.

Dowling, W. J. (1982). Melodic information processing and its development. In D. Deutsch (Ed.), *The psychology of music* (pp. 413–429). New York: Academic Press.

Dowling, W. J. (1984). Development of musical schemata in children's spontaneous singing. In W. R. Crozier & A. J. Chapman (Eds.), *Cognitive processes in the perception of art* (pp. 145–163). Amsterdam: Elsevier.

Dowling, W. J. (1988). Tonal structure and children's early learning of music. In J. Sloboda (Ed.), *Generative processes in music* (pp. 113–128). Oxford: Oxford University Press.

Dowling, W. J. (1991). Tonal strength and melody recognition after long and short delays. *Perception and Psychophysics, 50,* 305–313.

Dowling, W. J. (1999). The development of music perception and cognition. In D. Deutsch (Ed.), *The psychology of music* (pp. 603–625). San Diego, CA: Academic Press.

Dowling, W. J., & Fujitani, D. S. (1971). Contour, interval, and pitch recognition in memory for melodies. *Journal of the Acoustical Society of America, 49,* 524–431.

Dowling, W. J., & Harwood, D. L. (1986). *Music cognition.* New York: Academic Press.

Eng, H. (1931). *The psychology of children's drawings.* New York: Harcourt, Brace.

Farnsworth, P. R. (1928). The effects of nature and nurture on musicality. In *The 27th yearbook of the National Society for the Study of Education* (Pt. 2, pp. 233–247). Chicago: National Society for the Study of Education.

Fineberg, J. (1997). *The innocent eye.* Princeton, NJ: Princeton University Press.

Fox, D. B. (1990). An analysis of the pitch characteristics of infant vocalizations. *Psychomusicology, 9,* 21–30.

Frances, R. (1988). *The perception of music.* Hillsdale, NJ: Erlbaum.

Freeman, N. H. (1980). *Strategies of representation in young children: Analysis of spatial skills and drawing processes.* London: Academic Press.

Freeman, N. H. (1995). The emergence of a framework theory of pictorial reasoning. In C. Lange-Kuttner & G. V. Thomas (Eds.), *Drawing and looking: Theoretical approaches to pictorial representation in children* (pp. 135–146). New York: Harvester Wheatsheaf.

Freeman, N. H., & Sanger, D. (1993). Language and belief in critical thinking: Emerging explanations of pictures. *Exceptionality Education Canada, 3,* 43–58.

Gardner, H. (1970). Children's sensitivity to painting styles. *Child Development, 41,* 813–821.

Gardner, H. (1973). Children's sensitivity to musical style. *Merrill-Palmer Quarterly, 19,* 67–77.

Gardner, H. (1974). Metaphors and modalities: How children project polar adjectives onto diverse domains. *Child Development, 45,* 84–91.

Gardner, H. (1980). *Artful scribbles: The significance of children's drawings.* New York: Basic Books.

Gardner, H., & Gardner, J. K. (1973). Developmental trends in sensitivity to form and subject matter in paintings. *Studies in Art Education, 14,* 52–56.

Gardner, H., Winner, E., & Kircher, M. (1975). Children's conceptions of the arts. *Journal of Aesthetic Education, 9,* 60–77.

Gardner, H., & Wolf, D. (1983). Waves and streams of symbolization. In D. R. Rogers & J. A. Sloboda (Eds.), *The acquisition of symbolic skills* (pp. 19–42). London: Plenum Press.

Gardner, R., & Gardner, B. (1978). Comparative psychology and language acquisition. *Annals of the New York Academy of Sciences, 309,* 37–76.

Gentile, D. A., Pick, A. D., Flom, R. A., & Campos, J. J. (1994, April). *Adults' and preschoolers' perception of emotional meaning in music.* Poster presented at the 13th biennial conference on Human Development, Pittsburgh, PA.

Gerardi, G. M., & Gerken, L. (1995). The development of affective responses to modality and melodic contour. *Music Perception, 12,* 279–290.

Golomb, C. (1973). Children's representation of the human figure: The effects of models, media and instructions. *Genetic Psychology Monographs, 87,* 197–251.

Golomb, C. (1981). Representation and reality: The origins and determinants of young children's drawings. *Review of Research in Visual Art Education, 14,* 36–48.

Golomb, C. (1987). The development of compositional strategies in drawing. *Visual Arts Research, 13*(2), 42–52.

Golomb, C. (2002). *Child art in context: A cultural and comparative perspective.* Washington, DC: American Psychological Association.

Golomb, C. (2004). *The child's creation of a pictorial world* (2nd cd.). Mahwah, NJ: Erlbaum.

Golomb, C., & Dunnington, G. (1985, June). *Compositional development in children's drawings.* Paper presented at the annual Symposium of the Jean Piaget Society, Philadelphia.

Golomb, C., & Farmer, D. (1983). Children's graphic planning strategies and early principles of spatial organization in drawing. *Studies in Art Education, 24*(2), 87–100.

Gombrich, E. H. (1977). *Art and illusion: A study in the psychology of pictorial representation* (5th ed.). London: Phaidon Press.

Goodman, N. (1976). *Languages of art* (2nd ed.). Indianapolis, IN: Hackett.

Hagen, E. H., & Bryant, G. A. (2003). Music and dance as a coalition signaling system. *Human Nature, 14*(1), 21–51.

Hagen, M. A. (1986). *The varieties of realism.* Cambridge: Cambridge University Press.

Hardiman, G., & Zernich, T. (1985). Discrimination of style in painting: A developmental study. *Studies in Art Education, 26,* 157–162.

Hargreaves, D. J. (1982). The development of aesthetic reactions to music [Special issue]. *Psychology of Music,* 51–54.

Harris, D. B. (1971). The case method in art education. In G. Kensler (Ed.), *A report on preconference education research training program for descriptive research in art education* (pp. 29–49). Restow, VA: National Art Education Association.

Hartley, J. L., Somerville, S. C., Jensen, D. C., & Elifjua, C. C. (1982). Abstraction of individual styles from the drawings of 5-year-old children. *Child Development, 53,* 1193–1214.

Hauser, M. D., Chomsky, N., & Fitch, W. T. (2002). The faculty of language: What is it, who has it, and how did it evolve? *Science, 298,* 1569–1579.

Hauser, M. D., & McDermott, J. (2003). The evolution of the music faculty: A comparative perspective. *Nature Neuroscience, 6*(7), 663–668.

Hevner, K. (1936). Experimental studies of the elements of expression in music. *American Journal of Psychology, 48,* 246–268.

Hochberg, J., & Brooks, V. (1962). Pictorial recognition as an unlearned ability: A study of one child's performance. *American Journal of Psychology, 73,* 624–628.

Hussain, F. (1965). Quelques problèmes d'esthetique experimentale. *Sciences de l'Art, 2,* 103–114.

Ives, S. W. (1984). The development of expressivity in drawing. *British Journal of Educational Psychology, 54,* 152–159.

Jersild, A., & Bienstock, S. (1934). A study of the development of children's ability to sing. *Journal of Educational Psychology, 25,* 481–503.

Jolley, R. P., & Thomas, G. V. (1994). The development of sensitivity to metaphorical expression of moods in abstract art. *Educational Psychology, 14,* 437–450.

Jolley, R. P., & Thomas, G. V. (1995). Children's sensitivity to metaphorical expression of mood in line drawings. *British Journal of Developmental Psychology, 12,* 335–346.

Jolley, R. P., Zhi, C., & Thomas, G. V. (1998a). The development of understanding moods metaphorically expressed in pictures: A cross-cultural comparison. *Journal of Cross-Cultural Psychology, 29*(2), 358–376.

Jolley, R. P., Zhi, C., & Thomas, G. V. (1998b). How focus of interest in pictures changes with age: A cross-cultural comparison. *International Journal of Behavioural Development, 22,* 127–149.

Kaplan, B. (1967). Meditations on genesis. *Human Development, 10,* 65–87.

Karmiloff-Smith, A. (1992). *Beyond modularity: A developmental perspective on cognitive science.* Cambridge, MA: MIT Press.

Kastner, M. P., & Crowder, R. G. (1990). Perception of major/minor: Pt. 4. Emotional connotations in young children. *Music Perception, 8,* 189–202.

Kellogg, R. (1969). *Analyzing children's art.* Palo Alto, CA: National Press Books.

Kennedy, J. M. (1993). *Drawing and the blind.* New Haven, CT: Yale University Press.

Kerschensteiner, G. (1905). *Die entwicklung der zeichnerischen begabung.* Munich, Germany: Gerber.

Kessen, W., Levine, J., & Wendrich, K. A. (1979). The imitation of pitch in infants. *Infant Behavior and Development, 2,* 93–99.

Kratus, J. (1993). A developmental study of children's interpretation of emotion in music. *Psychology of Music, 21,* 3–19.

Krumhansl, C. L. (1979). The psychological representation of musical pitch in a tonal context. *Cognitive Psychology, 11,* 325–334.

Krumhansl, C. L. (1990). *Cognitive foundations of musical pitch.* New York: Oxford University Press.

Krumhansl, C. L., & Keil, F. C. (1982). Acquisition of the hierarchy of tonal functions in music. *Memory and Cognition, 10,* 243–251.

Kugler, K., & Savage-Rumbaugh, S. (2002, June). *Rhythmic drumming by Kanzi and adult male bonobo (Pan Paniscus) at the Language Research Center.* Poster presented at the 25th Meeting of the American Society of Primatologists, Oklahoma City, OK.

Kuhn, D., & Franklin, S. (2006). The second decade: What develops (and how). In W. Damon and R. M. Lerner (Series Eds.) & D. Kuhn & R. S. Siegler (Vol. Eds.), *Handbook of child psychology: Vol. 2. Cognitive language and perceptual development* (6th ed., pp. 953–993). Hoboken, NJ: Wiley.

Lawler, C., & Lawler, E. (1965). Color-mood associations in young children. *Journal of Genetic Psychology, 107,* 29–32.

Lerdahl, F., & Jackendoff, R. (1983). *A generative theory of tonal music.* Cambridge, MA: MIT Press.

Luquet, G. H. (1913). *Le dessin d'un enfant.* Paris: Alcan.

Luquet, G. H. (1927). *Le dessin enfantin.* Paris: Alcan.

Marr, D. (1982). *Vision: A computational investigation into the human representation and processing of visual information.* San Francisco: Freeman.

Masataka, N. (1999). Preference for infant-directed singing in 2-day-old hearing infants of deaf parents. *Developmental Psychology, 35,* 1001–1005.

Matthews, J. (1984). Children drawing: Are young children really scribbling? *Early Child Development and Care, 18,* 1–39.

Matthews, J. (1997). How children learn to draw the human figure: Studies from Singapore. *European Early Childhood Education Research Journal, 5*(1), 29–58.

Matthews, J. (1999). *The art of childhood and adolescence: The construction of meaning.* London: Falmer Press.

McKernon, P. (1979). The development of first songs in young children. *New Directions for Child Development, 3,* 43–58.

Meyer, L. B. (1956). *Emotion and meaning in music.* Chicago: University of Chicago Press.

Meyer, L. B. (1973). *Explaining music: Essays and explorations.* Berkeley: University of California Press.

Meyer, L. B. (1994). *Music, the arts and ideas: Patterns and predictions in twentieth-century culture.* Chicago: University of Chicago Press.

Millar, S. (1975). Visual experience or translation rules? Drawing the human figure by blind and sighted children. *Perception, 4,* 363–371.

Miller, G. F. (2000). *The mating mind.* New York: Doubleday.

Miyazaki, K. (1988). Musical pitch identification by absolute pitch possessors. *Perception and Psychophysics, 44,* 501–512.

Moog, H. (1976). *The musical experience of the preschool child.* London: Schott.

Moorhead, G. E., & Pond, D. (1978). *Music of young children.* Santa Barbara, CA: Pillsbury Foundation.

Moran, S., & Gardner, H. (2006). Extaordinary achievements: A developmental and systems analysis. In W. Damon & R. M. Lerner (Series Eds.) & D. Kuhn & R. S. Siegler (Vol. Eds.), *Handbook of child psychology: Vol. 2. Cognitive language and perceptual development* (6th ed., pp. 905–949). Hoboken, NJ: Wiley.

Morra, S. (1995). A neo-Piagetian approach to children's drawings. In C. Lange-Kuttner & G. V. Thomas (Eds.), *Drawing and looking: Theoretical approaches to pictorial representation in children* (pp. 93–106). New York: Harvester Wheatsheaf.

Morris, D. (1967). *The biology of art.* Chicago: Aldine-Atherton.

Mursell, J. L. (1937). *The psychology of music.* New York: Norton.

Nettl, B. (1956a). Infant musical development and primitive music. *Southwestern Journal of Anthropology, 12,* 87–91.

Nettl, B. (1956b). *Music in primitive culture.* Cambridge, MA: Harvard University Press.

Ninio, A., & Bruner, J. (1978). The achievement and antecedents of labeling. *Journal of Child Language, 5,* 1–15.

O'Hare, D., & Westwood, H. (1984). Features of style classification: A multivariate experimental analysis of children's response to drawing. *Developmental Psychology, 20,* 150–158.

Olson, R. K., & Boswell, S. L. (1976). Pictorial depth sensitivity in 2-year-old children. *Child Development, 47,* 1175–1178.

Ostwald, P. F. (1973). Musical behavior in early childhood. *Developmental Medicine and Child Neurology, 15*(3), 367–375.

Pariser, D., & van den Berg, A. (1997). Beholder beware: A reply to Jessica Davis. *Studies in Art Education, 38*(3), 186–192.

Patterson, F. G. (1978). The gesture of a gorilla: Language acquisition in another pongid. *Brain and Language, 5*(1), 72–97.

Phillips, W. A., Hobbs, S. B., & Pratt, F. R. (1978). Intellectual realism in children's drawings of cubes. *Cognition, 6*(1), 15–33.

Piaget, J. (1929). *The child's conception of the world.* New York: Harcourt Brace.

Piaget, J., & Inhelder, B. (1956). *The child's conception of space.* London: Routledge & Kegan Paul.

Pierroutsakos, S. L., & DeLoache, J. S. (2003). Infants' manual investigation of pictures objects varying in realism. *Infancy, 4,* 141–156.

Platt, W. (1933). Temperament and disposition revealed in young children's music. *Character and Personality, 2,* 246–251.

Premack, D. (1975). Putting a face together. *Science, 188,* 228–236.

Profita, J., & Bidder, T. G. (1988). Perfect pitch. *American Journal of Medical Genetics, 29,* 763–771.

Pufall, P. B., & Pesonen, T. (2000). Looking for the development of artistic style in children's artworlds. *New Directions for Child and Adolescent Development, 90,* 81–98.

Ramus, F., Hauser, M. D., Miller, C. T., Morris, D., & Mehler, J. (2000). Language discrimination by human newborns and cotton-top tamarins. *Science, 288,* 349–351.

Révész, G. (1954). *Introduction to the psychology of music.* Norman: University of Oklahoma Press.

Ricci, C. (1887). *L'arte dei bambini* [The art of children]. Bologna, Italy: Zanichelli.

Richert, R. A., & Lillard, A. A. (2002). Children's understanding of the knowledge prerequisites of drawing and pretending. *Developmental Psychology, 38*(6), 1004–1015.

Rose, S. A., Jankowski, J. J., & Senior, G. J. (1997). Infants' recognition of contour-deleted figures. *Journal of Experimental Psychology: Human Perception and Performance, 23*(4), 1206–1216.

Saffran, J. R., & Griepentrog, G. J. (2001). Absolute pitch in infant auditory learning: Evidence for developmental reorganization. *Developmental Psychology, 37,* 74–85.

Schaefer-Simmern, H. (1948). *The unfolding of artistic activity.* Berkeley: University of California Press.

Schellenberg, E. G., & Trehub, S. E. (1996). Natural musical intervals: Evidence from infant listeners. *Psychological Science, 7,* 272–277.

Schiller, P. (1951). Figural preferences in the drawings of a chimpanzee. *Journal of Comparative and Physiological Psychology, 44,* 101–111.

Seashore, C. E. (1919). *Psychology of musical talent.* New York: Silver Burdett.

Sergeant, D., & Roche, S. (1973). Perceptual shifts in the auditory information processing of young children. *Psychology of Music, 1*(2), 39–48.

Shepard, R. N. (1982). Structural representations of musical pitch. In D. Deutsch (Ed.), *The psychology of music* (pp. 343–390). New York: Academic Press.

Sloboda, J. A. (1985). *The musical mind: The cognitive psychology of music.* Oxford, England: Clarendon Press.

Steinberg, D., & DeLoache, J. S. (1986). Preschool children's sensitivity to artistic style in paintings. *Visual Arts Research, 12,* 1–10.

Takeuchi, A. H., & Hulse, S. H. (1993). Absolute pitch. *Psychological Bulletin, 113,* 345–361.

Thomas, G. V. (1995). The role of drawing strategies and skills. In C. Lange-Kuttner & G. V. Thomas (Eds.), *Drawing and looking: Theoretical approaches to pictorial representation in children* (pp. 107–122). New York: Harvester Wheatsheaf.

Thomas, G. V., Nye, R., & Robinson, E. J. (1994). How children view pictures: Children's responses to pictures as things in themselves and as representations of something else. *Cognitive Development, 9,* 141–144.

Thomas, G. V., & Silk, A. M. J. (1990). *An introduction to the psychology of children's drawings.* London: Harvester Wheatsheaf.

Trainor, L. J. (1996). Infant preferences for infant-directed versus non-infant-directed play songs and lullabies. *Infant Behavior and Development, 19,* 83–92.

Trainor, L. J., Clark, E. D., Huntley, A., & Adams, B. A. (1997). The acoustic basis of preferences for infant-directed singing. *Infant Behavior and Development, 20*(3), 383–396.

Trainor, L. J., & Heinmiller, B. M. (1998). The development of evaluative responses to music: Infants prefer to listen to consonance over dissonance. *Infant Behavior and Development, 21,* 77–88.

Trainor, L. J., & Trehub, S. E. (1992). A comparison of infants' and adults' sensitivity to Western tonal structure. *Journal of Experimental Psychology: Human Perception and Performance, 19,* 615–626.

Trainor, L. J., & Trehub, S. E. (1993). What mediates infants' and adults' superior processing of the major over the augmented triad? *Music Perception, 11,* 185–196.

Trainor, L. J., & Zacharias, C. A. (1998). Infants prefer higher-pitched singing. *Infant Behavior and Development, 21*(4), 799–805.

Trehub, S. E. (2001). Musical predispositions in infancy. *Annals of the New York Academy of Sciences, 930,* 1–16.

Trehub, S. E., & Schellenberg, E. (1995). Music: Its relevance to infants. *Annals of Child Development, 11,* 1–24.

Trehub, S. E., Schellenberg, E., & Hill, D. (1997). The origins of music perception and cognition: A developmental perspective. In I. Deliege & J. Sloboda (Eds.), *Perception and cognition of music* (Vol. 1, pp. 103–128). East Sussex, England: Psychology Press.

Trehub, S. E., & Thorpe, L. A. (1989). Infants' perception of rhythm: Categorization of auditory sequences by temporal structure. *Canadian Journal of Psychology, 43,* 217–229.

Trehub, S. E., Thorpe, L. A., & Trainor, L. J. (1990). Infants' perception of good and bad melodies. *Psychomusicology, 9,* 5–19.

Trehub, S. E., & Trainor, L. J. (1998). Singing to infants: Lullabies and play songs. In C. Rovee-Collier, L. Lipsitt, & H. Hayne (Eds.), *Advances in infancy research* (pp. 43–77). Stanford, CT: Ablex.

Trehub, S. E., Trainor, L. J., & Unyk, A. M. (1993). Music and speech processing in the first year of life. In H. W. Reese (Ed.), *Advances in child development and behavior* (Vol. 24, pp. 1–35). New York: Academic Press.

Trehub, S. E., Unyk, A. M., & Henderson, J. L. (1994). Children's songs to infant siblings: Parallels with speech. *Journal of Child Language, 21,* 735–744.

Trehub, S. E., Unyk, A. M., & Trainor, L. J. (1993a). Adults identify infant-directed music across cultures. *Infant Behavior and Development, 16,* 193–211.

Trehub, S. E., Unyk, A. M., & Trainor, L. J. (1993b). Maternal singing in cross-cultural perspective. *Infant Behavior and Development, 16,* 285–295.

Upitas, R. (1987). Children's understanding of rhythm: The relationship between development and music training. *Psychomusicology, 7*(1), 41–60.

Viola, W. (1936). *Child art and Franz Cizek.* Vienna: Austrian Red Cross.

Walk, R. D., Karusitis, K., Lebowitz, C., & Falbo, T. (1971). Artistic style as concept formation for children and adults. *Merrill-Palmer Quarterly of Behavior and Development, 17,* 347–356.

Wallin, N. L., Merker, B., & Brown, S. (2001). *The origins of music.* Cambridge, MA: Bradford Books.

Watson, M. W., & Schwartz, S. N. (2000). The development of individual styles in children's drawing. *New Directions for Child and Adolescent Development, 90,* 49–63.

Werner, H. (1961). *Comparative psychology of mental development.* New York: Wiley.

Willats, J. (1977). How children learn to draw realistic pictures. *Quarterly Journal of Experimental Psychology, 29*(3), 367–382.

Willats, J. (1984). Getting the drawing to look right as well as to be right. In W. R. Crozier & A. J. Chapman (Eds.), *Cognitive processes in the perception of art* (pp. 111–125). Amsterdam: North Holland.

Willats, J. (1995). An information-processing approach to drawing development. In C. Lange-Kuttner & G. V. Thomas (Eds.), *Drawing and looking: Theoretical approaches to pictorial representation in children* (pp. 27–43). New York: Harvester Wheatsheaf.

Winner, E., Blank, P., Massey, C., & Gardner, H. (1983). Children's sensitivity to aesthetic properties of line drawings. In D. Rogers & J. A. Sloboda (Eds.), *The acquisition of symbolic skills.* London: Plenum Press.

Winner, E., & Ettlinger, G. (1979). Do chimpanzees recognize photographs as representations of objects? *Neuropsychologia, 17,* 413–420.

Winner, E., & Gardner, H. (1981). First intimations of artistry. In S. Strauss (Ed.), *U-shaped behavioral growth* (pp. 147–168). New York: Academic Press.

Winner, E., Mendelsohn, E., & Garfunkel, G. (1981, April). *Are children's drawings balanced?* Paper presented at the Symposium of the Society for Research in Child Development: A New Look at Drawing, Aesthetic Aspects, Boston.

Winner, E., Rosenblatt, E., Windmueller, G., Davidson, L., & Gardner, H. (1986). Children's perception of "aesthetic" properties of the arts: Domain-specific or pan-artistic? *British Journal of Developmental Psychology, 4,* 149–160.

Winston, A. S., Kenyon, B., Stewardson, J., & Lepine, T. (1995). Children's sensitivity to expression of emotion in drawings. *Visual Arts Research, 21*(1), 1–14.

Wolf, D., & Perry, M. D. (1988). From endpoints to repertoires: Some new conclusions about drawing development. *Journal of Aesthetic Education, 22,* 17–34.

Wright, A. A., Rivera, J. J., Hulse, S. H., Shyan, M., & Neiworth, J. J. (2000). Music perception and octave generalization in rhesus monkeys. *Journal of Experimental Psychology: General, 129,* 291–307.

Zenatti, A. (1969). Le développement génétique de la perception musicale. *Monographies Francaises de Psychologie, 17.*

Zentner, M. R., & Kagan, J. (1996). Perception of music by infants. *Nature, 383,* 29.

Zentner, M. R., & Kagan, J. (1998). Infants' perception of consonance and dissonance in music. *Infant Behavior and Development, 21,* 483–492.

Zimmerman, R., & Hochberg, J. (1970). Responses of infant monkeys to pictorial representations of a learned discrimination. *Psychonomic Science, 18,* 307–308.

PART VI

EMOTION AND MOTIVATION

Chapter 11

Principles of Emotion and Emotional Competence

CAROLYN SAARNI, JOSEPH J. CAMPOS,
LINDA A. CAMRAS, and DAVID WITHERINGTON

This chapter is designed to reflect the major reconceptualizations that have taken place in emotion that place it at the center stage of psychology. In this review, we present one major approach to the conceptualization of emotion and its measurement, show its central relevance for communication between adult and child, and delineate some of the principles that account for emotional competence.

Conceptual Framework for Emotion

Emotions seem to be most closely linked to what a person is trying to do. One's perception and interpretation of events is never independent of the action that one can perform on them. Indeed, an event can be defined as an opportunity for action. However, not all events generate emotion—only those in which one has a stake in the outcome. Hence, we propose a working definition of emotion that emphasizes action, the preparation for action, and appraisal of the significance or relevance to concerns of person-environment transactions. This framework includes communication as a central aspect of action.

WORKING DEFINITION OF EMOTION

Emotion is the person's attempt or readiness to establish, maintain, or change the relation between the person and her or his changing circumstances, on matters of significance to that person (Campos, Frankel, & Camras, 2004). The definition may initially appear to be odd because of the absence of any reference to the traditional elements found in the most prevalent definitions of emotion. There is no allusion to feeling, vegetative states, facial indices of internal states, or other intrapersonal criteria. Instead, emotion is determined by the significance of a person-event transaction. Because the definition emphasizes what the person is trying to accomplish, and because it comes from a conception of emotion that stresses the consequences of emotional states, this working definition of emotion is often called a *functionalist* one (e.g., Campos, Mumme, Kermoian, & Campos, 1994; Frijda, 1986; Lazarus, 1991).

Not all emotions are generated by the relation of events to goals. A second way in which emotion can be generated is through the social signals of others, which have powerful capacities to render a person-environment transaction significant (e.g., Klinnert, Campos, Sorce, Emde, & Svejda, 1983). They do so because social signals can generate a contagious emotional response and tendency for action in the perceiver (Hatfield, Cacioppo, & Rapson, 1994). Social signals can also give meaning to a transaction associated with the signal (such as when an infant acquires the mother's fear of dogs and begins to avoid them). Finally, social signals play a central, though under-investigated, role in generating emotions such as pride, shame, and guilt through the enduring effects that they can have as accompaniments to the approval and disapproval of others.

A third source of significance comes about through hedonic processes—specifically, when hedonic stimulation is experienced and becomes the object of one's strivings (Frijda, 1986). Hedonic stimulation refers to the sights, sounds, tastes, smells, and tactile stimulations that intrinsically produce irreducible sensations of pleasure or pain. With pleasurable hedonic experience, we are more likely to want to repeat such experience and thus we approach objects and people. It is the opposite with painful experience. Pleasure and pain are affectogenic in the following way, taken from Frijda (1986): If, after one experiences pleasant stimulation and one wants to repeat the experience, the emotion of desire is generated; similarly, if one experiences pain and wants not to repeat the experience, the emotion of aversion is created. Desire and aversion, with further development, can become the core of much more complex emotional transactions, including envy, jealousy, and rage.

The fourth way that events become significant comes from memory of transactions from the past. Although all emotion theories stress the role of memory in generating affect, we would like to emphasize the importance of past experience for the selection of strategies for responding emotionally. Such a link is best represented in the research on working models in attachment. For example, as Cassidy (1994) has said, avoidantly attached infants typically have a history of interactions in which their attachment figure has ignored the infant's social signals such as bids for comfort. When these bids are consistently rejected by the caregiver, the child is predisposed toward muted affect during reunions with the caregiver. The past history of ignoring social bids makes the risk of present rejection too great. By contrast, infants who are classified as ambivalently attached have a history of interaction with a figure who has responded inconsistently to their social signals. When such children are reunited with the attachment figure following separation, they show exaggerated, rather than muted, emotional reactions. Such exaggeration serves the function, in part, of ensuring the parent's responsiveness and avoiding the parent's insensitivity. Thus, past experiences determine not only the precise nature of the emotion a child undergoes (as in the case of desire and aversion discussed earlier) but also the manner in which the child responds to, or copes with, contemporary interactions with significant others.

FACIAL EXPRESSIONS AND EMOTION

Facial expressions have been hypothesized to play a particularly important role in the emotion process. One historically influential emotion theorist (Tomkins, 1962) virtually equated emotion with facial responding. For preverbal infants, facial expressions have been proposed to have additional importance because they are presumed by some to be the sole means by which emotions can be communicated before the advent of language. Thus, some scholars have proposed a virtually one-to-one correspondence between emotion and facial expression for postneonatal infants (e.g., Izard, Ackerman, Schoff, & Fine, 2000) and developed coding systems for infant emotions that rest on the identification of prespecified facial configurations. Such an approach to emotion measurement would have considerable appeal because it provides an easy solution to the problem of identifying emotion in infants. However, we believe it is fundamentally flawed on both an empirical and conceptual level. Recent studies have documented numerous examples of nonconcordance between emotion and these prespecified facial expressions. For example, infants on the visual cliff display clear indications of fear (e.g., refusal to crawl) but do not show prototypic fear expressions. Indeed, they often smile. Conversely, infants typically produce the prototypic facial configuration of surprise (involving raised brow and open mouth) as they introduce an object into their mouth for oral exploration (Camras, Lambrecht, & Michel, 1996). Such mismatches do not imply that facial expressions are misleading or irrelevant to infant emotion. As we further argue, we believe that facial expressions serve as critically important components in a larger pattern of information that observers perceive and integrate in making an emotion judgment.

ACTION TENDENCIES AND THE FLEXIBLE MANIFESTATION OF EMOTION

In the course of studying blind infants, Fraiberg (1977) discovered that many parents of such children showed profound disappointment when they encountered low levels of facial responsiveness and eye contact in their children. The parents seemed to withdraw from their children and to lack the incentive to provide them with physical and social stimulation after noting their children's apparent unresponsiveness. Fraiberg (1977) discovered that although blind infants were indeed relatively unresponsive facially during social encounters, they seemed extraordinarily articulate in expressing their emotions and social responses through the actions of their fingers. When this responsiveness was pointed out to the parents, they dramatically increased their levels of interaction with the infants; the infants, in turn, were able to maintain their digitally mediated level of social responsiveness.

Fraiberg's observations document an important principle about emotions: Many different responses can be in the service of any given emotion—emotional responses exhibit the property of equipotentiality. To expect, as some theories do (e.g., Ekman, Levenson, & Friesen, 1983; Izard, 1977; Tomkins, 1962), a close correspondence between a given response or response pattern (e.g., a facial expression) and a given emotional state is likely to lead to errors of inference. The opposite is also true: The same response can be recruited to express many different emotions; for example, consider that the action of smiling can be in the service of joy, scorn, nurturance, embarrassment, and other emotions, or stereotyped social greeting. Similarly, the action of doing nothing can be in the service of sadness (as in depressive withdrawal), fear (as in keeping still to avoid detection), or anger (as in passive aggressiveness). Emotions are best considered as "syndromes"—alternative patterns of behavior, any of which can under the right circumstances specify the emotion (Lazarus, 1991). It is not possible to identify a priori an operational definition of a given emotion that can be applied in all circumstances, such that knowing the response or response pattern by itself one can predict the emotional state of a person. A discrete emotion thus lacks a gold standard—an ostensive definition. Neither the face, voice, gesture, specific instrumental behavior nor autonomic signatures are likely to have more than a probabilistic relation to an emotional state; even then, context must be taken into account to interpret the meaning of a response (see Camras et al., 2002).

MEASURING EMOTION VIA ACTION TENDENCIES

The absence of an ostensive criterion for a given emotional state creates serious problems of inference. One attempt to resolve this dilemma has been proposed by Frijda (1986) in his concept of action tendencies. Avoidance of threat, for instance, is the action tendency for fear; avoidance of social contact of the scrutinizing other is that for shame; devotion of effort to remove an obstacle is the action tendency for anger, and so on. For Frijda, the concept of action tendency in no way refers to a response that can be measured by electromyography or by operational definition of a given response. Rather, action tendency refers to any of a number of flexibly organized phenomena that serve the function of, for example, avoiding threat or overcoming an obstacle. In this sense, action tendency is similar to the ethologist's conception of a behavioral system—a conception that replaced notions of fixed action patterns with appreciation of the multiplicity of ways by which an animal can attain an end (Bischof, 1975). The behavioral system for the ethologist, like the concept of a specific emotion, is defined by the function those behaviors serve. How is function measured? The functionalist's answer is: (a) by inference from the organization of behavior, (b) by suppositions about what the person is trying to accomplish, and (c) by noting whether progress toward the inferred goal is proceeding smoothly or with difficulty. The identification of the operation of a discrete emotion is intimately tied in to the context in which the person is found and the types of behavior pattern the person shows in that setting.

Although the task of measuring emotion is much more difficult than initially thought when emotion was restored to its place in scientific study a few years ago, there is a major precedent for measuring the organization of behavior—a precedent that is both intellectually persuasive and highly influential (Sroufe & Waters, 1977). In attachment theory, Bowlby (1969) posited that attachment could be measured by proximity seeking in times of fear or distress. Although proximity seeking can be operationalized by measuring the physical distance of the child from the attachment figure (e.g., L. Cohen & Campos, 1974), such an approach reveals little in the way of stability of individual differences in attachment, nor is it an index that retains its manifestation as the child grows older and shows attachment patterns in a variety of different ways. Attachment theorists (e.g., Ainsworth, Blehar, Waters, & Wall, 1978) have solved this problem of measuring "proximity seeking" by noting first of all whether different behaviors shown by the child in the context of reunion with the caregiver are in the service of proximity-seeking, even though there may be no approach toward the caregiver. There are many alternative ways in which attachment security can be manifested: smiling at the caregiver, making pickup bids, sharing the joy of playing with a toy, and so on. These alternative behavioral strategies are taken as partial evidence for what Sroufe (1979) calls "the organization of behavior." The organization stems from the similar ends that morphologically quite different behaviors serve. The crucial factors of avoidance and ambivalence in attachment are similarly inferred by judging the many alternative ways that a child can give the parent the "cold shoulder treatment" specifying avoidance, or the "angry yet relieved" expression of ambivalence. In short, we think investigators of emotion can learn useful lessons from the literature on attachment, especially to the extent that both emotion and attachment exhibit the property of equipotentiality of responses.

This approach to measurement of the action tendencies related to attachment needs to be generalized to the study of other emotional states. It should not be thought that such flexibility of behavior organized around an emotion is limited to the older school-age child and the adult. Fraiberg's (1977) observations of blind infants' social responsiveness described earlier demonstrate this, and so do 8- to 9-month-old infants tested on the visual cliff, a highly reliable fear elicitor. At that age, infants can manifest fear by literal avoidance of descending onto the glass-covered deep side of the cliff, or they can approach the mother, but in a manner indicative of fear. The infants do this by detouring around the deep side, hitching along the sidewalls of the cliff table until they reach the mother (Campos, Hiatt, Ramsay, Henderson, & Svejda, 1978). Behavioral flexibility is the rule, not the exception, in the manifestation of emotion. Restriction of such flexibility in the interests of measuring one or more responses chosen a priori puts at risk the internal validity of a given study, as well as its external or ecological validity. This notion of ecological validity requires that we address the influence of culture, and we turn to that topic next.

CULTURE, EMOTION, AND EMOTIONAL DEVELOPMENT

Our attempts to understand how culture affects emotion and emotional development have changed considerably in the past 30 years. In the 1970s and 1980s, researchers were mostly concerned with universals in emotion expression. The search for universals generated impressive evidence on the similarity of recognition of facial expressions by preliterate tribes (e.g., Ekman, 1973) and judges in both Western and non-Western countries (Izard, 1972). In turn, this evidence led to the widespread use of facial expressions as the preferred indices of emotional states, and motivated the "emotion revolution" of the 1970s and 1980s. The apparent universality of recognition of facial expression also led to studies on the elicitation of facial expression patterns of anger and fear in infants of different cultures (Camras, Oster, Campos, & Bakeman, 2003; Camras et al., 1998; Camras, Oster, Campos, Miyake, & Bradshaw, 1992) and the development of methods of facial expression measurement based on anatomical criteria and judgments of emotion by coders (e.g., Izard & Dougherty, 1982; Oster, 1995). Although many criticisms have been leveled at research on universality of recognition (Fridlund, 1994; Russell, 1994), they have on the whole not proven entirely convincing (e.g., Izard, 1995). As a result, the search for universals continues in cross-cultural studies of patterns of appraisal (Mesquita & Frijda, 1992), speculations about child-rearing functions (Trevarthen, 1988), and attributional biases (Morris & Peng, 1994).

The study of culture and emotions has broadened considerably beyond the issue of universality to the role of culture in the generation, manifestation, and regulation of emotion (e.g., Kitayama & Markus, 1994; Lazarus, 1991). Because a complete review of culture and emotion is beyond the scope of this chapter, we limit ourselves to an illustration of how emotion communication accompanies and helps to inculcate cultural values, affects pre- and perinatal emotionality, determines the types of events to which an infant or child is exposed, and creates the emotional climate in which a person is immersed.

What Is Culture and Does Culture Influence Infants?

The concept of culture is rarely defined. For our purposes, culture refers to a set of traditional, explicit and implicit beliefs, values, actions, and material environments that are transmitted by language, symbol, and behavior in an enduring and interacting group of people. Because of the centrality of symbols, language, and values for culture, most studies of culture and emotion deal with adults, and especially the language of adults (Wierzbicka, 1992). Infants and children with minimal language skills are generally assumed to be beyond the pale of symbolic influence (Winn, Tronick, & Morelli, 1989). However, symbols, language, and values can have profound direct and indirect effects on the preverbal child. The direct effects result from diet, housing, and the material and physical implements of the culture that are used in child rearing. The indirect effects are largely mediated by two factors: (1) the physical/social context in which the infant is raised, and (2) the exposure of the child to the characteristic behavior patterns and nonverbal communication strategies of members of that culture (Gordon, 1989). So, subtle yet powerful are these direct and indirect effects that the infant can be said to be acculturated beginning at birth and maybe even before (Tronick, Morelli, & Ivey, 1992).

Parental Practices

Although the demand for provision and protection of infants and meeting their needs must be universal, the way in which those needs are defined and met varies enormously. One way that culture influences the infant is through the mother's selection of interventions for regulating social signaling, including the baby's crying and struggling. For this reason, swaddling methods have received a great deal of attention from anthropologists (e.g., Whiting, 1981). In the United States, by contrast, swaddling has been unpopular largely because it restricts freedom of movement and possibly produces undesired yet distinctive effects on the formation of characteristic emotional dispositions (Mead, 1954), some of which, such as passivity, are not valued in the United States (Chisholm, 1989).

Another cultural variation in parenting practice evident even in the neonatal period is that of co-sleeping. Co-sleeping has been proposed as a socialization mechanism that fosters attachment throughout life by creating a powerful motivation to remain close to the parent (Abbott, 1992). Although sleeping in separate beds and separate rooms is the norm in the United States, data collected in eastern Kentucky exemplifies the widespread regional variation that can occur in co-sleeping (Abbott, 1992). Co-sleeping occurred across all social classes in eastern Kentucky, but was less common among the college educated. Interview data suggested that co-sleeping did facilitate greater interdependence in the family and fostered close emotional ties early in life. Findings such as these contradict widespread beliefs that the effects of co-sleeping are uniformly negative (see discussion in Morelli, Rogoff, Oppenheim, & Goldsmith, 1992).

Physical activity and infant positioning are other examples of parenting practices related to emotional development and showing considerable variation across cultures. Compared to Americans, Gusii infants are exposed to more light tossing and vigorous handling. Provision of such vigorous stimulation has been proposed to explain how Gusii infants overcome fear by 3 to 4 months of age (Keefer, Dixon, Tronick, & Brazelton, 1991).

The Significance of Exposure to Events

Culture determines the types of events to which the child is exposed. Emotional reactions are determined not only by transactions taking place in the present but also by the history of prior encounters with similar events in the past. It is as if an adaptation level of experience is built up, and depending on the discrepancy of an event from that adaptation level, the child will show intense, moderate, or weak emotional reactions. This principle of adaptation level is well exemplified in the literature on culture and attachment patterns. In the attachment literature, there is evidence that infants from northern Germany show a preponderance of apparent avoidant patterns of attachment (Grossmann, Grossmann, Huber, & Wartner, 1981). By contrast, in Japan, there is a preponderance of apparently ambivalent and hard-to-soothe infants (Miyake, Chen, & Campos, 1985). In the kibbutzim in Israel, still another pattern of behavior is shown: Infants are extremely upset by the entry of strangers in the attachment testing situation (Sagi et al., 1985).

What accounts for such different patterns of behavior? Why do children in three different areas of the world react to the same events in such dramatically different ways? One interpretation is that the value system of different cultures affects what events infants are exposed to and thus to what events they become emotionally responsive. In northern Germany, for example, infants are frequently left alone outside of stores or supermarkets or in the home while the mother steps out briefly. The pattern of exposure (the adaptation level) to being alone renders maternal separations in attachment testing not a very great departure from that to which the infant is accustomed. As a result, infants with such a background may show little or no upset on a brief maternal separation and have little reason to give a strong response to the mother on reunion. Not surprisingly, 49% of infants tested in the Ainsworth Strange Situation in Germany show the "A" pattern of not directing much attention to the reentry of the mother (Grossmann et al., 1981). In Japan, there is a very different value system—one in which the mother desires very close proximity to her child. In Japan, babysitting is rare, and when it occurs, it is usually done by the grandparents. Accordingly, Japanese infants have very few experiences with separation from the mother. As a result, when the mother leaves the infant alone or with a stranger in the attachment test, the separation is extremely discrepant from the infant's past experience. As a result, the infant shows considerable upset, and it is thus no surprise that the infant is hard to console after experiencing intense distress on separation. The difficulty in consoling the child results in classifying the child as a "C" infant.

In the kibbutzim in Israel, security measures and the history of unexpected terrorist attacks make for a strong form of xenophobia. Strangers are looked on suspiciously, and they are typically not allowed to approach infants. Because infants are very sensitive to the emotional communication of significant others by 12 months of age, they have become sensitized to be wary of strangers themselves. As a result, when a stranger enters the room and initiates contact or approach to the child, the infant is set to become intensely fearful. Interestingly, in urban Israel, where the xenophobia is usually much less evident, infants do not show such intense negative reactions to strangers. The adaptation level of the kind of reaction that significant others typically give to the infants determines the intensity level of their negative responses. In sum, the value system of each culture (expectations of independence in northern Germany, desire for extreme proximity in Japan, and the need to protect the community in Israeli kibbutzim) leads to different levels of experience against which new experiences are compared. The culture thus determines both exposure to events and the context for differential emotional reactions.

CULTURE AND EMOTIONAL CLIMATE

Emotional climate refers to the characteristic patterning and intensity of verbal and nonverbal emotional communication that is within earshot and eyeshot of an audience. Cultures often differ in such emotional climates. In some cultures, loudness and extremes of gesticulation are encouraged or tolerated; in others, quiet and peaceful expression is the expectation. Such emotional climate may influence the emotional reaction of infants, children, and adults quite profoundly (Briggs, 1970).

It is now well known that the fetus can hear sounds in the womb from the seventh gestational month onward. As a result of the transmission of sounds through the amniotic fluid (e.g., Fifer & Moon, 1995), the unborn infant can acquire considerable experience about patterns and intensities of vocalic emotional communication. Just as the newborn can identify his or her mother's speech within 3 days of birth, it is possible that the newborn can come into the world with built-in expectations of what the typical emotional climate is in the society in which he or she is born.

In Japan, the emotional climate is one of soft vocalizations, few verbalizations, and much gentle stroking of the infant (Miyake, Campos, Kagan, & Bradshaw, 1986). This pattern of softness and low frequency and volume of speech has been attributed to the rice paper walls of the typical Japanese household, together with the Japanese value for harmony and tranquility in the home. To attain these cultural goals of harmony, mothers are charged with the responsibility of keeping volume of communication low and to keep the infant's crying to a minimum. Thus, Japanese mothers communicate with their infants much more by touch and less by vocalization than do American mothers.

In concluding this discussion of culture and emotion, the emphasis in this chapter should be clear: Emotions are relational and functional (in that they serve a purpose), they are embedded in social communicative relations, they are flexibly responsive to context, and they link our actions with our goals. Consistent with the preceding material on culture and emotional development and with a functionalist approach, in the remaining sections of the chapter we take a systems approach to emotional communication as multichannel (or multibehavioral), which includes facial expression, vocal quality, gesture, touch, eye contact, interpersonal distance, and so forth. With increased exposure and experience, young children's emotional-expressive behavior begins to resemble the normative emotional communicative patterns, as prescribed by the culture in which they live. Social referencing, which is reviewed in the next section, is a key interactive process for facilitating this learning of emotional meaningfulness.

In addition, a systems approach to communication is very useful for understanding the kinds of emotional-social phenomena that develop in the preschool and elementary school years, which are discussed in later sections. These phenomena include self presentation strategies, empathy-mediated prosocial behavior, emotion management, and coping strategies, among others. Systems communication theorists (e.g., Watzlawick, Beavin, & Jackson, 1967) emphasize further that what may be most important about communication is its involvement in the regulation of relationships, and their notion of metacommunication describes this regulatory function: A message, conveyed by nonverbal behavior, communicates how the content of what is said should be understood. In short, communication about communication is intended to influence us, and such communications are typically emotion laden. We turn next to a discussion of the early development of emotional communication, emphasizing social referencing, not only because it is a particularly well-investigated emotional communication process, but also because it illustrates this metacommunicative function of relationship.

Development of Emotional Communication in Early Life

In previous sections, we discussed the evocation of emotions in response to alterations in some significant aspect of the infant's relations in the environment. We now discuss how emotions provide signals indicating such a relational change and how such signals thereby can produce an effect on the infant. We consider emotional communication to occur whenever one person exhibits emotional behavior and another person witnesses and is affected by that emotional behavior. We look for three components in a thorough study of emotional communication: (1) on the input side, registration of the emotion signal by the perceiver; and (2) on the output side, a valenced response to that signal manifested in the recipient's own expressive or instrumental activity; and (3) in between, some degree of appraisal of the input such that the appraisal may change both the significance of the input and the nature of the emotional response. Registration refers to the perception of an expression of emotion (or some component of that expression) and includes the ability to distinguish among expressions of different emotions. (Habituation and preferential looking studies focus on the registration of emotion signals.) A valenced response is one that can be reasonably interpreted as reflecting the content of the internal appraisal and motivation processes on the part of the infant such as approach or avoidance, smiling or frowning. Valenced responses, whether expressive or instrumental, can be diffuse (oriented at no particular event in the world) or targeted at some specific object in the world or at one's own actions.

We delineate four phases of increasingly complex emotional communication between an adult and the infant. Phase 1 (prenatal to 6 weeks) describes the infant's initial valenced reactions to emotion signals. Phase 2 (6 weeks to 7 to 9 months) covers the developmental period preceding the advent of referentiality (i.e., understanding that a communicative signal may refer to some external aspect of the environment). Phase 3 (9 months to 18 months/2 years) focuses on the development of referential emotion communication, behavioral regulation (i.e., where the expressive and instrumental behaviors of the child are affected by the other's emotional expressions), and retention of the emotion signal's impact over progressively longer durations. Phase 4 (18 months/2 years and beyond) is marked by the development of what the literature calls self-conscious emotions, but which, following Watson (personal communication, April 1999), we call "other-conscious emotions" because they depend on the child's detecting the expressive and instrumental reactions of others to his or her own behaviors. We also hypothesize that during this period, marked improvements take place in the child's comprehension of the different "meanings" carried out by different negative emotional messages such as fear versus anger.

PHASE 1 (PRENATAL TO 6 WEEKS): INITIAL REACTIONS TO EMOTION SIGNALS

In the neonatal period that extends from birth to 4 to 6 weeks, rudimentary valenced responses to emotional messages clearly exist. As a consequence of prenatal exposure, for example, newborns respond to the valence of speech prosody produced in their mother's native language but not in nonmaternal languages (Mastropieri & Turkewitz, 1999). Specifically, neonates widen their eyes more in response to happy prosody than to sad or angry prosody. There is as yet no evidence for discrimination beyond the distinction between positive and neutral or negative vocalic emotion. Furthermore, newborns appear capable of responding with cries and negative facial expressions to the cries of another neonate (Dondi, Simion, & Caltran, 1999). The contagious crying phenomenon has been documented repeatedly, and constitutes a remarkable demonstration of the presence of emotional communication in the neonatal period (e.g., Martin & Clark, 1982).

PHASE 2 (6 WEEKS TO 9 MONTHS): PRE-REFERENTIAL COMMUNICATION

During this period, the infant can engage in synchronous dyadic interaction with the caregiver. This phenomenon indicates some limited ability to apprehend the caregiver's emotional valence, understand when the caregiver is targeting her or his emotion toward the infant, and then align her or his own emotional valence and behavior to be congruent with that exhibited by the caregiver. Two other phenomena appear to be well established about emotional communication in this time period. First, infants respond differentially to the valence of mothers' vocal contours (Fernald, 1993). Second, infants discriminate facial expressions as stimulus patterns but show no convincing evidence of comprehending their specific emotion meanings, although Fernald (1993) reported that 5-month-olds smiled more in response to infant-directed messages specifying "approval" and showed more negative affect in response to messages specifying "prohibition," irrespective of whether the message was produced in English or in an unfamiliar language (German or Italian). Thus, by 5 months of age, infants are able to discriminate the emotional valence of acoustic messages and to transform differential message content into congruent behavioral reactions that are either appropriately positive or negative.

A number of other studies investigated infants' differentially valenced responses in dyadic setting. Numerous investigations (e.g., Cohn & Tronick, 1988; Jaffe, Beebe, Feldstein, Crown, & Jasnow, 2001; Moore & Calkins, 2004) have demonstrated what many call "interactional synchrony"—contingencies in the timing of positive or negative expressions during face-to-face interactions between mothers and infants even younger than 3 months of age. Many of these studies claim to have demonstrated a process of direct and unmediated emotion contagion (e.g., Haviland & Lelwica, 1987). However, in our own view, what appears to be direct mutual mirroring between mother and child may instead result from the operation of two other powerful and rudimentary determinants of emotion—contingency and agency (or lack thereof). Michael Lewis and his colleagues (e.g., Lewis, Hitchcock, & Sullivan, 2004), following the pioneering work of J. S. Watson (1972), have unequivocally shown that infants as young as 2 months of age smile when their actions produce a contingent effect on the world and evidence distress when a previously operative contingency fails. Studies of affective synchrony may conclude erroneously that affective matching is being observed, when in fact the observed effects may be due instead to contingency and failure of contingency. Thus when contingent reciprocal smiling takes place, it might produce similar emotional responses in mother and baby. However, such shared emotion need not depend on either direct contagion or (alternatively) on the infant's in-depth comprehension of the emotional meaning of the smile. A simpler explanation is that the infant smiles contingently at the mother not because the baby sees a smile, but because the baby notices a contingent reaction that happens to be a smile. A related body of research on infants' ability to discriminate among discrete emotional cues also confounds discrimination with infants' recognition of emotion meaning (e.g., Walker-Andrews, 1997).

PHASE 3 (9 MONTHS TO 18 MONTHS): BEHAVIORAL REGULATION AND REFERENTIAL COMMUNICATION

The infant undergoes a major set of cognitive, social, emotional, agentic, and perceptual changes in this age period, and these changes have marked impact on the emotional communication of the infant. The most significant change for our purposes is the emergence of the infant's ability to engage in referential gestural communication (i.e., what it is that the mother is emoting about). Prior to 8 to 10 months, infants typically do not show any reliable tendency to follow the gaze or pointing gesture of the parent. By 9 months, infants begin to show such referential understanding, which becomes progressively more specific with the child's advancing age, and culminates in the baby being able to identify the approximate coordinates of where the experimenter or mother is looking or pointing (e.g., Campos et al., 2000; Mumme, Bushnell, DiCorcia, & Lariviere, in press). The implications of this new ability is that the infant becomes capable of engaging in what has been called a "two-person communication about a third event," becomes able to link quite precisely the target of the mother's or experimenter's pointing and gaze, and increasingly becomes able to retain the emotional impact of prior emotional messages (i.e., shows affective memory).

Onset of Emotional Communication Involving Environmental Objects

Two studies clearly document how the infant by 8.5 months of age becomes capable of reacting to the social signals of the mother directed at a third event. In one study (Boccia & Campos, 1989), the infant's reaction to strangers was markedly affected by whether the mother posed a stern or cheery greeting and facial expression when a stranger walked into the room. In the second study (see Campos, Thein, & Owen, 2003), the mother's vocalization of the baby's name followed by a nonsense phrase ("tat fobble") resulted in cessation of the infant's approach to a toy that was significantly longer when the vocalization was uttered in a fearful or angry manner than when it was uttered joyfully. These studies demonstrate that referential communication occurs in infants as young as 8.5 months of age for facial and vocal expressions combined and for vocal expressions produced alone. Regarding responses to facial expressions produced alone, while several studies have demonstrated regulatory effects in 12-month-olds (e.g., Camras & Sachs, 1991), none has investigated infants at younger ages. In addition, no studies to date have examined behavioral regulation in response to emotion signals produced in either modality by babies younger than 8.5 months of age. Thus, the precise age of onset for behavioral regulation with respect to environmental objects or events is not currently known.

Effects of Emotional Communication in Older Infants

In contrast to younger infants, there has been considerable research on older (10- to 14-month-old) infants' behavioral regulation in response to emotion signals. In an early and powerful demonstration of this phenomenon, Sorce, Emde, Campos, and Klinnert (1985) showed that 12-month-old infants referenced their mother (i.e., looked toward her) when they reached a mid-level drop-off on the visual cliff and most proceeded to cross if she displayed a facial expression of happiness or interest but not of sadness, anger, or fear. The mid-level drop-off induced a state of uncertainty in the infants and they therefore sought information from their mother to help them determine whether to proceed across the cliff. Through their actions, infants demonstrated that they did more than merely register their mothers' emotion signals; they displayed a valenced response reflecting an attempt to maintain or change their relation to the environment.

Evidence for responsiveness to facial and to vocal signals during this period exists, though controversy has arisen over the relative effectiveness of facial versus vocal signals (Mumme, Fernald, & Herrera, 1996; Sorce et al., 1985; Vaish & Striano, 2004), Recent work has moved beyond the face and voice to the modality of touch: Hertenstein and Campos (2001) showed that infants respond to maternal tactile behaviors that might be interpreted as indicating a negative emotional response (i.e., gently squeezing the abdomen as the infant reached toward a toy).

By 12 months, infants' behavioral regulation in response to emotion signals is referentially specific (e.g., Hertenstein & Campos, 2004; Mumme & Fernald, 2003). Referential specificity means that infants understand that an emotional expression is uniquely directed toward the object of the expresser's attention rather than to other objects in the environment or to no particular object at all. The issue of whether infants during this period can make qualitative distinctions among emotions of the same valence (e.g., distinguish anger from fear) is much less clear, as most studies of behavioral regulation have only compared reactions to positive versus negative emotional expressions (typically happiness versus fear or disgust). Sorce et al. (1985) found that almost no infants crossed the modified visual cliff when mothers displayed an expression of fear or anger, while approximately a third of the babies did proceed to cross in response to the sad expression. Although these findings suggest that 12-month-old infants distinguish among different negative emotions, one possible interpretation is that they distinguish on the basis of emotional intensity (i.e., degree of negativity) but do not understand the qualitatively different relational meanings and functional implications of fear versus anger versus sadness. Bingham, Campos, and Emde (1987), in fact, found no evidence for differential responding in either 13- or 15-month-olds to an experimenter's negative facial and vocal expressions of fear, sadness, disgust and anger in reference to a doll whose arm appeared to break and fall off when the infant touched it.

The authors concluded that perhaps infants at this age were not yet able to react differentially to emotional signals more specific than positive versus negative. They also cautioned for the need of further research to validate their tentative conclusion about the lack of differential behavioral regulation by discrete emotion signals.

PHASE 4 (18 MONTHS/2 YEARS AND BEYOND): THE RISE OF OTHER-CONSCIOUS EMOTIONS

In the next phase of the development of emotional communication, we believe that two significant changes take place in the infant's reactions to emotional signals from others. One is the establishment of differential expressive and instrumental behavioral responses to different emotion signals of the same valence (e.g., anger versus fear). The second is a major change in the infant's construal of the two-person communication about a third event leading to what are commonly called the "self-conscious" emotions (e.g., shame, guilt, pride), but which, the reader will recall, we prefer to call "other-conscious" emotions to note the importance of the emotional reactions of others in their generation. In contrast to the previous age periods, we acknowledge that our description of this phase includes considerable—albeit grounded—speculation. Therefore, several of our proposals regarding Phase 4 remain to be confirmed empirically.

Affect Specificity: Its Role in Generating Complex Emotions

To date, strong evidence demonstrating infants' abilities to make qualitative distinctions among emotions of the same valence is lacking. Nonetheless, in an exploratory study involving a small number of participants, E. Anderson (1994) observed a tendency for infants in this age range to respond differentially when an experimenter gazed at an unfamiliar food item while verbalizing "Look at that" using sad, angry, disgusted, fearful, or happy vocalizations and facial expressions. The results of that study were that 18-month-old female infants tended to give the food item to the experimenter in response to a sad emotion message, but behaved differently when other negative messages were given. As in other studies, there were major differences between positive and negative messages. Beyond such preliminary data, a survey of the infant literature suggests that by 18 months of age infants may indeed understand the specific meanings and implications of some negative emotions. Infants' affect vocabulary develops rapidly around this age (Dunn, Bretherton, & Munn, 1987) and includes words for several negative emotions (e.g., scary, yucky, mad). Furthermore, Zahn-Waxler and Radke-Yarrow (1990) found that by 2 years of age many infants show appropriate empathic/sympathetic responses to other persons' expressions of distress. In a study involving experimenter-produced expressions of disgust, Rapacholi (1998) showed that 18-month-old infants produced an emotionally appropriate response (i.e., avoiding the disgust-targeted food item when choosing a food item for the experimenter). However, data produced in all these studies are subject to possible interpretations that do not involve the necessary imputation of affect specificity in the infant's understanding of the emotion message. Therefore, this issue remains an important challenge in the area of emotion communication.

Development of Other-Conscious Emotions

The fourth phase in the development of emotional communication also involves the generation of complex emotions that may require, for their generation, the integration of a number of higher-order cognitive, perceptual, and retentive capacities. These emotions include embarrassment, shame, guilt, and pride. According to Lewis (1993) these emotions begin to develop between 15 and 18 months, and are in part the consequences of the development of self-recognition as indexed by the "rouge" task. In this well-known paradigm, an infant in this developmental phase will detect and respond appropriately to the sight of a dot of rouge surreptitiously placed on her nose and viewed only in a mirror reflection. Successful performance on the rouge/mirror self-recognition task is taken to indicate the origins of a reflective self that in turn permits the emergence of self-conscious emotions (e.g., Lewis & Ramsay, 2004). Lewis has called these emotions "self-conscious" because of the link between mirror self-recognition and other indices of self-development, on the one hand, and the onset of these emotions, on the other hand. As indicated earlier, we prefer to designate them as other-conscious emotions because they rest on the child's detecting other persons' reactions to the child or her behavior.

Emotional communication plays a necessary role in the development of these emotions. Indeed, as noted earlier, the emotions of embarrassment, guilt, shame, and pride may come about as a result of the emerging appreciation by the child of the meaning of the communication by others of anger, sadness, fear, contempt, and other emotions. In other words, the child must first perceive these emotions in others, differentiate them one from the other, know to whom these emotions are being targeted, and have a sense of responsibility by the child in the elicitation of these emotions in others. Some of these emotions, particularly anger and contempt, are likely to be part of the elicitation of some complex emotions (especially shame), but not of others (particularly guilt).

In conclusion, our focus has been on early development in illustrating the theoretical perspective taken in this essay. In the next section, we turn to an extended discussion of recent empirical research undertaken with preschoolers, school-age children, and adolescents. Much of the research with these older children and youth embeds emotional experience in social interaction, whether the focus is on socialization of emotional expression norms or on emotion knowledge as applied to social effectiveness. There is also a greater emphasis on the development of the self as related to emotional development, and we address this link in our discussion of "self-conscious" emotions (what we have argued should really be called "other-conscious" emotions) as well as in our discussion of adolescent "true self" development. Finally, we once again examine emotion regulation research in this older age group relative to temperament influence and the development of coping strategies. Throughout the next section, we also suggest topics for further research.

Emotional Development in Childhood and Adolescence: Social Effectiveness and Positive Adaptation

Noteworthy in recent research has been the greater emphasis given to how children's and youth's emotional development is manifest in their social competence. Although appraisal processes and the regulation of emotion continue to garner much scientific attention, our emphasis on the functional nature of emotional experience is especially relevant to how social goals are the fulcrum around which a great deal of emotion is elicited, experienced, and expressed.

Social psychologists have long examined the question of what constitutes well-being or positive adaptation, and a review of that literature is not appropriate here (for a brief review, see Diener & Lucas, 2000); however, what that research does consider is the extent to which social effectiveness and well-being are personality traits, deriving from temperament dispositions, or dependent on the situation a person finds her- or himself in. The research on children's emotion regulation suggests that a temperament-linked disposition to experience negative emotion may be related to social adjustment (for reviews, see Eisenberg & Morris, 2002; Swanson, Hemphill, & Smart, 2004). As an illustration of such research that attempts to tease apart the influences on children's resilience and adjustment, we briefly consider a recent longitudinal study by Eisenberg and colleagues (Eisenberg et al., 2004).

SOCIAL ADJUSTMENT AND EMOTION REGULATION

Eisenberg and her colleagues (2004) differentiate between effortful control—the ability to voluntarily inhibit or activate behavior—and reactive control—the relatively inflexible tendency to be either overly inhibited or impulsive. Although both types of control have their roots in children's temperament, the former construct is considered by Eisenberg and her colleagues as pivotal to their definition of effortful emotion regulation, whereas the latter construct, reactive control, is less accessible to voluntary control and is linked to temperamental reactivity. Reactive control is also more often linked to problems of adjustment when this characteristic is particularly pronounced in the individual child, in large part due to its involuntary nature. Eisenberg et al. (2004) examined how effortful control and reactive undercontrol were related to children's internalizing and externalizing problems over a 2-year period. The sample ranged from 4.5 to 8 years old, and they were reassessed 2 years later. The results were very complex, indicating that there is no simple path between emotion-laden qualities such as effortful control and reactive control to subsequent social adjustment. The clearest outcome was that impulsivity and insufficient effortful control were directly predictive of externalizing problems, and this relationship was even stronger if the children were rated by their teachers as high in dispositional anger.

A study undertaken with toddlers (Lawson & Ruff, 2004) used constructs similar to the Eisenberg et al. research. The results also indicated that negative emotionality and ability to sustain attention predicted later behavioral outcomes. More specifically, maternal ratings of emotional lability and proneness to irritability at age 2, defined by the authors as their index of "negative emotionality," and trained observers' ratings of attentiveness during frustrating play episodes with the mother combined to predict cognitive function (IQ) and problem behavior ratings (maternal ratings) at age 3.5 years. Their results indicated that when young children have both risk factors, low attentiveness and proneness to negative emotionality, at a young age, they are likely to obtain both lower IQ scores and be rated as significantly demonstrating more problem behavior. The authors refer to this as the "double hazard" of combined risk factors for both concurrent and predicted outcomes. Children who were prone to negative emotionality but had high attentiveness appeared to be protected against this deleterious outcome (especially for behavior problems).

Other studies undertaken by Eisenberg and her colleagues with preschoolers (e.g., Fabes, Hanish, Martin, & Eisenberg, 2002) suggest a continuity that may start relatively early in life (e.g., the Lawson and Ruff research), persist through the preschool years, continue through the elementary school years and extend into middle school as well (e.g., Gumora & Arsenio, 2002). Such research, albeit complex, does indicate that developmental psychologists have provided the preliminary data needed to inform public policy about early intervention, which may include parent guidance as well as appropriately structured preschool education for addressing the needs of children who are faced with the "double hazard" of low attentiveness and proneness to negative emotionality at a young age.

Emotional Competence

Another way to conceptualize children's emotional development relative to their overall psychological adjustment or well-being is to examine their level of functioning according to the degree to which they access the various skills characteristic of emotional competence. Similar to such constructs as well-being, social adjustment, and ego-resilience, the construct emotional competence is a superordinate term that subsumes a number of emotion-related skills. The definition of emotional competence is straightforward: It is the demonstration of self-efficacy in emotion-eliciting social transactions. Elsewhere one of us (Saarni, 1999) has extensively reviewed the developmental contributors to emotional competence; briefly, they include the self or ego identity, a moral sense or character, and a person's developmental history. The components of emotional competence are those skills necessary for self-efficacy in emotion-eliciting social transactions. Table 11.1 summarizes eight skills of emotional competence.

TABLE 11.1   Skills of Emotional Competence

1. Awareness of one's emotional state, including the possibility that one is experiencing multiple emotions, and at even more mature levels, awareness that one might also not be consciously aware of one's emotions due to unconscious dynamics or selective inattention.
2. Skill in discerning others' emotions, based on situational and expressive cues that have some degree of cultural consensus as to their emotional meaning.
3. Skill in using the vocabulary of emotion and expression terms commonly available in one's subculture, and at more mature levels, skill in acquiring cultural scripts that link emotion with social roles.
4. Capacity for empathic and sympathetic involvement in others' emotional experiences.
5. Skill in understanding that inner emotional state need not correspond to outer expression, both in oneself and in others, and at more mature levels, understanding that one's emotional-expressive behavior may impact on another and to take this into account in one's self-presentation strategies.
6. Skill in adaptive coping with aversive emotions and distressing circumstances by using self-regulatory strategies that ameliorate the intensity or temporal duration of such emotional states (e.g., stress hardiness) and by employing effective problem-solving strategies for dealing with problematic situations.
7. Awareness that the structure or nature of relationships is largely defined by how emotions are communicated in the relationship such as by the degree of emotional immediacy or genuineness of expressive display and by the degree of emotional reciprocity or symmetry in the relationship (e.g., mature intimacy is in part defined by mutual or reciprocal sharing of genuine emotions, but a parent-child relationship may have asymmetric sharing of genuine emotions).
8. Capacity for emotional self-efficacy: The individual views her- or himself as feeling, overall, the way he or she wants to feel. Emotional self-efficacy means that one accepts one's emotional experience, whether unique and eccentric or culturally conventional, and this acceptance is in alignment with the individual's beliefs about what constitutes desirable emotional balance. In essence, one is living in accord with one's personal theory of emotion and moral sense, when one demonstrates emotional self-efficacy.

Source: Emotional Development: Action, Communication, and Understanding (pp. 226–299), by C. Saarni, J. Campos, L. Camras, and D. Witherington, in *Handbook of Child Psychology: Vol. 3. Social, Emotional, and Personality Development,* sixth edition, W. Damon and R. M. Lerner (Series Eds.) and N. Eisenberg (Vol. Ed.), 2006, New York: Wiley.

The derivation of these eight skills was largely based on a survey of empirical investigations in the field of emotional development, although there is relatively less research that directly addresses the last two skills. However, these last two skills reflect implicit assumptions in many studies on emotional development in Western societies: We live in social-emotional systems (reflected in Skill 7) and emotional competence should ultimately address personal integrity—we can discern what works best for us, relative to our values (Skill 8). These last two skills have far less empirical developmental research associated with them, and in the interest of brevity, they will not be addressed in any detail. The reader is referred to Saarni, Campos, Camras, and Witherington (2006) and to Saarni (1999) for detailed discussions of these last two skills. Last, it is important to note that these skills of emotional competence also reflect a Western cultural bias, which is of concern, and thus caution should be exercised when trying to generalize these skills to non-Western societies. In what follows, we review a variety of studies that illustrate how each of the first six skills of emotional competence develops or is manifest, and we emphasize research that focuses on how the emotional competence skill facilitates an individual's effectiveness in relationships. In many cases, as children mature, their enhanced developmental functioning reveals itself in more complex manifestations of a given skill with concomitant advances in how interpersonal exchanges are negotiated.

SOCIAL EFFECTIVENESS AND SKILL 1: AWARENESS OF OUR EMOTIONS

On some very basic level, knowing what we feel clarifies what we want. Theorists who emphasize close links between emotion and motivation readily acknowledge that the intended target or goal is critical for how we understand our subjective experience of emotion (e.g., Lazarus, 1991). Likewise, our emphasis on the functional nature of emotion is consistent with this perspective. By the time children are 2 to 3 years of age, awareness of emotional state is usually empirically examined from the standpoint of how children use emotion labels or descriptive phrases to refer to their subjective feelings. A number of studies have shown that young children spontaneously talk about their own affective states as well as about others' emotions (e.g., Bloom, 1998). The conversations between these young children and their family members also imply that they have expectancies for how they *will* feel as well as memories for how they *did* feel. These everyday sorts of emotion-related communicative exchanges imply to young children that their emotions are part of a whole scenario of events, behaviors, and other people (Dunn, 2000). In short, emotional experience is contextualized.

Children who know what they feel are more able to negotiate with others when there is a conflict or a need to assert themselves. However, as Gottman, Katz, and Hooven (1997) argue, children are more likely to be effective negotiators when they can "down-regulate" or de-escalate their internal arousal sufficiently that they can attend to the social exchange and respond with useful social compromises to ease the impasse or conflict. Arsenio and Lemerise (2001) take this idea one step further in their model of social information processing, which is integrated with emotion processes such as encoding of affective cues from peers, the affective nature of the relationship a child has with the peer (e.g., hostile versus friendly), and empathic responsiveness. With this model, they suggest that a researcher can examine more effectively how and why children respond to some peer interactions with aggression and to others with social competence.

By early adolescence, well-functioning youth have the confidence to disclose their emotions and opinions to others, thereby revealing a "true self" to others in so far as they choose to express what their genuine emotions are, despite negative interpersonal consequences. Relevant research has been undertaken by Harter and her colleagues on adolescents' perceptions of their true self and under what conditions they present a dissembled self to others (Harter, 1999; Harter, Waters, Whitesell, & Dastelic, 1998). In addition, an early study (Saarni, 1988) found that some preadolescents recognized that although negative social consequences could occur if they revealed their genuine emotions, nonetheless, they contended that they would indeed express their genuine emotions because the emotions themselves were deemed important. With this kind of awareness of one's emotions, we can begin to understand how emotions themselves begin to constitute a part of a developing individual's definition of self (see Harter, 1999). As we noted previously in this chapter, referring to these emotions as "self-conscious" is a misnomer, because developmentally these emotions reflect the profound influence of others' reactions to the child, and it is the child's incorporation of those reactions that results in the development of pride, shame, guilt, embarrassment, and so forth. Indeed, we proposed using the term "other-conscious"; however, because there exists a significant literature that refers to these emotions as "self-conscious" emotions, we retain that term here for the sake of similarity.

Self-Conscious Emotions

Lewis' work (e.g., 2000) on the development of pride, hubris, shame, embarrassment, and guilt constitutes a cognitive appraisal view of how such emotions come about. According to Lewis, these self-conscious emotions require that an objective self has developed: Children can refer to themselves and have conscious awareness of themselves as distinct from others. The cognitive appraisals involved include (a) recognition that there are standards to be met, (b) evaluation of the self's performance relative to these standards, and (c) attribution of responsibility to the self on success or failure in meeting the standard. At around age 2 when children acquire objective self-awareness, they also become aware of parental standards for behavior, rules that they are expected to follow, and desirable goals for comportment. Children learn about these standards through their family's disciplinary practices, and over the next few years their increasing cognitive sophistication also allows them to gauge the degree to which they have met the standards.

The last cognitive appraisal that has to develop before self-conscious emotions are experienced is a focus on one's self from an evaluative standpoint such that either the whole self or a particular aspect of the self is considered the focus of the success or failure at living up to the standard, rule, or reaching a goal. Lewis (2000) contends that the more that the whole self is globally assumed to be responsible for the success or failure, the more that either hubris (arrogance) or shame will be felt, respectively. When specific aspects of the self are seen as leading to the success or failure, then pride or guilt will be felt, respectively. The prideful feelings of accomplishment and pleasure allow the individual to undertake still further challenges; the guilt felt on one's failure at a particular event or in a particular situation allows for interpersonal repair and future improvement (see also Barrett, Zahn-Waxler, & Cole, 1993 for a discussion of "avoiders versus amenders" in toddlerhood, with the "amenders" apparently experiencing guilt rather than shame or embarrassment).

There is also a critical interpersonal context that needs to be taken into account in distinguishing shame and guilt—whether we are observed or alone. We do not need social exposure to feel guilt (although it might help), but it is a significant feature in our feeling ashamed and wanting to hide from others' view (e.g., Barrett et al., 1993). Exposure contributes to another self-conscious emotion, embarrassment, which is not necessarily the same as shame. As an illustration of such research, Lewis and Ramsay (2002) proposed that there are two types of embarrassment, one is simply due to being the object of other's attention (exposure embarrassment) and the other is a more self-evaluative embarrassment that may be linked to shame. They studied 4-year-old children's reactions to a performance task (i.e., yielding success or failure) and a situation designed to emphasize focus on the self (e.g., receiving lavish compliments) and examined the children's cortisol responses after both conditions to see if they differed. The preschoolers who expressed behaviors indicative of shame or of evaluative embarrassment during failure at the task responded with higher cortisol levels, whereas the exposure to attention situation did not result in elevated cortisol responses. They concluded that shame and evaluative embarrassment are more stressful—as evidenced by the higher cortisol secretion—than feeling oneself to be the object of others' focused (and positive) attention.

The development and functioning of self-conscious emotions clearly needs more attention at all age levels. It would appear that the development of self-conscious emotions is especially relevant to clinical practice, whether it be the treatment of depression that occurs with a greater frequency among female adolescents or the development of effective interventions to facilitate a child's coping with the emotional aftermath of sexual abuse (see Tangney, Burggraf, & Wagner, 1995 for a review of shame, guilt, and psychopathology).

Awareness of Multiple Emotions

Also relevant to children's and adolescents' social effectiveness and adaptation is their ability to be aware of experiencing multiple emotions or conflicting emotions (as in ambivalence). This development may appear as early as 5 to 6 years of age (Stein, Trabasso, & Liwag, 2000) or not until late childhood (Harter & Whitesell, 1989), depending on the criteria and methods for eliciting such understanding from children. Stein and colleagues argued that children first focused on one situation to which they attached values and attributions, responded emotionally to its impact on them (e.g., "I don't like her because she took my Halloween candy"), and then focused on another situation with its accompanying values and attributions and respond emotionally to its impact (e.g., "But I like her when she plays with me"). Thus, ambivalence for Stein and colleagues was viewed as a sequential process with different appraisals attached to the different or polarized emotional responses.

Summary.   This first skill of emotional competence—the ability to be aware of an emotional experience—facilitates children's problem solving, for knowing how to respond emotionally to a particular eliciting encounter is crucial to deciding on a course of action, especially if a first impulse to action is potentially going to incur some undesirable consequences, and thus be less self-efficacious in the long term. In terms of social effectiveness, knowing how one's self tends to react, whether it is with shame or with a conflicted set of emotions leading to ambivalence, is still a source of important information for the developing child or teen to integrate into his or her self-definition, especially knowing that some emotional experiences render one's self acutely vulnerable in interpersonal situations.

SOCIAL EFFECTIVENESS AND SKILL 2: ABILITY TO DISCERN AND UNDERSTAND OTHERS' EMOTIONS

To understand others' emotions and motives, children need (a) to make sense of others' expressive behavior and action tendencies, (b) to understand common situational elicitors of emotions, and (c) to comprehend that others have minds, intentions, beliefs, and inner states. There is a fairly substantial research literature on these topics and the reader is referred to reviews in Denham (1999); Harris (2000); von Salisch (2001); and Thompson, Easterbrooks, and Padilla-Walker (2003). A variety of studies indicate that children who are more accurate in understanding others' emotional experience also tend to be more socially competent (see reviews in Halberstadt, Denham, & Dunsmore, 2001). Two studies have considerable potential for broadening research on this topic. In the first study, Barth and Bastiani (1997) investigated children's biases in labeling the expressions of their classmates' facial expression photos. Noteworthy among their results was that those children who had a bias for "seeing" angry facial expressions (contrary to what the familiar classmate was trying to produce expressively) were also the ones who had less satisfactory peer relations, and their teachers rated their adjustment more often as hostile dependent. This outcome is consistent with research with older children who used a hostile attribution bias in their peer relationships (e.g., Crick & Dodge, 1994). Similarly, Schultz, Izard, and Ackerman (2000) found that parental depression and family instability predicted preschool children's anger attribution bias, which in turn was associated with peer rejection. These children were also rated as aggressive by their teachers.

The second study was carried out by Hubbard (2001) who examined how rejected children behave when mildly interpersonally stressed. She had 7- and 8-year-olds rate their peers for "likeability" and aggressiveness and then observed the children in a rigged game with a confederate whom they did not know. Compared to well-liked children, the rejected children were more likely to express both facial and verbal anger during the game. They also expressed more happiness, but only when some game maneuver was to their advantage. Interestingly, aggressive children were not necessarily more likely to express anger (or happiness or sadness) than nonaggressive children.

Understanding Others' Feelings and Cognitive Development

The ability to understand what others are experiencing emotionally does not develop in isolation from other aspects of emotional development and cognitive development. Emerging insight into others' emotions develops in interaction with increasing awareness of an individual's own emotional experience, with the ability to empathize, and with the ability to conceptualize causes of emotions and their behavioral consequences. The more children learn about how and why people act as they do, the more they can infer their emotional state, even if it is not especially obvious or may even be counterintuitive. (For a review of children's cognitive understanding of emotions, see Harris, 2000.)

Facial Expressions and Emotion-Eliciting Situations. Facial expressions can have a dual function; they can be signs, in which case they bear a one-to-one correspondence to internal emotional state, or they can function as symbols, in which case they refer to something else. When facial expressions are symbolic, they are referring to metacommunicative processes, for example, placating someone, deterring someone, or presenting oneself in a more favorable light. The dissociation of facial expression from internal emotional experience is taken up in detail in the discussion of Skill 5.

By mid- to late-childhood, most children recognize and can verbalize that a person's expression may be both a social and an emotional response (e.g., Underwood & Hurley, 1999). Gross and Ballif (1991) reviewed the early research on children's understanding of emotions in others based on facial expression cues and situational elicitors of emotion. The easiest emotions to figure out were positive ones: Smiling faces and situations depicting pleasure and getting what one wants were readily comprehended as associated with happiness. Negative facial expressions depicting sadness, fear, or anger were more difficult for children to decode. However, if paired with a detailed emotion-eliciting situational context, children were much more likely to infer the negative emotion in question.

As children grow older, they combine both facial and situational cues as they attempt to discern and understand the emotional experience of others. Wiggers and van Lieshout (1985) suggested that when there was a contradiction between a facial expression and the emotion-eliciting situation, school-age children were more likely to opt for whichever cue was more clearly presented. Children also recognize that others might feel a mixture of feelings about a situation.

Social Competence and Discerning Others' Emotional States. A number of studies indicate that children with emotional problems or who have been abused show deficits in their understanding of links between facial expression and emotion, in producing facial expressions, and in discriminating emotion expressions (e.g., Camras, Sachs-Alter, & Ribordy, 1996; Pollak, Cicchetti, Hornung, & Reed, 2000; Shipman, Zeman, Penza, & Champion, 2000). The research by Pollak et al. (2000) warrants further description: These investigators found that neglected children had difficulties in discriminating emotions, whereas physically abused children appeared to have a bias to perceive angry facial expressions. Thus, the sorts of early emotion communication experiences that children receive influence how they construct their understanding of others' emotional expressions and emotional states.

Do children who are exceptionally socially competent show an enhancement of understanding emotion and expression linkages? Research undertaken by Walden and Knieps (1996) suggested that preschoolers who obtained high sociometric peer preferences as play partners were also those who tended to be better at discriminating among emotional facial displays and who tended to demonstrate high spontaneous expressivity (but they did not excel in posed expressions). An earlier study undertaken by Edwards, Manstead, and MacDonald (1984) with somewhat older children demonstrated a similar relation: Children's sociometric rating was positively related to their ability to recognize facial expressions of emotion. Further support for links between social effectiveness and emotion *knowledge* can be found in research undertaken by Denham, McKinley, Couchoud, and Holt (1990) on preschoolers' peer interaction: Those children who demonstrated greater knowledge of emotion in a puppet task were perceived by their peers as more likeable.

Summary

Children's social effectiveness is closely linked to their accurate appraisal of emotional states in others. Even if the expressive cues are ambiguous, they learn to infer what emotions others might be experiencing, based on their expanding knowledge of common elicitors of emotion relevant to their subculture. Preschoolers can anticipate others' emotional responses, if they are provided with fairly explicit cues. By the early school years, children take into account what they know about the circumstances to infer the target's emotional response.

SOCIAL EFFECTIVENESS AND SKILL 3: USE OF A VOCABULARY OF EMOTION AND EXPRESSION

With language and symbols, we can traverse time and space to communicate with others about our own and their emotions. Social psychologists have investigated why it is that we are so compelled to share our emotional experience with others, and one hypothesis has been the "stress and affiliation effect" (reviewed in Luminet, Bouts, Delie, Manstead, & Rimé, 2000): When we feel badly, we want the company of others, and, more specifically, we want to tell others how we are feeling (with the interesting exception of when we feel shame). This implies that communicating our feelings to another initiates change. Such change may be found in how we experience our subjective feeling state (e.g., internal emotion regulation is affected), or with the support of others, we may devise different ways to cope with a problematic situation.

From a developmental perspective, the "stress and affiliation" pattern is the hallmark of many attachment studies with young children. We also know that young children and their mothers are more likely to use emotion-laden language when there is a dispute or some negative event occurs (Denham, Mitchell-Copeland, Strandberg, Auerbach, & Blair, 1997; Dunn & Brown, 1991). Indeed, as Chambers' review indicates (1999), family discourse is critical to young children's learning about emotions, how to speak about feelings, and how to cope with emotion-laden situations. However, let us return to the beginning: how young children acquire a lexicon of emotion that permits them to represent their own and others' emotional experience.

Ability to Use Concepts, Lexicon, and Scripts Relevant to Emotion and Expression

The ability to represent emotional experience through words, imagery, and symbolism of varied sorts allows children to communicate to others what they want and what problems they are encountering as well as to describe their delight and pleasure. With words, the child can further elaborate these representations of emotional experience, integrate them across contexts, and compare them with others' representations about emotional experiences.

Development of Emotion Lexicon.   Bretherton, Fritz, Zahn-Waxler, and Ridgeway (1986) reviewed the relevant literature on children's acquisition of emotion words, and they noted that many toddlers could use emotion words toward the end of the second year. By 3 years of age, children could much more readily label the emotions of others in addition to their own feelings. Increasingly, they could also verbally address the consequences of emotional states as well as the situational causes of emotions; for example, "Grandma mad. I wrote on wall."

Children can also apply emotion terms to pretend play by age 2 to 3, and, indeed, listening to children talk as they enact fantasies with their figurative toys (e.g., dolls, action figures, stuffed animals) is an excellent way to observe a young child's competence with emotion language, for they construct both the causes of the figure's emotional response and the consequences of the emotion, including how the figure copes. Denham and Auerbach (1995) analyzed the emotional content of mothers and preschoolers' dialogues while looking at picture books together. They found that such an interaction was rich with adult-child exchanges that included affect labeling and causes and consequences of emotional experience. In addition, both mothers and children used their emotion-descriptive language in ways that suggested social influence of the other; for example, those mothers who made use of verbal explanation to a very great degree appeared to stimulate their children further to use more complex and elaborated emotion-descriptive language.

Conversations about Emotional Responses.   The classic research on this topic was undertaken by Dunn et al. (1987), who investigated naturally occurring conversations in the home between young children and their mothers and siblings. They were particularly interested in determining what sorts of functions conversations about emotional reactions had in the social exchange in the home and how children communicated causes of emotional reactions in their exchanges with others. Their results indicated that access to an adult who is interested in one's emotional reactions may be pivotal to children having opportunities both to talk about emotions and have their understanding of emotions elaborated.

A study by Dunn and Brown (1994) sheds further light on the effects of family emotional expression on children's acquisition of emotion-descriptive language. They documented that families characterized as high in frequency of anger and distress expression had children who were less likely to be engaged in discourse about emotional experience. However, if the families were low in frequency of negative emotional expression, when a negative emotional event did occur for the child, there was a greater likelihood of an emotion-related conversation to ensue between child and parent.

A study by Laible (2004) on mother-child discourse emphasized the role that the parent-child relationship plays in children's acquisition of emotion understanding and internalization of behavioral expectations. Attachment classification and proneness to negative emotional reactivity were evaluated in her preschool sample, and then conversations between the mother and her child were examined for elaborative style and discussion of negative emotions. Laible found that attachment security was related to maternal elaboration and the dyad's discussion of negative emotions. In turn, such maternal elaboration was associated with children demonstrating higher levels of behavioral internalization and higher levels of emotion understanding.

Emotion Script Learning.   Acquisition of emotion-descriptive concepts continues throughout childhood and into adolescence, but little research has examined these older age groups. Further development of emotion language in the school-age child and adolescent may be found in their greater ability to add variety, subtlety, nuance, and complexity to their use of emotion-descriptive words with others. Russell (1991) defines emotion scripts as "a knowledge structure for a type of event whereby the event is thought of as a sequence of subevents" (p. 442). Russell notes that even in the same culture scripts for the same emotions may differ from person to person because emotion scripts are linked to other belief networks. This is a significant point because, for example, if a script for anger is linked to a network of concepts about sex role, the anger script may well have additional emphases or omissions if a person's machismo or femininity is implicated in the anger episode.

Emotion scripts may merge with gender role socialization as suggested by some of the sex differences found for how anger and sadness are talked about in families. For example, gender differences in learning to talk about emotional experience were found by Dunn et al. (1987) in their study of young British children and their mothers. Little girls received more comments and inquiries about emotions from their mothers and from their older siblings than did little boys. In a similar vein, Fivush (1991) found that mothers of 3-year-old boys and girls tended to talk in a more elaborated fashion about sadness with their daughters and more about anger with their sons. The mothers also tended to embed their discussions of emotions in social frameworks more with their daughters than with their sons. Relative to script notions, she also found that when anger was involved, mothers emphasized relationship repair with their daughters and were more accepting of retaliation by their angry sons.

Last, cultural influence and the acquisition of an emotional lexicon are inseparable, for societies use language to regulate emotion in social interaction. Many societies emphasize some emotional responses over others by attaching special importance to certain emotion-descriptive words. Much anthropological research has been done that examines emotion-descriptive language. The reader is referred to an edited volume on this topic (Russell, Fernández-Dols, Manstead, & Wellenkamp, 1996).

Summary

Young children show a rapid increase in acquiring an emotion lexicon. Having words for their emotional experience allows for seeking support in distressing circumstances, for reciprocal sharing with others about emotional experience, and for being able to conceptualize lexically their emotions and how they came about as well as what the consequences for the self and others might be. This skill of emotional competence functions somewhat like a pivot for the other skills, for it is with access to the language of emotion concepts that children learn to predict how they themselves are likely to emotionally react, to understand others' emotional responses, and to respond empathically and sympathetically to others, as we discuss next.

SOCIAL EFFECTIVENESS AND SKILL 4: THE CAPACITY FOR EMPATHIC AND SYMPATHETIC INVOLVEMENT

Empathy and sympathy are emotional responses that connect us with others. Sympathy differs from empathy in that it can also be experienced when responding to purely symbolic information, such as reading about someone's distress or by hearing about someone's unfortunate circumstances. Empathy tends to be defined as a more immediate emotional response that is experienced by the observer on witnessing someone's emotional state. Empathy may include emotion contagion, but with older children and adults we more often assume that there is some ability to take the perspective of the distressed person, and, consequently, we experience vicariously what we believe the target person to be experiencing. Sympathy is an affective response that contains elements of sorrow or concern for the distressed person. When feeling sympathetic, we do not necessarily vicariously experience the same or similar negative affect of the target (Eisenberg, 2003).

In a number of well-conducted studies, Eisenberg and her colleagues found that children also need to establish psychological boundaries so that they can respond sympathetically and not become overwhelmed by another's distress (e.g., Eisenberg et al.,

1996). Such personal distress leads to a preoccupation with their own negative affective response, which then short-circuits their prosocial, sympathetic behavior. There has been considerable debate among social and developmental psychologists as to whether empathy is a mediator of altruistic and prosocial behavior. Readers are referred to Eisenberg (2003) for a review of the issues.

What seems critical to address in empathy research and its influence on children's and youths' relationships is how it combines with a sense of values to predict socially responsible behavior that is accompanied by a sense of compassion. Children who feel a sense of responsibility to help others are among those most likely to behave prosocially (Chapman, Zahn-Waxler, Cooperman, & Iannotti, 1987). There is also research that demonstrates that failures in empathy are implicated in adolescents with conduct disorders (D. Cohen & Strayer, 1996). Arsenio and Lemerise (2001) are particularly vocal in their call for the need to address moral values in research on aggression, and one of the pivotal mediators between values and prosocial behavior may well prove to be empathy.

We need to know more about the sources of individual differences in the capacity for empathic engagement without becoming overwhelmed by one's own personal distress. Eisenberg and colleagues (reviewed in Eisenberg, 2003) have provided data that show, for children to experience sympathy rather than personal distress in an emotion-evocative situation, they need to be capable of neurophysiological regulation, use attentional control processes, accurately appraise emotion-eliciting events, infer others' internal emotional states, and cope with situational demands. Eisenberg and her colleagues found that heart rate acceleration was associated with a personal distress response, but sympathy co-occurred with heart rate deceleration. They also found that children's heart rate and facial expressions were better predictors of their subsequent helpful overtures than their self-report.

Early Parental Attunement

Zahn-Waxler (1991) has argued that the origins of prosocial and altruistic behavior are to be found in the dynamic emotional exchanges of the attachment relationship between parent and infant. She notes that the processes of joint attention, social exchange, and cooperative turn taking between caregiver and infant "create a world of shared meaning, empathic understanding and appropriate linking of one's own emotions with those of others that then generalize beyond the parent-child dyad" (p. 156).

Influence of Socialization

A multimethod, multisource study on how parents might influence their children's empathy was carried out by Strayer and Roberts (2004a) who found paths between parents' empathy and their children's empathy, but the relationship was mediated by children's anger. More specifically, empathic parents had children who were less angry and who also demonstrated more empathy. Parents who were low in empathy were also more controlling, and they subsequently had children who were more angry and less empathic. This relationship between parental insensitivity and negative reactions toward their child and subsequent ineffective social behavior in the child was also substantiated by Snyder, Stoolmiller, Wilson, and Yamamoto (2003). In their observational study, they found that children's anger was associated with frequency of parental behaviors (e.g., displays of anger, contempt, threats) shown toward the child. The authors also found that the children displayed relatively less fear and sadness, and they suggested that a deficit in those more vulnerable feelings might also be associated with a deficit in empathy in these angry, belittled children.

Strayer and Roberts (2004b) also investigated more intensively how children's anger and aggression might be related to their empathy. They observed the play behavior of 5-year-olds and found that empathic children are less angry, less verbally and physically aggressive, and were involved in fewer object struggles with their peers. In terms of social effectiveness and the ability to be empathically engaged, this study suggests that more harmonious relationships with others are clearly associated with higher levels of empathy.

In terms of sympathy, both modeling and attitudes on the part of parents appear to be important factors in children showing more sympathy (see review by Eisenberg, Fabes, Carlo, & Karbon, 1992). In an investigation undertaken by Eisenberg, Fabes, Schaller, Carlo, and Miller (1991), parents' attitudes were assessed using the Parental Attitude toward Children's Expressiveness Scale (PACES; Saarni, 1990), which was modified for use with preschoolers. Parents of children who reported restrictive attitudes toward their children's emotional displays had children who seemed more inclined to experience personal distress rather than sympathetic concern when describing their reaction to another's distress. This effect was more noticeable when the parents espoused controlling beliefs about their children's emotional displays, even when the emotional displays simply expressed the child's own vulnerable feelings (e.g., sadness, anxiety) as opposed to showing one's genuine feelings without regard for whether they could also hurt someone else's feelings. Parents who restricted their children's emotional displays in circumstances where others' feelings might be hurt—but not when their children expressed vulnerable feelings—appeared to have more sympathy-oriented children.

Summary

Empathy and its derivative, sympathy, are critical to emotional communication; indeed, responsiveness to others' emotions is likely critical to human evolution. The development of empathy such that it becomes linked with altruistic, prosocial behavior obviously promotes the well-being of those who need support or help, but it also facilitates the well-being of individuals who respond sympathetically. The preceding discussion suggests that such individuals enjoy more favorable relations with their peers and are able to regulate their emotional arousal such that they can effectively intervene to assist another. The reviewed research also indicates that complex, often indirect, relationships exist between parenting behaviors and children's empathic, sympathetic, and prosocial behavior toward others.

SOCIAL EFFECTIVENESS AND SKILL 5: SKILL IN DIFFERENTIATING INTERNAL EMOTIONAL EXPERIENCE FROM EXTERNAL EMOTIONAL EXPRESSION

Whether a person is trying to protect his or her vulnerability, enhance some advantage to her- or himself, or promote the well-being of another about whom they care, being able to monitor individual emotional-expressive behavior and action tendencies strategically is adaptive, and children learn to do so with increasing finesse as they mature (Saarni, 1989b, 1999). In the following discussion emotion management will be used to refer to children's regulating their experience of emotion by monitoring their expressive behavior.

By the preschool years, if not earlier, young children learn how to introduce disparities between their internal emotional state and their external expressive behavior. Such discrepancies indicate that young children have begun to differentiate their inner emotional experience from what they express in their behavior—especially to others. Perhaps the earliest form of this differentiation between internal state and external expression is the exaggeration of emotional-expressive behavior to gain someone's attention (a trivial injury becomes the occasion to howl loudly and solicit comfort and attention; e.g., Blurton-Jones, 1967). Minimization may be the next to appear; it consists of dampening the intensity of emotional-expressive behavior, despite feeling otherwise. Neutralization describes the adoption of a "poker face," but it is probably relatively difficult to carry off, and, indeed, in early research by Ekman and Friesen (1975) it was found that substitution of another expression that differs from what one genuinely feels is probably a more successful strategy (e.g., smiling despite feeling anxious).

Children learn to manage their expressive behavior by taking into account relationship dimensions such as closeness of relationship, power or status similarity/difference, and the degree to which they are exposed (e.g., public versus private situations). Gottman and his colleagues (1997) demonstrated in their longitudinal research that children who were most effective with their peers knew how to regulate their external expressive behavior, but we contend that children believe that it is important to find an adaptive balance between self-presentation, which may require emotional dissemblance as well as genuine display of emotion. An early interview study indicated that school-age children believed that the display of genuine emotion was as regulated as the display of dissembled emotion (Saarni, 1989a).

Components of Emotional Dissemblance

As summarized some time ago by Shennum and Bugental (1982), children gradually acquire knowledge about when, where, with whom, and how to express behaviorally their emotional reactions. They also need to have the ability to control the skeletal muscles involved in emotional-expressive behavior. They need to have the motivation to manage their emotional-expressive behavior in the appropriate situations. They also need to have reached a certain complexity of cognitive representation. We address each of these components in turn as they are reflected in recent research.

Knowledge. Children can readily nominate reasons for showing their genuine emotions to others, and indeed, across all ages, the most common reason cited for when genuine emotions would be expressed was if they were experienced as very intense (i.e., and thus less controllable; Saarni, 1979). School-age children can also nominate reasons for dissembling their expressive behavior, and that early study found that the majority of their reasons referred to wanting to avoid embarrassment or derision from others for revealing vulnerable emotions such as hurt or fear. Avoiding getting into trouble and getting attention were also among the reasons mentioned for dissembling emotional expressive behavior. The older children were more likely to make reference to the degree of affiliation with an interactant, status differences, and controllability of both emotion and circumstances as contextual qualities that affected the genuine or dissembled display of emotion (see also Saarni, 1988).

Parker and her colleagues (Parker et al., 2001) examined children's knowledge of dissemblance strategies for anger in a hypothetical vignette about unfair treatment of one child by another and then compared their conceptual knowledge with their actual behavior in playing a competitive game with an unfamiliar peer confederate in which they were unfairly made to lose and the confederate overtly cheated. Their results were complex, but essentially what they found was that children reported they would feel angrier, be more likely to express their anger, and be less likely to dissemble their anger in the hypothetical story in contrast to what they reported and expressed after having lost to the cheating confederate in the unfair.

Another interesting study examined 6- to 8-year-olds' ability to conceptualize the difference between internal emotion state and facial expression and how this conceptualization might be related to their miniaturization of emotional expression when alone versus when engaged interpersonally (Holodynski, 2004). His results revealed that his oldest age group reliably reduced the intensity of their expressions when alone as opposed to being with the research assistant; the 6-year-olds revealed similarly intense expressions across both conditions.

Ability to Implement Emotional Dissemblance.   Control of skeletal muscles, especially in the face, is critical to being able to modify one's emotional-expressive behavior and thus dissemble the outward expression of one's emotional response. Children become capable of this modification voluntarily at a young age (2 to 3 years), and it is readily apparent in their pretend play; for example, they mimic postures, expressions, vocal qualities, and the like of assorted fantasy characters. Ceschi and Scherer (2003) examined children's ability to control their facial muscles when asked to suppress expressions of pleasure, which were elicited by a funny routine acted out by a clown. Seven- and 10-year-olds were interviewed about their knowledge of emotional expression control strategies and then divided into two groups: one group saw the clown routines without any instruction to suppress their expression and the second group were asked to try to conceal their amusement during the clown routine. Both groups apparently found the routine fairly intensely amusing, and thus the second group's ability to suppress their mirth was limited, although they were able to reduce the duration of their positive expressive behaviors to some extent. There was no noteworthy age difference in expressive behavior in the two groups or in the knowledge of emotion control strategies.

Motivation.   One of us has investigated children's knowledge of how to manage emotional-expressive behavior and their expectations about what motivated story characters to undertake such management strategies (Saarni, 1979). When the children were asked to explain why the story character's emotional reaction had not been genuinely expressed, four broad categories of motivation were apparent in their responses. These four motivation categories are elaborated as follows:

1. *Avoidance of negative situational outcomes or enhancement of positive situational outcomes:* This common motive is well illustrated in a study by Davis (1995), who had children play a game in which to get the attractive prize, they had to persuasively manage their expressive behavior so as to look positive about both attractive and unattractive prizes. The results showed that the girls were more successful at suppressing negative expressive behaviors toward the unattractive prize than the boys. The girls also revealed a greater number of social monitoring behaviors (e.g., rapid glancing at the experimenter) as well as tension

behaviors (e.g., touching one's face), and they appeared to monitor the social exchange more closely than the boys, which may have facilitated their expression management.

2. *Protection of one's self-esteem:* Meerum Terwogt and Olthof (1989) found that boys were reluctant to express fear because they worried they would be viewed as cowards by their peers. Fuchs and Thelen (1988) also reported that boys were loathe to reveal their sadness to their fathers but might consider doing so with their mothers. Maintenance of self-image appeared to be the chief motive for these boys and emotion management was sought by adoption of a stoic "emotional front." There is a great need for further research on how children's needs to self-protect or to enhance their self-image in the eyes of others are linked to emotion dissemblance strategies and self-presentation, but this topic, relative to children, has been underresearched.

3. *Maintenance or enhancement of relationships and concern for others' well-being:* As an illustration of this last motive for emotional dissemblance, von Salisch (1996) probed how children actually regulated a relationship by monitoring what they expressed. The participating children were 11 years old, and consisted of either best friends or of casual acquaintances who played together a rigged computer game that would "crash" randomly but seemingly caused by one of the players. With close friends, the incidence of smiling was even greater than with acquaintances, and among girls in close friend pairs, genuine smiles were especially notable in their reciprocity. In essence, these preadolescent boys and girls used their smiles to reassure their friend that the relationship was still on firm ground, despite their reproaching their friend for their "incompetence" in making the computer game "crash." What von Salisch's research shows us is that children are adept at using this social function of emotional-expressive behavior to manage their relationships, and they do so in a discriminating fashion.

4. *Observance of norms and conventions:* These are the cultural display rules that provide us with consensually agreed-on scripts for how to manage our emotions. Norms of etiquette, for example, "You should smile at the person who gives you something, even if you don't like the gift," are common examples of cultural display rules and illustrate scripts for the management of emotional-expressive behavior. It is probably noteworthy that cultural display rules often have "shoulds" associated with them. At least a couple of factors might account for why children do not consistently perform cultural display rule scripts, despite knowing them: First, the social stakes may not be sufficiently high for them to feel motivated to do so; second, their distressed, hurt, or angry emotional responses may be experienced as too intense to allow for emotional dissemblance (Saarni, 1989b).

These four categories for why we may be motivated to dissemble the expression of our emotional responses are not necessarily exhaustive nor are they mutually exclusive, but they all have one significant feature in common: They are concerned with interpersonal consequences, and it is the varying nature of these social consequences that yields the differences among motives. Even the self-esteem motive for dissemblance does not occur in a social vacuum, for the self is embedded in a history of social relationships.

Cognitive Representation.   As suggested by Josephs' (1994) research, a pragmatic or implicit knowledge of emotional dissemblance is likely to precede an articulated

person responds emotionally to evocative stimulation, we can examine the intensity of emotional response (both negative and positive valence), the threshold of arousal of emotional response, the duration (and other temporal aspects) of the emotional response, and even the proclivity for what sort of hedonic tone of emotional response is generated (i.e., negative versus positive reactions to change).

Using temperament in this fairly global fashion as having to do with how we dispositionally tend to modulate our emotional reactions, we can examine how individual differences in temperament may influence coping efficacy. This approach was taken by Eisenberg and her colleagues in several different research projects on preschoolers' coping efficacy relative to their social functioning. As an illustration, Eisenberg et al. (1993) investigated whether 4- to 6-year-old children's temperament-influenced emotional intensity level was related to their coping strategies and social competence. Among their very complex results was that high emotional intensity was associated with lower levels of constructive coping and with lower levels of attentional control (more distractable). Such children were also regarded by their teachers as less socially mature and by their peers as less attractive as playmates.

Coping Strategies and Development

It is not always clear whether coping is different from emotion regulation. Some researchers refer to coping as an aspect of self-regulation because effortful or purposeful responses may be involved when one copes with a challenging situation (e.g., Compas, 1987). Other investigators use the terms coping and emotion regulation interchangeably (e.g., Brenner & Salovey, 1997), arguing that both are implicated when children use available strategies to manage stressful encounters. Coping research has typically focused on strategies used to manage stress-provoking experience or aversive emotions that are evoked by challenging circumstances. From this perspective, coping follows emotion regulation in a temporal sense: first, a person modulates his or her emotional arousal and then seeks to resolve the stressful encounter to his or her benefit. However, given the dynamics of transactional and reciprocal relations in children's and youths' social worlds, it is unlikely that emotion regulation and coping are so simplistically distinguished according to a linear temporal path (e.g., Campos et al., 2004).

In examining what changes about coping strategies as children mature, we find that although use of situation-oriented problem solving is accessible throughout childhood, it becomes more targeted to the specific problem at hand, and children's repertoire of problem-solving strategies broadens with age (e.g., Altshuler & Ruble, 1989). With age, children's ability to consider a stressor from a number of different angles increases, thus older children can more readily consider different problem solutions relative to these different perspectives. They learn to recruit social support more effectively and subtly, for example, through effective self-presentation strategies that garner social approval. They expand their capacity to tolerate aversive emotion to the degree that appraisal processes can be redirected and thus reduce distress (e.g., Band & Weisz, 1988). If appraisal indicates that control over the situational stressor or conflict is minimal or extremely risky, effective emotional regulation may also involve distraction, cognitively reframing the meaning of the difficult situation, and use of cognitive blunting or sensitizing (Miller & Green, 1985). Denial and dissociation appear to be less adaptive coping strategies in that emotions are split off from their eliciting context for short-term gain but at long-term expense (e.g., Fischer & Ayoub, 1993).

Last, perceived control over the stressful situation is relevant to how coping efforts are undertaken. As children mature, they become better able to distinguish uncontrollable stressors from controllable ones (Wolchik & Sandler, 1997). For the uncontrollable situations, older children are more likely to nominate "secondary control" coping strategies, which include reframing, distraction, and avoidance through anticipatory planfulness (e.g., Marriage & Cummins, 2004). Younger children's avoidance is more often of the escape sort such as hiding under the bed to avoid an unpleasant event.

Family Influences on Children's Coping

Attachment. A potentially significant influence on children's coping strategies is their early attachment experience with significant caregivers. Cassidy (1994) has theorized how attachment history and emotion regulation may be linked; the reader is referred to her work for further detail and to the Handbook of Attachment (Cassidy & Shaver, 1999). Related research on infants' attachment classification and their propensity to experience different kinds of emotion was examined by Kochanska (2001). She found that over a 26-month period that (a) infants classified as avoidantly attached become progressively more fearful, (b) resistantly attached children appeared to have difficulty responding with joy or pleasure, (c) young children with disorganized attachment classifications became more angry, and (d) the securely attached children showed less fear and anger than children with the other attachment classifications, in spite of being placed in situations designed to elicit those emotions.

Family Conflict and Dysfunction. Given the relatively few studies that have tracked quality of attachment to children's subsequent coping competence, the ways that families contribute to individual children's coping competence are far from being well understood. There is a larger body of research that has examined the effects of marital conflict and anger on children's functioning—the latter having some links with how well children cope with the aversive feelings that they themselves experience. Cummings and his colleagues (e.g., Cummings, Goeke-Morey, Papp, & Dukewich, 2002) have conducted a number of investigations on this topic, and, not surprisingly, the general conclusion that they reach is that many children do not fare well when faced with frequent and intense marital conflict.

Parenting Style. Valiente, Fabes, Eisenberg, and Spinrad (2004) looked at mothers' and fathers' expressive style (self-reported) and their supportiveness toward their children as the latter coped with ordinary, daily stressors. Their results indicated that mothers who more often used "negative-dominant" expressive style, which included hostile and derogating expressive behavior, had children whose coping was less constructive. Mothers who reported using more supportive strategies had children who, in turn, were more able to access and use constructive coping strategies. An earlier study by Hardy, Power, and Jaedicke (1993) also found that parental supportiveness was significantly related to the breadth of repertoire of coping strategies. We infer that parental supportiveness is likely to be associated with an ongoing secure attachment between child and parent; thus, supportiveness may be a "proxy" for how attachment may mediate children's development of coping strategies.

As children mature, their growing cognitive sophistication, exposure to varied social models, and breadth of emotional-social experience contribute to their being able to generate more coping solutions to problematic situations. The older they are when faced with serious distress, the more able they are to see the situation from various perspectives and figure out a way to resolve it. With maturity, they become more accurate in their appraisals of how much control they really have over the situation and what risks might accompany taking control of a very difficult situation (e.g., intervening in a fight). Effective coping in Western cultures involves acknowledgment of one's emotional response, awareness of one's self as having some degree of agency, and a functional appraisal of the problematic situation and one's role in it.

Some Final Comments about Emotional Competence

As mentioned earlier, research and theory as related to the last two skills of emotional competence are not addressed in this chapter (see Saarni et al., 2006 or Saarni, 1999). Briefly, Skill 7 requires that the individual minimally recognize that emotions are communicated differently depending on a person's relationship with an interactant, but this particular skill goes beyond that of impression management or self-presentation strategies as defined in Skill 5. With this skill, we also want to include the awareness and use of emotional experience to differentiate the organization of a person's relations with others. The last skill of emotional competence, Skill 8, refers to the individual being able to access emotional self-efficacy, which entails an individual's acceptance of his or her emotional experience, whether eccentric or conventional, negative or positive. With this skill, individuals can tolerate and not feel overwhelmed by intense negative emotion (e.g., outrage or anguish) because they do not view their emotional responses as unjustified. They feel relatively in control of their emotional experience from the standpoint of mastery and positive self-regard. Indeed, a sense of global self-worth may lie at the heart of emotional self-efficacy (Harter, 1999). In our opinion, this sense of emotional self-efficacy is probably not achieved until adolescence, for it is undoubtedly dependent on cognitive development, including the ability to consider the realm of possibility and of reality.

In conclusion, further theoretical development of the construct of emotional competence is needed; for example, how does it differ from emotional intelligence (Mayer, Salovey, & Caruso, 2000; Saarni, 2007) and how might emotional competence skills be structured hierarchically. The skills of emotional competence are dynamic and transactional, for these skills are part of an interpersonal exchange that unfolds in a unique context. Indeed, one could design interesting studies simply by pairing together children or teens who differ in the degree to which they can employ the skills of emotional competence and then observe how their interpersonal negotiations unfold.

Some Final Thoughts about the Nature of Emotion

In science, progress is measured not so much by how many questions have been answered, but by how many new ones have been raised. Such is the case in the study of emotion, where there has been a plethora of significant contributions to knowledge in recent years. In conclusion, we review a few of the unresolved issues that we believe represent the frontier of research into emotional development.

Emotions as Organizers of Psychological Functions, Not Just Outward Signs of Internal States.   The functionalist perspective taken in this chapter is designed to liberalize the study of emotion. Many contemporary studies of emotions deal with them as outward signs of internal states; studies of emotions as antecedents and organizers of personal and social behaviors have been much less prevalent. When emotions are considered purely as responses, the tendency is to stop there, and not consider how those responses can be in the service of changing or maintaining person-environment relations. This imbalance between emotions considered as responses and emotions conceptualized as organizers generates a number of major new areas of research.

One of the areas in which emotions serve as organizers concerns emotional communication. Consider the wealth of information we have about individual differences in emotional *responding* (i.e., temperament), and individual differences in emotional *perception* and subsequent behavior regulation (a phenomenon for which we do not even have a noun, and about which there are consequently few studies). One of the first research questions we raised in several sections about emotional development concerned the little we know about how emotion perception originates, how such perceptions lead to functional consequences for the child, and how infants and children come to react, and subsequently to become dismissive, hyper-vigilant, or appropriately attuned, toward different cues of emotion expressed by others.

If emotions serve to organize human behavior, they must be social and relational. As a result, the boundary of social psychological research and developmental study becomes very permeable. For instance, the self, it has been said, develops under the watchful eye of the other. This statement captures our point that it is not just cognitive developments linked to the self that lead to so-called self-conscious emotions. The child must notice the presence of such watchful eyes, realize that the eyes reside in significant others, identify what emotion the eyes are communicating, and subsequently behave to have an appropriate effect on those eyes—such as by hiding from them in shame, or showing off to them in pride. The social context and the social signals (expressions) provided by significant others are thus constitutive of new emotions. This phenomenon has not been adequately studied, in comparison to studies of the relation between cognitive and emotional development. Put another way, rules and standards, and the construct of the self, may not be sufficient to generate later-appearing emotions like pride, shame, and guilt; these emotions may also require the affective sting of the emotional communications of others. If so, we need to study the value added by emotional signals to the imposition of rules and standards.

Another topic at the interface of developmental and social psychology is that of attention in dyadic and group settings. Basic issues such as the targeting of joint attention between two individuals and the quality of the emotional messages exchanged between them may determine the specific emotion generated in such interchanges. The meaning of a joyful reaction by a significant other in the presence of a child has different functional consequences depending on (a) whether the joy is targeted toward an action of the child (laying the basis for the child to experience pride), (b) whether the joy is merely witnessed by the child (leading to an empathic affect sharing but not pride), or (c) whether the joy is oriented toward the child himself or herself (resulting in the child developing affiliative or attachment bonds). Similarly, the quality of the emotion message manifested by the other in such social interactional exchanges (i.e., its fearful nature or its scornful nature) may have dramatically different results on the child. The first permits the child to "catch" the fear of an object expressed by another; the second potentially enters into the generation of shame (as noted before).

Are Emotions Always Social and Relational? The Interiorization of Emotions.
Emotions, on first consideration, do not seem to be relational. Indeed, they seem to be primarily intrapsychic and private events. For instance, we weep for the loss of a loved one in the privacy of our own room, with no one present, and no apparent social target

for the tears. We laugh at jokes while watching television alone, or become afraid when reading by ourselves. Is it the case that, contrary to the propositions of this chapter, emotions are primarily private and nonrelational? If they are relational, as we propose they are, how do they become private, and do such private events themselves have functional sequelae? Is it possible that, early in development, emotions are external and relational, and become internal and private at some later point in life? We know that in language speech shifts at 5 to 6 years of age from being primarily or exclusively external to potentially internal and private. Such interiorization has great relevance for the growth of self-regulation. Is there a similar process of interiorization that occurs for emotion? Does the interiorization of emotion take place at the same age as the interiorization of speech? And does such possible interiorization have implications for emotion regulation, by analogy to the consequences of the interiorization of speech for self-regulation? The recent work of Holodynski and Friedlmeier (2006) draws our attention to such interiorization processes. We believe that these authors have identified what may be a major yet unsuspected developmental transition in emotional life—one that takes place in the middle of the first decade of life.

Emotions as Flexible, Not Reflexive.   The approach to emotion we have taken is not only relational but also nonmechanistic. It considers emotions not as reflexive but as flexible, even in the very young infant. The functionalist approach stresses that the same event can produce quite different emotions, and the same emotion can result in quite different, indeed equipotential, transactions with the world. Equipotentiality of emotional behavior—the fact that the same emotion can be manifested in a multiplicity of functionally equivalent ways—rules out their being reflexive. However, most research on emotion to date has not done justice to the flexibility and equipotentiality of emotion. Our methods often constrain the possibility of observing flexibly manifested emotional behaviors, or of noting how the same event can be construed differently by different children. Moreover, the research objectives in most studies typically center on the search for the coherence of emotional behaviors—the more highly intercorrelated we find behaviors to be, the better we think our findings are. However, emotional behaviors are rarely highly intercorrelated. Such low-to-modest correlations are precisely what one would expect if emotional behaviors are equipotential. Low correlations due to equipotentiality of response would then reflect, not the presence of error variance, but a true state of affairs. How does one statistically and conceptually tease apart situations in which low correlations among behaviors are expectable from those in which there is error variance? This is a vexing problem for researchers to address, and our usual statistical models do not help disentangle the two possibilities. Only research designed to predict what behaviors are shown in what contexts can do so.

The Importance of Context in Understanding Emotion.   Another important issue in the functionalist approach is the critical role of context. One instantiation of the importance of context is again at the interface of social and developmental psychology. It relates to when and how children's disclosure of differently valenced emotions to different categories of people takes place (e.g., peers versus adults, close relationships versus distant ones, and so forth). Relevant individual differences to consider in such an investigation include personality disposition (e.g., degree of inhibition) and children's cognitive perspective-taking skills. Children's social cognitive expectancies about the reactions of others to emotion-laden disclosures are also relatively underinvestigated.

Also related to context is the process of how individual differences in the capacity for empathic engagement by the child without the child becoming overwhelmed by his or her own personal distress. Important contextual features of the relationship that exist between target and sufferer are also under investigated; such features can differentially contribute to personal distress reactions. For example, if the target is more dominant or powerful than the actor and now something affects the target to render her or him distressed, at what age will children intervene to assist sympathetically—and in a genuine manner, rather than instrumentally or strategically—as opposed to feeling personally distressed?

A central aspect of context in emotion is that of the role a person is expected to assume. One cannot understand many emotions without understanding the role a person is playing. However, we do not know very much about how children and youth integrate their knowledge about social roles (e.g., age roles, occupational roles, authority/leadership roles), how roles set the stage for different emotional reactions and different beliefs about emotional communication. Some research on gender roles exists, but it appears to be more related to socialization patterns (e.g., girls' conciliatory versus boys' coercive styles when faced with a conflict) or with attributions of propensity about which gender is more likely to experience what sort of emotion. We thus propose more of a focus on how children and youth organize their relationships with regard to how roles impact various dimensions of emotion.

What Develops in Emotional Development?

A final set of questions brings us full circle to the objective of this chapter: Emotional development is the development of what? We need to do research on how some emotions (or components of emotion) are present in some rudimentary form at birth or shortly thereafter. These nonemergent emotions develop in the sense that new events elicit them, or new motives are served by them, but the relation between the event and the motive stays invariant. However, what is the process by which different events in relation to different goals yield the same emotion? We do not know the answer to the question of how such totally different transactions yield the same or similar emotions. Other emotions are not present from birth but become organized due to the intercoordination of processes such as cognition, exposure to events in the world, the social reactions and attitudes of others, the biological constitution of the child, and the differentiation of the physical and social self. Do these emotions emerge? Or are they evident in some rudimentary, not-readily measurable form early in life. The possibility that emotions may be evident much earlier than the usual indices of emotion leads us to infer that this is an important question. We hope that future compendia on emotion may report answers to the unresolved issues we pose.

References

Abbott, S. (1992). Holding on and pushing away: Comparative perspectives on an eastern Kentucky child-rearing practice. *Ethos, 20,* 33–65.

Ainsworth, M., Blehar, M., Waters, E., & Wall, S. (1978). *Patterns of attachment.* Hillsdale, NJ: Erlbaum.

Altshuler, J., & Ruble, D. (1989). Developmental changes in children's awareness of strategies for coping with uncontrollable stress. *Child Development, 60,* 1337–1349.

Anderson, E. (1994). *Young children's understanding of facial and vocal expressions of emotion.* Unpublished doctoral dissertation, DePaul University, Chicago.

Arsenio, W., & Lemerise, E. (2001). Varieties of childhood bullying: Values, emotion processes, and social competence. *Social Development, 10,* 59–73.

Band, E., & Weisz, J. (1988). How to feel better when it feels bad: Children's perspectives on coping with everyday stress. *Developmental Psychology, 24,* 247–253.

Barrett, K. C., Zahn-Waxler, C., & Cole, P. M. (1993). Avoiders versus amenders: Implications for the investigation of guilt and shame during toddlerhood. *Cognition and Emotion, 7,* 481–505.

Barth, J., & Bastiani, A. (1997). A longitudinal study of emotion regulation and preschool children's social behavior. *Merrill-Palmer Quarterly, 43,* 107–128.

Bingham, R., Campos, J. J., & Emde, R. N. (1987 April). *Negative emotions in a social relationship context.* Paper presented at the Society for Research on Child Development, Baltimore.

Bischof, N. (1975). A systems approach toward the functional connections of attachment and fear. *Child Development, 46,* 801–817.

Bloom, L. (1998). Language acquisition in its developmental context. In W. Damon (Series Ed.) & D. Kuhn & R. S. Siegler (Vol. Eds.), *Handbook of child psychology: Vol. 2. Cognition, perception, and language* (5th ed., pp. 309–370). New York: Wiley.

Blurton-Jones, N. (1967). An ethological study of some aspects of social behaviour of children in nursery school. In D. Morris (Ed.), *Primate ethology* (pp. 347–368). London: Weidenfeld and Nicolson.

Boccia, M., & Campos, J. J. (1989). Maternal emotional signals, social referencing, and infants' reactions to strangers. In N. Eisenberg (Ed.), *New directions of child development* (Vol. 44, pp. 25–49). San Francisco: Jossey-Bass.

Bowlby, J. (1969). *Attachment and loss: Vol. 1. Attachment.* New York: Basic Books.

Brenner, E., & Salovey, P. (1997). Emotion regulation during childhood: Developmental, interpersonal, and individual considerations. In P. Salovey & D. Sluyter (Eds.), *Emotional literacy and emotional development* (pp. 168–192). New York: Basic Books.

Bretherton, I., Fritz, J., Zahn-Waxler, C., & Ridgeway, D. (1986). Learning to talk about emotions: A functionalist perspective. *Child Development, 57,* 529–548.

Briggs, J. (1970). *Never in anger.* Cambridge, MA: Harvard University Press.

Campos, J., Anderson, D. I., Barbu-Roth, M. A., Hubbard, E. M., Hertenstein, M. J., & Witherington, D. (2000). Travel broadens the mind. *Infancy, 1*(2), 149–219.

Campos, J., Frankel, C., & Camras, L. (2004). On the nature of emotion regulation. *Child Development, 75,* 377–394.

Campos, J., Hiatt, S., Ramsay, D., Henderson, C., & Svejda, M. (1978). The emergence of fear on the visual cliff. In M. Lewis & L. Rosenblum (Eds.), *The origins of affect* (pp. 149–182). New York: Wiley.

Campos, J., Mumme, D., Kermoian, R., & Campos, R. G. (1994). A functionalist perspective on the nature of emotion. In N. Fox (Ed.), *The development of emotion regulation* (pp. 284–303). Chicago: University of Chicago Press.

Campos, J., Thein, S., & Owen, D. (2003). A Darwinian legacy to understanding human infancy: Emotional expressions as behavior regulators. *Annals of the New York Academy of Sciences, 1000,* 110–134.

Camras, L. A., Lambrecht, L., & Michel, G. (1996). Infant "surprise" expressions as coordinative motor structures. *Journal of Nonverbal Behavior, 20,* 183–195.

Camras, L. A., Meng, Z., Ujiie, T., Dharamsi, S., Miyake, K., Oster, H., et al. (2002). Observing emotion in infants: Facial expression, body behavior, and rater judgments of responses to an expectancy-violating event. *Emotion, 2*(2), 179–193.

Camras, L. A., Oster, H., Campos, J. J., & Bakeman, R. (2003). Emotional facial expressions in European-American, Japanese, and Chinese Infants. In P. Ekman, J. Campos, R. Davidson, & F. de Waal (Eds.), *Annals of the New York Academy of Sciences: Vol. 1000. Emotions inside out* (pp. 135–151). New York: New York Academy of Sciences.

Camras, L. A., Oster, H., Campos, J., Campos, R., Ujiie, T., Miyake, K., et al. (1998). Production of emotional facial expressions in American, Japanese and Chinese infants. *Developmental Psychology, 34,* 616–628.

Camras, L. A., Oster, H., Campos, J., Miyake, K., & Bradshaw, D. (1992). Japanese and American infants' responses to arm restraint. *Developmental Psychology, 28,* 578–583.

Camras, L. A., & Sachs, V. B. (1991). Social referencing and caretaker expressive behavior in a day care setting. *Infant Behavior and Development, 14,* 27–36.

Camras, L., Sachs-Alter, E., & Ribordy, S. (1996). Emotion understanding in maltreated children: Recognition of facial expressions and integration with other emotion cues. In M. Lewis & M. W. Sullivan (Eds.), *Emotional development in atypical children* (pp. 203–225). Mahwah, NJ: Erlbaum.

Cassidy, J. (1994). Emotion regulation: Influences of attachment relationships. *Monographs of the Society for Research in Child Development, 59*(2/3, Serial No. 240), 228–249.

Cassidy, J., & Shaver, P. R. (Eds.). (1999). *Handbook of attachment.* New York: Guilford Press.

Ceschi, G., & Scherer, K. (2003). Children's ability to control the facial expression of laughter and smiling: Knowledge and behaviour. *Cognition and Emotion, 17,* 385–411.

Chambers, S. M. (1999). The effect of family talk on young children's development and coping. In E. Frydenberg (Ed.), *Learning to cope: Developing as a person in complex societies* (pp. 130–149). Oxford: Oxford University Press.

Chapman, M., Zahn-Waxler, C., Cooperman, G., & Iannotti, R. (1987). Empathy and responsibility in the motivation of children's helping. *Developmental Psychology, 23,* 140–145.

Chisholm, J. S. (1989). Biology, culture and the development of temperament: A Navajo example. In J. K. Nugent, B. Lester, & T. B. Brazelton (Eds.), *The cultural context of infancy: Vol. 1. Biology, culture, and infant development* (pp. 341–364). Norwood, NJ: Ablex.

Cohen, D., & Strayer, J. (1996). Empathy in conduct disordered and comparison youth. *Developmental Psychology, 32,* 988–998.

Cohen, L., & Campos, J. (1974). Father, mother and stranger as elicitors of attachment behaviors in infancy. *Developmental Psychology, 10,* 146–154.

Cohn, J. F., & Tronick, E. Z. (1988). Mother-infant face-to-face interaction: Influence is bidirectional and unrelated to periodic cycles in either partner's behavior. *Developmental Psychology, 24*(3), 386–392.

Compas, B. E. (1987). Coping with stress during childhood and adolescence. *Psychological Bulletin, 101,* 393–403.

Crick, N., & Dodge, K. (1994). A review of social-information processing mechanisms in children's social adjustment. *Psychological Bulletin, 115,* 74–101.

Cummings, E. M., Goeke-Morey, M. C., Papp, L. M., & Dukewich, T. L. (2002). Children's responses to mothers' and fathers' emotionality and tactics in marital conflict in the home. *Journal of Family Psychology, 16,* 478–492.

Davis, T. (1995). Gender differences in masking negative emotions: Ability or motivation? *Developmental Psychology, 31,* 660–667.

Denham, S. (1999). *Emotional development in young children.* New York: Guilford Press.

Denham, S., & Auerbach, S. (1995). Mother-child dialogue about emotions. *Genetic, Social, and General Psychology Monographs, 121,* 301–319.

Denham, S., McKinley, M., Couchoud, E., & Holt, R. (1990). Emotional and behavioral predictors of preschool peer ratings. *Child Development, 61,* 1145–1152.

Denham, S., Mitchell-Copeland, J., Strandberg, K., Auerbach, S., & Blair, K. (1997). Parental contributions to preschoolers' emotion competence: Direct and indirect effects. *Motivation and Emotion, 21,* 65–86.

Diener, E., & Lucas, R. E. (2000). Subjective emotional well-being. In M. Lewis & J. Haviland-Jones (Eds.), *Handbook of emotions* (2nd ed., pp. 325–337). New York: Guilford Press.

Dondi, M., Simion, F., & Caltran, G. (1999). Can newborns discriminate between their own cry and the cry of another newborn infant? *Developmental Psychology, 35*(2), 418–426.

Dunn, J. (2000). Mind-reading, emotion understanding, and relationships. *International Journal of Behavioral Development, 24,* 142–144.

Dunn, J., Bretherton, I., & Munn, P. (1987). Conversations about feeling states between mothers and their young children. *Developmental Psychology, 23,* 132–139.

Dunn, J., & Brown, J. (1991). Relationships, talk about feelings, and the development of affect regulation in early childhood. In J. Garber & K. Dodge (Eds.), *The development of emotion regulation and dysregulation* (pp. 89–108). Cambridge: Cambridge University Press.

Dunn, J., & Brown, J. (1994). Affect expression in the family, children's understanding of emotions, and their interactions with others. *Merrill-Palmer Quarterly, 40,* 120–137.

Edwards, R., Manstead, A., & MacDonald, C. J. (1984). The relationship between children's sociometric status and ability to recognize facial expressions of emotion. *European Journal of Social Psychology, 14,* 235–238.

Eisenberg, N. (2003). Prosocial behavior, empathy, and sympathy. In M. Bornstein & L. Davidson (Eds.), *Well-being: Positive development across the life course* (pp. 253–265). Mahwah, NJ: Erlbaum.

Eisenberg, N., Fabes, R., Bernzweig, J., Karbon, M., Poulin, R., & Hanish, L. (1993). The relations of emotionality and regulation to preschoolers' social skills and sociometric status. *Child Development, 64,* 1418–1438.

Eisenberg, N., Fabes, R., Carlo, G., & Karbon, M. (1992). Emotional responsivity to others: Behavioral correlates and socialization antecedents. In N. Eisenberg & R. Fabes (Eds.), *New directions in child development: Vol. 5. Emotion and its regulation in early development* (pp. 57–73). San Francisco: Jossey-Bass.

Eisenberg, N., Fabes, R., Murphy, B., Karbon, M., Smith, M., & Maszk, P. (1996). The relations of children's dispositional empathy-related responding to their emotionality, regulation, and social functioning. *Developmental Psychology, 32,* 195–209.

Eisenberg, N., Fabes, R., Schaller, M., Carlo, G., & Miller, P. A. (1991). The relations of parental characteristics and practices to children's vicarious emotional responding. *Child Development, 62,* 1393–1408.

Eisenberg, N., & Morris, A. S. (2002). Children's emotion-related regulation. *Advances in Child Development and Behavior, 30,* 190–229.

Eisenberg, N., Spinrad, T., Fabes, R., Reiser, M., Cumberland, A., Shepard, S., et al. (2004). The relations of effortful control and impulsivity to children's resiliency and adjustment. *Child Development, 75,* 25–46.

Ekman, P. (1973). *Darwin and facial expression.* New York: Academic Press.

Ekman, P., & Friesen, W. V. (1975). *Unmasking the face.* Englewood Cliffs, NJ: Prentice-Hall.

Ekman, P., Levenson, R. W., & Friesen, W. V. (1983). Autonomic nervous activity distinguishes between emotions. *Science* (221), 1208–1210.

Fabes, R., Hanish, L., Martin, C. L., & Eisenberg, N. (2002). Young children's negative emotionality and social isolation: A latent growth curve analysis. *Merrill-Palmer Quarterly, 48,* 284–307.

Fernald, A. (1993). Approval and disapproval: Infant responsiveness to vocal affect in familiar and unfamiliar languages. *Child Development, 64,* 657–674.

Fifer, W. P., & Moon, C. M. (1995). The effects of fetal experience with sound. In J.-P. Lecanuet, W. P. Fifer, N. A. Krasnegor, & W. P. Smotherman (Eds.), *Fetal development: A psychobiological perspective* (pp. 351–366). Hillsdale, NJ: Erlbaum.

Fischer, K., & Ayoub, C. (1993). Affective splitting and dissociation in normal and maltreated children: Developmental pathways for self in relationships. In D. Cicchetti & S. Toth (Eds.), *Rochester Symposium on Development and Psychopathology: Vol. 5. Disorders and dysfunctions of the self* (pp. 149–222). Rochester, NY: University of Rochester Press.

Fivush, R. (1991). The social construction of personal narratives. *Merrill-Palmer Quarterly, 37,* 59–82.

Fraiberg, S. (1977). *Insights from the blind.* New York: Basic Books.

Fridlund, A. (1994). *Human facial expressions: An evolutionary view.* New York: Academic Press.

Frijda, N. (1986). *The emotions.* Cambridge: Cambridge University Press.

Fuchs, D., & Thelen, M. (1988). Children's expected interpersonal consequences of communicating their affective states and reported likelihood of expression. *Child Development, 59,* 1314–1322.

Gordon, S. (1989). The socialization of children's emotions: Emotional culture, competence, and exposure. In C. Saarni & P. Harris (Eds.), *Children's understanding of emotions* (pp. 319–349). New York: Cambridge University Press.

Gottman, J. M., Katz, L. F., & Hooven, C. (1997). *Meta-emotion.* Hillsdale, NJ: Erlbaum.

Gross, A. L., & Ballif, B. (1991). Children's understanding of emotion from facial expressions and situations: A review. *Developmental Review, 11,* 368–398.

Grossmann, K. E., Grossmann, K., Huber, F., & Wartner, U. (1981). German children's behavior toward their mothers at 12 months and their fathers at 18 months in Ainsworth's Strange Situation. *International Journal of Behavioral Development, 4,* 157–181.

Gumora, G., & Arsenio, W. (2002). Emotionality, emotion regulation, and school performance in middle school children. *Journal of School Psychology, 40,* 395–413.

Halberstadt, A., Denham, S., & Dunsmore, J. (2001). Affective social competence. *Social Development, 10,* 79–119.

Hardy, D., Power, T., & Jaedicke, S. (1993). Examining the relation of parenting to children's coping with everyday stress. *Child Development, 64,* 1829–1841.

Harris, P. L. (2000). Understanding emotion. In M. Lewis & J. Haviland (Eds.), *Handbook of emotion* (2nd ed., pp. 281–292). New York: Guilford Press.

Harter, S. (1999). *The construction of the self.* New York: Guilford Press.

Harter, S., Waters, P. L., Whitesell, N., & Dastelic, D. (1998). Level of voice among female and male high school students: Relational context, support, and gender orientation. *Child Development, 34,* 892–901.

Harter, S., & Whitesell, N. R. (1989). Developmental changes in children's understanding of single, multiple, and blended emotion concepts. In C. Saarni & P. Harris (Eds.), *Children's understanding of emotion* (pp. 81–116). Cambridge: Cambridge University Press.

Hatfield, E., Cacioppo, J. T., & Rapson, R. L. (1994). *Emotional contagion.* Cambridge: Cambridge University Press.

Haviland, J. M., & Lelwica, M. (1987). The induced affect response: 10-week-old infants' responses to three emotional expressions. *Developmental Psychology, 23,* 97–104.

Hertenstein, M., & Campos, J. (2001). Emotion regulation via maternal touch. *Infancy, 2,* 549–566.

Hertenstein, M., & Campos, J. (2004). The retention effects of an adult's emotional displays on infant behavior. *Child Development, 75*(2), 595–613.

Holodynski, M. (2004). The miniaturization of expression in the development of emotional self-regulation. *Developmental Psychology, 40,* 16–28.

Holodynski, M., & Friedlmeier, W. (2006). *Development of emotions and emotion regulation.* New York: Springer.

Hubbard, J. (2001). Emotion expression processes in children's peer interaction: The role of peer rejection, aggression, and gender. *Child Development, 72,* 1426–1438.

Izard, C. E. (1972). *The face of emotion.* New York: Appleton-Century-Crofts.

Izard, C. E. (1977). *Human emotions.* New York: Plenum Press.

Izard, C. E. (1995). Innate and universal facial expressions: Evidence from developmental and cross-cultural research. *Psychological Bulletin, 115,* 288–299.

Izard, C. E., Ackerman, B., Schoff, K., & Fine, S. (2000). Self-organization of discrete emotions, emotion patterns and emotion-cognition relations. In M. Lewis & I. Granic (Eds.), *Emotion, development, and self-organization* (pp. 15–36). Cambridge: Cambridge University Press.

Izard, C. E., & Dougherty, L. (1982). Two complementary systems for measuring facial expressions in infants and children. In C. E. Izard (Ed.), *Measuring emotions in infants and children* (pp. 97–126). New York: Cambridge University Press.

Jaffe, J., Beebe, B., Feldstein, S., Crown, C. L., & Jasnow, M. D. (2001). Rhythms of dialogue in infancy: Coordinated timing in development. *Monographs of the Society for Research in Child Development, 66*(2), vi–131.

Josephs, I. E. (1994). Display rule behavior and understanding in preschool children. *Journal of Nonverbal Behavior, 18,* 301–326.

Keefer, C., Dixon, S., Tronick, E., & Brazelton, T. (1991). Cultural mediation between newborn behavior and later development: Implications for methodology in cross-cultural research. In J. Nugent, B. Lester, & T. Brazelton (Eds.), *The cultural context of infancy: Vol. 2. Multicultural and interdisciplinary approaches to parent-infant relations* (pp. 39–61). Norwood, NJ: Ablex.

Kitayama, S., & Markus, H. (1994). Introduction to cultural psychology and emotion research. In S. Kitayama & H. Markus (Eds.), *Emotion and culture* (pp. 1–19). Washington, DC: American Psychological Association.

Klinnert, M. D., Campos, J. J., Sorce, J. F., Emde, R. N., & Svejda, M. (1983). Emotions as behavior regulators: Social referencing in infancy. In R. Plutchik & H. Kellerman (Eds.), *Emotion: Theory, research and experience* (pp. 57–86). New York: Academic Press.

Kochanska, G. (2001). Emotional development in children with different attachment histories: The first three years. *Child Development, 72,* 474–490.

Laible, D. (2004). Mother-child discourse in two contexts: Links with child temperament, attachment security, and socioemotional competence. *Developmental Psychology, 40,* 979–992.

Lawson, K. R., & Ruff, H. A. (2004). Early attention and negative emotionality predict later cognitive and behavioural function. *International Journal of Behavioral Development, 28*(2), 157–165.

Lazarus, R. S. (1991). *Emotion and adaptation.* New York: Oxford University Press.

Lewis, M. (1993). Self-conscious emotions: Embarrassment, pride, shame, and guilt. In M. Lewis & J. Haviland (Eds.), *Handbook of emotions* (pp. 563–573). New York: Guilford Press.

Lewis, M. (2000). Self-conscious emotions: Embarrassment, pride, shame, and guilt. In M. Lewis & J. Haviland (Eds.), *Handbook of emotions* (2nd ed., pp. 623–636). New York: Guilford Press.

Lewis, M., Hitchcock, D. F., & Sullivan, M. W. (2004). Physiological and emotional reactivity to learning and frustration. *Infancy, 6,* 121–143.

Lewis, M., & Ramsay, D. (2002). Cortisol response to embarrassment and shame. *Child Development, 73,* 1034–1045.

Lewis, M., & Ramsay, D. (2004). Development of self-recognition, personal pronoun use, and pretend play during the 2nd year. *Child Development, 75,* 1821–1831.

Luminet, O., Bouts, P., Delie, F., Manstead, A., & Rimé, B. (2000). Social sharing of emotion following exposure to a negatively valenced situation. *Cognition and Emotion, 14,* 661–688.

Marriage, K., & Cummins, R. (2004). Subjective quality of life and self-esteem in children: The role of primary and secondary control in coping with everyday stress. *Social Indicators Research, 66,* 107–122.

Martin, G. B., & Clark, R. D. (1982). Distress crying in neonates: Species and peer specificity. *Developmental Psychology, 18,* 3–9.

Mastropieri, D., & Turkewitz, G. (1999). Prenatal experience and neonatal responsiveness to vocal expressions of emotion. *Developmental Psychobiology, 35*(3), 204–214.

Mayer, J. D., Salovey, P., & Caruso, D. (2000). Emotional intelligence as zeitgeist, as personality, and as a mental ability. In R. Bar-On & J. D. Parker (Eds.), *Handbook of emotional intelligence* (pp. 92–117). San Francisco: Jossey-Bass.

Mead, M. (1954). The swaddling hypothesis: Its reception. *American Anthropologist, 56,* 395–409.

Meerum Terwogt, M., & Olthof, T. (1989). Awareness and self-regulation of emotion in young children. In C. Saarni & P. Harris (Eds.), *Children's understanding of emotion* (pp. 209–237). Cambridge: Cambridge University Press.

Mesquita, B., & Frijda, N. (1992). Cultural variations in emotion: A review. *Psychological Bulletin, 112,* 179–204.

Miller, S. M., & Green, M. L. (1985). Coping with stress and frustration: Origins, nature, and development. In M. Lewis & C. Saarni (Eds.), *The socialization of emotions* (pp. 263–314). New York: Plenum Press.

Miyake, K., Campos, J., Kagan, J., & Bradshaw, D. (1986). Issues in socioemotional development in Japan. In H. Azuma, K. Hakuta, & H. Stevenson (Eds.), *Kodomo: Child development and education in Japan* (pp. 238–261). San Francisco: Freeman.

Miyake, K., Chen, S., & Campos, J. (1985). Infant temperament, mother's mode of interaction, and attachment in Japan. *Monographs of the Society for Research in Child Development, 50*(1/2, Serial No. 209) 276–297.

Moore, G. A., & Calkins, S. (2004). Infants' vagal regulation in the still-face paradigm is related to dyadic coordination of mother-infant interaction. *Developmental Psychology, 40,* 1068–1080.

Morelli, G., Rogoff, B., Oppenheim, D., & Goldsmith, D. (1992). Cultural variation in infants' sleeping arrangements: Questions of independence. *Developmental Psychology, 28,* 604–613.

Morris, M., & Peng, K. (1994). Culture and cause: American and Chinese attributions for social and physical events. *Journal of Personality and Social Psychology, 67,* 949–971.

Mumme, D., Bushnell, E., DiCorcia, J., & Lariviere, L. (in press). Infants' use of gaze cues to interpret others' actions and emotional reactions. In R. Flom, K. Lee, & D. Muir (Eds.), *The ontogeny of gaze following.* Mahwah, NJ: Erlbaum.

Mumme, D., & Fernald, A. (2003). The infant as onlooker: Learning from emotional reactions observed in a television scenario. *Child Development, 74,* 221–237.

Mumme, D., Fernald, A., & Herrera, C. (1996). Infants responses to facial and vocal emotional signals in a social referencing paradigm. *Child Development, 67,* 3219–3237.

Oster, H. (1995). *Baby FACS: Analyzing facial movement in infants.* Unpublished manuscript.

Parker, E. H., Hubbard, J., Ramsden, S., Relyea, N., Dearing, K., Smithmyer, C., et al. (2001). Children's use and knowledge of display rules for anger following hypothetical vignettes versus following live peer interaction. *Social Development, 10,* 528–557.

Pollak, S. D., Cicchetti, D., Hornung, K., & Reed, A. (2000). Recognizing emotion in faces: Developmental effects of child abuse and neglect. *Developmental Psychology, 36,* 679–688.

Rapacholi, B. (1998). Infants' use of attentional cue to identify the referent of another person's emotional expression. *Developmental Psychology, 34,* 1017–1025.

Rothbart, M., & Bates, J. E. (1998). Temperament. In N. Eisenberg (Ed.), *Social, emotional and personality development* (5th ed., Vol. 3, pp. 105–176). New York: Wiley.

Russell, J. A. (1991). Culture and the categorization of emotion. *Psychological Bulletin, 110,* 426–450.

Russell, J. A. (1994). Is there universal recognition of emotion from facial expression? A review of the cross-cultural studies. *Psychological Bulletin, 115,* 102–141.

Russell, J. A., Fernández-Dols, J. M., Manstead, A., & Wellenkamp, J. (Eds.). (1996). *Everyday conceptions of emotion: An introduction to the psychology, anthropology and linguistics of emotion.* Hingham, MA: Kluwer Press.

Saarni, C. (1979). Children's understanding of display rules for expressive behavior. *Developmental Psychology, 15,* 424–429.

Saarni, C. (1988). Children's understanding of the interpersonal consequences of dissemblance of nonverbal emotional-expressive behavior. *Journal of Nonverbal Behavior, 12,* 275–294.

Saarni, C. (1989a). Children's beliefs about emotion. In M. Luszez & T. Nettelbeck (Eds.), *Psychological development: Perspectives across the life-span* (pp. 69–78). Amsterdam: North-Holland.

Saarni, C. (1989b). Children's understanding of strategic control of emotional expression in social transactions. In C. Saarni & P. Harris (Eds.), *Children's understanding of emotion* (pp. 181–208). New York: Cambridge University Press.

Saarni, C. (1990). *Psychometric properties of the Parental Attitude toward Children's Expressiveness Scale* (PACES). Unpublished manuscript. (ERIC Document Reproduction Service No. ED317-301)

Saarni, C. (1999). *The development of emotional competence.* New York: Guilford Press.

Saarni, C. (2007). The development of emotional competence: Pathways for helping children become emotionally intelligent. In R. Bar-On, J. Maree, & M. J. Elias (Eds.), *Educating people to be emotionally intelligent* (pp. 15–35). Westport, CT: Praeger.

Saarni, C., Campos, J. J., Camras, L. A., & Witherington, D. (2006). Emotional development: Action, communication, and understanding. In W. Damon & R. M. Lerner (Series Ed.) & N. Eisenberg (Vol. Ed.), *Handbook of child psychology: Vol. 3. Social, emotional, and personal development* (6th ed., pp. 226–299). Hoboken, NJ: Wiley.

Sagi, A., Lamb, M., Lewkowicz, K., Shoham, R., Dvir, R., & Estes, D. (1985). Security of infant-mother, -father, and -metapelet attachments among kibbutz reared Israeli children. *Monographs of the Society for Research in Child Development, 50*(1/2, Serial No. 209) 257–275.

Schultz, D., Izard, C., & Ackerman, B. (2000). Children's anger attribution bias: Relations to family environment and social adjustment. *Social Development, 9,* 284–301.

Shennum, W. A., & Bugental, D. B. (1982). The development of control over affective expression in nonverbal behavior. In R. S. Feldman (Ed.), *Development of nonverbal behavior in children* (pp. 101–118). New York: Springer Verlag.

Shipman, K., Zeman, J., Penza, S., & Champion, K. (2000). Emotion management skills in sexually maltreated and nonmaltreated girls: A developmental psychopathology perspective. *Development and Psychopathology, 12,* 47–62.

Snyder, J., Stoolmiller, M., Wilson, M., & Yamamoto, M. (2003). Child anger regulation, parental responses to children's anger displays, and early child antisocial behavior. *Social Development, 12,* 335–360.

Sorce, J. F., Emde, R. N., Campos, J., & Klinnert, M. D. (1985). Maternal emotional signaling: Its effect on the visual cliff behavior of 1-year-olds. *Developmental Psychology, 21,* 195–200.

Sroufe, L. A. (1979). Socioemotional development. In J. Osofsky (Ed.), *Handbook of infant development* (pp. 462–516). New York: Wiley.

Sroufe, L. A., & Waters, E. (1977). Attachment as an organizational construct. *Child Development, 48,* 1184–1199.

Stein, N., Trabasso, T., & Liwag, M. (2000). A goal appraisal theory of emotional understanding: Implications for development and learning. In M. Lewis & J. Haviland (Eds.), *Handbook of emotions* (2nd ed., pp. 436–457). New York: Guilford Press.

Strayer, J., & Roberts, W. L. (2004a). Children's anger, emotional expressiveness, and empathy: Relations with parents' empathy, emotional expressiveness, and parenting practices. *Social Development, 13,* 229–254.

Strayer, J., & Roberts, W. L. (2004b). Empathy and observed anger and aggression in 5-year-olds. *Social Development, 13,* 1–13.

Swanson, A., Hemphill, S., & Smart, D. (2004). Connections between temperament and social development: A review. *Social Development, 13,* 142–170.

Tangney, J. P., Burggraf, S., & Wagner, P. (1995). Shame-proneness, guilt-proneness, and psychological symptoms. In J. P. Tangney & K. Fischer (Eds.), *Self-conscious emotions: The psychology of shame, guilt, embarrassment, and pride* (pp. 343–367). New York: Guilford Press.

Thompson, R., Easterbrooks, M. A., & Padilla-Walker, L. (2003). Social and emotional development in infancy. In R. Lerner, M. A. Easterbrooks, & J. Mistry (Eds.), *Handbook of psychology: Vol. 6. Developmental psychology* (pp. 91–112). Hoboken, NJ: Wiley.

Tomkins, S. (1962). *Affect, imagery, and consciousness: Vol. 1. The positive affects.* New York: Springer-Verlag.

Trevarthen, C. (1988). Universal cooperative motives: How infants begin to know the language and culture of their parents. In G. Johoda & I. M. Lewis (Eds.), *Acquiring culture: Cross-cultural studies in child development* (pp. 37–90). London: Croom Helm.

Trevarthen, C. (1993). The function of emotions in early infant communication and development. In J. Nadel & L. Cumaioni (Eds.), *New perspectives in early communicative development* (pp. 48–81). London: Routledge.

Tronick, E., Morelli, G., & Ivey, P. (1992). The Efe forager infant and toddler's pattern of social relationships: Multiple and simultaneous. *Developmental Psychology, 28,* 568–577.

Underwood, M., & Hurley, J. (1999). Emotion regulation and peer relationships during the middle childhood years. In C. Tamis-LeMonda & L. Balter (Eds.), *Child psychology: A handbook of contemporary issues* (pp. 237–258). Philadelphia: Psychology Press/Taylor & Francis.

Vaish, A., & Striano, T. (2004). Is visual reference necessary? Contributions of facial versus vocal cues in 12-month-old's social referencing behavior. *Developmental Science, 7*(3), 261–269.

Valiente, C., Eisenberg, N., Smith, C. L., Reiser, M., Fabes, R., Losoya, S., et al. (2003). The relations of effortful control and reactive control to children's externalizing problems: A longitudinal assessment. *Journal of Personality, 71,* 1171–1196.

Valiente, C., Fabes, R., Eisenberg, N., & Spinrad, T. (2004). The relations of parental expressivity and support to children's coping with daily stress. *Journal of Family Psychology, 18,* 97–106.

von Salisch, M. (1996). Relationships between children: Symmetry and asymmetry among peers, friends, and siblings. In A. E. Auhagen & M. von Salisch (Eds.), *The diversity of human relationships* (pp. 59–77). New York: Cambridge University Press.

von Salisch, M. (2001). Children's emotional development: Challenges in their relationships to parents, peers, and friends. *International Journal of Behavioral Development, 25,* 310–319.

Walden, T., & Knieps, L. (1996). Reading and responding to social signals. In M. Lewis & M. W. Sullivan (Eds.), *Emotional development in atypical children* (pp. 29–42). Hillsdale, NJ: Erlbaum.

Walker-Andrews, A. (1997). Infants' perception of expressive behaviors: Differentiation of multimodal information. *Psychological Bulletin, 121,* 437–456.

Watson, J. S. (1972). Smiling, cooing and "the game." *Merrill-Palmer Quarterly, 18,* 341–347.

Watzlawick, P., Beavin, J., & Jackson, D. (1967). *Pragmatics of human communication: A study of interactional patterns, pathologies, and paradoxes.* New York: Norton.

Whiting, J. (1981). Environmental constraint on infant care practices. In R. H. Munroe, R. L. Munroe, & B. Whiting (Eds.), *Handbook of cross-cultural human development* (pp. 155–179). New York: Garland STPM Press.

Wierzbicka, A. (1992). Talking about emotions: Semantics, culture, and cognition. *Cognition and Emotion, 6,* 285–319.

Wiggers, M., & van Lieshout, C. (1985). Development of recognition of emotions: Children's reliance on situational and facial expressive cues. *Developmental Psychology, 21,* 338–349.

Winn, S., Tronick, E. Z., & Morelli, G. A. (1989). The infant and the group: A look at Efe caretaking practices in Zaire. In J. K. Nugent, B. M. Lester, & T. B. Braelton (Eds.), *The cultural context of infancy: Vol. 1. Biology, culture, and infant development* (pp. 87–109). Norwood, NJ: Ablex.

Wolchik, S. A., & Sandler, I. N. (Eds.). (1997). *Handbook of children's coping: Linking theory and intervention.* New York: Plenum Press.

Zahn-Waxler, C. (1991). The case for empathy: A developmental review. *Psychological Inquiry, 2,* 155–158.

Zahn-Waxler, C., & Radke-Yarrow, M. (1990). The origins of empathic concern. *Motivation and Emotion, 14*(2), 107–130.

Zeman, J., & Shipman, K. (1997). Social-contextual influences on expectancies for managing anger and sadness: The transition from middle childhood to adolescence. *Developmental Psychology, 33,* 917–924.

Chapter 12

Development of Achievement Motivation

ALLAN WIGFIELD, JACQUELYNNE S. ECCLES,
ROBERT W. ROESER, and ULRICH SCHIEFELE

Motivational psychologists study what moves people to act and why people think and do what they do (Pintrich, 2003; Weiner, 1992). Motivation energizes and directs actions, and so it has great relevance to many important developmental outcomes. Achievement motivation refers more specifically to motivation relevant to performance on tasks in which standards of excellence are operative. Fundamentally, motivational theorists and researchers work to understand the motivational predictors of choice, persistence, and effort (Eccles, Wigfield, & Schiefele, 1998; Wigfield, Eccles, Schiefele, Roeser, & Davis-Kean, 2006).

Motivation is most directly observable in the level of energy in individuals' behaviors. Historically, drives, needs, and reinforcements were proposed as the primary sources (see Eccles et al., 1998; Pintrich & Schunk, 2002; Weiner, 1992), Much current theory and research on motivation focuses on individuals' beliefs, values, and goals as primary influences on motivation (Eccles & Wigfield, 2002). We focus in this abbreviated version of our chapter on current theories of achievement motivation, their development, and group differences in motivation. Because of space limitations, we do not discuss the important influences that socialization agents have on the development of motivation (see Wigfield et al., 2006, for review of the work on parents, schools, and peers as socialization agents affecting motivation).

Current Theoretical Perspectives on Motivation

Central constructs of interest to motivation theorists include (a) self-efficacy, perceptions of control, and other competence-related beliefs; (b) the goals (both specific and general) children have for learning and other activities; (c) children's interest and intrinsic motivation for learning; and (d) children's valuing of achievement. Although the study of beliefs, goals, and values remains strong, self-determination theorists continue to emphasize the role of basic psychological needs and how they influence motivation.

COMPETENCE-RELATED BELIEFS

Self-Efficacy Theory

Bandura's (1977, 1997) construct of self-efficacy is a major part of his broader social cognitive model of learning and development. Bandura defines self-efficacy as individuals' confidence in their ability to organize and execute a given course of action to solve a problem or accomplish a task and states that it has major influences on individuals' achievement strivings, including performance, choice, and persistence. Bandura (1997) characterizes self-efficacy as a multidimensional construct that can vary in strength (i.e., positive or negative), generality (i.e., relating to many situations or only a few), and level of difficulty (i.e., feeling efficacious for all tasks or only easy tasks). Bandura proposed that individuals' perceived self-efficacy is determined primarily by four things: Previous performance; vicarious learning; verbal encouragement by others; and one's physiological reactions. His stress on these four determinants reflects the link of this theory with both behaviorist and social learning traditions.

The self-efficacy construct has been applied to behavior in many domains, including school, health, sports, therapy, occupational choice, and even snake phobia (see Bandura, 1997, for a comprehensive review). The evidence is supportive of his theoretical predictions with respect to efficacy's influences on performance and choice, though there has been some criticism of the theory as too focused on one construct as the major predictor of performance and choice.

Attribution Theory and Theories about Beliefs about Intelligence and Ability

Attribution theory concerns individuals' explanations (or attributions) for their successes and failures and how these attributions influence subsequent motivation (Weiner, 1985, 2005). Weiner and his colleagues identified the most frequently used attributions (i.e., ability, effort, task difficulty, and luck), and classified these and other attributions into the different causal dimensions of stability (i.e., stable or unstable), locus of control (i.e., internal or external), and controllability (i.e., under one's volition or not). Each of these dimensions has important psychological consequences that influence subsequent motivation and behavior. The stability dimension relates most directly to expectancies for success and failure, locus of control to affective reactions to success and failure, and controllability to help giving. For instance, attributing failure to lack of ability leads to lowered expectancies for success and negative affect like shame (Weiner, 1985; see Eccles et al., 1998, for more detailed review).

Attribution theory was quite dominant in the motivation field for many years, but its influence has waned to an extent recently. Despite this, there still is great interest in the motivation field in perceptions of ability and also of effort. Dweck and her colleagues (e.g., Dweck, 2002; Dweck & Leggett, 1988; Dweck & Molden, 2005) posited that children can hold one of two views of intelligence or ability. Children holding an entity view of intelligence believe that intelligence is a stable trait. Children holding an incremental view of intelligence believe that intelligence is changeable, so that it can be increased through effort. These different beliefs have motivational consequences. Dweck

(2002) argued that children holding an entity view of intelligence are motivated to look smart and protect their sense of ability. Children holding an incremental view are motivated to work hard to improve their skills.

Control Theories

Building on the seminal early work of Rotter (1966) and Crandall, Katkovsky, and Crandall (1965) on internal and external locus of control, Connell (1985) added unknown control as a third control belief category and argued that younger children are particularly likely to use this category. He linked control beliefs to competence needs: Children who believe they control their achievement outcomes should feel more competent.

Skinner and her colleagues (e.g., Skinner, 1995; Skinner, Chapman, & Baltes, 1988) proposed a model of control beliefs including three critical control-related beliefs: (1) strategy beliefs, (2) control beliefs, and (3) capacity beliefs. Strategy beliefs concern the expectation that particular causes can produce certain outcomes; these causes include Weiner's (2005) various causal attributions and Connell's (1985) unknown control. Control beliefs are the expectations individuals have that they can produce desired events and prevent undesired ones. Capacity beliefs are the expectations that one has access to the means needed to produce various outcomes. Skinner (1995) proposed that control beliefs are a major determinant of actions, leading to outcomes that are interpreted by the individual and subsequently influence their control beliefs, starting the cycle again. Skinner, Connell, and their colleagues have broadened their discussion of perceived control and its influences by developing a model of the relations among context, the self, action, and outcomes (e.g., Connell, Spencer, & Aber, 1994).

Modern Expectancy-Value Theories

Modern expectancy-value theories (e.g., Eccles-Parsons et al., 1983; Pekrun, 1993; Wigfield & Eccles, 2000, 2002) are based on Atkinson's (1957, 1964) original expectancy-value model in that they link achievement performance, persistence, and choice most directly to individuals' expectancy-related and task-value beliefs. However, both the expectancy and value components are more elaborate and are linked to a broader array of psychological and social/cultural determinants. In this section, we focus on Eccles and colleague's expectancy-value model.

The Eccles et al. Expectancy-Value Model

Eccles-Parsons and her colleagues' expectancy-value model of achievement-related choices (see Eccles, 1987, 1993; Eccles & Wigfield, 1995; Eccles-Parsons et al., 1983; Wigfield & Eccles, 2000, 2002) focuses on the social psychological influences on choice and persistence. They defined expectancies for success as children's beliefs about how well they will do on upcoming tasks, either in the immediate or longer-term future and ability beliefs as beliefs about how good one is. Values are defined with respect to how important, interesting, or useful a given task or activity is to the individual (values are discussed in the next section).

Expectancies and values are assumed to directly influence performance, persistence, and task choice. Expectancies and values are assumed to be influenced by task-specific beliefs such as perceptions of competence, perceptions of the difficulty of different tasks, and individuals' goals and self-schema. These social cognitive variables are influenced by a variety of socialization agents and the cultural milieu.

THEORIES CONCERNED WITH TASK VALUES, INTRINSIC MOTIVATION, AND GOALS

The theories discussed in this section deal with why individuals do different tasks. Even if people are capable of doing a task, they may not want to engage in it, and so they may not be strongly motivated to approach it. Further, individuals often have different purposes or goals for doing different activities, which also can impact their motivation for doing the task.

Expectancy-Value Theories: Task Value

Eccles-Parsons and her colleagues (1983) defined four motivational components of task value: (1) attainment value, (2) intrinsic value, (3) utility value, and (4) cost. They defined attainment value as the personal importance of doing well on the task, intrinsic value as the enjoyment the individual gets from performing the activity, and utility value as how well a task relates to current and future goals, such as career goals. Cost refers to how doing one activity interferes with doing other possible activities; doing homework means one cannot call a friend.

Eccles and her colleagues and others (e.g., Bong, 2001) have assessed the links of expectancies and values to performance and choice (see Wigfield & Eccles, 2002, for review). They have shown that ability self-concepts and expectancies for success directly predict performance in mathematics, English, computer activities, and sport activities, even when previous performance is controlled. Children's task values predict course plans and enrollment decisions more strongly than do expectancy-related beliefs. Eccles (1994) found that both expectancies and values predict career choices.

Husman, Lens, and their colleagues have discussed another important values-related construct, future time perspective (FTP; Husman & Lens, 1999; Kauffman & Husman, 2004; Lens, 1986). They noted that much of the work in the motivation field focuses on motivation for immediate tasks and activities. This motivation obviously is important for students' engagement in learning, but students also know that a major purpose of education is to prepare them for the future. Therefore, if students believe that current educational activities are useful to them in the long run, they are more likely to be motivated to achieve.

Intrinsic Motivation Theories

There is a fundamental distinction in the motivation literature between intrinsic motivation and extrinsic motivation. When individuals are intrinsically motivated, they do activities for their own sake and out of interest in the activity. When extrinsically motivated, individuals do activities for instrumental or other reasons, such as receiving a reward (see Sansone & Harackiewicz, 2000). There is continuing debate about the pros and cons of intrinsic and extrinsic motivation, and a growing consensus that these two constructs should not be treated as polar opposites. Rather, they often both operate in different situations, and may even form a continuum.

Self-Determination Theory. Deci, Ryan, and their colleagues' self-determination theory (SDT) is an organismic theory of development that has a particular focus on the role of motivation in development and learning (e.g., Deci & Ryan, 1985, 2002b; Ryan & Deci, 2000). Broadly, self-determined behavior is behavior that originates from the self and that results from the individual utilizing his or her volition. When individuals' behavior is self-determined, they are psychologically healthier and tend to be intrinsically motivated. Deci, Ryan, and their colleagues propose that there are three basic or fundamental human psychological needs: (1) the need for competence, (2) the need for autonomy, and (3) the need for relatedness (Deci & Ryan, 2002b; Ryan & Deci, 2002). For healthy development to occur, these needs must be met.

Deci, Ryan, and colleagues go beyond the extrinsic-intrinsic motivation dichotomy in their discussion of internalization, which is the process of transferring the regulation of behavior from outside to inside the individual (see Deci, Koestner, & Ryan, 1999; Grolnick, Gurland, Jacob, & Decourcey, 2002). They developed a taxonomy to describe different types of motivation involved in the process of going from external to more internalized regulation of motivation. This taxonomy forms a continuum going from amotivation to intrinsic motivation, with intrinsic motivation being the most self-regulated kind of motivated behavior.

One major focus of this research and theorizing has been how extrinsic rewards can undermine intrinsically motivated behavior. They call this portion of their theory cognitive evaluation theory. There has been much debate in the field about the conditions under which this undermining occurs, but convincing evidence that it indeed does so (see Deci et al., 1999; Lepper & Henderlong, 2000; Ryan & Deci, 2000; Sansone & Harackiewicz, 2000).

Flow Theory.   Flow is defined as the immediate subjective experience that occurs when people are engaged in an activity. Interviews with climbers, dancers, chess players, basketball players, and composers revealed that these activities yield a specific form of experience—labeled flow—characterized by: (a) holistic feelings of being immersed in, and of being carried by, an activity; (b) merging of action and awareness; (c) focus of attention on a limited stimulus field; (d) lack of self-consciousness; and (e) feeling in control of one's actions and the environment (Csikszentmihalyi, 1988). Flow is only possible when people feel that the opportunities for action in a given situation match their ability to master the challenges. Further research has shown that both the challenges and skills must be relatively high before a flow experience becomes possible (Massimini & Carli, 1988).

Interest Theories

Closely related to the notion of intrinsic motivation is work on the concept of "interest" (P. A. Alexander, Kulikowich, & Jetton, 1994; Hidi, 2001; Krapp, 2002; Renninger, Hidi, & Krapp, 1992; Schiefele, 1991, 2001). Hidi and Harackiewicz (2000) propose that interest is more specific than intrinsic motivation, which is a broader motivational characteristic (see also Deci, 1992, 1998). Researchers studying interest differentiate between individual and situational interest. Individual interest is a relatively stable evaluative orientation toward certain domains; situational interest is an emotional state aroused by specific features of an activity or a task.

Much of the research on individual interest has focused on its relation to the quality of learning (see P. A. Alexander et al., 1994; Hidi, 2001; Renninger, Ewen, & Lasher, 2002; Schiefele, 1996, 1999). In general, there are significant but moderate relations between interest and text learning, particularly deeper-level learning.

Goal Theories

Work on achievement goals and goal orientations can be organized into three relatively distinct areas (see Pintrich, 2000a). One group of researchers has focused on the properties of goals for specific learning activities. These researchers (e.g., Bandura, 1986; Schunk, 1991) focus on goals' proximity, specificity, and level of challenge. A second group defined and investigated broader goal orientations students have toward their learning, focusing primarily on three broad orientations: (1) a mastery or learning orientation, (2) an ego or performance orientation, and (3) a work-avoidant orientation. These orientations refer to broader approaches children take to their learning, rather than goals for specific activities. A third group focuses on the content of children's goals, proposing that there are many different kinds of goals individuals can have in achievement settings, including both academic and social goals (e.g., Ford, 1992; Wentzel, 1991). We focus in this section on the work of the latter two groups.

Goal Orientation Theory. Researchers initially distinguished two broad goal orientations (e.g., Ames, 1992; Blumenfeld, 1992; Butler, 1993; Dweck & Leggett, 1988; Nicholls, 1984). The first has been called learning, task-involved, or mastery goal orientation and it occurs when children focus on improvement and mastery. The second is called performance or ego orientation and it occurs when children focus on maximizing favorable evaluations of their competence and minimizing negative evaluations of competence. Nicholls and his colleagues (e.g., Nicholls, Cobb, Yackel, Wood, & Wheatley, 1990) and Meece (1991, 1994) have described a work-avoidant goal orientation, which means that the child does not wish to engage in academic activities.

The different terms used to label these goal orientations occurred because different researchers were working on them simultaneously, with each having a somewhat distinctive view of each orientation (see Pintrich, 2000a; Thorkildsen & Nicholls, 1998). Although these distinctions are important, we also believe that the similarities are stronger than the distinctions between them (see Midgley, Kaplan, & Middleton, 2001; Pintrich, 2000a). We use the terms *mastery* and *performance goal orientations* in this chapter.

Theorists have separated these two broad goal orientations into approach and avoidance components, with the distinction first made for performance goals (Elliot, 1999, 2005; Elliot & Harackiewicz, 1996; Skaalvik, 1997). This occurred because empirically, findings concerning the outcomes of having a performance goal orientation were somewhat contradictory, leading researchers to wonder why this occurred. Theoretically, Elliot and Harackiewicz noted that traditional achievement motivation theories, such as Atkinson's (1957) expectancy-value model, included both approach and avoidance motives. Performance-approach goals refer to the students' desire to demonstrate competence and outperform others. Performance-avoidance goals involve the desire to avoid looking incompetent. Researchers began to disentangle the effects of these two kinds of performance orientations.

Elliot (1999; Elliott & McGregor, 2001) and Pintrich (2000b) proposed that the mastery goal orientation also may be divided into approach and avoid components. As Elliot and McGregor and Pintrich both note, perfectionists may be characterized as holding mastery-avoidance goals. Elliot and McGregor (2001) developed items to assess mastery-avoidance goals and found (in a study of college students) that these items factored separately from items measuring the other three kinds of goal orientations.

Research has documented consequences of adopting one or the other of these goal orientations. The results concerning mastery orientation are quite consistent and positive (see E. M. Anderman, Austin, & Johnson, 2002; Pintrich, 2000a, 2000b; Urdan, 1997, for review). When mastery-oriented children are more highly engaged in learning, use deeper cognitive strategies, and are intrinsically motivated to learn. Elliot and McGregor (2001) found that mastery-avoidance goals are associated with a mixture of outcomes, including subsequent test anxiety, mastery-approach goals, and performance-approach goals. Based on this and other work, researchers have proposed that schools should work to foster mastery goal orientations rather than performance goal orientations, and school reform efforts to do just that have been undertaken (e.g., Maehr & Midgley, 1996).

The research on performance goals is somewhat less consistent, in part because of the methodological confounding of performance-avoidance and performance-approach goals. When these two aspects of performance goals are unconfounded, researchers find that performance-avoidance goals have negative consequences for students' motivation and learning (e.g., Elliot & Harackiewicz, 1996; Middleton & Midgley, 1997; Skaalvik, 1997). Performance-approach goals relate positively to academic self-concept, task value, and performance (at least in college students) but not to intrinsic motivation to learn (see Harackiewicz, Barron, Pintrich, Elliot, & Thrash, 2002, for review).

The distinction between performance-approach and performance-avoidance goals, and evidence showing that performance-approach goals relate to positive motivational and achievement outcomes, led Harackiewicz, Barron, and Elliot (1998) and Pintrich (2000a, 2000b) to call for a revision of goal theory that acknowledges the positive effects of performance-approach goals, and also the need to look at how different goals relate to different outcomes. Traditional (or normative) goal theory argues for the benefits of mastery goals and the costs of performance goals. This led to a debate played out in the *Journal of Educational Psychology* about the relative benefits and costs of each kind of goal orientation (Harackiewicz et al., 2002; Kaplan & Middleton, 2002; Midgley et al., 2001; see also Roeser, 2004).

We believe the move beyond the perhaps too simplistic two-goal orientation theory is welcome, but acknowledge that more work is needed both on performance-approach and (especially) mastery-avoidance goals to evaluate their effects. Work on achievement goal orientations also needs to look more carefully at how different achievement domains (e.g., math, science, English) might impact achievement goal orientations and their effects (see Meece, 1991, 1994). Finally, Brophy (2005) noted that goal orientation theorists need to investigate further the frequency of occurrence of performance goals in school situations, arguing that students may not spontaneously generate such goals very frequently.

Goal Content Approach: Academic and Social Goals.   Building on Ford's (1992) work defining a taxonomy of human goals, Wentzel has examined the multiple goals of children in achievement settings (see Wentzel, 1991, 1993, 2002, for review of this work). Wentzel focused on the content of children's goals to guide and direct behavior, rather than the criteria a person uses to define success or failure (i.e., mastery versus performance). Wentzel primarily focused on academic and social goals and their relations to a variety of outcomes.

Wentzel demonstrated that both social and academic goals relate to adolescents' school performance and behavior (Wentzel, 2002). She also found positive relations between prosocial goals and children's grades and even IQ scores (Wentzel, 1989, 1996). Although it appears valuable to have multiple goals, Wentzel (2002) discussed the difficulty some children may have coordinating these multiple goals. Can students manage a variety of social and academic goals? This question also applies to the multiple goal perspective in goal orientation theory. Having multiple goals may be especially challenging for younger children, whose resources to manage such goals may be limited.

Building in part on Wentzel's work, researchers increasingly are interested in how social relations and the social context influence students' goals and other aspects of motivation (e.g., L. H. Anderman, 1999; Patrick, 1997). L. H. Anderman (1999) proposed a number of mechanisms by which students' social experiences in school relate to their motivation. These include the extent to which students feel a part of the school or at least some activities in the school, how much they endorse social responsibility goals, and the kinds of relationships they have with peers.

Motivation Development: Within-Person Change and Group Differences

Developmental and educational psychologists have done extensive work on how children's motivation changes across childhood and adolescence and how motivation differs across various groups.

WITHIN-PERSON CHANGE IN MOTIVATION

Young children's reactions to success and failure likely provide the foundation for the development of the different motivational beliefs, values, and goals discussed in this chapter. Heckhausen (1987) found that children between 2.5 and 3.5 years start to show self-evaluative, nonverbal facial expression reactions following a successful or unsuccessful action. When competing with others, 3- and 4-year-old children initially showed joy after winning and sadness after losing, and, after looking at their competitor, expressed pride or shame. Stipek, Recchia, and McClintic (1992) found that children younger than 22 months were neither concerned with others' evaluation of their performance nor self-reflective in their evaluations but showed positive emotional reactions to accomplishing a task and negative emotions when they did not. Two-year-olds reacted more to others' evaluations by seeking approval when they did well and turning away when they did poorly. After age 3, the children were able to evaluate their own performance.

Taken together, these studies show that reactions to success and failure begin early in the preschool years. The results concerning children's reactions to failure are particularly important because they suggest that children are more sensitive to failure in the preschool years than was once believed (see Dweck, 2002).

Development of Competence-Related Beliefs

Research on the development of competence beliefs has been extensive. We discuss three kinds of changes: (1) change in their factorial structure, (2) change in mean levels, and (3) change in children's understanding of them.

Eccles et al. (1998) reviewed factor analytic research showing that children as young as age 5 or 6 have distinctive competence perceptions among different academic and nonacademic domains of competence. Since that review researchers have studied even younger children and found that these children also have differentiated competence-related beliefs (Mantzicoupolus, French, & Maller, 2004; Marsh, Ellis, & Craven, 2002).

Another well-established finding in the literature is that children's competence beliefs for different tasks decline across the elementary school years and through the high school years (see Dweck & Elliott, 1983; Eccles et al., 1998; Stipek & Mac Iver, 1989, for review). Many young children are quite optimistic about their competencies in different areas, and this optimism changes to greater realism and (sometimes) pessimism for many children. Researchers in the United States and Australia have examined change over the entire elementary and secondary school years in children's competence beliefs for math, language arts, and sports (Fredericks & Eccles, 2002; Jacobs, Lanza, Osgood, Eccles, & Wigfield, 2002; Watt, 2004). Although there were some differences across domain with respect to when the strongest changes occurred, the dominant pattern was one of decline.

One caveat about this general "optimism early and realism later" pattern is that researchers observing children's reactions to failure find that some preschool children already reacted negatively to failure (see Dweck, 2002; Stipek et al., 1992). These early negative reactions to failure may not mean that children doubt their ability, as their views of ability still are taking shape. But the connection between these reactions and level of ability beliefs likely begins to develop early in the school years, and children reacting negatively to failure early on may be more likely to be pessimistic about their abilities later.

The negative changes in children's competence-related beliefs have been explained in two ways: (1) Because children become much better at understanding, interpreting, and integrating the evaluative feedback they receive, and engage in more social comparison with their peers, children become more accurate or realistic in their self-assessments, leading some to become relatively more negative (see Dweck & Elliott, 1983; Nicholls, 1984; Ruble, 1983; Stipek & Mac Iver, 1989); and (2) because school environment changes in ways that makes evaluation more salient and competition between students more likely, some children's self-assessments will decline as they get older (e.g., see Eccles & Midgley, 1989; Wigfield, Byrnes, & Eccles, 2006).

There are two important limitations to this work on mean-level change in the development of competence beliefs. First, most of it is normative. We thus know less about patterns of changes in different groups of children and adolescents, although there is some information about this (e.g., Harter, Whitesell, & Kowalski, 1992; Wigfield, Eccles, Mac Iver, Reuman, & Midgley, 1991). Wigfield et al. (1991) found that this pattern of change varied somewhat for children high or low in math ability. Second, the measures used in this work either are at the school level or (more frequently) at the domain-specific level. It is possible that children's beliefs about their competence for more particular activities may show different patterns of change, and we know little about this. We also know little about how children arrive at judgments of their competence in something as broad as reading or science (see Assor & Connell, 1992; Winne & Jamieson-Noel, 2002).

Finally, longitudinal studies looking at relations of children's competence beliefs over time show that these beliefs become increasingly stable as children get older (e.g., Eccles et al., 1989; Wigfield et al., 1997). Thus, by early adolescence there is much stability in these beliefs, even though the overall pattern of change is the decline just discussed. The implication of these findings is that individuals tend to maintain their relative position in their group, even as the group's mean declines.

There also are important developmental changes in children's understandings of ability (see Dweck, 2002). During preschool, children do not have a clear sense of ability as a characteristic that determines outcomes, but they do react to success and failure experiences. During the early school years, concepts of ability begin to emerge, and children see ability as distinct from other qualities and as just discussed also differentiate their ability across domains. They often think of ability as changeable, but some children begin to see ability as a stable characteristic. Social comparison takes on increasing importance. Children's beliefs about ability also become more accurate, in the sense of correlating more strongly with performance measures. Between ages 10 and 12, children differentiate more clearly ability, effort, and performance, but they also see how they interrelate. These children more often use comparative standards in judging ability. More children (at least in Western societies) come to view ability as capacity (or take an entity view of intelligence, to use Dweck's term), which means they are less likely to believe that with increased effort their ability will improve.

Nicholls and his colleagues found four relatively distinct levels of reasoning about ability, effort, and difficulty (Nicholls, 1978; Nicholls & Miller, 1984). At level one (ages 5 to 6), effort, ability, and performance are not clearly by cause and effect. At level two (ages 7 to 9), effort is seen as the primary cause of performance outcomes. At level three (ages 9 to 12), children begin to differentiate ability and effort as causes of outcomes, but they do not always apply this distinction. Finally, at level four, adolescents clearly differentiate ability and effort, and they understand the notion of ability as capacity.

These different views of ability and intelligence have important implications for children's motivation. Children with a stable view of ability are more likely to give up following failure, because they are less likely to believe that additional effort will improve their performance. By contrast, children believing ability is modifiable more likely continue to strive after failure because they think their ability can change.

Pomerantz and Saxon (2001) distinguished further between seeing ability as stable with respect to things external to the child, and ability as stable internally (like Dweck's entity notion). They argued that seeing ability as stable with respect to external forces actually is a positive belief for children to have because of the pattern of its relations with other motivational beliefs and performance. By contrast, believing that ability is stable with respect to internal forces has negative implications for motivation and performance.

Development of Efficacy Beliefs

There has not been extensive research on the development of efficacy beliefs per se. Instead, research on children's self-efficacy has focused primarily on interventions to enhance the self-efficacy and school performance of low-achieving children (e.g., see Schunk, 1994; Schunk & Pajares, 2002). Extant work on the development of efficacy shows that children's efficacy beliefs increase across age (Shell, Colvin, & Bruning, 1995; Zimmerman & Martinez-Pons, 1990). The inconsistency of these findings with those on children's competence beliefs just discussed likely reflects the self-efficacy measure used by Shell et al. Their instrument measured children's estimates of their efficacy on specific reading and writing skills rather than more general beliefs about competence reading and writing; the more specific beliefs should be higher among older children.

Bandura (1997) and Schunk and Pajares (2002) discussed factors influencing the development of self-efficacy. They proposed that children who have mastery experiences in which they exert some control over their environments develop the earliest sense of personal agency. Through these experiences, infants learn that they can influence their environments. Bandura argued that a more mature sense of self-efficacy should not emerge until children have at least a rudimentary self-concept and can recognize that they are distinct individuals, which happens sometime during the second year of life (see Harter, 2006). Through the preschool period, children are exposed to extensive performance information that is crucial to their emerging sense of self-efficacy. Schunk and Pajares also discuss the crucial role peers can play in the development, or demise, of self-efficacy. Finally, Schunk and Pajares (2002) and Bandura (1997) stressed the importance of school environments for developing and supporting a high sense of efficacy or possibly undermining it if support is not provided.

Development of Control Beliefs

Work on perceived control done in the 1980s and 1990s showed that there are developmental patterns in these beliefs. Weisz (1984) found that younger children actually believe they have greater control over chance events than do older children. Similarly, Connell (1985) found a decrease in the endorsement of all three of his locus of control constructs (internal control, powerful others control, and unknown control) from third through ninth grade.

Skinner, Gembeck-Zimmer, and Connell (1998) assessed the development of perceived control in children and early adolescents and how it predicted student engagement in school. Their cohort-sequential design encompassed third through seventh grade children. Skinner et al. (1998) found that perceived control showed a curvilinear pattern of change, being stable at first, increasing slightly through fourth grade, and then declining after fifth grade. Student engagement declined during middle school, as did students' perceptions that teachers provided structure and were involved with them. Children initially either high or low in perceived control decreased in their control perceptions if they perceived that teachers were providing less structure and were less involved with them.

Development of Subjective Task Values

Eccles, Wigfield, and their colleagues examined age-related changes in both the structure and mean levels of children's valuing of different activities. In Eccles, Wigfield, Harold, and Blumenfeld (1993) and Eccles and Wigfield (1995), children's competence-expectancy beliefs and subjective values within the domains of math, reading, and sports formed distinct factors at all grade levels from 1st through 12th. The distinction between various subcomponents of subjective task value appears to differentiate more gradually (Eccles & Wigfield, 1995; Eccles et al., 1993). Children in early elementary school differentiate task value into two components: (1) interest and (2) utility/importance. Children in grades 5 through 12 differentiate task value into the three major subcomponents (attainment value/personal importance, interest, and utility value) outlined by Eccles-Parsons et al. (1983). These results suggest that the interest component differentiates out first, followed later by the distinction between utility and attainment value. As with competence-related beliefs, studies generally show age-related decline in children's valuing of certain academic tasks (e.g., see Eccles et al., 1998; Wigfield & Eccles, 2002, Wigfield et al., 2006, for review).

Researchers have not addressed changes in children's understandings of the components of task value identified by Eccles-Parsons et al. (1983). There also may be age differences in which of the components of achievement values are most dominant. Wigfield and Eccles (1992) suggested that interest may be especially salient during the early elementary school grades with young children's activity choices being most directly related to their interests. As children get older, the perceived utility and personal importance of different tasks likely become more salient, particularly as they develop more stable self-schema and long-range goals and plans.

Another developmental question is how children's developing competence beliefs relate to their developing subjective task values. Eccles-Parsons et al. (1983) and Bandura (1997) both argued that ability self-concepts should influence the development of task values and interests. Mac Iver, Stipek, and Daniels (1991) found that changes in junior high school students' competence beliefs over a semester predicted change in children's interest much more strongly than vice versa. The developmental progression of these relations needs to be studied (see Wigfield, 1994).

Development of Interest and Intrinsic Motivation

Eccles et al. (1998) summarized work on the early development of children's interests, which shows that children have general or universal interests at first, which become more specific relatively quickly (see also Todt, 1990). This early differentiation eventually leads to individual differences in interests in different activities. Gender also shapes interest in important ways during childhood and adolescence (see Eccles, 1987; Ruble & Martin, 1998).

Changing needs or motives across the life span can influence the development of interests. A good example is the increasing interest in biology and psychology during puberty. The need to know oneself and to cope with rapid bodily and psychological changes seems to foster interest in biological and psychological domains of knowledge at adolescence (Todt, 1990).

Children's interest in different academic subject areas declines across the school years (Eccles et al., 1993; Gottfried, Fleming, & Gottfried, 2001; Harter, 1981; Wigfield et al., 1991). Pekrun (1993) found that intrinsic motivation stabilized after eighth grade, and Gottfried et al. (2001) reported surprisingly high stability coefficients for intrinsic motivation measured across a 1-year period for children ages 13 and above.

Development of Children's Goal Orientations

There still is not a large body of work on the development of children's goals and goal orientations (see E. M. Anderman et al., 2002, for review of extant work). Instead, most of the work has focused on relations of goals to ability beliefs and on how different instructional contexts influence achievement goals. L. H. Anderman and E. M. Anderman (1999) reported that adolescents endorse performance goals more than mastery goals. A major reason for this may be that schools increasingly emphasize performance goals as children get older. Midgley (2002) and colleagues' work has shown two major things with respect to this point: (1) Elementary school teachers focus on mastery-oriented goals to a greater extent than do middle school teachers, and (2) middle school students perceive school as more performance oriented than do elementary school students. Thus, any observed changes in children's goal orientations seem very bound up in changes in the school goal culture.

Some researchers have looked at goal orientations toward particular school activities. Meece and Miller (2001) studied the development during elementary school of students' goal orientations in reading and writing, looking at performance goals, mastery goals, and work-avoidant goals. They found that children's goal orientations were reasonably stable over a 1-year period; the lagged correlations were .44 for task-mastery goals, .58 for performance goals, and .45 for work-avoidant goals. With respect to change over time, following prediction children's mastery goals decreased over time. Contrary to prediction, performance goals did as well. The pattern of change in work-avoidant goals was less consistent.

Development and Remediation of Motivational Problems

Many children begin to experience motivational problems during the school years, including test anxiety, learned helplessness, and apathy. The first two of these problems are tied to beliefs about not being able to do different activities, whereas the third emerges when children devalue achievement related activities.

Anxiety.   Anxiety and test anxiety are estimated to interfere with the learning and performance of as many as 10 million children and adolescents in the United States (Hill & Wigfield, 1984; Tobias, 1985; Wigfield & Eccles, 1989). This problem likely is getting worse as evaluation and accountability become more emphasized in schools (Deci & Ryan, 2002a; Zeidner, 1998). Anxiety often is conceptualized as having two components—worry and emotionality—with worry referring to cognitive ruminations and emotionality referring to physiological reactions (see Morris, Davis, & Hutchings, 1981). Researchers have focused on the cognitive/worry aspect of anxiety because worry is more strongly and negatively related to performance than emotionality (e.g., Morris et al., 1981; Sarason, 1980).

Many programs have been developed to reduce anxiety (Denny, 1980; Wigfield & Eccles, 1989; Zeidner, 1998). Earlier intervention programs, emphasizing the emotionality aspect of anxiety, focused on relaxation and desensitization techniques. Although these programs did reduce anxiety, they did not always lead to improved performance, and the studies had serious methodological flaws. Anxiety intervention programs linked to the worry aspect of anxiety focus on changing the negative, self-deprecating thoughts of anxious individuals and replacing them with more positive, task-focused thoughts (e.g., see Denny, 1980; Meichenbaum & Butler, 1980). These programs have been more successful both in lowering anxiety and improving performance.

Learned Helplessness.   "Learned helplessness . . . exists when an individual perceives the termination of failure to be independent of his responses" (Dweck & Goetz, 1978, p. 157). Eccles et al. (1998) reviewed the early work (primarily by Dweck and her colleagues) on how helpless and mastery-oriented children differ in their responses to failure (see also Dweck & Elliott, 1983; Dweck & Leggett, 1988). When confronted by difficulty (or failure), mastery-oriented children persist, stay focused on the task, and sometimes even use more sophisticated strategies. In contrast, helpless children's performance deteriorates, they ruminate about their difficulties, and often begin to attribute their failures to lack of ability. Further, helpless children adopt the entity view that their intelligence is fixed, whereas mastery-oriented children adopt the incremental view of intelligence. Precursors to helplessness can develop even in preschool children (e.g., Burhans & Dweck, 1995). Dweck and Goetz (1978) discussed how learned helplessness can develop out of socializers' reactions to children's successes and failures and Dweck and Lennon (2001) showed that parents' views of children's ability as changeable or not influenced children's own views.

Various training techniques (including operant conditioning and providing specific attributional feedback) have been used successfully to change children's failure attributions from lack of ability to lack of effort, improving their task persistence and performance (e.g., Andrews & Debus, 1978; Dweck, 1975; Forsterling, 1985). Two problems with these approaches have been noted. First, what if the child is already trying very hard? Then, the attribution retraining may be counterproductive. Second, telling children to "try harder" without providing specific strategies designed to improve performance is likely to backfire if the children increase their efforts and still do not succeed. Therefore, some researchers advocate using strategy retraining in combination with attribution retraining to provide lower achieving and/or learned helpless children with specific ways to remedy their achievement problems (see Borkowski, Weyhing, & Carr, 1988).

Student Apathy.   Apathy has more to do with students' sense of the value of participating in different activities rather than their beliefs about whether they are capable of accomplishing the activity. Children who are apathetic about learning or participating in other activities do not find much worthwhile to do in school or in other situations; they may even be so alienated from these activities that they actively resist attempts to get them involved. Brophy (2004) contended that apathy is the most serious motivational problem that teachers must contend with in their students—more serious than learned helplessness or anxiety. The apathy construct has some overlap with the construct of amotivation in SDT (Vallerand et al., 1993).

There has not been a lot of research in the motivation literature on the development of apathy, but different researchers have discussed possible reasons for it. These range from broad social and cultural explanations to more psychologically oriented ones. Ogbu's (1992) discussion of why some minority children do well in school and others do not is an example of a broad cultural approach to this issue. Children who believe their ethnic or racial group is excluded from meaningful participation in the economic structure of this country may find little reason to engage in the school activities said to be needed to obtain good occupations. Ogbu has argued that such children often become oppositional to participation in school activities. A psychological perspective on apathy can be drawn from Markus and Nurius's (1986) work on possible selves. Markus and Nurius argued that possible selves provide an important motivational force for engagement in different activities such as school or sport activities. If children do not see much of a future for themselves in these or other domains, they may not see much reason to be involved in school or other activities designed to prepare them for the future, and so they may be very apathetic.

There may be different developmental trajectories for the development of apathy: (1) children who perceive few opportunities for themselves or for their group and so come to devalue school, or (2) children who begin to do poorly in school and so begin to devalue it as a way to protect their self-esteem. Another trajectory occurs for students doing well in school during the early school years and who come from backgrounds and cultural groups who generally have succeeded in our society, but who decide (for a variety of reasons) to no longer engage in school. These children may become alienated from school and therefore apathetic about participating in school activities (National Research Council [NRC], 2004). To date, there is little developmental work on any of these trajectories, but it should be undertaken. Researchers are focusing on ways to increase student engagement in school as a way to combat these kinds of problems (NRC, 2004).

Gender Differences in Motivation

Gender differences in achievement persist: females continue to be underrepresented in math, physical science, and technology courses and college majors; males continue to be overrepresented in all special learner categories and among high school and college drop outs (see McGillicuddy-De Lisi & De Lisi, 2002, for review). Males also continue to overrepresented in most competitive sport activities. Many different motivational models have emerged to explain these differences. Eccles and her colleagues originally proposed their expectancy-value model of achievement choices as an effort to organize this disparate research into a comprehensive theoretical framework (see Eccles-Parsons et al., 1983; Wigfield & Eccles, 2002). This model predicts that people will be most invested in those achievement activities (including academic courses, college majors, and leisure time achievement-related pursuits) that they think they will do well in and that have high task value for them. Processes linked to gender role socialization are likely to lead to sex differences in these beliefs. Existing evidence, reviewed next, supports this hypothesis.

GENDER DIFFERENCES IN COMPETENCE-RELATED BELIEFS, CAUSAL ATTRIBUTIONS, AND CONTROL BELIEFS

Gender differences (often favoring males) in competence beliefs are often reported, particularly in gender-role stereotyped domains and on novel tasks, and these differences are apparent as early as kindergarten or first grade, if not before. For example, gifted and high-achieving females are more likely to underestimate both their ability level and their class standing (Frome & Eccles, 1995). In other studies, the gender difference depends on the gender-role stereotyping of the activity. For example, boys hold higher competence beliefs than girls for math and sports, even after all relevant skill-level differences are controlled; in contrast, girls have higher competence beliefs than boys for reading and English, music and arts, and social studies. According to Jacobs et al. (2002), the gender differences in competence beliefs in math narrow during adolescence, but those in English remain. Further, the extent to which children endorse the cultural stereotypes regarding which sex is likely to be most talented in each domain predicts the extent to which girls and boys distort their ability, self-concepts, and expectations in the gender stereotypic direction (Eccles & Harold, 1991).

Gender differences are sometimes found for locus of control, with girls having higher internal locus of responsibility scores for both positive and negative achievement events and the older girls had higher internality for negative events than did the younger girls (Crandall et al., 1965). These two developmental patterns result in the older girls accepting more blame for negative events than the older boys (cf. Dweck & Goetz, 1978). Connell (1985) found that boys attributed their outcomes more than girls to either powerful others or unknown causes in both the cognitive and social domains.

This greater propensity for girls to take personal responsibility for their failures, coupled with their more frequent attribution of failure to lack of ability (a stable, uncontrollable cause) has been interpreted as evidence of greater learned helplessness in females (see Dweck & Licht, 1980). However, evidence for gender differences on behavioral indicators of learned helplessness is quite mixed. In most studies of underachievers, boys outnumber girls 2 to 1 (see McCall, Evahn, & Kratzer, 1992). Similarly, boys are more likely than girls to be referred by their teachers for motivational problems and are more likely to drop out of school before completing high school. More consistent evidence exists that females, compared to males, select easier laboratory tasks, avoid challenging and competitive situations, lower their expectations more following failure, shift more quickly to a different college major when their grades begin to drop, and perform more poorly than they are capable of on difficult, timed tests (see Dweck & Licht, 1980; S. J. Spencer, Steele, & Quinn, 1999).

Gender differences also emerge regularly in studies of anxiety (e.g., Hill & Sarason, 1966; Meece, Wigfield, & Eccles, 1990). However, Hill and Sarason suggested that boys may be more defensive than girls about admitting anxiety on questionnaires. In support of this suggestion, Lord, Eccles, and McCarthy (1994) found that test anxiety was a more significant predictor of poor adjustment to junior high school for boys even though the girls reported higher mean levels of anxiety. Closely related to the anxiety findings, S. J. Spencer et al. (1999) documented another motivational mechanism likely to undermine females' performance on difficult timed tests: stereotype vulnerability. Work by Shih and her colleagues clearly documents that Asian American girls do worse on timed math tests when their sex is primed and better when their Asian identity is primed (Shih, Pittinsky, & Ambady, 1999).

GENDER DIFFERENCES IN ACHIEVEMENT VALUES

Gender-role stereotypic differences in both children's and adolescents' valuing of sports, mathematics, physical science, and English emerge quite early during children's development and persist through adolescence (e.g., Eccles et al., 1989, 1993; Wigfield et al., 1991). European-American boys and girls are coming to value math equally during adolescence (Jacobs et al., 2002) even though the females remain less interested in physical science and engineering than males (see Wigfield, Battle, Keller, & Eccles, 2002, for review). Why? At the simplest level, internalizing gender-role norms are likely to lead to males and females to value different activities due to the gender-role stereotyping of these activities. At a deeper psychological level, processes associated with disidentification could be going on. Drawing on the writings of William James (1892/1963), we have suggested that children will lower the value they attach to particular activities or subject areas if they lack confidence in these areas to maintain their self-esteem (Eccles et al., 1998; see also Harter, 1990). S. J. Spencer et al. (1999) suggested a similar phenomenon related to stereotype vulnerability (see also Steele, 1997). They hypothesized that women will disidentify with those subject areas in which females are stereotyped as less competent than males. By disidentifying with these areas, the women will not only lower the value they attach to these subject areas, they will also be less likely to experience pride and positive affect when they are doing well in these subjects. Consequently, these subjects should become irrelevant to their self-esteem. A similar process could go on for males and reading and for low achieving males and schooling more generally.

Development of Group Differences in Motivation

As is the case in many areas of psychology (see Graham, 1992; McInerney & Van Etten, 2004), less is known about the motivation of children from racial and ethnic groups other than European Americans. However, work in this area is growing quickly, with much of it focusing on the academic problems and prospects of African American (see Hare, 1985; Meece & Kurtz-Costes, 2001; Slaughter-Defoe, Nakagawa, Takanishi, & Johnson, 1990), Mexican American (e.g., Padilla & Gonzalez, 2001; Portes & Rumbaut, 2001), and Asian American youth (Fuligni & Tseng, 1999; Lee, 1994). Understanding motivational dynamics behind these achievement differences is an important task. First we look at work directly growing out traditional motivational studies. Second we discuss a broader cultural approach to understanding group differences in motivation.

RACIAL AND ETHNIC GROUP DIFFERENCES IN CHILDREN'S COMPETENCE, CONTROL, AND ATTRIBUTION BELIEFS

Social group differences within the United States of America in children's specific motivational beliefs linked to competence, control and attributions are quite small (see Cooper & Dorr, 1995; Graham, 1994) but not very much comparative work has been done. Some research on competence beliefs and expectancies suggests greater optimism among African American children than among European American children, even when the European American children are achieving higher marks (e.g., Stevenson, Chen, & Uttal, 1990). But more important, the European American children's ratings of their ability related significantly to their performance but the African American children's did not. Graham (1994) suggested the following explanations: (a) African American and European American children may use different social comparison groups to help judge their own abilities; and (b) African American children may say they are doing well to protect their general self-esteem, and may also devalue or disidentify academic activities at which they do poorly to protect their self-esteem.

RACIAL AND ETHNIC GROUP DIFFERENCES IN ACHIEVEMENT VALUES AND GOALS

There are few ethnic comparative studies specifically focused on the kinds of achievement values measured by Eccles, Wigfield, and their colleagues, or of the kinds of goals measured by Nicholls, Dweck, Ames, and Wentzel. Researchers studying minority children's achievement values have focused instead on the broader valuing of school by minority children and their parents. In general, these researchers find that minority children and parents highly value school (particularly during the elementary school years) and have high educational aspirations for their children (e.g., Stevenson et al., 1990). However, the many difficulties associated with poverty may make these educational aspirations difficult to attain (see Duncan, Brooks-Gunn, & Klevbanov, 1994; Huston, McLoyd, & Coll, 1994; McLoyd, 1990).

Using a peer nomination method, Graham, Taylor, and Hudley (1998) and Graham and Taylor (2002) found that White, Latino, and African American girls chose high-achieving girls as those whom they admired, respected, and wanted to be like. For boys, this was only true for White boys; the other two groups of boys admired low achievers more. This sex-differentiated group difference pattern emerged sometime between fourth and seventh grades. So what it is about entering adolescent and puberty that seems to cause some African and Mexican American youth to endorse values and role-models that exclude school achievement (e.g., Tatum, 1997)?

Race, Ethnicity, and Motivation at the Interface between Expectancies and Values

Researchers interested in ethnic and racial differences in achievement have proposed models linking social roles, competence-related beliefs, and values. For example, Steele (1992, 1997) proposed stereotype vulnerability and disidentification to help explain the underachievement of African American students (see also Aronson, 2002; Aronson & Steele, 2005): Confronted throughout their school career with mixed messages about their competence and their potential and with the widespread negative cultural stereotypes about their academic potential and motivation, African American students should find it difficult to concentrate fully on their school work due to the anxiety induced by their stereotype vulnerability (for support see Steele & Aronson, 1995). In turn, to protect their self-esteem, they should disidentify with academic achievement leading to both a lowering of the value they attach to academic achievement and a detachment of their self-esteem from both positive and the negative academic experiences. In support, several researchers have found that academic self-concept of ability is less predictive of general self-esteem for some African American children (Winston, Eccles, Senior, & Vida, 1997). A key mediator of this process is African Americans beliefs about the nature of their intelligence (Dweck & Leggett, 1988). In a experimental intervention with college students, Aronson, Fried, and Good (2001) found that encouraging African American college students to adopt a mindset in which they viewed their own intelligence as malleable predicted increased enjoyment and engagement in academics as well as grades.

Fordham and Ogbu (1986) have made a similar argument linking African American students' perception of limited future job opportunities to lowered academic motivation: Because society and schools give African American youth the dual message that academic achievement is unlikely to lead to positive adult outcomes for them and that they are not valued by the system, some African American youth may create an oppositional culture that rejects the value of academic achievement. Contrary to this view, several investigators found no evidence of greater detachment from school among African American students (e.g., Eccles, 2004; M. B. Spencer, Noll, Stoltzfus, & Harpalani, 2001; Taylor, Casten, Flickinger, Roberts, & Fulmore, 1994; Wong, Eccles, & Sameroff, 2003). But several studies do show that experiences at school of inequitable and discriminatory treatment, as well as repeated failures coupled with little academic help, can undermine achievement and academic motivation (e.g., see Finn, 1989; Taylor et al., 1994; Wong et al., 2003). Unfortunately, some students, particularly members of disenfranchised "minority" groups, are quite likely to have such experiences as they pass through the secondary school system. Longitudinal studies of the process of disengagement from learning in school, and how to ameliorate it when it occurs, are needed.

MORE GENERAL CULTURAL APPROACHES TO MOTIVATION

Researchers interested in issues of culture, motivation, and achievement have examined the ways in which: (a) culture informs the development of self, motives, and behavioral scripts associated with achievement (e.g., Markus & Kitayama, 1991; Ogbu, 1981); (b) culture shapes group members' construal of the meaning of success and failure before and after achievement experiences (e.g., Grant & Dweck, 2001; Heine et al., 2001); (c) culture influences how universal and individual psychological needs are expressed (e.g., Chirkov, Ryan, Kim, & Kaplan, 2003); and (d) culture influences engagement in the classroom (e.g., Greeno, Collins, & Resnick, 1996; Hickey & McCaslin, 2001; Roeser, Peck, & Nasir, 2006).

Contemporary cultural psychology focuses on variation in the self linked to culture-specific socialization practices. Markus and Kitayama (1991) developed the notion of "cultural frame" as a way of describing how cultural socialization practices come to literally inform the self. Cultural frames are meaning systems comprised of language, tacit social understandings, and scripts for enacting these social understandings in daily life. Individual's self-construals (i.e., the individual's understandings about what it means to be a person in the world) are a critical component of these cultural frames. Markus and Kitayama (1991) outlined two different cultural frames, each associated with a specific self-construal: (1) independence and (2) interdependence. In the independent construal of self, individuals come to see themselves as autonomous, self-contained, unique from others, and assertive in pursuing personal goals and desires. In contrast, in the interdependent self-construal, individuals assign primary significance to others in defining the self, feel a fundamental sense of connectedness to others, and attend, first and foremost, to social roles, in-group norms, and obligations and responsibilities to others (see Oyserman, Coon, & Kemmelmeier, 2002). Self-construals are assumed to be the seedbed of goals and motives, including one's achievement-related goals and motives.

Although just beginning, research relating culture to motivation in this area tends to examine how (culturally informed) self-construals influence (a) the kinds of motivations that are prevalent for members of different cultural groups (the issue of approach and avoidance motivation), (b) the kinds of values and goals that are taken up into the self by members of different cultural groups (the issue of diversity in goal content), and (c) the kinds of meanings that individuals from different cultural groups make both before and after engaging with an achievement task (issues of meaning and appraisal). For example, Elliot, Chirkov, Kim, and Sheldon (2001) hypothesized that individualistic self-construals should promote approach motivation in which goals associated with self-assertion are focal; in contrast, interdependent self-construals should promote avoidance motivation in which goals associated with the reduction of group discord are focal. They found some support for these hypotheses in a cross-cultural study of college students. Other studies have also found that both the level and impact of avoidance motivation on achievement may be greater among individuals from cultural groups that emphasize interdependence and group membership. For instance, Eaton and Dembo (1997) found that the fear of failure (an avoidance motive) best predicted ninth grade Asian and Asian American students' performance on an intellectual task; in contrast, the non-Asian students' performance was best predicted by their beliefs about the incremental nature of intelligence, the importance of effort, and their self-efficacy.

Conclusions

Research on the development of children's achievement motivation remains vibrant. Research focused in several different theoretical traditions is giving us a more complete understanding of the development of motivation across the childhood and adolescent years. Over the past decade, we have learned much about contextual influences on motivation and how children's motivation varies across different contexts, such as in different kinds of families, and different school contexts. We have also learned much about the development of motivation in diverse groups of children in this country. Although much remains to be done in this area, motivation researchers increasingly include diverse samples in their work, revising their theories to incorporate culture more clearly in their models, and testing their theories in diverse groups (see McInerney & Van Etten, 2004, for good examples of this work). Further investigating relations among the different motivational beliefs, values, and goals; cognitive processes; and the regulation of behavior and affect is a major priority for the next several years (see Boekaerts, Pintrich, & Zeidner, 2000; Pintrich, 2003; Wigfield et al., 2006; Wolters, 2003).

References

Alexander, P. A., Kulikowich, J. M., & Jetton, T. L. (1994). The role of subject-matter knowledge and interest in the processing of linear and nonlinear texts. *Review of Educational Research, 64,* 201–252.

Ames, C. (1992). Classrooms: Goals, structures, and student motivation. *Journal of Educational Psychology, 84,* 261–271.

Anderman, E. M., Austin, C. C., & Johnson, D. M. (2002). The development of goal orientation. In A. Wigfield & J. S. Eccles (Eds.), *Development of achievement motivation* (pp. 197–220). San Diego, CA: Academic Press.

Anderman, L. H. (1999). Expanding the discussion of social perceptions and academic outcomes: Mechanisms and contextual influences. In T. Urdan (Ed.), *Advances in motivation and achievement* (Vol. 11, pp. 303–336). Greenwich, CT: JAI Press.

Anderman, L. H., & Anderman, E. M. (1999). Social predictors of changes in students' achievement goal orientations. *Contemporary Educational Psychology, 25,* 21–37.

Andrews, G. R., & Debus, R. L. (1978). Persistence and the causal perception of failure: Modifying cognitive attributions. *Journal of Educational Psychology, 70,* 154–166.

Aronson, J. (2002). Stereotype threat: Contending and coping with unnerving expectations. In J. Aronson (Ed.), *Improving academic achievement: Impact of psychological factors on education* (pp. 279–301). San Diego, CA: Academic Press.

Aronson, J., Fried, C. B., & Good, C. (2001). Reducing the effects of stereotype threat on African American college students by shaping theories of intelligence. *Journal of Experimental Social Psychology, 58,* 3–11.

Aronson, J., & Steele, C. M. (2005). Stereotypes and the fragility of academic competence, motivation, and self-concept. In A. J. Elliot & C. S. Dweck (Eds.), *Handbook of competence and motivation* (pp. 436–456). New York: Guilford Press.

Assor, A., & Connell, J. P. (1992). The validity of students' self-reports as measures of performance affecting self-appraisals. In D. H. Schunk & J. L. Meece (Eds.), *Student perceptions in the classroom* (pp. 25–47). Hillsdale, NJ: Erlbaum.

Atkinson, J. W. (1957). Motivational determinants of risk taking behavior. *Psychological Review, 64,* 359–372.

Atkinson, J. W. (1964). *An introduction to motivation.* Princeton, NJ: Van Nostrand.

Bandura, A. (1977). Self-efficacy: Toward a unifying theory of behavioral change. *Psychological Review, 84,* 191–215.

Bandura, A. (1986). *Social foundations of thought and action: A social cognitive theory.* Englewood Cliffs, NJ: Prentice Hall.

Bandura, A. (1997). *Self-efficacy: The exercise of control.* New York: Freeman.

Blumenfeld, P. C. (1992). Classroom learning and motivation: Clarifying and expanding goal theory. *Journal of Educational Psychology, 84,* 272–281.

Boekaerts, M., Pintrich, P. R., & Zeidner, M. (2000). *Handbook of self-regulation.* San Diego, CA: Academic Press.

Bong, M. (2001). Role of self-efficacy and task value in predicting college students' course enrollments and intentions. *Contemporary Educational Psychology, 26,* 553–570.

Borkowski, J. G., Weyhing, R. S., & Carr, M. (1988). Effects of attributional retraining on strategy-based reading comprehension in learning-disabled student. *Journal of Educational Psychology, 80,* 46–53.

Brophy, J. E. (2004). *Motivating students to learn* (2nd ed.). Mahwah, NJ: Erlbaum.

Brophy, J. E. (2005). Goal theorists should move on from performance goals. *Educational Psychologist, 40,* 167–176.

Burhans, K. K., & Dweck, C. S. (1995). Helplessness in early childhood: The role of contingent worth. *Child Development, 66,* 1719–1738.

Butler, R. (1993). Effects of task- and ego-achievement goals on information seeking during task engagement. *Journal of Personality and Social Psychology, 65,* 18–31.

Chirkov, V., Ryan, R. M., Kim, Y., & Kaplan, U. (2003). Differentiating autonomy from individualism and independence: A self-determination theory perspective on internalization of cultural orientations and well-being. *Journal of Personality and Social Psychology, 84,* 97–110.

Connell, J. P. (1985). A new multidimensional measure of children's perception of control. *Child Development, 56,* 1018–1041.

Connell, J. P., Spencer, M. B., & Aber, J. L. (1994). Educational risk and resilience in African American youth: Context, self, and action outcomes in school. *Child Development, 65,* 493–506.

Cooper, H., & Dorr, N. (1995). Race comparisons on need for achievement: A meta-analytic alternative to Graham's narrative review. *Review of Educational Research, 65,* 483–508.

Crandall, V. C., Katkovsky, W., & Crandall, V. J. (1965). Children's beliefs in their own control of reinforcements in intellectual-academic achievement situations. *Child Development, 36,* 91–109.

Csikszentmihalyi, M. (1988). The flow experience and its significance for human psychology. In M. Csikszentmihalyi & I. S. Csikszentmihalyi (Eds.), *Optimal experience* (pp. 15–35). Cambridge: Cambridge University Press.

Deci, E. L. (1992). The relation of interest to the motivation of behavior: A self-determination theory perspective. In K. A. Renninger, S. Hidi, & A. Krapp (Eds.), *The role of interest in learning and development* (pp. 43–70). Hillsdale, NJ: Erlbaum.

Deci, E. L. (1998). The relation to interest to motivation and human needs: The self-determination theory viewpoint. In L. Hoffman, A. Krapp, K. A. Renninger, & J. Baumert (Eds.), *Interest and learning* (pp. 146–162). Kiel, Germany: IPN Press.

Deci, E. L., Koestner, R., & Ryan, R. M. (1999). A meta-analytic review of experiments examining the effects of extrinsic motivation on intrinsic rewards. *Psychological Bulletin, 125,* 627–668.

Deci, E. L., & Ryan, R. M. (1985). *Intrinsic motivation and self-determination in human behavior.* New York: Plenum Press.

Deci, E. L., & Ryan, R. M. (2002a). The paradox of achievement: The harder you push, the worse it gets. In J. Aronson (Ed.), *Improving academic achievement: Impact of psychological factors on education* (pp. 61–87). San Diego, CA: Academic Press.

Deci, E. L., & Ryan, R. M. (2002b). Self-determination research: Reflections and future directions. In E. L. Deci & R. M. Ryan (Eds.), *Handbook of self-determination theory research* (pp. 431–441). Rochester, NY: University of Rochester Press.

Denny, D. R. (1980). Self-control approaches to the treatment of test anxiety. In I. G. Sarason (Ed.), *Test anxiety: Theory, research, and applications* (pp. 209–243). Hillsdale, NJ: Erlbaum.

Duncan, G. J., Brooks-Gunn, J., & Klevbanov, P. K. (1994). Economic deprivation and early childhood development. *Child Development, 65,* 296–318.

Dweck, C. S. (1975). The role of expectations and attributions in the alleviation of learned helplessness. *Journal of Personality and Social Psychology, 31,* 674–685.

Dweck, C. S. (2002). The development of ability conceptions. In A. Wigfield & J. S. Eccles (Eds.), *Development of achievement motivation* (pp. 57–88). San Diego, CA: Academic Press.

Dweck, C. S., & Elliott, E. S. (1983). Achievement motivation. In P. H. Mussen (Ed.), *Handbook of child psychology* (3rd ed., Vol. 4, pp. 643–691). New York: Wiley.

Dweck, C. S., & Goetz, T. E. (1978). Attributions and learned helplessness. In J. H. Harvey, W. Ickes, & R. F. Kidd (Eds.), *New directions in attribution research* (Vol. 2, pp. 155–179). Hillsdale, NJ: Erlbaum.

Dweck, C. S., & Leggett, E. (1988). A social-cognitive approach to motivation and personality. *Psychological Review, 95,* 256–273.

Dweck, C. S., & Lennon, C. (2001, April). *Person versus process focused parenting: Impact on achievement motivation.* Paper presented at the biennial meeting of the Society for Research in Child Development, Minneapolis, MN.

Dweck, C. S., & Licht, B. G. (1980). Learned helplessness and intellectual achievement. In J. Garber & M. E. P. Seligman (Eds.), *Human helplessness: Theory and applications.* New York: Academic Press.

Dweck, C. S., & Molden, D. C. (2005). Self theories: Their impact on competence motivation and acquisition. In A. Elliot & C. S. Dweck (Eds.), *Handbook of competence and motivation* (pp. 122–140). New York: Guilford Press.

Eaton, M. J., & Dembo, M. H. (1997). Differences in the motivational beliefs of Asian American and non-Asian students. *Journal of Educational Psychology, 89,* 433–440.

Eccles, J. S. (1987). Gender roles and women's achievement-related decisions. *Psychology of Women Quarterly, 11,* 135–172.

Eccles, J. S. (1993). School and family effects on the ontogeny of children's interests, self-perceptions, and activity choice. In J. Jacobs (Ed.), *Nebraska Symposium on Motivation: Vol. 40. Developmental perspectives on motivation* (pp. 145–208). Lincoln: University of Nebraska Press.

Eccles, J. S. (1994). Understanding women's educational and occupational choices: Applying the Eccles et al. model of achievement-related choices. *Psychology of Women Quarterly, 18,* 585–609.

Eccles, J. S. (2004). Schools, academic motivation, and stage-environment fit. In R. M. Lerner & L. Steinberg (Eds.), *Handbook of adolescent psychology* (2nd ed., pp. 125–153). Hoboken, NJ: Wiley.

Eccles, J. S., & Harold, R. D. (1991). Gender differences in sport involvement: Applying the Eccles' expectancy-value model. *Journal of Applied Sport Psychology, 3,* 7–35.

Eccles, J. S., & Midgley, C. (1989). Stage/environment fit: Developmentally appropriate classrooms for early adolescents. In R. Ames & C. Ames (Eds.), *Research on motivation in education* (Vol. 3, pp. 139–181). New York: Academic Press.

Eccles, J. S., & Wigfield, A. (1995). In the mind of the achiever: The structure of adolescents' academic achievement related-beliefs and self-perceptions. *Personality and Social Psychology Bulletin, 21,* 215–225.

Eccles, J. S., & Wigfield, A. (2002). Motivational beliefs, values, and goals. *Annual Review of Psychology, 53,* 109–132.

Eccles, J. S., Wigfield, A., Flanagan, C., Miller, C., Reuman, D., & Yee, D. (1989). Self-concepts, domain values, and self-esteem: Relations and changes at early adolescence. *Journal of Personality, 57,* 283–310.

Eccles, J. S., Wigfield, A., Harold, R., & Blumenfeld, P. B. (1993). Age and gender differences in children's self- and task perceptions during elementary school. *Child Development, 64,* 830–847.

Eccles, J. S., Wigfield, A., & Schiefele, U. (1998). Motivation to succeed. In W. Damon (Series Ed.) & N. Eisenberg (Vol. Ed.), *Handbook of child psychology: Vol. 3. Social, emotional, and personality development* (5th ed., pp. 1017–1095). New York: Wiley.

Eccles-Parsons, J., Adler, T. F., Futterman, R., Goff, S. B., Kaczala, C. M., Meece, J. L., et al. (1983). Expectancies, values, and academic behaviors. In J. T. Spence (Ed.), *Achievement and achievement motivation* (pp. 75–146). San Francisco: Freeman.

Elliot, A. J. (1999). Approach and avoidance motivation and achievement goals. *Educational Psychologist, 34,* 169–189.

Elliot, A. J. (2005). A conceptual history of the achievement goal construct. In A. J. Elliot & C. S. Dweck (Eds.), *Handbook of competence and motivation* (pp. 52–72). New York: Guilford Press.

Elliot, A. J., Chirkov, V. I., Kim, Y., & Sheldon, K. M. (2001). A cross-cultural analysis of avoidance (relative to approach) personal goals. *Psychological Science, 6,* 505–510.

Elliot, A. J., & Harackiewicz, J. M. (1996). Approach and avoidance goals and intrinsic motivation: A mediational analysis. *Journal of Personality and Social Psychology, 70,* 461–475.

Elliot, A. J., & McGregor, H. (2001). A 2 × 2 achievement goal framework. *Journal of Personality and Social Psychology, 80,* 501–509.

Finn, J. D. (1989). Withdrawing from school. *Review of Educational Research, 59,* 117–142.

Ford, M. E. (1992). *Human motivation: Goals, emotions, and personal agency beliefs.* Newbury Park, CA: Sage.

Fordham, S., & Ogbu, J. U. (1986). Black students' school success: Coping with "the burden of 'acting White.'" *Urban Review, 18,* 176–206.

Forsterling, F. (1985). Attributional retraining: A review. *Psychological Bulletin, 98,* 495–512.

Fredericks, J., & Eccles, J. S. (2002). Children's competence and value beliefs from childhood through adolescence: Growth trajectories in two male sex-typed domains. *Developmental Psychology, 38,* 519–533.

Frome, P., & Eccles, J. S. (1995, April). *Underestimation of academic ability in the middle school years.* Paper presented at the biennial meeting of the Society for Research in Child Development, Indianapolis, IN.

Fuligni, A. J., & Tseng, V. (1999). Family obligation and the academic motivation of adolescents from immigrant and American-born families. In T. Urdan (Ed.), *Advances in motivation and achievement: Vol. 11. The role of context* (pp. 159–183). Stamford, CT: JAI Press.

Gottfried, A. E., Fleming, J. S., & Gottfried, A. W. (2001). Continuity of academic intrinsic motivation from childhood through late adolescence: A longitudinal study. *Journal of Educational Psychology, 93,* 3–13.

Graham, S. (1992). Most of the subjects were European American and middle class: Trends in published research on African Americans in selected APA journals 1970–1989. *American Psychologist, 47,* 629–639.

Graham, S. (1994). Motivation in African Americans. *Review of Educational Research, 64,* 55–117.

Graham, S., & Taylor, A. Z. (2002). Ethnicity, gender, and the development of achievement values. In A. Wigfield & J. S. Eccles (Eds.), *Development of achievement motivation* (pp. 123–146). San Diego, CA: Academic Press.

Graham, S., Taylor, A. Z., & Hudley, C. (1998). Exploring achievement values among ethnic minority early adolescents. *Journal of Educational Psychology, 90,* 606–620.

Grant, H., & Dweck, C. S. (2001). Cross-cultural responses to failure: Considering outcome attributions with different goals. In F. Salili, C. Y. Chui, & Y. Y. Hong (Eds.), *Student motivation: The culture and context of learning* (pp. 203–219). New York: Plenum Press.

Greeno, J. G., Collins, A. M., & Resnick, L. B. (1996). Cognition and learning. In D. C. Berliner & R. C. Calfee (Eds.), *Handbook of educational psychology* (pp. 15–46). London: Prentice Hall International.

Grolnick, W. S., Gurland, S. T., Jacob, K. F., & Decourcey, W. (2002). The development of self-determination in middle childhood and adolescence. In A. Wigfield & J. S. Eccles (Eds.), *Development of achievement motivation* (pp. 147–171). San Diego, CA: Academic Press.

Harackiewicz, J. M., Barron, K. E., & Elliot, A. J. (1998). Rethinking achievement goals: When are they adaptive for college students and why? *Educational Psychologist, 33,* 1–21.

Harackiewicz, J. M., Barron, K. E., Pintrich, P. R., Elliot, A. J., & Thrash, T. M. (2002). Revision of achievement goal theory: Necessary and illuminating. *Journal of Educational Psychology, 94,* 638–645.

Hare, B. R. (1985). Stability and change in self-perceptions and achievement among African American adolescents: A longitudinal study. *Journal of African American Psychology, 11,* 29–42.

Harter, S. (1981). A new self-report scale of intrinsic versus extrinsic orientation in the classroom: Motivational and informational components. *Developmental Psychology, 17,* 300–312.

Harter, S. (1990). Causes, correlates, and the functional role of global self-worth: A life-span perspective. In J. Kolligian & R. Sternberg (Eds.), *Perceptions of competence and incompetence across the life-span* (pp. 67–98). New Haven, CT: Yale University Press.

Harter, S. (2006). Development of self-representations. In W. Damon and R. M. Lerner (Series Eds.) & N. Eisenberg (Vol. Ed.), *Handbook of child psychology: Vol. 3. Social, emotional, and personality development* (6th ed., pp. 505–570). Hoboken, NJ: Wiley.

Harter, S., Whitesell, N. R., & Kowalski, P. (1992). Individual differences in the effects of educational transitions on young adolescents' perceptions of competence and motivational orientation. *American Educational Research Journal, 29,* 809–835.

Heckhausen, H. (1987). Emotional components of action: Their ontogeny as reflected in achievement behavior. In D. Gîrlitz & J. F. Wohlwill (Eds.), *Curiosity, imagination, and play* (pp. 326–348). Hillsdale, NJ: Erlbaum.

Heine, S. J., Lehman, D. R., Ide, E., Leung, C., Kitayama, S., Takata, T., et al. (2001). Divergent consequences of success and failure in Japan and North America: An investigation of self-improving motivations and malleable selves. *Journal of Personality and Social Psychology, 81,* 599–615.

Hickey, D. T., & McCaslin, M. (2001). A comparative, sociocultural analysis of context and motivation. In S. Volet & S. Jarvela (Eds.), *Motivation in learning contexts: Theoretical advances and methodological implications* (pp. 33–55). Elmsford, NY: Pergamon Press.

Hidi, S. (2001). Interest, reading, and learning: Theoretical and practical considerations. *Educational Psychology Review, 13,* 191–209.

Hidi, S., & Harackiewicz, J. (2000). Motivating the academically unmotivated: A critical issue for the twenty-first century. *Review of Educational Research, 70,* 151–180.

Hill, K. T., & Sarason, S. B. (1966). The relation of test anxiety and defensiveness to test and school performance over the elementary school years: A further longitudinal study. *Monographs for the Society for Research in Child Development, 31*(2, Serial No. 104).

Hill, K. T., & Wigfield, A. (1984). Test anxiety: A major educational problem and what to do about it. *Elementary School Journal, 85,* 105–126.

Husman, J., & Lens, W. (1999). The role of the future in the study of motivation. *Educational Psychologist, 34,* 113–125.

Huston, A. C., McLoyd, V., & Coll, C. G. (1994). Children and poverty: Issues in contemporary research. *Child Development, 65,* 275–282.

Jacobs, J., Lanza, S., Osgood, D. W., Eccles, J. S., & Wigfield, A. (2002). Ontogeny of children's self-beliefs: Gender and domain differences across grades 1 through 12. *Child Development, 73,* 509–527.

James, W. (1963). *Psychology.* New York: Fawcett. (Original work published 1892)

Kaplan, A., & Middleton, M. (2002). Should childhood be a journey or a race? Response to Harackiewicz et al. *Journal of Educational Psychology, 94,* 646–648.

Kauffman, D. F., & Husman, J. (2004). Effects of time perspective on student motivation: Introduction to a special issue. *Educational Psychology Review, 16,* 1–7.

Krapp, A. (2002). Structural and dynamic aspects of interest development: Theoretical considerations from an ontogenetic perspective. *Learning and Instruction, 12,* 383–409.

Lee, S. J. (1994). Beyond the model-minority stereotype: Voices of high- and low-achieving Asian American students. *Anthropology and Education Quarterly, 25,* 413–429.

Lens, W. (1986). Future time perspective: A cognitive-motivational construct. In D. R. Brown & J. Veroff (Eds.), *Frontiers of motivational psychology* (pp. 173 190). New York: Springer-Verlag.

Lepper, M. R., & Henderlong, J. (2000). Turning "play" into "work": 25 years of research on intrinsic versus extrinsic motivation. In C. Sansone & J. M. Harackiewicz (Eds.), *Intrinsic and extrinsic motivation: The search for optimal motivation and performance* (pp. 257–307). San Diego, CA: Academic Press.

Lord, S., Eccles, J. S., & McCarthy, K. (1994). Risk and protective factors in the transition to junior high school. *Journal of Early Adolescence, 14,* 162–199.

Mac Iver, D. J., Stipek, D. J., & Daniels, D. H. (1991). Explaining within-semester changes in student effort in junior high school and senior high school courses. *Journal of Educational Psychology, 83,* 201–211.

Maehr, M. L., & Midgley, C. (1996). *Transforming school cultures.* Boulder, CO: Westview Press.

Mantzicopoulos, P., French, B. F., & Maller, S. J. (2004). Factor structure of the Pictorial Scale of Perceived Competence and Social Acceptance with two pre-elementary samples. *Child Development, 75,* 1214–1228.

Markus, H. R., & Kitayama, S. (1991). Culture and the self: Implications for cognition, emotion, and motivation. *Psychological Review, 98,* 224–253.

Markus, H. R., & Nurius, P. (1986). Possible selves. *American Psychologist, 41,* 954–969.

Marsh, H. W., Ellis, L. A., & Craven, R. G. (2002). How do preschool children feel about themselves? Unraveling measurement and multidimensional self-concept structure. *Developmental Psychology, 38,* 376–393.

Massimini, F., & Carli, M. (1988). The systematic assessment of flow in daily experience. In M. Csikszentmihalyi & I. S. Csikszentmihalyi (Eds.), *Optimal experience: Psychological studies of flow in consciousness* (pp. 266–287). New York: Cambridge University Press.

McCall, R. B., Evahn, C., & Kratzer, L. (1992). *High school underachievers: What do they achieve as adults?* Newbury Park, CA: Sage.

McGillicuddy-De Lisi, A., & De Lisi, R. (2002). Emergent themes in the development of sex differences in cognition. In A. McGillicuddy-De Lisi & R. De Lisi (Eds.), *Biology, society, and behavior: The development of sex differences in cognition* (pp. 243 258). Westport, CT: Ablex.

McInerney, D. M., & Van Etten, S. (2004). Big theories revisited: The challenge. In D. M. McInerney & S. Van Etten (Eds.), *Big theories revisited: Vol. 4. Research on sociocultural influences on motivation and learning* (pp. 1–13). Greenwich, CT: Information Age Press.

McLoyd, V. C. (1990). The impact of economic hardship on African American families and children: Psychological distress, parenting, and socioemotional development. *Child Development, 61,* 311–346.

Meece, J. L. (1991). The classroom context and students' motivational goals. In M. Maehr & P. Pintrich (Eds.), *Advances in motivation and achievement* (Vol. 7, pp. 261–286). Greenwich, CT: JAI Press.

Meece, J. L. (1994). The role of motivation in self-regulated learning. In D. H. Schunk & B. J. Zimmerman (Eds.), *Self-regulation of learning and performance* (pp. 25–44). Hillsdale, NJ: Erlbaum.

Meece, J. L., & Kurtz-Costes, B. (2001). Introduction: The schooling of ethnic minority children and youth. *Educational Psychologist, 36,* 1–7.

Meece, J. L., & Miller, S. D. (2001). A longitudinal analysis of elementary school students' achievement goals in literacy activities. *Contemporary Educational Psychology, 26,* 454–480.

Meece, J. L., Wigfield, A., & Eccles, J. S. (1990). Predictors of math anxiety and its consequences for young adolescents' course enrollment intentions and performances in mathematics. *Journal of Educational Psychology, 82,* 60–70.

Meichenbaum, D., & Butler, L. (1980). Toward a conceptual model of the treatment of test anxiety: Implications for research and treatment. In I. G. Sarason (Ed.), *Test anxiety: Theory, research, and applications.* Hillsdale, NJ: Erlbaum.

Middleton, M. J., & Midgley, C. (1997). Avoiding the demonstration of lack of ability: An unexplored aspect of goal theory. *Journal of Educational Psychology, 89,* 710–718.

Midgley, C. (2002). *Goals, goal structures, and adaptive learning.* Mahwah, NJ: Erlbaum.

Midgley, C., Kaplan, A., & Middleton, M. (2001). Performance-approach goals: Good for what, for whom, and under what circumstances? *Journal of Educational Psychology, 93,* 77–87.

Morris, L. W., Davis, M. A., & Hutchings, C. J. (1981). Cognitive and emotional components of anxiety: Literature review and a revised worry-emotionality scale. *Journal of Educational Psychology, 73,* 541–555.

National Research Council. (2004). *Engaging schools: Fostering high school students' motivation to learn.* Washington, DC: National Academies Press.

Nicholls, J. G. (1978). The development of the concepts of effort and ability, perceptions of academic attainment, and the understanding that difficult tasks require more ability. *Child Development, 49,* 800–814.

Nicholls, J. G. (1984). Achievement motivation: Conceptions of ability, subjective experience, task choice, and performance. *Psychological Review, 91,* 328–346.

Nicholls, J. G., Cobb, P., Yackel, E., Wood, T., & Wheatley, G. (1990). Students' theories of mathematics and their mathematical knowledge: Multiple dimensions of assessment. In G. Kulm (Ed.), *Assessing higher order thinking in mathematics* (pp. 137–154). Washington, DC: American Association for the Advancement of Science.

Nicholls, J. G., & Miller, A. T. (1984). The differentiation of the concepts of difficulty and ability. *Child Development, 54,* 951–959.

Ogbu, J. (1981). Origins of human competence: A cultural-ecological perspective. *Child Development, 52,* 413–429.

Ogbu, J. (1992). Understanding cultural diversity and learning. *Educational Researcher, 21,* 5–14.

Oyserman, D., Coon, H. M., & Kemmelmeier, M. (2002). Rethinking individualism and collectivism: Evaluation of theoretical assumptions and meta-analyses. *Psychological Bulletin, 128,* 3–72.

Padilla, A. M., & Gonzalez, R. (2001). Academic performance of immigrant and U.S. born Mexican heritage students: Effects of schooling in Mexico and Bilingual/English language instruction. *American Educational Research Journal, 38,* 727–742.

Patrick, H. (1997). Social self-regulation: Exploring the relations between children's social relationships, academic self-regulation, and school performance. *Educational Psychologist, 32,* 209–220.

Pekrun, R. (1993). Facets of adolescents' academic motivation: A longitudinal expectancy-value approach. In M. Maehr & P. Pintrich (Eds.), *Advances in motivation and achievement* (Vol. 8, pp. 139–189). Greenwich, CT: JAI Press.

Pintrich, P. R. (2000a). An achievement goal theory perspective on issues in motivation terminology, theory, and research. *Contemporary Educational Psychology, 25,* 92–104.

Pintrich, P. R. (2000b). The role of goal orientation in self-regulated learning. In M. Boekaerts, P. R. Pintrich, & M. Zeidner (Eds.), *Handbook of self-regulation* (pp. 451–502). San Diego, CA: Academic Press.

Pintrich, P. R. (2003). A motivational science perspective on the role of student motivation in learning and teaching contexts. *Journal of Educational Psychology, 95,* 667–686.

Pintrich, P. R., & Schunk, D. H. (2002). *Motivation in education: Theory, research, and application* (2nd ed.). Englewood Cliffs, NJ: Merrill-Prentice Hall.

Pomerantz, E. M., & Saxon, J. L. (2001). Conceptions of ability as stable and self-evaluative processes: A longitudinal examination. *Child Development, 72,* 152–173.

Portes, A., & Rumbaut, R. G. (2001). *Legacies: The story of the immigrant second generation.* Berkeley: University of California Press.

Renninger, K. A., Ewen, L., & Lasher, A. K. (2002). Individual interest as context in expository text and mathematical word problems. *Learning and Instruction, 12,* 467–491.

Renninger, K. A., Hidi, S., & Krapp, A. (Eds.). (1992). *The role of interest in learning and development.* Hillsdale, NJ: Erlbaum.

Roeser, R. W. (2004). Competing schools of thought in achievement goal theory. In M. L. Maehr & P. R. Pintrich (Eds.), *Advances in motivation and achievement: Vol. 13. Motivating students, improving schools* (pp. 265–299). New York: Elsevier.

Roeser, R. W., Peck, S. C., & Nasir, N. (2006). Self and identity processes in school motivation, learning, and achievement. In P. Alexander & P. H. Winne (Eds.), *Handbook of educational psychology* (2nd ed., pp. 391–424). Mahwah, NJ: Erlbaum.

Rotter, J. B. (1966). Generalized expectancies for internal versus external control of reinforcement. *Psychological Monographs, 80,* 1–28.

Ruble, D. N. (1983). The development of social comparison processes and their role in achievement-related self-socialization. In E. T. Higgins, D. N. Ruble, & W. W. Hartup (Eds.), *Social cognition and social development: A sociocultural perspective* (pp. 134–157). New York: Cambridge University Press.

Ruble, D. N., & Martin, C. L. (1998). Gender development. In W. Damon (Series Ed.) & N. Eisenberg (Vol. Ed.), *Handbook of child psychology: Vol. 3. Social, emotional, and personality development* (5th ed., pp. 933–1016). New York: Wiley.

Ryan, R. M., & Deci, E. L. (2000). Self-determination theory and the facilitation of intrinsic motivation, social development, and well-being. *American Psychologist, 55,* 68–78.

Ryan, R. M., & Deci, E. L. (2002). An overview of self-determination theory: An organismic-dialectical perspective. In E. L. Deci & R. M. Ryan (Eds.), *Handbook of self-determination theory research* (pp. 3–33). Rochester, NY: University of Rochester Press.

Sansone, C., & Harackiewicz, J. M. (2000). Looking beyond rewards: The problem and promise of intrinsic motivation. In C. Sansone & J. M. Harackiewicz (Eds.), *Intrinsic and extrinsic motivation: The search for optimal motivation and performance* (pp. 1–9). San Diego, CA: Academic Press.

Sarason, I. G. (1980). Introduction to the study of test anxiety. In I. G. Sarason (Ed.), *Test anxiety: Theory, research, and application* (pp. 3–14). Hillsdale, NJ: Erlbaum.

Schiefele, U. (1991). Interest, learning, and motivation. *Educational Psychologist, 26,* 299–323.

Schiefele, U. (1996). Topic interest, text representation, and quality of experience. *Contemporary Educational Psychology, 21,* 3–18.

Schiefele, U. (1999). Interest and learning from text. *Scientific Studies of Reading, 3,* 257–279.

Schiefele, U. (2001). The role of interest in motivation and learning. In J. M. Collis & S. Messick (Eds.), *Intelligence and personality: Bridging the gap in theory and measurement* (pp. 163–194). Mahwah, NJ: Erlbaum.

Schunk, D. H. (1991). Goal setting and self-evaluation: A social cognitive perspective on self-regulation. In M. L. Maehr & P. R. Pintrich (Eds.), *Advances in motivation and achievement* (Vol. 7, pp. 85–113). Greenwich, CT: JAI Press.

Schunk, D. H. (1994). Self-regulation of self-efficacy and attributions in academic settings. In D. H. Schunk & B. J. Zimmerman (Eds.), *Self-regulation of learning and performance* (pp. 75–99). Hillsdale, NJ: Erlbaum.

Schunk, D. H., & Pajares, F. (2002). The development of academic self-efficacy. In A. Wigfield & J. S. Eccles (Eds.), *Development of achievement motivation* (pp. 15–32). San Diego, CA: Academic Press.

Shell, D. F., Colvin, C., & Bruning, R. H. (1995). Self-efficacy, attribution, and outcome expectancy mechanisms in reading and writing achievement: Grade-level and achievement-level differences. *Journal of Educational Psychology, 87,* 386–398.

Shih, M., Pittinsky, T. L., & Ambady, N. (1999). Stereotype susceptibility: Identity salience and shifts in quantitative performance. *Psychological Science, 10,* 80–83.

Skaalvik, E. (1997). Self-enhancing and self-defeating ego orientation: Relations with task and task avoidance orientation, achievement, self-perceptions, and anxiety. *Journal of Educational Psychology, 89,* 71–81.

Skinner, E. A. (1995). *Perceived control, motivation, and coping.* Thousand Oaks, CA: Sage.

Skinner, E. A., Chapman, M., & Baltes, P. B. (1988). Control, means-ends, and agency beliefs: A new conceptualization and its measurement during childhood. *Journal of Personality and Social Psychology, 54,* 117–133.

Skinner, E. A., Gembeck-Zimmer, M. J., & Connell, J. P. (1998). Individual differences and the development of perceived control. *Monographs of the Society for Research in Child Development, 6*(2/3, Serial No. 254), 1–220.

Slaughter-Defoe, D. T., Nakagawa, K., Takanishi, R., & Johnson, D. J. (1990). Toward cultural/ecological perspectives on schooling and achievement in African- and Asian-American children. *Child Development, 61,* 363–383.

Spencer, M. B., Noll, E., Stoltzfus, J., & Harpalani, V. (2001). Identify and school adjustment: Revising the "Acting White" assumption. *Educational Psychologist, 36,* 31–44.

Spencer, S. J., Steele, M., & Quinn, D. M. (1999). Stereotype threat and women's math performance. *Journal of Experimental Social Psychology, 35,* 4–28.

Steele, C. M. (1992, April). Race and the schooling of Black Americans. *Atlantic Monthly, 269*(4), 68–78.

Steele, C. M. (1997). A threat in the air: How stereotypes shape intellectual identity and performance. *American Psychologist, 52,* 613–629.

Steele, C. M., & Aronson, J. (1995). Stereotype threat and the intellectual test performance of African-Americans. *Journal of Personality and Social Psychology, 69,* 797–811.

Stevenson, H. W., Chen, C., & Uttal, D. H. (1990). Beliefs and achievement: A study of Black, White, and Hispanic children. *Child Development, 61,* 508–523.

Stipek, D. J., & Mac Iver, D. (1989). Developmental change in children's assessment of intellectual competence. *Child Development, 60,* 521–538.

Stipek, D. J., Recchia, S., & McClintic, S. M. (1992). Self-evaluation in young children. *Monographs of the Society for Research in Child Development, 57*(2, Serial No. 226) 1–83.

Tatum, B. D. (1997). *"Why are all the Black kids sitting together in the cafeteria?" and other conversations about race.* New York: Basic Books.

Taylor, R. D., Casten, R., Flickinger, S., Roberts, D., & Fulmore, C. D. (1994). Explaining the school performance of African-American adolescents. *Journal of Research on Adolescence, 4,* 21–44.

Thorkildsen, T., & Nicholls, J. G. (1998). Fifth graders' achievement orientations and beliefs: Individual and classroom differences. *Journal of Educational Psychology, 90,* 179–201.

Tobias, S. (1985). Test anxiety: Interference, deficient skills, and cognitive capacity. *Educational Psychologist, 20,* 135–142.

Todt, E. (1990). Development of interest. In H. Hetzer (Ed.), *Applied developmental psychology of children and youth* (pp. 213–264). Wiesbaden, Germany: Quelle & Meyer.

Urdan, T. C. (1997). Achievement goal theory: Past results, future directions. In P. R. Pintrich & M. L. Maehr (Eds.), *Advances in motivation and achievement* (Vol. 10, pp. 99–142). Greenwich, CT: JAI Press.

Vallerand, R. J., Pelletier, L. G., Blais, M. R., Brière, N. M., Senécal, C. B., & Vallières, E. F. (1993). On the assessment of intrinsic, extrinsic, and amotivation in education: Evidence on the concurrent and construct validity of the Academic Motivation Scale. *Educational and Psychological Measurement, 53,* 159–172.

Watt, H. (2004). Development of adolescents' self-perceptions, values, and task perceptions. *Child Development, 75,* 1556–1574.

Weiner, B. (1985). An attributional theory of achievement motivation and emotion. *Psychological Review, 92,* 548–573.

Weiner, B. (1992). *Human motivation: Metaphors, theories, and research.* Newbury Park, CA: Sage.

Weiner, B. (2005). Motivation from an attribution perspective and the social psychology of perceived competence. In A. J. Elliot & C. S. Dweck (Eds.), *Handbook of competence and motivation* (pp. 73–84). New York: Guilford Press.

Weisz, J. P. (1984). Contingency judgments and achievement behavior: Deciding what is controllable and when to try. In J. G. Nicholls (Ed.), *The development of achievement motivation* (pp. 107–136). Greenwich, CT: JAI Press.

Wentzel, K. R. (1989). Adolescent classroom grades, standards for performance, and academic achievement: An interactionist perspective. *Journal of Educational Psychology, 81,* 131–142.

Wentzel, K. R. (1991). Social competence at school: Relation between social responsibility and academic achievement. *Review of Educational Research, 61,* 1–24.

Wentzel, K. R. (1993). Does being good make the grade? Social behavior and academic competence in middle school. *Journal of Educational Psychology, 85,* 357–364.

Wentzel, K. R. (1996). Social goals and social relationships as motivators of school adjustment. In J. Juvonen & K. R. Wentzel (Eds.), *Social motivation: Understanding school adjustment* (pp. 226–247). New York: Cambridge University Press.

Wentzel, K. R. (2002). The contribution of social goal setting to children's school adjustment. In A. Wigfield & J. S. Eccles (Eds.), *Development of achievement motivation* (pp. 222–246). San Diego, CA: Academic Press.

Wigfield, A. (1994). Expectancy: Value theory of achievement motivation—A developmental perspective. *Educational Psychology Review, 6,* 49–78.

Wigfield, A., Battle, A., Keller, L., & Eccles, J. S. (2002). Sex differences in motivation, self-concept, career aspirations, and career choice: Implications for cognitive development. In A. McGillicuddy-De Lisi & R. De Lisi (Eds.), *Biology, society, and behavior: The development of sex differences in cognition* (pp. 93–124). Greenwich, CT: Ablex.

Wigfield, A., Byrnes, J. B., & Eccles, J. S. (2006). Adolescent development. In P. A. Alexander & P. Winne (Eds.), *Handbook of educational psychology* (2nd ed., pp. 87–113). Mahwah, NJ: Erlbaum.

Wigfield, A., & Eccles, J. S. (1989). Test anxiety in elementary and secondary school students. *Educational Psychologist, 24,* 159–183.

Wigfield, A., & Eccles, J. S. (1992). The development of achievement task values: A theoretical analysis. *Developmental Review, 12,* 265–310.

Wigfield, A., & Eccles, J. S. (2000). Expectancy: Value theory of motivation. *Contemporary Educational Psychology, 25,* 68–81.

Wigfield, A., & Eccles, J. S. (2002). The development of competence beliefs and values from childhood through adolescence. In A. Wigfield & J. S. Eccles (Eds.), *Development of achievement motivation* (pp. 92–120). San Diego, CA: Academic Press.

Wigfield, A., Eccles, J. S., Mac Iver, D., Reuman, D., & Midgley, C. (1991). Transitions at early adolescence: Changes in children's domain-specific self-perceptions and general self-esteem across the transition to junior high school. *Developmental Psychology, 27,* 552–565.

Wigfield, A., Eccles, J. S., Schiefele, U., Roeser, R., & Davis-Kean, P. (2006). Development of achievement motivation. In W. Damon & R. M. Lerner (Series Eds.) & N. Eisenberg (Vol. Ed.) *Handbook of child psychology: Vol. 3. Social, emotional, and personality development* (6th ed., pp. 933–1002). Hoboken, NJ: Wiley.

Wigfield, A., Eccles, J. S., Yoon, K. S., Harold, R. D., Arbreton, A., Freedman-Doan, C., et al. (1997). Changes in children's competence beliefs and subjective task values across the elementary school years: A 3-year study. *Journal of Educational Psychology, 89,* 451–469.

Winne, P. H., & Jamieson-Noel, D. L. (2002). Exploring students' calibration of self-reports about study tactics and achievement. *Contemporary Educational Psychology, 27,* 551–572.

Winston, C., Eccles, J. S., Senior, A. M., & Vida, M. (1997). The utility of an expectancy/value model of achievement for understanding academic performance and self-esteem in African-American and European-American adolescents. *Zeitschrift Fur Padagogische Psychologie, 11,* 177–186.

Wolters, C. A. (2003). Regulation of motivation: Evaluating an underemphasized aspect of self-regulated learning. *Educational Psychologist, 38,* 189–206.

Wong, C. A., Eccles, J. S., & Sameroff, A. J. (2003). The influence of ethnic discrimination and ethnic identification on African-American adolescents' school and socioemotional adjustment. *Journal of Personality, 71,* 1197–1232.

Zeidner, M. (1998). *Test anxiety: The state of the art.* New York: Plenum Press.

Zimmerman, B. J., & Martinez-Pons, M. (1990). Student differences in self-regulated learning: Relating grade, sex, and giftedness to self-efficacy and strategy use. *Journal of Educational Psychology, 82,* 51–59.

PART VII

PROSOCIAL BEHAVIOR, ANTISOCIAL BEHAVIOR, AND MORAL DEVELOPMENT

Chapter 13

Aggression and Antisocial Behavior in Youth

Kenneth A. Dodge, John D. Coie, and Donald Lynam

Crime rates have risen steadily in nearly all countries that keep accurate records (Rutter, Giller, & Hagell, 1998). More dramatic has been the increase in violent crime by young juveniles in the United States. Since 1965, the homicide rate by juveniles aged 18 or under has increased by close to 400% (Blumstein, 2000). The annual aggregate burden of crime in the United States now exceeds $1 trillion (D. A. Anderson, 1999). Research in the past 2 decades has increasingly focused on the development of chronically antisocial individuals, in contrast to research on species-wide patterns in aggressive behavior. This shift in emphasis has grown from recognition that a small group of chronically violent youth are responsible for over half of all crimes (Howell, Krisberg, & Jones, 1995), that criminal careers can be charted across the life span beginning in childhood (Blumstein & Cohen, 1987), that career criminals cost society up to $2 million each (Cohen, 2005), and that citizens may be willing to pay a great deal in extra taxes for interventions that could confidently reduce crime (Cohen, Rust, Steen, & Tidd, 2004).

Dimensions of Aggression and Other Antisocial Behavior

Because antisocial or disruptive behavior is a heterogeneous set, attempts have been made to establish dimensions of antisocial behavior by factor-analytic or multi-dimensional scaling techniques. Frick et al. (1993) conducted a meta-analysis of

The authors wish to thank Lynda Harrison for her careful scrutiny of the text, Amber Runion for assembling over 1,000 references, Terrie Moffitt for her insightful review, and Nancy Eisenberg for her valuable editing. The first author is grateful for the support of Senior Research Scientist Award 5 K05 DA-015226.

factor-analytic studies of Oppositional Defiant Disorder and Conduct Disorder behaviors in over 23,000 youth and extracted two dimensions of antisocial behavior. One dimension runs from overt to covert behaviors, and the second dimension ranges in level of destructiveness. The resulting quadrants constitute categories of aggression (overt, high destructive), oppositional behavior (overt, low destructive), property violations (covert, high destructive), and status violations (covert, low destructive).

Aggressive behaviors can be further subcategorized into dimensions that reflect both forms and functions. The form varies as direct, involving verbal or physical attack, or relational, involving damage to the target's friendships or inclusion in the peer group (Crick & Grotpeter, 1995). The function is either instrumental, occurring in the anticipation of self-serving outcomes, or reactive, occurring as an angry defensive response to goal blocking or provocation (Little, Jones, Henrich, & Hawley, 2003). The perspective of this chapter is that human aggressive behavior, because of its many adaptive features, has evolved to be part of a broader social communication system (Tedeschi & Felson, 1994). Thus, aggression must be interpreted as a social event, with meaningful subtypes, topographies, antecedents, and functions.

Aggressive and Antisocial Development in the Human Species

EMERGENCE OF ANGER AND PHYSICAL AGGRESSION IN EARLY LIFE

The fundamental human emotion of anger prepares the body physiologically and psychologically to initiate self-protective and instrumental activity (Frijda, 1986) and may be an important reason for the adaptation and survival of the species (Lorenz, 1966). If anger is functional and innate, when does it emerge, and what are its earliest elicitors? Stenberg and Campos (1990) found that, following restraint, 1-month-olds turned their heads randomly, but 4-month-olds turned their heads toward the frustrator. Immediately following the onset of the first display of anger, 7-month-olds, but not 4-month-olds, turned their heads not toward the frustrator but toward their mothers. Stenberg and Campos (1990) concluded, "By at least 4 months anger facial displays may function as discrete social signals. These signals are at first directed proximally to the immediate source of frustration, but by 7 months they become expressed directly to social objects such as the mother" (pp. 270–271).

Trivers (1974) suggested that conflict, anger, and aggression increase in frequency and intensity across the second year of life in all mammalian species that undergo a prolonged period of symbiosis between mother and infant. Stable individual differences in anger expression emerge during the late first year and into the second year of life (Stifter, Spinrad, & Braungart-Rieker, 1999). Although physical aggression decreases, verbal aggression increases between 2 and 4 years of age (Cairns, 1979), coinciding with growth in expressive vocabulary. Although relatively few sex differences have been found in infancy and toddlerhood in the rate and form of aggressive behaviors, by the time that children interact in preschool groups, the differences become striking (Underwood, 2003), especially in physical aggression. One type of antisocial behavior for which girls score higher than boys (Crick & Zahn-Waxler, 2003) is social aggression (Underwood, 2003), variously labeled indirect aggression (Kaukiainen et al., 1999) or relational aggression (Crick & Grotpeter, 1995).

AGGRESSION DURING THE ELEMENTARY SCHOOL YEARS

Analyses of mothers' reports (National Institute of Child Health and Human Development Early Child Care Research Network, 2004) indicate "The most frequent form of early aggression, hits others, occurred in about 70% of the sample at ages 2 and 3, but declined to 20% by ages 4 and 5 (kindergarten), and to 12% by third grade" (p. 42). Keenan and Shaw (2003) have suggested that the development of emotion regulation is responsible for the decline in aggression during these years. Rapid neural development in the anterior cingulate gyrus during these years has been hypothesized by Posner and Rothbart (1998). Mischel (1974) suggested that the emerging ability to delay gratification is a crucial factor in declines in aggression during this period. Through interpersonal exchanges, children acquire cognitive strategies for delaying gratification (e.g., distraction, mentally representing delayed rewards) and effortful control (Eisenberg et al., 2004) that may help them avoid impulsive grabbing of others' possessions and hitting. The ability to delay gratification, in turn, may be aided by the corresponding development of broader representational abilities (Gelman & Baillargeon, 1983), emotion processing (Schultz, Izard, & Bear, 2004), and executive function.

With the decline in the rate of aggression comes a shift in its form and function. Aggressive behaviors become directed toward specific dyadic relationships (Coie et al., 1999), and its form becomes increasingly hostile, in contrast with the relatively nonsocial, instrumental nature of aggression in the preschool period. Aggressive behaviors also become more person-directed and relational (Crick & Bigbee, 1998). Finally, covert forms of antisocial behavior such as lying, cheating, and stealing emerge with greater frequency (Loeber, Farrington, Stouthamer-Loeber, & van Kammen, 1998).

Major elicitors of aggression come to include perceived threats and insults to one's ego (Schwartz, McFadden-Ketchum, Dodge, Pettit, & Bates, 1998). Children learn that some actions are unintended but others are under the volitional control of the actor; the result is that the attribution that a peer has acted with hostile intent has an inflammatory effect (Hubbard, Dodge, Cillessen, Coie, & Schwartz, 2001).

AGGRESSION DURING THE ADOLESCENT YEARS

Most longitudinal studies show decrements in ratings of aggressive behavior as children enter adolescence (Loeber et al., 1998). However, adolescence is a time when serious acts of violence increase, as age-crime curves regularly demonstrate (e.g., U.S. Department of Justice, 2003), when a second group of youth joins the early starting group in antisocial behavior, and when aggressive behavior broadens to new contexts, including romantic relationships.

Ethnic differences in aggression in the social context of the United States are almost negligible in the elementary school years (Achenbach, 1991) but are more pronounced in adolescence. Arrest record data indicate that even though African American youth make up 15% of the juvenile population, they account for 52% of those arrested for juvenile violent crimes (Dryfoos, 1990). The lifetime chances that an urban African American male will be arrested for an FBI "index" offense (murder, forcible rape, aggravated assault, robbery, burglary, larceny, and auto theft) is 50%, in contrast with 14% for urban White males (Blumstein & Cohen, 1987).

In American peer culture, physical aggression and delinquent deviance become more socially acceptable during adolescence (Coie, Terry, Zakriski, & Lochman, 1995). Moffitt (1993) hypothesized that early starting children contribute to the growth of a deviant peer culture by acting as role models and by offering opportunities for deviant behavior. Indeed, some deviant youth begin to hold positive status among peers (Miller-Johnson & Costanzo, 2004). As the contextual normativeness of antisocial behavior increases, the effects of this context are to increase the display of aggressive behavior by individual youth (Espelage, Holt, & Henkel, 2003). The new group of aggressors has been called adolescence-limited by Moffitt (1993), who asserted that this group engages in delinquent behavior only during adolescence.

AGGRESSION DURING ADULTHOOD

Most self-report studies indicate that between ages 18 and 25 the overall rate of aggressive behavior declines, and virtually no new cases of antisocial behavior begin in adulthood (Robins, 1966). Sampson and Laub (2003) found that further declines in crime are found after age 35 in all groups of early offenders in the Glueck sample. An important caveat to these findings is that almost all studies fail to include child abuse and spousal battery as instances of violence. Thus, it is misleading to conclude that adulthood brings about less violence. Straus and Gelles (1990) reported that 16% of American couples report physically assaulting each other, and 11% reported physically abusing their children, in the previous 12 months.

There is a second significant exception to the general pattern of decline in serious violence in adulthood (Coie, 2004). Among African American males, there is no decline in violence from age 22 to 30. Nearly twice as many African Americans continue their violent careers as do Whites; thus, the violent careers of African Americans last longer than they do for Whites (Elliott, 1994), in sharp contrast with the finding of few race differences in the propensity for initial violence. It seems that the underclass, especially poor African American males, are unable to escape the system of incarceration, labeling, unemployment, and negative identity once the course of violence begins.

Determinants of Individual Differences in Antisocial Behavior

Causes of individual differences in antisocial behavior range from genetic to socialization, and contemporary models integrate these factors through interactions, transactions, moderation, and mediation.

GENETICS

It is homiletic to say that antisocial behavior is the result of both nature and nurture. To move beyond homily, we must disentangle these effects and examine their interplay. This is the realm of behavior genetics, which relies on genetically sensitive designs (e.g., twin and adoption studies) to accomplish these goals. Genetically sensitive designs utilize the differing degrees of genetic similarity in relatives (e.g., monozygotic and dizygotic twins, parents and children, stepsiblings) to determine how much of the variance in a trait is due to variation in genetic similarity and environmental similarity. Contemporary behavior-genetics researchers provide estimates of four types of influences. The first two, additive and nonadditive genetic effects, constitute heritability. The third component, shared environment, indexes the degree to which environmental factors are responsible for the resemblance of family members. The fourth component, nonshared environment, indexes the degree to which environmental factors contribute to differences between family members. Furthermore, it is understood that genetic effects may be mediated environmentally through gene-environment transactions in which genes influence surrounding environments, which, in turn, influence phenotypic expression (cf., Scarr & McCartney, 1983). Also, all estimates are context specific. The influence of genes on behavior varies across social contexts, and a change in context may change the relative importance of genes and environment (cf., Dunne et al., 1997).

When measures of individual differences are summed across situations and time, large heritability estimates emerge, along with substantial nonshared environmental estimates. Arseneault et al. (2003) reported heritability estimates ranged from .42 for self-reports to .76 for teacher reports, nonshared environmental estimates ranged from .24 for teacher reports to .58 for child reports, and shared environmental estimates were zero. Rhee and Waldman's (2002) meta-analysis yielded a best-fitting model for the data that included additive genetic influences (.32), nonadditive genetic influences (.09), shared environmental influences (.16), and nonshared environmental influences (.43).

Studies of antisocial behavior were among the first to document interactions between genetic and environmental risk factors. Mednick and Christiansen (1977) reported that 14% of adoptees were convicted when neither their biological nor adoptive parents had been convicted of a crime; 15% were convicted if only their adoptive parent had been convicted; 20% were convicted if only their biological parent had been; finally, 25% were convicted if both their adoptive and biological parents had been convicted. The dynamic interaction effect was found to be even stronger in later studies. Cloninger, Sigvardsson, Bohman, and van Knoring (1982) found that 3% of adoptees were convicted as adults if both biological and rearing environments were normal; 7% offended if only rearing were abnormal; 12% offended in the face of offending in the biological parent; however, 40% offended if both the biological parent offended and the rearing environment was abnormal. Jaffee et al. (2005), in the E-risk twin study, showed that environmental risk interacted with genetic risk to predict Conduct Disorder (CD); physical maltreatment was associated with a 24% increase in the probability of CD among twins at high genetic risk (i.e., having a co-twin with CD), but only a 2% increase among twins at low risk. Thus, there is a stronger environmental impact among subgroups at higher genetic risk.

Caspi et al. (2002) provided evidence for the interaction between a specific gene and environmental risk in predicting antisocial behavior. These authors examined the interaction between childhood maltreatment and a functional polymorphism in the MAO-A gene in 442 males from the Dunedin Multidisciplinary Health and Development Study. The MAO-A gene was chosen because it encodes the MAO-A enzyme, which is responsible for metabolizing neurotransmitters, such as norepinephrine, dopamine, and serotonin, several of which have been linked with antisocial behavior. Caspi et al. reported a significant interaction between childhood maltreatment and MAO-A genotype, such that 85% of the males with the low-activity allele and a history of childhood maltreatment developed some form of antisocial outcome. Importantly, this finding was replicated in the 514 male twins from the Virginia Twin Study for Adolescent Behavioral Development (Foley et al., 2004). As in the Caspi et al. study, individuals with low MAO-A activity and an adverse childhood environment were the most likely to develop CD.

DISPOSITIONAL FACTORS

The evidence for the influence of both personality and temperament on antisocial outcomes is mounting. Large, prospective studies have shown that early temperament is predictive of antisocial behavior in the preschool period (Keenan, Shaw, Delliquadri, Giovanelli, & Walsh, 1998), childhood (Raine, Reynolds, Venables, Mednick, & Farrington, 1998), and even into adolescence (Caspi et al., 1994). Personality is robustly related to antisocial behavior in childhood (e.g., Krueger, Caspi, Moffitt, White, & Stouthamer-Loeber, 1996) and adulthood (Ball, Tennen, Poling, Kranzler, & Rounsaville, 1997).

There is also evidence for the interaction between temperament and the socialization context, particularly features of parenting. Coon, Carey, Corley, and Fulker (1992) found that among "difficult-temperament" young children, only those with conjoint maladaptive parenting were at risk for later conduct-disordered behavior. Kochanska (1997) has also reported an interaction between temperament and parenting style in producing compliance.

The dispositional construct of psychopathy has been studied intensively at the adult level. Interpersonally, the psychopath is grandiose, egocentric, manipulative, forceful, and cold-hearted; affectively, he or she displays shallow emotions, is unable to maintain close-relationships, and lacks empathy, anxiety, and remorse. Behaviorally, the psychopath commits more types of crime, more crimes of any type, and more violent crimes than nonpsychopathic counterparts (Hare, 2003). Juvenile psychopathy is moderately related to age at onset (Corrado, Vincent, Hart, & Cohen, 2004), number and variety of offenses (Kosson, Cyterski, Steuerwald, Neumann, & Walker-Matthews, 2002), stability of offending (Lynam, 1997), and quantity and quality of aggression (Murrie, Cornell, Kaplan, McConville, & Levy-Elkon, 2004).

NEUROPSYCHOLOGICAL AND EXECUTIVE FUNCTION FACTORS

One of the most robust correlates of severe conduct problems is impaired verbal ability. Verbal deficits have been found in aggressive toddlers, conduct-disordered children, serious adolescent delinquents, and adult criminals. There have been at least six comprehensive reviews since the first by Prentice and Kelly in 1963; each review includes additional confirming studies (see Lynam & Henry, 2001). Moffitt (1990) identified neuropsychological problems in young antisocial children that were as long-standing as their antisocial behavior. At ages 3 and 5, these boys had scored more than a standard deviation below the age-norm for boys on the Bayley and McCarthy tests of motor coordination; at each age (5, 7, 9, 11, and 13), these boys scored a more than .75 of a standard deviation below the age-norm for boys on verbal IQ (VIQ). The relation between poor verbal ability and antisocial behavior has also been found among clinic-referred children (Lahey et al., 1995).

Antisocial behavior has been associated with deficiencies in the brain's self-control or executive functions, which include operations such as sustaining attention and concentration, abstract reasoning and concept formation, formulating goals, anticipating and planning, programming and initiating purposive sequences of behavior, and inhibiting unsuccessful, inappropriate, or impulsive behaviors. Several studies have shown that executive functions discriminate between antisocial and nonantisocial children and adolescents (Lynam & Henry, 2001). Longitudinal studies have demonstrated that executive function deficits are associated with the stability and continuity of conduct problems (Seguin, Pihl, Harden, Tremblay, & Boulerice, 1995).

Researchers have employed brain-imaging methods that assess both the structural and functional characteristics of the brains of antisocial individuals (Lynam & Henry, 2001). Results have varied, but where significant findings do emerge, they generally involve dysfunction in the temporal and frontal regions among offenders, a pattern supportive of results found in studies using performance tests (Raine, Lencz, Bihrle, LaCasse, & Colletti, 2000). Lyoo, Lee, Jung, Noam, and Renshaw (2002) administered magnetic resonance imaging (MRI) assessments to over 400 children and adolescents with psychiatric disorders and found that the group with attention deficit disorder and CD had more severe levels of white matter signal hyperintensities in the frontal lobes than did controls. This literature, however, is far from complete. Reliance on small sample sizes, failure to use noncriminal control groups, and use of a wide variety of types of offenders precludes drawing firm conclusions.

BIOLOGICAL FACTORS

To the degree that temperament, personality, and neuropsychological health are based in biology, the evidence reviewed earlier demonstrates that biological variables are consistently related to antisocial behavior. In the sections that follow, we examine the relations between more direct indicators of biological function and antisocial behavior. Specifically, we review evidence that links antisocial behavior to pre- and perinatal complications, early exposure to nicotine, neurotransmitter activity, sex hormones, and autonomic reactivity. Perhaps most interesting, across many studies, the effects of these biological variables are strongest under adverse environmental circumstances.

At least six studies have found associations between minor physical anomalies (MPAs), presumed to be markers for fetal maldevelopment, and antisocial behavior in children (Raine, 2002). In several studies, MPAs have been found to interact with social factors to predict antisocial behavior. Brennan, Mednick, and Raine (1997) found that men with both MPAs and high family adversity had the highest rates of adult offending in a sample of male offspring of psychiatrically ill parents. Pine, Shaffer, Schonfeld, and Davies (1997) found that the presence of MPAs interacted with environmental disadvantage to predict CD at age 17. Studies from large, longitudinal studies in multiple countries have found that the relations between birth complications and antisocial behavior are stronger when other psychosocial risk factors are present. Raine, Brennan, and Mednick (1994) found that birth complications and maternal rejection at age 1 interacted to predict violent offending at age 18 in a sample of over 4,200 men from Copenhagen. In the follow-up at age 34, the interaction between biological and social risk predicted early onset, serious violent behavior.

In Utero Exposure to Nicotine

Several studies have shown that maternal smoking during pregnancy places the offspring at increased risk for later antisocial behavior. Fergusson, Woodward, and Horwood (1998) found that smoking during pregnancy almost doubled the risk for conduct problems in boys, even after controlling for antenatal and postnatal risk factors. Brennan, Grekin, and Mednick (1999) found a twofold increase in adult violent offending in the offspring of mothers who smoked in a birth cohort of over 4,000 men. These relations hold even after controlling many potentially confounding variables, including socioeconomic status, maternal education, mother's age at first birth, family size, parenting behaviors, parental psychopathology, birth weight, and perinatal complications (Maughan, Taylor, Caspi, & Moffitt, 2004). As with other biological variables, there is evidence that smoking during pregnancy interacts with social risks to increase the likelihood of antisocial behavior. Rasanen et al. (1999) found a 12-fold increase in recidivistic violent offending in offspring whose mothers smoked and who were born into single-parent families.

Autonomic Nervous System Activity

Raine (2002) calls low resting heart rate "the best-replicated biological correlate of antisocial behavior in child and adolescent samples" (p. 418). The relation is present in cross-sectional studies (e.g., Rogeness, Cepeda, Macedo, Fischer, & Harris, 1990) and prospective studies (e.g., Farrington, 1997). Low resting heart rate does not appear to interact with social adversity to increase offending. To the contrary, a single study reports that low resting heart rate is related to antisocial behavior only in children with nonadverse circumstances (Raine, Brennan, & Farrington, 1997). One possible explanation is that adverse environmental exposure may increase heart rate reactivity, which has been identified as a second (and independent) predictor of antisocial outcomes of a volatile reactive type (Lorber, 2004).

Sex Hormones

Theoretically, testosterone is a likely candidate factor in antisocial behavior. Both testosterone and antisocial behavior are more concentrated in men than women, and its level increases dramatically across adolescence, coincident with rises in severe violence. In nonhuman animals, the relation between testosterone and aggression has been unequivocally demonstrated through correlational and experimental studies (Turner, 1994). Despite the theoretical appeal, the evidence indicates that testosterone has, at best, a weak correlation with antisocial behavior in humans. Book, Starzyk, and Quinsey (2001) analyzed 45 independent studies that yielded 54 independent effect sizes. Their correlations ranged from .28 to .71, with a weighted mean correlation of .14. One study has examined the interaction between testosterone and environmental context. Rowe, Maughan, Worthman, Costello, and Angold (2004) examined the relations among testosterone, peer deviance, antisocial behavior, and social dominance in a large sample of boys from the Great Smoky Mountains Study and found that levels of testosterone were related to nonaggressive conduct problems, primarily among boys with deviant peers. Among boys with nondeviant peers, levels of testosterone were related to social dominance but not conduct problems.

Neurotransmitters

There is an extensive research literature indicating that the central serotonergic system is involved in the regulation of impulsive aggressive behavior (Herbert & Martinez, 2001). Decreased serotonergic functioning has been found among adults with past histories of aggressive acts including violent offenses and suicide (Asberg, 1994). Specifically, lower concentrations of cerebrospinal fluid (CSF) 5-HIAA, the major metabolite of serotonin, have been found among individuals with past histories of suicide attempts, in violent offenders, in individuals with personality disorders characterized by aggression, and in violent alcoholics (Virkkunen, Eggert, Rawlings, & Linnoila, 1996). Other studies have found opposite results. Castellanos et al. (1994) found that CSF 5-HIAA was positively correlated with aggression in 29 boys with attention-deficit hyperactivity disorder (ADHD). Increased prolactin response to fenfluramine challenge, indicating increased serotonergic activity, was related to increased aggression (Pine et al., 1997). One study examined the interaction between neurotransmitters and environments. Serotonergic activity interacted with a history of family conflict to predict violence at age 21 in the males of the Dunedin study (Moffitt, Caspi, & Fawcett, 1997). The nature of the interaction was such that men with high levels of whole blood serotonin, and therefore low levels of serotonin in the brain, and history of psychosocial adversity were the most violent by both official and self-report.

Other researchers have indexed platelet levels of monoamine oxidase (MAO), which is responsible for metabolizing both serotonin and dopamine. Although MAO activity is an indirect measure, results from studies using it are consistent with studies that have examined serotonin more directly. Low MAO activity in platelets has been shown to be associated with impulsivity, violent crime, and persistent criminality (Alm et al., 1994).

ECOLOGICAL FACTORS AND SOCIAL STRESSORS

As compelling as constitutional and biological factors are in leading to aggressive behavior, ecological factors play just as strong a role, and an even stronger role for certain indicators of aggression. The 600% increase in juvenile murder arrests between 1965 and 1994 (Blumstein, 2000) and wide variations across countries cannot be accounted for by genes and traits. Ecological contexts surely play a major role.

Culture, Laws, and Policies

Firearm homicide rates, including rates for children, are 12 to 16 times higher in the United States than in the average of 25 other industrialized countries, including Canada, simply because of differences in laws that allow gun ownership (U.S. Department of Health and Human Services, 1997). In the United States, children in the five states with the highest levels of gun ownership are three times more likely to die from firearm homicide as are children from the five states with the lowest levels of gun ownership (Miller, Azrael, & Hemenway, 2002).

Community Factors

C. Shaw and McKay (1942) argued that the three community structural variables of poverty, ethnic heterogeneity, and high residential mobility are associated with high violent crime rates that persist across time, even after the entire population in a community changes. Sampson, Raudenbush, and Earls (1997) found large variations in violent behaviors associated with structural characteristics across neighborhoods in Chicago. Neighborhood effects go well beyond structural characteristics to social factors such as disorganization and control. These latter factors have been called *collective efficacy* by Sampson et al. (1997) and are indexed by levels of trust among neighbors, supportive social networks, and the degree to which neighbors "look out for one another." These factors partially mediate the effects of structural factors but also operate independently (Ingoldsby & Shaw, 2002).

A problem in interpretation of neighborhood and community effects is the likelihood of self-migration into neighborhoods by families of varying background characteristics. As Jencks and Mayer (1990) noted, "the most fundamental problem confronting anyone who wants to estimate neighborhoods' effects on children is distinguishing between neighborhood effects and family effects" (p. 119), known as the *omitted variable bias* or *social selection*.

Within-Family Ecological Factors

Neighborhood factors influence a child's development at least partly through their effects on the family unit (McLoyd, 1990), and the family social context exerts its own independent effect on antisocial development.

Socioeconomic Status.   The most important of these factors is low socioeconomic status (SES). Controlling for other community variables, poverty in the family is associated with higher rates of peer-directed aggressive behavior by children (Bradley & Corwyn, 2002) and adults (Sampson & Laub, 1994). The potential problem of selection bias into poverty limits confidence in the causal role that family poverty plays in child conduct problems. Costello, Compton, Keeler, and Angold (2003) capitalized on the natural experiment afforded by a government policy enabling Native American families in western North Carolina to reap the financial benefits of a new casino in their community. Of the previously poor families, those that were suddenly thrust out of poverty (21.3% of all poor families) had children whose behavioral problem symptoms declined by 40%, whereas never-poor children in the same community displayed no change in symptoms across the same period. This finding is consistent with a causal role of family wealth in alleviating these symptoms. In an effort to understand mechanisms, Sampson and Laub (1994) reanalyzed the Glueck and Glueck (1950) longitudinal data set involving 1,000 Depression-era White families and found that the structural variable of family poverty influenced family processes of harsh discipline, low supervision, and poor parent-child attachment, which, in turn, influenced juvenile delinquency and accounted for two-thirds of the effect of poverty on delinquency.

Marital Conflict.   A second major family context factor is marital conflict. Cummings and Davies (2002) found that ambient conflict increases child aggression. The stress of child conduct problems can increase marital conflict, and so the issue of temporal ordering is crucial in understanding the role of this context factor in child behavior. Malone et al. (2004) followed 356 boys and girls across 10 years, as some of their families experienced divorce, and found that for boys (especially younger boys) the experience of parental divorce increased their externalizing problems for several years following divorce. Finally, Jaffee, Moffitt, Caspi, Taylor, and Arseneault (2002) employed a twin research design to find that adult domestic violence accounted for 5% of the variance in child antisocial behavior, even when genetic factors are controlled.

Other Environmental Conditions.   Other early environmental conditions that are associated with increases in children's aggression include being born to a teenage (Morash & Rucker, 1989) or single (Blum, Boyle, & Offord, 1988) parent, being raised in a large family (Rutter, Tizard, & Whitmore, 1970), and being parented by convicted felons (Farrington, 1992). These factors likely share a common pathway through effects on parenting quality. Furthermore, these risk factors are apparently not merely redundant in their impact on the developing child; rather, their effects are cumulative (Rutter & Garmezy, 1983).

Out-of-Home Child Care

The experience of early out-of-home group child care has been posited as a cause of child aggressive behavior (Belsky, 2001). However, families self-select into group child care for a variety of reasons, including attitudes about day care, availability, and ability to pay for other kinds of care (including a parent staying at home). The National Institute of Child Health and Human Development (NICHD) Early Child Care Research Network (2004) study of child care in the United States controlled for many potentially confounding variables and yielded a positive effect size of about one-fourth standard deviation of day-care experience on aggressive behavior at kindergarten as rated by mothers, caregivers, and teachers. Further analyses by Votruba-Drzal, Coley, and Chase-Lansdale (2004) indicated that the effect of group day care depends on the quality of that care. Furthermore, the effect of group care must be interpreted in light of the alternative type of care that is available to a child—the quality of available home-rearing may differ across families such that group day care might offer a better or worse experience for a child than available alternatives.

A Case of Pervasive Environmental Influence: The Effects of Media Violence

Perhaps no greater cultural influence on children's aggressive development can be found than the effects of viewing violence on television. Meta-analyses (Wood, Wong, & Chachere, 1991) indicate that television violence-viewing accounts for about 10% of the variance in child aggression, which approximately equals the magnitude of effect of cigarette smoking on lung cancer.

Field studies repeatedly demonstrate significant correlations between television-violence viewing and aggressiveness, even when self-selection factors, such as parental supervision and socioeconomic status, are controlled. Eron, Huesmann, Lefkowitz, and Walder (1972) found that boys' television-violence preferences at age 8 predicted aggressiveness at age 18. Follow-ups to age 30 showed that age 8 television violence predicted self-reported aggression and seriousness of criminal arrests, even when social class, intelligence, parenting, age 8 aggression, and age 30 TV violence viewing all were controlled statistically (Huesmann, 1986). Huesmann, Moise-Titus, Podolski, and Eron (2003) followed 450 6- to 10-year-old Chicagoan boys and girls for 15 years and found that childhood exposure to television violence predicted a composite adult aggression score, even when early parenting and socioeconomic status were controlled.

Perhaps even more threatening than passive viewing of television violence is the active experience of playing violent video games. C. A. Anderson (2004) has concluded that chronic experience playing video games that reward the shooting of victims increases children's future aggressive behavior.

Processes in Early Family Socialization

There is ample evidence of differences in discipline and parenting practices between families of aggressive children and nonproblem children, but the likelihood that aggressive children elicit higher levels of punitive discipline make a causal interpretation regarding parenting difficult from cross-sectional studies alone. Longitudinal, behavior-genetic, and intervention studies show convincingly the causal role of early family socialization.

Mother-Infant Attachment Relationships

Renken, Egeland, Marvinney, Mangelsdorf, and Sroufe (1989) found that insecure attachments between mother and infant predict childhood behavior problems in a sample from low-income and predominantly single-parent households. D. S. Shaw et al. (1995) found that insecure attachment, particularly disorganized attachment, predicted CBCL aggression scores at age 5. However, Bates, Bayles, Bennett, Ridge, and Brown (1991) failed to establish insecure attachment as a predictor of externalizing problems in a predominantly middle-class, two-parent sample followed from infancy into elementary school. Greenberg, Spelz, and Deklyen (1993) have argued that secure attachment is a protective factor for infants of low-income, highly stressed mothers but is less crucial to antisocial development in middle-class families.

Support for the interaction between parent-infant warmth and a biological factor comes from Raine, Brennan, and Mednick (1997), who found that Danish males with a history of birth complications and early rejection by the mother (unwanted pregnancy, attempt to abort fetus, and public institutional care of the infant) were at high risk for violent crime by age 19. Of children who had both risk factors, 47% became violent, compared to 20% of those who had just one factor. Thus, the strength of the mother-child bond protected children from later violence, but only for high biological-risk children.

Parental Warmth and Proactive Teaching

Closely related to the attachment construct is the concept of maternal warmth. Caspi et al. (2004) used a monozygotic twin study that controls for genetic differences to find that maternal expressed emotion (i.e., verbal statements of negative affect about a child) predicted children's antisocial behavior problems. Deater-Deckard (2000) used identical and fraternal twin pairs to reach the same conclusion. One social-learning explanation for the role of parental warmth is that for a parent to be effective in socializing a child to parental behavior standards, the parent must be seen by the child as a potential source of reward, which occurs through the exchange of warmth. Eisenberg et al. (2001) found support for a second possible mechanism, that parental negative emotion expression directly interferes with the child's normal development of self-regulation and regulation of emotion, which, in turn, mediate the child's development of externalizing problems. Zhou et al. (2002) found support for yet another pathway, that parental warmth leads to the child's development of empathy, which is known to protect a child from aggressive behavior.

Pettit, Bates, and Dodge (1997) have introduced the concept of proactive teaching by parents to indicate their positive attempts to teach their child appropriate behavior to prevent later discipline or conduct problems. They found that this construct is orthogonal to warmth and independently predicts child conduct problems.

Family Coercion and Inconsistent Discipline

In their classic longitudinal study of delinquency, Glueck and Glueck (1950) reported that parents of boys who became delinquent were less consistent in their discipline practices than parents of matched control boys who did not become delinquent. Patterson (Reid, Patterson, & Snyder, 2000) has offered a theory of coercive social learning that goes well beyond inconsistency in parenting as a core feature of antisocial development. Snyder, Reid, and Patterson (2003) describe coercion training as a four-step process that begins with the aversive intrusion of a family member into the child's activities (e.g., a mother may scold her child for not going to bed); followed by the child's counterattack (e.g., by whining, yelling, and complaining). The third step is the crucial one, for it involves the negative reinforcement that increases the likelihood of future aversive responding by the child: The adult stops her scolding and her demands for compliance. At the fourth step, the child stops the counterattack, thus reinforcing the mother's actions. According to this theory, it is the conditional probabilities in this sequence that distinguish the early parenting patterns of antisocial children from those of normal children.

Physical Punishment and Punitiveness

The role of physical punishment in promoting or reducing children's aggressive and antisocial behavior has long been a matter of dispute among professionals and laypersons (Straus, 2005). The practice of spanking children is almost ubiquitous in American culture: 94% of parents of 3- and 4-year-olds use spanking as a discipline technique (Straus & Stewart, 1999). Gershoff's (2002) meta-analysis has revealed a consistent correlation between corporal punishment and child aggressive behavior, although the interpretation of that correlation is still in doubt (Benjet & Kazdin, 2003). Longitudinal investigations have consistently supported the relation between early punishment and later antisocial behavior. Data from the 411 London males of the Cambridge Longitudinal Study (Farrington & Hawkins, 1991) point to harsh discipline practices at age 8 as an important predictor of the early onset of delinquency. Although robust, this correlation is moderated by other factors such as the quality of the parent-child relationship and the degree of parent-child warmth (Campbell, 1990). Deater-Deckard and Dodge (1997) reported that harsh physical discipline was positively correlated with later externalizing problems only among the subset of children who scored below the median in parent-child warmth. Thus, a warm parent-child relationship might buffer a child from deleterious effects of physical punishment.

The cultural context of parenting also moderates the impact of physical punishment. Deater-Deckard, Dodge, Bates, and Pettit (1996) found that physical punishment was positively correlated with later child aggressive behavior among European American families, in which this discipline style occurred relatively rarely. Among African American families, corporal punishment was more common (and normative) and was not correlated with child aggressive outcomes. Rather, it is the message that the child receives during the discipline event. Among European American families in which harsh discipline is nonnormative, for a child who receives harsh discipline, the message may be that the parent is rejecting the child. Among African American families for whom corporal punishment is normative and "good" parenting, the message may be that the parent cares about the child's development.

Abusive Parenting

The distinction between the use of physical punishment and physically abusive parenting is not simply one of degree. With abuse comes out-of-control, emotionally volatile, and nonnormative actions by a caregiver, which appear to have devastating effects on at least some children. Numerous studies have identified the experience of physical abuse as one of the most important parenting factors in antisocial development. Luntz and Widom (1994) found long-term effects of child abuse on antisocial behavior in a 20-year follow-up of children who had been reported as abused or neglected prior to age 11. Compared with control children matched for age, race, sex, and family socioeconomic status, the abused sample had twice the probability of being diagnosed as having an adult antisocial personality disorder. One of the problems with studies using children who have been identified as abused by child protective services (CPS) is that the experience of abuse is confounded with the actions taken by CPS, including being removed from the home, publicly labeled as abused, and aggregated with deviant children in foster and group-home settings. Dodge, Bates, and Pettit (1990) assessed physical maltreatment in a community sample of preschool children through extended clinical interviews and then followed this sample across childhood. They found short-term effects of maltreatment on aggressive behavior in kindergarten and long-term effects through late adolescence that included school suspensions and physical violence (Lansford et al., 2002).

Jaffee, Caspi, Moffitt, and Taylor (2004) studied 1,116 twin pairs in Great Britain and found that physical maltreatment plays a strong causal role in the development of children's antisocial behavior. At ages 5 and 7, mothers' and teachers' scores on the Child Behavior Checklist were .8 standard deviations higher for abused than nonabused children, controlling for genetic and other factors.

Childhood Peer Factors

The peer social context exerts yet another influence on the child's behavioral development. The ratio of peers who are aggressive in a child's classroom influences a child's growing tendency to become aggressive and to value aggression (Stormshak et al., 1999), and these influences last across several years of elementary school (Kellam, Ling, Merisca, Brown, & Ialongo, 1998).

There is substantial evidence that aggressive children are likely to become rejected by their peers (Kupersmidt & Dodge, 2004), but rejection, in turn, seems to exacerbate a child's growth in aggression (Haselager, Cillessen, Hartup, van Lieshout, & Riksen-Walraven, 2002). Dodge et al. (2003) found that rejection increases aggressive behavior, especially among children who are aggressive initially.

Adolescent Family Processes

Two aspects of parenting appear to be critical to controlling child antisocial activity in early adolescence: discipline practices and parental monitoring. Larzelere and Patterson (1990) used structural equation modeling to find that the linkage between family socioeconomic status, as measured when the boys were in fourth grade, and delinquency, measured in seventh grade from police records and self-report, is mediated by parent management practices measured in sixth grade.

Parental monitoring is particularly important in preventing adolescent involvement with deviant peers. Snyder, Dishion, and Patterson (1986) reported strong path relations between low levels of parental monitoring and increases in deviant peer associations in tenth grade. Problems in parental discipline practices (including poor monitoring, harsh discipline, lack of consistency, and ill-defined standards) in seventh grade predict increased deviant peer associations and police arrests and sanctions in ninth grade (Simons, Wu, Conger, & Lorenz, 1994). Not surprisingly, parental monitoring is more important in some circumstances and with some children than others. Positive effects of parental monitoring on keeping antisocial behavior in check were stronger for families living in dangerous neighborhoods than in safe neighborhoods and for children with previous histories of aggressive behavior than nonaggressive children (Pettit, Bates, Dodge, & Meece, 1999). Thus, youth who are at lower risk do not need, or benefit from, close monitoring as much as high-risk youth. This difference helps explain why parents of low-risk youth (and legislators who fund programs) are sometimes unable to grasp the importance of parent-training and supervised after-school programs for high-risk youth.

Several studies have demonstrated that it is difficult to monitor certain youth, especially high-risk antisocial youth who begin to engage in covert activities and learn to hide their deviance from their parents (Crouter & Head, 2002). Furthermore, parent-child conflict is extremely stressful for all parties involved, and monitoring can heighten conflict when the parent confronts the youth with evidence of misbehavior. Not surprisingly, early conduct problems lead to lower levels of parental monitoring in adolescence (Stattin & Kerr, 2000), but low monitoring subsequently increases adolescent delinquency beyond the levels that led to poor monitoring (Laird, Pettit, Bates, & Dodge, 2003).

An important validation of the causal role of parenting practices on adolescent antisocial activity comes from interventions designed to change these practices and reduce antisocial activity. Dishion, Patterson, and Kavanagh (1991) randomly assigned parents of preadolescents at risk for substance abuse to training in contingency management techniques and found significant reductions in teacher ratings of antisocial behavior compared with youth whose families were assigned to placebo control conditions. Of greatest significance for the validation of the causal role of parenting to antisocial behavior was the fact that improvements in behavior correlated significantly, controlling for baseline behavior, with improvements in observed discipline practices.

Adolescent Peer Processes

Whereas in earlier years when the major influence that peers had on antisocial development was to include or exclude a child from social acceptance, during adolescence the chief peer effect comes from the influence of particular kinds of peer groups. Children organize themselves into different peer cliques that have distinctive features (Bagwell, Coie, Terry, Lochman, 2000). Aggressive behavior is the primary factor associated with being a central member of deviant peer cliques. Deviant peer cliques offer both a home to attract like-minded antisocial youth (called homophily) and an opportunity to expand the range and severity of antisocial behaviors. The question of social selection versus social influence again looms as a methodological challenge, but current evidence supports both effects.

Highly visible antisocial peers come to be viewed positively by a large segment of the population during adolescence. Cillessen and Mayeux (2004) documented a general developmental trend for children to move from censuring aggressive peers during elementary school to giving those peers high social status in early adolescence. In turn, deviant peers come to influence other adolescents in a deviant direction, especially when those peers are central to one's peer clique or have stable friendships with a child. Berndt (2002) found that children who had a stable friendship with a deviant peer were at increased risk for growing in their own deviant behavior as they made the transition from elementary to junior high school. Involvement with deviant peers in sixth grade predicted subsequent delinquency even controlling for prior antisocial behavior (Patterson, Reid, & Dishion, 1992).

The relation between association with other deviant youth and delinquent activity is well-established in the literature on gangs. Gang members accelerated their illegal activity during the time they were associated with their gang and decelerated this activity when they left the gang and were not enmeshed in the gang environment (Thornberry, Krohn, Lizotte, & Chard-Wierschem, 1993).

Dishion and Dodge (2006) have proposed a general ecological model of the mechanisms of deviant peer influence that posits mechanisms at multiple levels, beginning with intrapersonal effects of association with deviant peers on cognitive processes of labeling, and stereotype threat. At the interpersonal level, modeling and positive reinforcement of deviant verbal statements during conversations (called *deviancy training*) occur in deviant peer groups, leading to increased deviant statements by a youth. Evidence for more specific social learning from deviant peers comes from analyses by Bayer, Pintoff, and Pozen (2004), who analyzed data from 15,000 juveniles serving sentences in 169 Florida correctional facilities. They used facility fixed effects to find that access to peers in prison who have histories of specific crimes (e.g., burglary, felony drug, or weapon-related) leads to facilitation of later crimes of that very same type. These effects are strongest for adolescents who have had initial experience with that type of crime (suggesting a facilitation effect rather than initial exposure effect) and who are exposed to older adolescents than younger adolescents.

Growing evidence indicates that peer effects on adolescent antisocial behavior occur not only in naturally formed peer groups but also in groups that are formed by government and interventionists. The frightening possibility that well-intentioned interventions can have harmful iatrogenic effects was proposed by Dishion, McCord, and Poulin (1999), with support from the domains of mental health, education, and juvenile justice. In all of these domains, deviant adolescents are routinely aggregated with each other for intervention purposes (e.g., through tracking and special education placement in education, group therapies and group residential homes in mental health, and incarceration and group placements such as boot camps in corrections). These effects provide strong evidence of deviant peer influences because self-selection biases are eliminated through institutional placements.

Cognitive-Emotional Processes as Mediators

A large body of evidence from laboratory, longitudinal, and intervention-experiment studies has accumulated to support the hypotheses that (a) cognitive-emotional processes contribute to antisocial behavioral responding in specific situations, (b) individual differences in cognitive-emotional processes account for a significant proportion of chronic individual differences in aggressive behavior, and (c) cognitive-emotional processes at least partially mediate the effects of socialization on aggressive behavior outcomes. These processes include a variety of constructs from online processing of current social stimuli to latent knowledge structures in memory.

SOCIAL-SITUATIONAL FACTORS THAT ALTER COGNITIVE-EMOTIONAL PROCESSES

One of the most consistent findings from laboratory studies is that provocation leads to retaliatory aggression (Ferguson & Rule, 1988), but the perception of provocation is far more important than the provocation itself in instigating aggression (Dodge, Murphy, & Buchsbaum, 1984). If a child interprets an environmental threat as malevolently intended and foreseeable, that child is likely to retaliate aggressively (Dodge et al., 2003). Environmental factors that facilitate a hostile attribution include information about the provocateur as acting consistently negatively over time, distinctively negatively toward the perceiver, and others consensually interpreting the provocateur's actions similarly (Kelley, 1973). Graham and Hudley (1994) demonstrated that "priming" the perception that others' negative actions are intentional can lead to hostile attributional biases, which, in turn, have been related to aggressive behavioral responses. Many factors influence the probability that a particular stimulus will prime aggressive responses. Aggressive script responses that are laid down in memory with great frequency, drama, and recency are likely to be at the top of the "storage bin" and primed (Wyer & Srull, 1989). Thus, growing up in an environment in which violence is normative will increase the accessibility of aggressive constructs in future situations.

Accessing aggressive behavior from memory is only partly a function of its salience and priming potential; it is also a function of the salience and accessibility of alternatives to aggression, enhanced by modeling. Furthermore, social learning theory stipulates that environments induce aggression by promoting the belief that aggression is normative, morally appropriate, and will lead to desired positive consequences (through reinforcement). According to Bandura (1983), "(In) societies that provide extensive training in aggression, attach prestige to it, and make its use functional, people spend a great deal of time threatening, fighting, maiming, and killing each other" (p. 11).

SOCIAL INFORMATION PROCESSING MODELS

Social information processing models of aggressive behavior were developed to describe at a proximal level how cognitive and emotional processes lead a child to engage in aggressive behavior in a social event (Dodge, 1986). According to current formulations (Dodge & Pettit, 2003), an individual comes to a social situation with a set of neural pathways that have been honed over time through genetic and experiential factors and a history of social experiences that are represented in memory. The individual is presented with a new set of social cues (e.g., peers gently tease a boy on the playground about his ugly shoes) and responds behaviorally as a function of how he or she processes those cues.

The first step of processing is encoding of the cues. Aggressive children are less able than nonaggressive children to recall relevant social cues (Dodge et al., 2003). Aggressive children have also been found to attend selectively to aggressive social cues in a stimulus array more than nonaggressive peers do and have difficulty diverting attention from aggressive cues (Gouze, 1987). Physically abused children (who are at risk for aggression) demonstrate selective attention to angry faces and reduced attention to happy faces (Pollak & Tolley-Schell, 2003).

As cues are encoded, they are interpreted, so the next step is mental representation of the meaning of the cues, particularly with regard to threat and others' intentions. Both biases (e.g., a hostile attributional bias, as dubbed by Nasby, Hayden, & DePaulo, 1979) and errors (e.g., misinterpreting a benign teasing stimulus as malicious) in mental representation could enhance the likelihood of aggressive responding. Positive correlations between hostile attributional biases and aggressive behavior have been found in many school-based samples, including 8- to 12-year-old white American children (Guerra & Slaby, 1989), African American middle school boys (Graham & Hudley, 1994), Latino children (Graham, Hudley, & Williams, 1992), and British 8- to 10-year-old children (Aydin & Markova, 1979). Hostile attributional biases have also been found in aggressive clinical samples, including children with diagnosed disruptive behavior disorders (MacBrayer, Milich, & Hundley, 2003), adolescent offenders (Dodge,

Price, Bachorowski, & Newman, 1990), incarcerated violent offenders (Slaby & Guerra, 1988), and aggressive boys in residential treatment (Nasby et al., 1979). Aggressive children also erroneously interpret hostile intent when the stimuli clearly depict benign intentions (Dodge et al., 1984), and statistical controls indicate that this intention-cue detection deficiency cannot be accounted for by impulsivity (Waldman, 1988) or verbal intelligence (Dodge, Price, et al., 1990). Prospective analyses by Dodge, Pettit, Bates, and Valente (1995) indicate that hostile attributional biases predict growth in aggressive behavior over time. Finally, experimental intervention with aggressive African American boys in which the focus was to reduce hostile attributional tendencies led to decreased aggressive behavior, relative to a control group (Hudley & Graham, 1993).

Once the stimulus is interpreted, a child formulates goals to guide responding. Aggressive behavior has been linked to present-oriented (versus future-oriented) goals (Caprara & Zimbardo, 1996), goals in friendships (Rose & Asher, 1998), less-social goals (Murphy & Eisenberg, 2002), and performance-competitive (rather than relational) goals (Asher & Renshaw, 1981). Taylor and Gabriel (1989) found that aggressive children have difficulty coordinating multiple goals.

The next step in processing is accessing of one or more possible behavioral responses from memory, as in a script (Huesmann, 1988). Shure and Spivack (1980) found that among preschool children, the number of responses that a child generates to hypothetical social problems is inversely related to that child's rate of aggressive behavior. Among children in elementary school, the quality, not quantity, of responses is linked to aggressive problems. Aggressive children generate high proportions of atypical responses (Ladd & Oden, 1979), bribery and affect manipulation responses (Rubin, Moller, & Emptage, 1987), direct physical aggression responses (Dodge et al., 2003), and adult intervention responses (Asher & Renshaw, 1981). They access fewer competent responses, including nonaggressive assertion (Deluty, 1981) and planning responses (Asarnow & Callan, 1985).

Accessing a response does not destine one to that course of action, so the next step of processing is response decision. The individual might evaluate a potential response by its moral acceptability and its instrumental, interpersonal, and intrapersonal outcomes, weight the values of those outcomes, and decide on a course of action. Wilson and Herrnstein (1985) proposed that criminal behavior (and aggression more broadly) involves a rational decision in which the participant considers the expectation of benefits and their probabilities (e.g., peer approval or instrumental gain) versus the expectation of costs and their probabilities (e.g., legal punishment or parental disapproval). Clarke and Cornish (1983) conducted a rational decision analysis of youthful burglary and found that important deciding factors included whether a house was occupied, whether it had a burglar alarm or dog, and whether it reflected affluence. Not surprisingly, Becker (1974) concluded that offenders typically estimate the risk of being caught as very low (whether valid or not); thus, a rational analysis can still lead to risky (and ill-informed) behavior by some individuals. When they are experimentally forced to make evaluations and consider consequences, aggressive children, relative to nonaggressive peers, evaluate aggressive responses as more legitimate (Erdley & Asher, 1998), less morally "bad" (Deluty, 1983), more "friendly" (Crick & Ladd, 1990), and globally more acceptable (Crick & Werner, 1998). They expect more positive instrumental outcomes (Egan, Monson, & Perry, 1998), more positive intrapersonal outcomes (Fontaine, Burks, & Dodge, 2002), fewer negative interpersonal outcomes (Quiggle, Panak, Garber, & Dodge, 1992), and fewer sanctional outcomes (Perry, Perry, & Rasmussen, 1986) for aggressing. One of the mental actions that can occur during decision making has been called moral disengagement by Bandura (2002). Through socialization, most children learn self-restraints on aggressive behavior that involve anticipatory self-censuring and evaluations that aggression will be punished. Bandura (2002) argued that otherwise moral children perform aggressive acts through processes that disengage the usual self-reactions from such conduct.

Finally, the selected response gets transformed into motor and verbal behavior. Skill deficiencies in enacting aggressive responses could inhibit those behaviors, whereas skill deficiencies in enacting competent, nonaggressive alternatives could enhance aggressive responding through default. Socially rejected and aggressive children have been shown to be less competent when asked to enact and role-play nonaggressive socially appropriate behaviors in laboratory settings (Burleson, 1982).

MEDIATION OF LIFE EXPERIENCES THROUGH ACQUIRED PROCESSING PATTERNS

Each of the processing-aggressive behavior correlations previously described is enhanced by considering the situational context, the type of aggressive behavior, and the profile of processing patterns. The correlation between processing and aggressive behavior is stronger in situations than across situations (i.e., processing about teasing events relates more strongly to aggressive behavior in response to teasing than to aggressive behavior in peer group entry situations; Dodge, Pettit, McClaskey, & Brown, 1986). Also, initial processing variables (i.e., encoding and hostile attributions) relate more strongly to reactive anger, whereas later-stage processing variables (i.e., response evaluations) relate more strongly to proactive aggression (Crick & Dodge, 1996). Finally, when profiles are assembled or multiple regression techniques are used, the predictability of aggressive behavior from aggregated processing measures is great (Dodge et al., 1986).

Several studies have found that the effects of adverse life experiences on growth in aggressive behavior are mediated by the child's development of patterns of processing social information. Dodge, Bates, et al. (1990) found that the experience of physical maltreatment is associated with an acquired tendency to become hypervigilant to hostile cues, to attribute hostile intent to others, to access aggressive responses readily, and to evaluate aggressive responses as instrumentally successful. In turn, these social information-processing patterns were found to lead to later aggressive behavior and to account for the effect of maltreatment on aggression in middle school (Dodge et al., 1995). Eisenberg et al. (2003) found that parents' negative expressed emotion influences the child's social adjustment through its mediating effects on the development of self-regulatory processes, including attention focusing, attention shifting, and inhibitory control. Snyder, Stoolmiller, Wilson, and Yamamoto (2003) found that parents' responses to child misbehavior lead to growth in the child's antisocial behavior through the mediating process of children's anger regulation.

LATENT KNOWLEDGE STRUCTURES

Social-cognitive theories in psychology (Bargh, Chaiken, Raymond, & Hymes, 1995) suggest that processing of social cues is guided by latent knowledge structures, variously called schemas and scripts that are stored in memory (Abelson, 1981). These structures are hypothesized to be the evolving representational products of experience, which guide processing of new cues. Huesmann (1998) has hypothesized that early development leads children to represent in memory scripts for aggression that include acceptable antecedents, details of context and action, and likely consequences. Graham and Hudley (1994) employed priming techniques from cognitive-social psychology to ascertain that aggressive children have highly accessible aggressive constructs represented in memory.

Self-concept is a knowledge structure that has been hypothesized to relate to aggression (Harter, 1982). However, despite the speculation of psychodynamic theorists (Keith, 1984) that aggressive children must have miserable self-concepts, empirical assessments have not borne out this hypothesis (Zakriski & Coie, 1996). Unpopular aggressive children received self-concept scores in academic, athletic, appearance, and social competence domains that were as high as those of average peers, even though objective assessments of their competence in these domains indicated otherwise (Hymel, Bowker, & Woody, 1993). Aggressive children appear to blame others rather than themselves for their negative outcomes (Cairns, 1991).

Huesmann (1998) proposed that children's beliefs about consensual social norms influence their aggressive behavior. Guerra, Huesmann, Tolan, Van Acker, and Eron (1995) assessed children's normative beliefs about the consequences of aggressing and found that normative beliefs and endorsement of aggression correlate with aggressive behavior.

Arsenio and Lemerise (2004) proposed that moral development acts as a distal latent knowledge structure to guide more proximal online processing of social information. Chandler (1973) found that aggressive children's social perspective-taking level, scored in terms of Piagetian developmental levels, was lower than their peers. Blasi (1980) reviewed studies testing the relation between moral judgment and moral action and concluded that a majority of these studies supported Kohlberg's (1986) thesis that higher moral reasoning would lead to personal honesty and altruism.

Treatment and Prevention of Antisocial Behavior

The past decade has witnessed an explosion of randomized trials testing interventions to prevent aggressive behavioral development and to treat conduct disorder. Intervention experiments also offer the opportunity to test the hypotheses that conduct problem behavior develops (or is maintained) by one or more of the developmental factors reviewed here and that intervention to alter those developmental factors will indirectly lead to the prevention or reduction of aggressive behavior.

STIMULANT MEDICATION

The success of psychostimulant medication in treating attention deficits (Frick, 2001), coupled with the known association between early biologically based attention deficits (ADHD) and conduct disorder has led to the hypothesis that psychostimulant medication could indirectly reduce conduct problems. The Multimodal Treatment Study of Children with Attention Deficit Hyperactivity Disorder (MTA) is the largest randomized trial test of this hypothesis, albeit with a subgroup of conduct-problem children who have comorbid ADHD. Although psychostimulant treatment (relative to no treatment) was found to be effective in altering attention deficits in this group of 7- to 10-year-olds, by itself it had no substantial impact on oppositional and aggressive behavior (MTA Cooperative Group, 1999).

PARENT-BASED APPROACHES

The bases for most of parent-training interventions are coercion theory by Patterson et al. (1992) and Forehand and McMahon's (1981) behavioral approach. The primary goal of Parent Management Training (PMT) is to alter the pattern of exchanges between parent and child during discipline events so that coercive behavior by each party is extinguished in favor of contingent, consistent, and clear rules that lead to compliance. Rigorous evaluations have proven this approach to be efficacious. "PMT is probably the most well-investigated therapy technique for children and adolescents . . . and has led to marked improvements in child behavior" (Kazdin, 2003, pp. 261–262). A meta-analysis by Serketich and Dumas (1996) yielded a large mean effect size of .86 standard deviations for programs with young children (up to age 10). Hinshaw et al. (2000) found that child disruptive behavior gains in school as a function of randomly assigned treatment could be accounted for by improvements in parenting practices.

For families facing extremely high levels of antisocial behavior in adolescents who are on the verge of incarceration, multisystemic therapy (MST) has proven efficacious (Henggeler, Schoenwald, Bourduin, Rowland, & Cunningham, 1998). It is an intensive home-based approach based on an ecological model of possible individual, family, peer, school, and community risk factors in antisocial behavior. A meta-analysis of 11 outcome studies revealed a mean effect size of .55 in reducing antisocial outcomes (Curtis, Ronan, & Bourduin, 2004).

For antisocial youth who are already in the child welfare system, multidimensional treatment foster care (MTFC) has been developed. In one randomized trial, MTFC boys had significantly lower rates of violent offending in a 24-month follow-up than did group-care youth (Eddy, Whaley, & Chamberlain, 2004). A second trial with adolescent girls found that MTFC girls spent fewer days in locked settings, had fewer parent-reported delinquent behaviors, and showed a trend toward fewer arrests at the 12-month follow-up (Leve & Chamberlain, 2005).

Webster-Stratton (1998) has brought these principles to preventive intervention with high-risk families of preschool-aged children (such as Head Start), with marked short-term success as evaluated by randomized trials. The Triple P-Positive Parenting Program by Sanders, Markie-Dadds, Tully, and Bor (2000) has been adapted for use in universal settings (media), on a selected basis for concerned parents, or in primary care settings, also with success. Olds et al. (1998) made weekly home visits by a nurse-practitioner to high-risk mothers beginning in pregnancy for 3 years. A randomized trial revealed no positive effects on children's conduct problems during elementary school (Kitzman et al., 1997), but, by age 15, 45% of the control group children had been arrested in contrast with just 20% of the intervention group children (Olds et al., 1998). Other home-visiting programs have yielded less favorable long-term effects (Stone, Bendell, & Field, 1988).

SCHOOL-BASED APPROACHES

The largest school-based approach to reducing aggressive behavior is that implemented by Olweus (1993), which involved the distribution of booklets and videos to teachers and parents in all schools in Norway, focusing on targeted parenting and discipline practices to reduce bullying behaviors. Cross-time evaluations suggest positive effects, but this program has not been evaluated by a randomized trial. The most well-known classroom-based approach is the Good Behavior Game (GBG), which is a behavior management program designed to reduce disruptive behavior and promote prosocial behavior by group-level contingencies. When implemented in first grade classrooms in randomized trials, it has proven efficacious in reducing disruptive behavior at both proximal (Ialongo et al., 1999) and distal (Ialongo, Poduska, Werthamer, & Kellam, 2001) time points.

Universally-administered classroom curricula have been developed to teach social-cognitive and social-emotional skills for the purpose of preventing aggressive behavior. Greenberg and Kusche (1993) have found success with their PATHS Program (Providing Alternative Thinking Strategies) in increasing prosocial behavior, and the Conduct Problems Prevention Research Group (1999b) has demonstrated classroom-level success in reducing aggressive behavior with its adaptation of this approach.

SOCIAL-COGNITIVE SKILLS TRAINING

A key component of developmental models of aggressive behavior is the child's social-cognitive skill deficits, including attributional biases, problem solving, and decision making. Graham and Hudley (1993) developed an intervention designed to reduce hostile attributional biases in African American children, with demonstrated short-term success in a randomized trial. Lochman developed the Coping Power Program, which is designed to enhance an array of social-cognitive skills in aggressive fourth- and fifth-grade boys. Lochman and Wells (2004) found positive effects of this program in reducing aggressive behavior as rated by school teachers, which persisted into the following school year, with an effect size of .42. Kazdin (2003) has developed Problem-Solving Skills Training (PSST) and has found success in reducing aggressive behavior in both home and school settings that lasts over 12 months.

COMBINING APPROACHES

In the MTA Study (Hinshaw et al., 2000), a combined program that included both stimulant medication and parent management training yielded more positive effects on child disruptive behavior than either approach alone. Lochman and Wells (2004) found that their child-focused Coping Power program with an enhanced program that added 16 parent-group sessions based on behavioral principles yielded more positive effects on child delinquency than either the child-focused program or a control. Likewise, Kazdin (2003) found that an intervention that combined parent management training with child problem-solving skills training tended to be more effective than either intervention alone. Tremblay, Mâsse, Vitaro, and Dobkin (1995) combined parent management training based on Patterson's principles with social and problem-solving skills training with groups of 7-year-old boys over a 2-year period. In contrast with a randomly assigned control group, by age 12 the intervention group committed fewer burglaries and were in fewer fights.

COMPREHENSIVE APPROACHES TO PREVENTION

Several interventions have gone beyond the simple combination of two approaches toward comprehensive approaches that last multiple years. These approaches tend to have greater and longer-lasting impact.

The Metropolitan Area Child Study (MACS; Metropolitan Area Child Study Research Group, 2002) nested interventions in a research design that contrasted no treatment, a classroom program, a classroom-plus-small-group peer-skills training program, and a classroom-plus-small-group plus family intervention program delivered in grades two and three and/or grades five and six. The peer-group component focused on altering normative beliefs about aggression and improving peer social skills, and the family intervention focused on parenting skills and parent-child communication. Outcome analyses revealed that only the fully combined intervention, when delivered in a community-rich context in the early grades, had a positive effect on reducing peer- and teacher-rated aggression, relative to a randomly assigned control group.

Hawkins, von Cleve, and Catalano (1991) combined parent training in behavior management, teacher training, and child interpersonal cognitive problem-solving skills training with first-grade children in the Social Development Model program. Hawkins, Catalano, Kosterman, Abbott, and Hill (1999) found that the full intervention group (receiving intervention for 6 years from grade one to grade six) reported less violence than a no-treatment control group and an intervention group that received intervention only in grades five and six.

The Conduct Problems Prevention Research Group (CPPRG) designed a 10-year-long intervention that combined family, peer, academic, classroom, and child social-cognitive skill-training components of the developmental model into a cohesive and comprehensive intervention called Fast Track. It was delivered to 445 first-grade children at high risk for adolescent violence and contrasted with a similar number of randomly assigned control-group children. After the 1st year of intervention, compared with the control group, the intervention group displayed higher levels of targeted skills in parenting, social cognition, and reading, and less aggressive behavior (CPPRG, 1999a). These effects on aggressive behavior persisted through third grade (CPPRG, 2002) and held equally well across gender, ethnic, and severity-level groups. Effects persisted through fifth grade, with a 25% reduction in cases that could be classified as clinically deviant (CPPRG, 2004).

Conclusions

PREDICTORS DIFFER ACROSS AGGRESSIVE ACTS, PERSONALITIES, AND PATTERNS

The first conclusion from this review is that it is necessary to distinguish among aggressive acts, aggressive personalities, and aggressive patterns. Aggressive acts are largely situationally and contextually determined. Individual acts of aggression are poorly predicted by heredity, however, stable and cross-situational patterns of aggression are well predicted by individual difference factors like heredity and dispositions. Furthermore, aggressive behavior occurs as a contingent pattern. Developmental studies suggest that life experiences alter a person's behavior in particular contexts for as long as the contextual parameters remain the same.

RISK FACTORS OPERATE IN BIOPSYCHOSOCIAL SYMBIOTIC DEVELOPMENT

Although risk factors cumulate (Rutter, 1989) to predict aggressive behavior, the positive correlation among risk factors suggests that they might share a common origin. Furthermore, a large portion of the variance in aggressive behavior is accounted for by interaction effects among risk factors. Merely cumulating nonredundant risk factors will not exhaustively account for the variation in aggressive behavior; rather, one of the most important findings of the past decade is that risk factors often exert their influence contingently—only in the context of another risk factor. Also, risk factors transact—they reciprocally influence each other across time.

A GENERAL CONSENSUS MODEL OF THE DEVELOPMENT OF AGGRESSIVE BEHAVIOR PATTERNS IS WITHIN REACH

Instead of a haphazard array of risk factors that may cumulate, interact, and transact in unknown ways, a rapidly growing body of theory is developing in the field such that a consensus model of the development of aggressive behavior patterns may well cohere in the next decade. The components of this model include genetic factors, sociocultural contexts, early life experiences (both biological exposures and psychosocial experiences in family and peer domains), middle childhood experiences (in family, peer, and school domains), adolescent experiences (in family, peer, school, and community domains) and transient situational stimuli. The mediating processes of these influences are likely to be intrapersonal, at both neuropsychological and cognitive-emotional levels.

MOST IMPORTANT DISCOVERIES IN THE NEXT DECADE WILL COME FROM STUDIES OF GENE-ENVIRONMENT INTERACTIONS, MODELING OF DEVELOPMENTAL TRAJECTORIES, AND PREVENTION EXPERIMENTS

This chapter points to three areas where the most exciting discoveries are likely to occur in the next decade. First, as technological advances make it easier and less expensive to identify specific genotypes, studies will test the correlation between various genotypes and indices of aggressive behavior and risk factors associated with aggression. These studies are likely to yield important findings if they are completed with samples for which the measurement of the environment is equally precise. It is anticipated that such studies will reveal interaction effects between genotypes and environmental factors. Replicating such findings and integrating them into coherent theories will challenge this field.

Second, methodological advances in the modeling of developmental trajectories and changes in latent classes across time will be applied to longitudinal data sets to reveal patterns in antisocial development, factors that predict trajectories, and life experiences that deflect individuals away from antisocial lives.

Finally, prevention science is maturing at a rapid rate. Randomized clinical trials provide opportunities to test developmental theories. These trials include both large-scale implementations of broad models of multiple risk factors and single-component trials designed to identify specific clinical techniques for achieving behavior change. Evidence is strong that changing parenting behavior and improving social-cognitive skills can alter trajectories of antisocial behavior, supporting the causal role of these factors. Future trials will refine developmental models through the rigor of experiments and will bring the fruits of developmental psychopathology to bear on the crucial problem of violence in children's lives.

References

Abelson, R. P. (1981). The psychological status of the script concept. *American Psychologist, 36,* 715–729.

Achenbach, T. M. (1991). *Manual for the Child Behavior Checklist and 1991 Profile.* Burlington: University of Vermont, Department of Psychiatry.

Alm, P. O., Alm, M., Humble, K., Leppert, J., Sörensen, S., Lidberg, L., et al. (1994). Criminality and platelet monoamine oxidase activity in former juvenile delinquents as adults. *Acta Psychiatrica Scandinavica, 89*(1), 41–45.

Anderson, C. A. (2004). An update on the effects of violent video games. *Journal of Adolescence, 27,* 113–122.

Anderson, D. A. (1999). The aggregate burden of crime. *Journal of Law and Economics, 42,* 611–642.

Arseneault, L., Moffitt, T. E., Capsi, A., Taylor, A., Rijsdijk, F. V., Jaffee, S. R., et al. (2003). Strong genetic effects on cross-situational antisocial behavior among 5-year-old children according to mothers, teachers, examiner-observers, and twins' self reports. *Journal of Child Psychology and Psychiatry, 44,* 832–848.

Arsenio, W. F., & Lemerise, E. A. (2004). Aggression and moral development: Integrating social information processing and moral domain models. *Child Development, 75,* 985–1002.

Asarnow, J. R., & Callan, J. W. (1985). Boys with peer adjustment problems: Social cognitive processes. *Journal of Consulting and Clinical Psychology, 53,* 80–87.

Asberg, M. (1994). Monoamine neurotransmitters in human aggressiveness and violence: A selected review. *Criminal Behaviour and Mental Health, 4*(4), 303–327.

Asher, S. R., & Renshaw, P. D. (1981). Children without friends: Social knowledge and social skill training. In S. R. Asher & J. M. Gottman (Eds.), *The development of children's friendships* (pp. 273–296). Cambridge: Cambridge University Press.

Aydin, O., & Markova, I. (1979). Attribution of popular and unpopular children. *British Journal of Social and Clinical Psychology, 18,* 291–298.

Bagwell, C. L., Coie, J. D., Terry, R. A., & Lochman, J. E. (2000). Peer clique participation in middle childhood: Associations with sociometric status and gender. *Merrill-Palmer Quarterly, 46,* 280–305.

Ball, S. A., Tennen, H., Poling, J. C., Kranzler, H. R., & Rounsaville, B. J. (1997). Personality, temperament, and character dimensions and the DSM-IV personality disorders in substance abusers. *Journal of Abnormal Psychology, 106,* 545–553.

Bandura, A. (1983). Psychological mechanisms of aggression. In R. G. Geen & E. Donnerstein (Eds.), *Aggression: Theoretical and empirical reviews* (pp. 1–24). New York: Academic Press.

Bandura, A. (2002). Selective moral disengagement in the exercise of moral agency. *Journal of Moral Education, 31,* 101–119.

Bargh, J. A., Chaiken, S., Raymond, P., & Hymes, C. (1995). The automatic evaluation effect: Unconditional automatic attitude activation with a pronunciation task. *Journal of Experimental Social Psychology, 31,* 221–232.

Bates, J. E., Bayles, K., Bennett, D. S., Ridge, B., & Brown, M. M. (1991). Origins of externalizing behavior problems at 8 years of age. In D. J. Pepler & K. H. Rubin (Eds.), *The development and treatment of childhood aggression* (pp. 3–120). Hillsdale, NJ: Erlbaum.

Bayer, P., Pintoff, R., & Pozen, D. (2004). *Building criminal capital behind bars: Social learning in juvenile corrections.* Unpublished manuscript, Yale University.

Becker, G. (1974). Crime and punishment: An economic approach. In G. Becker & W. Landes (Eds.), *Essays in the economics of crime and punishment* (pp. 1–54). New York: Macmillan.

Belsky, J. (2001). Emanuel Miller Lecture: Developmental risks (still) associated with early child care. *Journal of Child Psychology and Psychiatry, 42,* 845–859.

Benjet, C., & Kazdin, A. E. (2003). Spanking children: The controversies, findings, and new directions. *Clinical Psychology Review, 23,* 197–224.

Berndt, T. J. (2002). Friendship quality and social development. *Current Directions in Psychological Sciences, 11,* 7–10.

Blasi, A. (1980). Bridging moral cognition and moral action: A critical review of the literature. *Psychological Bulletin, 88,* 1–45.

Blum, H. M., Boyle, M. H., & Offord, D. R. (1988). Single-parent families: Child psychiatric disorder and school performance. *Journal of the American Academy of Child and Adolescent Psychiatry, 27,* 214–219.

Blumstein, A. (2000). Disaggregating the violence trends. In A. Blumstein & J. Wallman (Eds.), *The crime drop in America* (pp. 13–44). New York: Cambridge University Press.

Blumstein, A., & Cohen, J. (1987). Characterizing criminal careers. *Science, 237,* 985–991.

Book, A. S., Starzyk, K. B., & Quinsey, V. L. (2001). The relationship between testosterone and aggression: A meta-analysis. *Aggression and Violent Behavior, 6*(6), 579–599.

Bradley, R. H., & Corwyn, R. F. (2002). Socioeconomic status and child development. *Annual Review of Psychology, 53*(1), 371–399.

Brennan, P., Grekin, E. R., & Mednick, S. A. (1999). Maternal smoking during pregnancy and adult male criminal outcomes. *Archives of General Psychiatry, 56,* 215–219.

Brennan, P., Mednick, S. A., & Raine, A. (1997). Biosocial interactions and violence: A focus on perinatal factors. In A. Raine, P. Brennan, D. P. Farrington, & S. A. Mednick (Eds.), *Biosocial bases of violence* (pp. 163–174). New York: Plenum Press.

Burleson, B. R. (1982). The development of communication skills in childhood and adolescence. *Child Development, 53,* 1578–1588.

Cairns, R. B. (1979). *Social development: The origins and plasticity of interchanges.* San Francisco: Freeman.

Cairns, R. B. (1991). Multiple metaphors for a singular idea. *Developmental Psychology, 27,* 23–26.

Campbell, S. B. (1990). *Behavior problems in preschool children: Clinical and developmental issues.* New York: Guilford Press.

Caprara, G. V., & Zimbardo, P. G. (1996). Aggregation and amplification of marginal deviations in the social construction of personality and maladjustment. *European Journal of Personality, 10,* 79–110.

Caspi, A., McClay, J., Moffitt, T. E., Mill, J., Martin, J., Craig, I. W., et al. (2002). Role of genotype in the cycle of violence in maltreated children. *Science, 297,* 851–854.

Caspi, A., Moffitt, T. E., Silva, P. A., Stouthamer-Loeber, M., Krueger, F. F., & Schmutte, P. S. (1994). Are some people crime-prone? Replications of the personality-crime relationship across countries, genders, races, and methods. *Criminology, 32,* 163–195.

Caspi, A., Moffitt, T. E., Morgan, J., Rutter, M., Taylor, A., Arseneault, L., et al. (2004). Maternal expressed emotion predicts children's antisocial behavior: Using MZ-twin differences to identify environmental effects on behavioral development. *Developmental Psychology, 40,* 149–161.

Castellanos, F. X., Elia, J., Kruesi, M. J., Gulotta, C. S., Mefford, I. N., Potter, W. Z., et al. (1994). Cerebrospinal fluid monoamine metabolites in boys with attention deficit hyperactivity disorder. *Psychiatry Research, 52*(3), 305–316.

Chandler, M. J. (1973). Egocentrism and antisocial behavior: The assessment and training of social perspective-taking skills. *Developmental Psychology, 9,* 326–332.

Cillessen, A. H. N., & Mayeux, L. (2004). From censure to reinforcement: Developmental changes in the association between aggression and social status. *Child Development, 75,* 147–163.

Clarke, R. V., & Cornish, D. B. (1983). *Crime control in Britain: A review of policy research.* Albany: State University of New York Press.

Cloninger, C. R., Sigvardsson, S., Bohman, M., & van Knoring, A. L. (1982). Predisposition to petty criminality in Swedish adoptees: Pt. 2. Cross-fostering analyses of gene-environmental interactions. *Archives of General Psychiatry, 39,* 1242–1247.

Cohen, M. A. (2005). *The costs of crime and justice.* New York, NY: Routledge.

Cohen, M. A., Rust, R., Steen, S., & Tidd, S. (2004, February). Willingness-to-pay for Crime Control Programs. *Criminology, 42*(1), 86–106.

Coie, J. D. (2004). The impact of negative social experiences on the development of antisocial behavior. In J. B. Kupersmidt & K. A. Dodge (Eds.), *Children's peer relations: From development to intervention* (pp. 243–267). Washington, DC: American Psychological Association.

Coie, J. D., Cillessen, A., Dodge, K. A., Hubbard, J., Schwartz, D., Lemerise, E., et al. (1999). It takes two to fight: A test of relational factors and a method for assessing aggressive dyads. *Developmental Psychology, 35,* 1179–1185.

Coie, J. D., Terry, R., Zakriski, A., & Lochman, J. E. (1995). Early adolescent social influences on delinquent behavior. In J. McCord (Ed.), *Coercion and punishment in long-term perspectives* (pp. 229–244). New York: Cambridge University Press.

Conduct Problems Prevention Research Group. (1999a). Initial impact of the Fast Track prevention trial for conduct problems: Pt. 1. The high-risk sample. *Journal of Consulting and Clinical Psychology, 67,* 631–647.

Conduct Problems Prevention Research Group. (1999b). Initial impact of the Fast Track prevention trial for conduct problems: Pt. 2. Classroom effects. *Journal of Consulting and Clinical Psychology, 67,* 648–657.

Conduct Problems Prevention Research Group. (2002). Evaluation of the first 3 years of the Fast Track prevention trial with children at high risk for adolescent conduct problems. *Journal of Abnormal Child Psychology, 30,* 19–35.

Conduct Problems Prevention Research Group. (2004). The effects of the Fast Track program on serious problem outcomes at the end of elementary school. *Journal of Clinical Child and Adolescent Psychology, 33,* 650–661.

Coon, H., Carey, G., Corley, R., & Fulker, D. W. (1992). Identifying children in the Colorado Adoption Project at risk for conduct disorder. *Journal of the American Academy of Child and Adolescent Psychiatry, 31,* 503–511.

Corrado, R. R., Vincent, G. M., Hart, S. D., & Cohen, I. M. (2004). Predictive validity of the Psychopathy Checklist: Youth version for general and violent recidivism. *Behavioral Sciences and the Law, 22*(1), 5–22.

Costello, E. J., Compton, S. N., Keeler, G., & Angold, A. (2003). Relationships between poverty and psychopathology: A natural experiment. *Journal of the American Medical Association, 290,* 2023–2029.

Crick, N. R., & Bigbee, M. A. (1998). Relational and overt forms of peer victimization: A multi-informant approach. *Journal of Consulting and Clinical Psychology, 66,* 610–617.

Crick, N. R., & Dodge, K. A. (1996). Social-information-processing mechanisms in reactive and proactive aggression. *Child Development, 67,* 993–1002.

Crick, N. R., & Grotpeter, J. K. (1995). Relational aggression, gender, and social-psychological adjustment. *Child Development, 66,* 710–722.

Crick, N. R., & Ladd, G. W. (1990). Children's perceptions of the outcomes of aggressive strategies: Do the ends justify being mean? *Developmental Psychology, 26,* 612–620.

Crick, N. R., & Werner, N. (1998). Response decision processes in relational and overt aggression. *Child Development, 69,* 1630–1639.

Crick, N. R., & Zahn-Waxler, C. (2003). The development of psychopathology in females and males: Current progress and future challenges. *Development and Psychopathology, 15,* 719–742.

Crouter, A. C., & Head, M. R. (2002). Parental monitoring and knowledge of children. In M. Bornstein (Ed.), *Handbook on parenting* (2nd ed.). Mahwah, NJ: Erlbaum.

Cummings, E. M., & Davies, P. T. (2002). Effects of marital conflict on children: Recent advances and emerging themes in process-oriented research. *Journal of Child Psychology and Psychiatry and Allied Disciplines, 43,* 31–63.

Curtis, N. M., Ronan, K. R., & Bourduin, C. M. (2004). Multisystemic treatment: A meta-analysis of outcome studies. *Journal of Family Psychology, 18,* 411–419.

Deater-Deckard, K. (2000). Parenting and child behavioral adjustment in early childhood: A quantitative genetic approach to studying family processes. *Child Development, 71,* 468–484.

Deater-Deckard, K., & Dodge, K. A. (1997). Externalizing behavior problems and discipline revisited: Nonlinear effects and variation by culture, context, and gender. *Psychological Inquiry, 8,* 161–175.

Deater-Deckard, K., Dodge, K. A., Bates, J. E., & Pettit, G. S. (1996). Physical discipline among African-American and European-American mothers: Links to children's externalizing behaviors. *Developmental Psychology, 32,* 1065–1072.

Deluty, R. H. (1981). Alternative-thinking ability of aggressive, assertive, and submissive children. *Cognitive Therapy and Research, 5*, 309–312.

Deluty, R. H. (1983). Children's evaluations of aggressive, assertive, and submissive responses. *Journal of Clinical Child Psychology, 12*, 124–129.

Dishion, T. J., & Dodge, K. A. (2006). Deviant peer contagion within interventions and programs: An ecological framework for understanding influence mechanisms. In K. A. Dodge & T. J. Dishion (Eds.), *Deviant peer contagion in therapeutic interventions: From documentation to policy* (pp. 14–43). New York: Guilford Press.

Dishion, T. J., McCord, J., & Poulin, F. (1999). When interventions harm: Peer groups and problem behavior. *American Psychologist, 54*(9), 1–10.

Dishion, T. J., Patterson, G. R., & Kavanagh, K. (1991). An experimental test of the coercion model: Linking theory, measurement, and intervention. In J. McCord & R. Tremblay (Eds.), *Preventing antisocial behavior: Interventions from birth through adolescence* (pp. 253–282). New York: Guilford Press.

Dodge, K. A. (1986). A social information processing model of social competence in children. In M. Perlmutter (Ed.), *Minnesota Symposia on Child Psychology* (Vol. 18, pp. 77–125). Hillsdale, NJ: Erlbaum.

Dodge, K. A., Bates, J. E., & Pettit, G. S. (1990). Mechanisms in the cycle of violence. *Science, 250*, 1678–1683.

Dodge, K. A., Lansford, J. E., Burks, V. S., Bates, J. E., Pettit, G. S., Fontaine, R., et al. (2003). Peer rejection and social information-processing factors in the development of aggressive behavior problems in children. *Child Development, 74*, 374–393.

Dodge, K. A., Murphy, R. R., & Buchsbaum, K. (1984). The assessment of intention-cue detection skills in children: Implications for developmental psychopathology [Special issue]. *Child Development, 55*, 163–173.

Dodge, K. A., & Pettit, G. S. (2003). A biophychosocial model of the development of chronic conduct problems in adolescence. *Developmental Psychology, 39*(2), 349–371.

Dodge, K. A., Pettit, G. S., Bates, J. E., & Valente, E. (1995). Social information-processing patterns partially mediate the effect of early physical abuse on later conduct problems. *Journal of Abnormal Psychology, 104*, 632–643.

Dodge, K. A., Pettit, G. S., McClaskey, C. L., & Brown, M. (1986). Social competence in children. *Monographs of the Society for Research in Child Development, 51*(2, Serial No. 213).

Dodge, K. A., Price, J. M., Bachorowski, J. A., & Newman, J. P. (1990). Hostile attributional biases in severely aggressive adolescents. *Journal of Abnormal Psychology, 99*, 385–392.

Dryfoos, J. G. (1990). *Adolescents at risk: Prevalence and prevention.* New York: Oxford University Press.

Dunne, M., Martin, N., Statham, D., Slutske, W., Dinwiddie, S., Bucholz, K., et al. (1997). Genetic and environmental contributions to variance in age at first sexual intercourse. *Psychological Science, 8*, 211–216.

Eddy, J. M., Whaley, R. B., & Chamberlain, P. (2004). The prevention of violent behavior by chronic and serious male juvenile offenders: A 2-year follow-up of a randomized clinical trial. *Journal of Emotional and Behavioral Disorders, 12*, 2–8.

Egan, S., Monson, T., & Perry, D. (1998). Social-cognitive influences on change in aggression over time. *Developmental Psychology, 34*, 996–1006.

Eisenberg, N., Cumberland, A., Spinrad, T. L., Fabes, R. A., Shepard, S. A., Reiser, M., et al. (2001). The relations of regulation and emotionality to children's externalizing and internalizing problem behavior. *Development and Psychopathology, 72*, 1112–1134.

Eisenberg, N., Spinrad, T. L., Fabes, R. A., Reiser, M., Cumberland, A., Shepard, S. A., et al. (2004). The relations of effortful control and impulsivity to children's resiliency and adjustment. *Child Development, 75*, 1–22.

Eisenberg, N., Valiente, C., Morris, A. S., Fabes, R. A., Cumberland, A., Reiser, M., et al. (2003). Longitudinal relations among parental emotional expressivity, children's regulation, and quality of socioemotional functioning. *Developmental Psychology, 39*, 3–19.

Elliott, D. S. (1994). Serious violent offenders: Onset, developmental course, and termination—The American Society of Criminology 1993 Presidential Address. *Criminology, 32,* 1–21.

Erdley, C., & Asher, S. (1998). Linkages between children's beliefs about the legitimacy of aggression and their behavior. *Social Development, 7,* 321–339.

Eron, L. D., Huesmann, L. R., Lefkowitz, M. M., & Walder, L. O. (1972). Does television violence cause aggression? *American Psychologist, 27,* 253–263.

Espelage, D. L., Holt, M. K., & Henkel, R. R. (2003). Examination of peer-group contextual effects on aggression during early adolescence. *Child Development, 74,* 205–220.

Farrington, D. P. (1992). Juvenile delinquency. In J. C. Coleman (Ed.), *The school years* (2nd ed., pp. 123–163). London: Routledge & Kegan Paul.

Farrington, D. P. (1997). The relationship between low resting heart rate and violence. In A. Raine, P. A. Brennan, D. P. Farrington, & S. A. Mednick (Eds.), *Biosocial bases of violence* (pp. 89–106). New York: Plenum Press.

Farrington, D. P., & Hawkins, J. D. (1991). Predicting participation, early onset and later persistence in officially recorded offending. *Criminal Behavior and Mental Health, 1,* 1–33.

Ferguson, T., & Rule, B. (1988). Children's evaluations of retaliatory aggression. *Child Development, 59,* 961–968.

Fergusson, D. M., Woodward, L. J., & Horwood, J. (1998). Maternal smoking during pregnancy and psychiatric adjustment in late adolescence. *Archives of General Psychiatry, 55,* 721–727.

Foley, D. L., Eaves, L. J., Wormley, B., Silberg, J., Maes, H., Kuhn, J., et al. (2004). Childhood adversity, monoamine oxidase A genotype, and risk for conduct disorder. *Archives of General Psychiatry, 61,* 738–744.

Fontaine, R. G., Burks, V. S., & Dodge, K. A. (2002). Response decision processes and externalizing behavior problems in adolescents. *Development and Psychopathology, 14,* 107–122.

Forehand, R., & McMahon, R. (1981). *The noncompliant child.* New York: Guilford Press.

Frick, P. J. (2001). Effective interventions for children and adolescents with conduct disorder. *Canadian Journal of Psychiatry, 46,* 597–608.

Frick, P. J., Lahey, B. B., Loeber, R., Tannenbaum, L., Van Horn, Y., & Christ, M. A. G. (1993). Oppositional defiant disorder and conduct disorder: Pt. 1. Meta-analytic review of factor analyses. *Clinical Psychology Review, 13,* 319–340.

Frijda, N. (1986). *The emotions.* New York: Cambridge University Press.

Gelman, R., & Baillargeon, R. (1983). A review of some Piagetian concepts. In P. H. Mussen (Series Ed.) & J. H. Flavell & E. M. Markman (Vol. Eds.), *Handbook of child psychology: Vol. 3. Cognitive development* (4th ed., pp. 167–230). New York: Wiley.

Gershoff, E. T. (2002). Parental corporal punishment and associated child behaviors and experiences: A meta-analytic and theoretical review. *Psychological Bulletin, 128,* 539–579.

Glueck, S., & Glueck, E. (1950). *Unraveling juvenile delinquency.* Cambridge, MA: Harvard University Press.

Gouze, K. R. (1987). Attention and social problem solving as correlates of aggression in preschool males. *Journal of Abnormal Child Psychology, 15,* 181–197.

Graham, S., & Hudley, C. (1993). An attributional intervention to reduce peer-directed aggression among African-American boys. *Child Development, 64,* 124–138.

Graham, S., & Hudley, C. (1994). Attributions of aggressive and nonaggressive African-American male early adolescents: A study of construct accessibility. *Developmental Psychology, 30,* 365–373.

Graham, S., Hudley, C., & Williams, E. (1992). Attributional and emotional determinants of aggression among African-American and Latino young adolescents. *Developmental Psychology, 28,* 731–740.

Greenberg, M. T., & Kusche, C. A. (1993). *Promoting social and emotional development in deaf children: The PATHS Project.* Seattle: University of Washington Press.

Greenberg, M. T., Spelz, M. L., & Deklyen, M. (1993). The role of attachment in the early development of disruptive behavior problems. *Development and Psychopathology, 5,* 191–213.

Guerra, N. G., Huesmann, L. R., Tolan, P. H., Van Acker, R., & Eron, L. D. (1995). Stressful events and individual beliefs as correlates of economic disadvantage and aggression among urban children. *Journal of Consulting and Clinical Psychology, 63,* 518–528.

Guerra, N. G., & Slaby, R. G. (1989). Evaluative factors in social problem solving by aggressive boys. *Journal of Abnormal Child Psychology, 17,* 277–289.

Hare, R. D. (2003). *The Hare PCL-R* (2nd ed.). Toronto, Ontario, Canada: Multi-Health Systems.

Harter, S. (1982). The perceived competence scale for children. *Child Development, 53,* 89–97.

Haselager, G. J. T., Cillessen, A. H. N., Hartup, W. W., van Lieshout, C. F. M., & Riksen-Walraven, J. M. A. (2002). Heterogeneity among peer rejected boys across middle childhood: Developmental pathways of social behavior. *Developmental Psychology, 38,* 446–456.

Hawkins, J. D., Catalano, R. F., Kosterman, R., Abbott, R., & Hill, K. G. (1999). Preventing adolescent health-risk behaviors by strengthening protection during childhood. *Archives of Paediatrics and Adolescent Medicine, 153,* 226–234.

Hawkins, J. D., von Cleve, E., & Catalano, R. F. (1991). Reducing early childhood aggression: Results of a primary prevention programme. *Journal of the American Academy of Child and Adolescent Psychiatry, 30,* 208–217.

Henggeler, S. W., Schoenwald, S. K., Bourduin, C. M., Rowland, M. D., & Cunningham, P. B. (1998). *Multisystemic treatment of antisocial behavior in children and adolescents.* New York: Guilford Press.

Herbert, J., & Martinez, M. (2001). Neural mechanisms underlying aggressive behavior. In J. Hill & B. Maughan (Eds.), *Conduct disorders in childhood and adolescence* (pp. 43–67). Cambridge: Cambridge University Press.

Hinshaw, S. P., Owens, E. B., Wells, K. C., Kraemer, H. C., Abikoff, H. B., Arnold, L. E., et al. (2000). Family processes and treatment outcome in the MTA: Negative/ineffective parenting practices in relation to multimodal treatment. *Journal of Abnormal Child Psychology, 28,* 555–568.

Howell, J. C., Krisberg, B., & Jones, M. (1995). Trends in juvenile crime and youth violence. In J. C. Howell, B. Krisberg, J. D. Hawkins, & J. J. Wilson (Eds.), *Serious, violent, and chronic juvenile offenders* (pp. 1–35). Thousand Oaks, CA: Sage.

Hubbard, J. A., Dodge, K. A., Cillessen, A. H. N., Coie, J. D., & Schwartz D. (2001). The dyadic nature of social information-processing in boys' reactive and proactive aggression. *Journal of Personality and Social Psychology, 80*(2), 268–280.

Hudley, C. A., & Graham, S. (1993). An attributional intervention to reduce peer-directed aggression among African-American boys. *Child Development, 64,* 124–138.

Huesmann, L. R. (1986). Psychological processes promoting the relation between exposure to media violence and aggressive behavior by the viewer. *Journal of Social Issues, 42,* 125–139.

Huesmann, L. R. (1988). An information-processing model for the development of aggression. *Aggressive Behavior, 14,* 13–24.

Huesmann, L. R. (1998). The role of social information processing and cognitive schema in the acquisition and maintenance of habitual aggressive behavior. In R. Green & E. Donnerstein (Eds.), *Human aggression: Theories, research, and implications for social policy* (pp. 73–109). New York: Academic Press.

Huesmann, L. R., Moise-Titus, J., Podolski, C., & Eron, L. D. (2003). Longitudinal relations between children's exposure to TV violence and their aggressive and violent behavior in young adulthood: 1977–1992. *Developmental Psychology, 39,* 201–221.

Hymel, S., Bowker, A., & Woody, & E. (1993). Aggressive versus withdrawn unpopular children: Variations in peer and self-perceptions in multiple domains. *Child Development, 64,* 879–896.

Ialongo, N., Poduska, J., Werthamer, L., & Kellam, S. (2001). The distal impact of two first-grade preventive interventions on conduct problems and disorder in early adolescence. *Journal of Emotional and Behavioral Disorders, 9,* 146–160.

Ialongo, N., Werthamer, L., Kellam, S. G., Brown, C. H., Wang, S., & Lin, Y. (1999). Proximal impact of two first-grade preventive interventions on the early risk behaviors for later substance abuse, depression, and antisocial behavior. *American Journal of Community Psychology, 27,* 599–641.

Ingoldsby, E. M., & Shaw, D. S. (2002). Neighborhood contextual factors and early-starting antisocial pathways. *Clinical Child and Family Psychology Review, 5,* 21–55.

Jaffee, S. R., Caspi, A., Moffitt, T. E., Dodge, K. A., Rutter, M., Taylor, A., et al. (2005). Nature x nurture: Genetic vulnerabilities interact with physical maltreatment to promote conduct problems. *Development and Psychopathology, 17,* 67–84.

Jaffee, S. R., Caspi, A., Moffitt, T. E., & Taylor, A. (2004). Physical maltreatment victim to antisocial child: Evidence of an environmentally mediated process. *Journal of Abnormal Psychology, 113*(1), 44–55.

Jaffee, S. R., Moffitt, T. E., Caspi, A., Taylor, A., & Arseneault, L. (2002). Influence of adult domestic violence on children's internalizing and externalizing problems: An environmentally informative twin study. *Journal of the American Academy of Child and Adolescent Psychiatry, 41,* 1095–1103.

Jencks, C., & Mayer, S. E. (1990). The social consequences of growing up in a poor neighborhood. In L. E. Lynn & M. McGeary (Eds.), *Inner-city poverty in the United States* (pp. 117–135). Washington, DC: National Academy Press.

Kaukiainen, A., Bjorkqvist, K., Lagerspetz, K., Osterman, K., Salmivalli, C., Rothberg, S., et al. (1999). The relationship between social intelligence, empathy, and three types of aggression. *Aggressive Behavior, 25,* 81–89.

Kazdin, A. E. (2003). Problem-solving skills training and parent management training for conduct disorder. In A. E. Kazdin & J. R. Weisz (Eds.), *Evidence-based psychotherapies for children and adolescents* (pp. 241–262). New York: Guilford Press.

Keenan, K., & Shaw, D. S. (2003). Starting at the beginning: Exploring the etiology of antisocial behavior in the first years of life. In B. B. Lahey, T. E. Moffitt, & A. Caspi (Eds.), *Causes of conduct disorder and juvenile delinquency* (pp. 153–181). New York: Guilford Press.

Keenan, K., Shaw, D. S., Delliquadri, E., Giovanelli, J., & Walsh, B. (1998). Evidence for the continuity of early problem behaviors: Application of a developmental model. *Journal of Abnormal Child Psychology, 26,* 441–452.

Keith, C. R. (Ed.). (1984). *The aggressive adolescent: Clinical perspectives.* New York: Free Press.

Kellam, S., Ling, X., Merisca, R., Brown, C. H., & Ialongo, N. (1998). The effect of the level of aggression in the first grade classroom on the course and malleability of aggressive behavior into middle school. *Development and Psychopathology, 10,* 165–185.

Kelley, H. H. (1973). The processes of causal attribution. *American Psychologist, 28,* 107–128.

Kitzman, H., Olds, D. L., Henderson, C. R., Hanks, C., Cole, R., Tatelbaum, R., et al. (1997). Effect of prenatal and infancy home visitation by nurses on pregnancy outcomes, childhood injuries, and repeated childbearing: A randomized controlled trial. *Journal of the American Medical Association, 278,* 644–652.

Kochanska, G. (1997). Multiple pathways to conscience for children with different temperaments: From toddlerhood to age 5. *Developmental Psychology, 33,* 228–240.

Kohlberg, L. (1986). *The philosophy of moral development.* San Francisco: Harper & Row.

Kosson, D. S., Cyterski, T. D., Steuerwald, B. L., Neumann, C. S., & Walker-Matthews, S. (2002). The reliability and validity of the Psychopathy Checklist: Youth Version (PCL:YV) in nonincarcerated adolescent males. *Psychological Assessment, 14*(1), 97–109.

Krueger, R. F., Caspi, A., Moffitt, T. E., White, J., & Stouthamer-Loeber, M. (1996). Delay of gratification, psychopathology, and personality: Is low self-control specific to externalizing problems? *Journal of Personality, 64,* 107–129.

Kupersmidt, J., & Dodge, K. A. (Eds.). (2004). *Children's peer relations: From development to intervention to policy—A festschrift to honor John D. Coie.* Washington, DC: American Psychological Association.

Ladd, G. W., & Oden, S. (1979). The relationship between peer acceptance and children's ideas about helpfulness. *Child Development, 50,* 402–408.

Lahey, B. B., Loeber, R., Hart, E. L., Frick, P. J., Applegate, B., Zhang, Q., et al. (1995). Four-year longitudinal study of conduct disorder in boys: Patterns and predictors of persistence. *Journal of Abnormal Psychology, 104,* 83–93.

Laird, R. D., Pettit, G. S., Bates, J. E., & Dodge, K. A. (2003). Parents' monitoring-relevant knowledge and adolescents' delinquent behavior: Evidence of correlated developmental changes and reciprocal influences. *Child Development, 74,* 752–768.

Lansford, J. E., Dodge, K. A., Pettit, G. S., Bates, J. E., Crozier, J., & Kaplow, J. (2002). A 12-year prospective study of the long-term effects of early child physical maltreatment on psychological, behavioral, and academic problems in adolescence. *Archives of Pediatrics and Adolescent Medicine, 156,* 824–830.

Larzelere, R. E., & Patterson, G. R. (1990). Parental management: Mediators of the effect of socioeconomic status on early delinquency. *Criminology, 28,* 301–323.

Leve, L. D., & Chamberlain, P. (2005). Intervention outcomes for girls referred from Juvenile Justice: Effects on delinquency. *Journal of Abnormal Child Psychology, 33,* 339–347.

Little, T. D., Jones, S. M., Henrich, C. C., & Hawley, P. H. (2003). Disentangling the "whys" from the "whats" of aggressive behavior. *International Journal of Behavioral Development, 27,* 122–133.

Lochman, J. E., & Wells, K. C. (2004). The coping power program for preadolescent aggressive boys and their parents: Outcome effects at the 1-year follow-up. *Journal of Consulting and Clinical Psychology, 72,* 571–578.

Loeber, R., Farrington, D. P., Stouthamer-Loeber, M., & van Kammen, W. B. (1998). *Antisocial behavior and mental health problems: Explanatory factors in childhood and adolescence.* Mahwah, NJ: Erlbaum.

Lorber, M. F. (2004). Psychophysiology of aggression, psychopathy, and conduct problems: A meta-analysis. *Psychological Bulletin, 130*(4), 531–552.

Lorenz, K. (1966). *On aggression.* New York: Harcourt.

Luntz, B. K., & Widom, C. S. (1994). Antisocial personality disorders in abused and neglected children grown up. *American Journal of Psychiatry, 151,* 670–674.

Lynam, D. R. (1997). Pursuing the psychopath: Capturing the fledgling psychopath in a nomological net. *Journal of Abnormal Psychology, 106*(3), 425–438.

Lynam, D. R., & Henry, B. (2001). The role of neuropsychological deficits in conduct disorders. In J. Hill & B. Maughan (Eds.), *Conduct disorders in childhood and adolescence* (pp. 235–263). New York: Cambridge University Press.

Lyoo, I. K., Lee, H. K., Jung, J. H., Noam, G. G., & Renshaw, P. F. (2002). White matter hyperintensities on magnetic resonance imaging of the brain in children with psychiatric disorders. *Comprehensive Psychiatry, 43,* 361–368.

MacBrayer, E. K., Milich, R., & Hundley, M. (2003). Attributional biases in aggressive children and their mothers. *Journal of Abnormal Psychology, 112,* 698–708.

Malone, P. S., Lansford, J. E., Castellino, D. R., Berlin, L. J., Dodge, K. A., Bates, J. E., et al. (2004). Divorce and child behavior problems: Applying latent change score models to life event data. *Structural Equation Modeling, 11*(3), 401–423.

Maughan, B., Taylor, A., Caspi, A., & Moffitt, T. E. (2004). Prenatal smoking and early childhood conduct problems. *Archives of General Psychiatry, 61,* 836–843.

McLoyd, V. (1990). The impact of economic hardship on black families and children: Psychological distress, parenting, and socioemotional development. *Child Development, 61,* 311–346.

Mednick, S. A., & Christiansen, K. O. (1977). *Biosocial bases of criminal behavior.* Oxford, England: Gardner Press.

Metropolitan Area Child Study Research Group. (2002). A cognitive-ecological approach to preventing aggression in urban settings: Initial outcomes for high-risk children. *Journal of Consulting and Clinical Psychology, 70,* 179–194.

Miller, M., Azrael, D., & Hemenway, D. (2002). Firearm availability and unintentional firearm deaths, suicide, and homicide among 5- to 14-year-olds. *Journal of Trauma—Injury, Infection, and Critical Care, 52,* 267–275.

Miller-Johnson, S., & Costanzo, P. (2004). If you can't beat 'em . . . Induce them to join you: Peer-based interventions during adolescence. In J. Kupersmidt & K. A. Dodge (Eds.), *Children's peer relations: From development to intervention* (pp. 209–222). Washington, DC: American Psychological Association.

Mischel, W. (1974). Processes in delay of gratification. In L. Berkowitz (Ed.), *Advances in experimental social psychology* (Vol. 7, pp. 249–292). New York: Academic Press.

Moffitt, T. E. (1990). Juvenile delinquency and attention deficit disorders: Boys' developmental trajectories from age 3 to age 15. *Child Development, 61,* 893–910.

Moffitt, T. E. (1993). Adolescence-limited and life-course-persistent antisocial behavior: A development taxonomy. *Psychological Review, 100,* 674–701.

Moffitt, T. E., Caspi, A., & Fawcett, P. (1997). Whole blood serotonin and family background relate to male violence. In A. Raine, P. A. Brennan, D. P. Farrington, & S. A. Mednick (Eds.), *Biosocial bases of violence* (pp. 321–340). New York: Plenum Press.

Morash, M., & Rucker, L. (1989). An exploratory study of the connection of mother's age at child-bearing to her children's delinquency in four data sets. *Crime and Delinquency, 35,* 45–93.

Multimodal Treatment for Attention-Deficit/Hyperactivity Disorder Cooperative Group. (1999). Fourteen-month randomized clinical trial of treatment strategies for attention-deficit hyperactivity disorder. *Archives of General Psychiatry, 56,* 1073–1086.

Murphy, B. C., & Eisenberg, N. (2002). An integrative examination of peer conflict: Children's reported goals, emotions and behaviors. *Social Development, 11,* 534–557.

Murrie, D. C., Cornell, D. G., Kaplan, S., McConville, D., & Levy-Elkon, A. (2004). Psychopathy scores and violence among juvenile offenders: A multi-measure study. *Behavioral Sciences and the Law, 22*(1), 49–67.

Nasby, W., Hayden, B., & DePaulo, B. M. (1979). Attributional bias among aggressive boys to interpret un-ambiguous social stimuli as displays of hostility. *Journal of Abnormal Psychology, 89,* 459–468.

National Institute of Child Health and Human Development Early Child Care Research Network. (2004). Trajectories of physical aggression from toddlerhood to middle childhood. *Monographs of the Society for Research in Child Development, 69*(4, Serial No. 278).

Olds, D. L., Henderson, C. R., Cole, R., Eckenrode, J., Kizman, H., Luckey, D., et al. (1998). Long-term effects of nurse home visitation on children's criminal and antisocial behavior: 15-year follow-up of a randomized trial. *Journal of the American Medical Association, 280,* 1238–1244.

Olweus, D. (1993). *Bullying at school: What we know and what we can do.* Cambridge, MA: Blackwell.

Patterson, G. R., Reid, J. B., & Dishion, T. J. (1992). *A social learning approach: Vol. 4. Antisocial boys.* Eugene, OR: Castalia Press.

Perry, D. G., Perry, L. C., & Rasmussen, P. (1986). Cognitive social learning mediators of aggression. *Child Development, 57,* 700–711.

Pettit, G. S., Bates, J. E., & Dodge, K. A. (1997). Supportive parenting, ecological context, and children's adjustment. *Child Development, 68,* 908–923.

Pettit, G. S., Bates, J. E., Dodge, K. A., & Meece, D. W. (1999). The impact of after-school peer contact on early adolescent externalizing problems is moderated by parental monitoring, neighborhood safety, and prior adjustment. *Child Development, 70,* 768–778.

Pine, D. S., Coplan, J. D., Wasserman, G. A., Miller, L. S., Fried, J. E., Davies, M., et al. (1997). Neuroendocrine response to fenfluramine challenge in boys. *Archives of General Psychiatry, 54,* 839–846.

Pine, D. S., Shaffer, D., Schonfeld, I. S., & Davies, M. (1997). Minor physical anomalies: Modifiers of environmental risks for psychiatric impairment? *Journal of the American Academy of Child and Adolescent Psychiatry, 36,* 395–403.

Pollak, S. D., & Tolley-Schell, S. A. (2003). Selective attention to facial emotion in physically abused children. *Journal of Abnormal Psychology, 112,* 323–338.

Posner, M., & Rothbart, M. K. (1998). Attention, self-regulation, and consciousness. *Transactions of the Philosophical Society of London, B* 1915–1927.

Prentice, N. M., & Kelly, F. J. (1963). Intelligence and delinquency: A reconsideration. *Journal of Social Psychology, 60,* 327–337.

Quiggle, N., Panak, W. F., Garber, J., & Dodge, K. A. (1992). Social information processing in aggressive and depressed children. *Child Development, 63,* 1305–1320.

Raine, A. (2002). Biosocial studies of antisocial and violent behavior in children and adults: A review. *Journal of Abnormal Child Psychology, 30*(4), 311–326.

Raine, A., Brennan, P., & Farrington, D. P. (1997). Biosocial bases of violence: Conceptual and theoretical issues. In A. Raine, P. A. Brennan, D. P. Farrington, & S. A. Mednick (Eds.), *Biosocial bases of violence* (pp. 1–20). New York: Plenum Press.

Raine, A., Brennan, P., & Mednick, S. A. (1994). Birth complications combined with early maternal rejection at age 1 year predispose to violent crime at age 18 years. *Archives of General Psychiatry, 53,* 984–988.

Raine, A., Brennan, P., & Mednick, S. A. (1997). Interaction between birth complications and early maternal rejection in predisposing to adult violence: Specificity to serious, early onset violence. *American Journal of Psychiatry, 154,* 1265–1271.

Raine, A., Lencz, T., Bihrle, S., LaCasse, L., & Colletti, P. (2000). Reduced prefrontal gray matter volume and reduced autonomic activity in antisocial personality disorder. *Archives of General Psychiatry, 57,* 119–127.

Raine, A., Reynolds, C., Venables, P. H., Mednick, S. A., & Farrington, D. P. (1998). Fearlessness, stimulation-seeking, and large body size at age 3 years as early predispositions to childhood aggression at age 11 years. *Archives of General Psychiatry, 55,* 745–751.

Rasanen, P., Hakko, H., Isohanni, M., Hodgins, S., Jarvelin, M. R., & Tiihonen, J. (1999). Maternal smoking during pregnancy and risk of criminal behavior among adult male offspring in the northern Finland 1996 birth cohort. *American Journal of Psychiatry, 156,* 857–862.

Reid, J. B., Patterson, G. R., & Snyder, J. (Eds.). (2000). *Antisocial behavior in children and adolescents: A developmental analysis and model for intervention.* Washington, DC: American Psychological Association.

Renken, B., Egeland, B., Marvinney, D., Mangelsdorf, S., & Sroufe, L. A. (1989). Early childhood antecedents of aggression and passive-withdrawal in early elementary school. *Journal of Personality, 57,* 257–281.

Rhee, S. H., & Waldman, I. D. (2002). Genetic and environmental influences on antisocial behavior: A meta-analysis of twin and adoption studies. *Psychological Bulletin, 128,* 490–529.

Robins, L. N. (1966). *Deviant children grown up.* Baltimore: Williams & Wilkins.

Rogeness, G. A., Cepeda, C., Macedo, C. A., Fischer, C., & Harris, W. R. (1990). Differences in heart rate and blood pressure in children with conduct disorder, major depression, and separation anxiety. *Psychiatry Research, 33,* 199–206.

Rose, A., & Asher, S. (1998). Children's goals and strategies in response to conflicts within a friendship. *Developmental Psychology, 35,* 69–79.

Rowe, R., Maughan, B., Worthman, C. M., Costello, E. J., & Angold, A. (2004). Testosterone, antisocial behavior, and social dominance in boys: Pubertal development and biosocial interaction. *Biological Psychiatry, 55*(5), 546–552.

Rubin, K. H., Moller, L., & Emptage, A. (1987). The Preschool Behavior Questionnaire: A useful index of behavior problems in elementary school-age children. *Canadian Journal of Behavioral Science, 19,* 86–100.

Rutter, M. (1989). Pathways from childhood to adult life. *Journal of Child Psychology and Psychiatry, 30,* 25–31.

Rutter, M., & Garmezy, N. (1983). Developmental psychopathology. In P. H. Mussen (Series Ed.) & E. M. Hetherington (Vol. Ed.), *Handbook of child psychology: Vol. 4. Socialization, personality and social development* (4th ed., pp. 775–911). New York: Wiley.

Rutter, M., Giller, H., & Hagell, A. (1998). *Antisocial behavior by young people.* Cambridge: Cambridge University Press.

Rutter, M., Tizard, J., & Whitmore, K. (Eds.). (1970). *Education, health, and behavior.* London: Longmans.

Sampson, R. J., & Laub, J. H. (1994). Urban poverty and the family context of delinquency: A new look at structure and process in a classic study. *Child Development, 65,* 523–540.

Sampson, R. J., & Laub, J. H. (2003). Life-course desisters? Trajectories of crime among delinquent boys followed to age 70. *Criminology, 41*(3), 555–592.

Sampson, R. J., Raudenbush, S. W., & Earls, F. (1997). Neighborhoods and violent crime: A multi-level study of collective efficacy. *Science, 277,* 918–924.

Sanders, M. R., Markie-Dadds, C., Tully, L. A., & Bor, W. (2000). The Triple P-positive Parenting Intervention for parents of children with early onset conduct problems. *Journal of Consulting and Clinical Psychology, 68,* 624–640.

Scarr, S., & McCartney, K. (1983). How people make their own environments: A theory of genotype greater than environment effects. *Child Development, 54,* 424–435.

Schultz, D., Izard, C. E., & Bear, G. (2004). Children's emotion processing: Relations to emotionality and aggression. *Development and Psychopathology, 16,* 371–387.

Schwartz, D., McFadden-Ketchum, S. A., Dodge, K. A., Pettit, G. S., & Bates, J. E. (1998). Peer group victimization as a predictor of children's behavior problems at home and in school. *Development and Psychopathology, 10,* 87–99.

Seguin, J. R., Pihl, R. O., Harden, P. W., Tremblay, R. E., & Boulerice, B. (1995). Cognitive and neuropsychological characteristics of physically aggressive boys. *Journal of Abnormal Psychology, 104,* 614–624.

Serketich, W. J., & Dumas, J. E. (1996). The effectiveness of behavioral parent training to modify antisocial behavior in children: A meta-analysis. *Behavior Therapy, 27,* 171–186.

Shaw, C., & McKay, H. (1942). *Juvenile delinquency and urban areas.* Chicago: University of Chicago Press.

Shaw, D. S., Keenan, K., Owens, E. B., Winslow, E. B., Hood, N., & Garcia, M. (1995, April). *Developmental precursors of externalizing behavior among two samples of low-income families: Ages 1 to 5.* Paper presented at biennial meeting of the Society for Research in Child Development, Indianapolis, IN.

Shure, M. B., & Spivack, G. (1980). Interpersonal problem-solving as a mediator of behavioral adjustment in preschool and kindergarten children. *Journal of Applied Developmental Psychology, 1,* 29–44.

Simons, R. L., Wu, C. I., Conger, R. D., & Lorenz, F. O. (1994). Two routes to delinquency: Differences between early and late starters in the impact of parenting and deviant peers. *Criminology, 32,* 247–276.

Slaby, R. G., & Guerra, N. G. (1988). Cognitive mediators of aggression in adolescent offenders: Pt. 1. Assessment. *Developmental Psychology, 24,* 580–588.

Snyder, J., Dishion, T. J., & Patterson, G. R. (1986). Determinants and consequences of associating with deviant peers during preadolescence and adolescence. *Journal of Early Adolescence, 6,* 29–43.

Snyder, J., Reid, J., & Patterson, G. (2003). A social learning model of child and adolescent antisocial behavior. In B. B. Lahey, T. E. Moffitt, & A. Caspi (Eds.), *Causes of conduct disorder and juvenile delinquency* (pp. 27–48). New York: Guilford Press.

Snyder, J., Stoolmiller, M., Wilson, M., & Yamamoto, M. (2003). Child anger regulation, parental responses to children's anger displays, and early child antisocial behavior. *Social Development, 12,* 335–360.

Stattin, H., & Kerr, M. (2000). Parental monitoring: A reinterpretation. *Child Development, 71,* 1072–1085.

Stenberg, C., & Campos, J. (1990). The development of anger expressions in infancy. In N. Stein, T. Trabasso, & B. Leventhal (Eds.), *Concepts in emotion* (pp. 75–99). Hillsdale, NJ: Erlbaum.

Stifter, C. A., Spinrad, T. L., & Braungart-Rieker, J. M. (1999). Toward a developmental model of child compliance: The role of emotion regulation in infancy. *Child Development, 70,* 21–32.

Stone, W. L., Bendell, R. D., & Field, T. M. (1988). The impact of socioeconomic status on teenage mothers and children who received early intervention. *Journal of Applied Developmental Psychology, 9,* 391–408.

Stormshak, E. A., Bierman, K. L., Bruschi, C., Dodge, K. A., Coie, J. D., & the Conduct Problems Prevention Research Group. (1999). The relation between behavior problems and peer preference in different classroom contexts. *Child Development, 70,* 169–182.

Straus, M. A. (2005). *The primordial violence: Corporal punishment by parents, cognitive development, and crime.* Walnut Creek, CA: Alta Mira Press.

Straus, M. A., & Gelles, R. J. (1990). How violent are American families. In M. A. Straus & R. J. Gelles (Eds.), *Physical violence in American families* (pp. 95–112). New Brunswick, NJ: Transaction.

Straus, M. A., & Stewart, J. H. (1999). Corporal punishment by American parents: National data on prevalence, chronicity, severity, and duration, in relation to child and family characteristics. *Clinical Child and Family Psychology Review, 2,* 55–70.

Taylor, A. R., & Gabriel, S. W. (1989, April). *Cooperative versus competitive game-playing strategies of peer accepted and peer rejected children in a goal conflict situation.* Paper presented at the biennial meeting of the Society for Research in Child Development, Kansas City, MO.

Tedeschi, J. T., & Felson, R. B. (1994). *Violence, aggression, and coercive actions.* Washington, DC: American Psychological Association.

Thornberry, T. P., Krohn, M. D., Lizotte, A. J., & Chard-Wierschem, D. (1993). The role of juvenile gangs in facilitating delinquent behavior. *Journal of Research in Crime and Delinquency, 30,* 55–87.

Tremblay, R. E., Mâsse, L. C., Vitaro, F., & Dobkin, P. L. (1995). The impact of friend's deviant behavior on early onset of delinquency: Longitudinal data from 6 to 13 years of age. *Development and Psychopathology, 7,* 649–667.

Trivers, R. L. (1974). Parental-offspring conflict. *American Zoologist, 46,* 35–57.

Turner, A. K. (1994). Genetic and hormonal influences on male violence. In J. Archer (Ed.), *Male violence* (pp. 233–252). New York: Routledge.

Underwood, M. K. (2003). *Social aggression among girls.* New York: Guilford Press.

U.S. Department of Health and Human Services. (1997). *Morbidity and Mortality Weekly Report, 46*(5). Atlanta, GA: Centers for Disease Control and Prevention.

U.S. Department of Justice. (2003). *Crime in the United States: Uniform Crime Reports, 2002.* Washington, DC: U.S. Government Printing Office.

Virkkunen, M., Eggert, M., Rawlings, R., & Linnoila, M. (1996). A prospective follow-up study of alcoholic violent offenders and fire setters. *Archives of General Psychiatry, 53,* 523–529.

Votruba-Drzal, E., Coley, R. L., & Chase-Lansdale, P. L. (2004). Child care and low-income children's development: Direct and moderated effects. *Child Development, 75,* 296–312.

Waldman, I. D. (1988). *Relationships between noon-social information processing, social perception, and social status in 7- to 12-year-old boys.* Unpublished doctoral dissertation, University of Waterloo, Ontario, Canada.

Webster-Stratton, C. (1998). Preventing conduct problems in Head Start children: Strengthening parenting competencies. *Journal of Consulting and Clinical Psychology, 66,* 715–730.

Wilson, J. Q., & Herrnstein, R. (1985). *Crime and human nature.* New York: Simon & Schuster.

Wood, W., Wong, F. Y., & Chachere, G. (1991). Effects of media violence on viewers' aggression in unconstrained social interaction. *Psychological Bulletin, 109,* 371–383.

Wyer, R. S., Jr., & Srull, T. K. (1989). *Memory and cognition in its social context.* Hillsdale, NJ: Erlbaum.

Zakriski, A. L., & Coie, J. D. (1996). A comparison of aggressive-rejected and nonaggressive-rejected boys' interpretations of self-directed and other-directed rejection. *Child Development, 67,* 1048–1070.

Zhou, Q., Eisenberg, N., Losoya, S., Fabes, R. A., Reiser, M., Guthrie, I. K., et al. (2002). The relations of parental warmth and positive expressiveness to children's empathy-related responding and social functioning: A longitudinal study. *Child Development, 73,* 893–915.

Chapter 14

The Development of Morality

Elliot Turiel

Philosophers have been concerned with the topic of morality for a long time. Socrates is referred to as the "patron saint of moral philosophy" (Frankena, 1963, p. 1). The moral philosophies of Plato and Aristotle included concerns with how individuals acquire or develop morality and how to create the best educational conditions for its acquisition. Moral development has been of central concern in the major psychological theoretical perspectives since the beginning of the twentieth century. The major figures in these approaches, including Sigmund Freud, B. F. Skinner, and Jean Piaget, provided accounts of moral development. Many of the problems raised by them and by moral philosophers over the ages remain part of contemporary discussion.

Setting the Stage

Sigmund Freud wrote extensively about morality, incorporating it into his general formulations of individual development in society. Central to his view were the concepts of conscience and concomitant tension between an individual and society. Through the influences of society, particularly as reproduced in a family, the individual's needs for instinctual gratification become transformed and displaced in the developmental process to make room for internalized standards (via parents as representatives of society) and internalized emotional mechanisms for regulating behaviors. B. F. Skinner (1971, chap. 6), a behaviorist, proposed that morality reflects behaviors that have been reinforced by value judgments associated with cultural norms. Actions are not intrinsically good or bad but are acquired and performed as a consequence of contingencies of reinforcement. Certain contingencies, consistent with the mores of the group, are social in that they pertain to relationships with others and are governed by verbal reinforcers such as good, bad, right, and wrong.

473

Knowledge and judgments about social relationships were considered central to morality by Jean Piaget, who wrote about the topic mainly in the early part of his career (Piaget, 1932). In keeping with his general views of development as stemming from reciprocal interactions of individuals and multiple features of social experiences (entailing constructions of understandings of experiences), Piaget analyzed morality from the perspective of how experiences result in the formation of judgments about social relationships, rules, laws, authority, and social institutions. He proposed that moral development is influenced by a variety of experiences, including emotional reactions (e.g., sympathy, empathy, respect), relationships with adults, and relationships with other children.

Piaget proposed that as morality develops, there is a shift from a heteronomous to an autonomous orientation. Autonomy in this context does not mean that individuals' conceptions of morality are based on the independence of individuals. Indeed, the ideas of mutual respect and cooperation, key to Piaget's formulation, imply interdependence rather than independence. By autonomy, Piaget (1960/1995) meant "that the subject participates in the elaboration of norms instead of receiving them ready-made as happens in the case of the norms of unilateral respect that lie behind heteronomous morality" (p. 315). Therefore, Piaget used autonomy in reference to a process in which norms furthering interdependence are elaborated with the participation of the child.

The concept of autonomy, along with the propositions that obligatory moral judgments are applied with flexibility of thought in social contexts, makes for a fundamental contrast between Piagetian and Freudian or behaviorist approaches. In both the Freudian and behaviorist conceptions, the individual's morality is under some kind of psychological compulsion: In the Freudian view, an internalized conscience or superego compels behavior, and in the behaviorist conception, actions are compelled by habits of behavior. Contemporary analyses discussed in this chapter can also be contrasted on these dimensions as well. Contemporary researchers have examined moral judgments and how they are applied in situational and cultural contexts. There are also various psychological and/or biologically based explanations of moral functioning that are based on how psychological mechanisms compel actions. These include genetic traits and genetically based intuitions and emotions. Some explanations are based on propositions of internalized values, norms, or rules, such as from parents, society, and culture. Some of these explanations imply moral absolutism, such as genes are fixed and conscience or traits of character are regarded as unvarying. Other explanations imply a degree of moral relativism, such as different parents, societies, or cultural ways result in different groups being compelled in different ways.

Many of the issues put forth in the first part of the twentieth century by Freud, Piaget, and others had a major influence on later research on moral development. For a time, the dominant conceptions of morality were either based on psychoanalytic explanations of conscience and guilt or straightforward behaviorist explanations of moral learning. In either type of formulation, moral development was assumed to be a function of societal control over the individual's interests, needs, or impulses. Since then a major shift, brought about in no small measure by the work of Lawrence Kohlberg, has occurred in psychologists' approach to morality. Kohlberg critiqued the dominant behaviorist and psychoanalytic conceptions of morality, argued for the need to ground empirical study of moral development on sound philosophical definitions of the domain (Kohlberg, 1971), and presented his own formulations of the process of moral development (Kohlberg, 1969).

One of Kohlberg's major influences on research on moral development came from his call for its more adequate grounding in a substantive epistemology of the domain. Whereas morality was treated as a substantive epistemological category by many philosophers—from Plato and Aristotle to Hume, Mill, and Kant and contemporary philosophers (e.g., John Rawls)—psychologists attempted to explain its acquisition without considering the definition or meaning of that which is acquired. Kohlberg argued that we could not consider mechanisms of moral acquisition without concern with definitions, meanings, and the substance of morality. This idea was also based on psychological considerations. Kohlberg presumed that social scientists and philosophers were not the only ones who engage in systematic thinking about psychological, social, or moral matters: Laypersons do, too. He rejected the implied duality between the psychologist and the layperson evident in most psychological explanations.

Kohlberg studied moral development by focusing on how children and adolescents make judgments about conflicts, in hypothetical situations, around issues of life, interpersonal obligations, trust, law, authority, and retribution. He proposed a sequence of six stages, depicting a progression of judgments. Stages 1 and 2, grouped into a "preconventional" level, were primarily based on obedience, punishment avoidance, and instrumental need and exchange. Stages 3 and 4, grouped into a "conventional" level, were based on role obligations, stereotypical conceptions of good persons, and respect for the rules and authority legitimated in the social system. Stages 5 and 6, grouped into a "postconventional" level, were based on contractual agreements, established procedural arrangements for adjudicating conflicts, mutual respect, and differentiated concepts of justice and rights. This sequence was also a reformulation of Piaget's progression from heteronomy to autonomy. Kohlberg maintained that respect for rules and authority, which Piaget had attributed to young children at the heteronomous level, does not come about at least until adolescence (Kohlberg's conventional level), and that young children's moral judgments are characterized, instead, by a failure to distinguish moral value from power, sanctions, and instrumental needs. In turn, Kohlberg proposed that mutual respect and concepts of justice and rights as part of an autonomous system of thought, whose emergence Piaget had placed in late childhood or early adolescence, do not come about until, at the earliest, late adolescence and usually not until adulthood (Kohlberg's postconventional level).

Kohlberg's influence on subsequent research and theories is, in important respects, separate from the influence of his particular formulation of stages of moral development or even from the general theoretical viewpoint he espoused. Many advance alternative theoretical paradigms, including paradigms based on the idea of the internalization of conscience and values or the idea of culture-based morality. Among those who advance developmental positions influenced by Piaget's theory, many propose formulations divergent from that of Kohlberg. Yet, Kohlberg has influenced discourse about the psychology of moral development in several ways in addition to the need to ground psychological explanations in philosophical considerations about morality. Another influence is that in many current formulations morality is not framed by impositions on children due to conflicts between their needs or interests and the requirements of society or the group. Many now think that children are, in an active and positive sense, integrated into their social relationships with adults and peers and that morality is not solely or even primarily an external or unwanted imposition on them. Kohlberg had stressed children's constructions of moral judgments from social interactions and that emotions of sympathy for others, spontaneous interests in helping others, and respect were centrally involved in children's moral development. The scope of contemporary inquiry has also broadened to include and emphasize positive emotions; the intricacies of moral, social, and personal judgments as part of individuals' relations with the social world; and social interactions contributing to development, including with parents, peers, schooling, and culture. Debates now center on the roles of emotions and judgments, on the individual and the collectivity, on the contributions of constructions of moral understandings and culturally based meanings, and on how to distinguish between universally applicable and locally based moralities.

Issues, Emphases, and Theories

Discussions of moral development seem to involve strongly held and conflicting positions. It is frequently asserted that positions held by others exclude a particular feature of central importance—usually the feature emphasized by those characterizing the other's approach. The most frequent examples of this revolve around whether theorists account for emotions or judgments, for social influences or the individual's logical operations, for parental influences or peer influences, and for cultural or individual constructions. There is a tendency to mischaracterize positions as failing to account for this or that instead of recognizing that differences in theoretical perspectives have more to do with how different features (e.g., emotions and judgments) are explained and emphasized. Even when a theorist excludes a particular component regarded important by others, it is usually mistaken to say that there is a failure to account for the component. Often, the relevance of a component is explicitly and purposely excluded.

It is important, therefore, to consider how a theoretical perspective frames the relevant issues. In current theoretical perspectives and research programs, it is particularly important to consider how issues like emotion, culture, gender, judgment, social influences, and individual constructions are explained. Indeed, emphases placed on these issues serve to distinguish points of view on moral development. Whereas most explanations of moral development attempt to account for each of these issues, there are differences in the importance and roles given to them that result in varying explanations of morality and its development.

This chapter is organized around theoretical approaches to moral development, with the central issues emphasized. I first consider the concepts and research of developmental psychologists who emphasize emotions, influences of parental practices, and conscience. This is followed by discussion of approaches that, though including emotions and judgments, emphasize the role of gender and gender-related experiences in moral development. Then, I consider approaches in which culture is regarded as central and in which fairly sharp distinctions are drawn among moral orientations in different cultures. Next, I discuss approaches emphasizing moral judgments and reciprocal interactions in development. Finally, a perspective is presented based on reciprocal interactions; the domains of personal, social, and moral judgments; and their interplay with cultural practices.

In the course of this chapter, I review the different positions on moral development and comment on and evaluate the positions. Those evaluations are connected to my own views and positions. In the latter parts of the chapter, I discuss my positions, which are shared by a number of colleagues and collaborators.

Emphasizing Emotions

Emotions have been considered the basis for morality by some philosophers, and have been central in certain psychologists' formulations. The Freudian and behaviorist approaches viewed the acquisition of morally obligatory actions as a process by which aversive emotions of fear, anxiety, shame, and guilt as central to moral learning. However, a major shift in thinking about emotions in the late 1970s and through the 1980s entailed a focus on attachment, bonding, love, sympathy, and empathy. The emphasis on these emotions included continued concerns with the influences of the family, the role of aversive emotions, and a renewed interest in the evolutionary sources of emotions. Research demonstrating that very young children display positive emotions and affiliate and bond with others was particularly influential in the shift (e.g., Dunn, 1988; Hoffman, 1991a; Kochanska, 1993). Another set of relevant findings show that young children are sensitive to the interests and well-being of others, producing actions of an altruistic nature. Studies conducted in the home show that even children under 2 years of age share possessions (e.g., toys) with others, help mothers with household tasks, cooperate in games, and respond to the emotional distress of others (Radke-Yarrow, Zahn-Waxler, & Chapman, 1983). Toddlers and young children, in addition, show comfort and engage in caregiving of others. It also appears that reactions of empathy emerge by age 3 (Lennon & Eisenberg, 1987; Zahn-Waxler, Radke-Yarrow, Wagner, & Chapman, 1992).

The research findings on sympathy and prosocial actions are inconsistent with the idea that children, before they have internalized parental values, or societal standards, or have been taught to behave in socially sanctioned ways, will act solely in selfish and self-directed ways when they are not coerced or fearful of detection. The findings on sympathy and prosocial actions are not inconsistent with emotive positions on morality. In several formulations, it has been proposed that morality is directed more by emotions than reasoning (Dunn, 1988; Hoffman, 1991b; Kochanska, 1993).

A PRIMACY FOR EMPATHY

Empathy has been considered primary in moral development by some who do not rely heavily on associations of unpleasant and pleasant affect with morality. Hoffman (1991a, 2000) has put forth a formulation combining emotion due to evolution with internalization, in that "the society's moral norms and values [are made] part of the individual's personal motive system" (1991a, p. 106). His approach includes motives, cognition, moral principles of care and justice, and perspective taking, but it can be said that primacy is given to emotion because the linchpin is empathy.

Hoffman distinguishes his approach from those giving primacy to moral judgments in that he defines moral actions in motivational terms. A moral act is "a disposition to do something on behalf of another person, or to behave in accord with a moral norm or standard bearing on human welfare or justice" (Hoffman, 1991b, p. 276). The distinction between defining a moral act in terms of moral judgment or motives is not unambiguous (Turiel, 2003). It could be said that the moral judgments one makes—say that one should come to the aid of another in distress because it is wrong to allow suffering—motivates one to act. The key to the distinction is in the term disposition in the definition of a moral act—disposition referring to an emotional reaction that propels action. The main source of moral motives is the feeling of empathy, which is defined as an affective response that does not necessarily match another's affective state. By putting the matter in affective-motivational terms, Hoffman poses the question, "Why act morally?" and answers in terms of feelings that need to be acted on.

Empathy is characterized as developing through four stage-like manifestations that are partly determined by changing cognitive capabilities. The first stage is characterized by the "global" distress felt by infants (during the first year) entailing a confusion of the infant's own feelings with those of another. At the second stage of "egocentric" empathy (age of 1 year), the onset of object permanence allows for an awareness that other people are physically distinct from the self and a concern ("sympathetic distress") with another person who is in distress. However, children do not distinguish between their own or others' internal states.

Hoffman further asserts that role taking emerges at about 2 or 3 years of age (this, however, is a controversial issue), allowing for a differentiation of the child's own feelings from those of others. At the third stage, therefore, children are responsive to cues about the other person's feelings and empathize with a range of emotions other than distress (e.g., disappointment, feelings of betrayal). Whereas the third stage is labeled "empathy for another's feelings," the fourth stage, emerging in late childhood is labeled "empathy for another's life conditions." The relevant social cognitions for the fourth stage are children's awareness of self and others with separate identities. These conceptions allow for awareness that others feel pleasure and pain in their general life experiences. At this stage, empathy is felt in particular situations, as well as for more general life circumstances of others or of groups of people (e.g., the poor or the oppressed).

Whether this sequence of stages is an accurate representation of how children develop is undetermined because the stages were not, for the most part, based on empirical evidence. There is some evidence that infants respond to the actual crying of other infants to a greater extent than to sounds resembling the crying of human infants (Sagi & Hoffman, 1976). However, it is not entirely clear that this type of response is a form of very early empathy. The other stages have not been tested empirically and, instead, rely on illustrations with the types of anecdotal examples previously mentioned. Some research (Zahn-Waxler et al., 1992) does provide evidence that young children show empathic reactions to the distress of others and attempt to understand the nature of the distress.

In more recent writings, Hoffman (2000) identified situations in which empathic reactions and moral actions occur. He labeled these moral encounters and proposed that five "encompass most of the prosocial domain" (p. 3). These include situations in which a person is an innocent bystander (witnessing someone in pain or distress), a transgressor (harming or about to harm someone), or a "virtual transgressor" (an imagined harmful act). The two others are situations in which there are "multiple moral claimants" (where a person has to make choices about who to help) and in which there is a clash between caring and justice (between considering others and abstract issues of rights, duty, and reciprocity). These categories are meant to capture the situations that evoke guilt and empathic responses.

CONSCIENCE AND INTERNALIZATION

Some contemporary researchers have addressed hypotheses regarding moral internalization—defining morality through consensual norms—with the assumption that morality entails the acquisition of a conscience serving to internally regulate conduct consistent with societal values, norms, or rules (Kochanska, 1993). The concept of conscience, central to Freud's theory, was also central to behaviorist conceptions in which internalization was theorized to be acquired through the anxiety associated with punishments for transgressions (Aronfreed, 1968). Whether it be from a psychoanalytic or behaviorist perspective, the concept of conscience has been used to refer to a mechanism internalized by children for exerting control on needs that would otherwise be acted on.

In a contemporary formulation that has affinities with earlier positions on conscience and that includes elements of other socioemotional perspectives, Kochanska (1993) has examined conscience as regulation due to internalization marking successful socialization as "the gradual developmental shift from external to internal regulation that results in the child's ability to conform to societal standards of conduct and to restrain antisocial or destructive impulses, even in the absence of surveillance" (pp. 325–326). Moreover, the formation of conscience is functional from the societal perspective: "Without reliance on internalized consciences, societies would have to instill ever-present surveillance in all aspects of social life" (Kochanska, 1994, p. 20). This position includes a shift in balance away from natural moral propensities of concerns with the welfare of others back to more of an emphasis on the need to control antisocial and destructive tendencies. Ultimately, it is society that has to control the behavior of individuals, either by instilling control internally in children or through continual and all-encompassing ("in all aspects of social life") external control.

In keeping with the traditional conception of conscience, it was proposed that it is encompassed by "affective discomfort" or the various aversive emotional reactions to acts of transgression and "behavioral control." Reactions of sympathy and empathy contribute to the process of development, but they do so through the anxiety and distress they can arouse in a child. A significant aspect of this process is that parental socialization contributes greatly through arousal of children's anxiety.

Kochanska and her colleagues have continued this line of research in a series of studies aimed at examining what they refer to as bidirectional models of mother-child relationships. In these cases, the bidirectional conceptualizations of relationships remain within the context of a conception of conscience or morality as the internalization of values, norms, and behaviors established by parents. Some of these studies, for example, were designed to examine the role of children's temperament in the formation of conscience (Kochanska, 1997). Anxiety, fearfulness, and arousal (e.g., as found for shy children) underlie the affective component of conscience, and impulsivity and inhibition are related to behavioral control. Specifically, impulsive children are more likely to transgress and find it more difficult to internalize conscience than nonimpulsive children. Thus, parents' methods of socialization may work differently for children with different temperaments.

BEYOND FAMILY AND BEYOND INCORPORATION OF SOCIETAL STANDARDS

Findings on temperament are not consistent. A longitudinal study by Dunn, Brown, and Maguire (1995) showed, in contrast with the other studies, that shy children (i.e., inhibited, nonimpulsive, and anxious) scored lower on the same measures of moral orientation than children who were not shy. Dunn et al. found that in addition to parental practices, moral orientation was associated with factors like the quality of the child's relationships with older siblings (children who had friendlier, more positive relationships with siblings showed higher moral orientation scores) and the child's earlier level of understanding of emotions (children who had shown better emotional understandings at earlier ages scored higher on moral orientation at first grade). Moreover, Dunn et al. found differences among the stories used in the assessments. At kindergarten and first grade, children gave more empathic responses to a physical harm story than to a story dealing with cheating in a game. Correspondingly, more children gave guilt responses to the physical harm story than to the cheating story.

Findings in the Dunn et al. (1995) study suggest that influences on moral development extend beyond the practices of parents in disciplining children and that a child's reactions to transgressions are not uniform. Other research indicates that young children's development may proceed in several directions with regard to relationships with parents and in their orientations to morality. Along with an increased awareness of standards, at the age of 2 or 3 years, young children display increased teasing of their mothers, more physical aggression and destruction of objects, and greater interest in what is socially prohibited. Along with greater sympathy and empathy for others, with increasing age children begin to understand how to manipulate situations and upset others. This increasing complexity of young children's social relationships is also evident in their abilities, by 18 to 36 months, to engage in arguments and counterarguments in disputes with mothers (Dunn & Munn, 1987). Disputes occurred over issues such as rights and needs of persons, conventions (manners, etiquette), and destruction or aggression. Children's emotional reactions also varied by the different kinds of disputes; distress and anger were associated with disputes affecting children's rights and interests. These differentiations and extensions of the influences of social relationships are consistent with a reconceptualization of moral internalization presented by Grusec and Goodnow (1994).

Grusec and Goodnow maintained that the traditional view of internalization as the process by which children take over the values of society has significant limitations and is not consistent with existing data. A better understanding of the process requires accounting for additional factors, including the nature of the act (the misdeed or transgression), characteristics of parents, the child's perspective on the position of parents, and the child's perceptions of the misdeed. Furthermore, they argue that it is necessary to consider the child's ability to "move beyond the parent's specific position to one of his or her own, a consideration that points to successful socialization as more than an unquestioning adoption of another's position" (Grusec & Goodnow, 1994, p. 4).

In essence, they call for a reorientation in research that would take seriously the idea of reciprocal interactions in explanations of social development. There is evidence that the effectiveness of particular parental practices are not uniform and that parents do not consistently use one type of discipline. Mothers use different reasons for different kinds of transgressions. Smetana (1989) found that mothers of toddlers used explanations of needs and rights for acts entailing harm to others, whereas they used explanations pertaining to social order and conformity for violations of social conventions. It also appears that mothers vary their methods in accord with the types of standard violated (Chilamkurti & Milner, 1993). Other findings in accord with these propositions stem from studies of children's evaluations of parental discipline, as well as of correspondences between the judgments of children and adults (studies on parent-adolescent relationships are discussed later in the chapter). Research indicates both that mothers make discriminations in the ways discipline should be used and that by at least 10 years of age children make similar judgments about that type of discipline (Catron & Masters, 1993; Saltzstein, Weiner, & Munk, 1995).

These findings indicate that it is necessary to account for the child's perspective and, thereby, view the process of discipline as interactive. In particular, Grusec and colleagues maintained that because children's judgments differ for different types of misdeeds (e.g., moral as opposed to conventional transgressions; Turiel, 1983), they would evaluate and judge the appropriateness of the reasons given by parents, or others, when disciplining the child. It has been found that children are more responsive to adults' directives when the adults use reasons that correspond to the ways children classify moral actions. For example, when teachers simply point to rule violations in discussing acts like stealing or hitting, children are less responsive than when teachers underscore the welfare of others or fairness (Killen, 1991; Nucci, 1984). It has also been found that children are more likely to share with others when given reasons based on empathy and concern for others than when to adhere to norms (Eisenberg-Berg & Geisheker, 1979).

Unlike the traditional views of conscience or internalization, the model presented by Grusec and Goodnow includes the idea that internalization is not necessarily the sole desired goal of parents or the only positive outcome from the societal or individual perspectives. Parents may strive for flexibility and initiative on the part of the child rather than simply the adoption of parental standards. They may also be motivated by the goal that children acquire negotiation and thinking skills. Grusec and Goodnow raised the issue of noncompliance for positive goals and thereby raised the specter of social opposition and resistance. From the perspective of moral development as internalization of parental or societal norms, the good is defined as some form of compliance to the social environment. Social accommodation on the part of the child is thus regarded as the desirable end-state. In a later section, I consider research on opposition and resistance to social norms, societal arrangements, and cultural practices that stem from a moral standpoint.

Gender, Emotions, and Moral Judgments

The major issues considered thus far—emotion, socialization, and interaction—also have received scrutiny in theory and research on gender differences in moral development. The issue has been of particular controversy in the moral realm because in the early part of the century it was asserted (most notably by Freud) that the morality of females is less developed than that of males, and then, in the latter part of the century, that the morality of females is qualitatively different from that of males (Gilligan, 1982). Gilligan maintained that two moral injunctions define two sequences of moral development—the injunction not to treat others unfairly (justice) and the injunction to not turn away from someone in need (care). Gilligan argued that a morality of care, mainly linked to females, had been overlooked in favor of analyses of justice because mainly males had formulated explanations of moral development. These assertions, however, have generated controversy among students of moral development, as well as in other social scientific disciplines (Abu-Lughod, 1991; Okin, 1989), within feminist scholarship and in journalistic accounts (Pollitt, 1992).

In a way, Gilligan accepts Freud's (1925/1959) contention that women "show less sense of justice than men." She does not accept Freud's contention that women show less moral sense than men because women show more of a sense of the alternative form of care. A morality of justice fails to account for women's moral orientation because it focuses on rules and rights. The morality of care is one of fulfillment of responsibility and avoidance of exploitation and hurt and is linked to concepts of self as attached to social networks; the morality of justice is linked to concepts of self as autonomous and detached from social networks.

It would appear then that the formulation of a morality of care has affinities with those who emphasize emotions. Care entails avoidance of harm and concerns for the welfare of others (sympathy and empathy) and is applied mainly to those in close relationships. Although empathy and sympathy are relevant, this formulation differs in several respects from other perspectives emphasizing emotions. First, the central emotions for morality are defined differently from empathy, sympathy, shame, and guilt and are associated with a different set of experiences and mechanisms for the development of morality. Second, more emphasis is given to judgments in both moralities. And third, there is a sequence of development for the morality of care progressing toward increasing inclusiveness of moral judgments.

Gilligan (1982) argued that the study of the judgments of females serves to correct biases in influential theories of moral development put forth by males who largely overlooked females or who, when they addressed the issue, superficially relegated females' morality of care to a "lesser" form. Gilligan's propositions have received a good deal of attention, with some providing positive evaluations (Shweder & Haidt, 1993), and others pointing to inadequacies in sampling, procedures, research designs, and data analyses (e.g., Colby & Damon, 1983). Gilligan's formulation was not based on extensive research but initially on a combination of (a) the argument that a conception of morality as justice did not adequately characterize the moral judgments of females because they were usually assessed in stages lower than males, and (b) subjectively analyzed excerpts from a limited number of boys and girls responding to moral dilemmas in Kohlberg's interview (Gilligan, 1982, chap. 2). The construct of a morality of care was also based on the studies of women discussing abortion and of interviews of college students. Those studies were limited in that the samples were small and restricted to either pregnant women discussing one particular contested issue (abortion) or students in elite universities. Perhaps most important, the analyses of interview responses were neither based on systematic coding schemes nor analyzed statistically in extensive ways (Colby & Damon, 1983; Greeno & Maccoby, 1986; Luria, 1986). In subsequent research, a more circumscribed approach was taken, with a focus on defining the proposed orientations of care and justice and on coding (Lyons, 1983) the extent to which males and females use one or the other or combine the two. Studies assessing the distribution of care and justice orientations included male and female adolescents and adults responding to questions about moral conflicts in their lives (Gilligan & Attanucci, 1988). Varying results were obtained.

These types of studies have provided some evidence that care and justice tend to be associated with gender. However, the patterns are not clear-cut because studies also show shifts by context (Johnston, 1988). Perhaps because of the combinations of care and justice found in the reasoning of males and females, Gilligan and her colleagues appear, in later writings, to be inconsistent or ambiguous about sex differences, asserting that care and justice are concerns that can be part of the thinking of males or females. The conclusion drawn from a meta-analysis of research on care and justice orientations was that neither is used predominantly by women or men, though there is a tendency for females to use more care related reasoning than males (Jaffee & Hyde, 2000).

POLITICS, ECONOMICS, SOCIAL STRUCTURE, AND WOMEN'S PERSPECTIVES

The proposition that care and justice tend to be organized differently in males and females as a consequence of differences in childhood relationships carries a host of problems, including stereotyping of moral orientations, and the role of politics, economics, and social structure in possible inequalities and power relationships between men and women. Writing from her perspective as a journalist and feminist, Pollitt (1992) has critiqued characterizations of women as nurturing, caring individuals whose concerns are with relationships but not justice or logic. Not that Pollitt would exclude nurturing and caring from the purview of women by any means. Rather, it is that women neither have a monopoly on caring nor are they solely caring nurturers of others. Women are caring, cooperative, competitive, assertive of independence, and committed to rights and justice.

The characterization of women as caring and nurturing, according to Pollitt, stereotypes them in traditional and restrictive ways. It is restrictive because it limits real concern with justice, rights, and independence—just as it is restrictive to attribute characteristics of males solely to justice, rights, and autonomy. This stereotyping serves several ends for females and males. The positive end is that it provides women with an equal moral status to men and challenges the division of men as rational and women as irrational. Women are said to develop a type of rationality by which their morality is different and equal to that of men. Despite the greater concern with equality in moral orientations, Pollitt argues that the formulation constitutes a stereotype serving also to reinforce a status quo in which women retain positions subordinate to men. Men encourage the idea that women are concerned with care because men are, in addition to children, the main beneficiaries of women's nurturance.

Pollitt also argues that caring can be a consequence of economic dependence and subordination in the family. The role of caretaker and nurturer is, in part, imposed by a power structure in which men are in positions of influence and economic independence. Women appear less autonomous in the workplace as a consequence of discrimination serving ends of men in positions of power and influence.

The justice of distribution of resources, privileges, and burdens in the family, especially as it affects women, has been analyzed in depth by Okin (1989). She argues that moral philosophers and social scientists have either ignored the justice of gender relationships or accepted the legitimacy of unequal distributions and unjust treatment by relegating women to traditional roles. In that context, she also maintains that justice and rights are spheres relevant to women's thinking, and that the idea that women are oriented to care and not universally applicable concepts of rights and justice reinforces traditional stereotypes. In Okin's view, the distinction between care and justice has been overdrawn:

The best theorizing about justice, I argue, has integral to it the notions of care and empathy, of thinking of the interests and well-being of others who may be very different from ourselves. It is, therefore, misleading to draw a dichotomy as though they were two contrasting ethics. The best theorizing about justice is not some abstract "view from nowhere," but results from the carefully attentive consideration of everyone's point of view. (p. 15)

An implication of Okin's contention is that justice needs to be inclusive. Those emphasizing emotions argue that an inclusive or universal conception of morality is a Western one. In other cultures, and perhaps for ordinary people in Western cultures, morality is applied in a local and parochial fashion. Those who propose that integrated cultural patterns are central in the development of morality have taken a similar position.

Emphasizing Culture

The idea of cultures forming integrated cohesive patterns diverging from each other goes back at least to the formulations of cultural anthropologists of the early part of the twentieth century. Ruth Benedict (1934), one of the most influential proponents of the idea that cultures form integrated patterns, proclaimed "the diversity of cultures can be endlessly documented" (p. 45). Cultural anthropologists of the time also wrote about morality, often taking positions of cultural relativism, in reaction to predominant late-nineteenth-century anthropological assumptions that cultures could be classified in a hierarchy of lower to higher. Usually, Western cultures were placed at the apex of the hierarchy. Cultural anthropologists argued that the classifications of cultures in a hierarchy of progress or development were due to bias in favor of Western cultural values and to intolerance and lack of respect for the equally valid values of other cultures. Along with relativism, therefore, it was asserted that cultures should be treated as different and equal, and each accepted as functioning on its own moral standards with moral ends endemic to its system. Some critics of cultural relativism (e.g., Hatch, 1983) have pointed out that the position actually includes nonrelativistic moral prescriptions. In particular, relativists espouse the values of tolerance (that the validity of other cultures' values and perspectives should be accepted), freedom (that a culture should not be obstructed from following its moral standards), and equality (that a culture's moral standards should be regarded as of equal validity as those of any other).

In contemporary views of human development, the role of culture has once again been emphasized (Bruner, 1990; Shweder, Mahapatra, & Miller, 1987) and has become increasingly part of research on moral development. Some assert that culture must be given center stage (Markus & Kitayama, 1991; Shweder, Much, Mahapatra, & Park, 1997). In giving culture center stage, sharp distinctions are drawn between Western and non-Western cultures in morality and concepts of self. Westerners are said to place an emphasis on abstractions, justice, and the autonomy of individuals, whereas non-Westerners are said to place emphasis on concrete contexts, duties, and interdependence.

SOCIAL COMMUNICATION AND CULTURAL COHERENCE

In these positions cultures do not simply provide a series of isolated standards, values or codes. Some worlds of moral meaning emphasize rights and justice, others emphasize duties and obligations, each part of general orientations to individualistic (read Western cultures) and collectivistic (read non-Western cultures) conceptions of self, others, and society. The proposed contrast between individualistic and collectivistic cultural orientations is related to moral conceptions. However, these orientations encompass much more; they are the bases for cultural constructions of how persons are defined, how they interact with each other, how society is defined, and how the goals of persons and the group are established and met (e.g., Markus & Kitayama, 1991). In these formulations, the United States is often identified as the quintessential individualistic society, but individualism is also prevalent in other countries such as Australia, Canada, England, and New Zealand. Prototypical collectivistic cultures are found in

Japan, India, China, and the Middle East, as well as in Africa, Latin America, and southern Europe. The person conceived as an autonomous agent, with personal goals, is central in the individualistic frame, whereas the group as an interconnected and interdependent network of relationships is central in the collectivistic frame. A core feature of individualistic cultures is that the highest value is accorded to the person as detached from others and as independent of the social order. People are, therefore, oriented to self-sufficiency, self-reliance, independence, and resistance to social pressure for conformity or obedience to authority. Collectivistic cultures, by contrast, are oriented to tradition, duty, obedience to authority, interdependence, and social harmony (for a general review of evidence, see Oyserman, Coon, & Kemmelmeier, 2002).

A significant component of cultural meanings is the kind of moral orientation communicated to children and reproduced by them as they grow into adulthood. Shweder et al. (1987) proposed a distinction between "rights-based" and "duty-based" moralities in their comparisons between the United States and India. In Western cultures, moral authority resides in individuals who voluntarily enter into contracts and promises, with the idea of rights as fundamental (hence a "rights-based" morality). In a contrasting duty-based morality, the social order is the organizing feature of moral rationality. Customary social practices are viewed as part of the natural moral order, so that social practices are seen neither as within individual discretion nor as a function of social consensus (thus the concept of conventionality as agreement in a group is largely absent).

SOCIAL PRACTICES AND CULTURAL COHERENCE

Shweder et al. (1987) examined propositions regarding cultural divergence in "moral rationality" in a study conducted with samples of secular middle- and upper-middle-class children and adults from the United States (Hyde Park in Chicago), and samples of "untouchables" and Brahmans living in the old temple town of Bhubaneswar, Orissa, in India. In large measure, the research aimed at ascertaining whether a distinction could be drawn across the two cultures between morality, as based on concepts of justice, rights, and welfare, and conventionality, as based on context-specific uniformities serving goals of social coordination—a distinction that had been addressed by others and is considered further in subsequent sections of this chapter (e.g., Nucci, 1981; Smetana, 1981; Tisak, 1986; Turiel, 1979, 1983).

Shweder et al. (1987) hypothesized that a distinction between morality and convention is particular to cultures which structure social relationships through the concept of autonomous individuals free to choose by consensus. Accordingly, they included topics of consensual choice in Western cultures such as issues about food, dress, and terms of address. Whereas some items were straightforward (e.g., a son addressing his father by his first name) others included religious and metaphysical considerations for Indians because of their connections to ideas about an afterlife (e.g., a widow wearing jewelry and bright-colored clothing 6 months after the death of her husband, a widow eating fish 2 or 3 times a week). Also many of the items entailed acts on the part of women that might contradict the power and desires of men (e.g., a woman wanting to eat with her husband and elder brother, a son claiming an inheritance over his sister). Shweder et al. included items reflecting concepts they consider candidates for moral universals (e.g., a father breaking a promise to his son, cutting in line, refusing to treat an injured person) that dealt with justice, harm, reciprocity, theft, arbitrary assault, and discrimination. Still other issues dealt with family practices that might vary by culture, including those bearing on personal liberty, privacy, and equality (considered central themes for Americans), and sanctity, chastity, and respect for status (considered central themes for Indians).

The assessments were adapted, in modified form, from previous research on morality and convention (Turiel, 1983). Shweder et al. (1987) found that Americans and Indians rank the seriousness of transgressions in very different ways, such that there are high correlations among Americans and among Indians but little correlation between Americans and Indians. There was agreement in judgments about some moral issues between Indians and Americans and a good deal of disagreement on issues pertaining to conventions, liberty, equality, sanctity, chastity, and status.

In India, according to the findings, more things are regarded as wrong than in the United States. In particular, Indians regarded many breaches pertaining to food, dress, terms of address, and sex roles as wrong, as unalterable, and in some cases as universal. Shweder et al. (1987) maintained that conventional thinking "is almost a nonexistent form of thought in our Indian data" (p. 52). Although convention was existent in the American data, it was much less prevalent than found in many other studies conducted in the United States.

In addition to differences in judgments between the two cultural groups, on issues related to food, dress, terms of address, and sex roles, Shweder et al. (1987) found that a number of issues were judged as wrong by both Indians and Americans (these are the candidates for moral universals). Agreement occurred on issues pertaining to harm (e.g., hospital workers ignoring an accident victim, destroying another child's picture, kicking a harmless animal), injustice (e.g., cutting in line, discriminating against invalids), breaking promises, and incest. However, not all issues bearing on discrimination or harm were judged as wrong by Indians and Americans. Three issues, in particular, were judged as right by Indians and wrong by Americans. One of these depicted a father who canes his son for a misdeed. Two others pertained to gender relationships. One depicted a husband who beats his wife "black and blue" after she disobeys him by going to a movie alone without his permission, and a son who claims most of his deceased father's property, not allowing his sister to obtain much inheritance.

The overarching principle applied in the analyses of responses to these items is cultural meaning in a moral system. Not considered is that different and varying agendas may be at work in addition to "moral duties." For example, Indians may judge caning a son as right because of their psychological assumptions regarding the effectiveness of physical punishment on learning (see Wainryb, 1991). Also, exerting power and asserting personal entitlements may account for the acceptability, among Indians, of husbands beating their wives and sons claiming an inheritance over their sisters.

EMOTIONAL FORMS, INTUITIONS, AND RAPID PROCESSING

The emphasis on the dictates of roles, status, and hierarchy appears to leave little room for the types of moral concerns with justice, harm, and even rights (e.g., that it is wrong to discriminate against invalids) apparent in some of the findings of the Shweder et al. (1987) research. Recognizing that such judgments are made in that non-Western, "sociocentric" culture (as in their own findings and as in interpretations by Turiel, Killen, & Helwig, 1987), Shweder and his colleagues (1997) attenuated somewhat the proposition regarding the separation of a rights-based morality and a duty-based morality and elaborated on it. One elaboration is the proposition that three "ethics" are found the world over: the ethics of autonomy, community, and divinity. Although the inclusion of three ethics broadens the scope of the analyses beyond the dichotomy of rights and duties, it is still presumed that the social order determines the interplay of different types of "goods" in a worldview. Thus, in India, community and divinity are dominant, whereas in the United States autonomy prevails (Shweder et al., 1997). In Indian society, the ethics of autonomy, based on justice, harm, and rights, is subordinated to and in the service of the ethics of community, which refers to status, hierarchy, and social order, and the ethics of divinity based on concepts of sin, sanctity, duty, and natural order. In the United States, by contrast, there is a "specialization" in the ethics of autonomy, with community, and divinity in even smaller part, providing a background.

In India, the ethics of autonomy is linked to the idea of a soul, which obligates respect (souls include human and nonhuman animals). More dominant, however, is the ethic of community, in which a person's identity is associated with status and relationships to others to a much greater extent than individuality. Relationships are part of hierarchical orderings in which people in subordinate and dominant positions are obligated to protect and look after each other's interests (e.g., wives should be obedient to husbands and husbands should be responsive to the needs and desires of wives). Shweder et al. (1997) regard this as analogous to feudal ethics, where the feudal lord does for others as much as they do for him (an asymmetrical reciprocity because one person is in a position of dominance and control).

Along with the three types of morality, another set of modifications and extensions of the theory is that cultural content is communicated to individuals who are prepared by evolution with deep emotions to receive and rapidly process the content, making decisions intuitively (Haidt, 2001). In Haidt's view, rationality and reasoning are largely irrelevant in moral evaluations and decisions and it is immediate, reflexive reactions, such as revulsion, disgust, and sympathy that trigger moral reactions. Judging acts as wrong involves immediate "gut" reactions of intuitive kinds that do not involve reasoning. For Haidt, the defining feature of "intuitions" is quantitative: They occur rapidly, without effort, automatically, and without intentionality. Reasoning contrasts with intuitions in that it is slow, requires effort, and makes use of evidence. Moral reasoning is used mainly after the fact to justify to self and others why an act is intuitively grasped as wrong "when faced with a social demand for a verbal justification one becomes a lawyer building a case rather than a judge searching for the truth" (p. 814).

To the extent that evidence is provided for the proposition that moral evaluations are intuitive, it is from research in nonmoral realms. Haidt cites a number of studies from social psychology that appear to support the idea that people are biased, emotive, intuitive, and unconcerned with evidence. Moreover, Haidt proclaims that research on moral reasoning only reveals what people do in the way of justification to convince others or to rationalize, in a post hoc way, positions they hold for other reasons. However, he does not provide evidence as to how the moral reasoning investigated in so many studies fails to account for moral evaluations or how it is that such reasoning is mainly used for purposes of persuasion and rationalization. A good part of Haidt's argument is based on a few examples. One that he seems to regard as prototypical is that of incest—an example that could be viewed as shared within cultures, yet applicable across cultures, and an evolutionary adaptation. Incest is an act, even when it is specified that it is consensual and there is no risk of pregnancy occurring, to which people react immediately with a gut reaction that it is wrong and are unable to explain why. The specific example provided is of a brother and sister who go on vacation and, with all precautions, decide to make love. The act is intuitively grasped as wrong because most people say something like "I don't know, I can't explain it. I just know it's wrong."

A key question is the generality of this type of example and whether it applies to people's moral lives more generally and meaningfully. The research discussed in subsequent sections provides a good deal of evidence that children, adolescents, and adults explain many of their moral evaluations in ways that are very different from the way they approach an issue like incest. A number of features in social situations are taken into account, including what has been referred to as informational assumptions or assumptions about reality (see the discussion that follows; for a critique of the emotivist-intuitionist position, see Turiel, 2006a).

Emphasizing Judgment and Reciprocal Social Interactions

In several approaches considered thus far, it is, for the most part, proposed that children acquire morality from the family and/or the culture, and that this occurs very early in life. It is presumed that the necessary components of morality emerge very early in life—infants and very young children show positive social behaviors, react with positive emotions to others, and form attachments with them.

The findings that young children show positive moral emotions and actions toward others indicate that the foundations of morality are established in early childhood and do not solely entail the control and inhibition of children's tendencies toward gratifying needs or drives or acting on impulses. However, that the foundations of positive morality are established in early childhood does not necessarily establish that significant aspects of development do not occur beyond early childhood; that judgments, deliberations, and reflections are unimportant; or that many experiences, in addition to parental practices, do not contribute. As noted earlier, the theories and research of Piaget and Kohlberg have had much to do with the shift away from conceptualizing morality as entailing self-control over impulses through their demonstrations that children think about the social world, attempt to understand social relationships, form judgments of right and wrong, and thereby engage in reciprocal interactions with others. However, Piaget and Kohlberg thought that extrinsic features, such as basing right and wrong on obedience and sanctions, structure young children's moral judgments. As is discussed, it appears that Piaget and Kohlberg failed to uncover not only the positive nature of young children's moral feelings but also that young children form relatively complex judgments that are not based on extrinsic features.

Studies of moral development suggest alternatives to the propositions that emotions are primary in morality, that moral acquisition is mainly due to effects of parental practices on children, or that morality largely reflects the acquisition of societal standards. Dunn et al. (1995) found differences in the two types of situations they assessed (physical harm and cheating) and documented that relationships with siblings influence development. By 2 or 3 years of age, children display a fair amount of teasing of mothers, physical aggression, destruction of objects, and an increasing ability to engage in arguments and disputes with mothers (Dunn & Munn, 1987). This increasing variety in young children's social relationships is consistent with the findings reviewed by Grusec and Goodnow (1994) showing that parental practices are related to type of misdeed (e.g., moral or conventional), children judge the appropriateness of reasons given by parents when communicating with them, and parents may encourage ways of behaving that differ from those they engage in themselves.

An interactional perspective also needs to account for many aspects of social life in addition to family, including interactions among peers. It has been proposed that the effects of peer interactions are a consequence of "the coordinating of one's perspective and actions with those of another, rather than through the transmission of information and ideas" (Damon, 1981, p. 165).

CONSTRUCTION OF MORAL JUDGMENTS THROUGH SOCIAL INTERACTIONS

Conflicts, disputes, argumentation, and discussion are all part of social interactions. For many who emphasize the role of judgments in morality, such social interactions are involved in the individual's constructions of moral judgments that are not solely local or derived primarily from parental teachings or from an integrated, consistent cultural pattern. A significant aspect of approaches emphasizing judgments is to have an epistemological grounding with regard to the nature of the realm of morality. For a number of researchers, such grounding is provided by philosophical traditions that, as put by Nussbaum (1999), presume that "human beings are above all reasoning beings." Nussbaum also maintained that emotions are intertwined with moral reasoning. In this view, emotions involve evaluative appraisals so that "the entire distinction between reason and emotions begins to be called into question, and one can no longer assume that a thinker who focuses on reason is excluding emotion" (p. 72). From the psychological perspective, emotional experiences inform the development of thought and, reciprocally, thinking informs the development and maintenance of emotions.

MORAL JUDGMENTS IN EARLY CHILDHOOD AND BEYOND

Kohlberg's stage formulation, in which young children's moral judgments are based on obedience and sanctions, was derived from responses to complex situations in which competing and conflicting issues are depicted. As an example, the often-cited situation of a man who must decide whether to steal an overpriced drug that might save his wife's life includes considerations of the value of life, property rights, violating the law, interpersonal obligations, and personal responsibilities to each of these. In that sense, Kohlberg was attempting to study judgments in contexts. He constructed hypothetical situations in which the use of readily conceived values (e.g., it is wrong to steal; it is wrong to allow someone to die) would be complicated by situational circumstances (e.g., if you do not steal, you sacrifice a life; if you try to save a life, you violate another's property rights). These situations, however, presented multifaceted problems requiring children to weigh and coordinate competing moral considerations and nonmoral considerations (Turiel, 1978a). The complexity of the judgments required by those situations led to the appearance that young children's moral judgments are contingent on sanctions, are not based on understandings of morality as generalizable, and it is not until after progressing to the fourth stage (usually not until at least adolescence) that morality is distinguished from nonmoral issues (Turiel & Davidson, 1986). Research into several aspects of moral judgments indicates that starting at a young age children make moral judgments that are not based on extrinsic features like obedience and sanctions. These include judgments about distributive justice and prosocial actions.

Research on children's concepts of sharing and distribution revealed a developmental progression of moral judgments (Damon, 1977, 1980, 1988), with indications that very young children are somewhat attuned to sharing. In their second year, children take turns in playing with objects and show awareness that food or candy can be divided. Information regarding how children 4 to 5 years of age and older conceptualize sharing comes from research on children's judgments about hypothetical and real-life situations entailing the distribution of goods. For example, in one situation, children in a class that made paintings to sell at a school fair must decide how to distribute the proceeds. It was found that children's thinking about distributive justice progresses through four levels encompassing equality, merit, and benevolence (though not at the first level). At the first level, concepts of distribution initially are tied to the child's own desires and perspectives. After these initial judgments, children begin to bring in external criteria (such as size or ability). Although these external features ultimately are used to justify a person's desires and goals, this way of thinking leads to other-oriented concepts based on equality, merit, and benevolence. Elementary school-aged children, at the next level, base their judgments on equality; everyone should be given the same amount and receive the same treatment, regardless of merit or need. Next comes a shift to considerations of merit and reciprocity; distribution is based on the need to acknowledge good deeds, hard work, or personal attributes like intelligence. The next shift includes judgments that take benevolence into account, with greater awareness of competing claims and an understanding of the need for compromises to resolve claims in a fair manner. Therefore, by the ages of 10 or 11 years, children take into account merit (hard work, talent), advantages and disadvantages, and other factors (e.g., investment, inheritance).

Children's judgments about sharing or distribution pertain to actions beneficial to others and possibly entail sacrifice of self-interests. These are not the only types of positive social actions experienced by children. The term *prosocial moral reasoning* has been used (Eisenberg-Berg, 1979) with reference to judgments about positive social actions (e.g., helping, giving) serving to benefit others in contexts in which a person's actions are not based on rules, laws, or the dictates of authorities. Children were presented with hypothetical situations posing conflicts between the needs and desires of different actors and questioned about whether it would be right to help, give, or share with others at the expense of their own goals. One situation depicted people faced with deciding whether to help feed those of another town who had lost their food in a flood; doing so would present a hardship to them. Other situations included donating blood, helping another who is being mugged or bullied, and helping physically disabled children.

A sequence of five age-related levels in judgments about prosocial actions were identified—a sequence proposed to reflect developmental advances in "capabilities for complex perspective taking and for understanding abstract concepts" (Eisenberg, Miller, Shell, McNalley, & Shea, 1991, p. 849). At the first level, judgments are based on a "hedonistic," self-focused orientation (personal gain is linked to reciprocity with others, based in identification and relationship with another, or liking for the other), whereas at the next level there is an orientation to the needs of others. This is followed by judgments based on stereotypes of good or bad persons, along with concerns with the approval or disapproval of others. The fourth level is characterized by a self-reflective and empathetic orientation, including sympathetic concern and caring for others, and taking the perspective of others. At the fifth level, there is an internalization of affect linked to self-respect and an internalization of laws, norms, duties, and responsibilities, as well as abstract types of reasoning about society, rights, justice, and equality.

Domain Specificity: Emphasizing Distinctions in Judgments

Concepts of welfare and justice emerge as central in the development of morality across the diversity of theoretical approaches. Several theorists pursued hypotheses regarding other issues, but their research findings have pointed to welfare and justice as ubiquitous components of moral judgments [e.g., in Gilligan's (1982) transformed proposition that care and justice coexist; the transformed cultural proposition that non-Westerners maintain concepts of justice and welfare].

Philosophers, dating back to the formulations of Aristotle, have considered concepts of justice and welfare central to morality. Aristotle, like many philosophers after him (e.g., Dworkin, 1977; Gewirth, 1978; Habermas, 1990; Rawls, 1971), considered justice as "other-regarding," impartial, and as characterized by universality. As indicated, Piaget's research was consistent with moral epistemologies of this type. However, Piaget proposed that understandings of welfare, justice, and rights did not emerge until after a period in which right and wrong are judged by the word of authorities and the necessity of adhering to their rules (the "unilateral respect" in young children's heteronomous thinking). In this way of thinking, justice is subordinated to obeying rules and authority: "if distributive justice is brought into conflict with adult authority, the youngest subjects will believe authority right and justice wrong" (Piaget, 1932, p. 304). However, several studies conducted in the United States (e.g., Damon, 1977; Laupa, 1991; Laupa & Turiel, 1986; Tisak, 1986) and Korea (Kim, 1998; Kim & Turiel, 1996) have yielded a different portrayal of young children's understandings of authority relations and moral judgments. These studies have shown that young children, in evaluating commands by either adults or peers in positions of authority, account for the type of act commanded and the boundaries of the authority's jurisdiction in a social context. With acts entailing theft or physical harm to persons, young children (4 to 6 years) give priority to the act itself rather than the status of the person as in a position of authority. For example, whether they hold positions of authority, commands from peers or adults that children stop fighting were judged as legitimate. Moreover, commands from peers (with or without positions of authority in a school) that children stop fighting were judged as more legitimate than a conflicting command from an adult authority (e.g., a teacher) that children be allowed to continue fighting. By contrast, children do give priority to adult authority over children or other adults who are not in positions of authority for acts like turn-taking and interpretations of game rules.

Children's judgments are not based on respect or reverence for adult authority but on an act's harmful consequences to persons. Children's judgments about harmful consequences emerge early in life along with emotions of sympathy, empathy, and respect (Piaget, 1932; Turiel, 2006b); at young ages children go well beyond social impulses and the habitual or reflexive, attempting to understand emotions, other persons, the self, and interrelationships (Arsenio, 1988; Arsenio & Lemerise, 2004; Nucci, 1981; Turiel, 1983, 2007). A great deal of research has demonstrated that young children make moral judgments about harm, welfare, justice, and rights, which are different from their judgments about other social domains.

DOMAINS OF SOCIAL JUDGMENT

Distinguishing morality from other domains presupposes that individuals think about social relationships, emotions, social practices, and social order. It presupposes that thinking about morality has features distinctive from thinking about other aspects of the social world (hence the idea of domain specificity). It also presupposes that individuals' judgments about the social world include domains of importance, which need to be distinguished from morality. Individuals form judgments in the "personal" domain that pertain to actions considered outside the jurisdiction of moral concern or social regulation and legitimately in the jurisdiction of personal choice (Nucci, 2001). Individuals also form judgments about social systems, social organization, and the conventions that further the coordination of social interactions in social systems.

Morality, too, applies to social systems, but the contrast with convention is that it is not defined by existing social arrangements. In this perspective on morality, prescriptions are characterized as obligatory, generalizable, and impersonal to the extent that they stem from concepts of welfare, justice, and rights (Turiel et al., 1987). This type of definition of morality is, in part, derived from criteria given in philosophical analyses where concepts of welfare, justice, and rights are not seen as solely determined by consensus, agreement, or received wisdom. It is proposed that justice is universal, it is not legitimated by agreement (as opposed to convention), and it is impartial (not based on personal preference or individual inclinations).

These features of morality apply to laypersons' ways of thinking. It has been found that children and adolescents make judgments about welfare and justice that differ from their judgments about social convention in India (Bersoff & Miller, 1993), Korea (Song, Smetana, & Kim, 1987), Hong Kong (Yau & Smetana, 2003), Indonesia (Carey & Ford, 1983), Nigeria (Hollos, Leis, & Turiel, 1986), Zambia (Zimba, 1987), Brazil (Nucci, Camino, & Milnitsky-Sapiro, 1996), and Colombia (Ardila-Rey & Killen, 2001). A greater number of studies have evidenced that domain distinctions are made by children and adolescents in Western cultures. Well over 100 studies have examined and supported the validity of the domain distinctions (for reviews, see Smetana, 2006; Tisak, 1995; Turiel, 2002).

One direction of early research on domains was to examine how children make judgments about moral, conventional, and personal issues (e.g., Davidson, Turiel, & Black, 1983; Nucci, 1981; Smetana, 1981; Tisak & Turiel, 1984; Turiel, 1978b). Children were typically presented with a series of social acts or transgressions classified in accord with the distinctions among the domains. Thus, moral actions pertained to physical harm (e.g., hitting others or pushing them down), psychological harm (e.g., teasing, name-calling, or hurting feelings), and fairness or justice (e.g., failing to share, stealing, or destroying others' property). These acts were depicted as intentional and as resulting in negative consequences to others. Researchers also examined in more detail issues of psychological harm (Helwig, Hildebrandt, & Turiel, 1995) and fairness with regard to social exclusion (Killen, Lee-Kim, McGlothlin, & Stangor, 2002). By contrast, conventional issues pertained to uniformities or regulations serving functions of social coordination (e.g., modes of dress, forms of address, table manners, or forms of greeting). Actions that do not entail inflicting harm or violating fairness or rights and that are not regulated formally or informally are consistent with the definition of the personal domain (these issues, in Western cultures, include choices of friends, the content of personal correspondence, and recreational activities).

Two dimensions, in particular, have been examined. One pertains to the criteria by which thinking in domains is identified (referred to as criterion judgments); the second pertains to the ways individuals reason about courses of action (referred to as justifications). Assessments of criterion judgments have included questions as to whether the actions would be right or wrong in the absence of a rule or law, if the act would be all right if permitted by a person in authority (e.g., a teacher in a school context), whether an act would be all right if there were general agreement as to its acceptability, and whether the act would be all right if it were accepted in another group or culture. These studies consistently show that children and adolescents judge that moral issues are obligatory; that they are not contingent on authority dictates, rules or consensus (e.g., that the acts would be wrong even if no rule or law exists about it); or on accepted practices in a group or culture (e.g., the act is wrong even if it were an acceptable practice in another culture). Judgments about moral issues, based on these criteria, are structured by concepts of welfare, justice, and rights. Justifications for these judgments entail preventing harm and promoting welfare, fairness, and rights (Turiel, 1983, 2002).

Conventional issues are conceptualized as linked to existing social arrangements and contingent on rules, authority, and existing social or cultural practices. Justifications for judgments about conventional issues are based on understandings of social organization, including the role of authority, custom, and social coordination. Even when conventional transgressions are deemed very important, children still judge them by conventional criteria and justifications (Tisak & Turiel, 1988). Furthermore, nonmoral actions that are not part of the conventionally regulated system are judged to be part of the realm of personal jurisdiction, which defines the bounds of individual authority and establishes distinctions between the self and group (Nucci, 2001).

The findings on domain distinctions have far-reaching developmental implications. Because the domains are differentiated at fairly early ages and continue to be so into adulthood, development is not adequately characterized as entailing differentiations between domains. In addition, the domains provide the context for the study of developmental transformations. At least two types of analyses need to be drawn to better understand developmental changes. One would entail analyses of changes in judgments within domains and the other analyses of how the different domains are coordinated.

Research has been done on levels of thinking within the conventional domain (Turiel, 1983) and the personal domain (Nucci, 2001). Thus far, analyses of changes in thinking within the moral domain are limited. Levels of thinking about distributive justice identified by Damon (1977, 1980) have already been discussed. Other research indicates that young children's moral judgments are grounded in concepts of physical harm and welfare and that older children form greater understandings of psychological harm, fairness, justice, and equal treatment (Davidson et al., 1983). In early adolescence, there is also a greater concern with equity as part of fair treatment (Damon, 1977) and efforts to coordinate the fairness of equality and equity. (See Nucci, 2001, chap. 4, for a more extensive discussion of ways of characterizing developmental transformations in the moral domain.)

The research on domains shows that individuals' social judgments are multifaceted, including understandings of right and wrong based on concerns with welfare, justice, and rights that are not simply based on acceptance of societal values, along with understandings of the conventional system of social regulation and coordination judged as relative and context-specific. Starting in early childhood, differentiations are made among moral, conventional, and personal concepts whose origins appear to be based in early social experiences. This research indicates that a distinction between moral and conventional transgressions becomes more consistent and focused by about the ages of 4 or 5 years.

Just as children's judgments are multifaceted, their social experiences are varied. Some of those variations have already been considered—experiences with parents, siblings, and peers. Children also experience the substance of people's (adults' or children's) reactions to the events around them, including emotional responses to social interactions. Among young children's experiences are interactions that differ in the context of dealing with moral, conventional, or personal issues. A series of observational studies in schools, playgrounds, and homes (ages ranging from 2 and 3 years to late childhood) has shown that communications between adults and children, as well as other types of social interactions, are not uniform (e.g., Nucci & Nucci, 1982; Nucci & Turiel, 1978; Nucci & Weber, 1995).

Much more than exposure to directives about rules, standards, or norms is involved in children's social experiences. At the least, social interactions and social communications differ in accord with domains. Furthermore, the distinction between morality and social conventions has been shown to apply to situations actually experienced. An extensive study, conducted in the context of social interactions in elementary and junior high schools, showed that judgments about experienced moral and conventional events were similar to judgments about comparable hypothetical situations (Turiel, in press).

SOCIAL JUDGMENTS AND FAMILY INTERACTIONS

Differences among the domains of social judgment also have a bearing on social interactions in families. In addition to moral and conventional issues, the domain of personal jurisdiction is a salient aspect of social interactions across different age periods. As shown in a study (Nucci & Weber, 1995) of social interactions in the home between children (3 to 4 years of age) and mothers, children are given a fair amount of freedom and discretion with regard to aspects of behavior revolving around personal issues. Mothers allow their children choices in activities, show a willingness to negotiate, and accept challenges from them. Other studies have shown that mothers in the United States (Nucci & Smetana, 1996) and Japan (Yamada, 2004) believe that there are areas of personal jurisdiction to be granted to young children (e.g., clothes, recreational activities, or choices of playmates), but they also believe that control should be exercised over children's activities that have moral implications, that involve social conventions, and that might be unsafe. Therefore, the discretion mothers allow in the personal domain does not simply reflect a general permissive orientation.

The observational study by Nucci and Weber (1995), along with the research by Dunn and her colleagues (e.g., Dunn & Munn, 1987), show that relationships between parents and children, early on, include conflict and harmony, as well as domain differences in the extent to which parents are directive. This pattern of heterogeneity of social relationships is not, by any means, restricted to early childhood. It is generally accepted that conflicts occur between parents and adolescents (Smetana, 2002). Adolescence is a period in which parents have multiple goals for their children and in which personal decisions become more salient. The ways parents and adolescents think about moral, social-conventional, and personal issues in family interactions have been part of an extensive program of research by Smetana and her colleagues (see Smetana, 2002, for a review).

These studies consistently showed that morality is judged to be legitimately regulated and enforced by parents (Smetana, 2002), and that moral issues are not a frequent source of conflict. Adolescents also accept parental regulation over conventions. It is issues in the personal domain, as well as those entailing a combination of personal and conventional considerations, which produce disagreements and conflicts (Smetana, 1988; Smetana & Asquith, 1994). As with younger children, adolescents identify issues they consider part of personal jurisdiction (some of the issues examined in these studies include spending decisions, appearances, and friendship preferences). European American parents tend to believe that they should have authority to control these activities (judging the activities as part of social convention), whereas adolescents believe that the activities are not legitimately regulated and are part of the realm of personal choice.

These patterns of findings hold for African American families, with some differences. As one example, parents in African American families were more likely than European American families to insist on some degree of involvement in the decisions of adolescents as they grew older (Smetana, 2000; Smetana & Gaines, 1999). There also appears to be more concern among the middle-class African American parents with pragmatic and prudential issues (and less with conventional issues). More generally, African American parents are more restrictive of adolescents' freedom of choices over personal issues and issues that involve conventional and personal matters. Nevertheless, African American adolescents do assert their personal choices and oppose parents.

EMOTIONAL ATTRIBUTIONS AND SOCIAL JUDGMENTS

Observational studies also show that conflicts among siblings usually occur over morally relevant issues, such as possessions, rights, physical harm, and unkindness (Dunn & Munn, 1987). These interactions include feedback from siblings, which reveal negative reactions and feelings, as well as communications, especially from parents, about reasons as to why acts are wrong (Smetana, 2002). The observational studies suggest that the emotions surrounding moral transgressions may differ from those around conventional transgressions and those social events entail emotional reactions. Studies by Arsenio and his colleagues (Arsenio, 1988; Arsenio & Fleiss, 1996) have demonstrated that children associate different types of emotional outcomes with different types of social events. For instance, in one study (Arsenio, 1988), children from 5 to 12 years of age, who were presented with descriptions of several different types of acts, gave their assessments of the emotions that would be experienced by different participants (actors, recipients, and observers). For events entailing positive moral actions, such as helping and sharing, children generally attributed positive emotions, like happiness, to the actors. For conventional transgressions, children attributed neutral or somewhat negative emotions (sadness, anger) to the participants. In the case of moral transgressions entailing one person victimizing another (e.g., a child stealing a toy from another), children attributed very negative emotions to the recipients and observers, and attributed somewhat positive emotions to the perpetrators of the acts.

Children's reasons for characters in the events experiencing the emotions attributed to them, too, varied by domain of event and role of participants (Arsenio & Fleiss, 1996). The negative emotions expected of victims of moral transgressions were thought to occur because of the harm, loss, or injury resulting from the acts. For victimizers, however, it was thought that the material gains obtained by them would result in some feelings of happiness. With regard to conventional transgressions, it was thought that those in authority who tend not to want rules violated would feel negative emotions. Thus, children differentiate among the emotions attributed to people in different roles in an event. In particular, they attribute different emotions to victims and those who do the victimizing.

AMBIGUITIES, UNCERTAINTIES, AND DELIBERATIONS

Children, adolescents, and adults make moral judgments about many situations, such as harming another person for reasons of self-interest or stealing another's property (situations referred to as "prototypical," see Turiel et al., 1987), in an unambiguous way. However, not all situations are straightforward. Some situations include components from more than one domain (Turiel, 1989; Turiel & Davidson, 1986), so that the application of moral and social judgments is not entirely straightforward, entailing ambiguities, uncertainties, contradictions, and a good deal of disagreement. Many situations, studied naturalistically (Kelman & Hamilton, 1989) and experimentally (Haney, Banks, & Zimbardo, 1973; Milgram, 1974), pose conflicts between issues of harm and issues of authority, status, and social organization. Milgram's experiments on obedience to authority, which posed individuals with choices between avoiding harm and adhering to conventional authority-relations, have shown that moral and social decisions can entail uncertainties, emotional and cognitive conflicts, and belabored decision making (Turiel & Smetana, 1984).

Judgments about situations with salient features from more than one domain involve consideration of the different components, with expressions of conflict. The coordination of different domains applies to evaluations and decisions about social inclusion and exclusion (Killen et al., 2002). Some studies, conducted with preschoolers, children, and adolescents, examined judgments about social exclusion and gender stereotypes (e.g., in doll play or truck play) and racial stereotypes (e.g., in a basketball team or in a math club). The studies examined judgments about straightforward exclusion; these were situations in which a child is excluded because of gender or race. The studies also examined contextualized situations that depicted additional social or group considerations: information was provided about children's past experiences with the activity (child fitting the stereotype has more experience) or their qualifications (equally qualified or the child fitting the stereotype is better qualified). These assessments were made with regard to exclusion in friendships, peer groups, and school contexts. A central finding is that gender and racial exclusion were judged as wrong in straightforward situations. The judgments were based on moral reasons of fairness and equality. There was a greater tendency to accept exclusion in the contextualized situations. Moreover, these judgments included reasons based on conventional expectations and the need to maintain the goals of a social group (e.g., perform well in a basketball game or math competition).

INFORMATION, ASSUMPTIONS ABOUT REALITY, AND MORAL DECISIONS

The research discussed thus far indicates that there is a good deal of uniformity within and between cultures in the ways certain issues are morally evaluated. However, as is generally known and amply documented by many polls and surveys, sharp differences among people exist in positions taken on issues like abortion, homosexuality, and pornography (Turiel, Hildebrandt, & Wainryb, 1991). Research into the judgments of adolescents and adults also shows that individuals display inconsistencies and ambiguities. People differ in their judgments about these issues (and not about issues like killing or rape), in large measure, as a consequence of differences in assumptions about reality or aspects of nature. With regard to abortion, for example, differences were associated with assumptions about the origins of life, with those who assumed the fetus to be a life evaluating abortion as wrong.

Assumptions of an informational kind about persons, psychological states, biology, and nature represent an additional component to be added to the mix in analyses of social decision-making. Wainryb (1991) has shown that individuals may hold similar concepts about welfare, fairness, and rights but come to different decisions in situations where they apply different informational assumptions. An example is that assumptions about the effectiveness of parental punishment bears on evaluations of physical harm in the context of a parent disciplining a child, whereas, in other contexts, parents inflicting harm on children is commonly judged as unacceptable.

Possible variations in informational assumptions, especially those entailing assumptions about the natural and an afterlife, bear on cultural variations in moral decisions. It has been noted, not infrequently, that differences in such assumptions give the appearance of radical differences in moral concepts, when moral judgments or principles themselves may actually not vary (Asch, 1952; Hatch, 1983). Asch (1952) pointed out that beliefs about an afterlife bear on cultural practices. An example is the cultural practice of putting one's elderly parents to death because "there prevails the belief that people continue into the next world the same existence as in the present and that they maintain the same condition of health and vigor at the time of death" (Asch, 1952, p. 377). According to Asch, a concern with the welfare of one's parents underlies the practice. A similar view was proposed by Hatch (1983): "Judgments of value are always made against a background of existential beliefs and assumptions, consequently what appears to be a radical difference in values between societies may actually reflect different judgments of reality" (p. 67).

Most analyses of culture and morality, however, have not seriously considered the role of judgments of reality. Through consideration of such judgments the findings of Shweder et al. (1987) were reinterpreted by Turiel et al. (1987). In their comparative research of judgments about morality and convention in India and the United States, Shweder et al. presented individuals with some issues pertaining to matters like dress and eating (practices such as a son avoids eating chicken or getting a haircut the day after his father's death or a widow does not eat fish). These issues were supposedly conventional by U.S. standards, given their content, but treated as moral by Indians. Indians treat these as moral issues because of their assumptions about reality—especially about an after-life. As detailed elsewhere (Turiel et al., 1987), classifying acts solely on the basis of whether they involve matters like dress or food entails an overly literal interpretation of how to classify issues in domains (moral or otherwise) that fails to account for the intentions and goals of actors, the surrounding context of the actions, and informational assumptions. This literal interpretation would be akin to classifying any act that causes physical damage or pain to another person as a moral transgression. By that standard, a surgeon's thrust of the knife would be classified a moral transgression, as would the spanking of a child by a parent. Wainryb (1991) has shown that acts of hitting with the intent to harm are judged as morally wrong, whereas spanking is not judged as wrong because it is assumed that the actor's intent is to correct and guide a child's behavior and that he or she believes that spanking is effective.

For several "conventional" issues studied by Shweder et al. (1987), a different picture of their domain status emerges by considering the assumptions of reality surrounding the events. Those assumptions concern beliefs about an afterlife and actions on earth that can adversely affect unobservable entities such as souls and deceased ancestors. Several examples of practices in India involve events on earth that affect unobserved unearthly occurrences and beings, and illustrate how assumptions about an afterlife contextualize some issues to include potential harm. The cultural differences may thus reflect existential beliefs and not moral principles. A reanalysis by Turiel et al. (1987) showed that many issues of this kind pertaining to dress, food, and the like resulted in different judgments between Indians and Americans. By contrast, individuals in both cultures judged issues that directly depicted consequences of harm or unfairness to people on earth in the same ways.

THE PERSONAL AND THE SOCIAL

Most of the research comparing moral and conventional judgments with judgments in the personal domain has been conducted in Western cultures. From the viewpoint of the proposition that cultures can be divided according to orientations to collectivism and individualism, it would be expected that concepts of personal agency and jurisdiction are mainly part of Western individualism and not of non-Western collectivism. However, the findings from several studies (Ardila-Rey & Killen, 2001; Miller, Bersoff, & Harwood, 1990; Nucci et al., 1996; Yau & Smetana, 1996, 2003) in non-Western cultures showing that they distinguish areas of personal jurisdiction from moral and conventional regulations are consistent with fundamental propositions in the social theories and philosophical views of Habermas (1990). He argued that personal agency and individual freedom cannot be offset from collectivism or social solidarity, and that the self and the social, individual growth and social engagement, and personhood and social solidarity are not opposing orientations restricted to particular societies.

The development of personal boundaries and their connections to moral development have been elaborated by several researchers (e.g., Helwig, 1995; Nucci, 2001; Wainryb & Turiel, 1994). Beyond the identification of issues that individuals judge as part of personal jurisdiction, Nucci (2001) maintains that children attempt to establish boundaries between self and other, and that establishing such boundaries facilitates mutual respect and cooperation. Moreover, the process of coming to understand personal boundaries is social and includes interpersonal negotiations primarily around personal and not moral issues (Nucci & Weber, 1995). At a young age, children challenge parental authority to a greater extent in the personal than the moral realm.

Along with conceptions of philosophers (e.g., Dworkin, 1977), Nucci sees necessary links between the development of a personal sphere and concepts of rights. Concepts of the agency of self and others constitute the locus of the application of freedoms and rights. Indeed, if concepts of personal agency did not develop because persons were defined mainly through connections with the group and embeddedness in the collectivity (as in, e.g., Markus & Kitayama, 1991), it would follow that moral concepts of rights and freedoms would not apply.

Although many philosophers have regarded rights as universally significant, little research was conducted on the development of concepts of rights until recently. Helwig (1995), for instance, examined the judgments of American and Canadian children, adolescents, and adults about freedoms of speech and religion and about a series of situations entailing conflicts between the freedoms and other moral considerations. In response to general questions (e.g., Should people be allowed to express their views or engage in their religious practices? Would it be right or wrong for the government to institute laws restricting the freedoms?), most endorsed the freedoms and judged them as moral rights independent of existing laws that are generalizable to other cultural contexts. They based these judgments on psychological needs (e.g., self-expression, identity, and autonomy), social utility, and democratic principles. Along with the general judgments, however, individuals accepted restrictions on the freedoms when in conflict with other moral considerations (i.e., physical harm, psychological harm, or equality of opportunity). At younger ages, however, there was more likelihood of acceptance of restrictions than at older ages. The pattern of the application of rights by contexts is also found in Costa Rica, France, Italy, and Switzerland (Clémence, Doise, de Rosa, & Gonzalez, 1995). Moreover, these findings on rights, which were based on in-depth interviews, are consistent with findings of large-scale surveys of the attitudes of American adults toward civil liberties (McClosky & Brill, 1983).

All these studies indicate that there is a coexistence of concerns with the freedoms and rights of individuals and the welfare of the community. The findings support Habermas's contention that personal agency and social solidarity go together. Additional research, on the concepts of freedoms and rights of Druze Arabs living in northern Israel (Turiel & Wainryb, 1998), supports Habermas's (1993) view that the coexistence of personal agency and collectivism is not applicable "for Americans alone," and that it extends beyond those who are "heirs to the political thought of a Thomas Paine and a Thomas Jefferson" (p. 114).

The Druze community constitute a traditional hierarchical and patriarchal society, with strong sanctions for violations of societal norms (Wainryb & Turiel, 1994). Three types of freedoms were studied with adolescents and adults: speech, religion, and reproduction (i.e., freedom to bear the number of children desired). The Druze clearly judge, when put in general terms, that individuals should have noncontingent rights to each freedom. Individuals were also presented with conflicts depicting freedoms producing physical or psychological harm or having negative effects on community interests. Conflict situations also depicted ways that in the family the exercise of the freedoms by a son, daughter, or wife was in contradiction with the desires and directives of father or husband. The findings from the conflict situations showed that the Druze also think that freedoms should be, in certain situations, subordinated to other concerns, such as when they could cause harm to others. Similarly, in some situations (but not all) it is thought that considerations of community interest should take precedence over the right to exercise the freedoms. For the most part, however, freedoms and rights of sons, daughters, and wives were not subordinated to the authority of the father or husband.

Culture and Context Revisited

The research with the Druze, along with the other research in non-Western cultures, indicates that concepts of rights, welfare, and justice are found across cultures. In the context of these similarities among cultures, however, there are also differences.

In addition to differences in assumptions about reality, there are differences in the degree of hierarchically based distinctions in relationships between males and females and those of different social castes and classes. Many analyses of culture have focused on differences between cultures on these dimensions, interpreting them in accord with the proposition that cultures form integrated patterns represented either by an individualistic or collectivistic orientation. The hierarchical distinctions in gender or castes are said to be connected with the role designations of persons, through which persons are submerged in the group.

It is not at all clear, however, that the presumption of coherent, integrated cultural patterns and associated consistencies in individuals' judgments and actions are in line with other formulations central to the propositions of those emphasizing culture. In particular, the idea of coherence and consistency conflicts with the call for pluralism, and with the core ideas of cultural psychology that the mind is context-dependent, domain-specific, and local. With regard to pluralism, those emphasizing culture often have voiced that there be acceptance of a variety of moral perspectives. Shweder and Haidt (1993) asserted that Gilligan "won the argument for pluralism" (p. 362) by augmenting the traditional views on justice with the care orientation. They also argue that Gilligan's proposition does not go far enough in the quest for pluralism because it does not account for further variations among cultures.

These kinds of arguments are contradictory because descriptions of cultural orientations actually frame most of the elements in Gilligan's formulation of justice as part of Western (or individualistic) morality and most of the elements of the care orientation as part of non-Western (or collectivistic) morality. By describing cultures with integrated patterns of thought, a rather limited form of pluralism or heterogeneity is seen to be in differences between cultures while a unitary or homogeneous orientation (with a lack of pluralism) is imposed within cultures and for individuals. The evidence actually points in the other direction—that there is coexistence, not only within cultures but also for individuals, of care, interdependence, justice, and autonomy. As noted earlier, the research assessing those dimensions through Gilligan's formulations has shown that care (or collectivistic) and justice (or individualistic) judgments vary by context for females and males. The evidence suggests that the types of contextual distinctions drawn by Gilligan between females' and males' life circumstances are too broad and require further distinctions within each context.

Those emphasizing culture also have maintained that general, "abstract," universal moral principles are inadequate because they fail to account for variations among cultures. However, by locating contextual variations at the cultural level little consideration is given to variations that may be associated with contextual differences within cultures. For a given culture, therefore, constructs like individualism and collectivism end up functioning as general, abstract orientations that apply across contexts and fail to account for domain specificity. Distinctions in judgments by domain mean that individuals have heterogeneous orientations in social thought.

The coexistence of domains stems from a process of development that is not restricted to circumscribed experiences characterized by the family or parental child-rearing practices, more narrowly, or by culture, more broadly. As shown by much of the research considered thus far, social experiences influencing development are varied (with parents, siblings, peers, or social institutions). Through reciprocal interactions, children are engaged in communications, negotiations, compromises, disputes, and conflicts. The research has also shown that the diversity of children's social interactions includes concerns with the desires, goals, and interests of persons (self and others), as well as with the welfare of others and the group.

CULTURE AS CONTEXT OR CONTEXT AS CONTEXT?

Children's social interactions involve a dynamic interplay of personal goals and social goals, as well as interplay among different social goals. Reciprocity of social interactions means that individuals both participate in cultural practices and can stand apart from culture and take a critical approach to social practices. Typically, there are elements both of harmony and tension or conflict. Moreover, through the development of different domains of judgment, individuals deal with social situations from more than one perspective, taking into account varying features of situations and contexts.

The diversity in judgments of individuals includes domain specificity in people's thinking and contextual variations in the ways judgments are applied. People in so-called individualistic cultures have multiple social orientations, including concerns with social duties, the collective community, and interdependence, as well as independence, rights, freedoms, and equality. People in so-called traditional, collectivistic cultures endorse traditions, status, and role distinctions, but they also endorse individual freedoms and rights even when in contradiction with status and hierarchy.

Another issue of importance to moral and social functioning that involves contextual variations in judgments and actions is that of honesty. Honesty is often regarded as one of those moral matters that once acquired by the individual will be and should be applied consistently. In some analyses, honesty is a virtue or trait of character that children must be taught to always follow (Bennett, 1993). In other perspectives, honesty is linked to the need to maintain trust in social relationships.

Dishonest behavior can be self-serving and motivated for personal gain; however, issues of honesty are more complicated and are often weighed against other considerations so that there is much variability in the ways people act. For instance, honesty can be in conflict with desires to prevent harm to another. Some researchers who have recognized this type of conflict looked at so-called white lies—lies aimed at sparing the feelings of others (Lewis, 1993). There is only a little research on judgments about conflicts between honesty and preventing more serious harm. An example of how deception has been used to prevent harm is that during World War II many people lied and engaged in elaborate deceptions to save people from Nazi concentration camps. No doubt, they gave greater priority to preventing harm and deaths than to honesty.

Research addressing these issues shows that people systematically evaluate the consequences of telling the truth or engaging in deception in relation to furthering the welfare of persons, achieving justice, and promoting individual autonomy when it is perceived to be unfairly restricted. One study of this kind looked at how physicians evaluate deception of insurance companies when it is the only way to obtain approval for treatments or diagnostic procedures for medical conditions of different degrees of severity (Freeman, Rathore, Weinfurt, Schulman, & Sulmasy, 1999). With regard to severe conditions (life-threatening ones), the majority thought that the doctor was justified in engaging in deception. In other conditions, the percentages accepting deception were considerably lower, with the fewest (only 3%) judging that deception was legitimate for purposes of cosmetic surgery. Moreover, there is evidence that physicians actually do engage in deception of insurance companies (Wynia, Cummins, VanGeest, & Wilson, 2000).

Other research has shown a corresponding pattern of contextual differences in judgments of college undergraduates and adults about deception between husbands and wives (Turiel & Perkins, 2004). Participants were presented with situations entailing deception: One example is of a spouse who maintains a secret bank account; another example is of a spouse who, over the objections of the other, secretly attends meetings of a support group for a drinking problem. These acts were depicted as situations where only a husband works outside the home, with a wife engaging in deception; and the reverse, where only a wife works, with a husband engaging in deception. The large majority judged deception by wife or husband acceptable to attend meetings of a support group for a drinking problem. Most also judged it acceptable for the wife to maintain a secret bank account, but fewer judged it acceptable for a husband to engage in such deception even though it is the wife who works and controls the finances. It seems that the more general structure of power in society is taken into account in making these decisions. Males are accorded greater power and control over females, and family relationships are frequently based on the type of injustice that grants greater privileges and entitlements to men over women (Hochschild, 1989; Okin, 1989).

Another study (Perkins & Turiel, 2007) assessed judgments of adolescents who deceive parents or friends. The situations involved parents or peers telling an adolescent to act in ways that might be considered morally wrong (i.e., not to befriend another of a different race; to physically confront another who is teasing him or her); giving directives about issues of personal choice (not to date someone the parents or peers do not like; not to join a club because they think it is a waste of time); and directives about personal issues with prudential or pragmatic considerations (completing homework; not riding a motorcycle).

Most of the adolescents judged it acceptable to deceive parents about the demands considered morally wrong, viewing it necessary to prevent injustice or harm. The majority also thought that deception was justified when parents interfered with personal choices but that deception was not justified with regard to the prudential matters on the grounds that it is legitimate for parents to concern themselves with the welfare of their children (most thought the restrictions were not legitimate in the case of the moral and personal matters). Fewer judged deception of peers acceptable than deception of parents for the morally relevant and personal issues. Although the adolescents thought that the restrictions directed by peers were not legitimate, they were less likely to accept deception of peers than of parents because friends are in relationships of equality and mutuality and can confront each other about these matters without resorting to deception.

For these adolescents, honesty in social relationships is not a straightforward matter but they do not devalue honesty. Most said, in response to a general question, that lying is wrong, and the large majority thought that it is not justifiable to lie to parents or peers to cover up damage to property. A consistent finding across these studies is that deception and lying are judged wrong, but honesty is nevertheless evaluated in relation to competing moral claims. Social psychological experiments of morally relevant behaviors demonstrate the same phenomenon of variations by contexts. Although these experiments are well-known for their findings of group influences (Latanée & Darley, 1970), conformity (Asch, 1956), obedience (Milgram, 1974), and adherence to roles in social hierarchy (Haney et al., 1973), they actually show that individuals respond in several ways, often with conflict, and that different domains of judgment are used in interpreting the parameters of situations (Turiel, 2002). In each of these types of experiment, behaviors varied by context. In some experimental conditions, people generally obeyed an authority's directives to act in ways that caused physical pain to others (by administering electric shocks), but in other experimental conditions people generally defied the authority's directives to engage in similar acts (Milgram, 1974). Other experiments showed that individuals are influenced by group decisions as to whether to help someone in distress, helping in some situations but not in others (Latanée & Darley, 1970). Similarly, individuals "conform" to the judgments of a group in some situations but contradict the group in others (Asch, 1956).

The behaviors tapped in the experiments are not readily classified as independent and interdependent because of the interweaving of both types of judgment. Consider the research on whether bystanders intervene to help others in distress. An individual is more likely to intervene to help others when alone than when in the presence of others who do not intervene (Latanée & Darley, 1970). Thus, people seem to act in independent ways and take personal initiative when alone, but do so in the service of interdependence because the act furthers the welfare of others. Conversely, when in the presence of others, people are influenced socially in failing to intervene. This social influence, however, simultaneously works against interdependence in the sense that it is at the expense of the welfare of others. A similar analysis applies to experiments on obedience to an authority's commands to inflict pain on another person (Milgram, 1974). To the extent that participants in the experiments adhered to their assigned roles and accepted the authority's status and commands, they acted in ways consistent with a collectivistic orientation. In doing so, however, they acted against an interdependent concern with the welfare of the victim. To the extent that people defied the experimenter, and in that sense acted independently, they were acting in the service of the nonindividualistic goal of promoting the welfare of the victim. The overarching observation is that individuals do not simply obey or disobey nor act as conformists or nonconformists. Rather, they make judgments about the actions of others, social organizational features, and right and wrong.

Although it has been recognized that behaviors vary by situations (especially Mischel, 1973) and that research shows conformity, obedience to authority, and group influences among Americans (Kelman & Hamilton, 1989; Milgram, 1974), the import of these findings has not often been carried over to characterizations of culture. It seems that those who characterize Western cultures as individualistic attend mainly to one side of the picture.

TRADITION, SOCIAL HIERARCHY, HETEROGENEITY, AND SOCIAL OPPOSITION

Many of the findings considered thus far that document heterogeneous moral and social judgments come from research in the United States, but findings were reviewed from non-Western cultures showing that concepts of freedom and rights vary by context. Anthropological research yields direct evidence of contextual variations in the judgments of people in non-Western cultures, including variations in concepts of persons. Spiro's (1993) extensive review of anthropological research shows that concepts of self, as well as other social concepts, vary across individuals in the same society and across societies: "There is much more differentiation, individuation, and autonomy in the putative non-Western self, and much more dependence and interdependence in the putative Western self, than these binary opposite types allow" (p. 117). Ethnographic evidence also shows that self-interested goals and concerns with personal entitlements are part of the thinking of the Balinese, Indians, Pakistanis, Nepalese, and Japanese. Others have also documented that self-interest, personal goals, and autonomy are significant in the lives of Indians from various backgrounds (Neff, 2001), among the Toraja of Indonesia (Hollan, 1992), in China (Helwig, Arnold, Tan, & Boyd, 2003), Bangladesh (Chen, 1995), and Japan (e.g., Crystal, 2000).

In accord with these findings, several anthropologists (e.g., Abu-Lughod, 1991; Strauss, 1992; Wikan, 1996) have criticized conceptions of cultures as homogenous, coherent, and timeless or as embodying integrated, stable sets of meanings and practices readily reproduced in individuals through socialization. Abu-Lughod (1991) argued for the need to include, in analyses of culture, conflicts, disputes, arguments, contradictions, ambiguity, and changes in cultural understandings:

> *By focusing on particular individuals and their changing relationships, one would necessarily subvert the most problematic connotations of culture: homogeneity, coherence, and timelessness. Individuals are confronted with choices, struggle with others, make conflicting statements, argue about points of view on the same events, undergo ups and downs in various relationships and changes in their circumstances, and fail to predict what will happen to them or those around them. (p. 154)*

Several anthropologists and philosophers (Nussbaum, 1999; Okin, 1989; Strauss, 1992; Wikan, 1996) have stressed the need to explore the varying meanings individuals give to the dominant values and practices of the society, so as to ascertain if the actor's point of view looks different from the perspective of dominant institutions and ideologies.

Exploring the individual's understandings of dominant cultural values and practices was one of the aims of another study conducted with the Druze (Wainryb & Turiel, 1994). A second aim was to explore the hypothesis that there is more than one side to cultural practices. The varying perspectives individuals may take render cultural practices more nebulous and multifaceted; thus, a particular type of cultural practice is likely to contain differing messages. Cultural practices around social hierarchies are a case in point. One side of social hierarchy, which has been the focus of cultural analyses, is specified duties and roles, and the submergence of self into a network of interdependence. The other side, however, is that there is a strong sense of independence and personal entitlements embedded in hierarchical arrangements. Examples of where such entitlements hold are for those in higher castes and social classes relative to those in lower castes and classes (Turiel, 2002; Turiel & Wainryb, 2000), and in relationships between males and females. Whereas practices revolving around social hierarchical arrangements convey duties and role prescriptions, they also convey that those in dominant positions have personal autonomy and entitlements—especially due to them by those in subordinate positions.

The research with the Druze examined personal, social, and moral judgments, focusing on decision making in the family regarding various activities of relevance in the community (e.g., choices of occupational and educational activities, household tasks, friendships, or leisure activities). Family decisions were examined because the society is hierarchically organized, with a strong patriarchal tradition. Many restrictions are placed on the activities of females, including their education, work, dress, social affiliations, and leisure time. Men are in control of finances and can easily divorce their wives, while wives cannot easily divorce their husbands. Individuals were presented with conflicts between persons in dominant (i.e., husbands and fathers) and subordinate (i.e., wives, daughters, and sons) positions in the family structure. In one set of situations, a person in a dominant position objects to the choices of a person in a subordinate position (e.g., a husband objects to his wife's decision to take a job); in another set, the person in the subordinate position objects to the choices of the person who is in a dominant position (e.g., a wife objects to her husband's decision to change jobs).

The results showed that Druze males and females think men should have decision-making power and discretion. While most participants judged that wives or daughters should not engage in activities to which a father or husband objects, this was not reciprocal. Most judged that a man is free to choose his activities even if his wife, daughter, or son objects. It was also thought that sons should be able to make their own decisions over objections from their fathers. The inequality in decision making is based on different reasons for the decisions and on different ways of conceptualizing the relationships. In the context of objections from a man to the activities of his wife or daughter, relationships were viewed in interdependent and hierarchical terms. In the context of objections from a wife or daughter to the activities of her husband or father (as well as a father who objects to a son's activities), the relationships were conceptualized as ones of independence for a person choosing the activities (i.e., men). Males and females attributed interdependence to females and to males in some contexts and both attributed independence to males. However, Druze females were aware of the pragmatics of social relationships in the family and sometimes attributed decision-making authority to males because males have the power to inflict serious negative consequences to those in subordinate positions (e.g., abandonment and divorce). Moreover, females evaluated many of these practices giving men power over the activities of females as unfair. Similar findings were obtained in India (Neff, 2001), Colombia (Mensing, 2002), and Benin (Conry-Murray, 2006).

The findings of these studies demonstrate the multiple aspects of social hierarchy; in traditional cultures there is a complex picture of judgments about role obligations, prescribed activities, personal independence and entitlements, pragmatic concerns, and fairness. The multiplicity of individuals' perspectives brings with it both acceptance and opposition to cultural practices. Whereas persons in dominant and subordinate positions share orientations to duties, status, prescribed roles, and personal autonomy, those in subordinate positions are aware of the pragmatics of power relationships and view themselves as having legitimate claims to independence and unmet rights. The perspectives of those in subordinate positions are significant reflections of culture and provide windows into conflicts, struggles, below-the-surface activities, and the interplay of opposing orientations such as independence and interdependence, or conflict and harmony. Along with participation in cultural practices, there can be distancing and opposition to cultural practices (Turiel, 2002; Turiel & Wainryb, 2000; Wainryb, 2006).

Conflicts, struggles, and below-the-surface activities have been documented when social practices are examined from the perspective of those in subordinate positions. One example is Abu-Lughod's (1991) studies of Bedouin women in Egypt. Abu-Lughod reported that there are disagreements among group members, conflicts between people, efforts to alter existing practices, and struggles between wives and husbands, and parents and children. Women develop strategies, often hidden from men, to assert their interests. These strategies, which include deception, allow women to avoid unwanted arranged marriages, assert their will against restrictions imposed by men, attain some education, and engage in prohibited leisure activities. Similarly, Wikan (1996) found that in poor neighborhoods of Cairo there are conflicts, struggles, and efforts at subverting cultural practices. Women attempt to circumvent the effects of inequalities in their relationships with men and express unhappiness with practices like polygamy. Wikan's (1996) general conclusion is that "these lives I depict can be read as exercises in resistance against the state, against the family, against one's marriage, against the forces of tradition or change, against neighborhoods and society—even against oneself." (pp. 6–7; for additional examples of studies in India and Bangladesh, see Chen, 1995; Chowdry, 1994).

When we look beyond public characterizations of social practices and when analyses are not restricted to the perspectives of those in dominant positions, there is evidence for a conception of cultures as embodying variations in behaviors, diversity in orientations, and conflicting points of view resulting in disagreements, disputes, struggles among people, and acts of social opposition and resistance (Abu-Lughod, 1991; Turiel, 2002; Wikan, 1996). Conflicts over inequalities among persons of differing status are not restricted to traditional, hierarchically organized cultures. Gender relationships in Western cultures usually are not strictly hierarchical nor are the activities of females restricted in the same ways as in some traditional cultures. Despite the emphasis on equality in the culture, there is considerable evidence documenting inequalities and struggles between men and women in several spheres of life (see Hochschild, 1989; Okin, 1989). Unequal treatment of women is reflected in their underrepresentation in the political system, in positions of power and influence in business and the professions, and in fewer opportunities for paid work. In addition, in many fields, women are paid substantially less than men for similar work, even when their qualifications are the same (Okin, 1989). Studies of dual-career families document a pervasive pattern in which women are expected to do more of the undesired household tasks, and men have entitlements such as greater time for leisure activities (see Hochschild, 1989, for a review). These conditions provide another example of the interweaving of duties, roles, and assertion of rights and personal entitlements. Often conflicts occur over men's orientation to maintaining role distinctions and role responsibilities in the family and women's concerns that there be greater equality and fairness (Hochschild, 1989; Okin, 1989).

The existence of conflicts, opposition and below-the-surface activities in cultures that include the vantage points of those in subordinate positions as different from those in dominant positions casts a different light on the intersection of gender and cultures. Although there are commonalities and shared experiences between men and women in a culture, the issues are more complicated because women from different cultures also share certain perspectives based on their roles in a hierarchy, the status held, their burdens, and the unfairness experienced. Similarly, men from different cultures share perspectives based on their roles in the hierarchy, their privileges and burdens, and a sense of personal entitlements based on the extent to which they are in dominant positions relative to women.

However, aspects other than gender further complicate perspectives based on social hierarchy. Males and females share dominant or subordinate positions with regard to their status as members of social classes in the hierarchy. It is likely that the perspectives of men or women of lower classes in non-Western and Western cultures have some similarities (as would the perspectives of those of higher classes). Correspondingly, differences exist between people of different social classes in a culture (an interesting comparison, again, is between an upper-middle-class woman and a working-class man with regard to roles in the hierarchy). These considerations have received very little attention in research on social and moral development.

All these examples demonstrate that along with the cohesiveness usually ascribed to cultures, it is necessary to account for conflicts, struggles, ambiguities, and multiple perspectives. Multiple perspectives stem from both the varieties of social experiences and the differentiated domains of social thinking developed by individuals. Social and cultural practices can be nebulous, with many sides and connotations. They embody multiple messages and are carried out in multiple ways. It has been documented that experiences influencing social development go well beyond any one type (family, peers, culture) and must be viewed form the perspective of reciprocal interactions. The idea of development stemming from reciprocal interactions suggests that there are discrepancies between cultural ideologies, public documents, official pronouncements, or other manifestations of cultural orientations. More generally, the multiplicity of orientations in cultures, including conflicts and ambiguities, means that morality cannot be simply characterized through particular ideologies like that of individuals with rights and freedom to enter into contracts or that of persons as interconnected in a social order of involuntary duties and roles.

Conclusions

Heterogeneity and variability in social judgments and actions do not stem solely from the presence of different groups or cultures in a society. The types of variations documented pertain to given cultures and individual members of those cultures. However, those variations are not haphazard, nor do the features of situations simply determine how people will act. Rather, heterogeneity and variation suggest that the thinking of individuals is flexible and takes into account different and varied aspects of the social world. The variety of social experiences is relevant to an understanding of moral development because children attend to much more than one type or context of social experience. Moreover, these and other aspects of a vast social world affect development through reciprocal interactions that include a coordination of emotions, thoughts, and actions.

Very important social and psychological questions are embedded in the existence of social hierarchies within cultures. Do people accept their designated roles in a society even when they are in subordinate positions? Do people embrace cultural practices that grant greater power, control, and privileges to one group over another (such as males over females)? Do people in subordinate positions evaluate social hierarchies positively because of a respect for society or culture even though they hold an unequal status and are in subservient positions? Or do people in such positions perceive the inequalities as wrong and unjust and do they, in one way or another, critique societal arrangements and cultural practices through opposition, resistance, and subversion?

These questions go to the core of how cultures are to be characterized and to how individuals develop morally and socially. Research showing that people oppose cultural practices and act to resist and change societal arrangements and cultural practices they judge unfair leads to the view that morality does not involve compliance, and that its development is neither an accommodation to societal values or norms nor their internalization (Turiel, 2007).

There is evidence that the origins of opposition and resistance are in childhood (Turiel, 2006b). Children's social development involves a combination of what can be referred to as cooperative and oppositional orientations. Evidence of the origins of opposition and resistance in early childhood comes from studies showing that young children do not accept rules or authority dictates that are in contradiction with their judgments of what is morally right or wrong (Laupa, 1991; Laupa & Turiel, 1986). Moreover, there is a coexistence of positive, prosocial actions toward and conflicts with parents, siblings, and peers (e.g., Dunn, 1988; Dunn et al., 1995; Dunn & Munn, 1987). This combination reflects the multiple judgments that children develop. Children's moral judgments also produce acts of defiance or opposition when they perceive unfairness and harm. The research on deception discussed earlier and the research on family conflicts (Smetana, 2002) demonstrates that opposition and resistance are part of the lives of adolescents, as well.

As children interact with a varied social world, their development entails the formation of different but systematic types or domains of social reasoning. Whereas morality is an important domain, it needs to be understood alongside and in intersection with other aspects of understandings of the social world. Because the social world is varied, and because there are different domains of social judgment, moral prescriptions are not always applied in the same way. Social situations often require a balancing and coordination of different social and personal considerations related to features of the context. Consequently, although moral prescriptions dictate obligations based on right or wrong and how a person ought to act, they do not dictate rigid rules or maxims. There is more than one way to reach a particular set of goals. Habermas (1993) articulated this feature of morality, particularly in his analyses of how a traditional Kantian view failed to account for context. He argued that rational principles can take different forms in their application in contexts and are subject to change and elaboration through social discourse. However, those who critique abstract moral principles all too often postulate analogously abstract, decontextualized, and general cultural orientations.

Especially in the United States, the current political and intellectual climate seems to be one that de-emphasizes thought, reasoning, rationality, and reflective analyses and not infrequently places them under attack. Emotions, with assumptions about their underlying evolutionary biological bases, are frequently regarded as the central determinants of morality along with the authority of the group, religion, or culture. As important as emotions—especially sympathy, empathy, and respect—are for moral functioning, emotions occur in and among persons who can think about them with regard to other people and in relation to complicated social agendas, goals, and arrangements. The relationships among emotions, moral judgments, reflections, and deliberations require a great deal of attention in research and theoretical formulations. Of course, scholars critiquing the proposition of rational, deliberative, and reflective moral functioning, themselves engage in those very activities, attempting to persuade others though rational discourse. These human activities are not solely the province of scholars, however. Laypersons (children included), too, deliberate and reason systematically about emotions and morality and engage in discussion and argumentation.

References

Abu-Lughod, L. (1991). Writing against culture. In R. E. Fox (Ed.), *Recapturing anthropology: Working in the present* (pp. 137–162). Santa Fe, NM: School of American Research Press.

Ardila-Rey, A., & Killen, M. (2001). Middle-class Colombian children's evaluations of personal, moral, and social conventional interactions in the classroom. *International Journal of Behavioral Development, 25,* 246–255.

Aronfreed, J. (1968). *Conduct and conscience: The socialization of internalized control over behavior.* New York: Academic Press.

Arsenio, W. (1988). Children's conceptions of the situational affective consequences of sociomoral events. *Child Development, 59,* 1611–1622.

Arsenio, W., & Fleiss, K. (1996). Typical and behaviourally disruptive children's understanding of the emotional consequences of socio-moral events. *British Journal of Developmental Psychology, 14,* 173–186.

Arsenio, W., & Lemerise, E. A. (2004). Aggression and moral development: Integrating social information processing and moral domain models. *Child Development, 75,* 987–1002.

Asch, S. E. (1952). *Social psychology.* Englewood Cliffs, NJ: Prentice-Hall.

Asch, S. E. (1956). Studies of independence and conformity: A minority of one against a unanimous majority. *Psychological Monographs, 70*(Whole No. 416).

Benedict, R. (1934). *Patterns of culture.* Boston: Houghton Mifflin.

Bennett, W. J. (1993). *The book of virtues.* New York: Simon & Schuster.

Bersoff, D. M., & Miller, J. G. (1993). Culture, context, and the development of moral accountability judgments. *Developmental Psychology, 29,* 664–676.

Bruner, J. (1990). *Acts of meaning.* Cambridge, MA: Harvard University Press.

Carey, N., & Ford, M. (1983, August). *Domains of social and self-regulation: An Indonesian study.* Paper presented at the meeting of the American Psychological Association, Los Angeles, CA.

Catron, T. F., & Masters, J. C. (1993). Mothers' and children's conceptualizations of corporal punishment. *Child Development, 64,* 1815–1828.

Chen, M. (1995). A matter of survival: Women's right to employment in India and Bangladesh. In M. C. Nussbaum & J. Glover (Eds.), *Women, culture, and development: A study of human capabilities* (pp. 61–75). New York: Oxford University Press.

Chilamkurti, C., & Milner, J. S. (1993). Perceptions and evaluations of child transgressions and disciplinary techniques in high- and low-risk mothers and their children. *Child Development, 64,* 1801–1814.

Chowdry, P. (1994). *The veiled women: Shifting gender equations in rural Haryana 1880–1990.* Delhi, India: Oxford University Press.

Clémence, A., Doise, W., de Rosa, A. S., & Gonzalez, L. (1995). Le représentation sociale de droites de l'homme: Une recherche internationale sur l'étendue et les limites de l'universalité. *Journal Internationale de Psychologie, 30,* 181–212.

Colby, A., & Damon, W. (1983). Listening to a different voice: A review of Gilligan's "In a different voice." *Merrill-Palmer Quarterly, 29,* 473–481.

Conry-Murray, C. (2006). *Reasoning about gender hierarchy in Benin, West Africa: The role of informational assumptions and pragmatic concerns.* Unpublished doctoral dissertation, University of California, Berkeley.

Crystal, D. S. (2000). Concepts of deviance and disturbance in children and adolescents: A comparison between the United States and Japan. *International Journal of Psychology, 35,* 207–218.

Damon, W. (1977). *The social world of the child.* San Francisco: Jossey-Bass.

Damon, W. (1980). Patterns of change in children's social reasoning: A 2-year longitudinal study. *Child Development, 51,* 1010–1017.

Damon, W. (1981). Exploring children's social cognition on two fronts. In J. M. Flavell & L. Ross (Eds.), *Social cognitive development: Frontiers and possible futures* (pp. 154–175). Cambridge: Cambridge University Press.

Damon, W. (1988). *The moral child: Nurturing children's natural moral growth.* New York: Free Press.

Davidson, P., Turiel, E., & Black, A. (1983). The effect of stimulus familiarity on the use of criteria and justifications in children's social reasoning. *British Journal of Developmental Psychology, 1,* 49–65.

Dunn, J. (1988). *The beginnings of social understanding.* Cambridge, MA: Harvard University Press.

Dunn, J., Brown, J. R., & Maguire, M. (1995). The development of children's moral sensibility: Individual differences and emotion understanding. *Developmental Psychology, 31,* 649–659.

Dunn, J., & Munn, P. (1987). Development of justification in disputes with mother and sibling. *Developmental Psychology, 23,* 791–798.

Dworkin, R. M. (1977). *Taking rights seriously.* Cambridge, MA: Harvard University Press.

Eisenberg, N., Miller, P. A., Shell, R., McNalley, S., & Shea, C. (1991). Prosocial development in adolescence: A longitudinal study. *Developmental Psychology, 27,* 849–857.

Eisenberg-Berg, N. (1979). Development of children's prosocial moral judgment. *Developmental Psychology, 15,* 128–137.

Eisenberg-Berg, N., & Geisheker, E. (1979). Content of preachings and power of the model/preacher: The effect on children's generosity. *Developmental Psychology, 15,* 168–175.

Frankena, W. K. (1963). *Ethics.* Englewood Cliffs, NJ: Prentice-Hall.

Freeman, V. G., Rathore, S. S., Weinfurt, K. P., Schulman, K. A., & Sulmasy, D. P. (1999). Lying for patients: Physician deception of third-party payers. *Archives of Internal Medicine, 159,* 2263–2270.

Freud, S. (1959). Some psychological consequences of the anatomical distinction between the sexes. In S. Freud (Ed.), *Collected papers* (pp. 186–197). New York: Basic Books. (Original work published 1925)

Gewirth, A. (1978). *Reason and morality.* Chicago: University of Chicago Press.

Gilligan, C. (1982). *In a different voice: Psychological theory and women's development.* Cambridge, MA: Harvard University Press.

Gilligan, C., & Attanucci, J. (1988). Two moral orientations: Gender differences and similarities. *Merrill-Palmer Quarterly, 34,* 223–237.

Greeno, C. G., & Maccoby, E. E. (1986). How different is the "different voice?" *Signs, 11,* 313–314.

Grusec, J. E., & Goodnow, J. J. (1994). Impact of parental discipline methods on the child's internalization of values: A reconceptualization of current points of view. *Developmental Psychology, 30,* 4–19.

Habermas, J. (1990). *Moral consciousness and communicative action.* Cambridge, MA: MIT Press.

Habermas, J. (1993). *Justification and application.* Cambridge, MA: MIT Press.

Haidt, J. (2001). The emotional dog and its rational tail: A social intuitionist approach to moral judgment. *Psychological Review, 108,* 814–834.

Haney, C., Banks, C., & Zimbardo, P. (1973). Interpersonal dynamics in a simulated prison. *International Journal of Criminology and Penology, 1,* 69–97.

Hatch, E. (1983). *Culture and morality: The relativity of values in anthropology.* New York: Columbia University Press.

Helwig, C. C. (1995). Adolescents' and young adults' conceptions of civil liberties: Freedom of speech and religion. *Child Development, 66,* 152–166.

Helwig, C. C., Arnold, M. L., Tan, D., & Boyd, D. (2003). Chinese adolescents' reasoning about democratic and authority-based decision making in peer, family, and school contexts. *Child Development, 74,* 783–800.

Helwig, C. C., Hildebrandt, C., & Turiel, E. (1995). Children's judgments about psychological harm in social context. *Child Development, 66,* 1680–1693.

Hochschild, A. (1989). *The second shift.* New York: Avon.

Hoffman, M. L. (1991a). Commentary on: Toward an integration of Kohlberg's and Hoffman's moral development theories. *Human Development, 34,* 105–110.

Hoffman, M. L. (1991b). Empathy, social cognition, and moral action. In W. M. Kurtines & J. L. Gewirtz (Eds.), *Handbook of moral behavior and development: Vol. 1. Theory* (pp. 275–301). Hillsdale, NJ: Erlbaum.

Hoffman, M. L. (2000). *Empathy and moral development: Implications for caring and justice.* Cambridge: Cambridge University Press.

Hollan, D. (1992). Cross-cultural differences in the self. *Journal of Anthropological Research, 48,* 283–300.

Hollos, M., Leis, P. E., & Turiel, E. (1986). Social reasoning in Ijo children and adolescents in Nigerian communities. *Journal of Cross-Cultural Psychology, 17,* 352–374.

Jaffee, S., & Hyde, J. H. (2000). Gender differences in moral orientation: A meta-analysis. *Psychological Bulletin, 12,* 703–726.

Johnston, D. K. (1988). Adolescents' solutions to dilemmas in fables: Two moral orientations: Two problem solving strategies. In C. Gilligan, J. V. Ward, J. M. Taylor, & B. Bardige (Eds.), *Mapping the moral domain: A contribution of women's thinking to psychological theory and education* (pp. 49–71). Cambridge, MA: Harvard University Press.

Kelman, H. C., & Hamilton, V. L. (1989). *Crimes of obedience: Toward a social psychology of authority and responsibility.* New Haven, CT: Yale University Press.

Killen, M. (1991). Social and moral development in early childhood. In W. M. Kurtines & J. L. Gewirtz (Eds.), *Handbook of moral behavior and development: Vol. 2. Research* (pp. 115–138). Hillsdale, NJ: Erlbaum.

Killen, M., Lee-Kim, J., McGlothlin, H., & Stangor, C. (2002). How children and adolescents value gender and racial exclusion. *Monographs of the Society for Research in Child Development, 67*(4, Serial No. 271).

Kim, J. M. (1998). Korean children's concepts of adult and peer authority and moral reasoning. *Developmental Psychology, 34,* 947–955.

Kim, J. M., & Turiel, E. (1996). Korean and American children's concepts of adult and peer authority. *Social Development, 5,* 310–329.

Kochanska, G. (1993). Toward a synthesis of parental socialization and child temperament in early development of conscience. *Child Development, 64,* 325–347.

Kochanska, G. (1994). Beyond cognition: Expanding the search for the early roots of internalization, and conscience. *Developmental Psychology, 30,* 20–22.

Kochanska, G. (1997). Multiple pathways to conscience for children with different temperaments: From toddlerhood to age 5. *Developmental Psychology, 33,* 228–240.

Kohlberg, L. (1969). Stage and sequence: The cognitive-developmental approach to socialization. In D. Goslin (Ed.), *Handbook of socialization theory and research* (pp. 347–480). Chicago: Rand McNally.

Kohlberg, L. (1971). From is to ought: How to commit the naturalistic fallacy and get away with it in the study of moral development. In T. Mischel (Ed.), *Psychology and genetic epistemology* (pp. 151–235). New York: Academic Press.

Latanée, B., & Darley, J. M. (1970). *The unresponsive bystander: Why doesn't he help?* New York: Appleton-Crofts.

Laupa, M. (1991). Children's reasoning about three authority attributes: Adult status, knowledge, and social position. *Developmental Psychology, 27,* 321–329.

Laupa, M., & Turiel, E. (1986). Children's conceptions of adult and peer authority. *Child Development, 57,* 405–412.

Lennon, R., & Eisenberg, N. (1987). Gender and age differences in empathy and sympathy. In N. Eisenberg & J. Strayer (Eds.), *Empathy and its development* (pp. 195–217). New York: Cambridge University Press.

Lewis, M. (1993). The development of deception. In M. Lewis & C. Saarni (Eds.), *Lying and deception in everyday life* (pp. 90–105). New York: Guilford Press.

Luria, Z. (1986). A methodological critique. *Signs, 11,* 318.

Lyons, N. P. (1983). Two perspectives: On self, relationships, and morality. *Harvard Educational Review, 53,* 125–145.

Markus, H. R., & Kitayama, S. (1991). Culture and the self: Implications for cognition, emotion, and motivation. *Psychological Review, 98,* 224–253.

McClosky, M., & Brill, A. (1983). *Dimensions of tolerance: What Americans believe about civil liberties.* New York: Russell Sage.

Mensing, J. F. (2002). *Collectivism, individualism, and interpersonal responsibilities in families: Differences and similarities in social reasoning between individuals in poor, urban families in Colombia and the United States.* Unpublished doctoral dissertation, University of California, Berkeley.

Milgram, S. (1974). *Obedience to authority.* New York: Harper & Row.

Miller, J. G., Bersoff, D. M., & Harwood, R. L. (1990). Perceptions of social responsibilities in India and in the United States: Moral imperatives or personal decisions? *Journal of Personality and Social Psychology, 58,* 33–47.

Mischel, W. (1973). Toward a cognitive social learning reconceptualization of personality. *Psychological Review, 80,* 252–283.

Neff, K. D. (2001). Judgments of personal autonomy and interpersonal responsibility in the context of Indian spousal relationships: An examination of young people's reasoning in Mysore, India. *British Journal of Developmental Psychology, 19,* 233–257.

Nucci, L. P. (1981). The development of personal concepts: A domain distinct from moral or social concepts. *Child Development, 52,* 114–121.

Nucci, L. P. (1984). Evaluating teachers as social agents: Students' ratings of domain appropriate and domain inappropriate teacher responses to transgressions. *American Educational Research Journal, 21,* 367–378.

Nucci, L. P. (2001). *Education in the moral domain.* Cambridge: Cambridge University Press.

Nucci, L. P., Camino, C., & Milnitsky-Sapiro, C. (1996). Social class effects on Northeastern Brazilian children's conceptions of areas of personal choice and social regulation. *Child Development, 67,* 1223–1242.

Nucci, L. P., & Nucci, M. S. (1982). Children's responses to moral and social conventional transgressions in free-play settings. *Child Development, 53,* 1337–1342.

Nucci, L. P., & Smetana, J. G. (1996). Mother's concepts of young children's areas of personal freedom. *Child Development, 67,* 1870–1886.

Nucci, L. P., & Turiel, E. (1978). Social interactions and the development of social concepts in preschool children. *Child Development, 49,* 400–407.

Nucci, L. P., & Weber, E. (1995). Social interactions in the home and the development of young children's conceptions of the personal. *Child Development, 66,* 1438–1452.

Nussbaum, M. C. (1999). *Sex and social justice.* New York: Oxford University Press.

Okin, S. M. (1989). *Justice, gender, and the family.* New York: Basic Books.

Oyserman, D., Coon, H. M., & Kemmelmeier, M. (2002). Rethinking individualism and collectivism: Evaluation of theoretical assumptions and meta-analyses. *Psychological Bulletin, 128,* 3–72.

Perkins, S. A., & Turiel, E. (2007). To lie or not to lie: To whom and under what circumstances? *Child Development, 78,* 609–621.

Piaget, J. (1932). *The moral judgment of the child.* London: Routledge & Kegan Paul.

Piaget, J. (1995). *Sociological studies.* London: Routledge. (Original work published 1960)

Pollitt, K. L. (1992). Are women really superior to men? *Nation,* 799–807.

Radke-Yarrow, M., Zahn-Waxler, C., & Chapman, M. (1983). Children's prosocial dispositions and behavior. In P. Mussen (Series Ed.) & E. M. Hetherington (Vol. Ed.), *Handbook of child psychology: Vol. 4. Socialization, personality, and social development* (4th ed., pp. 469–545). New York: Wiley.

Rawls, J. (1971). *A theory of justice.* Cambridge, MA: Harvard University Press.

Sagi, A., & Hoffman, M. L. (1976). Empathic distress in the newborn. *Developmental Psychology, 32,* 720–729.

Saltzstein, H. D., Weiner, S., & Munk, J. (1995). *Children's judgments of the fairness of mothers who approve/disapprove good and bad intended acts.* Unpublished manuscript, City University of New York.

Shweder, R. A., & Haidt, J. (1993). The future of moral psychology: Truth, intuition, and the pluralist way. *Psychological Science, 4,* 360–356.

Shweder, R. A., Mahapatra, M., & Miller, J. G. (1987). Culture and moral development. In J. Kagan & S. Lamb (Eds.), *The emergence of morality in young children* (pp. 1–83). Chicago: University of Chicago Press.

Shweder, R. A., Much, N. C., Mahapatra, M., & Park, L. (1997). The "big three" of morality (autonomy, community, and divinity) and the "big three" explanations of suffering. In A. Brandt & P. Rozin (Eds.), *Morality and health* (pp. 119–169). Stanford, CA: Stanford University Press.

Skinner, B. F. (1971). *Beyond freedom and dignity.* New York: Knopf.

Smetana, J. G. (1981). Preschool conceptions of moral and social rules. *Child Development, 52,* 1333–1336.

Smetana, J. G. (1988). Adolescents' and parents' conceptions of parental authority. *Child Development, 59,* 321–335.

Smetana, J. G. (1989). Toddlers' social interactions in the context of moral and conventional transgressions in the home. *Developmental Psychology, 25,* 499–508.

Smetana, J. G. (2000). Middle class African American adolescents' and parents' conceptions of parental authority and parenting practices: A longitudinal investigation. *Child Development, 71,* 1672–1686.

Smetana, J. G. (2002). Culture, autonomy, and personal jurisdiction in adolescent-parent relationships. In H. W. Reese & R. Kail (Eds.), *Advances in child development and behavior* (Vol. 29, pp. 51–87). New York: Academic Press.

Smetana, J. G. (2006). Social domain theory: Consistencies and variations in children's moral and social judgments. In M. Killen & J. G. Smetana (Eds.), *Handbook of moral development* (pp. 119–153). Mahwah, NJ: Erlbaum.

Smetana, J. G., & Asquith, P. (1994). Adolescents' and parents' conceptions of parental authority and adolescent autonomy. *Child Development, 65,* 1147–1162.

Smetana, J. G., & Gaines, C. (1999). Adolescent-parent conflict in middle-class African-American families. *Child Development, 70,* 1447–1463.

Song, M. J., Smetana, J. G., & Kim, S. Y. (1987). Korean children's conceptions of moral and conventional transgressions. *Developmental Psychology, 23,* 577–582.

Spiro, M. (1993). Is the Western conception of the self "peculiar" within the context of the world cultures? *Ethos, 21,* 107–153.

Strauss, C. (1992). Models and motives. In R. G. D'Andrade & C. Strauss (Eds.), *Human motives and cultural models* (pp. 1–20). Cambridge: Cambridge University Press.

Tisak, M. S. (1986). Children's conceptions of parental authority. *Child Development, 57,* 166–176.

Tisak, M. S. (1995). Domains of social reasoning and beyond. In R. Vista (Ed.), *Annals of child development* (Vol. 11, pp. 95–130). London: Jessica Kingsley.

Tisak, M. S., & Turiel, E. (1988). Variation in seriousness of transgressions and children's moral and conventional concepts. *Developmental Psychology, 24,* 352–357.

Turiel, E. (1978a). The development of concepts of social structure: Social convention. In J. Glick & K. A. Clarke-Stewart (Eds.), *The development of social understanding* (pp. 25–107). New York: Gardner Press.

Turiel, E. (1978b). Social regulation and domains of social concepts. In W. Damon (Ed.), *Social cognition: New directions for child development* (pp. 45–74). San Francisco: Jossey- Bass.

Turiel, E. (1979). Distinct conceptual and developmental domains: Social convention and morality. In H. E. Howe & G. B. Keasey (Eds.), *Nebraska Symposium on Motivation: Vol. 25. Social cognitive development* (pp. 77–116). Lincoln: University of Nebraska Press.

Turiel, E. (1983). *The development of social knowledge: Morality and convention.* Cambridge: Cambridge University Press.

Turiel, E. (1989). Domain-specific social judgments and domain ambiguities. *Merril-Palmer Quarterly, 35,* 89–114.

Turiel, E. (2002). *The culture of morality: Social development, context, and conflict.* Cambridge: Cambridge University Press.

Turiel, E. (2003). Morals, motives, and actions. In L. Smith, C. Rogers, & P. Tomlinson (Eds.), *Development and motivation: Joint perspectives* (Monograph Series II, Serial No. 2, pp. 29–40). Leicester, England: British Journal of Educational Psychology.

Turiel, E. (2006a). The multiplicity of social norms: The case for psychological constructivism and social epistemologies. In L. Smith & J. Voneche (Eds.), *Norms in human development* (pp. 189–207). Cambridge: Cambridge University Press.

Turiel, E. (2006b). Thought, emotions, and social interactional processes in moral development. In M. Killen & J. G. Smetana (Eds.), *Handbook of moral development* (pp. 7–36). Mahwah, NJ: Erlbaum.

Turiel, E. (2007). The trouble with the ways morality is used and how they impede social equality and social justice. In C. Wainryb, J. Smetana, & E. Turiel (Eds.), *Social development, social inequalities, and social justice* (pp. 1–26). Mahwah, NJ: Erlbaum.

Turiel, E. (in press). Thought about actions in social domains: Morality, social conventions, and social interactions. *Cognitive Development.*

Turiel, E., & Davidson, P. (1986). Heterogeneity, inconsistency, and asynchrony in the development of cognitive structures. In I. Levin (Ed.), *Stage and structure: Reopening the debate* (pp. 106–143). Norwood, NJ: Ablex.

Turiel, E., Hildebrandt, C., & Wainryb, C. (1991). Judging social issues: Difficulties, inconsistencies and consistencies. *Monographs of the Society for Research in Child Development, 56*(Serial No. 224).

Turiel, E., Killen, M., & Helwig, C. C. (1987). Morality: Its structure, functions and vagaries. In J. Kagan & S. Lamb (Eds.), *The emergence of moral concepts in young children* (pp. 155–244). Chicago: University of Chicago Press.

Turiel, E., & Perkins, S. A. (2004). Flexibilities of mind: Conflict and culture. *Human Development, 47,* 158–178.

Turiel, E., & Smetana, J. G. (1984). Social knowledge and social action: The coordination of domains. In W. M. Kurtines & J. L. Gewirtz (Eds.), *Morality, moral behavior, and moral development: Basic issues in theory and research* (pp. 261–282). New York: Wiley.

Turiel, E., & Wainryb, C. (1998). Concepts of freedoms and rights in a traditional hierarchically organized society. *British Journal of Developmental Psychology, 16,* 375–395.

Turiel, E., & Wainryb, C. (2000). Social life in cultures: Judgments, conflicts, and subversion. *Child Development, 71,* 250–256.

Wainryb, C. (1991). Understanding differences in moral judgments: The role of informational assumptions. *Child Development, 62,* 840–851.

Wainryb, C. (2006). Moral development in culture: Diversity, tolerance, and justice. In M. Killen & J. G. Smetana (Eds.), *Handbook of moral development* (pp. 211–240). Mahwah, NJ: Erlbaum.

Wainryb, C., & Turiel, E. (1994). Dominance, subordination, and concepts of personal entitlements in cultural contexts. *Child Development, 65,* 1701–1722.

Wikan, U. (1996). *Tomorrow, God willing: Self-made destinies in Cairo.* Chicago: University of Chicago Press.

Wynia, M. K., Cummins, D. S., VanGeest, J. B., & Wilson, I. B. (2000). Physician manipulation of reimbursement rules for patients: Between a rock and a hard place. *Journal of the American Medical Association, 283,* 1858–1865.

Yamada, H. (2004). Japanese mothers' views of young children's areas of personal discretion. *Child Development, 75,* 164–179.

Yau, J., & Smetana, J. G. (1996). Adolescent-parent conflict among Chinese adolescents in Hong Kong. *Child Development, 67,* 1262–1275.

Yau, J., & Smetana, J. G. (2003). Conceptions of moral, social-conventional, and personal events among Chinese preschoolers in Hong Kong. *Child Development, 74,* 647–658.

Zahn-Waxler, C., Radke-Yarrow, M., Wagner, E., & Chapman, M. (1992). Development of concern for others. *Developmental Psychology, 28,* 126–136.

Zimba, R. F. (1987). *A study of forms of social knowledge in Zambia.* Unpublished doctoral dissertation, Purdue University, West Lafayette, IN.

PART VIII

ADOLESCENCE

Chapter 15

The Second Decade:
What Develops (and How)?

DEANNA KUHN and SAM FRANKLIN

Why do most researchers who study cognitive development focus their attention on the first decade, or even the first years or months, of life? One explanation is their wish to examine the earliest origins of later forms. If we can understand how something simple develops, we are arguably in the best position to understand the later development of its more complex instances. In this chapter, we make the case that there is much to learn from examining not just developmental origins but where development is headed and the patterns and processes entailed in getting there. It also becomes clear that cognitive development is by no means complete as children enter their second decade. Much continues to happen at all levels, from the neurological to the societal. Moreover, we need to ask not only, "What develops?" but also what the mechanisms of change are, and whether these mechanisms themselves undergo change—a possibility we pay particular attention to.

A major difference in the study of cognitive development in the first versus second decades of life, however, is that by middle childhood, researchers commonly encounter cognitive achievements that may or may not develop. As a result, enormous variability in cognitive functioning is apparent by adolescence, We probe the factors that contribute to this variability, among them not just environmental diversity but the greater role that older children and adolescents play in choosing what they will do, hence assuming the role of producers of their own development (Lerner, 2002).

What Develops? Abandoning the Simple Answer

Widespread interest in adolescent cognition as having unique characteristics absent in children's thinking began in the context of Piaget's stage theory. Inhelder and Piaget

(1958) proposed a final stage of formal operations as supported by a unique logical structure emerging at adolescence and manifesting itself in a number of different capabilities. In the context of stage theory, formal operations are significant as a reflection of the emergence of a structure that Piaget characterized as operations on operations. With attainment of this stage, according to Piaget, thought becomes able to take itself as its own object—adolescents become able to think about their own thinking, hence the term "operations on operations," or, more precisely, mental operations on the elementary operations of classification and relation characteristic of the preceding stage of concrete operations. The formal operational thinker becomes able, for example, not only to categorize animals according to physical characteristics and according to habitats but also to operate on these categorizations, that is, to put them into categories and on this basis to draw inferences regarding relations that hold among animals' physical characteristics and habitats. The formal operational thinker is thus said to reason at the level of *propositions* that specify relations between one category (or relation) and another. As aspects of this second-order operations structure, according to the theory, there emerge other reasoning capabilities, notably systematic combination and isolation of variables, and several others such as proportional and correlational reasoning, also thought to involve second-order operations.

Subsequent cross-sectional research generally upheld Inhelder and Piaget's (1958) claim that adolescents on average do better than children in tasks purported to assess these competencies (Keating, 1980, 2004; Neimark, 1975). Piaget, however, hypothesized these capabilities to appear in early adolescence as a tightly linked, integrated whole, a manifestation of the emergence of the formal operational stage structure. In this respect, subsequent research has been less supportive, yielding little evidence for a unified or abrupt transition from a childhood stage of concrete operations to an adolescent stage of formal operations.

Three kinds of variability contribute to this conclusion. One is inter-individual variability in the age of emergence of the different alleged behavioral manifestations of the formal operational structure, for example, combinatorial and isolation-of-variables reasoning. A second is intra-individual variability in the emergence of formal operations skills. There is little evidence to support the claim that these skills emerge synchronously within an individual. Third, and most serious, is task variability. As is the case with respect to virtually all reasoning skills, whether one is judged to possess or not possess the skill is very much a function of the manner in which it is assessed, in particular the amount of contextual support provided (Fischer & Bidell, 1991). Indeed, task variance is so pronounced that we confront in this chapter the phenomenon we call the paradox of early competence and later failures of competence. In other words, there are some tasks in which a particular form of reasoning can be identified as present in children as young as preschool age. In other forms of the same task, however, even adults appear deficient.

These findings make it doubtful that emergence of a singular cognitive structure at a specific point in time—whether Piaget's formal operational structure or some other structure—can account adequately for the progress along multiple fronts that we examine in this chapter. Nonetheless, to anticipate our conclusions, we shall end up maintaining that Piaget was on the right track in identifying thinking about one's own thought as a hallmark of cognitive development in the second decade of life. We can assign such a capability a modern-sounding name, like metacognition or executive control. But what needs to be abandoned is the idea that we can pinpoint its emergence to some narrow window of months or years in late childhood or early adolescence, or indeed any time. Even preschoolers can be metacognitive when, for example, they recognize an earlier false belief that they no longer hold, while examples of adults' failures to be sufficiently metacognitive are myriad.

In what has perhaps been a final blow to any "immaculate transition" (Siegler & Munakata, 1993) model of developmental change, microgenetic research (Kuhn, 1995; Kuhn & Phelps, 1982; Siegler, 2006; Siegler & Crowley, 1991) has revealed that individuals simultaneously have available not just one but multiple potential cognitive strategies they might apply to a problem, some more and others less advanced. Development, then, entails gradual shifts in the frequency of usage of various strategies, with better strategies being used more frequently and weaker strategies less frequently. The implication is that we must forego any simple account of emergence of a single structure that drives all of cognitive development, in favor of examining multiple strands of development that may have commonalities as well as unique characteristics.

Before we can abandon unitary accounts in favor of multidimensional ones, however, we must consider another very different kind of unitary account—one that explains development not in terms of emergence of a qualitatively new structure but rather in terms of quantitative change in the cognitive system, specifically quantitative increase in its processing ability. How far do hypotheses of this kind take us in accounting for cognitive development, and what evidence exists with respect to them?

Brain and Processing Growth

THE DEVELOPING BRAIN

Neuroimaging techniques are now available that allow precise longitudinal examination of changes in brain structure over time. These studies make it clear that the brain continues to develop into and through the adolescent years. The area of greatest change after puberty is the prefrontal cortex. It is implicated in what have come to be called "executive" functions (Nelson, Thomas, & deHaan, Chapter 2, this volume), which include monitoring, organizing, planning, strategizing—indeed any mental activity that entails managing one's own mental processes—and is also associated with increase in impulse control.

Modern longitudinal neuroimaging research reports two kinds of change, one in the so-called "gray matter," which undergoes a wave of overproduction (paralleling one occurring in the early years) at puberty, followed by a reduction, or "pruning," of those neuronal connections that do not continue to be used. A second change, in so-called "white matter," is enhanced myelination, that is, increased insulation of established neuronal connections, improving their efficiency (Giedd et al., 1999). By the end of adolescence, then, this evidence suggests, teens have fewer, more selective, but stronger, more effective neuronal connections than they did as children.

Notable about this neurological development is the fact that it is at least in part experience driven. It cannot be viewed in the traditional unidirectional manner simply as a necessary or enabling condition for cognitive or behavioral change. Instead, the activities a young adolescent chooses to engage in, and not to engage in, affect which neuronal connections will be strengthened and which will wither. These neurological changes in turn further support the activity specialization, in a genuinely interactive process that helps to explain the widening individual variation that appears in the second decade of life.

PROCESSING SPEED

What developments in cognitive function might these neurological advances support? Improvements in information processing may be of three major kinds. The clearest of the three is increase in processing speed. The most common measures of processing speed require naming a series of numbers or familiar words. Processing speed can also be measured simply as reaction time to a stimulus (Luna, Garver, Urban, Lazar, & Sweeney, 2004). In each of these cases, the pattern is clear. Response time has been found to decrease on measures of processing speed from early childhood roughly through mid-adolescence (Demetriou, Christou, Spanoudis, & Platsidou, 2002; Kail, 1991, 1993; Luna et al., 2004).

INHIBITION

While reaction time is a measure of how rapidly one can make a response, another cognitive function that is at least as important is the ability to inhibit a response. Although they are related, it is useful to make a distinction between two types of inhibition, especially because different research paradigms have been employed to investigate them.

In the first type, emphasis is on irrelevant stimuli that have the potential to interfere with processing and the challenge is to ignore them, that is, inhibit any attention to them, in favor of attending to stimuli relevant to the task at hand. This type of inhibition is typically referred to under the headings of selective attention. In an early classic study, Maccoby and Hagen (1965) demonstrated that the superior performance of adolescents over children on a learning task was attributable not only to their greater attention to the stimuli that were to be remembered but also to their reduced attention to irrelevant stimuli that were also present. Older participants performed more poorly than younger ones on a test of memory for the irrelevant stimuli. Increasing ability to ignore attention to irrelevant stimuli during the childhood years has also been reported in other studies (Hagen & Hale, 1973; Schiff & Knopf, 1985). A different kind of interference from competing stimuli arises not from simultaneous but from previously presented material. Kail (2002) reports a decline between middle childhood and adulthood in proactive interference— the interference of previously presented material in present recall. Adolescents and adults are better able than children to screen out and disregard the previous material.

A second type of inhibition has received less attention, despite its potential importance. It is the ability to inhibit an already established response in contexts where it is not appropriate to exhibit it. For example, an individual may be instructed to inhibit a response that has become routine whenever a particular signal is given. Performance on these tasks improves until mid-adolescence (Luna et al., 2004; Williams, Ponesse, Schacher, Logan, & Tannock, 1999). In another paradigm a "directed forgetting" technique has been used in studies of memorization of word lists. The individual is instructed to forget words that have already been presented and hence to inhibit them in subsequent free recall. During recall, improvement occurs across childhood in the ability to inhibit words under "forget" instructions, as well as to withhold production of incidentally learned words (Harnishfeger, 1995). Young children, in contrast, typically display no difference in frequencies of production of words they were instructed to forget and those they were instructed to remember.

In sum, the evidence is ample that both resistance to interfering stimuli and inhibition of undesired responses develop across the childhood years and into adolescence. It has even been suggested they may play a role in the developmental advances observed in basic memory tasks, notably digit span, that have been employed as measures of processing capacity (Bjorklund & Harnishfeger, 1990; Harnishfeger, 1995). It should be noted, however, that the evidence regarding inhibition of inappropriate responses comes from paradigms in which the individual is instructed to inhibit the undesirable response. We have less information about response inhibition in the important condition in which individuals must make their own decisions regarding the desirability of a response and hence which responses to exhibit and which to inhibit. We have more to say about this form of inhibition in examining the topic of executive control.

PROCESSING CAPACITY

In addition to speed and inhibition, a third processing dimension that may undergo developmental change is processing capacity. Here things become decidedly less clear, the primary reason being that different researchers operationalize this construct in different ways. At least two different components are involved. One, emphasized by Pascual-Leone (1970), is short-term storage space. The other, emphasized by Case (1992), is operating space, which arises when the individual must manipulate the information rather than only store and reproduce it. The familiar construct "working memory" in some contexts has been used in the operating space sense and in others in the storage sense.

Developmentally increasing processing speed, Case proposed (1992; Case, Kurland, & Goldberg, 1982; Case & Okamoto, 1996), reduces the space required for operations, leaving more space available for short-term storage. The net result is greater processing efficiency, rather than any absolute increase in capacity. Others (Cowan, 1997; Demetriou et al., 2002), however, dispute Case's claim that processing speed and processing capacity are causally related, as opposed to independently increasing or mediated by a third variable such as increasing knowledge.

Whether processing capacity increases in an absolute sense or only as a by-product of increased efficiency, there remains the question of how to measure it. Pascual-Leone (1970), Case (1992, 1998; Case & Okamoto, 1996), and, more recently Halford (Halford & Andrews, 2006; Halford, Wilson, & Phillips, 1998), have all proposed systems to identify the processing demands of a task, and, by implication, the processing capacity of an individual based on performance on the task. Case, for example, identified progress from tasks requiring attention to a single dimension to tasks requiring the coordination of two dimensions (Case & Okamoto, 1996). Halford and Andrews (2006) invoke a construct of structural complexity, indexed by the number of dimensions that must be simultaneously represented if their relations are to be understood. They present data for a number of tasks suggesting that this number increases developmentally from early childhood to early adolescence.

In sum, there is general agreement across studies that processing continues to improve in the second decade of life, but there is little agreement about the particulars. There are several distinct components of processing ability and there is no universal agreement as to how they are related. Do speed and capacity develop independently or do they influence one another? The same question can be asked with respect to speed and inhibition (Luna et al., 2004). Do processing improvements take place in a domain-general manner, as some researchers maintain (Gathercole, Pickering, Ambridge, & Wearing, 2004; Swanson, 1999), or do improvements differ across domains, as others claim (Demetriou et al., 2002)? Perhaps most importantly, the challenge of achieving widely agreed-on measures of processing capacity remains. Tasks involving capacities to represent versus store versus manipulate mental symbols are likely to produce divergent capacity estimates. Moreover, the goal of producing "pure" measures of capacity remains elusive. Supporting this conclusion is the fact that we have yet to identify conclusively the set of factors that contribute to developmentally increasing performance on what might appear to be the simplest, most straightforward measure of capacity of all—digit span. Indeed, all the factors we have noted—capacity, efficiency, speed, inhibition—as well as several others—familiarity, knowledge, strategy—have been implicated (Bjorklund & Harnishfeger, 1990; Case et al., 1982; Harnishfeger, 1995).

INFORMATION PROCESSING AND REASONING

In turning to the question of how processing improvement figures in the development of thinking and reasoning, it is hardly surprising that we encounter a similar degree of uncertainty. The claim is rarely made that development at the neurological level or an increase in the number of pieces of information that can be simultaneously processed is the direct and sole cause of a qualitatively new form of reasoning. The emergence and development of the new form must be accounted for at the psychological level. Still, processing increases may function as necessary conditions that create the potential for the emergence of new capabilities, allowing a child, for example, to solve a problem she was previously unable to or to devise a new approach to a familiar problem.

Demetriou et al. (2002) have undertaken the most wide-ranging empirical investigation to date of the relations between developing information-processing capacities and developing reasoning skills in a cross-sequential design in which children 8 to 14 years of age were assessed initially and again at two subsequent yearly intervals. Assessments included processing speed, capacity, and inhibition, as well as several kinds of reasoning; each skill was examined in three domains—verbal, numerical, and spatial. The authors' conclusion is that of a necessary-but-not-sufficient relation. Processing improvements, they say, "open possibilities for growth in other abilities. In other words, changes in these functions may be necessary but not sufficient for changes in functions residing at other levels of the mental architecture" (p. 97).

Unfortunately, however, the measurement uncertainties we have alluded to, make it difficult for the authors to definitively rule out any directions of causality. Performance improves with age on all of the various tasks they administer. But even the sophisticated analytic methods they use do not allow them to conclude with certainty what causal relations may exist. The reasoning tasks in particular are necessarily brief and arbitrarily chosen, for example four syllogisms and four analogies in the verbal domain, and even the authors acknowledge in their discussion that an improved "yardstick for specifying differences between concepts or problems" (p. 132) is needed. A further complication is the varying patterns they obtain in the three content domains, leading them to conclude that processing capabilities are specific to the kind of information being processed.

Demetriou et al. (2002) make it clear that processing capabilities can be no more than necessary conditions for thinking, and they stress the importance of what they label "top-down" as well as "bottom-up" influences. In particular they emphasize the role of a "hypercognitive" or executive operator which "may participate and contribute to the relations between all other processes and abilities" (p. 127). Thus, in turning now to an examination of these high-order forms of thinking, we must keep in mind developing information-processing capabilities without expecting that they will by themselves explain what is observed to develop in the higher-order realm.

Deductive Inference

In turning to higher-order cognition, we adopt a loosely historical approach, beginning with deductive inference not because it is the most important but because it was the first form of reasoning to be the topic of extensive systematic developmental research. The historical reason is in large part its connection to the theory of formal operations. Their theory was interpreted as claiming the formal operational stage to mark the advent of propositional reasoning, and drawing inferences from the propositions that make up formal syllogisms was taken as an index of this ability.

Most extensively studied have been classical syllogisms that assert conditional relations between categories, that is, *if p, then q*. In the traditional syllogistic reasoning task, the initial major premise—*if p, then q*—is presented, followed by one of four secondary premises, either *p* (known as the *modus ponens* form), *q, not-p,* or *not-q* (known as the *modus tollens* form). The respondent is asked if a conclusion follows. The *modus ponens* form allows the conclusion *q:* If *p* is asserted to be the case and it is known that *if p, then q*, it follows that *q* must be the case. Similarly, the *modus tollens* form allows the conclusion *not-p:* If *not-q* is asserted and it is known that *if p, then q*, it follows that *p* cannot be the case (because if it were, *q* would be the case and we know it is not). The other two forms, however, having *q* or *not-p* as secondary premises, allow no definite conclusion. Another extensively researched task is the selection task (Wason, 1966). In this case, instead of a secondary premise, the reasoner is asked to indicate which of the four cases (*p, not-p, q,* and *not-q*) would need to be examined in order to verify the truth of the major premise (*if p, then q*). (Here the answer is the two determinate cases—*p,* to verify that *q* follows, and *not-q,* to verify that *p* is not the case.)

In reviews of research on the development of deductive inference skills (Braine & Rumain, 1983; Klaczynski, 2004; Markovits & Barrouillet, 2002; O'Brien, 1987). Two conclusions emerge consistently. One reflects what we have referred to earlier as the paradox of early competence and later lack of competence. Provided the content and context are facilitative, even quite young children can respond correctly at least to the two determinate syllogism forms (Dias & Harris, 1988; Hawkins, Pea, Glick, & Scribner, 1984; Kuhn, 1977; Rumain, Connell, & Braine, 1983). The majority of adults, in contrast, do not respond correctly in the standard form of the selection task (Wason, 1966). The evidence, then, does not support any sudden onset, or even marked transition, in competence to engage in propositional reasoning.

The other consistent conclusion is the sizable effect of proposition content on performance. In short, what it is that is being reasoned about makes a great deal of difference (Klaczynski & Narasimham, 1998; Klaczynski, Schuneman, & Daniel, 2004; Markovits & Barrouillet, 2002). These consistent findings have led investigators to reject as implausible the acquisition of a general, content-free set of rules applicable across any content.

CRITICAL ROLE OF MEANING

Contemporary investigators have turned their efforts to theories in which problem content is critical and mediates performance. Klaczynski (2004), for example, claims that availability of mental representations of alternatives accounts for most of the performance variance.

Consider, for example, the two propositions, "If Tom studies, he'll pass the exam," and "If Tom cheats, he'll pass the exam." Respondents of all ages are more likely to respond correctly to the two indeterminate syllogism forms when they occur in an example like the second proposition, compared to the first. For affirming the consequent, *q* (Tom passed the exam), respondents may correctly note in the second example that it is indeterminate whether Tom cheated. In the example of the first proposition, by contrast, they are more likely to falsely conclude that Tom studied hard. The likely reason is that in the case of the cheating proposition they can readily represent alternative antecedents, that is, possible causes of Tom's success other than cheating, leading to recognition that the antecedent does not follow from the consequent and that the true antecedent remains indeterminate. In the first (Tom studies) proposition, these alternatives come to mind less readily. Similarly for the other indeterminate syllogism form, denying the antecedent (*not-p*)—Tom didn't study hard or Tom didn't cheat—respondents are more likely to recognize that no conclusion follows when presented the second proposition (because not cheating leaves open multiple alternative consequents). Thus, semantic content, or meaning significantly enhances or impedes deductive reasoning.

WHAT DEVELOPS?

An account of the factors determining success on indeterminate syllogism forms assumes the bulk of researchers' attention. On the two determinate forms (*modus ponens* and *modus tollens*), performance is very good (75% correct) by late childhood (Klaczynski et al., 2004). These forms, of course, are correctly answered by use of a simple biconditional (or mutual implication)—*if p, q* and *if q, p*—that is mastered even by young children: *p* and *q* simply "go together," such that if one is present so is the other and if one is absent so is the other.

On the indeterminate syllogism forms, in contrast, a low level of correctness in early adolescence increases modestly by late adolescence, although content effects remain strong and performance remains far from ceiling (Barrouillet, Markovits, & Quinn, 2001; Klaczynski & Narasimham, 1998; Klaczynski et al., 2004). To what should this improvement be attributed? One possibility is willingness to make an indeterminacy judgment. However, in contexts in which children have been assured that "it's okay not to be sure," school-aged children (Kuhn, Schauble, & Garcia-Mila, 1992) and even preschoolers (Fay & Klahr, 1996) have been shown to be willing to suspend judgment, so it does not appear to be the acknowledgment of indeterminacy itself that is the stumbling block.

Another possibility is increased availability of alternatives due to an expanding knowledge base (Klaczynski et al., 2004), which leads to the correct recognition of indeterminacy. This remains a potential contributor that cannot be excluded but, again, seems not to tell the whole story. It is worthy of note in this respect that content familiarity itself does not predict performance on syllogistic reasoning problems. Klaczynski (2004) offers the example of the two propositions, "If a person eats too much, she'll gain weight" and "If a person grows taller, she'll gain weight." The former is more familiar, but performance on the indeterminate syllogistic forms of the latter is superior, due to the greater availability of alternatives.

While task content and knowledge play a significant role, the determining factor must be the nature of the mental processing that occurs. One simple hypothesis is that incorrect responders terminate processing prematurely, with the tendency to do so diminishing into and through adolescence. That is, children rely first on the inference rule that is simplest and most readily available in their repertories, the biconditional—p and q "go together"—and consider the problem no further. Klaczynski (2004) points to more developed metacognitive skill as key in the adolescent's increasing likelihood of inhibiting premature termination and continuing processing long enough to contemplate alternatives and recognize their implications with respect to indeterminacy. Ready availability of such alternatives of course supports doing so.

WHEN KNOWLEDGE AND REASONING CONFLICT

Before concluding our examination of deductive reasoning, it remains to highlight another important factor that significantly affects deductive reasoning performance—the truth status of the premises (Markovits & Vachon, 1989; B. Morris & Sloutsky, 2002; Moshman & Franks, 1986). Children become increasingly able into and during adolescence to reason deductively irrespective of their belief in the truth or falsity of the premises being reasoned about. This capability extends beyond syllogistic reasoning and indeed was identified by Inhelder and Piaget (1958) as a foundation of the stage of formal operations. Consider an 8-year-old, for example, who is well able to perform a standard task assessing mastery of hierarchical classification, judging that in a vase containing roses and other flowers, all the roses are flowers. Now imagine asking this child to solve the following deductive inference problem:

All wrestlers are police officers.

All police officers are women.

Assume the two previous statements are true; is the following statement true or false?

All wrestlers are women.

Children rarely are able to judge such conclusions as valid deductions from the premises, despite their empirical falsity, and fail to see their logical necessity (Moshman & Franks, 1986; Pillow, 2002). By early adolescence, the distinction between truth and validity begins to appear. But even older adolescents and adults continue to make errors in deductive reasoning when the premises are counterfactual (Markovits & Vachon, 1989).

Inhelder and Piaget (1958) maintained categorically that children, having not reached the stage of formal operations, are unable to reason about the hypothetical and are confined to mental operations on the empirical world. But the distinction is not as clear-cut as they implied. Children are able to exercise their imaginative capabilities in creative ways: "Imagine a world in which . . ." and simple counterfactuals are a routine part of the school curriculum, for example, "Suppose you had 9 marbles and gave 4 to a friend." As the deductive operations get more complex, however, as in the above example, a conflict arises between trusting the deductive operations (which seem trustworthy enough when content is neutral) or trusting one's knowledge.

Overcoming this conflict implicates the executive, or metacognitive, processes that have been suggested play a role in improvements in performance on deductive reasoning problems involving indeterminacy. In the present case, two meta-level components may be involved. One is increasing meta-level understanding of the deductive inference form, that is, its validity, dependability, independence from content, and utility. The other is increasing meta-level awareness and management of one's own system of beliefs, making it possible to "bracket," that is, temporarily inhibit, these beliefs, in order to allow the deductive system to operate, with the understanding that this suspension of belief is only temporary. Response inhibition capacities are implicated here (Handley, Capon, Beveridge, Dennis, & Evans, 2004; Simoneau & Markovits, 2003), a fact we return to in further examination of executive processes.

The importance of belief inhibition is also supported by findings that deductive reasoning performance is susceptible to improvement in children by introducing a fantasy context (Dias & Harris, 1988; Kuhn, 1977; Leevers & Harris, 1999; A. Morris, 2000). If belief is suspended by the fantasy context, it can't conflict with the conclusions reached through deductive reasoning, and the practice in suspending belief stands to benefit the reasoning process once the fantasy context is withdrawn. From each of these perspectives, then, belief inhibition appears key.

DEDUCTION AND THINKING

A final question we must address is this: Is the development of deductive reasoning competence central to the development of mature, effective thinking? Does logic govern thought? The role of the deduction paradigm in research on thinking has been debated in recent years, leading one prominent researcher in the field of deductive reasoning to speculate that deductive tasks may involve simply the "application of strategic problem solving in which logic forms part of the problem definition" (Evans, 2002). Evans recommends that the deduction paradigm be supplemented with other methods of studying reasoning.

While Evans' recommendation seems sound, indeed hard to quarrel with, the extensive research literature on the development of deductive reasoning does point in several useful directions. One is toward the necessity of abandoning any view of deductive reasoning capability as a singular competence or one that emerges at a discrete point in the life cycle. The other direction is toward the role of executive processes that deploy, monitor, and manage inference rules, rather than simply execute them.

As for the specific findings from developmental research on deductive reasoning, we propose that mastery of the indeterminate syllogistic forms is secondary to development of ability to reason independently of the truth status of the premises—a broad, flexible, and powerful mental skill that allows one to disembed a representation of meaning from its context. With respect to mastery of the indeterminate syllogistic forms, adolescents and adults have learned to use these forms in practical, if not strictly logical, ways, drawing on their real-world knowledge to decide which interpretation applies. Thus, "If you drive too fast, you'll have an accident" readily invokes alternative antecedents and hence interpretation as the formal logical conditional. "If you drink too much, you'll have a hangover," in contrast, invokes the simpler (logically incorrect) biconditional. Little confusion arises over this difference in everyday reasoning.

When knowledge and deduction conflict, however, real-world knowledge does not scaffold reasoning. To the contrary, it must itself be managed and controlled, enabling the deductive system to function. Weak executive control, we see in the remainder of this chapter, makes it difficult to temporarily inhibit one's beliefs, so as to enable the reasoning process to operate independently of them, causing a number of different kinds of limitations. This skill does show improvement in the years between late childhood and late adolescence, but its absence remains an obstacle to good thinking throughout adolescence and adulthood. We turn now to inductive reasoning, where we find its role is crucial.

Inductive and Causal Inference

One of the final issues we addressed in examining deductive reasoning—its relevance in everyday thinking—is one we can bypass entirely in examining inductive reasoning. There is simply no question about the fundamental role that inductive reasoning plays in thinking and in cognitive development. Children (and adults) confront enormous amounts of data, some consistent and some inconsistent over time, and they must construct meaning out of this wealth of information. An extended, and we will argue ultimately unproductive, debate has existed as to whether children approach this task as empiricists or theorists. In other words, do they rely strictly on observed frequencies of associations to determine "what goes with what" as an indication of how the world is organized, or do they impose theoretical constructions on their encounters with data?

These are the same questions that Gelman and Kalish (Chapter 9, this volume) confront in asking how young children form their early concepts. The field has seen some evolution in this respect. Keil (1991), for example, at one time proposed that young children were initially empiricists, forming their concepts on an entirely associationist basis, and later overlaid a theoretical structure on this associational base. Subsequently, however, Keil rejected this view in favor of the position that children's thinking is from the very beginning theoretical. In other words, they try to make sense of a concept, rather than simply accept it as a statistical compilation of the features whose frequency associations define it. This sense-making effort influences the features they see as central versus peripheral to the concept, as much or more than statistical frequency of association. In Keil's (1998) words, "a system of covariation detection procedures must interact with a framework of expectations about causal patterns" (p. 378).

This is exactly the position we take here with respect to the formation of the more complex forms of understanding being constructed by older children, adolescents, and adults. Most often, their concern is with relations between concepts, relations that are commonly construed as causal. Does alcohol affect a person's judgment? Does this clothing style make one popular? A set of existing ideas is brought to contemplation of the topic, and the task becomes one of achieving coordination between these ideas and new information that becomes available. It is not a matter of identifying one or the other as more important (Koslowski, 1996).

There are thus two potentially problematic questions in examining inductive reasoning that we can set aside: Is it relevant? Does explanation *or* evidence govern it? Another question, however, that must be confronted squarely is the question of competence, and it appears to be a formidable one. Is the child on the cusp of adolescence a competent inductive reasoner? Here we face two strikingly disparate literatures. One, focused on infancy and early childhood, emphasizes the impressive causal inference skills evident in early childhood. The other, focused on adolescents and adults, highlights limitations in causal inference skill that remain characteristic into and throughout adulthood. Our task in this section, then, is to take account of both of these literatures and formulate a portrayal of the development of inductive inference skills in the years in between.

EVIDENCE FOR EARLY COMPETENCE

We begin by considering a study of early competence. Schulz and Gopnik (2004) present evidence of 4-year-olds' ability to isolate causes in a multivariable context (ones in which multiple events co-occur with an outcome and are potential causes). Children observed a monkey hand puppet sniff varying sets of three plastic flowers, one red, one yellow, and one blue. An adult first placed the red and blue flowers in a vase and brought the monkey puppet up to sniff them. The monkey sneezed. The monkey backed away, returned to sniff again, and again sneezed. The adult then removed the red flower and replaced it with the yellow one, leaving the yellow and blue flowers together in the vase. The monkey came up to smell the flowers twice and each time sneezed. The adult then removed the blue flower and replaced it with the yellow flower, leaving the red and yellow flowers together in the vase. The monkey came up to smell the flowers and this time did not sneeze. The child was then asked, "Can you give me the flower that makes Monkey sneeze?" Seventy-nine percent of 4-year-olds correctly chose the blue flower.

Our task is one of reconciling findings such as these with a sizable body of data on multivariable causal inference in older children, adolescents, and adults that portrays a more complex picture of causal reasoning skill. When individuals coordinate prior expectations with new information, as is usually the case, causal inference becomes more challenging and we see quite different patterns of performance. Here the findings of numerous investigators show the influence of theoretical expectation on the interpretation of data and the ubiquity of faulty causal inference (Ahn, Kalish, Medin, & Gelman, 1995; Amsel & Brock, 1996; Cheng & Novick, 1992; Chinn & Brewer, 2001; Klaczynski, 2000; Klahr, 2000; Klahr, Fay, & Dunbar, 1993; Koslowski, 1996; Kuhn, Amsel, & O'Loughlin, 1988; Kuhn, Garcia-Mila, Zohar, & Andersen, 1995; Kuhn et al., 1992; Schauble, 1990, 1996; Stanovich & West, 1997). When theoretical expectations are strong, individuals may ignore the evidence entirely and base inferences exclusively on theory. Or they may make reference to the evidence but represent it in a distorted manner, characterizing it as consistent with their theoretical expectations when it in fact is not. Or they may engage in "local interpretation" of the data (Klahr et al., 1993; Kuhn et al., 1992), recognizing only those pieces of data that fit their theory and failing to acknowledge the rest.

COORDINATING THEORY AND EVIDENCE

Biased processing of information about the world remains commonplace into and through adulthood. At the time of the 2004 presidential election, for example, three-fourths of Bush supporters, but less than a third of Kerry supporters, reported believing that Iraq provides substantial support to Al Qaeda, despite the findings of the 9/11 Commission that there was no evidence of significant support from Iraq ("Week in Review: When no fact goes unchecked," 2004).

Should it be assumed that people engage in intentional misrepresentation of the information they are exposed to? Most of the time, it appears, this is not the most likely explanation. A more likely one is insufficient control over the interaction of theory and evidence in one's thinking (Kuhn, 1989). Under such conditions of weak control, thinking is based on a singular representation of "the way things are" with respect to the phenomena being contemplated, and new information is seen only as supporting—or, more aptly, "illustrating"—this reality. New information is not encoded as distinct from what is already known.

Under such conditions, new information can still modify understanding, but the individual may not be aware that this has taken place. A consequence is that individuals remain largely unaware regarding the source of their knowledge. When asked, "How do you know (that A is the cause of O)?" they make mistakes in attributing the inference to the new information they are contemplating, versus their own prior understanding (Kuhn & Pearsall, 2000; Kuhn et al., 1988, 1992, 1995; Schauble, 1990, 1996).

Is there evidence of developmental progress in this respect? Kuhn et al. (1988) and Kuhn et al. (1995) compared children, early adolescents, and adults with respect to evidence evaluation and inference skills and found some improvement in the years between middle childhood and early adulthood, despite the far from ideal performance of adults. Among sixth graders, for example, the proportion of evidence-based inferences was about 25%, compared to roughly 50% for noncollege young adults.

INTERPRETING COVARIATION EVIDENCE

Even if the data are faithfully registered, the opportunity for inferential error remains strong. Much evidence exists of unjustified inductive inferences of a relation, usually causal, between two variables, based on minimal evidence, notably as minimal as a single co-occurrence of two events (Klahr et al., 1993; Kuhn et al., 1988, 1992, 1995; Schauble, 1990, 1996). Because the events occurred together in time and/or space, one is taken to be the cause of the other, despite the presence of other covariates. This "false inclusion" is of course common in everyday thought at all ages. Thus, when community college students were told about an effort to improve student performance in which a new curriculum, teacher aides, and reduced class size were all introduced in various combinations (Kuhn, Katz, & Dean, 2004), they sometimes relied on as little as a single instance in which multiple factors were introduced as evidence for the role that one or more of the factors had played in the outcome. A typical example: "Yes a new curriculum is beneficial because here where they had it the class did well."

False inclusion based on a single instance shows some decline in frequency in the years from late childhood to early adulthood (Kuhn et al., 1988, 1995, 2004). Adults are more likely than children to base their causal inferences on a comparison of two instances, rather than a single instance of co-occurrence of antecedent and outcome. Even inferences based on comparisons of multiple instances can be fallacious if additional covariates are not controlled and causality is attributed to the wrong variable, although again we see age-related improvement between late childhood and adulthood (Kuhn et al., 1988).

Notable, finally, is the extent to which the factors we have identified as important are similar to those we identified as important in the case of deductive inference. One is the ability to inhibit the premature responding that terminates processing and prevents considering alternatives (in this case, additional covariates). The other is the ability to "bracket," that is temporarily inhibit, one's beliefs, in order to accurately represent evidence and enable the inference system to operate. Both of these abilities, in turn, involve meta-level, or executive, control of mental processes, which we can accordingly hypothesize is increasing during the age period in which we see improvements in reasoning performance.

COORDINATING EFFECTS OF MULTIPLE VARIABLES

Inductive inference about causal status is one important kind of reasoning common in everyday life. Another is prediction of outcomes, based on causal knowledge. Here, an individual must consider the causal status not just of a single variable but of all relevant variables and integrate their individual (as well as interactive) effects in order to make an outcome prediction. Kuhn and colleagues (Keselman, 2003; Kuhn, Black, Keselman, & Kaplan, 2000; Kuhn & Dean, 2004; Kuhn & Pease, 2006; Kuhn, 2007; Kuhn et al., 2004); identify an inadequate mental model of multivariable causality as a further source of error affecting causal reasoning. (Here we use the "mental model" terminology in this more generic sense, rather than its typical usage referring to mental representations of particular physical phenomena.)

An implicit assumption underlying research in the adult causal inference literature is that people's understanding of multiple causality reflects a standard scientific model: Multiple effects contribute to an outcome in an *additive* manner; as long as background conditions remain constant, these effects are expected to be *consistent,* that is, the same antecedent does not affect an outcome on one occasion and fail to do so on another, or affect the same outcome differently on one occasion than another.

Data from the reasoning of both children and adults, however, bring that assumption into question. Keselman (2003) asked sixth graders to investigate and make inferences regarding the causal role of five variables on an outcome (earthquake risk), as well as asking them to make outcome predictions for two new cases representing unique combinations of levels of the variables. Three of the five variables had additive effects on the outcome and the remaining two had no influence. After each prediction, the question was asked, "Why did you predict this level of risk?" All five variables were listed and children were instructed to indicate as many of them as had influenced their prediction judgment.

Over half of the children justified one or more predictions by implicating a variable they had explicitly judged to be noncausal in making earlier judgments of causal status. More than 80% failed to implicate as contributing to the outcome one or more variables they had previously explicitly judged to be causal. Overall, fewer features were implicated as contributing to a prediction than had been explicitly stated to be causal and attributions were inconsistent across predictions. Most often, children justified their predictions by appealing to the effect of only a single (usually shifting) variable. Kuhn (2007) reports similar findings for fourth and fifth graders. Adults do better in each of these respects (Kuhn & Dean, 2004), but their performance remains far from the normative scientific model of multivariable causality.

We can thus point to an inadequate mental model of multivariable causality as a constraint on children's and even many adults' ability to reason about the simultaneous, additive effects of multiple variables. Additional challenges, we have seen, come into play when individuals bring new evidence to bear on their causal models and to coordinate them with theoretical expectations. Does experience in coordinating effects of multiple variables improve this mental model? This question is one part of the more general question to which we now turn. As children progress into and through adolescence, do they improve in their ability to integrate the new information they encounter with their existing understandings? In other words, do children become better learners?

Learning and Knowledge Acquisition

COMPARING ADULTS AND CHILDREN

A study by Kuhn and Pease (2006) asks most directly the question of concern to us in this section: Do children and adults learn differently? Sixth graders and young adults were shown a teddy bear that they helped the interviewer in outfit with seven accessories, for example, jacket, backpack, and keychain. The interviewer presented the situation of a charity group raising funds and having teddy bears to give to donors as token gifts. To improve donations, it was explained, the charity wanted to try dressing the bears up a bit. They could afford to add a few accessories and had to choose which ones. Participants were asked to choose two they thought most likely to increase donations and the two least likely to do so. This content domain was selected to make it unlikely that either age group could be regarded as more knowledgeable in making these choices.

The participant was then presented results of some "test runs" involving these four accessories. A sequence of five instances, presented cumulatively, involving different combinations of the accessories, established that two accessories (one the participant believed effective and one the participant believed ineffective) increased donations and the other two did not. The most successful combination was presented as the fifth instance, such that the correct answer could simply be "read off" from this instance and no complex inferential reasoning was required. Nonetheless, neither group was entirely successful in learning the information presented. Adults, however, showed a higher rate of success than the 12-year-olds: 75% reported the correct answer, versus 35% of the younger group.

Kuhn and Pease's (2006) findings of less effective learning by preadolescents compared to adults were substantiated in a more extensive microgenetic study (Kuhn et al., 1995). Participants were observed over multiple occasions spanning several months as they sought to learn which variables were effective and which were not in contexts involving both physical content (e.g., the speed of model boats down a canal) and social content (e.g., the popularity of children's TV programs). Again, in both physical and social domains, an adult group was more effective in acquiring the new information than was a young adolescent group. Both children and adults drew conclusions virtually from the outset, on the basis of minimal or no data, and then changed their minds repeatedly. But the children remained more strongly wedded to their initial theories and drew on them more than on the new evidence they accessed as a basis for their conclusions.

How, then, should one account for superior learning on the part of adults? Kuhn and Pease (2006) propose that the older participants made better use of a meta-level executive to monitor and manage learning. This executive allowed them to maintain dual representations, one of their own understanding (of the relations they expect or see as most plausible) and the other of new information to be registered. It is this executive control that enables one to temporarily set aside or "bracket" existing beliefs and thereby effectively inhibit their influence on the interpretation of new data. In the absence of this executive, there exists only a singular experience—of "the way things are"—as a framework for understanding the world. This executive control, manifested in response inhibition and bracketing, is exactly what we identified earlier as a central factor in the development of deductive and inductive inference.

Microgenetic analysis in the Kuhn et al. (1995) research made possible the dual objectives of tracing not only the acquisition of knowledge over time but, also, the evolution of the knowledge-acquisition strategies that were responsible for generating that knowledge. Here the now widely observed findings from microgenetic research emerge (Kuhn et al., 1995; Siegler, 2006). At both ages, individuals displayed not just one but a variety of different strategies, ranging from less to more effective. Over time, what changes is the frequency of usage of these strategies, with a general decline over time in the usage of less effective strategies and increase in the use of more powerful ones.

DEVELOPMENT OF LEARNING

Should it be concluded, then, that the learning process undergoes developmental change? Some years ago, Carey (1985) answered this question with a categorical no, claiming there was no reason to believe that the learning process operated any differently in children than in adults. The findings described here suggest that Carey's sweeping claim, while likely true with respect to some kinds of learning, is not categorically correct. A great deal of the learning children and adults engage in, both in and out of school, is simple associative learning. It is not mindful learning, and there is no evidence to indicate that the nature of associative learning processes undergoes developmental change. Learning that is conceptual, in contrast—that is, involves change in understanding—requires cognitive engagement on the part of the learner, and hence an executive that must allocate, monitor, and otherwise manage the mental resources involved. These executive functions, and the learning that requires them, do show evidence of developing, although Kuhn and Pease's data show that developmental change of this sort is highly variable. Some 12-year-olds performed as well as the typical adult, and some adults performed no better than most 12-year-olds.

The microgenetic method of examining repeated engagement with a task over time has been held responsible for blurring the distinction between development and learning (Kuhn, 1995, 2001a; Siegler, 2006). While the distinction between the two may not be as rigid as theorists of the Piagetian era in the 1960s and 1970s held it to be, it does not follow that there remain no useful distinctions at all. Learning what recordings are on this week's "Top 100" List and learning that conflicting ideas can both be right are different kinds of learning in numerous important respects (among them generalizability, reversibility, and universality of occurrence). What is important is recognizing the process of change as one that has multiple parameters. When the process is examined microgenetically, it becomes possible to begin to characterize it in terms of many such parameters. It is more research of this sort that is required to support the claim that these change processes themselves undergo change as individuals mature.

Inquiry and Scientific Thinking

Modern research in developmental psychology on the development of scientific thinking began very narrowly, in the form of replication studies seeking to confirm the findings reported by Inhelder and Piaget (1958). The bulk of these replication studies focused even more narrowly on the "isolation of variables" or "controlled comparison" investigative strategy, which, recall, Inhelder and Piaget reported did not appear until adolescence. Using Piagetian tasks in which participants were required to investigate simple physical phenomena such as a pendulum or the flexibility of rods, Inhelder and Piaget's findings were upheld with respect to children's difficulty with these tasks and evidence of improvement from childhood to adolescence, but it was also found that even older adolescents and adults did not always perform successfully (Keating, 1980). Relatively little discussion occurred, however, regarding the broader educational or practical significance of these findings. Assuming these tasks were valid indicators of the ability to engage in scientific thinking, was it important for most people to be able to think scientifically?

DOES CHILDREN'S THINKING NEED TO BECOME "SCIENTIFIC?"

In the early twenty-first century, the picture could not be more different. What has come to be called "inquiry" has found its way into the American national curriculum standards for science for every grade beginning with second or third through twelfth and appears in a large majority of state standards as well. Inquiry often appears in social studies and even language arts standards as well (Levstik & Barton, 2001). In the national science standards, the goals of inquiry learning for grades 5 to 8, for example, are the following (National Research Council, 1996):

- Identify questions that can be answered through scientific investigations.
- Design and conduct a scientific investigation.
- Use appropriate tools and techniques to gather, analyze, and interpret data.
- Develop descriptions, explanations, predictions, and models using evidence.
- Think critically and logically to make the relationships between evidence and explanations.

Under "Design and conduct a scientific investigation," subskills identified include "systematic observation, making accurate measurements, and identifying and controlling variables."

It is worth asking, then, what scientific thinking is and why it is so important, such that, within a few decades, it has come to be so widely embraced as an educational goal. Defining scientific thinking as "what scientists do" does not work very well, since very few children will grow up to become professional scientists, few enough certainly that educating all children toward this end in elementary school seems scarcely appropriate or worth the effort involved. Nor is defining scientific thinking operationally in terms of the control-of-variables strategy satisfactory, since few people, children or adults, have the opportunities or inclination to conduct controlled experiments in the course of their everyday activities.

The position we take here is to regard scientific thinking as central to science but not specific to it. The definition of scientific thinking we adopt is *intentional knowledge seeking* (Kuhn, 2002). This definition encompasses any instance of purposeful thinking that has the goal of enhancing the seeker's knowledge. As such, scientific thinking is a human activity engaged in by most people, rather than a rarefied few. It connects to other forms of thinking studied by psychologists, such as inference and problem solving. We characterize its goals and purposes as more closely aligned with argument than with experimentation (Kuhn, 1993; Lehrer, Schauble, & Petrosino, 2001). Scientific thinking is frequently social in nature, rather than a phenomenon that occurs only inside people's heads.

From their earliest years, children construct implicit theories that enable them to make sense of and organize their experiences. In a process that has come to be referred to as *conceptual change,* these theories are revised as new evidence is encountered bearing on them. Unlike scientific thinking, early theory revision occurs implicitly and effortlessly, with little indication of conscious awareness or intent. Young children think *with* their theories, rather than about them. In the course of so doing they may revise these theories, but they are unlikely to be aware that they are doing so. As a result, as we noted earlier in the discussion of inductive reasoning, they are typically uncertain regarding the source of their knowledge.

It is the intention to seek knowledge that transforms implicit theory revision into scientific thinking. Theory revision becomes something one *does,* rather than something that happens to one outside of conscious awareness. To seek knowledge is to recognize that one's existing knowledge is incomplete, possibly incorrect—that there is something new to know. The process of theory-evidence coordination accordingly becomes explicit and intentional. Newly available evidence is examined with regard to its implications for a theory, with awareness that the theory is susceptible to revision and that its modification may be an outcome of the process.

In this framework, it becomes possible to reconcile the shortcomings in scientific thinking identified in this chapter with the "child as scientist" perspective adopted by authors such as Gelman and Kalish (Chapter 9, this volume) and Gopnik, Meltzoff, and Kuhl (1999). As theory builders, children are indeed young scientists (or scientists big children) virtually from the beginning. There is no evidence to indicate that children's construction and elaboration of theories as means of understanding the world take place in a qualitatively different way than they do for lay adults or scientists (although this is not a question that has been thoroughly researched). Where the difference arises is in the intentional, consciously controlled coordination of these theories with new evidence. Here the research evidence is plentiful that children execute this process less skillfully than most adults and certainly less skillfully than professional scientists.

PROCESS OF INQUIRY

As Klahr (2000) notes, very few studies of scientific thinking encompass the entire cycle of scientific investigation, a cycle we characterize as consisting of four major phases: inquiry, analysis, inference, and argument. A number of researchers have confined their studies to only a portion of the cycle, most often the evaluation of evidence (Amsel & Brock, 1996; Klaczynski, 2000; Koslowski, 1996), a research design that links the study of scientific reasoning to research on inductive causal inference. We postpone discussion of argument to a later section, and we focus here on studies in which participants direct their own investigations and seek their own data as a basis for their inferences, hence involving at least the first three phases of the cycle (Keselman, 2003; Klahr, 2000; Klahr et al., 1993; Kuhn et al., 1992, 1995, 2000; Kuhn & Phelps, 1982; Kuhn & Pease, in press; Penner & Klahr, 1996; Schauble, 1990, 1996). These studies offer a picture of how the strategies associated with each phase of scientific investigation are situated within a context of all the others and how they influence one another.

The studies by Klahr and his associates (Klahr, 2000; Klahr et al., 1993) have followed children and adults asked to conduct investigations of the function of a particular key in controlling the behavior of an electronic robot toy, or, in another version, the behavior of a dancer who performs various movements in a computer simulation. To do this, individuals need to coordinate hypotheses about this function with data they generate, or, in Klahr's (2000) terminology, to coordinate searches of an hypothesis space and an experiment space.

The microgenetic studies by Kuhn and associates, as well as those by Schauble (1990, 1996), Keselman (2003), and Penner and Klahr (1996) examine what we regard as a prototypical form of scientific inquiry—the situation in which a number of variables have potential causal connections to an outcome and the investigative task is to choose instances for examination and on this basis to identify causal and noncausal variables, with the goals of predicting and explaining variations in outcome. Examined in these studies in their simplest, most generic form, at the same time these are common objectives of professional scientists engaged in authentic scientific inquiry.

Studies originating in both Klahr's and Kuhn's laboratories have portrayed very similar overall pictures. Adults on average exhibit more skill than children or young adolescents at each stage of the process. The younger group is more likely to seek to investigate all factors at once, to focus on producing outcomes rather than analysis of effects, to fail to control variables and, hence, to choose uninformative data for examination, and to engage in what Klahr refers to as "local interpretation" of fragments of data, ignoring other data that may be contradictory. Klahr (2000) concludes that, "adult superiority appears to come from a set of domain-general skills that . . . deal with the coordination of search in two spaces" (p. 119).

Kuhn et al. (1995) compared the progress of children and adults as they continued their investigations in multiple content domains over a period of months. Although the strategies of both groups improved, adults both started at a slightly higher level and progressed further. Yet microgenetic analysis of the change process confirmed the now common finding that individuals of both ages displayed not just one but a variety of different strategies ranging from less to more effective. Kuhn et al. (1995) concluded, "Rather than a unidimensional transition from a to b, the change process must be conceptualized in terms of multiple components following individual (although not independent) paths" (p. vi). This was the case with respect to *inquiry* strategies, which range from "generate outcomes" to "assess the effect of X on outcome"; with respect to *analysis* strategies, which range from "ignore evidence" to "choose instances that allow an informative comparison"; and with respect to *inference* strategies, which range from "unsupported claims" to "representations in relation to both consistent and inconsistent evidence" (Kuhn, 2002).

Consistent with other microgenetic research (Siegler, 2006), over time the frequency of usage of less effective strategies diminished and the frequency of more effective strategies increased. In postulating mechanisms underlying this change, Siegler (2006) emphasizes the need for associations with the more frequent, less effective strategies to be weakened. While similarly emphasizing the relinquishment of less effective strategies as a more formidable obstacle than strengthening new ones, Kuhn (2001a) proposed that knowledge at the meta-level is as important as that at the performance level and plays a major role in what happens there. Feedback from the performance level should enhance meta-level understanding, further enhancing performance, in a continuous process.

Strategic progress with continued engagement not only occurred in both age groups, Kuhn et al. (1995) found, but was maintained when new problem content was introduced midway through the sessions. And, importantly, the most prevalent change to occur overall was not the emergence of any new strategies but the decline of ineffective ones, in particular the inhibition of invalid causal inference.

Supporting the Development of Inquiry Skills

Inquiry skills, we noted, have become a focus of very wide concern to educators. As a result, growing attention is being devoted to how these skills might be promoted. Exercise in a rich problem environment, as we have noted, is usually effective over time (Dean & Kuhn, 2007). And weaknesses in the inquiry process arise long before one gets to the phase of designing and interpreting experiments. A first, critical phase is formulating a question to be asked. Unless the student understands the purpose of the activity as seeking information that will bear on a question whose answer is not already known, inquiry often degenerates into an empty activity of securing observations for the purpose of illustrating what is already known to be true (Kuhn, 2002). Students may initially pose ineffective questions, for example by intending to discover the effects of all variables at once. And it may be this ineffective intention that then leads them to experimentation flaws, for example, simultaneously manipulate multiple variables (in effect overattending to them, rather than underattending by failing to control them, as is often assumed).

Kuhn and Dean (2005) in the context of an extended intervention otherwise confined to exercise, added the simple suggestion to students that they choose a single variable to try to find out about. This simple intervention had a pronounced effect on their investigation and inference strategies, greatly enhancing frequency of controlled comparison and valid inference. This finding highlights the complex multifaceted nature of inquiry and the fact that more is involved in mastery than ability to execute effective strategies.

The understanding associated with the initial phase of the inquiry process is most critical because it gives meaning and direction to what follows. If a question is identified that seems worth asking and the ensuing activity seems capable of answering, the stage is set for what is to follow. In the multivariable context of isolation of variables and controlled comparison, the individual may cease to vary other variables across two-instance comparisons because of an increasing sense that they are not relevant to the comparison being made. Once they are left alone, and thereby "neutralized" as Inhelder and Piaget (1958) described it, the way is prepared for increased usage and increasing metastrategic understanding of the power of controlled comparison. But the most important message here is that we need to look beyond the control-of-variables strategy as a narrow procedure to teach students to execute. Rather, it should be conveyed as a tool that serves as a resource for them to draw on in seeking answers to the questions that they may pose.

Argument

Even more than inquiry, argument brings us squarely into the realm of everyday, informal reasoning. Yet, there has been comparatively little work on the development of argument skills.

The terms *argument* and *argumentation* reflect the two senses in which the term *argument* is used, as both product and process. An individual constructs an argument to support a claim. The dialogic process in which two or more people engage in debate of opposing claims can be referred to as *argumentation* or *argumentive discourse* to distinguish it from argument as product. Nonetheless, implicit in argument as product is the advancement of a claim in a framework of evidence and counterclaims that is characteristic of argumentive discourse, and the two kinds of argument are intricately related (Billig, 1987; Kuhn, 1991). Most empirical research has been devoted to argument as product and we begin with it.

INDIVIDUAL ARGUMENTS

Producing Arguments

Educators at all levels have long lamented students' weaknesses in producing a cogent argument in support of a claim in their expository writing. By asking adolescents and adults to generate arguments in individual verbal interviews, Kuhn (1991) probed whether these weaknesses reflect poorly developed writing skills or deficits that are more cognitive in nature. Individual argument skills remained poor among adolescents even when the possibly inhibiting factor of producing written text was removed. Only on average about a third of a teen sample was able to offer a valid supporting argument for their claim regarding an everyday topic (e.g., why prisoners return to crime when they're released), a percentage that increased only very modestly to near one half among adults. Others tended to offer pseudoevidence for their claims, in the form of an example or script (e.g., of a prisoner returning to crime), rather than any genuine evidence to support the claim. Similarly in the minority were those adolescents or adults who were able to envision counterarguments or rebuttals to their claims. Although chronological age (from adolescence through the sixties) was not a strong predictor of skill, education level was a significant predictor.

Other research is consistent with a picture of poorly developed argument skills (Brem & Rips, 2000; Glassner, Weinstock, & Neuman, 2005; Knudson, 1992; Means & Voss, 1996; Perkins, 1985; Voss & Means, 1991). In particular there is a consistent picture of arguments that are confined to the merits of one's own position, without attention to alternatives or opposing arguments. Kuhn, Shaw, and Felton (1997) compared young teens' and young adults' arguments for or against capital punishment. The two groups were equally likely to address both sides of the argument (31% of teens and 34% of adults did so); the remainder confined their arguments to supporting their own position. Overall, the available research indicates at most slight improvement during adolescent years in ability to produce sound arguments.

Evaluating Arguments

In other studies, participants have been asked to evaluate the strength or soundness of arguments presented to them (Kuhn, 2001a; Neuman, 2002; Weinstock, Neuman, & Tabak, 2004). Kuhn (2001a) reported a tendency on the part of eighth graders to focus on the content of the claim rather than the nature of the argument supporting it, hence producing the typical justification, "This is a good argument because it [the claim] is true." A comparison group of community college students were better able to separate their belief in the truth or falsity of the claim from their evaluation of the strength of the argument.

Several authors have examined the influence of one's belief regarding the claim on the evaluation of arguments supporting or opposing it (Klaczynski, 2000; Koslowski, 1996; Stanovich & West, 1997). These studies report that the same arguments are scrutinized more thoroughly and evaluated more stringently if they contradict the evaluator's beliefs than if they are supportive of these beliefs, paralleling findings from the scientific reasoning literature that individuals evaluate identical evidence differently if it is belief-supportive versus belief-contradictory (Kuhn et al., 1988, 1995; Schauble, 1990, 1996). Klaczynski (2000), for example, studied early adolescents (mean age 13.4) and middle adolescents (mean age 16.8) classified by self-reported social class and religion. They were asked to evaluate fictitious studies concluding that one social class or one religion was superior to another on some variable. At least one major and several minor validity threats were present in each study. The older group was superior in critiquing the studies. Both groups, however, exhibited a positive bias toward studies that portrayed their group favorably, critiquing these studies less severely, although only for the religion grouping—a bias that did not diminish with age.

ARGUMENTIVE DISCOURSE

Why do skills in producing or identifying sound arguments generally remain poor throughout adolescence? Graff (2003) makes the claim that developing arguments to support a thesis in expository writing is difficult for students because the task fails to reproduce the conditions of real-world argument, which is dialogic. In the absence of a physically present interlocutor, the student takes the writing task to be one of stringing together a sequence of true statements, avoiding the complication of stating anything that might not be true. The result is often a communication in which both reader and writer are left uncertain as to why the argument needs to be made at all. Who would want to claim otherwise? If students plant a "naysayer"—an imaginary opponent—in their written arguments, Graff suggests, as a scaffold for the missing interlocutor, their argumentive essays become more like authentic arguments and hence more meaningful.

Felton and Kuhn (2001) asked junior high school and community college students to engage in a discussion of the merits of capital punishment with a peer whose view opposed theirs. Each of the utterances in the dialog was classified according to whether its function was (a) to advance exposition of the speaker's claims or arguments, or (b) in some way to. Among teens, an average of 11% of utterances address the partner's claims or arguments, compared to 24% among adults. Thus, while some improvement appears during adolescence, the weaknesses observed in dialogic argument resemble those observed in individual arguments, with only a minority of arguers going beyond exposition of their own position. Why might this be? Felton and Kuhn (2001) suggest that attention to the other's ideas and their merits may create cognitive overload, or it simply may not be recognized as part of the task. Supporting the latter explanation, Kuhn and Udell (2007) found that young teens had no difficulty producing arguments against the opposing position when these were explicitly solicited. Thus, they had the competence to address opposing positions, but did not see a need to do so. Most likely, then, meta-level, as well as procedural, limitations constrain performance.

SUPPORTING THE DEVELOPMENT OF ARGUMENT SKILLS

Efforts to enhance teens' argument skills, where these can be distinguished and addressed apart from students' broader academic skills in verbal and written expression, have been focused on dialogic argument as the most promising context.

Kuhn et al. (1997) asked young teens to engage in dialogic arguments on capital punishment with a series of different classmates over a period of weeks. Felton (2004) had students alternate roles of dialog participants and peer advisors, the latter role intended to heighten students' reflective awareness of their argumentive discourse. Prepost differences in both studies were encouraging, especially as they mirrored the cross-sectional differences between teens and adults observed by Felton and Kuhn (2001). Gains transferred to dialogs on a new topic, as well as to individual arguments—the latter a finding also reported by Reznitskaya et al. (2001) in a study of group discourse among younger children.

One limitation of this dialogic practice method is that it engages young people in the relevant activity without offering them a reason to be engaged in it. Kuhn and Udell (2003) thus devised a more structured intervention in which students were organized into pro and con teams (based on their initial opinions) and engaged in various activities over a 10-week period toward a goal of a "showdown" debate with the opposing team. After several sessions devoted to developing and evaluating their own arguments, the teams exchanged arguments and then generated counterarguments to the opposing team's arguments, related evidence to both their own and the opposing team's arguments, and, finally, generated rebuttals to the opposing team's counterarguments. Progress occurred in the same directions as observed in the preceding studies, particularly a sizeable increase in counterargument against the opponents' claims. A comparison group who participated only in the initial phase of developing their own arguments showed some, but more limited, progress. Udell (2007) extended this design to a topic of personal relevance (teen pregnancy) as well as a more impersonal one (capital punishment) and found that gains following the personal-topic intervention transferred to the impersonal topic, but transfer did not occur in the reverse direction.

At the beginning of this intervention, students clearly wanted to win. By the end, they still wanted to win, but by now they cared deeply about their topic and had developed a richer understanding surrounding it, even though none of the participants had much initial knowledge. But had students learned anything about argument itself? Had they come to see a point to arguing, beyond prevailing, being the winner? Had they progressed from winning to knowing as a conceptual justification for their activity? Had they constructed an understanding of argument itself? The only possible answer is incompletely, at best. But to address the question more fully, we turn to our final topic—young people's developing understanding of knowledge and knowing.

Understanding and Valuing Knowing

We begin our summary of developing understanding of knowing and valuing knowledge with preschoolers' attainment of false belief understanding because we maintain this early development is fundamental to the developments that follow. Three-year-olds regard beliefs as faithful copies of reality; they are received directly from the external world, rather than constructed by the knower. Hence, there are no inaccurate renderings of events, nor any possibility of conflicting beliefs, since everyone perceives the same external reality. Thus, children of this age make the classic false-belief error of unwillingness to attribute to another person a belief they themselves know to be false (Perner, 1991). For such a child, theory and evidence do not exist as distinct epistemological categories, making genuine scientific thinking (the coordination of theory and evidence) impossible.

Later in the preschool years, the human knower, and knowledge as mental representations produced by knowers, finally come to life. Once it is recognized that assertions are produced by human minds and need not necessarily correspond to reality, assertions become susceptible to evaluation vis-à-vis the reality from which they are now distinguished.

The products of knowing, however, for a time still remain more firmly attached to the known object than to the knower. Hence, while inadequate or incorrect information can produce false beliefs, these errors are easily correctable by reference to an external reality—the known object. To be wrong is simply to be misinformed, mistaken, in a way that is readily correctable once the appropriate information is revealed. At this *absolutist* level of epistemological understanding, knowledge is thus regarded as an accumulating set of certain facts.

Researchers studying the development of epistemological understanding have characterized childhood as a period when the absolutist level of thought prevails. Although details vary across researchers, there is broad agreement that further development proceeds toward transition to a *multiplist* (or *relativist*) level, sometime during adolescence, followed by, in at least some individuals, an *evaluativist* level (Hofer & Pintrich, 1997, 2002). This further progress in epistemological understanding can be characterized as an extended task of coordinating the subjective and the objective elements of knowing (Kuhn, Cheney, & Weinstock, 2000; Kuhn, Iordanou, Pease, & Wirkala, in press). At the realist and absolutist levels, the objective dominates. In adolescence, the discovery that reasonable people—even experts—disagree is a likely source of coming to recognize the uncertain, subjective aspect of knowing. This recognition initially assumes such proportions, however, that it eclipses recognition of any objective standard that could serve as a basis for evaluating conflicting claims. Knowledge comes to consist not of facts but of opinions, freely chosen by their holders as personal possessions and accordingly not open to challenge.

Knowledge is now clearly seen as emanating from the knower, rather than the known, but at the significant cost of any discriminability among competing knowledge claims. By adulthood, many, though by no means all, adolescents will have reintegrated the objective dimension of knowing and achieved the understanding that while everyone has a right to their opinion, some opinions are in fact more right than others, to the extent they are better supported by argument and evidence. Rather than facts or opinions, knowledge at the evaluativist level consists of judgments, which require support in a framework of alternatives, evidence, and argument.

Developmentally, progress (from absolutist to multiplist to evaluativist) appears between early and late adolescence. But here again, we encounter a domain in which development is far from universal. Less than half of 12th graders had achieved evaluativist thinking in any domain (Kuhn, Cheney, et al., 2000). This same lack of universality appeared in dimensions of cognitive development examined in previous sections—the development of skills of argument, certainly, and also of inquiry. It is here that the interests of developmentalists and of educators converge. Attention turns to what might support the development in question.

Several authors have focused on the relation between level of epistemological understanding and argument skill, reporting a relation between the two (Kuhn, 1991; Mason & Boscolo, 2004; Weinstock & Cronin, 2003; Weinstock et al., 2004). This relation is not surprising. If facts can be ascertained with certainty and are readily available to anyone who seeks them, as the absolutist understands, or, alternatively, if any claim is as valid as any other, as the multiplist understands, there is little reason to expend the intellectual effort that argument entails. One must see the point of arguing to engage in it. This connection extends well beyond but certainly includes science, and in the field of science education a number of authors have made the case for the connection between productive science learning and a mature epistemological understanding of science as more than accumulation of facts (Carey & Smith, 1993; Metz, 2004). In order for scientific inquiry to be valued as a worthwhile enterprise, it must be understood to occupy an epistemological ground other than the accumulation of undisputed facts dictated by absolutism or the suspension of judgment dictated by multiplism.

Kuhn and Park (2005) further propose that advancement in epistemological understanding supports development of intellectual values, specifically the commitment to intellectual discussion and debate as the soundest basis for choosing between competing claims and resolving conflicts. Across cultural and subcultural groups of children and parents, level of epistemological understanding was (inversely) related to endorsement of items like this one:

Many social issues, like the death penalty, gun control, or medical care, are pretty much matters of personal opinion, and there is no basis for saying that one person's opinion is any better than another's. So there's not much point in people having discussions about these kinds of issues.

In sum, after years of relative orphan status, the study of epistemological understanding has undergone a surge of attention that appears well deserved. Understanding of the intellectual activities of thinking and knowing is not of interest only to philosophers. To the contrary, it may provide a foundation that is critical in influencing what both adolescents and adults are disposed to do intellectually, as opposed to what they are competent to do—a distinction that has itself begun to receive broader attention (Perkins, Jay, & Tishman, 1993; Stanovich & West, 1999, 2000). By the second decade of life, disposition becomes a construct that cannot be ignored.

Conclusions

WHAT DEVELOPS?

During the second decade of life, individuals continue to learn and to develop, in universal but also increasingly individual directions. Although the boundaries between development and learning have become blurred, there remain important distinctions between the two kinds of change. Development is generally progressive, irreversible, and generalizable, while learning need have none of these characteristics. Where development and learning come together is in similarities in process, and hence the microgenetic method is useful in studying both. This is so largely because earlier conceptions of learning as formation of S-R bonds or strengthening of habits have been replaced by contemporary models in which learning is more likely to be defined as "change in understanding" (Schoenfeld, 1999). We thus need models more like those of development to characterize the process—that is, models that characterize change in terms of reorganization of patterns of thought, rather than strengthening of associations or habits.

What do we know about the nature of the change process? The phenomena reviewed in this chapter are consistent with a process in which multiple forms (of varying strengths and hence probabilities of occurrence) co-exist over extended periods of time. Over time this distribution of probabilities shifts, as less effective forms are exercised less often and more effective ones more frequently (Kuhn, 1995, 2001b; Kuhn et al., 1995; Siegler, 2000, 2006). Although new forms, of course, do emerge, first emergence rarely indicates the beginning of consistent usage, and the majority of change is thus of this shifting-frequency variety.

Two other features of this change process are of particular significance during the years of transition from childhood to adulthood. One is the fact that exercise (of existing forms) is often a sufficient condition for change (Kuhn, 1995). An implication, which we return to, is that adolescents are likely to get even better at what they are already good at, thus increasing the range and diversity of developmental pathways. The other is the importance of abandoning old, less effective forms, a challenge that in many cases exceeds that of adopting new, more effective ones. Interestingly, in a psychotherapeutic context, when a client finally abandons a self-limiting behavior, we do not hesitate to regard this event as an instance of positive change. In the case of cognitive development, however, we tend to focus only on attainment of new forms as markers of progressive change.

Finally, worthy of special note is the change that may occur in the change process itself. Evidence we have examined here suggests that as children enter their second decade, an increasingly strong executive may begin to develop. This executive assumes a role of monitoring and managing the deployment of cognitive resources as a function of task demands, making thinking and learning more effective.

Emergence and strengthening of this executive is arguably the single most consequential intellectual development to occur in the second decade of life. Young adolescents begin to acquire much more control over their activities and lives than they experienced as children. Hence, they have more discretion over how and where their cognitive resources will be deployed. Modern culture has introduced them to the art of dividing attention among multiple kinds of input. The executive thus fills a much needed role in determining how that attention will be allocated.

The developing executive also affords increasing ability to inhibit initial responses and to process further, when one judges doing so to be worth the effort. And finally, and critically, it affords a level of metacognitive awareness that makes it possible to temporarily "bracket" the perspective dictated by one's own beliefs or understanding, in order to extract decontextualized representations, disembedded from a particular context, and to determine their implications. Without this skill, deductive, inductive, and argumentive reasoning are all impaired.

A stronger executive implies that development is increasingly governed from the "top down." This is not to say that most adults, as well as children and teens, don't apply "bottom-up" habitual patterns of thinking and behaving much of the time. But during the second decade of life young people, we have claimed, increasingly develop the potential to manage and deploy their cognitive resources in consciously controlled and purposefully chosen ways. A major implication is that disposition—to do or not to do X or Y—becomes increasingly important (Kuhn, 2001a; Perkins et al., 1993; Stanovich & West, 1997, 1998, 2000). And disposition is governed by more than the competence to execute procedures. For these reasons, we have emphasized the larger picture that includes meta-level *understanding* of strategies—what they do or do not buy one—in relation to task *goals,* as well as *values* as a critical link mediating understanding and disposition. This larger structure presents a considerably more complex picture of what it is that needs to develop. Unsurprisingly, no simple change mechanism exists that can assume the entire explanatory burden.

EARLY ADOLESCENCE AS A SECOND CRITICAL PERIOD

Stronger executive control of intellectual processes, we have suggested, differentiates the second decade of life from the first. Another difference is the extent and range of individual variability, which greatly increase in the second decade. All children within the normal intellectual range can be counted on to have exhibited certain universal developmental progressions in their thinking by age 10. They will also have learned a great deal about the world, much of it universally shared; many, however, will also have acquired expertise within domains of individual interest, although even here there are certain asymptotes—10-year-olds very rarely master calculus.

After the first decade of life, however, development along universal pathways does not continue to the most advanced levels for everyone. Many adults cease to show any development beyond the level achieved by the typical early adolescent. Variation in positions along developmental pathways becomes pronounced. In addition, within specific content domains the range and depth of individually acquired expertise becomes much greater than it was in childhood. The processes involved in learning in "core domains," which all people encounter, and "noncore domains," which only some individuals choose to explore, may nonetheless be similar (Gelman, 2002).

How should we explain this heightened variability, and what are its implications? One level of explanation lies in the brain. Early adolescence, we noted, is a second developmental period during which a sequence of overproduction and pruning of neuronal connections occurs. This pruning of unused connections is guided by the activities in which the young teen engages. Both brain and behavior, then, together begin to become more specialized. To this evolution, we add teens' increasing freedom and personal control—on the one hand in managing and deploying their intellectual resources to accomplish a task, and, on the other, more broadly, in choosing the activities in which they will invest themselves and in managing their lives.

With concentrated engagement in the activities they choose, adolescents get even better at what they are already good at, thus increasing the range and diversity of individual pathways. By early adolescence, individuals are indeed producers of their own development (Lerner, 2002). One consequence of these choices is an increasingly firm sense of personal identity—"this is who I am"—and, particularly, "this is what I'm good at" (and its even more potent complement, "this is what I'm no good at"). Evidence suggests that what happens at this age may be as influential as what happens in the first years of life (Feinstein & Bynner, 2004). Potential attainment in both core and noncore domains—in both universal and individual directions—can be encouraged and supported or left to wither, with enormously disparate results.

During this second critical period, it is arguably disposition, as much or more than competence, that ought to be the focus of those concerned with supporting adolescents' intellectual development. To a greater extent than children, teens attribute meaning and value (both positive and negative) to what they do and draw on this meaning to define a self. Positively valued activities lead to behavioral investment that leads to greater expertise and hence greater valuing, in a circular process that has taken hold by early adolescence. The selfless curiosity and exploration characteristic of the early childhood critical period have likely gone underground and are difficult to detect. An implication is that the valuing of intellectual engagement can certainly be supported by those who work with young adolescents, but better results can be expected to the extent the way has been laid by activities involving genuine intellectual engagement in the years leading up to the second decade (Kuhn, 2005).

UNDERSTANDING DEVELOPMENT BY STUDYING BOTH ORIGINS AND ENDPOINTS

What are the implications for those seeking to investigate intellectual development during the second decade of life? One that follows fairly directly from what has just been said is the need to conduct more studies of adolescent cognition in the situated contexts of the activities in which teens choose to invest their intellectual resources. We are certainly taking a risk in drawing conclusions from investigations confined to artificial problems, constructed for research purposes, that bear no clear relation to the kinds of thinking that adolescents do in their daily lives. At the same time, the ability to decontextualize—to extract a generalized representation distinct from its specific context—remains a critical developmental achievement that needs to be studied further.

An emphasis on disposition, in addition to competence, suggests the importance of continued study of mechanism. We are dealing with a decade of life in which not everything that has the potential to develop does. Yet, continued development is more likely in this second decade than in the decades thereafter. The "good enough" intellectual environment that suffices to support the basic transitions characteristic of childhood cognitive development is apparently not good enough to support universal attainment of the cognitive capabilities that have the potential to develop during the second decade of life. The implications are strong ones in terms of both social policy and research. With respect to policy, investment of resources may have dividends at this life stage greater than at any other. With respect to research, the need to understand mechanism is, at this level, arguably even more urgent. Research has a fundamental role to play in identifying developmental pathways. But its role is equally critical in identifying the factors that make this development more likely to occur.

We noted early that the current focus in cognitive development research is on earliest origins in the first years of life. In time, the pendulum may well swing back toward greater interest in older children and adolescents and what they have to tell us about development. Diamond and Kirkham (2005), noting that early modes of responding are not outgrown or discarded but rather need to be overcome and managed, assert that we need to study the extremes of early childhood to fully understand adults. Arguably, the reverse is fully as true. We need to study its entire path and endpoint—to know where it's headed—in order to fully understand the significance of an early form. Indeed, that is exactly what developmental analysis is all about. We hope to have made the case here that it can be worthwhile to look beyond the earliest years in seeking to understand the what and how of cognitive development.

References

Ahn, W., Kalish, C., Medin, D., & Gelman, S. (1995). The role of covariation versus mechanism information in causal attribution. *Cognition, 54,* 299–352.

Amsel, E., & Brock, S. (1996). Developmental changes in children's evaluation of evidence. *Cognitive Development, 11,* 523–550.

Barrouillet, P., Markovits, H., & Quinn, S. (2001). Developmental and content effects in reasoning with causal conditionals. *Journal of Experimental Child Psychology, 81,* 235–248.

Billig, M. (1987). *Arguing and thinking: A rhetorical approach to social psychology.* Cambridge: Cambridge University Press.

Bjorklund, D., & Harnishfeger, K. (1990). The resources construct in cognitive development: Diverse sources of evidence and a theory of inefficient inhibition. *Developmental Review, 10,* 48–71.

Braine, M., & Rumain, B. (1983). Logical reasoning. In P. H. Munsen (Series Ed.) & J. Flavell & E. Markman (Vol. Eds.), *Handbook of child psychology: Vol. 3. Cognitive development* (4th ed.). New York: Wiley.

Brem, S., & Rips, L. (2000). Explanation and evidence in informal argument. *Cognitive Science, 24,* 573–604.

Carey, S. (1985). Are children fundamentally different kinds of thinkers and learners than adults. In S. Chipman, J. Segal, & R. Glaser (Eds.), *Thinking and learning skills* (Vol. 2). Hillsdale, NJ: Erlbaum.

Carey, S., & Smith, C. (1993). On understanding the nature of scientific knowledge. *Educational Psychologist, 28,* 235–251.

Case, R. (1992). *The mind's staircase: Exploring the conceptual underpinnings of children's thought and knowledge.* Hillsdale, NJ: Erlbaum.

Case, R. (1998). The development of conceptual structures. In W. Damon (Series Ed.) & D. Kuhn & R. Siegler (Vol. Eds.), *Handbook of child psychology: Vol. 2. Cognition, perception, and language* (5th ed.). New York: Wiley.

Case, R., Kurland, D., & Goldberg, J. (1982). Operational efficiency and the growth of short-term memory span. *Journal of Experimental Child Psychology, 33*(3), 386–404.

Case, R., & Okamoto, Y. (1996). The role of central conceptual structures in the development of children's thought. *Monographs of the Society for Research in Child Development* (Vol. 61, Whole No. 246).

Cheng, P., & Novick, L. (1992). Covariation in natural causal induction. *Psychological Review, 99,* 365–382.

Chinn, C., & Brewer, W. (2001). Models of data: A theory of how people evaluate data. *Cognition and Instruction, 19,* 323–393.

Cowan, N. (1997). The development of working memory. In N. Cowan (Ed.), *The development of memory in childhood.* East Sussex, England: Psychology Press.

Dean, D., & Kuhn, D. (2007). Direct instruction vs. discovery: The long view. *Science Education.*

Demetriou, A., Christou, C., Spanoudis, G., & Platsidou, M. (2002). The development of mental processing: Efficiency, working memory, and thinking. *Monographs of the Society for Research in Child Development* (Vol. 67, Serial No. xxx).

Diamond, A., & Kirkham, N. (2005). Not quite as grown-up as we like to think: Parallels between cognition in childhood and adulthood. *Psychological Science, 16,* 291–297.

Dias, M., & Harris, P. (1988). The effect of make-believe play on deductive reasoning. *British Journal of Developmental Psychology, 6,* 207–221.

Evans, J., St. (2002). Logic and human reasoning: An assessment of the deduction paradigm. *Psychological Bulletin, 128*(6), 978–996.

Fay, A., & Klahr, D. (1996). Knowing about guessing and guessing about knowing: Preschoolers' understanding of indeterminacy. *Child Development, 67*(2), 689–716.

Feinstein, L., & Bynner, J. (2004). The importance of cognitive development in middle childhood for adulthood socioeconomic status, mental health, and problem behavior. *Child Development, 75,* 1329–1339.

Felton, M. (2004). The development of discourse strategies in adolescent argumentation. *Cognitive Development, 19,* 35–52.

Felton, M., & Kuhn, D. (2001). The development of argumentive discourse skills. *Discourse Processes, 32,* 135–153.

Fischer, K., & Bidell, T. (1991). Constraining nativist inferences about cognitive capacities. In S. Carey & R. Gelman (Eds.), *The epigenesis of mind: Essays on biology and cognition* (pp. 199–235). Hillsdale, NJ: Erlbaum.

Gathercole, S., Pickering, S., Ambridge, B., & Wearing, H. (2004). The structure of working memory from 4 to 15 years of age. *Developmental Psychology, 40*(2), 177–190.

Gelman, R. (2002). Cognitive development. In H. Pashler & D. Medin (Eds.), *Stevens' handbook of experimental psychology* (3rd ed., Vol. 2). Hoboken, NJ: Wiley.

Giedd, J., Blumenthal, J., Jeffries, N., Castellanos, F., Lui, H., Zijdenbos, A., et al. (1999). Brain development during childhood and adolescence: A longitudinal MRI study. *Nature Neuroscience, 2,* 861–863.

Glassner, A., Weinstock, M., & Neuman, Y. (2005). Pupils' evaluation and generation of evidence and explanation in argumentation. *British Journal of Educational Psychology, 75,* 105–118.

Gopnik, A., Meltzoff, A., & Kuhl, P. (1999). *The scientist in the crib: Minds, brains, and how children learn.* New York: HarperCollins.

Graff, G. (2003). *Clueless in academe: How schooling obscures the life of the mind.* New Haven, CT: Yale University Press.

Hagen, J., & Hale, G. (1973). The development of attention in children. In A. Pick (Ed.), *Minnesota Symposium on Child Psychology* (Vol. 7). Minneapolis: University of Minnesota Press.

Halford, G. S., & Andrews, G. (2006). Reasoning and problem solving. In W. Damon & R. M. Lerner (Series Eds.) & D. Kuhn & R. S. Siegler (Vol. Eds.), *Handbook of child psychology: Vol. 2. Cognition, perception, and language* (6th ed., pp. 557–608). Hoboken, NJ: Wiley.

Halford, G. S., Wilson, W. H., & Phillips, S. (1998). Processing capacity defined by relational complexity: Implications for comparative, developmental, and cognitive psychology. *Behavioral and Brain Sciences, 21,* 803–864.

Handley, S., Capon, A., Beveridge, M., Dennis, I., & Evans, J. (2004). Working memory, inhibitory control and the development of children's reasoning. *Thinking and Reasoning, 10,* 175–196.

Harnishfeger, K. (1995). The development of cognitive inhibition: Theories, definition, and research evidence. In F. Dempster & C. Brainerd (Eds.), *Interference and inhibition in cognition.* San Diego, CA: Academic Press.

Hawkins, J., Pea, R., Glick, J., & Scribner, S. (1984). "Merds that laugh don't like mushrooms": Evidence for deductive reasoning by preschoolers. *Developmental Psychology, 20*(4), 584–594.

Hofer, B., & Pintrich, P. (1997). The development of epistemological theories: Beliefs about knowledge and knowing and their relation to learning. *Review of Educational Research, 67,* 88–140.

Hofer, B., & Pintrich, P. (2002). *Epistemology: The psychology of beliefs about knowledge and knowing.* Mahwah, NJ: Erlbaum.

Inhelder, B., & Piaget, J. (1958). *The growth of logical thinking from childhood to adolescence.* New York: Basic Books.

Kail, R. (1991). Development of processing speed in childhood and adolescence. In R. Hayne (Ed.), *Advances in child development and behavior* (Vol. 23). San Diego, CA: Academic Press.

Kail, R. (1993). Processing time decreases globally at an exponential rate during childhood and adolescence. *Journal of Experimental Child Psychology, 56,* 254–265.

Kail, R. (2002). Developmental change in proactive interference. *Child Development, 73,* 1703–1714.

Keating, D. (1980). Thinking processes in adolescence. In J. Adelson (Ed.), *Handbook of adolescent psychology.* New York: Wiley.

Keating, D. (2004). Cognitive and brain development. In R. Lerner & L. Steinberg (Eds.), *Handbook of adolescent psychology.* Chichester, West Sussex, England: Wiley.

Keil, F. (1991). The emergence of theoretical beliefs as constraints on concepts. In S. Carey & R. Gelman (Eds.), *The epigenesis of mind: Essays on biology and cognition* (pp. 237–256). Hillsdale, NJ: Erlbaum.

Keil, F. (1998). Cognitive science and the origins of thought and knowledge. In W. Damon (Series Ed.) & R. Lerner (Vol. Ed.), *Handbook of child psychology: Vol. 1. Theoretical models of human development* (5th ed.). New York: Wiley.

Keselman, A. (2003). Supporting inquiry learning by promoting normative understanding of multivariable causality. *Journal of Research in Science Teaching, 40*(9), 898–921.

Klaczynski, P. (2000). Motivated scientific reasoning biases, epistemological beliefs, and theory polarization: A two-process approach to adolescent cognition. *Child Development, 71*(5), 1347–1366.

Klaczynski, P. (2004). A dual-process model of adolescent development: Implications for decision making, reasoning, and identity. In R. Kail (Ed.), *Advances in child development and behavior* (Vol. 31). San Diego, CA: Academic Press.

Klaczynski, P., & Narasimham, G. (1998). Representations as mediators of adolescent deductive reasoning. *Developmental Psychology, 5,* 865–881.

Klaczynski, P., Schuneman, M., & Daniel, D. (2004). Development of conditional reasoning: A test of competing theories. *Developmental Psychology, 40,* 559–571.

Klahr, D. (2000). *Exploring science: The cognition and development of discovery processes.* Cambridge, MA: MIT Press.

Klahr, D., Fay, A., & Dunbar, K. (1993). Heuristics for scientific experimentation: A developmental study. *Cognitive Psychology, 25*(1), 111–146.

Knudson, R. (1992). Analysis of argumentative writing at two grade levels. *Journal of Educational Research, 85,* 169–179.

Koslowski, B. (1996). *Theory and evidence: The development of scientific reasoning.* Cambridge, MA: MIT Press.

Kuhn, D. (1977). Conditional reasoning in children. *Developmental Psychology, 13*(4), 342–353.

Kuhn, D. (1989). Children and adults as intuitive scientists. *Psychological Review, 96,* 674–689.

Kuhn, D. (1991). *The skills of argument.* Cambridge: Cambridge University Press.

Kuhn, D. (1993). Science as argument: Implications for teaching and learning scientific thinking. *Science Education, 77*(3), 319–337.

Kuhn, D. (1995). Microgenetic study of change: What has it told us? *Psychological Science, 6,* 133–139.

Kuhn, D. (2001a). How do people know? *Psychological Science, 12,* 1–8.

Kuhn, D. (2001b). Why development does (and doesn't) occur: Evidence from the domain of inductive reasoning. In R. Siegler & J. McClelland (Eds.), *Mechanisms of cognitive development: Neural and behavioral perspectives.* Mahwah, NJ: Erlbaum.

Kuhn, D. (2002). What is scientific thinking and how does it develop. In U. Goswami (Ed.), *Handbook of childhood cognitive development.* Oxford, England: Blackwell.

Kuhn, D. (2005). *Education for thinking.* Cambridge, MA: Harvard University Press.

Kuhn, D. (2007). Reasoning about multiple variables: Control of variables is not the only challenge. *Science Education.*

Kuhn, D., Amsel, E., & O'Loughlin, M. (1988). *The development of scientific thinking skills.* San Diego, CA: Academic Press.

Kuhn, D., Black, J., Keselman, A., & Kaplan, D. (2000). The development of cognitive skills to support inquiry learning. *Cognition and Instruction, 18,* 495–523.

Kuhn, D., Cheney, R., & Weinstock, M. (2000). The development of epistemological understanding. *Cognitive Development, 15,* 309–328.

Kuhn, D., & Dean, D. (2004). Connecting scientific reasoning and causal inference. *Journal of Cognition and Development, 5*(2), 261–288.

Kuhn, D., & Dean, D. (2005). Is developing scientific thinking all about learning to control variables? *Psychological Science, 16,* 866–870.

Kuhn, D., Garcia-Mila, M., Zohar, A., & Andersen, C. (1995). Strategies of knowledge acquisition. *Society for Research in Child Development Monographs, 60*(4, Serial No. 245).

Kuhn, D., Iordanou, K., Pease, M., & Wirkala, C. (in press). Beyond control of variables: What needs to develop to achieve skilled scientific thinking? [Special issue]. *Cognitive Development.*

Kuhn, D., Katz, J., & Dean, D. (2004). Developing reason. *Thinking and Reasoning, 10*(2), 197–219.

Kuhn, D., & Park, S. (2005). Epistemological understanding and the development of intellectual values. *International Journal of Educational Research, 43,* 111–124.

Kuhn, D., & Pearsall, S. (2000). Developmental origins of scientific thinking. *Journal of Cognition and Development, 1,* 113–129.

Kuhn, D., & Pease, M. (2006). Do children and adults learn differently? *Journal of Cognition and Development, 7,* 279–293.

Kuhn, D., & Pease, M. (in press). What needs to develop in the development of inquiry skills? *Cognition and Instruction.*

Kuhn, D., & Phelps, E. (1982). The development of problem-solving strategies. In H. Reese (Ed.), *Advances in child development and behavior* (Vol. 17). New York: Academic Press.

Kuhn, D., Schauble, L., & Garcia-Mila, M. (1992). Cross-domain development of scientific reasoning. *Cognition and Instruction, 9,* 285–332.

Kuhn, D., Shaw, V., & Felton, M. (1997). Effects of dyadic interaction on argumentive reasoning. *Cognition and Instruction, 15,* 287–315.

Kuhn, D., & Udell, W. (2003). The development of argument skills. *Child Development, 74,* 1245–1260.

Kuhn, D., & Udell, W. (2007). Coordinating own and other perspectives in argument. *Thinking and Reasoning, 13,* 90–104.

Leevers, H., & Harris, P. (1999). Transient and persisting effects of instruction on young children's syllogistic reasoning with incongruent and abstract premises. *Thinking and Reasoning, 5,* 145–174.

Lehrer, R., Schauble, L., & Petrosino, A. J. (2001). Reconsidering the role of experiment in science education. In K. Crowley, C. Schunn, & T. Okada (Eds.), *Designing for science: Implications from everyday, classroom, and professional settings* (pp. 251–277). Mahwah, NJ: Erlbaum.

Lerner, R. (2002). *Concepts and theories of human development* (3rd ed.). Mahwah, NJ: Erlbaum.

Levstik, L., & Barton, K. (2001). *Doing history: Investigating with children in elementary and middle schools.* Mahwah, NJ: Erlbaum.

Luna, B., Garver, K., Urban, T., Lazar, N., & Sweeney, J. (2004). Maturation of cognitive processes from late childhood to adulthood. *Child Development, 75*(5), 1357–1372.

Maccoby, E., & Hagen, J. (1965). Effects of distraction upon central versus incidental recall: Developmental trends. *Journal of Experimental Child Psychology, 2*(3), 280–289.

Markovits, H., & Barrouillet, P. (2002). The development of conditional reasoning: A mental model account. *Developmental Review, 22,* 5–36.

Markovits, H., & Vachon, R. (1989). Reasoning with contrary-to-fact propositions. *Journal of Experimental Child Psychology, 47*(3), 398–412.

Mason, L., & Boscolo, P. (2004). Role of epistemological understanding and interest in interpreting a controversy and in topic-specific belief change. *Contemporary Educational Psychology, 29,* 103–128.

Means, M., & Voss, J. (1996). Who reasons well? Two studies of informal reasoning among students of different grade, ability, and knowledge levels. *Cognition and Instruction, 14,* 139–178.

Metz, K. (2004). Children's understanding of scientific inquiry: Their conceptualization of uncertainty in investigations of their own design. *Cognition and Instruction, 22,* 219–290.

Morris, A. (2000). Development of logical reasoning: Children's ability to verbally explain the nature of the distinction between logical and nonlogical forms of argument. *Developmental Psychology, 36,* 741–758.

Morris, B., & Sloutsky, V. (2002). Children's solutions of logical versus empirical problems: What's missing and what develops? *Cognitive Development, 116,* 907–928.

Moshman, D., & Franks, B. A. (1986). Development of the concept of inferential validity. *Child Development, 57*(1), 153–165.

National Research Council. (1996). *The National Science Education Standards.* Washington, DC: National Academy Press.

Neimark, E. (1975). Intellectual development during adolescence. In F. Horowitz (Ed.), *Review of child development research* (Vol. 4). Chicago: Chicago University Press.

Neuman, Y. (2002). Go ahead, prove that God does not exist! On students' ability to deal with fallacious arguments. *Learning and Instruction, 13,* 367–380.

O'Brien, D. (1987). The development of conditional reasoning: An iffy proposition. In H. Reese (Ed.), *Advances in child development and behavior* (Vol. 20). Orlando, FL: Academic Press.

Pascual-Leone, J. (1970). A mathematical model for transition in Piaget's developmental stages. *Acta Psychologica, 32,* 301–345.

Penner, D., & Klahr, D. (1996). The interaction of domain-specific knowledge and domain-general discovery strategies: A study with sinking objects. *Child Development, 67*(6), 2709–2727.

Perkins, D. (1985). Postprimary education has little impact on informal reasoning. *Journal of Educational Psychology, 77*(5), 562–571.

Perkins, D., Jay, E., & Tishman, S. (1993). Beyond abilities: A dispositional theory of thinking. *Merrill-Palmer Quarterly, 39,* 1–21.

Perner, J. (1991). *Understanding the representational mind.* Cambridge, MA: MIT Press.

Pillow, B. (2002). Children's and adults' evaluation of the certainty of deductive inferences, inductive inferences, and guesses. *Child Development, 73,* 779–792.

Reznitskaya, A., Anderson, R., McNurlen, B., Nguyen-Jahiel, K., Archodidou, A., & Kim, S. (2001). Influence of oral discussion on written argument. *Discourse Processes, 32,* 155–175.

Rumain, B., Connell, J., & Braine, M. (1983). Conversational comprehension processes are responsible for reasoning fallacies in children as well as adults: It is not the biconditional. *Developmental Psychology, 19*(4), 471–481.

Schauble, L. (1990). Belief revision in children: The role of prior knowledge and strategies for generating evidence. *Journal of Experimental Child Psychology, 49,* 31–57.

Schauble, L. (1996). The development of scientific reasoning in knowledge-rich contexts. *Developmental Psychology, 32,* 102–119.

Schiff, A., & Knopf, I. (1985). The effect of task demands on attention allocation in children of different ages. *Child Development, 56,* 621–630.

Schoenfeld, A. (1999). Looking toward the 21st century: Challenges of educational theory and practice. *Educational Researcher, 28,* 4–14.

Schulz, L., & Gopnik, A. (2004). Causal learning across domains. *Developmental Psychology, 40*(2), 162–176.

Siegler, R. (2000). The rebirth of children's learning. *Child Development, 71,* 26–35.

Siegler, R. (2006). Microgenetic analyses of learning. In W. Damon & R. M. Lerner (Series Eds.) & D. Kuhn & R. Siegler (Vol. Eds.), *Handbook of child psychology: Vol. 2. Cognition, perception, and language* (6th ed., pp. 464–510). Hoboken, NJ: Wiley.

Siegler, R., & Crowley, K. (1991). The microgenetic method: A direct means for studying cognitive development. *American Psychologist, 46*(6), 606–620.

Siegler, R., & Munakata, Y. (1993, Winter). Beyond the immaculate transition: Advances in the understanding of change. *SRCD Newsletter,* pp. 3, 10–11, 13.

Simoneau, M., & Markovits, H. (2003). Reasoning with premises that are not empirically true: Evidence for the role of inhibition and retrieval. *Developmental Psychology, 39*(6), 964–975.

Stanovich, K., & West, R. (1997). Reasoning independently of prior belief and individual differences in actively open-minded thinking. *Journal of Educational Psychology, 89,* 342–357.

Stanovich, K., & West, R. (1998). Individual differences in rational thought. *Journal of Experimental Psychology: General, 127,* 161–188.

Stanovich, K., & West, R. (1999). Individual differences in reasoning and the heuristics and biases debate. In P. Ackerman & P. Kyllonen (Eds.), *Learning and individual differences: Process, trait, and content determinants* (pp. 389–411). Washington, DC: American Psychological Association.

Stanovich, K., & West, R. (2000). Individual differences in reasoning: Implications for the rationality debate? *Behavioral and Brain Sciences, 23,* 645–665.

Swanson, H. L. (1999). What develops in working memory? A life span perspective. *Developmental Psychology, 35*(4), 986–1000.

Udell, W. (2007). Enhancing adolescent girls' argument skills in reasoning about personal and non-personal decisions. *Cognitive Development, 22,* 341–352.

Voss, J., & Means, M. (1991). Learning to reason via instruction in argumentation. *Learning and Instruction, 1,* 337–350.

Wason, P. (1966). Reasoning. In B. Foss (Ed.), *New horizons in psychology.* London: Penguin.

Week in Review: When no fact goes unchecked. (2004, October 31). *New York Times,* Section 4, p. 5.

Weinstock, M., & Cronin, M. (2003). The everyday production of knowledge: Individual differences in epistemological understanding and juror-reasoning skill. *Applied Cognitive Psychology, 17*(2), 161–181.

Weinstock, M., Neuman, Y., & Tabak, I. (2004). Missing the point or missing the norms? Epistemological norms as predictors of students' ability to identify fallacious arguments. *Contemporary Educational Psychology, 29,* 77–94.

Williams, B., Ponesse, J., Schacher, R., Logan, G., & Tannock, R. (1999). Development of inhibitory control across the life span. *Developmental Psychology, 35,* 205–213.

Chapter 16

Adolescent Development in Interpersonal Context

W. ANDREW COLLINS and LAURENCE STEINBERG

The study of adolescence began with Hall's (1904) two-volume work, *Adolescence: Its Psychology and Its Relations to Physiology, Anthropology, Sociology, Sex, Crime, Religion, and Education.* Hall's vision blended attention to individual and contextual factors, as well as basic and applied concerns, and this breadth of perspective continues to characterize research on adolescence today. As the twentieth century came to an end, the individualistic orientation and dominance of family influences characteristic of the first 50 years of empirical research in the period gradually broadened to include *relational* processes in development (Collins & Laursen, 2004). Researchers began to attend to adolescents' abilities for high-quality affiliations, to seek support effectively from others, and to cooperate and collaborate on formal and informal tasks (e.g., Collins, Gleason, & Sesma, 1997). Researchers also recognized that extrafamilial interpersonal relationships contributed significantly to both individual and relational competence in childhood and adolescence (Collins, Maccoby, Steinberg, Hetherington, & Bornstein, 2000). Socialization and acculturation increasingly were viewed as occurring in networks of relationships in diverse contexts (Cooper, 1994). Researchers now recognize that adolescents of different ages differ in their capacities as relationship partners and that social contacts during adolescence differ from those of childhood. Although family relationships remain salient, the proportion of time that adolescents spend with persons outside of the family increases, and these extrafamilial relationships serve many of the same functions that previously were considered the exclusive province of family relationships during childhood (Collins & Laursen, 2004). Research on adolescents' social relationships has been refocused to include interest in interpersonal *transformations* in which the properties and conditions of relationships within and outside of the family change without subverting the bond between parent and child (Collins, 1995).

An increased emphasis on relationships has altered perspectives on the nature and course of psychosocial achievements that long have been regarded as touchstones of adolescent development. One is the development of a sense of *independence,* including both behavioral and emotional autonomy from parents. The other is the development of *interdependence* by forming connections with others in which mutual influence and support can occur. Increasingly, research is encompassing the facilitating role of both familial and extrafamilial relationships in achieving age-appropriate independence, as well as the formation and maintenance of effective relations with others (Collins & Laursen, 2004).

Significant Interpersonal Relationships during Adolescence

The psychosocial challenges of adolescence arise in rapidly diversifying personal and social contexts. This section addresses both relationships established in earlier life periods (e.g., with family members, long-time peers) and those that emerge during adolescence (e.g., with secondary school classmates, romantic interests, extrafamilial adult mentors). In each case, we give particular attention to the importance of differing relationships for accomplishing the psychosocial tasks of independence and interdependence.

FAMILIAL RELATIONSHIPS AND INFLUENCES

The role of the family in social development is arguably the most studied topic in the field of adolescence (Steinberg, 2001). Because the literature on parent-adolescent relations has been reviewed so frequently, so extensively, and so recently (Collins & Laursen, 2004), our brief discussion is oriented toward articulating the major themes and conclusions on the topic. Scholars interested in parent-adolescent relationships generally have asked two related questions:

1. How do family relationships change over the course of adolescence (i.e., What is the impact of adolescence on the family)?
2. How does adolescent adjustment vary as a function of variations in the parent-adolescent relationship (i.e., What is the impact of the family on the adolescent)?

Transformations in Family Relationships

Researchers have tracked changes in parent-child relations across three different dimensions: (1) autonomy (the extent to which the adolescent is under the control of the parents), (2) conflict (the extent to which the parent-adolescent relationship is contentious or hostile), and (3) harmony (the extent to which the parent-adolescent relationship is warm, involved, and emotionally close; Collins & Laursen, 2004). Generally, the most important transformations in family relationships occur during the early portion of the period. Many theorists have argued that the biological, cognitive, and social changes of early adolescence disturb an equilibrium that had been established during middle childhood and that it is not until middle or even late adolescence that a new equilibrium is in place (Collins, 1995).

Autonomy-related changes are probably the most salient of the relational transformations in the family context during adolescence. Adolescents' early attempts at establishing behavioral autonomy in the family frequently precipitate conflict between parents and teenagers, especially during early adolescence. During adolescence, a shift occurs from patterns of influence and interaction that are asymmetrical and unequal to ones in which parents and their adolescent children are on a more equal footing (Collins, 1995).

Despite firmly held popular notions and pervasive media portrayals of conflict as the hallmark of family relations during this period, research has established that frequent, high-intensity, angry fighting is not normative during adolescence (Collins & Laursen, 2004; Steinberg, 1990). Although fighting is not a central feature of normative family relationships in adolescence, however, nattering or bickering is. Early and middle adolescence are characterized by a decline in the frequency of parent-adolescent conflict but an increase in its intensity (Laursen, Coy, & Collins, 1998). Much parent-adolescent conflict results from changes in the adolescent's reasoning about the legitimacy of parental authority (Smetana, 1995). Parents and adolescents often squabble over matters that are defined by parents as moral or prudential issues but by adolescents as questions of personal choice and, accordingly, as less appropriate for parental regulation. With increasingly more sophisticated reasoning abilities, adolescents gradually better appreciate distinctions among the personal, the prudential, and the moral, and they begin to challenge parental authority when they believe it is not legitimate (Smetana & Daddis, 2002).

Many of the frustrations associated with parent-adolescent conflict may be related less to the content of the conflict and more to the manner in which conflict is typically resolved. Conflicts between teenagers and parents tend to be resolved not through compromise but through submission (i.e., giving in) or disengagement (i.e., walking away; Laursen & Collins, 1994). Compared with conflicts between adolescents and their friends, conflicts between adolescents and their parents are more apt to involve neutral or angry affect and less likely to involve positive affect (Adams & Laursen, 2001).

Although there is less research on the extent of changes in positive affect than on autonomy or conflict, existing evidence suggests that subjective feelings of closeness and objective measures of interdependence decrease across the adolescent years (Collins & Repinski, 2001; Laursen & Williams, 1997), as does the amount of time parents and adolescents spend together (Larson, Richards, Moneta, Holmbeck, & Duckett, 1996). Although perceptions of relationships remain generally warm and supportive, both adolescents and parents report less frequent expressions of positive emotions and more frequent expressions of negative emotions when compared with parents and preadolescent children. After a decrease in early adolescence, older teens report more positive affect during family interactions (Larson et al., 1996). Children who had warm relationships with their parents during preadolescence are likely to remain close and connected with their parents during adolescence, even though the frequency and quantity of positive interactions may be somewhat diminished (Collins & Laursen, 2004).

Influence of Parenting on Adjustment

Many researchers employ a typological approach to the study of parenting style in which families are categorized into one of several groups based on multiple dimensions of the parent-child relationship. The most influential and well-known approach groups parents into four categories based on levels of responsiveness and demandingness: (1) authoritative (responsive and demanding), (2) authoritarian (demanding but not responsive), (3) indulgent (responsive but not demanding), and (4) indifferent (neither responsive nor demanding; Maccoby & Martin, 1983). A vast literature has linked higher levels of psychosocial competence to rearing by authoritative parents than to rearing by authoritarian, indulgent, or indifferent parents. Adolescents from authoritative homes are relatively more responsible, more self-assured, and more socially and instrumentally competent. In contrast, adolescents from authoritarian homes are typically more dependent, more passive, less socially adept, less self-assured, and less intellectually curious; those from indulgent households are often less mature, more irresponsible, more conforming to their peers, and less able to assume positions of leadership; and those reared in indifferent homes are disproportionately impulsive and more likely to be involved in delinquent behavior and in precocious experiments with sex, drugs, and alcohol (Steinberg & Silk, 2002). Although occasional exceptions to these general patterns have been noted, the evidence linking authoritative parenting and healthy adolescent development is remarkably strong, and it comes from studies of a wide range of ethnicities, social classes, and family structures, not only in the United States, but around the world (Steinberg, 2001). Research also consistently indicates that adolescents who have experienced indifferent, neglectful, or abusive parenting disproportionately experience problems in mental health and development, such as depression and a variety of behavior problems, including, in cases of physical abuse, aggression toward others (Steinberg & Silk, 2002).

It is important to acknowledge possible bidirectional influence in these associations (C. Lewis, 1981). Adolescents who are aggressive, dependent, or less psychosocially mature in other ways may provoke parental behavior that is excessively harsh, passive, or distant (Rueter & Conger, 1998), whereas adolescents who are responsible, self-directed, curious, and self-assured may elicit from their parents warmth, flexible guidance, and verbal give-and-take. In all likelihood, links between adolescent competence and authoritative parenting may be the result of a reciprocal cycle in which the child's psychosocial maturity leads to authoritative parenting, which in turn leads to the further development of maturity (J. Lerner, Castellino, & Perkins, 1994).

Studies of the independent, additive, and interactive effects of variations in autonomy, harmony, and conflict on adolescent adjustment have yielded remarkably consistent findings. Across a variety of outcomes, adolescents fare best in households characterized by a climate of warmth, in which they are encouraged both to be "connected" to their parents and to express their own individuality (e.g., McElhaney & Allen, 2001). Adolescents who report feeling relatively closer to their parents score higher than other adolescents on measures of psychosocial development, including self-reliance; behavioral competence, including school performance; and psychological well-being, including self-esteem, whereas adolescents who report feeling close to their parents also score lower than comparison groups on measures of psychological or social problems, such as drug use, depression, and antisocial behavior (Steinberg & Silk, 2002). The benefits of a balance between autonomy and connectedness also are evident in research on family decision making. Adolescents fare better when their families engage in joint decision making in which the adolescent plays an important role but parents remain involved in the eventual resolution, rather than unilateral decision making by the parent or adolescent (Lamborn, Dornbusch, & Steinberg, 1996).

Problems in psychosocial adjustment commonly occur when parents are either highly constraining or insufficiently involved. Adolescents whose parents are intrusive or overprotective, for example, may have difficulty individuating from them, which may lead to depression, anxiety, and diminished social competence (McElhaney & Allen, 2001). Alternatively, adolescents who are granted autonomy but who feel distant or detached from their parents score poorly on measures of psychological adjustment (Ryan & Lynch, 1989).

An important vehicle through which parents remain connected to adolescents without constraining them unduly is monitoring (Crouter & Head, 2002). Parental monitoring and supervision are correlated highly with positive adjustment and academic achievement among adolescents (Patterson & Stouthamer-Loeber, 1984). Stättin and Kerr recently have argued that the beneficial outcomes often attributed by researchers to effective parental monitoring may actually have little to do with monitoring and may merely be the end result of a parent-adolescent relationship in which the adolescent willingly discloses information to the parent (Stättin & Kerr, 2000). Although one recent analysis suggests that parental monitoring is a deterrent to adolescent problem behavior above and beyond that attributable to knowledge derived from other sources (Fletcher, Steinberg, & Williams-Wheeler, 2004), Stättin and Kerr's work points up the importance of distinguishing between what parents do and what they know. It is especially important that researchers interested in parental monitoring take care to ensure that the measurement of this construct is precise and that, perhaps, parental knowledge of their adolescent's behavior (and how the knowledge is obtained) be measured separately.

Ethnic Variations.   Authoritative parenting is less prevalent among African American, Asian American, or Hispanic American families than among White families, no doubt reflecting the fact that parenting practices are often linked to cultural values and beliefs (Steinberg, Dornbusch, & Brown, 1992). Nevertheless, even though authoritative parenting is less common in ethnic minority families, its links to adolescent adjustment appear to be positive in all ethnic groups (Steinberg, 2001).

Research also has indicated that authoritarian parenting is more prevalent among ethnic minority than among White families, even after taking ethnic differences in socioeconomic status into account (e.g., Steinberg, Lamborn, Dornbusch, & Darling, 1992). In contrast to research on authoritative parenting, which suggests similar effects across ethnic groups, research on authoritarian parenting indicates that the adverse effects of this style of parenting may be greater among White youngsters than among ethnic minority youth (Steinberg, 2001).

In addition, ethnic minority American adolescents, more than White adolescents, are likely to believe that it is important to respect, assist, and support their family (Fuligni, Tseng, & Lam, 1999), although ethnic differences in adolescents' beliefs and expectations appear to be more sizable than ethnic differences in how adolescents and their parents actually interact. Indeed, except for families who are recent immigrants to the United States, relations between American adolescents and their parents appear surprisingly similar across ethnic groups (Fuligni, 1998).

Relationships with Siblings

Less is known about adolescents' relations with their brothers and sisters than with their parents. During adolescence relationships with siblings, and especially with younger siblings, generally become more egalitarian but also more distant and less emotionally intense (Buhrmester & Furman, 1990). Early adolescents commonly describe their relationships with siblings and with parents similarly in terms of power differentials and the degree to which the relationship provides assistance and satisfaction (Furman & Buhrmester, 1985). By contrast, sibling relationships are perceived as more similar to friendships than to parent-adolescent relationships with respect to the provision of companionship and the importance of the relationship (Furman & Buhrmester, 1985). As children mature from childhood to early adolescence, conflict increasingly typifies sibling relationships (Brody, Stoneman, & McCoy, 1994), with adolescents reporting more negativity in their sibling relationships compared to their relationships with friends (Buhrmester & Furman, 1990). Like conflicts in parent-adolescent relationships, high levels of sibling conflict in early adolescence gradually diminish as adolescents move into middle and late adolescence. As siblings mature, relations become more egalitarian and supportive, but siblings become less influential as adolescents expand their relations outside the family (Hetherington, Henderson, & Reiss, 1999).

Several researchers have uncovered important connections among parent-child, sibling, and peer relationships in adolescence. The quality of parent-adolescent relationships may influence the quality of relations among adolescent siblings, which in turn influences adolescents' relationships with peers (e.g., MacKinnon-Lewis, Starnes, Volling, & Johnson, 1997), though the causal status of these interrelations has yet to be conclusively documented. Children and adolescents learn much about social relationships from sibling interactions, and they may bring this knowledge and experience to friendships outside the family (McCoy, Brody, & Stoneman, 1994). In poorly functioning families, aggression between unsupervised siblings may provide a training ground for learning, practicing, and perfecting antisocial and aggressive behavior (Bank, Reid, & Greenley, 1994).

The quality of sibling relationships has been linked not only to adolescents' peer relations but also to their adjustment in general (Stocker, Burwell, & Briggs, 2002). Positive sibling relationships contribute to adolescents' academic competence, sociability, autonomy, and self-worth (e.g., Hetherington et al., 1999). A close sibling relationship can partially ameliorate the negative effects of not having friends in school (East & Rook, 1992), and siblings can serve as sources of advice and guidance (Tucker, McHale, & Crouter, 2001). At the same time, siblings are often similar in problem behaviors (K. Conger, Conger, & Elder, 1997; Slomkowski, Rende, Conger, Simons, & Conger, 2001), such as early sexual activity, early pregnancy (e.g., East & Jacobson, 2001), drug use, and antisocial behavior (e.g., Rowe, Rodgers, Meseck-Bushey, & St. John, 1989).

EXTRAFAMILIAL RELATIONSHIPS AND INFLUENCES

Relationships with peers differ from those with family members in the distribution of power between participants and the permanence of the affiliation (Laursen & Bukowski, 1997). Peer relationships, moreover, are voluntary and transitory; participants freely initiate and dissolve interconnections. Whether an affiliation persists hinges on mutually satisfactory terms and outcomes (Laursen & Hartup, 2002). These distinctive features of relationships among peers provide potentially important that differ from the socialization experiences that families provide. This section emphasizes the nature and significance of friendships and of romantic relationships during adolescence and the extent and implications of interrelations among personal relationships.

Social Networks and Social Status

Adolescents typically affiliate with one or more peer groups, which are commonly distinguished as cliques (relatively small networks of friends or persons sharing common interests or activities) or crowds (loose aggregations based on members' common reputations for certain attitudes, interests, or behaviors). According to estimates, almost half of high school students are associated with one crowd, about one-third are associated with two or more crowds, and about one-sixth do not fit into any crowd (Strouse, 1999). Although common interests and shared activities are important determinants of clique membership at all ages, cliques during adolescence also are important in establishing individuals' status in the social hierarchy of the high school (Eder, 1985). Adolescents who feel relatively more confident in their identity may consider crowd affiliations less important than those who are more uncertain. By high school, many adolescents report that being part of a crowd stifles identity and self-expression (Larkin, 1979; Varenne, 1982)—a perception that may account partly for the instability in crowd identification during middle and late adolescence. Research with a national sample showed that two-thirds of individuals changed crowds between grades 10 and 12 (Kinney, 1993; Strouse, 1999).

Little is known about the long-term implications of identifying with particular crowds, with the exception of youth who belong to delinquent crowds (e.g., Brown, Mounts, Lamborn, & Steinberg, 1993; Cairns & Cairns, 1994; Dishion, 2000; Patterson, DeBaryshe, & Ramsey, 1989). Some writers argue that the tendency of group members to exaggerate the positive features of their own group while disparaging the features of others groups may be beneficial to identity development, whereas others deplore the same process as perpetuating socially dysfunctional in-group versus out-group patterns (e.g., Stone & Brown, 1998). Crowd membership has been linked to academic success and failure, which may constrain later developmentally important opportunities (Brown et al., 1993).

Friendships

Adolescents commonly report that friends are their most important extrafamilial resources and influences, and relationships with friends consistently are implicated in variations in adolescent competence and well-being (for reviews, see Brown, 2004; Hartup & Abecassis, 2002). Moreover, self-perceived competence in friendships is a significant component of overall competence during adolescence (Masten et al., 1995). Experiences with friends appear both to influence and moderate social adaptation and academic competence (Cairns & Cairns, 1994) and provide a prototype for later close relationships (Furman & Wehner, 1994; Sullivan, 1953).

Identity of Friends.   Adolescents choose as friends other adolescents who are similar to them on some dimensions and dissimilar on others. For example, European Americans and Asian Americans have friends who are similar in substance use and academic orientation but dissimilar in the importance given to ethnicity in self-definition, whereas African American adolescents show the reverse pattern (Hamm, 2000). Affiliative preferences may be somewhat fluid as adolescents engage and resolve identity issues. This fluidity, as well as school transitions and more diverse involvement in school and extracurricular activities (e.g., choices of courses, sports, or other activities), almost certainly contributes to the considerable instability in friendships during adolescence (Hardy, Bukowski, & Sippola, 2002; Way, Cowal, Gingold, Pahl, & Bissessar, 2001). Changing friends can be beneficial if new associates are more prosocial or espouse more positive goals than former associates did (e.g., Berndt, Hawkins, & Jiao, 1999; Mulvey & Aber, 1988).

Though less often studied than same-sex friendships, cross-sex friendships are a common experience in adolescence, with slightly fewer than half (47%) of adolescents reporting a cross-sex friendship (Kuttler, La Greca, & Prinstein, 1999). Acknowledging mixed-gender friendships in social groups is more common in adolescence than in middle childhood, when gender segregation is the norm in mixed-gender groups (Maccoby, 1990). Affiliations with other-sex, as well as same-sex, friends are correlated with self-perceived competence (Darling, Dowdy, Van Horn, & Caldwell, 1999).

Concepts of Friendship.   The changing features of friendships during adolescence parallel increasingly complex and sophisticated beliefs about and expectations of friendships (Furman & Wehner, 1994; Selman, 1980; Youniss & Smollar, 1985). Adolescents increasingly regard companionship and sharing as a necessary, but no longer sufficient, condition for closeness in friendships; commitment and intimacy are expected as well, especially among females (Youniss & Smollar, 1985). Friendships become more intimate during adolescence in ways that imply improved perspective taking, abstract thinking, and meta-cognition (Savin-Williams & Berndt, 1990), but no study has yet made these connections explicit. Similarly, links between adolescents' understanding of the structure and organization of cliques and crowds undoubtedly depends on cognitive advances (Brown, 2004), although this relation has not been examined directly (Barry & Wigfield, 2002; Eisenberg & Morris, 2004).

Friendship Quality.   Mutuality, self-disclosure, and intimacy (defined as reciprocal feelings of self-disclosure and shared activities) increase markedly (Furman & Buhrmester, 1992; Sharabany, Gershoni, & Hofmann, 1981) during adolescence. Intimacy in particular is related to satisfaction with friendships during early and middle adolescence (Hartup, 1996). Paradoxically, conflicts also are more likely between friends than between acquaintances in both childhood and adolescence. Among adolescents, topics of conflict reflect current concerns, with older adolescents reporting more conflicts regarding disrespect in private interactions with peers, and young adolescents voicing more concern about instances of disrespect and undependability that occur in public (Shulman & Laursen, 2002). Still, compared to middle childhood conflicts with friends, conflicts decline during adolescence, and those that occur are increasingly likely to be resolved effectively and are less likely to disrupt relationships (Laursen & Collins, 1994; Laursen, Finkelstein, & Betts, 2001).

Developmental Significance.   Friendships are primary settings for the acquisition of skills, ranging from social competencies to motor performance (e.g., athletics, dancing) to cognitive abilities (Hartup, 1996). Poor quality adolescent friendships (e.g., those low in supportiveness and intimacy) are associated with multiple outcomes, including incidence of loneliness, depression, and decreases in achievement in school and work settings (Hartup, 1996). Difficult, conflictful relations with peers, especially if chronic in an individual's history, have been linked persistently to negative personal and social characteristics of the individuals involved (e.g., Abecassis, Hartup, Haselager, Scholte, & van Lieshout, 2002).

During adolescence, perceptions of parents as primary sources of support decline and perceived support from friends increases, such that friendships are perceived as providing roughly the same (Helsen, Vollebergh, & Meeus, 2000; Scholte, van Lieshout, & van Aken, 2001) or greater (Furman & Buhrmester, 1992) support as parental relationships. High-quality friendships become increasingly important as sources of support for adolescents' experiencing emotional problems. Adolescents receiving little support from parents and greater support from friends report more emotional problems (Helsen et al., 2000). These results are consonant with other findings showing stronger contributions of parental than peer relationships to increased risk for depression among youth at risk for affective problems (Aseltine, Gore, & Colten, 1994). In an area long dominated by simplistic views of parent-peer cross-pressures on adolescent behavior, more nuanced views are both eminently plausible and badly needed.

Gender-Related Patterns. Gender differences are integral to friendship expectations of both children and adolescents (Markovits, Benenson, & Dolenszky, 2001). Indeed, girls typically report greater companionship, intimacy, prosocial support and esteem support in their close friendships than boys do (Kuttler et al., 1999). Closeness to friends, however, may create a vulnerability that could account for some negative features of girls' relationships. For example, females' current friendships tend to be of shorter duration than males' friendships, and more females than males report both actions that have harmed existing friendships and histories of dissolved friendships (Benenson & Christakos, 2003). The greater emotional intensity of girls', as compared to boys', friendships and the resulting potential vulnerability when friendship ends have been hypothesized as risk factors for depression and as one explanation for the emergence of gender differences in internalized distress during adolescence (Cyranowski, Frank, Young, & Shear, 2000).

Romantic Relationships

Romantic interests are both normative and salient during the adolescent years. In the United States, 25% of 12-year-olds report having had a romantic relationship in the past 18 months; by age 18, more than 70% do (Carver, Joyner, & Udry, 2003). Zani (1991) reported similar rates of involvement for studies of European youth. Despite the obvious centrality of these relationships, however, research on adolescent romantic relationships was both meager and superficial until the last decade of the twentieth century. This section distills key points from this currently burgeoning area of study.

Contexts of Romantic Development. Romantic feelings and the initiation of dating commonly have been attributed to hormonal changes. Most current findings imply that, however, the growing nature and significance of romantic relationships during adolescence and early adulthood stem as much from a culture that emphasizes and hallows romance and sexuality as from physical maturation. Social and cultural expectations, especially age-graded behavioral norms, independently influence the initiation of dating (Dornbusch et al., 1981; Feldman, Turner, & Araujo, 1999; Meschke & Silbereisen, 1997).

Relationships with peers are a primary context for the transmission and realization of these expectations (Brown, 2004; Giordano, 2003). Adolescents regard being in a romantic relationship as central to "belonging" and status in the peer group (Connolly, Craig, Goldberg, & Pepler, 1999; Levesque, 1993). The link may be a transactional one: Peer networks support early romantic coupling, and romantic relationships facilitate connections with other peers (Connolly, Furman, & Konarski, 2000; Milardo, 1982; for reviews, see Brown, 2004; Furman, 1999; Giordano, 2003). Other studies have documented the impact of the extensiveness of peer networks for involvement in dating (Connolly & Johnson, 1996; Taradash, Connolly, Pepler, Craig, & Costa, 2001).

Mixed-gender peer groups appear to be especially significant settings for the development of romantic relationships. Several scholars have recently documented the role of these groups (Connolly, Craig, Goldberg, & Pepler, 2004; Connolly et al., 2000; Feiring, 1999; for reviews, see Brown, 2004; Collins & Van Dulmen, 2006b; Giordano, 2003). According to Connolly et al. (2004), among fifth and eighth graders, participation in mixed-gender peer groups normatively preceded involvement in dyadic romantic relationships. This progression partly reflects the tendency to incorporate dating activities with mixed-gender affiliations. For these young adolescents, group-based romantic activities were more stable than other dating contexts. At the same time, being with mixed-gender groups promotes proximity and common ground that enhance two adolescents' attraction to each other (Connolly & Goldberg, 1999).

Developmental Course.   By middle adolescence, most individuals have been involved in at least one romantic relationship; and, by the early years of early adulthood, most are currently participating in an ongoing romantic relationship (Carver et al., 2003). Middle and late adolescents (approximately, ages 14 to 18) balance time spent with romantic partners with continued participation in same-sex cliques, gradually decreasing time in mixed-sex groups; by early adulthood, time with romantic partners increases further at the expense of involvement with friends and crowds (Reis, Lin, Bennett, & Nezlek, 1993).

Most current findings portray normative experiences of adolescent romance as part of a continuous progression toward the romantic relationships of adulthood. After age 17, adolescents, however, tend to emphasize personal compatibility rather than focusing solely on superficial features of appearance and social status (Levesque, 1993); and couple interactions often are marked by greater interdependence and more communal orientations than was the case in early adolescent relationships (Laursen & Jensen-Campbell, 1999). In general, differences between mid-adolescents and 25-year-olds reflect increasing differentiation and complexity of thoughts about romantic relationships but continuity in relationship motives, concerns, and expectations. In a longitudinal analysis of relationship narratives (Waldinger et al., 2002), the structure and complexity of narratives increased between middle adolescence and age 25, whereas narrative themes were surprisingly similar across the 8- to 10-year gap between waves of the study. A desire for closeness was a dominant theme in the relationships of participants at both ages.

Developmental Significance.   Variations in qualities of dating and romantic relationships are associated with psychosocial development during adolescence (Furman & Shaffer, 2003). Variations in the timing of involvement in both romantic relationships and sexual activity also have been linked to adolescent behavior and development. Findings typically have identified early dating and sexual activity as risk factors for current and later problem behaviors and social and emotional difficulties (e.g., Davies & Windle, 2000; Zimmer-Gembeck, Siebenbruner, & Collins, 2001). At the same time, having a romantic relationship and having a relationship of high quality are associated positively with romantic self-concept and, in turn, with feelings of self-worth (Connolly & Konarski, 1994; Kuttler et al., 1999); longitudinal evidence indicates that, by late adolescence, self-perceived competence in romantic relationships emerges as a reliable component of general competence (Masten et al., 1995). Several writers have suggested that romantic relationships may be implicated in key processes of identity formation during adolescence, though no research currently supports this hypothesis (e.g., Furman & Shaffer, 2003; Sullivan, 1953). The findings linking adolescent romantic relationships and psychosocial development generally do not substantiate causal connections between the two, though correlational findings document associations that should be explained. For example, longitudinal research with a German sample (Seiffge-Krenke & Lang, 2002) showed that quality of romantic relationships in middle adolescence was significantly and positively related to commitment in other relationships in early adulthood.

The developmental significance of romantic relationships depends more heavily on the behavioral, cognitive, and emotional processes that occur in the relationship than on the age of initiation and the degree of dating activity that a young person experiences (Collins, 2003). Interactions with romantic partners are associated with distinctive patterns of experience for adolescents. Adolescents in romantic relationships, for example, report experiencing more conflict than other adolescents (Laursen, 1995). Moreover, conflict resolution between late-adolescent romantic partners more often involves compromise than does conflict resolution in early adolescent romantic pairs (Feldman & Gowen, 1998). Mood swings, a stereotype of adolescent emotional life, are more extreme for those involved in romantic relationships (Larson, Clore, & Wood, 1999). Participants in the National Longitudinal Study of Adolescent Health who had begun romantic relationships in the past year manifested more symptoms of depression than adolescents not in romantic relationships (Joyner & Udry, 2000). This elevation may be due to breakups, rather than to involvement in a romantic relationship per se. Indeed, the most common trigger of the first episode of a major depressive disorder is a romantic breakup (Monroe, Rohde, Seeley, & Lewinsohn, 1999).

Little information is available on how time devoted to romantic relationships is spent or how teenage romantic partners behave toward one another. Without such information, it is difficult to identify possible functions of the relationships, whether positive or negative, for long-term growth (Collins, 2003).

Individual Differences. Variations in relationship expectancies reflect prior relationship experiences. Adolescents who have poor relationships with parents and peers appear to be at risk for later physical and relational aggression with romantic partners (Linder & Collins, 2005). Similarly, individual differences in the history of attachment security in relationships with caregivers in early life and in accounts of those relationships in early adulthood are correlated with characteristics of romantic relationships in early adulthood (Collins & Van Dulmen, 2006b). Other individual differences play a role as well. Initial findings (e.g., Connolly & Konarski, 1994) imply that adolescent relationships parallel adult relationships in the relevance of individual partners' self-esteem, self-confidence, and physical attractiveness to the timing, frequency, duration, and quality of relationships (Long, 1989).

Interpersonal Contexts and the Psychosocial Tasks of Adolescence

Adolescence has long been viewed as a period of tension between two developmental tasks: (1) increasing connections to others beyond the family and conformity to societal expectations, while simultaneously (2) attaining individual competence and autonomy from the influence of others. Implicitly, researchers have weighted questions of how adolescents separate themselves from others more heavily than questions of how they form connections and close relationships. Balance has been restored partially by research on intimate and romantic relationships in adolescence (e.g., Collins, 2003; Furman, Brown, & Feiring, 1999), but studies of autonomy and identity still far exceed studies of close relationships.

DEVELOPING A SENSE OF INDEPENDENCE

Independence is a multifaceted construct that refers, somewhat loosely, to a lengthy list of phenomena that vary in their interrelatedness. The definition of adolescent autonomy suggested by Douvan and Adelson (1966) remains a helpful starting point for discussing what it means to become "independent." These writers identified three broad types of autonomy: emotional autonomy, which refers to the subjective feelings of independence, especially in relation to parents; behavioral autonomy, which refers to the capacity for independent decision making and self-governance; and value autonomy, which refers to the development of an independent world view that is grounded in a set of overarching principles and beliefs. This subsection emphasizes research on emotional and behavioral autonomy. Research on the development of value autonomy in adolescence, generally discussed with reference to moral development, has been extensively reviewed elsewhere (Eisenberg & Morris, 2004; Rest, 1983).

We begin with three introductory observations about the study of independence in adolescence. First, although the development of independence is usually cast as an individual accomplishment (i.e., the adolescent becomes "an autonomous person"), the development of autonomy almost always implies independence from or in relation to some person (e.g., a parent), group, or institution. Second, independence is both a process and an outcome. Relative to research on independence as an outcome, however, research on independence as a process is relatively sparse; consequently, we know far more about the characteristics of adolescents who are individuated, capable of independent decision making, or principled in their beliefs, than we do about the interpersonal and intraindividual transformations that facilitated these outcomes. Third, independence, as defined here, is valued differently in different cultural contexts (Feldman & Quatman, 1988). Among cultural and socioeconomic groups that value individual autonomy more than demonstrations of collective responsibility (e.g., middle-class European Americans), the capacity to function without depending on parents, to make personal decisions that contradict the desire of the group, and to voice one's own opinions, even if they challenge those of one's elders, are highly desirable traits, and adolescents who do not demonstrate sufficient emotional or behavioral autonomy are viewed as psychosocially immature. Among groups in which attending to the good of the larger collective is more important than the exercise of personal choice (e.g., middle-class Japanese, working-class Mexican Americans), however, establishing emotional independence from parents, making decisions without the input of one's elders, and endorsing values or beliefs that go against those of one's family often are seen in a negative light (e.g., Rothbaum, Pott, Azuma, Miyake, & Weisz, 2000). One interesting but relatively unstudied question is whether the correlates and consequences of independence in adolescence vary across groups that differ in their views of its value.

Emotional Autonomy

The development of emotional autonomy involves increases in adolescents' subjective sense of his or her independence, especially in relation to parents or parental figures.

At least in the early stages of adolescence, feeling emotionally autonomous is achieved in part by separating oneself from and arguing with one's parents; through this process, the relationship is transformed and the adolescent develops both a new behavioral repertoire and a new image of his or her parents (Steinberg, 1990). In this sense, the development of emotional autonomy is not primarily an intrapsychic transformation in which the adolescent comes to see him- or herself as more grown up, but an interpersonal transformation, in which patterns of interaction between the adolescent and parents shift through a process of mutual (if not always willing) renegotiation. At the end of this transformative process are three interrelated outcomes: a changed adolescent, who now views him- or herself in a different light; a changed parent, who now views his or her child (and perhaps him- or herself) in a different light; and a changed parent-child relationship, which is likely to be somewhat more egalitarian (Collins, 1995).

The starting point for most discussions of emotional autonomy and its development is the psychodynamic perspective on adolescence. In this perspective, the development of emotional independence during adolescence is conceptualized as independence from parents, parent-adolescent conflict is seen as a normative manifestation of the detachment process, and parent-adolescent harmony, at least in the extreme, is viewed as developmentally stunting and symptomatic of intrapsychic immaturity (Freud, 1958). Orthodox analytic views of the detachment process gave way in the last quarter of the twentieth century to more tempered, neoanalytic theories that cast the development of emotional independence in terms of the adolescent's individuation or sense of identity rather than limiting the phenomenon to his or her detachment from parents. The development of emotional autonomy begins with individuation from parents (Blos, 1979) and ends with the achievement of a sense of identity (Erikson, 1968).

Theory and research recently have shifted toward the idea that emotional autonomy results from a progressive negotiation between adolescent and parents over issues related to the granting and exercise of adolescent autonomy (Collins et al., 1997). Thus, the process of individuation is less about the adolescent's attempt to separate from his or her parents than about a transformation in the implicit and explicit assumptions and beliefs that shape interactions among family members. This is not to say that all elements of this negotiation process are conscious or deliberate, the involved parties are always agreeable participants, or the everyday experience of renegotiating the terms of the parent-adolescent relationship is necessarily pleasant. This new view of emotional autonomy, however, emphasizes the different ways in which adolescents and parents construe their relationship, the different expectations that they bring to the kitchen table, the different frames they use to interpret their experiences with one another, and the ways in which these cognitions shape patterns of interaction among family members (Larson & Richards, 1994). Empirical research on the development of emotional autonomy implies a reciprocal process of intra-individual and interpersonal change in which the adolescents' growing sense of emotional independence affects, is affected by, and manifests itself in their relations with others. Several conclusions have emerged from work in this area. First, over the course of adolescence, individuals' subjective sense of independence increases significantly, as indicated by feelings of separateness from their parents and changes in their perceptions of them, with older adolescents less likely than preadolescents to idealize their parents or believe in their omnipotence (Steinberg & Silverberg, 1986). Notably, although this process begins early in adolescence, typically with the de-idealization of parents and challenges to parental authority, it unfolds over the entire adolescent period, and fully mature images of one's parents do not begin to appear until very late in adolescence, around the time that the adolescent is likely to be in the midst of the identity crisis described by Erikson (Smollar & Youniss, 1985).

Second, the development of emotional autonomy is far more gradual and far less dramatic than originally suggested in "storm and stress" perspectives on adolescence (Collins & Laursen, 2004). No studies suggest that active rebellion or unrelenting oppositionalism is necessary to later healthy psychosocial development, and many studies indicate that the overt repudiation of parents by the adolescent likely forecasts problems, not success, in the development of emotional independence (Steinberg, 1990).

Third, whereas the process of individuation appears to be especially significant during early adolescence, identity development is salient in late adolescence and early adulthood. Indeed, research on identity development indicates few age differences in early, or even middle, adolescence; rather, the end of the adolescent decade appears to be the critical time for the development of a coherent sense of identity (Nurmi, 2004). Thus, the process of discovering that one has a separate identity (the process of individuation) precedes the process of discovering what that identity is (the process of identity development). Middle adolescence is important as the time during which the psychosocial concerns of adolescence shift from individuation from parents to the establishment of a sense of identity. Peers, in close relationships as well as in groups, undoubtedly play a crucial role in this transition (Brown, 2004).

Fourth, the early adolescent timing of these changed family patterns suggests that interpersonal changes that reflect the development of emotional autonomy precede some of the intrapsychic changes associated with gains in self-governance, which may not take place until the middle portion of the period, or with the development of a sense of identity, which takes place relatively late in adolescence. Although more longitudinal studies of the links between intrapsychic and interpersonal aspects of emotional autonomy are needed, one plausible hypothesis is that changes in the parent-adolescent relationship lead to, rather than follow from, changes in the adolescent's subjective sense of self-reliance (Steinberg, 1990). In other words, the interpersonal may drive the intrapsychic, rather than the reverse.

Finally, there are sizable individual differences in the extent to which significant others in the adolescent's life permit or encourage the development of emotional independence, and these differences are meaningfully related to measures of adolescent psychosocial adjustment, especially in the realms of self-reliance, self-perceptions, and mental health. Many studies, involving both observational and self-report measures, indicate that the development of emotional independence is facilitated by parents who are warm but not intrusive. Extreme psychological control, including various forms of love withdrawal and guilt induction, has been shown to be especially incompatible with the development of emotional autonomy (Barber, 1996; Pomerantz, 2001). The same factors that are associated with the development of healthy individuation—parental warmth, involvement, and the tolerance of expressions of individuality—also appear to contribute to the development of a healthy sense of identity, lending further support to the notion that these phenomena are interrelated (Grotevant & Cooper, 1986; Perosa, Perosa, & Tam, 1996).

Behavioral Autonomy

Behavioral autonomy encompasses multiple capacities involved with self-reliance, but the construct of behavioral independence has appeared in two very different forms in research on adolescence (see Hill & Holmbeck, 1986). In one, behavioral autonomy refers to the capacity for competent self-governance in the absence of external guidance or monitoring, as when, for example, an adolescent is able to function on his or her own without parents in a new or challenging situation or behave ethically when outside the purview of adult supervision. In the other, behavioral autonomy also refers to the capacity to function independently in the face of excessive external influence, when, for example, the adolescent must be able to resist peer pressure to behave in a way that goes against his or her better judgment or personal preferences. Both of these situations require self-reliance, but whether these very different aspects of behavioral independence (i.e., the ability to function responsibly without guidance or in the presence of strong external influence) develop concomitantly has not received adequate research attention, nor has the broader issue of whether the expression of behavioral autonomy is stable across contexts. It is quite easy to imagine, for example, a young person who functions competently while alone but who behaves irresponsibly when in the presence of peers or one who is slavishly dependent on parents when around the house but who stands up for herself when with friends.

Research on the development of behavioral autonomy has for the most part been conducted in the broader framework of socialization research, guided mainly by social learning theory. Investigators have studied features of family contexts that covary with responsible independence, manifested in self-reliance, personal accountability, and appropriate responses to social influence. Two specific lines of work have dominated: studies of the development of responsibility (e.g., Cauffman & Steinberg, 2000; Greenberger & Sorenson, 1974; Lamborn, Mounts, Steinberg, & Dornbusch, 1991; Steinberg, Lamborn, Darling, Mounts, & Dornbusch, 1994) and studies of resistance to peer pressure, especially in antisocial situations (Berndt, 1979; Brown, Clasen, & Eicher, 1986; Erickson, Crosnoe, & Dornbusch, 2000; Krosnick & Judd, 1982; Steinberg & Silverberg, 1986). According to these socialization models, parents facilitate the development of behavioral autonomy in four chief ways: (1) by serving as models of competent decision makers; (2) by encouraging independent decision making in the family context; (3) by rewarding independent decision making outside the family context; and (4) by instilling in the adolescent a more general sense of self-efficacy through the use of parenting that is both responsive and demanding (Darling & Steinberg, 1993). Unfortunately, the sizable intercorrelations among these features of parenting make it impossible to specify which of these processes is most important.

As with research on emotional autonomy, behavioral autonomy sometimes has been examined as a quality of the adolescent's psychological capability or functioning (e.g., studies of age or gender differences in self-reliance) and sometimes as a quality of the adolescent's relationships with parents (e.g., studies of independence seeking or independence granting) or peers (e.g., studies of resistance to peer influence). Studies of behavioral autonomy as a quality of the parent-child relationship generally rely on questionnaires requiring parents and, independently, adolescents to report on how familial decisions are made (e.g., unilaterally by parents, jointly, or unilaterally by the adolescent; e.g., Dornbusch, Ritter, Liederman, Roberts, & Fraleigh, 1987).

The fact that expressions of behavioral autonomy likely vary as a function of who else is present at the time (e.g., parents, peers) makes it difficult to draw generalizations about the developmental course of behavioral independence as an overall capacity. Most studies that ask adolescents to gauge their own level of self-reliance (e.g., Steinberg & Silverberg, 1986) find a linear increase in this trait over the course of adolescence, but it is not clear whether adolescents' own appraisal of their capacity for responsible autonomy is consistent with their actual performance across varied situations. For example, whereas the period between age 11 and 14 is characterized by gains in subjective reports of responsibility, the same period is characterized by a decline in resistance to peer influence. Indeed, even in research on susceptibility to social influence, studies indicate different developmental timetables with respect to resistance to parental influence (which tends to increase linearly over the course of adolescence) and resistance to peer influence (which, at least in the realm of antisocial peer pressure, follows an U-shaped pattern, declining between ages 11 and 14 but increasing thereafter; Berndt, 1979). Although few studies have charted developmental changes in parental autonomy-granting, early adolescence is likely to be an important time for changes, with most parents relinquishing unilateral control over an increasingly wider array of everyday issues involving the adolescent and most families undergoing the sorts of transformations in family relations described in the previous section on emotional autonomy. Because they appear to progress along similar developmental timetables, adolescents' reports of their own sense of self-reliance may more closely reflect their assessment of their growing emotional and behavioral independence in relation to their parents rather than changes in their relations with peers.

The period between early and middle adolescence, from around age 13 until 15, appears to be an important transitional time in the development of behavioral autonomy, because adolescents become increasingly motivated to seek independence from parents during this period, while not yet having the psychosocial maturity for mature self-regulation when alone or in the company of their friends. Recent advances in developmental neuroscience have led several writers to link findings from studies of brain maturation to findings from studies of self-governance (e.g., Steinberg et al., 2006). Changes in the limbic system that impel the adolescent toward sensation seeking and risk taking, both of which require greater independence from parental control, precede the maturation of the prefrontal cortex, which undergirds various aspects of executive function, affecting self-regulation, impulse control, planning, and foresight. This disjunction creates a gap that some writers have likened to "starting the engines with an unskilled driver" (C. Nelson et al., 2002, p. 515). This gap between the degree of autonomy adolescents seek and are granted, on the one hand, and their actual capacity for self-governance, on the other, may leave individuals prone to poor judgment, so that they place themselves in difficult or challenging situations before having developed the capacity for mature self-regulation (Steinberg & Scott, 2003).

Several investigators have examined ethnic and cross-cultural differences in adolescents' and parents' expectations for behavioral autonomy. Feldman and her colleagues, for example, have examined this issue by asking parents and adolescents from both Asian and Anglo cultural groups to fill out a "teen timetable"—a questionnaire that asks at what age one would expect an adolescent to be permitted to engage in various behaviors that signal autonomy (e.g., "spend money however you want," "go out on dates," "go to rock concerts with friends"; Feldman & Wood, 1994). In general, Anglo adolescents and their parents living in America, Australia, or Hong Kong have earlier expectations for adolescent autonomy than do Asian adolescents and parents from these same countries (Feldman & Quatman, 1988; Rosenthal & Feldman, 1990). Because of this, adolescents from Asian families may be less likely to seek autonomy from their parents than are their Anglo counterparts. In general, adolescents' mental health is most positive when their desires for autonomy match their expectations for what their parents are willing to grant (Juang, Lerner, McKinney, & von Eye, 1999).

Not surprisingly, adolescents believe that individuals should be granted autonomy earlier than parents do (Ruck, Peterson-Badali, & Day, 2002).

Studies of expectations for behavioral autonomy have failed to find consistent sex or birth-order differences in age expectations for behavioral independence, contrary to the popular belief that boys expect more autonomy than girls or that later-born adolescents are granted earlier freedom because their older siblings have paved the way. Sex and birth-order differences in the extent to which parents grant autonomy do exist, though the pattern varies depending on the particular constellation of sons and daughters in the household and the parents' attitudes toward sex roles. Although parents are generally thought to be more controlling of daughters than sons, this is relatively more likely in households where parents have traditional views of gender roles (Bumpus, Crouter, & McHale, 2001). Gender differences in the extent to which adolescents are granted independence appear to be especially pronounced in African American households. Relative to other ethnic groups, African American boys are given relatively more freedom but girls are given less (Bulcroft, Carmody, & Bulcroft, 1996). Contrary to expectation, parents grant more autonomy to first-borns than to second-borns, especially when the first-born is a girl and the second-born is a boy (Bumpus et al., 2001). Adolescents' expectations for autonomy may be highly influenced by the ways in which peers are treated by parents. Consistent with this, adolescents who "feel" older seek more independence than their same-aged peers who "feel" younger (Galambos, Kolaric, Sears, & Maggs, 1999).

Summary Comment

The purportedly individual process of developing independence is embedded in the interpersonal contexts of family and peer relationships. Though rarely conceptualized as a systemic phenomenon, the emergence of evidence on the likely interacting processes of brain development, transformations in parent-child relationships, and the ascendance of extrafamilial networks implies that a developmental systems perspective is the minimum adequate conceptual framework for studying the development of autonomy.

DEVELOPING A SENSE OF INTERDEPENDENCE

Interdependence is the norm in societies throughout the world. The emphasis on independence in industrialized cultures is relative not absolute (Goodnow, 2002). The significance of interdependence for developing adolescents is apparent in several ways. Adolescents in diverse industrialized societies generally now enjoy more discretionary time than in other historical periods; in many cultures (e.g., East Asian countries or Hispanic communities in the United States), a large proportion of the time not devoted to schooling is spent with family members (Cooper, 1994; Larson & Verma, 1999; Rothbaum et al., 2000). Although European American middle-class adolescents in the United States spend less time with family members during adolescence than before, the amount of time actually spent talking with family members declines negligibly over these years (Larson et al., 1996) and appears to exceed the time that non-Western youth typically spend talking with their families (Stevenson et al., 1990; Whiting & Edwards, 1988). In addition, time with peers increases gradually during adolescence (Larson & Richards, 1991), and most adolescents claim to have several good friends and one or more best friends (Hartup & Abecassis, 2002). The centrality of interdependence is also apparent in the importance adolescents assign to interpersonal competence during the adolescent years. Longitudinal findings indicate that, by late adolescence, self-perceived competence in close relationships (e.g., with romantic partners) emerges as a reliable component of self-perceptions of general competence (Masten et al., 1995).

Developmental task analyses imply that achieving interdependence in adolescence is part of a process begun at birth (Buhrmester & Furman, 1987). Attachment to caregivers forms a substrate on which other attachments can be built, and the processes of forming and transforming attachments continues into adulthood as a component of interdependence. Same-gender peer relationships during childhood provide initial experiences of intimacy, but intimate relationships with opposite-sex peers typically first develop during adolescence (Savin-Williams & Berndt, 1990; Sullivan, 1953). Some rudiments of sexuality are present in infancy and childhood, but sexual activity itself generally begins during adolescence, bringing with it issues of relationships, social and personal responsibility, health, and safety (Brooks-Gunn & Paikoff, 1997; Simon & Gagnon, 1969; Udry, 1990). The focus of this section is the three psychosocial goals comprising the task of interdependence: (1) attachment, (2) intimacy, and (3) sexuality.

Attachment

The construct of attachment in infant-caregiver relationships refers to a relatively unique or distinct connection, which supports infants' efforts to feel safe from threatening conditions and to be regulated emotionally. These internal emotional experiences are manifested in the organization of the infant's behavior to maintain proximity with the caregiver, especially in novel or threatening circumstances. According to M. Ainsworth (1989), infant behaviors with attachment partners are prototypes of attachments at every age, including those that occur outside of the biological family. Two largely compatible explanations have been offered for links between attachments with caregivers and those in later extrafamilial relationships. One is a carry-forward model, in which functions and representations of caregiver-child attachment relationships (internal working models) organize expectations and behaviors in later relationships (e.g., Waters & Cummings, 2000). Research findings document correspondences between early insecure attachment and poor peer relationships in adolescence (e.g., Weinfield, Ogawa, & Sroufe, 1997) and between security, as assessed in the Adult Attachment Interview, and peers' reports of resiliency, undercontrol, hostility, and anxiety (Kobak & Sceery, 1988). A second explanation is that relationships with caregivers prior to adolescence expose individuals to components of effective relating, such as empathy, reciprocity, and self-confidence, which shape interactions in other, later relationships (e.g., Collins & Sroufe, 1999). In turn, childhood and adolescent friendships serve as templates for subsequent close relationships outside of the family (Furman & Wehner, 1994; Sullivan, 1953; Youniss, 1980). For example, findings substantiate links between representations of romantic relationships and representations of other close relationships, especially relationships with friends; and these interrelated expectancies parallel interrelations in features like support and control (Furman, Simon, Shaffer, & Bouchey, 2002; Furman & Wehner, 1994). Studies of the same individuals from birth to age 19 suggest that these two pathways may be part of a single process. In longitudinal studies, representations of attachment throughout childhood and also social behavior during the same period both have been predicted by early attachment relationships, and interactions between behavior and representations across time in turn have been found to predict social competence at age 19 (Carlson, Sroufe, & Egeland, 2004).

Maintaining interdependence in adolescence and early adulthood, however, involves relative redistributions of relationship functions. Adolescents' perceptions of parents as primary sources of support generally decline, whereas perceived support from friends increases, such that friendships are seen as providing roughly the same (Helsen et al., 2000; Scholte et al., 2001) or greater (Furman & Buhrmester, 1992) support as parental relationships. This process especially implicates friends and romantic interests, the individuals with whom early adults most like to spend time (proximity seeking) and with whom they most want to be when feeling down (safe-haven function; Ainsworth, 1989; Cassidy, 2001; Waters & Cummings, 2000). This shift in attachments requires a cognitive and emotional maturity that rarely is achieved before late adolescence (Ainsworth, 1989). In the process, attachment is transformed from caregiving of one partner by the other to that of mutual caregiving between the two partners (Allen & Land, 1999; Cassidy, 2001; Waters & Cummings, 2000). Although parents are just as likely as friends to be the primary source from which late adolescents and early adults seek advice and on which they depend (Fraley & Davis, 1997), Hazan and Zeifman (1994) have suggested that the apparent overlap among relationships at this time implies that components of attachment relationships (namely, maintaining proximity, using the other as a safe haven, and using the other as a secure base) also become characteristic of relationships with extrafamilial partners.

The significance of attachment for individuals and their relationships both before and during adolescence is apparent in longitudinal findings. For example, secure early attachment in caregiving relationships predicts the features of relationships with extrafamilial partners during adolescence (Sroufe & Fleeson, 1988). Similarly, early attachment security predicts competence with peers both during middle childhood (the elementary school years) and during adolescence. The combination of early experiences of caregiving and competence in peer relationships in preschool and middle childhood predicts adolescent competence more strongly than any of these assessments alone (Sroufe, Egeland, & Carlson, 1999). Likewise, early caregiving experiences significantly predict hostility in interactions with romantic partners in early adulthood over and above the contributions of proximal relationships with peers and parents (Collins & Van Dulmen, 2006b).

Attachments assessed during adolescence and early adulthood also predict quality of relationships. Representations of attachment in earlier life, as assessed by the Adult Attachment Interview (AAI; Main, Kaplan, & Cassidy, 1985; see also Kobak, Cole, Ferenz-Gillies, Fleming, & Gamble, 1993) have been linked significantly to characteristics of relationships with parents in adolescence and early adulthood (Becker-Stoll & Fremmer-Bombik, 1997). Researchers also have documented remarkable correspondence between AAI classifications and an individual's actual manifestations of security in relationships with their caregiver in infancy, as assessed by the Strange Situation (Waters, Merrick, Treboux, Crowell, & Albersheim, 2000). Exceptions to this general continuity also are consistent with the hypothesis that current functioning reflects a combination of relationship history and current experiences (Carlson et al., 2004; Sroufe, Egeland, Carlson, & Collins, 2005; for a critical perspective, see M. Lewis, Feiring, & Rosenthal, 2000). For example, Weinfield, Sroufe, and Egeland (2000) reported that disruptive life events often undermine continuity from early attachment assessments to early adult attachment assessments in a risk sample, whereas Waters et al. (2000) found significant continuities in a largely stable middle-class sample. Finally, individuals' security in caregiver relationships during infancy significantly predicted representations of romantic relationships, as assessed by the Current Relationships Interview (CRI; Crowell & Owens, 1996), at age 21. Other things being equal, a foundation of interdependence in early life appears to be a significant forerunner of continued interdependence in one's closest relationships in adolescence and adulthood.

Whether adolescent attachments contribute uniquely to future adaptation and well-being is still largely unknown. More extensive evidence is accumulating slowly, partly because few valid, reliable measures of adolescents' current attachments exist. Conceptually sound, well-validated measures of attachment, such as the AAI (Main et al., 1985), are of questionable validity for some samples of adolescents. Moreover, some instruments carry the label "attachment," but do not systematically assess Ainsworth's (1989) criteria for distinguishing attachment relationships from other close relationships. Nor have these instruments been validated longitudinally against attachment measures that do address these criteria, such as the Strange Situation or the AAI (Crowell, Fraley, & Shaver, 1999). The most widely used such instrument, Armsden and Greenberg's Inventory of Parent and Peer Attachment (IPPA; Armsden, & Greenberg, 1984), reliably measures certain features of relationships that overlap with the features of secure attachments, such as degree of mutual trust, quality of communication between partners, and degree of anger and alienation. Although IPPA scores cannot substitute for valid measures of attachment, the scores have yielded interesting age-related patterns that are relevant to interdependence during adolescence and even into early adulthood. For example, in a study linking IPPA scores with measures of romantic relationships, relationship quality with mothers and decreasing quality of relationships with father during adolescence were associated with greater expectations of rejection in relationships with friends and romantic partners (Ho, 2004). Other researchers have documented significant positive correlations between poor quality relationships with parents and peers, as assessed by the IPPA, and aggression and victimization toward partners in romantic relationships in early adulthood (Linder & Collins, 2005).

In summary, achieving the psychosocial tasks of interdependence implies building on earlier relationship patterns to form and maintain further stable interdependencies during and beyond adolescence. Attachment perspectives have yielded compelling evidence that interpersonal contexts are significant not only in achieving adolescents' interdependence goals but also in providing a foundation for competent independent functioning as well (Allen & Land, 1999; R. Thompson, 1999).

Intimacy

Intimacy has been defined in several ways. In the widely accepted definition proposed by Reis and Shaver (1988; see also Reis & Patrick, 1996):

Intimacy is an interpersonal process within which two interaction partners experience and express feelings, communicate verbally and nonverbally, satisfy social motives, augment or reduce social fears, talk and learn about themselves and their unique characteristics, and become "close" (psychologically and often physically). (p. 387)

As a psychosocial task of adolescence, intimacy refers to experiencing this mutual openness and responsiveness in at least some relationships with age-mates. Interdependence is a necessary, but not sufficient, condition for intimacy. If interdependence declines, intimacy may be less likely or less satisfying (Prager, 2000; Reis & Patrick, 1996).

The development of capabilities for intimacy during adolescence undoubtedly builds on the hallmark physical, cognitive, and social changes of the period. Concepts of friendship first incorporate notions of intimacy in early adolescence (Furman & Bierman, 1984). In contrast to the relatively large number of studies linking these changes to the growth of independence, few studies have examined their links to changing patterns of intimacy with peers. Nevertheless, many scholars speculate that adolescents become increasingly capable of intimate relationships as more sophisticated understanding of social relations emerges and as adolescents' ability to infer the thoughts of feelings of others sharpens (e.g., Selman, 1980).

The interpersonal roots of emerging intimacy during adolescence have been studied more extensively. Generally, findings confirm links between the quality of adolescents' relationships (i.e., the degree of openness and support experienced with close associates) and the nature of family relationships in earlier periods, as well as changes in the abilities of relationship partners during adolescence (Collins & Van Dulmen, 2006a). For example, in one longitudinal study parent involvement during childhood predicted closeness to parents during adolescence, with stronger links between childhood father involvement in childhood and closeness to father at age 16 for girls than for boys (Flouri & Buchanan, 2002). Furthermore, the degree of flexible control, cohesion, and respect for privacy experienced in families has been linked positively to intimacy in late-adolescent romantic relationships, with especially strong associations emerging for women (Feldman, Gowen, & Fisher, 1998). In contrast, degree of negative emotionality in parent-adolescent dyads predicted degree of negative emotionality and poor quality interactions with romantic partners in late adolescence (Kim, Conger, Lorenz, & Elder, 2001). This association appears to be mediated by negative affect and ineffective monitoring and discipline in parent-adolescent relationships (R. D. Conger, Cui, Bryant, & Elder, 2000).

In relationships with peers, larger amounts of time with peers and correspondingly less time with adults during adolescence may contribute to the development of intimacy by increasing comfort with peers and encouraging self-disclosure, as well as openness to others' self-revelations. Shared interest in mastering the distinctive contexts and social systems of adolescence also stimulates a desire to communicate with peers, and biological changes associated with puberty also may occasion more frequent discussion with peers, who may offer a more comfortable arena than parent-child relationships for discussing issues of physical changes, sex, and dating. Opportunities for intimacy may be one reason why friendships occupy increasing amounts of time during adolescence. The superficial sharing of activities that sufficed between childhood friends is supplanted, during adolescence, by the potential for mutual responsiveness, concern, loyalty, trustworthiness, and respect for confidence between adolescent friends (Furman & Bierman, 1984; Newcomb & Bagwell, 1995). According to Sullivan (1953), the theoretical fountainhead of research in the area, friendship in preadolescence and adolescence meets a basic psychological need to overcome loneliness, an idea that is similar to Baumeister and Leary's (1995) proposal that humans have an evolved need to belong. In Sullivan's view, same-sex peers develop the psychological capacity to achieve intimacy by overcoming loneliness through close friendships with same-sex peers (chumships).

Increases during adolescence in mutuality, self-disclosure, and intimacy with friends (defined as reciprocal feelings of self-disclosure and engagement in activities) have been documented in several studies (e.g., Furman & Buhrmester, 1992). Sharabany et al. (1981) reported, from age 10 to age 16, adolescents increasingly reported frankness, spontaneity, knowing, and sensitivity toward friends. Trust and loyalty, as well as taking and imposing, were characteristics of communication with friends throughout this age range.

Gender differences in both extent and significance of intimacy are both common and widely discussed. During adolescence, girls' friendships consistently involve more knowing and sensitivity, more giving and sharing, and more taking and imposing than boys' friendships do (e.g., Sharabany et al., 1981; Youniss & Smollar, 1985). McNelles and Connolly (1999) found that with increasing age both girls and boys in grades 9, 10, and 11 in a Canadian sample increasingly engaged in discussion and self-disclosure with close friends and were equally successful in sustaining shared affect between them. In this study, the two genders differed primarily in the manner in which intimacy was established, with boys more often manifesting intimacy in the context of shared activities than girls did and girls more likely than boys to attain intimacy through discussion and self-disclosure. One interesting by-product of this gender difference is the relatively greater tendency for adolescent girls to engage in "co-rumination," which may leave them more susceptible than boys to the development of depressive symptomatology (Rose, 2002).

Intimacy in opposite-sex friendships, although not uncommon among late adolescents (Kuttler et al., 1999), emerges relatively late. Sharabany et al. (1981) found that not until the 9th and 11th grades were opposite-sex friendships rated very high in intimacy. Little is known about the intimacy of these friendships relative to those of same-gender pairs (but see Sippola, 1999, for relevant evidence), the typical role of intimacy in networks of same-gender and opposite-gender friends, or the developmental significance of placing high relative importance on opposite-gender over same-gender friendships.

Adolescent friendships appear to provide critical interpersonal experiences for both genders that both shape later close relationships and support individual psychosocial growth (Furman & Wehner, 1994; Sullivan, 1953). Qualities of friendships in middle and late adolescence appear to be linked to concurrent qualities of romantic relationships (Collins & Van Dulmen, 2006a, 2006b; Furman et al., 2002). Representations of friendships and romantic relationships are interrelated as well. Displaying safe-haven and secure-base behaviors with best friends is correlated positively with these behaviors in dating relationships (Treboux, Crowell, Owens, & Pan, 1994). Perhaps the growing importance of romantic relationships calls attention to the commonalities across types of relationships. It is equally likely that the parallels between early adults' relationships reflect their common similarity to prior relationships with parents and peers (Collins & Van Dulmen, 2006a; R. D. Conger et al., 2000; Owens, Crowell, Treboux, O'Connor, & Pan, 1995; Waters et al., 2000).

Intimacy also may enhance other aspects of psychosocial development. In particular, intimacy with peers has been implicated in identity development. In an influential early essay, Elkind (1967) depicted the opportunity to share perceptions and feelings with other adolescents as one of the main ways in which adolescents overcome egocentric beliefs that others are preoccupied with their behavior (the imaginary audience) or that their experiences are unique (the personal fable). Erikson (1968) regarded intimacy in early adulthood as emerging from identity achievement, which enables individuals to engage in sharing with others without feeling excessively vulnerable personally. Little evidence bears on either Elkind's or Erikson's predictions. Some studies have shown that young adults who are relatively advanced in identity achievement, as assessed in Marcia's (1980) classification scheme, also are more likely than those in less advanced classifications to have formed intimate relationships (Dyk & Adams, 1990; Fitch & G. Adams, 1983; Orlofsky, Marcia, & Lesser, 1973; Tesch & Whitbourne, 1982). Although these correlational findings do not address the causal implications of Erikson's developmental formulation, multiple findings imply that high-quality friendships—those that are intimate and in which the adolescent feels supported and cared for—are associated with a range of positive outcomes, including school engagement and positive self-esteem and mental health, and poor-quality relationships consistently are associated with the converse (for reviews, see Brown, 2004; Hartup, 1996).

In summary, intimacy as an aspect of interdependence, though rooted in key family experiences and same-sex friendships prior to adolescence, is largely an emergent of adolescent development. Research findings, however, have revealed more about the observable characteristics of adolescent friendships than about the meaning of deeper, less discernible qualities like intimacy.

Sexuality

The psychosocial task of sexuality refers to adjusting to a sexually maturing body, managing sexual desires, forming sexual attitudes and values and learning about others' expectations, experimenting with sexual behaviors, and integrating these dimensions into one's sense of self (Crockett, Raffaelli, & Moilanen, 2003). As with other aspects of physical and psychological change during adolescence, psychosocial sexuality reflects complex exposure to social roles, behaviors, mores, and values, as well as biological changes. The focus of this section is social, attitudinal, and emotional aspects of sexuality rather than sexual behavior per se (e.g., patterns of sexual behavior, rates of sexual intercourse, or contraceptive use; for a comprehensive review of these topics, see Savin-Williams & Diamond, 2004).

Key elements of sexual response are present well before gonadal puberty. For example, sexual attraction is evident in diverse societies by the age of 10, the age at which adrenal puberty (adrenarche) occurs (Herdt & McClintock, 2000). The main developmental issues of psychosocial sexuality during the adolescent period, thus, are not biological ones but social ones. Pubertal changes and their endocrinological antecedents mainly affect the frequency and intensity of sexual arousal in both sexes. These latter sequelae are highly correlated with sexual activity of various kinds among both females and males, although their significance is moderated by social relationships and social context, especially among females (B. Miller, Norton, Fan, & Christopherson, 1998).

Sexual fantasizing typically appears earliest and remains the most common adolescent sexual experience (Halpern, Udry, Campbell, & Suchindran, 1993; Katchadourian, 1990). Erotic fantasies appear to be followed by the initiation of masturbation, "making out," and sexual intercourse of various kinds (B. Miller et al., 1998; E. Smith & Udry, 1985). This sequence appears to be typical of European American youth, whereas the order in which these sexual experiences occur is less predictable for African American youth (E. Smith & Udry, 1985). Ethnic and racial differences are especially marked in the prevalence of intercourse and in the speed with which adolescents progress to intercourse from other sexual activity (Blum et al., 2000; Katchadourian, 1990).

Other generalizations about the normative development of psychosocial sexuality are difficult, because expectations, attitudes, and values vary considerably across cultural, societal, and ethnic-racial contexts (Eyre, Auerswald, Hoffman, & Millstein, 1998; T. W. Smith, 1994), and even across neighborhoods (for reviews, see Crockett et al., 2003; Savin-Williams & Diamond, 2004). For example, societal indicators of sexual behavior, contraceptive practices, sexually transmitted diseases, and early pregnancy among the United States and other Western nations parallel variations between those countries in prevalent attitudes about the desirability and appropriateness of sexual experimentation during adolescence and the proper goals of sexuality education (Fine, 1988), the impact of family relationships on sexual behavior (e.g., Weinstein & Thornton, 1989; for a review, see B. Miller, Benson, & Galbraith, 2001), and processes and peer norms of sexual behavior (e.g., Billy & Udry, 1985; for a review, see Crockett et al., 2003).

In the United States, social and cultural expectations account partly for changes in attitudes and values regarding sexuality since the middle of the twentieth century: (a) An increased proportion of both males and females now express approval of premarital intercourse when it occurs in the context of an affectionate relationship; and (b) a larger proportion of females now engage in sexual activity during the middle adolescent years than had done so in past decades (Moore & Rosenthal, 1993). Though often attributed to a "sexual revolution," the changes have occurred so gradually that the term sexual evolution may be more appropriate.

Social and interpersonal processes undoubtedly also contribute to persistent differences between the genders and between adolescents with heterosexual versus homosexual preferences in component tasks of achieving maturity in psychosocial sexuality. Evidence on these comparisons is not adequately balanced in that studies of girls' subjective experiences of sexuality are more numerous than studies of boys' experiences and many more studies focus on heterosexual adolescents than on homosexual or bisexual youth. Nevertheless, contrasting challenges are apparent. For example, girls, who are judged more harshly than boys for engaging in some types of sexual activities, are more likely than boys to express ambivalence about their sexuality and to fear harsh judgments if they are viewed as sexually active (Graber, Brooks-Gunn, & Galen, 1999). Similarly, in contrast to females with heterosexual orientations, females with preferences for same-gender partners appear to experience more fluidity in their sexual-identity labels during adolescence (Diamond, 2000; for other research on bisexual attractions, see Weinberg, Williams, & Pryor, 1994).

Understanding the development of psychosocial sexuality is complicated further by the sizable individual differences in attitudes and values pertaining to relationships and sexual expression. Evidence of such differences comes from research showing that a sample of Australian adolescents could be differentiated according to five "styles" of psychosocial sexuality: (1) sexually naive, (2) sexually unassured, (3) sexually competent, (4) sexually adventurous, and (5) sexually driven (Buzwell & Rosenthal, 1996). These clusters varied correspondingly in tendencies toward sexual risk taking, a finding that implies that appropriate differentiation might be needed for interventions such as sex-education programs and campaigns to reduce the risk of teenage pregnancy or to promote safe sexual practices. Gender and sexual-orientation variations also are apparent. Females generally appear to emphasize emotional aspects of relationships as contexts for sexual behavior, whereas males more often emphasize physical satisfaction and release (Moore & Rosenthal, 1993), though within-gender views are highly variable (S. Thompson, 1995). Similarly, current evidence implies that the risk of social and emotional isolation in sexual relationships may be relatively greater for gay, lesbian, and bisexual adolescents of both genders than for adolescents with heterosexual orientations. Sanctions against explicit displays of same-sex romance in adolescence may make the maintenance of a more "normalized" emotional relationship difficult because sexual-minority youth often find it difficult to engage in many of the social and interpersonal activities that their heterosexual peers are permitted to enjoy (Diamond & Savin-Williams, 2003).

Further sources of individual variation in the development of psychosocial sexuality include significant others, especially relationships and processes involving family members, best friends, and romantic partners. Longitudinal and cross-sectional evidence alike implicates positive parent-adolescent relationships in delayed initiation of intercourse, less frequent intercourse, and fewer sexual partners (e.g., K. E. Miller, Sabo, Farrell, Barnes, & Melnick, 1998; for reviews, see Brooks-Gunn & Paikoff, 1997; Savin-Williams & Diamond, 2004). Peers, especially best friends, also contribute to individual differences in sexual expectations, attitudes, and behaviors, albeit more so among girls than boys (e.g., East, Felice, & Morgan, 1993; Whitbeck, Conger, & Kao, 1993). For European American males, though apparently not for African American males, a similar association may reflect selection of friends with similar activities and values (e.g., Bauman & Ennett, 1996; Billy, Rodgers, & Udry, 1984; Rowe et al., 1989).

Sexuality most often has been regarded as a source of developmental difficulties and risks during adolescence. This assumption stems partly from a concern about the impact of precocious sexual experience on normative developmental timetables and abilities and prevailing moral values regarding sexuality outside of marriage, especially for the very young, and partly from concerns about sexual exploitation, pregnancy, and health risks from early sexual activity (Brooks-Gunn & Paikoff, 1997; Savin-Williams & Diamond, 2004). Most studies have emphasized these and other dysfunctional outcomes; research findings consistently have shown that adolescents who become sexually active at a young age (typically, initiating intercourse before age 16) generally exhibit relatively greater risk for problematic outcomes, compared to adolescents who defer sexual activity. Indeed, early onset of sexual activity, rather than sexual activity per se, appears to account for the association between sexual activity and problematic psychosocial development. The link almost certainly is mediated by relative psychosocial immaturity and by a general orientation to unconventionality among early active teenagers (Jessor, Costa, Jessor, & Donovan, 1983). As a group, these adolescents tend to be less achievement oriented, more alienated from their parents, and more likely to exhibit other problem behaviors such as drug or alcohol abuse (e.g., Davies & Windle, 2000; Zimmer-Gembeck et al., 2001).

Several theoretical formulations, bolstered by supportive findings from empirical research, view these associations as part of a cluster of behaviors defined as problems because they represent "transition proneness," or a pattern of earlier-than-usual transitions to behaviors that are typically expected of adults but not of adolescents (e.g., Bingham & Crockett, 1996; Capaldi, Crosby, & Stoolmiller, 1996; Tubman, Windle, & Windle, 1996). This inference is bolstered by findings that later initiation of intercourse and less frequent intercourse for those who do begin early are inversely related to both religiosity (Rostosky, Wilcox, Comer Wright, & Randall, 2004; Whitbeck, Yoder, Hoyt, & Conger, 1999) and high levels of educational aspirations and achievement (Jessor et al., 1983; Ohannessian & Crockett, 1993; Whitbeck et al., 1999). In a 4-year longitudinal study, self-restraint at age 10 to 11 predicted having had fewer sexual partners at the later time (Feldman & Brown, 1993). By contrast, sexual activity is associated with risk proneness (Rawlings, Boldero, & Wiseman, 1995). Contrary to common expectations, however, correlations between delayed intercourse and self-esteem generally have been negligible (e.g., Crockett, Bingham, Chopak, & Vicary, 1996; Whitbeck et al., 1999), although more depressed girls are at risk for higher levels for sexual activity (Whitbeck et al., 1999).

One concern about early sexual behavior is that a premature focus on sexual expression may interfere with successful integration of physical sexuality with attitudinal, emotional, and identity components. For example, Maccoby (1998) has observed that sexually adventurous female adolescents, unlike their male counterparts, may experience social condemnation, peer derision, and stereotyping that interfere with more positive developmental opportunities. Savin-Williams (1996) has suggested that negative social sanctions, stigmatization, and personal identity struggles may account partly for current findings showing a high rate of attempted suicide, emotional distress, school problems, and alcohol and drug abuse among self-identified gay, lesbian, and bisexual youth. Although some researchers question the validity of these findings (Savin-Williams, personal communication, October 22, 2004), many adolescents, regardless of sexual orientation, report negative experiences stemming from perceived pressure to engage in sexual activity, which they did not desire or for which they felt unready. These individuals disproportionately reported guilt and self-doubt following sexual experimentation, which colored feelings about subsequent sexual experiences (Moore & Rosenthal, 1993; Savin-Williams, 1996; Zani, 1991).

Unfortunately, relatively little research has been devoted to examining the hypothesized psychological advantages of integrating physical and psychosocial aspects of sexuality during adolescence, especially for sexual-minority youth. Contemporary views regard mature sexuality in the psychosocial sense as developmentally healthy rather than problematic (e.g., Brooks-Gunn & Paikoff, 1997; Carpenter, 2001; Savin-Williams & Diamond, 2004; Tolman, Spencer, Rosen-Reynoso, & Porche, 2004). Accordingly, many observers have advocated that public school sex-education efforts include more detailed and comprehensive programs that directly address issues of attitudes, values, and responsible sexual decision making (including decisions to abstain from sexual activity), in contrast to the largely ineffective current models based exclusively on abstinence (Landry, Kaeser, & Richards, 1999). Some experts are cautiously optimistic that a combination of school-based sex education and community-based health clinics could reduce the rate of teenage pregnancy by providing the information about contraception, sex, and pregnancy that sexually active adolescents need (e.g., Frost & Forrest, 1995; Tiezzi, Lipshutz, Wrobleski, Vaughan, & McCarthy, 1997). Even more broadly based programs may be needed, as in one highly effective combination of service learning with classroom discussions about life options (Allen, Philliber, Herrling, & Kuperminc, 1997). Efforts like these integrate sexuality into a framework of healthy interdependence (i.e., focused on the relational aspects of sexuality) and independence (i.e., focused on responsible and self-governed sexual behavior).

Summary Comment

Interdependence implies a cluster of interrelated psychosocial competencies. Thus far, researchers have focused primarily on the separate tasks of attachment, intimacy, and sexuality but have given little attention to the interrelations among them. Isolated findings suggest that, for example, questions about the role of attachment in the development of intimacy (e.g., Cassidy, 2001; Collins & Sroufe, 1999) and the degree to which sexuality is integrated with intimacy and commitment in early adulthood (e.g.,

Bogaert & Sadava, 2002; Zimmer-Gembeck et al., 2001) deserve further attention. These and other questions regarding the extent of such linkages and the processes by which they occur promise to illuminate the nature of adolescent development in relational contexts.

Conclusions

Research on adolescence, which was moribund halfway through the twentieth century, now is a vital and productive area of developmental psychology. As in other vital subfields of psychology, research on adolescence reflects significant theoretical and empirical themes in psychology generally and developmental psychology in particular. One such theme, the importance of contextual as well as traditionally intra-individual forces in human functioning, has become a hallmark of research on adolescence during the past 2 decades (e.g., Grotevant, 1998; Larson & Wilson, 2004; R. Lerner & Steinberg, 2004). Initially focused largely on institutional, economic, and cultural conditions, contemporary interest in context is now realizing the vision of developmental systems theorists (e.g., Bronfenbrenner, 1979; Magnusson & Stättin, 1998; Sameroff, 1983). The emphasis has shifted from external, often distal forces as moderating influences on intrapersonal processes to processes by which intra-individual processes are engaged in dynamic interplay with both proximal (e.g., interpersonal) and distal (e.g., economic systems) environments.

This chapter underscores how this more inclusive view is expanding understanding of the nature and significance of psychological functioning during adolescence. Extensive findings substantiate long-standing speculations that perceptions and expectancies emanating from society and culture, via interactions with salient members of social networks, mediate the psychological and behavioral impact of pubertal changes. Expanded knowledge of brain development and function is clarifying many previously veiled processes that contribute to this interactive nexus of influences. Likewise, the extent and nature of interrelated social processes in diverse interpersonal contexts, from those typifying relationships with parents and siblings to those more typical of expanding networks of peers, is moving the field beyond simplistic notions of the distinctiveness and separateness of family and extrafamilial influences that characterized the writings of adolescent researchers for three quarters of a century (Collins & Laursen, 2004). Full-fledged realizations of developmental systems formulations in research designs and statistical analyses remain a goal for the future, but an appreciation of the extensive interconnections among individual and contextual factors has contributed greatly to the creative thrust in contemporary research with adolescents.

Although the overall level of activity and the gains accrued from studying phenomena of adolescence are impressive, some topics have received less attention and less rigorous investigation than others. Whereas the study of social influences has advanced remarkably, cognitive development and intellectual performance in adolescence have been addressed in relatively few recent studies. Similarly, emotional development and self-regulation, both key elements in the transition from childhood to adulthood, have attracted only tangential attention from adolescence researchers. These topics represent a growing interest in the development of positive competence as a complement to the long-standing emphasis on deficits in competence as factors in maladaptation during and beyond adolescence. Several of the key psychosocial tasks that for decades have served as theoretical and conceptual hallmarks of adolescence, such as the development of the capacity for mature intimacy in close relationships, are the focus of only a minority of the research findings reported each year. Autonomy and identity arguably are exceptions to this generalization, but even when these widely studied aspects of adolescent functioning are brought into research, the purpose is to assess an adolescent's current status rather than to examine the nature and course of development toward mature functioning during adolescence and beyond.

This unevenness in research emphases challenges researchers to complement the vigorous attention to contexts of adolescent development with renewed attention to developmental issues. From questions of how adolescents function differently in relationships with different partners, in varying ethnic or cultural milieu, or in relatively disadvantaged versus relatively more advantaged environments, research should move to questions of how variations in self-regulatory competence or in capacities for seeking gratification for one's partner as well as oneself in sexual relationships emerge from characteristic interpersonal experiences in families, peer networks, school, and community experiences. In addition to greater emphasis on developmental processes, more attention to psychological processes generally would enhance research on adolescence. At present, studies focus heavily on individual and relational correlates of antecedent and contemporaneous aspects of development (e.g., behavior problems in relation to parental styles or peer-group values) or as contributors to later competence (e.g., parent-adolescent interactions as predictors of later interactions with dating partners). Relatively few studies examine the mediating processes that account for these links (for exemplary exceptions, see Brown et al., 1993; Carlson et al., 2004; R. D. Conger et al., 2000; Kim et al., 2001). Greater attention to biopsychosocial processes derived from current theories would move research beyond the descriptive level toward more comprehensive understanding of adolescent functioning. In the next decade, a more comprehensive understanding of the nature and course of achieving maturity promises to come from extending the question of which influences to questions of how and through what processes adolescents develop the capacities for healthy independence and healthy interdependence in a complex world.

References

Abecassis, M., Hartup, W. W., Haselager, G. J. T., Scholte, R. H. J., & van Lieshout, C. F. M. (2002). Mutual antipathies and their significance in middle childhood and adolescence. *Child Development, 75*(5), 1543–1556.

Adams, R., & Laursen, B. (2001). The organization and dynamics of adolescent conflict with parents and friends. *Journal of Marriage and the Family, 63,* 97–110.

Ainsworth, M. S. (1989). Attachments beyond infancy. *American Psychologist, 44*(4), 709–716.

Allen, J. P., & Land, D. (1999). Attachment in adolescence. In J. Cassidy & P. R. Shaver (Eds.), *Handbook of attachment: Theory, research, and clinical applications* (pp. 319–335). New York: Guilford Press.

Allen, J. P., Philliber, S., Herrling, S., & Kuperminc, G. P. (1997). Preventing teen pregnancy and academic failure: Experimental evaluation of a developmentally based approach. *Child Development, 68*(4), 729–742.

Armsden, G., & Greenberg, M. T. (1984). *The inventory of parent and peer attachment: Individual differences and their relationship to psychological well-being in adolescence.* Unpublished manuscript, University of Washington.

Aseltine, R. H., Gore, S., & Colten, M. E. (1994). Depression and the social developmental context of adolescence. *Journal of Personality and Social Psychology, 67*(2), 252–263.

Bank, L., Reid, J., & Greenley, K. (1994, February). *Middle childhood predictors of adolescent and early adult aggression.* Paper presented at the biennial meeting of the Society for Research on Adolescence, San Diego, CA.

Barber, B. (1996). Parental psychological control: Revisiting a neglected construct. *Child Development, 67,* 3296–3319.

Barry, C. M., & Wigfield, A. (2002). Self-perceptions of friendship-making ability and perceptions of friends' deviant behavior: Childhood to adolescence. *Journal of Early Adolescence, 22*(2), 143–172.

Bauman, K. E., & Ennett, S. T. (1996). On the importance of peer influence for adolescent drug use: Commonly neglected considerations. *Addiction, 91*(2), 185–198.

Baumeister, R. F., & Leary, M. R. (1995). The need to belong: Desire for interpersonal attachments as a fundamental human motivation. *Psychological Bulletin, 117*(3), 497–529.

Becker-Stoll, F., & Fremmer-Bombik, E. (1997, April). *Adolescent-mother interaction and attachment: A longitudinal study.* Paper presented at the biennial meeting of the Society for Research in Child Development, Washington, DC.

Benenson, J. F., & Christakos, A. (2003). The greater fragility of females' versus males' closest same-sex friendships. *Child Development, 74*(4), 1123–1129.

Berndt, T. J. (1979). Developmental changes in conformity to peers and parents. *Developmental Psychology, 15,* 608–616.

Berndt, T. J., Hawkins, J. A., & Jiao, Z. (1999). Influences of friends and friendships on adjustment to junior high school. *Merrill-Palmer Quarterly, 45*(1), 13–41.

Billy, J. O. G., Rodgers, J. L., & Udry, J. R. (1984). Adolescent sexual behavior and friendship choice. *Social Forces, 62,* 653–678.

Billy, J. O. G., & Udry, J. R. (1985). The influence of male and female best friends on adolescents' sexual behavior. *Adolescence, 20,* 21–32.

Bingham, C. R., & Crockett, L. J. (1996). Longitudinal adjustment patterns of boys and girls experiencing early, middle, and late sexual intercourse. *Developmental Psychology, 32,* 647–658.

Blos, P. (1979). *The adolescent passage.* New York: International Universities Press.

Blum, R. W., Beuhring, T., Shew, M. L., Bearinger, L. H., Sieving, R. E., & Resnick, M. D. (2000). The effects of race/ethnicity, income, and family structure on adolescent risk behaviors. *American Journal of Public Health, 90*(12), 1879–1884.

Bogaert, A. F., & Sadava, S. (2002). Adult attachment and sexual behavior. *Personal Relationships, 9*(2), 191–204.

Brody, G., Stoneman, Z., & McCoy, J. (1994). Forecasting sibling relationships in early adolescence from child temperaments and family processes in middle childhood. *Child Development, 65,* 771–784.

Bronfenbrenner, U. (1979). *The ecology of human development.* Cambridge, MA: Harvard University Press.

Brooks-Gunn, J., & Paikoff, R. (1997). Sexuality and developmental transitions during adolescence. In J. Schulenberg & J. L. Maggs (Eds.), *Health risks and developmental transitions during adolescence* (pp. 190–219). New York: Cambridge University Press.

Brown, B. (2004). Adolescents' relationships with peers. In R. Lerner & L. Steinberg (Eds.), *Handbook of adolescent psychology* (2nd ed., pp. 363–394). Hoboken, NJ: Wiley.

Brown, B., Clasen, D., & Eicher, S. (1986). Perceptions of peer pressure, peer conformity dispositions, and self-reported behavior among adolescents. *Developmental Psychology, 22,* 521–530.

Brown, B., Mounts, N., Lamborn, S., & Steinberg, L. (1993). Parenting practices and peer group affiliation in adolescence. *Child Development, 64,* 467–482.

Buhrmester, D., & Furman, W. (1987). The development of companionship and intimacy. *Child Development, 58,* 1101–1113.

Buhrmester, D., & Furman, W. (1990). Perceptions of sibling relationships during middle childhood and adolescence. *Child Development, 61,* 1387–1396.

Bulcroft, R., Carmody, D., & Bulcroft, K. (1996). Patterns of parental independence giving to adolescents: Variations by race, age, and gender of child. *Journal of Marriage and the Family, 58,* 866–883.

Bumpus, M. F., Crouter, A. C., & McHale, S. M. (2001). Parental autonomy granting during adolescence: Exploring gender differences in context. *Developmental Psychology, 37*(2), 163–173.

Buzwell, S., & Rosenthal, D. (1996). Constructing a sexual self: Adolescents' sexual self-perceptions and sexual risk-taking. *Journal of Research on Adolescence, 6*(4), 489–513.

Cairns, R. B., & Cairns, B. D. (1994). *Lifelines and risks: Pathways of youth in our time.* New York: Cambridge University Press.

Capaldi, D. M., Crosby, L., & Stoolmiller, M. (1996). Predicting the timing of first sexual intercourse for at-risk adolescent males. *Child Development, 67*(2), 344–359.

Carlson, E. A., Sroufe, L. A., & Egeland, B. (2004). The construction of experience: A longitudinal study of representation and behavior. *Child Development, 75*(1), 66–83.

Carpenter, L. M. (2001). The ambiguity of "having sex": The subjective experience of virginity loss in the United States. *Journal of Sex Research, 38,* 127–139.

Carver, K., Joyner, K., & Udry, J. R. (2003). National estimates of adolescent romantic relationships. In P. Florsheim (Ed.), *Adolescent romantic relations and sexual behavior: Theory, research, and practical implications* (pp. 23–56). Mahwah, NJ: Erlbaum.

Cassidy, J. (2001). Truth, lies, and intimacy: An attachment perspective. *Attachment and Human Development, 3*(2), 121–155.

Cauffman, E., & Steinberg, L. (2000). (Im)maturity of judgment in adolescence: Why adolescents may be less culpable than adults. *Behavioral Sciences and the Law, 18,* 1–21.

Collins, W. A. (1995). Relationships and development: Family adaptation to individual change. In S. Shulman (Ed.), *Close relationships and socioemotional development* (pp. 128–154). New York: Ablex.

Collins, W. A. (2003). More than a myth: The developmental significance of romantic relationships during adolescence. *Journal of Research on Adolescence, 13*(1), 1–24.

Collins, W. A., Gleason, T., & Sesma, A., Jr. (1997). Internalization, autonomy, and relationships: Development during adolescence. In J. E. Grusec & L. Kuczynski (Eds.), *Parenting and children's internalization of values* (pp. 78–102). New York: Wiley.

Collins, W. A., & Laursen, B. (2004). Parent-adolescent relationships and influences. In R. Lerner & L. Steinberg (Eds.), *Handbook of adolescent psychology* (2nd ed., pp. 331–361). Hoboken, NJ: Wiley.

Collins, W. A., Maccoby, E., Steinberg, L., Hetherington, E. M., & Bornstein, M. (2000). Contemporary research on parenting: The case for nature and nurture. *American Psychologist, 55,* 218–232.

Collins, W. A., & Repinski, D. J. (2001). Parents and adolescents as transformers of relationships: Dyadic adaptations to developmental change. In J. R. M. Gerris (Ed.), *Dynamics of parenting: International perspectives on nature and sources of parenting* (pp. 429–443). Leuven, The Netherlands: Garant.

Collins, W. A., & Sroufe, L. A. (1999). Capacity for intimate relationships: A developmental construction. In W. Furman, C. Feiring, & B. B. Brown (Eds.), *Contemporary perspectives on adolescent romantic relationships* (pp. 123–147). New York: Cambridge University Press.

Collins, W. A., & Van Dulmen, M. (2006a). Friendships and romantic relationships in emerging adulthood: Continuities and discontinuities. In J. J. Arnett & J. Tanner (Eds.), *Emerging adults in America: Coming of age in the 21st century* (pp. 219–234). Washington, DC: American Psychological Association.

Collins, W. A., & Van Dulmen, M. (2006b). "The course of true love(s) . . .": Origins and pathways in the development of romantic relationships. In A. Booth & A. Crouter (Eds.), *Romance and sex in adolescence and emerging adulthood: Risks and opportunities* (pp. 63–86). Mahwah, NJ: Erlbaum.

Conger, K., Conger, R. D., & Elder, G., Jr. (1997). Parents, siblings, psychological control, and adolescent adjustment. *Journal of Adolescent Research, 12,* 113–138.

Conger, R. D., Cui, M., Bryant, C. M., & Elder, G. H., Jr. (2000). Competence in early adult romantic relationships: A developmental perspective on family influences. *Journal of Personality and Social Psychology, 79,* 224–237.

Connolly, J. A., Craig, W., Goldberg, A., & Pepler, D. (1999). Conceptions of cross-sex friendships and romantic relationships in early adolescence. *Journal of Youth and Adolescence, 28,* 481–494.

Connolly, J. A., Craig, W., Goldberg, A., & Pepler, D. (2004). Mixed-gender groups, dating, and romantic relationships in early adolescence. *Journal of Research on Adolescence, 14,* 185–207.

Connolly, J. A., Furman, W., & Konarski, R. (2000). The role of peers in the emergence of heterosexual romantic relationships in adolescence. *Child Development, 71*(5), 1395–1408.

Connolly, J. A., & Goldberg, A. (1999). Romantic relationships in adolescence: The role of friends and peers in their emergence and development. In W. Furman, B. B. Brown, & C. Feiring (Eds.), *The development of romantic relationships in adolescence* (pp. 266–290). New York: Cambridge University Press.

Connolly, J. A., & Johnson, A. (1996). Adolescents' romantic relationships and the structure and quality of their close interpersonal ties. *Personal Relationships, 3,* 185–195.

Connolly, J. A., & Konarski, R. (1994). Peer self-concept in adolescence: Analysis of factor structure and of associations with peer experience. *Journal of Research on Adolescence, 4*(3), 385–403.

Cooper, C. R. (1994). Cultural perspectives on continuity and change in adolescents' relationships. In R. Montemayor, G. R. Adams, & T. P. Gullotta (Eds.), *Personal relationships during adolescence* (pp. 78–100). Thousand Oaks, CA: Sage.

Crockett, L. J., Bingham, C., Chopak, J., & Vicary, J. (1996). Timing of first sexual intercourse: The role of social control, social learning and problem behavior. *Journal of Youth and Adolescence, 25,* 89–111.

Crockett, L. J., Raffaelli, M., & Moilanen, K. L. (2003). Adolescent sexuality: Behavior and meaning. In G. R. Adams & M. D. Berzonsky (Eds.), *Blackwell handbook of adolescence* (pp. 371–392). Malden, MA: Blackwell.

Crouter, A. C., & Head, M. R. (2002). Parental monitoring and knowledge of children. In M. Bornstein (Ed.), *Handbook on parenting* (2nd ed., pp. 461–484). Mahwah, NJ: Erlbaum.

Crowell, J. A., Fraley, R. C., & Shaver, P. R. (1999). Measurement of individual differences in adolescent and adult attachment. In J. Cassidy & P. R. Shaver (Eds.), *Handbook of attachment: Theory, research, and clinical applications* (pp. 434–465). New York: Guilford Press.

Crowell, J. A., & Owens, G. (1996). *Current relationship interview and scoring system* (Version 2). Unpublished manuscript, State University of New York at Stony Brook.

Cyranowski, J., Frank, E., Young, E., & Shear, K. (2000). Adolescent onset of the gender difference in lifetime rates of major depression. *Archives of General Psychiatry, 57,* 21–27.

Darling, N., Dowdy, B. B., Van Horn, M. L., & Caldwell, L. L. (1999). Mixed-sex settings and the perception of competence. *Journal of Youth and Adolescence, 28*(4), 461–480.

Darling, N., & Steinberg, L. (1993). Parenting style as context: An integrative model. *Psychological Bulletin, 113,* 487–496.

Davies, P. T., & Windle, M. (2000). Middle adolescents' dating pathways and psychosocial adjustment. *Merrill-Palmer Quarterly, 46*(1), 90–118.

Diamond, L. M. (2000). Passionate friendships among adolescent sexual-minority women. *Journal of Research on Adolescence, 10,* 191–209.

Diamond, L. M., & Savin-Williams, R. C. (2003). Explaining diversity in the development of same-sex sexuality among young women. In L. D. Garnets & D. C. Kimmel (Eds.), *Psychological perspectives on lesbian, gay, and bisexual experiences* (2nd ed., pp. 130–148). New York: Columbia University Press.

Dishion, T. J. (2000). Cross-setting consistency in early adolescent psychopathology: Deviant friendships and problem behavior sequelae. *Journal of Personality, 68,* 1109–1126.

Dornbusch, S., Carlsmith, J., Gross, R., Martin, J., Jennings, D., Rosenberg, A., et al. (1981). Sexual development, age, and dating: A comparison of biological and social influences upon one set of behaviors. *Child Development, 52,* 179–185.

Dornbusch, S., Ritter, P., Liederman, P., Roberts, D., & Fraleigh, M. (1987). The relation of parenting style to adolescent school performance. *Child Development, 58,* 1244–1257.

Douvan, E., & Adelson, J. (1966). *The adolescent experience.* New York: Wiley.

Dyk, P. H., & Adams, G. R. (1990). Identity and intimacy: An initial investigation of three theoretical models using cross-lag panel correlations. *Journal of Youth and Adolescence, 19*(2), 91–110.

East, P. L., Felice, M. E., & Morgan, M. C. (1993). Sisters' and girlfriends' sexual and childbearing behavior: Effects on early adolescent girls' sexual outcomes. *Journal of Marriage and the Family, 55*(4), 953–963.

East, P. L., & Jacobson, L. J. (2001). The younger siblings of teenage mothers: A follow-up of their pregnancy risk. *Developmental Psychology, 37*(2), 254–264.

East, P. L., & Rook, K. (1992). Compensatory patterns of support among children's peer relationships: A test using school friends, nonschool friends, and siblings. *Developmental Psychology, 28,* 163–172.

Eder, D. (1985). The cycle of popularity: Interpersonal relations among female adolescence. *Sociology of Education, 58,* 154–165.

Eisenberg, N., & Morris, A. (2004). Moral cognitions and prosocial responding in adolescence. In R. Lerner & L. Steinberg (Eds.), *Handbook of adolescent psychology* (2nd ed., pp. 155–188). Hoboken, NJ: Wiley.

Elkind, D. (1967). Egocentrism in adolescence. *Child Development, 38,* 1025–1034.

Erickson, K., Crosnoe, R., & Dornbusch, S. M. (2000). A social process model of adolescent deviance: Combining social control and differential association perspectives. *Journal of Youth and Adolescence, 29*(4), 395–425.

Erikson, E. (1968). *Identity: Youth and crisis.* New York: Norton.

Eyre, S. L., Auerswald, C., Hoffman, V., & Millstein, S. G. (1998). Fidelity management: African-American adolescents' attempts to control the sexual behavior of their partners. *Journal of Health Psychology, 3*(3), 393–406.

Feiring, C. (1999). Gender identity and the development of romantic relationships in adolescence. In W. Furman, B. B. Brown, & C. Feiring (Eds.), *The development of romantic relationships in adolescence* (pp. 175–210). New York: Cambridge University Press.

Feldman, S. S., & Brown, N. L. (1993). Family influences on adolescent male sexuality: The mediational role of self-restraint. *Social Development, 2*(1), 15–35.

Feldman, S. S., & Gowen, L. K. (1998). Conflict negotiation tactics in romantic relationships in high school students. *Journal of Youth and Adolescence, 27*(6), 691–717.

Feldman, S. S., Gowen, L. K., & Fisher, L. (1998). Family relationships and gender as predictors of romantic intimacy in young adults: A longitudinal study. *Journal of Research on Adolescence, 8*(2), 263–286.

Feldman, S. S., & Quatman, T. (1988). Factors influencing age expectations for adolescent autonomy: A study of early adolescents and parents. *Journal of Early Adolescence, 8,* 325–343.

Feldman, S. S., Turner, R., & Araujo, K. (1999). Interpersonal context as an influence on sexual timetables of youths: Gender and ethnic effects. *Journal of Research on Adolescence, 9,* 25–52.

Feldman, S. S., & Wood, D. (1994). Parents' expectations for preadolescent sons' behavioral autonomy: A longitudinal study of correlates and outcomes. *Journal of Research on Adolescence, 4,* 45–70.

Fine, M. (1988). Sexuality, schooling, and adolescent females: The missing discourse of desire. *Harvard Educational Review, 58*(1), 29–53.

Fitch, S., & Adams, G. (1983). Ego identity and intimacy statuses: Replication and extension. *Developmental Psychology, 19,* 839–845.

Fletcher, A. C., Steinberg, L., & Williams-Wheeler, M. (2004). Parental influences on adolescent problem behavior: A response to Stattin and Kerr. *Child Development, 75,* 781–796.

Flouri, E., & Buchanan, A. (2002). What predicts good relationships with parents in adolescence and partners in adult life: Findings from the 1958 British birth cohort. *Journal of Family Psychology, 16,* 186–198.

Fraley, R. C., & Davis, K. E. (1997). Attachment formation and transfer in young adults' close friendships and romantic relationships. *Personal Relationships, 4*(2), 131–144.

Freud, A. (1958). Adolescence. In R. Eissler, A. Freud, H. Hartman, & M. Kris (Eds.), *Psychoanalytic study of the child* (Vol. 13, pp. 255–278). New York: International Universities Press.

Frost, J., & Forrest, J. (1995). Understanding the impact of effective teenage pregnancy prevention programs. *Family Planning Perspectives, 27,* 188–195.

Fuligni, A. (1998). Authority, autonomy, and parent-adolescent conflict and cohesion: A study of adolescents from Mexican, Chinese, Filipino, and European backgrounds. *Developmental Psychology, 34,* 782–792.

Fuligni, A., Tseng, V., & Lam, M. (1999). Attitudes toward family obligations among American adolescents from Asian, Latin American, and European backgrounds. *Child Development, 70,* 1030–1044.

Furman, W. (1999). Friends and lovers: The role of peer relationships in adolescent romantic relationships. In W. A. Collins & B. Laursen (Eds.), *Minnesota Symposia on Child Psychology: Vol. 30. Relationships as developmental contexts* (pp. 133–154). Hillsdale, NJ: Erlbaum.

Furman, W., & Bierman, K. L. (1984). Children's conceptions of friendship: A multimethod study of developmental changes. *Developmental Psychology, 20*(5), 925–931.

Furman, W., Brown, B., & Feiring, C. (Eds.). (1999). *Contemporary perspectives on adolescent romantic relationships.* New York: Cambridge University Press.

Furman, W., & Buhrmester, D. (1985). Children's perceptions of the personal relationships in their social networks. *Developmental Psychology, 21,* 1016–1024.

Furman, W., & Buhrmester, D. (1992). Age and sex differences in perceptions of networks of personal relationships. *Child Development, 63,* 103–115.

Furman, W., & Shaffer, L. (2003). The role of romantic relationships in adolescent development. In P. Florsheim (Ed.), *Adolescent romantic relations and sexual behavior: Theory, research, and practical implications* (pp. 3–22). Mahwah, NJ: Erlbaum.

Furman, W., Simon, V. A., Shaffer, L., & Bouchey, H. A. (2002). Adolescents' working models and styles for relationships with parents, friends, and romantic partners. *Child Development, 73*(1), 241–255.

Furman, W., & Wehner, E. A. (1994). Romantic views: Toward a theory of adolescent romantic relationships. In R. Montemayor, G. R. Adams, & T. Gullotta (Eds.), *Personal relationships during adolescence* (pp. 168–195). Thousand Oaks, CA: Sage.

Galambos, N., Kolaric, G., Sears, H., & Maggs, J. (1999). Adolescents' subjective age: An indicator of perceived maturity. *Journal of Research on Adolescence, 9,* 309–337.

Giordano, P. C. (2003). Relationships in adolescence. *Annual Review of Sociology, 29,* 257–281.

Goodnow, J. J. (2002). Adding culture to studies of development: Toward changes in procedure and theory. *Human Development, 45*(4), 237–245.

Graber, J. A., Brooks-Gunn, J., & Galen, B. R. (1999). Betwixt and between: Sexuality in the context of adolescent transitions. In R. Jessor (Ed.), *New perspectives on adolescent risk behavior* (pp. 270–316). New York: Cambridge University Press.

Greenberger, E., & Sorenson, A. (1974). Toward a concept of psychosocial maturity. *Journal of Youth and Adolescence, 3,* 329–358.

Grotevant, H. D. (1998). Adolescent development in family contexts. In W. Damon (Series Ed.) & N. Eisenberg (Vol. Ed.), *Handbook of child psychology: Vol. 3. Social, emotional, and personality development* (5th ed., pp. 1097–1149). New York: Wiley.

Grotevant, H. D., & Cooper, C. R. (1986). Individuation in family relationships: A perspective on individual differences in the development of identity and role-taking skill in adolescence. *Human Development, 29,* 82–100.

Hall, G. S. (1904). *Adolescence: Its psychology and its relations to physiology, anthropology, sociology, sex, crime, religion, and education* (Vols. 1–2). Englewood Cliffs, NJ: Prentice-Hall.

Halpern, C. T., Udry, J. R., Campbell, B., & Suchindran, C. (1993). Relationships between aggression and pubertal increases in testosterone: A panel analysis of adolescent males. *Social Biology, 40*(1/2), 8–24.

Hamm, J. V. (2000). Do birds of a feather flock together? The variable bases for African American, Asian American, and European American adolescents' selection of similar friends. *Developmental Psychology, 36*(2), 209–219.

Hardy, C. L., Bukowski, W. M., & Sippola, L. K. (2002). Stability and change in peer relationships during the transition to middle-level school. *Journal of Early Adolescence, 22,* 117–142.

Hartup, W. W. (1996). The company they keep: Friendships and their developmental significance. *Child Development, 67*(1), 1–13.

Hartup, W. W., & Abecassis, M. (2002). Friends and enemies. In P. K. Smith & C. H. Hart (Eds.), *Blackwell handbook of childhood and social development* (pp. 286–306). Malden, MA: Blackwell.

Hazan, C., & Zeifman, D. (1994). Sex and the psychological tether. In K. Bartholomew & D. Perlman (Eds.), *Attachment processes in adulthood* (pp. 151–178). London: Jessica Kingsley.

Helsen, M., Vollebergh, W., & Meeus, W. (2000). Social support from parents and friends and emotional problems in adolescence. *Journal of Youth and Adolescence, 29*(3), 319–335.

Herdt, G., & McClintock, M. (2000). The magical age of 10. *Archives of Sexual Behavior, 29*(6), 587–606.

Hetherington, E. M., Henderson, S., & Reiss, D. (1999). Adolescent siblings in stepfamilies: Family functioning and adolescent adjustment. *Monographs of the Society for Research in Child Development, 64*(Serial No. 259).

Hill, J. P., & Holmbeck, G. (1986). Attachment and autonomy during adolescence. In G. Whitehurst (Ed.), *Annals of child development* (Vol. 3, pp. 145–189). Greenwich, CT: JAI Press.

Ho, M. J. (2004, April). Adolescent attachment to parents: Predicting later rejection sensitivity. In D. Welsh (Chair), *The development of adolescent romantic relationships: The role of attachment.* Symposium conducted at the conference of the Society for Research on Adolescence, Baltimore.

Jessor, R., Costa, F., Jessor, L., & Donovan, J. E. (1983). Time of first intercourse: A prospective study. *Journal of Personality and Social Psychology, 44,* 608–620.

Joyner, K., & Udry, J. R. (2000). "You don't bring me anything but down": Adolescent romance and depression. *Journal of Health and Social Behavior, 41,* 369–391.

Juang, L., Lerner, J., McKinney, J., & von Eye, A. (1999). The goodness of fit in autonomy timetable expectations between Asian-Americans late adolescents and their parents. *International Journal of Behavioral Development, 23,* 1023–1048.

Katchadourian, H. (1990). Sexuality. In S. S. Feldman & G. R. Elliott (Eds.), *At the threshold: The developing adolescent* (pp. 330–351). Cambridge, MA: Harvard University Press.

Kim, K., Conger, R. D., Lorenz, F. O., & Elder, G. H., Jr. (2001). Parent-adolescent reciprocity in negative affect and its relation to early adult social development. *Developmental Psychology, 37*(6), 775–790.

Kinney, D. A. (1993). From nerds to normals: The recovery of identity among adolescents from middle school to high school. *Sociology of Education, 66,* 21–40.

Kobak, R. R., Cole, H. E., Ferenz-Gillies, R., Fleming, W. S., & Gamble, W. (1993). Attachment and emotion regulation during mother-teen problem solving: A control theory analysis. *Child Development, 64*(1), 231–245.

Kobak, R. R., & Sceery, A. (1988). Attachment in late adolescence: Working models, affect regulation, and representations of self and others. *Child Development, 59*(1), 135–146.

Krosnick, J., & Judd, C. (1982). Transitions in social influence at adolescence: Who induces cigarette smoking? *Developmental Psychology, 18,* 359–368.

Kuttler, A., La Greca, A. M., & Prinstein, M. J. (1999). Friendship qualities and social-emotional functioning of adolescents with close, cross-sex friendships. *Journal of Research on Adolescence, 9*(3), 339–366.

Lamborn, S., Dornbusch, S., & Steinberg, L. (1996). Ethnicity and community context as moderators of the relation between family decision-making and adolescent adjustment. *Child Development, 66,* 283–301.

Lamborn, S., Mounts, N., Steinberg, L., & Dornbusch, S. (1991). Patterns of competence and adjustment among adolescents from authoritative, authoritarian, indulgent, and neglectful families. *Child Development, 62,* 1049–1065.

Landry, D., Kaeser, L., & Richards, C. (1999). Abstinence promotion and the provision of information about contraception in public school district sexuality education policies. *Family Planning Perspectives, 31,* 280–286.

Larkin, R. W. (1979). *Suburban youth in cultural crisis.* New York: Oxford University Press.

Larson, R. W., Clore, G. L., & Wood, G. A. (1999). The emotions of romantic relationships. In W. Furman, B. B. Brown, & C. Feiring (Eds.), *Contemporary perspectives on romantic relationships* (pp. 19–49). New York: Cambridge University Press.

Larson, R. W., & Richards, M. (1991). Daily companionship in late childhood and early adolescence: Changing developmental contexts. *Child Development, 62,* 284–300.

Larson, R. W., & Richards, M. (1994). *Divergent realities: The emotional lives of mothers, fathers, and adolescents.* New York: Basic Books.

Larson, R. W., Richards, M. H., Moneta, G., Holmbeck, G., & Duckett, E. (1996). Changes in adolescents' daily interactions with their families from 10 to 18: Disengagement and transformation. *Developmental Psychology, 32,* 744–754.

Larson, R. W., & Verma, S. (1999). How children and adolescents spend time across the world: Work, play, and developmental opportunities. *Psychological Bulletin, 125,* 701–736.

Larson, R. W., & Wilson, S. (2004). Adolescence across place and time: Globalization and the changing pathways to adulthood. In R. Lerner & L. Steinberg (Eds.), *Handbook of adolescent psychology* (2nd ed., pp. 299–330). Hoboken, NJ: Wiley.

Laursen, B. (1995). Conflict and social interaction in adolescent relationships. *Journal of Research on Adolescence, 5*(1), 55–70.

Laursen, B., & Bukowski, W. M. (1997). A developmental guide to the organization of close relationships. *International Journal of Behavioral Development, 21*(4), 747–770.

Laursen, B., & Collins, W. (1994). Interpersonal conflict during adolescence. *Psychological Bulletin, 115,* 197–209.

Laursen, B., Coy, K., & Collins, W. A. (1998). Reconsidering changes in parent-child conflict across adolescence: A meta-analysis. *Child Development, 69,* 817–832.

Laursen, B., Finkelstein, B. D., & Betts, N. (2001). A developmental meta-analysis of peer conflict resolution. *Developmental Review, 21*(4), 423–449.

Laursen, B., & Hartup, W. W. (2002). The origins of reciprocity and social exchange in friendships. In W. G. Graziano & B. Laursen (Eds.), *New directions for child and adolescent development: Vol. 95. Social exchange in development* (pp. 27–40). San Francisco: Jossey-Bass.

Laursen, B., & Jensen-Campbell, L. A. (1999). The nature and functions of social exchange in adolescent romantic relationships. In W. Furman, B. B. Brown, & C. Feiring (Eds.), *The development of romantic relationships in adolescence* (pp. 50–74). New York: Cambridge University Press.

Laursen, B., & Williams, V. (1997). Perceptions of interdependence and closeness in family and peer relationships among adolescents with and without romantic partners. In S. Shulman & W. A. Collins (Eds.), *Romantic relationships in adolescence* (pp. 3–20). San Francisco: Jossey-Bass.

Lerner, J., Castellino, D., & Perkins, D. (1994, February). *The influence of adolescent behavioral and psychosocial characteristics on maternal behaviors and satisfaction.* Paper presented at the biennial meeting of the Society for Research on Adolescence, San Diego, CA.

Lerner, R., & Steinberg, L. (2004). The scientific study of adolescence: Past, present, and future. In R. Lerner & L. Steinberg (Eds.), *Handbook of adolescent psychology* (2nd ed., pp. 1–12). Hoboken, NJ: Wiley.

Levesque, R. J. R. (1993). The romantic experience of adolescents in satisfying love relationships. *Journal of Youth and Adolescence, 22,* 219–251.

Lewis, C. (1981). The effects of parental firm control. *Psychological Bulletin, 90,* 547–563.

Lewis, M., Feiring, C., & Rosenthal, S. (2000). Attachment over time. *Child Development, 71*(3), 707–720.

Linder, J. R., & Collins, W. A. (2005). Parent and peer predictors of physical aggression and conflict management in romantic relationships in early adulthood. *Journal of Family Psychology, 19,* 252–262.

Long, B. H. (1989). Heterosexual involvement of unmarried undergraduate females in relation to self-evaluations. *Journal of Youth and Adolescence, 18,* 489–500.

Maccoby, E. E. (1990). Gender and relationships. *American Psychologist, 45,* 513–520.

Maccoby, E. E. (1998). *The two sexes: Growing up apart, coming together.* Cambridge, MA: Harvard University Press.

Maccoby, E. E., & Martin, J. (1983). Socialization in the context of the family: Parent-child interaction. In P. H. Munsen (Series Ed.) & E. M. Hetherington (Vol. Ed.), *Handbook of child psychology: Vol. 4. Socialization, personality, and social development* (4th ed., pp. 1–101). New York: Wiley.

MacKinnon-Lewis, C., Starnes, R., Volling, B., & Johnson, S. (1997). Perceptions of parenting as predictors of boys' sibling and peer relations. *Developmental Psychology, 33,* 1024–1031.

Magnusson, D., & Stättin, H. (1998). Person-context interaction theories. In W. Damon (Series Ed.) & R. M. Lerner (Vol. Ed.), *Handbook of child psychology: Vol. 1. Theoretical models of human development* (5th ed., pp. 685–760). New York: Wiley.

Main, M., Kaplan, N., & Cassidy, J. (1985). Security in infancy, childhood, and adulthood: A move to the level of representation. *Monographs of the Society for Research in Child Development, 50*(1/2, Serial No. 209), 66–104.

Marcia, J. (1980). Ego identity development. In J. Adelson (Ed.), *Handbook of adolescent psychology* (pp. 159–187). New York: Wiley.

Markovits, H., Benenson, J., & Dolenszky, E. (2001). Evidence that children and adolescents have internal models of peer interactions that are gender differentiated. *Child Development, 72*(3), 879–886.

Masten, A. S., Coatsworth, J. D., Neeman, J., Gest, S. D., Tellegen, A., & Garmezy, N. (1995). The structure and coherence of competence from childhood through adolescence. *Child Development, 66*(6), 1635–1659.

McCoy, J., Brody, G., & Stoneman, Z. (1994). A longitudinal analysis of sibling relationships as mediators of the link between family processes and youths' best friendships. *Family Relations: Journal of Applied Family and Child Studies, 43*(4), 400–408.

McElhaney, K. B., & Allen, J. P. (2001). Autonomy and adolescent social functioning: The moderating effect of risk. *Child Development, 72,* 220–231.

McNelles, L. R., & Connolly, J. A. (1999). Intimacy between adolescent friends: Age and gender differences in intimate affect and intimate behaviors. *Journal of Research on Adolescence, 9*(2), 143–159.

Meschke, L. L., & Silbereisen, R. K. (1997). The influence of puberty, family processes, and leisure activities on the timing of first experience. *Journal of Adolescence, 20*(4), 403–418.

Milardo, R. M. (1982). Friendship networks in developing relationships: Converging and diverging social environments. *Social Psychology Quarterly, 45,* 162–172.

Miller, B., Benson, B., & Galbraith, K. A. (2001). Family relationships and adolescent pregnancy risk: A research synthesis. *Developmental Review, 21,* 1–38.

Miller, B., Norton, M., Fan, X., & Christopherson, C. (1998). Pubertal development, parental communication, and sexual values in relation to adolescent sexual behaviors. *Journal of Early Adolescence, 18,* 27–52.

Miller, K. E., Sabo, D. F., Farrell, M. P., Barnes, G. M., & Melnick, M. J. (1998). Athletic participation and sexual behavior in adolescents: The different worlds of boys and girls. *Journal of Health and Social Behavior, 39*(2), 108–123.

Monroe, S. M., Rohde, P., Seeley, J. R., & Lewinsohn, P. M. (1999). Life events and depression in adolescence: Relationship loss as a prospective risk factor for first onset of major depressive disorder. *Journal of Abnormal Psychology, 108*(4), 606–614.

Moore, S., & Rosenthal, D. (1993). *Sexuality in adolescence.* New York: Routledge.

Mulvey, E. P., & Aber, M. S. (1988). Growing out of delinquency: Development and desistance. In R. Jerkins & W. Brown (Eds.), *The abandonment of delinquent behavior: Promoting the turn-around* (pp. 99–116). New York: Praeger.

Nelson, C., Bloom, F., Cameron, J., Amaral, D., Dahl, R., & Pine, D. (2002). An integrative, multidisciplinary approach to the study of brain-behavior relations in the context of typical and atypical development. *Development and Psychopathology, 14,* 499–520.

Newcomb, A. F., & Bagwell, C. L. (1995). Children's friendship relations: A meta-analytic review. *Psychological Bulletin, 117*(2), 306–347.

Nurmi, J.-E. (2004). Socialization and self-development: Channeling, selection, adjustment, and reflection. In R. Lerner & L. Steinberg (Eds.), *Handbook of adolescent psychology* (2nd ed., pp. 85–124). Hoboken, NJ: Wiley.

Ohannessian, C. M., & Crockett, L. J. (1993). A longitudinal investigation of the relationship between educational investment and adolescent sexual activity. *Journal of Adolescent Research, 8*(2), 167–182.

Orlofsky, J., Marcia, J., & Lesser, I. (1973). Ego identity status and the intimacy versus isolation crisis of young adulthood. *Journal of Personality and Social Psychology, 27,* 73–88.

Owens, G., Crowell, J., Treboux, D., O'Connor, E., & Pan, H. (1995). The prototype hypothesis and the origins of attachment working models: Adult relationships with parents and romantic partners. *Monographs of the Society for Research in Child Development, 60*(2/3, Serial No. 244), 216–233.

Patterson, G. R., DeBaryshe, B. D., & Ramsey, E. (1989). A developmental perspective on antisocial behavior. *American Psychologist, 44,* 329–335.

Patterson, G. R., & Stouthamer-Loeber, M. (1984). The correlation of family management practices and delinquency. *Child Development, 55,* 1299–1307.

Perosa, L., Perosa, S., & Tam, H. (1996). The contribution of family structure and differentiation to identity development in females. *Journal of Youth and Adolescence, 25,* 817–837.

Pomerantz, E. (2001). Parent child socialization: Implications for the development of depressive symptoms. *Journal of Family Psychology, 15*(3), 510–525.

Prager, K. J. (2000). Intimacy in personal relationships. In C. Hendrick & S. S. Hendrick (Eds.), *Close relationships: A sourcebook* (pp. 229–242). Thousand Oaks, CA: Sage.

Rawlings, D., Boldero, J., & Wiseman, F. (1995). The interaction of age with impulsiveness and venturesomeness in the prediction of adolescent sexual behavior. *Personality and Individual Differences, 19*(1), 117–120.

Reis, H. T., Lin, Y., Bennett, M. E., & Nezlek, J. B. (1993). Change and consistency in social participation during early adulthood. *Developmental Psychopathology, 29,* 633–645.

Reis, H. T., & Patrick, B. C. (1996). Attachment and intimacy: Component processes. In E. T. Higgins & A. Kruglanski (Eds.), *Social psychology: Handbook of basic principles* (pp. 367–389). New York: Guilford Press.

Reis, H. T., & Shaver, P. (1988). Intimacy as an interpersonal process. In S. Duck (Ed.), *Handbook of personal relationships: Theory, research, and interventions* (pp. 367–389). Chichester, West Sussex, England: Wiley.

Rest, J. (1983). Morality. In P. H. Mussen (Series Ed.) & J. Flavell & E. Markman (Vol. Eds.), *Handbook of child psychology: Vol. 3. Cognitive development* (4th ed., pp. 556–629). New York: Wiley.

Rose, A. (2002). Co-rumination in friendships of girls and boys. *Child Development, 73,* 1830–1843.

Rosenthal, D., & Feldman, S. (1990). The acculturation of Chinese immigrants: The effects on family functioning of length of residence in two cultural contexts. *Journal of Genetic Psychology, 151,* 493–514.

Rostosky, S. S., Wilcox, B. L., Comer Wright, M. L., & Randall, B. A. (2004). The impact of religiosity on adolescent sexual behavior: A review of the evidence. *Journal of Adolescent Research, 19,* 677–697.

Rothbaum, F., Pott, M., Azuma, H., Miyake, K., & Weisz, J. (2000). The development of close relationships in Japan and the United States: Paths of symbiotic harmony and generative tension. *Child Development, 71,* 1121–1142.

Rowe, D. C., Rodgers, J. L., Meseck-Bushey, S., & St. John, C. (1989). Sexual behavior and nonsexual deviance: A sibling study of their relationship. *Developmental Psychopathology, 25*(1), 61–69.

Ruck, M., Peterson-Badali, M., & Day, D. M. (2002). Adolescents' and mothers' understanding of children's rights in the home. *Journal of Research on Adolescence, 12*(3), 373–398.

Rueter, M., & Conger, R. D. (1998). Reciprocal influences between parenting and adolescent problem-solving behavior. *Developmental Psychology, 34,* 1470–1482.

Ryan, R., & Lynch, J. (1989). Emotional autonomy versus detachment: Revisiting the vicissitudes of adolescence and young adulthood. *Child Development, 60,* 340–356.

Sameroff, A. J. (1983). Developmental systems: Contexts and evolution. In P. H. Mussen (Series Ed.) & W. Kessen (Vol. Ed.), *Handbook of child psychology: Vol. 1. History, theory, and methods* (4th ed., pp. 237–294). New York: Wiley.

Savin-Williams, R. C. (1996). Dating and romantic relationships among gay, lesbian, and bisexual youths. In R. C. Savin-Williams & K. M. Cohen (Eds.), *The lives of lesbians, gays, and bisexuals: Children to adults* (pp. 166–180). Fort Worth, TX: Harcourt Brace Jovanovich.

Savin-Williams, R. C., & Berndt, T. J. (1990). Friendship and peer relations. In S. S. Feldman & G. R. Elliott (Eds.), *At the threshold: The developing adolescent* (pp. 277–307). Cambridge, MA: Harvard University Press.

Savin-Williams, R. C., & Diamond, L. (2004). Sex. In R. Lerner & L. Steinberg (Eds.), *Handbook of adolescent psychology* (2nd ed., pp. 189–231). Hoboken, NJ: Wiley.

Scholte, R. H. J., van Lieshout, C. F. M., & van Aken, M. A. G. (2001). Perceived relationship support in adolescence: Dimensions, configurations, and adolescent adjustment. *Journal of Research on Adolescence, 11*(1), 71–94.

Seiffge-Krenke, I., & Lang, J. (2002, April). Forming and maintaining romantic relations from early adolescence to young adulthood: Evidence of a developmental sequence. In S. Shulman & I. Seiffge-Krenke (Co-chairs), *Antecedents of the quality and stability of adolescent romantic relationships.* Symposium conducted at the biennial meeting of the Society for Research on Adolescence, New Orleans, LA.

Selman, R. (1980). *The growth of interpersonal understanding.* New York: Academic Press.

Sharabany, R., Gershoni, R., & Hofmann, J. (1981). Girlfriend, boyfriend: Age and sex differences in intimate friendship. *Developmental Psychology, 17,* 800–808.

Shulman, S., & Laursen, B. (2002). Adolescent perceptions of conflict in interdependent and disengaged friendships. *Journal of Research on Adolescence, 12*(3), 353–372.

Simon, W., & Gagnon, J. (1969). On psychosexual development. In D. Goslin (Ed.), *Handbook of socialization theory and research* (pp. 733–752). Chicago: Rand McNally.

Sippola, L. K. (1999). Getting to know the "other": The characteristics and developmental significance of other-sex relationships in adolescence. *Journal of Youth and Adolescence, 28,* 407–418.

Slomkowski, C., Rende, R., Conger, K. J., Simons, R. L., & Conger, R. D. (2001). Sisters, brothers, and delinquency: Social influence during early and middle adolescence. *Child Development, 72,* 271–283.

Smetana, J. (1995). Parenting styles and conceptions of parental authority during adolescence. *Child Development, 66,* 299–316.

Smetana, J., & Daddis, C. (2002). Domain-specific antecedents of parental psychological control and monitoring: The role of parenting beliefs and practices. *Child Development, 73*(2), 563–580.

Smith, E., & Udry, J. R. (1985). Coital and noncoital sexual behaviors of White and Black adolescents. *American Journal of Public Health, 75,* 1200–1203.

Smith, T. W. (1994). Attitudes towards sexual permissiveness: Trends, correlates, and behavioral connections. In A. S. Rossi (Ed.), *Sexuality across the life course* (pp. 63–97). Chicago: University of Chicago Press.

Smollar, J., & Youniss, J. (1985, April). *Transformation in adolescents' perceptions of parents.* Paper presented at the biennial meeting of the Society for Research in Child Development, Baltimore.

Sroufe, L. A., Egeland, B., & Carlson, E. A. (1999). One social world: The integrated development of parent-child and peer relationships. In W. A. Collins & B. Laursen (Eds.), *Minnesota Symposia on Child Psychology: Vol. 30. Relationships as developmental context* (pp. 241–262). Hillsdale, NJ: Erlbaum.

Sroufe, L. A., Egeland, B., Carlson, E., & Collins, W. A. (2005). *The development of the person.* New York: Guilford Press.

Sroufe, L. A., & Fleeson, J. (1988). The coherence of family relationships. In R. A. Hinde & J. Stevenson-Hinde (Eds.), *Relationships within families: Mutual influences* (pp. 27–47). Oxford: Oxford University Press.

Stättin, H., & Kerr, M. (2000). Parental monitoring: A reinterpretation. *Child Development, 71*(4), 1072–1085.

Steinberg, L. (1990). Autonomy, conflict, and harmony in the family relationship. In S. S. Feldman & G. R. Elliott (Eds.), *At the threshold: The developing adolescent* (pp. 255–276). Cambridge, MA: Harvard University Press.

Steinberg, L. (2001). We know some things: Adolescent-parent relationships in retrospect and prospect. *Journal of Research on Adolescence, 11,* 1–19.

Steinberg, L., Dahl, R., Keating, D., Kupfer, D., Masten, A., & Pine, D. (2006). The study of developmental psychopathology in adolescence: Integrating affective neuroscience with the study of context. In D. Cicchetti & D. J. Cohen (Eds.), *Developmental psychopathology: Vol. 2. Developmental neuroscience* (2nd ed., pp. 710–741). Hoboken, NJ: Wiley.

Steinberg, L., Dornbusch, S., & Brown, B. (1992). Ethnic differences in adolescent achievement: An ecological perspective. *American Psychologist, 47,* 723–729.

Steinberg, L., Lamborn, S., Darling, N., Mounts, N., & Dornbusch, S. (1994). Over-time changes in adjustment and competence among adolescents from authoritative, authoritarian, indulgent, and neglectful families. *Child Development, 65,* 754–770.

Steinberg, L., Lamborn, S., Dornbusch, S., & Darling, N. (1992). Impact of parenting practices on adolescent achievement: Authoritative parenting, school involvement, and encouragement to succeed. *Child Development, 63,* 1266–1281.

Steinberg, L., & Scott, E. S. (2003). Less guilty by reason of adolescence: Developmental immaturity, diminished responsibility, and the juvenile death penalty. *American Psychologist, 58*(12), 1009–1018.

Steinberg, L., & Silk, J. (2002). Parenting adolescents. In M. Bornstein (Ed.), *Handbook of parenting: Vol. 1. Children and parenting* (2nd ed., pp. 103–133). Mahwah, NJ: Erlbaum.

Steinberg, L., & Silverberg, S. (1986). The vicissitudes of autonomy in early adolescence. *Child Development, 57,* 841–851.

Stevenson, H. W., Lee, S., Chen, C., Stigler, J. W., Hsu, C.-C., Kitamura, S., et al. (1990). Contexts of achievement: A study of American, Chinese, and Japanese children. *Monographs of the Society for Research in Child Development, 55*(1/2, Serial No. 221).

Stocker, C. M., Burwell, R. A., & Briggs, M. L. (2002). Sibling conflict in middle childhood predicts children's adjustment in early adolescence. *Journal of Family Psychology, 16*(1), 50–57.

Stone, M. R., & Brown, B. B. (1998). In the eye of the beholder: Adolescents' perceptions of peer crowd stereotypes. In R. E. Muuss & H. D. Porton (Eds.), *Adolescent behavior and society: A book of readings* (5th ed., pp. 158–169). New York: McGraw-Hill.

Strouse, D. L. (1999). Adolescent crowd orientations: A social and temporal analysis. In J. A. McLellan & M. J. V. Pugh (Eds.), *The role of peer groups in adolescent social identity: Exploring the importance of stability and change* (pp. 37–54). San Francisco: Jossey-Bass.

Sullivan, H. S. (1953). *The interpersonal theory of psychiatry.* New York: Norton.

Taradash, A., Connolly, J. A., Pepler, D., Craig, W., & Costa, M. (2001). The interpersonal context of romantic autonomy in adolescence. *Journal of Adolescence, 24*(3), 365–377.

Tesch, S. A., & Whitbourne, S. K. (1982). Intimacy and identity status in young adults. *Journal of Personality and Social Psychology, 43*(5), 1041–1051.

Thompson, R. (1999). Early attachment and later development. In J. Cassidy & P. R. Shaver (Eds.), *Handbook of attachment: Theory, research, and clinical applications* (pp. 265–286). New York: Guilford Press.

Thompson, S. (1995). *Going all the way: Teenage girls' tales of sex, romance and pregnancy.* New York: Hill & Wang.

Tiezzi, L., Lipshutz, J., Wrobleski, N., Vaughan, R., & McCarthy, J. (1997). Pregnancy prevention among urban adolescents younger than 15: Results of the "In Your Face" program. *Family Planning Perspectives, 29,* 173–176, 197.

Tolman, D. L., Spencer, R., Rosen-Reynoso, M., & Porche, M. V. (2004). Sowing the seeds of violence in heterosexual relationships: Early adolescents narrate compulsory heterosexuality. *Journal of Social Issues, 59*(1), 159–178.

Treboux, D., Crowell, J. A., Owens, G., & Pan, H. S. (1994, February). *Attachment behaviors and working models: Relations to best friendship and romantic relationships.* Paper presented at the Society for Research on Adolescence, San Diego, CA.

Tubman, J. G., Windle, M., & Windle, R. C. (1996). Cumulative sexual intercourse patterns among middle adolescents: Problem behavior precursors and concurrent health risk behaviors. *Journal of Adolescent Health, 18*(3), 182–191.

Tucker, C., McHale, S. M., & Crouter, A. C. (2001). Conditions of sibling support in adolescence. *Journal of Family Psychology, 15*(2), 254–271.

Udry, J. R. (1990). Hormonal and social determinants of adolescent sexual initiation. In J. Bancroft & J. Reinisch (Eds.), *Adolescence and puberty* (pp. 70–87). New York: Oxford University Press.

Varenne, H. (1982). Jocks and freaks: The symbolic structure of the expression of social interaction among American senior high school students. In G. Spindler (Ed.), *Doing the ethnography of schooling* (pp. 213–235). New York: Holt, Rinehart and Winston.

Waldinger, R. J., Diguer, L., Guastella, F., Lefebvre, R., Allen, J., Luborsky, L., et al. (2002). The same old song?—Stability and change in relationship schemas from adolescence to young adulthood. *Journal of Youth and Adolescence, 31*(1), 17–29.

Waters, E., & Cummings, E. M. (2000). A secure base from which to explore close relationships. *Child Development, 71*(1), 164–172.

Waters, E., Merrick, S., Treboux, D., Crowell, J., & Albersheim, L. (2000). Attachment security in infancy and early adulthood: A 20-year longitudinal study. *Child Development, 71*(3), 684–689.

Way, N., Cowal, K., Gingold, R., Pahl, K., & Bissessar, N. (2001). Friendship patterns among African American, Asian American, and Latino adolescents from low-income families. *Journal of Social and Personal Relationships, 18,* 29–53.

Weinberg, M. S., Williams, C. J., & Pryor, D. W. (1994). *Dual attraction: Understanding bisexuality.* New York: Oxford University Press.

Weinfield, N. S., Ogawa, J., & Sroufe, L. A. (1997). Early attachment as a pathway to adolescent peer competence. *Journal of Research on Adolescence, 7,* 241–265.

Weinfield, N. S., Sroufe, L. A., & Egeland, B. (2000). Attachment from infancy to young adulthood in a high-risk sample: Continuity, discontinuity and their correlates. *Child Development, 71*(3), 695–702.

Weinstein, M., & Thornton, A. (1989). Mother-child relations and adolescent sexual attitudes and behaviors. *Demography, 26*(4), 563–577.

Whitbeck, L. B., Conger, R. D., & Kao, M. (1993). The influence of parental support, depressed affect, and peers on the sexual behaviors of adolescent girls. *Journal of Family Issues, 14*(2), 261–278.

Whitbeck, L. B., Yoder, K. A., Hoyt, D. R., & Conger, R. D. (1999). Early adolescent sexual activity: A developmental study. *Journal of Marriage and the Family, 61*(4), 934–946.

Whiting, B. B., & Edwards, C. P. (1988). *Children of different worlds.* Cambridge, MA: Harvard University Press.

Youniss, J. (1980). *Parents and peers in the social environment: A Sullivan Piaget perspective.* Chicago: University of Chicago Press.

Youniss, J., & Smollar, J. (1985). *Adolescent relations with mothers, fathers, and friends.* Chicago: University of Chicago Press.

Zani, B. (1991). Male and female patterns in the discovery of sexuality during adolescence. *Journal of Adolescence, 14,* 163–178.

Zimmer-Gembeck, M. J., Siebenbruner, J., & Collins, W. A. (2001). Diverse aspects of dating: Associations with psychosocial functioning from early to middle adolescence. *Journal of Adolescence, 24,* 1–24.

PART IX

DIVERSITY IN DEVELOPMENT

Chapter 17

Culture and Cognitive Development in Phylogenetic, Historical, and Ontogenetic Perspective

MICHAEL COLE

In light of the increasing attention being given to culture's role in development (see Greenfield, Maynard, & Childs, 2000; and Shweder et al., 1998), my goal is to comple- ment this chapter complements these contributions by broadening the issue of culture and cognitive *ontogeny* to place the question of culture and cognitive development in a broad evolutionary and historical framework.

This expanded analysis of culture in development seems an important task at this moment in the development of the field. No one writing on this topic denies that human development is heavily constrained by our species' phylogenetic heritage. In fact, Shweder and his colleagues explicitly state that human beings are creatures with a long, common phylogenetic past that provides constraints on ontogenetic development. They also invoke ideas about the influence of experience that come directly from work in developmental neuroscience. However, they do not explore how these phylogenetic factors are linked to culture and human ontogeny, restricting themselves to pointing out that whatever these primeval, shared characteristics are, they "only gain character, sub- stance, definition and motivational force . . . when . . . translated and transformed into, and through, the concrete actualities of some particular practice, activity setting, or way of life" (Shweder et al., 1998, p. 871). This perspective provides a good starting point, but if it is not elaborated on, it de facto places human phylogeny and cultural his- tory so far into the background that the ongoing inter-relationships between these dif- ferent developmental spheres during ontogeny go unexamined.

My approach reflects my long-term interest in the work of the Russian cultural- historical school of psychology, for which human development was seen as the emergent outcome of phylogenetic, cultural-historical, ontogenetic, and microgenetic processes all acting simultaneously on the developing person (Vygotsky, 1997; Wertsch, 1985). This position makes contact with increasingly popular work in the field of evolutionary developmental psychology (e.g., Bjorklund & Pellegrini, 2002), which focuses on the relationship between phylogeny and ontogeny. Unfortunately, however, the evolutionary developmental perspective pays little attention to the role of cultural history, particularly with respect to the issue of *cognitive* development. Consequently, one of my goals is to bring cultural-history into the study of human development without abandoning a commitment to an evolutionary perspective.

Definitional Issues: Culture, Cognitive Development, and Allied Concepts

Because this chapter links the study of biological history, cultural history, and cognitive ontogeny, a brief discussion of the meanings of the terms *culture* and *cognition* as they appear in the different disciplines that I must draw upon (e.g., anthropology, paleontology, primatology, and psychology) seems necessary.

CULTURE

In its most general sense, the term "*culture*" refers to the socially inherited body of past human accomplishments that serves as the resources for the current life of a social group ordinarily thought of as the inhabitants of a country or region (D'Andrade, 1996). However, several issues perennially spur debate concerning the concept of culture as it relates to the study of cognitive development: Is culture a unique property of human beings? Can human cultures be ranked in terms of "level of development"? What is the relationship between mental/ideal and material aspects of culture? To what extent can culture be assumed to be shared by members of a social group?

Is Culture Unique to Humans?

In recent years, many primatologists have argued that the core notion of culture is "group-specific behavior that is acquired, at least in part, through social influences" (McGrew, 1998, p. 305) or "behavioral conformity spread or maintained by nongenetic means" through processes of social learning (Whitten, 2000, p. 284). By this minimalist definition, culture is not specific to human beings. Not only many primates, but members of other species display behavioral conformities that they have been acquired by nongenetic means, although precisely what those means are is widely debated.

Even those who argue for the presence of culture, so defined, among nonhuman primates generally agree that there is more to human culture than nongenetically transmitted behavioral patterns, just as there is more to human cognition than is found in nonhuman primates. However, disagreements about precisely what this "more" is and what the differences in the nature of culture among species tell us about the role of culture in human cognitive development have produced a massive and contentious literature (Byrne et al., 2004).

Culture, Cultural History, and Development

During the nineteenth century, culture was used more or less as a synonym for civilization, referring roughly to the progressive improvement of human creativity—in the industrial arts including the manufacturing techniques for metal tools and agricultural practices, the extent of scientific knowledge, the complexity of social organization, the refinement of manners and various customs, as well as control over nature and oneself (Cole, 1996; Stocking, 1968).

During the twentieth century, owing to the work of Franz Boas and his colleagues, the notion of culture-as-progress was gradually replaced by the idea that all cultures are the products of local adaptations to the circumstances of the social group during its history up to the present. Consequently, anthropologists have generally resisted the idea that different cultures could be scaled with respect to overall value or virtue, since such judgments are historically and ecologically contingent. However, there remain those who emphasize that cultures can be ranked in terms of lower and higher levels of complexity, if not virtue. The question then becomes how such cultural variations are associated with variations in psychological processes (e.g., Damerow, 1996; Hallpike, 1979; Feinman, 2000).

Cultural Patterns: Shared or Distributed?

When early ethnographers such as Margaret Mead went to far-off, relatively isolated, nonliterate societies to study culture and development, they generally made the additional assumption that culture is highly patterned, interconnected, homogeneously experienced, and pervasive. The heavy emphasis placed on cultures as monolithic, gestalt-like configurations gave way over subsequent decades to appreciation of internal heterogeneity at both the cultural and individual levels and to the consequent need for people actively to create and recreate their culture for it to exist at all (Schwartz, 1978).

At present, the degree to which particular cultural elements are shared has become an important topic in anthropology in general and the study of culture and cognition in particular. Kim Romney and his colleagues have proposed what they refer to as a "cultural consensus model" to characterize the degree to which users of a culture share particular understandings (Romney & Moore, 2001; Romney, Weller, & Batchelder, 1986). Medin and Atran (2004) apply this model to characterize how different subgroups within a society think differently about particular domains (e.g., how they conceive of nature and consequently, how they act with respect to it). Such a "distributed" notion of culture finds its natural counterpart in distributed theories of cognition (e.g., Hutchins, 1995).

The Relation of the Ideal and Material in Culture

The proliferation of conceptions of culture by the middle of the twentieth century was sufficient to induce Alfred Kroeber and Clyde Kluckhohn (1952) to offer a famous omnibus definition that provided greater specification to the general "social learning" approach adopted by primatologists or the "social inheritance" approach noted by D'Andrade for the human case:

Culture consists of patterns, explicit and implicit, of and for behavior acquired and transmitted by symbols, constituting the distinctive achievements of human groups, including their embodiment in artifacts; the essential core of culture consists of traditional (i.e., historically derived and selected) ideas and especially their attached values; cultural systems may on the one hand be considered as products of action, on the other as conditioning elements of further action. (p. 181)

This definition contains a mixture of elements, some of which appear to be material things "out there in the world," others of which appear to be mental entities (ideas and values), which are "in here," in the human mind. This division between material culture and symbolic culture represents a major cleavage line in the field to this day. Moreover, Kroeber and Kluckhohn provide at least a crude evaluation of the relative importance of the ideal and material aspects of culture when they pick out ideas and values as the "essential core" of culture. This is not an innocent preference, but rather reflects the fact that in the middle of the twentieth century there began a steady movement in anthropology away from definitions of culture that emphasize its behavioral/material aspects toward definitions that emphasize its ideational/mental aspects.

In recent years, there have been efforts to combine the "culture is out there/material" and the "culture is in here/mental" views in definitions of culture. For example, Shweder and his colleagues (1998) define human culture as *both* a symbolic *and* a behavioral inheritance:

The symbolic inheritance of a cultural community consists of its received ideas and understandings . . . about persons, society, nature, and divinity. . . . The "behavioral inheritance" of a cultural community consists of its routine or institutionalized family life and social practices. (p. 868)

There are a great many suggestions about how culture operates as a constituent of human social practices. For example, in the early 1970s, Geertz (1973) cited with approval Max Weber's image of humankind as "an animal suspended in webs of significance he himself has spun," declaring "I take culture to be those webs" (p. 5). Owing to this metaphor, Geertz is often read as an anthropologist who adopts the conception of culture as exclusively inside-the-head-knowledge (e.g., Berry, 2000). However, Geertz (1973) explicitly rejected this strictly idealist approach by suggesting that culture should be conceived of by analogy to a recipe or a computer program, which he referred to as "control mechanisms":

The "control mechanism" view of culture begins with the assumption that human thought is basically both social and public—that its natural habitat is the house yard, the marketplace, and the town square. Thinking consists not of "happenings in the head" (though happenings there and elsewhere are necessary for it to occur) but of traffic in what have been called, by G. H. Mead and others, significant symbols—words for the most part but also gestures, drawings, musical sounds, mechanical devices like clocks. (p. 45)

In this chapter, I adopt the view that symbols and meanings embodied in artifacts, and made up of, historically accumulated practices, constitute human culture.

DEVELOPMENT

Because this chapter is intended for an audience dominated by developmental psychologists, the theory-laden nature of definitions of development requires far less exposition. If you thumb through leading introductory texts on child development, it is apparent that many of them simply assume its meaning and focus on particular content domains or methods or analysis. Other texts offer "least common denominator" definitions that are filled in later through examinations of theory and data (e.g., "the sequence of changes that children undergo as they grow older—changes that begin with conception and continue throughout life"; Cole, Cole, & Lightfoot, 2004, p. 2). Still others provide definitions that are clearly theory laden (e.g., "development involves age-related, qualitative changes and behavioral reorganization that are orderly, cumulative, and directional"; Sroufe, Cooper, & DeHart, 1996, p. 6).

The same problem arises when we turn to the more specialized topic of culture and cognitive development. Rogoff (2003) for example, treats the terms *"learning* and *development"* as synonymous. Others, including myself, see learning and development as interleaved, but distinct processes involved in the cognitive change as children grow older Learning implies accumulation of knowledge and skills, while development implies qualitative reorganization of different constituents of such knowledge and skills and a corresponding reorganization of the relationship between persons and their environments (Cole, 1996; R. Gelman & Lucariello, 2002; Vygotsky, 1978). Diagnosis of the notion of development implied in any given treatment of culture and cognitive development is often most readily inferred from the specific tasks that are used as indexes of cognition, drawn as they are from different theoretical traditions of developmental psychology.

Culture and Cognition: A Synthetic Framework

As noted earlier, the cultural-historical perspective from which I approach the question of culture and cognitive development requires not only that psychologists study ontogenetic change but phylogenetic and historical change as well, all in relation to one another (Wertsch, 1985). According to the initiators of the cultural-historical perspective, each new "level of history," in their view, was associated with a new "critical turning point":

Every critical turning point is viewed primarily from the standpoint of something new introduced by this stage into the process of development. Thus we treated each stage as a starting point for further processes of evolution. (Vygotsky & Luria, 1993, p. 37)

The turning point in phylogeny is the appearance of tool use in apes. The turning point in human history is the appearance of labor and symbolic mediation. The turning point in ontogeny is the convergence of cultural history and phylogeny with the acquisition of language. The products of these fusions of different "streams of history" are distinctly human, higher psychological function.

In bringing this perspective up to date, I begin by reviewing current data and speculation about the phylogenic perspective of human biological, cultural, and cognitive characteristics in phylogenetic perspective. Next I turn to research on cultural-historical change, then age-related changes in children's thinking as mediated by culture, and the microgenetic changes through which ontogenies are constructed.

CULTURE AND PHYLOGENETIC DEVELOPMENT

I present the "knot" of phylogenetic issues in terms of two evolutionary lines. The first spans the several million years of human evolution beginning with the appearance of *Australopithecus* approximately 4 million years ago and ending with *homo sapiens sapiens,* perhaps 60,000 years ago. The second focuses on the other branch of our phylogenetic tree, the great apes, especially contemporary chimpanzees and bonobos.

The logic uniting these two lines of investigation is the assumption that human beings and apes share a common ancestor some 4 to 5 million years ago (Noble & Davidson, 1996). The successors to that common ancestor that lead to *homo sapiens* underwent massive changes not only in the brain and in physical morphology of the body (bipedalism, the structure of the arms, hands, fingers, the vocal tract, etc.), but in physical ecology, cognitive capacities, and the accumulation of the products of the past in the form of human culture. By contrast, among nonhuman primates, the anatomy, body size, physical morphology, behavior, cognitive abilities, and modes of life have not changed markedly over the past several million years. Hence, a three-way analysis of change, one that follows the homid line, one that follows the nonhuman primate line, and a third which compares the two should provide a "guesstimate" of the initial capacities of archaic human predecessors, the processes of homid physical and mental evolution, and in particular, the role of culture in those processes. The results of this analysis then provide the essential foundations for considering human ontogeny and its relationship to human culture in evolutionary context.

Culture and Hominization

There are a few relatively uncontroversial "facts" that serve as anchors for more detailed accounts of hominid evolution prior to the advent of modern human beings. First, there is the evident increase in the size of the brain in the sequence of species leading to *homo sapiens sapiens.* There are various ways of calculating this growth in brain size but since the work of Jerrison (1973), brain size has in some way been treated in relation to overall body size, which he referred to as an encephalization quotient (EQ; Falk & Gibson, 2001). Jerison demonstrated that the EQs of species from the great apes through the hominid line increase markedly, so that the EQ of modern humans is almost three times that of the chimpanzee and other great apes.

Although the overall and relative brain size of later hominids increased following the line from *Australopithecus* to *homo sapiens sapiens,* this growth appears to have been especially pronounced in the frontal and prefrontal cortices, hippocampus, and cerebellum, all heavily implicated in cognitive changes both in phylogeny and ontogeny. Of special interest has been the evidence for increased brain volume in Broca's area that appears with the advent of *homo erectus* because of the relationship of Broca's area to language in normally developing modern humans.

Also widely studied have been morphological changes in other parts of the body that are associated with species changes following divergence from a common ancestor. Such changes include bipedalism and various changes in anatomy with significance for hominization such as changes in the hand implicated in fine motor control (especially the opposable thumb), the pelvic region (which is crucial to the timing of birth and the length of infancy), and the vocal apparatus necessary for rapid fluent speech. (See Lewin & Foley, 2004, for a summary.)

Data relevant to the cultural sphere, particularly the evidence of changes in material artifacts, are perhaps the second most reliable source of evidence concerning cognition-culture relations (Foley & Lahr, 2003). The first, crude tools are often said to appear with *homo habilis.* These tools were made of stone and appear, according to most interpreters, to have been made by shattering small rocks to make sharp-edged implements (choppers) and additional tools, such as knives made by chipping off flakes from the remaining stone core. With *homo erectus,* there is generally believed to have been a quantum increase in size and the complexity of the tool kit. According to this line of interpreting the fossil record, tools now included hand axes with two cutting edges that required a much more complex manufacturing process. While change in the hominid tool kit was initially exceedingly slow, lasting perhaps a million years, the rate of change, the variety, and the complexity of tools increased in the course of human evolution, although the timing of changes is disputed (Foley & Lahr, 2003; Lewin & Foley, 2004).

With respect to behavior, which is inferred from the tools and the uses to which they were presumably put (e.g., cutting up large animals for meat and later for skins to be used as clothing) as well as evidence of group size and patterns of food consumption, *homo erectus* appears to have been a "critical turning point." For the first time, there is evidence of creatures that lived in relatively permanent base camps, had stone tools that clearly differed from any claimed for other species, and ventured out to hunt and gather; later in their one and a half million year existence, the use of fire makes its appearance. It is also *homo erectus* that ventures out of Africa and makes its appearance in Asia and Europe.

When we get to *homo erectus,* the increased complexity of the tool kit (in particular, the appearance of symmetrical, clearly crafted implements) is evidence of greater cultural complexity and implies more complex cognitive abilities although it is uncertain what this increased cognitive complexity consisted of. Some scholars argue language was one such constituent (Bickerton, 1990; Deacon, 1997); according to this view, special selective pressures for language development began early in evolution along the line to *homo Sapiens* perhaps resulting from the need for increased cooperation in larger social groups, as with the appearance of *homo sapiens* (Dunbar, 2004). Others argue that language came very late, with the advent of *homo sapiens sapiens* owing to the development of a specialized vocal tract that could produce rapid speech (Lieberman, 1984). Whether early or late in hominization, symbolic language is agreed to be essential to the emergence of modern humans.

Suggestions for important cognitive changes that may (or may not) have accompanied language include increased ability to coordinate motor and spatial processing (Stout, Toth, Schick, Stout, & Hutchins, 2000; Wynn, 1989), increased ability to cooperate with others over extended periods of time to produce standardized products (Foley & Lahr, 2003), and an increased ability to imitate the behavior of conspecifics (Donald, 1991, 2001). (For discussion of Donald's views, pro and con, see Renfrew & Scarre, 1998.)

In some ways, the most well-documented developmental change, from *homo sapiens* to *homo sapiens sapiens* is the most mysterious. Except for continued brain growth and some development in tools, there appears to be no clear reason for the sudden flowering of symbolic culture and the rapid expansion of human culture, including elaborate burial with clear symbolic content, cave art and ornamentation that appear to have no direct utilitarian significance. The apparent discontinuity some 40 to 60 thousand years ago has led some to suggest a genetic mutation controlling the operation of a language module as *the* event leading to the appearance of modern humans (Berlim, Mattevi, Belmonte-de-Abreu, & Crow, 2003). But this discontinuity position has been challenged by evidence of a great many species whose remains have been found in Africa that bespeak the presence of various elements of the "human revolution" (new technologies, long-distance trading, systematic use of pigment for art and decoration) tens of thousands of years earlier than previously thought but never fully developed in one place (McBrearty & Brooks, 2000). By this latter account, the "human revolution" was simply "human evolution" in which many isolated changes in different species came together with the changes in climate and population that brought disparate peoples together 40,000 years ago in Europe as it emerged from the latest Ice Age that had served to keep human groups apart, blocking the conditions of cultural and biological interaction among groups from which modern humans emerged.

If we seek to rise above the myriad disagreements among those who seek to synthesize the processes of development at the phylogenetic level of analysis, the most important conclusion for our purposes is that the relations between biological, cultural, and cognitive change are reciprocal. The "virtuous circle" that the evidence most strongly supports is that changes in anatomy (increased relative brain volume) results from a change in diet, in particular, greater intake of protein from the killing and ingestion of animals. The ability to kill and eat animals was the result of concomitant anatomical changes (the ability to run long distances that evolved following the evolution of the ability to work upright, which also freed the hands and was accompanied by greater dexterity of the fingers). These biological changes were both cause and result of increased sophistication of the cultural tool kit, including the control of fire (a clearly cultural practice, but one whose origins are disputed across a million year margin). This richer diet and the way of life associated with it enabled the growth of new cognitive capacities that further enriched the cultural tool, which in turn further supported growth of the brain, and so on. In Henry Plotkin's (2001) felicitous phrasing, "Human evolution and cultural evolution are two-way streets of causal interactions" (p. 93).

Living Primates

Virtually all attempts to arrive at plausible speculations about cognitive change in phylogeny incorporate information from a variety of currently living species of non-human primates as an indirect way to make educated guesses about all of the questions that arise when dealing solely with archeological evidence. (See Joulian, 1996, for a discussion of this approach.) Collectively, a number of remarkable events linking evolutionary biology, primatology, and developmental psychology in recent decades have revolutionized our ideas about the relationship between chimpanzees and/or bonobos (our closest primate kin) and modern humans (de Waal, 2001; Parker & McKinney, 1999).

I first examine current evidence concerning cognitive achievements and then the presence of culture among nonhuman primates before turning to the question of culture-cognition relations in these species and what issues those relations pose for scholars interested in culture-cognition relations in human ontogeny.

Cognitive Achievements.   Some of the primate literature grows out of, or is conducted in connection with, ontogenetic studies of such processes as imitation, numeration, self-awareness, attributions of intentionality, active teaching, and tools use, all of which have been implicated in the acquisition of cognitive capacities and the acquisition of human culture (Parker, Langer, & McKinney, 2000; Tomasello & Rakoczy, 2003; see also Boysen & Hallberg the special issue of *Cognitive Science,* 2000).

Language.   Current enthusiasm for the idea that chimpanzees have the capacity to understand and produce language has been inspired by the work of Duane Rumbaugh & Sue Savage-Rumbaugh (Rumbaugh, Savage-Rumbaugh, & Sevcik, 1994; Savage-Rumbaugh, Fields, & Taglialatela, 2001). These researchers provided their chimpanzees with a "lexical keyboard" whose keys bear symbols that stand for words, and they used standard reinforcement learning techniques to teach the chimpanzees the basic vocabulary symbols (e.g., "banana," "give"). In addition, the people who worked with the chimpanzees used natural language in everyday, routine activities such as feeding.

The Rumbaughs' most successful student has been Kanzi, a bonobo ape who initially learned to use the lexical keyboard by being present when his mother was being trained to use it. Kanzi is able to use the keyboard to ask for things and he can comprehend the meanings of lexical symbols created by others. He has also learned to understand some spoken English words and produce phrases of his own (Rumbaugh & Washburn, 2003).

For example, Kanzi correctly acted out the spoken request to "feed your ball some tomato" (he picked up a tomato and placed it in the mouth of a soft sponge ball with a face embedded in it). He also responded correctly when asked to "give the shot [syringe] to Liz" and then to "give Liz a shot": in the first instance, he handed the syringe to the girl, and in the second, he touched the syringe to the girl's arm.

Kanzi's ability to produce language is not as impressive as his comprehension, however. Most of his "utterances" on the lexical keyboard are single words that are closely linked to his current actions. Most of them are requests. He uses two-word utterances in a wide variety of combinations, however, and occasionally makes observations. For example, he produced the request "car trailer" on one occasion when he was in the car and wanted (or so his caretakers believed) to be taken to the trailer rather than to walk there. He has created such requests as "play yard Austin" when he wanted to visit a chimpanzee named Austin in the play yard. When a researcher put oil on him while he was eating a potato, he commented, "potato oil."

At present, it appears that bonobos and chimpanzees can produce many aspects of language roughly at the level of a 2-year-old child using the lexical keyboard. In their productions, they form telegraphic utterances that encode the same semantic relations as young children (e.g., a two-symbol combination relating an agent to its action—"Kanzi eat"). These telegraphic utterances can either combine visual symbols or combine gestures with symbols (Savage-Rumbaugh, Murphy, Sevcik, & Brakke, 1993).

Piagetian Developmental Milestones. An extensive line of work yielded evidence modeled on sensorimotor tasks favored by Piagetians to make the case for evolutionary continuity (e.g., Parker & McKinney, 1999). This research indicates that chimpanzees go through the same sequence of sensorimotor changes as human children, passing Piagetian sensorimotor tasks in various domains up to, and sometimes into, substage 6, the achievement of representational thought. Further evidence that substage 6 Piagetian understanding provides a meeting point of chimpanzee and human ontogenetic development comes from the work of Kuhlmeir and Boysen (2002) who have shown that that chimpanzees can recognize spatial and object correspondences between a scale model and its referent at a level of complexity roughly equivalent to 3-year-olds.

Tool Use and Tool Creation. At least from the time of Kohler's classic studies of problem solving, a great deal of attention has been focused on chimpanzee tool use and tool creation. McGrew's (1998) summary regarding tool use is worth quoting at length because it indicates clearly current claims for chimpanzee tool use and tool making capabilities:

Each chimpanzee population has its own customary tool kit, made mostly of vegetation, that functions in subsistence, defense, self-maintenance, and social relations . . . many have tools sets, in which two or more different tools are used as composites to solve a problem. . . . The same raw material serves multiple functions: A leaf may be a drinking vessel, napkin, fishing probe, grooming stimulator, courtship signaler, or medication. . . . Conversely, a fishing probe may be made of bark, stem, twig, vine, or the midrib of a leaf. An archeologist would have no difficulty classifying the cross-cultural data in typological terms, based on artifacts alone; for example, only the far western subspecies . . . uses stone hammer stone hammers and anvils to crack nuts. . . . Given this ethnographic record, it is difficult to differentiate, based on material culture, living chimpanzees from earliest Homo . . . or even from the simplest living human foragers. (pp. 317–318)

In line with McGrew's views, in at least one case it has been claimed that chimpanzees carry different tools with them to accomplish different goals (Boesch & Boesch, 1984). The chimpanzees in question lived in the Ivory Coast. They encountered two kinds of nuts in their foraging, one with hard shells, the other with softer shells. For the harder nuts, they transported harder, heavier hammers (mostly stones) from their home base. They seemed to remember the location of stones and to choose the stones so as to keep the transport distance minimal.

Theory of Mind.   The domain of social cognition has received special attention because it appears to indicate that chimpanzees interpret correctly the state of mind of conspecifics. This work is thoroughly reviewed elsewhere. Just a few points deserve highlighting to maintain continuity in the current context.

    Boesch and Tomasello (1998) argue that chimpanzees acquire some parts of theory of mind, but not others (they understand some things about what others see or have seen in the recent past, and some aspects of others' goal-directed activities, but do not appear to distinguish gaze direction from attention or prior intentions that are no longer perceptually present). Most recently, Tomasello and his colleagues (Tomasello, Carpenter, Call, Behne, & Moll, 2005) have argued that the key cognitive difference is the adult human ability to engage in *shared* intentionally that permits engagement in complex collaborative activities and requires powerful skills of intention-reading as well as for a motivation to share psychological states with others, an ensemble of abilities that gives rise to what they refer to as "dialogical cognitive representations." Additional examples of cognitive domains could be reviewed in which it has been claimed that chimpanzees exhibit at least the rudiments of cognitive abilities once believed to be the sole possession of human beings (myriad examples are provided by Bekoff, Allen, & Burghardt, 2002, and by de Waal, 2001). However, extending such examples still leaves us with the question of how such cognitive similarities are related to the issue of central concern in this chapter—the relation of culture and cognition in development. To address this issue, we need to look more closely at treatments of culture among the great apes and then return to examine the relation of culture to cognition in nonhuman species and humans.

Culture among Apes.   Belief in a narrow, quantitative gap between humans and nonhuman primate cognition is paralleled by belief in a narrow gap with respect to culture (Wrangham, McGrew, de Waal, & Heltne, 1994). Recall that in approaching the issue of primate culture, researchers define culture as behavioral traditions spread or maintained by nongenetic means through processes of social learning. This kind of definition does not presuppose characteristics that are themselves arguably specifically human (e.g., religious beliefs, aesthetic values, social institutions). Hence, the analyst can remain agnostic with respect to culture-cognition relationships in different species (Byrne et al., 2004). At the same time, the definition allows examination of the extent to which cognitive characteristics claimed to be necessary for acquisition of human culture are present in displays of nonhuman primate behavioral traditions (cultures), such as deliberate teaching or tool making and use. I will focus here on chimpanzees, for which the most extensive evidence is available, but I include other well-researched examples as well (see McGrew, 1998).

The textbook example of a social tradition for which we know the origin and have data on its spread comes from sweet-potato-washing by Japanese macaque monkeys on Koshima Island (Matsuzawa, 2001). In 1953, a juvenile female monkey was observed washing a muddy sweet potato in a stream. This behavior first spread to peers and then to older kin. Ten years later it was observed among more than 50% of the population and 30 years later by 71%. A few years later the same monkey invented a form of "wheat-sluicing," in which wheat that had been mixed with sand was cast upon the sea so that the floating bits of wheat could be easily sorted from the sinking sand. Within 30 years, 93% of this group engaged in this behavior.

McGrew (1998) draws attention to other important characteristics of Japanese macaque cultural traditions. First, they do not remain entirely static. Koshima monkeys began by washing their potatoes in fresh water, but later adopted washing in seawater (presumably to add to the taste). A group of monkeys living in the far north adopted the tradition of bathing in warm springs in winter; initially the mothers left their offspring on the edge of the pools, but the young monkeys can now be seen swimming under water. Second, cultural traditions develop with no discernable relation to subsistence activities; several groups of macaques routinely handle small stones in a variety of ways (rolling, rubbing, piling) that are not related to any discernable adaptive function. These observations blunt attempts to find restrictions of the observed cultural behaviors to subsistence constraints.

The behavioral traditions involved have included ways of using probes for termites and ants, nut cracking using sticks and stones by various means, hunting strategies, nest building, and styles of grooming behavior (Matsuzawa, 2001; McGrew, 1998; Whitten, 2000; Wrangham et al., 1994). Interestingly, in light of their importance in discussions of both primate language and cognition, bonobos in the wild appear to display no evidence of tool use. This species difference should serve to block any simple equation between tool use and either cognitive development or the nature of social traditions.

Culture, Cognition, and Non-Human Primate Development. With respect to both cognition and culture considered separately, current evidence appears to support the idea that members of the great ape family, particularly chimpanzees, attain levels of cognitive development that bring them to the threshold of the corresponding human accomplishments. In the cultural realm, they form within-group social traditions through processes of social learning; these traditions include elementary kinds of tool use. In effect, nonhuman primates attain levels of cultural and cognitive development that terminate at approximately the transition from infancy to early childhood among human children. This brings us to the question of how cognition and culture are related among nonhuman primates.

Attempts to answer this question have focused on the question of the cognitive mechanisms of social learning. The general answer given is that social learning requires some form of mimesis broadly interpreted as a process in which the behavior of one individual comes to be like another through some form of contact. But this broad an understanding of mimesis is little more than restating what one means by a social tradition, since many different processes can lead to behavioral conformity. Consequently, the task of further specifying the processes of mimesis has garnered the bulk of scholarly attention (Byrne, 2002; Meltzoff & Prinz, 2002; Tomasello & Rakoczy, 2003; Whitten, 2000).

The most complex (and most controversial) claims about the source of acquiring social traditions in nonhuman primates center on *imitation,* when the infant attempts to copy the goal-directed strategies of the mother. There is as yet no consensus on whether nonhuman primates raised in the wild engage in this form of imitation (Byrne, 2002).

For those who believe that true imitation is present among the great apes, there is little to distinguish the resulting forms of culture and their cognitive underpinnings among species (Russon & Begun, 2002; Parker & McKinney, 1999). However, note that we are again faced with a "threshold" phenomenon; whether the threshold involves the presence of symbolic representation arising in substage 6 of Piaget's sensorimotor period or the extent to which chimpanzees are engaged in interpreting the intentions of conspecifics. The resulting form of culture, while meeting the minimal definition of culture as socially acquired behavior pattern, does not involve either symbolic mediation of thought. It is also noteworthy that there are no claims for the ways in which chimpanzee culture influences chimpanzee cognition. The most that has been claimed is that chimpanzees raised by humans are likely to be poorly adapted to life in the wild, a perfectly reasonable conclusion that implicates learning of various kinds, but no cultural influences on the development of chimpanzee thought processes.

The one clear set of circumstances where immersion in culture *does* reveal clear consequences on the cognitive and linguistic development of nonhuman primates is the one in which primates are raised by human beings who seek to promote their cognitive development using all the (human) cultural means at their disposal. This point has been emphasized by Tomasello (1994) who has suggested that "a humanlike social-cognitive environment is essential to the development of human-like social-cognitive and imitative learning skills. . . . More specifically, for a learner to understand intentions of another individual requires that the learner be treated as an intentional agent" (pp. 310–311). As might be expected, those who attribute more mental capacities to nonhuman primates than does Tomasello dispute this idea and, to buttress their argument, point to observational evidence that primates raised by humans undergo hardships when introduced into their natural environment precisely because they have not been exposed to the appropriate culture (Parker & McKinney, 1999; Russon & Begun, 2002).

CULTURAL HISTORY

Although there are innumerable differing explanations for the causes of the transition to *Homo Sapiens Sapiens* (a genetic change, a change in climate, a change in interactivity among *homo sapiens* creating a critical mass of cultural isolates, some combination of the above, etc.), there is reasonable agreement that something special emerged in the hominid line between 40,000 to 50,000 years ago, the "high Paleolithic" period of paleontology. The following set of changes is among those widely believed to have occurred (Cheyne, n.d.):

1. Semeiosis. The act of creating signs that stand for objects. The production of figurative and nonfigurative marks on stones, bones, plaques, cave walls, and so on.
2. Production of second-order tools. This refers to the production and use of tools to work bone, ivory, antler, and similar materials into a great variety of new tools such as points, awls, needles, pins, spear-throwers, and so on.
3. Production and use of simple "machines" that exploited mechanical advantage (e.g., the spear thrower and perhaps the so-called baton-de commandment).
4. An ability to visualize the complex action of tools or simple machines. The production and use of fish-hooks and harpoons appeared at this time. The mechanics

of these devices required that the makers be able to visualize and understand or predict the sequence of remote events such as those of penetration, withdrawal, and secondary penetration of a barb.

5. Spatial structural organization of living sites.
6. Long-distance transport of raw materials such as stones and shells over tens or even hundreds of kilometers.

These psychological and cultural developments were associated with other changes of enduring significance. These included:

1. A rapid expansion of human populations into all territories previously occupied by earlier developed forms of humans and the extremely rapid replacement of the indigenous populations.
2. Further expansion into territories not previously inhabited by humans.
3. An increase in population densities to levels comparable to those of hunting and gathering societies of historical times (Cheyne, n.d.).

Here, it appears, is the beginning of modern humans, the "cave men" and "hunter-gatherers" of anthropological, paleontological, and historical lore.

I assume the following "common" story of change following the emergence of biologically modern humans to be roughly true (c.f. Diamond, 1997; Donald, 1991; Gellner, 1988). Some of the hunter-gatherers who inhabited many parts of the earth and lived in small bands went on to engage in sedentary agriculture. From that way of life there emerged in some places conglomerations of people larger than the small groups that preceded them; older ways of life disappeared or continued in very much the same way for millennia. In others there was a marked increase in sociocultural complexity (Feinman, 2000).

As a number of scholars interested in culture and cognitive development in prehistory have emphasized, a defining characteristic of the Paleolithic era was the appearance of external systems of symbolic, representational cave art, statuary, and perhaps elementary counting devices (Donald, 2001). While the symbolic nature of such artifacts and their probable incorporation in symbolically mediated rituals including burial practices is generally agreed to provide convincing proof of the evolution of symbolic activity among *homo sapiens sapiens,* the precise cognitive mechanisms involved are not yet agreed upon. According to Damerow (1998), it seems most reasonable to consider the many millennia between the beginning of the Paleolithic period and the Neolithic period around 8000 B.C. (when people began to domesticate plants and animals and live in permanent villages) as an historical equivalent of the transition from sensori-motor to preoperational thinking. If, as McGrew (1987) argues, such societies approximate the level encountered in small face-to-face societies during the European age of exploration, it provides evidence in favor of the assumption that the cognitive processes of such peoples are best characterized as preoperational (Hallpike, 1979).

According to both Damerow (1998) and Donald (2001), it is with the urban revolution coinciding with the elaboration of tools, agricultural techniques, the smelting of copper and then bronze that one sees the transition from preoperational to operational thinking in human history. Two important lessons for the study of contemporary studies of culture and human ontogeny are emphasized by this literature. First, when concrete operational thinking begins to make an appearance, it is tightly bound to particular domains of culturally organized activity. Cuneiform writing, Damerow writes, represented mental models of the administrative activities that they mediated. Although they in-volved proto-numerical systems, such systems did not themselves embody principles of concrete operations and did not conclusively imply that their users could engage in re-versible mental operations. Second, the causal relations between the development of culture and the development of cognition were reciprocal. Like Plotkin, quoted earlier, who was referring to a much earlier period of hominization, Donald (2001) is emphatic in his conclusion that the brain and culture "have evolved so closely that the form of each is greatly constrained by the other." Moreover, with the advent of literacy espe-cially, "Culture actually configures the complex symbolic systems needed to support it by engineering the functional capture of the brain for epigenesis" (p. 23).

The difficulty with using prehistoric and even historical materials that have survived only in writing is that we have too little information about their contexts of use to make refined inferences about culture and cognitive development in ontogeny. For this rea-son, psychologists especially value studies enabled by rapid cultural-historical change in most parts of the world over the past several decades. Conditions of rapid change make it easier to tease apart relations between cultural-historical and ontogenetic change because there are co-existing generations close to each other in age who en-gaged in markedly different culturally organized activities.

Cross-Sectional Cultural-Historical Comparisons

Perhaps the most well known study to focus on the relation of rapid cultural-historical change to cognitive change was carried out by Alexander Luria in the early 1930s, al-though the work was not fully published in Russian or any other language until the middle of the 1970s (Luria, 1976). Luria studied a cohort of people under conditions of rapid change in remotes parts of the Kirghizia and Uzbekistan.

The historical occasion was the collectivization of agricultural labor under state con-trol, which brought with it changes such as formal schooling and exposure to bureau-cratic state agencies, during what can fairly be described as a revolutionary period in that part of the world. Luria concluded that the new modes of life deeply affected the dominant modes of thought, such that the "premodern" group was restricted to a form of "graphical/functional" reasoning based on common experience, while moderniza-tion brought with it access to scientific concepts which subsumed and dominated the everyday modes of thought foundations, replacing graphical/functional thinking.

Luria's research was not developmental in the sense of studying the impact of the historical changes on people of different ages. He relied primarily on psychological test data collected from adults with different degrees of exposure to Soviet collec-tivization. His conclusions are open to a series of criticisms, two of which are most im-portant. First, data from tests and clinical interviews were generalized very broadly to activity-dependent experience, but there was no in-situ evaluation of such connections. The interview situation itself was an alien form of activity to the traditional pastoralists who served as subjects in Luria's experiments so that their responses may have re-flected as much the alien nature of the modes of discourse as the influence of their own cultural experience employed in indigenous activities. Second, this same abstraction from the theoretical site of change, the activities themselves, both made it difficult to grasp the processes at work in the course of change and made it appear that the changes from concrete-graphic to theoretical thinking were of a general nature. In this respect, Luria's research was typical of a good deal of cross-cultural work. However, it is still valued for its clever use of interview methods similar to those used by Piaget, rather than settling for simple, unchallenged test responses, and for Luria's use of a broad range of tests ranging from perception, through classification, logical reasoning, and reasoning about oneself.

Modern research by King Beach in an area of Nepal undergoing rapid historical change uses methods that appear to overcome some of the shortcomings of Luria's work (Beach, 1995). Beach studied changing forms of arithmetic calculations in a Nepalese village that underwent rapid socioeconomic and cultural change in the 1960s and 1970s. Roads from India moved closer to the village, schooling was introduced for the first time and continued to expand over ensuing decades, and shops that exchanged merchandise for money appeared during the same period and rapidly increased in number. As a result, at the time the research was initiated in the late 1980s, there were two co-existing generations of men who experienced different relations between their experience of traditional farming, shop keeping, and schooling. What all groups shared was some experience with subsistence agriculture and the need to buy and sell in the shops using traditional nonmetric units to measure a given length of cloth and then calculate price in terms of meters and centimeters, to which the monetary price was linked. The traditional system relied on using the length from the elbow to the tip of the middle finger while the newly introduced system involved use of a ruler and the metric system.

Senior high school students were apprenticed to shopkeepers in the village, and shopkeepers who had never had the opportunity to attend school were enrolled in an adult literacy/numeracy class. Farmers who had never attended school and had never worked in a shop also completed a shop-keeping apprenticeship, or were enrolled in the adult education class. The transitions between education and work activities that were induced as a part of the study simulated larger-scale changes taking place in rural Nepali society. Some of the problems posed by Beach to track changes in arithmetic during the shop apprenticeship involved purchases requiring translation and calculation between the two measurement systems. Problems presented to those enrolled in the adult education class were arithmetic problems of the kind typically encountered in school mathematics classes.

Traditionally, shopkeepers used arithmetic forms based on indigenous systems that bear little surface relationship to either metric measurement (arm lengths versus a metric measuring stick) or the methods of calculating amounts and prices (the use of objects and other artifacts and decomposition strategies versus the use of paper and pencil to write equations and calculate with column algorithms). Those students becoming shopkeepers continued to use the written form they had learned in school after they entered the shops, even though reliable traditional methods long in use were prevalent there. Over time and with much pressure from the shopkeeper and customers, the students adapted the written form for use with the calculation strategies championed by the shopkeepers. Those who began as shopkeepers and were studying in the adult education class used their arms and traditional measurement objects to carry out their calculations, but eventually adopted a flexible approach of sometimes using traditional measurement units and calculation strategies and other times doing written calculations adapted to the problem at hand. Why?

From interviews with the participants, Beach was able to determine that students who were becoming shopkeepers viewed themselves as engaged in two activities, displays of school learning and shopkeeping that were initially in contradiction with each other. The status of schooling and of "being educated" made it difficult for them give up the written form of calculation, though the speed and adaptability of the shopkeeper's calculations eventually induced them to adapt the written form to the shopkeeper's calculation strategies. In this way, their status as formally educated adults was retained, marked by their use of the written form, but they could use the written form to do the calculations they needed to do quickly and accurately as shopkeepers. The shopkeepers, however, even though they were in an evening school, always thought of themselves as engaged in shopkeeping activities, their own shopkeeping activities, and did not shift over to the school-based system except when they saw it as facilitating their ongoing work as shopkeepers. Both by virtue of the tasks he presented and the way in which he presented them, Beach verified the linkage between cultural-historical and ontogenetic change, but one that depended on both the history of relations between the activities and the individuals' developmental history at the point of participation in those activities. This leads to a process of ontogenesis that is much more variable and more content/artifact-specific than Luria's results would suggest.

A Longitudinal Study of Cultural-Historical Change

Despite differences in methods, the research by Beach and Luria involved people with different amounts of exposure to new cultural practices.[1] A central feature of the study discussed in this section is that the same developmentalist returned after many years to the same place, using the same general methods, so that it is possible to document the course of cognitive development under changed sociocultural conditions for the same people at two disparate times.

The study I review here covers three generations: adults and children 30 to 40 years ago and grandparents, parents, and children recently. This relatively long time scale (in ontogenetic terms) meant that children in earlier studies could be studied as parents in the second, while their children became the new child subjects in the contemporary study.

Historical Change and Cognitive Change in Zinacantan.   Patricia Greenfield and her colleagues in the late 1960s went to the Zinacantan, a Mayan group living in the state of Chiapas, Mexico, where they began to study the cognitive and social consequences of learning to weave (Greenfield & Childs, 1977). Their work included experimental tests of categorizing ability by both boys and girls, careful descriptions of the apprenticing of young girls into weaving, of the weaving process "itself," and analysis of the products produced. In the 1990s, they returned to the same village and conducted parallel observations of parents (former child subjects) inducting their children into weaving and the products of this work (Greenfield, 1999; Greenfield, Maynard, & Childs, 2000).

In her recent writing comparing the relation between cultural change, modes of weaving, and modes of weaving instruction, Greenfield has emphasized the interconnectedness of historical change in economic activity, exposure to new products and practices from contact with people from the modern sector of Mexican society, socialization practices (in particular, modes of socializing girls into weaving), and cognitive processes involving the mental representation of the patterns in woven cloth (Greenfield, 2002, 2004; Greenfield et al., 2000). These changes are viewed as interconnected:

---

[1] Beach's students were in their early 20s, his shopkeepers in their 40s, but this age difference was not the object of his research and all were treated as adults.

- *Historical changes.* The analysis begins with historical changes in general modes of living. In contrast with the late 1960s, in the mid-1990s this Mayan community shifted from an economy based primarily on subsistence agriculture and relatively secluded from the modern state to one based more heavily on involvement in the money economy, trade, and much more frequent interaction with people and trade from outside of the village and the local region.

- *Socialization.* The instructional mode characterizing the mother-child weaving sessions in 1970 emphasized a long process of gradual apprenticeship involving many roles preparatory to weaving itself. When children first began to weave, mothers hovered close by and guided children with their own hands and bodies, using little verbal instruction. The entire system appeared to focus on maintenance of tradition and is characterized as "interdependent cultural learning."[2] In the 1990s, mothers who were more involved in the modern economy (e.g., by weaving products for sale) instructed their children verbally from a distance, sometimes using older siblings to take over instruction, and the children learned by a process that Greenfield and her colleagues characterize as "independent cultural learning" characterized by a good deal more trial and error and self-correction of errors.

- The variety of *products changed.* In the late 1960s the variety of products was limited, reflecting a very small set of "right ways to weave cloth." By the 1990's there was no longer a small set of simple, "correct" patterns, but an efflorescence of patterns, indicating the increased respect paid to individual innovation which comes with a trial-and-error approach to learning. This proliferation in turn depended on, and contributed to, changes in weaving practices.

- *Changing modes of mentally representing patterns.* Accompanying the historical changes were changes in the way children represented weaving patterns in an experimental task that used sticks of varying width and color that could be inserted into a rack to reproduce model patterns from woven models. Instead of using, for example, three white sticks to represent a broad band of white cloth, a single broad white stick was more likely to be used in the later historical period and those who attended school were more likely to be able to create novel patterns. Importantly, these historical changes were accompanied by an unchanging pattern of representational development related to age: older children in both historical periods were more able than younger children to represent more complex visual patterns, a fact that Greenfield et al. interpret as an indication of universal developmental processes accompanying culturally contingent ones. (I return to examine other results from this extensive research program in the section on ontogenetic developmental change.)

Based on her decades long involvement with a Mayan community in the Yucatan, Suzanne Gaskins (1999, 2000, and 2003) notes the same economic changes observed by Greenfield and her associates but provides a different, although compatible, explanation of the causal factors involved. Gaskins focuses on how the changing economic circumstances change maternal work patterns, suggesting that reduced time spent on

---

[2] The importance of getting an early start on learning to weave reveals itself in the fact that when American psychologists such as Greenfield and Rogoff have sought to learn to weave, one of the major hurdles was the great difficulty they experienced being able to maintain the postural position required. This pervasively experienced fact is a clear reminder of how cultural practice shapes biological capacity during ontogeny.

traditional chores (hauling water, for example, because there is running water, or having a longer day because of electricity) and time spent in the commercial sector outside the home, shift the division of labor inside the house in a variety of ways that reduce direct parental involvement with children's socialization in general, not just with respect to weaving. She also suggests that the efflorescence of weaving patterns may arise as much from copying models and parts of models imported by truck and the availability of money for "foreign" cultural goods as from any individual increase in creativity engendered by different modes of teaching.

Differences in interpretation of the underlying process notwithstanding, the Greenfield et al. multigenerational study brings a whole new range of data to bear on the question of the mechanisms of cultural change and accumulation, suggesting a strong link between cultural change resulting from the interaction of cultures and the development of new means of teaching and learning that accompanies the shift to more intensively commercially mediated forms of life.

History, Social Differentiation, and "Education"

An example of change at the cultural-historical level with clear implications for cognitive development is the historical development of formal schooling based on literacy and numeracy (Cole, 2005; Rogoff, Correa-Chávez, & Cotuc, 2005). Among academics, policy makers, and the general public, it is widely believed that education makes one more developed cognitively, either generally (Olson, 1994; United Nations Educational, Scientific, and Cultural Organization, 1951) or with respect to some more specific range of cognitive skills (Rogoff, 1981; Serpell & Hatano, 1997). Hence, historical changes in this form of culturally organized activity are an especially important example of the relationship between cultural change and cognitive development.

Although it is sometimes argued that the term, "*education,*" applies equally across all societies at all times because all human groups must prepare the next generation if the social group is to continue (Reagan, 2000), I find it more helpful to think of education as a particular form of schooling and schooling as a particular form of institutionalized enculturation. Tracing the process of education thus interpreted over historical time serves to concretize this ordering from enculturation (induction into the cultural order of the society), to schooling (deliberate instruction for specific skills), to education (an organized effort to "bring out" [educe] the full potential of the individual).

Small, Face-to-Face Societies.   Reminiscent of arguments that arise in the literature on culture formation in nonhuman primates, Jerome Bruner, in an influential monograph on culture and cognitive development, remarked that in watching "thousands of feet of film (about life among the Kung San Bushmen), one sees no explicit teaching in the sense of a 'session' out of the context of action to teach the child a particular thing. It is all implicit" (Bruner, 1966, p. 59). Elsewhere in the same essay he comments that "the process by which implicit culture is 'acquired' by the individual . . . is such that awareness and verbal formulation are intrinsically difficult" (p. 58).

Rudimentary Forms of Separation between Enculturation and Schooling.   Even granting such a starting point, one encounters small societies where agriculture has displaced hunting and gathering as the mode of life, but they remain small in size and relatively isolated from each other. In such conditions one witnesses the beginnings of differentiation of child and adult life involving forms of deliberate teaching that usually include a good deal of training. In many societies in rural Africa, for example, what are referred to casually as *rites de passage* may be institutionalized activities that last for several years, and teaching is certainly involved. For example, among the Kpelle and Vai peoples of Liberia, where I worked in the 1960s and 1970s, children were separated from their communities for 4 or 5 years in an institution referred to in Liberian pidgin as "bush school." There, children were instructed by selected elders in the essential skills of making a living as well as the foundational ideologies of the society, embodied in ritual and song. Some began there a years-long apprenticeship that would later qualify them to be specialists in bone setting, midwifery, and other valued arcane knowledge.

Social Accumulation, Differentiation, and the Advent of Schooling.   It appears that it is primarily, if not only, when a society's population grows numerous and it develops elaborate technologies enabling the accumulation of substantial material goods, that the form of enculturation to which we apply the term, schooling, emerges. As a part of the sea change in human life pattern associated with the transition from the Bronze Age to the Iron Age in what is now referred to as the Middle East, the organization of human life began a cascade of changes, which while unevenly distributed in time and space, appear to be widely, if not universally, associated with the advent of formal schooling. In the Euphrates valley, the smelting of bronze revolutionized economic and social life. With bronze, it became possible to till the earth in more productive ways, to build canals to control the flow of water, to equip armies with more effective weapons, and so on. Under these conditions, one part of the population could grow enough food to support large numbers beside themselves. This combination of factors made possible a substantial division of labor and development of the first city states (Schmandt-Besserat, 1996).

Another essential technology which enabled this new mode of life was the elaboration of a previously existing, but highly restricted mode of representing objects by inscriptions on tokens and the elaboration of the first writing system, cuneiform, which evolved slowly over time. Initially the system was used almost exclusively for record keeping, but it evolved to represent not only objects but the sounds of language, enabling letter writing and the recording of religious texts (Larsen, 1986; Schmandt-Besserat, 1996).

The new system of cuneiform writing could only be mastered after long and systematic study, but record keeping was so essential to the coordination of activities in relatively large and complex societies, where crop sizes, taxes, troop provisioning, and multiple forms of exchange need to be kept track of for the society to exist, that these societies began to create a new institution and devote resources to support selected young men for the explicit purpose of making them scribes, people who could write. The places where young men were brought together for this purpose were the earliest formal schools.

Not only the interactional patterns of the activities that took place in these schools, but the architecture, the organization of activities, and the reigning ideologies within them were in many respects startlingly modern. The classrooms consisted of rows of desks, facing forward to a single location where a teacher stood, guiding students in repetitive practice of the means of writing and calculating as well as the operations that accompanied them. Instead of inkwells, the classrooms contained bowls where wet clay could be obtained to refresh current clay tablets. In many such schools, the compiling of quantified lists of valued items (not unlike listing states of the Union or capitals of the world) was a major past time, although some letter writing also occurred. These lists were often viewed as evidence of extraordinary cognitive achievements (Goody, 1977).[3]

Evidence concerning early schooling indicates that more than socially neutral, technical, literacy, and numeracy skills were thought to be acquired there. Learning esoteric lists and the means for creating them were imbued with special powers such as are currently ascribed to those who are "civilized," and it was clearly recognized that socioeconomic value flowed from this knowledge.

In the Middle Ages, the focus of elementary schooling shifted to what LeVine and White (1986) refer to as "the acquisition of virtue" through familiarity with sacred texts, but a certain number of students were taught essential recordkeeping skills commensurate with the forms of economic and political activity that needed to be coordinated through written records. Such is the state of schooling in many Muslim societies to this day, although there is great variation in Islamic schooling depending on whether the local population speaks Arabic and how formal schooling articulates with the state and religion in the country in question. (See Serpell & Hatano, 1997, for a discussion of these variations and their implications.)

As characterized by LeVine and White (1986), the shift from schools in large agrarian societies to the dominant forms found in most contemporary industrialized and industrializing societies manifests the following set of common features:

- Internal organization to include age grading, permanent buildings designed for this purpose, with sequentially organized curricula based on level of difficulty.
- Incorporation of schools into larger bureaucratic institutions so that the teacher is effectively demoted from "master" to a low-level functionary in an explicitly standardized form of instruction.
- Re-definition of schooling as an instrument of public policy and preparation for specific forms of economic activity—"manpower development."
- Extension of schooling to previously excluded populations, most notably women and the poor.

Serpell and Hatano (1997) have dubbed this form of schooling "institutionalized public basic schooling" (IPBS). They point out that this European model evolved in the nineteenth century and followed conquering European armies into other parts of the world (LeVine, LeVine, & Schnell, 2001; LeVine & White, 1986; Serpell & Hatano, 1997). However, local forms of enculturation, even of schooling, have by no means been obliterated, sometimes, preceding (Wagner, 1993), sometimes co-existing with (LeVine & White, 1986), the more or less universal "culture of formal schooling" supported by, and supportive of, the nation state. Often these more traditional forms emphasize local religious and ethical values (Serpell & Hatano, 1997). Nonetheless, these alternatives still retain many of the structural features already evident in the large agrarian societies of the Middle Ages.

As a consequence of these historical trends, the institutional form, referred to as IPBS, has become an ideal if not a reality in most of the world (the Islamic world providing one alternative in favor of adherence to religious/social laws, as written in the *Q'uaran,* a word which means "recitation" in Arabic). The IPBS approach operates in the service of the secular state, economic development, the bureaucratic structures

---

[3] Although some features differ, a similar story could be told for China, where bureaucratized schooling arose a thousand or so years later, and in Egypt, as well as in many of the civilizations that followed.

through which rationalization of this process is attempted, and exists as a pervasive fact of contemporary life. According to a survey conducted by United Nations Educational, Scientific, and Cultural Organization in 2003, during the 1990s more than 80% of children in Latin America, Asia (outside of Japan), and Africa were enrolled in public school, although there are large disparities among regions and many children only complete a few years of schooling. Nonetheless, experience of IPBS has become a pervasive fact of growing up the world over (Serpell & Hatano, 1997).

The Consequences of Formal Schooling in the IPBS Mode. The reader interested in a comprehensive survey or the intellectual and social consequences of school is referred to summaries by Cole (2005), Rogoff et al. (2005), and Serpell and Hatano (1997).

In brief, accumulated evidence from comparisons of children who have or have not attended formal schools indicates that on a variety of measures of intellectual development covering a broad range of cognitive domains, performance increases as a function of years of schooling rather than as a function of age (at least for the age of 6 years and up when formal schooling generally begins). Evidence from three cognitive domains that have received a good deal of attention in studies of cognitive development: organization of word meaning, memory, and metacognitive skills, illustrate key kinds of evidence for cognitive-developmental consequences of schooling:

1. *Organization of word meaning.* Donald Sharp and his co-workers studied the potential impact of schooling on the way Mayan Indians on the Yucatan peninsula of Mexico organize their mental lexicons (Sharp, Cole, & Lave, 1979). When adolescents who had attended high school one or more years were asked which words they associated with the word "duck," they responded with other words in the same taxonomic category, such as "fowl," "goose," "chicken," and "turkey." But when adolescents in the same area who had not attended school were presented with the same word, their responses were dominated by words that describe what ducks do ("swim," "fly") or what people do with ducks ("eat"). Such word associations are often used as a subscale on IQ tests, with duck-goose accorded a higher score than duck-fly. In addition, a good deal of developmental research shows that in the course of development, young children are more likely to produced duck-fly than duck-goose. The results of this study and findings from other parts of the world (Cole, Gay, Glick, & Sharp, 1971) suggest that schooling sensitizes children to the abstract, categorical meanings of words, in addition to building up their general knowledge.

2. *Spatio-temporal memory.* A meticulous study by Daniel Wagner suggested that children who attend school gain memory—enhancing skills (Wagner, 1974). His methods replicated those of Hagen, Meacham, and Mesibov (1970), who had demonstrated a marked increase in children's ability to remember the locations of cards after they reached middle childhood. But was this increase a result of universal maturational changes or participation in IPBS? To find out, Wagner also conducted his study among educated and uneducated Maya in the Yucatan, where the amount of schooling available to children varied from 0 to 16 years depending up whether or not the government had built a school with 3, 6, 9, 12, or 16 years of instruction available in the locale where they live. Wagner asked a large number of people varying in age from 6 years to adulthood who had experienced

different levels of schooling to recall the positions of picture cards laid out in a linear array. The items pictured on the cards were taken from a popular local version of bingo called *lotería,* which uses pictures instead of numbers, so Wagner could be certain that all the pictures were familiar to all of his subjects. On repeated trials, each of seven cards was displayed for two seconds and then turned face down. As soon as all seven cards had been presented, a duplicate of a picture on one of the cards was shown and people had to point to the position where they thought its twin was located. By selecting different duplicate pictures, Wagner in effect manipulated the length of time between the first presentation of a picture and the moment it was to be recalled.

Wagner found that the performance of children who were attending school improved with age, just as in the earlier study by Hagen and his colleagues. However, older children and adults who did not attend school remembered no better than young children, leading Wagner to conclude that it was schooling that made the difference. Additional analyses of the data revealed that those who attended school systematically rehearsed the items as they were presented leading to the improvement in their performance.

3. *Metacognitive skills.* Schooling appears to influence the ability to reflect on and talk about one's own thought processes (Rogoff, 2003; Tulviste, 1991). When children have been asked to explain how they arrived at the answer to a logical problem or what they did to make themselves remember something, those who have not attended school are likely to say something like "I did what my sense told me" or to offer no explanation at all. Schoolchildren, on the other hand, are likely to talk about the mental activities and logic that underlie their responses. The same results apply to metalinguistic knowledge. Scribner and Cole (1981) asked schooled and unschooled Vai people in Liberia to judge the grammatical correctness of several sentences spoken in Vai. Some of the sentences were grammatical, some not. Education had no effect on the interviewees' ability to identify the ungrammatical sentences; but schooled people could generally explain just what it was about a sentence that made it ungrammatical, whereas unschooled people could not.

Questioning the Evidence

Although these findings are typical, there are serious reasons to doubt that differences obtained with standard psychological testing methods provide evidence for *generalized* changes in classical categories of cognitive functioning. For example, it is not plausible to believe that word meaning fails to develop among children who have not attended school. Nonliterate Mayan farmers studied by Sharp and his colleagues (1973) knew perfectly well that ducks are a kind of fowl. Although they did not refer to this fact in the artificial circumstances of the free-association task, they readily displayed awareness of it when they talked about the kinds of animals their families kept and the prices brought by different categories at the market. Similarly, in studies of the development of memory, when materials to be remembered were part of a locally meaningful setting, such as a folk story or by placing objects in a diorama of the subjects' town, the effects of schooling on memory performance disappear (Mandler, Scribner, Cole, & De Forest, 1980; Rogoff & Waddell, 1982). Consequently, demonstrations of the impact of schooling using more-or-less standard cognitive tasks imported from Euro-American psychological traditions led some to conclude that when schooling appeared to induce new cognitive abilities, it might well be because the entire structure of standardized testing procedures served as a covert model of schooling practices (Rogoff, 1981; Sharp, Cole, & Lave, 1973). It was noted that virtually all of the experimental tasks used in such research, modified or not, bear a strong resemblance to the tasks children encounter in school, but bear little or no relation to the structure of the intellectual demands they face outside of school.

The logic of this sort of comparative work appeared to demand the identification of tasks that schooled and unschooled children from the same town encounter with equal frequency, followed by a demonstration that children who go to school solve such tasks in more sophisticated ways than their nonschooled peers and that these are tied specifically to their schooling. Failure to find tasks of equal familiarity, in effect, meant that we were treating psychological tasks as neutral with respect to their contexts of use, when this was patently false. But identifying cognitive tasks in everyday life circumstances not constructed by the research is a problematic undertaking (Cole, 1996).

At the same time, the finding of school/nonschool differences on more or less standard psychological tasks, if treated as specific forms of skill acquisition, does not mean that schooling exerts no significant impact on children. First, as many have noted, schools are places where children's activity is mediated through print, adding not only a new mode of representation to the child's repertoire, but also introducing a whole new mode of discourse (Olson, 1994) that clearly has counterparts in everyday life. At a minimum, it seems certain that practice in representing language using writing symbols improves children's and adults' ability to analyze the sound structure and grammar of their language (Morais & Kolinsky, 2001), a finding that Peter Bryant and his colleagues have made good use of in the design of programs for the teaching of reading (Bryant, 1995; Bryant & Nunes, 1998).

Support for the view that acquiring literacy in school leads to long-term, but highly language specific, consequences has been carried out by Aleandre Castro-Caldas, Feggy Ostrosky, Alfredo Ardila, their colleagues, and others (see, for example, Ardila, Rosselli, & Puente, 1994; Castro-Caldas, 2004; Ostrosky et al., 1986). These studies contrast the brain morphology and functions of people who have or have not been to school with those of nonschooled people. Collectively, they have involved a variety of populations ranging from cases in cultural practices in a Portuguese study where older girls being kept at home while second-borns went to school and both were tested decades later, to cross-sectional studies of adults who had experienced various levels of education and come from different parts of the same country. Their testing methods were heavily grouped around functions where the impact of cultural practice and plausible brain regions could be identified, for example, those mediated by print in some fashion. They used functional magnetic resonance imaging (fMRI), magneticoenchephelogray (MEG) and positron emission tomography (PET) scans to identify areas of brain activity.

Castro-Caldes (2004) summarizes the results as follows:

Results concerning visual processing, cross-modal operations (audiovisual and visuotactile), and interhemispheric crossing of information are reported. Studies with magnetoencephalography, with positron emission tomography, and with functional magnetic resonance provided evidence that the absence of school attendance at the usual age constitutes a handicap for the development of certain biological processes that serve behavioral functioning. Differences between groups of literate and illiterate subjects were found in several areas: while dealing with phonology a complex pattern of brain activation was only present in literate subjects; the corpus callosum in the segment where the parietal lobe fibres cross was thinner in the illiterate group; the parietal lobe processing of both hemispheres was different between groups; and the occipital lobe processed information more slowly in cases that learned to read as adults compared to those that learned at the usual age. (2004, p. 7)

Taken individually, various of these studies could be faulted in terms of the extent to which the comparison groups not chosen at random, a problem in all such comparative work (Cole & Means, 1981). Taken as an ensemble, they lead Castro-Caldas to conclude that it is possible to identify brain structures that can be identified with the functions of reading and writing, both from the functional and from the anatomical points of view.

These effects, while not necessarily trivial, do not indicate that education produces any general influence on children's mental processes that can be considered superior to the kind of enculturation that has existed in all societies throughout human history.

Intergenerational Studies of the Impact of Schooling.   As noted above, the difficulty with cross-sectional studies comparing schooled and nonschooled people is that the logic of comparison requires that we identify situations equally experienced by both groups, with the cognitive skills and modes of discourse (such as those learned in elementary school) finding application outside of school. Although they did not pursue this issue, Sharp and his colleagues (1979) suggested an answer that has been followed up subsequently in their monograph on the consequences of education in the Yucatan:

. . . the information-processing skills which school attendance seems to foster could be useful in a variety of tasks demanded by modern states, including clerical and management skills in bureaucratic enterprises, or the lower-level skills of record keeping in an agricultural cooperative or a well-baby clinic. (Sharp et al., 1979, p. 84)

In recent decades, Robert LeVine and his colleagues pursued this path in a program of research that provides convincing evidence of the cognitive and social consequences of schooling. These researchers focused on the ways in which formal schooling changes the behavior of mothers toward their offspring and their interactions with people in modern, bureaucratic institutions, as well as the subsequent impacts on their children (LeVine et al., 2001; LeVine & White, 1986). These researchers propose a set of plausible habits, preferences, and skills that children acquire in school which they retain into adulthood and apply in the course of raising their own children. Raising one's children can reasonably be considered a task with many cognitive elements that is common to schooled and nonschooled adults. These changes in parenting behavior include, in addition to use of rudimentary literacy and numeracy skills:

- Discourse skills involved using written texts for purposes of understanding and using oral communication that is directly relevant to the negotiation of interactions in health and educational settings involving their children.
- Models of teaching and learning based on the scripted activities and authority structures of schooling, such that when in subordinate positions schooled women adopt and employ behaviors appropriate to the student role and, when in superordinate positions, adopt behaviors appropriate to the teacher role.
- An ability and willingness to acquire and accept information from the mass media, such as following health prescriptions more obediently.

As a consequence of these changes in the maternal behavior of young women who have attended school at least through elementary school, LeVine and his colleagues find that the children of women who have attended elementary school experience a lower level of infant mortality, better health during childhood, and greater academic achievement. Hence, while schooling may or may not produced measurable cognitive affects at the time, such experience does produce context-specific changes in behavior that has quite general consequences with respect to the task of child rearing, which in turn produces general consequences in the next generation.

The work of these researchers has been supported by direct observations of the teaching styles of Mayan mothers who have, or have not, been to school. Pablo Chava-jay and Barbara Rogoff found that mothers who had experienced 12 years of schooling used school-like teaching styles when asked to teach their young children to complete a puzzle, while those with 0 to 2 years of schooling participated *with* their children in completing the puzzle and did not explicitly teach them (Chavajay & Rogoff, 2002). There is, of course, nothing inherently wrong with the unschooled mothers' teaching style, but it does not prepare their children well for schools, which rely heavily on the recitation script as the mode of instruction.

In sum, when the effects on health-related behaviors that affect the child's biological well-being are combined with changes in maternal ability to use modern social welfare institutions and to adopt new ways of interacting with their children, the effects of schooling appear to go well beyond "cognitive effects" to become general in the society.

Ontogeny

When we come to the question of the ontogeny of culture and cognitive development against the background of evidence concerning hominization, primatology, and cultural history, several basic points stand out. First, the development of human beings at the beginning of the twenty-first century is but the most recent manifestation of a variety of life processes that at a minimum trace their origins back several million years (assuming that we begin with consideration of the common ancestor of *homo sapiens sapiens* and the great apes).

Second, cultural resources and constraints have co-evolved with the biological structure of *homo sapiens* "from the beginning." Culture is, quite literally, a phylogenetic property of human beings.

Third, while biological changes may have been minimal in the "eyeblink" of phylogenetic time separating the Paleolithic period from the twenty-first century, cultural historical change, driven in significant measure by the invention and deployment of cultural artifacts, especially externalized symbol systems, has markedly increased the complexity and power of the human cultural tool kit, thereby changing the conditions of ontogenetic (and particularly) cognitive development in ways that re-configure phylogeny-ontogeny relations.

Fourth, claims for marked discontinuities between human beings and near neighbors among the great apes must be tempered in comparison with views that ascribe entirely unique cultural and cognitive processes to human beings.

Unfortunately, while these points are currently receiving wide acceptance, research that incorporates them into the study of human ontogeny is relatively sparse and concentrated within a few parts of the vast domain of culture and cognitive development. Overall, research on cognitive development in recent years has tended to focus on younger and younger age groups so that, for example, middle childhood, which received the lion's share of attention 20 years ago is sparsely represented in contemporary research, while the opposite situation holds for infancy (see also Kuhn & Franklin, Chapter 15, this volume). At the same time, research on infancy that considers cultural influences is more likely to be concentrated on socioemotional and physical than cognitive development, particularly research that uses cross-cultural methods. Even in cases where the same topic (e.g., the development of concept formation or memory) continues to yield new evidence, psychologists' theoretical preferences and the specific methods they use to gather evidence have changed, so that it is not possible to report the results of further research on topics formulated at an earlier period. These circumstances restrict the relevant data upon which I can draw to summarize research conducted in recent years.

I have adopted two strategies in response to these difficulties. First, at certain points, I summarize culture-development relationships that spill beyond the cognitive domain, narrowly conceived, but which illustrate phylogeny-culture-ontogeny relationships with clear implications for cognitive development. Second, when dealing with cultural variations and cognitive development, I concentrate my attention on two areas of research where there has been relatively dense interest and hence a good deal of new data—conceptual development and autobiographical memory. Current research on conceptual development is particularly rich in implications for the intertwining of phylogenetic and cultural constraints in cognitive development. Autobiographical memory, by contrast, connects the study of cognitive development to presumed society-wide contrasts in broad cultural themes, thereby making contact with both earlier and contemporary research on culture and cognitive styles.

THE PROXIMAL LOCUS OF DEVELOPMENT: ACTIVITY SETTINGS AND CULTURAL PRACTICES

An important lesson from the primate literature on the process of acquiring culture is that the young must be in close enough proximity to older members of the community who engage in commonly patterned forms of behavior to acquire those patterns during postnatal development. Human beings are, of course, notable for the fact that their young are born in an extremely immature state and require many years of extraordinary support from their parents and community to survive into adulthood and acquire the cultural knowledge necessary for the social reproduction of the group (Bogin, 2001; Bruner, 1966).

As noted earlier, developmentalists who study cultural and development have highlighted the fact that the arrangements made in all societies to support the postnatal development of young children be conceived of as a "developmental niche" that merges practices to support physical care with parental beliefs about future requirements. This emergent sociocultural system, or "developmental niche" as Super (1987) commented, implies that "environments have their own structure and internal rules of operation, and thus, . . . what the environment contributes to development is not only isolated, unidimensional pushes and pulls but also structure" (p. 5).

Moreover, the nature of this niche within societies changes with the age of the child. Whiting and Edwards (1988), following Mead (1935), early on suggested a periodization of childhood that corresponded with the physical constraints on children's behavior. She referred to early infancy as the period of the "lap" child, the period between 2- to 3-years as the "knee child," who are kept close at hand but not continuously on the mother's lap or in a crib; 4- to 5-year-olds are referred to as "yard children," because they can leave their mothers' sides but are not allowed to wander far. In many modern, industrialized countries, children between 3 and 5 to 6 years of age spend part of every day in an environment designed to prepare them for school, which has led this time of life to be called the preschool period, after which they become neighborhood children, free to roam, but not beyond the confines of the community.

Cultural differences in the organization of children's developmental niches are almost certainly more variable than the physical environments in which they live. So, for example, infants among the Aka foragers in the Central African Republic are held by their parents while the parents' hunt, butcher, and share game (Hewlett, 1992). Quechua infants high in the Andes spend their early months wrapped in layers of woolen cloth strapped to their mothers' backs that forms a "*manchua* pouch" in order to survive the exceedingly cold, thin, dry air surrounding them, greatly restricting their vision and movement. Ache infants living in the rain forests of eastern Paraguay spend 80% to 100% of their time in physical contact with their parents and are almost never more than 3 feet away because this hunter-gatherer group does not make permanent camps in the forest, but only clear a space adequate that has stumps and roots remaining that are hazardous for the children (Kaplan & Dove, 1987). Contrast these niches with those of American children with their own bedroom and play areas, time spent in daycare or preschool among many children the same age and one or two stranger-caretakers, while *Sesame Street* is playing on the television; or other American children living two families to a room in a crowded slum, reality TV playing on the television, and single, unemployed mothers trying to keep order and their sanity. The range of developmental niches in contemporary human development is clearly obvious.

As a number of researchers have pointed out, these variations in developmental niches create a variety of experiential patterns that make it difficult to reduce them to a single dimension, although clusters of attributes are discernable. For example, according to Morelli and her colleagues, the Efe of the Democratic Republic of Congo (formerly Zaire) live in small groups of one or more extended families who forage with bow and arrow and work for members of nearby farm communities. Children are free to wander where they wish around their small camp to watch adults making tools, cook, and are allowed to entertain themselves; they may enter, uninvited into most huts. From the age of at least three they accompany their parents to gather food, collect firewood, and work in gardens. Although they were only 2 to 4 years of age, Efe children were at least present when adults were working in 74 of the observations periods and participated in specialized child-focused activities by adults only 5% of the time. A similar pattern was observed in San Pedro, an agricultural town in Guatemala, where people engage in agriculture and small business, family sizes are larger, the total number of the community members is far greater, and older children spend part of their time in school (Morelli, Rogoff, & Angellilo, 2003).

As different as they are from each other, these two communities exhibited relatively similar patterns of adult arrangement of 2- to 4-year-old children's activities in many ways. In contrast with two middle-class communities in the United States (one in Utah and one in Massachusetts, so they also differed in many ways) children were present when adults were engaged in work only during 30% of the observations. When Efe and San Pedro children were observed playing by themselves, their play almost always consisted of emulation of adult activities, but the play of the American children rarely emulated that of adult activities. In the two American samples, children were often engaged by adults in specialized child-focused activities including lessons or play that often mimicked schooling. The American adults also engaged their young children as conversational partners on child-focused topics in approximately 15% of the interactions observed, a category that was very rare in either of the other two communities.

Those engaged in the study of children's development in the activity settings they inhabit in nonindustrialized societies have accrued a variety of evidence to show that such children develop a special proclivity or ability for learning through keen observation, although it is not entirely clear if such skills involve higher order forms of imitation, motivation to emulate others, or some combination of such factors. For example, Bloch (1989) reports that Senegalese children 2 to 6 years of age observed other people more than twice as much as European-American children in the same age-range. Rogoff et al. (1993) and Chavajay and Rogoff (1999) found that Guatemalan Mayan mothers and toddlers were more likely than middle-class European-American counterparts to attend simultaneously to several ongoing events, a practice that, they argue, supports learning by observing.

Rogoff and her colleagues (Rogoff, Paradise, Arauz, Correa-Chavez, & Angelillo, 2003) include observational learning in their notion of "intent participation," in which keen observation is motivated by the expectation that at a later time, the observer will be responsible for the action in question. Intent participation may involve more experienced participants facilitating a learner's participation and participating along with the learner, or it may involve direct verbal instruction (Maynard, 2002). But it does place a heavy role on observation relative to verbal instruction of the sort characteristic of developmental processes that are prominent in formal schooling. A variety of studies indicate that intent participation is a special form of learning by observation and contributing to ongoing activities that has cultural roots.

For example, Mejia-Arauz, Rogoff, and Paradise (2005) arranged for Mexican- and European-heritage children whose parents had either a relatively high or low level of education to observe an "Origami lady" make two origami figures, after which they made figures of their own to keep. They found that all the children keenly observed the Origami lady's demonstration, but the children whose parents had little education completed their own origami figures without asking for further information while those whose parents had experienced more education were likely to ask for help.

I will not repeat here the material on the influences of schooling, which I sketched out in the earlier section on cultural-historically organized forms of activity. Suffice it to say that in study after study mothers who have experienced higher levels of schooling are more likely to organize children's activities in ways that place less emphasis on intent participation and more emphasis on verbal explanation. Clearly, both the content of what children gain deep knowledge about and the way they attain that knowledge are influenced by the range of activities that adults arrange for them and the way that those activities are carried out. Further, these contents and ranges are strongly affected by the physical and social ecology of the groups in question.

THE INTERTWINING OF BIOLOGY AND CULTURAL PRACTICES IN CONCEPTUAL DEVELOPMENT

For many years the dominant line of cross-cultural research employed tasks in which children of different ages and backgrounds were presented sets of objects or drawings that could be classified along various dimensions (color, form, number, function, taxonomic category were most frequently studied). (See Cole & Scribner, 1974; Laboratory of Comparative Human Cognition, 1983 for reviews.)

During the past 2 decades, this line of work has withered away, in part because the evidence seemed to indicate that there are a number of difficult-to-pin-down factors closely associated with the particular stimuli and experimental procedures used that differentially influenced the performance of schooled and nonschooled populations in uncontrolled and uninterpretable ways, and in part because the general approach to concept development it represented fell from favor. One of the new lines of research that arose to take its place focused on the *categorization of natural kinds.* Categorization of natural kinds was presumed to be constrained to a great extent by phylogenetically based cognitive predispositions. In addition, inductive judgments about new instances rather than sorting by similarity became the essential criterion of categorical knowledge (see Gelman & Kalish, Chapter 9, this volume; R. Gelman & Williams, 1998, for relevant reviews).

The concepts that have been featured in this recent work are often identified with cognitive domains, where *domain* is defined as "a body of knowledge that identifies and interprets a class of phenomena assumed to share certain properties and to be of a distinct and general type" (Hirschfeld & Gelman, 1994, p. 21). Current disagreements focus on what these initial constraints are and how they limit or shape the role of experience (including culturally organized experience) in conceptual development. (See Gelman and Kalish, Chapter 9, this volume, for a more extensive account focused on ontogenetic change.)

Many developmentalists are currently convinced of the existence of domain-specific, biological constraints on conceptual development that constitute "core" or "privileged" domains of knowledge, where biological constraints may provide "skeletal principles" that constrain how developing children's attend to relevant features of the domain, but are not entirely encapsulated; rather, they require the infusion of cultural input and continued learning to develop past a rudimentary starting point (Baillargeon, 2004; Chen & Siegler, 2000; Gelman & Kalish, this volume; R. Gelman & Lucariello, 2002; Hatano, 1997). Various investigators differ from each other in precisely how to construe the role of environmental factors and the ways in which phylogenetic and environmental factors combine to produce development. Among those who argue for the combined roles of biological constraints and culturally organized experience in concept development believe that environmental contingencies not dissimilar to those proposed by S-R theorists of earlier generations are essential (Elman et al., 1996), while others argue that domain-general cognitive mechanisms such as analogizing are key mechanisms in moving beyond initial states to more mature forms of conceptual thought (Springer, 1999).[4]

To further complicate matters, it appears plausible that the degree to which "highly specific innate constraints + minimal experience," versus "skeletal constraints + a good deal of culturally organized experience," are needed to account for development may differ with the domain in question. For example, in the domain of physics it appears that

---

[4] As Gelman and Kalish (Chapter 9, this volume) point out, even those who deny the need to posit strong phylogenetic, domain-specific constraints, assume that phylogenetic factors play a role in cognitive development, including concept formation; the disagreements center on how to characterize those phylogenetic constraints and the extent to which they are domain specific.

within months after birth children have some grasp of at least a few very basic physical principles, including expectations that two objects cannot occupy the same location at the same time or cannot pass through physical obstructions (Spelke, 1994). As a result, of such findings, Spelke has argued that knowledge in the domain of physics is innate, domain-specific, encompasses constraints that apply to all entities in the domain, forms the core of mature knowledge, and is task specific. Similar claims have been made for the domain of number (Feigenson, Dehaene, & Spelke, 2004), agency (Gergely, 2002; Gopnik & Meltzoff, 1997), biology (Atran, 1998) and theory of mind (Leslie, 1994), although in each case, there are others who argue for hybrid positions that include domain-general reasoning abilities (Astuti, Solomon, & Carey, 2004; Springer, 1999).

Research on the influence of the environment, particularly cultural variations in environmental influence; have not been evenly distributed across the full range of conceptual domains that have preoccupied developmentalists. For example, there is apparently no research on cultural differences in the development of naïve physics, although even those who favor strong nativist claims have an interest in determining whether development beyond initial, core, principles does in fact continue to adhere to the initial constraints they hypothesize on the basis of research with very young infants. There is, however, some cross-cultural research in the domain of number (the work of Saxe reviewed earlier with respect to cultural-historical change is relevant in this regard), and there is a good deal of research on the domains of psychology and biology. Consequently, I focus my review largely on these three domains.

Number

In recent decades, there has been a good deal of evidence accumulated for elementary numerical abilities involving small quantities, including counting, addition, and subtraction in both very young human infants and in primates, although there is controversy about the precise processes involved (Boysen & Hallberg, 2000; R. Gelman & Gallistel, 2004; Hauser & Carey, 1998). For example, R. Gelman and Williams (1998) conclude that the pattern of errors evidenced by young infants asked to perform numerical operations on set sizes of three or less objects may indicate the presence of a "common preverbal counting mechanism similar to the one used in animals" (p. 588). Hauser and Carey (1998) go somewhat further, concluding that:

Early primate evolution (and probably earlier), and early in the conceptual history of children, several of the building blocks for a representation of number are firmly in place. [These include] criteria for individuation and numerical identity (the sortal object, more specific sortals like cup and carrot, and quantifiers such as one and another). Furthermore, there are conceptual abilities . . . such as the capacity to construct one to one correspondence and the capacity to represent serial order relations. (p. 82)

Studies of numerical reasoning in early childhood indicate that it builds upon these early starting conditions in an orderly fashion. Thus, for example, Zur and Gelman (2004) report that when 3-year-olds who had not attended preschool viewed the addition or subtraction of N objects from a known number and were asked to predict the answer and then check their prediction, they provided reasonable cardinal values as predictions and accurate counting procedures to test their predictions. Such rapid learning in the absence of explicit instruction, Zur and Gelman argue, supports the idea that there are "skeletal mental structures that expedite the assimilation and use of domain-relevant knowledge (p. 135)." Data such as these, despite uncertainties about mechanism, support the argument for number reasoning as a core domain, and hence a human universal.

Evidence from number development in other cultures, however, appears, at least at first glance, to cast doubt on the universality of elementary number reasoning and leaves little doubt that Hatano and Inagaki (2002) are correct in arguing that because innately specified knowledge is still skeletal, it is essential to study the ways in which cultural experience interacts with phylogenetic constraints to produce adult forms of numerical reasoning.

To begin with, there are a good many societies in the world that appear to have at most a few count words on the order of "one, two, many" (Gordon, 2004; Pica, Lemer, Izard, & Dehaene, 2004). While no research has been conducted with infants in such societies using procedures comparable to those used by modularity and core-domain theorists, it is not clear how such an impoverished system could be considered evidence of a universal set of numerical knowledge. R. Gelman and Williams (1998) argue that this appearance may be deceiving. They cite evidence from a South African hunter-gatherer group which has only two numerical lexemes but report that this does not stop them, for example, from counting to ten by using the additional operation to generate successively larger cardinal numbers, so that the word corresponding to eight translates as 2+2+2+2. However, Gordon (2004) has recently reported that while Pirahã adults living in a remote area of the Amazon jungle display elementary arithmetic abilities for very small arrays, their performance quickly deteriorates with larger numbers. But Pirahã children who learn Portuguese number words do not display the same limitations as their parents. Similar results are reported for another Amazonian group (Pica et al., 2004). While the presence of number reasoning beyond the level achieved by some nonhuman primates and infants may be in doubt for some hunter-gather groups, this same evidence underscores how important cultural influences are for the elaboration of core numerical knowledge. A key factor appears to be the appearance of lexicalized arithmetic knowledge when economic activities begin to produce sufficient surplus to necessitate recordkeeping and trade. Recall that traditional Oksapmin number practices appear to have been at the very beginnings of such reasoning because, according to Saxe (1981), small amounts were traded and one-to-one correspondence often sufficed as a mechanism to mediate exchange.

Taking an example from two societies, both of which engaged in agricultural production, Jill Posner (1982) compared children from two neighboring groups in the Ivory Coast. The first she characterized as farmers using primitive agricultural methods to eek out a subsistence living; the second also farmed, but in addition engaged in trades such as tailoring and peddling which required frequent participation in the money economy. The children in both groups displayed knowledge of relative quantity, a skeletal principle, but the children from the subsistence farming group displayed far weaker counting skills and calculation skills than those from the group with more involvement in the money economy, a difference that was compensated for by schooling.

Overall, the research on development in the domain of number provides strong support for the "core domain plus cultural practice" perspective proposed by Hatano and Inagaki (2002). (See also the discussion of cognitive development in the chapter by Shweder et al., 2006, and the position adopted by Gelman and Kalish, Chapter 1, in this volume, although they do not speak of culture as the source of empirical input.)

Research in two other domains where there is greater disagreement about their status as core domains and the experiential factors that may affect development offer a more challenging picture in which phylogenetic and cultural contributions to development may not dovetail so neatly.

Naïve Psychology and Theory of Mind

As applied to humans, the term, *theory of mind* "refers to the tendency to construe people in terms of their mental states and traits" (Lillard & Skibbe, 2004). It is referred to as a theory because people use these inferences based on invisible entities (desire, beliefs, thoughts, emotion) to guide their action, and to predict the behaviors of others.

As indicated in the earlier section on chimpanzee cognition, Tomasello and Rakoczy's (2003) assertion that there is no evidence that chimpanzees or bonobos can think about the beliefs of others can stand as an agreed-on point of differentiation because there is no doubt that human children growing up in industrialized countries where the requisite research has been done to develop a "belief-desire" psychology of mind by about 4 years of age. The question then becomes one of whether this ability is universal in both its timing and nature. Again, because the role of culture on the ontogenetic course of theory of mind is extensively reviewed by Harris (2006). I confine myself to summarizing his thorough treatment in order to maintain continuity in the present discussion.

To begin with, research conducted in industrialized countries indicates that in the transition from infancy to early childhood, and all during early childhood, children gain a more comprehensive idea about how other peoples' desires and beliefs are related to how they act in the world. Even at the age of 2, children are able to distinguish between their own desires and those of others. From studies of American children's spontaneous speech in a wide variety of settings, it has been established that by the age of 2 years, children are already capable of using terms such as "*want*" and "*like*" correctly (Wellman, Phillips, & Rodriguez, 2000; Wellman & Woolley, 1990). As discussed by Harris (2006), the favorite experimental method for diagnosing the development of the ability to think about other people's beliefs and the relations of their beliefs to their actions is the "false belief" task which is presented in various ways.

By the time they are three, children can engage in deception in collaboration with an adult. As Lillard and Skibbe (2004) summarize the matter, "mentalizing abilities thus appear to begin during infancy." By the age of 5, children master the ability to reason about a false belief and mental representations in tasks that apply to others. Later, their theory grows to encompass secondary emotions such as surprise and pride.

This sequential, developmental progression of theory of mind capabilities led quickly to the suggestion that such a theory is a mental module (Leslie, 1994), which is part of the common inheritance of some nonhuman primates. Among humans, it appears to develop within a narrow age range, 3 to 5 years, and it appears to be a kind of rapid, unconscious, inference-generating device. Links between the asocial nature of autistic children and modularity are used as evidence favoring the nativist argument.

If theory of mind were modular, one would expect it to be impervious to cultural variation; it would develop on a universal time scale, much as does losing one's baby teeth. This expectation has not been tested for the full set of relevant age ranges, but there is reasonable consistency in how children deal with a key test of achieving a more adult-like form of thinking—the false-belief task.

The result has by no means yielded a forgone conclusion. There is ample evidence from cultures around the world that there is enormous variety in the extent and ways that mental states and actions are spoken about and presumably how they are conceived

(Lillard, 1998a, 1998b; Vinden, 1999, 2002). In terms of sheer number, English is at one extreme of the continuum, possessing more than 5,000 words for emotion words alone. By contrast, Howell (1984) reports that the Chewong people of Malaysia are reported to have only five terms to cover the entire range of mental processes, translated as *want, want very much, know, forget, miss,* or *remember.* Anthropologists have also reported that in many societies there is a positive avoidance of talking about other people's minds (Paul, 1995).

At present, opinion about cultural variation using locally adapted versions of theory-of-mind tasks is divided (Harris, 2006; Lillard & Skibbe, 2004). As Harris notes, ambiguities arise because people in some cultures are unlikely to talk in terms of psychological states in the head and in some cases success on the theory-of-mind tasks was absent or partial (Vinden, 1999, 2002). But was performance poor because people lacked the vocabulary or inclination, or was it that they could not describe their intuitive understanding in words?

Callaghan et al. (2005) conducted a study that sought to avoid the issue of language by using a minimally verbal procedure where it was unnecessary to use difficult-to-translate words such as belief and emotion. With two experimenters present, they hid a toy under one of three bowls. Then one experimenter left and the other induced the child to put the toy under a different bowl before asking the child to point to which bowl the first experimenter would pick up when she returned. Notice that the procedure uses language at the level of behavior (picking up a bowl) with no reference to mental terms, so the prediction that the absent experimenter would look where the toy had been when she left would be indicative of presence of ability to think about others' beliefs without using the term.

Under these conditions, a large number of children 3 to 6 years of age were tested in Canada, India, Samoa, and Peru. Performance improved with age, with 4 to 5 years of age being the point at which 50% of the children performed correctly, and 5 to 6 years of age being the point at which all the children responded correctly. Here is a case where careful standardization of the precise, same procedure conducted in such a way that performance does not depend on the ability to communicate about mental language with people who do not use such terms produces universality (in line with a modularity view). But note that this invariance taps into the most skeletal core of theory of mind behavior, devoid as it is of enrichment by the local vocabulary of any information about how the children would respond if they were asked to reason about beliefs. Thus, for example, Vinden (1999) found that while children from a variety of small-scale, low technology groups in Cameroon and New Guinea were able to understand how belief affects behavior, they had difficulty predicting an emotion based upon a false belief.

Using a different task, in which children were asked to explain the bad behavior of a story character, Lillard, Skibbe, Zeljo, and Harlan (2003) found culture, regional, and class differences in whether children attributed the behavior to an internal, psychological trait or external circumstances, a plausible element in any theory of mind a person uses to predict and interpret someone else's behavior. Lillard and her colleagues make the important point that "cultural differences are usually a matter of degrees, of different patterns and frequencies of behaviors in different cultural contexts" (p. 73), a view put forward early on by Cole et al., 1971. Children in all groups gave both kinds of responses, internal and situational; it was the frequency and patterns of use that differed. They attribute the average results in this case to language socialization practices in different communities, noting, for example, that low SES children or rural children are more likely to have parents who make situational attributions of behavior and model this form of interpretation for their children, while high SES/urban parents are more likely to use an internal model of interpretation which they embody in their interactions with their children. It has also been shown that children's theory of mind appears more rapidly if they have older siblings, who presumably provide them with extensive experience in mind reading and mind-interpreting talk (Ruffman, Perner, Naito, Parkin, & Clements, 1998).

Both universality and cultural specificity appear to characterize the development of theories of minds. Given evidence that many (but not all) elements of a human theory of mind can be found, using suitable procedures, among chimpanzees (Tomasello & Rakoczy, 2003), it should not come as a surprise that when a carefully stripped-down version of false-belief tasks are presented to people of widely different cultural backgrounds, they perform the same, while cultural variations appear when language and explanation are made part of the assessment. This pattern of results supports the idea of Hatano and Inagaki (2002) that both phylogeny and cultural history are necessary contributors to the development of an adult mode of thinking about the thoughts and situations of oneself and others.

The Biological Domain

Among the domains considered here, the possibility of a core domain of biological knowledge has generated special controversy about the degree to which biology is a core domain and the extent to which the development of biological understanding is influenced by culturally organized experience. In an influential book, Carey (1985) argued that children's understanding of biological phenomena grows out of a naïve psychology. Children interpret other living things by reference to, and by analogy with, human beings whose behavior is governed by their intentional beliefs and desires. They do not accept the idea that our bodily organs function independent of our intentions, and in so far as other entities are similar to humans, the same intentional causality should apply to them. Carey used a technique in which children are asked to judge whether a particular kind of entity shares a property with a target stimulus (if humans breathe do dogs breathe? do plants breathe? do rocks breathe?). According to her results, it is not until after the age of seven that children begin to develop a theory that treats humans as one of many kinds of living things sharing many causal principles (in particular, a mechanistic causality of bodily organs). This change gives rise to a naïve biology, which is a derivative domain.

In their work on the domain of biology, Hatano and Inagaki (2002) argued that biology is a core domain that does not arise from psychology but does use the human body as a cornerstone for interpreting other biological entities. According to their view, naïve biology uses a mode of explanation (a naïve theory) of living things in terms of their similarity to human beings (personification) and the idea that living phenomena are produced by a special form of causation, vital principle, as distinct from a purely chemical or physical force (vitalism).

This form of domain-specific reasoning is based on a three-way relationship between food/water, activeness/liveliness (actively taking in vital power from food), and growth in size or number (the ingestion of vital power produces individual growth and production of offspring). This mode of reasoning is also assumed to be universal across cultures. While the cross-cultural data are somewhat sparse, evidence in favor of this proposition has been found in Australia and North America, as well as Japan, where children exhibit such reasoning by 6 years of age (see Hatano & Inagaki, 2002, for more details).

However, Hatano and Inagaki also believe that participation in local cultural practices is important to development of biological thinking beyond the most skeletal knowledge. This kind of developmental process is illustrated by Inagaki (1990), who arranged for some 5-year-old Japanese children to raise goldfish at home while a comparison group had no such experience. The goldfish raisers soon displayed far richer knowledge about the development of fish than their counterparts who had not raised fish. They could even generalize what they had learned about fish to frogs. If asked, for example, "Can you keep the frog in its bowl forever?" they answered, "No, we can't, because frogs grow bigger. My goldfish were small before and now they are big" (quoted in Hatano & Inagaki, 2002, p. 272).

Additional evidence in favor of cultural involvement in the development of biological knowledge comes from the work of Atran and his colleagues on the growth of biological classifications. Atran (1998) once adopted the view with respect to biological categories that the taxonomy of living kinds is universal because it is a product of "an autonomous, natural classification scheme of the human mind" (p. 567). However, at present he and his colleagues acknowledge that factors such as density of experience and local ecological significance contribute to the development of biological understanding beyond early childhood (Medin, Ross, Atran, Burnett, & Blok, 2002; Ross, Medin, Coley, & Atran, 2003). Moreover, they demonstrate that biological thinking does not universally begin by using one's own body as the foundation of reasoning.

In some of their studies, Atran, Medin, and their colleagues used a version of the procedure developed by Carey. For example, the child might be shown a picture of a wolf and asked, "Now, there's this stuff called andro. Andro is found inside some kinds of things. One kind of thing that has andro inside is wolves. Now, I'm going to show you some pictures of other kinds of things, and I want you to tell me if you think they have andro inside like wolves do."

This questioning frame was then used with a number of "inferential bases" (in this case, human, wolf, bee, goldenrod, water) and a larger number of "target objects" from each of the taxonomic categories represented by the bases (e.g., raccoon, eagle, rock, bicycle) in order to see if the child believes that "andro" (or some other fictitious property) found in the base will also be found in the target object. Two questions were of primary interest: Does inference of the presence of a property ("andro") decrease as the biological similarity of the target object decreases, and do children appear to use human beings as a unique base of inference when judging biological similarity (i.e., is personification a universal feature of the development of biological classification)?

This group of researchers conducted one such study with populations they term "urban majority culture children" and "rural majority children," and rural Native American (Menominee) children between the ages of 6 to 10 years. With respect to the first question, they found, like Carey, that the urban majority children generalized on the basis of the similarity of the comparison entity to human beings. But even the youngest rural children generalized in terms of biological affinity according to adult expert taxonomies (they did not use humans as a unique foundation of their reasoning). In addition, all ages of Native American children and the older rural majority culture children manifested ecological (systems) reasoning as well; they made inferences of the relations between the entities being compared on the basis of their relationships in an ecological system, such as a pond or forest.

With respect to the second question, they found that urban children displayed a bias toward using humans as a base of comparison, but the rural children, and particularly the rural Menominee children, did not, contradicting Carey's claim of anthropomorphism as a universal characteristic of folk theories of biology. Such results show that both culture and expertise (exposure to nature) play a role in the development of biological thought. Such evidence fits well with the views of Hatano and Inagaki, as well as Geertz (1973), that culturally organized experience is essential for completing the work of phylogeny.

The same experimental paradigm was used to study the development of biological induction among Yucatec Mayan children and adults (Atran et al., 2001). Adults decreased their inductions from humans to other living kinds and then to nonliving kinds, following the pattern predicted by standard biological taxonomies. But when the bee was the base, they often made inferences of shared properties not only to other invertebrates, but to trees and humans. According to Atran et al., this pattern of inference is based on ecological reasoning: Bees build their nests in trees and bees are sought after by humans for their honey. Adults often explicitly used such ecological justifications in their responses.

Most important with respect to the issue of cultural influences on development, the Yucatec children's responses were very similar to those of adults. Whatever the base concept, inductive inferences decrease as the target moves from mammals to trees. And, like Yucatec adults, the children showed no indication of personification: Inferences from humans did not differ from inferences beginning with animals or trees and they did not appear to favor humans as a basis of inference. If anything, the children preferred dogs as a basis of inference, perhaps based on their affection for and familiarity with this common household pet. Again, the evidence speaks to the importance of culturally organized experience in the development of inferences in the domain of biology.

A recent, extensive, and instructive study of phylogenetic and cultural influences on the development of biological understanding comes from a series of studies conducted in Madagascar by Rita Astuti and her colleagues (2004). Astuti and her colleagues assert that a core domain of biological knowledge should include concepts of birth, birth parent, biological inheritance, and innate potential. As these authors point out, claims for a core domain of biology are contentious. For example, evidence in favor of a core domain of biology comes from evidence obtained from preschool children, not infants. And cross-cultural evidence from North American and Nigerian children indicated that before the age of 7 to 9 years of age, children would not agree that if a raccoon (in the American case) gave birth to a certain animal and that this animal then gave birth to more raccoons, then the newborn animal was a raccoon, even if it looked like and acted like a skunk (Keil, 1989). Madagascar is a strategically interesting place to study biological understanding because it is one of the places in the world where people emphasize the importance of postnatal experience in determining kinship and similarity among people. For example, when adults are asked why some babies appear or behave as they do, they give reasons such as "the mother spent a lot of time with a person who looks just like the baby" or that the baby was tampered with by a wandering spirit. Consequently, according to Astuti and her colleagues, it is difficult, from a Malagasy point of view, to differentiate between the baby as a biological organism and the baby as a social being.

These researchers carried out studies among three groups of people. The first two groups were the Vezo, who live on the coast and make their livelihood as fishermen, and the Masikoro who live inland, farm, and raise cattle. Both of these groups are ethnically Malagasy, having arrived on the island a thousand or more years ago. They share traditional religious beliefs, a form of "ancestor worship," as well as a common language. The third group, the Karany, are descendents of Indo-Pakistani immigrants who are town dwellers; they are generally shopkeepers and moneylenders who are relatively wealthy and well educated. At birth, Vezo and Masikoro babies are indistinguishable, but Karany babies are easily distinguished by their lighter skin and straighter hair. The major questions were whether people of different ages would attribute similarities between a child and its parents to biological inheritance or social circumstances. Comparisons were made when the birth and adopted parents were from the same group, or one of the other two groups. Three types of traits were queried: bodily traits (e.g., wide feet or narrow feet), beliefs (do cows have strong teeth than horses), and skills (knows how to be a carpenter or a mechanic). The specific questions differed depending on whether the adoptive and birth parents were from the same or a different group in order to tease out conditions under which biological or social inference modes would display themselves.

When Vezo adults answered questions about the babies' bodily characteristics, they overwhelmingly chose biological inheritance as the crucial factor. When asked about what social group the child would belong to, the children were judged to be members of the groups into which they were adopted, whether Masikoro or Karany—group identity depends on what people do, not who their parents were. When asked about beliefs and skills, they again selected the adoptive parents' group as the one's the child would acquire.

In two follow-up studies, Astuti and her colleagues presented the same task to groups of children (6- to 13-years-old) and youth (17- to 20-year-olds). Contrary to the adults, the children were likely to say that the children's bodily characteristics, beliefs, and skills would all be determined primarily by their adoptive parents. The adolescents were most likely to follow the adult pattern, ascribing bodily characteristics to birth parents while beliefs and skills were more like the adult pattern that ascribed bodily characteristics to biology while beliefs and skills were ascribed to cultural experience.

In a final study, children and adults were asked to make judgments about properties of baby birds that were adopted into a new mother bird. In this case, both adults and children ascribed the characteristics of the birds to their birth parents and gave biological inheritance reasons for doing so.

There are many other interesting findings in this set of studies, but for present purposes they raise two key issues. First, under some conditions (e.g., when reasoning about birds) young Malagasy children, like young children in Tokyo or Boston appear to understand basic biological principles of inheritance. Second, when reasoning about humans, Malagasy adults show that they understand these laws of inheritance, but in their everyday lives, they staunchly deny their significance.

Such results greatly complicate conclusions one can draw about biology as a core domain. While it seems reasonable to conclude that understanding of basic biological principles is universal when probed in an appropriate manner, it is difficult to understand how adults can elaborate a complex set of cultural beliefs, which have great force in people's everyday lives, that contradict this same core biological knowledge. That Malagasy children should be slow to acquire the (universal) adult system of core biological understanding is easy enough to understand: They are constantly exposed to adults whose interpretations of their everyday experience deny principles of naïve biology. But how does it come about that adults acquire that same knowledge while at the same time acquiring the cultural knowledge about kinship, ancestors, and sources of group similarity that contradict the skeletal principles of the core domain?

There is clearly more to the organization of culturally organized belief and action than is captured by evidence of a core domain of biology. Astuti and her colleagues suggest that because the highest value of Malagasy society is to reach old age surrounded by a vast number of descendents, Malagasy systematically de-value and de-emphasize biological ties in favor of social ties that make children the descendants of the entire village, not the birth parents alone. Whatever the case, the effect of this research is to emphasize the complex interweaving of biological constraints and cultural practices on the development of reasoning.

BEYOND CORE DOMAINS

As R. Gelman and Lucariello (2002) note, a great deal of knowledge that children must master does not fall within any recognized core domain. With respect to objects in the world, a major class of such objects is the class of artifacts, which I defined earlier as aspects of the material world that have been transformed in order to carry out some goal-directed human action.

Ample evidence indicates that American children differentiate between artifacts and natural objects at an early age, although the conditions under which they differentiate these two categories of objects may vary (Keil, 1989; Kemler Nelson, Frankenfield, Morris, & Blair, 2000). For example, when children were told that an item was a kind of food and taught a name for it and then were shown a novel item and told it was a kind of food, they generalized the name they had learned on the basis of color. However, if they were told that the original object was a tool and the new object a tool, they generalized the name for it based on its shape. Another line of evidence for differentiation of artifacts and natural kinds comes from, among other places, studies in which the object in question undergoes a transformation of some kind and the child is asked whether or not it is the same or a different object, and why. If, for example, a young child is told about a goat that has had its horns removed and its hair curled and been trained to say "baaah baaaah" like a sheep, and is shown a picture of this transformed animal, very young children will maintain that it remains a goat because its insides haven't changed. Children assume there is something essential about the goat that cannot be changed by changing its external appearance (S. A. Gelman & Opfer, 2002). This is the sort of response we would expect given the data on the development of knowledge in core domains, such as biology. Moreover, it is also well established that very early in life, children distinguish animate and inanimate objects, a central criterion distinguishing natural and artificial kinds.

When it comes to categorizing artificial objects, resorting to essential, inner properties as an indicator of an object's category membership no longer holds. A coin that is melted down and made into an ice pick no longer remains a coin. Faced with such transformations, young children are unlikely to say that the object retains its identity. Consequently, interest has focused on the criteria that children use to judge whether two artificial objects belong to the same category or not. Some believe that before the age of 3 to 4 years, most children categorize such objects according to a perceptual criterion: how similar do they look (in particular, whether they are the same shape or the same color).

According to this view, at about 4 years of age, the criterion changes to one of function, which is the criterion ordinarily used by adults, since by definition, an artifact is an object designed to achieve some goal. However, under some conditions, American children as young as 2 have been shown to generalize names learned for one artifact to another of the same function (e.g., two dissimilar looking objects that both functioned as a hinge; Kemler Nelson et al., 2000) and reasoning based on categories of artifacts continues to develop over childhood and probably beyond (R. Gelman & Lucariello, 2002).

As Keil (2003, p. 369) comments, "most people seem to live in worlds of the artificial," which immediately poses a problem. While people may be able to make inferences about function from observing someone using an artifact and making inferences about their intentions, there appear to be no straightforward, domain-specific "core principles" that will help them draw proper inferences about the categories of artifacts involved and the functions they fulfill.

Within the framework presented here, as indicated above, formal instruction is a subset of the general category of historically evolved cultural practices. Consequently, the constraints that arise from the patterned forms of interaction that structure a great variety of cultural activities may serve to enable concept formation in noncore domains. Unfortunately, to date, relatively little developmental research has been conducted with these issues in mind although some relevant research can be gleaned from what has come to be known as the study of "everyday cognition" (Rogoff & Lave, 1984; Schliemann, Carraher, & Ceci, 1997). The acquisition of concepts involved in learning to weave provides one example.

I have already presented some information about the acquisition of weaving in Zinacantan in considering research that integrates the study of cultural history and ontogenetic development. Here I return to a portion of that research project, headed by Patricia Greenfield, which focuses on contemporary cultural practices involved in weaving. These practices involve a number of artifacts including the production and dying of thread, the backstrap loom and its constituents (e.g., the warping frame), dowels that hold threads in place, and so on.

Whereas previously I highlighted different forms of interpersonal interaction involved in the organization of learning to weave, over recent decades and changes in the products of weaving, here the focus changes to the closely related issue of the organization of the artifacts provided children at different ages and the way in which they reveal an implicit, indigenous theory of how to promote knowledge of the functions of the artifacts and skills in their use during ontogeny. What makes this story especially interesting is that the implicit ethnotheory embodied in the artifacts and their deployment is well aligned with a Piagetian stage theory of cognitive development.

Maynard and her colleagues (Maynard, 2002; Maynard, Greenfield, & Childs, 2003) report that before they begin to engage in the adult practice of weaving (perhaps at the age of 9 to 10), young girls are provided with simplified weaving tools of two levels of complexity. The simpler of the two is a tool for winding thread that maintains the orientation of the threads that will later be used in weaving the cloth; the more complex tool involves doubling the long (warp) threads around a dowel. This more complex approach requires the weaver to visualize the extended warp (undoubled) rather than simply seeing it. Threads on opposite sides of the dowel will end up at different ends of the loom, and the length of cloth produced is twice the length of the frame.

These researchers argue that the complex warping frame requires the ability to engage in mental transformations while the simplified winding frame does not ("the weaver simply winds the warp from top . . . to bottom of the loom. . . . : What you see is what you get."). They note that parents and weaving teachers assign the simpler tool to 3- to 4-year-old children, and the more complex tool to 7- to 8-year-old children, corresponding to the canonical ages for Piagetian preoperational and concrete operational stages.

To test out this correspondence, the researchers compared performance on a task requiring children to match patterns on looms to patterns of cloth and in addition asked them to perform a perceptual matching task based on Piaget and Inhelder's (1956) research on the development of spatial thinking. The task involved six different colored beads strung as a necklace that were laid out as a necklace (requiring only a simple perceptual match), or as a figure eight, such that when the figure eight was "unfolded" as a circle, two pairs of beads in the middle of the figure were reversed, requiring a mental transformation to arrive at a match between a necklace laid out as a necklace or a figure eight. These tests were presented to both boys and girls ranging in age from 4 to 13 years in both Zinacantan and Los Angeles.

Among the many interesting results of this study, most germane to this chapter are the following:

- Both Zinacantecan and North American children showed a developmental progression on both tasks that corresponded to expectations from Piagetian theory.
- While the progressions were the same in the two cultural groups, the American children had higher average scores on the bead matching/transformation tasks while the Zinacantecan children outperformed the American children on weaving tasks. This is the pattern of results that one would expect on the basis of local familiarity.
- Correspondingly, Zinacantecan girls outperformed Zinacantecan boys on the weaving tasks and the Zinacantecan boys, who were at least familiar with the cloth patterns used and had seen weaving occur although they did not participate, outperformed the same-age children in Los Angeles.

Overall, these results fit well with Greenfield's theoretical claim that cultural practices build upon species-wide patterns of maturation. They also provide evidence of the way in which cultural practices can provide the necessary constraints on learning in non-core domains.

CULTURE AND THE ONTOGENY OF AUTOBIOGRAPHICAL MEMORY

Although the topic of cultural influence on the development of remembering has a long history, the kinds of studies carried out at the time of prior reviews, like those on concept development, appear to have gone out of fashion. This earlier research was divided into studies for coherent stories and memory for arbitrary word lists which were then fashionable in experimental psychology.

Those approaches that focused on memory for coherent stories converged on the conclusion, consistent with theoretical claims made by Bartlett (1932), that people would remember parts of the story consistent with important local cultural themes, but inconsistent with Bartlett's idea that nonliterate people would be prone to remember events in a rote, serial order. In addition, cultural variations in overall amount of remembering for coherent stories were found to be minimal or absent. Studies that used lists of words or objects to be remembered often produced wide variations among populations, but when such differences appeared, they seemed to be associated with amount of schooling. (For a review, see Cole, 1996, chap. 2.) No substantial body of work has followed up on either of these traditions.

Coincident with the decline of interest in story recall and such questions as the influence of literacy on the way people remember arbitrary word lists has been a marked increase in studies that examine cultural influences on the development of autobiographical memory—"explicit memory of an event that occurred in a specific time and place in one's personal past" (Fivush & Haden, 2003; C. A. Nelson & Fivush, 2004).

In addition to the fact that there is a relatively substantial amount of research to make it worth reviewing in this venue, there are other reasons that motivate discussion of culture and the development of autobiographical memory. First, people are asked to remember events in their own lives that are likely to be of significance to them rather than verbal or pictorial materials imported by researchers. Second, the topic of autobiographical memory makes theoretical links to the currently fashionable research on comparisons of societies characterized as independent or interdependent, which I have chosen not to include here because little of the accompanying research is developmental in nature. (See however, the chapter by Greenfield and her colleagues, 1998, for a discussion of independence-interdependence in relation to schooling.)

Several additional reasons motivate discussion of research on autobiographical memory in the context of this chapter. First, the onset as well as developmental increases in the quantity and quality of autobiographical memory have repeatedly been linked to ways that adults engage children in talk about the past, in particular past events experienced by the child (and usually, by the parent as well). Second, there have been several studies (unfortunately involving only a few distinctively different cultures) that indicate cultural variations in parental reminiscing practices, and onset of autobiographical memories. Third, in contrast with earlier research on culture and memory linked up most distinctively with questions of literacy and schooling, the study of autobiographical memory links up most distinctively with questions of the development of the self and personality, providing a bridge to areas of research on culture and development that ordinarily fall outside the purview of cognitive development. (See the Shweder et al., 1998, for a view of the landscape on the other side of this bridge.)

In Nelson and Fivush's account of the development of autobiographical memory, for example, it is assumed that there is a species-general set of basic memory processes for events, people, and objects that are supported by species-general neuro-cognitive maturation. These basic processes enable the acquisition of an understanding of intentionality and those understandings of others with regard to the self that were discussed earlier in terms of core domains. Language is added to these early infantile processes along with the new forms of culturally mediated, social experiences that are required for its emergence and which in turn enable further cognitive development. Especially important in this regard is the emergence of various genres of narrative, especially talk about personal episodes that come enmeshed in emotions and the entanglement of each child with those among whom the child develops. Nelson and Fivush (2004) summarize the centrality of narrative to autobiographical memory in these terms:

Narrative adds layers of comprehensibility to events above and beyond what is available from direct experience by linking events together through causal, conditional, and temporal markers.

Narratives are structured around meanings, emphasizing goals and plans, motivations and emotions, successful and failed outcomes, and their meaningful relation to the teller as well as to the other players. . . . Perhaps most important, through the use of evaluative devices, narratives provide for the expression of and reflection on personal meaning and significance that in turn allows for a more complex understanding of psychological motivation and causation. (p. 494)

In short, narratives constitute important, rather general purpose, tools for thinking, acting, and feeling in the world.

For purposes of thinking about autobiographical memory and culture, the first central compelling line of evidence is that there are significant individual differences in the ways that U.S. parents organize conversations about the past with their young children and that these differences significantly influence the children's autobiographical memories. In their review of this literature, Nelson and Fivush (2004) differentiate maternal styles of reminiscing about past events in terms of "elaborativeness," by which they mean the frequency and degree of embellishment in their reminiscing conversations with their children. (It is important to note that elaborativeness is not the same as talkativeness: highly elaborative parents may not be talkative in other circumstances.) The major finding of their review, which includes longitudinal as well as cross-sectional evidence, is that greater parental elaborativeness produces better autobiographical remembering (measured by amount and coherence). This effect is found as much as 2 years after a particular reminiscing episode. Over time, the relationship between maternal and child remembering in these episodes shifts as children begin to contribute as much to what the parents recall in the conversations as the children.

When we turn to research on cultural variation, a number of interesting findings have been reported. First, as summarized by Leichtman, Wang, and Pillemer (2003), a number of studies have reported cultural variations in the dominant forms of parent-child conversations about the past. These variations occur both in the degree to which parents engage in elaborative conversational patterns and the cultural values that they emphasize. Moreover, for Korean, Chinese, and Indian societies, where the bulk of the cross-cultural research has been carried out, these two aspects of parent-child discourse covary; compared to middle-class Americans, parents in these cultures where low-elaborative styles dominate, parents are more likely to emphasize hierarchy, proper social relations, and good behavior. Second, consistent with results concerning the relation between conversational style and autobiographical memory, the earliest memories in the three non-U.S. societies were significantly later than those obtained in U.S. samples. This result was particularly striking in India, where only 12% of rural adults and 30% of urban adults reported *any* specific events about their childhoods and for a subset of those who did report events and the age at which they occurred, the range was between 6 and 11 years of age, far later than is characteristic in U.S. samples.

Researchers engaged in this work have linked such results to the distinction between cultures that privilege an interdependent versus an independent social orientation. The latter encourages a focus on oneself or others in construing one's self in relation to others (Markus & Kitayama, 1991; see also Shweder et al., 1998). Without pretending to do justice to this line of theorizing, in the present context the distinction is captured by Mullen and Yi's (1995) idea that in interdependently oriented societies children are taught to see themselves as a collection of roles in a social network, while in independent societies children are taught to see themselves as a collection of individual attributes. The elaborative reminiscing style and relative lack of emphasis on social hierarchy with which it is associated thus promote the construction of coherent autobiographical narratives while the nonelaborative style blurs the distinction between self and group, in effect, diminishing the "auto" in the term autobiographical.

Research by Hayne and MacDonald (2003) reveals another cultural factor that influences autobiographical memory—the extent to which a society values narrative accounts of its own past. These researchers compared the autobiographical memories of Maori and European-descent New Zealanders, as well as the discourse styles of mothers from the two groups when talking with their children about the past.

The first interesting finding was that Maori adult women's earliest memories occurred at just under 3 years of age, while their European-descent counterparts' earliest memories occurred a year later, on average. This difference led the authors to the assumption, based on the work previously cited, that the Maori mothers would use a more elaborative style than European-descent mothers. But they found instead that the European-descent mothers were more likely to use an elaborative style that focused on the larger context of the event and salient details about people and objects present, while the Maori mothers were more like to focus on a limited aspect of the event and repeatedly ask the same questions about it as if they were trying to elicit a particular response. It thus appears that early autobiographical memory can come about via more than one path. These results provide strong support for K. Nelson's (2003) "functional systems" approach to development "wherein memory is seen not as a singular structure but as a set of functions that employ similar processes to achieve different ends" (p. 14).

Conclusions

It is fair to say that never before have the chapters in the *Handbook of Child Psychology* reflected as great an interest in the role of culture and development as do the chapters in the present edition. Not only is the role of culturally organized experience examined in two other chapters that have the word "culture" in the title, but in chapters that are focused on more or less traditional categories such as concept development and social cognition (and perhaps others to which I have not had advance access).

Most heartening from my perspective is that there seems to be a growing number of scholars who are rejecting the bedeviling nature-nurture controversy and beginning to treat culture as a phylogenetically evolved property of human beings. To be sure, programmatic statements of such a position have been discernable for many decades. To take two prominent examples from anthropology and psychology, consider the following:

[M]an's nervous system does not merely enable him to acquire culture, it positively demands that he do so if it is going to function at all. Rather than culture acting only to supplement, develop, and extend organically based capacities logically and genetically prior to it, it would seem to be ingredient to those capacities themselves. A cultureless human being would probably turn out to be not an intrinsically talented, though unfulfilled ape, but a wholly mindless and consequently unworkable monstrosity. (Geertz, 1973, p. 68)

Recall Sir Peter Medewar's bon mot about nature and nurture: each contributes 100% to the variance of the phenotype. Man is not free of either his genome or his culture. (Bruner, 1986, p. 135)

Since these lines were written, they have begun to resonate far beyond anthropology. I have already quoted the psychobiologist Henry Plotkin's remark that there is bidirectional causation between biology and culture. Even more pointed are the assertions of neuroscientists Steven Quartz and Terrence Sejnowski, who assert that culture "contains part of the developmental program that works with genes to build the brain that underlies who you are" (2002). They emphasize, especially, the fact that the prefrontal cortex, which is the latest brain structure to develop in both phylogeny and ontogeny, and which is central to planning functions and complex social interaction, depends crucially on culture for its development. They refer to the emerging discipline required to bring these ideas to fruition as "cultural biology." As indicated earlier in this chapter, I arrive at the same perspective from the broad theoretical framework referred to as cultural-historical activity theory, which traces its origins back to Vygotsky and his students.

Whether approaching the task of developing a view of human ontogeny as the emergent process of development resulting from the intertwining of culture and phylogeny from the perspective of cultural biology or cultural-historical activity theory, one is driven to take seriously the need to conduct such an inquiry in light of the different "streams of history" or "genetic domains" that have organized this chapter.

To initiate this task, I note the conclusions suggested by my review of the literature on hominization, comparisons of human and nonhuman primates, and cultural history. Against this backdrop, it should be possible to evaluate the new lines of research on conceptual and memory development reviewed earlier and to suggest other lines of research that appear to hold promise for theoretical progress.

OVERALL LESSONS FROM PHYLOGENY AND CULTURAL HISTORY RELEVANT TO HUMAN ONTOGENY

My reading of the literature on the paleological and primatological branches of human phylogenetic research suggests that each has a special contribution to make in thinking about culture and cognitive development in humans. What stands out in the literature on hominization is the reciprocal relations between anatomical changes, changes in behavior that involve the creation and use of culture, and relations of individual organisms to each other and their environment. In particular, the influence of culture on biological change, seemingly so obscure in the case of modern humans, is particularly clear.

Several points stand out in the research on modern nonhuman primates. First, this work renders it plausible that who or whatever the common ancestor of contemporary humans and apes was, there was a small gap indeed between that progenitor and the earliest human beings. Nonetheless, that tiny difference was (to use Bateson's, 1972, phrase) a difference that made a difference—it started a complex dialect of change in which biological, cultural, cognitive, and behavioral changes accumulated to produce *homo sapiens sapiens* and made development through culture a defining characteristic of the species. Second, current research with nonhuman primates has contributed materially to deeper appreciation of such basic psychological mechanisms as imitation in the process of cognitive development of human beings.

In addition, research on culture understood as group-level social traditions turns attention to new questions about human culture. Now the question becomes: Why did culture appear to accumulate among early hominids and why has it become so central to humans, dominating their worlds, intertwining with their thinking, while it does not appear to do so at all in chimpanzees in the wild (Boesch & Tomasello, 1998)? It appears characteristic of human cultures that, except in unusual circumstances (Tasmania being cut off from Australia and isolated), among human beings there is a proclivity for cultural accumulation and increased complexity, both in the sphere of tool manufacture and design and the complexity of social practices and institutions. Tomasello (1999) has termed this tendency "the ratchet effect," and he has argued that innovation, true imitation (e.g., imitation based on understanding others' intentions), and perhaps deliberate instruction are essential in this process. But the ratchet effect does not always work and it certainly does not always work rapidly. Boesch and Tomasello (1998) attribute this failure to "slippage," but aside from the issue of specifying what makes a cultural ratchet durable or subject to slippage, there seems to be more to the issue of the conditions of (relatively pervasive) cultural evolution among *homo sapiens sapiens.*

Two factors, often working together, appear essential. One is the use of external symbol-systems and the other is group interaction (both within groups and between groups). Each promotes vertical and horizontal cultural transmission. The case for the centrality of external symbol systems has been made persuasively by Donald (1991) and does not require review here. The Tasmanian case, and as well as the flowering of modern *homo sapiens sapiens,* point to intergroup interaction as an important factor in cumulative human cultural change because the frequent interaction of human groups provides rich opportunities for exogenously introduced innovation, a process that nineteenth and early twentieth century anthropologists referred to as diffusion. Such intergroup exchanges were infrequent during the Ice Age that preceded the appearance of modern humans and are infrequent among nonhuman primates. Study of the phylogenetic and cultural-historical foundations of contemporary human cognitive abilities requires us to remember the cardinal importance of trying to keep in mind the *scale* of time involved in the processes of organic and cultural change. It is a difficult task. I can write *4 million years,* but I cannot, in any deep sense, comprehend it. Yet the evidence indicates that cultural changes along the hominid line over the past 4 million years have been staggering in their accelerating rate and their transformation of the environment, for better and for worse.

Unfortunately, even in the case of the study of cultural change among anatomically modern humans, the injunction to "study behaviors over time to see how they change" is easier said than done because culture among anatomically modern humans dates back at least 40,000 years and existing cultures characteristic of entire social groups ordinarily exceed the lifetime of the researcher. These circumstances motivate research in those rare cases where it has proven possible to study changes in human cognition associated with rapid changes in cultures that are associated with specific historical circumstances.

The research by Beach, Greenfield, Luria, and Saxe provides a much closer look at the dynamics relating individual ontogenetic and microgenetic change to society-level collective cultural-historical change. So long as one studies such processes using tests of presumably general psychological functioning, or relies on the broad historical record, it is difficult if not impossible to gain access to the uneven, historically contingent interplay between microgenetic, ontogenetic, and cultural-historical levels of analysis that seem so central to the process of developmental change. But as soon as one focuses on specific culturally organized activities and traces the changing location of these activities within the ways of life of which they are a part, processes of change appear to be linked proximally to specific forms of interaction involving people seeking to achieve their goals, or discovering new goals, under specifiable conditions using specifiable combinations of artifacts.

The cultural-historical line of research also highlights the importance of specialized institutions for the propagation of culture, such as modern schools, and the specialized cognitive artifacts, written language and notation systems in particular, which mediate activities within those institutions and the society at large.

Cultural Variation in Ontogeny

Serious consideration of culture-cognition relations in phylogeny and cultural history brings us to the study of cognitive development in ontogeny prepared to assume that maturational factors constrained heavily by phylogenetic history will be closely inter-twined with cultural factors that are essential in the organization of social life in the society into which each child is born. However, given the relatively short duration of a single life (all the more so, a single childhood) relative to the long duration of a society's cultural history, let alone the unimaginably long time span of human evolution since the appearance of *homo sapiens,* there is a strong, and almost irresistible, tendency of psychologists to treat phylogeny as invariant, and hence irrelevant, and to use cross-sectional studies (culturally speaking) of children growing up in different cultures as a means of understanding culture-ontogeny relationships.

The historical obstacles that cross-cultural research has posed are well summarized in the Laboratory of Comparative Human Cognition (1983) *Handbook* chapter and elsewhere (e.g., Berry, Poortinga, & Pandey, 1997) and entered my earlier discussion of the difficulties of seeking to determine the impact of schooling on cognitive development in this chapter, so they need no review here. It is thus interesting that with some exceptions (to be noted later), two lines of ontogenetic research reviewed in this chapter—concept development and memory—use methods that minimize those difficulties. With respect to the issue of the role of culture in conceptual developments, the key seems to be that instead of seeking directly to establish category membership or similarity relations by asking people to engage in sorting artificially constructed objects according to preset criteria, the experimenter gets at similarity relations by asking people to make inductions using question-asking discourse frames that are reasonable in local terms. For example, questions aimed at revealing conceptions about the causes of growth such as "Can you keep the frog in its bowl forever?" can pass as natural for young Japanese children who have been given frogs and other creatures to raise. To give another example from the concept formation work, children in all cultures are used to hearing words they do not understand, so when told that a wolf has "andro" inside and asked if a bird also has "andro" inside, the question can "pass as reasonable."

In an analogous manner, questions about memory for early events do not have the odd characteristic of being "known-answer questions" that pervade so much of the research on memory development (and schooling). Researchers (and as a rule parents) have no idea what children will claim to be their earliest memories. While not totally immune to misinterpretation owing to features of the local language and culture, this verisimilitude that locates the crucial questions in a familiar cultural context go a good distance toward establishing their cultural-ecological validity. In like manner, the work of Greenfield and Saxe gains plausibility to the extent that they embed procedures in familiar cultural activities, modified only in sufficient degree to isolate crucial comparisons of theoretical interest.

Unsurprisingly, then, it is when experimental procedures have the "feel" of artificiality that controversies over the validity of cross-cultural comparisons arises. With respect to the data on cultural variations in development of core domains, for example, this is what occurs in efforts to use false-belief tasks where questions of language ordinarily play a large (and, many would argue, key) role in children's performance. It is only when the procedure used is reduced to its behavioral core that cultural invariance appears but at the cost of being unable to explore important concomitants of children's theories of mind, such as the connections between false beliefs and emotions. It appears that decades of effort to satisfy the demands of cross-cultural comparison and ecological validity are beginning to yield some evidence of success.

Less progress has been made, however, in demonstrating the role of culture in forms of cognitive development that are assumed to have a strong biological foundation. Perhaps the most promising arena for pursuit of this kind of research are cases of children who experience brain insults early in life and then undergo different forms of culturally organized environmental intervention by adults, operating on evidence of the activity-dependent nature of many forms of brain development. For example, Antonio Battro (2000), took advantage of modern fMRI technologies and computer programs to provide a child who had undergone a right hemispherectomy at the age of 3 years with dense, culturally organized, experience designed to build compensatory functional brain systems in the remaining cortex. He reports that the child attained a high level of cognitive accomplishment as a result of this "neuroeducation." In light of our current discussion, he also demonstrated the important role of culturally organized experience on brain development.

Other data combining variations in culturally organized activities that correspond to differences in the brain organization of behavior have been reported for adult abacus experts (Hanakawa et al., 2003; Tanaka, Michimata, Kaminaga, Honda, & Sadato, 2002). When tested for digit memory or mental arithmetic, fMRI recordings of abacus experts show right hemisphere activation of the parietal area and other structures related to spatial processing. The fMRI activity in nonexperts engaged in such tasks is in the left hemisphere, including Broca's area, indicating that they are solving the task by language-mediated, temporally sequential processing. When compared engaged in verbal tasks, experts and nonexperts display the same forms of left-hemisphere-dominated fMRI activity. Although research that traces shifting brain localization of psychological processes is only beginning, existing cases nicely illustrate the ways in which cultural artifacts, incorporated into cultural practices, react back on the human brain so that nurture becomes nature.

In sum, a perspective on culture and cognitive development that takes seriously the simultaneous relevance of phylogenetic history, cultural history, and culturally organized activity during ontogeny promises to bring culture into the mainstream of developmental research without forcing us once again into the untenable bifurcation of nature and nurture. Our way of nurturing *is* our nature. The sooner we embrace this reality and begin to use it to organize our environments and ourselves, the brighter the future of human development.

References

Ardila, A., Rosselli, M., & Puente, A. E. (1994). *Neuropsychological evaluation of the Spanish speaker.* New York: Plenum Press.

Astuti, R., Solomon, G. E. A., & Carey, S. (2004). Constraints on conceptual development: A case study of the acquisition of folkbiological and folksociological knowledge in Madagascar. *Monographs of the Society for Research in Child Development, 277, 69*(3), vii–135.

Atran, S. (1998). Folk biology and the anthropology of science: Cognitive universals and cultural particulars. *Behavioral and Brain Sciences, 21*(4), 547–609.

Atran, S. Medin, D., Lynch, E., Vapnarsky, V., Ek, E. U., & Soursa, P. (2001). Folkbiology does not come from Folkpschology: Evidence from Yukatek Maya in cross-cultural perspective. *Journal of Cognition and Culture, 1*(1), 3–41.

Baillargeon, R. (2004). Infants' physical world. *Current directions in psychological science, 13*(3), 89–94.

Bartlett, F. C. (1932). *Remembering.* Cambridge: Cambridge University Press.

Bateson, G. (1972). *Steps to an ecology of mind.* New York: Ballentine.

Beach, K. (1995). Activity as a mediator of sociocultural change and individual development: The case of school-work transition in Nepal. *Mind, Culture and Activity, 2,* 285–302.

Bekoff, M., Allen, C., & Burghardt, G. M. (Eds.). (2002). *The cognitive animal: Empirical and theoretical perspectives on animal cognition.* Cambridge, MA: MIT Press.

Berlim, M. T., Mattevi, B. S., Belmonte-de-Abreu, P., & Crow, T. J. (2003). The etiology of schizophrenia and the origin of language: Overview of a theory. *Comprehensive Psychiatry, 44*(1), 7–14.

Berry, J. W. (2000). Cross-cultural psychology: A symbiosis of cultural and comparative approaches. *Asian Journal of Social Psychology, 3*(3), 197–205.

Berry, J. W., Poortinga, W. H., & Pandey, J. (Eds.). (1997). *Handbook of cross-cultural psychology: Vol. 1. Theory and method* (2nd ed.). Boston: Allyn & Bacon.

Bickerton, D. (1990). *Language and species.* Chicago: University of Chicago Press.

Bjorklund, D. F., & Pellegrini, A. D. (2002). *The origins of human nature: Evolutionary developmental psychology.* Washington, DC: American Psychological Association.

Bloch, M. N. (1989). Young boys' and girls' play at home and in the community. In M. N. Bloch & A. D. Pellegrini (Eds.), *The ecological context of children's play* (pp. 120–154). Norwood, NJ: Ablex.

Boesch, C., & Boesch, H. (1984). Mental map in wild chimpanzees: An analysis of hammer transports for nut cracking. *Primates, 25,* 160–170.

Boesch, C., & Tomasello, M. (1998). Chimpanzee and human cultures. *Current Anthropology, 39*(5), 591–614.

Bogin, B. (2001). *The growth of humanity.* New York: Wiley-Liss.

Boysen, S. T., & Hallberg, K. I. (2000). Primate numerical competence: Contributions toward understanding nonhuman cognition. *Cognitive Science, 24*(3), 423–443.

Bruner, J. S. (1966). On culture and cognitive growth II. In J. S. Bruner, R. Olver, & P. M. Greenfield (Eds.), *Studies in cognitive growth* (pp. 30–67). New York: Wiley.

Bruner, J. S. (1986). *Actual minds, possible worlds.* Cambridge, MA: Harvard University Press.

Bryant, P. (1995). Phonological and grammatical skills in learning to read. In B. D. Gelder & J. Morais (Eds.), *Speech and reading: A comparative approach* (pp. 249–256). Hove, England: Erlbaum.

Bryant, P., & Nunes, T. (1998). Learning about the orthography: A cross-linguistic approach. In H. M. Wellman (Ed.), *Global prospects for education: Development, culture, and schooling* (pp. 171–191). Washington, DC: American Psychological Association.

Byrne, R. (2002). Seeing actions as hierarchically organized structures: Great ape manual skills. In A. N. Meltzoff & W. Prinz (Eds.), *The imitative mind: Development, evolution, and brain bases—Cambridge studies in cognitive perceptual development* (pp. 122–140). New York: Cambridge University Press.

Byrne, R. W., Barnard, P. H., Davidson, I., Janik, V. M., McGrew, W. C., Miklósi, Á, & Wiessner, P. (2004). Understanding culture across species. *Trends in Cognitive Sciences, 8*(8), 341–346.

Callaghan, T., Rochat, P., Lillard, A., Claux, M. L., Odden, H., Itakura, S., et al. (2005). Universal onset of mental state reasoning: Evidence from 5 cultures. *Psychological Science, 16*(5), 378–384.

Carey, S. (1985). *Conceptual change in childhood.* Cambridge, MA: MIT Press.

Castro-Caldas, A. (2004). Targeting regions of interest for the study of the illiterate brain. *International Journal of Psychology, 39*(1), 5–17.

Chavajay, P., & Rogoff, B. (2002). Schooling and traditional collaborative social organization of problem solving by Mayan mothers and children. *Developmental Psychology, 38*(1), 55–66.

Chen, Z., & Siegler, R. S. (2000). Intellectual development in childhood. In R. Sternberg (Ed.), *Handbook of intelligence* (pp. 92–116). New York: Cambridge University Press.

Cheyne, J. A. (n.d.). *Signs of consciousness: Speculations on the psychology of Paleolithic graphics.* Available from www.arts.uwaterloo.ca/~acheyne/signcon.html.

Cole, M. (1996). *Cultural psychology.* Cambridge, MA: Harvard University Press.

Cole, M. (2005). Cross-cultural and historical perspectives on the developmental consequences of education: Implications for the future. *Human Development, 48*(4), 195–216.

Cole, M., Cole, S., & Lightfoot, C. (2004). *The development of children* (5th ed.). New York: Scientific American.

Cole, M., Gay, J., Glick, J. A., & Sharp, D. W. (1971). *The cultural context of learning and thinking.* New York: Basic Books.

Cole, M., & Means, B. (1981). *Comparative studies of how people think.* Cambridge, MA: Harvard University Press.

Cole, M., & Scribner, S. (Eds.). (1974). *Culture and thought: A psychological introduction.* New York: Wiley.

Damerow, P. (1996). *Abstraction and representation: Essays on the cultural evolution of thinking.* Boston: Kluwer Academic.

Damerow, P. (1998). Prehistory and cognitive development. In J. Langer & M. Killen (Eds.), *Piaget, evolution and development* (pp. 247–270). Mahwah, NJ: Erlbaum.

D'Andrade, R. (1996). Culture. In A. Kuper & J. Kuper (Eds.), *Social science encyclopedia* (pp. 161–163). London: Routledge.

Deacon, T. W. (1997). *The symbolic species: The co-evolution of language and the brain.* New York: Norton.

de Waal, F. (2001). *The ape and the sushi master.* New York: Basic Books.

Diamond, J. (1997). *Guns, germs, and steel: The fates of human societies.* New York: Norton.

Donald, M. (1991). *Origins of the modern mind: Three stages in the evolution of culture and cognition.* Cambridge, MA: Harvard University Press.

Donald, M. (2001). *A mind so rare: The evolution of human consciousness.* New York: Norton.

Dunbar, R. I. (2004). *The human story: A new history of mankind's evolution.* London: Faber & Faber.

Elman, J., Bates, E., Johnson, M. H., Karmiloff-Smith, A., Parisi, D., & Plunkett, K. (1996). *Rethinking innateness: A connectionist perspective on development.* Cambridge, MA: MIT Press.

Falk, D., & Gibson, K. (Eds.) (2001). *Evolutionary anatomy of the primate cerebral cortex.* New York: Cambridge University Press.

Feigenson, L., Dehaene, S., & Spelke, E. (2004, July). *Trends in Cognitive Sciences, 8*(7), 307–314.

Fivush, R., & Haden, C. A. (Eds.). (2003). *Autobiographical memory and the construction of a narrative self.* Mahwah, NJ: Erlbaum.

Foley, R. A., & Lahr, M. M. (2003). On stony ground: Lithic technology, human evolution, and the emergence of culture. *Evolutionary anthropology, 12*(3), 109–122.

Gaskins, S. (1999). Children's daily lives in a Mayan village: A case study of culturally constructed roles and activities. In A. Goncu (Ed.), *Children's engagement in the world: Sociocultural perspectives* (pp. 25–60). New York: Cambridge University Press.

Gaskins, S. (2000). Children's daily activities in a Mayan village: A culturally grounded description. *Cross-Cultural Research, 34*(4), 375–389.

Gaskins, S. (2003). From corn to cash: Change and continuity within Mayan families. *Ethos, 31*(2), 248–273.

Geertz, C. (1973). *The interpretation of culture.* New York: Basic Books.

Gellner, E. (1988). *Plough, sword, and book: The structure of human history.* London: Collins Harvill.

Gelman, R., & Gallistel, R. (2004). Language and the origin of numerical concepts. *Science, 306*(5695), 441–443.

Gelman, R., & Lucariello, J. (2002). The role of learning in cognitive development. In H. Pashler & R. Gallistel (Eds.), *Steven's handbook of experimental psychology: Vol. 3. Learning, motivation, and emotion* (3rd ed., pp. 395–443). Hoboken, NJ: Wiley.

Gelman, R., & Williams, E. M. (1998). Enabling constraints for cognitive development and learning: Domain specificity and epigenesis. In W. Damon (Series Ed.) & D. Kuhn & R. S. Siegler (Eds.), *Handbook of child psychology: Vol. 2. Cognition, perception and language* (5th ed., pp. 575–630). New York: Wiley.

Gelman, S. A., & Opfer, J. E. (2002). Development of the animate-inanimate distinction. In U. Goswami (Ed.), *Blackwell handbook of childhood cognitive development* (pp. 151–166). Malden, MA: Blackwell.

Gergely, G. (2002). The development of understanding self and agency. In U. Goswami (Ed.), *Blackwell handbook of childhood cognitive development* (pp. 26–46). Malden, MA: Blackwell.

Goody, J. (1977). *Domestication of the savage mind.* Cambridge: Cambridge University Press.

Gopnik, A., & Meltzoff, A. (1997). *The scientist in the crib: Minds, brains, and how children learn.* New York: Morrow.

Gordon, P. (2004). Numerical cognition without words: Evidence from Amazonia. *Sciencexpress,* 1–6. Available from www.sciencexpress.org.

Greenfield, P. M. (1999). Historical change and cognitive change: A two-decade follow-up study in Zinacantan, a Maya community in Chiapas, Mexico. *Mind, Culture, and Activity, 6*(2), 92–108.

Greenfield, P. M. (2002). The mutual definition of culture and biology in development. In H. Keller, Y. H. Poortinga, & A. Schömerick (Eds,). *Between culture and biology: Perspectives on ontogenetic development* (pp. 57–76). New York: Cambridge University Press.

Greenfield, P. M. (2004). *Weaving generations together: Evolving creativity in the Maya of Chiapas.* Santa Fe, NM: School of American Research.

Greenfield, P. M., & Childs, C. P. (1977). Weaving, color terms and pattern representation: Cultural influences and cognitive development among the Zinacantecos of Southern Mexico. *Inter-American Journal of Psychology, 11,* 23–28.

Greenfield, P. M., Maynard, A. E., & Childs, C. P. (2000). History, culture, learning, and development. *Cross-Cultural Research: Journal of Comparative Social Science, 34*(4), 351–374.

Greenfield, P. M., Suzuki, L. K., Rothstein-Fisch, C. (2006). Cultural pathways through human development. In W. Damon & R. M. Lerner (Series Eds.) & A. K. Renninger & I. E. Sigel (Vol. Eds.) *Handbook of child psychology: Vol 4. Child psychology in practice* (6th ed., pp. 655–699). Hoboken, NJ: Wiley.

Hagen, J. W., Meacham, J. A., Mesibov, G. (1970). Verbal labeling, rehearsal, and short-term memory. *Cognitive Psychology, 1,* 47–58.

Hallpike, C. R. (1979). *The foundations of primitive thought.* Oxford, England: Clarendon Press.

Hanakawa, T., Immisch, I., Toma, K., Dimyan, M. A., van Gelderen, P., & Hallett, M. (2003). Neural correlates underlying mental calculations in abacus experts: A functional magnetic resonance imaging study. *NeuroImage, 19,* 296–307.

Harris, P. (2006). Social cognition. In W. Damon & R. M. Lerner (Series Eds.) & D. Kuhn & R. S. Siegler (Vol. Eds.), *Handbook of child psychology: Vol 2. Cognition, perception, and language* (6th ed., pp. 811–858). Hoboken, NJ: Wiley.

Hatano, G. (1997). Commentary: Core domains of thought, innate constraints, and sociocultural contexts. In H. M. Wellman & K. Inagaki (Eds.), *The emergence of core domains of thought: Children's reasoning about physical, psychological, and biological phenomena* (pp. 71–78). San Francisco: Jossey-Bass.

Hatano, G., & Inagaki, K. (2002). Domain-specific constraints in cognitive development. In W. W. Hartup & R. K. Silbereisen (Eds.), *Growing points in developmental science: An introduction* (pp. 123–142). Philadelphia: Psychology Press.

Hauser, M. D., & Carey, S. (1998). Building a cognitive creature from a set of primitives: Evolutionary and developmental insights. In D. Cummins Dellarosa & C. Allen (Eds.), *The evolution of mind* (pp. 51–106). London: Oxford University Press.

Hayne, H., & MacDonald, S. (2003). The socialization of autobiographical memory in children and adults: The roles of culture and gender. In R. Fivush & C. A. Haden (Eds.), *Autobiographical memory and the construction of a narrative self* (pp. 99–120). Mahwah, NJ: Erlbaum.

Hewlett.B. (1992). *Father-child relations: Cultural and biosocial contexts.* New York: Aldine de Gruyter.

Hirschfeld, L., & Gelman, S. A. (Eds.). (1994). *Mapping the mind: Domain specificity in cognition and culture.* New York: Cambridge University Press.

Howell, S. (1984). *Society and cosmos.* Oxford: Oxford University Press.

Hutchins, E. (1995). *Cognition in the wild.* Cambridge, MA: MIT Press.

Inagaki, K. (1990). Children's use of knowledge in everyday biology. *British Journal of Developmental Psychology, 8*(3), 281–288.

Jerison, H. (1973). *Evolution of the brain and intelligence.* New York: Academic Press.

Joulian, F. (1996). Comparing chimpanzee and early hominid techniques: Some contributions to cultural and cognitive questions. In P. Mellars & K. Gibson (Eds.), *Modelling the early human mind* (pp. 173–189). Cambridge, England: University of Cambridge, McDonald Institute for Archaeological Research.

Kaplan, H., & Dove, H. (1987). Infant development among the Ache of eastern Paraguay. *Developmental Psychology, 23*(2), 190–198.

Keil, F. (1989). *Concepts, kinds, and cognitive development.* Cambridge, MA: MIT Press.

Keil, F. (2003). That's life: Coming to understand biology. *Human Development, 46*(6), 369–377.

Kemler Nelson, D. G., Frankenfield, A., Morris, C., & Blair, E. (2000). Young children's use of functional information to categorize artifacts: Three factors that matter. *Cognition, 77*(2), 133–168.

Kroeber, A. L., & Kluckhohn, C. (1952). *Culture: A critical review of concepts and definitions.* Cambridge, MA: Harvard University Peabody Museum of American Archeology and Ethnology Papers 47.

Kuhlmeir, V. A., & Boysen, S. T. (2002). Chimpanzees (Pan troglodytes) recognize spatial and object correspondences between a scale model and its referent. *Psychological Science, 13*(1), 60–63.

Laboratory of Comparative Human Cognition. (1983). Culture and development. In P. H. Mussen (Series Ed.) & W. Kessen (Vol. Ed.), *Handbook of child psychology: Vol. 1. History, theory, and methods* (4th ed., pp. 295–356). New York: Wiley.

Larsen, M. T. (1986). "Writing on clay from pictograph to alphabet." *Newsletter of the Laboratory of Comparative Human Cognition, 8*(1), 3–7.

Leichtman, M. D., Wang, Q., & Pillemer, D. B. (2003). Cultural variations in interdependence and autobiographical memory: Lessons from Korea, China, India, and the United States. In R. Fivush & C. A. Haden (Eds.), *Autobiographical memory and the construction of a narrative self* (pp. 73–97). Mahwah, NJ: Erlbaum.

Leslie, A. M. (1994). ToMM, ToBy, and Agency: Core architecture and domain specificity. In L. Hirschfeld & S. A. Gelman (Eds.), *Mapping the mind: Domain specificity in cognition and culture* (pp. 119–148). New York: Cambridge University Press.

LeVine, R. A., LeVine, S. E., & Schnell, B. (2001). "Improve the women": Mass schooling, female literacy, and worldwide social change. *Harvard Educational Review, 71*(1), 1–50.

LeVine, R. A., & White, M. I. (1986). *Human conditions: The cultural basis of educational development.* Boston: Routledge & Kegan Paul.

Lewin, R., & Foley, R. A. (2004). *Principles of human evolution.* Malden, MA: Blackwell.

Lieberman, P. (1984). *The biology and evolution of language.* Cambridge, MA: Harvard University Press.

Lillard, A. S. (1998a). Ethnopsychologies: Cultural variations in theories of mind. *Psychological Bulletin, 123*(1), 3–32.

Lillard, A. S. (1998b). The socialisation of theory of mind: Cultural and social class differences in behavior explanation. In A. Antonietti, O. Liverta-Sempio, & A. Marchetti (Eds.), *Theory of mind and language in different developmental contexts* (pp. 65–76). Amsterdam: Wolters Kluwer.

Lillard, A. S., & Skibbe, L. (2004). Theory of mind: Conscious attribution and spontaneous trait inference. In R. Hassin, J. S. Uleman, & J. A. Bargh (Eds.), *The new unconscious* (pp. 277–305). Oxford: Oxford University Press.

Lillard, A. S., Skibbe, L. L., Zeljo, A., & Harlan, D. (2003). *Developing explanations for behavior in different communities and cultures.* Charlottesville: University of Virginia.

Luria, A. R. (1976). *Cognitive development.* Cambridge, MA: Harvard University Press.

Mandler, J., Scribner, S., Cole, M., & De Forest, M. (1980). Cross-cultural invariance in story recall. *Child Development, 51,* 19–26.

Markus, H., & Kitayama, S. (1991). Culture and the self: Implications for cognition, emotion, and motivation. *Psychological Review, 98*(2), 224–253.

Matsuzawa, T. (Ed.). (2001). *Primate origins of human cognition and behavior.* Tokyo: Springer Verlag.

Maynard, A. E. (2002). Cultural teaching: The development of teaching skills in a Maya sibling interaction. *Child Development, 73*(3), 969–982.

Maynard, A. E., Greenfield, P. M., & Childs, C. P. (2000). Culture, history, biology, and body: Native and non-native acquisition of technological skill. *Ethos, 27*(3), 379–402.

McBrearty, S., & Brooks, A. S. (2000). The revolution that wasn't: A new interpretation of the origin of modern human behavior. *Journal of Human Evolution, 39*(5), 453–563.

McGrew, W. C. (1987). Tools to get food: The subsistants of Tasmanian aborigines and Tanzanian chimpanzees compared. *Journal of Anthropological Research, 43*(3), 247–258.

McGrew, W. C. (1998). Culture in nonhuman primates? *Annual Review of Anthropology, 27,* 301–328.

Mead, M. (1935). *Sex and temperament in three primitive societies.* New York: Morrow.

Medin, D. L., & Atran, S. (2004). The native mind: Biological categorization and reasoning in development and across cultures. *Psychological Review, 111*(4), 960–983.

Medin, D. L., Ross, N., Atran, S., Burnett, R. C., & Blok, S. V. (2002). Categorization and reasoning in relation to culture and expertise. In B. H. Ross (Ed.), *The psychology of learning and motivation: Vol. 41. Advances in research and theory* (pp. 1–41). San Diego, CA: Academic Press.

Mejía-Arauz, R., Rogoff, B., & Paradise, R. (2005). Cultural variation in children's observation during a demonstration. *International Journal of Behavioral Development, 29*(4), 282–291.

Meltzoff, A. N., & Prinz, W. (Eds.). (2002). *The imitative mind: Development, evolution, and brain bases—Cambridge studies in cognitive perceptual development.* New York: Cambridge University Press.

Morais, J., & Kolinsky, R. (2001). The literate mind and the universal human mind. In E. Dupoux (Ed.), *Language, brain, and cognitive development: Essays in honor of Jacques Mehler* (pp. 463–480). Cambridge, MA: MIT Press.

Morelli, G. A., Rogoff, B., & Angellilo, C. (2003). Cultural variation in young children's access to work or involvement in specialised child-focused activities. *International Journal of Behavioral Development, 27*(3), 264–274.

Mullen, M. K., & Yi, S. (1995). The cultural context of talk about the past: Implications for the development of autobiographical memory. *Cognitive Development, 10*(3), 407–419.

Nelson, C. A., & Fivush, R. (2004). The emergence of autobiographical memory: A social cultural developmental theory. *Psychological Review, 111*(2), 486–511.

Nelson, K. (2003b). Narrative and self, myth and memory. In R. Fivush & C. A. Haden (Eds.), *Autobiographical memory and the construction of a narrative self* (pp. 3–28). Mahwah, NJ: Erlbaum.

Noble, W., & Davidson, I. (1996). *Human evolution, language, and mind.* Cambridge: Cambridge University Press.

Olson, D. (1994). *The world on paper.* New York: Cambridge University Press.

Ostrosky, F., Quintanar, L., Canseco, E., Meneses, S., Navarro, E., & Ardila, A. (1986). Habilidades cognoscitivas y nivel sociocultural (Cognitive abilities and sociocultural level). *Revista de Investigacin Clinica, 38,* 37–42.

Parker, S., Langer, J., & McKinney, M. L. (Eds.). (2000). *Biology, brains, and behavior: The evolution of human development.* Santa Fe, NM: School of American Research Press.

Parker, S., & McKinney, M. L. (1999). *Origins of intelligence: The evolution of cognitive development in monkeys, apes, and humans.* Baltimore, MD: Johns Hopkins University Press.

Paul, R. A. (1995). Act and intention in Sherpa culture and society. In L. Rosen (Ed.), *Other intentions: Cultural contexts and the attribution of inner states* (pp. 15–45). Santa Fe, NM: School of American Research Press.

Piaget, J., & Inhelder, B. (1956). *The child's conception of space.* New York: Humanities Press.

Pica, P., Lemer, C., Izard, V., & Dehaene, S. (2004). Exact and approximate arithmetic in an Amazonian indigeneous group. *Science, 306*(5695), 499–503.

Plotkin, H. (2001). Some elements of a science of culture. In E. Whitehouse (Ed.), *The debated mind: Evolutionary psychology versus ethnography* (pp. 91–109). New York: Berg.

Posner, J. K. (1982). The development of mathematical knowledge in two west African societies. *Child Development, 53,* 200–208.

Quartz, S. R., & Sejnowski, T. J. (2002). *Liars, lovers, and heroes: What the new brain science reveals about how we become who we are.* New York: Morrow.

Reagan, T. (2000). *Non-Western educational traditions: Alternative approaches to educational thought and practice.* Mahwah, NJ: Erlbaum.

Renfrew, C., & Scarre, C. (Eds.). (1998). *Cognition and material culture: The archeology of symbolic storage.* Oxford, England: Oxbow Books, McDonald Institute for Archeological Research, University of Cambridge.

Rogoff, B. (1981). Schooling and the development of cognitive skills. In H. C. Triandis & A. Heron (Eds.), *Handbook of cross-cultural psychology* (Vol. 4, pp. 233–294). Boston: Allyn & Bacon.

Rogoff, B. (2003). *The cultural nature of human development.* New York: Oxford University Press.

Rogoff, B., Correa-Chávez, M., & Cotuc, M. (2005). A cultural/historical view of schooling in human development. In D. Pillemer & S. H. White (Eds.), *Developmental psychology and social change* (pp. 225–264). New York: Cambridge University Press.

Rogoff, B., & Lave, J. C. (1984). *Everyday cognition: Its development in social context.* Cambridge, MA: Harvard University Press.

Rogoff, B., Paradise, R., Arauz, R. M., Correa-Chávez, M., & Angelillo, C. (2003). Firsthand learning through intent participation. *Annual Review of Psychology, 54,* 175–203.

Rogoff, B., & Waddell, K. (1982). Memory for information organized in a scene by children from two cultures. *Child Development, 53,* 1224–1228.

Romney, A. K., & Moore, C. C. (2001). Systemic culture patterns as basic units of cultural transmission and evolution [Special issue]. *Cross-Cultural Research: Journal of Comparative Social Science, 35*(2), 154–178.

Romney, A. K., Weller, S. C., & Batchelder, W. H. (1986). Culture as consensus: A theory of culture and informant accuracy. *American Anthropologist, 88*(2), 313–338.

Ross, N., Medin, D., Coley, J. D., & Atran, S. (2003). Cultural and experimental differences in the development of folkbiological induction. *Cognitive Development, 18,* 25–47.

Ruffman, T., Perner, J., Naito, M., Parkin, L., & Clements, W. A. (1998). Older (but not younger) siblings facilitate false belief understanding. *Developmental Psychology, 34*(1), 161–174.

Rumbaugh, D. M., Savage-Rumbaugh, S., & Sevcik, R. (1994). Biobehavioral roots of language: A comparative perspective of chimpanzee, child, and culture. In R. W. Wrangham, W. C. McGrew, F. de Waal, & Heltne, P. (Eds.), *Chimpanzee cultures* (pp. 319–334). Cambridge, MA: Harvard University Press.

Rumbaugh, D. M., & Washburn, D. A. (Eds.). (2003). *Intelligence of apes and other rational beings: Current perspectives in psychology.* New Haven, CT: Yale University Press.

Russon, A., & Begun, D. R. (2004). *The evolution of though: Evolutionary origins of great ape intelligence.* New York: Cambridge University Press.

Savage-Rumbaugh, S., Fields, W. M., & Taglialatela, J. P. (2001). Language, speech, tools and writing: A cultural imperative. *Journal of Consciousness Studies, 8*(5/7), 273–292.

Savage-Rumbaugh, S., Murphy, J., Sevcik, R. A., & Brakke, K. E. (1993). Language comprehension in ape and child. *Monographs of the Society for Research in Child Development, 58*(3/4), v–221.

Saxe, G. B. (1981). Body parts as numerals: A developmental analysis of numeration among the Oksapmin in Papua New Guinea. *Child Development, 52*(1), 306–316.

Schliemann, A. Carraher, D., &Ceci, S .J. (1997). Everyday cognition. In J. W. Berry, P. R. Dasen, Saraswathi, T. S. (Eds.), *Handbook of cross-cultural psychology: Vol. 2. Basic processes and human development* (2nd ed., pp. 117–216). Needham Heights, MA: Allyn & Bacon.

Schmandt-Besserat, D. (1996). *How writing came about.* Austin: University of Texas Press.

Schwartz, T. (1978). The size and shape of culture. In F. Barth (Ed.), *Scale and social organization* (pp. 215–222). Oslo, Norway: Universitetforgalet.

Scribner, S., & Cole, M. (1981). *The psychology of literacy.* Cambridge, MA: Harvard University Press.

Serpell, R., & Hatano, G. (1997). Education, schooling, and literacy. In J. W. Berry, P. R. Dasen, Saraswathi, T. S. (Eds.), *Handbook of cross-cultural psychology: Vol. 2. Basic processes and human development* (2nd ed., pp. 339–376). Needham Heights, MA: Allyn & Bacon.

Sharp, D. W., Cole, M., & Lave, C. A. (1979). "Education and cognitive development: The evidence from experimental research." *Monographs of the Society for Research in Child Development, 44*(1/2), 1–112.

Shweder, R., Goodnow, J., Hatano, G., LeVine, R., Markus, H., & Miller, P. (1998). The cultural psychology of development: One mind, many mentalities. In W. Damon (Series Ed.) & R. M. Lerner (Ed.), *Handbook of child psychology: Vol. 1. Theoretical models of human development* (5th ed., pp. 865–938). New York: Wiley.

Spelke, E. (1994). Initial knowledge: Six suggestions. *Cognition, 50*(1/3), 431–445.

Springer, K. (1999). How a naïve theory of biology is acquired. In M. Siegal & C. Peterson (Eds.), *Children's understanding of biology and health* (pp. 45–70). Cambridge: Cambridge University Press.

Sroufe, L. A., Cooper, R. G., & DeHart, G. B. (1996). *Child development: Its nature and course.* New York: McGraw-Hill.

Stocking, G. (1968). *Race, culture, and evolution.* New York: Free Press.

Stout, D., Toth, N., Schick, K., Stout, J., & Hutchins, G. (2000). Stone tool-making and brain activation: Positron tomography (PET) studies. *Journal of Archeological Science, 27*(12), 1215–1233.

Super, C. M. (Ed.). (1987). *The role of culture in developmental disorder.* San Diego, CA: Academic Press.

Tanaka, S., Michimata, C., Kaminaga, T., Honda, M., & Sadato, N. (2002). "Superior digit memory of abacus experts: An event-related functional MRI study." *NeuroReport, 13*(17), 2187–2191.

Tomasello, M. (1994). The question of chimpanzee culture. In R. W. Wrangham, W. C. McGrew, F. B. M. de Waal, & P. G. Heltne (Eds.), *Chimpanzee cultures* (pp. 301–317). Cambridge, MA: Harvard University Press.

Tomasello, M. (1999). *The cultural origins of human cognition.* Cambridge, MA: Harvard University Press.

Tomasello, M., Carpenter, M., Call, J., Behne, T., & Moll, H. (2005). Understanding and sharing intentions: The origins of cultural cognition. *Behavioral and Brain Sciences, 28*(5), 675–735.

Tomasello, M., & Rakoczy, H. (2003). What makes human cognition unique? From individual to shared to collective intentionality. *Mind and Language, 18,* 121–147.

Tulviste, P. (1991). *The cultural-historical development of verbal thinking.* Commack, NY: Nova Science.

United Nations Educational, Scientific, and Cultural Organization. (1951). *Learn and live: A way out of ignorance of 1,200,000,000 people.* Paris: Author.

United Nations Educational, Scientific, and Cultural Organization. (2003). *Gross net and gross enrollment ratios: Secondary education.* Montreal, Canada: Institute of Statistics.

Vinden, P. G. (1996). Junín Quechua children's understanding of mind. *Child Development, 67*(4), 1707–1716.

Vinden, P. G. (1999). Children's understanding of mind and emotion: A multi-culture study. *Cognition and Emotion, 13*(1), 19–48.

Vinden, P. G. (2002). Understanding minds and evidence for belief: A study of Mofu children in Cameroon. *International Journal of Behavioral Development, 26*(5), 445–452.

Vygotsky, L. S. (1978). *Mind in society.* Cambridge, MA: Harvard University Press.

Vygotsky, L. S. (1997). *The collected works of L. S. Vygotsky: Problems of general psychology.* New York: Plenum Press.

Vygotsky, L. S., & Luria, A. R. (1993). *Studies on the history of behavior: Ape, primitive, and child.* Mahwah, NJ: Erlbaum. (Original work published 1931)

Wagner, D. A. (1974). The development of short-term and incidental memory: A cross-cultural study. *Child Development, 48*(2), 389–396.

Wagner, D. A. (1993). *Literacy, culture, and development: Becoming literate in Morocco.* New York: Cambridge University Press.

Wellman, H. M., Phillips, A. T., & Rodriguez, T. (2000). Young children's understanding of perception, desire, and emotion. *Child Development, 71*(4), 895–912.

Wellman, H. M., & Woolley, J. D. (1990). From simple desires to ordinary beliefs: The early development of everyday psychology. *Cognition, 35*(3), 245–275.

Wertsch, J. (1985). *Vygotsky and the social formation of mind.* Cambridge, MA: Harvard University Press.

Whiting, B. B., & Edwards, C. P. (1988). *Children of different worlds: The formation of social behavior.* Cambridge, MA: Harvard University Press.

Whitten, A. (2000). Primate culture and social learning. *Cognitive Science, 24*(3), 477–508.

Wrangham, R. W., McGrew, W. C., de Waal, F. B. M., & Heltne, P. G. (Eds.). (1994). *Chimpanzee cultures.* Cambridge, MA: Harvard University Press.

Wynn, T. G. (1989). *The evolution of spatial competence.* Urbana: University of Illinois Press.

Zur, O., & Gelman, R. (2004, Spring). Young children can add and subtract by predicting and checking. *Early Childhood Research Quarterly, 19*(1), 121–137.

Chapter 18

Gender Development

SHERI A. BERENBAUM, CAROL LYNN MARTIN,
and DIANE N. RUBLE

Being born a girl or a boy has implications that carry considerably beyond chromosomal, hormonal, and genital differences. Virtually all of human functioning has a gendered cast—appearance, mannerisms, communication, temperament, activities at home and outside, aspirations, and values. In this chapter, we consider the developmental processes involved in sustaining this gender system. How docs a girl come to think of herself as a girl? Do children's beliefs about the sexes influence their own behavior?

The issues surrounding gender span many controversial topics, and we focus on summarizing recent work and the theoretical positions underlying these topics. This chapter is a condensed version of a chapter in the multivolume *Handbook of Child Psychology*. To explore details of topics covered, see Ruble, Martin, and Berenbaum (2006); for historical perspectives and details on central conceptual and methodological issues, see Ruble and Martin (1998).

This chapter is organized in three major sections: (1) a summary of aspects of gender that change across age, including sex differences; (2) a concise description and discussion of the three major theoretical perspectives on gender development: biological, socialization, and cognitive; and (3) conclusions and future directions.

This chapter is dedicated with love to our mothers, Edith Berenbaum, and in memory to Marjorie W. Nelesen and Carolyn I. Martin. We are grateful to Faith Greulich and Matthew DiDonato for assistance in gathering materials and organizing references. We are also grateful to Meredith Bachman, David Perry, and Martin Trautner for a number of very helpful suggestions, and to Elaine Blakemore for sharing her reviews of the literature on sex differences in physical skills, cognitive abilities, personality, and social behavior. Preparation of this chapter was facilitated by grants from the National Institutes of Health to Diane Ruble (MH37215, HD049994), Carol Martin (HD45816), and Sheri Berenbaum (HD19644, HD044398).

Development of Gender-Related Constructs and Content

We first describe current information about the developmental course of the components of gender, using the multidimensional matrix shown in Table 18.1, with four constructs and six content areas; definitions and examples are provided. The matrix, developed by Huston (1983) and modified by Ruble and Martin (1998; Ruble et al., 2006) has proven useful in several ways. It permits organization and reveals consistencies and variations in each domain, pinpoints areas needing research, provides clear

TABLE 18.1   A Matrix of Gender-Typing: Examples of Constructs by Content

Content Area	A. Concepts or Beliefs	B. Identity or Self-Perception	C. Preferences	D. Behavioral Enactment
1. Biological/ Categorical sex	A1. Gender labeling and constancy	B1. Inner sense of maleness or femaleness or self-perception of masculinity or femininity	C1. Wish to be male or female	D1. Displaying bodily attributes of one's gender (e.g., clothing, body type, or hair); transvestism, transsexualism
2. Activities and interests: Toys, play activities, occupations, household roles, or tasks	A2. Knowledge of gender stereotypes or concepts about toys, activities, etc.	B2. Self-perception of interests	C2. Preference for toys, games, activities	D2. Engaging in play, activities, occupations, or achievement tasks that are gender typed
3. Personal-social attributes: Personality traits; social behaviors and abilities	A3. Concepts about gender stereotypes of personality or role-appropriate social behavior	B3. Perception of own traits and abilities (e.g., on self-rating questionnaires)	C3. Preference or wish to have certain attributes	D3. Displaying gender-typed traits (e.g., aggression, dependence) and abilities (e.g., math)
4. Social relationships: Sex of peers, friends, lovers, preferred parent, models, and play qualities	A4. Concepts about norms for gender-based relations	B4. Self-perception of own patterns of friendships, relationships, or sexual orientation	C4. Preference for friends, parents, and models, or judgments of popularity based on sex or gender	D4. Engaging in social activity with others on the basis of sex or gender (e.g., same-sex peer play)
5. Styles and symbols: Gestures, speech patterns (e.g., tempo), or fantasy	A5. Awareness of gender-related symbols or styles	B5. Self-perception of nonverbal stylistic characteristics	C5. Preference for stylistic or symbolic objects or personal characteristics	D5. Manifesting gender-typed verbal and nonverbal behavior or fantasy
6. Values regarding gender	A6. Knowledge of greater value attached to one sex or gender role over the other	B6. Biased self-perceptions associated with group identification	C6. In-group/out-group biases, prejudice, attitudes toward egalitarian roles	D6. In-group/out-group discrimination

distinctions among aspects of gender-typing and thus reinforces the multidimensional nature of gender development. It has some limitations, however: It is fine-grained and atheoretical, and it can be difficult to distinguish among cells to ensure that common developmental trends across cells are identified. In introducing each content area, we highlight specific topics of theoretical or empirical interest.

BIOLOGICAL/CATEGORICAL SEX (1)

Work on biological/categorical sex includes gender identity, gender constancy, and disorders of sex development (previously called intersex conditions). A key issue concerns how and when children learn about their placement in a gender group.

Concepts or Beliefs (1A)

Making Gender Distinctions.   How early can children discriminate the sexes? When do they use labels to do so? What cues do they use? Before children can walk or talk, they have perceptual categories that distinguish "male" from "female." The ability to distinguish the sexes occurs at 3 to 4 months of age (e.g., Quinn, Yahr, Kuhn, Slater, & Pascalis, 2002), and finer discriminations occur at 9 to 11 months (e.g., intermodal associations among female faces and voices; see Martin, Ruble, & Szkrybalo, 2002). Children's labeling of males and females was long thought to occur at 30 months of age (S. K. Thompson, 1975), but data show that many children understand and use gender labels earlier—at least by their second birthday (e.g., Zosuls, Greulich, Haddad, Ruble, & Tamis-LeMonda, 2007) and perhaps even as early as 18 months for some children (Poulin-Dubois, Serbin, & Derbyshire, 1998). Cues used to discriminate the sexes may change with age; these cues include biological (e.g., genitalia) and social correlates (e.g., hair length; Ruble et al., 2006).

Gender Constancy.   A controversial and compelling aspect of gender concerns "gender constancy," first described by Kohlberg (1966). Children's sense of the permanence of categorical sex ("I am a girl and will always be a girl") develops in stages (Slaby & Frey, 1975). Children first learn to identify their own and others' sex (basic gender identity or labeling) by age 3 and likely before; they then learn that gender remains stable over time (gender stability) generally between ages 3 and 5 in the United States but maybe later in other countries (Ruble, Trautner, Shrout, & Cyphers, 2007); and finally they learn that gender is a fixed and immutable characteristic not altered by superficial transformations in appearance or activities (gender consistency), with controversy about when this occurs. From a cognitive developmental perspective, children would not be expected to show a complete understanding of constancy until they mastered conservation, particularly the distinction between appearance and reality, during the concrete operational period (5 to 7 years of age; Trautner, Gervai, & Nemeth, 2003). It is unclear when constancy is acquired: some research suggests 3 to 4 years of age (Bem, 1989); other research suggests around 7 years (De Lisi & Gallagher, 1991), with discrepancies reflecting methodological and theoretical issues (e.g., Ruble, Taylor, et al., 2007).

Identity or Self-Perception (1B)

Gender identity is a person's sense of self as a male or female (Zucker & Bradley, 1995). This understanding is anatomical, but also includes feelings about a person's biological sex and behavioral self-presentation as male or female. Research on gender identity has generally followed two paths differing in emphases: (1) developmental patterns of self-awareness as male or female, and (2) variations in feelings about core gender identity.

Typical Developmental Course.   A child's awareness of being a boy or a girl is considered by cognitive theorists to motivate gender-typed behavior (Constantinople, 1979; Martin et al., 2002). Most children accurately label their sex and place a picture of themselves with same-sex children by 27 to 30 months, and some probably earlier (e.g., Zosuls et al., 2007).

Variations in Core Gender Identity.   Children vary in their feelings about themselves as boys or girls, with implications for adjustment (see 1C, 2B). Gender identity is not determined simply by biology or rearing alone, and gender identity may change even in adulthood (see Biological Approaches). About 2 to 5% of children meet psychiatric criteria for Gender Identity Disorder of Childhood (GIDC) or have subclinical variants. They show both identity problems (e.g., wishing to be the other sex) and cross-gender behavior (e.g., wearing clothes and playing with toys typical of the other sex; Zucker & Bradley, 1995). Boys are referred for treatment more than girls, which may reflect referral biases (e.g., less tolerance of cross-gender behavior in boys). Children with GIDC show gender-atypical behavior early in life that may lead to peer ostracism. The causes of GIDC are unknown but may include hormones, temperament, family dysfunction, and encouragement of cross-sex behaviors.

Is GIDC truly a psychiatric disorder? A distinction has been made between discomfort with one's biological sex and discomfort with the gender role prescribed for one's sex, with GIDC to be reserved only for the former (Bartlett, Vasey, & Bukowski, 2000), but there is disagreement about whether most children with GIDC truly wish to be the other sex (Bartlett, Vasey, & Bukowski, 2003; Zucker, 2002).

Preferences (1C)

How satisfied are children with their sex? Very few children in Western cultures say they want to be the other sex, although more girls wish to be boys than vice versa, with this difference increasing into adolescence but decreasing from the 1950s to the 1980s.

Behavioral Enactment (1D)

Despite wide varieties of socialization pressures, cultural differences, and even biological influences, most children master the roles generally associated with their assigned sex. Individuals with gender identity disorder (GID) display gender-atypical feelings and behavior, and as adults may have sex-reassignment surgery. Adult males with GID show heterogeneity in other aspects of gender-related behavior, such as sexual orientation (Blanchard, 1989).

ACTIVITIES AND INTERESTS (2)

Exploring parallels in the development of children's concepts and beliefs about gender-related activities and interests, and their self-perceptions, preferences, and behaviors provides insights into the mechanisms driving children's behavior. Processes governing verbally reported choices may be different from those governing behavior.

Concepts or Beliefs (2A)

Stereotypes about clothing, activities, toys, and games are known as early as age 2.5 and probably as early as 18 months (Martin et al., 2002; C. F. Miller, Trautner, & Ruble, 2006), but the level of understanding varies by measure, stereotype, and child sex. For example, on a preferential looking-time task, 18- and 24-month-old girls (but not boys) matched gender-typed toys with the face of a boy or a girl (Serbin, Poulin-Dubois, Colburne, Sen, & Eichstedt, 2001). Stereotype knowledge of child and adult activities and occupations increases rapidly between ages 3 and 5 (e.g., Blakemore, 2003). Meta-analysis (Signorella, Bigler, & Liben, 1993) shows that simple gender stereotypes (e.g., boys like cars) are well developed at the end of preschool. Sophisticated stereotype knowledge continues to develop with age (Ruble & Martin, 1998).

Limited evidence suggests that around 26 months children are most aware of gender associations with adult possessions (e.g., shirt and tie), roles, physical appearance, and abstract characteristics (e.g., softness), and soon become aware of toy stereotypes (Ruble & Martin, 1998). In middle childhood, the range of stereotypes regarding occupations, sports, and school tasks or subjects expands (C. F. Miller, Lurye, Zosuls, & Ruble, 2007; Ruble & Martin, 1998).

Do stereotypes become more flexible with age? Clear developmental trends are difficult to describe because flexibility means many things, for example, the willingness to apply an attribute to both sexes rather than just to one, the recognition of the relativity of stereotypes across cultures, or to personal acceptance of stereotypes, with the latter being closer in meaning to attitudes or values that the sexes "should" be different. "Flexible" is used for any nonrigid application of stereotypes, whether because of knowledge or because of personal attitudes.

Around 7 years of age, children's range of stereotypes continues to increase, as does their flexibility (Huston, 1983; Ruble & Martin, 1998). Meta-analysis of stereotype attitudes and knowledge shows that, when asked "who can" or "who should" engage in an activity, responses of "both" increase with age among elementary school children (Signorella et al., 1993). Longitudinal studies show similar patterns. Children studied annually from ages 5 to 10 showed a peak in rigidity at either 5 or 6 years of age and then a dramatic increase in flexibility 2 years later (Trautner et al., 2005); neither level nor timing of peak rigidity affected the developmental trajectory, suggesting that all children follow the same basic developmental path of stereotype rigidity and flexibility across development, despite variations in when it begins and what level it reaches.

Development of stereotypes varies by sex and culture. Some studies suggest that, after the preschool years, girls are more flexible in their personal acceptance of gender stereotypes, whereas boys hold stereotypic views more rigidly and are held to them more by others. Limited data on ethnicity suggest that, relative to children of European origin, Hispanic/Latino children (e.g., B. A. Bailey & Nihlen, 1990) and Asian children (Lobel, Gruber, Govrin, & Mashraki-Pedhatzur, 2001) show greater stereotyping, whereas African American children show less (e.g., Albert & Porter, 1988; see Liben & Bigler, 2002, for an exception). Even countries that share a European background vary with respect to degree of stereotyping (Zammuner, 1987).

Changes in flexibility during adolescence are not clearly specified. Most indexes of stereotype flexibility show an increase through early adolescence (Liben & Bigler, 2002), but later changes are unclear, varying by the nature of the stereotype, the measure, and the sex of the participants (Ruble & Martin, 1998).

Identity or Self-Perception (2B)

Understanding connections between self-perceptions/identities and activities and interests is important for theories of gender development, especially concerning whether self-perceptions and identities precede or follow from activities and interests. For example, do children like certain activities because they are consistent with their sex or is the direction from interests to identity? Few studies address the direction of these effects.

Self-concept and academic interests are differentially linked for the sexes (e.g., Marsh, Byrne, & Yeung, 1999): Boys' academic self-concept is correlated more strongly with math than with verbal self-perceptions, and the reverse is true for girls (Skaalvik & Rankin, 1990). Young children show gendered self-beliefs: math is relevant for boys' self-concepts but not for girls' (Entwisle, Alexander, Pallas, & Cadigan, 1987). Such relations are important because children may avoid courses or occupations believed to be unimportant or irrelevant for their academic self-concept (e.g., girls may decreasingly like math, and then do not enroll in physics classes; Eccles, 1989). Students' views of future selves involve stereotypic interests: with boys emphasizing science, numbers, reasoning, and girls emphasizing people, culture, and self-expression (Lips, 2004).

Preferences (2C)

A key question has been whether preferences parallel stereotypes. Clear developmental trends for activity and interest preferences are difficult to see because of methodological variations: some studies examine developmental trends between the sexes and others focus on within-sex comparisons (e.g., female typical, male typical), and the nature of gendered activities changes with age. Such interpretational difficulties also apply to behavioral engagement in gender-typical activities (2D). Conclusions drawn about developmental changes depend on which comparison is made (e.g., see McHale, Shanahan, Updegraff, Crouter, & Booth, 2004).

Using nonverbal methods, there is some evidence that gender-typed preferences begin before age 2 (A. Campbell, Shirley, Heywood, & Crook, 2000; Serbin et al., 2001), but methodological issues suggest caution because girls' and boys' activities are not always made equally appealing. In preschool, development of gender-typed toy and activity preferences parallels that for stereotypes: they increase and are well established by age 5, with more gender-typed preferences for boys than for girls (Ruble & Martin, 1998). In middle childhood, there is some inconsistency about the extent to which the development of activity/interests parallels aspects of stereotyping (which become less rigid and more elaborated). When a sex difference is observed, it is likely to show that boys are more rigidly gender-typed during the middle grades (Ruble et al., 2006). Preferences generally become more flexible between middle childhood and early adolescence (e.g., Katz & Ksansnak, 1994), but flexibility regarding certain kinds of interests may decline during this period.

Behavioral Enactment (2D)

Children's engagement in gender-stereotypical activities has been examined in a wide range of settings, including free-play in home, school, and laboratory observations. Some evidence shows sex-differential play as early 2 years of age (e.g., A. Campbell, Shirley, & Caygill, 2002), but whether these differences occur earlier is unclear (Martin et al., 2002). Gender-typed toy play increases dramatically between ages 2 and 3; by

3, both boys and girls play more with gender-typical toys. During preschool, the two sexes engage in very different activities: girls play more with dolls, kitchen sets, dress-up, and engage in fantasy play involving household roles, glamour, and romance, whereas boys play with transportation and construction toys, and engage in fantasy play involving action heroes, aggression, and themes of danger (Dunn & Hughes, 2001; Maccoby, 1998). Gender-typical activity involvement increases dramatically during the preschool years (Golombok & Rust, 1993). Sex differences persist into middle childhood and adolescence across a variety of domains: sports, household jobs, toys owned, interests/hobbies (Ruble et al., 2006).

PERSONAL-SOCIAL ATTRIBUTES (3)

What traits do children ascribe to themselves and do these show parallel trends to gender-typed beliefs about the traits that girls and boys should have? We focus on developmental changes in characteristics examined in the literature on sex differences.

Concepts or Beliefs (3A)

Gender stereotype knowledge of personal-social attributes emerges at approximately 5 years of age and increases steadily throughout childhood (e.g., Powlishta, Sen, Serbin, Poulin-Dubois, & Eichstedt, 2001; Signorella et al., 1993). Effects are found across cultures and varying stereotype content (Gibbons, 2000; Zammuner, 1987). Children (and adults) apply trait stereotypes more strongly to children than to adults (Powlishta, 2000). The extent of trait stereotyping varies across methods; for example, stereotypes were stronger when direct comparisons between males and females were made than when they were not (Heyman & Legare, 2004). Although preschool children do not use many trait stereotypes, instead attributing positive characteristics to their own sex and negative characteristics to the other (Ruble & Martin, 1998), they do use some, particularly related to power differentials. For example, children stereotype the sexes on some traits (e.g., cruel), emotions (e.g., fearful), or behaviors (e.g., hits; Ruble & Martin, 1998), and have sophisticated knowledge about aggression (Giles & Heyman, 2005). Children also use a general evaluative dimension: males are labeled negatively (e.g., aggressive) and females are labeled positively (e.g., nice; C. F. Miller et al., 2007; Serbin, Powlishta, & Gulko, 1993).

  As with concrete activities and objects, flexibility in beliefs about gender-typed traits increases following a period of rigidity after they are learned (Trautner et al., 2005). Developmental trends for traits appear similar to those for activities and interests with a peak in rigidity as children enter school and a subsequent increase in flexibility with age (Signorella et al., 1993). Flexibility increases through early adolescence (Ruble & Martin, 1998) and is often higher for girls (Antill, Cotton, Russell, & Goodnow, 1996), and may stabilize or decline during high school (e.g., Neff & Terry-Schmitt, 2002).

Identity or Self-Perception (3B)

How early do children view themselves in terms of gendered personality traits (instrumental versus expressive) and do these patterns change over time? Limited evidence suggests that 3- to 4-year-olds of both sexes endorse socially desirable characteristics, but 8- to 9-year-olds rate themselves in terms of gender-typed traits (Ruble & Martin, 1998), and this continues into adolescence (Klingenspor, 2002; Washburn-Ormachea,

Hillman, & Sawilowsky, 2004). These gendered personality characteristics may account for sex differences in adjustment (Ruble et al., 2006). For example, in adolescents, instrumentality partially mediated the relationship between sex and internalizing symptoms, and expressivity fully mediated the relation between sex and externalizing symptoms (Hoffman, Powlishta, & White, 2004).

Sex differences in self-concept are small and follow expected patterns (e.g., Wilgenbusch & Merrell, 1999), with boys' self-concepts higher in math, sports, and physical appearance, and girls' self-concepts higher in music, and verbal/reading ability, and sometimes social competence (Klomsten, Skaalvik, & Espnes, 2004; Watt, 2004). Sex differences develop early and remain relatively consistent over time with a few exceptions (Cole et al., 2001; Jacobs, Lanza, Osgood, Eccles, & Wigfield, 2002).

Preferences (3C)

Do children prefer certain kinds of gender-linked personality traits for themselves? In the previous section (3B), we discussed a closely related issue: how children perceive their current or actual selves in terms of such traits—that is, their identity. Few researchers have examined trait preferences, even though preferred characteristics may influence children's future behavior. In one relevant study (Intons-Peterson, 1988b), Swedish boys and girls aged 11 to 18 years endorsed several instrumental qualities (e.g., never gives up) and several expressive qualities (e.g., kind), and only 19 of 59 characteristics showed sex differences. With age, the importance of expressive characteristics increased and instrumental traits decreased.

Behavioral Enactment (3D)

There is a voluminous literature on sex differences in behaviors and abilities. Here we provide a brief summary, relying heavily on Blakemore's recent summary of sex differences in physical skills, cognition, personality, and social behavior, which includes empirical studies and meta-analyses (which are quantitative summaries of empirical work; Blakemore, Berenbaum, & Liben, 2008; for details, see Ruble et al., 2006).

The sex differences reported by Maccoby and Jacklin (1974) in their landmark comprehensive review have been well documented, and work since has expanded the range of sex differences. Differences are found for aspects of spatial, mathematical, and verbal skills, with effects largest for spatial abilities and on standardized tests, but questions remain about the age at which these differences first appear. Males are more physically aggressive than females and more likely to take risks. Females are better at expressing and decoding emotions than are males. There are also strong and consistent sex differences in activity level and physical and motor skills. Overall, sex-difference patterns vary considerably by content area, developmental level, and context. In general, personal-social behaviors show negligible to moderate differences but no large differences, whereas interests and abilities show differences across the full range of effect sizes (for details, see Blakemore et al., 2008; Halpern, 2000; Ruble et al., 2006).

SOCIAL RELATIONSHIPS (4)

Children's gendered social relationships include peer relationships and friendships and sexual relationships. To what extent do children's concepts, self-perceptions, preferences, and enactment show parallels in this domain? What is the developmental course of children's preferences and behaviors regarding same- and other-sex relationships?

Concepts or Beliefs (4A)

Children have different conceptions of relationships with girls and boys and these views change developmentally. Young children understand that certain relationships are more acceptable than others (i.e., same-sex play and friendships are more acceptable than other-sex play and friendships; Martin, Fabes, Evans, & Wyman, 1999). Knowledge and beliefs about gendered social relationships increase with age (Ruble et al., 2006).

Boys and girls have different conceptions of friendship (Ladd, 2005). In childhood, girls regard friendships as higher in positive qualities (e.g., intimacy and closeness) than do boys. The sexes have similar levels of relationship conflict, but deal with it differently: girls place greater priority on maintaining a friendship, whereas boys are more likely to try to seek control over friends (Rose & Asher, 1999). In adolescence, girls' friendships focus on issues of intimacy, love, and communion, whereas boys' friendships tend to focus on agency, power, and excitement (Rose, 2002). Because of greater intimacy, girls' relationships are more fragile and prone to disruption through divulging of confidential information (Benenson & Christakos, 2003).

Identity or Self-Perception (4B)

Although gender is best studied as it is constructed in social context, little attention has been paid to how children incorporate stereotypic beliefs into their self-concepts about their relationships, and how gender identity relates to relationship choices. There is some evidence from gender-atypical children. For example, tomboys and children with GIDC report preferences for other-sex playmates (J. M. Bailey, Bechtold, & Berenbaum, 2002; Zucker & Bradley, 1995). Further, sexual identity is often but not always related to sexual behavior, with women more likely than men to show discordance and to change their sexual identity (Diamond, 2000; Savin-Williams & Diamond, 2000).

Preferences (4C)

Children's self-reported preferences for same-sex peers have been widely documented (see 4D for behavioral data). Children like same-sex (known or unknown) peers and prefer them as friends over other-sex peers, with this preference increasing until adolescence when interest in other-sex others develops (Lobel, Bar-David, Gruber, Lau, & Bar-Tal, 2000; Serbin et al., 1993; Sippola, Bukowski, & Noll, 1997).

Behavioral Enactment (4D)

Children enact their strong preferences for relationships with same-sex others, and there are sex differences in the qualities of these relationships. As children grow older, their relationships increasingly reflect sexual interests.

Play Qualities of Girls and Boys. There are marked differences in the qualities of boys' and girls' play, evident in even young children. Interactions among boys are characterized by rough-and-tumble play, activity, and attempts to attain dominance, whereas interactions among girls are more often cooperative and enabling of others (Di Pietro, 1981; Eaton & Enns, 1986; Pellegrini & Smith, 1998). Boys often play further away from adults than do girls (Benenson, Morash, & Petrakos, 1998), so their play may be more peer- than adult-oriented (Martin & Fabes, 2001). Boys are more likely than girls to associate in larger groups (Maccoby, 2002), and sex differences in play are exaggerated in groups versus dyads (Fabes, Martin, & Hanish, 2003). These differences continue and increase with age: In middle childhood, boys more than girls are involved in physical and fantasy games and aggression, whereas girls more than boys are involved in conversations, verbal games, and emotional exchange (Buhrmester, 1996; Lansford & Parker, 1999).

Children's play is influenced by their play partners. Boylike behavior may result not from the direct influence of individual boys' personalities but from boys' tendencies to respond in particular ways in boy groups (Maccoby, 2002), whereas girls' behavior is more similar than boys' across play contexts (Benenson et al., 2002). Both boys and girls engage in more active play with boys than with girls. Both sexes adjust their behavior somewhat to fit their play partners' styles, but other-sex group encounters are relatively rare, so may have little overall impact on children (Fabes, Martin, & Hanish, 2003).

Development of Sex Segregation.   One of the most pervasive sex differences concerns children's play partners (Maccoby, 1998). Children and adolescents spend more time with same-sex peers and siblings (McHale, Kim, Whiteman, & Crouter, 2004), with the sex difference extremely large (sex accounts for 70% to 85% of the variance in children's play partners, Martin & Fabes, 2001). Sex segregation is universal, occurring in nonhuman primates (Wallen, 1996), and in Western and non-Western societies, although its extent depends on the children available (e.g., Whiting & Edwards, 1988), and setting (Maccoby, 1998). Stable individual differences are found in preferences (Martin & Fabes, 2001).

Sex segregation emerges early: for girls, by 27 months; for boys, by 36 months (La Freniere, Strayer, & Gauthier, 1984). By preschool, children spend most of their time with same-sex peers. Sex-segregation is especially pronounced during middle childhood (Maccoby, 1998): only about 15% of children have other-sex friends (Kovacs, Parker, & Hoffman, 1996).

During adolescence, peer networks change. Small cliques of same-sex peers in early adolescence (Bukowski, Sippola, & Hoza, 1999) give way to both same-sex friendships and heterosexual dating couples and other types of other-sex relationships (Sippola, 1999). About 40% to 50% of youth in mid-adolescence have romantic relationships, increasing to almost 100% by late adolescence (e.g., Connolly, Craig, Goldberg, & Pepler, 1999). Girls (but not boys) still report feeling more comfortable with same-sex peers (Lundy, Field, & McBride, 1998).

Sibling interactions influence adolescent friendships, especially for girls. Girls with a brother are more likely to report using control strategies with friends than girls with a sister (Updegraff, McHale, & Crouter, 2000). Sibling interactions provide opportunities unavailable in school for learning about other-sex interactions (McHale, Crouter, & Tucker, 1999).

Few children report preferences for other-sex relationships. Girls with gender-atypical interests have some preference for other-sex peers (J. M. Bailey et al., 2002; Berenbaum & Snyder, 1995). Sexual minority youth report predominantly same-sex peers, but both sexes report more friendships with girls than boys (Diamond & Dube, 2002).

Causes of Sex Segregation.   Children may segregate because of behavioral similarity, for example, physiology, temperament (e.g., Fabes, 1994; Serbin, Moller, Gulko, Powlishta, & Colburne, 1994), shared interests, and/or their gender theories or cognitions (Martin, 1994; Martin et al., 2002). Furthermore, interaction patterns are complexly determined and a dynamic system in which partner choices are influenced by many small and large forces working in concert (Martin, Fabes, Hanish, & Hollenstein, 2005).

Development of Sexual Behavior and Orientation. In 4B, we discussed how sexual identity can be discrepant from sexual behavior. Here we focus on developmental patterns of sexual attraction and behavior (for details, see Diamond, 2003b). With few exceptions (e.g., Hyde & Jaffee, 2000), most work concerns sexual minorities, although a complete picture requires understanding sexual development in all individuals (Diamond, 2003a). On average, sexual attraction begins at age 10, but varies by sex, culture, and sexual orientation (Herdt & McClintock, 2000). Same-sex sexual orientation has been suggested to develop in stages marked by awareness of same-sex attractions in late childhood/early adolescence, followed by testing and exploration, and finally the adoption of a sexual minority label, disclosing sexual identity to others, and involvement in same-sex romantic relationships. Different models are needed to describe the development of sexual orientation in men versus women (Diamond, 2000; Savin-Williams & Diamond, 2000). Interesting precursors to sexual orientation have been identified: early gender atypicality is apparent in individuals who grow up to identify themselves as homosexual or bisexual (J. M. Bailey & Zucker, 1995).

STYLES AND SYMBOLS (5)

Gendered styles and symbols range from body image and hairstyles to speech patterns and communication. Do children know the gendered meanings of voices, interaction and communication styles, gestures, hairstyles, and clothing? To what extent are their self-perceptions, preferences, and behavioral patterns in these domains gender-typed?

Concepts or Beliefs (5A)

Young children know gender-related symbolic associations. They have stereotypes about colors, associate colors to gender-typed interests in others (e.g., Picariello, Greenberg, & Pillemer, 1990), attribute qualities based on associations they have to boys and girls (e.g., angular and soft, respectively), know hairstyles and clothing associated with gender (Blakemore, 2003), and associate certain speech patterns and roles with the sexes (Andersen, 1996). Body image stereotypes develop around age 5, with respect to weight (Hendy, Gustitus, & Leitzel-Schwalm, 2001) and muscularity in men (Spitzer, Henderson, & Zivian, 1999), and these relate to children's own body perceptions (5B).

Identity or Self-Perception (5B)

Evidence concerning clothing preferences, types of mannerisms, and body image is sparse, although recent work on body image provides a picture of how identity and self-perception are evidenced through stylistic and symbolic markers.

Body Image. Body image predicts depression, eating disorders, and low self-esteem, especially in adolescent girls (e.g., J. K. Thompson, Heinberg, Altabe, & Tantleff-Dunn, 1999). At age 5, the sexes are similar in body image (Hendy et al., 2001), but between 6 and 8 years, girls show more dissatisfaction with their bodies than do boys, and more desire to be thin (e.g., Ricciardelli & McCabe, 2001; Schur, Sanders, & Steiner,

2000); these differences relate to disordered eating behavior and eating attitudes (Davison, Markey, & Birch, 2002; Ricciardelli & McCabe, 2001). Preadolescent girls continue to be more dissatisfied than are boys about weight (Thomas, Ricciardelli, & Williams, 2000), and boys focus on being muscular (McCabe & Ricciardelli, 2003; Smolak, Levine, & Thompson, 2001).

Sex differences in body image continue in adolescence (Byely, Archibald, Graber, & Brooks-Gunn, 2000), with dissatisfaction in many girls linked to emotional problems and unnecessary cosmetic surgery (e.g., Ohring, Graber, & Brooks-Gunn, 2002; Stice & Whitenton, 2002). Body image has been linked to media and societal pressures (e.g., Smolak et al., 2001; J. K. Thompson & Stice, 2001), to peer pressure (Carlson-Jones, 2001, 2004), to pubertal timing (Ohring et al., 2002) and to pressure to lose weight (Ricciardelli & McCabe, 2001).

Preferences (5C)

Despite anecdotal data about children's preferences in dress, few studies have addressed children's verbal preferences for clothing (see 4D for adoption of styles of dress). Children aged 5 to 10 years preferred same-sex peers dressed in stereotypic or neutral clothing over children dressed in counterstereotypic clothing and associated play activities with clothing styles (Albers, 1998). Young adults often show stereotypic color preferences: Females prefer pinks but not darker reds, and males prefer shades of blues (Ellis & Ficek, 2001).

Behavioral Enactment (5D)

Sex differences in the use of language and nonverbal communication styles may reflect power and status and appear to depend on context.

Communication Styles.   There are consistent stylistic differences, although there are many similarities between the sexes. Girls tend to use strategies to demonstrate attentiveness, responsiveness, and support, and use affiliative and help-seeking speech acts, whereas boys tend to use strategies to demand attention and establish dominance, and use controlling and domineering exchanges (Leaper, Tenenbaum, & Shaffer, 1999; Leman, Ahmed, & Ozarow, 2005). Meta-analysis shows small sex differences in language use (Leaper & Smith, 2004), with girls tending to be more talkative (but only in early childhood), and using more affiliative and less self-assertive speech. But, sex differences depend on context (larger in same-sex than mixed-sex interactions and in unstructured than in structured situations) and culture (less gendered communication in African American than in White adolescent girls; Leaper et al., 1999).

Nonverbal Communication.   In terms of mannerisms and gestures, girls are more likely than boys to use limp wrists, arm flutters, and flexed elbows when walking, and less likely to put hands-on-hips; gender nonnormative boys exhibit feminine mannerisms (Ruble & Martin, 1998). In college students, observed gender-related physical characteristics and mannerisms (e.g., deep voice, broad shoulders) are linked to personality traits, interests, roles, and gender identity in men but not women (Aube, Norcliffe, & Koestner, 1995). Infant and toddler boys and girls differ in their use of communicative gestures (Fenson et al., 1994; Stennes, Burch, Sen, & Bauer, 2005).

Clothing and Appearance.   Clothing, jewelry, cosmetics, and hairstyles provide a wealth of information about a person's sex, socioeconomic background, status, lifestyle, nationality, and age. Parents use clothing to mark the sex of their children, and these cues are usually accurately interpreted (Ruble & Martin, 1998). Adult women are thought to actively construct identity through the "gendering" of clothing, but there has been little parallel work in children, perhaps because of the assumption that parents choose children's clothing.

Do children construct gender through appearance? Are they are aware of clothing as markers of gender? Children prefer to dress in sex-appropriate clothing, and girls particularly prefer feminine clothing. Girls aged 3 to 6 years often insist on wearing clothes that are highly female stereotypic, such as pink frilly dresses, a phenomenon Ruble has labeled PFD (Greulich, Ruble, Khuri, & Cyphers, 2001; Ruble, Lurye, & Zosuls, 2007). This may be one of the strongest gender effects found in childhood. Children's clothing choices may signal their gender-related interests or roles: Tomboys' clothing is more masculine than that of nontomboys (Dinella & Martin, 2003), and children with GIDC wear clothing typically associated with the other sex. But, it is unclear whether clothing choices are practical or serve as signals for others. Interesting questions remain about the consequences of clothing choices. Girls who dress in feminine styles may not engage in active or dirty activities because of their clothing, and may rigidly adhere to gender norms (Ruble & Martin, 1998). A cycle may develop in which clothing choices modify behavior, decreasing competence for certain activities over time, leading to even less interest in those activities. Any factor that modifies children's interests may have a large impact on later abilities and behavior.

VALUES REGARDING GENDER (6)

What are children and adolescents' evaluative beliefs and preferences about gender? At what age do they become aware that males and females may be differentially valued, and how does that affect their self-perceptions, personal preferences, and behaviors such as discrimination?

Concepts or Beliefs (6A)

When do children become aware that, in many cultures, more positive evaluations are applied to men and masculine activities than to women and feminine activities (e.g., Berscheid, 1993)? There are distinctions between personal evaluations (i.e., private regard) about a social group and perceptions of others' evaluations (i.e., public regard; Sellers, Smith, Shelton, Rowley, & Chavous, 1998). Little research has examined children's public regard for gender (see Ruble et al., 2004, for review). Research on stereotype knowledge suggests that children are attentive to sex differences in power (Kohlberg, 1966). Children perceive that females are devalued, beginning after age 10 (Intons-Peterson, 1988a), and they may be aware of gender discrimination as early as 5 to 7 years, but more so at 8 to 10 years (Brown & Bigler, 2004).

Identity or Self-Perception (6B)

As children begin to recognize that males and females are differentially valued, their own self-perceptions may be affected. Although girls evaluate themselves more negatively than boys in many situations (Ruble, Greulich, Pomerantz, & Gochberg, 1993), the specific link to gender values is not clear. There is some suggestion that as 5- to 8-year-old children learn about positive and negative traits associated with the sexes, they gradually begin to view themselves in terms of such traits (Aubry, Ruble, & Silverman, 1999). Moreover, recent work shows a positive relation between regard

660   DIVERSITY IN DEVELOPMENT

for one's own sex, as measured by gender contentedness (e.g., liking to be a girl), and adjustment among third to eighth graders (Carver, Yunger, & Perry, 2003; Egan & Perry, 2001).

Preferences (6C)

How do children personally evaluate gender categories and related activities and interests? Do they view males and masculine activities as somehow better or more valued? Do they view cross-gender behavior or traits as wrong? Unfortunately, personal values about gender are rarely measured directly.

In-Group/Out-Group Biases. According to cognitive theories, children's growing awareness of their membership in one sex category is likely to create a number of identity validation processes, one of which is to view one's own sex, the "in-group," more favorably than the other (Martin & Halverson, 1981; Tajfel, 1978). There is considerable evidence of in-group evaluative biases. For example, 5-year-old girls and boys were more positive about their own sex than about the other sex, and even 3-year-old girls (but not boys) showed significant in-group favoritism (Yee & Brown, 1994); children also assign more positive than negative traits to their own sex in the early and middle school years (Ruble & Martin, 1998). The positivity bias declines with age, at least after age 4 to 5 years (e.g., Heyman & Legare, 2004) and often more so for girls (Yee & Brown, 1994).

Prejudice against Women. Is there any evidence that children value males more than females, and if so, how early does this begin? Interestingly, despite general cultural biases attributing greater prestige and power to males (and children's awareness of such status differences, see 6A), most evidence suggests that young children are more likely to derogate males than females (e.g., Heyman, 2001; Yee & Brown, 1994). This pattern might reflect attention to attributes implying moral goodness, such as helpfulness (Ruble & Dweck, 1995), often stereotypically associated with females. After preschool, children's judgments begin to incorporate stereotypically masculine attributes of prestige and power: 5- to 7-year-old children view males as more competent overall (Levy, Sadovsky, & Troseth, 2000); 11- to 12-year-olds but not 6- to 8-year-olds evaluated novel occupations portrayed with male workers as higher in prestige than identical jobs portrayed with female workers (Liben, Bigler, & Krogh, 2001).

Egalitarian Attitudes. Do children think it is desirable for individuals to engage in whatever behaviors they prefer, or are cross-gender activities considered inappropriate? There are several types of relevant data. First, studies that ask what males, females, or both "should" be like or do (Section 2A) show that values about gender increase in rigidity until 5 to 7 years of age but then become more flexible (Signorella et al., 1993). Second, attitudes become more egalitarian with age (Ruble et al., 2006). Gender-related attitudes may become intensified in adolescence as sexual identity emerges, heightening concerns about gender norms (Hill & Lynch, 1983). Such gender intensification of attitudes is stronger for boys and varies by birth order and family traditionality (Crouter, Whiteman, McHale, & Osgood, 2007). Third, children's personal evaluations (good or bad) of individuals who engage in cross-gender behavior show curvilinear developmental trends similar to those described previously for stereotypic attitudes (Ruble, Taylor, et al., 2007). But, such effects are not always found: some negative reactions are relatively stable (Levy, Taylor, & Gelman, 1995) or increase in childhood (Carter & McCloskey, 1984). Developmental trends in children's reactions to atypical behavior vary with the sex of target (boys judged more negatively for violating norms), the target behavior, and the reaction assessed—but the reasons for those variations are unclear.

Behavioral Enactment, Adoption (6D)

Values are expressed in behavior through preferential or discriminatory treatment. In a reward allocation task in which individuals distribute resources on the basis of performance and personal attributes, young girls used in-group favoritism and boys used equity (Yee & Brown, 1994). Values are also expressed responses to cross-gender behavior. Children, especially boys, who deviate from gender norms suffer peer ridicule and rejection (Cohen-Kettenis, Owen, Kaijser, Bradley, & Zucker, 2003; Zucker, 1990).

SUMMARY OF DEVELOPMENTAL TRENDS

The extensive data base on gender development produces the following portrait. Before 1 year of age, infants respond to some gender cues. By 2 to 2.5 years of age, children have rudimentary gender stereotypes, label themselves and others by sex, play more often with same- rather than other-sex toys, and affiliate more with same- rather than other-sex peers. Early indications of GIDC may be seen at this age. Three-year-old children master gender stability; stereotype children's toys and activities, colors, and certain traitlike characteristics; and exhibit gender-typed play preferences. From 4 to 5, gender knowledge and behavior increase dramatically. Many children show complete gender constancy understanding, link power and evaluative traits to gender, show in-group positivity biases, heightened gender rigidity, and expect same-sex peers to play together. In addition, sex differences are apparent in aggression and decoding facial expressions.

A number of important changes in gender development occur during the elementary school years. Children develop more complex and extensive stereotypes, become aware of male-favored status differences, show increasingly flexible stereotypic beliefs, and girls often become flexible in their activity preferences and behaviors. A few indices do not show increasing flexibility, however, such as children's sex segregation, which remains high during elementary school. Sex differences in certain spatial skills and emotional perception and expression are seen in middle childhood and increase with age.

Finally, further changes are found during adolescence. A few studies suggest that attitudes become somewhat less flexible. Trends for preferences are less clear and appear to diverge for males and females, with boys less likely to become flexible. However, in middle adolescence, both sexes show gender-typed activities and interests in many contexts (e.g., home, school) and sexual identity generally emerges. In addition, sex differences in mathematical problem solving, physical skills, and depression emerge or increase during adolescence. Taken together, the various trends show a number of parallel developments among cognitions, preferences, and behavior.

What is the state of the field regarding the unity of gender-typing constructs? The multidimensionality of gender-typing (e.g., Hort, Leinbach, & Fagot, 1991; Serbin et al., 1993) has been inferred from failures to find relations among gender-related variables. The likelihood of finding expected correlations is influenced by many factors (Aubry et al., 1999; C. F. Miller et al., 2006), so it is important to specify the nature and moderators of expected links. Nevertheless, it appears that basic knowledge about one's own and others' sex develops at about the same time as gendered behavior and may influence that behavior (see Cognitive Approaches section).

It is also informative to examine links among subsets of variables. For instance, much of gender differentiation may be thought of as a set of self variables, and it may be productive to examine to coherence among such variables as categorical gender, gender identity, preferences for same-sex playmates, preferences for gender-typed activities, and later preferences for other-sex sexual partners. Many of these components in the matrix do show parallel developmental trends, but it is unclear whether they cohere within individuals, so associations and causal relations need to be assessed in longitudinal or, in some cases, experimental studies. It would also be productive to examine the stability of individual differences over time. Are 3-year-old girls who dress in pink frilly dresses, and play primarily with girls likely to become 9-year-olds who avoid sports, and show feminine interpersonal characteristics? To date, there has been relatively little research about such issues (Maccoby, 2002; McHale, Crouter, & Whiteman, 2003), but one retrospective study suggests that some early gender-typed interests have stability into adolescence (e.g., Giuliano, Popp, & Knight, 2000).

Theoretical Analysis of Gender Development

Most explanations of gender development fit into one of three broad approaches: (1) biological, (2) socialization, and (3) cognitive. These theories posit consistencies across certain cells of the matrix. For instance, several theories hold that concepts or beliefs about a content area, such as stereotypes about activities and interests, influence preferences and adoption of these attributes. Some theories suggest that gender identity influences preferences and adoption of attributes more broadly.

BIOLOGICAL APPROACHES

Biological perspectives are increasingly visible and accepted. Converging data from multiple methods (facilitated by methodological and technological advances) provide compelling support for biological contributors to gender development. The nature-nurture debate has given way to questions about the mechanisms by which biology and the social environment work together to produce behavior. Political and social implications of sex differences are not dependent on their causes. Biological factors do not imply determinism because behaviors with a strong biological influence may be relatively easy to modify (e.g., using diet to prevent retardation in children with phenylketonuria). Environmental factors do not imply easy malleability, because social forces may be difficult to counteract, as exemplified by racism. Biological approaches to gender development emphasize the parallels between physical and psychological sexual differentiation, and focus on both distal evolutionary explanations and proximal mechanisms mediated by genes and hormones.

Evolutionary Psychology

Evolutionary psychologists view behavior as the result of adaptive pressures, so that our brains—and, therefore, our behaviors—developed to solve problems faced by our ancestors, and good solutions enabled them to survive and reproduce. The sexes have faced different adaptive pressures related to differences in reproduction, and these are hypothesized to result in behavioral sex differences seen today, including females' greater interest in babies and males' greater aggression and preferences for multiple sex partners (Buss, 2000; Geary, 1998).

Although there are many appeals to evolutionary approaches, they are currently incomplete as explanations of gender development. These approaches have been criticized because they do not make unique predictions (results often can be explained by other theories), are difficult to falsify (there are no methods available to decide whether a behavior "evolved" because it was adaptive or a by-product of another trait), and do not explain within-sex variations (not all men and women behave in ways predicted by evolutionary theory).

Comparative Approaches

Another perspective relies on cross-species comparisons to understand the origins of behavior, as illustrated in two recent papers. The first described a sex difference in wild chimpanzees in learning to use tools to fish for termites. Compared to males, female chimps learned at a younger age and were more likely to use techniques resembling those of their mothers (Lonsdorf, Eberly, & Pusey, 2004). The second paper described a study of toy preferences in vervet monkeys, showing sex differences paralleling those seen in children (Alexander & Hines, 2002).

A comparative approach seems promising for examining gender development, given that primates, and perhaps other animals, learn from others in their social groups and that they form and use cognitive categories and concepts that can be generalized and adapted to new circumstances (E. K. Miller, Nieder, Freedman, & Wallis, 2003). It is important to know, for example, whether juvenile monkeys sex segregate (Maccoby, 1998), what gender concepts they have, and how they use knowledge of sex membership (their own and other's). Comparative studies can also provide information about proximal mechanisms that can be studied in human beings, such as characteristics underlying toy preferences.

Parallels between Physical and Psychological Sexual Differentiation

Evolutionary and comparative approaches put human gender development into context. Proximal explanations focus on biological mechanisms accounting for differences between males and females, specifically processes of physical sexual differentiation.

Genetic sex is determined at conception by the sex chromosomes (XX or XY). The sexes start out with the same sets of structures that differentiate into male or female gonads, internal reproductive organs, and genitals (Grumbach, Hughes, & Conte, 2002). Male development is initiated by a gene on the Y-chromosome, SRY (for sex-determining region), which causes the indifferent gonad to develop into testes at about weeks 6 to 7 of gestation. Subsequently, sexual differentiation largely depends on hormones secreted by the gonads, particularly androgens; estrogens have little role during prenatal development. Both sexes produce and respond to androgens and estrogens, but they differ in their concentrations of these hormones. External genitalia start out the same in the two sexes; high levels of androgen beginning at prenatal weeks 7 to 8 cause male external genitalia to develop. Females can develop masculinized genitalia if they are exposed to high levels of androgen early in development. Female-typical development is largely a default process, occurring when SRY is absent and androgen is low, but completely normal female development requires other genes. Complete masculinization requires both high levels of androgen and functioning androgen receptors.

Hormonal Influences on Behavior and Brain in Nonhuman Animals

Hormones are also responsible for sexual differentiation of the brain and behavior. Evidence from nonhuman species regarding behavioral and neural effects of sex hormones have implications for human gender development (see Becker, Breedlove, Crews, & McCarthy, 2002; Cohen-Bendahan, van de Beek, & Berenbaum, 2005; Wallen, 2005). Hormones affect behavior in two ways: by producing permanent changes to brain structures and the behaviors they subserve, usually early in life ("organizational" effects) and by producing temporary alterations to the brain and behavior (through ongoing changes to neural circuitry) as the hormones circulate in the body, primarily throughout adolescence and adulthood ("activational" effects); the distinction between organizational and activational hormone effects is not absolute. There are multiple sensitive periods for permanent effects of hormones, and these periods may differ for the brain and the genitals. The human sex difference in testosterone is largest during prenatal weeks 8 to 24, postnatal months 1 to 5, and puberty through adulthood (Smail, Reyes, Winter, & Faiman, 1981). The key sensitive period for human brain and behavioral sexual differentiation has been considered to occur right after the genitals differentiate, but other times may be important.

Human Behavioral Effects of Prenatal Hormones

It is not possible to investigate the effects of hormones in people by manipulating their levels, but much has been learned from children and adults whose hormone levels were atypical for their sex during early development as a result of genetic disease or maternal ingestion of drugs during pregnancy to prevent miscarriage. Evidence from these natural experiments has been supplemented by data from normal individuals with typical variations in hormones. In light of space limitations, we only discuss a sample of this work (for additional information, see Berenbaum, 2006; Cohen-Bendahan et al., 2005; Ruble et al., 2006).

Congenital Adrenal Hyperplasia.   The most extensively studied natural experiment, congenital adrenal hyperplasia (CAH) is a genetic disease that results in exposure to high levels of androgens beginning early in gestation because of an enzyme defect affecting cortisol production. Females with CAH have external genitalia masculinized to varying degrees, but they have ovaries and a uterus and are fertile. Most girls are diagnosed at birth and treated with cortisol to reduce androgen excess (or they will experience rapid growth and early puberty) and surgically to feminize their genitalia. If sexual differentiation of human behavior is affected by androgens present during critical periods of development, females with CAH should be behaviorally more masculine and less feminine than a comparison group of females without CAH. Males with CAH have few prenatal effects and are treated postnatally with cortisol to maintain growth and prevent early puberty and other consequences of the disease. They are reared as boys, develop male gender identity, and generally display male-typical behavior. (For reviews, see Berenbaum, 2001; Cohen-Bendahan et al., 2005.)

Girls with CAH are masculinized and defeminized in aspects of their feelings, preferences, and behavior. In childhood and adolescence, girls with CAH report being more interested in male-typical occupations than in female-typical occupations (Berenbaum, 1999; Servin, Nordenström, Larsson, & Bohlin, 2003), and they report liking and engaging more with boys' toys and activities and less with girls' toys and activities than do typical girls and report preferences for boys as playmates (e.g., Berenbaum, 1999; Berenbaum & Snyder, 1995; Servin et al., 2003). Observational studies confirm boy-typical toy preferences for girls with CAH (e.g., Berenbaum & Snyder, 1995; Nordenström, Servin, Bohlin, Larsson, & Wedell, 2002).

Masculinized preferences and play in girls with CAH appear to result directly from prenatal androgen: Play with boys' toys is related to degree of prenatal androgen excess (Berenbaum, Duck, & Bryk, 2000; Nordenström et al., 2002). Parents' socialization influences on play have not been demonstrated: The amount of time that girls with CAH played with boys' toys was not increased when parents were present (Nordenström et al., 2002), and parents encourage their daughters to play with girls' toys (Pasterski et al., 2005). Although these results strongly suggest prenatal androgen effects, it is possible that differential parent treatment is subtle and best detected in within-family designs (McHale et al., 1999).

Females with CAH appear to be masculinized and defeminized in other domains (reviewed in Cohen-Bendahan et al., 2005). Compared to typical females, females with CAH are more aggressive and less interested in babies. At several ages (childhood to adulthood), females with CAH scored higher on spatial tasks than unaffected females (Berenbaum, 2001; Hines et al., 2003). These findings are less firmly established than those on activities and interests and have not been studied in relation to prenatal androgen exposure or parental treatment.

Gender identity is typical in the majority of girls and women with CAH, although degree of identification may be reduced compared to typical females (Berenbaum & Bailey, 2003). Degree of prenatal androgen excess and genital appearance do not appear to contribute to variations in gender identity. Sex change in females with CAH is uncommon but still more common than in the general population (Dessens, Slijper, & Drop, 2005). Finally, women with CAH are more likely than typical women to have bisexual or homosexual orientation, although most are exclusively heterosexual (Zucker et al., 1996).

Boys without a Penis. Much attention has been directed to rare clinical conditions in which boys are lacking a penis (e.g., because of congenital defect or mishandled circumcision) but all other aspects of sexual differentiation are male-typical. These children have usually been reared as females, because it was believed that gender identity is determined by rearing and that normal psychological development depends on having normal-looking genitalia (although some surgical correction is now possible, the penis will never look or function normally; Money & Ehrhardt, 1972).

A small number of such individuals with male gender identity (i.e., identity inconsistent with rearing) have been used to argue for the primacy of biology in determining gender identity (e.g., Reiner & Gearhart, 2004). Systematic review of the world's cases, however, shows that most of these children develop gender identity consistent with rearing sex (Meyer-Bahlburg, 2005), although their interests are masculinized, consistent with their prenatal androgen exposure.

Normal Variations in Prenatal Hormones. Considerable progress has been made in examining the generalizability of results obtained in clinical populations, through studies of gender-related behavior in relation to prenatal hormones obtained from amniotic fluid or mother's blood during pregnancy (none directly measure fetal hormones) or to markers of prenatal hormones (see Cohen-Bendahan et al., 2005). Associations between indicators of amniotic prenatal hormones and postnatal behavior are found sometimes (e.g., Lutchmaya, Baron-Cohen, & Raggatt, 2002) but not always (e.g., Knickmeyer et al., 2005). It is unclear whether negative findings indicate lack of association between behavior and testosterone within the normal range or study limitations (e.g., small samples, single measure, limited variability in testosterone).

Hormones in mother's blood during pregnancy has been linked to behavior in daughters (Hines et al., 2002; Udry, 2000). In children aged 3.5 years, involvement in boy-typical activities was highest in girls whose mothers had high levels of testosterone in blood samples collected between weeks 5 and 36 of gestation (Hines et al., 2002).

Increasingly, studies in typical samples have examined associations between behavior and morphological measures considered markers of prenatal hormone exposure. For example, fingerprint patterns, relative finger lengths, and otoacoustic emissions (sounds produced by the ear) have been related to sexual orientation, spatial ability, personality, and activity interests. Potentially valuable as nonintrusive, easily collected, retrospective measures of prenatal hormone exposure that can be used at all ages, these markers await further validation (Cohen-Bendahan et al., 2005).

Hormone Influences in Adolescence

Do the changes in sex hormones and physical appearance at adolescence contribute to gender development? Research has focused on characteristics that emerge or become increasingly sex-differentiated in adolescence, such as emotion and cognition.

Emotion, Aggression, and Problem Behavior. Hormonal increases at pubertal onset generally appear to increase girls' risk for serious depression, especially for those with genetic vulnerability (Angold, Costello, Erkanli, & Worthman, 1999), but not to increase negative affect in the normal range (Buchanan, Eccles, & Becker, 1992). Associations between hormones and affect across the entire pubertal transition are neither simple nor large (see Brooks-Gunn, Petersen, & Compas, 1995; Buchanan et al., 1992).

Hormone effects are clearer in studies linking hormones to aggression and behavior problems, particularly in boys (Buchanan et al., 1992; Susman et al., 1998). Hormones both affect and are affected by behavior. For example, testosterone levels increase in adult sports players who win and in their fans (e.g., Bernhardt, Dabbs, Fielden, & Lutter, 1998). Behavioral effects of testosterone also depend on social context (Rowe, Maughan, Worthman, Costello, & Angold, 2004).

Timing of pubertal onset has behavioral significance (reviewed in Susman & Rogol, 2004). Early-maturing girls have more emotional distress and problem behavior (e.g., delinquency, substance use, early sexuality) than on-time peers (e.g., Ge, Conger, & Elder, 1996) and these problems persist into adulthood (Weichold, Silbereisen, & Schmitt-Rodermund, 2003). Among boys, late maturers have low self-esteem compared to on-time peers, whereas early maturers are more popular and have better self-image (Ruble & Martin, 1998) but are more likely to engage in delinquent, antisocial, and sexual behaviors and substance use (Williams & Dunlop, 1999). Social factors that mediate and moderate these effects, especially in girls, include association with older and other-sex peers, childhood problems, parenting practices, and neighborhoods (Ge, Brody, Conger, Simons, & Murry, 2002; Weichold et al., 2003).

Cognition. Circulating hormones relate to patterns of cognitive abilities. Most evidence comes from observational studies in adults (Hampson, 2002). Verbal fluency and memory are enhanced by circulating estrogens beginning in adolescence. Spatial ability is enhanced by moderate levels of androgen in adults (i.e., levels high for normal females, low for normal males).

Interpretive Issues in Studying Hormone Effects in Adolescence. Some of the inconsistencies about effects of hormones in adolescence reflect their complexity and the challenges of assessing pubertal hormones and the physical changes that accompany them (Dorn, Dahl, Woodward, & Biro, 2006). Even direct hormone assays are limited unless they are repeated to capture intraindividual variability. It is important to study how biological factors exert effects indirectly and interact with social factors to produce gender-related changes during adolescence (e.g., Ruble & Martin, 1998; Susman, 1997). For instance, school transitions affect children's self-perceptions and mood, especially for girls, and gender identification or socialization processes prior to adolescence may affect reactions to adolescent transitions.

Brain Structure and Function

Ultimately, all aspects of gender development are mediated through the brain. The brain changes in response to the environment, but there has been less study of the ways in which brain sex differences are shaped by behavioral differences than the reverse. Knowledge of male and female brains has increased dramatically with the availability of imaging techniques, including structural magnetic resonance imaging (MRI) to observe fine-grained details of brain structure and functional MRI (fMRI) to measure brain activation to specific tasks (e.g., looking at emotional pictures; see Resnick, 2006).

Overall Brain Structure. Sex differences in brain size (about 10% to 15% larger in men than in women) are largely attributable to differences in body size (Halpern, 2000). Beyond that, there are sex differences in specific brain regions that may underlie differences in behavior and abilities (see Resnick, 2006). Some studies suggest that females have more cortical gray matter (containing cell bodies), whereas males have more white matter (containing fiber tracts), differences that might have implications for processes involving coordination among multiple brain areas.

Organization of the Cerebral Hemispheres. In most people, the left hemisphere is specialized for language tasks and the right for perceptual and spatial processing, with some variation among individuals in brain lateralization. Women are somewhat less lateralized than men (Voyer, 1996) both functionally and structurally (Resnick, 2006), and sex differences may be found in brain organization within hemispheres (Kimura, 1999).

Regional Brain Structures. Sex differences in brain structure are suggested to underlie cognitive and behavioral sex differences. Two aspects of brain structure garnered early attention: The preoptic area of the anterior hypothalamus has been associated with sex and sexual orientation in people (e.g., LeVay, 1993); the corpus callosum, which connects the hemispheres and allows information transfer, has been suggested to be larger in women than in men, but studies are inconsistent (Resnick, 2006). Recent studies have focused on brain regions associated with specific behaviors; for example, differences in the size of the temporal lobe that might account for differences in language (e.g., Goldstein et al., 2001; Resnick, 2006). Brain sex differences are generally small and a large brain size does not always mean optimal function; further, brain size differences have seldom been explicitly related to behavioral differences. Developmental changes in the brain, including sex differences, are only beginning to be understood (e.g., Gogtay et al., 2004).

Regional Brain Function.   Functional MRI studies have been used to examine sex differences in the activation of specific regions in response to psychologically relevant stimuli or tasks. For example, when navigating a virtual-reality maze, men and women activated different regions, and men performed more quickly than women; processing differences may reflect men's use of geometric cues versus women's use of landmarks (Grön, Wunderlich, Spitzer, Tomczak, & Riepe, 2000).

The amygdala has been a focus because of its role in processing emotion (Hamann & Canli, 2004). Meta-analysis (Wager, Phan, Liberzon, & Taylor, 2003) revealed no sex difference in overall activation to emotional stimuli, but men show greater lateralized activation. They may be sex differences in specific aspects of emotional processing (e.g., sexual arousal; Hamann & Canli, 2004; Hamann, Herman, Nolan, & Wallen, 2004).

Integration and Conclusions

The biologically oriented work of the past few years has enhanced knowledge about hormonal influences on gender development and potential neural mechanisms that mediate both hormone effects and environmental input. Just as sex hormones affect the body, they also influence behavior. Hormones present during early development (organizational effects) play a substantial role in aspects of gender development, particularly self-perception, preferences, and behavioral enactment of some matrix content areas. Many important questions remain unanswered about hormone effects on gender development. Do prenatal hormones affect gender-related styles and values or concepts and beliefs? What are the psychological mechanisms that mediate the behavioral effects of hormones? For example, what is it about boys' toys that makes them attractive to children who have been exposed to high prenatal androgen levels? What neural mechanisms mediate the psychological effects of early hormones?

Sex hormone increases during adolescence do not have many direct behavioral effects within the normal range, but may increase girls' depression and boys' aggressiveness and behavior problems. Hormone-behavior links are complex, mediated and moderated by social and psychological changes. Sex hormones circulating in the body throughout adolescence and adulthood influence gender-related behavior, but generally different aspects than are influenced by prenatal hormones.

Brain structure and function also differ in some ways between the sexes, including regions involved in gender-related behavior. But it is necessary to make the explicit link between the brain and behavior and to show how the links are forged—for example, how structural differences are produced by prenatal exposure to sex hormones, and how patterns of brain activation are affected by sex-differential experience and circulating sex hormones at puberty.

There is increasingly sophisticated understanding of biological effects and recognition that they are not immutable. Genes are activated or suppressed by environmental factors. Hormones and brain functioning are almost certainly influenced by the different environments in which girls and boys are raised, by their different toy and activity choices, and by joint effects of genes and the social environment.

SOCIALIZATION APPROACHES

Gender permeates every aspect of a child's social environment. In Bronfenbrenner's (1977) terms, gender is communicated through the cultural values and practices of the macrosystem (e.g., power and economic differentials between men and women), which in turn influence the microsystems a child experiences at home, school, and neighborhood (Leaper, 2002). But how do we conceptualize the effects of these various influences? Which environmental features are noticed and incorporated into gender development, and by what processes? These questions are at the heart of socialization approaches.

Socialization Processes

Early applications of social learning theory (Mischel, 1970) viewed gender development as proceeding through direct reinforcement for conformity to gender norms and observational learning. Social learning perspectives have since been modified and elaborated (Bandura, 1986), with particular focus on cognitive processes (e.g., attention, memory). For example, when children observe same-sex models, they are assumed to extract information about how behaviors are enacted, the sequencing of events, and consequences associated with enacting behavior.

These formulations provide increased explanation of gender learning. First, children imitate behavior under some circumstances but not others (e.g., imitation of multiple same-sex models is more likely than single ones). Second, observational learning is not confined to imitation of same-sex models. Children learn abstract rules and styles of modeled behaviors, constructing notions of "appropriate" appearance, occupations, and behavior for each sex, and use these stereotypes to develop complex concepts about gender-appropriate behavior. Learning depends on the incentives and sanctions associated with the outcomes of engaging in these behaviors. These experiences lead children to develop outcome expectancies and self-efficacy beliefs that become linked to gender-related behaviors, serving to motivate and regulate gender role conduct. Although such regulatory processes are originally environmentally determined, they become internalized as children administer self-praise or self-sanctions in relation to a set of personal standards for gender conduct. Third, gender learning results from three reciprocal influences: the person (i.e., cognitive, affective, and biological factors), behavior, and the environment (see Bandura, 1986; Bussey & Bandura, 1999, for details).

Most work on socialization of gender development focuses on the influences of the family, peers, school, and the media through the processes of reinforcement and observational learning, as described next. The only study directly examining the shift from external to internal regulation suggested that this develops between 3 to 4 years of age (Bussey & Bandura, 1992), but the lack of longitudinal data and other limitations preclude definitive conclusions.

Gender Socialization in the Family

The family provides many types of socialization experiences, including models of gender roles and differences in the ways sons and daughters are raised.

Encouragement of Gender-Typed Activities and Interests. Caregivers provide boys and girls with different toys and room furnishings (Pomerleau, Bolduc, Malcuit, & Cossette, 1990; Rheingold & Cook, 1975), which may channel children's preferences and engagement in activities. Meta-analysis of parents' differential treatment of boys and girls (Lytton & Romney, 1991) showed the clearest effect for encouragement of gender-typed activities (versus areas such as personality traits). For example, parents offer gender-stereotypic toys to children during free play, and are more responsive to gender-typical than to gender-atypical play; the effect is somewhat stronger for fathers than for mothers, and decreases with the child's age. It is found in cultures other than middle-class Caucasian (e.g., Raffaelli & Ontai, 2004), and relates to parent-child communication patterns (Leaper, 2000). But, parents also treat young children in nonstereotypic ways, including the purchase of gender neutral toys when they are not requested by the child (e.g., Fisher-Thompson, 1993). Thus, contemporary efforts to foster sex-differentiated play may often be subtle or limited, and many parents make efforts to be egalitarian.

What is the effect of encouraging gender-typed play? Parents' encouragement of gender-typed play in very young children may promote learning of gender distinctions (Ruble & Martin, 1998). Parents' provision of specific experiences may also foster different skills in daughters versus sons (Leaper, 2002), for example, boys receive more explanations of scientific content in museums than do girls, which may foster boys' interest in and knowledge about science (Crowley, Callanan, Tenenbaum, & Allen, 2001).

Little is known about how these parent behaviors affect children's play preferences and behaviors (Ruble & Martin, 1998). There appear to be significant but weak correlations between parent behaviors and children's preferences and behaviors (Lindsey & Mize, 2001). An important "tool" of gender socialization is channeling or shaping, with socializing agents structuring the environment in ways to limits choices, such as providing only dolls for girls and trucks for boys (Eisenberg, Wolchik, Hernandez, & Pasternack, 1985). Thus, desired behavior may result from the situation, and not from parents' direct encouragement of specific activities.

Encouragement of Gender-Typed Personal-Social Attributes. It is unclear whether parental socialization practices influence the development of gender-typed personality characteristics in children, with some reviews indicating that there are effects (Huston, 1983) but a meta-analysis suggesting that there are not (Lytton & Romney, 1991). Some of the discrepancy may be due to the subtlety and context-dependence of socialization. Parents provide greater gender socialization to children in mixed-sex than same-sex sibling dyads (McHale et al., 2003); siblings with an other-sex sibling and a traditional father exhibited the most sex-typed leisure activities and parent-child activities (McHale et al., 1999). Gender socialization practices may involve subtleties in gender-related language and communication, for example, mothers in one study explicitly espoused egalitarian views but implicitly made gender concepts salient through labeling of gender and contrasting males and females (Gelman Taylor, & Nguyen, 2004).

Parents show different treatment of sons and daughters in important ways beyond the assignments of chores or encouragement of activities or traits (Leaper, 2002). The nature and frequency of parents' communications differ for sons versus daughters (e.g., Fivush, Brotman, Buckner, & Goodman, 2000; Leaper, Anderson, & Sanders, 1998). Parents also believe that boys and girls have different attributes and skills, even when they do not. For example, mothers of 11-month-olds underestimated girls' motor skills and overestimated boys' skills, but the sexes did not differ in motor performance (Mondschein, Adolph, & Tamis-LeMonda, 2000). Such beliefs and expectations influence both adults' perceptions and behaviors toward their children, and the children's own perceptions and behaviors. In an impressive research program, Eccles and colleagues (e.g., Fredricks & Eccles, 2002) found that parents who hold stronger stereotypes regarding the capabilities of boys and girls in English, math, and sports had differential expectations regarding their own children's abilities in these subjects, which were in turn related to the children's performance and self-perceptions of competence, even when actual ability levels were controlled. Such relations are mediated, in part, by parents' tendencies to provide different experiences for sons and daughters (e.g., enrolling sons in sports programs). Further, differential treatment may occur because parents feel greater commonality and responsibility for socializing same-sex children, and thereby exert closer control over them (Huston, 1983; Ruble & Martin, 1998).

Role Models in the Home.   In what ways do parents act as role models, thereby influencing their children's attitudes and behaviors? Maternal employment has been associated with less stereotyped concepts and beliefs in both girls and boys and fewer gender-typed preferences and behaviors in girls (Ruble & Martin, 1998), although the processes that mediate the associations are not clear. Family roles affect children's gender development: egalitarian division of labor in the home (or father involvement) is associated with less traditional occupational and peer preferences (Serbin et al., 1993), and less traditional gender role attitudes and behaviors (McHale et al., 2003), although such effects are not consistently found (e.g., Weisner, Garnier, & Loucky, 1994).

Parental Attitudes and Values.   To what extent are children's gender concepts related to general measures of gender orientation in the home, such as parents' attitudes about equality or nonegalitarian lifestyles? Parental attitudes have been associated with children's gender-typing, including the distribution of gender-typed chores to sons and daughters (e.g., Blair, 1992) and children's own gender attitudes (e.g., McHale et al., 1999). Such relations vary across measures of gender-typing, even in the same study, and are often moderated by other factors such as birth order (McHale et al., 1999). For example, meta-analysis of the relation between parents' gender schemas and child outcomes (Tenenbaum & Leaper, 2002) showed larger effects for parent-daughter pairs and for parents of older children and adolescents. Research would benefit from an approach recognizing cultural and historical variations in gendered attitudes (Leaper, 2002; McHale et al., 2003).

Alternative Family Structures: Single Parenting and Gay and Lesbian Parenting.
Evidence suggests small differences at best between children in traditional versus nontraditional families, such as single-parent or lesbian households (e.g., Patterson, 2006; Stevens, Golombok, Beveridge, & Avon Longitudinal Study of Parents and Children Study Team, 2002; Stevenson & Black, 1988), but effects may be subtle or selective. It is probably more productive to look at specific processes in the home (e.g., division of labor, parental attitudes) than the family structure itself (McHale et al., 2003).

Sibling Effects.   Siblings may promote stronger gender socialization than do parents, but sibling effects vary by age, birth order, and whether they are the same sex (Crouter, Manke, & McHale, 1995; McHale et al., 2003). Although sibling effects have generally been conceptualized in terms of modeling, attempts to be different from siblings may also be involved (McHale, Updegraff, Helms-Erikson, & Crouter, 2001).

Gender Socialization at School

Schools provide a wide array of gender-related messages to children through the different positions held by men and women, teachers' differential treatment of boys and girls, and opportunities to learn about the consequences of behavior through observing peers.

Role Models in School.   Schools provide children with gender-related information through roles played by men and women. Men are disproportionately represented in positions of power and administration, whereas women are often teachers, particularly in the early grades. Only in older grades are children likely to have male teachers, and these are often in male-typical content areas (e.g., mathematics, science). But it is not clear how these role models affect gender development and whether same-sex education is better than coed-education (Ruble & Martin, 1998; Ruble et al., 2006).

Differential Treatment.   Some research suggests that teachers influence gender development in several ways: by interacting differently with girls and boys, reinforcing stereotypic expectations about girls' and boys' behavior, encouraging gender-appropriate play and discouraging gender-inappropriate play, attending more to boys than to girls and interrupting them less (see Ruble & Martin, 1998). Effects are biggest in the early years, except that high school boys receive more criticism from teachers than do girls. Teacher responsiveness might reflect bias or students' willingness to volunteer answers. Elementary school teachers called on boys more than girls, but girls and boys were equally likely to be called on when they volunteered (Altermatt, Jovanovic, & Perry, 1998), whereas high school teachers' greater interactions with male students were not driven by boys' verbal comments to teachers (Duffy, Warren, & Walsh, 2002).

Teachers hold differentiated views of girls and boys, believing that the sexes differ in science and math (e.g., Tiedemann, 2000) and in having different expectations for their classroom behavior (Borg, 1998). However, some evidence suggests that teachers form relatively accurate perceptions of students based on children's characteristics (e.g., achievement and motivation) and only occasionally rely on stereotypes about sex (Madon et al., 1998).

Gender Socialization by Peers

Peers serve as socialization agents through reinforcement and role modeling. Through extensive exposure to same-sex others (due to sex-segregation), children selectively learn behaviors and interaction styles associated with their sex (Leaper, 1994; Maccoby, 1998).

Differential Treatment.   Classic studies show that, by age 3, children respond differentially to gender-typed behavior in others (e.g., Fagot, 1977; reviewed in Huston, 1983; Ruble & Martin, 1998), for example, negatively to boys engaging in female-typical behaviors. Research shows that children are evaluated (and rejected, for example) on their gender-typed behavior (Waas & Graczyk, 1999).

Peer Models.   Children learn standards for gender-appropriate behavior through observation, but it is unclear whether peer modeling of gender-inconsistent behavior can
promote change. Simple observation of peer models engaging in gender-inconsistent
behavior did not change young children's behavior unless the model's behavior was reinforced (Katz & Walsh, 1991). Other-sex role models can sometimes dissuade children from "own-sex appropriate" preferences, but children also consider the perceived
appropriateness of the activities encouraged (Harrison & O'Neill, 2000). Children and
adolescents may also try to behave in ways that are "cool" or popular and this varies by
sex and ethnicity (Graham, Taylor, & Hudley, 1998).

Socialization in Sex-Segregated Play.   Because children spend so much time in sex-
segregated play, their same-sex peers provide opportunities to learn gender-typed interactional styles and behaviors (see Ladd, 2005; Leaper, 1994; Maccoby, 1998 for
reviews); in fact, sex-segregated play has been suggested to produce "separate cultures," which may narrow children's behavioral repertoires and influence their attitudes
(Maccoby, 1998). The evidence shows that sex segregation effects depend on age. In
older children, it may lessen gender-stereotypes; for example, all-female schools and
math classes may promote nontraditional attitudes (e.g., Lee & Bryk, 1986), allow
greater exposure to successful role models, and reduce differential teacher responsiveness and peer pressures compared to mixed-sex groupings (Ruble & Martin, 1998).
But, in young children, sex segregated play has a different effect. In one study (Martin
& Fabes, 2001), preschool children with higher "social dosage" of same-sex play early
in the school year increased in gender-typed behaviors later in the school year more
than children who had lower levels of same-sex play. Sex-segregated play also influences school readiness (Fabes, Martin, Hanish, Anders, et al., 2003; Martin & Dinella,
2002) and can facilitate or exacerbate existing behavioral tendencies. For example,
highly arousable children who play with same-sex peers show changes in behavior
problems—increased for boys and decreased for girls. Playing with other arousable
boys may not help with behavior regulation, but girls' calm play may help arousable
girls learn control (Fabes, Shepard, Guthrie, & Martin, 1997). It is difficult to disentangle the consequences of peer socialization from the selection factors that draw children
together; a transactional pattern is likely (Hanish, Martin, Fabes, Leonard, & Herzog,
2005; Martin et al., 2005).

Observational Learning from the Media

Children spend much of their free time watching television and using other media (e.g.,
DVDs, the Internet), which provides them with messages about gender (Subrahmanyam, Kraut, Greenfield, & Gross, 2001). Boys and girls watch somewhat different
programs, for example, video games and sports versus relationship and comedy programming, with differences increasing across childhood (Huston, Wright, Marquis, &
Green, 1999; Subrahmanyam et al., 2001; Wright et al., 2001) and in adolescence
(Roberts & Foehr, 2004). Despite some changes over time, all forms of media—television, other electronic media, books, music—still convey stereotypic messages, teaching and reinforcing traditional roles (Ruble et al., 2006).

Influence of Gender-Stereotypic Portrayals of the Sexes.   How do these stereotyped
media presentations affect children's gender development? It is very difficult to study
the causal influence of something so pervasive in our culture. Some correlational studies

show that exposure to media is associated with stereotypic beliefs, but it is unclear whether the media influence beliefs or children choose media that are consistent with their beliefs (Ruble et al., 2006). Meta-analyses of experimental and nonexperimental studies show a small association between frequent television viewing and more stereotypic beliefs about gender roles (e.g., Morgan & Shanahan, 1997). Longitudinal data suggest that television viewing at one time is linked to gender-related attitudes and behavior later in time; for example, messages counter to gender-typed norms have longer-term effects than gender-typed messages (Anderson, Huston, Schmitt, Linebarger, & Wright, 2001). The most convincing evidence for television's impact comes from a natural experiment in Canada: the introduction of television into towns that had been unable to receive it. Children held less traditional gender attitudes than comparison children before television was introduced, but increased in traditional attitudes 2 years after television was introduced (Kimball, 1986).

Integration and Conclusions

Gender socialization processes at home, at school, with peers, and through the media all contribute to gender differentiation in most areas identified in Table 18.1—concepts, preferences, behaviors, and values. The social world is gender-typed, but it is less clear how this influences gender development and by what processes. For example, studies using social learning principles to change stereotypic beliefs and behaviors have met with little success (Ruble & Martin, 1998). Although traditional role modeling in the home is associated with encouragement of gender-differentiated play, it is unclear what it is about the home that matters, for example, differential responding, traditional attitudes, or the father's lack of involvement in activities.

COGNITIVE APPROACHES

There is a rapidly growing body of work showing how cognitions affect gender development. Although cognitive approaches have similarities (see Martin et al., 2002, for a review), different theories focus on different cognitions and mechanisms linking cognitions to beliefs and behavior. We examine three cognitive approaches to gender development: (1) cognitive developmental theory, (2) gender schema theory, and (3) social identification theory.

Cognitive Developmental Theory and the Role of Gender Constancy

Kohlberg (1966) first posited the importance of developmental changes in children's gender category understanding for organizing gender development. He proposed that gender development involves an active construction of the meaning of gender categories, initiated internally by the child rather than externally by socializing agents. This idea that children socialize themselves into gender roles was pioneering, but the mechanisms driving this socialization were not articulated (Huston, 1983; Martin & Little, 1990).

Review of the Evidence. Over the years, cognitive developmental theory (CDT) has been elaborated (Ruble & Martin, 1998). A key aspect is the role of gender constancy in increasing responsiveness to gender-related information and application of gender norms. Many studies show positive relationships between level of gender constancy and aspects of gender development: selective attention to same-sex models; same-sex imitation; same-sex activity, clothing, and peer preferences; gender stereotype knowledge; and heightened responsiveness to gender cues (see Martin et al., 2002). But, not all results are consistent (e.g., Levy, 1998; Zucker et al., 1999). Comparisons across studies are difficult because of varying operationalizations of constancy (see 1A).

Increased responsiveness to gendered information is found more often to relate to early stages of gender constancy such as gender stability (over time) or basic identity. Only rarely has the highest level of constancy, gender consistency (consistency across different situations, e.g., appearance changes), been associated with other indices of gender development (Ruble & Martin, 1998). These findings support Kohlberg's idea about the motivational significance of knowledge and identification with gender categories (Maccoby, 1990), but suggest that the process begins earlier than he thought. In support, two recent studies show associations between understanding of stability and increases in gender-typed beliefs (Ruble, Taylor, et al., 2007; Ruble, Trautner, et al., 2007). It is unclear what psychological processes underlie relations between different components of constancy and gender-related outcomes (e.g., Does gender identity elicit group identification or reflect the motivational attachment to one's group?).

Does gender consistency have any important consequences for gender development? Firm conclusions are difficult to draw because of methodological issues, but the evidence suggests that children show strongest adherence to gender-related behaviors prior to attainment of gender consistency, perhaps because they fear that cross-sex behaviors may transform them to the other sex (Huston, 1983). Recent research suggests that consistency relates to decreased rather than increased rigidity (Ruble, Taylor, et al., 2007). Thus, gender constancy may function differently than initially suggested: A complete understanding of constancy does not serve the initial organizing function that Kohlberg (1966) proposed but may serve other important functions, such as promoting an increase in flexibility. Early stages of constancy—identity and sometimes stability—do show some of the predicted associations.

Gender Schema Theory

A consistent theme in gender schema theory (GST; Bem, 1981; Liben & Signorella, 1980; Martin & Halverson, 1981) is that children are actively involved in gender development. Gender schemas are interrelated networks of mental associations representing information about the sexes. Schemas are active constructions and not passive copies of the environment, prone to errors and distortions. Contemporary refinements to GST (Martin et al., 2002) clarify the role of self- and other-schemas (Hannover, 2000), emphasize the interplay between gender schemas and social environments (Martin & Dinella, 2001, 2002) and the dynamic nature of gender schemas (Martin, 2000), and delineate the processes that influence stereotyping (Barbera, 2003) and contribute to schema maintenance (Hughes & Seta, 2003).

Schematic consistency refers to children's tendencies to bring their attention, actions, and memories in line with their gender schemas. Once they identify themselves as boys or girls, children seek details and scripts for same-sex activities, show in-group biases, and become more sensitive to sex differences. Children are motivated to behave according to gender norms to define themselves and attain cognitive consistency. The links between gender cognitions and behavior are presumed to occur through selective attention to and memory for own-sex relevant information and through motivation to be similar to same-sex others. Gender schemas are considered to be organizers of gender development but not the sole causes of gendered behavior (Martin et al., 2002).

That is, children may show gendered behavior prior to development of gender identity and for reasons other than that a behavior is appropriate for their sex.

Developing Gender Schemas.   The development of gender schemas involves learning actual gender-related regularities in the environment while also constructing other gender-related patterns, some of which may not exist in reality. Infants attend to statistical regularities and form categories and concepts based on them. For gender, sex differences in physical appearance (e.g., body shape) and styles (e.g., clothing) make learning even easier and increase the salience of gender categories. Furthermore, parents, media, peers, and the culture highlight the functional utility of gender categories and transmit information about sex-related differences (e.g., boys don't wear pink). Research shows that children are more likely to use categories to make judgments of others when the categories are both physically salient and functional (e.g., teachers line children up by groups; Bigler, Brown, & Markell, 2001; Bigler, Jones, & Lobliner, 1997).

Children expand schemas by using processes that are less veridical, for instance, by forming illusory correlations (see next section), exaggerating between-group differences and within-group similarities (see section on identification with social categories), and drawing inferences from limited information. Schemas may also be modified by children's preferences (Liben & Bigler, 2002; Martin, Eisenbud, & Rose, 1995).

Individual Differences in Gender Schemas.   The content and application of gender schemas varies across situations and children (e.g., Spence, 1999). Children vary in how fully developed, elaborated, and accessible their gender schemas are (Hannover, 2000; Liben & Bigler, 2002), which relates to how schemas influence behavior and thinking (Bem, 1981). By middle childhood, children develop ideas about gender typicality, and these cognitions have consequences for adjustment (Egan & Perry, 2001; Perry, 2004).

Gender Schemas and Inferences.   Gender schemas guide children's gender-based inferences and judgments. Children rely on gender schemas to make social judgments, such as deciding on a play partner; interest, liking and activity preferences of unfamiliar girls and boys (see Ruble et al., 2006). Applications can be subtle: By age 8 or 9, children use gender schemas to judge which sex will play particular musical instruments, and their own preferences are similar to their stereotypes (Harrison & O'Neill, 2000, 2003). Children use sex and other social categories to make judgments in novel and ambiguous situations and to make generalizations about unfamiliar characteristics (Gelman, Collman, & Maccoby, 1986). For example, 3.5-year-olds told the preferences of a girl and a boy for nongender-typed objects (e.g., pizza) projected these preferences to sex-unspecified others based only on their proper names (Bauer & Coyne, 1997). Children also use gender schemas to evaluate and explain behavior (Giles & Heyman, 2004; Heyman, 2001; Heyman & Gelman, 2000). This reliance on gender schemas provides missing information, and feeds the formation and expansion of gender schemas.

Memory and Illusory Correlations.   Children selectively attend to and remember schematically consistent information (e.g., remember own-sex objects better than other-sex objects, Cherney & Ryalls, 1999), and they distort information that does not fit their schemas into schema-consistent information, for instance, remembering a woman firefighter as a man (Ruble et al., 2006). Furthermore, children show illusory correlations, believing that schema-consistent information occurred more frequently than schema-inconsistent or neutral information, even when each is presented an equal number of times (Susskind, 2003). Selective memory, distortions, and illusory correlations contribute to the formation and maintenance of gender schemas, and give schemas a resiliency even in the face of contradictory information.

Role of Identification with a Social Category

Social categorization approaches emphasize gender identification occurring at a group level, in which social groupings provide a system of orientation for self-reference (Tajfel & Turner, 1979). Social or collective identities are socially meaningful categories that individuals consider descriptive of themselves or their group (Ashmore, Deaux, & McLaughlin-Volpe, 2004; Thoits & Virshup, 1997).

Much work has suggested that identification with a particular social category (involving a comparison with other social categories) promotes a sense of belonging and connectedness but also may lead to stereotyping of out-group members, prejudice, and intergroup conflict (Hewstone, Rubin, & Willis, 2002; Tajfel & Turner, 1979). But, little is known about the development of social category beliefs in young children (Ruble et al., 2004). Three elements of collective identity are particularly relevant to a developmental analysis of gender: (1) the consequences of a sense of "we," (2) the multidimensional nature of collective identity, and (3) contextual influences on collective identity.

Consequences.   Collective identities have significant personal and interpersonal consequences (Brewer & Brown, 1998; Hewstone et al., 2002), which takes many forms. Group membership shapes personal values and interests, in turn influencing effort and performance. Individuals whose gender identity is central to their self-definitions may value tasks associated with their sex and devalue those associated with the other sex (e.g., Wigfield & Eccles, 2000). Simply labeling an ambiguous activity as associated with one sex affects performance (Martin & Dinella, 2002; C. F. Miller et al., 2006). The mere act of categorizing individuals into social groups changes the nature of interpersonal perceptions and behaviors (Tajfel, 1978) by increasing perception of between-group differences and within-group similarity, and increasing in-group favoritism. Social categorization and in-group positivity are probably universal aspects of human social groups, but out-group hostility requires social-structural and motivational conditions not inherent to collective identity formation (Brewer, 2001). For example, prejudice against women is more likely when they violate gender stereotypes or participate in male-dominated domains (Eagly & Mladinic, 1994).

Gender is one of the earliest and most salient social categories available, so children's self-identification as members of the group of males or females is likely to affect their self-concepts, preferences, and behaviors. The emergence of this sense of "we boys" or "we girls" (Maccoby, 1998) probably begins by 2 to 3 years of age, when children recognize and label the sexes, and is clearly evident by age 5, when children spontaneously categorize people by sex (Bennett, Sani, Hopkins, Agostini, & Mallucchi, 2000). Children evaluate their own group positively and out-groups negatively (see 6C), but it is unclear whether this directly reflects the emergence of collective identity.

Multidimensional Nature.   Group identity depends on more than simple self-labeling (e.g., Ashmore et al., 2004) and includes the centrality/importance of gender to self-concept, personal evaluation of one's gender, and feelings about oneself in relation to gender (i.e., typicality, contentedness, or felt pressure for gender conformity; Egan & Perry, 2001; Ruble et al., 2004). There is little work on the emergence of these components of identity, but gender appears to be central to young children relative to other social identities (Ruble et al., 2004). Certain combinations of identity components may create problems: Children who feel gender atypical but also feel pressure for gender conformity are particularly likely to have low self-esteem (e.g., Egan & Perry, 2001).

Context.   There are several ways in which context influences collective identity related to gender. First, gender salience varies by group composition (e.g., the only girl in a group; e.g., McGuire, McGuire, Child, & Fujioka, 1978). Second, categories are more likely used for processing information when they have functional value, perceptual salience (e.g., distinctive clothing), and group-to-attribute links (e.g., observing that boys' do X; e.g., Bigler et al., 1997). Third, stereotypes are representations of social groups formed in context and depend on specific comparisons rather than being stored concepts waiting to be activated (Sani & Bennett, 2001). For example, boys described boys as strong when compared to girls, but as talkative when compared to men (Sani, Bennett, Mullally, & MacPherson, 2003). Fourth, context-dependent collective gender identity may emerge in preschool, with gender qualities constructed and maintained at the level of the group ("we girls" and "we boys") rather than the individual (Maccoby, 2002).

Integration and Conclusions

The three cognitive approaches have commonalities, but differ in emphases. First, all hypothesize that gender cognitions act to organize and interpret information and provide standards to guide behavior, but they have historically emphasized different cognitions. Early versions of CDT emphasized gender stability and constancy, but there is similarity in new versions of CDT, gender schema, and category identification theories as they all emphasize the importance of basic categorization as a girl or boy. The theories also have different perspectives: the relation of individuals to social groups (category identification), the stability and consistency of gender understanding (CDT), and the range of gender-related knowledge structures that influence gender development (GST).

Second, all cognitive theories view children as actively seeking and constructing rules about gender at an early age, being motivated to build on their schemas and to develop gendered standards for their own behavior as they strive to understand the significance of their gender category. "Gender construction" processes are assumed to permit the collection and organization of accurate and inaccurate information about the sexes, but questions remain about exactly how this happens.

Third, these cognitive approaches focus on development—the relative waxing and waning of gender knowledge and its use and implications for behavior. Children move from awareness of gender categorical distinctions (construction/information gathering) to rigid application of those distinctions during "consolidation" (Ruble, 1994) or "schema confirmation" (Welch-Ross & Schmidt, 1996) to later flexibility in applying gender knowledge (integration and schema deployment; Trautner et al., 2005). It is unclear whether these phase-like shifts in gender knowledge and application parallel other elements of gender development (e.g., Ruble, 1994) and link to changes in broad cognitive skills (Bigler, 1995).

Cognitive theories have sometimes been misunderstood (see Martin et al., 2002; Martin, Ruble, & Szkrybalo, 2004, for detailed review), with criticisms focusing on the temporal sequence of cognitions and gendered behavior, and with links between cognitions and behavior. With regard to temporal sequencing, there is a widespread but erroneous assumption that cognitions must not affect gender development if their appearance has a later onset than gendered behavior (e.g., Bandura & Bussey, 2004; A. Campbell et al., 2002). Cognitive theories allow for this, instead focusing on the organizational and motivational function of gender concepts (see Martin et al., 2004). Moreover, there is good evidence that gender cognitions develop early (e.g., Martin et al., 2002).

Links between cognitions (gender identity/labeling and gender stereotypes) and behavior have not always been found. Few studies have examined correlates of *gender identity* (group membership), and most assumed (without evidence) that gender labeling reflects gender identity understanding. In very young children, gender labeling is related to preferences for same-sex peers and some behaviors, but shows mixed relations with toy play (e.g., Fagot, Leinbach, & Hagan, 1986; O'Brien & Huston, 1985); in preschoolers, gender labeling/membership is related to preferences and stereotype knowledge (Martin & Little, 1990). Limited longitudinal data provide the clearest support: Children who use gender labels early show increased gender-typed play in the toddler years relative to those who use labels later (Fagot & Leinbach, 1989; Zosuls et al., 2007). Children's gender cognitions and beliefs about play partners relate to their observed play patterns, for example, how much time they spend with same-sex peers (Martin et al., 1999; Martin, Fabes, Hanish, Leonard, & Dinella, 2007). *Gender stereotypes* are sometimes found to correlate with behavior (Aubry et al., 1999; C. F. Miller et al., 2006; Serbin et al., 1993), but the direction of causation is unclear (Liben & Bigler, 2002). Stronger evidence comes from experimental studies showing gender stereotypes to influence behavior, motivation and interests, and memory for information (see Martin & Dinella, 2002; Martin et al., 2002). When children are shown novel toys given gender-typed labels ("boys like the things in this box better than girls do"), their behavior and memory reflect the stated gender-typing of the toy (e.g., Bradbard, Martin, Endsley, & Halverson, 1986). These findings are consistent across laboratories, labels, age, and efforts to reduce demand characteristics.

AN INTEGRATION OF PERSPECTIVES

The three broad approaches to gender development—biological, socialization, and cognitive—generally focus on specific topics and concerns unique to each approach. To fully understand gender-typing, however, we need to listen to messages from each perspective and devise ways to integrate the three approaches in meaningful ways. Huston's (1983) plea for biological and social psychologically oriented researchers to combine their efforts is beginning to be realized in conversation, if not yet in data. Research findings are accumulating about the wide range of influences on particular gendered behaviors, suggesting several promising avenues for future research using multiple approaches.

Children come into this world with certain predispositions that are manifested and exaggerated or suppressed by the environment in which they are reared, and those with sex-atypical predispositions provide a unique opportunity to examine gender development. For example, hypotheses derived from cognitive/schema and socialization theories could be tested in girls with CAH or typical girls with high levels of prenatal testosterone. Doing so makes clear that biology is a process, unfolding across development, manifested through and moderated by the social environment.

Consider some outstanding questions about gender development that can be informed by such studies. What is the role of gender identity and awareness in gender-typing—how do girls with CAH develop female gender identity but interest in boys' toys? How does socialization occur—do girls with CAH model others who share their identity (female-typical) or their interests (male-typical)? What is the basis of their interactional patterns—do girls with CAH play with girls because they have the same gender identity, with boys because they have similar interests, or with children who have similar play styles or strategies for influencing others?

The key questions about gender development—for example, how do gender identity and gendered behaviors develop and how does gender socialization operate—require creative thinking across disciplinary boundaries and perspectives. Answers require a willingness to suspend narrow conceptualizations of gender and old biases. Using multidisciplinary teams, multiple perspectives, and broader conceptualizations of underlying mechanisms and processes should enable significant strides in understanding the complexities of gender differentiation.

Conclusions

One of the difficulties about summarizing research on gender is that it cuts across areas and is relevant to virtually every topic, ranging from brain sex differences to children's identification with gender to play styles and sexuality. Controversies frequently arise that do not often occur in other areas, such as the questioning of the research enterprise itself, confusion about terms for major constructs, and the political implications of the findings. Despite, or perhaps because of the controversies, the study of gender attracts scientists from many disciplines, each bringing to the enterprise different interests and strategies. The pluralism of views provides insights into the diverse issues covered in gender studies.

Several broad themes are apparent from research work on gender development. First, there is increasing interest in biological factors and evidence that they play a prominent role in gendered behavior, thinking, and identity. Second, social and cognitive theories have moved more closely together but continue to disagree about some issues, and these theoretical debates drive a surprising amount of gender-typing research. Third, there is increasing recognition of the multidimensionality of gender development (Huston, 1983): researchers draw fewer broad inferences about gender-typing from a single measure; and more careful consideration has been made of distinctions among various content domains and constructs. Fourth, there are exciting new methods available, including some that allow us to understand what infants and young children know about gender.

Many intriguing ideas are emerging. There is renewed interest in process and change in gender development. Social learning theorists have concentrated efforts on cognitive mechanisms underlying observational learning (Bussey & Bandura, 1999). Cognitive theorists have considered how shifts from early gender concepts to consolidated ones influence information processing and memory (Martin et al., 2002; Ruble, 1994). There is increasing interest in the changing nature of gendered personal identities and stereotypes in context (e.g., Sani & Bennett, 2001). Biological perspectives also encourage the study of change because predispositions are manifested and moderated by the organism's transactions with the environment.

The construction of gender in a social context has many interesting possibilities for future research. We need to investigate not only how we see others in gendered ways, but how individuals construct their own gender cues and how they believe these cues work in social interactions. For instance, do individuals strive for balance in their gender cues to present a particular image? Appearance, clothing, adornment, mannerisms all become important to study, given that they are visible cues used to construct gender.

Questions about mental health and self-esteem also require more research efforts. Work has shifted from perspectives about mental health benefits of androgyny to notions that different elements of gender identity relate differentially to adjustment beyond gender-linked competencies (e.g., Egan & Perry, 2001). Do particular domains of gender influence self-regard? Why are preadolescent girls more likely than boys to show declines in self-esteem? Which factors related to gender increase risk or provide buffers?

Gender in relationships has been an interesting focus of research. Peers and parents continue to be studied as agents of socialization, but the processes involved in socialization are assumed to be broader and more subtle than initially expected. More research is needed on the processes involved in socialization, and on individual characteristics related to socialization susceptibility.

Finally, there has been a disproportionate amount of work on younger children and a relative dearth of research on adolescents and adolescent transitions. This is puzzling given the significance of changes during adolescence for gender development (e.g., acceptance of one's male or female body and reproductive functions, forming a sexual orientation, establishing new forms of relationships with same-sex and other-sex peers, decisions regarding future gender roles). Although many researchers have been intrigued by notions of gender intensification during adolescence, empirical research (including suitable measures) has been relatively rare. Future theorizing about gender development would benefit from greater attention to adolescence (Eccles & Barber, 1999; Eckes, Trautner, & Behrendt, 2005).

In conclusion, the study of gender is a monumental undertaking, shared by individuals from many fields. Constantinople (1979) used the metaphor about four blind men studying an elephant to describe how gender researchers have focused on individual parts of the elephant, with each assuming that the animal was best described by the part he was studying. No one recognized the whole animal. Gender researchers must continue to be careful about building global concepts based on partial information. However, we now have some sense of the size of the animal, its capacities, and its general framework. The picture is far from complete but the process of identification continues to be intriguing.

References

Albers, S. M. (1998). The effect of gender-typed clothing on children's social judgments. *Child Study Journal, 28,* 137–159.

Albert, A. A., & Porter, J. R. (1988). Children's gender-role stereotypes: A sociological investigation of psychological models. *Sociological Forum, 3,* 184–210.

Alexander, G. M., & Hines, M. (2002). Sex differences in response to children's toys in nonhuman primates (Cercopithecus aethiops sabaeus). *Evolution and Human Behavior, 23,* 467–479.

Altermatt, E. R., Jovanovic, J., & Perry, M. (1998). Bias or responsivity? Sex and achievement-level effects on teachers' classroom questioning practices. *Journal of Educational Psychology, 90,* 516–527.

Anderson, D. R., Huston, A. C., Schmitt, K. L., Linebarger, D. L., & Wright, J. C. (2001). Early childhood television viewing and adolescent behavior: The recontact study. *Monographs of the Society for Research in Child Development, 66,* 1–147.

Andersen, E. S. (1996). A cross-cultural study of children's register knowledge. In D. I. Slobin, J. Gerhardt, A. Kyratzis, & J. Guo (Eds.), *Social interaction, social context, and language: Essays in honor of Susan Ervin-Tripp* (pp. 125–142). Hillsdale, NJ: Erlbaum.

Angold, A., Costello, E. J., Erkanli, A., & Worthman, C. M. (1999). Pubertal changes in hormone levels and depression in girls. *Psychological Medicine, 29,* 1043–1053.

Antill, J. K., Cotton, S., Russell, G., & Goodnow, J. J. (1996). Measures of children's sex-typing in middle childhood: Pt. II. *Australian Journal of Psychology, 48,* 35–44.

Ashmore, R. D., Deaux, K., & McLaughlin-Volpe, T. (2004). An organizing framework for collective identity: Articulation and significance of multidimensionality. *Psychological Bulletin, 130,* 80–114.

Aube, J., Norcliffe, H., & Koestner, R. (1995). Physical characteristics and the multifactorial approach to the study of gender characteristics. *Social Behavior and Personality, 23,* 69–82.

Aubry, S., Ruble, D. N., & Silverman, L. B. (1999). The role of gender knowledge in children's gender-typed preferences. In L. Balter & C. S. Tamis-LeMonda (Eds.), *Child psychology: A handbook of contemporary issues* (pp. 363–390). New York: Psychology Press.

Bailey, B. A., & Nihlen, A. S. (1990). Effect of experience with nontraditional workers on psychological and social dimensions of occupational sex-role stereotyping by elementary school children. *Psychological Reports, 66,* 1273–1282.

Bailey, J. M., Bechtold, K. T., & Berenbaum, S. A. (2002). Who are tomboys and why should we study them? *Archives of Sexual Behavior, 31,* 333–341.

Bailey, J. M., & Zucker, K. J. (1995). Childhood sex-typed behavior and sexual orientation: A conceptual and quantitative review. *Developmental Psychology, 31,* 43–55.

Bandura, A. (1986). *Social foundations of thought and action: A social cognitive theory.* Englewood Cliffs, NJ: Prentice-Hall.

Bandura, A., & Bussey, K. (2004). On broadening the cognitive, motivational, and sociocultural scope of theorizing about gender development and functioning: Comment on Martin, Ruble, and Szkrybalo (2002). *Psychological Bulletin, 130,* 691–701.

Barbera, E. (2003). Gender schemas: Configuration and activation processes. *Canadian Journal of Behavioural Science, 35,* 176–184.

Bartlett, N. H., Vasey, P. L., & Bukowski, W. M. (2000). Is gender identity disorder in children a mental disorder? *Sex Roles, 43,* 753–785.

Bartlett, N. H., Vasey, P. L., & Bukowski, W. M. (2003). Cross-sex wishes and gender identity disorder in children: A reply to Zucker, 2002. *Sex Roles, 49,* 191–192.

Bauer, P. J., & Coyne, M. J. (1997). When the name says it all: Preschoolers' recognition and use of the gendered nature of common proper names. *Social Development, 6,* 271–291.

Becker, J. B., Breedlove, S. M., Crews, D., & McCarthy, M. M. (Eds.). (2002). *Behavioral endocrinology* (2nd ed.). Cambridge, MA: MIT Press.

Bem, S. L. (1981). Gender schema theory: A cognitive account of sex typing. *Psychological Review, 88,* 354–364.

Bem, S. L. (1989). Genital knowledge and gender constancy in preschool children. *Child Development, 60,* 649–662.

Benenson, J. F., & Christakos, A. (2003). The greater fragility of females' versus males' closest same-sex friendships. *Child Development, 74,* 1123–1129.

Benenson, J. F., Meaiese, R., Dolenszky, E., Dolensky, N., Sinclair, N., & Simpson, A. (2002). Group size regulates self-assertive versus self-deprecating responses to interpersonal competition. *Child Development, 73,* 1818–1829.

Benenson, J. F., Morash, D., & Petrakos, H. (1998). Gender differences in emotional closeness between preschool children and their mothers. *Sex Roles, 38,* 975–985.

Bennett, M., Sani, F., Hopkins, N., Agostini, L., & Mallucchi, L. (2000). Children's gender categorization: An investigation of automatic processing. *British Journal of Developmental Psychology, 18,* 97–102.

Berenbaum, S. A. (1999). Effects of early androgens on sex-typed activities and interests in adolescents with congenital adrenal hyperplasia. *Hormones and Behavior, 35,* 102–110.

Berenbaum, S. A. (2001). Cognitive function in congenital adrenal hyperplasia. *Endocrinology and Metabolism Clinics of North America, 30,* 173–192.

Berenbaum, S. A. (2006). Psychological outcome in children with disorders of sex development: Implications for treatment and understanding typical development. *Annual Review of Sex Research, 17,* 1–38.

Berenbaum, S. A., & Bailey, J. M. (2003). Effects on gender identity of prenatal androgens and genital appearance: Evidence from girls with congenital adrenal hyperplasia. *Journal of Clinical Endocrinology and Metabolism, 88,* 1102–1106.

Berenbaum, S. A., Duck, S. C., & Bryk, K. (2000). Behavioral effects of prenatal versus postnatal androgen excess in children with 21-hydroxylase-deficient congenital adrenal hyperplasia. *Journal of Clinical Endocrinology and Metabolism, 85,* 727–733.

Berenbaum, S. A., & Snyder, E. (1995). Early hormonal influences on childhood sex-typed activity and playmate preferences: Implications for the development of sexual orientation. *Developmental Psychology, 31,* 31–42.

Bernhardt, P. C., Dabbs, J. M., Fielden, J. A., & Lutter, C. D. (1998). Testosterone changes during vicarious experiences of winning and losing among fans at sporting events. *Physiology and Behavior, 65,* 59–62.

Berscheid, E. (1993). Forward. In A. E. Beall & R. J. Sternberg (Eds.), *The psychology of gender* (pp. i–xvii). New York: Guilford Press.

Bigler, R. S. (1995). The role of classification skill in moderating environmental effects on children's gender stereotyping: A study of the functional use of gender in the classroom. *Child Development, 66,* 1072–1087.

Bigler, R. S., Brown, C. S., & Markell, M. (2001). When groups are not created equal: Effects of group status on the formation of intergroup attitudes in children. *Child Development, 72,* 1151–1162.

Bigler, R. S., Jones, L. C., & Lobliner, D. B. (1997). Social categorization and the formation of intergroup attitudes in children. *Child Development, 68,* 530–543.

Blair, S. L. (1992). The sex-typing of children's household labor: Parental influences on daughters' and sons' housework. *Youth and Society, 24,* 178–203.

Blakemore, J. E. O. (2003). Children's beliefs about violating gender norms: Boys shouldn't look like girls and girls shouldn't act like boys. *Sex Roles, 48,* 411–419.

Blakemore, J. E. O., Berenbaum, S. A., & Liben, L. S. (2008). *Gender development.* Manuscript in preparation.

Blanchard, R. (1989). The classification and labeling of nonhomosexual gender dysphorias. *Archives of Sexual Behavior, 18,* 315–334.

Borg, M. G. (1998). Secondary school teachers' perception of pupils' undesirable behaviours. *British Journal of Educational Psychology, 68,* 67–79.

Bradbard, M. R., Martin, C. L., Endsley, R. C., & Halverson, C. F. (1986). Influence of sex stereotypes on children's exploration and memory: A competence versus performance distinction. *Developmental Psychology, 22,* 481–486.

Brewer, M. B. (2001). Ingroup identification and intergroup conflict: When does ingroup love become outgroup hate. In R. D. Ashmore, L. Jussim, & D. Wilder (Eds.), *Social identity, intergroup conflict, and conflict reduction* (pp. 2–41). New York: Oxford University Press.

Brewer, M. B., & Brown, R. J. (1998). Intergroup relations. In P. H. Munset (Series Ed.) & D. T. Gilbert, S. T. Fiske, & G. Lindzey (Vol. Eds.), *Handbook of social psychology* (4th ed., Vol. 2, pp. 554–594). New York: McGraw-Hill.

Bronfenbrenner, U. (1977). Toward an experimental ecology of human development. *American Psychologist, 32,* 513–531.

Brooks-Gunn, J., Petersen, A. C., & Compas, B. E. (1995). Physiological processes and the development of childhood and adolescent depression. In I. M. Goodyear (Ed.), *The depressed child and adolescent: Developmental and clinical perspectives* (pp. 91–109). New York: Cambridge University Press.

Brown, C. S., & Bigler, R. S. (2004). Children's perceptions of gender discrimination. *Developmental Psychology, 40,* 714–726.

Buchanan, C. M., Eccles, J. S., & Becker, J. B. (1992). Are adolescents the victims of raging hormones: Evidence for activational effects of hormones on moods and behavior at adolescence. *Psychological Bulletin, 111,* 62–107.

Buhrmester, D. (1996). Need fulfillment, interpersonal competence and the developmental contexts of early adolescent friendship. In W. M. Bukowski, A. F. Newcomb, & W. W. Hartup (Eds.), *The company they keep: Friendship in childhood and adolescence* (pp. 158–185). New York: Cambridge University Press.

Bukowski, W. M., Sippola, L. K., & Hoza, B. (1999). Same and other: Interdependency between participation in same- and other-sex friendships. *Journal of Youth and Adolescence, 28,* 439–459.

Buss, D. M. (2000). Desires in human mating. *Annals of the New York Academy of Sciences, 907,* 39–49.

Bussey, K., & Bandura, A. (1992). Self-regulatory mechanisms governing gender development. *Child Development, 63,* 1236–1250.

Bussey, K., & Bandura, A. (1999). Social cognitive theory of gender development and differentiation. *Psychological Review, 106,* 676–713.

Byely, L., Archibald, A. B., Graber, J., & Brooks-Gunn, J. (2000). A prospective study of familial and social influences on girls' body image and dieting. *International Journal of Eating Disorders, 28,* 155–164.

Campbell, A., Shirley, L., & Caygill, L. (2002). Sex-typed preferences in three domains: Do 2-year-olds need cognitive variables? *British Journal of Psychology, 50,* 590–593.

Campbell, A., Shirley, L., Heywood, C., & Crook, C. (2000). Infants' visual preference for sex-congruent babies, children, toys and activities: A longitudinal study. *British Journal of Developmental Psychology, 18,* 479–498.

Carlson-Jones, D. (2001). Social comparison and body image: Attractiveness comparisons to models and peers among adolescent girls and boys. *Sex Roles, 45,* 645–664.

Carlson-Jones, D. (2004). Body image among adolescent girls and boys: A longitudinal study. *Developmental Psychology, 40,* 823–835.

Carter, D. B., & McCloskey, L. A. (1984). Peers and the maintenance of sex-typed behavior: The development of children's conceptions of cross-gender behavior in their peers. *Social Cognition, 2,* 294–314.

Carver, P. R., Yunger, J. L., & Perry, D. G. (2003). Gender identity and adjustment in middle childhood. *Sex Roles, 49,* 95–109.

Cherney, I. D., & Ryalls, B. O. (1999). Gender-linked differences in the incidental memory of children and adults. *Journal of Experimental Child Psychology, 72,* 305–328.

Cohen-Bendahan, C. C., van de Beek, C., & Berenbaum, S. A. (2005). Prenatal sex hormone effects on child and adult sex-typed behavior: Methods and findings. *Neuroscience and Biobehavioral Reviews, 29,* 353–384.

Cohen-Kettenis, P. T., Owen, A., Kaijser, V. G., Bradley, S. J., & Zucker, K. J. (2003). Demographic characteristics, social competence, and behavior problems in children with gender identity disorder: A cross-national, cross-clinic comparative analysis. *Journal of Abnormal Child Psychology, 31,* 41–53.

Cole, D. A., Maxwell, S. E., Martin, J. M., Peeke, L. G., Seroczynski, A. D., Tram, J. M., et al. (2001). The development of multiple domains of child and adolescent self-concept: A cohort sequential longitudinal design. *Child Development, 72,* 1723–1746.

Connolly, J., Craig, W., Goldberg, A., & Pepler, D. (1999). Conceptions of cross-sex friendships and romantic relationships in early adolescence. *Journal of Youth and Adolescence, 28,* 481–494.

Constantinople, A. (1979). Sex-role acquisition: In search of the elephant. *Sex Roles, 5,* 121–132.

Crouter, A. C., Manke, B. A., & McHale, S. M. (1995). The family context of gender intensification in early adolescence. *Child Development, 66,* 317–329.

Crouter, A. C., Whiteman, S. D., McHale, S. M., & Osgood, D. W. (2007). Development of gender attitude traditionality across middle childhood and adolescence. *Child Development, 78,* 911–926.

Crowley, K., Callanan, M. A., Tenenbaum, H. R., & Allen, E. (2001). Parents explain more often to boys than to girls during shared scientific thinking. *Psychological Science, 12,* 258–261.

Davison, K. K., Markey, C. N., & Birch, L. L. (2002). A longitudinal examination of patterns in girls' weight concerns and body dissatisfaction from age 5 to 9 years. *International Journal of Eating Disorders, 33,* 320–332.

De Lisi, R., & Gallagher, A. M. (1991). Understanding of gender stability and constancy in Argentinean children. *Merrill-Palmer Quarterly, 37,* 483–502.

Dessens, A. B., Slijper, F. M., & Drop, S. L. (2005). Gender dysphoria and gender change in chromosomal females with congenital adrenal hyperplasia. *Archives of Sexual Behavior, 34,* 389–397.

Diamond, L. M. (2000). Sexual identity attractions, and behavior among young sexual-minority women over a 2-year period. *Developmental Psychology, 36,* 241–250.

Diamond, L. M. (2003a). New paradigms for research on sexual-minority and heterosexual youth. *Journal of Clinical Child and Adolescent Psychology, 32,* 490–498.

Diamond, L. M. (2003b). What does sexual orientation orient? A biobehavioral model distinguishing romantic love and sexual desire. *Psychological Review, 110,* 173–192.

Diamond, L. M., & Dube, E. M. (2002). Friendship and attachment among heterosexual and sexual-minority youths: Does the gender of your friend matter? *Journal of Youth and Adolescence, 31,* 155–166.

Dinella, L., & Martin, C. L. (2003, April). *Gender stereotypes, gender identity, and preferences of self-identified tomboys and traditional girls.* Paper presented at the meetings of the Society for Research in Child Development, Tampa, FL.

Di Pietro, J. A. (1981). Rough and tumble play: A function of gender. *Developmental Psychology, 17,* 50–58.

Dorn, L. D., Dahl, R. E., Woodward, H. R., & Biro, F. (2006). Defining the boundaries of early adolescence: A user's guide to assessing pubertal status and pubertal timing in research with adolescents. *Applied Developmental Science, 10,* 30–56.

Duffy, J., Warren, K., & Walsh, M. (2002). Classroom interactions: Gender of teacher, gender of student, and classroom subject. *Sex Roles, 45,* 579–593.

Dunn, J., & Hughes, C. (2001). "I got some swords and you're dead!": Violent fantasy, antisocial behavior, friendship, and moral sensibility in young children. *Child Development, 72,* 491–505.

Eagly, A. H., & Mladinic, A. (1994). Are people prejudiced against women? Some answers from research on attitudes, gender stereotypes, and judgments of competence. In W. Stroebe & M. Hewstone (Eds.), *European review of social psychology* (Vol. 5, pp. 1–35). New York: Wiley.

Eaton, W. O., & Enns, L. R. (1986). Sex differences in human motor activity level. *Psychological Bulletin, 100,* 19–28.

Eccles, J. S. (1989). Bringing young women to math and science. In M. Crawford & M. Gentry (Eds.), *Gender and thought* (pp. 36–58). New York: Springer-Verlag.

Eccles, J. S., & Barber, B. L. (1999). Student council, volunteering, basketball, or marching band: What kinds of extracurricular involvement matters? *Journal of Adolescent Research, 14,* 10–43.

Eckes, T., Trautner, H. M., & Behrendt, R. (2005). Gender subgroups and intergroup perception: Adolescents' views of own-gender and other-gender groups. *Journal of Social Psychology, 145,* 85–111.

Egan, S. K., & Perry, D. G. (2001). Gender identity: A multidimensional analysis with implications for psychosocial adjustment. *Developmental Psychology, 37,* 451–463.

Eisenberg, N., Wolchik, S. A., Hernandez, R., & Pasternack, J. (1985). Parental socialization of young children's play: A short-term longitudinal study. *Child Development, 56,* 1506–1513.

Ellis, L., & Ficek, C. (2001). Color preferences according to gender and sexual orientation. *Personality and Individual Differences, 31,* 1375–1379.

Entwisle, D. R., Alexander, K. L., Pallas, A. M., & Cadigan, D. (1987). The emergence of academic self-image of first graders: Its response to social structure. *Child Development, 58,* 1190–1206.

Fabes, R. A. (1994). Physiological, emotional, and behavioral correlates of gender segregation. In C. Leaper (Ed.), *New directions for child development: Vol. 65. Childhood gender segregation—Causes and consequences* (pp. 19–34). San Francisco: Jossey-Bass.

Fabes, R. A., Martin, C. L., & Hanish, L. D. (2003). Young children's play qualities in same-, other-, and mixed-sex peer groups. *Child Development, 74,* 921–932.

Fabes, R. A., Martin, C. L., Hanish, L. D., Anders, M. C., & Madden-Derdich, D. A. (2003). Early school competence: The roles of sex-segregated play and effortful control. *Developmental Psychology, 39,* 848–858.

Fabes, R. A., Shepard, A. S., Guthrie, I. K., & Martin, C. L. (1997). Roles of temperamental arousal and gender segregated play in young children's social adjustment. *Developmental Psychology, 33,* 693–702.

Fagot, B. I. (1977). Consequences of moderate cross-gender behavior in preschool children. *Child Development, 48,* 902–907.

Fagot, B. I., & Leinbach, M. (1989). The young child's gender schema: Environmental input, internal organization. *Child Development, 60,* 663–672.

Fagot, B. I., Leinbach, M. D., & Hagan, R. (1986). Gender labeling and the adoption of sex-typed behaviors. *Developmental Psychology, 22,* 440–443.

Fenson, L., Dale, P. S., Resznick, J. S., Bates, E., Thale, D. J., & Pethick, S. J. (1994). Variability in early communicative development. *Monographs of the Society for Research in Child Development, 59,* v–173.

Fisher-Thompson, D. (1993). Adult toy purchase for children: Factors affecting sex-typed toy selection. *Journal of Applied Developmental Psychology, 14,* 385–406.

Fivush, R., Brotman, M. A., Buckner, J. P., & Goodman, S. H. (2000). Gender differences in parent-child emotion narratives. *Sex Roles, 42,* 233–253.

Fredricks, J. A., & Eccles, J. S. (2002). Children's competence and value beliefs from childhood through adolescence: Growth trajectories in two male-sex-typed domains. *Developmental Psychology, 38,* 519–533.

Ge, X., Brody, G. H., Conger, R. D., Simons, R. L., & Murry, V. M. (2002). Contextual amplification of pubertal transition effects on deviant peer affiliation and externalizing behavior among African American children. *Developmental Psychology, 38,* 42–54.

Ge, X., Conger, R. D., & Elder, G. H. (1996). Coming of age too early: Pubertal influences on girls' vulnerability to psychological distress. *Child Development, 67,* 386–400.

Geary, D. C. (1998). *Male, female: The evolution of human sex differences.* Washington, DC: American Psychological Association.

Gelman, S. A., Collman, P., & Maccoby, E. E. (1986). Inferring properties from categories versus inferring categories from properties: The case of gender. *Child Development, 57,* 396–404.

Gelman, S. A., Taylor, M. G., & Nguyen, S. P. (2004). Mother-child conversations about gender. *Monographs of the Society for Research in Child Development, 69*(1), vii–127.

Gibbons, J. L. (2000). Gender development in cross-cultural perspective. In T. Eckes & H. S. Trautner (Eds.), *The developmental social psychology of gender* (pp. 389–415). Mahwah, NJ: Erlbaum.

Giles, J. W., & Heyman, G. D. (2004). When to cry over spilled milk: Young children's use of category information to guide inferences about ambiguous behavior. *Journal of Cognition and Development, 5,* 359–386.

Giles, J. W., & Heyman, G. D. (2005). Young children's beliefs about the relationship between gender and aggressive behavior. *Child Development, 76,* 107–121.

Giuliano, T. A., Popp, K. E., & Knight, J. L. (2000). Footballs versus Barbies: Childhood play activities as predictors of sport participation by women. *Sex Roles, 42,* 159–181.

Gogtay, N., Giedd, J. N., Lusk, L., Hayashi, K. M., Greenstein, D., Vaituzis, A. C., et al. (2004). Dynamic mapping of human cortical development during childhood through early adulthood. *Proceedings of the National Academy of Sciences, 101,* 8174–8179.

Goldstein, J. M., Seidman, L. J., Horton, N. J., Makris, N., Kennedy, D. N., Caviness, V. S., et al. (2001). Normal sexual dimorphism of the adult human brain assessed by in vivo magnetic resonance imaging. *Cerebral Cortex, 11,* 490–497.

Golombok, S., & Rust, J. (1993). The pre-school activities inventory: A standardized assessment of gender role in children. *Psychological Assessment, 5,* 131–136.

Graham, S., Taylor, A. Z., & Hudley, C. (1998). Exploring achievement values among ethnic minority early adolescents. *Journal of Educational Psychology, 90,* 606–620.

Greulich, F. K., Ruble, D. N., Khuri, J., & Cyphers, L. (2001, April). *What parents say about children's gender-typed behavior.* Poster presentation at the Society for Research in Child Development Conference, Minneapolis, MN.

Grön, G., Wunderlich, A. P., Spitzer, M., Tomczak, R., & Riepe, M. W. (2000). Brain activation during human navigation: Gender-different neural networks as substrate of performance. *Nature Neuroscience, 3,* 404–408.

Grumbach, M. M., Hughes, I. A., & Conte, F. A. (2002). Disorders of sex differentiation. In P. R. Larsen, H. M. Kronenberg, S. Melmed, & K. S. Polonsky (Eds.), *Williams textbook of endocrinology* (10th ed., pp. 842–1002). Philadelphia: Saunders.

Halpern, D. F. (2000). *Sex differences in cognitive abilities* (3rd ed.). Mahwah, NJ: Erlbaum.

Hamann, S., & Canli, T. (2004). Individual differences in emotional processing. *Current Opinion in Neurobiology, 14,* 233–238.

Hamann, S., Herman, R. A., Nolan, C. L., & Wallen, K. (2004). Men and women differ in amygdala response to visual sexual stimuli. *Nature Neuroscience, 7,* 411–416.

Hampson, E. (2002). Sex differences in human brain and cognition: The influence of sex steroids in early and adult life. In J. B. Becker, S. M. Breedlove, D. Crews, & M. M. McCarthy (Eds.), *Behavioral endocrinology* (2nd ed., pp. 579–628). Cambridge, MA: MIT Press.

Hanish, L. D., Martin, C. L., Fabes, R. A., Leonard, S., & Herzog, M. (2005). Peer contagion effects on young children's externalizing symptomatology. *Journal of Abnormal Child Psychology, 33*(3), 267–281.

Hannover, B. (2000). Development of the self in gendered contexts. In T. Eckes & H. M. Trautner (Eds.), *The developmental social psychology of gender* (pp. 177–206). Mahwah, NJ: Erlbaum.

Harrison, A. C., & O'Neill, S. A. (2000). Children's gender-typed preferences for musical instruments: An intervention study. *Psychology of Music, 28,* 81–97.

Harrison, A. C., & O'Neill, S. A. (2003). Preferences and children's use of gender-stereotyped knowledge about musical instruments: Making judgments about other children's preferences. *Sex Roles, 49,* 389–400.

Hendy, H. M., Gustitus, C., & Leitzel-Schwalm, J. (2001). Social cognitive predictors of body image in preschool children. *Sex Roles, 44,* 557–569.

Herdt, G., & McClintock, M. (2000). The magical age of 10. *Archives of Sexual Behavior, 29,* 587–606.

Hewstone, M., Rubin, M., & Willis, H. (2002). Intergroup bias. *Annual Review of Psychology, 53*(1), 575–604.

Heyman, G. D. (2001). Children's interpretation of ambiguous behavior: Evidence for a "boys are bad" bias. *Social Development, 10,* 230–247.

Heyman, G. D., & Gelman, S. A. (2000). Preschool children's use of trait labels to make inductive inferences. *Journal of Experimental Child Psychology, 77,* 1–19.

Heyman, G. D., & Legare, C. H. (2004). Children's beliefs about gender differences in the academic and social domains. *Sex Roles, 50,* 227–239.

Hill, J. P., & Lynch, M. E. (1983). The intensification of gender-related role expectations during early adolescence. In J. Brooks-Gunn & A. C. Petersen (Eds.), *Girls at puberty: Biological and psychosocial perspectives* (pp. 201–228). New York: Plenum Press.

Hines, M., Fane, B. A., Pasterski, V. L., Mathews, G. A., Conway, G. S., & Brook, C. (2003). Spatial abilities following prenatal androgen abnormality: Targeting and mental rotations performance in individuals with congenital adrenal hyperplasia. *Psychoneuroendocrinology, 28,* 1010–1026.

Hines, M., Golombok, S., Rust, J., Johnston, K. J., Golding, J., & Avon Longitudinal Study of Parents and Children Study Team. (2002). Testosterone during pregnancy and gender role behavior of preschool children: A longitudinal, population study. *Child Development, 73,* 1678–1687.

Hoffman, M. L., Powlishta, K. K., & White, K. J. (2004). An examination of gender differences in adolescent adjustment: The effect of competence on gender role differences in symptoms of psychopathology. *Sex Roles, 50,* 795–810.

Hort, B. E., Leinbach, M. D., & Fagot, B. I. (1991). Is there coherence among components of gender acquisition? *Sex Roles, 24,* 195–208.

Hughes, F. M., & Seta, C. E. (2003). Gender stereotypes: Children's perceptions of future compensatory behavior following violations of gender roles. *Sex Roles, 49,* 685–691.

Huston, A. C. (1983). Sex-typing. In P. H. Munsen (Series Ed.) & E. M. Hetherington (Vol. Ed.), *Handbook of child psychology: Vol. 4. Socialization, personality, and social development* (4th ed., pp. 387–467). New York: Wiley.

Huston, A. C., Wright, J. C., Marquis, J., & Green, S. B. (1999). How young children spend their time: Television and other activities. *Developmental Psychology, 35,* 921–925.

Hyde, J. S., & Jaffee, S. R. (2000). Becoming a heterosexual adult: The experiences of young women. *Journal of Social Issues, 56,* 283–296.

Intons-Peterson, M. J. (1988a). *Children's concepts of gender.* Norwood, NJ: Ablex.

Intons-Peterson, M. J. (1988b). *Gender concepts of Swedish and American youth.* Hillsdale, NJ: Erlbaum.

Jacobs, J. E., Lanza, S., Osgood, D. W., Eccles, J. S., & Wigfield, A. (2002). Changes in children's self-competence and values: Gender and domain differences across grades 1 through 12. *Child Development, 73,* 509–527.

Katz, P. A., & Ksansnak, K. R. (1994). Developmental aspects of gender role flexibility and traditionality in middle childhood and adolescence. *Developmental Psychology, 30,* 272–282.

Katz, P. A., & Walsh, V. (1991). Modification of children's gender-stereotyped behavior. *Child Development, 62,* 338–351.

Kimball, M. M. (1986). Television and sex-role attitudes. In T. M. Williams (Ed.), *The impact of television: A natural experiment in three communities* (pp. 265–301). Orlando, FL: Academic Press.

Kimura, D. (1999). *Sex and cognition.* Cambridge, MA: MIT Press.

Klingenspor, B. (2002). Gender-related self discrepancies and bulimic eating behavior. *Sex Roles, 47,* 51–64.

Klomsten, A. T., Skaalvik, E. M., & Espnes, G. A. (2004). Physical self-concept and sports: Do gender differences still exist? *Sex Roles, 50,* 119–127.

Knickmeyer, R. C., Wheelwright, S., Taylor, K., Raggatt, P., Hackett, G., & Baron-Cohen, S. (2005). Gender-typed play and amniotic testosterone. *Developmental Psychology, 41,* 517–528.

Kohlberg, L. A. (1966). A cognitive-developmental analysis of children's sex role concepts and attitudes. In E. E. Maccoby (Ed.), *The development of sex differences* (pp. 82–173). Stanford, CA: Stanford University Press.

Kovacs, D. M., Parker, J. G., & Hoffman, L. W. (1996). Behavioral, affective, and social correlates of involvement in cross-sex friendship in elementary school. *Child Development, 67,* 2269–2286.

Ladd, G. W. (2005). *Peer relationships and social competence of children and adolescents.* New Haven, CT: Yale University Press.

La Freniere, P., Strayer, F. F., & Gauthier, R. (1984). The emergence of same-sex affiliative preferences among preschool peers: A developmental/ethological perspective. *Child Development, 55*(5), 1958–1965.

Lansford, J. E., & Parker, J. G. (1999). Children' interactions in triads: Behavioral profiles and effects of gender and patterns of friendships among members. *Developmental Psychology, 35,* 80–93.

Leaper, C. (1994). Exploring the consequences of gender segregation on social relationships. In C. Leaper (Ed.), *Childhood gender segregation: Causes and consequences* (pp. 67–86). San Francisco: Jossey-Bass.

Leaper, C. (2000). The social construction and socialization of gender during development. In P. H. Miller & E. K. Scholnick (Eds.), *Toward a feminist developmental psychology* (pp. 127–152). New York City: Routledge.

Leaper, C. (2002). Parenting girls and boys. In M. H. Bornstein (Ed.), *Handbook of parenting: Children and parenting* (pp. 189–225). Mahwah, NJ: Erlbaum.

Leaper, C., Anderson, K. J., & Sanders, P. (1998). Moderators of gender effects on parents' talk to their children: A meta-analysis. *Developmental Psychology, 34,* 3–27.

Leaper, C., & Smith, T. E. (2004). A meta-analytic review of gender variations in children's language use: Talkativeness, affiliative speech, and assertive speech. *Developmental Psychology, 40,* 993–1027.

Leaper, C., Tenenbaum, H. R., & Shaffer, T. G. (1999). Communication patterns of African American girls and boys from low-income, urban backgrounds. *Child Development, 70,* 1489–1503.

Lee, V. E., & Bryk, A. S. (1986). Effects of single-sex secondary schools on student achievement and attitudes. *Journal of Educational Psychology, 78,* 381–395.

Leman, P. J., Ahmed, S., & Ozarow, L. (2005). Gender, gender relations, and the social dynamics of children's conversations. *Developmental Psychology, 41,* 64–74.

LeVay, S. (1993). *The sexual brain.* Cambridge, MA: MIT Press.

Levy, G. D. (1998). Effects of gender constancy and figure's height and sex on young children's gender-typed attributions. *Journal of General Psychology, 125,* 65–88.

Levy, G. D., Sadovsky, A. L., & Troseth, G. L. (2000). Aspects of young children's perceptions of gender-typed occupations. *Sex Roles, 42,* 993–1006.

Levy, G. D., Taylor, M. G., & Gelman, S. A. (1995). Traditional and evaluative aspects of flexibility in gender roles, social conventions, moral rules, and physical laws. *Child Development, 66,* 515–531.

Liben, L. S., & Bigler, R. S. (2002). The developmental course of gender differentiation. *Monographs of the Society for Research in Child Development, 67,* 1–147.

Liben, L. S., Bigler, R. S., & Krogh, H. R. (2001). Pink and blue collar jobs: Children's judgments of job status and job aspirations in relation to sex of worker. *Journal of Experimental Child Psychology, 79,* 346–363.

Liben, L. S., & Signorella, M. L. (1980). Gender-related schemata and constructive memory in children. *Child Development, 51,* 11–18.

Lindsey, E. W., & Mize, J. (2001). Contextual differences in parent-child play: Implications for children's gender role development. *Sex Roles, 44,* 155–176.

Lips, H. M. (2004). The gender gap in possible selves: Divergence of academic self-views among high school and university students. *Sex Roles, 50,* 357–371.

Lobel, T. E., Bar-David, E., Gruber, R., Lau, S., & Bar-Tal, Y. (2000). Gender schema and social judgments: A developmental study of children from Hong Kong. *Sex Roles, 43,* 19–42.

Lobel, T. E., Gruber, R., Govrin, N., & Mashraki-Pedhatzur, S. (2001). Children's gender-related inferences and judgments: A cross-cultural study. *Developmental Psychology, 37,* 839–846.

Lonsdorf, E. V., Eberly, L. E., & Pusey, A. E. (2004). Sex differences in learning in chimpanzees. *Nature, 428,* 715–716.

Lundy, B., Field, T., & McBride, C. K. (1998). Same-sex and opposite-sex best friend interactions among high school juniors and seniors. *Adolescence, 33,* 279–289.

Lutchmaya, S., Baron-Cohen, S., & Raggatt, P. (2002). Foetal testosterone and eye contact in 12-month-old human infants. *Infant Behavior and Development, 25,* 327–335.

Lytton, H., & Romney, D. M. (1991). Parents' differential socialization of boys and girls: A meta-analysis. *Psychological Bulletin, 109,* 267–296.

Maccoby, E. E. (1990). The role of gender identity and gender constancy in sex-differentiated development. In D. Schroder (Ed.), *The legacy of Lawrence Kohlberg: New directions for child development* (pp. 5–20). San Francisco: Jossey-Bass.

Maccoby, E. E. (1998). *The two sexes: Growing apart and coming together.* Cambridge, MA: Harvard University Press.

Maccoby, E. E. (2002). Gender and group process: A developmental perspective. *Current Directions in Psychological Sciences, 11,* 54–58.

Maccoby, E. E., & Jacklin, C. N. (1974). *The psychology of sex differences.* Stanford, CA: Stanford University Press.

Madon, S., Jussim, L., Keiper, S., Eccles, J. S., Smith, A., & Palumbo, P. (1998). The accuracy and power of sex, social class, and ethnic stereotypes: A naturalistic study in person perception. *Personality and Social Psychology Bulletin, 24,* 1304–1318.

Marsh, H. W., Byrne, B. M., & Yeung, A. S. (1999). Causal ordering of academic self-concept and achievement: Reanalysis of a pioneering study and revised recommendations. *Educational Psychologist, 34,* 154–157.

Martin, C. L. (1994). Cognitive influences on the development and maintenance of gender segregation. In L. Campbell (Ed.), *New directions for child development: Vol. 65. Childhood gender segregation—Causes and consequences* (pp. 35–51). San Francisco: Jossey-Bass.

Martin, C. L. (2000). Cognitive theories of gender development. In T. Eckes & H. M. Trautner (Eds.), *The developmental social psychology of gender* (pp. 91–121). Mahwah, NJ: Erlbaum.

Martin, C. L., & Dinella, L. M. (2001). Gender development: Gender schema theory. In J. Worell (Ed.), *Encyclopedia of women and gender* (Vol. 1, pp. 507–521). New York: Academic Press.

Martin, C. L., & Dinella, L. M. (2002). Children's gender cognitions, the social environment, and sex differences in cognitive domains. In A. McGillicuddy-De Lisi & R. De Lisi (Eds.), *Biology, society, and behavior: The development of sex differences in cognition* (pp. 207–239). Westport, CT: Ablex.

Martin, C. L., Eisenbud, L., & Rose, H. (1995). Children's gender-based reasoning about toys. *Child Development, 66,* 1453–1471.

Martin, C. L., & Fabes, R. A. (2001). The stability and consequences of young children's same-sex peer interactions. *Developmental Psychology, 37,* 431–446.

Martin, C. L., Fabes, R. A., Evans, S. M., & Wyman, H. (1999). Social cognition on the playground: Children's beliefs about playing with girls versus boys and their relations to sex segregated play. *Journal of Social and Personal Relationships, 16,* 751–771.

Martin, C. L., Fabes, R. A., Hanish, L. D., & Hollenstein, T. (2005). Social dynamics in the preschool. *Developmental Review, 25,* 299–327.

Martin, C. L., Fabes, R. A., Hanish, L. D., Leonard, S., & Dinella, L. (2007). *The role of gender cognitions in children's peer play.* Unpublished manuscript.

Martin, C. L., & Halverson, C. (1981). A schematic processing model of sex typing and stereotyping in children. *Child Development, 52,* 1119–1134.

Martin, C. L., & Little, J. K. (1990). The relation of gender understanding to children's sex-typed preferences and gender stereotypes. *Child Development, 61,* 1427–1439.

Martin, C. L., Ruble, D. N., & Szkrybalo, J. (2002). Cognitive theories of early gender development. *Psychological Bulletin, 128,* 903–933.

Martin, C. L., Ruble, D. N., & Szkrybalo, J. (2004). Recognizing the centrality of gender identity and stereotype knowledge in gender development and moving toward theoretical integration: Reply to Bandura and Bussey. *Psychological Bulletin, 130,* 702–710.

McCabe, M. P., & Ricciardelli, L. A. (2003). Body image and strategies to lose weight and increase muscle among boys and girls. *Health Psychology, 22,* 39–46.

McGuire, W. J., McGuire, C. V., Child, P., & Fujioka, T. (1978). Salience of ethnicity in the spontaneous self-concept as a function of one's ethnic distinctiveness in the social environment. *Journal of Personality and Social Psychology, 36,* 511–520.

McHale, S. M., Crouter, A. C., & Tucker, C. J. (1999). Family context and gender role socialization in middle childhood: Comparing girls to boys and sisters to brothers. *Child Development, 70,* 990–1004.

McHale, S. M., Crouter, A. C., & Whiteman, S. D. (2003). The family contexts of gender development in childhood and adolescence. *Social Development, 12,* 125–148.

McHale, S. M., Kim, J., Whiteman, S., & Crouter, A. C. (2004). Links between sex-typed time use in middle-childhood and gender development in early adolescence. *Developmental Psychology, 40,* 868–881.

McHale, S. M., Shanahan, L., Updegraff, K. A., Crouter, A. C., & Booth, A. (2004). Developmental and individual differences in girls' sex-typed activities in middle childhood and adolescence. *Child Development, 75,* 1575–1593.

McHale, S. M., Updegraff, K. A., Helms-Erikson, H., & Crouter, A. C. (2001). Sibling influence on gender development in middle childhood and early adolescence: A longitudinal study. *Developmental Psychology, 37,* 115–125.

Meyer-Bahlburg, H. F. L. (2005). Gender identity outcome in female-raised 46, XY persons with penile agenesis, cloacal exstrophy of the bladder, or penile ablation. *Archives of Sexual Behavior, 34,* 423–438.

Miller, C. F., Lurye, L., Zosuls, K., & Ruble, D. N. (2007). *Developmental changes in the accessibility of gender stereotypes.* Manuscript in preparation.

Miller, C. F., Trautner, H. M., & Ruble, D. N. (2006). The role of gender stereotypes in children's preferences and behavior. In C. Tamis-LeMonda & L. Balter (Eds.), *Child psychology: A handbook of contemporary issues* (2nd ed., pp. 292–323). Philadelphia: Psychology Press.

Miller, E. K., Nieder, A., Freedman, D. J., & Wallis, J. D. (2003). Neural correlates of categories and concepts. *Current Opinion in Neurobiology, 13,* 198–203.

Mischel, W. (1970). Sex typing and socialization. In P. H. Mussen (Ed.), *Carmichael's handbook of child psychology* (Vol. 2, pp. 3–72). New York: Wiley.

Mondschein, E. R., Adolph, K. E., & Tamis-LeMonda, C. S. (2000). Gender bias in mothers' expectations about infant crawling. *Journal of Experimental Child Psychology, 77,* 304–316.

Money, J., & Ehrhardt, A. A. (1972). *Man and woman, boy and girl.* Baltimore: Johns Hopkins University Press.

Morgan, M., & Shanahan, J. (1997). Two decades of cultivation research: An appraisal and meta-analysis. In B. R. Burleson (Ed.), *Communication yearbook* (Vol. 20, pp. 1–46). Thousand Oaks, CA: Sage.

Neff, K. D., & Terry-Schmitt, L. N. (2002). Youths' attributions for power-related gender differences: Nature, nurture, or God? *Cognitive Development, 17,* 1185–1202.

Nordenström, A., Servin, A., Bohlin, G., Larsson, A., & Wedell, A. (2002). Sex-typed toy play behavior correlates with the degree of prenatal androgen exposure assessed by CYP21 genotype in girls with congenital adrenal hyperplasia. *Journal of Clinical Endocrinology and Metabolism, 87,* 5119–5124.

O'Brien, M. H., & Huston, A. C. (1985). Development of sex-typed play behavior in toddlers. *Developmental Psychology, 21,* 866–871.

Ohring, R., Graber, J. A., & Brooks-Gunn, J. (2002). Girls' recurrent and concurrent body dissatisfaction: Correlates and consequences over 8 years. *International Journal of Eating Disorders, 31,* 404–415.

Pasterski, V. L., Geffner, M. E., Brain, C., Hindmarsh, P., Brook, C., & Hines, M. (2005). Prenatal hormones and postnatal socialization by parents as determinants of male-typical toy play in girls with congenital adrenal hyperplasia. *Child Development, 76,* 264–278.

Patterson, C. J. (2006). Children of lesbian and gay parents. *Current Directions in Psychological Science, 15,* 241–244.

Pellegrini, A. D., & Smith, P. K. (1998). Physical active play: The nature and function of a neglected aspect of play. *Child Development, 69,* 577–598.

Perry, D. G. (2004, April). *Gender identity and gender relevance beliefs: Two components of a causal cognitive system underlying gender differentiation?* Paper presented at the Gender Development Conference, San Francisco.

Picariello, M. L., Greenberg, D. N., & Pillemer, D. B. (1990). Children's sex-related stereotyping of colors. *Child Development, 61,* 1453–1460.

Pomerleau, A., Bolduc, D., Malcuit, G., & Cossette, L. (1990). Pink or blue: Environmental gender stereotypes in the first 2 years of life. *Sex Roles, 22,* 359–367.

Poulin-Dubois, D., Serbin, L. A., & Derbyshire, A. (1998). Toddlers' intermodal and verbal knowledge about gender. *Merrill-Palmer Quarterly, 44,* 338–354.

Powlishta, K. K. (2000). The effect of target age on the activation of gender stereotypes. *Sex Roles, 42,* 271–282.

Powlishta, K. K., Sen, M. G., Serbin, L. A., Poulin-Dubois, D., & Eichstedt, J. A. (2001). From infancy through middle childhood: The role of cognitive and social factors in becoming gendered. In R. K. Unger (Ed.), *Handbook of the psychology of women and gender* (pp. 116–132). New York: Wiley.

Quinn, P. C., Yahr, J., Kuhn, A., Slater, A. M., & Pascalis, O. (2002). Representation of the gender of human faces by infants: A preference for female. *Perception, 31,* 1109–1121.

Raffaelli, M., & Ontai, L. L. (2004). Gender socialization in Latino/a families: Results from two retrospective studies. *Sex Roles, 50,* 287–299.

Reiner, W. G., & Gearhart, J. P. (2004). Discordant sexual identity in some genetic males with cloacal exstrophy assigned to female sex at birth. *New England Journal of Medicine, 350,* 333–341.

Resnick, S. M. (2006). Sex differences in regional brain structure and function. In P. W. Kapan (Ed.), *Neurologic disease in women* (2nd ed., pp. 15–26). New York: Demos Medical.

Rheingold, H. L., & Cook, K. V. (1975). The contents of boys' and girls' rooms as an index of parents' behavior. *Child Development, 46,* 445–463.

Ricciardelli, L. A., & McCabe, M. P. (2001). Children's body image concerns and eating disturbance: A review of the literature. *Clinical Psychology Review, 21,* 325–344.

Roberts, D., & Foehr, U. (2004). *Kids and media in America.* Cambridge: Cambridge University Press.

Rose, A. J. (2002). Co-rumination in the friendships of girls and boys. *Child Development, 73,* 1830–1843.

Rose, A. J., & Asher, S. R. (1999). Children's goals and strategies in response to conflicts within a friendship. *Developmental Psychology, 35,* 69–79.

Rowe, R., Maughan, B., Worthman, C. M., Costello, E. J., & Angold, A. (2004). Testosterone, antisocial behavior, and social dominance in boys: Pubertal development and biosocial interaction. *Biological Psychiatry, 55,* 546–552.

Ruble, D. N. (1994). A phase model of transitions: Cognitive and motivational consequences. *Advances in Experimental Social Psychology, 26,* 163–214.

Ruble, D. N., Alvarez, J. M., Bachman, M., Cameron, J. A., Fuligni, A. J., Garcia Coll, C., et al. (2004). The development of a sense of "we": The emergence and implications of children's collective identity. In M. Bennett & F. Sani (Eds.), *The development of the social self* (pp. 29–76). East Sussex, England: Psychology Press.

Ruble, D. N., & Dweck, C. (1995). Self-conceptions, person conceptions, and their development. In N. Eisenberg (Ed.), *Review of personality and social psychology: Vol. 15. Social development* (pp. 109–135). Thousand Oaks, CA: Sage.

Ruble, D. N., Greulich, F., Pomerantz, E. M., & Gochberg, G. (1993). The role of gender-related processes in the development of sex differences in self-evaluation and depression. *Journal of Affective Disorders, 29,* 97–128.

Ruble, D. N., Lurye, L. E., & Zosuls, K. M. (2007). Pink frilly dresses (PFD) and early gender identity. *Princeton Report on Knowledge (P-ROK), 2*(2).

Ruble, D. N., & Martin, C. (1998). Gender development. In W. Damon (Series Ed.) & N. Eisenberg (Vol. Ed.), *Handbook of child psychology: Vol. 3. Personality and social development* (5th ed., pp. 933–1016). New York: Wiley.

Ruble, D. N., Martin, C. L., & Berenbaum, S. A. (2006). Gender development. In W. Damon & R. M. Lerner (Series Eds.) & N. Eisenberg (Vol. Ed.), *Handbook of child psychology: Vol 3. Social, emotional, and personality development* (6th ed., pp. 858–932). Hoboken, NJ: Wiley.

Ruble, D. N., Taylor, L. J., Cyphers, L., Greulich, F. K., Lurye, L. E., & Shrout, P. E. (2007). The role of gender constancy in early gender development. *Child Development, 78,* 1121–1136.

Ruble, D. N., Trautner, H. M., Shrout, P., & Cyphers, L. (2007). *Longitudinal analysis of the consequences of children's understanding of gender stability.* Manuscript in preparation.

Sani, F., & Bennett, M. (2001). Contextual variability in young children's gender in group stereotypes. *Social Development, 10,* 221–229.

Sani, F., Bennett, M., Mullally, S., & MacPherson, J. (2003). On the assumption of fixity in children's stereotypes: A reappraisal. *British Journal of Developmental Psychology, 99,* 113–124.

Savin-Williams, R. C., & Diamond, L. (2000). Sexual identity trajectories among sexual-minority youths: Gender comparisons. *Archives of Sexual Behavior, 29,* 607–627.

Schur, E. A., Sanders, M., & Steiner, H. (2000). Body dissatisfaction and dieting in young children. *International Journal of Eating Disorders, 27,* 74–82.

Sellers, R. M., Smith, M., Shelton, J. N., Rowley, S. A. J., & Chavous, T. M. (1998). Multidimensional model of racial identity: A reconceptualization of African American racial identity. *Personality and Social Psychology Review, 2,* 18–39.

Serbin, L. A., Moller, L. C., Gulko, J., Powlishta, K. K., & Colburne, K. A. (1994). The emergence of gender segregation in toddler playgroups. In W. Damon (Series Ed.) & C. Leaper (Vol. Ed.), *New directions for child development: Vol. 65. Childhood gender segregation—Causes and consequences* (pp. 7–18). San Francisco: Jossey-Bass.

Serbin, L. A., Poulin-Dubois, D., Colburne, K. A., Sen, M. G., & Eichstedt, J. A. (2001). Gender stereotyping in infancy: Visual preferences for and knowledge of gender-stereotyped toys in the second year. *International Journal of Behavioral Development, 25*(1), 7–15.

Serbin, L. A., Powlishta, K. K., & Gulko, J. (1993). The development of sex-typing in middle childhood. *Monographs of the Society for Research in Child Development, 58*(Serial No. 232, Whole issue).

Servin, A., Nordenström, A., Larsson, A., & Bohlin, G. (2003). Prenatal androgens and gender-typed behavior: A study of girls with mild and severe forms of congenital adrenal hyperplasia. *Developmental Psychology, 39,* 440–450.

Signorella, M. L., Bigler, R. S., & Liben, L. S. (1993). Developmental differences in children's gender schemata about others: A meta-analytic review. *Developmental Review, 13,* 147–183.

Sippola, L. K. (1999). Getting to know the "other": The characteristics and developmental significance of other-sex relationships in adolescence. *Journal of Youth and Adolescence, 28,* 407–418.

Sippola, L. K., Bukowski, W. M., & Noll, R. B. (1997). Dimensions of liking and disliking underlying the same-sex preference in childhood and early adolescence. *Merrill-Palmer Quarterly, 43,* 591–609.

Skaalvik, E. M., & Rankin, R. J. (1990). Math, verbal, and general academic self-concept: The internal/external frame of reference model and gender differences in self-concept structure. *Journal of Educational Psychology, 82,* 546–554.

Slaby, R. G., & Frey, K. S. (1975). Development of gender constancy and selective attention to same-sex models. *Child Development, 52,* 849–856.

Smail, P. J., Reyes, F. I., Winter, J. S. D., & Faiman, C. (1981). The fetal hormone environment and its effect on the morphogenesis of the genital system. In S. J. Kogan & E. S. E. Hafez (Eds.), *Pediatric andrology* (pp. 9–19). Den Haag, The Netherlands: Martinus Nijhoff.

Smolak, L., Levine, M. P., & Thompson, J. K. (2001). The use of the sociocultural attitudes towards appearance questionnaire with middle school boys and girls. *International Journal of Eating Disorders, 29,* 216–223.

Spence, J. T. (1999). Thirty years of gender research: A personal chronicle. In W. B. Swann, J. H. Langlois, & L. A. Gilbert (Eds.), *Sexism and stereotypes in modern society: The gender science of Janet Taylor Spence* (pp. 255–289). Washington, DC: American Psychological Association.

Spitzer, B. L., Henderson, K. A., & Zivian, M. T. (1999). Gender differences in population versus media body sizes: A comparison over 4 decades. *Sex Roles, 40,* 545–565.

Stennes, L. M., Burch, M. M., Sen, M. G., & Bauer, P. J. (2005). A longitudinal study of gendered vocabulary and communicative action in young children. *Developmental Psychology, 41,* 75–88.

Stevens, M., Golombok, S., Beveridge, M., & Avon Longitudinal Study of Parents and Children Study Team. (2002). Does father absence influence children's gender development? Findings from a general population study of preschool children. *Parenting: Science and Practice, 2,* 47–60.

Stevenson, M. R., & Black, K. N. (1988). Paternal absence and sex-role development: A meta-analysis. *Child Development, 59,* 793–814.

Stice, E., & Whitenton, K. (2002). Risk factors for body dissatisfaction in adolescent girls: A longitudinal investigation. *Developmental Psychology, 38,* 669–678.

Subrahmanyam, K., Kraut, R., Greenfield, P., & Gross, E. (2001). New forms of electronic media: The impact of interactive games and the internet on cognition, socialization, and behavior. In D. Singer & J. Singer (Eds.), *Handbook of children and the media* (pp. 73–99). Thousand Oaks, CA: Sage.

Susman, E. J. (1997). Modeling developmental complexity in adolescence: Hormones and behavior in context. *Journal of Research on Adolescence, 7,* 283–306.

Susman, E. J., Finkelstein, J. W., Chinchilli, V. M., Schwab, J., Liben, L. S., D'Arcangelo, M. R., et al. (1998). The effect of sex hormone replacement therapy on behavior problems and moods in adolescents with delayed puberty. *Journal of Pediatrics, 133,* 521–525.

Susman, E. J., & Rogol, A. D. (2004). Puberty and psychological development. In R. M. Lerner & L. Steinberg (Eds.), *Handbook of adolescent psychology* (2nd ed., pp. 15–44)). Hoboken, NJ: Wiley.

Susskind, J. E. (2003). Children's perception of gender-based illusory correlations: Enhancing preexisting relationships between gender and behavior. *Sex Roles, 48,* 483–494.

Tajfel, H. (1978). Social categorization, social identity and social comparison. In H. Tajfel (Ed.), *Differentiation between social groups: Studies in the social psychology of intergroup relations* (pp. 61–76). London: Academic Press.

Tajfel, H., & Turner, J. (1979). An integrative theory of intergroup conflict. In W. Austin & S. Wochel (Eds.), *The social psychology of intergroup relations* (pp. 33–47). Monterey, CA: Brooks/Cole.

Tenenbaum, H. R., & Leaper, C. (2002). Are parents' gender schemas related to their children's gender-related cognitions? A meta-analysis. *Developmental Psychology, 38,* 615–630.

Thoits, P. A., & Virshup, L. K. (1997). Me's and we's: Forms and functions of social identities. In R. D. Ashmore & L. J. Jussim (Eds.), *Self and identity: Vol. 1. Fundamental issues—Rutgers series on self and social identity* (pp. 106–133). New York: Oxford University Press.

Thomas, K., Ricciardelli, L. A., & Williams, R. J. (2000). Gender traits and self-concept as indicators of problem eating and body dissatisfaction among children. *Sex Roles, 43,* 441–458.

Thompson, J. K., Heinberg, L. J., Altabe, M., & Tantleff-Dunn, S. (1999). *Exacting beauty: Theory, assessment, and treatment of body image disturbances.* Washington, DC: American Psychological Association.

Thompson, J. K., & Stice, E. (2001). Thin-ideal internalization: Mounting evidence for a new risk factor for body-image disturbance and eating pathology. *Current Directions in Psychological Science, 10,* 181–183.

Thompson, S. K. (1975). Gender labels and early sex-role development. *Child Development, 46,* 339–347.

Tiedemann, J. (2000). Parents' gender stereotypes and teachers' beliefs as predictors of children's concept of their mathematical ability in elementary school. *Journal of Educational Psychology, 92,* 144–151.

Trautner, H. M., Gervai, J., & Nemeth, R. (2003). Appearance-reality distinction and development of gender constancy understanding in children. *International Journal of Behavioral Development, 27*(3), 275–283.

Trautner, H. M., Ruble, D. N., Cyphers, L., Kirsten, B., Behrendt, R., & Hartmann, P. (2005). Rigidity and flexibility of gender stereotypes in children: Developmental or differential? *Infant and Child Development, 14,* 365–380.

Udry, J. R. (2000). Biological limits of gender construction. *American Sociological Review, 65,* 443–457.

Updegraff, K. A., McHale, S. M., & Crouter, A. C. (2000). Adolescents' sex-typed friendship experiences: Does having a sister versus a brother matter? *Child Development, 71,* 1597–1610.

Voyer, D. (1996). On the magnitude of laterality effects and sex differences in functional lateralities. *Laterality, 1,* 51–83.

Waas, G. A., & Graczyk, P. A. (1999). Child behaviors leading to peer rejection: A view from the peer group. *Child Study Journal, 29,* 291–307.

Wager, T. D., Phan, K. L., Liberzon, I., & Taylor, S. F. (2003). Valence, gender, and lateralization of functional brain anatomy in emotion: A meta-analysis of findings from neuroimaging. *NeuroImage, 19,* 513–531.

Wallen, K. (1996). Nature needs nurture: The interaction of hormonal and social influences on the development of behavioral sex differences in rhesus monkeys. *Hormones and Behavior, 30,* 364–378.

Wallen, K. (2005). Hormonal influences on sexually differentiated behavior in nonhuman primates. *Frontiers in Neuroendocrinology, 26,* 7–26.

Washburn-Ormachea, J. M., Hillman, S. B., & Sawilowsky, S. S. (2004). Gender and gender-role orientation differences on adolescents' coping with peer stressors. *Journal of Youth and Adolescence, 33,* 31–40.

Watt, H. M. G. (2004). Development of adolescents' self-perception, values, and task perceptions according to gender and domain in 7th- through 11th-grade Australian students. *Child Development, 75,* 1556–1572.

Weichold, K., Silbereisen, R. K., & Schmitt-Rodermund, E. (2003). Short-and long-term consequences of early versus late physical maturation in adolescents. In C. Hayward (Ed.), *Puberty and psychopathology* (pp. 241–276). Cambridge: Cambridge University Press.

Weisner, T. S., Garnier, H., & Loucky, J. (1994). Domestic tasks, gender egalitarian values and children's gender typing in current and nonconventional families. *Sex Roles, 30,* 23–54.

Welch-Ross, M. K., & Schmidt, E. R. (1996). Gender-schema development and children's constructive story memory: Evidence for a developmental model. *Child Development, 67,* 820–835.

Whiting, B. B., & Edwards, C. P. (1988). *Children of different worlds.* Cambridge, MA: Harvard University Press.

Wigfield, A., & Eccles, J. S. (2000). Expectancy-value theory of achievement motivation. *Contemporary Educational Psychology, 25,* 68–81.

Wilgenbusch, T., & Merrell, K. W. (1999). Gender differences in self-concept among children and adolescents: A meta-analysis of multidimensional studies. *School Psychology Quarterly, 14,* 101–120.

Williams, J. M., & Dunlop, L. C. (1999). Pubertal timing and self-reported delinquency among male adolescents. *Journal of Adolescence, 22,* 157–171.

Wright, J. C., Huston, A. C., Vandewater, E. A., Bickham, D. S., Scantlin, R. M., Kotler, J. A., et al. (2001). American children's use of electronic media in 1997: A national study. *Journal of Applied Developmental Psychology, 22,* 31–47.

Yee, M., & Brown, R. (1994). The development of gender differentiation in young children. *British Journal of Social Psychology, 33,* 183–196.

Zammuner, V. L. (1987). Children's sex-role stereotypes: A cross-cultural analysis. In P. Shaver & C. Hendrick (Eds.), *Review of personality and social psychology: Sex and gender* (pp. 272–293). Newbury Park, CA: Sage.

Zosuls, K. M., Greulich, F., Haddad, M. E., Ruble, D. N., & Tamis-LeMonda, C. (2007). *Understanding gender labels and sex-typed play behavior before two years of age: A longitudinal analysis.* Manuscript submitted for publication.

Zucker, K. J. (1990). Psychosocial and erotic development in cross-gender identified children. *Canadian Journal of Psychiatry, 35,* 487–495.

Zucker, K. J. (2002). A factual correction to Bartlett, Vasey, and Bukowski's (2000) "Is gender identity disorder in children a mental disorder?" *Sex Roles, 46,* 263–264.

Zucker, K. J., & Bradley, S. J. (1995). *Gender identity disorder and psychosexual problems in children and adolescents.* New York: Guilford Press.

Zucker, K. J., Bradley, S. J., Kuksis, M., Pecore, K., Birkenfeld-Adams, A., Doering, R. W., et al. (1999). Gender constancy judgments in children with gender identity disorder: Evidence for a developmental lag. *Archives of Sexual Behavior, 28,* 475–502.

Zucker, K. J., Bradley, S. J., Oliver, G., Blake, J., Fleming, S., & Hood, J. (1996). Psychosexual development of women with congenital adrenal hyperplasia. *Hormones and Behavior, 30,* 300–318.

Chapter 19

Phenomenology and Ecological Systems Theory: Development of Diverse Groups

MARGARET BEALE SPENCER

Variability *and* consistency typify processes of life-course human development. As lives unfold, human development and learning occur in wide-ranging social and physical contexts. Diverse settings provide unique and repetitive as well as positive and challenging experiences, depending on an individual's physical and personal characteristics. Thus, the degree of "fit" between an individual's physical and social contexts and his or her personal characteristics becomes important because it influences not only the nature of social interactions but the makeup of attitudes and beliefs about "self" and others. Socially constructed environments are communicated both formally, through language and social-cultural traditions, as well as informally, and require constant processing and interpretation. Thus, "meaning making" is an ever-present aspect of the human development process, and as such, deserves to be unpacked and examined for fully grasping its relevance to life-course human development.

Introduction of Theory and Foundational Assumptions

From the beginning, life-course human development experiences are unavoidably shaped by both objective reality and perception. Individuals come to understand and respond to their world through interactions with others, although it is not the interactions themselves that determine life outcomes but rather the meaning that individuals make from their social encounters (i.e., their perceptions). The meanings construed have important implications for actions since individuals perceive and act on their perceptions. In other words, they infer meanings, engage in responsive coping processes, and construct both formal and informal "action plans." These processes are unavoidably associated with emotions since human variability represents both successes and failures of human coping processes. Thus, within the social contexts of development, the character of perceptions made, or meaning making inferred, contributes to the variability of human coping and identity formation outcomes as lives unfold across the life course. Assumptions gleaned, inferences made, and subsequent coping patterns enacted result from the quality of fit between the individual and the diverse contexts encountered. It is these unavoidable and life-course processes that signal the need to combine *fundamental human development thinking with basic phenomenological tenets and ecological perspectives.*

WHY PHENOMENOLOGY AND ECOLOGY?

The study of phenomenology has been around for centuries and embraced across continents, as any simple web search or dictionary exercise demonstrates. It includes significant controversies around meanings and research applications across disciplines. However, as used here and synthesized from a broad array of philosophers and translations, phenomenology is conceived as the study of "phenomena"—literally, *appearances* as opposed to *reality.*

A synthesis by Wilson (2002) posits that phenomenology is a branch of philosophy that attempts to understand how individuals make meaning from their diverse experiences. A fundamental component includes the concept intersubjectivity, which suggests that we experience the world with and through others. Given the significant role of cognition, affect, and biology in the social interactions and interpersonal experiences of humans, phenomenology communicates important opportunities for understanding differences in human "meaning making" as lives open up across the life course. This is noteworthy because categories describing human diversity often represent socially constructed meanings. And, due to the social construction of race-defined (and still salient!) social groupings, the framework is helpful because it provides a way to interpret and understand how behavioral outcomes and coping strategies are linked to the social experiences and meaning making processes of humans given their intersubjective and relevant encounters with others.

Human perception is important, and, whether taking a basic social cognitive perspective (e.g., Flavell, 1968) or a traditional phenomenology point of view (e.g., see Rogers & Kelly as reviewed in Schultz, 1976), *individual-context interactions matter.* A basic role taking or social cognition perspective assumes that perceptual processes begin at birth and gain acuity across the life course due to problem-solving of progressively complex sets of social experiences (e.g., maturation dependent cognitive processes contribute to *a growing awareness of different perspectives or points of view*). How one describes and labels this process may differ by discipline since sociologists might label the phenomenon "role enactment," while psychologists might discuss social perspective taking. However, the basic notion from either a phenomenology or social cognition standpoint is that basic perceptual processes are active and contribute to how people "make sense" of situations and experiences as one negotiates progressively complex social interactions over time and place (i.e., their meaning making processes). Thus, an individual's perceptions about settings and their experiences in them matter.

Social settings are important whether one most appreciates the individual-context interaction perspective offered by Bronfenbrenner's ecological systems theory (1985) or the more basic view provided by the early ecological psychologists (e.g., Barker &

Wright, 1954) who emphasized the character of settings (e.g., size and arrangement). The unavoidable fact is that *one's point of view matters* and is associated with the character of the environment. This highlights the potential for a wide variety of bidirectional, individual-context interactions that, in turn, contribute to diverse and patterned outcomes. It is unavoidable, then, that individuals have experiences, perceptions, and coping processes that represent active *meaning making* as a function of the quality of individual-context interactions. As such, *the conceptual combination of phenomenology with ecological systems perspectives* serves to improve one's appreciation of the "how" of development. Emphasizing the "how" of development is very different from the traditional and linear acknowledging of the "what" (i.e., individuals' patterned *outcomes*), and demands the introduction of a new framework that can help illuminate the phenomenological quality of individual-context interactions. Phenomenological variant of ecological systems theory—pronounced as the acronym, PVEST (Spencer, 1995, 2006b; Spencer, Dupree, & Hartman, 1997; Spencer et al., 2006)—is a dynamic and recursive framework that was developed to encourage the critical analysis of human development processes that unfold in multilevel contexts over time. To name but a few advantages of the PVEST framework, the process-focused or "how" oriented perspective contributes understandings about individual-context interactions. To cite a few examples, the diverse processes and outcomes emphasis is associated with (a) inescapable and diverse phenotypic expressions of the human genotype such as biology dependent maturational processes (e.g., cognition-dependent perceptual processes, early versus late pubertal development, genotype influenced body type), (b) biologically influenced temperament, (c) outcomes of socially constructed human categories [e.g., stereotypes about race, definitions of beauty] and, of course, (d) interactions with the multiple characteristics of physical and psychological contexts.

PVEST combines social cognition relevant phenomenology themes with ecological systems theory to provide a heuristic device for understanding the unique experiences of diverse group members as had at varying developmental periods. As suggested, *outcomes are often compared between and among members of diverse groups;* too frequently, stereotypic assumptions and interpretations follow. Conversely, PVEST considers the unique and cumulative individual-context interactions, such as the interaction between maturational influences and social experience-based cognitions (e.g., cognition linked comparisons made between self and others along with stressful self-consciousness). Additionally, social inequalities that may impact context experiences are not only seen as a potential category of risk but also as a source of daily challenge (i.e., dealing with disseminated stereotypes such as body type, skin color, racial categorization, stereotypic definitions of physical attractiveness, economic status disadvantage, age discrimination). Accordingly, another advantage in introducing the new framework is that it improves our understanding about unique and patterned processes and outcomes given human variability, cognition supported perceptual variations, and unavoidable individual-context interaction differences. As a systems theoretical framework, PVEST combines social-cognition linked perceptions with unavoidable context features, and acknowledges the critical role of coping processes in identity formation and affords a way to frame context-linked life-course experiences and explain patterned outcomes for diverse humans.

CONTRIBUTIONS OF HUMAN DEVELOPMENT THEORIZING

From our earliest years of life, we make efforts to make sense of the world, its people, its objects, and their stability (e.g., early person and object permanence). Our ability to conceptually organize and make sense out of social phenomena (i.e., social cognition) is a key and gradual process that develops and is made use of from the "cradle to the coffin." This ability is critical for helping individuals interpret their context-linked experiences. Given the many sources of human vulnerability (i.e., the balance between risks and protective factors), behavioral responses and emergent patterns of coping are unavoidable. Moreover, the propensity to produce behavior in social contexts and to engage in human development-linked normative activities (e.g., as developmental tasks; see Havighurst, 1953) is shared by all and is independent of age, gender, race, ethnicity, socioeconomic status, nativity, faith group, immigration status, body type, and skin color. Particularly when it comes to diverse humans living in both similar and varied settings, it is the meanings individuals make of their experiences (i.e., given the noted human characteristics and manner in which they are perceived and evaluated) that are important and require acknowledgment. For maximizing good science, individuals' meaning-making processes should represent the constructs that are actually tested and explored by scientists rather than using narrowly determined constructs based on scientists' unexamined perceptions of "social realities."

As a theory of human development applicable to diverse individuals who are acknowledged as having unique features and varying levels of vulnerability (i.e., both protective factors including privileges as well as risk factors), PVEST has distinct characteristics. The theoretical framework focuses on acknowledging and considering human similarities and differences as they are experienced by individuals growing and functioning in diverse *and* similar social ecologies; accordingly, the conceptual orientation suggests a particular perspective and approach. As a systems theory of life-course human development, the framework *considers and integrates developmental processes as inextricably linked with unavoidable context characteristics.* The consequent processes and outcomes are *not independent of individual distinctiveness.* Thus, while beginning with the acknowledgment and contributions of basic human development perspectives (i.e., cognitive, social, emotional and biological considerations), PVEST emphasizes and combines them with two significant scholarly traditions, classic phenomenology and ecological systems perspectives. The framework synthesizes and considers the long-term and critical contributions of ecological theorists such as Roger Barker, Herbert Wright, and Paul Gump (i.e., published in the mid-1940s through the 1960s), space psychologists such as Joachim Wohlwill (i.e., published in the 1970s), and the very salient contributions of the ecological system's theorist, Urie Bronfenbrenner (i.e., published in the 1970s through today). Accordingly, PVEST enjoys enormous conceptual benefits. As an integrated theoretical formulation and systems framework, it provides a mechanism for synthesizing ontological insights about human experience, perceptions, and development with cultural and anthropological studies (e.g., Jablonski, 2004, 2006; Lee, Spencer, & Harpalani, 2003; Nanda, 1974; Rogoff, 2003), as joined with ecological formulations (Barker & Wright, 1949, 1954; Bronfenbrenner, 1977, 1979, 1985, 1989, 1992, 1993; Bronfenbrenner & Ceci, 1993, 1994; Bronfebrenner & Crouter, 1983; Gump & Sutton-Smith, 1955; Wohlwill, 1985; Wohlwill & Heft, 1987). Further, as a function of the oft political nature of individual-context interactions given the socially constructed character of racial groupings, insights from critical race (CRT) theorists (e.g., Bell, 1992, 1995, 2000a, 2000b; Bonilla-Silva, 2001; Delgado & Stefancic, 2000, 2001; Hall, 2002; McIntosh, 1989) and contributions from Whiteness studies (e.g., Roediger, 1991, 1994, 2001), considered together, continue to be vital.

CONCEPTUAL TASKS OF THE FRAMEWORK

Individuals' phenomenological experiences and interactions within their social contexts matter both for the nature of behavioral outcomes and coping processes and for their influence on the character and nature of identity formation. Thus, relative to social relationships and shared environmental experiences, individuals may, at one level, appear to be very similar. In fact, children may be born into the same family with equivalent objective assets evident and ostensibly available to each. Further, context-sharing youth may appear to confront comparable experiences (e.g., parental childrearing efforts), social conditions (e.g., neighborhoods risks or privileges), and developmental hurdles (e.g., adolescent stereotypes associated with hormonal fluctuations as well as ageism and employment assumptions often reported by healthy senior citizens). Additionally, youth may be schoolmates, close community associates, and long-term friends. They may appear to have enjoyed parallel child-rearing experiences, had access to equal opportunities, espouse commitments to similar goals and activities but, none the less, embody quite different life pathways when reunited 20 years later. Thus, irrespective of assumptions about shared environments, youth may embody *quite different life-course trajectories* 20 years afterward when united again at a family gathering or school reunion event. In fact, those close neighborhood friends or schoolmates may represent both *life-course likenesses* (e.g., as adults engaged in various fields of work, confronting normative adult developmental tasks, and the enactment of multiple societal social roles) as well as *distinctively dissimilar outcomes* (e.g., fragile marital relations, unexpected wealth, enactment of a satisfying career, or untoward encounters with the justice system). As opposed to ease and success, individuals may struggle valiantly with traditional adult roles given the impact of life challenges, experienced differences in access to opportunities, and patterned coping responses. Accordingly, contributing to explanations about the "how" and the "why" regarding the multiple life-course trajectories and myriad expressions of human diversity is the undertaking of Phenomenological Variant of Ecological Systems Theory.

Framework Overview

As a theoretical perspective and heuristic device, Phenomenological Variant of Ecological Systems Theory (PEVST) represents both an *inclusive and process-oriented* human development framework. The life-course relevant conceptual system considers, unpacks and recasts the many life-stage specific expressions of human diversity as individuals interact with the physical and psychological ecologies where growth and development take place. Research findings that report differences between and within diverse humans frequently describe less optimum outcomes as problems or deficiencies. Too often, unproductive outcomes are frequently presented narrowly as primarily situated within an individual, family, community or demographic group (e.g., lower-income societal members or recent immigrants). Conversely, as a *systems explanatory framework,* PVEST functions differently in that it "unpacks" and considers diverse individual-context interactions as worthwhile contributors to *the sources and pathways of both productive and less productive coping processes, which, in turn, result in patterned life stage-specific outcomes* frequently sensationalized in the media.

To name a few illustrative outcomes, the media frequently rivets attention on "hard to miss" patterns of under-achievement, adverse life patterns of low wage earning families, gender- or ethnicity-associated health disparities, school truancy and low graduation rates. Phenomenological variant of ecological systems theory (PVEST) functions to disaggregate the multiple *sources and pathways of less than stellar outcomes* as well as to accentuate *the many expressions of positive outcomes obtained under conditions of systematic inequality;* thus, given the latter's contribution, the framework acknowledges, accommodates and proactively explores the attainment of *resiliency or good outcomes obtained in the face of significant and frequently overlooked challenges.* The conceptual approach is consistent with and, in fact, borrows from James Anthony's (1974, 1987) foundational notion of human vulnerability. Not only are significant risk factors traditionally associated with patterned outcomes for any given developmental period of interest noted, but moreover, the presence, salience, and function of *protective factors* are similarly highlighted. As indicated in Figure 19.1 and as relevant to any point in the life course, PVEST draws attention to the links between human vulnerability (i.e., the presence of risks *as well as* protective factors) and the fact of myriad life stage specific (i.e., coping) outcomes.

From our alternative perspective that underscores the need to both expect and explain diverse life outcomes (i.e., given individual-context variations), coping outcomes can represent both *unproductive* as well as *productive* developmental stage specific patterns.

In varying contexts of development as individuals live out their lives, protective factors are experienced as sources of support as individuals confront both normative and unique life-course tasks and crises. Protective factors serve to balance against the impact of risk factor presence. A core view and foundational premise of the framework emanating from Anthony's perspective (1974, 1987) is that *all humans are vulnerable;* that is, exposure both to risks and protective factors is part of the human experience. The notions of Frantz Fanon are particularly cogent at this junction since he surmises that human experience is synonymous with occurrences of oppression associated either as its source or its target (see Bulhan, 1985). Because of its subjective character, Fanon's notions about oppression are important when considering the contributions of ecology, phenomenology and intersubjectivity for unpacking the processes of human development. Going back to the women's suffrage movement in America's history, the notion of oppression has continued to have a clear function for understanding and addressing access to social opportunities and emergent roles for women. Unfortunately, its acknowledgment, deliberation, and embracement for understanding human development outcomes and processes when considered for socially constructed societal

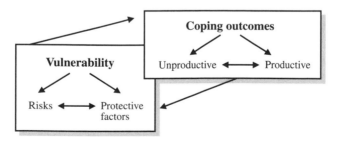

FIGURE 19.1 Traditional and Deterministic View about an Individual's Characteristics and Outcomes.

groupings based on race, socioeconomic status, privilege, and immigration status have been less transparent than ideal when reviewing twentieth-century research efforts (Spencer, 2006a, 2006c). Accordingly, the topic remains under-addressed in meaningful ways; given the pattern of omissions and subsequent misunderstandings apparent in the developmental literature and popular media, the situation of not so "blind and benign neglect" increases the relevance of the notion for contemporary basic science.

In fact—consistent with our inferences about vulnerability (Anthony, 1974, 1987), ecology, and basic human development themes when also connected with the life work of Frantz Fanon—Bulhan (1985) considers that "few human encounters are exempt from oppression of one kind or another. For by the virtue of our race, sex, or class, each of us happens to be a victim and/or perpetrator of oppression" (p. vii). Accordingly, as a function of one's victim or perpetrator societal role, risk level may be associated with *oppression* and *victim status.* Further, we posit that the level of one's protective factor character and presence may suggest either one's functioning as a source of others' risk status or, perhaps on the other hand, represent a "silent toleration" of others' victimization. The latter invariably functions as the "elephant in the room" phenomenon: There may be a tacit agreement to ignore relevant factors affecting others' life status experiences endured either as victim or oppressor; most important, the outcome of the "derived social climate" results in either high-risk levels for some and, at the same time, significant protective factor presence for others. A relevant and contemporary experimental illustration of this social dilemma, conceptualized as stereotype threat, represents findings from sets of elegantly designed studies with varied manipulations conducted in the field of social psychology both individually and collectively by Claude Steele and Joshua Aaronson (e.g., see Steele 1997, 2004; Steele & Aaronson, 1995). The experiences constructed as context features unavoidably matter for the quality of individual-context interactions, individuals' meaning-making processes (e.g., relevant intersubjective inference making process), and performance outcomes. As a function of basic social cognition, the character and content of human insights (e.g., attitudes, beliefs, assumptions and expectations) are affected and have consequences for context-specific coping behaviors (including decision making) and identity processes.

Thus, unlike other theories that focus mainly on risk factors for some individuals or groups and highlight or infer mainly protective factors for others, PVEST is different. It cautions against unbalanced research designs (see Spencer, 2006c) and espouses an approach consistent with Anthony's (1974) by *considering simultaneously* both risk factor and protective factor presence; thus, the conceptual strategy reinforces the view that humans always represent some *net level of vulnerability.* In keeping with the logic of Fanon in describing human discourse and the selective use of knowledge, Bulhan (1985) adds that, "Although we know a great deal about the economics and politics of oppression, the *psychology of oppression* is neglected and, at best, indirectly broached as a topic" (p. vii). Accordingly and as suggested by Fanon's reasoning (see Bulhan, 1985), the global and long-term reality of race, sex, or class means that everyone can be both a victim and/or perpetrator of oppression. Fanon's analysis of global human propensities and the fact of human development reaffirm our view that *everyone is vulnerable* given that we serve as the context for others' experiences; thus, the approach practices the assumptions of intersubjectivity (i.e., we experience the world both through and with others), which is a fundamental assumption of phenomenology.

Hence, PVEST provides a mechanism for considering, designing, and introducing authentic (i.e., perceptually relevant) and contextually linked constructs to the study of life-course human development. The theory's intent is to offer opportunities for specifying and demonstrating the nature and impact of "traditional" (e.g., perceived threat of psychological and/or physical violence; see Cunningham, 1993; Swanson, Cunningham, & Spencer, 2003) along with more "novel" risk factors (e.g., manifestations of the "downside of privilege"; see Luthar & Becker, 2002; Luthar & Latendresse, 2002). Consequently, the approach acknowledges and explores variables generally underresearched as constructs functioning as salient protective factors (e.g., cultural socialization, meditation, spirituality, cultural identity, physical and artistic aesthetics [e.g., music performance and dance; art appreciation], physical [e.g., walking, jogging] activity, "outsider experiences" [e.g., growing up with a "special needs" parent or sibling], and political socialization). Their function, character, use, and significance may differ as a consequence of the particular developmental period.

Given the variation and intensity of life experiences as a function of the different developmental periods, also relevant is the role of unique characteristics of humans as each navigates life and confronts normative developmental tasks (see Havighurst, 1953). There are few times when "innuendos" about disparate experiences, outcomes, and circumstances are as relevant, evident, and "interesting" as those retrieved at reunion events. Insights and information are gleaned (or inferred) from the banter and social comparison processes of peers or family members reconnecting after returning "home" after a decade or two of absence to attend a school function or family reunion. A qualitative analysis of "overheard party discussions" would affirm that decision-making outcomes linked to cognitive functioning (e.g., inferred beliefs), individuals' perceptual acuity, and cognition based awareness of socially constructed social conditions *matter*. Challenging experiences as themes of oppression (i.e., as either the perpetrator or victim) are not novel. For example, a woman recognizes at a reunion 20-years postgraduation that strongly held and inadequately addressed assumptions about prom night sexual promiscuity (i.e., often subscribed to for "short-term" popularity gains), in fact, had changed the direction of her life. In parallel fashion, bowing to adults' and peers' narrow recognition of his early maturation and physical prowess, a youth may opt to focus narrowly on athletics rather than to commit equally to parallel and significant academic interests; acknowledged years later, a college sophomore year injury underscores the significant impact and academic losses sustained and potentially associated with early, adult reinforced, and narrowly focused athletic interests. A basic definition of the term *oppression* refers to an unjust use of persuasion or force. In each example (i.e., given an understanding about the fragile character of adolescence), absent significant protective factors such as parental and school level socialization supports and acknowledged and reinforced healthy social options, the intersubjectivity of experienced risk factors such as peer pressure and reinforced beliefs concerning "fame and fortune," the absence of protective factors function oppressively to compromise productive and best possible outcomes. As a final example and as illustrated and supported by the experimental studies of Steele (1997, 2004) and Steele and Aaronson (1995), marginalized youth of color, without the availability of effective and apropos protective factors, may succumb to the risk factors (i.e., social stereotypes) associated with underperformance assumptions, which are widely held for minorities and women. In addition, the situation is made worse by unchallenged and prevalent media-hyped performance gaps statements and the inability of most educators and school systems to address the "hidden curriculum" of schools as sources of socialization (see Jackson, 1968). Left unchallenged, social stereotypes function as oppressive expectations and contexts, which undermine youthful performance. These problematic and oppression relevant assumptions are implicit when confronting gender-based performance differences and achievement more generally (e.g., see Dweck, 1978); although the theme has been more explicitly, substantively, and specifically confronted by Boykin and colleagues when addressed for African American male youth both relative to schooling (e.g., Allen, 1985; Boykin, 1986; Boykin & Ellison, 1995; Hare & Castenell, 1985) and efforts to obtain authentic support (e.g., Boyd-Franklin, 1989; A. J. Franklin, 2004; Stevenson, 1997).

Unfortunately, albeit elegantly (and globally) described by Fanon (1967), constructs apropos to oppression *are ignored* in *psychology more generally and in developmental science, specifically.* In laying the groundwork for highlighting Fanon's perspective and detailing the sources of social tensions and unrest, Bulhan (1985) posits that experiences of oppression may be unavoidable given that "People often hurl stones, steel, and insults at one another in order to own, to control, and to secure privileges" (p. vii). He specifies that, "In reality, few human encounters are exempt from oppression of one kind or another" (p. vii). Constructs sensitive to the perspective of human susceptibility to oppression (and its sources), unfortunately and as suggested, are not included in programs of research nor, more generally, assimilated into formulations of theory. The obvious exception, of course, is the myriad representations of social class and social marginalization assumed to be narrowly associated with poverty, caste status or disability. Further and unfortunately, the general and published perspective taken is that its etiology is located primarily in the individual or group as opposed to its association with historical conditions of oppression (e.g., see Gould, 1981). Alternatively, the theoretical approach taken here, and akin to Fanon's perspective, is that human growth and development themes should be approached with an awareness of the unavoidability of oppression; thus, by definition, the PVEST perspective allows for the expectation of disparate outcomes (i.e., the "what" of developmental outcomes). Equally salient, integrating the perspective and acknowledging its foundational relevance provides a needed mechanism for understanding and accounting for the "how" and "why" of human coping and identity process products. Stated differently, the theoretical perspective forwarded recognizes the variation of outcomes as the "what" (i.e., the coping product); however, at the same time it focuses on and explores the "how" of mediating identity and coping processes. The premise is that in identifying and understanding the "how" (i.e., as mediating processes that also acknowledge the shared human experience of oppression), *empirical demonstrations of the theoretical insights obtained should facilitate and afford the design and implementation of authentic and research-demonstrated supports of salience to supportive social policy.* Several empirical studies provide helpful demonstrations.

Stevenson's (1997) clinical research approach and analytic perspective, considered together, are instructive. Given the stereotypes about Black males that abound, his program of research, in fact, details the impact of daily "micro-aggressions" as a persistent state of oppression on the daily experiences of youth of color . . . specifically males. Quite interesting is that, on the one hand, Robert White's (1959, 1960) notions that it is important for people to be afforded opportunities to show competence are of general psychological relevance (i.e., individuals have a need to benefit from the residual effects of demonstrated competence, which he calls "effectance motivation"); as suggested by Stevenson (1997), Black male youth are denied the opportunity, are aware of the fact, and, thus, know they are "missed." As a consequence, according to Stevenson who describes how youths are generally "missed" and "dissed" by mainstream American society, the oppressive experiences along with neighborhood factors have signal implications for becoming "pissed" while managing their anger. The "how" scenario proposed by PVEST and consistent with the intersubjectivity assumptions of phenomenology, calls for different ameliorative solutions; the identification of authentic corrective strategies as structured protective factors and their transformation into mandated supports would be required for obtaining real outcome (i.e., "what") changes. Stated differently, the "how" themes of relevance for understanding youths' feelings about being "missed" and "dissed" by mainstream America, merit quite different strategies for impacting and supporting youths' resiliency efforts. Accordingly, the "how" or mediating factor approach introduces a very different view from the traditional and narrow outcome (i.e., "what" focus) emphasis. In fact, the latter or "what" focus too frequently exacerbates stereotypes concerning youths' underachievement and difficult relationships with the American crime and delinquency sector. In sum and from a competence-based perspective, youths' inaccessibility to opportunities that would provide options to positively shape their environments and lives has implications for frustration and anger expression. In similar fashion, Phelan, Davidson, and Cao (1991) afford parallel demonstrations of the dissonance evident between micro-system character (i.e., such as schools and neighborhoods), and their impingement on policy and practice, which potentially undermine the manifestation of resiliency and healthy development. The two examples clearly demonstrate the basic premise of Chestang (1972) who charges that for marginalized youth of color, the human development task is best framed as the dilemma of character formation undertaken in a hostile environment. On the other hand, Luthar and colleagues posit that for other youth, human development alternatively unfurls in a context of unacknowledged privilege (see Luthar, 2003; Luthar & Latendresse, 2002). Thus, the idea of "fit" between the character of research undertaken and its role for useful policy is important; policies intended to provide support, in fact, may not be actually experienced as supportive. Medicaid legislation and its implementation provide a case in point given the ever-increasing longevity of America's senior citizens.

An important function of Medicaid health-care benefits for physically fragile and vulnerable senior citizens is to diminish the extraordinary financial burdens associated with the delivery of effective health care (i.e., *diminished risk*) by providing health relevant protective factors (i.e., *as reduced health-care costs including good accessibility and improved delivery*). Illustrative comments from 83-year-old octogenerarian and recently widowed Doris D. (2007) provide helpful albeit disturbing reflections. She describes the fiscal consequences associated with family-level financial contributions required for the receipt of Medicaid assistance for an ailing spouse. As lamented by Doris D. and when assessed "down the line" following the spouse's death, all "advertised" Medicaid program support delivered to the ailing spouse is not actually experienced as supportive for the surviving member of a middle-income couple. In fact, if candid information about family finances is actually provided by the caregiving spouse to the Medicaid program representative in a bid to receive needed Medicaid support, the underadvertised economic consequences may ultimately be grim. More to the point and evident following the patient's demise, the health-care "protection" promised by successful Medicaid health benefits receipt, assessed at one point, may inadvertently result in extreme economic risk, emotional turmoil, and financial instability for the surviving spouse. The financial contributions required of a "middle-income," elderly, American couple seeking Medicaid support and analyzed after the patient's demise may indicate "unintended injury" to the surviving spouse. The survivor may appear "pauperized." From the patient's perspective as immediate beneficiary of the program's advertised benefits, actual health-care support may have been experienced as such (and even indirectly felt "in the moment" by the nonpatient spouse given the affective relief of having orchestrated health-care assistance delivery). However, due to the required level of financial disclosure and contributions from the family's resources, the actual cost to the surviving spouse may be fiscal destitution. More to the point and as poignantly reported by Mrs. Doris D., "Medicaid was helpful to Jimmy [the deceased spouse] but has made a pauper out of me!" (personal communication from a recently widowed spouse, August 8, 2007). Thus, promised health care delivery as Medicaid to an elderly couple may have been conceptualized as a source of support but not actually *experienced as supportive, in fact, when considering the subsequent economic status of a surviving and grieving spouse.* It would appear that the background research supporting passage of the Medicaid legislation for elderly families, given the financial participation criteria, may not have considered its consequent high-risk and stressful impact for the grieving spouse. The underlying research used in setting policy may have been focused narrowly on health supports to be provided for the patient; however, for the surviving spouse it was an underestimate of its impact as implemented policy (i.e., given required financial disclosure of the couple's economic status). Accordingly, following the demise of the targeted patient and taking an economic stability perspective, the policy's implementation is not actually "supportive" for the surviving spouse. In sum, and to illustrate the potential lack of fit between research questions posed (i.e., given constructs considered and character of study designs) and implemented health-care policy decisions, unfortunately, satisfying required criteria for program participation *intended to support* America's senior citizens may inadvertently function as a significant *source of risk* by pauperizing the survivor. The use of a vulnerability relevant perspective may diminish the possibility and frequency of such a conundrum.

Important, and as suggested, the intensity of the net vulnerability level experienced at a particular period of the life course is associated with the balance between *risk factor burdens* pitted against *protective factor presence.* As afforded by the Doris D. case study and illustrated in Figure 19.1, net vulnerability is bidirectionally associated with coping products (i.e., given years of health support needed before death for the patient although an unknown amount of dire economic straits experienced into the future for the surviving spouse). Additionally, Figure 19.2 suggests that between net vulnerability level and a particular developmental period's net coping outcomes achieved, there are mediating processes or moderating influences that are generally overlooked or ignored.

Considered from a life-span perspective, including Fanon's ideas concerning oppression (Bulhan, 1985) and the bidirectional relationship between *Net Vulnerability Level* and *Net Coping Outcomes,* the linkages highlighted in Figure 19.2 suggest a variety of relevant individual and policy relevant opportunities (i.e., both as processes and outcomes). Specifically, the outcome patterns salient for mediating moral, ethical, and health-relevant decisions and behavioral themes have relevance to psychology, psychiatry, philosophy, public health, political science, medicine, economics, education, and sociology (i.e., to name but a few disciplines and fields). It is apparent that positive coping products achieved at one point have implications for subsequent periods of net vulnerability; they also contribute to context as a function of one's status as either a victim or perpetrator of oppression. The bidirectional perspective suggests that net vulnerability has implications for the character of an individual's net coping outcomes; further, coping products inform the subsequent period's character of net vulnerability

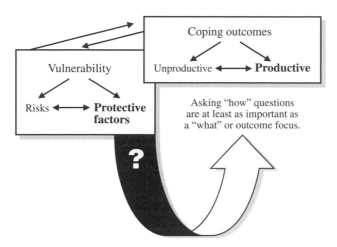

FIGURE 19.2 *Nondeterministic Theorizing:* Acknowledges Intervening Mediating Processes and Moderating Influences, Which Illustrate the Potential for Diverse Outcomes (i.e., given unique and patterned individual-context interactions).

(e.g., as cogently illustrated in the reflections by Doris D.) regarding having been "pauperized" by having accepted Medicaid support for her spouse (Doris D., 2007, personal communication).

FEATURES OF THE PHENOMENOLOGICAL VARIANT OF ECOLOGICAL SYSTEMS THEORY (PVEST)

As suggested, one of the *over-arching premises of* PVEST represents Anthony's (1974, 1987) core views concerning the fact of human vulnerability. The underlying and foundational assumption provides the opportunity to neatly fold in Fanon's perspective (Bulhan, 1985), which says that *everyone is vulnerable,* at one level or another, to the vicissitudes of oppression. Considered together, the combined presupposition fits well with the view that *lives unfold in diverse contexts as humans confront normal developmental tasks* (Havighurst, 1953). In summarizing a few key characteristics of the framework, it is evident that the *first* and most important feature of PVEST establishes *joint contributors* to one's net vulnerability level (i.e., risks and protective factors matter). Accordingly, the framework reinforces the possibility of *both unproductive* and *productive* outcomes. *Second,* the bidirectional links between the core components of the theory acknowledges that each bidirectionally influences the other; it underscores the fact of the theory's recursive character. As illustrated in Figure 19.2, the recursive relationships between net vulnerability level and coping consequences at a particular time imply salient mediating processes and moderating effects. As suggested by the question mark in Figure 19.2 and detailed elsewhere (see Spencer & Harpalani, 2004), in fact, a variety of interim forces and processes are possible when one considers several descriptive illustrations. Figure 19.3 illustrates that the framework *progresses from* the simplistic, deterministic, and linear model suggested by Figure 19.2, and alternatively, provides a focus on human development *processes.*

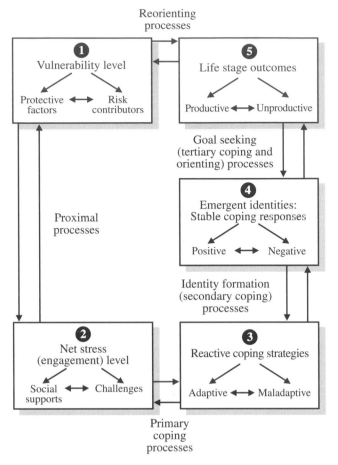

FIGURE 19.3   Processes Emphasizing: Phenomenological Variant of Ecological Systems Theory (PVEST). (*Source:* "Nature, Nurture, and the Question of 'How?': A Phenomenological Variant of Ecological Systems Theory" (pp. 53–77), by M. B. Spencer and V. Harpalani, in *Nature and Nurture: The Complex Interplay of Genetic and Environmental Influences on Human Behavior and Development,* C. Garcia-Coll, K. Kearer, and R. Lerner (Eds.), 2004, Mahwah, NJ: Erlbaum.)

Mediating processes and moderating influences are believed to make important differences in shaping human vulnerability and, thus, contribute insights concerning human coping outcomes. Fanon's perspective implicates the mediating role of scientists as reported in Bulhan's (1985) biographic treatment of Fanon's life and theoretical offerings: "Among the contributions of Fanon was the obligation placed on Western scientists to consider their role in the creation, perpetuation, and consequences of racism and colonialism" (p. v). Accordingly, PVEST recognizes that mediating and moderating influences are not independent of human characteristics and social circumstances . . . as fashioned from human distinctiveness, individual behavior, and historical conditions, as well as those that are socially constructed.

For example, the presence of an infant's siblings (e.g., including their access to and feelings about involvement) may impact the acquisition rate and point at which the family's 9-month-old baby copes with developmental tasks and achievement of person and object permanence (i.e., awareness that a person or an object, respectively, does not "disappear" when no longer in one's visual field). Similarly, the ease and actual achievement of sphincter control by 2-year-olds in the throes of potty-training may vary both within and/or between children who are cared for at home versus those attending a group day-care facility. Further, the fifth grade student's successful and straightforward acquisition of conservation and other cognitive attainments may be supported by the protective character and supports afforded by good schools, culturally sensitive teachers, engaged parents, and small classrooms. Research has shown that culturally inclusive teaching strategies matter although infrequently addressed in a substantive manner in most teacher training programs. Pedagogy enhances learning by acknowledging the reality and validity of cultural group specific social experiences, unavoidable social perceptions, values, and beliefs (e.g., see Steele, 1997, 2005; Steele & Aaronson, 1995; Stevenson, 1997). At the same time, effective teaching strategies facilitate students' broad ego identity processes such as academic self-concept (i.e., view of self as a learner) and school engagement. To illustrate the possibilities, the abstract thinking accomplished by a seventh grader in under-resourced urban classrooms may be due to an adolescent's proactive transformation of neighborhood risk conditions into more abstract representations such as community mapping (i.e., the cognitive mapping of neighborhoods for determining safe "neighborhood" routes). In fact, this safety relevant coping strategy described and frequently engaged in by urban youth and their families may assist students' safe and confident navigation from home to school and, thus, have implications for attendance statistics in addition to participation rates for after school programming options. Further, being able to acknowledge and utilize one's neighborhood "distractions" in proactive and positive ways (e.g., such as cognitive mapping) potentially contributes to a sense of empowerment, "effectance motivation" and increased school engagement. As referenced previously relative to Robert White's contributions to competence theory (1959, 1960), "effectance motivation" suggests that there are positive affective consequences for being effective around some task or experience! An individual's emotionally positive feelings accrued by demonstrating competence or showing that one has made a positive impact on a task or a situation has implications for subsequent efforts "to make a difference." That is, effectance motivation, as used by R. White's competence motivation theorizing, suggests that there is an exhilarating or motivating consequence experienced from successful efforts to impact the world. R. White's (1959, 1960) view is that the need to show an effect or to make a difference is virtually a biological need. Communicating the same level of salience about the construct's importance, DeCharms (1968) refers to it as personal causation. The underlying assumption is that humans have a need to feel that they can "make a difference" and can have an impact. As a motivational perspective for explaining the energy or motivation for the systemic character of development and achievement across the life course, the theoretical contributions of Robert White and DeCharms demonstrate that opportunities to make a difference have affective implications of relevance for beliefs concerning the nature of "becoming" and the formation of the self. Stated differently, the efforts expended in responding to the multiple and unique challenges in pursuit of "making a difference" have salient cognitive, social, and affective consequences. All have implications for normative identity processes. That is, as suggested by Figure 19.3, there are important *proximal processes,* which link transformed net vulnerability factors into net stress level (i.e., the balance between social supports versus challenges). There are important *primary coping processes,* which represent how the net stress is handled "in the moment" given unavoidable developmental tasks (i.e., reactive coping strategies suggest a balance between adaptive versus maladaptive solutions). As suggested from Figure 19.3, there are secondary coping efforts, which herald important psychosocial or identity processes that, given their patterned character or stability, have important life-course implications analogous to the themes described by Erikson (1959, 1968) and other more contemporary theorists. Given the latter, stable emergent identity processes serve to guide behavioral "next steps" as tertiary coping and orienting behaviors that speak to specific goal seeing processes given the period's normative developmental tasks. Given our discussion of diverse humans, the fact of human vulnerability, and the ever-presence of oppression, the implications of the previous ideas for assorted humans is needed. This is particularly important given R. White's (1959, 1960) notions concerning the motivational under-girding of competence formation and the role of effectance motivation for the process.

Anthony's (1987) ideas concerning resiliency along with more contemporary perspectives suggest that confronting challenges with success have important implications for positive growth and development (e.g., see Connell, Spencer, & Aber, 1994; Luthar, 2003; Luthar & Cicchetti, 2000; Spencer, 1986, 1987, 2001; Spencer, Cole, Dupree, Glymph, & Pierre, 1993; Spencer & Dupree, 1996; Spencer et al., 2006 [a review]; Spencer & Swanson, 2000; Swanson & Spencer, 1991; Swanson, Spencer, Dell'Angleo, Harpalani, & Spencer, 2002). Since challenges are transformed risk factors, achieving resiliency and a balance of the challenges with significant supports matters. The various papers cited suggest the myriad examples of effective supports (i.e., transformed protective factors), which aid positive outcomes such as adaptive reactive coping, positive identities and productive stage specific developmental products. Accordingly, experiencing some challenge should be construed as a positive experience. Of course, an important two-part query is "How much challenge is constructive and helpful in the pursuit of 'self-comparing' competence goals and resiliency, versus how much risk and adversity, as challenge, in fact, undermines psychological health and well-being?" On the other hand, other posed questions are relevant to issues concerning the "downside of privilege" (i.e., as conspicuous consumption and high levels of unacknowledged access). More specifically, "Do the efforts of highly resourced parents to provide everything humanly possible for their offspring, in fact, represent a disadvantaging parenting strategy?" In fact, "Do such strategies ultimately function to undermine effectance motivation and authentic psychosocial processes for the establishment of a healthy and purpose-focused identity?" The latter is particularly important since absent a healthy and earned level of self-esteem, maintaining a positive sense of earned self-worth and self-respect may be compromised. That is, given one's unprecedented access to resources and supports and the artificiality of the constructed self, efforts to maintain the resource-linked sense of self-conception and its attendant self-esteem may be fragile. In fact, the intersubjective relevant coping processes (i.e., coping strategies as interpersonal behaviors and social relationships that are comparatively filtered through others and their evaluative judgments concerning what is valued and important), may well contribute to the ever-present state of oppressive conditions alluded to by Fanon (i.e., theoretical notions concerning the psychology of oppression [see Bulhan, 1985]) and suggested by Chestang's (1972) formulation; the latter, using the post *Brown v. Education* 1954 era as a demonstration model, unpacks the problem of youths' character formation processes taking place in a hostile environment.

Additionally, and of relevance to protective factors and supports that might serve to nullify the "downside of privilege" alluded to in the previous example for communities that herald significant economic advantages, other problems emerge. Problems emerge when conspicuous resources are used to substitute for parental supports (i.e., in-depth and extensive use of hired household staff members or entertainment technology to substitute for consistent parental involvement as proactive socializing agents; Luthar & Becker, 2002; McIntosh, 1989). Hired help may be less likely to be concerned with or the best judge for determining how and under what conditions developmentally appropriate "challenges" are needed. The affluent social dilemmas of the perpetrators of the Columbine High School massacre provide a case in point. The news media and attendant educators are quick to recognize and characterize the problem of "missing parents" from school-based activities when reporting on students who attend low-resource schools. Unfortunately, very little is said about and examined when confronting the problems of highly affluent youth (Luthar & Becker, 2002; Luther & Latendresse, 2002). Teachers are a critical part of the youth socialization process although they are less apt to provide disparaging or critical analyses of affluent youth's challenges and needs. Of course, the supportive school climate and experience of individual-context "consonance" (i.e., individual-context "fit") had by affluent youth in schools is quite different from the "dissonance" frequently experienced by culturally marginal or economically impoverished youth with their teachers.

A culturally competent and non-stereotyping teaching orientation potentially functions as a source of support for students; it also represents a protective factor for teachers (i.e., functioning as a culturally inclusive pedagogy) since it would be expected to undermine teachers' fearfulness of students (see Hafiz, 2007); conversely in more affluent schools, teachers may have some trepidation for professional parents and their ability to impact systems. Such under-investigated teacher competencies, beliefs, practices and pedagogy have implications for youths' ultimate demonstrated confidence, social and academic competence, school engagement, sense of purpose, and school attendance (see Seaton, Dell'Angelo, Spencer, & Youngblood, 2007; Dell'Angelo, 2007; Hafiz, 2007). The type of pedagogy suggested and needed in each case would be consistent with Fanon's perspective and acknowledges the necessity that teacher training participants experience "self discovery"; the recommendation is consistent with the idea that, unintended or not, people can serve as the sources of oppressive conditions for young people (i.e., experienced either as benign neglect or as fear-based and competence undermining values and beliefs).

Such insights and programming efforts aid what Fanon calls social reconstruction and self-reconstitution (Bulhan, 1985). The various components of the teacher skill set described, if incorporated into programs of teacher training, might have implications for the off cited and dire teacher retention statistics (e.g., see Ingersoll, 2002). Without the framing of teacher training in this way (i.e., the psychosocial and foundational inclusion of self-reflection and self examination), low teacher retention rate statistics lack transparency and may inadvertently feed into furthering the public's stereotyping and internalizing of problematic beliefs concerning "other peoples' children" (see Darling-Hammond, 2004; Delpit, 1988; Ladson-Billings, 1994; Lee et al., 2003). Unfortunately, traditional perspectives about pedagogy and retention issues do not provide guidance for improved and coherent teacher training nor offer insights for improved student outcomes; that is, although hypotheses concerning environmental character (e.g., stereotype threat) are posed (see Steele, 1997, 2004; Steele & Aaronson, 1995), the self-appraisal relevant linked processes needed for social reconstruction and self-reconstitution are infrequently broached (see Bulhan, 1985). The situation is carefully described by a teacher who notes that her altered perspective and social approach results in "My teaching becomes a stewardship and not a totalitarian regime" (Cruesoe, 1999).

Undoubtedly, and as illustrated by Cruesoe's perspective as a practice teacher, teachers' underpinning values, attitudes and beliefs are salient. As the above examples demonstrate, significant numbers of mediating intervening processes, moderating influences, and social experiences are possible. Acknowledging and drawing attention to them serves to explicate and more accurately account for the recursive links between net vulnerability level and the prior stage's specific coping outcomes as suggested by Figures 19.2 and 19.3. As previously noted, the inserted question mark in Figure 19.2 between vulnerability level and coping addresses the "how" for particular outcomes as well as providing explanations as to "why." Accordingly, and as illustrated in Figure 19.3, a special feature of a PVEST perspective is its ability to explore processes and explanations that potentially inform constructive change. This is quite different from the traditional "what" question, which narrowly focuses on *outcome comparisons*—and frequently compares unequal samples or individuals that represent very different conditions (i.e., the consistent and problematic comparisons between lower-income students versus affluent youth; see Spencer, 2006a, 2006c). Specifically, too frequently, conclusions are based on analyses of research and program designs representing either between group contrasts of impoverished individuals versus high-resource youth or, alternatively, between White privileged youth versus ethnically diverse youth of color from under-resourced families. Moreover, the research and inferences based on findings from the more traditional group comparisons generally occur without an acknowledgment of either *color associated risks or privileges*. The invalid comparisons, although the subject of thorough, long-term and classic critiques (e.g., see Banks, 1976; Gould, 1981; Guthrie, 1976), continue to appear in published reports of highly acclaimed journals (see critiques in Spencer, 2006a, 2006c).

The critiques described and their significance for intervention/prevention efforts, culturally relevant research questions, effective programming efforts, and innovative training opportunities suggest that the Phenomenological Variant of Ecological Systems Theory (PVEST) is different from traditionally formulated human development frameworks. The underlying goal of PVEST is to improve the formulation of science and its application to programming efforts and practice by its attention to context-linked perspectives and speculations about diverse humans. It has the potential to improve the interpretation and explanation of findings by hypothesizing about and testing mediating human processes of conjectured salience for *productive* stage specific outcomes (refer to Figure 19.3). It is applicable to diverse humans who represent some level of vulnerability. It acknowledges that humans cope with a variety of conditions and social contexts including oppression as described by Fanon (see Bulhan, 1985). In fact, the framework is robust enough to consider the multiple sources of and expressions of *resiliency,* an under-explored coping outcome of diverse humans.

FUNCTION AND ASSUMPTIONS OF RESILIENCY AND PRIVILEGE

For Anthony (1974), resiliency hypothesizes about the attainment of good outcomes accrued in the context of significant challenge and contributes to the foundational premises of PVEST. The idea is reinforced by Fanon's (see Bulhan, 1985) analysis of and theorizing about the psychology of oppression (i.e., all humans are vulnerable). Achieving *resiliency* (i.e., positive outcomes achieved in the presence of persistent and significant difficulty) is relevant to all periods of life. Obviously, given the relationship between coping outcomes and subsequent vulnerability level, resiliency may function as a coping outcome at one point or represent a protective factor vis-à-vis net vulnerability level at a consequent stage. In fact and as conceded when discussing the unique experiences of affluent students, one might surmise that some level of challenge experienced is a "good thing" given its potential contributions to demonstrated resiliency. Further and as alluded to when stating the several hypothetical questions, it is important to ascertain how much challenge substantiates and supports resilient outcomes versus how much challenge contributes to *significant imbalance given significant levels of consequent stress* (i.e., given an extreme challenge versus support imbalance; Figure 19.3).

Stress is a natural outcome given one's net vulnerability and youths' ongoing confrontation of normal developmental tasks. Thus, the net balance between challenges versus supports, as illustrated in Figure 19.3, is another unique feature of the framework's capacity to recognize, explore and the implications of disproportionately high levels of accessible supports for particular individuals and a state of significant imbalance due to the salient under-abundance or, in fact, inadequate level of resources experienced by others.

Thus, PVEST provides a mechanism for addressing *unacknowledged conditions of privilege* as well as exploring needed protective factors that may contribute to resiliency and are required for offsetting significant levels of risk. Another evident strength of PVEST is its potential for representing both the stable presence of inequality for some (i.e., excessive risks), and at the same time, addressing the impact of the cumulative and over-abundant affluence available to selected others. The latter situation (i.e., disproportionate presence of accessible protective factors) opens the possibility of experiencing the "downside of privilege" given the lack of opportunity to hone competence-building skills through the opportunity of expending efforts that result from the reciprocated positive feelings that accompany making a difference; as suggested, Robert White (1959, 1960) refers to the process as effectance motivation while for DeCharms (1968) the process is akin to what he refers to as personal causation. Both conceptual devices suggest an affective consequence for successfully addressing challenges of one type or another. The honed skill sets achieved as an outcome are consistent with R. White's (1959, 1960) competence notion.

Accordingly, even though frequently overlooked in the social sciences, more generally, the disparate context of human development, due to conditions of inequality of social opportunities, is important. Its recognition as a salient scholarly focus, unfortunately, continues as the mainstay of legal scholars and is addressed under the rubric of Critical Race Theory (CRT; Bell, 1992, 1995, 2000a, 2000b; Hall, 2002) and whiteness studies (e.g., see McIntosh, 1989; Roediger, 1991, 1994). The dilemma is presented as an examination of the downside of affluence and privilege and has been addressed fairly recently by a few developmental researchers (see Luthar & Becker, 2002; Luthar & Latendresse, 2002). Considered collectively from the several perspectives then, the downside of privilege relates to the fact that in the absence of challenge, there are too few opportunities to develop, and thus hone through practice, and adaptive coping strategies; the problem is that you are "protected" from coping opportunities by parents who consistently "step in" and take care of all potentially dissonance producing situations or problems (i.e., contemporarily referred to in the media as "helicopter parents"). Accordingly, there is very little independent and adaptive coping, just acceptance of the status quo. In sum, the first time you encounter what you perceive as a challenge or threat to self, there is nothing to fall back on (i.e., accumulated experiences of adaptive problem-solving skills are absent). As a consequence, the individual may then be *more vulnerable* than someone who has had to cope with myriad challenges throughout life—hence, one experiences the downside of privilege. As illustrated by the media coverage of Hollywood's privileged young adult women (e.g., Lohan, Hilton, & Richie) and illustrated as component three of PVEST (see Figure 19.3 component three, reactive coping processes). Accordingly, there may be inordinate preoccupation with "problematic efforts" or maladaptive reactive coping strategies exercised to establish a positive sense of self; the reactive coping efforts may in turn foster dangerous or problematic situations for self and others who may share aspects of context (e.g., as car crash victims of "hit and runs" or due to exposure to media exploiting distorted body images). We suggest that there may be adverse consequences to the "downside of privilege" for unknown others as a consequence of privileged and unacknowledged recklessness. Given the level of privilege and power of such individuals and, over the life course, the psychological energy expended in efforts to sustain "inauthentic self-esteem" provide illustrations of what Chestang (1972) refers to as an unacknowledged but unmistakably hostile environment. It also illustrates the nation's income bifurcation and ever increasing disparity described by Darity and Myers (1998) in their seminal economic analysis, *Persistent disparity: Race and economic inequality in the United States since 1945.* Accordingly, such analyses of privilege more widely opens the door for proposing effective responses to patterns of inequality and to applying Fanon's globally relevant views concerning the psychology of oppression (see Bulhan, 1985).

Inequality of Opportunity, Access, and Social Contextual Experiences

Another foundational premise of PVEST is consistent with Chestang's (1972) position concerning the post-*Brown v. Education* 1954, 1955 era and its continuing social context salience for contemporary American life (*Brown I,* 1954; *Brown II,* 1955). The theory's attentiveness to and recognition of the social fact of inequality introduces and demonstrates myriad sources of dissonance. Often personalized and viewed as an individual experience of inferred psychological assault with inferences about racism, parallel construct's to Chestang's (1972) context relevant theme (i.e., specifically, the dilemma of character formation in a hostile environment) continues to be ignored; the oversight suggests a perception that the topic is too uncomfortable to address in the psychological sciences; accordingly, its intersubjective reality for many and phenomenological relevance, too frequently, is ignored. Interesting, of course, is that many individuals can discuss, research and publish "broad-minded" analyses about gender bias although unable to address the continuing role of color consciousness in the foundational experience of American racial inequality. Accordingly, another advantage of PVEST is that it provides the mechanism for addressing the net stress individuals feel as a consequence of *imbalance* between challenges encountered versus the availability of supports; as suggested from several disciplinary perspectives, the noted sources of imbalance have been analyzed by Chestang (1972), Fanon (see Bulhan, 1985), and Darity and Myers (1998) and associated with social class, nativity, gender, race, color, immigration status or faith group membership.

Given the vulnerability level associated with the risks or protective factors linked to any of the demographic categories noted, the challenges one encounters on a day-to-day basis may unavoidably vary although their *impact can be alleviated by the transformation of protective factors into broad, multilevel and ecologically associated supports* (refer to Figure 19.3). Although not previously noted as an important demographic category, the experiences of special needs individuals are also important and provide another illustrative example of the utility of PVEST.

Public Law 94-142 (Education of All Handicapped Children Act, Pub. L. No. 94-142, 1975) was designed to guarantee that special needs individuals have access to education in the least restrictive environment; its passage influences the macro-level of the ecology as social policy (see Bronfebrenner, 1979, 1985). Unfortunately, its regulation and implementation have not been without problems and controversy but continue to have a significant impact on educational access for special needs students. Before passage of the public law, the learning context and opportunities for many special needs youngsters and their families were uncertain, at best. The probability of failure was high for youth needing classroom immersion experience. For some, the national implementation of the edict functions as a protective factor and provides for a broad array of supports. However, for others, the decree's failure is thought to stem from the oft mis-direction of students into special education programming. The actual problem may be linked to the continuing dilemma affecting culturally diverse youth of color taught by inadequately trained teachers (see Darling-Hammond, 2004; Delpit, 1988; Ladson-Billings, 1994; Lee et al., 2003). Frequently, youth neither connect with nor grasp the particular teaching style used by traditionally trained teachers. That is, pedagogy may be uncritically used with culturally unique students; moreover and quite frequently, the failed outcomes are blamed narrowly on students and their families; in fact, one is reminded of Cruesoe's (1999) comment about needing her teaching to represent stewardship versus the semblance to a totalitarian regime.

The actual context specific tensions of inadequate teacher training along with the questionable content of implemented programming are overlooked (e.g., due to the lack of cultural scaffolding or the teacher's use of the children's own culturally specific experiences to explain and demonstrate school lesson relevant phenomena). One well-experienced school consultant's report of the student-teacher "mis-match" is informative. Williams (the school consultant) describes a teacher's perceptual failure that is evident in her explanation for the high rate of "special education referrals" for removing African American youth from her classroom. As the teacher explains, "I thought my job was to teach children who 'got it' and to refer out (i.e., to special education) all students who did not" (Belinda Williams, 2000, personal communication; Williams, 2003). The teacher's perception of her role as a teacher potentially contributes to a context of risk for many students and a source of unnecessary special education referrals for others. The lack of student-teacher match functions in at least two ways: (1) it represents a source of inadequate support and, at the same time, can inadvertently contribute to an oppressive state of affairs consistent with and reminiscent of Fanon's perspective about the omnipresence of oppression (Bulhan, 1985); and (2) the circumstances also speaks to a potential "system injury" situation. Most salient, because it is not recognized as such, the infrequent attention by social scientists leaves it both unmonitored and impervious to correction and change. Again, the dilemma noted is akin to Frantz Fanon's notion that everyone has the potential both to be oppressed and to serve as the perpetrator of others' oppression (see Bulhan, 1985). Most significant, the accurate identification of "the problem" needing to be addressed is overlooked. The consequent and continuing predicament of school climate concerns functions as the "elephant in the room" (i.e., unacknowledged and uncomfortable social dilemma) as experienced by many students, their families, enlightened educators, and responsible policy analysts. Infrequently acknowledged is the dilemma of school personnel who lack effective teaching strategies, cultural sensitivity, instructional innovations, and, thus, teacher competence. As implicated previously, the latter is frequently due to ineffective pedagogy and training, which contributes to a lack of teaching confidence and sense of efficacy.

Of course, for students having legitimate special needs, without the policy, their particular requirements remain inadequately attended to or unaddressed. Public Law 94-142 was designed to provide significant sources of support and in many cases functions as such. However, for others and as suggested, special education programming provides a referral option for some teachers who are either unprepared for or choose not to teach. Inadvertently and generally not unacknowledged as such, the policy *makes a referral option available for those actually incapable of addressing the needs of particular youth and families.* The conundrum is never approached as one that contributes system injury and the perpetuation of oppression for some and significant entitlement for others (see Bulhan, 1985).

Accordingly, the educational needs of diverse learners from families living cultural traditions not recognized or valued by the school culture, too frequently and unfortunately, do not easily benefit from traditional American schooling opportunities and implemented policies. However, from a PVEST perspective and considered as a source of student benefit and support, students can potentially profit from the supporting conceptual scaffolding provided by teachers who, in fact, recognize and respect the unique cultural traditions of diverse students (Lee, Spencer, & Harpalani, 2003). In fact, culturally distinct students in mono-cultural classrooms may experience challenges as "cultural divides," which often separate them from recognizing, accessing and using educational opportunities mandated and made available by macro-system level public edicts (e.g., see Phelan et al., 1991). Given the No Child Left Behind federal mandate, youth are expected to perform under generally unacknowledged, academically bereft and, in fact, oppressive conditions (Seaton et al., 2007). The perspective suggests significantly different research designs and relevant constructs for consideration given the inferred net vulnerability level (i.e., both protective and risk factors), stress level (i.e., specific sets of supports and challenges) and need for responsive coping processes. The implications for the training of professionals along with the design and implementation of intervention options might be quite different from those normally assumed.

At the same time, proximal media exposure heralds affluent conditions (e.g., conspicuous consumption and unlimited resource access) and ignores inequalities experienced as socioeconomic associated disparities. Further, attention to themes of purpose, positive youth development and spirituality continue to elicit attention in the developmental and social science literatures; however, the moral, psychosocial and ethical *dilemmas resulting from unacknowledged protective factor presence as disproportionate access to supports* (i.e., privileging conditions for some and socially constructed inequalities for others) *are frequently overlooked*. It is this dilemma and its general invisibility in the social sciences that buttresses Fanon's perspective that scholarship and practices become unwitting participants in the same historical violence and captivity as those they actually seek to heal (Bulhan, 1985, p. viii). Accordingly, the PVEST framework draws attention to opportunities for considering context sensitive constructs, which are currently infrequently addressed in the conduct of social science. For example, exploring the impact of unacknowledged privileges for particular youth while narrowly analyzing sources of deviations and problems for other youth obfuscates the need to consider the individual's unique "meaning making" and basic perceptual processes as a function of vulnerability level, stress level, reactive coping methods and models available, and internalized self-identifications (refer to Figure 19.3). Integration of a Fanonian perspective concerning the fact of human vulnerability and oppressive conditions, along with evident varying mediating processes made more complex by the fact of developmental status, suggests the need for a formulation such as that provided by PVEST.

To illustrate, adolescents may be unprepared to confront and productively cope with the persistence of unjust conditions. In fact, youths' affective responses to these unacknowledged but highly stressful conditions are not unlike the chronic psychological stress responses reminiscent of posttraumatic stress disorder (PTSD; see Dupree, Spencer, & Bell, 1997; Spencer, Dupree, Cunningham, Harpalani, & Munoz-Miller, 2003; Spencer, Dobbs, & Swanson, 1988). PTSD is a debilitating condition caused by a terrifying physical or emotional event; it results in the individual having unrelenting, alarming and intrusive thoughts often experienced as frightening feelings, memories or flashbacks. Most important, the individual may feel chronically numb. The disorder has been referred to as "shell shock" or "battle fatigue." In such situations, the net level of stress produced has implications for a student's patterns of coping. Intrusions into youths' learning capacity and more general academic prowess would be expected and, in fact, difficult to avoid.

At each stage, the expected developmental tasks engaged in by youth may be thought of as the confronting of challenges in response to normative responsibilities including academic performance, school attendance, apprenticeship training (i.e., in preparation for taking on adult roles), healthy peer relationships and good citizenship. Too frequently, given the latter, each is pursued under conditions of unappreciated inequality. On the other hand, available protective factors may be called on and transformed into accessible supports; they serve to offset the level of challenge confronted and residual stress experienced. As illustrated in Figure 19.3, the level of net stress experienced is not independent of attendant vulnerability level; thus, the level of net stress experienced and manifested represents the balance between the challenges confronted (i.e., given a particular risk level) versus the supports available and accessible (i.e., transformed protective factor presence). Accordingly and consistent with Anthony's (1974, 1987) notions and insert Fanon's views about society (see Bulhan, 1985), one always struggles with some level of stress given that, as noted, *all humans* experience some level of vulnerability.

STRESS, VULNERABILITY, CONTEXT CHARACTER, AND IDENTITY

Unfortunately, and too frequently, the term *vulnerability* is used interchangeably with risk, which then ignores the powerful reality of protective factor presence. Potentially overlooked are the many ways that transformed protective factors (a) impact lives as a *stress reducer* (i.e., given the presence of supports), (b) facilitate *constructive reactive coping patterns* (i.e., *as adaptive coping options*), and (c) contribute to *beneficial emergent identities* (i.e., as positive identity options). This, then, increases the likelihood of success for stage-specific coping effects (i.e., as productive outcomes given the developmental tasks of concern for the particular period of the life course). The bidirectional and recursive relationships between the five components of PVEST evident in Figures 19.3 and 19.4 illustrate the sources of individual and group consistencies and dissimilarities given the key role of individual meaning making, perceptions, and the diverse character of social contexts. Figure 19.4 provides examples of the probable constructs available for assessing the component elements of PVEST.

As suggested, environments differ in accessibility and resource availability (i.e., as both recognized and reachable supports). Thus, even for children sharing child-rearing environments, the degree to which one sibling views the family's situation as having available and sustainable assets matters and affects behavior. Differences in beliefs about accessibility to resources have implications for one youth's perceptions of supports, coping efforts to access them, adaptive use of them, internalized positive identification with them, and productive coping outcomes. Thus, independent of the developmental period of concern, an individual's experiences with, perceptions of, and responses to performance expectations matter. Equally importantly is our consideration of the extent to which a young person does or does not navigate neighborhoods and other contexts onto a path of *patterned productive coping processes* (i.e., as accessed supports, their adaptive use in time of immediate need, and internalization as an ever-present option). The outcomes may reinforce and support the protective factors available for reducing levels of vulnerability. As such, the recursive and bidirectional aspects of PVEST demonstrate why one sibling can end up on a productive path and the second, having shared the same physical and family childrearing context, can be firmly off onto an opposite trajectory.

Evident from Figure 19.4 is that the redundant use of a particular reactive coping strategy (i.e., as a function of secondary coping processes illustrated in Figure 19.3) becomes internalized as a stable emergent identity (i.e., either negative or positive). Further, it should be noted that component four (emergent identities: stable coping responses) of PVEST is illustrated as specific coping processes linking it with components 3 and 5 as depicted in Figure 19.3; additionally, component four lists exemplar identity constructs and appears in Figure 19.4 (e.g., self as learner, role identity with family, or exaggerated sex role presentation [e.g., hypermasculinity]). The consequences and impact of the stable emergent identity processes achieved across a variety of settings, developmental periods and attendant tasks, then, result in the life-stage specific outcomes, which may represent either productive or unproductive coping products (refer to Component Five as illustrated in Figure 19.4). The evaluative character of the outcomes has to do with the degree of match between the result expected (i.e., given the specific tasks required for that particular developmental stage in question; see Havighurst, 1953), and the coping outcome actually produced. For example, as suggested, stereotyping may be exacerbated by media reporting of disparities without acknowledging the myriad socially constructed inequalities. Considered together and as suggested, Figures 19.3 and 19.4 illustrate the recursively organized and linked five-component processes of PVEST.

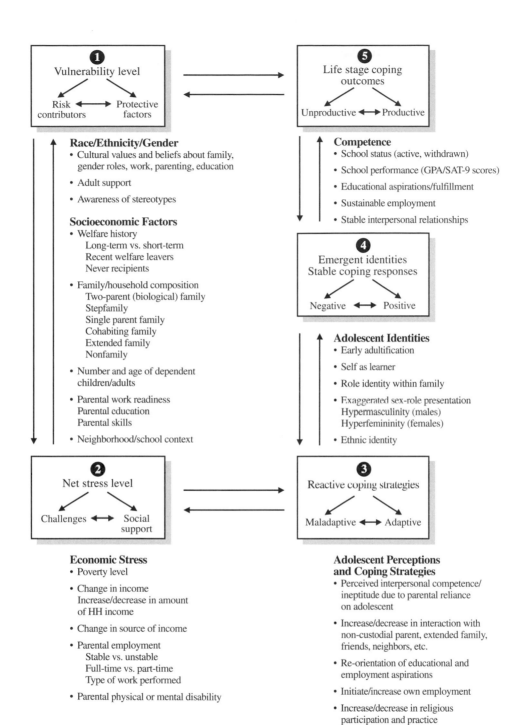

FIGURE 19.4 Using PVEST to Consider the Effects of Specific Economic Policies and Requirements for Parents on Adolescent Academic and Employment Outcomes.

PVEST Rationale and Need for New Theory

The continuing shortcomings of efforts to understand the development of diverse youngsters as a function of socialization experiences in varying contexts suggest the need for new theory. Proposed is that systems thinking about the development of diverse humans and their efforts to demonstrate competence and achieve a healthy sense of self should have important implications for training, practice, and policy.

THEORY RATIONALE

Access to a multifaceted, context-linked, and systems-oriented human development framework is essential for understanding the broad array of contributions to human vulnerability as well as the essential ingredients for obtaining resilient outcomes. Dynamic systems theories aid our appreciation of both resiliency and unproductive outcomes. As a development-sensitive and context-linked recursive systems framework, PVEST demonstrates how positive outcomes or coping features at one point in the life course may be transformed into protective factors of value for diminishing vulnerability level at subsequent stages. PVEST allows for speculations about how a poor developmental outcome at one point (i.e., including its a priori and attendant risk factors) can still result in productive outcomes (Figures 19.3 and 19.4). Recognizing an array of potential *protective factors as transformed supports, the analytic approach provides a strategy for explaining "the how" of improved outcomes at subsequent developmental stages.* Turecki's (1989) descriptive analysis of the difficult child syndrome (i.e., as it relates to temperament) provides a helpful illustration of some of the framework's unique and needed aspects. Temperament is generally acknowledged as the biologically based or "wired-in" aspect of personality. Its more vulnerable manifestations are evident in people as seen across a variety of individual difference characteristics including race, ethnicity, social class, and faith groups: The possession of a difficult temperament represents an "equal opportunity trait." Turecki's (1989) essay on the topic describes the needed parenting supports for altering the childrearing context of temperamentally difficult children; the analysis demonstrates how parenting can be proactively and strategically used as a significant source of support. As a primary intervention technique, such strategies are important for obtaining good outcomes for this under-acknowledged syndrome present across diverse groups of families. He emphasizes that a family's experience of a difficult child's temperament need not result in poor child outcomes. Parent-implemented supports change the course of individual-context interactions for the child *and the family* (see Turecki, 1989; refer to component 3 of Figure 19.4). The family's reactive coping strategies introduced for understanding and supporting a temperamentally difficult child have implications for lowering child risk and, thus, degree of vulnerability as experienced for subsequent periods. Accordingly, the life-course relevant mediated transformations of the temperamentally difficult child, as described by Turecki, contribute to subsequent experiences of *lowered vulnerability* due to an increase in protective factor presence; the net vulnerability posited by Anthony (1974) and depicted in Figure 19.3 represents the balance between risk and protective factor presence. The reactive coping strategies provided to parents as sources of primary support for difficult children as expressed by Turecki have implications for significantly *lowered levels* of child vulnerability and net stress (i.e., both for the child and the parent[s]).

The PVEST framework's recursive and systemic character aids in explaining and interpreting individual-context interactions as lives unfold across developmental periods. To illustrate, relative to Turecki's approach to supporting parents and families of a difficult child, the PVEST framework pushes for the consideration of a virtual host of options for primary (i.e., parental and family) prevention efforts. However, alterations in secondary prevention efforts (i.e., social service-, health-, or school-level system supports) are also possible and important. This could include alterations in (a) the design of exo- and meso-systems, (b) the character of staff training, and (c) the design of innovative practices and service-delivery policies. Accordingly, as considered either individually or collectively, any one would contribute to or diminish the likelihood of unintentional systems injury (i.e., as experienced by families purportedly seeking support).

In fact, as another system-level (meso- and exo-ecological) illustration, the theoretical framework has significant currency for analyzing and characterizing the impact of maternal full-time work on the quality of life for families and children. As described in the National Academy of Sciences Report (1990: Who Cares for America's Children), family-supporting social policies such as maternity leave, the availability of part-time work, and job sharing opportunities are viewed as important family friendly resources and supports (i.e., protective factors experienced as specific supports; see Spencer, Blumenthal, & Richards, 1995). At the same time, a requirement of employment is the system-level response to poor and low-income workers who depend on state and federally subsidized sources of family support; additionally, available minimum wage and entry-level jobs generally lack family leave benefits. Thus, as a function of socioeconomic status and related factors, family-supporting policies serve as a *source of support* for one group albeit a source of *challenge* for other groups. Accordingly, also applicable at the policy level, PVEST provides an option for analyzing youth outcome disparities as associated with policy implementation impact (i.e., individual and family experiences of policy as a risk versus protective factor). This dilemma is also apparent for the health and human services sector (see Silver, 2007); policies purportedly designed as youth- and family-friendly edicts, in fact, show differential impact for low- and high-resource families. Accordingly, it is possible that a policy designed and intended to serve as an asset or protective factor for the functioning of children and families in one situation, actually represents a deleterious factor or risk condition for another group seeking help with a special needs child or a youth possessing a difficult child syndrome.

Not surprising, the sets of assets described by Turecki (1989) indeed explain how the increasingly segmented social support networks (i.e., advertised as available to children and families), in fact, potentially mitigate outcomes. Additionally, the broad and diverse social systems through which youth frequently and independently navigate (i.e., as they move from middle childhood and on into adolescence) further complicate the process. More to the point, the situation may place a young person with a difficult child syndrome at great risk for manifesting higher levels of vulnerability if parents are unable to provide adequate, appropriate and significant numbers of support. Of course, potentially, the situation becomes increasingly more conceptually dense when individuals are members of marginalized groups. A quick scan of published research demonstrates the continuing problem of narrowly conceptualized human development research and application efforts when considering the experiences of culturally diverse groups of color.

To illustrate, there may be significant within and between group similarities when looking at the social encounters of youth reared in Spanish-speaking families (e.g., Spanish-speaking Puerto Ricans, Costa Ricans, and Mexicans have significantly different social experiences from those had by Spaniards). At the same time, although not sharing a common language, Asian ethnic groups (e.g., Chinese, Korean, Hmong, and Japanese Americans) may equally benefit from the general positive stereotyping often ascribed to Americans of Asian descent, more generally. Accordingly, a benefit of the framework is its consideration of the individual's own perceptions (i.e., one's phenomenology or "meaning making processes"), which may vary significantly and independently from the assumptions imposed on the entire group (see Spencer et al., 2006).

IMPLICATIONS FOR RESEARCH METHODS

The sources of within- and between-group variation increase as a function of the group's designated socioeconomic status. For example, low-income, European American youth are as under-represented in the normal human development emphasizing literature as are diverse youth of color. The explanation for this continuing situation may be due to the use of school-level data although speculations are made about individual functioning. That is, the percentage of free lunch participation of schools is used as the level of analysis and socioeconomic status designations. The scenario is made increasingly complicated when race is also considered.

PVEST is unique in that it provides a strategy for proactively addressing the socially constructed and continually uncomfortable race variable. Often, race as a variable is either ignored, considered beyond the scope of normative developmental science efforts, or is included only if questions of deficits, deviance, social problems or individual pathology are the focus. Further, when twenty-first century research is designed by many students trained by faculty who themselves earned degrees within the past 30 to 35 years, too many young scholars are unaware of standard research methodology critiques concerning ethnicity salient sampling bias (e.g., Banks, 1976; Gould, 1981; Guthrie, 1976). The critiques illustrate and explain the redundant and faulty character of research efforts that continue to *compare middle-income Whites* with *low-resource Blacks and Hispanics.* The critiques also cite the parallel major problems of ignoring low-income and working class European Americans and overlooking the existence of middle-income ethnic groups of color (e.g., African American and Hispanics). Qualitative reports by Sullivan (1989), addressing the adolescent to young adulthood transition for ethnically diverse young adults, draw attention to the latter concern and afford a useful exception. It is the case that sample identification often requires significant effort for obtaining individual level social economic class designations from school-level data. For example, attempts to infer accurate family level information from school-level statistics (i.e., the percentage of children in the school that qualify for free lunch) virtually guarantee inadequate information and confused data interpretation. Impoverished and working-class White youth and their families may live, at the same time, *both socially isolated from* but still *scattered within* working class and middle-income White community enclaves. Thus, although sharing aspects of risks that contribute to vulnerability, they potentially benefit from accessible community level social and economic resources, which function as potential supports (e.g., apprenticeship opportunities as available work options, which have relevance for adolescent identity issues). Additionally, the absence of harassing experiences with police officers may protect them from social risks, which are virtually normative for low-income youth of color growing up in urban, under-resourced areas; at the same time, middle-income youth of color living in predominately white neighborhoods are not protected from risks more often found in low-resource predominately Black communities. The critical point emphasized is that low- and working-class European American youths' social experiences in neighborhood and school settings are, for the most part, missing from the developmental literature; unpacking such youths' identity and coping given assumptions about "White privilege" and the fact of working class or lower-income status deserve careful study. Considered from a vulnerability and mental health perspective, the findings should have important implications for understanding youths' reactive coping tendencies, identity processes and life stage coping efforts. The suggested inclusive and race-sensitive perspective is important but remains inadequately addressed in developmental science although the themes continue to be addressed in the critical race literature as whiteness studies (see Ignatiev, 1995; Roediger, 1991, 1994, 2001). As suggested, the stereotypes and themes associated with "Whiteness" are generally addressed by legal scholars under the rubric of critical race studies (Delgado & Stefancic, 2001; Ignatiev, 1995; McIntosh, 1989). Unfortunately, developmental conceptual perspectives are outside their spheres of interest and expertise and, thus, are infrequently considered. As such, it becomes difficult to address issues of vulnerability for low- and working-class Whites, which may leave youth highly vulnerable to reactive coping strategies, and identity patterns that lead to marginalized lives and/or behaviors and beliefs that marginalize others.

As reviewed by Allen, Spencer, and Brookins (1985) and the several multidisciplinary contributions to the edited volume by Spencer, Brookins, and Allen (1985), the long-standing need for an inclusive focus in developmental science is either disregarded or treated descriptively as a demographic listing much like age, gender, and social class (i.e., as one's social address). Considered long-term, the traditional approach tells us little about how race functions either as a risk factor or protective feature. The oversight in considering the analysis of race in developmental science means that it is costly for policy, training, practice, and basic research efforts; not taking into account social variables associated with racial stratification continues to leave a void in most theories of *normal human functioning*. Instead, racial stratification relevant constructs are considered in disciplines, fields, and research efforts concerned with discerning problems, characterizing deviance, reporting on pathology, and listing disparities (see review by Spencer, Brookins, & Allen, 1985). Consequently, traditional programs of research consider race in conceptually narrow and deficit-focused ways. There are few contemporary led discussions of *diverse human patterns* that are highlighted more frequently than those having to do with the socially constructed "*race*" status variable.

Slaughter-Defoe, Johnson and Spencer's recent (in press) synthesis reiterates the principle that more diversity exists *within* than *between* groups. Research strategies and media attention often choose to highlight between group "gap findings" as "the day's newsworthy disparity insight" (e.g., school achievement, crime statistics, health outcomes, living standards, longevity). A major advantage of PVEST is that it acknowledges and unpacks the role of phenotypic differences such as body type, skin tone and maturational rate as well as social status hierarchies. As noted, although clearly not comfortable for many researchers, recognizing and analyzing the environment-associated coping processes required by youth given the varied levels of human vulnerability is a useful exercise. It provides insights about the changeable individual-context interactions that emanate from disparities in resource distribution and, which are frequently associated with developmental outcomes and "gap" findings.

In like manner, efforts to bring attention to persistent thematic social injustices are viewed as problematic and, thus, are frequently ignored. Examples include the lack of adequate housing and affordable health care in addition to the chronic absence of teen work opportunities; the latter has critical implications for adolescent identity processes and youths' preparation for the world of work. Suburban communities provide important apprenticeship opportunities; youth are able to learn the habits of work, including acquiring feedback concerning errors, albeit without future defining consequences. Similarly, disproportionate minority police department contact, and inadequate teacher and administrator training for diverse learners are other contributors that support media communicated gap outcomes. Each individual-context incongruent relationship becomes patterned over time and, indeed, matters for diminishing human risk. Neighborhood features as basic as supermarket presence with competitive prices and quality products are ignored when reporting obesity statistics; similarly, the presence of well-kept and safe recreational outlets remains at issue although the importance of physical activity is a consistent media disseminated theme. Further, the lack of culturally sensitive and well-trained police cadets continues to be under-recognized in addition to parallel deficiencies relative to the training of teachers and educational administrators. Traditional programs of training are not actually supportive if race stratification factors (i.e., multiple levels of persistent risks) are ignored but, in fact, represent a significantly greater impact than recognized. In sum, consistent with Anthony's perspective (1974, 1987), everyone is vulnerable and struggles to obtain balance between risk factor presence versus the availability of protective factors. Unfortunately, invisibly treated racial stratification variables significantly increase the risk for some and, thus, require significant and appropriate levels of support for offsetting high oppression levels of risk. Disparate conditions matter in significant ways. As suggested, infrequently acknowledged but very salient for affluent youth is their exposure to transmitted conditions of intergenerational privilege, and to unacknowledged exposure to models, which communicate *tolerance for social injustice.* Thus, published accounts describe *unproductive outcomes in racial* terms without also conceding the overlooked and inequitable conditions that contribute to disparities (i.e., referred to are conditions of privilege and inequality).

The Slaughter-Defoe et al. (in press) perspective affirms the lack of biogenetic evidence for many media emphasizing performance differences. Their review reaffirms that human biological diversity is due to the *interaction between culture and ethnicity, not race.* Simply phrased, culture represents the ways in which individuals live in contexts (e.g., Lee et al., 2003). Unfortunately, the fact that race is socially constructed is *infrequently* made explicit; nonetheless, reported racial patterns frequently function as social stereotypes and, given the intersubjective quality of lived experience, unavoidably determine the daily lives for many. Accordingly and consistent with Fanon's (see Bulhan, 1985) views concerning the omnipresence of oppression, contemporarily considered, *race continues to stratify American life.* It influences behavioral conduct in socially determined settings where humans interact. As a U.S. tradition through the legacy of legal social stratification, the very quality of cultural contexts is affected (see Slaughter, Johnson, & Spencer, in press). Too frequently and unlike the PVEST analytic approach advanced, traditional models of human development ignore the legacy of racial stratification for members of diverse groups (e.g., diverse youth of color and

Whites). The consequences of the oversight vary for different developmental periods. For example, variations include assumptions about preschoolers' play (e.g., the mis-interpretation of Black boys' rough-and-tumble play behaviors) to the inferences made about late adolescent pursuits as youth confront developmental tasks in preparation for adult roles (see Havighurst, 1953).

As an illustration, the dilemma of "motivated misunderstandings" about long-term race stratification concerns is made evident by recent international press coverage of efforts by Korean World War II "comfort women" to pursue justice. The women continue their efforts to secure monetary retributions and formal acknowledgment and apologies from the Japanese government for wrongs committed over 50 years ago, and from which they report continuing psychological harm. Similarly, reminders that the second Iraqi War is made complex due to the fact that it is also an ethnic war plagues the media and public discourse while fomenting distrust. Unfortunately, the nation's apparent "motivated oversight" of the continuing residuals and transformed character of slavery's impact on American life is less enthusiastically recognized. Instead, as the unacknowledged "elephant in the room," it remains a critical aspect of the fabric of twenty-first century American life both for long-term diverse people of color, new immigrants, and the nation's European Americans (i.e., given the underacknowledged problem of the "downside" of privilege).

Considered collectively, the omission of lingering race/ethnicity concerns includes failing to acknowledge the possibility that, for some, life-course character development occurs in a hostile environment (see Chestang, 1972). Conversely, for others, processes of concern for psychological well-being and good health take place under conditions of unacknowledged privilege (see Luthar & Becker, 2002; Luthar & Latendresse, 2002). Between-group outcomes are frequently compared and promoted in the media, which suggest the need for new theory helpful for unpacking research findings and for determining the impact adverse context quality contributes to the omnipresence of proliferated stereotypes. Failing to acknowledge, analyze and monitor how social stratification contributes to (a) stereotyping, (b) underdevelopment of particular youth, and (c) underattentiveness to problematic environmental blight, considered collectively, further exacerbates environmental risk. The consequent underservicing of settings where socialization takes place compromises and undermines human life-course efforts to successfully address developmental tasks (Havighurst, 1953); the situation compromises positive affective consequences; it undermines efforts to show personal causation (see DeCharms, 1968) and, thus, undercuts the demonstration of stage specific competencies (see R. White, 1959, 1960). Accordingly, use of a *systems framework* for understanding individual-context interactions over time provides a meaningful addition for describing and demonstrating the recursive and dynamic character of life-course human development had in varying cultural contexts by diverse individuals in their attempt to arrive at positive identity processes. As indicated in Figure 19.5 as the contemporary, recursive, and cyclical systems framework, phenomenological variant of ecological systems theory (PVEST) provides a way of understanding outcome determining identity processes from a context-linked and culturally aware perspective.

Accordingly, as an identity-focused culturally ecological (ICE) perspective, PVEST provides a heuristic conceptual device for capturing the processes of life-course development for diverse humans. The themes delineated and shortcomings that persist underscore the need for new conceptually dynamic formulations.

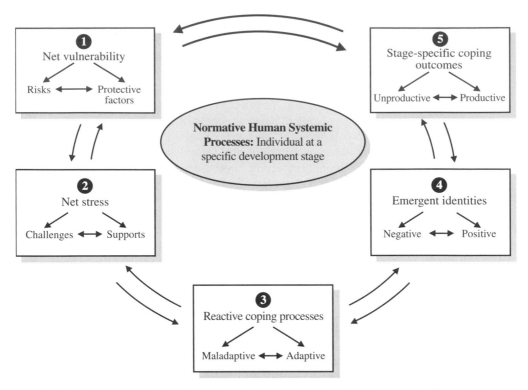

FIGURE 19.5   Phenomenological Variant of Ecological Systems Theory (PVEST; 2004 Revised Process Version). (*Source:* "Old Issues and New Theorizing about African American Youth: A Phenomenological Variant of Ecological Systems Theory" (pp. 37–70), by M. B. Spencer, in *Black Youth: Perspectives on Their Status in the United States,* R. L. Taylor (Ed.), 1995, Westport, CT: Praeger.)

PVEST: An Identity-Focused Cultural-Ecological Perspective

The systems developmental framework introduced and reviewed provides a context-sensitive and culture-ethnicity interaction focus. Consistent with the views of Erikson (1968) and others, identity processes are viewed as key to life course human development. As opposed to ignoring the existence of social stratification, PVEST explores the ways in which race, as a socially constructed and social organizational construct, dictates the quality of life for cultural niches located within ecologically defined systems (refer to Bronfenbrenner, 1977, 1979, 1985; and ecological psychologists such as Barker & Wright, 1949, 1954; Wright, 1967); an example would certainly be the organization and practices of urban schools. Race, racial stratification, and their multiple and institutional expressions co-exist at the macro-level as *social variables* (Slaughter-Defoe, Johnson, & Spencer, in press). As suggested and relevant to the issue of vulnerability, individuals and groups experience the noted social variables as either significant challenges or unacknowledged privileges. However, whether recognized as challenges or privileges, children and their families are profoundly affected in their everyday lives. The recent analysis by Slaughter-Defoe et al. (in press) reaffirms lingering legacy affects of legal social stratification suggesting important implications across domains of human development. For example, the recently published neuropsychology paper by Robertson et al. (2007) introduces brain imaging findings confirming that moral decisions and actions are related to self-identity and self-interest. Thus, one implication inferred from Robertson et al. is that the degree to which one thinks, functions and identifies oneself as "privileged" may have implications for behavior (i.e., moral sensitivity, behavior, and the social structuring of contexts for others). Additionally and still relevant, although published some 40 years earlier, J. H. Franklin's (1968) historical analysis of color and race demonstrates the stratifying role of race and its entrenched presence across a host of diverse countries. The strength and salience of racial stratification is reported as conspicuously evident not only by sighted individuals but also by those without sight (Isaacs, as included in J. H. Franklin, 1968).

By appreciating the stridency of race as a socially constructed and common aspect of American life (i.e., independent of whether its impact is actually acknowledged), PVEST fills a conceptual void; it acknowledges the salience of the noted social variables and explores their impact as represented by race and racial stratification variables. The inclusive perspective forwarded explains the persistent and entrenched social organizational character of racial stratification as experienced in people's everyday lives (irrespective of race/ethnicity). The theory's formulation recognizes the habit of most perspectives either *to use deficit explanations for "race" differences* or *to ignore the resistant twenty-first century American legacy of racial stratification.* Conversely, as a conceptual strategy, PVEST takes into account the character of culture-ethnicity encounters experienced by individuals . . . or not (i.e., at varying developmental stages and reasoning) as each navigates the several levels of social contexts as described by Bronfenbrenner and others (1979, 1985).

Additional PVEST advantages include recognizing the broad spectrum of diverse humans' individual-context behavioral expressions while also demonstrating an *inclusive* or more open perspective for interpreting outcomes. As used here the term *inclusive* is instructive and assists theory-building that contributes to (a) programs of research, (b) implementation strategies supporting intervention/prevention programming designs, and (c) conceptual framing of culturally authentic policy efforts and initiatives. As an example of the latter (i.e., improving policy design and application), Children and Youth Services (CYS) policies might require that low resource adolescent girls in supervised independent living (SIL) situations not have boy friends. However, in many instances, the "forbidden males" are frequently present for purposes of protection given frequently unacknowledged and *extreme environmental risk conditions* generally overlooked by those designing policy or by service-level individuals responsible for implementing its intent (see Silver, 2007). In parallel fashion, privileged youngsters have significant access to personal computers and other technology-based resources although inadequate Internet policies leave them underprotected. In both cases of needed context scrutiny, inadequate child welfare and Internet system administration policies and practices require that youth design coping devices, which themselves represent varying levels of risk (e.g., unintended pregnancies, abuse, and abductions). Context-linked considerations are needed in both cases; generally promulgated in the media are the "system breakdown consequences" (e.g., rates of teen pregnancy) for low-resource youth even though privilege does not necessarily protect those considered high-resource and low-risk.

As illustrated and used here then, the term *inclusive* refers to the broad experiences of *diverse* human groups; for example, it holds that along some criterion such as race or developmental stage, individuals are organized into socially constructed groupings (e.g., Black, White, Hispanic, Asian, biracial as well as infants, preschoolers, adolescents, and the elderly). Additional organizational methods with varying levels of identifiable groupings include *ethnicity* (Italian, Irish, Mexican American, Puerto Rican); *gender; socioeconomic class; immigration status* (e.g., first-, 1.5-, or second generation status); *faith community* (e.g., Christian, Islam, Jewish); *skin tone*; and *sexual orientation.* Given the illustration of youth in SIL situations versus youth at risk for cyberspace-linked predators, the SIL example is exacerbated for youth lacking access to (race-defined) communities with better housing stock and educational programming options. Thus, the example shared might result in less positive outcomes for poor Black or Hispanic youngsters in the youth serving system versus poor White or middle-income youth more generally. Any disparities obtained having to do with school completion, job training success, and lack of adjudication might be contributed to by differences in context character, system access options, advocacy availability, and quality of supports (see Silver, 2007). On the other hand, policies that protect against cyberspace predators may not display, at the same level, parallel disparities by ethnicity, race, gender, and so on. Any disparate outcomes having to do with cyberspace risk encounters, if evident at all, might be attributable to access level issues: The degree to which one has unlimited and private access to contemporary technology might alter level of risk. On the other hand, considered as a learning tool, the lack of consistent access to cutting-edge technology might diminish the research and knowledge exposure opportunities to which youth have differential access.

Accordingly, as a systems perspective that acknowledges culture-ethnicity and context interactions, the framework addresses the conundrum regarding the use of the idiom, *diversity.* The term is narrowly and, thus, erroneously, applied exclusively to *persons of color or members of minority status groups.* Conversely, PVEST posits that "*diverse youth*" refers to the context-relevant and broad experiences of *all individuals.* The conceptual strategy advocated fosters the consideration of context experiences from the vantage point of the individual or group of focus (i.e., as opposed to some "standard."). However, we make clear that this chapter's use of the term *"diverse youth of color,"* signifies non-Caucasians (e.g., African American, Asian Americans, Hispanics, or other minority status individuals). Caucasian individuals are labeled and referred to as Whites, European Americans or privileged individuals (i.e., the history of American race stratification and positive group stereotyping justifies the assumption of privilege). The term privilege denotes specific advantaging circumstances; as suggested, these include daily experiences emanating as the legacy from American legal racial stratification systems that were intended to have been addressed by *Brown v. Board of Education* I and II. Accordingly, taking advantage of extant conceptual efforts, the experiences of Whites are approached from a critical race theory (CRT) perspective (see Delgado & Stefancic, 2001; Luthar & Latendresse, 2002; McIntosh, 1989; Roediger, 1991, 1994). Further, the extensive contributions from legal scholarship specify that a privilege designation for Whites implies quite different culture-ethnicity contextual interactions when compared against those had by diverse persons of color who enjoy economic privilege. For example, when considering an African American male youth wearing "contemporary teen (Hip Hop) dress," most adults do not infer that the youth is either an academically high-performing African American student lacking an adjudication history or an individual from an upper income professional family. Social class assets do not protect male youth of color from destabilizing stereotypes generally held for most low-resource inner-city neighborhood youths. There are assumptions of commonality (i.e., beliefs that the young man in "traditional teen attire" is a thug, a delinquent, physically and sexually aggressive, thus generally speaking, a dangerous person); the situation is made worse if the male youth is also physically large or is an early maturing preadolescent person (see Cunningham, Swanson, Spencer, & Dupree, 2003; Spencer, Dupree, Swanson, & Cunningham, 1998). Economic privilege means different things as a function of race, ethnicity, skin color, maturational rate, and gender. Insights from critical race theorizing are instructive as we consider youths' needs at different developmental periods.

Contemporary Experiences of Contemporary African American Males and Contributions of Critical Race Theory

CRT suggests that white privilege provides intergenerational benefits from power disparities; the designation implies *minimal exposure to* daily destabilizing psychological and physical challenges (i.e., hostile environments; see Chestang, 1972; Phelan et al., 1991; Steele & Aaronson, 1995). Not absent but less evident for privileged individuals are the redundant and subtle, patterned and context-linked barriers (e.g., "glass ceilings," media disseminated social stereotyping) experienced as daily challenges by individuals of color. The patterned risk conditions transform into daily challenges requiring social policies and multilevel (i.e., federal, state and local) protective legislation to support positive life-course human coping efforts and sought-after desired outcomes (e.g., Delgado & Stefancic, 2001; Hall, 2002; McIntosh, 1989; Roediger, 1991, 1994). The extremely impoverished youth participants in the monetary incentive-based (stipend) program (see Spencer, Noll, & Cassidy, 2005) illustrate the power of monetary resources for urban youth. For example, a mother notes her student's reaction to receiving a monetary stipend for obtaining high grades: "I could honestly say that it's been a real motivator for my son, because first of all, he said that somebody's actually interested in his education. Somebody cares. The stipend has motivated my child to 'hang in there.'" As an identified "academic scholar" and under the special conditions and privilege that participating in a monetary incentive linked academic performance program provides, the finding that the incentives impacted academic outcomes was not unexpected; however, it was not expected that the impact of receiving a stipend and being known as an academic scholar had its major effect primarily during the first year of the program. That is, receiving a stipend after the first year did not matter to youths' continuing high performance. The findings suggest an important effect due to the identification of youths as an achiever and the persistence of the effect independent of subsequent years of stipend receipt (see Spencer et al., 2005).

As regards race at the level of the macro-ecology, providing equal access to educational opportunity was the purpose for *Brown v. Board of Education* I and II. However, skin-tone defining assumptions further moderate actual social experiences and are frequently underacknowledged given skin color research findings. Dissonance around skin color continues to be evident in studies of children from the preschool years as well as evident in adult studies. The experiences of biracial individuals are informative. For example, biracial individuals may have varied generational histories (e.g., having one Black and one White parent, or one Asian and one Black parent). It is the role and valued status of White skin tone in a race-conscious nation that suggests varying outcomes (see Spencer, Brookins, & Allen, 1985; Spencer & Markstrom-Adams, 1990; Fegley, Spencer, & Dupree, 2008). The phenotypic expression of one's biracial parentage and the attendant character of context-linked social interactions produce different individual-context experiences (i.e., including challenges versus support). This is the case even for siblings or dizygotic twins sharing the same child-rearing context since phenomenology or basic perceptual processes may differ (e.g., the lighter skin youngster might infer different evaluative judgments of support than the darker skinned toned sibling).

Thus, social inequities experienced by some members but conspicuously absent for others are one source of between group differences. Understanding variation as either between or within groups is improved when combined with phenomenology and ecological systems perspectives. More to the point, the conceptual strategy accomplishes three major tasks: It focuses attention on (a) cognition linked perceptions (i.e., historically addressed as phenomenology), (b) unique "meaning making processes" associated with constantly changing and widening social experiences, and (c) character of human coping in response to unavoidable human vulnerability. People move across unique and shared contexts at different developmental stages and are made aware of expectations for accomplishing developmental tasks as associated with specific social settings such as home, school, community, peer groups, work/apprenticeships, and so on (see Havighurst, 1953). In the example of the stipend-receiving program recipients described in the analyses reported in Spencer et al. (2005), the mother reported that the receipt of a monetary stipend by her son reinforced his interest "to hang in there" (i.e., continue to persist and resist) because he felt that it meant that someone cared about him. Thus, although academic performance is a developmental task of school-aged youth, however, the availability of monetary resources may not be an issue for privileged youth but makes a difference for *academic persistence, school engagement,* and perceptions of *emotional caring.* The first two might be particularly salient for male youth who infer a need to contribute to the "household economy," which then might contribute to truancy, underattentiveness, or decisions about truancy. It is important to test some of the foundational assumptions of the theory. Thus, a model is provided for the specific purpose of testing the theoretical assumptions put forth by PVEST.

Testing of the Phenomenological Variant of Ecological Systems Theory as a Dual Axis Coping Formulation

As illustrated in Figure 19.3, too few conceptual frameworks are process-focused and consider human vulnerability as experienced by diverse humans in social contexts and, which include a focus both on risks and protective factors (refer back to Figure 19.3). The perspective is even less frequently acknowledged when one includes the experiences of diverse individuals of color and diverse individuals of privilege. Further, too infrequently are there emphases that include positive outcomes, resiliency prediction, and an unpacking of human vulnerability more generally.

PREDICTING POSITIVE OUTCOMES IN THE FACE OF CHALLENGE

One of the many strengths of Anthony's (1974) formulation of resiliency is its acknowledgment of the simultaneous juxtaposing of protective factors with risks for understanding *net vulnerability level.* As described in this chapter, Anthony defines resiliency as the attainment of positive outcomes in the face of significant risk. Adapted from Anthony's theorizing as a process-oriented theoretical framework and conceptualized for our use as a dual axis coping formulation, PVEST can be empirically tested as to the hypothesized links between net vulnerability level (i.e., component one of PVEST: *Protective factor presence versus risk level comparisons*) with (a) net stress [engagement] level [i.e., component two of PVEST: *Social Supports versus Challenges*]; (b) reactive coping strategies [i.e., component three of PVEST: *Adaptive versus Maladaptive Coping strategies*]; (c) emergent identities (i.e., stable coping responses [i.e., component four] of PVEST: *Positive versus Negative Identification* responses]); and (d) life stage outcomes [i.e., component five of PVEST: *Productive versus Unproductive coping products*].

Thus, Figure 19.6 is an adaptation of Anthony's perspective, with four quadrants of individuals identified.

The four quadrants can be empirically compared with specific dependent variables as constructs hypothesized as associated with components two through five of PVEST. Accordingly, if one is interested in looking at a sample's vulnerability as a function of stress level, one would list a set of constructs of relevance to experienced supports (e.g., cultural socialization measurement) and challenges (e.g., decrease in family economy; Refer to Figure 19.4 for a list of exemplar and component relevant constructs). In parallel fashion, if one were interested in vulnerability level as linked to emergent (stable) identities, negative constructs might include exaggerated hypermasculinity, sexual promiscuity or positive measures such as academic self-concept or faith group identification.

Thus, as the empirically testable dual axis coping formulation of PVEST, the relationship between risk level and protective factor presence (i.e., vulnerability level) is explored. Each of the consequent four quadrants represents a particular character of *net vulnerability* (i.e., risks versus protective factor balance).

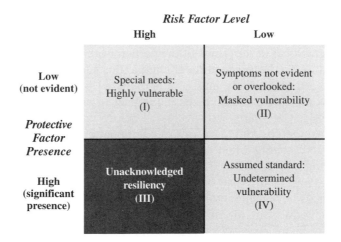

FIGURE 19.6 Spencer's Dual Axis Coping Formulation of PVEST. (*Source:* "Phenomenology and Ecological Systems Theory: Development of Diverse Groups" pp. 829–893, by M. B. Spencer, in *Handbook of Child Psychology: Vol. 1. Theoretical Models of Human Development,* sixth edition, W. Damon (Series Ed.) & R. Lerner (Vol. Ed), 2006b, Hoboken, NJ: Wiley.)

FOUR QUADRANTS OF VULNERABILITY LEVEL REPRESENTING THE DUAL AXIS FORMULATION OF PVEST

Accordingly, the first task is to determine the available measures for defining the sample's vulnerability level. The risk factor construct might be a measure of high family density as combined with low family economic resources. The protective factor construct could be measures of parental work readiness or parental years or completed education. Exemplar constructs are listed by component in Figure 19.4. After determining the high-low split for each vulnerability component (i.e., risk versus protective factor level) in a defensible manner, the four quadrants can be defined and are illustrated in Figure 19.6.

Quadrant I: High Risk and Low Protective Factor Presence

Quadrant I individuals are viewed as *highly vulnerable individuals* and are assumed to have *special needs* (refer to Figure 19.6). The group is characterized as having high risks although lacking in protective factor presence (i.e., protective factors are not evident). Too frequently, *Vulnerability Group I* members when considered from a Dual Axis Coping Formulation would have been assumed to represent individuals who are either poor and and/or members of marginalized groups (e.g., Blacks, Hispanics, immigrants of color). Given the role of women in America's history along with the gender-linked theorizing about human development, females would have been assigned a priori to Group I membership (i.e., Highly Vulnerable and Special Needs).

Quadrant II: Low Risk and Low Protective Factor Presence

Quadrant II Individuals are defined as being low in risk although also low in protective factor presence. This group is generally underrepresented in the human development literature given that significant symptoms of problems are not very obvious and, thus, they tend to appear invisible or demonstrate "masked vulnerability"; that is, a low risk status tends to mask their special needs. Most important, they are more often at risk for receiving little special attention until something "explosive occurs" when their level of risk and perceived sense of support changes. The change might be due to an adverse experience and, thus, increase in risk level or altered perceptions of support. In many ways, the biographical descriptions of the perpetrators of the Columbine High School massacre in Littleton, Colorado certainly mimic this scenario. More recently, the April 2007 West Virginia University massacre perpetrated by the student, Seung Hui Cho, more saliently introduces the exacerbating impact of cultural variables. Given reports from Korean relatives where Cho was reared before immigrating to the United States with his parents, there were indications of emotional difficulties. It is unclear whether the positive stereotyping often afforded Asian youth in American schools further masked his vulnerability status. Thus, Seung Cho lacked significant attention until 32 fellow students and faculty had been killed. Most important and as suggested, Quadrant II individuals have generally been ignored in the developmental literature. In sum, Quadrant II individuals are low on risk factor level although generally lacking high levels of protective factor presence; accordingly, Figure 19.6 describes them as lacking in significant symptomatology but show overall "masked vulnerability."

Quadrant III: High Risk and High Protective Factor Presence

Quadrant III considers resilient individuals (i.e., positive outcomes are expected in the face of high risk and challenge). That is, like Quadrant II representatives, Quadrant III individuals are generally unacknowledged as healthy, productive individuals. Thus, they have been frequently ignored in the design of studies and the formulation of research questions and program designs. These individuals are also important from a policy perspective since it would take less support to maintain their healthy status since there are clearly protective factors in place that are effective in balancing out their high levels of risk. The group is also important for careful study since the unpacking of their experiences allows one to determine how much risk is facilitative (i.e., provides a sense of personal causation or effectance motivation as conceptualized by DeCharms, 1968, and Robert White, 1959, 1960, respectively), and how much risk (i.e., given specified levels of protective factor presence) undermines positive health and development (i.e., pushing individuals from functioning as Quadrant III members and, instead, deteriorate into Quadrant I level of high vulnerability). The dual axis coping formulation allows that level of testing of the PVEST framework. As suggested and illustrated in Figure 19.6, Quadrant IV is recognizable.

Quadrant IV: Low Risk and High Protective Factor Presence

Quadrant IV individuals represent the majority of studies in developmental science who are narrowly compared against Quadrant I (i.e., highly vulnerable individuals). Most important, Quadrant IV member are assumed to be the "normal standard" against whom all others are compared. In fact, in general, they are infrequently conceptualized as being high in protective factor presence but, instead, are presented as the "normal individual." The inferences are consistent with the concerns aired by Slaughter-Defoe, Spencer, and Johnson (in press) concerning our failure to understand the ways in which social stratification is defined. From a primary prevention perspective (i.e., given the unacknowledged fact of the group's high level of protective factor presence) there is a potential for the group to show heightened and masked vulnerability. More specifically, if their unacknowledged but generally accepted protective factor level changes (e.g., drops), these youngsters may be in need of significant support since the protection afforded by their Quadrant IV status means that their mettle has been untested under extreme conditions. The media accounts of unexpected problems occurring for Quadrant IV youths in their family or community contexts always begin with the statement that the adverse outcome "was not expected in this neighborhood." Thus, from a humanist and prevention perspective certainly alluded to by Luthar and her colleagues, specific questions that speak to the group's undetermined vulnerability deserves attention.

Considered carefully from the theoretical perspective of James Anthony, as a major contributor to the PVEST framework, "resiliency" can only be expected for Quadrant III members because, as defined by Anthony, resiliency is associated with those experiencing significant levels of risk but concomitantly have access to high levels of protective factors. As indicated, we believe that this dual axis model provides a helpful heuristic device for maximizing our insights about levels of vulnerability and resiliency prediction estimates without engaging in unfair and stigmatizing analyses.

Unfortunately, this is not the orientation of most theories of human development that consider the experiences of diverse youth; a priori placements into Quadrant I is a frequent "given." Importantly and as suggested, PVEST is not only applicable to identifiable diverse young people but is also sensitive to their unique cultural and contextual niches. As such, it serves as a broad life-course theory of human development, which analyzes the systemic relationships between vulnerability, stress level, coping processes (i.e., reactive, stable coping as emergent identities), and stage-specific coping outcomes as lives unfold across the life course, irrespective of group membership (including privilege) and its socially structured social standing.

In sum, considered together, PVEST and its dual axis coping formulation of vulnerability level provide conceptual tools and heuristic devices for accounting for the diverse expressions of human development in cultural context. As illustrated in process focuses noted in Figures 19.3, 19.4 and 19.5, in general, traditional and limited views of human development may consider risk level and protective factor intensity for understanding human vulnerability. However, the approach is still generally underdeveloped when considering the experiences of diverse youth of color.

As suggested by the literatures reviewed and synthesized, high-risk assessments without the consideration of available protective factors have generally represented the analyses of youth of color and economically vulnerable individuals. At the same time, unacknowledged White privileging views about European Americans are generally not associated with estimates of vulnerability (i.e., only protective factors such as social class are considered and the advantaging role of "Whiteness" is inferred). As suggested and problematic, the high performance often associated with middle-income European Americans is assumed to be the expected norm for all youth (i.e., irrespective of the social circumstances and risk level of others); outliers are considered deviant or atypical. As suggested, two groups (i.e., Quadrants I and IV) are usually compared when conducting research with diverse youth; middle-income Whites are invariably compared (i.e., as Quadrant IV) with a group or groups of low-resource marginalized youth (i.e., assumed to narrowly represent Quadrant I). This problem of lack of sample equivalency when comparing groups, described in previous sections of the paper, remains a significant conundrum in the developmental literature. Use of dual axis analyses of vulnerability is believed to provide an alternative approach and needed opportunity.

To sum and as suggested, as a dual axis model of vulnerability, too frequently Quadrant I is assumed to be poor and minority; on the one hand, Quadrant IV is assumed to be individuals of middle-income (or model minority) status. However, Quadrant II individuals are generally ignored in the literature except for recent efforts by Luthar (2003) with extremely affluent suburban European Americans. When considering Quadrant III (unacknowledged resilient individuals), the major publication patterns particularly in child psychology have overwhelmingly ignored this high-risk and high-protective factor level group or assumed its nonexistence. There are a few theorists that explore protective factors such as parental monitoring, cultural socialization, specific achievement enhancing programming, and reference group identity as protective factors (e.g., Spencer, 1983; Spencer, Fegley, & Harpalani, 2003; Spencer, Noll, Stoltzfus, & Harpalani, 2001; Swanson et al., 2002; Youngblood & Spencer, 2002). A recent publication and demonstration of the dual axis model provides a helpful guide (Fegley, Spencer, & Dupree, 2008; Fegley, Spencer, Goss, Harpalani, & Charles, 2008). When collectively considered, it appears that as a specific outcome-oriented and hypothesis-testing perspective of the PVEST framework, Figure 19.6 provides important opportunities for testing the framework and for determining and interpreting resiliency patterns in the spirit as conceptualized by Anthony (1987).

Conclusions

The abridged form of this chapter was structured to delineate the advantages and contributions of PVEST for maximizing the applicability of human development theorizing for many ethnicities or diverse groups of humans (both youth of color and European Americans). One major conclusion to be inferred from the multidisciplinary literatures integrated and analyses provided in demonstrating the benefits of PVEST is that any inclusive theory of human development *should bear a particular burden.* Specifically, not only should the framework acknowledge and incorporate the major objectively identifiable expressions of human variation (e.g., race, gender, ethnicity, and unique life-course placement—an infant versus an elder) that may differentially interface with context, but also provide an adequate explanation of the "how" of human development processes that leads to the "what" or particularly patterned outcomes.

The uniquely structured and experienced processes of human development are inextricably linked to the tensions produced between nuanced developmental tasks pursued by the individual given context character and influences of the psychohistorical moment, along with expectations for competence. However, unavoidable tensions are also produced as a function of individuals' characteristics such as group membership and context quality; although infrequently noted, the latter continues to be linked to structural conditions associated with race, racism, and White privilege. As suggested, this unchanging dilemma is overlooked in the child psychology literature except for a priori assumptions of deviance, psychopathology, or problems associated with youth of color. Further, this stigma-reinforcing situation is linked to historical conditions and is perpetuated as values, beliefs, attitudes, contextual inequalities, and psychosocial experiences. Our introduction of PVEST as an identity-focused cultural ecological (ICE) perspective suggests that the unfolding coping processes and consequent coping products experienced at one stage serves as the major source of the individual's net vulnerability at the next stage given the ongoing experiences of individual-context interface. Thus, as a dynamic recursive theoretical framework, PVEST moves beyond narrow deterministic perspectives of human development and provides, instead, opportunities for meaningful support and effective programs for needed improvements and change.

References

Allen, W. R. (1985). Race, income and family dynamics: A study of adolescent male socialization processes and outcomes. In M. B. Spencer, G. K. Brookins, & W. R. Allen (Eds.), *Beginnings: The social and affective development of Black children* (pp. 273–292). Hillsdale, NJ: Erlbaum.

Allen, W. R., Spencer, M. B., & Brookins, G. K. (1985). Synthesis: Black children keep on growing. In M. B. Spencer, G. K. Brookins, & W. R. Allen (Eds.), *Beginnings: The social and affective development of Black children* (pp. 301–314). Hillsdale, NJ: Erlbaum.

Anthony, E. J. (1974). Introduction: The syndrome of the psychologically vulnerable child. In E. J. Anthony & C. Koupernik (Eds.), *The child in his family: Children at psychiatric risk* (pp. 3–10). New York: Wiley.

Anthony, E. J. (1987). Risk, vulnerability, and resilience: An overview. In E. J. Anthony & B. J. Cohler (Eds.), *The invulnerable child* (pp. 3–48). New York: Guilford Press.

Banks, W. C. (1976). White preference in Blacks: A paradigm in search of phenomenon. *Psychological Bulletin, 83,* 1179–1186.

Barker, R. G., & Wright, H. F. (1949). Psychological ecology and the problem of psychosocial development. *Child Development, 20,* 131–143.

Barker, R. G., & Wright, H. F. (1954). *Midwest and its children: The psychological ecology of an American town.* Evanston, IL: Row, Peterson.

Bell, D. A. (1992). *Faces at the bottom of the well: The permanence of racism.* New York: Basic Books.

Bell, D. A. (1995). Brown v. Board of Education and the interest convergence dilemma. In K. Crenshaw, N. Gotanda, G. Peller, & K. Thomas (Eds.), *Critical race theory: The key writings that formed the movement* (pp. 20–28). New York: New Press.

Bell, D. A. (2000a). After we've gone: Prudent speculations on America in a post-racial epoch. In R. Delgado & J. Stefancic (Eds.), *Critical race theory: The cutting edge* (pp. 2–8). Philadelphia: Temple University Press.

Bell, D. A. (2000b). Serving two masters: Integration ideals and client interests in school desegregation litigation. In R. Delgado & J. Stefancic (Eds.), *Critical race theory: The cutting edge* (pp. 236–246). Philadelphia: Temple University Press.

Bonilla-Silva, E. (2001). *White supremacy and racism in the post-civil rights era.* Boulder, CO: Lynne Rienner.

Boyd-Franklin, N. (1989). *Black families in therapy: A multisystems approach.* New York: Guilford Press.

Boykin, A. W. (1986). The triple quandary and the schooling of Afro-American children. In U. Neisser (Ed.), *The school achievement of minority children* (pp. 57–92). Hillsdale, NJ: Erlbaum.

Boykin, A. W., & Ellison, C. M. (1995). The multiple ecologies of Black youth socialization: An afrographic analysis. In R. L. Taylor (Ed.), *African-American youth: Perspectives on their status in the United States* (pp. 93–128). Westport, CT: Praeger.

Bronfenbrenner, U. (1977). Toward an experimental ecology of human development. *American Psychologist, 32,* 513–531.

Bronfenbrenner, U. (1979). *The ecology of human development: Experiments by nature and design.* Cambridge, MA: Harvard University Press.

Bronfenbrenner, U. (1985). Summary. In M. B. Spencer, G. K. Brookins, & W. R. Allen (Eds.), *Beginnings: Social and affective development of Black children* (pp. 67–73). Hillsdale, NJ: Erlbaum.

Bronfenbrenner, U. (1989). Ecological systems theory. In R. I. Vasta (Ed.), *Annals of child development: Vol. 6. Six theories of child development* (pp. 187–249). Greenwich, CT: JAI Press.

Bronfenbrenner, U. (1992). *The process-person-context model in development research: Principles, applications and implications.* Unpublished manuscript, Cornell University, Department of Human Development and Family Studies, Ithaca, NY.

Bronfenbrenner, U. (1993). The ecology of cognitive development. In R. H. Wozniak & K. W. Fischer (Eds.), *Development in context: Acting and thinking is specific environments* (pp. 3–44). Hillsdale, NJ: Erlbaum.

Bronfenbrenner, U., & Ceci, S. J. (1993). Heredity, environment, and the question "How?": A first approximation. In R. Plomin & G. E. McClearn (Eds.), *Nature, nurture, and psychology* (pp. 313–324). Washington, DC: American Psychological Association.

Bronfenbrenner, U., & Ceci, S. J. (1994). Nature-nurture reconceptualized in developmental perspective: A bioecological mode. *Psychological Review, 101*(4), 568–586.

Bronfenbrenner, U., & Crouter, A. C. (1983). The evolution of environmental models in developmental research. In P. H. Mussen (Series Ed.) & W. Kessen (Vol. Ed.), *Handbook of child psychology: Vol. I. History, theory, and methods* (4th ed., pp. 357–414). New York: Wiley.

Brown I. 347 U.S. 483 (1954).

Brown II. 349 U.S. 294 (1955).

Bulhan, H. A. (1985). *Frantz Fanon and the psychology of oppression.* New York: Plenum Press.

Chestang, L. W. (1972). *Character development in a hostile environment* (Occasional Paper No. 3). Chicago: University of Chicago, School of Social Service Administration.

Connell, J. P., Spencer, M. B., & Aber, J. L. (1994). Educational risk and resilience in African-American youth: Context, self, action and outcomes in school. *Child Development, 65,* 493–506.

Cruesoe, M. (1999). *Critical theory as it relates to power in a multicultural classroom.* Retrieved August 7, 2007, from http://home.earthlink.net/~rcrusoe/musings/critical.html.

Cunningham, M. (1993). Sex role influences of African American adolescent males: A literature review. *Journal of African American Male Studies, 1,* 30–37.

Cunningham, M., Swanson, D. P., Spencer, M. B., & Dupree, D. (2003). The association of physical maturation with family hassles in African American adolescent males. *Journal of Cultural Diversity and Ethnic Minority Psychology, 9,* 274–276.

Darity, W. A., Jr., & Myers, S. L., Jr. (1998). *Persistent disparity: Race and economic inequality in the United States since 1945.* Northampton, MA: E. Elgar.

Darling-Hammond, L. (2004). Inequality and the right to learn: Access to qualified teachers in California Public Schools. *Teachers College Record, 106*(10), 1936–1966.

DeCharms, R. (1968). *Personal causation: The internal affective determinant of behavior.* New York: Academy Press.

Delgado, R., & Stefancic, J. (2000). Introduction. In R. Delgado & J. Stefancic (Eds.), *Critical race theory: The cutting edge* (pp. xv–xix). Philadelphia: Temple University Press.

Delgado, R., & Stefancic, J. (2001). *Critical race theory: An introduction.* New York: New York University Press.

Dell'Angelo, T. (2007). *Teacher-principal trust: Cognitive and affective influences on teacher self-efficacy and student achievement.* Unpublished dissertation abstract, University of Pennsylvania.

Delpit, L. (1988). The silenced dialogue: Power and pedagogy in educating other people's children. *Harvard Educational Review, 58*(3), 280–298.

Dupree, D., Spencer, M. B., & Bell, S. (1997). The ecology of African American child development: Normative and non-normative outcomes. In G. Johnson-Powell & Y. Yamamoto (Eds.), *Transcultural child psychiatry: A portrait of America's children* (pp. 237–268). New York: Wiley.

Dweck, C. S. (1978). Achievement. In M. Lamb (Ed.), *Social and personality development* (pp. 114–130). New York: Holt, Reinhart and Winston.

Education of All Handicapped Children Act, Pub. L. No. 94-142 (1975).

Erikson, E. H. (1959). Identity and the life cycle. *Psychological Issues, 1,* 1–171.

Erikson, E. H. (1968). *Identity: Youth and crisis.* New York: Norton.

Fanon, F. (1967). *Black skin, white masks* (C. L. Markmann, Trans.). New York: Grove Press.

Fegley, S. G., Spencer, M. B., & Dupree, D. (2008). *Skin color status and coping processes among adolescent immigrants: The effect of skin color dissonance on the identity processes of high performing adolescent immigrants.* Manuscript submitted for publication.

Fegley, S. G., Spencer, M. B., Goss, T. N., Harpalani, V., & Charles, N. (2008). Bodily self-awareness: Skin color and psychosocial well-being in adolescence. In W. Overton & U. Mueller (Eds.), *Developmental perspectives on embodiment and consciousness* (pp. 281–312). Mahwah, NJ: Erlbaum.

Flavell, J. H. (1968). *The development of role-taking and communication skills in children.* New York: Wiley.

Franklin, A. J. (2004). *From brotherhood to manhood: How Black men rescue their relationships and dreams from the invisibility syndrome.* Hoboken, NJ: Wiley.

Franklin, J. H. (1968). *Color and race.* Boston: Houghton Mifflin.

Gould, S. J. (1981). *The mismeasure of man.* New York: Norton.

Gump, P. V., & Sutton-Smith, B. (1955). The "It" in children's games. *Group, 17,* 3–8.

Guthrie, R. (1976). *Even the rat was White: A historical view of psychology.* New York: Harper & Row.

Hafiz, F. (2007). *Fear and the pedagogy of care: A study of teacher emotional resilience in urban schools.* Unpublished dissertation abstract, Temple University.

Hall, S. (2002). Race, articulation, and societies structured in dominance. In P. Essed & D. T. Goldberg (Eds.), *Race critical theories: Text and context* (pp. 38–68). Malden, MA: Blackwell.

Hare, B. R., & Castenell, L. A., Jr. (1985). No place to run, no place to hide: Comparative status and future prospects of Black boys. In M. B. Spencer, G. K Brookins, & W. R. Allen (Eds.), *Beginnings: The social and affective development of Black children* (pp. 201–214). Hillsdale, NJ: Erlbaum.

Havighurst, R. J. (1953). *Human development and education.* New York: McKay.

Ignatiev, N. (1995). *How the Irish became White.* New York: Routledge & Kegan Paul.

Ingersoll, R. M. (2002). The teacher shortage: A case of wrong diagnosis and wrong prescription. *National Association of Secondary School Principals [NASSP] Bulletin, 86*(631), 16–31.

Isaacs, H. R. (1968). Group identity and political change: The role of color and physical characteristics. In J. H. Franklin (Ed.), *Color and race* (pp. 75–97). Boston: Houghton Mifflin.

Jablonski, N. G. (2004). The evolution of human skin and skin coloration. *Annual Review of Anthropology, 33,* 585–623.

Jablonski, N. G. (2006). *Skin: A natural history.* Berkeley: University of California Press.

Jackson, P. (1968). *Life in classrooms.* New York: Holt, Rinehart and Winston.

Ladson-Billings, G. (1994). *The dream keepers: Successful teachers of African-American children.* San Francisco: Jossey-Bass.

Lee, C., Spencer, M. B., & Harpalani, V. (2003). Every shut eye ain't sleep: Studying how people live culturally. *Educational Researcher, 32,* 6–13.

Luthar, S. S. (2003). *Resilience and vulnerability: Adaptation in the context of childhood adversities.* Cambridge: Cambridge University Press.

Luthar, S. S., & Becker, B. E. (2002). Privileged but pressured? A study of affluent youth. *Child Development, 73,* 1593–1610.

Luthar, S. S., & Cicchetti, D. (2000). The construct of resilience: Implications for interventions and social policies. *Development and Psychopathology, 12,* 857–885.

Luthar, S. S., & Latendresse, S. J. (2002). Adolescent risk: The cost of affluence. *New Directions in Youth Development, 95,* 101–121.

McIntosh, P. (1989). White privilege: Unpacking the invisible knapsack. *Peace and Freedom,* 10–12.

Nanda, S. (1974). *Cultural anthropology.* New York: VanNostrand.

National Academy of Sciences. (1990). *National Academy of Sciences Report: Who cares for America's children?* Washington, DC: National Academy Press.

Phelan, P., Davidson, A. L., & Cao, H. T. (1991). Students' multiple worlds: Negotiating the boundaries of family, peer, and school cultures. *Anthropology and Education Quarterly, 22,* 224–250.

Robertson, D., Snarey, J., Ousley, O., Bowman, D., Harenski, Gilky, R. F., et al. (2007). The neural basis of moral reasoning: An fMRI study. *Neuropsychology, 45,* 755–766.

Roediger, D. R. (1991). *The wages of whiteness: Race and the making of the American working class.* New York: Verso.

Roediger, D. R. (1994). *The abolition of whiteness.* New York: Verso.

Roediger, D. R. (2001). Whiteness and ethnicity in the history of "White Ethnics" in the United States. In P. Essed & D. T. Goldberg (Eds.), *Race critical theories: Text and context* (pp. 325–343). Malden, MA: Blackwell.

Rogoff, B. (2003). *The cultural nature of human development.* Oxford: Oxford University Press.

Schultz, D. (1976). *Theories of personality.* Monterey, CA: Brooks/Cole.

Seaton, G., Dell' Angelo, T., Spencer, M. B., & Youngblood, J. (2007, Spring). Moving beyond the dichotomy: Meeting the needs of urban students through contextually-relevant education practices. *Teachers Education Quarterly,* 163–183.

Silver, L. (2007). *Navigating child welfare: Adolescent mothers and the politics of regulation.* Unpublished dissertation, University of Pennsylvania.

Slaughter-Defoe, D., Johnson, D., & Spencer, M. B. (in press). *Race and children's development entry.* Chicago: Companion to the Child.

Spencer, M. B. (1983). Children's cultural values and parental child rearing strategies. *Developmental Review, 3,* 351–370.

Spencer, M. B. (1986). Risk and resilience: How Black children cope with stress. *Social Science, 71*(1), 22–26.

Spencer, M. B. (1987). Black children's ethnic identity formation: Risk and resilience of castelike minorities. In K. S. Phinney & M. J. Rotheram (Eds.), *Children's ethnic socialization* (pp. 103–116). Beverly Hills, CA: Sage.

Spencer, M. B. (1995). Old issues and new theorizing about African American youth: A phenomenological variant of ecological systems theory. In R. L. Taylor (Ed.), *Black youth: Perspectives on their status in the United States* (pp. 37–70). Westport, CT: Praeger.

Spencer, M. B. (2001). Resiliency and fragility factors associated with the contextual experiences of low resource urban African American male youth and families. In A. Booth & A. Crouter (Eds.), *Does it take a village?: Community effects in children, adolescents and families* (pp. 51–71). Mahwah, NJ: Erlbaum.

Spencer, M. B. (2006a). Commentary. *Research in Human Development, 3*(4), pp. 271–280.

Spencer, M. B. (2006b). Phenomenology and ecological systems theory: Development of diverse groups. In W. Damon & R. M. Lerner (Series Eds.) & R. M. Lerner (Vol. Ed.), *Handbook of child psychology: Vol. 1. Theoretical models of human development* (6th ed., pp. 829–893). Hoboken, NJ: Wiley.

Spencer, M. B. (2006c, September/October). Invited editorial: Revisiting the 1990 Special issue on minority children: An editorial perspective 15 years later. *Child Development, 77*(5), 1149–1154.

Spencer, M. B., Blumenthal, J., & Richards, E. (1995). Child care and children of color. In J. Brooks-Gunn & P. Lindsay Chase-Lansdale (Eds.), *Escape from poverty: What makes a difference for children* (pp. 138–156). New York: Cambridge University Press.

Spencer, M. B., Brookins, G. K., & Allen, W. R. (Eds.). (1985). *Beginnings: Social and affective development of Black children.* Hillsdale, NJ: Erlbaum.

Spencer, M. B., Cole, S. P., Dupree, D., Glymph, A., & Pierre, P. (1993). Self-efficacy among urban African American early adolescents: Exploring issues of risk, vulnerability and resilience [Special issue]. *Development and Psychopathology, 5,* 719–739.

Spencer, M. B., Dobbs, B., & Swanson, D. P. (1988). African American adolescents: Adaptational processes and socioeconomic diversity in behavioral outcomes. *Journal of Adolescence, 11,* 117–137.

Spencer, M. B., & Dupree, D. (1996). African American youths' eco-cultural challenges and psychosocial opportunities: An alternative analysis of problem behavior outcomes. In D. Cicchetti & S. Toth (Eds.), *Rochester Symposium on Developmental Psychopathology: Vol. 7. Adolescence: Opportunities and challenges* (pp. 259–282). Rochester, NY: University of Rochester Press.

Spencer, M. B., Dupree, D., Cunningham, M., Harpalani, V., & Munoz-Miller, M. (2003). Vulnerability to violence: A contextually-sensitive, developmental perspective on African American adolescents. *Journal of Social Issues, 59*(1), 33–49.

Spencer, M. B., Dupree, D., & Hartmann, T. T. (1997). A Phenomenological Variant of Ecological Systems Theory (PVEST): A self-organization perspective in context. *Development and Psychopathology, 9,* 817–833.

Spencer, M. B., Dupree, D., Swanson, D. P., & Cunningham, M. (1998). The influence of physical maturation and hassles on African American adolescents' learning behaviors. *Journal of Comparative Family Studies, 29,* 189–200.

Spencer, M. B., Fegley, S., & Harpalani, V. (2003). A theoretical and empirical examination of identity as coping: Linking coping resources to the self processes of African American youth. *Journal of Applied Developmental Science, 7*(3), 181–187.

Spencer, M. B., & Harpalani, V. (2004). Nature, nurture, and the question of "How?": A phenomenological variant of ecological systems theory. In C. Garcia-Coll, K. Kearer, & R. Lerner (Eds.), *Nature and nurture: The complex interplay of genetic and environmental influences on human behavior and development* (pp. 53–77). Mahwah, NJ: Erlbaum.

Spencer, M. B., Harpalani, V., Cassidy, E., Jacobs, C., Donde, S., Goss, T., et al. (2006). Understanding vulnerability and resilience from a normative development perspective. In D. Cicchetti & E. Cohen (Eds.), *Handbook of development and psychopathology: Vol. 1. Implications for racially and ethnically diverse youth* (pp. 627–672). Hoboken, NJ: Wiley.

Spencer, M. B., & Markstrom-Adams, C. (1990). Identity processes among racial and ethnic minority children in America. *Child Development, 61,* 290–310.

Spencer, M. B., Noll, E., & Cassidy, E. (2005). Monetary incentives in support of academic achievement: Results of a randomized field trial involving high-achieving, low-resource, ethnically diverse urban adolescents, *Evaluation Research, 29*(3), 199–222.

Spencer, M. B., Noll, E., Stoltzfus, J., & Harpalani, V. (2001). Identity and school adjustment: Revisiting the "acting White" assumption. *Educational Psychologist, 36*(1), 21–30.

Spencer, M. B., & Swanson, D. P. (2000). Promoting positive outcomes for youth: Resourceful families and communities. In S. Danziger & J. Waldfogel (Eds.), *Securing the future* (pp. 182–204). New York: Russell Sage Foundation.

Steele, C. (1997). A threat in the air: How stereotypes shape intellectual identity and performance. *American Psychologist, 52,* 613–629.

Steele, C. (2004, April). *Endowed lectureship on stereotype threat.* Sponsored by the Provost Office, University of Michigan.

Steele, C., & Aaronson, J. (1995). Stereotype threat and the intellectual test performance of African-Americans. *Journal of Personality and Social Psychology, 69,* 797–811.

Stevenson, H. C. (1997). Missed, dissed and pissed: Making meaning of neighborhood risk, fear and anger management in urban Black youth. *Cultural Diversity and Mental Health, 3,* 37–52.

Sullivan, M. (1989). *Getting paid: Youth, crime and work in the inner city.* Ithaca, NY: Cornell University Press.

Swanson, D. P., Cunningham, M., & Spencer, M. B. (2003). Black males' structural conditions, achievement patterns, normative needs, and "opportunities." *Urban Education, 38,* 605–633.

Swanson, D. P., & Spencer, M. B. (1991). Youth policy, poverty, and African-Americans: Implications for resilience. *Education and Urban Society, 24*(1), 148–161.

Swanson, D. P., Spencer, M. B., Dell'Angleo, T., Harpalani, V., & Spencer, T. (2002). Identity processes and the positive youth development of African Americans: An explanatory framework. In G. Noam (Series Ed.) & C. S. Taylor, R. M. Lerner, & A. von Eye (Eds.), *Pathways to positive youth development among gang and non-gang youth: New directions for youth development* (No. 95, pp. 73–99). San Francisco: Jossey-Bass.

Turecki, S. (with Leslie Toma). (1989). *The difficult child.* New York: Bantam Books.

White, R. (1959). Motivation reconsidered: The concept of competence. *Psychological Review, 66,* 297–333.

White, R. (1960). Competence and psychosexual development. In M. R. Riley (Ed.), *Nebraska Symposium on Motivation* (pp. 3–32). Lincoln: University of Nebraska Press.

Williams, B. (2003). *Closing the achievement gap: The reform agenda revisited.* Alexandra, VA: Association for Supervision and Curriculum.

Wilson, T. D. (2002, September). *Alfred Schutz, phenomenology and research methodology for information behaviour research.* A paper delivered at ISIC4-Fourth International Confernce on Information Seeking in Context, Universidade Lusiada, Lisbon, Portugal.

Wohlwill, J. F. (1985). The confluence of environmental and developmental psychology: Signpost to an ecology of development? *Human Development, 23,* 354–358.

Wohlwill, J. F., & Heft, H. (1987). The physical environment and the development of the child. In D. Stokols & I. Altman (Eds.), *Handbook of environmental psychology* (Vol.1, pp. 281–328). New York: Wiley.

Wright, H. F. (1967). *Recording and analyzing child behavior.* New York: Harper & Row.

Youngblood, J., & Spencer, M. B. (2002). Integrating normative identity processes and academic support requirements for special needs adolescents: The application of an Identity-Focused Cultural Ecological (ICE) Perspective. *Journal of Applied Developmental Science, 6,* 95–108.

Author Index

Subject Index

Ability:
  children's understandings of, 415
  theories about beliefs about, 407–408
Absolute pitch, 349
Abstract analogies, 285
Abstract constructions, 279–284
"Abstract mappings," 242, 243
Abuse:
  during early adolescence, 239
  during late adolescence/early adulthood, 249
  during middle adolescence, 245
  by socializing agents, 230
Abused children, response bias for anger in, 38
Abusive parenting, role in antisocial behavior,
  449–450
Abusive relationships, 205
Academic adjustment, childhood peer experiences
  and, 167–168
Academic goals, 412–413
Academic motivation, of African-American
  students, 423
Academic outcomes, parental involvement and,
  106
Academic stipends, 729, 730
Academic subject areas, interest in, 417
Access:
  educational, 715
  inequality of, 714–717
Acculturation, 118–119
  role in family relationships, 126
Achievement:
  expectancy-value model of, 420
  gender differences in, 420
Achievement goal orientations, 412
Achievement motivation, 191. *See also* Motivation
  development of, 406–434
  research on, 424–425
Achievement-related choices, expectancy-value
  model of, 408
Achievement settings, multiple goals of children in,
  412
Achievement values:
  gender differences in, 421
  racial and ethnic group differences in, 422–423
Acquired processing patterns, life experience
  mediation through, 455
Action representations, in pictures, 330

Action tendencies:
  emotion manifestation and, 363–364
  measuring emotion via, 364–365
Activational hormone effects, 664
"Active niche-picking," 206
Activity, gender-role stereotyping of, 420
Activity level trait, 185
Adaptation level principle, 367
Adaptive coping, social effectiveness and,
  390–397
Adaptive outcomes:
  during middle adolescence, 244–245
  during middle to late childhood, 232–234
  during toddlerhood and early childhood,
  226–228
Adaptive self-processes, during late
  adolescence/early adulthood, 248–249
Adaptive strategies, in ethnic/racial minority
  families, 117
Adjustment:
  childhood peer experiences and, 167–169
  influence of parenting on, 553–555
  temperament and, 71–81
  temperament as predictive of, 71–72
Adolescence:
  aggression during, 439–440
  attachment in, 568–570
  cognition during, 517–518
  developing a sense of interdependence in,
  567–577
  emotional development in, 374–376
  friendships during, 557–559
  hormone influences in, 666
  independence in, 562–567
  interpersonal contexts and psychosocial tasks of,
  561–577
  intimacy in, 570–573
  peer interactions during, 153–156
  psychodynamic perspective on, 563
  psychological functioning during, 577
  psychosocial challenges of, 552
  research on, 577–578
  romantic relationships during, 559–561
  self-representations during, 234–235
  significant interpersonal relationships during,
  552–561
  studying hormone effects in, 667

Depression, 190
during middle adolescence, 245
parenting behavior and, 111–112
Depth, representing, 334–336
"Deselection pressures," 206
Development:
children's influences on, 56
cognitive approach focus on, 678
contributions of temperament to, 65
coping strategies and, 392–393
diversity of, 8
versus learning, 541–542
origins and endpoints in, 544–545
positive, 11–12
proximal locus of, 618–620
psycholinguistic processes of, 290–291
temperament and, 64–69
theory-laden definitions of, 596–597
transactional models of, 170
variation in, 543
Developmental approach, to biology and
neuroscience, 9–10
Developmental changes, during late adolescence,
247–248
Developmental cognitive neuroscience, advances
in, 43
Developmental disorders, 41
Developmental elaboration, of personality traits,
195–198
Developmental neuroscience, 9–10
"Developmental niches," 618–619
cultural variations in, 619–620
Developmental pathways, early-emerging
personality differences and, 204–208
Developmental readiness hypothesis, 250
Developmental research, temperament-related, 83
Developmental science, 4, 6
inclusive focus in, 723
key substantive themes in, 12
Developmental scientists, "job description" of, 12
Developmental systems theories, 5–6
defining features of, 7–8
Developmental task analyses, 568
Developmental theory, 312–313
Developmental trajectories, modeling of, 460
Deviancy training, 149, 452
Deviant peer cliques, 451
Deviant peer influence, ecological model of, 452
"Dialogical cognitive representations," 602
Dialogic practice method, 539
Diatonic structure, sensitivity to, 343
Diatonic tonal scale, 340, 344
Differential continuity/change, 201–202

Differential linkage model, 76
Difficult child syndrome, 720, 721
Difficult temperament, 75, 78, 162–163, 196
Dimensional card sorting task, 43
"Directed forgetting" technique, 520
Direct linkage model, 72–73
Disagreeableness, 205
disease and, 206–207
Disciplinary responses, by parents, 79–80
Discipline:
inconsistent, 448–449
as interactive, 481
Discomfort trait, 185
Disengaged parents, 100
Dishonest behavior, 501
Disidentification processes, 421
Disordered behavior, 240–241
Disorganized-disoriented infants, 230
Disposition, emphasis on, 544
Dispositional factors, role in antisocial behavior, 442
Disruptive behaviors, 157
"Dissociation" coping strategy, 230
Dissociative identity disorder, 249
Distress, mental habits involving, 69
Distressing circumstances, adaptive coping with,
390–397
Distributional analyses, 292
functionally based, 290
Distributive justice, children's thinking about, 490
Ditransitives, 280–281
Diverse human patterns, discussions of, 723
Diverse learners, educational needs of, 716
Diverse life outcomes, 701
Diverse methodologies, 10–11
"Diverse youth," 728
"Diverse youth of color," 728
Diversity:
complexity of, 116
as a feature of human development, 8
within-group, 723
Divinity, ethics of, 487
Dizygotic (DZ) twins, 198–199
Domain-relevant knowledge, skeletal mental
structures and, 622–623
Domain-specific evaluations, of self, 219
Domain-specific reasoning, 626–627
Domain-specific self-evaluations, gender
differences in, 251–252
Dominance hierarchies, 148–149
Dopamine genes, 64
Dopamine receptor D4 (DRD4), 63–64
Dorsolateral prefrontal cortex (DLPFC), 39, 40, 41,
42

Ethnic group differences:
  in achievement values and goals, 422–423
  in competence, control, and attribution beliefs,
      422
Ethnicity, parenting style and, 555
Ethnicity issues, family socialization and,
      115–126
Ethnic minorities, 115
  effects of prejudice and discrimination on, 126
Ethnic minority families, socialization in, 117,
      121–126
Ethnic minority youth, 243
Ethnic/racial focus groups, 116
Ethnic/racial minority families, status of, 117
Ethnic/racial pride, 122
Ethnographic approaches, 127
Event-related potentials (ERPs), 26, 28–29. See
      also ERP face processing studies
Event-related potential studies, 35–36
Events:
  significance of exposure to, 367–368
  varying reactions to, 367–368
Evolutionary psychology, gender development and,
      663
Executive control:
  development of, 542–543
  of intellectual processes, 543
Executive function factors, role in antisocial
      behavior, 442–443
Executive functions, 38–43
  domains of, 39–43
Expectancy/value interface, race, ethnicity, and
      motivation at, 423
Expectancy-value model, 408
  of achievement, 420
Expectancy-value theories, 409
  modern, 408
Experience, role in face processing, 38
Experience-independent functions, 20
Experimental strategies, 127
Explicit memory, 26–28
  evaluation of, 30
Exposure embarrassment, 379
Expression:
  as an aesthetic property of music, 344–345
  as an aesthetic property of pictures, 328–329
  in drawings, 336
Expressions, 269
Extended-family system, American Indian, 122
Extended-kin systems, African-American, 121
Externalizing problems, peer rejection and, 168
Extrafamilial relationships, during adolescence,
      556–561

Extraversion, 186, 188
  pattern of change in, 202
Extraversion/surgency, versus shyness and
      behavioral inhibition, 66
Extraversion trait, models explaining, 189

"Face-biased" input, 35
Face/object recognition, 33
Face processing:
  gradual specialization of, 36–37
  impairments to, 33
  neuroimaging study of, 35
  pathways in, 34–35
  role of experience in, 38
Facial expression(s):
  emotion and, 363, 365–366
  emotion-eliciting situations and, 380–381
  infant discrimination of, 370–371
Facial expression processing, amygdala in, 37–38
Facial signals, responsiveness to, 372
Factor analysis, 56
Factor analytic research, 413–414
Failed realism phase, 324
Failure:
  personal responsibility for, 420
  reactions to, 413, 414
Failure attributions, changing, 419
False-belief error, 539–540
"False belief" task, 624
"False inclusion," 529
False self, 239
False-self behavior, 226–227
Familial relationships, during adolescence,
      552–556
Families:
  contribution to children's socialization, 109–110
  contribution to socialization outcomes, 128
  gender socialization in, 670–672
  impact of secular shifts on, 97
  individual differences among, 127
  influences on children's coping, 393–394
  models of relationships in, 96
  role in Latino adaptation, 125–126
Families of color, growth of, 117
Family coercion, role in antisocial behavior,
      448–449
Family conflict, dysfunction and, 393
Family emotional expression, effects of, 383
Family interactions, social judgments and, 494–495
Family members:
  differences among, 199
  direct and indirect impact of, 96
Family myths, 110

Institute of Child Health and Human Development. *See* National Institute of Child Health and Human Development (NICHD)

Institutionalized public basic schooling (IPBS), 612–613. *See also* IPBS mode

Instructional materials, requirements for, xi–xii

Integrative developmental analysis, 10

Intellectual engagement, valuing of, 544

Intellectual processes, executive control of, 543

Intellectual realism, 324

Intelligence:
theories about beliefs about, 407–408
varying views of, 415

Intentional knowledge seeking, 533–534

"Intention cue bias," 159

Intention-reading, 290

Intentions, detection of, 314

"Intent participation," 620

"Interactional synchrony," 370

Interaction effects, 78

Interactions, peer, 141, 142

Interdependence:
developing a sense of, 567–577
development of, 552
psychosocial competencies in, 576–577

Interdependent self-construal, 424

Interests, development of, 417

Interest theories, 410

Interkinetic nuclear migration, 22

Internalization:
conscience and, 478–479
moral development as, 481
traditional view of, 480

Internalized standards, 473

Internalizing problems, peer rejection and, 168–169

Interpersonal competence, 567–568

Interpersonal relationships:
during adolescence, 551–561
Latino, 124–125

"Interrelational development," 224

"Interrelational" self-descriptions, 222

Intersubjectivity, 147, 697, 702

Intervention studies, 127

Intimacy:
during adolescence, 570–573
interpersonal roots of, 571
role in psychosocial development, 572–573

Intimate relationships, personality and, 204–205

Intracultural research, problems in, 116

Intransitives, simple, 280

Intraventricular hemorrhage (IVH), 33

Intrinsic motivation, development of, 417

Intrinsic motivation theories, 409–410

Intrinsic value, 409

Invented musical notations, 348

Inventory of Parent and Peer Attachment (IPPA), 570

Inversion errors, 283–284

IPBS mode, formal schooling in, 613–614. *See also* Institutionalized public basic schooling (IPBS)

Irritability, adaptive difficulties and, 73

Irritability/anger/frustration trait, 185

I-self, 218–219, 219, 254

I-self processes, cognitive, 242

"Isolation of variables" investigative strategy, 533

Israel, infant adaptation level in, 368

Item-based constructions, 285
linguistic, 269–273
syntactically marked, 270, 271

Japan:
emotional climate in, 368
infant adaptation level in, 367

Japanese macaque cultural traditions, 603

"Jingle-jangle" fallacy, 185–186

Job quality, family socialization and, 114–115

Judgment(s). *See also* Moral judgments
age-related levels of, 490–491
contextual differences in, 501–502
in moral development, 488–491

Junior high school, adjustment to, 167

Justice, as a component of morality, 491

Juveniles, violent crime by, 437

Knock-in/out genes, 22

Knowledge:
conflict with reasoning, 525–526
emotional dissemblance and, 387
generic, 306
ontological, 308–309
"privileged" domains of, 621–622
sources of, 529
understanding and valuing, 539–541

Knowledge acquisition, during the second decade, 531–532

Knowledge seeking, intentional, 533–534

Labeling effect, 303

Laboratory temperament, measures, 61–62

Language. *See also* Linguistic entries
that children hear, 266–267
concepts encoded in, 302–304
determining the effects of, 303
earliest, 267–269

Language *(Continued)*
  early ontogeny of, 266–279
  false-self behavior and, 226–227
  generics in, 306
  grammatical dimension of, 265
  later ontogeny of, 279–288
  research on, 600–601
Language acquisition:
  multiple factors in, 292
  processes in, 288–291
Language brokers, children as, 120
Language cues, 303
Language development research, 126
Language-learning child, task of, 267
Late adolescence:
  adaptive and maladaptive self-processes in, 248–249
  normative liabilities during, 248
  self-representations and self-evaluations in, 245–248
Late childhood:
  individual differences in, 232–234
  liabilities for self-development during, 231–232
  self-representations and self-evaluations in, 230–231
Latent knowledge structures, 455–456
Latino adaptation, role of family in, 125–126
Latino Catholic ideology, 125
Latino culture, status and roles in, 125
Latino families, socialization concerns in, 124–126
Latino fathers, role in socialization, 126
Latino populations, growth of, 117
Latinos, identification with family, community, and ethnic group, 124
Laws, role in antisocial behavior, 445
Learned helplessness, 418–419, 420–421
Learning:
  development of, 532
  gender, 669–669
  implicit, 30–31
  implicit-sequence, 31–33
  during the second decade, 531–532
Learning processes, temperament differences and, 195, 196
Lesbian parenting, 671
"Lexicalized" concepts, 302
Life course, personality and, 204–208
Life-course charting, 204
Life-course human development, 696–697
Life-course perspective, 96
Life-course tasks, parental management of, 127
Life-course trajectories, differences in, 700

Life experience mediation, through acquired processing patterns, 455
Life span, personality structure across, 184–186
Life-span developmental perspective, 202
Life stage-specific outcomes, 700–701
Linguistic abstractions, constraints on, 286–288
Linguistic categories, creation of, 270
Linguistic competence, 266
Linguistic construction(s):
  abstract, 285–286
  acquiring, 263–297
  defined, 265–266
  growing abstractness of, 288–290
  item-based, 269–273
  as meaningful linguistic symbols, 265
  symbolic elements in, 273
Linguistic ordering patterns, 270
Linguistic schemas, 292
Linguistic symbols, 263
Literacy, acquiring in school, 615
"Local cues," 278
"Local interpretation," 528, 535
Locative alternation, 287
Locatives, 281
Locus of control, gender differences for, 420
Longitudinal assessments, 10
Longitudinal research, 208
"Looking glass self," 220
Low agreeableness, 193
Lower-order personality traits, proposed taxonomy of, 188
Low risk/high protective factor presence vulnerability level, 733–734
Low risk/low protective factor presence vulnerability level, 732

Machismo, 126
Magnetic resonance imaging (MRI), 25
  assessments via, 443
"Making a difference," opportunities for, 709
Maladaptive outcomes:
  during middle adolescence, 244–245
  during middle to late childhood, 232–234
  during toddlerhood and early childhood, 226–228
Maladaptive reactive coping strategies, 714
Maladaptive self-processes, during late adolescence/early adulthood, 248–249
MAO-A genotype, 441. *See also* Monoamine oxidase (MAO) activity
Marital conflict, role in antisocial behavior, 446
Marital satisfaction/discord, influence on child outcomes, 107–108

Marital subsystem, as a contributor to child
socialization, 107–110
"Masked vulnerability," 732
Mastery-avoidance goals, 411–412
Mastery goal orientation, 411, 412
Mastery-oriented goals, 417
Maternal acculturation, among Mexican American
families, 126
Maternal employment, effects of, 114
Maternal utterances, 267
Maturation, species-wide patterns of, 632
Mayan community, economic changes in,
609–610
Meaning, critical role of, 524
"Meaning making," 696, 697, 698
Mean-level continuity/change, 202–203
Measurement contamination, 71
Measurement error, 76–77
Media, observational learning from, 673
Media violence, role in antisocial behavior, 447
Medicaid health-care benefits, 705–706
Melodies:
awareness of proper structure of, 344
relational processing of, 342
rhythmic and tonal organization of, 346–347
Melody structure, sensitivity to, 342
Memory, 26–28
autobiographical, 632–635
cultural variations in, 632–633
in gender development, 676–677
nondeclarative, 30–31
role in generating affect, 362
Memory development, research on, 638
Memory processes, species-general set of, 633
Memory systems, development of, 26
Men, standards of appearance for, 252. *See also*
Fathers
Men's employment patterns, family socialization
and, 114
"Mental combinations," 272
Mental habits, 69–70
development of, 70
Mental processing, during the second decade, 525
Me-self, 219–220, 233, 254
Metacognitive processes, 526
Metacognitive skills, formal schooling and, 614
"Metaphorical exemplification," 328
Methodological rigor, 98
Methodologies, diverse and innovative, 10–11
Metric notations, 350
Metropolitan Area Child Study (MACS), 458–459
Mexican American family ecologies, generational
differences in, 118

Mexican Americans, academic problems and
prospects of, 422
"Micro-aggressions," 704
Microgenetic analysis, 532, 535
Microgenetic research, 519
Middle adolescence, 564
adaptive and maladaptive outcomes in, 244–245
normative liabilities during, 243–244
self-representations and self-evaluations in,
241–243
Middle childhood:
groups during, 152–153
individual differences in, 232–234
liabilities for self-development during, 231–232
peer interactions during, 149–153
self-representations and self-evaluations in,
230–231
Middle voice constructions, 283
Mind, theory of, 602
Minnesota Multiphasic Personality Inventory
(MMPI), 61
Minor physical anomalies (MPAs), antisocial
behavior and, 443
Mitosis, S phase of, 22
Mixed-gender peer groups, 560
Mixed-sex cliques, 155
Moderated linkage, between temperament and
adjustment, 77–79
Modern expectancy-value theories, 408
Modern humans, beginning of, 605–606
Molecular genetics, 63–64
Monoamine oxidase (MAO) activity, 445. *See also*
MAO-A genotype
Monoamine oxidase A (MAOA) gene, 64
Monozygotic (MZ) twins, 198–199
Moral absolutism, 474
Moral acquisition, mechanisms of, 475
Moral actions, 477
Moral decisions, 496–498
Moral development, 456, 473–514
Freudian view of, 474
gender differences in, 481
influences on, 480
interactional perspective on, 489
issues, emphases, and theories related to, 476
judgment and reciprocal social interactions in,
488–491
primacy of empathy in, 477–478
role of culture in, 484–488
social judgment and, 491–499
stages of, 475
theoretical approaches to, 476
Moral disengagement, 455

Problem behavior, hormonal increases and, 666–667
Problem solving, situation-oriented, 392–393
Problem-Solving Skills Training (PSST), 458
Processing-aggressive behavior correlations, 455
Processing capacity, 521–522
Processing improvement, role in thinking and reasoning, 522
Projective systems, in drawing, 334
Pronouns, overgeneralization of, 277
Prosocial actions, research findings on, 477
Prosocial behaviors, 79–80, 147, 193
Prosocial moral reasoning, 490
Protective factors, 701, 702
  disproportionate, 713
  from positive outcomes/coping features, 720
  transformation of, 718
Providing Alternative Thinking Strategies (PATHS) program, 458
Provocative victim, 150
Proximal processes, 709
"Proximity seeking," 364, 365
Psychobiological research approaches, to temperament, 62–64
Psychodynamic perspective, on adolescence, 563
Psycholinguistic processes, 290–291
Psychological adjustment, childhood peer experiences and, 168–169
Psychological boundaries, 384–385
Psychological needs, fundamental, 410
Psychological perspective, on apathy, 419
Psychological sexual differentiation, parallels with physical sexual differentiation, 663–664
Psychological tasks, school/nonschool differences on, 615
Psychopathology, theories of, 73
Psychopathy, dispositional construct of, 442
Psychosocial adjustment:
  adolescent, 564
  problems in, 554–555
Psychosocial sexuality:
  normative development of, 573–574
  variation in the development of, 574–575
Psychosocial tasks, of adolescence, 561–577
Pubertal change experience, gender differences in, 252
Punitiveness, role in antisocial behavior, 449

Qualitative assessment methods, 10–11
Quantitative assessment methods, 10
Questions, 283–284

Race empowerment strategies, 122
Race issues, family socialization and, 115–126

Race-sensitive perspective, 723
Race variable, proactively addressing, 722–723
Racial differences:
  in achievement values and goals, 422–423
  in competence, control, and attribution beliefs, 422
Racial stratification, 723, 724–725, 727
Radial cell migration, 23
Rank-order stability, of personality traits, 201
"Ratchet effect," 637
Rational decision analysis, 454
Reactive attention, 66
Reactive control, 375
Reactive coping strategies, redundant use of, 718
Reactivity, 54, 162
Realism, 326
  phases in the development of, 324
Reality, judgments of, 497–498
Reasoning:
  conflict with knowledge, 525–526
  during the second decade, 522–523
Reasoning levels, about ability, effort, and difficulty, 415
Reciprocal social interactions, in moral development, 488–491
Reciprocity, in friendships, 143
Recognition memory, 28
"Recruitment" effects, 206
Referential specificity, 372
Reflexives, 283
Rejected-aggressive children, 159
Rejected children, 157
  behavior of, 380
Rejection:
  chronic, 160
  externalizing problems and, 168
  internalizing problems and, 169
Rejection sensitivity (RS), 69
Relational aggression, 161
Relational processes, 551
Relational processing, of rhythm and melody, 342
Relations, during middle childhood, 150–152
Relationship functions, redistributions of, 569
Relationships:
  during adolescence, 154–155
  cognitive models of, 103
  cultivating, 204–205
  during early childhood, 148
  gender in, 681
  during infant and toddler years, 146
  maintenance or enhancement of, 389
  parental influence on, 104–105
Religious organizations, involvement in, 106

Vulnerability level:
  challenges associated with, 715
  quadrants of, 732–734
Vulnerability model, 72

Welfare:
  community, 499
  as a component of morality, 491
"Well adjusted" preschool children, 68
Well-being, 374–375
Willfulness, 193
Wisconsin Card Sorting Task (WCST), 42
Within-family ecological factors, role in antisocial
    behavior, 446
Within-person change in motivation, 413–419
Women. *See also* Females
  characterization of, 483
  prejudice against, 660
  unequal treatment of, 506
Women's employment patterns, family socialization
    and, 114
Word combinations, 269
  producing, 272

Word meaning organization, formal schooling and,
    613
Word order, 273–277
  comprehension of, 270–271
Words:
  learning, 266
  pivot-type, 270
Words and rules approach, 264
Working memory, 39, 40, 521
Work quality, family socialization and, 114–115
Worry, motivation and, 418

Youth development:
  community networking and, 112
Youth of color:
  human development task for, 705
  "micro-aggressions" against, 704–705
  risk factors for, 703

Zinacantan, historical and cognitive change in,
    608–610